W9-BOB-993

CANADA
Osoyoos
Grand Forks
Oroville
Okanogan National Forest
Colville National Forest
Columbia River
Metaline Falls
Tonasket
Republic
Kettle Falls
Colville
Priest Lake
Winthrop
Omak
Colville
Franklin D. Roosevelt Lake
Kaniksu National Forest
Cusick
Twisp
Okanogan
Indian Reservation
Lake Roosevelt Nat. Rec. Area
Chewelah
Newport
Brewster
Lake Chelan
Columbia River
Franklin D. Roosevelt Lake
Spokane Indian Reservation
Deer Park
IDAHO
Coulee Dam
Chelan
Banks Lake
Wilbur
Davenport
Coeur d'Alene
Waterville
Spokane
Coulee City
Wenatchee
Soap Lake
Ephrata
Odessa
Coeur d'Alene Lake
Moses Lake
Moses Lake
Ritzville
Potholes Reservoir
Vantage
Othello
Colfax
Pullman
Columbia River
Snake River
Clarkston
Lewiston
Sunnyside
Richland
Pasco
Dayton
Kennewick
Walla Walla
Umatilla National Forest
OREGON
Columbia River
Pendleton
0 25 mi
0 25 km

Contents

- **Discover Washington** 6
  - Planning Your Trip 8
  - Explore Washington 11
    - The Best of Washington 11
    - Weekend Getaways 14
    - Plate and Barrel 17
    - The Olympiad 18
    - Four Seasons 19
    - Washington's Five Corners 20
- **Seattle** 21
  - Sights 28
  - Entertainment and Events 47
  - Shopping 54
  - Sports and Recreation 57
  - Accommodations 60
  - Food 65
  - Information and Services 81
  - Getting There 82
  - Getting Around 83
- **The Eastside** 88
  - Bellevue and Mercer Island 91
  - Kirkland 100
  - Redmond 105
  - Issaquah 110
  - Woodinville and Bothell 115
- **North Puget Sound** 118
  - Edmonds and Mukilteo 121
  - Whidbey Island 126
  - Everett 144
  - Northern Snohomish County 150
  - Skagit Valley and Mount Vernon 155
  - La Conner 160
  - Burlington to Bellingham 164
  - Bellingham 166
  - North to Canada 179
- **South Puget Sound** 186
  - Olympia 189
  - Tacoma 200
  - Kitsap Peninsula 215
  - Islands and Inlets 227
  - Puyallup Valley to White River Valley 236
  - Sea-Tac Corridor 239
- **San Juan Islands** 244
  - Anacortes 249
  - San Juan Island 256
  - Orcas Island 270
  - Lopez Island 281
  - Other Islands 287
- **Olympic Peninsula and the Coast** 290
  - Olympic National Park 292
  - Hood Canal and Vicinity 295
  - Port Townsend 305
  - Oak Bay Area 314
  - Sequim 316
  - Port Angeles 322
  - Port Angeles to Sol Duc 331
  - Olympic Coast and Hoh Rain Forest 337
  - Queets and Quinault 345
  - North Beach 348
  - Grays Harbor and Vicinity 356
  - Long Beach Peninsula 366
  - Longview and Kelso Vicinity 379

Columbia Gorge and Wine Country **383**
Vancouver 386
The Columbia Gorge 395
Tri-Cities 412
Walla Walla 421
Yakima Valley 430
Ellensburg 443
Wenatchee 449

North Cascades **459**
Mount Baker and Vicinity 463
The Mountain Loop: Granite Falls to Darrington 469
North Cascades Highway 477
Methow Valley 491
Chelan and Vicinity 502
Cashmere 515
Leavenworth 516
Stevens Pass and Skykomish Valley .. 527

South Cascades **535**
Snoqualmie Valley and Snoqualmie Pass 538
Cle Elum and Vicinity 544
Eatonville and Elbe 550
Ashford 553
Mount Rainier National Park 555
Chinook Pass and Highway 410 571
White Pass Scenic Byway 574
Approaching Mount St. Helens 580
Mount St. Helens National Volcanic Monument 585
Mount Adams and Gifford-Pinchot 592

Eastern Washington **596**
Columbia Basin 600
Grand Coulee Dam and Vicinity 610
Omak and Okanogan 623
Okanogan Valley 625
Okanogan Highlands 628
The Northeast Corner 632
Spokane 644
Palouse Country 658
Pullman 660
Clarkston and Vicinity 667
Snake River and Blue Mountains Country 671

Background **676**
The Land 677
Flora and Fauna 679
History 686
Industry and Economy 694

Essentials **698**
Getting There 698
Getting Around 699
Sports and Recreation 701
Accommodations and Food 705
Tips for Travelers 708
Health and Safety 709
Information and Services 711

Resources **713**
Suggested Reading 713
Internet Resources 716

Index **718**

List of Maps **750**

Discover Washington

Washington engages the senses – all of them.

Catch a whiff of bracing salt air along the wild and scenic coast, or the fragrant aroma of blackberries along the Puget Sound.

Feel the ice tickle your eyelashes through the flurries of the Northern Cascades, or the sweat trickle down your back under the hot sun in the high desert of Eastern Washington.

Experience the joy of seeing Mount Rainier rise over Lake Washington on a brilliant summer day, or watching raindrops break the foam of a perfect cappuccino when the drizzle sets in.

Listen for the mournful, deep booming of train horns through the Columbia Gorge, or the quiet swishing of skis on the backcountry trails of the Cascades.

Or try tasting Washington – the sweetness of wild blueberries in August, the smoky richness of freshly caught and grilled salmon, the robust complexities of a Columbia River cabernet sauvignon – they're all here waiting to be experienced.

Tromp through rain forests, raft on rivers, and clamber up rocky outcroppings long enough and you'll be won over by the natural charms of the state. During Washington's long summer days, an after-work hike is *de rigeur* for the locals, with a striking and well-maintained trail never far away. Turquoise-colored alpine lakes beckon fly-fishing anglers in

their peaceful art. Miles of bike-friendly roads and trails await those of the two-wheeled persuasion, while horse lovers can take their four-footed companions far from the maddening crowds.

But these aren't the state's only draws – Washington is also a hub of art and culture, engineering and history. The region is home to historic lighthouses, impressive skyscrapers, and great works of art, such as the outdoor designs at the Seattle Olympic Sculpture Park. You're likely to be equally impressed by the dizzying heights of Seattle's Columbia Center tower and Mount Rainier.

The Evergreen State isn't just a destination for the body and mind, but for the soul, too. If you don't try too hard, the secret Zen of this place just might open up to you. It might come standing atop mountain peaks hewn over thousands of years, under trees that took root before the birth of Columbus, or maybe amid the rolling solitude of golden wheat fields planted last spring. Wherever you are, be ready for it. Washington has a way of rewarding those who come ready to embrace it.

Planning Your Trip

▶ WHERE TO GO

Seattle

Washington's largest city and cultural centerpiece, Seattle is known as the Emerald City for good reason. The city is awash in green spaces and parks such as the Washington Arboretum and Discovery Park, which balance well with the sleekly engineered Space Needle and city high-rises like the Columbia Tower. Seattle is surrounded by water, so don't forget the boat shoes. Enjoy Lake Union by kayak or floatplane, Elliot Bay by ferry, or Lake Washington by canoe.

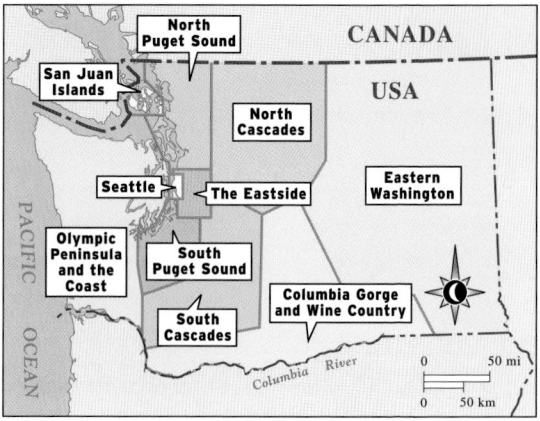

The Eastside

Seattle's tony bedroom communities lie east of Lake Washington in an expanse that is part rural, part subdivision, and part outdoor park. Sip a little vino at the boutique wineries in Woodinville, take a sailing lesson at the Kirkland marina, hike to the top of the Issaquah Alps, or enjoy a good meal and some upscale shopping in Bellevue.

North Puget Sound

North of Seattle, cities line up along the Sound until development gives way first to suburb, then to country. See where Boeing builds its jumbo-liners in Everett. Or for some solitude, pedal the farm roads past the loamy soil of Skagit County. Motor along Chuckanut Drive, which careens by coves and bays along the wooded edge of the Sound until you reach historic Fairhaven in Bellingham. Northernmost along I-5 is Washington's portal to Canada, Blaine, home to the symbolic white arch at the border.

South Puget Sound

The southern stretch of the Puget Sound is a craggy puzzle of inlets, islands, and peninsulas. Explore the industrial center–turned–cultural mecca of Tacoma, with its well-preserved historic brick buildings and an amazing collection of art and history museums. Travel even farther south to Olympia, home of the state capitol campus, with its whitewashed legislative building, gardens, and parks. In between them, a curious traveler can find nature preserves and historic parks galore.

San Juan Islands

Puget Sound's prominent archipelago lies east of Anacortes. At low tide there are more than 786 islands, but the four serviced by Washington State Ferries are San Juan Island, Orcas Island, Lopez Island, and

Shaw Island. The largest of the four, San Juan offers the widest variety of historic sites, restaurants and lodging. Orcas features the most rugged landscapes and the best trails. Lopez is a favorite for bicycling and Shaw is the most pastoral.

Olympic Peninsula and the Coast

Surf-pounded sea stacks, steaming hot springs, and crystal clear rivers all greet the traveler out in the Olympic Peninsula and Washington's coast. Crowning the interior of the peninsula are the majestic Olympic Mountains, reachable only by foot. At the southernmost point, at the mouth of the Columbia River, lies Long Beach peninsula, the longest stretch of sandy beach in the state, which protects Willapa Bay, known for its oysters.

Columbia Gorge and Wine Country

East of Vancouver, road-trippers will find a stretch of road seemingly made just for Sunday afternoons. Rumble alongside the deep gorge cut by the mighty Columbia River through basaltic rock. Peer over craggy cliffs plunging down to the swift river waters, often dotted with windsurfers and kiteboarders. Walk the vineyards here, or veer northeast to the sunny orchards and wine fields of the Yakima Valley and Walla Walla.

IF YOU HAVE . . .

A weekend: Visit Seattle, the Eastside, and the Puget Sound.

A week: Add a trip to Mount Rainier and Mount St. Helens.

Two weeks: Drive the Olympic Peninsula and Coast, then drive the Columbia River Gorge to the wine country.

A month: Add a trip to Eastern Washington, stopping in Spokane and the Grand Coulee Dam. Drive the North Cascades Highway. Spend a weekend in the San Juan Islands.

North Cascades

The northern spires of the Cascades reach all the way up to the Canadian border in a network of glacial lakes, trout-filled rivers, twisty mountain roads, alpine meadows, and wooded trails. The highlight of the region is the pristine North Cascades National Park. Nearby is the miles-long Lake Chelan, a

Tatoosh Wilderness from Mount Rainier National Park

summer destination for all Washingtonians. Also in the region is the Bavarian look-alike town of Leavenworth, a favorite among hikers in summer and skiers when the snow flies.

South Cascades

From the state line all the way up to the I-90 corridor, rolling through Snoqualmie Pass, the Cascade mountains cut a wide swath across the middle of the state. Most notable among them is the tallest mountain in the continental United States, Mount Rainier. Contrast the tall and complete snowcaps on Rainier to the craggy, gaping hole left in Mount St. Helens. And the oft-overlooked but rugged Mount Adams is surrounded by public forest-land, just waiting to be explored.

Eastern Washington

Wind your way up and over any one of Washington's passes from the Puget Sound and you're likely to find Seattle's precious commodity in abundant supply: sunshine. Enjoy the weather at giant reservoirs out here, including the granddaddy of them all, Lake Roosevelt, formed by the massive Grand Coulee Dam. If all the rural, arid, rocky landscape gets too lonely for you, get a taste of city life in Spokane, home of one of the nicest city parks in the state, Riverfront Park.

▶ WHEN TO GO

Mount Vernon Tulip Festival

There's no doubt about it, there is nothing so sublime as late summer in Washington, particularly the month of August. During this time, visitors have the best chance of catching sunshine throughout the state, even in rainy Puget Sound. All of the snow has usually melted from mountain trails by then, replaced by blossoms kissing the alpine meadows. And hot Eastern Washington beckons sun lizards looking to hang out by its innumerable lakes under the late afternoon light.

Of course, other times of year bring their own joys. In spring, the tulips burst forth in the Skagit Valley and hearty rhododendron blossoms explode from seemingly every street-side bush in the Puget Sound.

In much of Washington, fall is harvest time. Take a drive along the back roads of the Palouse hills in Eastern Washington to see farmers working away at the golden sea of wheat or tour wine country during the grape harvest to see what it takes to perfect those vintages. This is also one of the most dramatic times to watch the surf pound the ocean along the coast or revel in the water dripping off the Olympic rainforest leaves.

And though the drizzle descends pretty unceasingly onto the Puget Sound in winter, the season is far from gloomy to those willing to strap on skis or snowshoes. The Cascade mountain range is painted white each year, easily reachable in as little as a half hour from Seattle. If that isn't your thing, this is the also the perfect time to huddle up in a Seattle coffee shop and enjoy the museums around the region.

Explore Washington

▶ THE BEST OF WASHINGTON

Washington is filled with mountain vistas, remote beaches, country roads, and urban hideaways. Enjoy the very best the state has to offer on this whirlwind tour.

Day 1

From Seattle, take a meandering drive up to Mount Rainier, soaking up the views from the lovely flower-filled meadows at aptly named Paradise and then from the stunning alpine ridges high up at Sunrise. On the way back from Sunrise, stop in for a short hike to the towering ancient trees at Grove of the Patriarchs. Settle in for a soak in the hot tub and maybe even a massage at Wellspring in Ashford.

Day 2

Today is an early day. Head to Castle Rock, gateway to the Mount St. Helens National Volcanic Monument. You'll wind your way up the Spirit Lake Memorial Highway, past areas once ravaged by the mountain's explosive force. At the end of the road lies the Johnston Ridge Observatory, the closest viewpoint reachable by car, with vistas of the mountain and of log-strewn Spirit Lake. Stay the night at Eco Park at Mount St. Helens, the only lodging within the mountain's blast zone.

Day 3

Motor south on I-5 to Vancouver, sister city to Portland, Oregon, just across the mighty Columbia. Spend the day exploring the orderly barracks, officers' rows, and marching grounds at Fort Vancouver National Historic Reserve before catching a late lunch at Grant's Grill. Then check out the rebuilt wooden stockades and grounds at old Fort Vancouver and the prop-driven relics at Pearson Air Museum, both also on the reserve.

meadows at Paradise in Mount Rainier National Park

Day 4

Put on the driving gloves again for a leisurely drive along the dramatic banks of the Columbia. Take the time to climb up to the top of Beacon Rock, and imagine the thrill Lewis and Clark felt navigating the river below. Continue on to Maryhill Winery for a glass of wine, and enjoy the sunset as you look over the Gorge and Mount Hood. Then continue up to Goldendale Observatory for a nighttime star show through the looking glass.

Day 5

Drive up and over the Cascade foothills to reach the heart of wine country, the Yakima Valley. Start with a quick stop in Toppenish, a genuine western town known for its amazing murals. Then take a drive around the wineries in the Rattlesnake Hills. Finally, cruise by the apple and fruit orchards around Wapato. Settle down for the evening in Yakima.

Day 6

Take the scenic route up to I-90 along the Yakima River on Highway 821. Then blast over the asphalt eastward toward Spokane. Take a long break along the way, stopping to check out the trees made of stone at Ginko Petrified Forest State Park. Finish the day with a relaxing spa treatment at the luxurious Davenport Hotel, your home for the evening.

Day 7

Start the day off with a gondola ride over Spokane Falls at Riverfront Park, enjoying a leisurely lunch at nearby Clinkerdagger's Restaurant. Then hop in the car up to Grand Coulee Dam for a late-afternoon tour of the grounds. Stay the night here so you can enjoy the laser light show at the dam later in the evening.

Day 8

Travel to the marvelously sunny Methow Valley and explore the faux-Western town of Winthrop, being sure to stop off at Sheri's Sweet Shop for treats. Rent a mountain bike and explore the valley's trails, hike Hart's Pass, or just stick around town and visit Shafer Museum.

Day 9

Experience one of the most breathtaking ribbons of asphalt in the state, rambling right

downtown Yakima

by the glaciated spires and turquoise lakes of North Cascades National Park. Stop for vistas at the Washington Pass Viewpoint, Ross Lake Overlook and Diablo Lake Overlook. In Diablo, catch the speedboat to unique floating cabins at Ross Lake Resort for a couple of nights of R&R.

Day 10

Time to take it easy. Relax dockside with a book or rent a boat and fish Ross Lake for rainbow trout. If you're really feeling ambitious, hike the nearly seven-mile trail to the top of Desolation Peak, where writer Jack Kerouac once stood watch at the fire lookout that still stands there today.

Day 11

Catch the ferry and hit the North Cascades Highway eastward again. Stop in Marblemount, grab a paddle and life vest, and climb aboard a guided rafting trip down the Skagit River. Once you've had your fun, continue on the highway until the landscape opens up into the wide open fields of the Skagit Valley and head north to Bow, where you'll stay in a restored 1914 farmhouse at Benson's Farmstead.

Day 12

Today you have a choice. You'll be making the short drive south to Deception Pass, over the arching green-trussed Deception Pass Bridge and onto Whidbey Island. You can spend the day exploring the numerous trails and lakes in Deception Pass State Park and even catch a boat under the bridge. Or you can continue south and enjoy the rolling pastoral land in Ebey's Landing National Historical Reserve, examine museum artifacts and a blockhouse in Coupeville, and enjoy a slice of loganberry pie and pet the llamas at Greenbank Farm. Either way, end the day with a ferry ride to Mukilteo and stay the night in Seattle.

Day 13

Enjoy a quintessential day in Seattle. Pick through the wares at Pike Place Market and watch the fish fly. Then travel up to Ballard to see the fishies in their own environment, making their way up the fish ladder at Hiram M. Chittenden Locks. Cap off the touring with an elevator ride to the top of the Space Needle for a 360-degree view of the city. Finally, finish your last evening in Seattle off with a dinner downtown or in Belltown. If

Capitol Lake in Olympia

you haven't had Northwest salmon yet, now's your chance.

Day 14

Grab your camera and explore the state's capitol in Olympia. Visit the grand dome of Washington, the Legislative Building, then watch the kids run through the dancing waters of Heritage Fountain at Heritage Park. Enjoy lunch by Tumwater Falls at Falls Terrace Restaurant on the south end of Capitol Lake. Then drive north to Tacoma and check into the swanky Hotel Murano, home to a kaleidoscope of one-of-a-kind glass art.

Day 15

From your downtown digs, walk to Tacoma's museum row and start by touring the interactive exhibits at one of the state's finest, the Washington State History Museum. Cross native son Dale Chihuly's Bridge of Glass to the International Museum of Glass and watch glassmaking demonstrations in its theater hot shop.

▶ WEEKEND GETAWAYS

The Puget Sound region has so much to offer visitors and residents alike that it is really most fun to explore in small chunks. Here are a few weekend itineraries to get you started.

Jet City

Seattle has enough sights to keep the curious occupied for weeks. The following trip highlights the very best the city has to offer.

DAY 1

Take a little drive to the southern part of the city and start the day at the Museum of Flight with a tour of the aviation industry that first put Seattle on the map. Then park your car in the hotel garage for the rest of the weekend — you'll be able to walk or take alternative means of transportation after that. Grab a camera and take a ride on the monorail from Westlake Center to Seattle Center and spend some time atop the Space Needle. Bundle up — it gets cold on that observation deck!

DAY 2

The weekends are the best time of the week to visit Pike Place Market, which absolutely teems with activity on these days. Try an Asian pear or some fresh honeycomb, listen to street buskers croon, and pet Rachel, the bronze pig. Then take the stairs all the way down the Pike Street Hill Climb to the Waterfront. Enjoy the octopus, sea urchins, and sea mammals at the Seattle Aquarium. Check out Sylvester, the mummy, at Ye Olde Curiosity Shop. Enjoy some fish and chips from restaurant stalls lined up by the piers. And then, if you've still got some life in you, walk it all off with a long stroll all the way down to Olympic Sculpture Park.

Pike Place Market

DAY 3

Take the Elliot Bay Taxi over to West Seattle and enjoy one of the best Sunday brunches in the state at Salty's on Alki, feasting on crab legs, prime rib, and dainty little desserts. Then relax by the water with a walk along Alki Beach, taking in the Seattle view from a distance.

DAY 4

Enjoy your last morning on the water. Take the Lake Union Trolley down to South Lake Union and then trek a mile up Westlake Avenue, or take bus 17 over to NorthWest Outdoor Center. Hop in a kayak for a close-up look at the houseboats made famous by the film *Sleepless in Seattle*. Check out the giant structures at Gasworks Park and watch the seaplanes zip over the water.

History and Culture

History and art buffs will be in heaven in and around the Puget Sound, which acts as the cultural hub for the entire Pacific Northwest.

DAY 1

Learn about the exploding toilets, the seedy houses of ill repute, and the Great Fire at the lively Seattle Underground Tour. Once above ground again, check out the Klondike Gold Rush National Historic Park and the brick facades of historic Pioneer Square. Spend the evening enjoying a performance by the symphony at Benaroya Hall or the impressive Seattle Opera.

DAY 2

Learn the art and craft of glassblowing in the fiery hot Tacoma Glassblowing Studio. Then compare your handiwork with that of Tacoma's master glass artist, Dale Chihuly, who has donated some of his most original work to the Tacoma Art Museum. Spend time exploring the museum's other works, including a fantastic European collection featuring masters such as Degas, Renoir, and Pissarro.

DAY 3

Travel to Olympia to learn the ins and outs of Washington's early years. Enjoy the pioneer and Native American artifacts at the Washington State Capitol Museum. While on campus, be sure to make time to admire the sculptures, paintings, and other artwork created by Northwest artists and housed

Tacoma Glassblowing Studio

San Juan Islands

inside the State Library. Finally, travel to the southern end of Capitol Lake to explore the Tumwater Historical District.

Island Hopper

Escape city life on a trip to the Puget Sound's premier weekend destination, the San Juan Islands. This trip can also be taken by car and ferry, departing from Anacortes.

DAY 1

Make your getaway from Seattle to the San Juan Islands aboard a floatplane. Have the pilot touch down near Friday Harbor on San Juan Island. Rent a moped to explore the back roads of the island. Stop for a wine-tasting at San Juan Vineyard, pet the alpacas and buy a sweater at Krystal Acres, and wander the fragrant flower fields at Pelindaba Lavender Farm. Be sure to also check out American Camp and British Camp on opposite sides of the island, both a part of the San Juan Islands National Historic Park, which memorializes an international scuffle started over a pig.

DAY 2

Spend the morning whale-watching, either on a motorboat or on a kayak tour, in search of breaching and spyhopping killer whales. Then jump aboard the ferry to Orcas Island and take the shuttle bus to Moran State Park. Set up camp for the night, or stay at the park's guesthouse, then explore. Ply the park's lakes for fish, or hike up to the rumbling Cascades Falls.

DAY 3

Moran State Park is home to the island chain's highest peak, Mount Constitution. Wake early and trek four miles up to the top for an unbeatable view of the Sound. Then pack up and head out for a ferry over to the flat, bike-friendly terrain of Lopez Island. Arrange for Lopez Bicycle Works to bring you bike rentals and tour the island on two wheels. Stay the night on Lopez and hitch a floatplane back to Seattle in the morning.

Over the River and Through the Woods

You don't have to drive hours from Seattle to experience the great outdoors. There are loads of natural wonders right out the doorstep from the Puget Sound.

PLATE AND BARREL

Don't just *see* Washington, *taste* it, too! The Evergreen State is bountiful with culinary delights. It's enough to bring tears to a foodie's eyes. Here are the 10 best culinary experiences across the state.

VINEYARD TOURS

In the center of the state, **Yakima Valley** has the most variety of wineries, vineyards, tasting rooms, and cellars in a 50-mile stretch.

BLAKE ISLAND SALMON DINNER

Hop aboard the **Tillicum Village** tour boat for a ticket to cedar-plank cooked salmon accompanied by tribal dance.

ORCHARD TOURS

Wenatchee is the self-professed Apple Capital of the world. Stretch your legs under the shade of the area orchards and taste a few unique heirloom varieties.

COUNTRYSIDE TOUR

The cloistered **San Juan Islands** still lives by its own produce, dairy, and meat. Taste farm-fresh food sold at countryside stands, and get the freshest stuff at the bed-and-breakfasts and restaurants that support their neighbors.

PIKE PLACE MARKET TOUR

Stop for an espresso at the very first **Starbucks** and then hit up **Seattle Food Tours** (www.seattlefoodtours) for a journey of the taste buds through the Emerald City's hub of all things culinary.

DIM SUM

Take a chance in the **International District,** and grab a few dishes you don't recognize from the carts those nice ladies push by your table.

DINNER AT HERBFARM

The ultimate multi-course dining experience is tucked away near the **Woodinville** wineries.

SLURPING UP OYSTERS

Washingtonians love their shellfish, especially the kind known for love. The oyster beds along Chuckanut Drive supply two of the finest purveyors of oysters on the half shell in the state, **The Oyster Bar** and **Chuckanut Manor.**

CAMPFIRE-FRIED TROUT

Nothing beats fresh-caught trout cooked over open coals. The wooded expanse of the **Okanogan and Colville National Forests** offer some of the best mountain lakes and streams, with plenty of campsites nearby to build the fire.

MUNCHING FRESH-PICKED BERRIES

Western Washington is redolent with the scent of blackberries and blueberries in late summer. You have to work harder for the blueberries – they typically grow alongside mountain trails around July and August. But blackberries are everywhere around the Puget Sound in August. Try **Discovery Park** in Seattle for a surefire picking spot.

Washingtonians have a love affair with oysters.

DAY 1

Drive up to the thundering water of Snoqualmie Falls, the waterfall made famous as the backdrop for the TV series *Twin Peaks.* Take a short hike down to the bottom of the falls and then splurge on a gourmet meal in the Salish Lodge overlooking the scenery here.

DAY 2

Enjoy the Issaquah Alps today, with a nice hike up to the top of Tiger Mountain for fantastic views of Seattle and the Eastside. Then drive over to the unique Cougar Mountain Zoo and visit the menagerie of endangered animals there.

DAY 3

Take a drive to Kanasket-Palmer State Park and put-in with a guided rafting trip over the white water of the Green River. Experience class IV rapids with quirky names like the Nozzle and the Ledge Drop as you float by the hanging gardens along the river until you reach Flaming Geyser State Park.

▶ THE OLYMPIAD

Take a rugged tour around the Olympic Peninsula's US 101 loop and the Olympic National Park.

Day 1

Start the Highway 101 loop heading north between the Olympic mountains and Hood Canal. If you've got dive experience, rent equipment from Mike's Dive Resort and search the murky depths for giant octopus. Or just take a short hike at Dosewallips State Park. Enjoy a lunch of Hood Canal oysters in Hoodsport, and take it easy for the night in Port Townsend.

Day 2

Enjoy the history in Port Townsend with a visit to Fort Worden State Park. Then head east to Sequim for a brisk hike along the longest natural sand spit in the United States, Dungeness Spit. Head west on 101 to Port Angeles. Learn about the wilderness on the peninsula at the Olympic National Park Visitors Center and find a local bed-and-breakfast to rest for the evening.

Day 3

Start the morning by taking a drive to one of the best viewpoints in Washington, Hurricane Ridge. Then continue east to the Sol Duc River Valley. Take a hike up to Sol Duc Falls and soak in the hot spring waters at Sol Duc Resort, where you'll rest for the evening.

Day 4

Continue east on 101, and you'll be greeted by the neon blue waters of Lake Crescent. Stop for an interpretive hike at Barnes Point by the lakeshore. Stay the night in La Push and enjoy a walk along the log-strewn beach here.

Day 5

Get back on 101 going south, until you reach Upper Hoh Road. This will take you east along the Hoh River, deep into the lush Hoh Rain Forest. Pick one of the many trails to tramp between the towering pines drooped with moss here. Then continue on to the bluffs of Kalaloch for a look at the rugged Washington coast.

Day 6

Today you'll explore Lake Quinault, less than an hour south of Kalaloch along Highway 101. Take the 30-mile loop around the lake—numerous trails butt up against the road if you're eager to stretch your legs. Take it easy by the lake at Lake Quinault Resort.

Day 7

From Lake Quinault, sneak back over to the coast on Moclips-Quinault Road, and take a leisurely scenic drive down Highway 109. Stop at Pacific Beach State Park or Griffiths-Priday State Park to fly a kite or cast a fishing line. Then keep driving south until you hit Ocean Shores, to enjoy the last hours of sunlight riding horseback along the beach.

▶ FOUR SEASONS

Washington offers a full spectrum of outdoor adventures, no matter the time of year.

Spring

Spring is the best time to trek to the eastern half of the state. The sun shines brightly over recreational paradises like Steamboat Rock State Park, a fun spot for fishing, boating, and waterskiing.

Also enjoyable in late spring is the Yakima River Canyon, an anglers' favorite and a great spot for rafting. The area is also an ideal hiking ground when most other areas are still snow-covered.

Or, if you don't mind the rain and want to keep close to Seattle, pedal up, down, and 'round the hills of Whidbey Island. Stop in at the boutiques and bed-and-breakfasts in Langley or Coupeville and make it a fun overnight trip.

Summer

Summer in Washington is recreational heaven for most folks. Water rats can go gangbusters kayaking in the San Juan Islands, or whizzing a speedboat up Lake Chelan.

Mountain climbers can make ascents up Mount Rainier, Mount Adams, or Mount Saint Helens. Hikers will find most passes open after the fourth of July, making this a prime time for epic backpacking trips on the Wonderland Trail around Mount Rainier or Elwha River Trail through Olympic National Park. Or just opt for a day hike up to Heather Meadows near Mount Baker, the

kayaks waiting to be rented

WASHINGTON'S FIVE CORNERS

Gas up the car and head deep into this oddly-shaped state's five corners. You'll discover some hidden gems that are well worth the drive.

BLAINE

You'll get the chance to put one foot in Canada and the other in the United States on the lawn of **Peace Arch State Park,** a lovely park right on the border with British Columbia. The giant white arch here symbolizes the friendship between Americans and Canadians.

NEAH BAY

The blustery tip of land at **Cape Flattery** in Neah Bay is the northwesternmost point in the continental United States and a deliciously remote spot to explore. Hike around the Cape and then head south to **Shi Shi Beach,** one of the most peaceful stretches of sand along the entire Washington Coast.

CAPE DISAPPOINTMENT

Get a glimpse of the Pacific Ocean from the same vantage point as Lewis and Clark did more than 200 years ago. Where the Columbia River meets the ocean is home to the popular **Cape Disappointment State Park,** which offers an old military fort, scenic beaches and lighthouses, trails for exploration, and an interpretive center about America's favorite transcontinental explorers.

PALOUSE COUNTRY

The undulating golden wheat hillsides of the Palouse greet travelers to the lonely rural countryside of the southeast corner of the state. Road-trippers are rewarded with historic sites and classy vineyards in **Walla Walla,** as well as the thundering waters of the state's mightiest cataract, **Palouse Falls.**

PEND OREILLE

Enjoy the satisfying crunch of pine needles and cones underfoot in the quiet backcountry of the state's northeastern corner. This is a land of solitude, blessed still mountain lakes, serene campgrounds, and miles of trails. It is also home to the **Pend Oreille River,** the only river in the states to flow north, looping up into Canada until it reaches the Columbia.

Big Four Ice Caves on the Mountain Loop Highway, or the dramatic Kendall Katwalk along the longer Pacific Crest Trail.

Fall

Fly fishers love the fall, a prime time for catching trout and other cool-water fish. Try your hand in the Pend Oreille River near Colville National Forest or Bogachiel River in the Olympics to catch a limit's worth of lunkers.

Very early fall is also when area river rafters gear up to enjoy the Tieton River, which rages after the Bureau of Reclamation releases a torrent of dam water in what locals call the "flip-flop."

Winter

Downhill skiers have a full spectrum of resorts and ski areas to choose among in the state. Most convenient to Seattle is Snoqualmie Pass, less than an hour away from the city, with a decent range of runs. Better yet, travel just a bit farther up to Stevens Pass for one of the best all-around ski areas in the state.

Hard-core skiers will do well to make the trek up north to Mount Baker, down south to Crystal Mountain, or toward Wenatchee's Mission Ridge for the most challenging runs, even if they are a bit out of the way.

Those who prefer to ski on level ground can also sweat it out on the miles of cross-country trails offered by the Methow Valley Sport Trails Association, near Winthrop, which offers small camping huts along the trail for a multi-day adventure. Similar hut-to-hut skiing can be found along the Mount Tahoma Trails Association network of trails near Mount Rainier.

SEATTLE

Newcomers to Seattle are inevitably impressed by this big but still friendly home to 560,000 people, where the various monikers that have been applied—America's Most Livable City, Emerald City, Latte Land, and City of Niceness—all seem to fit. The obvious charms of Seattle and the Puget Sound region draw more tourists each year, many of whom come back to stay.

Seattle's appeal comes from its beautiful setting, its friendly and creative people, and the way the city has grown up along the shores of Puget Sound and Lake Washington. Oddly shaped towers and preserved historical districts stand alongside modern skyscrapers and the busy waterfront in jaunty disharmony. Every major event in the city's short life span, from Yesler's 1850s sawmill to the 1962 World's Fair to the 1990s high-tech boom (and subsequent bust) has left its legacy; the resulting mishmash of periods gives the city a flavor absent in showpieces of urban renewal.

History doesn't make a city livable, though, and no one event or attraction can ever take that credit. Rather, it's a thousand incidents, enjoyed daily: dining at the waterfront, watching the sun set behind the Olympics as sailboats head home; reading the paper on your early-morning ferry commute, accompanied by a lively porpoise escort service; listening to a free outdoor lunchtime concert in the heart of downtown; stopping for fresh vegetables or fish at Pike Place Market; cleansing your lungs with fresh, rain-rinsed air as you dodge slugs and puddles on your morning run; attending a summertime party on a harbor tour boat; and

© WASHINGTON STATE TOURISM/JIM POTH

HIGHLIGHTS

Seattle Underground: Learn Seattle's colorful history on this tour of the underground formed when Seattle was rebuilt after the Great Fire of 1889 (page 32).

Seattle Art Museum: Explore a world of artwork that ranges from Renaissance masterpieces to delicate painted porcelain to tribal ritual art (page 32).

LOOK FOR TO FIND RECOMMENDED SIGHTS, ACTIVITIES, DINING, AND LODGING.

Pike Place Market: Experience the buzz of farmers hawking their produce, flying fish, and scrumptious treats at the oldest continually operating market in the country (page 33).

Seattle Aquarium: Explore the depths of the Puget Sound without even getting wet (page 34).

Space Needle: Seattle's iconic landmark, this tower offers stellar views from the observation deck (page 35).

Experience Music Project: Check out the guitars, the concert jumpsuits, the street flyers, and all sorts of ephemera from the rock 'n' roll age (page 37).

Discovery Park: This is Seattle's largest park, a big slice of nature sitting on a bluff overlooking the Sound (page 40).

Chittenden Locks: See the boats navigate from the Puget Sound to the Lake Washington Ship Canal, watch the fish push up the salmon ladder from the viewing windows, and take in the flowers in the gardens at this Ballard favorite (page 42).

Arboretum and Japanese Garden: Green thumbs and garden lovers will admire the foliage and plant diversity at Seattle's premier botanic reserve (page 45).

Museum of Flight: Follow the history of flight and aviation and learn about Seattle's contribution to the skies at this extremely well-curated museum (page 46).

being surprised by a clear view of bashful Mt. Rainier from the highway or the University of Washington campus.

Seattle maintains a justified reputation for kindness and open-mindedness. It's the little things that immediately impress visitors: drivers waiting for other cars to pull out ahead of them, the almost total lack of horn-honking, the easy acceptance of long lines at an espresso bar, the friendly bus drivers who don't charge for a short ride, and the pedestrians waiting for the Walk sign before crossing a deserted street. Sometimes this laid-back nature approaches the annoying stage—such as the times clerks stop to chat with a customer about her kids while a long queue waits patiently—but Seattleites take it all in stride. Maybe it's the Northwest heritage of acceptance and community; maybe it's the on-again off-again rain that teaches patience...or maybe it's something they put in the coffee.

HISTORY

The First Inhabitants

The original residents of present-day Seattle were the Duwamish and Suquamish tribes, seminomadic people who relied on salmon and seasonal plants for sustenance. It was the chief of both of these tribes who contributed his name to the city, Chief Seattle, sometimes spelled Sealth. Today a bronze sculpture of Chief Seattle stands at the corner of 5th and Denny Way; his burial site, a peaceful Suquamish cemetery across the Sound, overlooks his namesake's skyline.

Early White Settlers

David Denny and Lee Terry are credited as the first white men to arrive at the site that would become Seattle. Denny, Terry, and their 22 compatriots left Cherry Grove, Illinois, in wagons bound for Portland, Oregon. There, they boarded a schooner and sailed to the banks of Elliott Bay, where in 1851, they established their town site at the exposed and unfavorable Alki Point. What they lacked in planning, they made up for in ambition, hoping to establish "the New York of the Pacific Coast." Time spent in the blustery Seattle weather convinced them to move down the bay to the much more sheltered area now known as Pioneer Square.

It wasn't long before the town fathers realized the cash crop they had in the gigantic coniferous trees that grew everywhere. Logs were skidded down the original "Skid Road," now Yesler Way, to Henry Yesler's steam-powered sawmill. Still, getting these goods to market was a problem. The city's position west of the intimidating Cascade Mountain range left expensive and slow boat transport the only option. The situation changed for the better in 1893, when the Great Northern Line railroad added Seattle as a terminus. Suddenly, the coal and lumber business had an economically viable outlet, and the population boomed to over 10 times its pre-railroad numbers. With the new townsfolk came the grading and planking of streets and sidewalks, the installation of sewer systems, electric lights, telephones, and home mail delivery. Seattleites were living high on the hog, and it seemed like nothing could stop the party.

The Great Fire

In the mid-19th-century American West, fortunes could turn very quickly, however. On June 6, 1889, 58 city blocks—the entire downtown area—were destroyed by fire when a burning pot of glue tipped over inside a cabinet shop. Within a half hour the entire young city was threatened. The town contained the conflagration by 8:30 that night, but its effects were to last a long, long time. The next morning it was decreed unanimously that the burnt district must be rebuilt in considerably less-flammable

SKID ROW

Seattle has the dubious distinction of coining the term "skid row." The phrase started out innocently enough. Local loggers used it to refer to the corduroy road they built along Yesler Way using rows of timber. It was set up that way so they could skid logs from the top of First Hill down to Henry Yesler's sawmill on the waterfront.

As time went on, many of the city's well-to-do denizens migrated to other parts of the city, and the timber industry dried up somewhat. The fortunes of Pioneer Square began to slide as surely as the timber once did, and Yesler Way grew into a seedy part of town.

The term became synonymous with a neighborhood down on its luck early in the 20th century, when a teetotaling local preacher proclaimed: "Yesler Way was once a skid road down which logs were pushed to Henry Yesler's sawmill on the waterfront. Today it is a skid road down which human souls go sliding to hell!"

brick. Today, several of those buildings are still in use in Pioneer Square and beyond.

Other problems had yet to be solved. Building a town on mudflats has its disadvantages. Flooding was an annual event, and toilets and sewers tended to back up during high tides. A massive engineering project was proposed to solve the problem. The whole town was to be regraded—raised from its present level. Streets and sidewalks were raised, leaving storefronts below ground and forcing shopowners to cut doorways in what used to be their second story. As you walk through downtown, look out for purple squares of glass in the sidewalk—these are essentially skylights into the "Underground."

The Klondike Gold Rush

As if timber, coal, and salmon weren't enough of a blessing, Seattle was soon to see the mother lode of economic stimulus. On August 16, 1896, George Washington Carmack and two friends, Skookum Jim and Tagish Charley, discovered gold deep in Canada's Yukon on a creek that fed into the Klondike River. A year later, when the first 68 wealthy prospectors and their gold arrived in the Lower 48, the "Klondike Gold Rush" was off and running. Fathers left their families, workmen left their jobs, and even Seattle's mayor quit to go seek his fortune in the Klondike.

The trip to the Klondike was a rough one, and the North West Mounted Police required that each prospector carry a year's supply of food plus necessary tools and clothing. Erastus Brainerd, a former newspaperman, tirelessly (and successfully) promoted Seattle as *the* place to get outfitted for the Klondike. Hoteliers, outfitters, saloons, and brothels all thrived even as the streets of Seattle become open markets. Some prospectors did strike it rich, but it was Seattle that emerged as the real winner. It's said that half the $200 million in Klondike gold ended up in Seattle. More than any other event in the city's history, the Klondike Gold Rush made Seattle the major city in America's Northwest corner and the last bastion of civilization before the barren wastes of Alaska.

Modern Seattle

It's impossible to dismiss the role of the Boeing Company in the growth and sustainability of Seattle. Prior to World War II, the Boeing Airplane Company eked out a living with a modest 4,000 workers at its Renton plant. With the outbreak of the war and the impressive success rates of Boeing's B-17 bomber, employment swelled to 30,000 in 1942, soon to peak at 50,000. After the Allied victory in 1945, the factory saw an inevitable slowdown, resulting in massive layoffs. While production would pick up again briefly during the Korean conflict and Cold War, William M. Allen, Boeing's postwar president, hoped for something more dependable. That innovation came in the form of the 707, the commercial jet-powered plane that changed the face of civilian air travel forever. Later successful developments—the 727, 737, and jumbo 747—helped establish Boeing as a worldwide leader in aviation and, for a time, giving Seattle fame as the "Jet City."

In 1962, the city of Seattle decided to show off its success to the rest of the world and throw itself a party in the process. "Century 21" was a World's Fair without peer. Drawing almost 10 million people, the event not only made Seattle an international destination, but also left behind the iconic Space Needle, as well as the Monorail, Pacific Science Center, and Opera House.

Today, the Seattle area is known for its individuality and entrepreneurship, supported by such major corporations as Starbucks, Boeing, Microsoft, Costco, and Weyerhaeuser, but also by thousands of smaller businesses.

CLIMATE

Yes, it's true. In 1898, a boy actually drowned on a downtown Seattle street. Apparently he was trying to cross an enormous sinkhole on a raft, fell off, and couldn't swim. Despite what you may have heard, however, it doesn't normally rain enough to drown folks in Seattle. The city actually gets less annual rainfall than New York City—it just falls more slowly. Gray and drizzly skies are standard fare from

October to May; when it does rain, it's frequently a who-needs-an-umbrella sprinkle. One of Seattle's oddest facts is that more pairs of sunglasses are sold there per capita than any other American city, yet umbrella and raincoat sales are no higher than average. The winter weather pattern remains nearly constant; storms off the Pacific coast send swirling clouds over Seattle for months, leading you to suspect the TV weather forecaster uses the same satellite photo all season.

Nearly all of the precipitation is rain; less than an inch of snow per month is the average, so plows are few . . . and generally in disrepair. When snowstorms dropped 17 inches on Seattle in November 1985, only four of the city's seven snowplows worked. Commuters, who have little experience driving in snow, relied on chains to traverse the I-5 snowfield; while some actually reached their destinations, most simply abandoned their cars and turned the freeway into a disorderly parking lot.

Seattle and other western Washington residents have learned to expect these three seasonal events: a windstorm on Thanksgiving that knocks out electrical power while the turkey is in the oven; floods on the Snohomish and Skagit Rivers around Christmas and New Year's that force farmers to evacuate their homes built on the floodplain; and perfect Santa Barbara weather the weekend of July 4th. You could almost make a living betting on these meteorological events.

When spring arrives the clouds move more quickly; rain comes in unpredictable spurts. Summer convinces many visitors to move here, with low humidity, temperatures in the high 70s to 80s, and cloudless skies; sometimes two entire months pass without a drop of rain. Then, as suddenly as it began, summer ends: Clouds return, temperatures drop to average in the 40s, and residents stockpile firewood, books, hot chocolate, and party invitations for the soggy season ahead.

ORIENTATION

See the Seattle map to get an idea of the major neighborhoods and thoroughfares. The city's street numbering system takes a little time to understand. Avenues run north and south and streets run east and west, but street names get more complex than this. Example: N.E. 63rd Street is in the Ravenna District east of 1st Avenue NE, and 63 blocks north of Yesler Way; 63rd Avenue SW is in West Seattle, south of Yesler Way and 63 blocks west of the Duwamish Waterway. Fortunately, the system starts to make a bit of sense after awhile and is used throughout King County (named for Martin Luther King Jr.), making it easier to find addresses in neighboring cities such as Bellevue or Renton.

As an aside, King County was originally named for William R. King, elected in 1852 as vice president under President Franklin Pierce (for whom adjacent Pierce County is named). King died just six weeks into his term of office. In the 1970s his legacy as an Alabama slaveowner made Seattleites uncomfortable, and the county was officially renamed for a more politically acceptable King, slain civil rights leader Martin Luther King Jr.

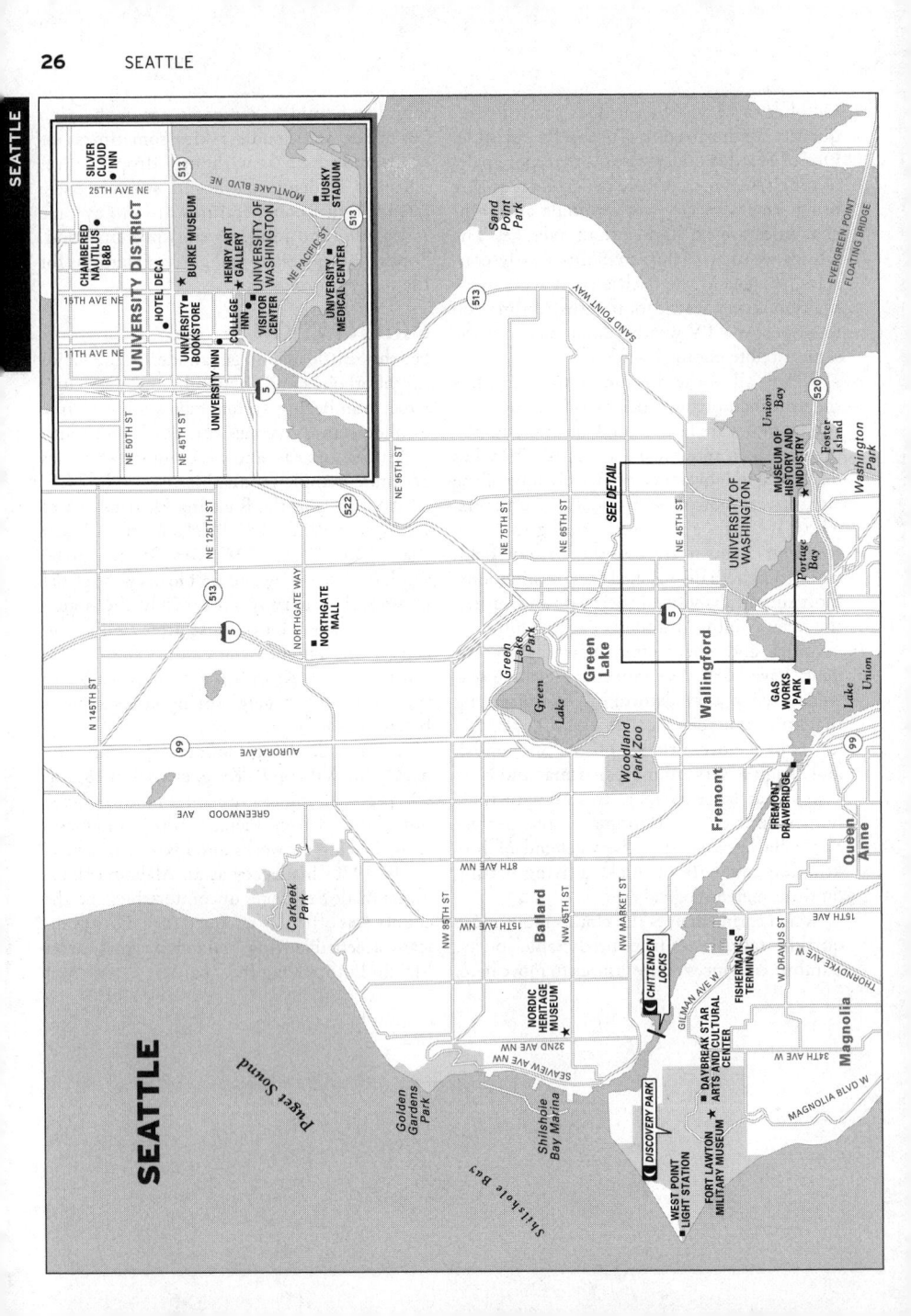
SEATTLE
Puget Sound
Shilshole Bay
Golden Gardens Park
Shilshole Bay Marina
Carkeek Park
Ballard
Fremont
Wallingford
Green Lake
Green Lake Park
Woodland Park Zoo
Sand Point Park
Union Bay
Portage Bay
Lake Union
Queen Anne
Magnolia
Foster Island
Washington Park
UNIVERSITY DISTRICT
SEE DETAIL
UNIVERSITY OF WASHINGTON
MUSEUM OF HISTORY AND INDUSTRY
GAS WORKS PARK
FREMONT DRAWBRIDGE
FISHERMAN'S TERMINAL
CHITTENDEN LOCKS
DISCOVERY PARK
WEST POINT LIGHT STATION
FORT LAWTON MILITARY MUSEUM
DAYBREAK STAR ARTS AND CULTURAL CENTER
NORDIC HERITAGE MUSEUM
NORTHGATE MALL
UNIVERSITY INN
UNIVERSITY BOOKSTORE
HOTEL DECA
BURKE MUSEUM
CHAMBERED NAUTILUS B&B
SILVER CLOUD INN
COLLEGE INN
HENRY ART GALLERY
VISITOR CENTER
UNIVERSITY OF WASHINGTON
UNIVERSITY MEDICAL CENTER
HUSKY STADIUM
NE 50TH ST
NE 45TH ST
11TH AVE NE
15TH AVE NE
25TH AVE NE
MONTLAKE BLVD NE
NE PACIFIC ST
NE 125TH ST
N 145TH ST
NORTHGATE WAY
AURORA AVE
GREENWOOD AVE
NE 95TH ST
NE 75TH ST
NE 65TH ST
NE 45TH ST
SAND POINT WAY
EVERGREEN POINT FLOATING BRIDGE
8TH AVE NW
15TH AVE NW
NW 85TH ST
NW 65TH ST
NW MARKET ST
32ND AVE NW
SEAVIEW AVE NW
GILMAN AVE W
W DRAVUS ST
15TH AVE
THORNDYKE AVE W
34TH AVE W
MAGNOLIA BLVD W
5
99
513
522
520

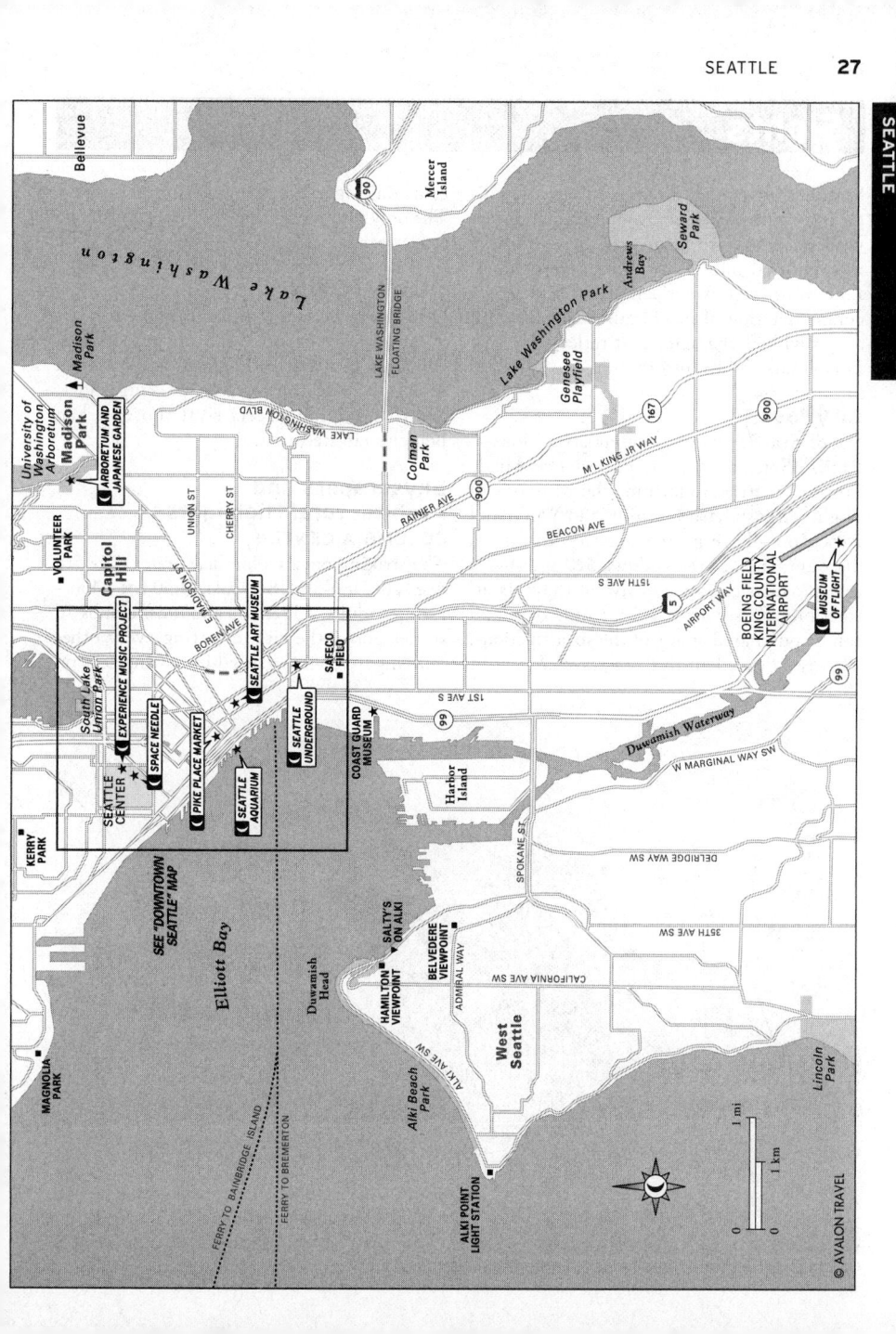
Bellevue
Lake Washington
Mercer Island
Seward Park
Andrews Bay
Lake Washington Park
Genesee Playfield
Madison Park
University of Washington Arboretum
Madison Park
ARBORETUM AND JAPANESE GARDEN
LAKE WASHINGTON FLOATING BRIDGE
LAKE WASHINGTON BLVD
Colman Park
M L KING JR WAY
RAINIER AVE
BEACON AVE
15TH AVE S
AIRPORT WAY
BOEING FIELD KING COUNTY INTERNATIONAL AIRPORT
MUSEUM OF FLIGHT
VOLUNTEER PARK
Capitol Hill
UNION ST
CHERRY ST
E MADISON ST
BOREN AVE
SEATTLE ART MUSEUM
SAFECO FIELD
South Lake Union Park
EXPERIENCE MUSIC PROJECT
SEATTLE CENTER
SPACE NEEDLE
PIKE PLACE MARKET
SEATTLE AQUARIUM
SEATTLE UNDERGROUND
1ST AVE S
COAST GUARD MUSEUM
Duwamish Waterway
W MARGINAL WAY SW
Harbor Island
SPOKANE ST
DELRIDGE WAY SW
KERRY PARK
SEE "DOWNTOWN SEATTLE" MAP
Elliott Bay
SALTY'S ON ALKI
BELVEDERE VIEWPOINT
ADMIRAL WAY
CALIFORNIA AVE SW
37TH AVE SW
HAMILTON VIEWPOINT
Duwamish Head
West Seattle
ALKI AVE SW
Alki Beach Park
Lincoln Park
MAGNOLIA PARK
FERRY TO BAINBRIDGE ISLAND
FERRY TO BREMERTON
ALKI POINT LIGHT STATION
0 1 mi
0 1 km
© AVALON TRAVEL

Sights

Seattle is big enough to keep an intrepid visitor busy with weeks of explorations, and even residents who have spent years here still have not ventured into all its nooks and crannies. Like most large American cities, Seattle is a conglomeration of neighborhoods, each with an individual character that reflects both its inhabitants and its history.

CityPass

Six of Seattle's most popular attractions—Pacific Science Center, Experience Music Project, Seattle Aquarium, the Museum of Flight, Argosy harbor cruise, and Woodland Park Zoo—have gotten together to offer a discount CityPass ($44 adults, $29 ages 4–12) that provides entrance to five of these six attractions. Passes are valid for nine days and can be purchased at any of the six attractions. This is an excellent deal for travelers, and it beats waiting in lines for tickets at each venue. The only bummer is that the Space Needle no longer participates.

DOWNTOWN

Downtown Seattle is a busy, almost frenetic place, with the expected mix of stuffed shirts, confused tourists, and pierced-and-tattooed hipsters. Pack comfortable walking shoes. Seattle's sloping streets rival those of San Francisco in steepness.

Skyscrapers and Architectural Highlights

COLUMBIA CENTER

The striking onyx Columbia Center (701 5th Ave., 206/386-5151, 8:30 A.M.–4:30 P.M. Mon.–Fri., $5 adults, $3 seniors and kids) climbs 76 stories above the city, dwarfing every other building in town. A glassed-in viewing deck on

© ERICKA CHICKOWSKI

Outdoor art abounds in city parks and public spaces.

the 73rd floor provides a panorama of the entire region. Ask at the information desk in the lobby for access. With a view like this, it's hard to imagine a better locale to watch the traffic.

SMITH TOWER

The 42-story Smith Tower (Yesler Way and 2nd Ave., 206/622-4004, www.smithtower.com) was the tallest building west of the Mississippi when completed in 1914, and it remained Seattle's highest for several decades. Now dwarfed by neighboring skyscrapers, it is still an interesting place, with elevator rides—run by some of the last elevator operators on the West Coast—to a 35th-floor outdoor observation deck (10 A.M.–sunset daily Apr.–Aug., 10 A.M.–7 P.M. daily Sept., 10 A.M.–5 P.M. daily Oct., 10 A.M.–4 P.M. Sat.–Sun. Nov.–Mar., $7.50 adults, $6 seniors and students, $5 kids). Also on this floor is the ornately furnished Chinese Room, a popular place for meetings and wedding receptions.

OTHER BUILDINGS

Another attention-grabbing skyscraper is the **Rainier Tower** (4th Ave. and University St.), a unique edifice that seems to balance on the tip of an upside-down pyramid. The **Washington Mutual Tower** (3rd and Seneca) is perhaps best known as the home of a pair of nesting peregrine falcons, while the **US Bank Centre** (5th Avenue and Union St.) contains a marvelous collection of colorful glass art, including a 12-foot-high piece by Dale Chihuly.

Another local landmark is the tall Venetian-style clock tower of Amtrak's **King Street Station** at the intersection of S. King Street and 3rd Avenue South.

Freeway Park

At 6th Avenue and Seneca *over* I-5, the aptly named Freeway Park is a solution to the blight of a freeway roaring through the heart of a city. Located just outside of the Washington State Convention Center, the park was built on a lid over part of that freeway and has greenery, waterfalls, fountains, and free summertime lunch concerts.

TOTEM THIEVES

When you walk around Pioneer Square, be sure to take a gander at the towering **Tlingit totem** in the middle of it all. This is a replica of a pole destroyed by an arsonist in 1938. The original pole was stolen on a fateful night in 1890 from Southeast Alaska's Tongass Island by a group of Seattle's leaders who believed the village deserted. Legend holds that after the original was burned, the city sent a check for $5,000 to carve a new one; the Tlingits cashed the check, and then sent a note saying, "Thanks for finally paying for the first one. A new pole will cost another $5,000."

Pioneer Square

Pioneer Square offers a striking clash of cultures. High-end art galleries, Oriental-carpet stores, and sidewalk cafés are nestled between corner missions; executives in tailored suits and young couples out for a night on the town pass Occidental Park's homeless residents.

Pioneer Square is the oldest section of Seattle, although the center of activity has long since migrated north a half mile or so. After the great fire of 1889, the area was rebuilt in magnificent brick buildings, many of which are still standing.

In spite of frequent complaints about the aggressiveness of the panhandlers and drunks who reside in nearby flophouses and missions (or on the street), the 20-block restored historical district along 1st Avenue, Yesler Way, and S. Main Street, south of downtown, is also home to upscale boutique hotels, fine restaurants, galleries, and a busy nightlife.

The center of Pioneer Square activity—for better and worse—is at **Occidental Square Park** (Occidental Ave. S and S. Main St.), a cobblestone space with several totem poles and park benches shared by tourists waiting for the Underground Tour, suited people noshing on lunch, cooing pigeons, and a rotating crew of street musicians and homeless folk.

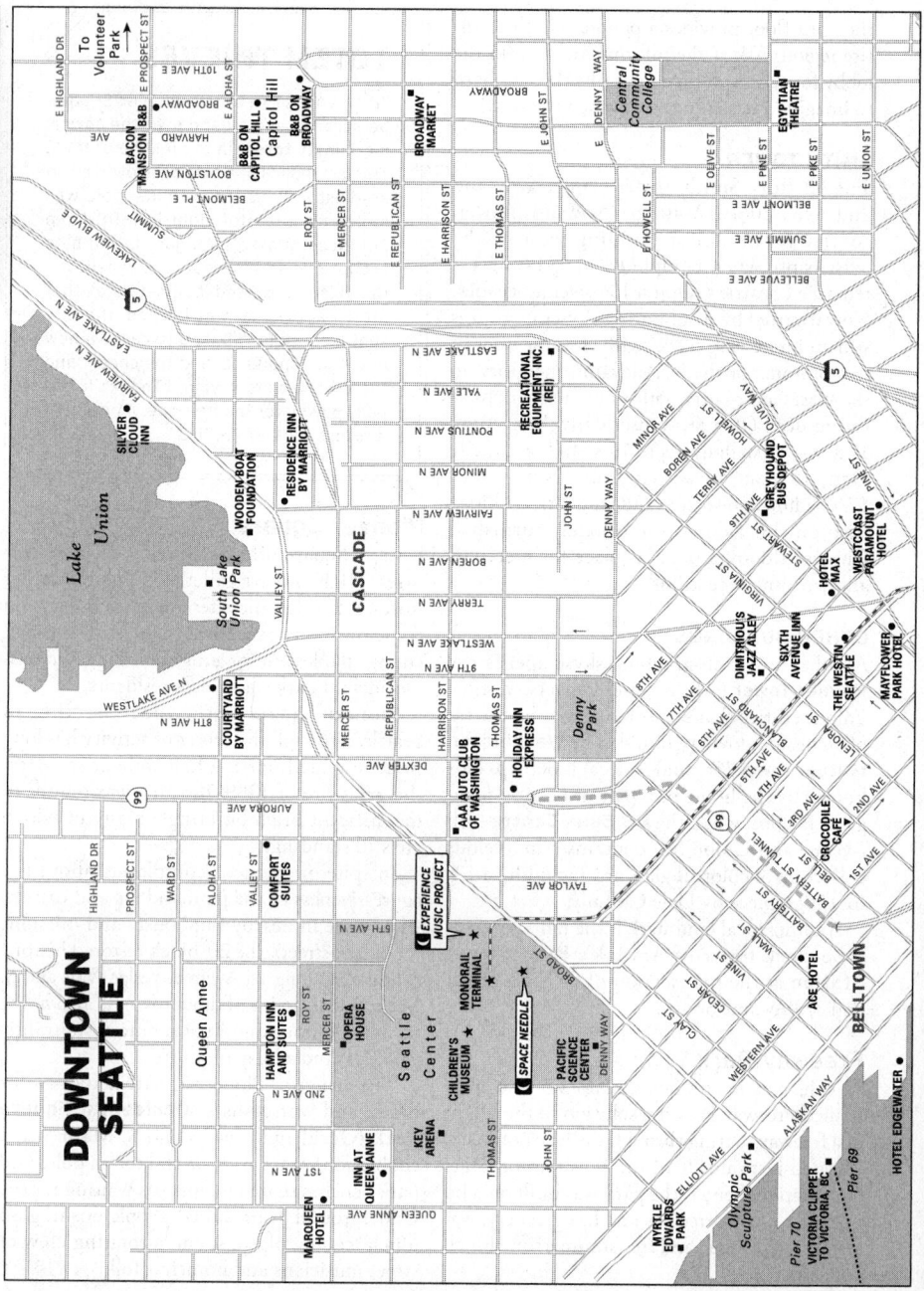
DOWNTOWN SEATTLE
Lake Union
South Lake Union Park
Queen Anne
Seattle Center
CASCADE
Denny Park
BELLTOWN
Olympic Sculpture Park
Pier 70
Pier 69
To Volunteer Park
Capitol Hill
Central Community College
SILVER CLOUD INN
WOODEN BOAT FOUNDATION
RESIDENCE INN BY MARRIOTT
COURTYARD BY MARRIOTT
COMFORT SUITES
HAMPTON INN AND SUITES
INN AT QUEEN ANNE
MARQUEEN HOTEL
OPERA HOUSE
KEY ARENA
CHILDREN'S MUSEUM
MONORAIL TERMINAL
EXPERIENCE MUSIC PROJECT
SPACE NEEDLE
PACIFIC SCIENCE CENTER
AAA AUTO CLUB OF WASHINGTON
HOLIDAY INN EXPRESS
RECREATIONAL EQUIPMENT INC. (REI)
BACON MANSION B&B
B&B ON CAPITOL HILL
B&B ON BROADWAY
BROADWAY MARKET
EGYPTIAN THEATRE
GREYHOUND BUS DEPOT
HOTEL MAX
WESTCOAST PARAMOUNT HOTEL
SIXTH AVENUE INN
THE WESTIN SEATTLE
MAYFLOWER PARK HOTEL
DIMITRIOU'S JAZZ ALLEY
CROCODILE CAFE
ACE HOTEL
HOTEL EDGEWATER
MYRTLE EDWARDS PARK
VICTORIA CLIPPER TO VICTORIA, BC
HIGHLAND DR
PROSPECT ST
WARD ST
ALOHA ST
VALLEY ST
AURORA AVE
ROY ST
MERCER ST
2ND AVE N
1ST AVE N
QUEEN ANNE AVE
THOMAS ST
JOHN ST
DENNY WAY
TAYLOR AVE
BROAD ST
5TH AVE N
8TH AVE N
WESTLAKE AVE N
REPUBLICAN ST
HARRISON ST
DEXTER AVE
9TH AVE N
WESTLAKE AVE N
TERRY AVE N
BOREN AVE N
FAIRVIEW AVE N
MINOR AVE N
PONTIUS AVE N
VALE AVE N
EASTLAKE AVE N
LAKEVIEW BLVD E
EASTLAKE AVE N
FAIRVIEW AVE N
SUMMIT
10TH AVE E
E HIGHLAND DR
E PROSPECT ST
E ALOHA ST
BROADWAY
HARVARD AVE
BOYLSTON AVE
BELMONT PL E
E ROY ST
E MERCER ST
E REPUBLICAN ST
E HARRISON ST
E THOMAS ST
BROADWAY
E JOHN ST
E DENNY WAY
E HOWELL ST
E OLIVE ST
E PINE ST
E PIKE ST
E UNION ST
BELMONT AVE E
SUMMIT AVE E
BELLEVUE AVE E
MINOR AVE
BOREN AVE
TERRY AVE
9TH AVE
HOWELL ST
OLIVE WAY
STEWART ST
VIRGINIA ST
PINE ST
6TH AVE
7TH AVE
6TH AVE
5TH AVE
4TH AVE
3RD AVE
2ND AVE
1ST AVE
BLANCHARD ST
LENORA ST
BELL ST
BATTERY ST TUNNEL
BATTERY ST
WALL ST
VINE ST
CEDAR ST
CLAY ST
WESTERN AVE
ALASKAN WAY
ELLIOTT AVE
5
99

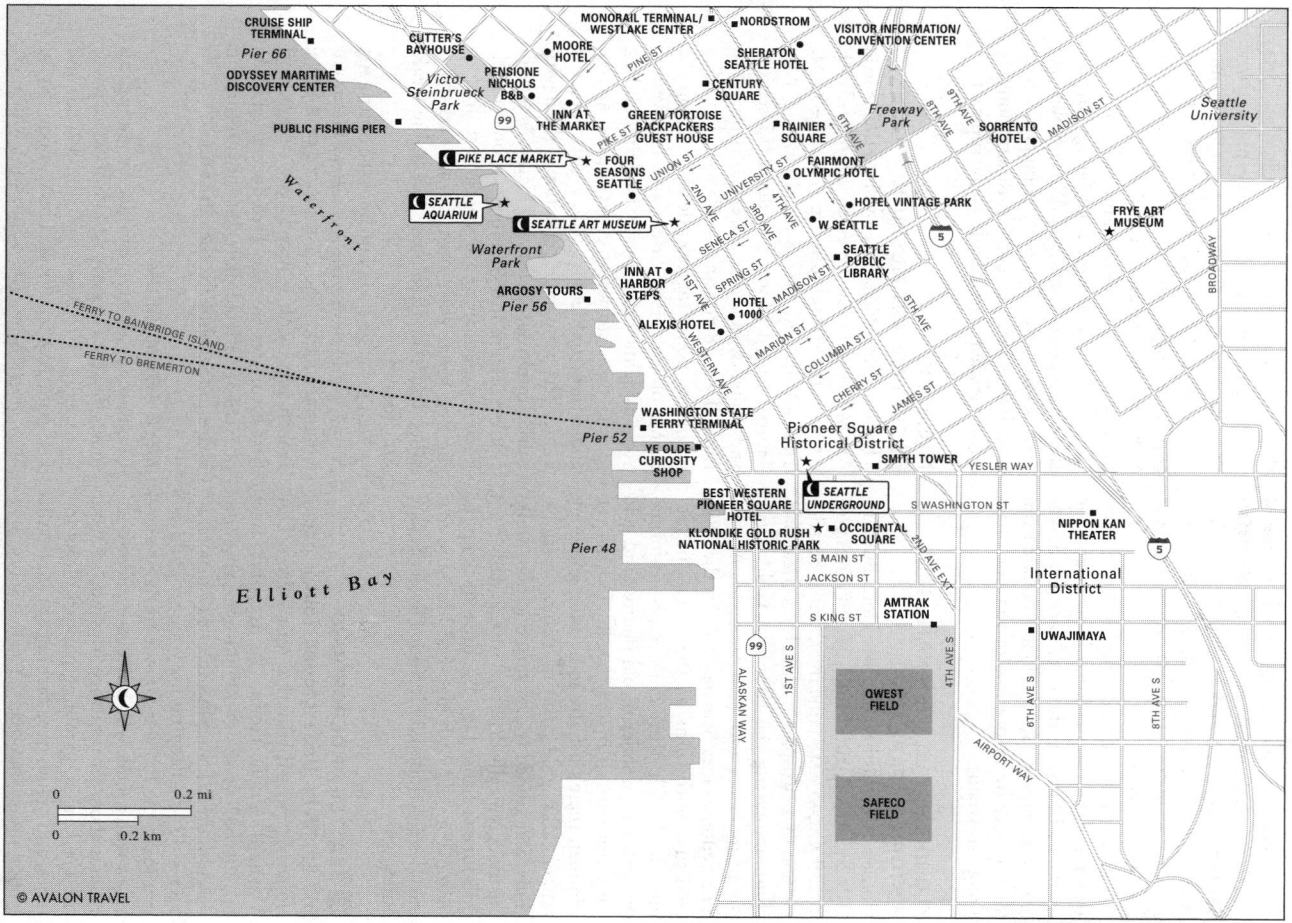
CRUISE SHIP TERMINAL
Pier 66
ODYSSEY MARITIME DISCOVERY CENTER
PUBLIC FISHING PIER
CUTTER'S BAYHOUSE
MOORE HOTEL
PENSIONE NICHOLS B&B
Victor Steinbrueck Park
MONORAIL TERMINAL/ WESTLAKE CENTER
NORDSTROM
VISITOR INFORMATION/ CONVENTION CENTER
SHERATON SEATTLE HOTEL
CENTURY SQUARE
INN AT THE MARKET
GREEN TORTOISE BACKPACKERS GUEST HOUSE
RAINIER SQUARE
Freeway Park
SORRENTO HOTEL
Seattle University
PIKE PLACE MARKET
FOUR SEASONS SEATTLE
FAIRMONT OLYMPIC HOTEL
HOTEL VINTAGE PARK
SEATTLE AQUARIUM
SEATTLE ART MUSEUM
W SEATTLE
FRYE ART MUSEUM
Waterfront
Waterfront Park
SEATTLE PUBLIC LIBRARY
INN AT HARBOR STEPS
ARGOSY TOURS
Pier 56
HOTEL 1000
ALEXIS HOTEL
FERRY TO BAINBRIDGE ISLAND
FERRY TO BREMERTON
WASHINGTON STATE FERRY TERMINAL
Pier 52
YE OLDE CURIOSITY SHOP
Pioneer Square Historical District
SMITH TOWER
YESLER WAY
BEST WESTERN PIONEER SQUARE HOTEL
SEATTLE UNDERGROUND
S WASHINGTON ST
NIPPON KAN THEATER
KLONDIKE GOLD RUSH NATIONAL HISTORIC PARK
OCCIDENTAL SQUARE
Pier 48
S MAIN ST
JACKSON ST
International District
Elliott Bay
AMTRAK STATION
S KING ST
UWAJIMAYA
QWEST FIELD
SAFECO FIELD
AIRPORT WAY
PINE ST
PIKE ST
UNION ST
UNIVERSITY ST
SENECA ST
SPRING ST
MADISON ST
MARION ST
COLUMBIA ST
CHERRY ST
JAMES ST
2ND AVE EXT
1ST AVE
2ND AVE
3RD AVE
4TH AVE
5TH AVE
6TH AVE
7TH AVE
8TH AVE
WESTERN AVE
ALASKAN WAY
1ST AVE S
4TH AVE S
6TH AVE S
8TH AVE S
BROADWAY
99
5
0
0.2 mi
0
0.2 km
© AVALON TRAVEL

The neighborhood is also home to one of Seattle's most tranquil urban parks, **Waterfall Garden** (2nd Ave. S and S. Main St.). Tucked away between several buildings, visitors find a secret cascade of water that provides a break from the street noise.

The southern edge of the Pioneer Square area abuts the International District and the sports stadiums; to the north are the downtown skyscrapers. Get to Pioneer Square from town center by riding one of the free buses along 1st Avenue.

KLONDIKE GOLD RUSH NATIONAL HISTORICAL PARK

Housed in the historic Cadillac Hotel Building (319 2nd Ave. S, 206/553-7220, www.nps.gov/klse, 9 A.M.–5 P.M. daily, free), this is Seattle's portion of a two-part national historical park commemorating the Klondike Gold Rush; the primary section is in Skagway, Alaska. The center traces Seattle's role in the 1897 gold rush with films on the event—including Charlie Chaplin's *Gold Rush*—informative exhibits, wonderful old photos, and gold rush and natural history books. During the summer, there's usually something going on: ranger talks, gold-panning demonstrations, films, and guided walks. Free one-hour walking tours typically depart at 10 A.M. daily from mid-June to Labor Day. Be sure to pick up the interesting gold rush map and brochure that includes descriptions of historic Pioneer Square buildings.

SEATTLE UNDERGROUND

Bill Speidel's Underground Tour is one of the city's most distinctive tours. From Doc Maynard's Public House (1st Ave. and James St., 206/682-4646 or 888/608-6337, www.undergroundtour.com, $15 adults, $12 seniors, $7 ages 7–12, challenging for younger children) you roam the Pioneer Square area above and below with a guide who provides humorous anecdotes about local history. You'll learn about the speakeasies, gambling parlors, illegal lotteries, and opium dens that once occupied this section under the streets. You'll also hear how the city's tidewater location created all sorts of problems for early residents—particularly those who tried to flush toilets on an incoming tide—and how the "seamstress tax" was applied to single women working out of the Sweet Home Boarding House in the red-light district. The tour ends shamelessly in a museum/gift shop where you're encouraged to purchase such practical items as deluxe rubber rats and cockroaches. These very popular 1.5-hour tours leave several times daily. Reservations are recommended, particularly in the summer.

Museums

SEATTLE ART MUSEUM

The first thing you see in a visit to the Seattle Art Museum (1300 1st Ave., 206/654-3100, www.seattleartmuseum.org, 10 A.M.–5 P.M. Tues.–Wed. and Fri.–Sun., 10 A.M.–9 P.M. Thurs., closed Mon., $7 adults, $5 seniors and students, free kids under 12) is Jonathan Borofsky's 48-foot-high *Hammering Man* sculpture, pounding relentlessly away on the corner of University Street and 1st Avenue. Step inside the dramatically modern building to find three stories of gallery space, a large auditorium and lecture hall, a gift shop, and a café. The permanent collection is filled with works from Asia, Africa, and Native American cultures. You're also guaranteed a look at well-known American and European art, including one room with avant-garde works that range from the frivolously fun to the freakishly foolish.

Your ticket gets you into both the Seattle Art Museum and the Seattle Asian Art Museum in Volunteer Park. The first Thursday of every month admission is just $3 per person, and first Saturdays are free. Free docent-led tours of SAM are offered daily; see the information board in the lobby for the next tour.

FRYE ART MUSEUM

Connoisseurs are well rewarded by visiting this museum (704 Terry Ave., 206/622-9250, www.fryeart.org, 10 A.M.–5 P.M. Tues.–Wed. and Fri.–Sat., 10 A.M.–8 P.M. Thurs., noon–5 P.M. Sun., closed Mon., free admission), which features significant 19th-century German artists from the Munich School. Interestingly, the emphasis on these works came by happenstance—the founding collection and museum itself was endowed by Charles and Emma Frye, who made some of their millions selling lard to the Germans after World War I and taking oil paintings as partial payment. Today, this collection of melodramatic oils in gilded frames may well be a relief to traditionalists weary of the contemporary conceptual art scene. Among the museum's well-regarded collection is Alexander Max Koester's *Ducks.* Other galleries at the recently expanded Frye contain changing exhibits, and a café offers light meals.

SEATTLE POLICE MUSEUM

You may want to also take a peek into the Seattle Police Museum (317 3rd Ave. S, 206/748-9991, 11 A.M.–4 P.M. Tues.–Sat., $3 adults, $1 kids). It's the largest police museum in the western states, with badges, uniforms, antique firearms, and other artifacts from as far back as the 1860s.

THE MARKET AND WATERFRONT

Pike Place Market

The Space Needle might be Seattle's iconographic symbol, but Pike Place Market (www.pikeplacemarket.org, 9 A.M.–6 P.M. Mon.–Sat., 11 A.M.–5 P.M. Sun.) is—as more than one writer has called it—the true heart and soul of Seattle, a sensory and social statement of why the city is such a livable place. Mingle with the locals here to buy the freshest fish and produce in town, listen to colorful street musicians, enjoy the parade of humanity, and explore a myriad of shops. It's hard not to love it.

Initial appearances can be deceiving in Pike Place Market. It's much larger than you might think, spreading over three levels in the Main Arcade, and up several blocks to include half a dozen other large buildings, each filled with additional shops. All told, the market contains more than 250 businesses covering nine acres. Early risers have the advantage; things are pretty slow early in the morning, giving you more time to explore without having to fight your way through the crowds.

The main focal point is beneath the famous "Public Market Center" neon sign. Enter here to meet **Rachel,** the fat bronze charity piggy bank that has been here since 1986.

Follow the throngs of tourists to **Pike Place Fish** (www.pikeplacefish.com), right behind Rachel. You can't miss the famous flying fish (watch your head!), the raucous repartee, and the clowning around. It helps to be part showman to work here. Despite a competitor's complaint that "I can't see how throwing fish makes them taste any better," everything here is fresh.

INFORMATION AND SERVICES

For a market map and newsletter, head to the tiny **Pike Place Information Booth** (10 A.M.–6 P.M. daily) near the market entrance on the corner of Pike Street and 1st Avenue; you can also purchase half-price tickets here for concerts and plays on the day of the show.

In-depth **Pike Place Market Heritage Tours** (206/682-7453, www.pikelplacemarket.org, $10 adults, $5 seniors and kids) are offered Wednesday–Sunday. These three-hour traipses blend history with quirky anecdotes, led by knowledgeable insiders.

GETTING THERE

It's nearly impossible to drive up Pike Place Street with lunch-hour pedestrians overflowing the sidewalks, and parking spaces are harder to find than a conservative Seattleite. Your best bet is to take the bus around town—it's free throughout downtown Seattle—but you can always find parking in the Market Parking Garage downhill from Pike Place. Get your ticket validated at market merchants.

Along the Waterfront

Generally a sightseer's first waterfront stop, Elliott Bay's Piers 48–70 represent the main waterfront: fish-and-chip eateries, gift shops, museums, the aquarium, and harbor-tour departure points. Washington State Ferries

(206/464-6400, 888/808-7977, or 800/843-3779 for automated info, www.wsdot.wa.gov/ferries) depart Pier 52 for Bainbridge Island and Bremerton across the sound.

Ye Olde Curiosity Shop (206/682-5844, www.yeoldecuriosityshop.com), a combination museum/gift shop on Pier 54, specializes in the bizarre: shrunken heads and the mummified body of "Sylvester," a two-headed calf, plus inane souvenirs and tacky curios. Nearby is **Exclusively Washington,** 206/624-2600, a small shop filled with collectibles, books, and other Washington items.

Next door at Pier 57 is **Bay Pavilion,** with touristy restaurants, an indoor carousel ($1) popular with young children, and a plethora of video games for the older ones. Public fishing is allowed at **Waterfront Park** on Pier 57, but I wouldn't eat fish from such polluted water.

In the summer, the historic tugboat *Arthur Foss* ties up at nearby Pier 69. Continue north to the outdoor creations of **Olympic Sculpture Park** (Alaskan Way and Broad St.), an outdoor public area hosted by the Seattle Art Museum. Just beyond the sculptures lies **Myrtle Edwards Park** (Alaskan Way and Broad St.), where a one-mile path follows the bay to Grain Terminal.

SEATTLE AQUARIUM

A visit to Pier 59's Seattle Aquarium (206/386-4320, www.seattleaquarium.org, 9:30 A.M.–5 P.M. daily, open limited hours Thanksgiving, Christmas Eve, Christmas, and New Year's Day, $15 adults, $10 ages 4–12, free ages 3 and under) will give you an appreciation for the incredible diversity of sealife swimming right below your feet. The traditional part of the aquarium leads you past a "touch tank" filled with various tidepool creatures, and aquariums containing everything from an octopus to an electric eel. Displays tell about the creatures and how humans are affecting their survival. A tropical coral reef exhibit makes you want to hop on a plane for Fiji. The real treat is outside, where you'll find large tanks containing harbor seals, sea otters, and northern fur seals, along with a salmon ladder and hatchery. Check the board for the next feeding time for the sea mammals and diving birds. Ducks and shorebirds occupy another noisy section, but the star feature is an underwater dome where you sit surrounded by fish from the Sound. It's as if the tables have been turned and the humans are in a giant fishbowl looking outward at salmon, skates, halibut, rockfish, and other creatures. The last entrance ticket is sold an hour before closing time.

MUSEUMS

On the south end of the waterfront, Pier 36 hosts the **Coast Guard Museum** (206/217-6993, 9 A.M.–3 P.M. Mon., Wed., and Fri. and 1–5 P.M. Sat.–Sun., free) with nautical artifacts, models of Coast Guard cutters, historic photographs, and a 15-minute slide show. The Coast Guard has three 400-foot icebreakers and two 378-foot cutters that are homeported at Pier 36.

Odyssey, the Maritime Discovery Center (206/374-4000, www.ody.org, 10 A.M.–9 P.M. Sun.–Wed., 10 A.M.–5 P.M. Thurs.–Sat., $7 for adults, $5 for students and seniors, free kids under 5) at Pier 66, houses fun and educational exhibits in a large and little-visited space. Try your hand at loading containers onto a ship, paddle a kayak through a virtual bay, listen to vessel radio traffic from Elliott Bay, learn how fish are caught and processed in Alaska, explore the lives of sea creatures, and learn how ships move through the water.

PARKING

Park your car under the Alaskan Way Viaduct and try for a metered space; as a last resort, pay the exorbitant fees at parking lots. The meters cost a minimum of $1 an hour, which is cause enough to leave your car at a suburban park-and-ride. You can also find a lot on the north end at Myrtle Edwards Park.

INTERNATIONAL DISTRICT

This part of Seattle has long been home to people from all over Asia, including those of Japanese, Korean, Chinese, Filipino, and Vietnamese ancestry. The International

District is easy to reach; just catch one of the free buses and ride through the tunnel to the International District bus tunnel station, where outsized origami pieces decorate the walls.

All roads lead to **Hing Hay Park,** a small city park with a colorful pagoda-style Chinese pavilion donated by the city of Taipei. Watch out for the hundreds of pigeons that get fed here and coat the pavilion with their droppings.

The **Wing Luke Asian Museum** (719 South King St., 206/623-5124, www.wingluke.org, 10 A.M.–5 P.M. Tues.–Sun., $8 adults, $6 seniors and students, $5 ages 5–12) has artifacts from early Asian businesses, memorabilia of all types, hand-painted kites, a 35-foot Chinese dragon, plus many historic photos. The museum also displays changing exhibits of Asian art and history. Admission is free on the first Thursday and third Saturday of the month.

King Street is the heart of the district, with Chinese shops lining both sides. The International District lacks the crowded intensity of San Francisco's Chinatown, but the streets are bordered with hole-in-the-wall restaurants, shops selling imported goods, and Asian grocers (some of the biggest are up the hill near the corner of S. Jackson Street and 12th Avenue). You can easily find a filling lunch for $8. **Kobe Terrace Park,** a community garden, follows the hillside above the International District; it is capped by a concrete lantern given to Seattle by its sister city of Kobe, Japan.

Chinese-American Vi Mar leads interesting **Chinatown Discovery Tours** (425/885-3085, www.seattlechinatowntour.com) of the International District. A variety of walking tours are offered, including one with lunch at a dim sum restaurant.

SEATTLE CENTER AND BELLTOWN

Seattle Center (206/684-7200, www.seattlecenter.com), sandwiched between Belltown to the south and the Queen Anne neighborhood to the north, is an odd mishmash of attractions designed with the *Jetsons*-style architecture of the early 1960s. Although it attracts many adults, this legacy of the 1962 World's Fair is also a favorite of children.

Seattle Center is in the first stages of a decades-long redevelopment project, so the rickety amusement park rides that surround the Center House and the Space Needle are no longer lit up. Visitors will see these rides dismantled in favor of more green spaces, as well as a splash pool and ice rink as construction moves on in the coming years.

THE DENNY REGRADE

One of the prominent features of Seattle is its steep hills, which make walking and driving difficult. Many schemes have been hatched to eliminate them, but only one ever came to fruition: the Denny Regrade project. Beginning in 1902, the city engineer directed high-pressure hoses that pumped water from Lake Union onto the steep slopes of Denny Hill in an area now called Belltown, washing the soil into Elliott Bay and creating the waterfront of today. It took eight years to complete the project, but this is now one of the few relatively level parts of this otherwise hilly city.

Seattle Monorail

The best way to venture into this space-age world is aboard the kitschy **Monorail** (206/441-6038, www.seattlemonorail.com, 9 A.M.–11 P.M. daily, $2 each way), the elevated train that connects trendy Westlake Center at 5th and Pine with passé Seattle Center. This strange contraption was considered a model for transportation in its day but never really caught on. The 90-second ride departs every 15 minutes.

Space Needle

The Space Needle (400 Broad St., 206/443-2111 or 800/937-9582, www.spaceneedle.com, 9 A.M.11 P.M. Sun.–Thurs., 9 A.M.–midnight Fri.–Sat., $16 adults, $14 for seniors, $8 for

© ERICKA CHICKOWSKI

Seattle skyline from Pike Street

ages 4–113, free for younger kids) is one of Seattle's trademarks, a 605-foot tower topped by a flying saucer viewing deck and restaurant. Elevators levitate you to the top, where you can walk out on the observation deck for a 360-degree view of downtown Seattle, of planes flying by, and of the Cascades, Mt. Rainier, and the Olympics on a clear day. On a rainy day you may be able to make out downtown. Detailed signboards describe the buildings and other surrounding features.

The Space Needle is privately owned and highly commercialized, but the spectacular view makes you forget the make-a-buck setting. If you have restaurant reservations, the ride is free.

Pacific Science Center

The Pacific Science Center (206/443-2001 or 866/414-1912, www.pacsci.org, 10 A.M.–6 P.M. daily mid-June through Labor Day, 10 A.M.–5 P.M. Mon.–Fri., 10 A.M.–6 P.M. Sat.–Sun. the rest of the year, $15 adults, $13.50 seniors, $12 ages 6–12, $10 kids 3–5, free under age 3) began as the U.S. Science Pavilion at the 1962 World's Fair and is showing its age a bit gracelessly. The dated architecture stands in marked contrast to the glitzy, high-tech Experience Music Project just a short walk away. Despite this, the Science Center is a wonderful place to take kids for a day of learning and fun. Distinctive white concrete arches rise over pools and fountains at this hugely popular family museum that attracts almost two million visitors annually. The five buildings are filled with hands-on exhibits: virtual reality voyages, a planetarium, a menagerie of mechanized Mesozoic dinosaurs, a tropical butterfly house, a colony of naked mole rats, plus fun and educational exhibits of all types. The fountains outside are filled with water toys that blast jets of water at all sorts of objects; there's even a spinning two-ton granite ball. Look for the high-rail bike demonstrations most days. Two big IMAX screens here create unforgettably dramatic first-run movies; one even shows high-tech 3-D IMAX films. Since the IMAX Dome closed down in 2005, this has been the only mega-screen option in town. The Science Center also has a changing series of exhibits and special events, including a popular (and decidedly low-tech) **Model Railroad Show** on Thanksgiving weekend and the kids'-favorite **Bubble Festival** in mid-August.

Admission to the Pacific Science Center includes IMAX films. It is closed on Thanksgiving and Christmas. If you don't want to wait in long lines for the featured attractions, try to come Sunday morning or Monday through Wednesday afternoons, when things tend to be quieter.

EMP RADIO

Experience Music Project even has its own radio station. **KEXP** (FM 90.3, www.kexp.org) is a great local radio station with an amazing mix of music and no ads. Although owned by the University of Washington, it is connected to the EMP.

Experience Music Project

With a wildly curvy exterior of multicolored aluminum—said to mimic the shape of an electric guitar—it's pretty hard to miss this outlandish building plunked on the edge of Seattle Center (5th Ave. and Harrison St., 206/367-5483 or 877/367-5483, www.empsfm.org, $15 adults, $12 for seniors, military, and kids, free under age 4). Experience Music Project (EMP) is the brainchild of Microsoft billionaire Paul Allen, whose fascination with Seattle-born Jimi Hendrix led him to bankroll much of this 140,000-square-foot homage to rock. The museum opened in 2000 and was an immediate hit, though many folks still complain about its bizarre exterior.

Inside EMP, visitors are treated to an amazing array of displays and interactive exhibits on musicians and their music. The first level contains Sky Church, which boasts the world's largest indoor video screen; it's used for musical performances on Friday and Saturday nights. The Hendrix Gallery is another centerpiece, with the Fender Stratocaster that Hendrix used to play "The Star-Spangled Banner" at Woodstock and other artifacts. Other attractions include an on-stage section where kids can pretend they're rock stars ($10 including a poster of them in performance), a sound lab where you can join others in loud and fun musical attempts, plus exhibits describing punk, grunge, hip-hop, reggae, and other variations on the theme. One of the most popular EMP features is Artist's Journey, a multimedia ride with a dumb plot and Hollywood special effects. Also at EMP are educational collections that encompass oral histories (from Ann and Nancy Wilson to Dr. Dré), Kurt Cobain's handwritten song lyrics, Paul Revere and the Raiders' stage uniforms and instruments, Elvis Presley's black leather jacket, a pink feather boa worn by Janis Joplin, and lots of other obscure memorabilia. A gift shop, restaurant, lounge (great mixed drinks), and movie theater are here as well.

Since first opening, EMP made room for SFM—the Science Fiction Museum and Hall of Fame, which shares the building with a collection of memorabilia that even music geeks see as a little nerdy. But Sci-Fi enthusiasts will love it for its assortment of props and costumes from the sets of famous shows and movies such as *Star Trek, Planet of the Apes,* and *Blade Runner,* as well as the interpretive exhibits that explore the origins of sci-fi and examine the innate human desire to explain the unknown and prognosticate the future. The hours are the same as EMP and admission gets you into both.

The last ticket is sold 90 minutes prior to closing. Museum visitors are each given an electronic Museum Exhibit Guide to carry around, with complete details on virtually everything you'll see. Many folks find these annoying after a short time and turn them off, but rock enthusiasts will discover 16 hours worth of information on these gizmos.

Center House

The Center House started life as an armory but was reborn as a shopping and food mall for the 1962 World's Fair. Today, the interior is lined on two levels with 18 different fast-food eateries. A three-ton slab of the **Berlin Wall** stands inside Center House, a gift from a German businessman in 1991.

Downstairs in Center House is the delightful **Seattle Children's Museum** (305 Harrison St., 206/441-1768, www.thechildrensmuseum.org, 10 A.M.–5 P.M. Mon.–Fri. and 10 A.M.–6 P.M. Sat.–Sun., $5.50 for anyone over age 1), filled with wacky and fun exhibits that manage to educate children. Each year, more than 200,000 kids drag their parents through the 32,000 square feet of play space. The exhibits change all the time, but there's always something fun to do here, including hands-on workshops. Kids love this place—the average stay is three hours (try getting any child to do anything for three hours!). The gift shop sells educational toys. Adults must accompany children under 12.

Other Sights

The deceptively simple **International Fountain** (6–11 P.M. Mon.–Fri. and 2–11 P.M. Sat.–Sun.) never ceases to delight kids trying to escape the random jets of water and amuse adults when the inevitable happens. The fountain erupts in an on-the-hour frenzy of action complete with music pumped through loudspeakers.

Seattle Center also houses the **Bagley Wright Theater,** where the Seattle Repertory Theater performs, and the **Opera House,** home of the Seattle Opera, Seattle Youth Symphony, and Pacific Northwest Ballet.

LAKE UNION AND VICINITY

Lake Union is a natural lake that was transformed early in this century when canals were dug linking Lake Washington, Lake Union, and Puget Sound. The Chittenden Locks provide boat access from Puget Sound into Lake Union. For many years, Lake Union was treated mostly as an industrial area that floated.

Today Lake Union is an urban neighborhood transformed. The old gas plant has become Gasworks Park, one of the most imaginative parks in America. Most of the debris has been removed from the lakeshore, and where once you saw only greasy clutter you now see people—lots of people.

The southern end is now primarily a mix of restaurants, historical boats, kayak rentals, expensive yachts for sale, and seaplane rides, all connected by a shoreline boardwalk. With the city's acquisition of South Lake Union Park from the Navy, Steve Allen supplying millions in real estate investment dollars, and a new trolley from downtown to the area chugging along, South Lake Union has emerged as one of Seattle's hottest neighborhoods on the rise. Learn about it at the **South Lake Union Discovery Center** (101 Westlake Avenue N., 11 A.M.–6 P.M. daily), which has a pretty cool scale model of Lake Union for folks who dig that kind of thing.

South Lake Union Park

Picked up by the city from the Navy in 2000, South Lake Union Park (860 Terry Ave. N) has turned out to be one of Seattle's prettiest waterfront spot, with plenty of grassy areas to loll about and watch kayakers paddle, motorboats putt-putt along, and seaplanes swoop over Lake Union.

Maritime History

Run by volunteers, the **Center for Wooden Boats** (1010 Valley St., 206/382-2628, www.cwb.org, 10 A.M.–5 P.M. Tues.–Sun. Nov.–mid-Mar., 10 A.M.–6 P.M. daily mid-Mar.–mid-May and Sept.–Nov., 10 A.M.–8 P.M. daily mid-May–Aug., free) restores and maintains a fleet of historic rowboats and sailboats. Take a class here to learn about wooden boat building, or rent one of its boats to sail or row around the lake for an afternoon. Right next door is the small **Maritime Heritage Center** (206/447-9800, www.nwseaport.org) with vintage wooden boats and programs detailing maritime restoration.

Chandler's Cove houses the small and free **Puget Sound Maritime Museum** (901 Fairview Ave. N, 206/938-2397, www.puget-maritime.org, 11 A.M.–7 P.M. Mon.–Sat. and noon–5 P.M. Sun.), with historic maritime photos and ship models on display.

Gasworks Park

Built on the site of a former gas plant, Gasworks Park (N. Northlake Way and Meridian Ave. N) is the world's only industrial site conversion park. Much of the original rusting gas equipment was incorporated into the park's landscaping, including a play barn that kids (and the homeless) love. Enjoy the views of Seattle and Lake Union from the industrial equipment and fly a kite from the hills here. The paved and very popular **Burke-Gilman Trail** begins west of Gasworks, skirts Lake Washington, connects to the Sammamish River Trail, and ends in Redmond's Marymoor Park, 24 miles away.

CAPITOL HILL

Capitol Hill is a study in sharp contrasts. The hill itself is one of the most prestigious old neighborhoods in Seattle, with countless mansions and stately older homes, quite a few of which are now elaborate bed-and-breakfast inns. At one time local politicians dreamed of making this the location for Washington's capitol building—hence the name. Today the campuses of Seattle Central Community College and Seattle University mark the southern edge, while two commercial centers attract visitors: a small, fairly quiet strip along 15th Avenue East, and the busy, on-the-edge Broadway Avenue East stretch.

Broadway

Because of a strong gay and lesbian presence, Broadway has been likened to San Francisco's Castro District, but it could also be Berkeley's Telegraph Avenue. It's a great place to people-watch and catch up on the latest fashion statements from the youthful art crowd. You're guaranteed to see more black leather skirts and jackets, frenzied fluorescent green hair, tattoos, nose rings, and pink triangles here than anywhere else in Seattle. Walk down the street in either direction and you'll discover artist Jack Mackie's amusing ***Dancers Series: Steps,*** bronze footprints of various dances embedded in the sidewalk.

Volunteer Park

This Capitol Hill park (enter from 14th or 15th Ave. E, 206/684-4743, www.ci.seattle.wa.us/parks, 10 A.M.–4 P.M. daily Oct.–Apr., 10 A.M.–7 P.M. daily May–mid-Sept.) has 44 acres of lawn, a concrete reservoir, and a number of interesting attractions. Completed in 1912, the park is one of many famous sites—including New York's Central Park and the University of Washington campus—designed by the famed Olmsted Brothers landscape architectural firm. Climb the long spiral staircase up the 75-foot brick **water tower** for a grand view across the city. On the other side of the park is the glass **Conservatory,** built in 1912 and filled with colorful plants of all kinds. One room houses cacti; others contain ferns, bromeliads, and seasonal displays. The central space features a gorgeous collection of orchids, along with a banana palm and fig tree. There's always something in bloom at the Conservatory, making this a great, steamy place to visit on a rainy winter day.

SEATTLE ASIAN ART MUSEUM

The centerpiece of Volunteer Park is the Seattle Asian Art Museum (1400 E. Prospect St., 206/654-3100, www.seattleartmuseum.org, 10 A.M.–5 P.M. Tues.–Sun., 10 A.M.–9 P.M. Thurs., closed Mon., $7 adults, $5 seniors and students, free kids under 12) a 1933 art-deco building. Exhibits cover two spacious wings, including rooms with Japanese folk art, Native American Mughal art, Qing dynasty Chinese art, and Korean art. Of particular interest are the beautiful Japanese screens, the bronze Buddhist sculptures, and the collection of intricate Chinese snuff bottles.

Free tours are offered daily, or borrow an audiotape for a do-it-yourself tour. Admission gets you in to both the Asian Art Museum and the Seattle Art Museum downtown on the same day. The first Thursday of every month is just $3 per person, and first Saturdays are free. A small gift shop sells books and other items, and the Kado Teagarden Café (206/729-1070) serves light lunches and more than 55 different teas from around the world.

LAKEVIEW CEMETERY

Just north of Volunteer Park is Lakeview Cemetery (206/322-1582), where many of the city's early residents are buried, including Doc Maynard (the doctor who named Seattle after Chief Seattle) and the daughter of Chief Seattle. Most folks come here, however, to visit the grave of martial artist and actor Bruce Lee, who died in 1973. His son, Brandon Lee, also a martial artist and actor, is buried here as well. He was accidentally killed in 1993 while filming *The Crow.*

QUEEN ANNE AND MAGNOLIA

Queen Anne is a small neighborhood crowning the tallest hill in Seattle. Given the commanding vistas from this location, it comes as no surprise that the captains of industry built mansions here at the turn of the 20th century. Many of these spacious and grand old homes are still here, along with a few cobblestone streets, but alongside are other, less ostentatious homes that give Queen Anne a comfortable atmosphere.

West of Queen Anne is the similar Magnolia neighborhood, with a wonderful shoreside route (Magnolia Drive) along the north edge of Elliott Bay to Discovery Park.

Discovery Park

Located five miles northwest of downtown in the Magnolia District, this 535-acre park (206/386-4236, www.ci.seattle.wa.us/parks) juts out into Puget Sound. In Discovery—Seattle's largest city park—you'll discover an "urban wilderness" with a wild feeling that belies its location next to two million people. The park features a 2.8-mile loop trail through forest and meadow, with access to two miles of Puget Sound beaches, plus the half-mile interpretive **Wolf Tree Nature Trail.** Discovery Park's West Point is reputedly Seattle's best bird-watching spot, with more than 150 kinds of birds, including frequent sightings of loons, grebes, cormorants, terns, and other marine birds.

Discovery Park is located on what was originally **Fort Lawton,** a defensive base established in the late 1890s to protect Puget Sound. It served mainly as a shipping center in the early 1900s; in World War II it was a vital processing base for more than a million troops en route to the Pacific—the second busiest point of embarkation on the West Coast. At its peak, the fort contained a small city's worth of buildings, and the mess hall bragged that it could feed 12,000 troops in an hour. After World War II and the Korean War, the fort was declared surplus property and given to the city of Seattle. In March 1970, 500 Native Americans invaded the grounds, claiming the old fort site as a cultural center. It took two battalions of Army troops and 119 arrests (including actress Jane Fonda) to quell the protest. Eventually, the city agreed to set aside 20 acres for what is now the **Daybreak Star Arts and Cultural Center** (206/285-4425). A small collection of art is inside, but the building is mainly used for Native American events. The rest of Fort Lawton became Discovery Park in 1972. Quite a few of the fort's structures remain, including more than a dozen from the earliest days. An interesting walking tour booklet detailing the fort and its history is available at the park's visitors center (8:30 A.M.–5 P.M. daily). The city offers free 90-minute Saturday nature walks at 2 P.M., along with a variety of classes and special events.

Other Parks

Magnolia Park, perched upon a high bluff along Magnolia Drive, is a great place for views of Puget Sound and the Olympics and a favorite spot to watch a sunset.

Mount Rainier, downtown Seattle, the Olympics, and the harbor can all be seen from tiny **Kerry Park** (W. Highland Dr. and 2nd Ave. W) on the south slope of Queen Anne Hill. It's especially popular with photographers in search of picture-postcard shots of Seattle and the Space Needle.

BALLARD AND SHILSHOLE BAY

Ballard and nearby Shilshole Bay were the Nordic section of Seattle when immigration from Norway and Sweden peaked from 1890 to 1910. Ballard still retains a trace of its Scandinavian heritage, although with the influx of new condos and other developments the ethnic lines have blurred considerably—the old Scandie's shop is now an Indian restaurant!

Downtown Ballard still has Norwegian and Swedish flags along Market Street, plus a few remnants of its Nordic past, including **Olsen's Scandinavian Foods** (2248 N.W. Market St., 206/783-8288), where you can still swing by to pick up some lutefisk. Ballard's **Syttende Mai Parade** takes place on May 17, Norwegian Constitution Day; this is the largest Syttende Mai parade outside Norway.

Nordic Heritage Museum

An early 1900s redbrick grade school has been transformed into the Nordic Heritage Museum (3014 N.W. 67th St., 206/789-5707, www.nordicmuseum.com, 10 A.M.–4 P.M. Tues.–Sat., noon–4 P.M. Sun., $6 adults, $5 seniors and students, $4 ages 6–16 years, and free for kids under 6), the only museum of its kind in America. The first floor opens with a lengthy and educational Dream of America exhibit, including the factors that pushed people to emigrate here in the 19th century. Upper levels cover the new life—in tenement slums, logging camps, and aboard fishing boats—with more exhibits on explorations by the Vikings, changing art and craft displays, and a gift shop with books on the homeland. The third floor has individual spaces for each of the Nordic countries: Norway, Sweden, Finland, Denmark, and Iceland. The museum is also home to Norwegian rosemaling classes; music, theater, and children's programs; a research library; and the **Scandinavian Language Institute** (www.sliseattle.com), where you can join classes in Danish, Norwegian, or Swedish. The museum is free on the first Tuesday of each month.

Come to the museum on the weekend after the 4th of July for the **Tivoli Festival** with a pancake breakfast, food and craft booths, entertainment, and a beer garden. Return on the weekend after Thanksgiving for **Yulefest,** with traditional carols, Nordic crafts, and food.

© ERICKA CHICKOWSKI

Part blue-collar Scandanavian, part Seattle hipster, Ballard is fast becoming Seattle's trendiest neighborhood.

Chittenden Locks

At the west end of Ballard, Hiram M. Chittenden Locks (N.W. 54th St., 206/783-7059, www.nws.usace.army.mil, 7 A.M.–9 P.M. daily) connect saltwater Puget Sound with freshwater Lake Washington via Lake Union. The locks (also known as the Ballard Locks) serve various functions: a passageway for some 90,000 ships each year, a way to prevent saltwater intrusion into the lakes, and a fish ladder. Built between 1911 and 1917, they are managed by the U.S. Army Corps of Engineers, which has a visitors center (10 A.M.–6 P.M. daily mid-May to mid-Sept., and 10 A.M.–4 P.M. Thurs.–Mon. rest of the year) here. Films are shown here every half hour. Attend free hour-long guided tours every day at 1 P.M. and 3 P.M. in the summer, and on Saturday and Sunday at 2 P.M. in the winter months, or join the throngs and figure it out for yourself. Chittenden Locks are one of Seattle's most-visited attractions; over a million people come here each year to watch container ships, tugs, tour boats, fishing boats, and pleasure craft make the transition between saltwater and freshwater. They also come to see the salmon return home to spawn via big underwater windows along the fish ladder—the best time to look for the salmon is late June to early September.

On the bank overlooking the locks are the **Carl S. English Jr. Botanical Gardens,** with more than 500 species of plants that English collected from around the world, plus native Northwest species. Included are pines, palms, oaks, dawn redwood, swamp flowers, and trees, and a great collection of rhododendrons. A brochure details a self-guided tour through the gardens.

Along the Water

Across the Ballard Bridge in Salmon Bay is the **Fishermen's Terminal,** a bustling marina—largest in the Northwest—packed with some 700 commercial fishing boats. Ask around to buy seafood directly from the fishermen, or head to **Wild Salmon Seafood Market** (1900 W. Nickerson St., 206/283-3366) on the water's edge.

West of the Chittenden Locks, Seaview Avenue curves north along the shore past Shilshole Bay with several popular seafood restaurants—most notably Ray's Boathouse and Anthony's HomePort—and Seattle's major pleasure-boat moorage, **Shilshole Marina.** Continue north to the enormously popular **Golden Gardens Park,** with one of the Sound's best bathing beaches. North beyond this is **Carkeek Park** (N.W. 110th St.), where you'll find a beautiful picnic area and playground, enjoyable hiking trails, and walks and talks at the Environmental Education Center (206/684-0877). Puget Sound is accessible via a footbridge over the railroad tracks. If the tide's in, chances are the beach will be out.

FREMONT

Long known as Seattle's quirkiest neighborhood, the "Republic of Fremont" has its own troll and a Lenin monument, plus an official motto that proclaims the "Freedom to be Peculiar." Several of the offbeat businesses that most epitomized this quirkiness have folded, but Fremont is still a delightful place to spend an afternoon. The best way to reach the neighborhood is across the **Fremont Drawbridge,** the world's most active drawbridge according to the *Guinness Book.* Be ready to wait; on busy summer weekends it often opens every 10 minutes or so.

Public Art

Once you cross the bridge, you'll meet one of Seattle's most famous pieces of public art, Richard Beyer's life-size group of commuters and a dog, *Waiting for the Interurban.* They are often decked out in used hats, balloons, or umbrellas contributed by passersby.

Head one block east and turn up the road beneath the Aurora Bridge that towers above you. Two blocks uphill you'll meet the locally famous ***Aurora Bridge Troll*** in the act of devouring a VW bug.

From here, walk to the official "Center of the Universe" at the corner of N. 35th Street and Evanston Avenue, where a 53-foot-high **Russian rocket** prepares to blast off from one building. Nearby stands ***Lenin*** in heroic pose. This statue originally stood in Slovakia until the 1989 revolution, when it was toppled and sold to capitalists. Lenin is now available to the first person with $150,000 to spend.

WALLINGFORD AND GREEN LAKE

Wallingford consists of a busy strip of shops just west of I-5 along North 45th Street. This attractive neighborhood is close enough to the university to have a strong student flavor, but far enough away to mix in a more upscale atmosphere. Just north of Wallingford is Green Lake, almost a mile wide and the center for recreation in the area. On the south side of the lake is the Woodland Park Zoo.

Woodland Park Zoo

Ranked among the nation's best, the Woodland Park Zoo (601 N. 59th St., 206/684-4800, www.zoo.org, 9:30 A.M.–4 P.M. daily Oct.–Apr., 9:30 A.M.–6 P.M. daily May–Sept., $15 adults, $13 seniors, $10 ages 3–12, free 2 and under, parking $4.50) has re-created wildlife habitats from around the world. The nocturnal house is home to bats, sloths, and other creatures of the night. Also included are a tropical Asian habitat and elephant forest where you can watch daily elephant logging demonstrations during the summer, and a Northern Trail section that leads past brown bears, river otters, bald eagles, mountain goats, gray wolves, and snowy owls, all in a relatively realistic setting (even the plants are native to Alaska). Bug World reveals the secret lives of singing katydids, Brazilian cockroaches, New Guinea walkingsticks, and assassin bugs. Raptor demonstrations are given on summer weekends, and the big field in the middle is a good place for a lunch break. The newest zoo exhibit is African village, where you enjoy music, dancing, and storytelling while watching animals from the African savanna.

Next to the zoo is the **Woodland Park Rose Garden** (206/684-4880) with hundreds of rose varieties spread over two acres.

Green Lake

An extremely popular three-mile paved bicycle, jogging, and skating loop—watch out for errant skateboards—hugs Green Lake (7201 E. Green Lake Dr. N), where you can also sail and swim or rent a paddleboat, canoe, kayak, sailboard, or rowboat. A kids-only fishing pier is at the east end of the lake. Crocodile hunting was popular here in 1986, when assorted reports of a lake creature took on the proportions of a Loch Ness Monster. The "monster" turned out to be a three-pound, 28-inch caiman, which was shipped to a private breeder in Kansas City; the lake is now believed crocodile-free.

UNIVERSITY DISTRICT

The University District (better known as "The U District") is a somewhat gritty center for student activity near the University of Washington's campus. The U District covers several blocks near the intersection of University Way NE ("The Ave") and N.E. 45th Street, with inexpensive restaurants, used CD and book stores, pizza joints, copy centers, Internet cafés, coffeehouses, and other student-oriented places. This is probably the best place in Seattle to get a quick lunch or an ethnic dinner for just a few bucks. To find the best spots, follow your nose and the students. If it's packed, it's probably tasty—or it serves cheap beer. Either way, you're golden.

University of Washington

The University of Washington (www.washington.edu) is the largest and best-known institute of higher education in the state and home to tens of thousands of students, staff, and faculty members.

The university began on a 10-acre downtown site in 1861, when Seattle was little more than a cow town, closing several times before it was firmly established. After statehood in 1889, the school began to grow rapidly, and the campus was relocated to the present site. (The original location on University Street downtown is still university property.) The Alaska-Yukon-Pacific Exposition of 1909 was held on the UW campus; in exchange for use of the

U-DUB

Outsiders may scratch their heads in wonder when a local refers to some place called "U-Dub." This is just a tender shortening of the already shortened acronym for University of Washington.

Even though the nickname may be informal, UW takes learning very seriously. This is the state's biggest and best school – a major center for research in the fields of Asian languages, zoology, astronomy, cell biology, forestry, fisheries, physics, and many other areas of study. UW's medical school and teaching hospital frequently rank in the nation's top 10. Three UW faculty members have won Nobel Prizes in physics and medicine, and five others have been awarded the MacArthur Foundation "genius grants." The school is highly competitive; incoming freshmen collectively have a 3.5 grade point average, and the graduate programs are widely acknowledged as some of the strongest in America. The UW library system contains 5.5 million volumes spread over two dozen campus libraries, making it one of the largest in the nation. The university's football and basketball teams often rank in the nation's top 20. Walk down University Way on the day of a football game, and you'll quickly learn that the team colors are purple and gold, and the mascot for the Huskies is an Alaskan malamute. By the way, the shorthand term for the Huskies is "Dawg" – never "Dog."

campus, the fair's promoters constructed several permanent buildings and landscaped the grounds, making UW one of the nation's prettiest campuses.

The campus is an attractive place, with tall brick buildings, springtime cherry blossoms, fountains, views of Lake Washington, and shady, landscaped grounds. For a taste of the good life, head to Red Square on a sunny spring day and join the throngs of sunseekers, skateboarders, Frisbee players, musicians, and brown-baggers as they check out Mount Rainier from this prime vantage point. Also of interest is **Denny Hall,** the oldest building on campus; it was completed in 1895. The center of campus activity is the **Husky Union Building** (the HUB) with a bookstore, newsstand, food and coffee, bowling lanes, pool tables, and more.

The **UW Visitors Information Center** (4014 University Way NE, 206/543-9198, www.depts.washington.edu/visitors, 8 A.M.–5 P.M. Mon.–Fri.). Stop here for school information, campus bus schedules, maps, upcoming sporting events, and other activities. Ninety-minute campus tours depart the visitors center at 10:30 A.M. Monday–Friday. Potential students and their families may be more interested in separate tours that leave from the admissions office (Room 320 in Schmitz Hall, 1410 N.E. Campus Parkway, at 2:30 P.M. Mon.–Fri.). Both of these tours are free and led by students. You can also pick up a self-guided walking tour brochure at the visitors center if you want to head out on your own.

BURKE MUSEUM

The Burke Museum (N.E. 45th St. and 17th Ave., 206/543-5590, www.washington.edu/burkemuseum, 10 A.M.–5 P.M. daily, $8 adults, $6.50 seniors, $5 ages 5–18, and free to kids under 6 and UW students and staff) stands just inside the north entrance to the campus and features an extraordinary collection of anthropological and natural-history displays. As you enter the museum you face a "treasures case" with Tlingit potlatch masks, a feathered Pomo basket, and even a ceramic horse from China's Wei dynasty. Permanent exhibits focus on Washington's geological, paleontological, and biological history, and on various Pacific cultures. The museum also features outstanding changing exhibitions, a gift shop, and totem poles out front. Downstairs is a fine little coffeehouse—it becomes a study hall during the school year.

HENRY ART GALLERY

Founded in 1927 and greatly expanded in the 1990s, the Henry Art Gallery (206/543-2280, www.henryart.org, 11 A.M.–5 P.M. Tues., Wed., Fri.–Sun., 11 A.M.–8 P.M. Thurs., closed Mon., $10 adults, $6 seniors, students and under 14 free, free to all on Thursday), occupies a 46,000-square-foot building on the west edge of the campus. It is a major facility for traveling exhibits and always features something innovative.

Ravenna Park

All but hidden from view in a ravine under the 15th Avenue Northeast bridge, Ravenna Park has 52 acres of woodlands and a babbling brook, accessible via a series of beautiful trails, plus a children's play area and soccer field, all in a most unlikely location. Douglas fir, Pacific madrone, western red cedar, bigleaf maple, and English and Pacific yew line the nature trail. It's a wonderful place for a morning jog.

MADISON PARK AND LAKE WASHINGTON

Arboretum and Japanese Garden

Trees and shrubs from all over the world thrive at the 267-acre University of Washington Arboretum (Lake Washington Blvd., dawn–dusk daily, free). A half-mile trail leads visitors past lodgepole pine, Oregon crabapple, huckleberry, Pacific dogwood, madrone, and more than 5,500 other varieties of plants. The 0.75-mile Azalea Way path winds through cherry, Japanese maple, azalea, dogwood, and rhododendron trees and bushes; it's a gorgeous place in the spring when everything is in bloom. In the off-season, head to the Joseph A. Witt Winter Garden.

The Waterfront Trail is a 1.5-mile round-trip stroll through wooded islands and Union Bay's shores at the north end of the arboretum, passing through the largest remaining wetland in Seattle (duck sightings guaranteed). The woodchip and boardwalk trail is level, with numerous benches for resting. Pick up a nature guide at the west end, at the Museum of History and Industry, or at the arboretum visitors center. The **Graham Visitors Center** (206/543-8800, www.depts.washington.edu/wpa, 10 A.M.–4 P.M. daily) on the north end of the park has a shop with gardening books and knickknacks for sale. Stop here for free hour-long guided tours at 1 P.M. Saturday and Sunday (Sunday only in winter). A greenhouse near the visitors center sells plants propagated from the arboretum collection.

At the south end of the arboretum (near Lake Washington Blvd. E) is the 3.5-acre **Japanese Tea Garden** (206/684-4725, opens at 10 A.M. daily Mar.–Nov., closes at varying times depending upon the season and weather, $5 adults, $3 kids and seniors, kids under 6 free), with manicured ornamental trees, a secluded pond, and an authentic teahouse given to Seattle by its sister city, Kobe, in the 1960s. A popular tea ceremony takes place at 1:30 P.M. on the third Saturday of each month.

Museum of History and Industry

Hidden away on the south side of Union Bay and just across the Montlake Bridge from the university, MOHAI (2700 24th Ave. E, 206/324-1126, www.seattlehistory.org, 10 A.M.–5 P.M. daily, $8 adults, $7 seniors, students, and military, $6 ages 5–17, and free for

BRIDGES TO NOWHERE

Anyone who's ever paddled a canoe or taken a walk near where the Aboretum meets Lake Washington has probably taken note of a curious sight. Two huge freeway appendages hanging off of Highway 520 appear to be bridges to nowhere. These two offshoots were the start of the R. H. Thomson Expressway, a freeway meant to link the Interstate 90 and Highway 520 routes. After realizing what the expressway would do to the Arboretum and their quiet neighborhoods, citizens rose up to put the kibosh on the project, but not before the interchanges were built. Today, these bridges are popular spots for thrill-seeking bridge jumpers who like to get their kicks cannonballing into Lake Washington from the edge.

kids under 5, free to all on Tuesday) is the city's finest historical museum and a great place for kids. The museum's primary exhibit focuses on Seattle's 150-plus years of history through artifacts, photos, and interactive displays. A noisy and fun exhibit on salmon fishing includes historical photos, a climb-aboard fishing boat, an "iron chink," and a hilarious "industrial fish." Other ongoing exhibits include a walk-through 1880s Seattle street, displays on the great Seattle fire of 1889, and ornately carved figureheads from old sailing vessels. Additional exhibits change periodically.

Other Sights

The **Northwest Puppet Center** (9123 15th Ave. NE, 206/523-2579, www.nwpuppet.org) is a fun place for kids, with weekend shows October through May, and a puppet museum offering changing exhibits of puppets from around the globe.

Jutting into Lake Washington on a forested peninsula is **Seward Park** (Lake Washington Blvd. S and S. Juneau Street). It features trails, picnic areas, fishing, swimming, and Mt. Rainier views. A one-mile loop trail takes you past Douglas firs six feet in diameter, madronas, bigleaf maples, and the shores of Lake Washington.

WEST SEATTLE

A high bridge spans the Duwamish Waterway, which separates industrial South Seattle's docks, warehouses, factories, and train tracks from quiet West Seattle. Once over the bridge you'll discover a neighborhood of simple homes and apartments with views across Puget Sound. Several shoreside parks provide places to ride bikes, walk the beaches, and enjoy the view. For photography buffs, **Hamilton Viewpoint** (California Way SW) offers a panoramic view of Seattle's skyline, the Cascades, and Elliott Bay, as does **Belvedere Viewpoint** (S.W. Admiral Way and 36th Ave. SW).

Alki Beach Park

For a leisurely scenic drive, head along the water on Harbor Avenue SW to Duwamish Head, then west on Alki Avenue SW to **Alki Beach Park,** a long, narrow, sandy stretch—as close to a real beach (outside Golden Gardens) as you'll find on this part of Puget Sound. In warm weather a whole beach culture emerges here—cruising cars, illegally parked vehicles, bonfires, suntan goop, the works—even though the water rarely gets above 55°F. Keep going on Alki Avenue to the **Alki Point Lighthouse** (206/286-5423). Tours of the station are available weekdays by reservation.

Lincoln Park

Traveling south on Beach Drive SW you'll reach the wonderful Lincoln Park, where you'll find great trails, playgrounds, and a long beach facing Puget Sound. A bike path follows the same scenic route. Just south of here is the **Fauntleroy** state ferry dock, with connections to Vashon Island and Southworth.

SOUTH SEATTLE

The south end of Seattle is dominated by industrial developments, especially an enormous Boeing plant. The area is not especially attractive but does feature one of Seattle's most enjoyable sights, the fabulous Museum of Flight.

Museum of Flight

This world-class museum (9404 E. Marginal Way S, 206/764-5720, www.museumofflight.org, 10 A.M.–5 P.M. daily, $14 adults, $13 seniors, $7.50 kids ages 5–17, kids under 5 free) is one of Seattle's premier attractions, and the largest air and space museum on the West Coast. The main focal point is a dramatic steel-and-glass **Great Gallery** packed with more than 50 planes, many of which appear to be flying in formation. Everything here has been meticulously restored. Suspended overhead are a Douglas DC-3, a replica of the Wright Brothers' glider, the human-powered Gossamer Albatross II, and 18 other aircraft. An additional 40 planes sit on the tarmac below, including a Russian MiG-21, an F4C Phantom II, and the famous M/D-21 Blackbird, officially the fastest plane ever to fly. Also on the ground level is a 1950s-era Aerocar III. Built by Moulton B. Taylor for the fly-and-drive crowd, the Aerocar could fly at 105 mph and convert into a car in 10 minutes. Visitors can also listen in on air traffic from busy Boeing Field at the full-size control tower exhibit here. Highly knowledgeable docents lead tours; stop by the desk to see when the next one begins. Throughout the day, the theater screens various films about flying. Outside, visitors can walk through the first **Air Force One,** used by Presidents Eisenhower, Kennedy, Johnson, and Nixon.

A second large exhibit space at the Museum of Flight is the **Red Barn,** a lovingly restored structure that was the Boeing Company's original manufacturing plant. It traces the history of flight through fascinating exhibits on two floors, including a restored 1917 Curtiss Jenny biplane and a replica of the Wright Brothers' wind tunnel. Also at the Museum of Flight are a hands-on area where kids pretend to pilot their own miniature aircraft, a Challenger Learning Center where school groups launch the space shuttle into orbit, a gift shop, library, and Wings Café. More planes are arranged outside the museum. Set aside at least three hours for this extraordinary museum, especially if you're a pilot! And, yes, it's OK to take photos.

Get to the museum by taking exit 158 from I-5, turning right at the first light on E. Marginal Way S, and following the signs, or by taking the No. 174 bus from downtown or the airport. Get in free 5–9 P.M. on the first Thursday of each month. On Father's Day there's free admission to the museum, an outdoor barbecue, and biplane rides. Stop by during Seafair to view the Blue Angels' F/A-18 Hornets.

Entertainment and Events

In the early 1990s Seattle gained a reputation as a center for alternative/grunge music, with local bands such as Nirvana, Pearl Jam, Soundgarden, Alice in Chains, and Foo Fighters achieving an international following. Seattle's music scene continues to change, and by the time you read this it will be off in yet another direction.

The best entertainment guides are the several free weekly papers available at stores and in newspaper boxes throughout the city. ***The Seattle Weekly*** has articles on politics and Seattle goings-on, plus concert information, club dates, restaurant reviews, movie, lecture, sports, dance, and theater listings—not to mention the phone sex and singles ads. Find the same information online at www.seattleweekly.com. Another freebie, ***The Stranger*** (www.thestranger.com), has a youthful edge and is the best source for upcoming music.

The mainstream ***Seattle Times*** (www.seattletimes.com) Thursday edition and ***Seattle Post-Intelligencer*** Friday edition (www.seattlep-i.com) have entertainment sections packed with details on dance, dining, theater, movies, and literary events.

NIGHTLIFE

Bars

BREWERIES AND PUBS

The Northwest has become a center for high-quality handcrafted ales. Though many folks still swill down Rainier or Budweiser, microbrewed specialty beers have gained in popularity as people discover the difference between quantity and quality.

Pike Pub & Brewery (1415 1st Ave., 206/622-6044, www.pikebrewing.com) is a popular and friendly place in the heart of the market, with some of the best micros anywhere, including XXXXX Stout.

In existence since 1981, **Redhook Ale Brewery** (3400 Phinney Ave. N, 206/483-3232, www.redhook.com) is one of the largest microbreweries in America (though Anheuser-Busch has a 34 percent ownership stake). Stop by corporate headquarters in Fremont to taste its ales, check out the gift shop and tasting room, or enjoy a light meal at the popular **Trolleyman Pub.** Redhook beers aren't brewed in Fremont, but you can tour the big brewery in Woodinville.

A much smaller operation is **Dad Watsons Restaurant & Brewery** (3601 Fremont Ave. N, 206/632-6505, www.mcmenamins.com). This attractive brewpub has ales on tap and an enjoyably diverse menu; it's part of the McMenamins chain of brewpubs.

Just west of Redhook—and right off the bike path—is **Hale's Ales Brewery** (4301 Leary Way NW, 206/706-1544, www.halesales.com, 11 A.M.–10 P.M. Sun.–Thurs., 11 A.M.–midnight Fri.–Sat.), which cranks out seven different draft-only beers and serves meals in the cozy pub or outside on the small deck. There are no scheduled tours, but the staff will describe the brewing process.

Out in the U District, **Big Time Brewery and Alehouse** (4133 University Way NE, 206/545-4509, www.bigtimebrewery.com) features several fresh-brewed ales on tap and an antique back bar where you can enjoy the passing scene through the big front windows.

With its fireplace and comfy sofas, **College Inn Pub** (4006 University Way NE, 206/634-2307) is a favorite place to catch a beer with the grad students and profs around UW.

DIVE BARS

In keeping with Seattle's informal nature, the best joints in town to throw back a few drinks are the hidden, hole-in-the-wall bars made for a night in T-shirt and jeans.

The U District's **Blue Moon Tavern** (712 N.E. 45th St., 206/675-9116) is one of the most famous old-time hangouts in Seattle, the sort of place that once attracted the likes of Allen Ginsberg, Jack Kerouac, and Tom Robbins. It still brings in the Deadheads on Sunday nights for a jukebox jam. Monday is opera night, and the first Wednesday of every month is poetry night.

Grab a handful of peanuts from the endless free bowls at **Hooverville Bar** (1721 1st Ave. S, 206/264-2428, www.hoovervilleseattle.com) and don't worry about the shells—just throw 'em on the ground. Situated near the stadiums, this lovable bar borders on the edge of poseur, maybe just slightly too conscious of its diveyness. But, hey, there's Pabst Blue Ribbon on tap and pinball machines waiting for a new high score. Who can argue with that?

The view of Elliott Bay is great at **Alki Tavern** (1321 Harbor Ave. SW, 206/932-9970), as long as you look out the open doors—the windows are pretty grimy and tiny, a symbol of this place's dive status. The drinks are plentiful and cheap and the barkeeps are friendly, making this place a keeper. Visit on Tuesday night for $1 burgers.

The unpretentious ***Nite Lite*** (1926 2nd Ave., 206/443-0899) serves drinks strong enough to put a little kink in a writer's step. This dark den is right downtown next to the Moore Theater, a secret favorite among comics and other artists who like to visit after their shows.

GAY AND LESBIAN BARS

Check out the ***Seattle Gay News*** (www.sgn.com), a free weekly newspaper, for the latest in events and music. Otherwise, direct yourself to **Neighbours** (1509 Broadway, 206/324-5358) on Capitol Hill, Seattle's definitive gay bar, complete with sharp young men, drag queens, and straights who love them. It's loud, crowded, and perfect for an all-night dance party. Thursday night brings out the crowd with "Rock Lobster" and other 1980s tunes. Lesbians (and some hopeful dudes) head to **The Wild Rose** (1021 E. Pike St., 206/324-9210) with its dartboards, pool tables, jukebox, and karaoke on Wednesday night; there's DJ dance music on Saturday night.

Timberline Tavern (2015 Boren Ave., 206/622-6220) features a huge maple dance floor and country music (with free two-step lessons) on Tuesday nights, with more country (and disco!) tunes on Friday and Saturday night. The clientele is mixed but always includes a substantial component of gays and lesbians. On Sunday afternoons it attracts the young crowd for dance tunes; other nights you might see "lube wrestling" or karaoke. Not far away is **Re-Bar** (1114 E. Howell St., 206/233-9873), a predominately gay dance club with DJs spinning disco, hip-hop, and techno music Friday–Sunday (and sometimes shows or other types of music on other nights).

On Capitol Hill, **Vogue** (1516 11th Ave., 206/324-5778) is a center for the fringe and gay crowd. Fetish night is every Sunday and Gothic night comes on Wednesdays, plus reggae, industrial, and alternative music or CDs other nights. Lots of other queer hangouts crowd the Capitol Hill area.

Live Music

HEADLINERS

The city's most elaborate music venue is **Sky Church,** located within Experience Music Project (325 5th Ave. N, 206/770-2777, www.emplive.com). Well-known performers often come here, though space for the audience is limited—meaning there's barely room to stand. You also can't carry drinks into the performance area. But the enormous high-tech video screen is an attraction in its own right.

You'll also find a lot of national acts at the **Showbox** (1426 1st Ave., 206/628-3151), near Pike Place Market. This decades-old venue has such a rep for good performances that it had to open an annex in Pioneer Square (1700 1st Ave. S.) to satisfy Seattle's thirst for rockin' shows.

The Belltown area north of downtown has several popular clubs. **Crocodile Café** (2200 2nd Ave., 206/441-5611, www.thecrocodile.com) is a fun club that acted as the alternative scene's incubator for years. It's a good place to look for rock stars passing through town.

One of Seattle's most unusual nightspots is **Sit & Spin** (2219 4th Ave., 206/441-9484) a Belltown laundry/bar/restaurant where you can watch the clothes go 'round in the front or head back for dancing, eating, playing board games, or surfing the Web.

Worth checking out is the stylish **Watertown** (106 1st Ave. N, 206/284-5003), with a music mix that romps all over the place, from alternative to dance music. Tasty food, too.

COUNTRY

Head north for nightclubs that attract big alt-country and honky-tonk acts. Click those boots on over to the **Tractor Tavern** (5213 Ballard Ave., 206/789-3599, www.tractortavern.com) in Ballard or **Little Red Hen** (7115 Woodlawn Ave. NE, 206/522-1168, www.littleredhen.com) in Greenlake.

ALL AGES

Old and young flock to **El Corazon** (109 Eastlake Ave. E, 206/381-3094), which dishes up some of the area's hottest bands in a mixed setting that gives the under-21 set a chance to get a taste of the music scene. This has been the city's best all-ages venue for years now, albeit under a spate of different names.

JAZZ, BLUES, FOLK, AND MORE

The most popular place for Seattle jazz buffs is **Dimitriou's Jazz Alley** (2033 6th Ave., 206/441-9729, www.jazzalley.com) where big-time national acts and up-and-coming talent can be heard. This is an elegant, dress-up place. More authentic is my favorite, **Tulas Jazz Club** (2214 2nd Ave., 206/443-4221), an old-fashioned speak-easy-type lounge that is only missing the bouncer asking for a code word. Quarters are cramped, service is surly, and the music is like honey. That's the way it's supposed to be, you dig?

Find more live jazz at the **Seattle Art Museum** (206/654-3100, www.seattleartmuseum.org) on the second Thursday of the month January through June.

The unpretentious **Owl 'n' Thistle Irish Pub** (808 Post Ave., 206/621-7777, www.owlnthistle.com) is Seattle's most famous Irish pub, with world-class Celtic tunes from the house band on weekends, and a wide range of other styles the rest of the week—from blues to jazz to rock. There's no cover charge, and the back room has pool and darts. Needless to say, Guinness is the drink of choice.

In Pioneer Square, there are a number of places to find live tunes. **New Orleans Restaurant** (114 1st St., 206/622-2563) serves up spicy Creole meals plus Dixieland

SMELLS LIKE SEATTLE BANDS

The city of Seattle has a long and storied musical history. Local legends include:

Jimi Hendrix: The guitar virtuoso was born in Seattle and learned to play his instrument here, belonging to various local bands in his youth. Hendrix left the area in 1961 and never lived here again, although he is buried at Greenwood Memorial Park in Renton.

Queensrÿche: This Bellevue progressive-metal band experienced some celebrity in 1990.

Heart: Ann and Nancy Wilson, the founding sisters of this iconic rock group, are both from Seattle.

Kenny G: The mellow saxophonist was born in Seattle and is a graduate of the University of Washington.

Quincy Jones: Producer, singer, composer, musician, the legendary Quincy Jones lived in Seattle through much of his childhood.

Sir Mix-a-lot: The man behind Posse on Broadway and Baby Got Back was born in Seattle and still calls the city home. The reference to Broadway is actually the street in Seattle's Capitol Hill area, not the better known one in New York.

Grunge Music: The Seattle area is still most closely associated with the "grunge" movement of the early 1990s. Characterized by distorted electric instrumentation, a fashion sense borrowed from local lumberjacks, and angsty, lamenting lyrics, grunge is undeniably Northwestern. Must be the rain. The dean of all grunge acts, Nirvana, was formed by two Aberdeen locals, Kurt Cobain and Krist Novoselic. It was in the Lake Washington area of Seattle that Cobain killed himself in 1994. Pearl Jam, Alice in Chains, and Screaming Trees are all Seattle bands, as is Soundgarden, whose breakthrough hit Spoonman was written about a street performer who once frequented Pike Place Market.

Murder City Devils: These hard-edge punk rockers were the yin to grunge's yang in the 1990s and are just now seeing a resurgence in the national club scene.

Harvey Danger: This band was best known for its late-1990s post-grunge anthem Flagpole Sitta.

Modest Mouse and Death Cab for Cutie: Both of these emo superbands played the local club circuit for years before recently hitting the big time.

Sub Pop and Kill Rock Stars: These two legendary labels are based in Washington, the former in Seattle and the latter in Olympia.

jazz, blues, and zydeco. Seattle's oldest bar, **Central Saloon** (207 1st Ave., 206/622-0209) offers great blues, jazz, funk, and reggae bands seven nights a week. **Doc Maynard's** (610 1st Ave., 206/682-4649, www.docmaynards.com) is a restored 1890s saloon with loud rock and roll.

Nightclubs

It is no Miami Beach, but Seattle does have a healthy mix of dance clubs for those looking to get their groove on. **Polly Esther's Culture Club** (332 5th Ave. N, 206/441-1970) is an extremely popular downtown club that attracts dance fiends, horny college kids, and others who come out for fun. It gets packed on weekends. **Last Supper Club** (124 S. Washington St., 206/748-9975) is another college hangout, and one of the town's place-to-be-seen spots. Perhaps the best place for some booty-shakin', bump-and-grindin' action is over in Pioneer Square: The aptly named **Trinity** (111 Yesler Way, 206/447-4140, trinitynightclub.com) spreads the music vibes over three levels, offering different jams on each floor.

For some truly high-class partying, round up your peeps and head to **Heaven** (172 S. Washington St., 206/622-1863, http://heavenseattle.com), a swank Pioneer Square club with VIP tables and bottle service at the ready.

For something completely different, the **Century Ballroom** (915 E. Pine St., 206/324-7263, www.centuryballroom.com) on Capitol Hill is a snazzy spot for swing and salsa dance enthusiasts. It has one of the largest dance floors in the state.

Comedy Clubs

Seattle's biggest comedy club, **Comedy Underground** (222 S. Main St., 206/622-4550, www.comedyunderground.com) in Pioneer Square is one of the top West Coast destinations for national comedy acts. Expect capacity crowds in a crowded setting when attending headliner acts. See both local and big-time acts at **Giggles** (5220 Roosevelt Way NE, 206/526-5347, www.gigglescomedyclub.com) in the U District, which offers cheap food and beer to go with the show.

Check out theater sports and improv acts at one of two venues. Near Pike Place Market, **Unexpected Productions** (1428 Post Alley, 206/587-2414) offers quirky competitions between quick-thinking thespians à la *Who's Line is it Anyway?*, and in the U District, **Jet City Improv** (5031 University Way NE, 206/781-3879, www.jetcityimprov.com) performs from-the-hip sketches and bits on Friday and Saturday nights.

THE ARTS

Much of Seattle's cultural action—at least when it comes to live theater, classical music, opera, and ballet—happens at Seattle Center (better known as "that place with the Space Needle"). For an up-to-date recording of arts events in Seattle, call 206/447-2787. The Friday edition of both the ***Seattle Times*** (www.seattletimes.com) and ***Seattle Post-Intelligencer*** (www.seattlep-i.com) newspapers, along with the ***Seattle Weekly*** (www.seattleweekly.com), all have a complete listing of upcoming productions, as does the **Seattle/King County Convention and Visitors Bureau** (www.visitseattle.org).

Get event tickets from **Ticketmaster** (206/628-0888, www.ticketmaster.com). For half-price concert, comedy, and dance performance tickets the day of the show, stop by **Ticket/Ticket** (www.ticketwindowonline.com) booths at Pike Place Market and in Broadway Market (401 Broadway Ave. E, 206/324-2744).

Live Theater

Nobody is quite sure why—maybe it really is the weather—but live theater has always done very well in Seattle. Consequently, if you can't find a good movie, you will have a wide choice of plays and musicals to try. Much of the action takes place in Seattle Center's theaters; check local papers for current activities. **Seattle Repertory Theatre** (206/443-2210, www.seattlerep.org) produces classic and contemporary plays October through May at Seattle Center. A Contemporary Theatre, or **ACT** (700 Union St., 206/292-7676, www.acttheatre.org), fills out the other half of the year, performing downtown. **Book-It Repertory Theatre** (206/216-0833, www.book-it.org) has year-round performances of classic literature, from Jane Austen to James Purdy. The **Intiman Theatre Company** does classic dramatic productions May–Novemer at Seattle Center's Intiman Theatre (201 Mercer St., 206/269-1901, www.intiman.org), while the **Seattle Public Theater** (7312 W. Greenlake Dr. N, 206/524-1300, www.seattlepublictheater.org) presents a wide range of plays at the refurbished bathhouse along Green Lake. Also of note is **On the Boards** (100 W. Roy St., 206/217-9888, www.ontheboards.org) in Queen Anne.

For multicultural productions, check out the historic **Nippon Kan Theater** (628 S. Washington St., 206/467-6807), well known for its Japanese performing arts productions. Also popular are offbeat and provocative productions from **Empty Space Theatre** (3509 Fremont Ave., 206/547-7500, www.emptyspace.org).

Two Seattle theaters provide a venue for Broadway-style musicals: the **5th Avenue Theatre** (1308 5th Ave., 206/625-1418, www.5thavenuetheatre.org) and the beautifully restored, historic **Paramount Theater** (Pine St. near 9th Ave., 206/292-2787, www.theparamount.com).

America's largest—and perhaps finest—kids' theater, the **Seattle Children's Theater** (206/441-3322, www.sct.org) is housed within the impressive Charlotte Martin Theatre at

Seattle Center. Productions and classes include both the silly and the serious.

Music and Dance

Just uphill from the Seattle Art Museum, the marvelous Benaroya Hall is home to the **Seattle Symphony** (2nd Ave. and University St., 206/215-4747 www.seattlesymphony.org). The largest employer of artists in the Pacific Northwest, the symphony has gained international attention under conductor Gerard Schwartz, with more than a dozen compact discs and at least 10 Grammy nominations. Performances take place in the state-of-the-art auditorium September–June, with more than 100 concerts a year. On Sunday afternoons, the Musically Speaking series mixes the classics with commentary about the music and the composers. Tours are available. The **Seattle Youth Symphony** (206/362-2300, www.syso.org) is another notable organization for younger artists, who also perform frequently at Benaroya. Benaroya Hall is open 10 A.M.–6 P.M. weekdays, with one-hour tours starting at noon.

Seattle Center Opera House hosts the **Seattle Opera** (206/389-7676, www.seattleopera.org), whose September–May regular season almost always sells out. It presents five productions annually, including Wagner's famous four-opera Ring cycle every four years—the next one's scheduled in 2010.

The **Pacific Northwest Ballet** (206/628-0888, www.pnb.org), whose season is October–May, produces the traditional *Nutcracker* for Christmas. A number of contemporary dance companies help fill out the offerings in Seattle.

Film

Seattle has earned an international reputation among filmmakers as having one of the most discriminating audiences in America. Movies are often tested on this urban market before being released, and Seattle viewers have often made a little-known film a winner. If you are in town in May and June, be sure to take in a flick at the outstanding **Seattle International Film Festival** (206/324-9997, www.seattlefilm.com). It's the largest of its kind in America, attracting more than 100,000 filmgoers.

On a smaller scale, the **Fremont Outdoor Cinema** (N. 34th St. and Phinney Ave. N, 206/781-4230, www.fremontoutdoormovies.com, $5) is held on summer Saturday nights across from the Redhook Brewery. Bring your lawn chair to join in the fun of watching old B movies and cult classics.

For the ultimate movie experience, join the crowds at downtown's **Cinerama Theatre** (2100 4th Ave., 206/441-3080) where billionaire Paul Allen's money is once again in evidence. This 800-seat remodeled classic is *the* place to see a flick in Seattle. The screen is enormous, the sound and projection systems are state-of-the-art, and the first-run blockbuster movies are just plain fun.

Off-the-beaten-path cinemas with art-house films include **Grand Illusion Cinema** (N.E. 50th St. and University Way NE, 206/523-3935) and **Varsity Theatre** (4329 University Way NE, 206/632-3131) in the U District, **Guild 45th** (2115 N. 45th St., 206/781-5755) in Wallingford, and **Egyptian Theatre** (801 E. Pine, 206/323-4978) on Capitol Hill. Looking for a cheap flick? Head out to the **Crest Cinema Center** (16505 5th Ave. NE, 206/363-6338) in North Seattle, where all shows are only $3.

FESTIVALS AND EVENTS

The Seattle/King County Convention and Visitors Bureau (206/461-5840, www.seeseattle.org) can provide details on year-round events, starting with a big fireworks show from the Space Needle on **New Year's Eve** and lots of partying downtown.

Winter

King 5 Winterfest is a five-week holiday festival with decorations, children's entertainers, choirs, an ice rink, lighting ceremony, and New Year's Eve celebration at Seattle Center (206/684-8582, www.seattlecenter.com).

The last festival of the year is the multi-day **Christmas Ships Parade** (206/461-5840) a lighted flotilla that cruises Lake Washington in mid-December.

Chinese New Year (206/382-1197, www.nwasianweekly.com) is celebrated in late January or early February, when the International District comes alive with parades and colorful displays.

Seattle's weeklong **Mardi Gras** celebration in February at Pioneer Square features jazz and Cajun music, arts and crafts, and a parade. Unfortunately, in 2001, drunken rioters (many apparently from local gangs) left one person dead and 70 others injured. Mardi Gras continues to be celebrated annually in Seattle, but it has been much scaled down since then.

Spring

The first Saturday of May brings the **Opening Day of Boating Season** (206/527-3801, www.seattleyachtclub.org) with a big parade of boats and the **Windermere Cup Races,** where top university rowing teams from around the world compete on the Montlake Cut. This is the top event of its kind in the nation.

On the third weekend of May, the **University District Street Fair** (206/547-4417, www.udistrictchamber.org) attracts hundreds of artists who display their wares on University Way Northeast—also known as The Ave. Also here are food booths and live music. More than 6,000 musicians, dancers, and craftspeople display their talents while enormous amounts of food are consumed at the **Northwest Folklife Festival** (206/684-7300, www.nwfolklife.org), held at Seattle Center on Memorial Day weekend. In late May, the **Pike Place Market Festival** (206/587-0351, www.pikeplacemarket.com) has free entertainment and music, a beer garden, chalk art, and a kids' area.

Summer

In June the **Pioneer Square Fire Festival** (206/622-6235) recalls Seattle's Great Fire of 1889 (any excuse for a party, right?) with free activities in the park, a parade of classic firefighting equipment, contests, and entertainment.

In late June, the funky "Republic of Fremont" holds the **Summer Solstice Parade and Fair** (206/547-7440, www.fremontfair.com) with booths, live music, ethnic food and drink, and assorted street performers and residents from the fringe. These are not your standard productions, but instead visual and performance works from new artists that push the envelope. The events could be bizarre, disconcerting, funny, psychedelic, and haunting all at the same time. A handful of nude participants are always there for a bit of spice.

The 4th of July brings twin fireworks displays, one on Lake Union and the other at Myrtle Edwards Park on Elliott Bay. The latter—called **4th of Jul-Ivar's** (206/587-6500, www.ivarsrestaurants.com)—is sponsored by Ivar's Acre of Clams and is said to be one of the largest in America. It also features food booths and entertainment, plus a fly-over of antique and modern aircraft. Also in early July, the **Lake Union Wooden Boat Festival** (206/382-2628, www.cwb.org) takes place at the south end of Lake Union, where you'll see some of the most beautiful boats on Puget Sound.

SEAFAIR

Held over the whole month of July, Seafair is the annual celebration of all things Seattle. Events include a marathon, a triathlon, a fun run, hydroplane races, fireworks, and a traditional performance by the Air Force's precision flyers, the Blue Angels.

The festival begins with the Seafair Pirate's Landing, in which many city leaders, dressed as pirates and acting the role to the hilt, "sack" Seattle and are handed the keys to the city by the mayor. The fair's centerpiece is the signature Torchlight Parade, held at the end of the month. This long-running event brings upwards of 300,000 onlookers to watch the clowning pirates as well as local drill teams, equestrians, floats, and bands as they march through the streets of downtown.

Most events are extremely family friendly and do a fantastic job of conveying the flavor of this unique city.

In mid-July the **Bite of Seattle** (206/232-2982, www.biteofseattle.com) comes to Seattle Center, giving more than 60 fine restaurants an opportunity to show their products. It attracts nearly a half-million participants in three days! Across the way in Ballard, **Seafoodfest** (206/784-9705, www.ballardchamber.com) arrives in late July, with a street festival, salmon barbecue, food and crafts booths, beer garden, and children's games.

Seattle's biggest fair of the year, **Seafair** (206/728-0123, www.seafair.com) starts on the 4th of July and packs in a month of crafts, more than a dozen parades, along with triathlons, ethnic festivals, live music, a milk-carton boat race, ship tours, and demonstrations by the Navy's Blue Angels, culminating in the unlimited **General Motors Cup Hydroplane Races** on Lake Washington in early August.

One of the more unusual events is the **Bubble Festival** (206/443-2001, www.pacsci.org) held in mid-August at the Pacific Science Center. Professional bubble blowers create bubbles in every imaginable shape. Also in August, the **Seattle Music Fest** (206/664-1000, www.seattlemusicfest.org) brings 20 or so bands to Alki Beach.

A Labor Day weekend arts extravaganza, **Bumbershoot** (206/281-7788, www.bumbershoot.org) brings together top-billed musicians, writers, and craftspeople for a huge end-of-summer blowout at Seattle Center. Bumbershoot attracts more than a quarter million visitors annually and features internationally known musicians, along with local talents. All told, more than 2,500 artists perform! Find the full schedule at bumbershoot.org/lineup, available in the spring prior to the festival.

Shopping

SHOPPING CENTERS

Unlike most other cities around the Sound, Seattle's downtown shopping district has not died out under the pressure of surrounding suburban malls. In fact, downtown shopping is more alive than ever, with popular **Westlake Center** (5th Ave. and Pine St.) and **Century Square** (4th Ave. and Pike St.) among the highlights. Top-shelf jewelry, perfume, art, leather goods, and clothing stores abound in these two small centers. Westlake is the endpoint for the Monorail from Seattle Center, and it has a Ticketmaster booth for discounted day-of-performance tickets. Downstairs, you'll find the entrance to the bus tunnel; upstairs is a food court with plenty of quick-eat choices.

Nearby is **Pacific Place** (600 Pine St., 206/405-2655 www.pacificplaceseattle.com), a retail and entertainment center with five levels of retail shops, three restaurants, and an 11-plex movie theater. The complex has underground parking and is connected by skywalk to Seattle's flagship **Nordstrom** store (5th Ave. between Pike and Pine St., www.nordstrom.com).

Another downtown shopping center with small shops—this one underground—is **Rainier Square** (4th and 5th Aves. and Union St.) The underground concourse has bookstores and restaurants and serves as an entrance to **Eddie Bauer,** another store founded in Seattle that became global.

The waterfront and **Pike Place Market** are loaded with tiny wine shops, boutiques, and craft stores, plus the big, obvious produce stands and tourist traps. Plan to get lost in the maze of crowds for at least a couple of hours!

The center of Capitol Hill buzz is **Broadway Market** (401 Broadway E, 206/322-1610, www.shopbroadwaymarket.com, 10 A.M.–9 P.M. Mon.–Sat., noon–6 P.M. Sun.), a thriving set of offbeat shops with—for some reason—a Fred Meyer store occupying the back half. Buy magazines at Bulldog News, get a glass of wheatgrass juice at the arty Gravity Bar, buy half-price concert tickets at Ticket/Ticket, or get a blast of latte at B&O Espresso. Interesting artworks are displayed on the upper level.

Malls abound in the Seattle area; the largest is **Northgate Shopping Mall,** seven miles north of downtown Seattle (exit 173 from I-5). The attractive **University Village Mall** (25th Ave. NE) near campus down N.E. 45th St. is another good neighborhood mall, with numerous boutiques, a Barnes and Noble, loads of restaurants, and a grocery store. There are a number of additional suburban area malls in the vicinity of Seattle.

GALLERIES

The fine arts are alive in Seattle, as will be immediately obvious even to those who visit briefly. For the latest fine arts exhibitions throughout Puget Sound, pick up a copy of ***Art Access*** (www.artaccess.com) from a local gallery.

Downtown, **Phoenix Rising Gallery** (2030 Western Ave., 206/728-2332, www.phoenixrisinggallery.com) is packed with glass pieces, jewelry, gifts, and other artwork. Other downtown galleries worth seeing include **Lisa Harris Gallery** (1922 Pike Pl., 206/443-3315, www.lisaharrisgallery.com) and **William Traver Gallery** (110 Union St., 206/587-6501, www.williamtraver.com).

Several galleries fill a pedestrian-only stretch of Occidental Street just north of the sports stadiums, and along 1st Avenue S. Particularly notable ones include **Bryan Ohno Gallery** (155 S. Main St., 206/667-9572, www.bryanohnogallery.com), **Greg Kucera Gallery** (212 3rd Ave. S, 206/624-0770, www.gregkucera.com), **D'Adamo/Hill Gallery** (307 Occidental Ave. S, 206/652-4414, www.artforte.com), **Esther Claypool Gallery** (617 Western Ave., 206/264-1586, www.estherclaypool.com), **Foster/White Gallery** (311½ Occidental S, 206/622-2833, www.fosterwhite.com), **Davidson Galleries** (313 Occidental Ave. S, 206/624-7684, www.davidsongalleries.com), and **Northwest Gallery of Fine Woodworking** (101 S. Jackson St., 206/625-0542, www.nwfinewoodworking.com). Join the Pioneer Square throngs on the **first Thursday** of each month, when the galleries all stage opening receptions. It has become a big event and is a good opportunity to mingle with artists and art connoisseurs; bargain hunters appreciate the free munchies and drinks.

Pike Place Market (www.pikeplacemarket.org) always has photographers, painters, jewelers, and craftspeople selling their pieces for reasonable prices.

Also noteworthy for items from around the world is **La Tienda Folk Art Gallery** (4138 University Way NE, 206/632-1796, www.latienda-folkart.com) in the U District.

In Fremont, try **Frank & Dunya** (3418 Fremont Ave. N, 206/547-6760), a fun gallery of "functional art" by Washington artists, or **Edge of Glass Gallery** (513 N. 36th St., 206/632-7807, www.edgeofglass.com, 11 A.M.–6 P.M. Wed.–Sun.) where you can watch students and teachers blowing glass. Also worth seeing is **Elliott Brown Gallery** (215 Westlake Ave. N, 206/340-8000, www.elliottbrowngallery.com).

A monthly **First Saturday Art Walk** showcases artists at work and is one of Fremont's many attractions for art lovers.

OUTDOOR GEAR

In business since 1938, **REI** is America's most successful cooperatively run company, with more than 60 stores scattered across the country. Its 80,000-square-foot flagship store (222 Yale Ave., 206/223-1944 or 800/426-4840, www.rei.com) is a favorite of locals and visitors. The building's main attraction is a 65-foot indoor climbing wall—the world's tallest—just inside the entrance. It's open to all levels of ability; ask the belay experts for help. Test hiking boots or mountain bikes on the loop trail outside, enjoy an espresso next to the waterfall, try out Gore-Tex jackets in the rain room, plan trips with the help of Park Service or Forest Service personnel at the in-store Outdoor Recreation Information Center, or simply wander through the clothing and gear. REI also rents all sorts of outdoor equipment, including backpacks, climbing shoes, tents, sleeping bags, ice axes, and skis. The store features an auditorium where you can watch outdoor presentations and clinics most evenings. Below the store are three levels of free underground parking.

A lifetime REI membership ($20) entitles you to yearly rebates of around 8 percent of full-price purchases. **REI Adventures** (800/622-2236) leads treks all over the world, including such close-in places as the Olympics, San Juan Islands, and Mount Rainier.

Other major outdoor outfitters include **The North Face** (1023 1st Ave., 206/622-4111, www.thenorthface.com), **Eddie Bauer** (1330 5th Ave., 206/622-2766, www.eddiebauer.com) and **Patagonia** (2100 1st Ave., 206/622-9700, www.patagonia.com).

BOOKS AND MAGAZINES

Seattleites spend more money on books per capita than any other American city—almost twice the national average. Given this, you can be assured that the city has lots of choices when it comes to buying books. With more than 150,000 titles on the shelves, a comfortable atmosphere, knowledgeable staff, and a café and almost nightly readings by acclaimed authors and poets, the **Elliott Bay Book Company** (101 S. Main St., 206/624-6600, www.elliottbaybook.com) is a local legend. This Pioneer Square bookstore is *the* quintessential place for Seattle bibliophiles. Pick up its quarterly *Elliott Bay Booknotes* for detailed book reviews and articles about the craft of writing.

The **University Bookstore** (4326 University Way NE, 206/634-3400 or 800/335-7323, www.bookstore.washington.edu) competes with Harvard's book shop for the nation's largest university bookstore, carrying an impressive array of titles, plus office supplies, "go-Huskies" clothing, cameras, CDs, and more. Just down the block is a place at the opposite end of the spectrum, **Twice Sold Tales** (4501 University Way NE, 206/545-4226), with two cats and a funky collection of used books. It has other shops in Fremont and on Capitol Hill.

Bulldog News (4208 University Way NE, 206/632-6397) is the best magazine and newspaper store in town, with over 2,000 titles, including quite a few foreign magazines. Almost any night you're bound to find several dozen folks scanning the issues (and doing quite a bit of reading). Bulldog also has a smaller shop at Broadway Market on Capitol Hill. Another excellent place for magazines and out-of-town

© ERICKA CHICKOWSKI

When the weather turns for the worst, there's always a bookstore nearby.

newspapers is the **Read All About It** (206/624-0140) newsstand at Pike Place Market—it is on the corridor just to the left of the flying fish.

For a great selection of travel books, visit **Wide World Books and Maps** (1911 N. 45th Ave., 206/634-3453, www.wideworldtravels.com, 10 A.M.–9 P.M. Mon.–Sat., 11 A.M.–6 P.M. Sun.) in Wallingford. Established in 1976, it was the first travel-only bookshop in America. The tea shop next door is a fine place to read about Asia while sipping Chinese tea.

On Capitol Hill, **Bailey/Coy Books** (414 Broadway Ave. E, 206/323-8842, http://bailycoybooks.com, 10 A.M.–10 P.M. Mon.–Sat., 10 A.M.–8 P.M. Sun.) offers a large selection of gay and lesbian titles. Unrepentant leftists, socialists, and radicals love **Left Bank Books** in the Pike Place Market (206/322-2868, www.leftbankbooks.com, 10 A.M.–7 P.M. Mon.–Sat., 11 A.M.–6 P.M. Sun.). Other distinctive bookstores include the appropriately named **Peter Miller Architecture and Design Books** (1930 1st Ave., 206/441-4114, www.petermiller.com, 10 A.M.–6 P.M. Mon.–Fri., 10 A.M.–5:30 P.M. Sat., closed Sun.) and **Cinema Books** (4753 Roosevelt Way NE, 206/547-7667, http://cinema.net, 10 A.M.–7 P.M. daily).

East West Book Shop (1032 N.E. 65th St., 206/523-3726, www.eastwest.com) is the place for the crystal, channeling, and pyramid-power crowd. For something more down to earth (literally), be sure to visit **Flora and Fauna** (121 1st Ave., 206/623-4727, www.ffbooks.com), the biggest purveyor of natural history volumes in the West. Lots of other bookstore choices are in town, including a big **Barnes and Noble** store in University Village Mall (206/517-4107) and another downtown (600 Pine St., 206/264-0156).

PHOTOGRAPHY

Photographers can stock up on supplies at **Cameras West** (1908 4th Ave., 206/622-0066). Professionals head to **Glazer's Camera Supply** (430 8th Ave. N, 206/624-1100 or 888/531-3232, www.glazerscamera.com), where the shelves are crammed with lighting gear, darkroom supplies, tripods, and other supplies. Its digital photography shop is right across the street. Also of note is **Photo-Tronics** (513 Dexter Ave. N, 206/682-2646), which offers a large professional camera shop, as well as quick camera repair. It is the only place downtown that will clean a digital sensor within a day.

Photographic Center Northwest (900 12th Ave., 206/720-7222, www.pcnw.org) offers a wide range of classes and workshops for photographers at all levels, along with darkroom rentals.

Sports and Recreation

BOATING

Rent wooden rowboats and sailboats and learn about building these classics at the **Center for Wooden Boats** (1010 Valley St., 206/382-2628, www.cwb.org), on the south end of Lake Union. Or, rent sea kayaks from the **Northwest Outdoor Center** (2100 Westlake Ave. N, 206/281-9694 or 800/683-0637, www.nwoc.com) on the southwest side of the lake. This is an outstanding place to learn about sea kayaking from the experts, with classes at all levels. It also sells kayaks and provides guided tours. Also on the south end of Lake Union, **Moss Bay Rowing & Kayak Center** (1001 Fairview N., 206/682-2031, www.mossbay.net) offers kayak rentals and lessons, plus sculling lessons and teams.

Rent sailboards, surfboards, and in-line skates from **Urban Surf** (2100 N. Northlake Way, 206/545-9463, www.urbansurf.com). Washington's largest rafting store, **Swiftwater** (206/547-3377) sells and rents rafts and non-motorized inflatable boats of all types.

In the summer you can rent kayaks, rowboats, pedalboats, sailboards, and canoes to play around the warm waters of Green Lake from **Green Lake Boat Rentals** (7351 E. Green Lake Dr., 206/527-0171).

Over on Lake Washington, head to **University of Washington Waterfront Activities Center** (just east of the Montlake Bridge, 206/543-9433) for canoe or rowboat rentals. Take rowing, sailing, canoeing, or kayaking lessons on Lake Washington from **Mount Baker Rowing and Sailing Center** (3800 Lake Washington Blvd., 206/386-1913).

BICYCLING AND RUNNING

Bikes are a favorite way to get around Seattle, even on rainy winter days. For an easy and level ride, walk, run, or skate, join the throngs at **Green Lake,** where a 2.8-mile paved path circles the duck-filled lake. On sunny spring weekends you're likely to meet hundreds if not thousands of other folks out for fun in the sun.

One of Seattle's most popular bike/running paths is an old railroad route, the **Burke-Gilman Trail.** This 14-mile-long paved path begins in Fremont at 8th Avenue NW, cuts through Gasworks Park on the north shore of Lake Union, and follows along Lake Washington all the way to the north end in Kenmore. From here, the 10-mile-long **Sammamish River Trail** continues to Marymoor Park in Redmond for a total of 24 miles of bike riding, in-line skating, running, or walking pleasure.

© ERICKA CHICKOWSKI

Shred the obstacles under the freeway at Colonnade Park.

Another favorite ride is the six-mile **Alki Trail,** which follows the shore of Puget Sound at Alki Point. It begins at the intersection of Harbor Avenue SW and S.W. Florida Street and curves around the north tip and then west to Alki Point Lighthouse.

Lake Washington Boulevard through the Arboretum and south along Lake Washington to Madrona Park makes for a scenic bike ride, but traffic can get heavy. Other popular cycling places include Bainbridge Island, Mercer Island, Seward Park (in south Lake Washington), and Elliott Bay Trail (just northwest of downtown off Alaskan Way).

Maps

Get an excellent free map detailing the various cycling routes around Seattle from the city's **Bicycle and Pedestrian Program** (600 4th Ave., 206/684-7570); it's also available in Seattle visitors centers. Also free and useful is the **King County Bicycle Guidemap,** which covers the areas surrounding Seattle. It is available from the county RoadShare Program (206/263-4741, www.metrokc.gov/kcdot).

Cycling Clubs

Three regional cycling organizations lead rides and are involved in cycling issues: **Cascade Bicycle Club** (206/522-2453, www.cascade.org), **Seattle Bicycle Club** (www.seattlebike.org), and the **Bicycle Alliance of Washington** (206/224-9252, www.bicyclealliance.org).

Bike Rentals

Tougher insurance regulations have really put a dent in the number of city shops that offer bike rentals these days. Your best bet is one of two shops in the U District. Budget riders should check out **Recycled Cycles** (1007 N.E. Boat

St., 206/547-4491, $40 per day), which rents decent road bikes, mountain bikes, comfort bikes, and trailers. Bike snobs might be happier at **Montlake Bicycle Shop** (2223 24th Ave. E., 206/329-7333, $35–125 per day), which offers a fuller range of rentals, including some of the top mountain and road bikes around.

Gregg's Greenlake Cycle (7007 Woodlawn Ave. NE, 206/523-1822, www.greggscycles.com) no longer rents bikes, but it is still a good spot to pick up tubes and other repair supplies.

SWIMMING

Swimmers will find eight city-run indoor pools around town (www.ci.seattle.wa.us/parks): **Ballard** (1417 N.W. 67th St., 206/684-4094), **Evans** (7201 E. Green Lake Dr. N, 206/684-4961), **Helene Madison** (13401 Meridian Ave. N, 206/684-4979), **Meadowbrook** (10515 35th Ave. NE, 206/684-4989), **Medgar Evers** (500 23rd Ave., 206/684-4766), **Queen Anne** (1920 1st Ave. W, 206/386-4282), **Rainier Beach** (8825 Rainier Ave. S, 206/386-1944), and **Southwest** (2801 S.W. Thistle St., 206/684-7440). The very popular outdoor **Colman Pool** (8603 Fauntleroy Way SW, 206/684-7494) is open summers only for saltwater bathing. The pools at Evans, Queen Anne, and Southwest have saunas, and the Ballard and Southwest pools have hot tubs.

Green Lake is a favorite summertime swimming hole, but the water gets a bit rank by the end of the season with algae (lots of nutrients from all the duck and goose poop). Other beaches with lifeguards in the summer include Madison Park, Madrona Park, Magnuson Park, Matthews Beach, Mount Baker Park, Pritchard Beach, and Seward Park. You can also enjoy Lake Washington from numerous Eastside parks in Kirkland and Bellevue.

MOUNTAINEERING AND CLIMBING

Backcountry enthusiasts should contact the **Washington Alpine Club** (206/467-3042, www.washingtonalpineclub.org), in existence since 1916. Monthly meetings include slide shows and discussions, and the group also offers climbing and skiing classes. A good place to practice rock climbing is the 65-foot artificial pinnacle at the REI store (222 Yale Ave., 206/223-1944 or 800/426-4840, www.rei.com). Several other indoor climbing facilities are available, including America's original indoor climbing gym—**Vertical World** in Magnolia (2123 W. Elmore St., 206/283-4497, www.verticalworld.com). More climbing is available at **The Stone Gardens** in Ballard (2839 N.W. Market St., 206/781-9828, www.stonegardens.com). **Mountain Madness** (4218 S.W. Alaska St., 206/937-8389 800/328-5925, www.mountainmadness.com) offers courses in rock climbing, mountaineering, and ski mountaineering, and staff leads technical climbs up several North Cascades peaks.

SPECTATOR SPORTS

The **Seattle Mariners** (206/346-4001 or 800/696-2746, www.mariners.mlb.com) play Major League Baseball at the striking **Safeco Field** (1250 1st Ave. S.), located just south of Pioneer Square. Sports fans will appreciate the retractable roof, real grass, state-of-the-art video board, excellent sight lines, family barbecue area, kids' zone, and the 47,000 made-for-baseball seats. Hour-long ballpark tours (206/622-4487, $3) are given daily in the summer or Tues.–Sun. in winter.

The NFL's **Seattle Seahawks** (206/628-0888, www.seahawks.com) play right next door at the equally popular **Qwest Field** (800 Occidental Ave. S, 206/381-7848), an open-air gridiron stadium that also hosts the **Seattle Sounders FC** (206/622-3415, www.seattlesounders.net), a professional soccer team that joins the Major League Soccer ranks in 2009 for the first time.

Seattle basketball fans are currently mourning the loss of their beloved SuperSonics to a very controversial move to the Midwest. The only professional basketball action in town these days is the championship-winning (2004 **Seattle Storm** (206/217-9622, www.storm.wnba.com) women's professional team, which plays in KeyArena during the summer months.

The **Seattle Thunderbirds** (206/448-7825, www.seattle-thunderbirds.com) also play at KeyArena. The team competes in minor-league hockey October through May for the Western Hockey League.

College sports are big here, particularly the University of Washington's Husky football (206/543-2200, www.gohuskies.com) and men's and women's basketball teams (206/543-2200, www.gohuskies.com).

Accommodations

Anyone willing to spend $150 or more will find a wide range of options close to the heart of the action, including many of the large chain hotels. Note, however, that you are paying dearly for the location; the same room in Edmonds (a 15-mile drive) would cost half these rates.

Finding a Room

The Seattle-King County Convention and Visitors Bureau offers a free **Seattle Hotel hotline** (206/461-5882 or 800/535-7071, www.visitseattle.org), through which you can make reservations at local hotels. It's a good one-stop place to find a room in your price range. Its online lodging guide is categorized by location and price, with direct links to hundreds of local places; it's an excellent starting place if you have Web access. In addition, the Convention and Visitors Bureau publishes a free calendar of events booklet with discount coupons for many local hotels. Find it at visitors centers or call to request one prior to your arrival in Seattle. Many hotels and motels offer special discount rates for business travelers or members of various organizations (such as AAA), so be sure to ask.

Summer travelers to Seattle should make advance hotel reservations. For longer-term accommodations, check the *Yellow Pages* or local newspapers for places offering apartments and other rentals.

DOWNTOWN

Under $100

A well-run historic place close to Pike Place Market, **Moore Hotel** (1926 2nd Ave., 206/448-4851 or 800/421-5508, www.moorehotel.com, $39 s or $49 d shared bath, $59 s or $67 d private bath) offers bath-down-the-hall rooms, but it also has rooms with private baths; all contain TVs and phones. Parking is available in local lots for $12 per day.

Seattle's only private hostel, **Green Tortoise Backpacker's Guest House** (1525 2nd Ave., 206/282-1222 or 888/424-6873, www.greentortoise.com, $32–36 pp, $90 d private room) has 38 rooms right in the center of town. It's near Pike Place, but the neighborhood also has its share of sleaze. The hostel itself is clean, well managed, and friendly. The hostel has storage lockers, a full kitchen, free Internet access, and daily walking tours. There is no curfew, and alcohol is permitted; there is even free beer on Fridays! Parking is available in local parking garages for around $14 per day. As with other Seattle lodging places, the Green Tortoise fills up quickly in the summer; call ahead for reservations. For longer-term lodging, Green Tortoise offers **A Backpacker's Garden Apartments** (715 2nd Ave. N, 206/340-1222), where you can stay in four-bed dorms for $300 a month; it's a popular place for young folks relocating to Seattle. The hostel is connected with the Green Tortoise Bus (415/956-7500 or 800/867-8647), a great and inexpensive way to explore the country. Trips run all over the continent, even north to Alaska or south to Central America.

$100-150

The renovated and historic **Best Western Pioneer Square Hotel** (77 Yesler Way, 206/340-1234 or 800/800-5514, www.pioneersquare.com, $139–209 s or d) features tastefully appointed rooms and continental breakfast, plus convenient shopping in nearby

FINDING THE PERFECT B&B

Seattle has a number of outstanding B&Bs, particularly in the Capitol Hill neighborhood, home of many stately historic mansions. If you want to simplify your search, contact a reservation service. Two good ones are the **Seattle Bed and Breakfast Association** (206/547-1020 or 800/348-5630, www.seattlebandbs.com) and **A Pacific Reservation Service** (206/439-7677 or 800/684-2932, www.seattlebedandbreakfast.com).

art galleries or the chance to see a Seattle Mariners ball game, whose stadium is just a few blocks away. Parking costs $20.

$200-250

A couple of posh Seattle hotels well worth investigating include **The Paramount Hotel** (724 Pine St., 206/292-9500 or 800/426-0670, www.westcoasthotels.com, $199–239) near the famed theater and downtown's **Hotel Vintage Park** (1100 5th Ave., 206/624-8000 or 800/853-3914, www.kimptonhotels.com, $219–259), a boutique hotel that's serious about wine.

Over $250

Ask for a room with a view at **Alexis Hotel** (1007 1st Ave., 206/624-4844 or 800/264-8482, www.alexishotel.com, $295–335 d, suites $525–825 d) and watch the sun set over the Puget Sound. The sumptuous rooms here feature 300-thread-count linens, flat-screen TVs, and plush furnishings. The themed decor revolves around the arts, and each room is decorated with unique work, as are public areas such as the lobby, where you can sit and sip a cup of complimentary coffee in the morning. Guests can also enjoy complimentary wine-tasting each afternoon downstairs at the acclaimed Library Bistro, which serves Northwest fare in its bookshelf-paneled nooks, as well as one of the better breakfasts on 1st Avenue. The property has a full spa, fitness center, and steam room. It is also pet friendly—the front desk will even watch your pooch for you while you explore downtown or grab a bite to eat. Valet parking costs $30.

One of the city's most stylish hotels is the 26-story **W Seattle Hotel** (1112 4th Ave., 206/264-6000 or 877/946-8357, www.whotels.com). Little touches abound here, from the library of CDs and goose down comforters to the snazzy lobby and attentive service. Everything about the W speaks of elegance and style. Rightly so: most of the rooms start around $400 (less on weekends) and the swankiest suite will set you back $950. Valet parking costs $34.

Fairmont Olympic Hotel (411 University St., 206/621-1700, 800/821-8106 in Washington, 800/223-8772 outside Washington, www.fourseasons.com/seattle, $295–435 s or d, $900 suites) is one of Seattle's grande dames of hospitality, here since 1924 and still a center of luxury. The service is tops, and features include two upscale restaurants (Shuckers and The Georgian), an indoor pool, hot tub, saunas, health club, and self-parking ($35).

The Westin Seattle (1900 5th Ave., 206/728-1000 or 800/228-3000, www.westin.com, $399 s or d) fills two cylindrical towers with its 891 rooms. It offers upmarket accommodations throughout, with all the amenities you expect: a large indoor pool, hot tub, saunas, sundeck, and fitness center. Valet parking is $38.

Classy but not stuffy, **Hotel 1000** (1000 First Ave., 206/957-1000, www.hotel1000.com, $325–$400 d) is one of downtown's finest upscale lodging establishments. Décor is modern, but not uncomfortably so, with muted dark furnishings accented by colorful lighting and art. Rooms are well appointed, the highlights being the large marbled bathrooms featuring waterfall showerheads. The hotel features all of the business amenities you'd expect of a hotel of this caliber, plus a spa and a unique virtual "golf course" just steps away from the lobby that allows you to unwind with a driver without ever putting on your golf shoes.

Another of Seattle's mega-hotels (1,258 rooms) is the **Sheraton Seattle Hotel & Towers** (1400 6th Ave., 206/621-9000 or 800/325-3535, www.sheraton.com, $245–345 s or d). The Sheraton is popular with business and convention travelers and features dramatic vistas from the upper levels of this 35-story building. An indoor pool, hot tub, sauna, and concierge are all available. Parking is an additional $38.

As soon as you walk into the lobby and see the giant photo mural of a model in the nude it becomes pretty clear that the boutique **Hotel Max** (620 Stewart St., 206/728-6299, www.hotelmaxseattle.com, $269 d) is not your mom and dad's luxury hotel. This artsy hotel offers modern furnishings and edgy photos and paintings in the public spaces and in rooms, a spiritual menu of holy books that far surpass that lonely Gideon Bible in most hotel drawers, and a pillow menu for choosy sleepers. It's also pet friendly — tell them you're checking in with your pooch and they'll leave you a dog bed, some treats, and even doggie bottled water.

THE MARKET AND WATERFRONT

$100-150

In the heart of Pike Place Market, **Pensione Nichols B&B** (1923 1st Ave., 206/441-7125 or 800/440-7125, www.seattle-bed-breakfast.com, $90 s or $110 d) is a European-style place with 10 antique-furnished guest rooms with shared baths, plus two suites ($195 for four people). The B&B has great views across Puget Sound. A continental breakfast is served, and kids are welcome in the suites. Pets welcome, too.

$200-250

Seattle's only waterfront lodging on Elliot Bay, the modern 233-room **Hotel Edgewater** (2411 Alaskan Way, 206/728-7000 or 800/624-0670, www.edgewaterhotel.com, $209–309 s or d) sits on Pier 67. Decorated in a mountain-lodge style with in-room fireplaces and pine furniture, the hotel fronts Elliott Bay and the Olympic Mountains, so be sure to ask for a waterside room. Valet parking is $26.

If you want to be in the heart of the action, it's hard to beat the elegant **Inn at the Market** (86 Pine St., 206/443-3600 or 800/446-4484, www.innatthemarket.com), just a few steps from bustling Pike Place Market. The 70 beautifully appointed rooms start at $235 d, spiraling up to a $625 parlor suite. Amenities include a complimentary shuttle, concierge, twice-daily maid service, and robes. Valet parking is $25 per day.

Inn at Harbor Steps (1221 1st Ave., 206/748-0973 or 888/728-8910, www.foursisters.com, $199–240 s or d) is an elegant 28-room urban inn popular with corporate travelers who appreciate the indoor lap pool, hot tub, sauna, fitness facility, fireplaces, wet bars, fridges, full breakfasts, and hors d'oeuvres. Secure parking is another $18.

SEATTLE CENTER AND BELLTOWN

$100-150

Sixth Avenue Inn (2000 6th Ave., 206/441-8300 or 800/648-6440, www.sixthavenueinn.com, $139 s or $151 d) offers clean and updated downtown rooms, including free parking.

One of Seattle's newer downtown hotels, **Hampton Inn and Suites** (700 5th Ave. N, 206/282-7700 or 800/476-7866, www.hamptonsuites.com, $129 d) is on the north side of Seattle Center. A breakfast buffet is included each morning, and parking is free. All suites ($149–199 d) feature fireplaces and kitchens, with some accommodating up to six people.

Not far away is another newer motel with the same ownership: **Comfort Suites-Downtown Seattle Center** (601 Roy St., 206/282-2600 or 800/517-4000, www.comfortsuites.com, $109–149 s or d). Here you will find fridges and microwaves in all rooms, plus an exercise facility and free parking garage. Also available are mini-suites ($119–159), one-bedroom suites ($129–169), and two-bedroom suites ($139–179).

$150-200

The well-cared-for **Holiday Inn Express** (226 Aurora Ave. N, 206/441-7222 or 800/465-

4329, www.holiday-inn.com, $159 s or d) provides clean rooms and amenities such as free parking, an indoor pool, exercise room, and a breakfast buffet.

$200-250

Built in 1918 and beautifully restored eight decades later, the 53-room **MarQueen Hotel** (600 Queen Ave. N, 206/282-7407 or 888/445-3076, www.marqueen.com, $215–389 s or d) is close to Seattle Center. The spacious rooms feature period-style furnishings, hardwood floors, Internet ports, elegant artwork, and full kitchens. Its brochures rightly describe it as "old world charm with new world amenities." Valet parking is $20.

LAKE UNION AND VICINITY

$150-200

Over in South Lake Union, **Courtyard by Marriott-Lake Union** (925 Westlake Ave. N, 206/213-0100 or 800/321-2211, www.courtyard.com, $159–189 s or d) is a good bet, convenient to the lake, the freeway, and Seattle Center. Rooms are what you would expect from this chain, complemented by amenities including an outdoor pool, hot tub, and exercise room.

$200-250

A couple of other mid-priced lodging options are worth a look: The best place to perch your noggin for the night in South Lake Union is **Silver Cloud Inn-Seattle Downtown Lake Union** (1150 Fairview Ave. N, 206/447-9500 or 800/551-7207, www.scinns.com, $209–229 d). Well-appointed rooms come equipped with plush beds, plasma-screen TVs, and free wireless Internet.

Houseboat Rentals

The *Sleepless in Seattle* fans will be disappointed to find that updated city ordinances have all but ended short-term houseboat rentals on Lake Union. The only way you can get your own little floating cottage is to stay three months or longer. Contact Seattle Houseboat Rentals (www.seattlehouseboatrentals.com) for details.

CAPITOL HILL

One of Seattle's oldest and most desirable neighborhoods, the quiet residential streets of Capitol Hill are home to nearly a dozen classic bed-and-breakfasts.

Under $100

Bed and Breakfast on Capitol Hill (739 Broadway E, 206/325-0320, $68–115 s or d) has three guest rooms with shared or private baths; rooms include a self-serve "continental plus" breakfast. The Foursquare home was built in 1903 and contains family antiques. No kids under 16 are permitted.

$100-150

Built in 1904, **Salisbury House B&B** (750 16th Ave. E, 206/328-8682, www.salisburyhouse.com, $139–185 d) is a grand Capitol Hill home with a wraparound porch and a flowery backyard. The public rooms are large and bright, and the four guest rooms and a suite all have private baths.

Bed & Breakfast on Broadway (722 Broadway E, 206/329-8933 or 888/329-8933, www.bbonbroadway.com, $105–135 s or $135–175 d is a 1906 home with the original stained glass windows, oriental rugs, a fireplace, and a grand piano. The three guest rooms have private baths. A continental breakfast is served, and no children under 16 are allowed.

Housed in a historic 1905 home, the stately **Gaslight Inn** (1727 15th Ave., 206/325-3654, www.gaslight-inn.com, $88–159 s or d) is one of the larger B&Bs in Seattle, with eight rooms (private or shared baths), a library, outdoor pool, and continental breakfast. It frequently books up far ahead, so reserve early for the summer. No kids are allowed here.

Thankfully for B&B-loving families, several places do welcome the little ones. One of the most impressive is **Bacon Mansion B&B** (959 Broadway E, 206/329-1864 or 800/240-1864, www.baconmansion.com, $99–179 s or d). This superb 1909 Tudor mansion sprawls over four levels, with an adjacent carriage house. Inside the mansion you'll find marble fireplaces, a crystal chandelier, grand piano, and 11 guest rooms, nine with private baths. An expanded continental breakfast is served.

Built in 1890, **Mildred's B&B** (1202 15th Ave. E, 206/325-6072 or 800/889-2110, www.mildredsbnb.com, $90–165 s or d) is an attractive Capitol Hill Victorian with a wraparound porch facing Volunteer Park. It has four guest rooms with private baths, and the living room contains a grand piano and fireplace. Guests also have fun on the little putting green on the front lawn. Kids are welcome here.

$150-200

The stately **Shafer-Baillie Mansion Guest House** (907 14th Ave. E, 206/322-4654 or 800/922-4654, www.shafer-baillie.com, $149–219 s or d for the guest rooms, or $195 d for the master suite) sits along "Millionaire's Row" on Capitol Hill, with five attractively decorated guest rooms, most with private baths. This English manor–style mansion was built in 1914 and is popular for weddings. A continental breakfast is served, and kids are welcome.

QUEEN ANNE AND MAGNOLIA

$100-150

The **Inn at Queen Anne** (505 1st Ave. N, 206/282-7357 or 800/952-5043, www.innatqueenanne.com) features charming downtown studios ($99–109 d) and suites ($119–159 d), all with kitchens and continental breakfasts. The great location near Seattle Center, moderate rates, and apartment-style units make Inn at Queen Anne popular with families. Book well ahead for the summer. Parking is $10 daily.

Inn of Twin Gables (3258 14th Ave. W, 206/284-3979 or 866/466-3979, www.innoftwingables.com, $100–180 s or d) is a classic Craftsman home built in 1915. Inside, you will find an enclosed sun porch, plus a cozy living room with fireplace and overstuffed furniture. One room has its own bath, and the other two share the master bath. Rates include a substantial gourmet breakfast. No children are allowed here.

BALLARD AND SHILSHOLE BAY

Under $100

Dibble House B&B (7301 Dibble Ave. NW, 206/783-0320, $60–70 s or d) has five guest rooms with shared or private baths in a 1920s Ballard home. The owner runs a catering service, so you know her breakfasts are notable. Room rates are among the lowest in Seattle, and kids are welcome.

$100-150

Chez Sharon B&B (8068 26th Ave. NW, 206/789-6660, www.chezsharoninseattle.com, $105 d) has a quiet Ballard district suite facing a flower-filled garden. A continental breakfast is served. This is an adults-only establishment.

UNIVERSITY DISTRICT

Under $100

College Inn (4000 University Way NE, 206/633-4441, www.collegeinnseattle.com, $55–85 d) is a historic 1909 University District hotel with down-the-hall baths and a European feeling. The owners are friendly. A generous continental breakfast is included, but there are no elevators in this four-story building, so pack light. You'll also need to find a nearby lot to park your car overnight.

University Motel (4731 12th Ave. NE, 206/522-4724 or 800/522-4720, $93–121 d) has dated motel accommodations that will do just fine for visiting students. All rooms contain full kitchens—a real plus for travelers—and parking is free, but there is no elevator at this three-story motel.

Eastlake Inn (2215 Eastlake Ave., 206/322-7726, $89 s or d, suites $160 for up to six people) is a little family-run motel just five minutes by car south of the University, near Lake Union. The decor is rather plain in this older motel, but all rooms contain kitchenettes.

$100-150

University Inn (4140 Roosevelt Way NE, 206/632-5055 or 800/733-3855, www.universityinnseattle.com, $105–129 s or $115–139

d) is just a five-minute walk from the campus. The property has an outdoor pool, hot tub, fitness room, continental breakfast, and free parking. Some rooms contain fridges and microwaves; all are nonsmoking.

Hotel Deca (4507 Brooklyn Ave. NE, 206/634-2000 or 800/899-0251, www.universitytowerhotel.com, $139–169) is the swankiest spot to sleep in the U District, and one of the best bargains in the city. This 15-story luxury hotel is the product of a $2 million renovation that installed art deco decor with a colorful modern flair. The tower is within easy walking distance of all campus sights and restaurants; amenities include a complimentary breakfast and newspaper, exercise room, and free parking.

$150-200

The modern **Silver Cloud Inn-University Village** (5036 25th Ave. NE, 206/526-5200 or 800/205-6940, www.scinns.com, $189 d) is just a short distance from University Village Mall, one of the nicer local places to shop. The campus is a few uphill blocks away, though not really walkable. Guests enjoy the use of an indoor pool, hot tub, exercise room, continental breakfast, and free parking.

The Chambered Nautilus B&B (5005 22nd Ave. NE, 206/522-2536 or 800/545-8459, www.chamberednautilus.com, $139–204 s or d) offers Cascade views on a hill just four blocks north of the university. This Georgian Colonial home was built in 1915 and is the only B&B close to campus. There's a library and pleasant sun porch, and the six large guest rooms all have private baths, TVs, and phones. The Chambered Nautilus fills fast, so book early. Kids over eight are accepted. Next to the B&B, the owners have a newer four-plex building called **University Suites** with one- and two-bedroom apartments—all with full kitchens ($129–184 d one-bedroom or $134–204 d two-bedroom). Guests at Chambered Nautilus and University Suites are served a gourmet three-course breakfast.

CAMPING

There are no public campgrounds in the immediate vicinity of Seattle, but **Fay-Bainbridge State Park** has year-round campsites on Bainbridge Island, just a short ferry ride away. You'll need a car or bike to get to the park from the ferry dock on Bainbridge, six miles away. Other state park campgrounds around Seattle are in Federal Way (Dash Point State Park), Enumclaw (Kanaskat-Palmer Recreation Area), and Des Moines (Saltwater State Park). The closest Forest Service campgrounds are in the Cascades, at least 35 miles east on I-90.

As for private RV parks, the best bets for centrally located urban parks are the Issaquah, Lynnwood, and Renton areas.

Food

The options listed herein are only a minuscule sampling of Seattle's food and drink establishments. If you are serious about your meals out, take a gander at a specific guide to Seattle dining.

DOWNTOWN

Cafés and Delis

A classy restaurant based out of the Alexis Hotel, **Library Bistro** (92 Madison St., 206/624-3646, www.paintedtableseattle.com, 7–10 A.M. and 11:30A.M.–2 P.M. Mon.–Fri., 8 A.M.–1 P.M. Sat.–Sun., $15) features breakfasts, brunches, and lunches that favor Northwest cuisine with a flair. Kids and kids-at-heart will love the book-filled shelving and the butcher-paper and crayons at each table.

Stop by **13 Coins** (125 Boren Ave. N., 206/682-2513, www.13coins.com, $20), Seattle's classic 24-hour restaurant and gathering place for both the famous and the infamous. It offers more than 130 menu items.

COFFEEHOUSES

If you can't find an espresso café within a block of any Seattle shopping district, your eyes are closed and you've lost your sense of smell. It's hard to know where to begin when it comes to coffee in this place where coffee consumption tops that of any other American city. With hundreds of espresso bars, carts, and drive-throughs all over Seattle, you would be hard-pressed to *not* find a great cup of java. The most famous, of course, is **Starbucks** (www.starbucks.com), with dozens of shops scattered across the city. The original shop is in the Pike Place Market – note the company's original and rather risqué logo on the front window – you won't see this at other Starbucks. Named for the first mate in Herman Melville's *Moby Dick,* Starbucks is considered by many the godfather of quality coffee in the Northwest. That first store opened in 1971, offering dark-roasted beans and a commitment to quality; roasted beans more than a week old are given to charities.

Also of note are **Tully's Coffee** (www.tullys.com) and **Seattle's Best Coffee** (www.seattlesbest.com), both of which have a dozen or so Seattle shops. Tully's took over the old Rainier brewery in Seattle a few years back, while Seattle's Best Coffee is actually owned by Starbucks! Even when you think they don't have ya, they do . . .

Roasteria (321 Broadway E., Capitol Hill, 206/860-5869, www.espressovivace.com, 6:30 A.M.-11 P.M. daily) is a great little walk-up spot for espresso in the heart of Capitol Hill. It also has a second, larger shop downtown (901 E. Denny Way, 206/860-5869, same hours). **Cafe Septieme** (214 Broadway E., 206/860-8858, www.cafeseptieme.com, 9 A.M.-11:45 P.M. daily) has the charm of a Parisian café and is a romantic place to enjoy a big bowl of cappuccino.

Other great places to sip espresso are **Caffe Ladro** (600 Queen Anne Ave. N., 206/282-1549, www.caffeladro.com, 5:30 A.M.-11 P.M. daily) in Queen Anne, **Diva Espresso Bar** (7916 Greenwood Ave. N., 206/781-1213. 7 A.M.-10 P.M. Mon.-Sat., 8 A.M.-8 P.M. Sun.) and **Caffè Umbria** (320 Occidental Ave. S., 206/624-5847, www.caffeumbria.com) in Pioneer Square.

The Bistro (709 N. 35th St., 206/547-9850) is a wonderful espresso house that also serves healthy sandwiches, rich soups, and chocolate desserts in a bright and oft-crowded café.

A rambling old home at contains one of the U District's classic places, **Grand Illusion Coffeehouse** (NE 50th St. and University Way NE, 206/523-3935). The student crowd sprawls in the funky chairs and couches, sipping coffee, reading books, and waiting for films in the adjacent art-house theater. Another old favorite – it opened in 1975 – is just a few blocks down. **Cafe Allegro** (4214½ University Way NE, facing the alley on 15th St., 206/633-3030, www.cafeallegro.com, 6 A.M.-10:30 P.M. Mon.-Fri., 7 A.M.-10:30 P.M. Sat., 7:30 A.M.-10:30 P.M. Sun.) is a popular sit-down-and-stay-awhile espresso house with three rooms spread over two floors.

Those with bigger appetites will rave over the cheesesteaks at **Tat's Delicatessen** (115 Occidental Ave. S., 206/264-8287, www.tatsdeli.com, 7 A.M.–4 P.M. Mon.–Fri., $10). These sandwiches "wit Whiz" are the closest you're gonna get to Philly around these parts.

Contemporary Northwest

Sitting in the Fairmont Olympic Hotel, the **Georgian Room** (411 University St., 206/621-7889, www.fairmont.com/seattle, 6 A.M.–2:30 P.M. and 5:30–10 P.M. Tues.–Sat., $40) is an elegant dining room with a Renaissance look and Northwest cuisine. The food is very expensive but much lighter than what you might expect in a luxury hotel. The salmon, sturgeon, rabbit, lamb, veal, and steaks are cooked to a creative perfection, and the menu also includes a five-course vegetarian dinner that has garnered national praise. Expect to pay at least $150 for a dinner for two with wine and dessert.

Sleek and sexy, **Union** (400 1st Ave., 206/838-8000, www.unionseattle.com, 5–10 P.M.

© ERICKA CHICKOWSKI

Seattle's coffee scene is alive and well.

daily, $50) still manages to maintain its hip vibe even now that it's well past the two-to-three-year shelf life of "hot" Seattle restaurants. You see, this one is a keeper. The kitchen keeps it fresh but simple with a daily changing menu that highlights the Northwest's best ingredients, using everything from chanterelle mushrooms to fresh geoduck. Best of all, the wait staff here are some of the most professional, kind, and attentive among Seattle's best restaurants. Ask for their wine and food recommendation and run with it; they won't steer you wrong.

Steak and Seafood

Metropolitan Grill (820 2nd Ave., 206/624-3287, 11 A.M.–10:30 P.M. Mon.–Fri., 4–10:45 P.M. Sat., 4–10 P.M. Sun., $50) is one of the best places in town for steak, and it fills up with business folk at lunch. Seafood (including great clam chowder), pork, lamb, and pastas are also on the menu. Expensive, but worth it.

Located a short stroll from Safeco Field and Qwest Field, **F.X. McRory's Steak, Chop & Oyster House** (419 Occidental Ave. S., 206/623-4800, www.fxmcrorys.com, 11:30 A.M.–1 A.M. daily, $18) is the ideal place for a post-game party with friends. The fun-loving young crowd is loud, and the menu includes prime rib and salmon, along with six types of raw oysters on the half-shell. Beer isn't brewed here, but more than two dozen different Northwest microbrews are on tap.

Conventioners seeking an impressive and close-by establishment to wine and dine clients should book their reservations at **Union Square Grill** (621 Union St., 206/224-4321, www.unionsquaregrill.com, 11 A.M.–3 P.M. Mon.–Fri. and 5–10 P.M. Sun.–Thurs., 5–11 P.M. Fri.–Sat., $40), which far surpasses the run-of-the-mill eateries that surround the convention center. Featuring quality cuts of beef and lamb, fresh seafood, nicely presented cheese platters, and drool-worthy desserts, the grill is a definite crowd pleaser. And if you don't get the sale, no worries. The bartenders here pour a stiff drink.

Asian

Pan-Asian fare has a strong following in Seattle, and trendy noodle houses are as plentiful as coffee beans and Goretex. One of the best of the bunch, **Wild Ginger** (1401 3rd Ave., 206/623-4450, www.wildginger.net, 11:30 A.M.–3 P.M. and 5–11 P.M. Mon.–Thurs., 11:30 A.M.–2 P.M. and 5 P.M.–midnight Fri., 4:30 P.M.–midnight Sat., 4–11 P.M. Sun., $17) jumps all over Asia: Vietnamese, Thai, Indonesian, and Szechuan Chinese dishes all come out of this creative kitchen. Wild Ginger is best known for its *satay* bar, which features skewered and grilled seafood, chicken, pork, and vegetables, but it also offers delicious curries, soups, and crab. The menu changes seasonally.

Also worth a look is the arty Thai **Typhoon** (1400 Western Ave., 206/262-9797, www.typhoonrestaurants.com, 4–9:30 P.M. Mon.–Fri., 5–9:30 P.M. Sat.–Sun., $14). The menu is much more expensive than the average hole-in-the-wall Thai restaurant about town, but then again, its noodles, curries, and satays are a cut above the rest. Come 'round with the after-work crowd to take advantage of one of the best happy hour menus downtown.

Italian

Il Terrazzo Carmine (411 1st Ave. S., 206/467-7797, www.ilterrazzocarmine.com, 11:30 A.M.–2:30 P.M. and 5:30–10:30 P.M. Mon.–Fri., 5:30–10:30 P.M. Sat., $28) is a delightful Pioneer Square restaurant perfect for a romantic dinner. Choose from homemade pastas, creamy risottos, and fantastic meat dishes, including a fall-off-the-bone osso bucco.

Al Boccalino (1 Yesler Way, 206/622-7688, www.alboccalino.com, 11:30 A.M.–2:30 P.M. and 5–10 P.M. Mon.–Fri., 5 P.M.–10 P.M. Sat., $14) is another longtime Pioneer Square favorite. Especially notable are the prawns and garlic served over a bed of sautéed spinach, and the saddle of lamb. Whatever you choose, pair it with a silky glass of wine from this restaurant's amply stocked cellar.

Bakeries

Pick up a big, chewy bagel slathered in house-made whipped cream cheese at **Seattle Bagel Bakery** (804 Howell St., 206/667-9327, $4), which offers a range of bagel and schmear flavors. It also serves up lots of bagel sandwich offerings come lunchtime.

Enjoy a croissant or another fluffy treat from **Chez Dominique European Pastries & Café** (77 Spring St., 206/623-2219, 6:30 A.M.–4:45 P.M. Mon.–Fri., closed Sat.–Sun., $5).

The suits love to tuck the napkins into their shirts at **Grand Central Bakery** (214 1st Ave. S., 206/622-3644, www.grandcentralbakery.com, 7 A.M.–5 P.M. Mon.–Fri., 8 A.M.–4 P.M. Sat., $8), which offers ample choices of soups, salads, and healthy sandwiches at lunch and some tasty breakfast plates to boot.

Markets

The tiny brick **Esquin Wine Merchants** (2700 4th Ave., 206/682-7374, www.esquin.com) shop is big on Italian wines but also carries Northwest varieties and offers tastings, classes, and reasonable prices.

THE MARKET AND WATERFRONT

Cafés and Delis

Right in Pike Place Market is **Cafe Campagne** (1600 Post Alley, 206/728-2233, www.campagnerestaurant.com, 11 A.M.–10 P.M. Mon.–Fri., 5:30 A.M.–10 P.M. Sat.–Sun., $22), the downstairs neighbor of the more upscale Campagne. The café serves all three meals, but its breakfasts are a relative bargain. Try the Provençal eggs at breakfast and at dinner go for the French 101, a three-course prix fixe for $33.

Foodies love **Steelhead Diner** (95 Pine St., 206/625-0129, www.steelheaddiner.com, 11 A.M.–10 P.M. Tues.–Sat., 10 A.M.–3 P.M. Sun., $20) for its inventive take on counter-and-stool roadhouse fare. Nosh on delicious eggs served with andouille sausage and potato latkes, veggie "meat" loaf, delectable roast chicken with wilted spinach, and dozens more dishes that will make your eyes roll back into your head. Don't skip this one.

Contemporary Northwest

OK, so you've just strolled the market's main arcade and taken in the sights and smells whirling about the kaleidoscope of fresh food. You'd love to taste it, too, but you just don't have a kitchen or the inclination to cook with the market's bounty, right? Get thee immediately to **Matt's in the Market** (94 Pike St., Ste. 32, 206/467-7909, 11:30 A.M.–2:30 P.M. and 5:30–10 P.M. Mon.–Sat., closed Sun., $30), a charming bistro whose staff crafts the menu each day based on what's freshest in the stalls. Trust them to be your culinary guides. From your perch in this second story eatery you can watch the crowds bustle below and enjoy your meal 'neath the glow of the market's iconic clock display.

Seafood

Given its waterfront location, it should come as no surprise that Seattle's specialty is fresh seafood of all types. The city is jammed with fishy restaurants, from takeout fish-and-chips joints to luxury dining that will set you back $60 per person and more.

With five species of oysters grown in Puget Sound waters—including the native Olympia oyster—Seattle has a reputation as one of the best places to slurp fresh oysters on the half-shell. **Emmett Watson's Oyster Bar** (1916 Pike Pl., 206/448-7721, 11:30 A.M.–7 P.M. Mon.–Thurs., 11:30 A.M.–8 P.M. Fri.–Sat., 11:30 A.M.–6 P.M. Sun., $12) is one of the best of these, a relaxed little place in the Soames-Dunn Building at Pike Place Market, with reasonable prices and ultra-fresh oysters, plus great salmon soup or fish and chips. **Elliott's Oyster House & Seafood Restaurant** (Pier 56, 206/623-4340, 11:30 A.M.–8 P.M. Mon.–Sat., 11:30 A.M.–6 P.M. Sun., $22) is one of the better waterfront seafood restaurants, with crab, clams, and freshly shucked oysters. Expensive, but it's a fantastic location.

You will not go wrong at **Etta's Seafood** (2020 Western Ave., 206/443-6000, www.tomdouglas.com, 11:30 A.M.–9:30 P.M. Mon.–Thurs., 11:30 A.M.–10 P.M. Fri., 9 A.M.–3 P.M. and 4–10 P.M. Sat., 9 A.M.–3 P.M. Sun., $27–34) in Pike Place Market. The mixed drinks are great.

Ivar's Acres of Clams (on the waterfront at Pier 54, 206/624-6852, www.ivars.net, 11 A.M.–10 P.M. daily, $22) was folk singer Ivar Haglund's original restaurant (open since 1938). The restaurant is an unpretentious, quality seafood restaurant that often surprises diners who only know Ivars for the tourist-friendly takeout bar out front ($7.50 for four-piece cod and chips).

A bright and elegant waterfront place, **Anthony's Pier 66** (2201 Alaskan Way, 206/448-6688, www.anthonys.com, 11 A.M.–3 P.M. and 5–10 P.M. daily, $30) serves a seafood menu that includes award-winning clam chowder, fresh mahimahi, scallops, crab fettuccine, and other favorites. Downstairs at the more casual **Bell St. Diner** the menu also focuses on fresh seafood, but prices are lower and the wine list is smaller. Both places have delightful patios overlooking Elliott Bay.

Just up the street from Pike Place Market, **Cutter's Bayhouse** (2001 Western Ave., 206/448-4884, www.cuttersbayhouse.com, 11 A.M.–10 P.M. Sun.–Thurs., 9:30 A.M.–10 P.M. Fri.–Sat., $16–40) has a lively bar with a long list of hors d'oeuvres; its specialties—fresh fish, pasta, and prime rib dishes—are accompanied by an extensive wine-by-the-glass list. Sunsets over the Olympics are even more notable than the food.

French

Impress your sweetheart and secure a table upstairs at **Place Pigalle** (81 Pike St., 206/624-1756, www.placepigalle-seattle.com, 11:30 A.M.–2:30 P.M. Mon.–Fri., 11:30 A.M.–3 P.M. Sat. and 5:30–9:30 P.M. Mon.–Thurs., 5:30–10 P.M. Fri.–Sat., closed Sun., $26), a cozy bistro with a certain *je ne sais quoi*. Its entrance is hidden in a market nook just between the flying fish and the movie memorabilia shop. Come during happy hour, when the menu is really affordable and tasty and you can watch the sun sink down behind the Olympics from the bank of windows looking out over the Sound.

Campagne (86 Pine St., 206/728-2800, www.campagnerestaurant.com, 5–10 P.M. daily, $24–30) is an elegant bistro with a French-inspired Northwest menu. The food is priced to match the quality. The restaurant sits in the heart of Pike Place Market.

Another classic Pike Place restaurant with French inspirations is **Maximilien in the Market** (206/682-7270, www.maximilien-restaurant.com, 11:30 A.M.–9 P.M. daily, $30) with stunning views across Elliott Bay and lamb, fish, veal, and beef entrées.

Bakeries

For a taste of old England, don't miss **The Crumpet Shop** (1503 1st Ave., 206/682-1598, 7 A.M.–5 P.M. Mon.–Wed. and Fri., 7:30 A.M.–5 P.M. Sat.–Sun., closed Thurs., $5) in the Sanitary Market building, where you can get delicious fresh crumpets and a steaming pot of tea. Don't miss the fluffy scones, either. They'll make you forever swear off those lumpy rocks most coffee shops masquerade as scones these days.

Some hungers, though, just can't be satisfied with scones and crumpets alone. If you're looking for something a little more substantial stop in for a piping hot meat pastry at **Piroshky Piroshky** (1908 Pike Pl., 206/441-6068, www.piroshkybakery.com, 7:30 A.M.–7:30 P.M. daily in summer, 8 A.M.–6:30 P.M. daily in fall–spring, $5). This is a long-time personal favorite, a little food stand with just a table or two in front of its displays packed full with its namesake pastry, an Eastern European pocket of cheeses, veggies, meats, and delicious spices.

Markets

The stalls at **Pike Place Market** are the place to go for fresh fruit, veggies, nuts, and even jalapeño jelly. Pick up some flowers for your honey while you're at it—and maybe even some honey, too! Those big bears full of the golden stuff sold at the day stalls in the North Arcade will make you swear off grocery store honey forever. Most of the following markets are open during the market's peak hours of 10 A.M.–6 P.M. Monday through Saturday and 11 A.M.–5 P.M. Sunday.

You can find the pepper jelly at **Mick's Peppouri** (1531 Pike Pl., 206/233-0128) a permanent fixture in the Main Arcade that mixes up unique blends featuring horseradish, lime, garlic, and more. It might sound a little weird to the uninitiated, but wander over here for a taste — they've always got samples out — and you'll likely be hooked for life!

Pick a pinch of penne at **Pappardelle's Pasta of Pike Place Market** (1519 Pike Pl., Ste. 8, 206/340-4114, www.pappardellespasta.com), right in the Main Arcade. With dozens of lusciously fresh pastas on hand at all times, this place is a must when looking for a starchy accompaniment for seafood snagged at the market.

Even though Pike Place is best associated with the flying fish guys over at **Pike Place Fish,** that's far from the only quality fishmon-

TEAHOUSES

Although Seattle is best known for its lattes, the city also has a number of quality tea shops. **Seattle Best Tea** (504 S. King St., 206/749-9855) is a little shop across from Uwajimaya in the International District with an excellent selection of Asian teas. The **Teacup** (2207 Queen Anne N., 206/283-5931, www.tearanch.com) in Queen Anne sells 150 varieties of black, green, and herb teas from all over the globe and always has something interesting to taste. The Chinese-style **Teahouse Kuan Yin** (1911 N. 45th St., 206/632-2055, www.teahousechoice.com, 9 A.M.–11 P.M. daily) is connected to Wide World Books and offers a taste of Asian teas, along with light meals. Also visit the **Kado Teagarden Café** (206/729-1070, 11 A.M.–4:30 P.M. Thurs.–Sun.) inside the Seattle Asian Art Museum in Volunteer Park, and the **Japanese Tea Garden** (206/684-4725, 10 A.M.–7 P.M. daily) at the University of Washington Arboretum.

The best place for a formal afternoon high tea is at **Queen Mary Tea Room** (2912 NE 55th St., 206/527-2770, www.queenmarytearoom.com, 9 A.M.–4 P.M. daily).

ger at the market. Try **Pure Food Fish** (1511 Pike Pl., 206/622-5765, www.freshseafood.com) for cheaper prices and some of the best shellfish at the market.

If you really want to walk on the wild side, why not pair up those mussels you just bought with some artisan-crafted andouille? You'll find the best sausage in the shop right next to Pure Food at **Uli's Famous Sausage** (1511 Pike Pl., 206/839-1100, www.ulisfamoussausage.com), a market fixture and a favorite among award-winning chefs around the city.

You can also find a number of shops across the street from the Main Arcade with plenty of specialty goodies, including **DeLaurenti Market** (1435 1st Ave., 206/622-0141), filled with gourmet imported groceries and wines from Europe. **Pike and Western Wine Merchants** (1934 Pike Pl., 206/441-1307, www.pikeandwestern.com) at the Pike Place Market has groceries, along with a diverse choice of Northwest wines.

The cheese is out of this world and so are the prices at ☾ **Beechers Handmade Cheese** (1600 Pike Pl., 206/956-1964, www.beechershandmadecheese.com), where it is not impossible to plunk down $25 or more for a little wedge. But I'm telling you, it is worth it, particularly if you're already spending a mint on some good Washington wine. The specialty is the Flagship cheese, aged one year.

For something on the sweeter side, pop into Post Alley and pick out a selection of cocoa-laden treats at **Rose's Chocolate Treasures** (1906 Post Alley, 206/441-2936, www.roseschocolatetreasures.com), which not only offers artisan bonbons and truffles but also spicy chocolate ideal for whipping up a perfect mole sauce.

INTERNATIONAL DISTRICT

Chinese

As you might guess, the International District is laden with Chinese restaurants. Among the best is ☾ **House of Hong** (409 8th Ave. S., 206/622-7997, www.houseofhong.com, 9:30 A.M.–10 P.M. SUN.–THURS., 9:30 A.M.–11 P.M. Fri.–Sat., $10) with dim sum, seafood, chicken, and Hong Kong barbecue. Things get crowded in the evening, but the dim sum carts always have something appealing on board.

Tai Tung (655 S. King St., 206/622-7372, 10 A.M.–11 P.M. Sun.–Thurs., 10 A.M.–1:30 A.M. Fri.–Sun., $9) is the real thing, packed with Chinese from the neighborhood and longtime Seattleites who consistently rate it an International District favorite. The food can be inconsistent and heavy on the sauces, so your best bet is to look around and see what others are eating for a clue on what to order.

Sea Garden Restaurant (509 7th Ave. S., 206/623-2100, http://fourseasrestaurant.com, 11 A.M.–2 A.M. daily, $12) serves Cantonese meals, but the food isn't the bland chow mein you might expect. Instead, the menu offers a wide range of soups, seafood specialties, and perfectly cooked vegetables.

Vietnamese

Pho Bac (415 7th Ave. S., 206/323-4387, 9 A.M.–7 P.M. daily) is a haven for those of us who love the Vietnamese staple, a flavorful soup called *pho.* It's all they serve, so you know they do it right here! The setting is budget, and so are the prices—$6.50 for a large bowl.

If *pho* isn't your game, don't give up on Vietnamese food! Try the delicious *bahn mi,* or Vietnamese sandwiches, at **Saigon Vietnam Deli** (1200 S. Jackson St., 206/328-2357, 7 A.M.–8P.M. daily) for something completely different. Consisting of soft baguettes, crispy veggies, and meats such as shredded pork, ham, and pate, these make for a cheap and filling meal — most sandwiches clock in at a miniscule $2.

Markets

The International District has a quite a few small markets selling Asian groceries, but none compare to the sprawling **Uwajimaya** (600 5th Ave., 206/624-6248, www.uwajimaya.com). The largest Asian supermarket in the Northwest, it sells everything from high-quality groceries to Japanese furniture. Step inside for an eye-opening venture across the Pacific, plus excellent light meals in the Japanese deli.

Snag the tastiest — and sometimes funniest — fortune cookies at **Tsue Chong Co. Inc.** (800 S. Weller St., 206/623-0801, 9:30 A.M.–5:30 P.M. Mon.–Fri., 10 A.M.–2 P.M. Sat., closed Sun.), where you can buy bags of uniquely flavored fortune cookies, witty "misfortune" cookies stuffed with predictions unseen in most Chinese desserts, as well as the standard fare. Tsue Chong also sells scrumptious egg noodles.

SEATTLE CENTER AND BELLTOWN

Cafés and Diners

The food won't knock your socks off at **Whym Diner** (101 Denny Way, 206/269-9496, 24 hours daily, $10), but after a night of partying in Belltown, this is a clean, well-lighted place perfect for satisfying that middle-of-the-night urge to binge.

You won't find a traditional grinder on a hoagie here, so I can't say it's *completely* authentic, but **Mike's East Coast Sandwiches** (113 Cedar St., 206/818-1744, www.mikeseastcoast.com, 8 A.M.–6 P.M. Mon.–Fri., 9 A.M.–5 P.M. Sat., $6) does serve a darned good reuben on rye, plus unique creations. Try the meat and potato sandwich, which puts potato salad right in there with the meat and other sandwich fillings. Nutella fanatics will also dig the Nutella fluffernutter, served with the cocoa and hazelnut spread, marshmallow fluff, and peanut butter.

Artists, wanna-be artists, folks on the fringe, and even the button-down set jam the counter at **Two Bells Tavern** (2313 4th Ave., 206/441-3050, 11 A.M.–10 P.M. daily, $10) They all come here for some of the best and biggest burgers in Seattle, served on sourdough rolls and topped with fried onions. The menu expands to include tasty soups, salads, and other well-prepared pub grub.

Contemporary Northwest

Marco's Supperclub (2510 1st Ave., 206/441-7801, www.marcossupperclub.com, 5–10 P.M. Mon.–Sat., $18) is a bright and arty Belltown place with a menu that bumps from grilled salmon to Jamaican jerk chicken to fried sage-leaf appetizers (far better than it sounds). The food is always creative, and the atmosphere is relaxed.

Dahlia Lounge (2001 4th Ave., 206/682-4142, www.tomdouglas.com, 11 A.M.–2:30 P.M. Mon.–Fri. and 5–10 P.M. Mon.–Thurs., 5–11 P.M. Fri.–Sat., 5–p P.M. Sun. $28) is a trendy eatery with widely varied and spicy fare created by famed chef/owner Tom Douglas. It's a wonderful place for a memorable meal.

The food is beautifully presented and the atmosphere is raucous at Belltown's **Flying Fish** (2234 1st Ave., 206/728-8595, www.flyingfishrestaurant.com, 11:30 A.M.–2 P.M. and 5–11 P.M. Mon.–Fri., 5–11 P.M. Sat.–Sun., $28). Take a seat in the bar to survey the crowd below.

Located atop the Space Needle, **SkyCity Restaurant** (206/443-2111, www.spaceneedle.com, 11:30 A.M.–2 P.M. and 5–8:45 P.M. Mon.–Thurs., 11:30 A.M.–2 P.M. and 5–9:45 P.M. Fri., 10 A.M.–2:45 P.M. and 5–9:45 P.M. Sat., 10 A.M.–2:45 P.M. and 5–8:45 P.M. Sun., $45) is a top-of-the-world dining experience at 500 feet, very popular with tourists, visiting relatives, and teens on prom night. The food is mediocre and expensive, but the view is unsurpassed, as the revolving restaurant completes a 360-degree turn by the time your dessert arrives.

Asian

In Belltown, the popular **Noodle Ranch** (2228 2nd Ave., 206/728-0463, 11 A.M.–10 P.M. Mon.–Fri., noon–10 P.M. Sat., closed Sun., $8) offers up a snazzy decor, with a variety of noodle soups, satays, curries, udons, grilled meats, and spring rolls. Reasonable prices, too.

Owned by one of Seattle's most revered sushi chefs, Shiro Kashiba, **Shiro's** (2401 2nd Ave., 206/443-9844, www.shiros.com, 5–10 P.M. daily, $20) serves the freshest sushi, with daily specials.

French

Le Pichet (1933 1st Ave., 206/256-1499, 8 A.M.–midnight Sun.–Thurs., 8 A.M.–2 A.M. Fri.–Sat.) is a wonderful Belltown café with a fun atmosphere, exquisite French meals, and fine wine selection (including many by the glass). Sit at the bar if the tables are all taken.

Bakeries

In the land of latte, the lowly doughnut has fallen out of favor among epicurean elitists. However, there still remains a place where fried dough in the round reigns supreme. Located at several strategic spots about town, **Top Pot Doughnuts** (2124 5th Ave., 206/728-1966, www.toppotdoughnuts.com, 6 A.M.–7 P.M. Mon.–Fri., 7 A.M.–7 P.M. Sat.–Sun., $3) is most easily found in its spacious two-story Belltown castle. Choose between 40 types of doughnuts including cake doughnuts, bear claws, and Boston crème pies.

Macrina Bakery and Café (2408 1st Ave., 206/448-4032, www.macrinabakery.com, 7 A.M.–10 P.M. Mon–Sat., 8 A.M.–6 P.M. Sun., $10) is an absolutely wonderful Belltown bakery and café with delicious breads, light lunches, and perfect lattes. It's a comfy place to hang out Seattle-style.

LAKE UNION AND VICINITY

Cafés and Delis

There's no Soup Nazi at **Soup Daddy** (211 Fairview Ave. N., 206/682-7202, www.soupdaddysoups.com, 9 A.M.–4 P.M. Mon.–Fri., $7), and thank goodness for that, because I would have a meltdown if I were ever denied its stunning soup selection. Choose among five or so different soups each day. Pair it with a bread bowl, sandwich, or salad to make the perfect midday meal. Operating for years out of Pioneer Square, Daddy done moved on over to the hip South Lake Union neighborhood.

Seafood

The Ivar's chain has several other locations, the most notable **Ivar's Salmon House** (401 NE Northlake Way, 206/632-7223, 11 A.M.–10 P.M. Sun.–Thurs., 11 A.M.–11 P.M. Fri.–Sat., $22) on Lake Union. It's in a cedar facsimile of a Native American longhouse, with historic photos and Tlingit carvings on the walls and dugout canoes hanging from the rafters. This is a fantastic waterside location with an outside deck (summers only) looking across the lake to downtown Seattle. If you're only looking for nibbles stop by the Whale Maker Lounge at the Salmon House for happy hour (free hors d'oeuvres 4–6:30 P.M. Mon.–Fri.), and to check out the rather intimidating (for men at least) killer whale "whalemakers." You're more likely to get a window seat here than in the restaurant.

Chandler's Crabhouse (901 Fairview Ave. N., 206/223-2722, 11 A.M.–3 P.M. and 4–9 P.M. Sun.–Thurs., 4–10 P.M. Fri.–Sat., $40) is on the south shore of Lake Union with views north across the lake. The specialties here are crab dishes of all sorts, including a flavorful whiskey crab bisque. This is dependably good seafood in a busy waterfront setting. It's a great place to watch the seaplanes landing and taking off.

Japanese

My favorite sushi counter is in South Lake Union at **I Love Sushi** (1001 Fairview Ave. N., 206/625-9604, www.ilovesushi.com, $25), where the experienced chefs will do well by you if you bring some cash and just ask them to make whatever they think you will like until you're full.

CAPITOL HILL

Cafés and Delis

No place fills the morning urge for hearty grub more than **Coastal Kitchen** (429 15th Ave. E., 206/322-1145, www.chowfoods.com/coastal, 8 A.M.–11 P.M. daily, $9). Among the highlights are out-of-this-world pancakes. Or try **Glo's** (1621 E. Olive Way, 206/324-2577, 7 A.M.–3 P.M. Mon.–Fri., 7 A.M.–4 P.M. Sat.–Sun., $10), a fun little place with great eggs Benedict and Belgian waffles for breakfast.

For a light dinner or a wonderful weekend brunch, try Capitol Hill's **Table 219** (219 Broadway Ave. E., 206/328-4604, www.table219.com, 4:30–10 P.M. Tues.–Thurs., 9 A.M.–10 P.M. Fri.–Sat., 9 A.M.–3 P.M. Sun., $9), which serves inventive dishes such as andouille corndogs, bread salad, and a sandwich made with roasted garlic, gorgonzola, and sherry shallot marmalade.

When it comes to chocolates, it is pretty hard to beat **Dilettante Chocolates** (416 Broadway E., 206/329-6463, www.dilettante.com, $10), where you'll also find a light menu of soups, salads, and sandwiches. Dilettante has three other shops scattered around Seattle.

Contemporary Northwest

Embued with the quiet bustle of a European bistro, **Lark** (926 12th Ave., 206/323-5275, www.larkseattle.com, 5 P.M.–10:30 P.M. Tues.–Sun., $30) invites languorous meals underneath its exposed-beam ceilings and soft lighting. The menu is made for grazing, with generous selections of cheese, charcuteries, and small plates carefully crafted by the eatery's James Beard Award-winning chef.

Established by some of the gastronomic geniuses behind the renowned Herb Farm in Woodinville, **Poppy** (622 Broadway E., 206/324-1108, www.poppyseattle.com, 5:30–10 P.M. Sun., Tues.–Thurs., 5:30–11 P.M. Fri.–Sat., closed Mon.) draws in diners with the prospect of its eclectic "thali" plates. For $32, these dinner collections consist of about 10 different petite dishes, some no larger than what other restaurants serve as *muse bouche,* but all packing in plenty of creativity and flavor.

Asian

Set in a post-modern great room, **Boom Noodle** (1121 E. Pike St., 206/701-9130, www.boomnoodle.com, 11:30 A.M.–10 P.M. Mon.–Thurs., noon–midnight Fri.–Sat., noon–10 P.M. Sun., $15) offers a trendy take on cafeteria-style seating, minus the buffet line or the mustached lunch lady. Sit at one of the banks of long communal tables in the boisterously loud dining room to partake in stylishly presented Asian fusion, including a dizzying array of ramens, sobas, and udons.

Try the substantial Vietnamese fare at **Monsoon** (615 19th Ave. E., 206/325-2111, 10 A.M.–2:30 P.M. and 5–10 P.M. daily, $18), which, most impressively, offers up banana-leaf wrapped halibut. This place is delightfully different.

Fill up on *bento* box lunches, salmon teriyaki, sushi, sashimi, tempura, and other simple Japanese meals at **Hana Restaurant** (219 Broadway Ave. E., 206/328-1187, 11 A.M.–10 P.M. daily, $15).

Pub Grub

Seattle has embraced the gastropub movement with open, albeit pint-holding, arms. No establishment in the genre garners better reception than **Quinn's** (1001 E. Pike St., 206/325-7711, www.quinnspubseattle.com, 11 A.M.–3 P.M. Mon.–Sat. and 5 P.M.–midnight Mon.–Thurs., 5 P.M.–1 A.M. Fri.–Sat., 5–10 P.M. Sun., $15), a hideaway on the hill that revels in good beer and the food that makes you thirst for it. The menu is awash in a sea of tantalizingly exotic choices designed for the most hearty food explorers ready to set sail toward a new horizon of taste. Find beef tongue hash, fried frog legs, and even wild boar sloppy joes.

If you're looking for a fun saloon serving up the more traditional bar-food standard bearers, opt instead for **The Buck** (1506 E. Olive Way, 206/329-2493, 5 P.M.–2 A.M. daily, $9). Somewhere halfway between an old hunting lodge and a country honky-tonk, this raucous canteen offers delicious pizzas and tasty nacho skillets on the cheap.

QUEEN ANNE AND MAGNOLIA

Cafés

Queen Anne's **5 Spot** (1502 Queen Anne Ave. N., 206/285-7768, 8:30 A.M.–midnight Mon.–Fri., 8:30 A.M.–3 P.M. and 5 P.M.–midnight Sat.–Sun., $14). The 5 Spot emphasizes all-American comfort food. You will not go wrong here, but be ready for a mob scene if you wake up after 9 A.M. on Sunday morning. All of these also offer down-home American cooking for lunch and dinner. Highly recommended.

Steak and Seafood

A long-time Seattle favorite perched high above Lake Union, **Canlis** (2576 Aurora Ave. N., www.canlis.com, 5:30 P.M.–midnight Mon.–Sat., $45) is where the hip go to dig into juicy steaks and a tasty house salad that has had patrons raving for 50 years. The pastry chef here is one of the tops in the city, so do not skip that last course.

One of my favorite special-event restaurants in the city is hidden away in Magnolia over the Elliott Bay Marina. With a Southern Seas-type decor and incredibly tasty steaks, seafood, and Northwest cuisine touched with a bit of Polynesia, **Palisade** (2601 West Marina Pl., 206/285-1000, 9:30 A.M.–2 P.M. and 4–9 P.M. Sun., 11:15 A.M.–2 P.M. and 5–9 P.M. Mon.–Thurs., 11:15 A.M.–2 P.M. and 5–10 P.M. Fri., 4–10 P.M. Sat., $45) never fails to impress. The best parts of the menu bookend your entrees: the appetizer pupu platters and delicious desserts. If you're with a group, don't miss The Captain's Tower Pupu with seared teriyaki tenderloins, tiger prawns, and Dungeness crab. And finish the meal off with the trio of flavored crème brulees. Yum.

Asian

Bamboo Garden Vegetarian Cuisine (364 Roy St., 206/282-6616, www.bamboogarden.net, 11 A.M.–10 P.M. daily, $11) is a popular Chinese vegetarian restaurant near Seattle Center. It isn't appealing outside, but the interior is considerably more inviting.

Take your pick: **Orrapin Thai Cuisine** (10 Boston St. in Queen Anne, 206/283-7118, www.orrapin.com, 11 A.M.–10 P.M. daily, $11) and **Bahn Thai** (409 Roy St., 206/283-0444, www.bahnthaimenu.com, $11) are inexpensive and both offer fantastic Thai specials. Orrapin offers better Tom Kah and curries, and Bahn better noodle dishes such as Phad See Ew.

For Asian fusion try **Asian Breeze** (366 Roy St., 206/285-6713, 5–10 P.M., $14) where the food is always packed with garlic, and the portions are enormous. It's excellent and reasonable.

Other International

Specializing in small-plate, Northwest-with-an-Italian-twist fare, **How to Cook a Wolf** (2208 Queen Anne Ave. N., 206/838-8090, www.howtocookawolf.com, 5 P.M.–midnight Thurs.–Mon., $35) is a fantastic choice for those who enjoy the simple pleasure of fresh and innovative dishes but who are turned off by the eccentricities of many fine dining establishments. Unpretentious and extremely attentive, the servers here are generously scattered in a high wait staff-to-table ratio. Diners are seated first come, first serve — no reservations taken here. And, best of all, the kitchen lets the delicious Northwest ingredients speak for themselves.

BALLARD AND SHILSHOLE BAY

Cafés

The crowds line up around the corner on weekend mornings at **The Dish** (4358 Leary Way NW, 206/782-9985, 7 A.M.–1:45 P.M. daily, $12) for good reason. This tiny little diner griddles up the best breakfasts in town. The place is cramped, so if you're serious about your morning meal, stop in during the weekdays.

When the wait is too long at Dish, walk down the block to **Vera's** (5417 22nd Ave. NW, 206/782-9966, 7 A.M.–2:30 P.M. Mon.–Fri., 8 A.M.–2:30 P.M. Sat., 8 A.M.–2 P.M. Sun., $12), a classic stool-and-counter diner that's been flipping flapjacks for locals since the name Sven was more common than John 'round these parts. Just be prepared with some of the green stuff — this place is so old-school that it still works on the cash-only model.

A home-away-from-home kind of neighborhood joint, **Kiss Café** (2817 NW Market St., 206/789-5477, 11 A.M.–10 P.M. daily, $8) offers up a slate of sandwiches, salads, and comfortable café faves in a spot equally perfect for sipping coffee or beer.

If Dr. Frankenstein had opened up a restaurant it very well may have looked a lot like **Lunchbox Laboratory** (7302 15th Ave. NW, 206/706-3092, www.lunchboxlaboratory.com, 11:30 A.M.–8 P.M. Wed.–Sun., $18), a haven for monstrously sized burgers custom designed by diners. Pick between a choice of meats such as prime rib, buffalo, lamb, and even "dork", a duck-pork combo. Then add on a range of cheeses, rolls, veggies, and sauces to make a creation of your very own. Just be prepared; science is not cheap and the Lab isn't either. Once you've picked out all those add-ons it is possible to have created a $20 burger. And that's without fries.

Seafood

Some of Seattle's finest seafood is supped at **Ray's Boathouse** (6049 Seaview Ave. W., 206/789-3770, www.rays.com, 5–9 P.M. Mon.–Thurs., 4:30–9 P.M. Sat.–Sun., $28). North of the Ship Canal along Shilshole Bay, with outstanding views over Puget Sound at sunset (be sure to reserve a window table) and perfectly prepared oysters, fish, and other fresh seafood, this large and attractive place has a nautical design with wooden floors and beams like an old boat shed. It is a bit expensive (expect a bill of $35 per person), but the seafood is great. Reservations are a must. You can save money and avoid the crowds by arriving weeknights 5–6 P.M. Upstairs is a spacious and equally popular café serving a lighter menu that includes oysters and fish and chips.

© ERICKA CHICKOWSKI

Ray's Boathouse

If you can't get in at Ray's, **Anthony's HomePort** (6135 Seaview Ave. W., 206/783-0780, www.anthonys.com, 11 A.M.–3 P.M. and 4:30–9:30 P.M. Wed.–Sat.) is just up the road, with moderately priced fresh fish and a saucy cioppino ranging $16–29. Also popular are the Sunday brunch and all-you-can-eat crab feed on Sunday afternoons.

Pub Grub

Anyone bestowed with a healthy appetite and a fast metabolism will appreciate the honkin' servings of chili doled out at **Mike's Chili Parlour** (1447 NW Ballard Way, 206/782-2808, www.mikeschiliparlor.com, 11 A.M.–11 P.M. Mon.–Thurs., 11 A.M.–midnight Fri.–Sat., noon–8 P.M. Sun., $5) , a Ballard classic that's been ladling chili over dogs, fries, spaghetti, and more for decades. The stout of heart can dig into the satellite dish-size Big Ass Bowl for $10.

Housed in a building with a bordello past, **Madame K's Pizza Bistro** (5327 Ballard Ave. NW, 206/783-9710, 5–10 P.M. Mon.–Thurs., 5–11 P.M. Fri., 2–11 P.M. Sat., 2–9 P.M. Sun., $15) plays up the place's history with a bawdy but fun theme woven into everything from the décor (corsets hang on scarlet red walls) to the dish names (Screaming Orgasm dessert, anyone?), all the way down to the lipstick-kissed check at the end of the meal. Better yet, the restaurant doesn't hang its hat solely on the theme, either. All the food's good, especially the gourmet pizzas and the decadent desserts.

Bakeries

Eating cake in small bites doesn't count for as many calories, right? Whatever your cupcake philosophy, **Cupcake Royale** (2052 NW Market St., 206/782-9557, www.cupcakeroyale.com, 6:30 A.M.–10 P.M. Mon.–Thurs., 6:30 A.M.–11 P.M. Fri.–Sat., 7:30 A.M.–10 P.M. Sun.) in Ballard is there to fulfill the snacking urge with moist little creations topped with a heavenly buttercream whip. Pair that with a smooth cappuccino to combat that inevitable sugar crash about 15 minutes later.

Or you can lose the guilt altogether and

© ERICKA CHICKOWSKI

Enjoy a cupcake with your cappuccino at Cupcake Royale.

instead visit **Tall Grass Bakery** (5907 24th St. NW, 206/706-0991, 9 A.M.–7 P.M. Mon.–Fri.), which emphasizes hearty, organic breads. Find everything from well-crafted baguettes to spongy sourdough to dark rye.

FREMONT, WALLINGFORD, AND GREEN LAKE

Cafés and Diners

Mae's Phinney Ridge Café (6412 Phinney Ave. N., 206/782-1222, www.maescafe.com, 7 A.M.–3 P.M. daily, $8) is a cow-infested place complete with a "Moo Room" for milk shakes and displays of cow paraphernalia. The food is all made from scratch and includes big, sticky cinnamon rolls and scrumptious hash browns. And, yes, it gets jammed on weekends.

Another great place where you'll have to fend off the weekend brunch crowd is **Julia's** (4401 Wallingford Ave., 206/633-1175, www.eatatjulias.com, 7 A.M.–9 P.M. daily, $17). The food is tasty, with lots of vegetarian items and a lively atmosphere.

For something a little different, join the Sunday morning queue at **Beth's Café** (7311 Aurora Ave. N., 206/782-5588, www.bethscafe.com, 24 hours daily, $9). A Green Lake establishment since 1957, this 24-hour diner remains a hit with those who like old-fashioned American breakfasts. Infamous 12-egg omelettes, greasy hash browns, loud jukebox music, reasonable prices, and sometimes-cranky waitresses keep 'em coming back.

You'll have to grin-and-bear-it through the surly New York–style service at **Bagel Oasis** (2112 NE 65th St., 206/526-0525; and 462 N. 36th St., 206/633-2676, 6 A.M.–5 P.M. Mon.–Fri., 6 A.M.–4 P.M. Sat.–Sun., $5) in order to get your mitts on the best New York–style bagels in the Northwest.

Looking for the best burger in Seattle? The argument rages, but the public votes with their feet (and mouths) for **Dick's Drive-In** (111 NE 45th St., 206/632-5125, www.ddir.com, 10:30 A.M.–2 A.M. daily, $5). The food at this straight-from-the-1950s joint consists of marvelously greasy fries, fat burgers, and wonderful chocolate milk shakes. There's usually a line out front on a summer evening. You can also find Dick's in Queen Anne and on Capitol Hill.

Contemporary Northwest

The food at **Art of the Table** (1054 N. 39th St., 206/282-0942, www.artofthetable.net) is a celebration of the earth, Seattle's seminal tribute to the farm-to-table movement. Chef Dustin Ronspies establishes convivial bonhomie amongst his diners at the Weekend Supper Club, regularly walking and talking with eager participants who sit for his prix fixe four-course meals (7 P.M., $55) fashioned with ingredients hand-plucked from weekend markets around the city. For something a little less formal, stop by for Happy Mondays, an evening-long happy hour (5–10P.M.) with no reservations required.

The rotating list of mouthwatering dishes at **Tilth** (1411 N. 45th St., 206/633-0801, www.tilthrestaurant.com, 10 A.M.–2 P.M. Sat.–Sun. and 5–10 P.M. Sun.–Thurs., 5–10:30 P.M. Fri.–Sat., $26) prominently feature organic fresh fruits, veggies, meats, and seafood grown in the Northwest, a seasonal tour of the state served tableside.

International

Musashi's Sushi & Grill (1400 N. 45th St., 206/633-0212, 11 A.M.–10 P.M. Mon.–Sat., 4–10 P.M. Sun., $15) is an always-crowded, friendly little place with inexpensive fresh sushi (the main attraction), chicken teriyaki, and *bento* box lunches.

Kabul (2301 N. 45th St., 206/545-9000, www.kabulrestaurant.com, 5–11 P.M. daily, $18) creates reasonably priced Afghan cuisine, including quite a few vegetarian dishes such as sautéed eggplant with a tomato, yogurt, and mint sauce. The food has obvious Indian influences but is distinctively different. The basmati rice spiced with saffron and pepper and topped with raisins and nuts is a treat in itself.

Fremont's **El Camino Restaurant** (607 N. 35th St., 206/632-7303, www.elcaminorestaurant.com, 5–10 P.M. Tues.–Thurs., 5–11 P.M. Fri.–Sat., 5–9 P.M. Sun., happy hour 5–6 P.M. Tues.–Fri. and 3–5 P.M. Sat.–Sun., closed Mon., $15) is a great little nouvelle Mexican place that serves chiles rellenos, baby back ribs, and fantastic margaritas.

Vegetarian

Check out **Carmelita** (7314 Greenwood Ave. N., 206/706-7703, www.carmelita.net, 5–9 P.M. Tues.–Thurs. and Sun., 5–10 P.M. Fri.–Sat., $18), a hip little Green Lake vegetarian dinner spot. Even carnivores will go away impressed at flavorful dishes such as the carrot-mascarpone gnocci or the artisanal polenta cake. Try the lemon pound cake for dessert.

Bakeries

Bar none, Seattle's most unusual bakery is in Fremont, where you'll find X-rated cakes, pastries, and other goodies rising from the oven at **The Erotic Bakery** (2323 N. 45th St., 206/545-6969, 10 A.M.–7 P.M. Mon.–Sat.). This is a favorite among not-so-PC co-workers, maids of honor, and anyone else looking to shock and titillate their friends.

For more traditionally shaped goodies, **The Urban Bakery** (7850 E. Greenlake Dr. N, 206/524-7951, 7 A.M.–10 P.M. Mon.–Sat., 8 A.M.–6 P.M. Sun.) is a great spot for fresh-from-the-oven baked treats, including scrumptious chocolate cakes, cheesecakes, and pies. The espresso bar is a favorite stopping place for the Green Lake post-jogging crowd.

Markets

As might be expected, Seattle has quite a few natural and organic grocers. The oldest is **Puget Consumers' Co-op Natural Markets,** a.k.a. PCC, with seven stores around Seattle offering bulk foods, organic produce, and other healthy edibles. You don't have to be a member to shop here, though prices are a bit lower if you join. Several of the markets—notably the one in Fremont (716 N. 34th St., 206/632-6811, www.pccnaturalmarkets.com, 6 A.M.–midnight daily)—have fine delis with both vegetarian and meat dishes.

Fremont Sunday Market brings a farmers market, jewelry, flea market, and live music to N. 34th Street in Fremont between late April and Christmas. During the winter months it moves inside a parking garage at 400 N. 34th Street. It takes place 10 A.M.–4 P.M. Sunday.

UNIVERSITY DISTRICT AND MADISON PARK

Cafés

Hi-Spot Café (1410 34th Ave., 206/325-7905, 8 A.M.–2:30 P.M. Mon.–Fri., $12) is a popular place for burgers and BLTs—along with delightful breakfasts and famous cinnamon rolls.

Chinese

The U District has a big cluster of cheap student-oriented places with heaping helpings of Asian comestibles. Just walk up The Ave to see what looks good. A personal favorite is **Mandarin Chef** (5022 University Way NE, 206/528-7596, www.mandarinchef.com, 11 A.M.–10 P.M. Mon.–Sat., closed Sun., $8) with homemade noodles and dumplings for practically nothing. Tasty mu shu dishes, too.

For Chinese food with a difference, head to the always-crowded **Black Pearl** (7347 35th Avenue NE, 206/283-9030, 11 A.M.–9:30 P.M. Mon.–Thurs., 11 A.M.–10 P.M. Fri.–Sat., 4–9:30 P.M. Sun., $10) just north of the U District in Wedgwood. Watch the busy cooks in the open kitchen, and enjoy the friendly service and distinctive dishes such as a batter-fried eggplant with vegetables, or green onion and smoked salmon pancakes. But be ready for a wait most evenings. Save time and order out; there's free delivery to the north end of town (including the U District).

Japanese

One of the most popular student eateries in the U District, ☾ **Kiku Tempura House** (5018 University Way NE, 206/524-1125, 11 A.M.–10 P.M. daily, $8) whips up tempura and teriyaki that's quick, delicious, and served up in huge portions. Great for a quick lunch or evening meal; order at the counter and wait for them to call your number.

For the ultimate in sushi—even diehard fans from Tokyo are impressed—be sure to make reservations for a meal at **Nishino** (3130 E. Madison St., 206/322-5800, www.nishinorestaurant.com, 5:30–10:30 P.M. Mon.–Sat., 10:30 A.M.–9:30 P.M. Sun., $25). It's a busy and sometimes-noisy place, but the food is impeccable and perfectly prepared. For a real treat, request the chef's menu (a fixed-price six-course meal, $60) when you reserve a table. Nishino is expensive, but worth every dollar.

Other Asian

A notable U District place for inexpensive and tasty Vietnamese lunches is **My's Restaurant** (4220 University Way NE, 206/634-3526, 11 A.M.–10 P.M. daily, $8). This immensely popular student eatery dishes up huge portions of pho and fried noodles, including several vegetarian specialties.

Neelam Authentic Indian Cuisine (4735 University Way NE, 206/523-6830, 10 A.M.–10 P.M. daily, $15) lives up to its name with outstanding and very spicy East Indian meals. It has tandoori and vegetarian specialties, plus wonderful curries. The onion *kulcha* bread is hard to beat.

Another extremely popular and reasonable UW hangout is **Tandoor Indian Restaurant** (5024 University Way NE, 206/523-7477, www.tandoor-india.com, 4:30–10 P.M. Mon.–Thurs., 11 A.M.–2:30 A.M. Fri.–Sat., $12), which offers decent dishes at slightly more student-friendly prices.

Italian

An excellent southern Italian eatery, **Salvatore Ristorante Italiano** (6100 Roosevelt Way NE, 206/527-9301, 5–10 P.M. Tues.–Thurs., 5–10:30 P.M. Fri.–Sat., closed Sun.–Mon., $18) in Ravenna dishes up favorites such as veal, linguine with clams, and pasta with red hot peppers, tomatoes, capers, anchovies, and olives. There's also a fine choice of antipastos and Italian wines. No reservations are accepted, so be prepared to wait if you come late.

Other International

☾ **Continental Restaurant** (4549 University Way NE, 206/632-4700, 7 A.M.–9:30 P.M. daily, $12) on the Ave. is a longtime favorite for inexpensive Greek meals and friendly service. Go there often enough and they'll treat you like family. If you come in the morning, any omelette with feta will satisfy. Visit later and be sure to finish the meal off with some of the best baklava on the planet. There's also a deli here.

For impressive French cuisine, you will not go wrong at Madison Park's **Rover's** (2808 E. Madison St., 206/325-7442, www.rovers-seattle.com, 5–10 P.M. Tues.–Sat., 10 A.M.–2 P.M. Sun., $22), where the food, service, and setting win uniform praise. The outstanding wine list is a nice accompaniment. Many people regard this as Seattle's finest restaurant. Complete five-course menus are typically $95 per person.

Over by the Arboretum, **Cactus** (4220 E. Madison St., 206/324-4140, Www.cactusrestaurants.com, 11:30 A.M.–3 P.M. and 5–10 P.M. Mon.–Thurs., 11:30 A.M.–3 P.M. and 5–11 P.M. Fri.–Sat., $15) is another popular place with a blend of Spanish and Southwest dishes. You'll find a fun tapas bar, Indian fry bread, fajitas, enchiladas, and lots of unusual dishes. A personal fave is the grilled jalapeños, stuffed with goat cheese and wrapped in bacon.

Pizzerias

Seattle's best quick pizza place is **Pizzeria Pagliacci** (www.pagliacci.com), with three sit-down locations around town, including one on the Ave (4529 University Way NE, 206/632-0421, 5–11 P.M. Mon.–Fri., 4–midnight Sat.–Sun.). This is about as close as you can get to real New York–style pizzas: perfect thin crusts and distinctive toppings. Several types of pizzas are always available by the slice at this location, along with calzones and lasagna.

Northlake Tavern & Pizza House (660 NE Northlake Way, 206/633-5317, 11 A.M.–10 P.M. Sun.–Thurs., 11 A.M.–11 P.M. Fri., 11 A.M.–midnight Sat.) mixes three American favorites: great pizza, beer, and sports on the television. The place is a favorite haunt of University of Washington sports fans, but nobody under 21 is allowed because it's a bar.

Vegetarian

Cash-poor students absolutely flock to **Flowers** (4247 University Way NE, 206/633-1903, 11 A.M.–2 P.M. daily) on the Ave. during lunch hours for its famous vegetarian buffet, an unlimited feast of veggies that can be had for around $8 during the week and $10 on the weekends. Just be prepared to invest a little time to reap the benefits of cheap food — the service is notoriously bad here.

If you prefer a more grown up dining experience, **Cafe Flora** (2901 E. Madison St., 206/325-9100, www.cafeflora.com, 11 A.M.–10 P.M. Mon.–Fri., 9 A.M.–2 P.M. and 5–9 P.M. Sat.–Sun., $15) in Madison Park is one of the city's best-loved vegetarian restaurants. The rustic polenta is especially notable, and it also offers offbeat pizzas and portobello Wellington (grilled portobello mushrooms) on the ever-changing menu. The kitchen can get noisy at times, and service may be uneven.

WEST SEATTLE

Cafés

Pies aren't just for dessert at **Shoofly Pie Company** (4444 California Ave. SW, 206/938-0680, 10 A.M.–8 P.M. Wed.–Thurs., 10 A.M.–9 P.M. Fri.–Sat., 10 A.M.–5 P.M. Sun., closed Mon.–Tues., $5), which specializes in everything from sweet to savory. Dig into slices of cheesy quiches, carmelized onion galletes, creamy pot pies, and sublime tarts. Don't forget to try the namesake, a classic Pennsylvania Dutch molasses pie that's sweet enough to put the dentist on call.

Contemporary Northwest

Escape the pretension of downtown's fine dining scene at **Spring Hill** (4437 California Ave. SW, 206/935-1075, www.springhillnorthwest.com, 10 A.M.–2 P.M. Sat.–Sun. and 5 –9 P.M. Mon., 5:45–10 P.M. Sun. and Tues.–Thurs., 5:45–11 P.M. Fri.–Sat., $25) a chic little place tucked away in West Seattle where you can order high-brow meals minus the self-absorbed attitude. You'll find a warm and friendly atmosphere in this dining room bedecked with modern light woods, glazed cement flooring and plenty of light streaming in through the floor-to-ceiling windows up front. The food's the real star, though. The menu allows you to go as casual or fancy as you like — order anything along the spectrum from the gigantic and juicy burgers to the roasted duck with quinoa waffle.

Steak and Seafood

Undoubtedly the best view of the Seattle skyline is from a window-side seat in **Salty's on Alki** (1936 Harbor Ave. SW, 206/937-1600, www.saltys.com, 11:30 A.M.–3 P.M. and 5–9 P.M. Mon.–Fri., 9 A.M.–1 P.M. and 4–9 P.M. Sat.–Sun., $30). Situated on West Seattle's Alki Point, this offers the choicest glimpse of the glimmering lights reflected off Eliott Bay. Best of all, the food is worthy of the view, with plenty of seafood offerings and a few decent cuts of meat thrown in for good measure. On Saturday and Sunday, Salty's lays out the best brunch buffet in Seattle, with unlimited platters of shellfish, prime rib, and pastries all served up with your choice of mimosas or Bloody Marys.

If that all sounds a little extravagant to you, then try another West Seattle classic, **Spud Fish and Chips** (2666 Alki Ave. SW, 206/938-0606, 11 A.M.–9 P.M. daily), which has been frying up fishies by Alki Beach since 1935.

Asian

Extremely popular — and justifiably so — are a couple of Asian offerings: **Pailin Thai Cuisine** (2223 California Ave. SW, 206/937-8807, 11:30 A.M.–10 P.M. Mon.–Thurs., 11 A.M.–10 P.M. Fri., 5–10 P.M. Sat.–Sun.) and **Mashiko Japanese Restaurant** (4725 California Ave. SW, 206/935-4339, 5–9:30 P.M. Sun.–Thurs., 5–11 P.M. Fri.–Sat.).

Information and Services

INFORMATION CENTERS

For information on Seattle attractions and events, plus maps and other assistance, contact the **Seattle/King County Convention and Visitors Bureau** (800 Convention Place in the Washington State Convention and Trade Center, on the Galleria level, www.seeseattle.org, 8:30 A.M.–5 P.M. Mon.–Fri., 10 A.M.–4 P.M. Sat.–Sun. April–Oct.; 8:30 A.M.–5 P.M. Mon.–Fri. the rest of the year). While there, be sure to pick up the ***Seattle Visitors Guide,*** a compendium of local entertainment, restaurants, shopping, and sights. Call 206/461-5840 ahead of your visit for a big packet of Seattle information, including the helpful *Seattle Visitors Guide.* Also in the convention center are various shops, changing displays of fine artwork along the walls, and access to **Freeway Park,** built over part of I-5, with greenery, waterfalls, and fountains. At Sea-Tac Airport, the **Visitor Information Booth** has additional local information and brochures.

Located inside the REI store, the **Outdoor Recreation Information Center** (222 Yale Ave. N., 206/470-4060, www.nps.gov/ccso, 10:30 A.M.–7 P.M. Tues.–Fri., 9 A.M.–7 P.M. Sat., and 11 A.M.–6 P.M. Sun., closed Mon.) has complete details on Forest Service and Park Service lands throughout Washington, along with Washington State Park and Department of Natural Resources lands. Stop here to ask about hiking trails, campgrounds, and backcountry access. You can't make campground or backcountry reservations here, but you can buy Northwest Forest Passes.

If you're a member, the **AAA Travel Store** (1523 15th Ave. W., 206/218-1222, www.aaawa.com, 8:30 A.M.–5:30 P.M. Mon.–Fri.) is a good source of free maps and area information plus travel guidebooks, luggage, and other travel-related accessories.

WEB ACCESS

Free Internet access is available from any of the **Seattle Public Library** (www.spl.org) branches. In addition, many copy shops (including Kinko's) rent computer time by the minute or hour for Web surfing or to check your email.

Some good Internet cafés (free if you buy a coffee) are **Bulldog News** (4208 University Way NE, 206/632-6397), **Cafe Allegro** (4214 University Way NE, 206/633-3030), **Alibi Room** (85 Pike St., Pike Place Market, 206/623-3180), and **Speakeasy Café** (2304 2nd Ave., Belltown, 206/728-9770).

FOREIGN CURRENCY EXCHANGE

Thomas Cook (206/248-0401 or 800/287-7362, www.us.thomascook.com) has currency exchange booths at the airport and Westlake Center (4th and Pine). Other options are **American Express** (600 Stewart St., 206/441-8622, www.americanexpress.com), **AllWorld Currency Exchange** (1411 4th Ave., suite 1401, 206/464-0204 or 888/335-0204) and **Custom House Currency Exchange** (1900 5th Ave., 206/269-6353).

LIBRARIES

The **Seattle Public Library's** main branch (1000 4th Ave., 206/386-4636) is perhaps the coolest downtown library in the entire country, a giant glass-and-steel masterpiece well worth a couple of hours of exploration on a rainy day. Another 23 neighborhood libraries are scattered around Seattle; call 206/386-4636 for the information line.

The University of Washington has collections totaling more than five million volumes in its various campus libraries (206/543-0242 for details, www.lib.washington.edu), the majority of which are housed in the sprawling **Suzzallo and Allen Libraries,** both on Red Square.

Situated in Ballard, the **Metaphysical Library** (2220 NW Market St., L-05, 206/329-1794, www.seattlemetaphysical.org)—a.k.a. the As You Like It Library—is certainly Seattle's most unusual place to borrow books. This collection of 12,000 books covers the metaphysical spectrum, including astrology, magic, reiki, parapsychology, telepathy, and tarot. Anyone can come here to read, but to check out books you'll need to pay a $30 annual fee.

Getting There

BY AIR

Seattle's airport is 12 miles south of town and midway between Seattle and Tacoma, hence the name **Sea-Tac Airport** (www.portseattle.org, or call 206/431-4444 or 800/544-1965). All the major domestic and many international airlines fly into Sea-Tac. Foreign travelers can change money at the Thomas Cook booth in the main terminal. Storage lockers are scattered around the airport, but you'll need to pass through security first. Another option is **Ken's Baggage and Frozen Food Storage** (located near the baggage claim area, 206/433-5333, open 5:30 A.M.–12:30 A.M. daily). Also near the baggage claim is a volunteer-staffed **Visitor Information Booth** (open 9:30 A.M.–7:30 P.M. daily in the summer; brochures available at other times), along with car-rental counters and kiosks with information on Metro buses, shuttle buses, and limo services.

Getting to Seattle

The least expensive way to reach Seattle from the airport is aboard one of **Metro Transit's** (206/447-4800 or 800/542-7876; http://transit.metrokc.gov city, one-way $1.25 off-peak or $2 peak) buses. Numbers 174, 184, and 194 run between Sea-Tac and downtown Seattle about every half hour. Buses leave from outside the lower-level baggage claim area of the domestic terminal (turn right as you exit), or catch them downtown if you're headed out. It takes approximately 50 minutes to reach downtown from Sea-Tac. Make sure you catch the bus heading north to Seattle, not south to Federal Way! Metro buses travel along the Pacific Highway and provide the cheapest access for the many motels close to the airport.

To do it the easy (and expensive) way, grab a cab on the airport's second level; they charge around $30–35 to downtown Seattle.

Gray Line Airport Express (206/626-6088 or 800/426-7505, www.graylineofseattle.com, 5 A.M.–11:30 P.M., $11 adults, $8.25 kids) has airport pick-up service to 10 downtown hotels every half hour. No reservations needed, just board the bus outside the baggage claim area.

Shuttle Express (206/622-1424 or 800/942-7433, www.shuttleexpress.com) runs door-to-door van service between Sea-Tac and Seattle ($27), as well as Bellevue and points north to Everett and south to Tacoma. Reserve ahead for a pickup. It also offers scheduled service to hotels in Seattle and Bellevue.

Quick Shuttle Service (604/244-3744 or 800/665-2122, www.quickcoach.com, $55) provides scheduled connections between Sea-Tac and Vancouver, British Columbia. **Olympic Bus Lines** (360/417-0700 or 800/457-4492, www.olympicbuslines.com) has shuttle vans to Edmonds, Sequim, and Port Angeles. **Airporter Shuttle** (360/380-8800 or 866/235-5247, www.airporter.com) has connections between Sea-Tac and Marysville, Mount Vernon, Anacortes, Oak Harbor, Bellingham (including the Alaska Ferry terminal), and the town of Blaine on the Canadian border. **Capital Aeroporter** (253/838-7431 or 800/962-3579, www.capair.com) provides connections to Tacoma, Puyallup, Olympia, Centralia/Chehalis, and Hoodsport. The **Bremerton-Kitsap Airporter** (206/876-1737 or 800/562-7948, www.kitsapairporter.com) shuttles passengers to Bremerton, Port Orchard, Poulsbo, Gig Harbor, and northwest Tacoma. **Centralia-SeaTac Airport Express** (360/786-0636 or 800/773-9490) serves Olympia and Centralia.

BY TRAIN AND BUS

Amtrak

Amtrak serves Seattle from its historic King Street Station (3rd Ave. S and S. King St., 206/464-1930 or 800/872-7245, www.amtrak.com). The **Coast Starlight** has service four times a day, connecting Seattle with Tacoma, Olympia, Centralia, Kelso-Longview, Vancouver, Portland, and south to Oakland and Los Angeles. The **Empire Builder** provides daily service from Seattle to Edmonds, Everett, Wenatchee, Ephrata, and Spokane, and continuing eastward to Minneapolis and Chicago. The futuristic-looking **Cascades** provides daily train connections to Vancouver, B.C., via Edmonds, Everett, Mount Vernon, and Bellingham; it continues south as far as Eugene, Oregon.

Intercity Bus Service

Transportation Connections is a private, nonprofit agency whose excellent website (www.transconnect.org) contains links to a wide range of public transportation in Washington. In addition to buses, options include car sharing, cycling organizations, Amtrak, and the state ferries.

Greyhound (9th Ave. and Stewart St., 206/628-5508 or 800/231-2222, www.greyhound.com) has daily bus service throughout the lower 48 and to Vancouver, B.C., from its bus terminal downtown. **Northwest Trailways** (206/728-5955 or 800/366-3830, www.nwadv.com/northw) operates from both the Greyhound station and the Amtrak depot, with service to Everett, Tacoma, Spokane, Pullman, and points between.

Getting Around

Getting around downtown is easy—all Metro buses here are free every day between the hours of 6 A.M. and 7 P.M. The boundaries for this free area are S. Jackson Street, I-5, Pine Street, Battery Street, and Alaskan Way. A bus tunnel runs through the center of the city, with downtown stops at Convention Place (9th and Pine St.), Westlake Center (4th and Pine), University Street (3rd and University), Pioneer Square, and the International District (5th Ave. and S. Jackson St.). The Monorail connects Westlake Center with Seattle Center.

BY BUS

Seattle's **Metro** (206/553-3000 or 800/542-7876, http://transit.metrokc.gov) bus system provides connections throughout the area. Metro buses run 6 A.M.–1 A.M. every day, about every 30 minutes on the city routes. Customer service offices are at 821 2nd Avenue and in the Westlake Station. Fares cost $1.25 off-peak, $1.50 peak within the city; or $1.25 off-peak and $2 peak if you ride through two zones (beyond Seattle city limits). For $2.50 on weekends, you can purchase a pass that gives you unlimited rides on Metro buses and the streetcars; get it from the bus driver when you board. Call. All Metro buses carry bikes at no extra charge, but bikes are not carried within the Ride Free area of downtown.

Pierce Transit (253/581-8000 or 800/562-8109, www.piercetransit.org) operates southern

Puget Sound bus service connecting downtown Seattle with Tacoma. **Community Transit** (800/562-1375, www.commtrans.org) provides commuter bus service connecting Everett, Edmonds, and other Snohomish County cities with downtown Seattle and the University District.

BY FERRY

Washington State Ferries

One of the best ways to see Seattle is from the water. Washington State Ferries (206/464-6400, 888/808-7977, or 800/843-3779 for automated info, www.wsdot.wa.gov/ferries) operate almost continuously from before sunrise to after 1 A.M. daily, leaving from the main terminal at Pier 52 for Bainbridge Island and Bremerton. To either destination, summertime car-and-driver fares are $14.45 each way; passengers and walk-ons pay only $6.70 round-trip. A passenger-only **Seattle-Vashon Island** ferry ($4.30 round-trip) has daily departures from Pier 50 in the summer, with Mon.–Sat. departures in the winter.

The Fauntleroy ferry dock in West Seattle serves Southworth on the Kitsap Peninsula and Vashon Island about every 20–50 minutes daily. Summertime car-and-driver fares are $14.80 one-way; passengers and walk-ons pay just $4.30 round-trip. The crossing to Southworth takes approximately 35 minutes, while the **Fauntleroy-Vashon Island** takes 15 minutes. Get to the Fauntleroy dock by heading south on I-5 to exit 163; follow the signs from there.

There is a $1 surcharge to carry bikes on all these ferry runs. Fares for vehicles are lower in the off-season (mid-October to mid-May), and discounts are available for seniors, children, and people with disabilities. If you're going to be traveling a lot on the ferries, ask about frequent-user coupon books. There are no state ferry connections from Seattle to the San Juan Islands; you must leave from Anacortes or Sidney, B.C., or take the *Victoria Clipper.*

Victoria and San Juan Islands Ferries

Car ferries no longer operate between Seattle and Victoria; you will need to drive north to Anacortes, where you can catch a state ferry through the San Juan Islands to Vancouver Island. For a daylong excursion to Canada, take the passenger-only ***Victoria Clipper*** (206/448-5000 or 800/888-2535, www.victoriaclipper.com, $149) from Pier 63 to Ogden Point in Victoria. Reservations are required for this high-speed catamaran cruise, and it takes two hours to reach Victoria. The round-trip cruise can be completed in one day (8:30 A.M. departure and 9:30 P.M. return) while allowing a brief stay in Olde English Victoria. For variety, take the *Clipper* to Victoria and fly back on Kenmore Air (206/486-1257 or 800/543-9595, www.kenmoreair.com). The *Clipper* also offers optional one- or two-night stays in Victoria, a "triple play" that includes a night each in Victoria and Vancouver, and a wide range of other tours into British Columbia. In addition, it has service between Seattle and the San Juan Islands, and between Victoria and the San Juans ($59–69).

BY CAR

According to one recent study, Seattle's traffic was the third worst in the United States (after Los Angeles and San Francisco); the average Seattleite spends over 50 hours per year stuck in traffic jams! If possible, try to stay on public transit, both for your own sanity and for the environment. By all means avoid the 3–7 P.M. weekday rush hour, when I-5 and the I-90 and Highway 520 floating bridges are often virtual parking lots.

One of the more difficult aspects of Seattle city driving isn't getting there, but getting back: Finding an I-5 entrance ramp can be frustrating, especially after you zigzag over and under the highway a few times. One sure cure: Head down 5th Avenue, because entrances to both north- and southbound traffic are along it. Another good, although very busy, way to approach the freeway is on Mercer Street; get in the right lanes for southbound, left lanes for northbound.

Driving around downtown Seattle is much more difficult than walking, and sometimes almost as expensive as flying to Portland, because at some point you've got to park the car. Parking downtown is difficult on weekdays—

and costly: meters (if you can find one) are $1.50 per hour ($1.25 in South Lake Union), and private lots cost $9–16 a day. Be warned that the vigilant meter readers seem always to be waiting for your sticker to expire so they can stick you with a $20 ticket.

Car Rental

Seattle has all the major national car rental companies, along with several smaller operators; surf their websites or call their 800 numbers for specifics. The big operators have desks near baggage claim at Sea-Tac Airport. It often pays to make an initial reservation online, using the 800 number, or with www.travelocity.com, www.expedia.com, or www.orbitz.com, and then do additional checking at the counters when you arrive. AAA or Costco members should be sure to also ask about any special discounts. The best rates are often from locations away from the airport such as Bellevue; sometimes the company will provide a shuttle van to its office. I've found that **Thrifty Car Rental** (800/847-4389, www. www.thrifty.com) typically has some of the lowest rates and is a good starting point for price comparisons. For wheelchair-friendly van rentals, contact **Wheelchair Getaways** (425/788-7318 or 888/376-1500, www.wheelchairgetaways.com).

TOURS

When it comes to tours, Seattle has every possible option, from the standard drive-'em-around-in-the-bus type to the goofy, tongue-planted-firmly-in-cheek version.

Flightseeing Tours

To see the city from about 1,500 feet, try one of **Seattle Seaplanes'** (206/329-9638 or 800/637-5553, www.seattleseaplanes.com, $58 pp, two-person minimum) 20-minute scenic floatplane rides over Seattle. Longer flights are available to Mt. St. Helens, Mt. Rainier, or the San Juan Islands. Flights take off and land at Lake Union.

In business since 1946, **Kenmore Air** (206/486-1257 or 800/543-9595, www.kenmoreair.com) flies year-round scheduled floatplane flights from Lake Union or the north shore of Lake Washington. Destinations include the San Juan Islands ($159–183 round-trip), Gulf Islands ($220), Victoria ($162–192), and onward to several Vancouver Island destinations. A 24-pound baggage weight limit is in effect for these flights, with excess baggage charged at $1 per pound. In addition, Kenmore offers more standard flightseeing trips over Seattle at $198 for up to three people on a quick 20-minute flight.

The most distinctive way to see Seattle is aboard a classic biplane from **Olde Thyme Aviation** (206/730-1412, www.oldethymeaviation.com). Flights start at $135 for two people on a 20-minute trip. They operate from the Museum of Flight at Boeing Field throughout the spring and summer, and passengers suit up in old-fashioned barnstorming regalia.

Bus and Van Tours

Gray Line of Seattle (206/626-5208 or 800/426-7532, www.graylineofseattle.com) offers a variety of Puget Sound tours. Its 3.5-hour city tour ($35) highlights Ballard Locks, the University of Washington, and Pioneer Square. The Double Decker tour ($21) includes eight stops around downtown and Seattle Center. Riders are given a narrated tour and can get off and on at any of the stops. Or save your money by riding the free Metro buses around downtown and let local drunks provide the narration. Gray Line has several other sightseeing trips, including Everett's Boeing plant ($48) and day trips to Mt. Rainier ($59).

Several other companies offer more specialized tours. At **Private Eye Tours** (206/622-0590, www.privateeyetours.com), a semi-retired private detective takes you on a murder and mystery exploration of Seattle. **Scenic Bound Tours** (206/433-6907 or 888/293-1404, www.seattlecitytours.com, $79) takes you on all-day van trips to the wild places around Puget Sound, including both Mt. St. Helens and Mt. Rainier. **The Will and the Way Travel** (206/713-2745) is set up for travelers with disabilities.

Ride the Ducks (206/441-3825 or 800/817-1116, www.seattleducktours.net) is probably the strangest (and most annoying) tour company; it cruises through town—and into Lake Union—in a restored World War II landing craft, with tourists quacking loudly all the way at passersby. Any gimmick for a tourist buck.

Excellent **Viewpoints Discover Tours** (206/667-9186, www.seattlearchitecture.org, $15) take place on summer Saturdays, focusing on Seattle's architectural heritage. These last 1.5 hours and are led by members of the Seattle Architectural Foundation.

Argosy Cruises

A number of boat tours and ferry services depart from Seattle's waterfront, providing a relaxing, scenic change of pace for the foot-weary traveler. The most popular ones are offered year-round by **Argosy Cruises** (206/623-4252 or 206/623-1445, www.argosycruises.com, $19–35) with a fleet of a dozen cruise vessels. Reservations are recommended for all of these, but they usually have space for walk-ups. The one-hour informative tour of Elliott Bay and the waterfront describes the hows and whys of containerized shipping, along with historical background. The tours depart daily from Piers 55 and 56. Argosy also has Lake Washington cruises from Lake Union or Kirkland.

One of Argosy's most popular tours takes you from Elliott Bay through the Chittenden Locks into Lake Union, and then back by bus. The *Royal Argosy,* the company's flagship, offers lunch and dinner cruises ($40–46 lunch, $80–99 dinner). Argosy also offers cruises to Tillicum Village, jetboat trips, and special event cruises throughout the year.

Other Boat Tours

Let's Go Sailing (206/624-3931, www.sailingseattle.com) offers 1.5-hour sails during the day ($25), and 2.5-hour sunset sailing trips ($40) aboard two 70-foot sloops. They depart Pier 54 several times a day during the summer. Sail on Lake Union aboard a 33-foot sloop from **Sailing in Seattle** (206/298-0094, www.sailing-in-seattle.com, $100/hour). And if you're really serious, take weekend or evening sailing classes from the **Seattle Sailing Club** (Shilshole Bay, 206/782-5100, www.seattlesailing.com).

For something different, take a guided sunset or moonlight tour of Lake Union and Ballard Locks by sea kayak. These are offered periodically in the summer by **Northwest Outdoor Center** (2100 Westlake Ave. N, 206/281-96949694 or 800/683-0637, www.nwoc.com). **Outdoor Odysseys** (206/361-0717 or 200/647-4621, www.outdoorodysseys.com) offers sea kayak tours around various parts of the Sound and to the San Juan Islands.

Discover Houseboating (206/322-9157, www.discoverhouseboating.com) leads specialized tours of Lake Union houseboats—from the funky to the fabulous—including the home where *Sleepless in Seattle* was filmed. Prices start at $25.

Walking and Biking Tours

Several notable walking tours are described under *Sights* in this chapter: the Park Service's free gold rush historical walks around Pioneer Square; the three-hour walking tours of Pike

TILLICUM VILLAGE TOUR

This trip into history has been one of Washington's premier tours since 1962. Visitors ride an Argosy boat to Blake Island State Park, where they enjoy a salmon bake inside a cedar longhouse, dances, nature trails, and a gift gallery. Departing from Pier 55 on the Seattle waterfront, these four-hour tours are available daily from May to early October, with weekend-only sailings the rest of the year. The cost is $79.95 for adults, $72.95 for seniors, $30 for ages 5-12, and free for kids under five. Reservations are required (206/443-1244, www.tillicumvillage.com). For those who want more time to explore Blake Island's hiking paths, the company offers 6.5-hour trips on Saturday from mid-June to mid-September, plus weekdays in July and August.

Place Market; the walking/eating tours of International District offered by Chinatown Discovery Tours; and Bill Speidel's Underground Tours. All are interesting and educational, but the last of these is particularly popular; guides cover the Pioneer Square area, providing humorous anecdotes (often at the expense of Tacoma), along with dollops of local history.

Some of the finest local walking tours are offered by the Museum of History and Industry (206/324-1126 for upcoming treks, or visit www.seattlehistory.org) on summer Sundays. These two-hour tours offer a great way to learn local history.

Several private companies lead guided walking tours of Seattle on a daily basis, including **Seattle Walking Tours** (206/885-3173, www.seattlewalkingtours.com, $15) and **See Seattle Walking Tours** (425/226-7641, www.see-seattle.com, $20).

THE EASTSIDE

Head east across the glistening waters of Lake Washington on either of Seattle's famous floating bridges and you'll stumble across what locals refer to as "The Eastside." This chain of suburban cousins to the Emerald City is where you'll find Microsoft millionaires tap-tap-tapping on their laptops at coffeehouse hot spots and see their husbands schlepping the kids off to soccer practice in BMW minivans. Look hard enough, though, and you'll also discover outdoors nuts enjoying some of the finest urban trails in the country, wine aficionados sipping reds and whites in area tasting rooms, equestrian lovers enjoying open pastures on horseback, and cyclists spinning along stream-lined bike paths and lazy waterfront roads.

The Eastside may not be as exciting as Seattle to some travelers, but it is hardly the one-dimensional enclave it is often painted to be by certain city dwellers across the lake.

Sure, there are McMansions and high-tech business parks galore. And shopping does seem to be a favorite activity among the locals, who love to roam the upscale shopping malls and kitschy little boutiques out here. But, really, if there is something suburbanites and tourists have in common, it' s a mutual love of browsing wares.

And between all of these stereotypical Eastside trappings, the curious traveler will discover plenty of unexpected sights. Here you'll find everything from pastoral farmlands to lakeshore beaches to lowland forests. There's an art museum touted as one of the region's best and a lesser-known pair of quirky little zoos. And when the sun is

© WILLIAM PERRY/DREAMSTIME.COM

HIGHLIGHTS

Bellevue Arts Museum: This unique gallery focuses on the arts of craft and design (page 91).

Bellevue Botanical Garden: Stop and smell the rhododendrons, the dahlias, and all the flowers in between at this colorful park (page 92).

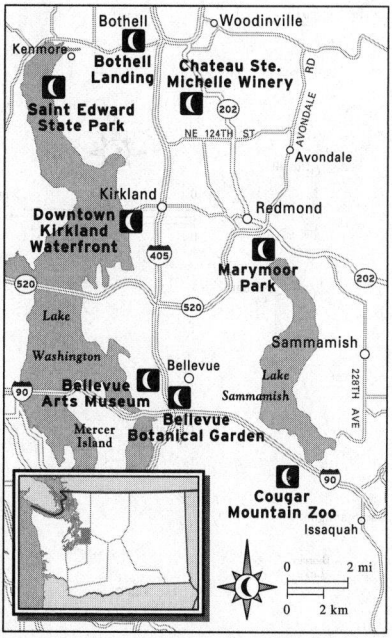

Downtown Kirkland Waterfront: Spend an afternoon window shopping, strolling the grassy lakeside parks, and maybe even taking a sail from Kirkland's charming village center (page 100).

Saint Edward State Park: Once home to a Catholic seminary, this wooded retreat still offers plenty of space along its waterfront and its trails for thoughtful contemplation and recreational healing (page 100).

Marymoor Park: Tucked away on the northern end of Lake Sammamish, this green space is made for activity. It features an enormous off-leash dog park, an acclaimed velodrome, tennis courts, a remote-control plane field, playgrounds, and more (page 105).

Cougar Mountain Zoo: This small zoo offers a much more intimate animal experience than at your typical city zoo (page 111).

Bothell Landing: Set along the Sammamish River Trail, this spot is a hub for recreation, shopping, and relaxation (page 115).

Chateau Ste. Michelle Winery: Washington's oldest winery and Puget Sound's finest, this elegant destination offers cellar tours and barrel tasting (page 115).

LOOK FOR TO FIND RECOMMENDED SIGHTS, ACTIVITIES, DINING, AND LODGING.

shining, the Eastside shines even brighter, with its enviable collection of eclectic parks for picnickers, dog walkers, swimmers, lollygaggers, and everyone in between. So don't let the clichés hold you back—those bridges really are worth crossing.

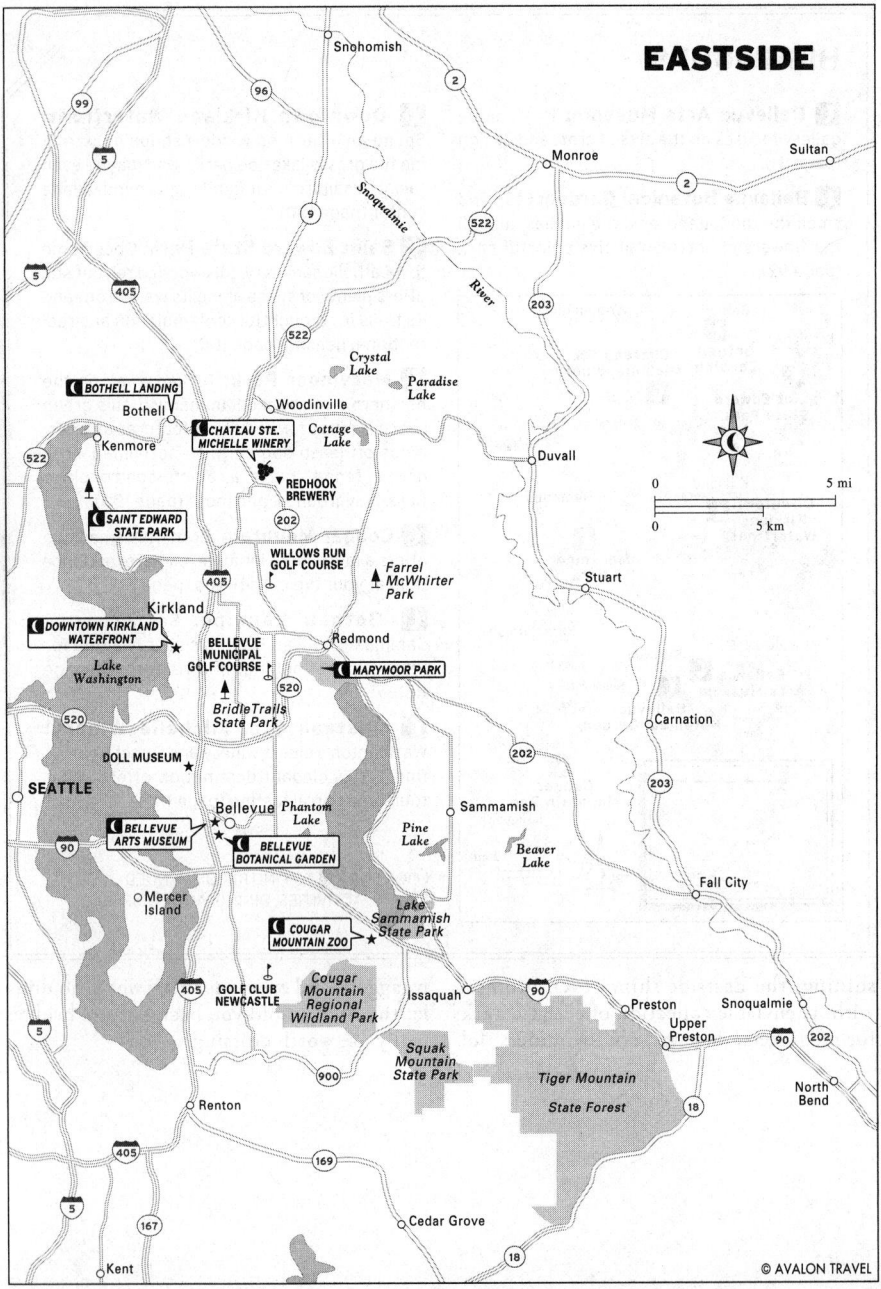
EASTSIDE
Snohomish
Monroe
Sultan
Snoqualmie
River
Crystal Lake
Paradise Lake
BOTHELL LANDING
Bothell
Woodinville
CHATEAU STE. MICHELLE WINERY
Cottage Lake
Kenmore
Duvall
REDHOOK BREWERY
SAINT EDWARD STATE PARK
WILLOWS RUN GOLF COURSE
Farrel McWhirter Park
Stuart
Kirkland
DOWNTOWN KIRKLAND WATERFRONT
Redmond
BELLEVUE MUNICIPAL GOLF COURSE
MARYMOOR PARK
Lake Washington
Bridle Trails State Park
Carnation
DOLL MUSEUM
SEATTLE
Bellevue
Phantom Lake
Sammamish
BELLEVUE ARTS MUSEUM
BELLEVUE BOTANICAL GARDEN
Pine Lake
Beaver Lake
Fall City
Mercer Island
Lake Sammamish State Park
COUGAR MOUNTAIN ZOO
GOLF CLUB NEWCASTLE
Cougar Mountain Regional Wildland Park
Issaquah
Preston
Snoqualmie
Upper Preston
Squak Mountain State Park
Tiger Mountain State Forest
North Bend
Renton
Cedar Grove
Kent
0 5 mi
0 5 km
© AVALON TRAVEL

Bellevue and Mercer Island

Directly across Lake Washington, Bellevue has certainly grown up from the sleepy Seattle suburb it used to be. When the city was incorporated in 1953, the surrounding land was primarily strawberry fields, and Bellevue's streets were simple gravel roads. These days visitors are likely to see more towering construction cranes here than in downtown Seattle. As the home to many rapidly expanding high-tech industries, Bellevue now has its own high-rise downtown, with a well-respected art museum, crowded nightspots, and one of the fanciest shopping malls in the Northwest.

It is here and in the nearby bedroom community of Mercer Island that the stereotype of hoity-toity Eastsiders blossomed. Teenagers drive around Bellevue in brand-new luxury cars and a little fixer-upper of a home can go for well over $1 million. Here is where you'll find Bill Gates' $125 million digs. He lives just west of Bellevue in the exclusive Medina neighborhood on the shore of Lake Washington. His 20,000-square-foot mansion is visible from the Evergreen Point Floating Bridge. Microsoft cofounder and high-profile philanthropist Paul Allen lives just across the water on Mercer Island's southwest shore. Hop in a kayak and you can check out his floating helicopter pad bobbing in the lake.

THE FLOATING BRIDGES

How do you build a bridge over a glacier lake that sinks down to depths of more than 200 feet? Simple: build above the water, not below. As you drive across Lake Washington on either the Interstate 90 Lake Washington Floating Bridge or the State Route 520 Evergreen Floating Bridge, you might be impressed to know that you're essentially driving on a very elaborate barge. Both bridges were designed by adapting concrete cell technology first developed for World War I barges and are made up of numerous hollow pontoons cabled together and then anchored with weights dropped down to the lake's muddy bottom.

Now if only they could develop technology to make all of those cars that crowd the bridges when we're headed across during rush hour disappear...

SIGHTS

Bellevue Arts Museum

You won't find classical paintings at the Bellevue Arts Museum (510 Bellevue Way NE, 425/519-0770, www.bellevuearts.org, 10 A.M.–5 P.M. Tues., Wed., Fri., and Sat., 10 A.M.–8 P.M. Thurs., noon–5 P.M. Sun., closed Mon., $6 adults, $4 seniors and students, free for kids under 6). This organization eschews the traditional with its constant rotation of exhibits dedicated to the arts of crafts and design. Sculpture, carvings, glasswork, fabric art, and other unique pieces that might be considered novelties at other art museums are rather the norm here. Because there are no permanent exhibits on display here, the collection can be hit or miss. But since the museum revitalized its mission in 2005, curation has generally been spot on.

Designed by the internationally acclaimed architect Steven Holl, the facility stands as a piece of artwork itself, with a particularly pleasing outdoor court on the rooftop featuring a wall that follows the curve of the 48th parallel. It perfectly captures the sun's movement during summer solstice.

In addition to exhibitions, the museum offers an artist-in-residence studio, an art school, and a wide range of talks and programs. The museum extends hours to 9 P.M. and offers free admission on the first Friday of every month.

Doll Museum

Housed in an elaborate Victorian fantasy structure, the **Rosalie Whyel Museum of Doll Art** (1116 108th Ave. NE, 425/455-1116

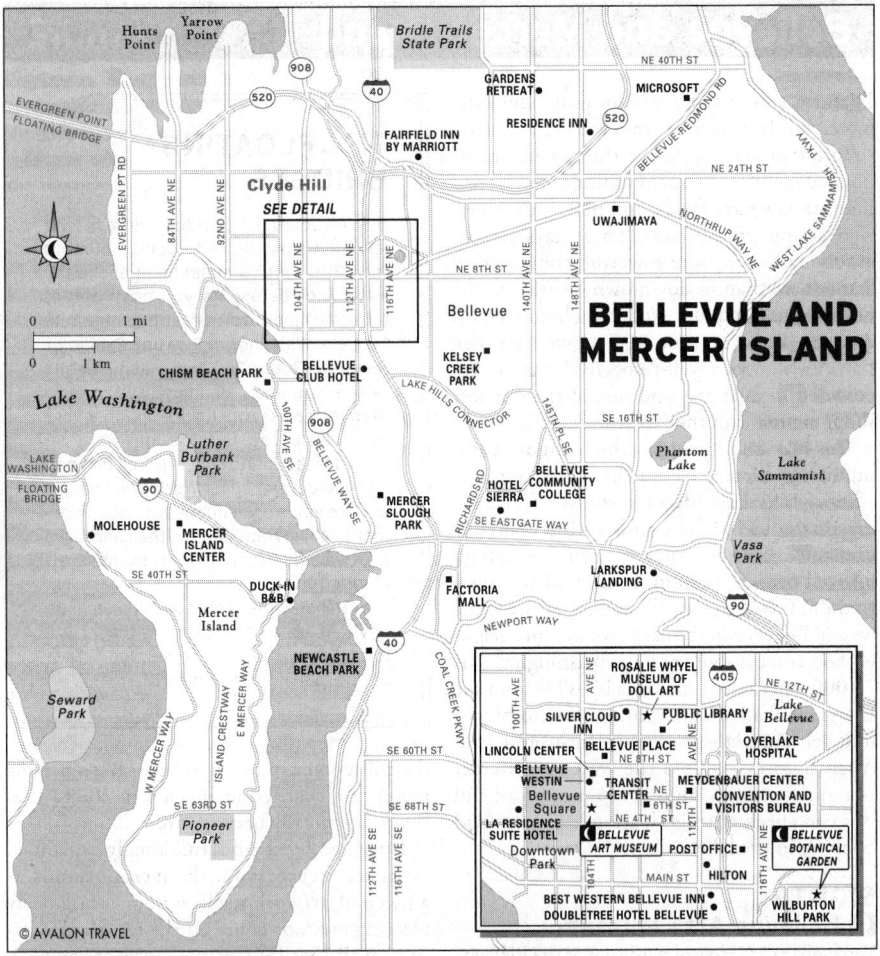

or 800/440-3655, www.dollart.com, 10 A.M.–5 P.M. Mon.–Sat., 1–5 P.M. Sun., $7 adults, $6 seniors, $5 ages 5–17, free for kids under 5) is home to one of the world's largest collections of dolls and is guaranteed to bring a smile to every four-year-old girl. The museum covers two expansive floors with professional presentations and more than 1,000 dolls on display. Start out with a five-minute video explaining the history of dollmaking, then head upstairs to check out the diverse collection that includes thumbnail-sized Egyptian tomb dolls and other antique dolls. Downstairs are 20th-century dolls, including mechanical dolls, authentically detailed dollhouses, Barbies, GI Joes, teddy bears, and even Elvis figures. Also downstairs is a gift shop filled with dolls and doll paraphernalia. The museum is especially popular with the over-60 set, and busloads roll in from senior centers all over the state.

Bellevue Botanical Garden

Stroll the grounds at Bellevue Botanical Garden (12001 Main St., 425/462-2750, www

.bellevuebotanical.org, dawn–dusk daily, free) to take in over 53 acres of floral displays and native greenery. Garden highlights include an alpine rock garden with high elevation varietals, a tranquil Japanese garden, and a 19-acre botanical reserve featuring forest, wetlands, and meadowland. An army of enthusiastic volunteers help run the visitors center (10 A.M.–6 P.M. daily May–Sept., 10 A.M.–4 P.M. daily Oct.–Apr.) on the grounds. Tours can be caught here at 2 P.M. on Saturday and Sunday April–October.

The garden is beautiful year-round, but its dahlia bloom in summer is the marquee draw. Over 40 varieties surround the historic Sharp Cabin in a kaleidoscopic display. Park volunteers also take advantage of the short days of winter each year to put on a display of Christmas lights fashioned as flowers during its Garden d'Lights festival. From the end of November through the beginning of January the park is open until 9:30 P.M. each night for visitors to admire the sparkling spectacle.

Bellevue Parks

The 79-acre **Kelsey Creek Farm and Park** (13204 S.E. 8th Pl., 425/455-7688, 7 A.M.–6 P.M. daily, free) is a choice destination for animal-lovin' youngsters. The main attraction here is a welcoming petting zoo with cows, rabbits, sheep, pigs, and ponies galore.

The property offers primo opportunities for the enthusiastic shutterbug. On premises, visitors can aim a lens at two enormous hip-roofed barns, an 1888 pioneer log cabin, a Japanese garden, a rustic farmhouse, and, of course, the animals.

Mercer Slough covers 320 acres of marsh habitat just south of downtown Bellevue. Here you'll discover 10 miles of trails, as well as four miles of waterways perfect for exploring in a canoe or kayak. It's fine place to watch for deer, muskrats, ducks, herons, and other critters. This entire area was underwater until 1917, when Seattle's Chittenden Locks were completed, lowering the level of Lake Washington by nine feet.

Mercer Island Parks

Mercer Island's postage-stamp 10 square miles is dominated by nearly 500 acres of parks and green spaces just ripe for exploration. Most prized among them is **Luther Burbank Park** (2040 84th Ave. SE). This is the island's best waterfront park, featuring nearly a mile of shoreline, public boat docks, a roped-in swimming beach and plenty of spots to plunk down a lure. Visitors can dip their toes in the chilly waters or just stroll the shore to work up an appetite before grilling up some dogs in the barbecue area. There's also a fun playground and swings to let the shoulder monkeys loose and even an off-leash dog park.

Those who seek a little solitude should wander into **Pioneer Park.** This undeveloped park is an homage to the island's wilder days, before sprawling estates and $5 lattes. It features over six miles of multiuse trails that wander through stands of old-growth cedar, Douglas fir, bigleaf maple, and alder.

One of the most novel parks on the island, **The Park on the Lid** is a slice of greenery known less for what is on park grounds than for what the park grounds are on—namely, the I-90 tunnel lid. Check out the big white stovepipe-looking tubes set amid the well-manicured picnic lawns. These are the vents that filter out fumes from the freeway below.

ENTERTAINMENT AND EVENTS

Nightlife

As downtown Bellevue grows up, so does the surrounding nightlife. Though it doesn't rival Seattle's scene, Bellevue's collection of nightspots offers enough variety to keep most people happy for an evening or two.

Besides, happy hour is so much happier when you don't have to contend with traffic over the bridges. Bellevue has some particularly attractive spots come happy hour, including Taphouse Grill (550 106th Avenue NE, 425/467-1730, www.taphousegrill.com, 11 A.M.–10 P.M. Sun.–Thurs., 11 A.M.–11 P.M. Fri.–Sat.) in the Galleria shopping center. This upscale brewhouse has more than 160 beers on tap; during happy hour drinkers can nosh on a number of finger foods for under $5 a plate. During peak weekend evenings, this is a very popular gathering spot for the flirty 20-something crowd.

Just a few blocks west, the **520 Bar and Grill** (10138 Main St., 425/450-0520, www.520barandgrill.com) is another favorite happy hour hangout, particularly among the well-heeled middle-aged set. The trick is to get there early, as happy hour runs 2–5:20 P.M.; specials are also good all day on Sunday. Set slightly away from the Bellevue Square rush, this bar prides itself on its uniqueness. Happy hour appetizers are distinctive, and there isn't a whiff of chain-bar flair—just classy walnut columns and oak floors, handmade furniture, and a genuine public-house vibe.

Those looking to impress a date should look to the Bellevue skies for help. Set atop the 989 Elements High Rise, **Vertigo Lounge and Grill** (989 112th Avenue NE, 425/467-6767, www.vertigobellevue.com) is a big-city-style establishment with sleek modern furnishings and plenty of jet-setters to fill them. Vertigo is best known for its jazz lineup, generally putting on shows Wednesday through Saturday night each week.

Finally, Bellevue also has options for the restless type who prefer doing something while they drink. Lincoln Center plays host to a pair of fun sporting nightspots. **The Parlor** (700 Bellevue Way NE Ste. 300, 425/289-7000, www.parlorbilliards.com, 11 A.M.–2 A.M. Mon.–Sat., 11 A.M.–midnight Sun., tables $10–18 per hour) is an upscale pool hall where the players come dressed to impress. **Lucky Strike Lanes** (700 Bellevue Way NE, Ste. 250, 425/453-5137, www.bowlluckystrike.com, noon–midnight Mon.–Thurs., noon–2 A.M. Fri., 11 A.M.–2 A.M. Sat., 11 A.M.–midnight Sun.) is a posh bowling alley. Its chic decor pays homage to the mid-20th-century stylings popular during bowling's heyday, without the gross 50-year-old bowling shoes.

The Arts

You won't find anything approaching the Seattle music scene in Bellevue, but **Crossroads Shopping Center** (15600 N.E. 8th Ave., 425/644-1111, www.crossroadsbellevue.com) does put on free concerts of all types on Friday and Saturday nights.

The **Bellevue Philharmonic Orchestra** (425/455-4171, www.bellevuephilharmonic.com) performs classical and pop concerts at various local venues, including the state-of-the-art **Meydenbauer Center** (112th Ave. NE and N.E. 6th St., www.meydenbauer.com). The Meydenbauer also hosts theatrical and musical productions from a variety of Eastside companies, including the **Bellevue Chamber Chorus** (425/881-0445, www.bellevuechamberchorus.net), a group of 30 singers who perform October–May. The **Bellevue Civic Theatre** (4038 Factoria Blvd. #165, 425/235-5087, www.bellevuecivic.org) is the city's professional acting company.

Bellevue Arts Fair

Bellevue Arts Museum sponsors the annual Bellevue Arts Fair (425/519-0742 or www.bellevuearts.org), held on the last full weekend of July. One of the state's largest art fairs, this one has been going on since 1947 and usually features more than 300 booths. The juried show and crowds that top 300,000 have helped many artists' careers along.

SHOPPING

Bellevue's motto might be best expressed by a bumper sticker seen on local cars: "When the going gets tough, the tough go shopping."

Shopping Malls

Bellevue Square (N.E. 8th St. and Bellevue Way NE, 9:30 A.M.–9:30 P.M. Mon.–Sat., 11 A.M.–7 P.M. Sun.) has been around the longest among Bellevue's shopping meccas, and it still reigns as the king of 'em all. It is one of the Northwest's largest shopping malls—more than 200 stores and a dozen restaurants around a big atrium. Locals crow that this upscale shopping center attracts more visitors than Disneyland. Luxe stores on the premises include Armani Exchange, bebe, Brooks Brothers, Burberry, and Lacoste.

GEARING UP

Heading from Seattle, Eastside cities are often the last stop in civilization before driving into the wilderness for a bit of outdoor fun. Here are some of the best shops around the area to buy or rent gear and grab trail food and the like on your way to the woods or the slopes.

Marmot Mountain Works (827 Bellevue Way NE, Bellevue, 425/453-1515, 10 A.M.-8 P.M. Mon., Thurs., and Fri., 10 A.M.-6 P.M. Tues., Wed., and Sat., noon-6 P.M. Sun.) specializes in hard-to-find climbing, skiing, and backpacking gear and parts, as well as apparel, outerwear, and maps. Its rental shop offers climbing, camping, and skiing gear.

Gerk's Alpine Hut (7875 Leary Way, Redmond, 425/650-6752, www.gerksalpinehut.com, 10 A.M.-7 P.M. Mon.-Fri., 10 A.M.-5 P.M. Sat., noon-5 P.M. Sun.) is a small, local shop with mountain biking, cycling, and ski gear. Daily, weekly, and seasonal ski rentals available.

REI (7500 166th Ave. NE, Redmond, 425/882-1158, 10 A.M.-9 P.M. Mon.-Fri., 10 A.M.-8 P.M. Sat., 11 A.M.-6 P.M. Sun.) offers two stories of all nature of outdoor gear. The larger of two REI stores on the Eastside, the Redmond outpost has a rental shop with camping, climbing, mountaineering, and snow sports gear. **REI** (735 Northwest Gilman Blvd., Issaquah, 425/313-1660, 9 A.M.-9 P.M. Mon.-Fri., 9 A.M.-8 P.M. Sat., 10 A.M.-6 P.M. Sun.) in Issaquah is smaller than the Redmond store but closer to Snoqualmie Pass. The rental shop here only offers snowshoes.

Montlake Bike Shop (208 Kirkland Ave., Kirkland, 425/828-3800, 10 A.M.-7 P.M. Mon.-Fri., 9 A.M.-5 P.M. Sat., 10 A.M.-4 P.M. Sun.) is one of the best bike shops on the Eastside, offering a full range of bike rentals on a daily and weekly basis.

Just across the street, **Lincoln Square** (700 Bellevue Way NE, 425/450-9100, www.lincolnsquare.com) expands on "Belle Square's" shopping range with more stores, including Ex Officio, Henredon, and Vino 100. It also houses a billiards parlor, bowling alley, luxury cinema, and a spa. A convenient footbridge connects Bellevue and Lincoln Squares together, and both are open the same hours.

Shoppers who prefer to save a buck or two might want to run over to **Crossroads Mall** (15600 NE 8th St., 425/644-1111, www.crossroadsbellevue.com, 10 A.M.–9 P.M. Mon.–Sat., 11 A.M.–6:00 P.M. Sun.), about 10 minutes away from the hotsy-totsy downtown area. This shopping complex has an Old Navy, Sports Authority, Shoe Pavilion, and Bed, Bath and Beyond, among others. It also has an extensive food court that serves up delicious ethnic food from around the world.

Old Bellevue Boutiques

Shoppers who prefer those one-of-a-kind items that make friends ask enviously, "Where'd you find *that?*" should skip the mall and trek a few blocks to Old Bellevue's restored business district on Main Street between 100th and Bellevue Way.

Don't miss **Cuttysark** (10237 Main St., 425/453-1265, www.cuttysark.net), a store that is almost a museum, with intricate old ship models, marine antiques of all sorts, and flags from around the globe. Next door is **Ming's Asian Gallery** (425/462-4008), with antique Asian pieces.

Fashonistas will love this stretch as well. Ladies looking for sleek designer apparel and accessories should make it a point to hit **La Ree** (11 103rd Ave. NE, 425/453-7866, www.lareeboutique.com, 10 A.M.–7 P.M. Mon.–Sat., 11 A.M.–6 P.M. Sun.), a New York–style specialty shop that loads up on lines such as Alexander Wang, Mint, and Proportion of Blue.

You'll have endless options for matching pumps, sandals, or flats at not one but two specialty shoe stores nearby. **Gotta Have Shoes** (10047 Main St. #101, 425/460-8316, 10 A.M.–6 P.M. Mon.–Sat., 11 A.M.–5 P.M. Sun.) and **Posh on Main** (10245 Main St., 425/454-2022, www.poshonmain.com, 10 A.M.–6 P.M.

Mon.–Sat., noon–5 P.M. Sun.) both offer a fetishist's dream supply of high-end foot fashions and handbags to boot.

Bookstores

Bellevue also is home to several surprisingly large bookstores, including **Barnes and Noble** (626 106th Ave. NE, 425/451-8463, www.bn.com) and **University Book Store** (990 102nd Ave. NE, 425/632-9500, www.bookstore.washington.edu).

SPORTS AND RECREATION

Bridle Trails State Park

As the name attests, Bridle Trails State Park (116th Ave. NE, www.parks.wa.gov, no camping) is an urban retreat for equestrian lovers. Settled in a wooded plot resting between Bellevue and Kirkland, the park offers 28 miles of equestrian and hiking trails, as well as a riding arena that hosts regular shows and competitions during the summer months. Riders and hikers can also extend their exploration over the **Bridle Crest Trail,** which continues on to Redmond's Marymoor Park.

Walking and Running

Bellevue's **Lake Hills Greenbelt** (off 156th Ave. SE) features five miles of trails through 100 acres of wetlands and pines in the heart of the city. Open to joggers, cyclists, wheelchairs, and hikers, the greenbelt trail links Larsen and Phantom Lakes. A ranger station has information on the area's natural history.

If that isn't enough land to roam, take to the **Lake to Lake Parkway Trail,** a paved cycling and running path connecting Lake Sammamish with Lake Washington.

Water Sports

Cascade Canoe & Kayak Center (425/637-8838, www.canoe-kayak.com) offers sea kayak tours, lessons, and rentals on Lake Washington at **Enatai Beach Park** (108th Ave. SE at 35th Ave.). It is affiliated with REI.

Located along Lake Washington, both **Chism Beach Park** (off 100th Ave. SE) and **Newcastle Beach Park** (off Lake Washington Blvd. SE) have picnic areas, trails, and swimming beaches with summertime lifeguards.

Golf

Just south of Bellevue in the onetime coal mining settlement of Newcastle, **The Golf Club at Newcastle** (15500 Six Penny Lane, 425/793-5566, www.newcastlegolf.com) has been called one of the top 10 courses in America. Short of the peaks of the Issaquah Alps, the greens and fairways here offer the most stunning Eastside vistas of Seattle and the Cascades on a clear day.

Camping

Although the nearest public campground is many miles away in the Cascades, Bellevue does have tent and vehicle spaces at two private RV parks: **Trailers Inn RV Park** (exit 11 west from I-90, 15531 S.E. 37th St., 425/747-9181 or 800/659-4684, open year-round) and **Vasa Park Resort** (2560 W. Lake Sammamish Rd. SE, 425/746-3260, mid-May–Sept.). Vasa is right along Lake Sammamish and features a fun dock and slide that dumps kids right into the lake.

ACCOMMODATIONS

As Bellevue continues to gentrify, the city's budget lodging options have dwindled considerably. Those travelers wishing stay close to the city in cheap lodging under $100 should motor south on I-405 for the most options. Renton and its environs are only a few minutes away and will have a number of chain hotels that fetch a much more modest price than comparable digs within Bellevue's high-demand zip codes.

$100-150

That's not to say that the Bellevue area doesn't have a few lodging deals waiting to be snagged. For example, right downtown on the west side of Bellevue Square, **La Residence Suite Hotel** (475 100th Ave. NE, 425/455-1475, www.bellevuelodging.com, $125 one bedroom, $165 two bedroom) offers guests who stay for at least seven days a super rate of $105 per night in its one-room suites. The rooms here are converted condos, so every room comes complete with full kitchen, dining room, and living room. The furnishings are a bit tired, but for the price and the location it is a steal.

Both Bellevue and Mercer Island play host to a few surprisingly reasonable B&Bs. Just 10 minutes from the heart of downtown Bellevue's high-rises and shopping centers, **Gardens Retreat** (3444 140th Ave. NE, 206/370-2484, www.gardensretreat.com, $95–110 s, $110–135 d) is cozied up near the little pastures and barns of Bellevue's quaint Bridle Trails neighborhood. The inn has two rooms, one with private bathroom, a lovely backyard garden, and a cozy library for lounging. Full breakfast is served each morning. Both rooms have wireless Internet, and there is a printer and fax in the library for business travelers.

In Mercer Island, **Molehouse** (3308 West Mercer Way, 206/232-1611, www.molehouse.com, $120 s or d) has a winsome private suite perched atop the innkeeper's three-story home. Guests can gaze out to Lake Washington from the private balcony here. Breakfast is do-it-yourself, with all the necessary accoutrements stocked in the suite's refrigerator and pantry.

For just a few dollars more than the Molehouse, the **Duck-In B&B** (4118 100th Ave. SE, 206/232-2554, www.seattlebestbandb.com/duckin, $135 d) in Mercer Island is probably the best B&B deal in the area. This romantic, two-bedroom, 1920s-era cottage is settled right on the shore of Lake Washington, with a big grassy lawn leading out to the water. A continental breakfast is provided, and kids are welcome.

$150-200

Conveniently located just off of I-90 in Bellevue's Eastgate neighborhood, **Larkspur Landing** (15805 S.E. 37th St., 425/373-1212, www.larkspurlanding.com, $169–189 s or d) is a new hotel built in pleasing Craftsman-style architecture. This is a great spot for those who mix long business trips with pleasure—all rooms come with fully equipped kitchens, deliciously comfy feather-top beds, large desks, and high-speed Internet. The place is kid and pet friendly, laundry facilities are free to use, and continental breakfast is served each morning. Plus, there's a pool and a well-appointed gym. Best of all, freshly baked cookies are served every afternoon.

Hotel Sierra (3244 139th Ave SE, 425/747-2705, www.hotel-sierra.com, s or d $179) is another of Bellevue's newly renovated hotels, gussied up to accommodate travelers expecting luxurious digs. Rooms feature plush furniture and plasma TVs, and there's an indoor pool and fitness center on premises. Stay comes with complimentary breakfast in the morning, including a made-to-order omelette bar, and an evening wine hour with appetizers.

Over $250

Because Bellevue accommodates so many business travelers, many luxury room-rate schedules are the reverse of a typical tourist resort—weekdays are the most expensive days to stay. Some of downtown's nicest hotels are nearly half the rack rate on weekend nights.

This is true of the **Bellevue Westin** (600 Bellevue Way NE, 425/638-1000, www.westin.com, $369 s or d), arguably downtown's nicest luxury chain hotel. The rooms are impeccable here, and one can stay for as little as $159 on some weekends. Try to get a room above the sixth floor, as many below that have obstructed views.

The city's classiest lodging is **Bellevue Club Hotel** (11200 S.E. 6th St., 425/454-4424 or 800/579-1110, www.bellevueclub.com, $250–310 s or d), where you'll find all the amenities: indoor pool, sauna, hot tub, racquetball courts, tennis courts, a complete athletic facility, twice-daily housekeeping, and private minibars.

FOOD

Steak and Seafood

Located 21 floors up in the Bank of America Building at Bellevue Place, **Daniel's Broiler** (10500 NE 8th St., 425/462-4662, www.schwartzbros.com/daniels, 4:30 P.M.–10 P.M. Sun.–Thurs., 4:30 P.M.–11 P.M. Fri.–Sat., $50) has good seafood chowder and steaks, and extraordinary views. The lounge serves wines by the glass, oysters on the half-shell, and a variety of light meals and desserts, plus jazz or piano music nightly.

Asian

Golkonda South Indian Cuisine (15600 NE 8th Ave., 425/649-0355, 11:30 A.M.–2:15 P.M. and 5:30 P.M.–10 P.M. Mon.–Fri., 11:30 A.M.–10:30 P.M. Sat., 11:30 A.M.–9P.M. Sun., $10) is a popular destination for Microsoft employees who appreciate the excellent $9 weekday lunch buffet. **Thai Ginger** (3717 Factoria Blvd. SE, 425/641-4008, www.thaiginger.com, 11 A.M.–9:30 P.M. Sun.–Thurs., 11 A.M.–10 P.M. Fri.–Sat., $10) is a fine place for Thai food, prepared in the open kitchen. Try the garlic prawns or chicken satay.

The best local Chinese restaurant is **Yeas Wok** (6969 Coal Creek Parkway SE, 425/644-5546, http://yeaswokwa.com, 11 A.M.–9:30 P.M. Mon.–Thurs., 11 A.M.–10:30 P.M. Fri., 10:30 A.M.–10:30 P.M. Sat., 10:30 A.M.–9:30 P.M. Sun., $11) in Newcastle, where specialties include Hunan, Szechuan, and Mandarin dishes, notably the crispy shrimp. It's in a strip mall, but don't let that put you off; the food is authentic and the menu vast. **Noble Court** (1644 140th Ave. NE, 425/641-6011, www.thenoblecourt.com, 11 A.M.–9:30 P.M. Mon.–Thurs., 11 A.M.–10:30 P.M. Fri., 10 A.M.–10:30 P.M. Sat., 10 A.M.–5 P.M. Sun., $9) has the tastiest dim sum on the Eastside, along with many unusual offerings.

Nigiri lovers would do well to swing by **I Love Sushi** (11818 NE 8th St., 425/454-5706, www.ilovesushi.com, 11 A.M.–2 P.M. Mon–Sat. and 5 P.M.–10 P.M. Sun.–Thurs., 5 P.M.–10:30 P.M. Fri.–Sat., $15), an excellent Japanese restaurant and sushi bar with some of the best knife-wielding chefs this side of Lake Washington.

Mercer Island has two great Thai restaurants, **Pon Preom Restaurant** (3039 78th Ave. SE, 206/236-8424, 11 A.M.–3 P.M. and 5 P.M.–9 P.M. daily, $11) and the more Americanized **Thai on Mercer** (7691 SE 27th St., 206/236-9990, 11:30 A.M.–2 P.M. Mon.–Fri. and 5–9 P.M. Mon.–Thurs. and Sun., 5–10 P.M. Fri.–Sat., $11), both worth a visit if you've worked up a good appetite for noodles or spring rolls after a day at Luther Burbank Park.

Uwajimaya (15555 NE 24th St., 425/747-9012, www.uwajimaya.com, 9 A.M.–10 P.M. Mon.–Sat., 9 A.M.–9 P.M. Sun.) is the local outpost of the Asian grocery chain, featuring fresh seafood, high-quality produce, a deli with sushi and other many Asian specialties, plus Japanese books and gifts.

Continental and Mediterranean

BIS on Main (10213 Main St., 425/455-2033, www.bisonmain.com, 11:30 A.M.–11 P.M. Mon.–Thurs., 11:30 A.M.–midnight Fri., 5:30 P.M.–MIDNIGHT SAT., 5–9 P.M. Sun., $38), is *the* place to be seen in downtown Bellevue, with a great service and wonderful continental cuisine and seafood. It's where locals go to impress a business client. Try the whipped potatoes with wasabi or the savory fish soup.

Pogacha (119 106th Ave. NE, 425/455-5670, www.pogacha.com, 11:30 A.M.–2:30 P.M. Mon.–Fri. and 5 P.M.–8:30P.M. Sun.–Mon., 5 P.M.–9 P.M. Tues.–Thurs., 5 P.M.–10 P.M. Fri., 5 P.M.–9:30 P.M. Sat., $15) is certainly one of the more unusual Bellevue restaurants, with flavorful toppings on Croatian-style pizzas and delightfully crunchy breads.

Spazzo (10655 NE 4th St., 425/454-8255, www.schwartzbros.com/spazzo, 11 A.M.–9 P.M. Mon.–Thurs., 11 A.M.–10 P.M. Fri., 11:30 A.M.–10 P.M. Sat., 11:30 A.M.–9 P.M. Sun., $21) offers impressive vistas from the top of the Key Bank Building. The Mediterranean menu includes well-prepared food from North Africa, Turkey, and Greece.

Tucked away into an unassuming strip mall in Overlake, **Tosoni's** (14320 NE 20th St., 425/644-1668, 5–10 P.M. Tues.–Sat., closed Sun.–Mon., $25) is actually one of the nicest eateries on the Eastside. Step inside and you're greeted by a cozily romantic bistro with white tablecloths, flickering candles, and a window into the kitchen. The rosy-cheeked chef often comes out to greet guests after he cooks his heart out, serving creative and hearty servings of Italian and Eastern European fare. The wait staff is very knowledgeable, so you can always trust in them to find a great wine pairing for your meal from the amply stocked reserve.

If you're on Mercer Island and craving wholesome food with a bit of French and Italian flair, **Bennett's Pure Food Bistro** (7650 SE 27th St., Mercer 206/232-2759, www.bennettsbistro.com, 11:30 A.M.–2 P.M. Mon.–Fri., 10 A.M.–3 P.M. Sat.–Sun. and 4:30–9:30 P.M. Sun.–Thurs., 4:30–10:30 P.M. Fri.–Sat., $22) serves only fresh, local foods with an emphasis on whole foods and handmade artisan meats, cheeses, and breads. Cheese fans will be happy to note that this well-regarded restaurant is a sister establishment to Pike Place icon Beecher's Handmade Cheese.

Brunch

The luxurious **Calcutta Grill** (15500 Six Penny Lane, 425/793-4646, www.newcastlegolf.com, 11 A.M.–10 P.M. Mon.–Thurs., 11 A.M.–11 P.M. Fri.–Sat., 10 A.M.–10 P.M. Sun., $32), located in The Golf Club at Newcastle, is known for its popular Sunday brunch spread. Come for the gourmet omelettes, prime rib, and desserts, and stay for the sweeping vistas of the Seattle skyline. It's also open for lunch and dinner daily. Reservations are highly recommended at any time of day.

INFORMATION AND SERVICES

For additional information on Bellevue and the surrounding area, contact the helpful **East King County Convention and Visitors Bureau** (520 112th Ave. NE, Suite 101, 425/450-5640 or 800/252-1926, www.eastkingcounty.org, 8:30 A.M.–5 P.M. Mon.–Fri., plus some summer weekends).

The modern **Bellevue Public Library** (11501 Main, 425/455-6889, www.kcls.org) is the largest in King County.

Visit **Mercer Island Chamber of Commerce** (7601 S.E. 27th St., 206/232-3404, www.mercerislandchamber.org) in the island's "downtown" district for local information. The main annual event is **Summer Celebration,** held in mid-July, with a street fair, fireworks, concerts, and more fun.

GETTING THERE AND AROUND

Both east ends of Lake Washington's floating bridges land in Bellevue. Downtown Bellevue is closer to Highway 520 by a hair, and generally it is a toss-up between routes from Seattle. Sometimes, though, one bridge will definitely have the traffic advantage over another. Check the state Department of Transportation website (www.wsdot.wa.gov/traffic/seattle/) for a color-coded traffic map and web cams to help you make up your mind. The only way to drive to Mercer Island is to take I-90 over the Lake Washington Floating Bridge. Mercer's small business district is located on the north end of the island and just off I-90.

Metro Transit (800/542-7876, http://transit.metrokc.gov) has several buses serving Bellevue and Mercer Island from Seattle, plus numerous local routes. The main stop is the Bellevue Transit Center, on N.E. 6th Street downtown.

Kirkland

The oldest city on the east side of Lake Washington, Kirkland's gentrified neighborhoods may never have been what they are today if the town's namesake had his way. Back around 1886, Peter Kirk hoped to turn the town into the "Pittsburgh of the West" with a giant steel mill along Lake Washington that never came to fruition. Instead, early town pioneers depended on lumber for subsistence, and eventually the town blossomed into the charming lakeside community it is today.

The centerpiece of Kirkland is its real estate along Lake Washington. Many area boutiques, art galleries, cafés, parks, and houses line the lake, and downtown directly abuts its lapping water.

SIGHTS

Downtown Kirkland Waterfront

Kirkland's charms are particularly evident along **Lake Street,** in the city's village-like downtown. Just a skipped stone away from the shores of Lake Washington, this quaint commercial district is a fun place to do some window shopping, grab a bite to eat, or sit down with a cup of joe for an afternoon of people-watching.

Much of Kirkland's waterfront activity centers on **Marina Park,** a welcoming shore-side haven that features a sandy beach and ample grass for lounging while checking out the views of downtown Seattle and the Olympic Mountains. In the summer it seems as if the rigging of nearby docked boats ping against their masts in time with the music from the park's regularly held community concerts.

Saint Edward State Park

Head farther north on N.E. 145th Street to Saint Edward State Park (425/296-2970, www.parks.wa.gov), a 316-acre retreat from civilization. This quiet piece of property was part of a

© ERICKA CHICKOWSKI

Kirkland's waterfront is an ideal spot for a picnic when the weather is right.

Catholic seminary until 1977. When the seminary closed, the diocese sold the land to the state and the park opened the following summer. St. Edward boasts almost a mile of forested, undeveloped Lake Washington shoreline and five miles of hiking and mountain biking trails, plus picnic areas, a gymnasium, and an indoor pool.

Other Parks

A cluster of city parks provide much-needed open space on the shore of Lake Washington. Right downtown, **Waverly Beach Park** has a lovely swimming area and a great across-the-lake views. Keep driving north and you'll eventually hit upon **Juanita Bay Park** (425/828-1217), an old golf course now transformed with scenic hiking trails and guided walks in the summer, and **Juanita Beach Park,** with an impressively long pier, picnic tables, and one of the area's best swimming beaches. Northwest of Juanita, **Denny Park** on Holmes Point Drive has a small beach, picnic area, and hiking trail leading to King County's largest Douglas fir. Standing 255 feet high and eight feet in diameter, the tree is estimated to be 600 years old.

ENTERTAINMENT AND EVENTS

Nightlife

Waldo's Tavern (12657 N.E. 85th St., 425/827-9292) is a big place with dance bands on weekends and pool tables all the time. More music and dancing can be had at **Dynamite Lounge** (15 Lake St., 425/822-3474), **The Shark Club** (52 Lakeshore Plaza, 425/803-3003), and **Kirkland Roaster and Ale House** (111 Central Way, 425/827-4400).

The Arts

Downtown Kirkland is sprinkled with fun public sculptures, including *Cow and the Coyote* on Central Way. **Kirkland Arts Center** (620 Market St., 425/822-7161, www.kirklandartscenter.org) presents exhibits and classes in the historic Peter Kirk Building, built in 1891. The second Thursday of each month, Kirkland galleries open for **Art Walk** (425/889-8212, 6–9 P.M.), featuring artist receptions and shows.

The modern and spacious **Kirkland Performance Center** (350 Kirkland Ave., 425/893-9900, www.kpcenter.org) is home to theater, dance, classical and pop music concerts, and family programs.

Festivals and Events

On Father's Day weekend, the **Washington Summer Microbrew Festival** (206/706-9869, www.washingtonbrewfest.com) brings beer lovers to Saint Edward State Park. Most regional microbreweries are here, along with food and craft booths, live music, and activities for kids.

Summerfest (425/822-7161), on the second weekend in July, attracts crowds of people for local arts and crafts. Also in July **Kirkland Uncorked** (www.kirklanduncorked.com) celebrates good wine, food, and art at Marina Park.

Kirkland Farmers Market (425/893-8766) fills Park Lane East between 3rd Street and Main with vegetables, flowers, sweets, and crafts 1–7 P.M. on summertime Wednesdays.

SHOPPING

The **Kirkland Antique Gallery** (151 3rd St., 425/828-4993) is a collector's paradise, containing 80 shops filled with antiques. **Eastside Trains** (217 Central Way, 425/828-4098, www.eastsidetrains.com) is a surprisingly large place where 40-something men play with model trains and pretend to be buying trains for their kids.

A dozen art galleries are right downtown on Central Way NE and Park Lane. Three of the best are **Berozkina Gallery** (9 Lake St., 425/803-5032, www.berozkina.com), **Foster/White Gallery** (126 Central Way, 425/822-2308, www.fosterwhite.com), and **Lakeshore Gallery** (15 Lake St., 425/827-0606).

SPORTS AND RECREATION

Boating

Kirkland is a natural jumping-off point for Lake Washington boaters hoping to get a closer look at area estates and wetland parks along the lake's perimeter. The **Kirkland Marina** is the only public dock with overnight moorage available; the nearby boat launch is a popular spot to ease craft into the water. A $10 permit is required to access the launch. Permits can be picked up at the Kirkland Parks and Community Services office (505 Market St.) 8 A.M.–5 P.M., Monday–Friday. The office is closed on weekends and holidays, so plan ahead.

Nearby, Yarrow Bay Marina is a convenient place to fuel up vessels from the water. It is also a good spot to quell a little bit of boat envy. Yarrow rents 19- to 21-foot runabouts for $75 per two hours.

For a more quiet time on the water, pick up a paddle and join the sea kayak tours led by **Upper Left-Hand Corner Kayak Tours** (10823 NE 60 St., 425/828-4772, www.kayak-wa.com) out on the lake.

Cycling and Mountain Biking

Mountain bikers and cyclists love Kirkland for its endless spaghetti bowl of quiet surface streets and its cornucopia of fat tire–friendly trails. Most popular among roadies is a curvy 15-mile out-and-back along Lake Washington. To take this route, park at St. Edward State Park and ride south along Juanita Drive Northeast. The road will curve to the northeast and eventually you'll need to turn right to head south on 98th Avenue Northeast, which turns into Market Street. From there, continue south on Lake Street, which turns into Lake Washington Boulevard and takes you to the doorsteps of Carillon Point, your turnaround spot. This commercial plaza is a good lunch spot, either in its bistros or sack-lunch style in its central plaza. Listen for the six ringing carillon bells that toll every half hour. St. Edward is also a popular stop among mountain bikers, who zigzag and bunny-hop along the wooded trails here.

If your bike is hung up in the garage back home, or if you'd simply like to give these routes a go on something other than an old beater, try **Montlake Bicycle Shop** (208 Kirkland Ave., 425/828-3800, www.montlakebike.com, 10 A.M.–7 P.M. Mon.–Fri., 9 A.M.–5 P.M. Sat., 10 A.M.–4 P.M. Sun.). It offers a range of premium road and mountain bikes for $25 to $125 per day.

ACCOMMODATIONS

$100-150

Kirkland's most affordable lodging is situated near the strip malls in Totem Lake. Though they generally lack many amenities or ambiance, the motels around here are safe, close to I-405 and are usually reasonably priced. One of the better deals can be found at **Baymont Inn** (12223 N.E. 116th St., 425/229-6668, $120 s or d), which has clean rooms, an indoor spa, and continental breakfast served each morning. It is right next to the freeway, so come with earplugs or be prepared to imagine there's a very loud river nearby.

$150-200

A step up from most Totem Lake motels, the **Carlton Inn** (12233 NE Totem Lake Way, 425/821-2202, $149–169 s or d) has a much nicer interior than its shabby exterior suggests. This comfortable budget-to-midrange hotel's rooms can sometimes be had for less than $100 during non-peak times. Amenities include an outdoor heated pool, indoor spa, and fitness center. Plus, it's got interior entry halls, a safety feature that many motels, such as the Baymont, lack.

Over $200

Arguably the Eastside's nicest hotel, the **Heathman Hotel** (220 Kirkland Ave., 425/284-5800 or 800/551-0011 or, www.heathmankirkland.com, $239–899 s or d) gets all of the details right. There's no front desk here because staff greets guests at the front doorstep and personally walks them through check-in at small kiosks before whisking them away to their rooms. Not only is there a pillow menu, there's a mattress menu here as well—each floor has a different kind of mattress for guests to choose among. The new hotel was built green from the ground up; smart rooms automatically switch vents off when windows are opened and turn lights off after you've left the room. If money is no object, the suites are big enough to spend a whole vacation in without darkening the doorstep—some even have jetted tubs out on their private patios.

The **Woodmark Hotel** (1200 Carillon Pt., 425/822-3700 or 800/822-3700, www.thewoodmark.com, $205–1,800 s or d), doesn't look that impressive from the outside but is actually one of the finest lodging places in the area, with every possible amenity (grand piano, stocked minibars, terry robes, TV in the bathroom, and full breakfast) and rooms overlooking Lake Washington. This is the only hotel on the shores of the lake, and rates are commensurate with the amenities.

FOOD

Kirkland is blessed with a mix of quick eateries and fine restaurants, many of which are right downtown.

Cafés and Diners

With its comfy leather sofas and trendy red interior, **Terra Bite Lounge** (Kirkland Ave. and State St., www.terrabite.org, 5 A.M.–10 P.M. Mon.–Fri., 7 A.M.–10 P.M. Sat., 7 A.M.–9 P.M. Sun.) is a great café to linger over a cup of coffee or surf the Internet with free Wi-Fi. It is also a grand social experiment. Founded by a lead engineer at Google's local offices, Terra Bite has no set prices and no barista tip jar. Patrons pay what they think is fair or what they can afford, slipping payments into an anonymous drop box near the counter. Surprisingly, the honor system brings out the best among Terra Bite's patrons, and there is a definite sense of community cultivated here.

Closer to the waterfront, **Kahili Coffee** (105 Lake St. S., 425/576-5600, www.kahilicoffee.com, 6 A.M.–10 P.M. Mon.–Thurs., 6 A.M.–11 P.M. Fri.–Sat., 6:30 A.M.–10 P.M. Sun.) is a real treat for lovers of Hawaiian coffee blends. Kahili serves dark and robust Kona coffees alongside a small assortment of pastries and baked goods. The space is quite large for a coffeehouse, offering a number of sofas to sink into and a row of barstools facing the bustle of Lake Street.

Just steps away from Marina Park, **Coffee & Cone** (1 Lake Shore Plaza, 425/827-7098) is ideal for those craving a simple cup of drip coffee. It is also a great place to grab some ice cream before lounging by the lake.

Downtown's best breakfast place is **Hector's Restaurant** (112 Lake St., 425/827-4811, www.hectorskirkland.com, 7:30 A.M.–4 P.M. Mon.–Fri., 8 A.M.–4 P.M. Sat.–Sun. and 5 P.M.–10 P.M. Mon.–Thurs., 5 P.M.–11 P.M. Fri.–Sat., 5 P.M.–9 P.M. Sun., $25), with an array of unique home-style breakfasts. Try the Hobo Scramble ($10.50) with potatoes, caramelized onions, mushrooms, and tomatoes. The restaurant also has a tasty lobster bisque at lunch.

Brown Bag Café (12217 NE 116th St., 425/822-9462, www.brownbagcafes.com, 6:30 A.M.–3 P.M. daily, $10) is another favorite breakfast spot, particularly good if you're staying in a nearby Totem Lake motel whose continental breakfast won't satisfy the growling tummy. Servings are substantial, and all the usual favorites are here, along with such specialties as cinnamon roll French toast and shrimp omelettes. Be prepared to wait on the weekend, when crowds throng to eat here.

Contemporary Northwest

Third Floor Fish Café (205 Lake St. S., 425/822-3553, www.fishcafe.com, 5–9 P.M. daily, $29) on the marina is a trendy and spendy place specializing in perfectly prepared seafood and dramatic Lake Washington views.

Another expensive place with lake vistas is **Yarrow Bay Grill and Beach Café** (1270 Carillon Point, 425/889-9052, www.ybgrill.com, 5:30–9:30 P.M. Sun.–Thurs., 5:30–10 P.M. Fri.–Sat., $32), where the food blends new American cookery with Asian influences. The menu changes every two months.

Szmania (148 Lake St., 425/803-3310, www.szmanias.com, 11:30 A.M.–2 P.M. Fri. and 4:45–9:30 P.M. Tues.–Sun., $26) is another Northwest/continental restaurant with a cadre of loyal fans. The grilled mahimahi is especially good.

Asian

Izumi (Totem Lake West Shopping Center, 425/821-1959, 11:30A.M.–1:30 P.M. and 5–9 P.M. daily, $20) has fine Japanese sushi, tempura, teriyaki, and other specialties. Reasonable prices, too.

Another treat is the extremely popular **Shamiana Restaurant** (10724 NE 68th St., 425/827-4902, 11 A.M.–2:30 P.M. daily and 5–9:30 P.M. Sun.–Thurs., 5–10 P.M. Fri.–Sat., $15), a great place for Indian and Pakistani food, including a number of vegetarian specials. Lunch is an especially good deal, and there's live sitar music on Sunday and Monday evenings. **Raga Cuisine of India** (212 Central Way, 425/827-3300, www.ragarestaurant.com, 11:30 A.M.–3 P.M. daily and 5 P.M.–10 P.M. Mon.–Sat., 3–9 P.M. Sun., $12) offers classical Indian food, with tandoori, lamb, and vegetarian specialties, plus a popular luncheon buffet.

The Thin Pan (170 Lake St., 425/827-4000, 11 A.M.–10:30 P.M. daily, $12) is the place to go if you can't afford a visit to Thailand. Choose between spicy curries and tangy noodle dishes including the tasty specialty, Thin Pan Noodles, which features a thick noodle stir-fried with veggies and your choice of meat. The location is right in Kirkland's downtown district.

Italian

Ristorante Paradiso (120 A Park Lane, 425/889-8601, www.ristoranteparadiso.com, 11 A.M.–10:30 P.M. Mon.–Fri., 3–10:30 P.M. Sat.–Sun., $18) offers outstanding nouvelle cuisine with an Italian twist, including fresh seafood, lamb chops, and veal.

Also of note is **Cafe Juanita** (9702 NE 120th Pl., 425/823-1505, www.cafejuanita.com, 5–10 P.M. Tues.–Sat., 5–9 P.M. Sun.–Mon., $28), which offers up highly innovative fresh pastas in a scenic setting along Lake Washington just north of Kirkland. The food is dependably great, and the selection of Italian wines is notable.

INFORMATION

For maps and a limited amount of other information, drop by the **Kirkland Chamber of Commerce** (upstairs in Parkplace Mall, 425/822-7066, www.kirklandchamber.org, 9 A.M.–5 P.M. Mon.–Fri.).

GETTING THERE AND AROUND

By Bus

Metro Transit (425/447-4800 or 800/542-7876, http://transit.metrokc.gov) provides daily bus service to Kirkland from Seattle and other points in King County.

Boat Tours

Argosy Cruises (425/623-1445 or 800/642-7816, www.argosycruises.com, $26 adults, $24 seniors, $14 kids, free kids under 5) offers scenic 1.5-hour boat tours of Lake Washington, departing from Kirkland's Marina Park daily May–September. These take place onboard the MV *Kirkland,* a 110-foot wooden ferry built in 1924, and feature the lake and surrounding sights (including homes of the rich and famous).

Redmond

Redmond began as a boat landing along the Sammamish Slough, the slow-moving stream that links Lake Washington and Lake Sammamish. Foot travel in pioneer days was almost impossible due to the dense forests and extensive marshland, so most inland travel was accomplished via river. Today the city moves more quickly than that, acting as the official epicenter of the state's technology industry. The city is home to a number of tech companies, including Nintendo America and—most famously—software giant Microsoft. The Microsoft campus now encompasses more than 8 million square feet of office space in Redmond and has additional facilities in nearby Eastside cities and in Seattle.

MICROSOFT HQ

One of the largest employers in the region, Microsoft has done a lot to shape the Eastside. Nearly everyone knows of some Microsoft millionaire who made it big when the company went gangbusters in the 1990s. Nowadays it is much harder to make a million as a Microsoftie, but the company still pours a lot of wealth into Eastside communities: The sheer number of German luxury vehicles up and down Highway 520 can attest to that.

MICROSOFT FAST FACTS

- Founded: 1975
- Moved to Puget Sound: 1979
- Redmond Headquarters Established: 1986
- Puget Sound Sites: 120
- Puget Sound Employees: 40,797
- Net Income in 2008: $17.68 billion

SIGHTS

Museums and Churches

The **Microsoft Museum** (4420 148th Ave. NE., 425/703-6214, www.microsoft.com/museum, 9 A.M.–7 P.M. Mon.–Fri., free) houses a few items from the company's quarter century of history, along with the expected high-tech exhibits. You can even play computer games or check your email. It's housed in one of the company's multitude of buildings.

The striking **Ling Shen Ching Tze Temple** (17012 N.E. 40th Ct., 425/882-0916, 9:30 A.M.–6 P.M. Mon.–Sat.) is the largest and most impressive Buddhist temple in Washington. Guests are invited to check out the temple with meditations at 8 P.M. Saturday.

Marymoor Park

Marymoor Park on the West Lake Sammamish Parkway has 533 acres of open space on Seattle banker James Clise's 1905 estate. The Marymoor Museum used to occupy half of the furnished 28-room mansion; it closed in 2002 due to county budget shortfalls. It is now used exclusively for wedding receptions and other gatherings. Marymoor Park is known for its **Velodrome** (425/389-5825), a banked 400-meter bike-racing track that draws competitors from across the United States. Bike races are held Friday evenings April–November. The park also features a one-mile interpretive trail, soccer fields, tennis courts, a model airplane field, dog training grounds, and picnic shelters.

Other Parks

South of Marymoor Park along the west shore of Lake Sammamish, **Idylwood Park** (3650 West Lake Sammamish Pkwy. NE) is a neighborhood secret, a waterfront park treasured by the locals for quiet grassy picnics, a lazy game of catch, or a dip in the lake's cold waters.

Kids love the 68-acre **Farrel-McWhirter Park** (10400 192nd Ave. NE) for its barnyard zoo and horse arena. The park makes

© ERICKA CHICKOWSKI

Marymoor's off-leash dog park is one of the state's finest.

for a great family afternoon, with plenty of equestrian and hiking trails, plus a paved path called Charlotte's Trail that extends around the length of the park and is a perfect spot to test out the little one's first bike, with streamers flying and training wheels skidding along the pavement in all their glory.

ENTERTAINMENT AND EVENTS

Nightlife

For such a small city, Redmond has a surprising number of fun watering holes. Perhaps it is the Microsoft influence—many early-retiring Microsofties tend to get their kicks opening up places they would like to enjoy themselves.

That was the case for **Celtic Bayou** (7281 W. Lake Sammamish Pkwy. NE, 425/869-5933, www.celticbayou.com), opened by an enterprising tech millionaire who thought it would be cool to marry an Irish pub with Cajun cookin'. The bizarre combo works, as the place is thronged most every weekend and on some weeknights, too.

Just down Leary Way, **Matador** (7824 Leary Way NE, 425/883-2855, www.matadorseattle.com) offers a safer Tex-Mex menu to pair with its cocktails. Happy hour is peak time at this bar, which is set within Redmond's historic brick Brown Building. Legend has it the second story here was once the town's house of ill repute back in the 19th century. Nowadays the crowd is a little more law abiding, but the place does have an ornate saloon bar worthy of such historic surroundings.

If wine is your thing, then saunter over to **Jerzy's Wine Bar** (16727 Redmond Way, 425/702-8575, www.jerzyswinebar.com). Located in a cute two-story house on the fringe of downtown Redmond's central core, this place has a cozy atmosphere, if a somewhat limited wine list for a bar that specializes in vino. The interior is swathed in tapestries and accented with lots of wrought-iron furniture, plush barstools, and artistic blown-glass light fixtures.

Live Music

Marymoor Amphitheater (206/205-3661, www.concertsatmarymoor.com), a relative

© ERICKA CHICKOWSKI

You can find Tex-Mex repast and plenty of libations at the trendy Matador.

newcomer to Seattle's cadre of outdoor music venues, has quickly established itself as one of the best. Set next to the grassy area near Clise Mansion, this stage is frequently trod by A-list acts such as Sheryl Crow, the Doobie Brothers, Erykah Badu, G-Love and Special Sauce, and Willie Nelson. During the summer it is also the venue for a series of free movie nights.

Festivals and Events

Head to Marymoor Park on the 4th of July weekend for the very popular **Heritage Festival** (425/296-2964) with arts and crafts, music, ethnic dancing, and food booths.

The **Redmond Bicycle Derby Days** (425/885-4014, www.derbydays.net) in mid-July is a major cycling event with street criterion bike races, a carnival, an antique car show, parades, arts and crafts, and plenty of food. It has been going on since 1939. The year's biggest event is **World of Music Arts and Dance (WOMAD)** (206/633-6282, www.womad.org), which comes to Marymoor Park in late July, attracting thousands of revelers for a weekend of multicultural music. Past performers have included Peter Gabriel (a WOMAD founder), the Neville Brothers, Joan Osborne, Steel Pulse, Taj Mahal, Bonnie Raitt, Youssou N'Dour, and many world music bands. This is one of 11 WOMAD festivals held annually around the globe, and the only one in North America.

The **Redmond Saturday Market** (7730 Leary Way, 425/556-0636, 8 A.M.–2 P.M. Sat. May–Oct.) brings fresh veggies, flowers, crafts, fruit, honey, and more downtown.

The **Evergreen Classic Horse Show** (www.evergreenclassic.com)—one of the top 10 equestrian shows in the nation—takes place at Marymoor Park each September.

SHOPPING

Redmond's shopping centerpiece is **Redmond Town Center** (16495 NE 74th St., 425/867-0808, www.redmondtowncenter.com), an outdoor mall with 110 stores. Most shops are smaller boutiques, with only a couple of large anchors, including Macy's, REI, and a two-story Borders bookstore.

SPORTS AND RECREATION

Sammamish River Trail

The paved 13-mile Sammamish River Trail begins in Marymoor Park and follows the river through Redmond, Woodinville, and on to Kenmore. There it connects with Seattle's Burke-Gilman Trail, which continues all the way to Fremont, a total distance of approximately 27 miles. This immensely popular path provides Mt. Rainier and Lake Washington views and passes the Chateau Ste. Michelle and Columbia wineries, favorite stopping places. The **Puget Power-Redmond Trail** is a three-mile gravel path (great for mountain bikes) that connects the Sammamish River Trail to Farrel-McWhirter Park.

Cycling

As the self-professed bicycle capital of the Northwest, Redmond is home to a number of bike shops, but only one of them rents bikes. **Redmond Cycle** (16205 Redmond Way, 425/885-6363, www.redmondcycle.com) offers an assortment of mountain bikes and hybrids for $30 a day. It also has a fine selection of steeds for sale, along with a repair shop, parts, and tools.

If you don't see the accessories or other bike ephemera your pedaling little heart desires, then check out **Sammamish Valley Cycle** (8451 164th Ave. NE, 425/881-8442, www.sammamishcycle.com) or **Gerk's Alpine Hut** (7875 Leary Way, 425/883-7544, www.gerksalpinehut.com). All three are within an easy five-minute ride of one another.

Golf

Known as one of the Eastside's best public links, **Willows Run** (10402 Willows Rd. NE, 425/883-1200, www.willowsrun.com) is a first-class facility with a little something for every type of golfer. The grounds are home to two challenging 18-hole courses with tall grass and water hazards lurking around every dogleg. There's also a shorter, nine-hole, family pitch-and-putt course, as well as a fun putting course that puts the average miniature golf course to shame.

If tee-times are in short supply at Willows, give **Trilogy Golf Club** (11825 Trilogy Pkwy NE, 425/836-1510, www.trilogygolfclub.com) at Redmond Ridge a try. Situated within an enormous planned suburban development, Trilogy's par-70 course is well known for its meticulously groomed greens and fairways.

Hot-Air Ballooning

The Balloon Depot (16138 N.E. 87th St., 425/881-9699 or 877/881-9699, www.balloondepot.com) lifts off with hot-air balloon rides most mornings and evenings.

ACCOMMODATIONS

Cottage Creek Inn B&B (425/881-5606, www.cottagecreekinn.com, $89–125 s or d) is a Tudor-style manor home in a beautiful country setting with an attractive garden and hot tub. The four guest rooms include private baths, and full breakfasts are served each morning.

Redmond Inn (15304 N.E. 21st St., 425/883-4900 or 800/634-8080, www.redmondinn.com, $103–129 s or d) features an outdoor pool and hot tub. Rates include a continental breakfast.

Surrounded by the stores and restaurants of Redmond Town Center, **Redmond Marriott** (7401 164th Ave. NE, 425/498-4000, $239 d) is a favorite among business travelers working with Microsoft, which means weekenders can usually sneak in with some pretty amazing rates (as low as $100 a night). The business-class amenities can be a nice change of pace for those used to humbler digs. Rooms come with huge bathrooms, oversized flat-screen TVs, and fluffy quilted-top beds. There's a fee for Internet, but for around $10 you'll get unlimited local long distance and local calls, plus wired or wireless connectivity. Downstairs, next to the fireplace lobby, saunter in for a glass of wine and appetizer at the wine bar. There's also a fitness center and business center on premises.

FOOD

Cafés and Delis

Redmond doesn't have a very good coffeehouse scene, with one big exception. **Victor's Coffee**

(7993 Gilman St., 425/881-6451, www.victorscelticcoffee.com, 5:30 A.M.–7 P.M. Mon.–Fri., 7 A.M.–7 P.M. Sat., 8 A.M.–6 P.M. Sun.) is one of the best coffee joints on the Eastside. The clanking and hissing of espresso making reverberates throughout the cozy confines, and stacks of roasted coffee wait to be ground or bagged for sale. This is the type of place that won't chase you off right after your cup has run dry, even going so far as to offer a stash of board games and paperbacks for lingering patrons.

Popular for Sunday brunch is **Village Square Café** (16150 NE 85th, 425/885-7287, 6 A.M.–3 P.M. Mon.–Sat., 7 A.M.–3 P.M. Sun., $11). **Mikie's Brooklyn Bagel Deli** (16640 Redmond Way, 425/881-3344, 6:30A.M.–4 P.M. Mon.–Fri., 7:30 A.M.–3:30 P.M. Sat., closed Sun., $6) has fresh-baked breads and deli meats from New York; locals call the bagels here the most authentic on the Eastside.

Asian

Microsoft and other tech companies have brought an influx of Indian and Pakistani workers into Redmond on temporary work visas. That's good news for foodies hankering for a good curry or tandoori chicken, as numerous Indian places have cropped up in recent years to satisfy demand. Perhaps the best Indian place on the Eastside, if not the entire Seattle area, is **Kanishka** (16101 Redmond Way, 425/869-9182, www.kanishkaofredmond.com, 11 A.M.–3 P.M. Mon.–Fri., 11:30 A.M.–3 P.M. Sat.–Sun. and 5–10 P.M. daily, $12) in downtown Redmond. Flavors are evocative and complex, ingredients are fresh, and the steady procession of Indians through the door attest to the fact that the genuine article is served here.

Kikuya (8105 161st Ave. NE, 425/881-8771, 11:30 A.M.–2 P.M. and 5–9 P.M. daily, $16) is a wonderful small Japanese restaurant with friendly service and high-quality food. But don't come here on a weekend evening unless you're ready to wait. No need to dress up to sup on Redmond's best teriyaki. **Yummy Teriyaki** (17218 Redmond Way, 425/861-1010, 10:30 A.M.–9 P.M. daily, $8) is a nice and comfy jeans-and-t-shirt kind of place where you order up front and take a plastic number to your table. Dishes are huge, so come with an appetite or a partner to share.

Italian

Don't let the strip mall location at **Tropea Ristorante Italiano** (8042 161st Ave. NE, 425/867-1082, www.ristorantetropea.com, 11 A.M.–2 P.M. Mon.–Fri. and 4:30–9:30 P.M. Sun.–Thurs., 4:30–10 P.M. Fri.–Sat., $18) fool you. Inside, just past the cultivated bushes grown by the door as a screen, there is a charming grotto serving up Southwestern Italian fare. The seafood pastas are especially scrumptious. Portions are huge, so be sure to take some of your dinner home to save room for dessert. The homemade fruit sorbets are to die for and beautifully presented in the flavor's corresponding fruit rind.

INFORMATION

The **Greater Redmond Chamber of Commerce** (16210 N.E. 80th St., 425/885-4014, www.redmondchamber.org, 9 A.M.–5 P.M. Mon.–Fri.) has local information.

GETTING THERE AND AROUND

Metro Transit (800/542-7876, http://transit.metrokc.gov) has daily bus service around Redmond, on to Seattle and Bellevue, and throughout King County.

Issaquah

Settled between the foot of an impressive set of Cascade foothills and the southern tip of Lake Sammamish, Issaquah (ISS-a-kwa) offers an escape to country-fresh air in a fast-growing town loaded with history. This land has been attractive for a long time—prior to Anglo settlement in the 1860s, it was home to many Native Americans who fished the lake and picked berries on nearby hillsides. These first inhabitants called this place "Squak," after the sound made by the thousands of ducks and cranes that passed through each spring and fall. To white settlers, the Native American word sounded something like "Issaquah."

Today, some of the town's past is slowly slipping away in favor of housing developments, office parks, and shopping centers built for all of the newcomers drawn to the area's centuries-old charm. But the impressive Issaquah Alps remain unblemished, preserved in their forested state for all to enjoy. These very old, worn-down mountains are at a lower elevation that keeps them hikeably snow-free virtually year-round. The town itself is a pleasant place to enjoy the blend of old and new. Historic buildings are next to shiny new office complexes. There's even traces of Issaquah's farming legacy at the Darigold creamery in town, which produces all the company's yogurt sold in the Northwest.

HISTORICAL TOUR

Several buildings from Issaquah's turn-of-the-20th-century coal mining days are still in use, and remains from the mine are evident. Go down Newport Way to Park Boulevard and turn right onto Wildwood for a look at the original miners' homes, preserved and still occupied. At the end of the block, a depression in the ground near a grove marks the entrance to the mine's first shaft; to the right is the concrete bulkhead used to anchor the mine's hauling machinery.

Downtown, a number of historically significant buildings face Front Street. **Odd Fellows Hall** is the oldest, built in 1888. The second-oldest commercial building is the **Grand Central Hotel,** dating from 1903; today it houses offices and apartments. Adjacent to the railroad tracks on Sunset Way, the lovingly restored **Railroad Depot** was built in 1889 (the year Washington became a state), out of Washington Territory timber – note the "W.T." symbol. Issaquah's downtown streets have been planted with all sorts of fruit trees and berry bushes; get here in late summer to pick apples, cherries, pears, plums, or blueberries as you stroll along.

SIGHTS

Museums

The **Gilman Town Hall Museum** (165 S.E. Andrews, 425/392-3500, www.issaquahhistory.org, 11 A.M.–3 P.M. Thurs. and Sat., free) building, built in the 1890s, served as the original town hall, back when Issaquah was known as Gilman. Railroad tools, children's toys, a pioneer kitchen and grocery store, artifacts, and many historical photographs are on display inside. Out back is the old two-cell town jail.

Issaquah Train Depot Museum (Front and Sunset Streets, 425/392-2322, 11 A.M.–3 P.M. Sat., $2) in the restored 1889 train depot also has historical photos and artifacts. Be sure to check out the vintage caboose and other railcars on display outside the station.

Boehms Candies

For chocolate, visit the Swiss-style building that houses Boehm's Candies (255 N.E. Gilman Blvd., 425/392-6652, www.boehms.com, 9 A.M.–6 P.M. Mon.–Sat. and 10 A.M.–6 P.M. Sun.). Free candy factory tours are offered July to mid-September; call ahead for reservations. If you can't get on a tour, just walk outside and peek in the side windows.

Adjacent to the chocolate factory is a shady garden with a replica of a Swiss chapel.

Cougar Mountain Zoo

Issaquah's zoo (19525 S.E. 54th St., 425/391-5508, www.cougarmountainzoo.org, 10 A.M.–5 P.M. Fri.–Sun. Mar.–Oct., $8 adults, $6.50 seniors, $5.50 ages 4–15, $4 ages 2–3) is one of the more unusual in Washington, emphasizing threatened or endangered animals from around the globe, including the Formosa Sika elk and hyacinthine macaw. The real attraction, however, is the cougars. Visitors to the zoo are treated to highly informative tours by the docents and staff.

Issaquah State Salmon Hatchery

The Issaquah State Salmon Hatchery (125 W. Sunset Way, 425/392-3180, www.issaquahfish.org) raises five million chinook and one million coho salmon annually for release into Issaquah Creek. In existence since 1936, the hatchery is a good place to learn about the life cycle of salmon and how they are raised. The grounds are open dawn–dusk daily, with tours in late summer.

Wineries

Established in 1987, **Hedges Cellars** (195 N.E. Gilman Blvd., 425/391-6056 or 800/859-9463, www.hedgescellars.com, 11 A.M.–5 P.M. Mon.–Sat.) originally made wines exclusively for the Swedish market. Today it has grown to become Washington's fifth-largest winery, producing three wines from its Yakima Valley winery.

ENTERTAINMENT AND EVENTS

The Arts

The semiprofessional **Village Theatre** (120 Front St. N, 425/392-2202, www.villagetheatre.org) puts on first-rate productions in its modern 488-seat theater (complete with a soundproof room for screaming babies). Theatrical productions are generally on the light side, with a heavy dose of musical favorites.

NIKE MISSILE BASES

In the early days of the Cold War, the heightened fear that the Soviets would "just do it" and bomb the daylights out of America's West Coast lead to a novel program. The U.S. Army stationed a series of bases across the country equipped with so-called Nike missiles, which were developed to intercept the heavy Soviet bombers that, in those pre-ICBM days, were the only means of carrying out nuclear holocaust. By the mid-1960s, the proliferation of high-altitude ballistic missiles made these bases seem quaint at best. Most were decommissioned and given to civilian authorities to handle as they liked. Today, many of these interesting historical relics are on display as parks throughout the state of Washington.

Site S-20 is at the end of a short hike to the peak of Issaquah's Cougar Mountain. While there are no interpretive displays, it's fun to tromp around atop the former silos or wait out the rain in the guard shack. Nearby Redmond is home to sites S-13 and S-14, which are now, respectively, school buildings and a nice grassy park, aptly named Nike Park. Even on swanky Vashon Island, you can visit site S-61, the outbuildings of which now house a variety of local businesses and the field of which has been transformed into a horse park.

Events

Issaquah's **Down Home 4th of July Parade** is fun for everyone, with all the usual events. Every fall, salmon return to their birthplace at the state salmon hatchery, and Issaquah doesn't miss the opportunity for a celebration. The two-day **Issaquah Salmon Days** (206/270-2532, www.salmondays.org) comes around the first weekend in October with a parade, kids' fair, 350 arts and crafts booths, live music, a pancake feed, fun run, and hatchery tours. More than 200,000 people crowd downtown Issaquah for the festival. The **Issaquah**

Reindeer Festival (425/391-5508, www.cougarmountainzoo.org) takes place at Cougar Mountain Zoo in December, with thousands of twinkling lights, plus Santa and his herd of reindeer.

SHOPPING

Gilman Village

Issaquah's Gilman Village (317 N.W. Gilman Blvd., 425/392-6802, www.gilmanvillage.com) is a collection of 40 or so century-old homes, all moved and restored to form a quaint cluster of boutiques selling clothing, crafts, gifts, kitchenware, jewelry, and food. If you're into lacy froufrou, you'll love these boardwalk-linked places. Several shops offer something more substantial, including a number of restaurants. Be sure to drop by **Evolution** (425/392-6963), an artists' cooperative that sells high quality works, including many pieces made from recycled products. A **Made in Washington** shop (425/392-4819, www.madeinwashington.com) is filled with locally made items.

SPORTS AND RECREATION

The Issaquah Alps

As the "Trailhead City," Issaquah takes pride in a chain of nearby mountains—the Issaquah Alps—a range older than the Cascades that includes Tiger, Cougar, and Squak Mountains. Just two exits east of Renton on I-90, these venerable hills are within an easy half-hour drive of Seattle and Tacoma. The Tiger Mountain area is Washington's most popular hiking area, attracting hundreds of hikers and mountain bikers on sunny summer days. Also here are many shallow talus caves that are fun to explore.

The **Issaquah Alps Trails Club** (425/328-0480, www.issaquahalps.org) organizes hikes every Saturday and Sunday, plus twice during the week, all year, to points of interest along 200 miles of trails in these mountains. No membership or previous registration is necessary. If you want to step out on your own, stop by the city-run **Issaquah Trails Center** (110 S.E. Bush St.) for maps and hiking information.

Tiger Mountain State Forest covers 13,500 acres of forested lands and is capped by 3,004-foot **East Tiger Mountain,** the highest peak in the range. The hike up East Side Road to the summit provides spectacular views of the surrounding country. To reach the trailhead, take I-90 exit 25; go right onto Highway 18 and drive three miles to a dirt road on the right; proceed to the power line and park. Start your seven-mile hike on the uphill road under the power line.

Cougar Mountain Regional Wildland Park (www.metrokc.gov/parks) encompasses second-growth forests surrounding this 1,595-foot peak, with well-marked trails climbing past an old mining camp and waterfalls.

Squak Mountain State Park covers 613 acres of forested land just south of Issaquah

CARRYING COALS TO NEWCASTLE

When people think of American coal mining, they usually imagine the hill country of Kentucky, Pennsylvania, and West Virginia. Even many lifetime Seattleites don't realize that the Eastside cities of Issaquah and Newcastle once had their own coal boom. Between the mid-19th century, with the arrival of the railroad, and the mid-20th century, when the cost of mining increased and the value of coal decreased, the mountains east of the Puget Sound produced tens of thousands of tons of coal. Underground mines operated throughout the region, with the richest veins located on Squak and Cougar Mountains, now part of what is commonly called the Issaquah Alps.

Fans of enormous holes and rusting metal can see plenty of both along the 36-mile trail system that ribbons its way though Cougar Mountain. Several interpretive markers provide useful background, and the remaining machinery and building foundations cause one to truly marvel at the effort that went into extracting this valuable resource from such tricky terrain.

and contains a maze of poorly maintained trails. Access is a bit tricky; ask locally for directions or learn more at www.parks.wa.gov. No camping is available at Squak Mountain.

Horseback Riding

Even if you've had no prior experience, riding a horse along wooded trails can be a relaxing, enjoyable way to view the scenery. **Tiger Mountain Stables** (132nd Ave., 425/392-5090) offers guided three-hour trips in Tiger Mountain State Forest. **High Country Outfitters** (23836 S.E. 24th, 425/392-0111, www.highcountry-outfitters.com) leads trail rides and overnight trips into the Cascades.

Water Sports

Just over 1.5 miles northwest of Issaquah, **Lake Sammamish State Park** (425/455-7010, www.parks.wa.gov, no camping) is one of the more popular Puget Sound area parks. Facilities include a big sandy beach for sunbathing and swimming, a swimming float, bathhouses, boat ramps, picnic tables, hiking trails, and a concession stand selling fast food. The area is popular with boaters and water-skiers; get here on a sunny weekend morning and you'll find long traffic jams at the boat launch. **Klub Kayak** (425/453-5363 or 888/765-2925, www.klubkayak.com) offers sea kayak tours, lessons, and summertime rentals on Lake Sammamish.

Owners of smaller motorboats, canoes, and rafts may prefer **Pine Lake** (off 228th Ave. SE), a nearby county park with a five-mph speed limit on its lake and lots of fish willing to rise for bait.

Campgrounds

Although there are no public campgrounds near Issaquah, you can camp in comfort at the 120-acre **Issaquah Highlands Camping Club** (10610 Renton-Issaquah Rd. SE, 425/392-2351). Other private campgrounds include **Issaquah Village RV Park** (50 1st Ave. NE, 425/392-9233 or 800/258-9233) and **Blue Sky RV Park** (9002 302nd Ave. SE, 425/222-7910).

RAINDROPS ARE FALLIN' ON MY SKIN

Tiger Mountain is home to a unique local park, **Fraternity Snoqualmie Nudist Park** (425/392-NUDE), a 40-acre family place to let it all hang out, so to speak. This is the oldest (in existence since 1931) and largest nudist park in the Northwest. It sponsors a clothing-optional Bare Buns Fun Run in early July, followed in mid-August by a summer music festival called **Nudestock.** Thousands of nudists show up. Fun for the whole naked family!

ACCOMMODATIONS

Under $100

Two motels are available on the east side of Issaquah. Standard, inexpensive motel rooms can be found at **Motel 6** (1885 15th Pl. NW at I-90 exit 15, 425/392-8405 or 800/466-8356, www.motel6.com, $60 s or $66 d) including an outdoor pool. You'll find more refined accommodations at **Issaquah Holiday Inn** (1801 12th Ave. NW, 425/392-6421 or 800/465-4329, www.hi.com, $99–107 s or d). Amenities include a salmon-shaped outdoor pool, sauna, and hot tub.

$100-200

The Issaquah area has two charming lakefront bed-and-breakfasts. Located near the quiet waters of Pine Lake, **Water's Edge Guesthouse** (2736 222nd Ave. SE, 425/392-7727, www.watersedgeonpinelake.com, $130–160 s or d) has a private suite facing the lake. Visitors can use the canoe and rowboat, and kids are welcome. A continental breakfast is served, and there is a two-night minimum stay.

Lakehouse Bed & Breakfast (415 E. Lake Sammamish Pkwy., 425/868-7536, www.bbonline.com/wa/lakehouse, $120–200 d, additional $10 fee for a one-night stay) is also lakeside, only on the much larger Lake Sammamish. Innkeepers emphasize organic and in-season ingredients in their breakfast dishes, and guests are encouraged to take advantage of the property's row boat to work it all off after indulging. There are three rooms here, the best of which features French doors opening up directly out to the lake.

FOOD

Issaquah has a surprising diversity of restaurants serving everything from fast food to gourmet fare. Several of the best are in Gilman Village (317 NW Gilman Blvd.), where the historic buildings add to the ambience. Notable Gilman Village eateries include **Tantalus Restaurant** (425/391-6090, 11:15 A.M.–9 P.M. daily, $14), featuring Greek specialties, and **Ristorante Nicolino Italiano** (425/391-8077, 11:30 A.M.–2 P.M. Mon.–Fri., noon–2 P.M. Sat.–Sun. and 5–9 P.M. Sun.–Thurs., 5–10 P.M. Fri.–Sat., $16), with deliciously authentic southern Italian dinners. For lunch, join the crowds at **The Sweet Addition** (425/392-5661, 9 A.M.–4 P.M. Mon.–Fri., 8 A.M.–4 P.M. Sat., 9 A.M.–4 P.M. Sun., $9), where the salads and sandwiches, shrimp linguine, and grilled trout are always well prepared, and the decadent cakes, truffles, and pies are a real temptation. Also good for breakfast and lunch is **Snow Goose Café** (425/391-4671, 10 A.M.–5 P.M. Mon.–Wed., 10 A.M.–8 P.M. Thurs.–Fri., closed Sat.–Sun.).

Fine restaurants can also be found elsewhere in Issaquah. Housed in the Village Theatre building, **Fins Bistro Seafood Restaurant** (303 Front St. N., 425/392-0109, 11 A.M.–9 P.M. Tues.–Fri., 9 A.M.–10 P.M. Sat.–Sun, closed Mon., $19) is an elegant café with fresh-from-the-sea specials.

The Chinese food is tasty at **Mandarin Garden** (40 E. Sunset Way, 425/392-9476, 11 A.M.–9:30 P.M. Sun.–Thurs., 11 A.M.–10 P.M. Fri.–Sat., $9).

Issaquah Brewhouse (35 W. Sunset Way, 425/557-1911, 11:30 A.M.–10:30 P.M. daily, $12) has 10 or so brewed-on-the-premises beers on tap, and a surprisingly good pub menu of salads, burgers, sandwiches, Cajun gumbo, and Thai grilled chicken.

XXX Drive-In (98 NE Holly St., 425/392-1266, 11 A.M.–9 P.M. daily, $6) is a real old-time favorite, with burgers, shakes, and the best root beer around. On summer weekends, the parking lot overflows with dozens of vintage cars.

Markets

The **Issaquah Public Market** (425/837-3321, 9 A.M.–2 P.M. Sat. mid-Apr.–Oct.), located in the Pickering Barn off 10th Avenue, features all sorts of handicrafts in addition to fresh produce.

Get quality cuts of meat and fresh smoked salmon at **Fischer's Meats and Seafoods** (85 Front St. N, 425/392-3131), in existence since 1910.

INFORMATION

For maps and information, contact the **Issaquah Visitor Information Center** (155 N.W. Gilman Blvd., 425/392-7024, www.issaquah.org, 9 A.M.–5 P.M. daily). It's housed in the beautiful historic Alexander house surrounded by rose bushes (but across the busy highway from the now-standard strip malls).

The impressively modern **Issaquah Library** (Front St. and Sunset Way, 425/392-5430, www.kcls.org) is located in the heart of downtown.

GETTING THERE AND AROUND

You can get to and from Seattle, Bellevue, and other points in King County via **Metro Transit** (425/447-4800 or 800/542-7876, http://transit.metrokc.gov).

Woodinville and Bothell

Woodinville is a rapidly growing suburban town that still maintains its pastoral atmosphere with plenty of stables and bridle trails still maintained around town. This is a popular cycling destination, with easy access from Seattle via the Burke-Gilman and Sammamish River Trails that pass right by several wineries and a big brewery.

Neighboring Bothell was founded in 1884 by David Bothell and his family. Apparently without competition, they logged the area, built a hotel, platted the town, and sold lots to pioneers who wanted to get away from the bustle of the city. Now it is primarily a Seattle bedroom community and is home to a large Microsoft campus and a burgeoning biotech corridor along I-405.

SIGHTS

Bothell Landing

The featured attraction in Bothell is **Bothell Landing** (18120 N.E. Bothell Way), where a park, small shopping complex, and the **Bothell Historical Museum** (425/486-1889, 1–4 P.M. Sun. Mar.–mid-Dec.) mark the original steamboat berth along the Sammamish Slough. The museum is housed in the 1893 William Hannan cabin. Cross the footbridge behind the museum to pick up the **Sammamish River Trail** and follow it east to Marymoor Park in Redmond, or head west on the **Burke-Gilman Trail** to Seattle.

Chateau Ste. Michelle Winery

Woodinville is home to the state's largest winery, Chateau Ste. Michelle (14111 N.E. 145th St., 425/415-3300, www.ste-michelle.com). Established in 1934 as the National Wine Company—shortly after the end of Prohibition—and renamed Ste. Michelle Vintners in 1965, it has come to represent the Washington wine industry across the country. Though the wine grapes are grown (and most of the wine is produced) in eastern Washington, this winery is among the nicest to visit in Washington.

The original 1912 residence—once owned by Seattle lumber baron Fred Stimson—is surrounded by 87 acres of manicured grounds that include experimental vineyards, an arboretum, and trout ponds. The amphitheater is home to the **Summer Festival on the Green** a full summer of music and arts events with picnics on the lawn; get tickets from Ticketmaster (206/628-0888, www.ticketmaster.com). The crowds gather outside the impressive French-chateau winery building, built in 1976.

Informative cellar tours and free tastings are offered every half-hour 10 A.M.–4:30 P.M. daily, except Christmas and New Year's Day. Avoid the summer mob scene by visiting on Monday or Tuesday; weekends can get pretty hectic. Those who take the tours can taste four different wines, but if you don't take a tour you can sample a wider variety. The gift shop sells wines, books, cheese, and more.

Columbia Winery

A modern Victorian-style building directly across the road from Chateau Ste. Michelle houses the Columbia Winery (425/488-2776 or 800/488-2347, www.columbiawinery.com, 10 A.M.–7 P.M. daily, closed holidays). Founded in 1962 by a group of University of Washington professors, Columbia produces award-winning chardonnay, semillon, cabernet sauvignon, and merlot, among others.

Tours are given two or more times each day. Sample five regular wines free, or five reserve wines for $5 (a bargain). The best time to visit is during the grape crush in September and October.

Other Winery Tours

Two small wineries are also located in Woodinville. **Silver Lake Winery** (17721 132nd Ave. NE, 425/486-1900 or 800/318-9463, www.washingtonwine.com, noon–5 P.M. Mon.–Fri.) is the only customer-owned winery in Washington. **Facelli Winery** (16120 Woodinville-Redmond Rd., 425/488-1020, www.facelliwinery.com, noon–4 P.M. Sat.–Sun.) is a small family operation with a tasting room (in a business park).

Washington Wine Tours (206/794-0562 or 877/689-8687, www.washingtonwinetours.com) leads half-day tours from Seattle that include time at Chateau Ste. Michelle, Columbia Winery, and Silver Lake Winery, plus a lunch and wine-tasting for $53.

Redhook Ale Brewery

Right next door to the Columbia Winery is the Redhook Ale Brewery (14300 NE 145th St., 425/483-3232, www.redhook.com). This large facility is one of three owned by Redhook (the others are in Portsmouth, New Hampshire, and the Fremont district of Seattle). Forty-minute tours are offered at 1, 3, and 4 P.M. Monday–Friday and every hour noon–5 P.M. Saturday and Sunday. You can taste a half dozen brews for $1, and you get to keep the shot glass. The immensely popular pub here, **Forecasters Public House** (11 A.M.–10 P.M. Mon.–Thurs., 11 A.M.–midnight Fri.–Sat., 11 A.M.–8 P.M. Sun., open one hour later on Sundays btwn. Memorial Day and Labor Day) has all Redhook's beers on tap, a tasty menu with the best burgers around, plus live blues and pop tunes on Friday and Saturday nights. The patio is popular with weekend cyclists.

EVENTS

In Woodinville, local events include the bizarre **All Fool's Day Parade and Basset Bash** in late March, and the very popular **Woodinville Wine Festival** in September. Chateau Ste. Michelle hosts famous **Summer Concerts on the Green;** tickets are available from Ticketmaster (206/628-0888, www.ticketmaster.com). In addition, free **Summer Concerts** take place at noon on Thursday in DeYoung Park (downtown), with evening concerts on Sundays at City Hall Plaza (425/398-9327).

The **Woodinville Farmers Market** comes to old city hall (13209 N.E. 175th, 425/485-1042, 9 A.M.–4 P.M. Sat.) April–mid-October.

Bothell's **4th of July** celebration is a fun event, with two parades through town. Also popular is the free **Music in the Park** series on Friday evenings in July and August.

SPORTS AND RECREATION

For a bit of fresh Woodinville air try the **Tolt Pipeline Trail,** an 11-mile hiking and horse trail that passes through town and extends to Snoqualmie Valley near Duvall. Find the trailhead just around the corner from Chateau Ste. Michelle. The paved **Sammamish River Trail** passes through on the other side of Ste. Michelle on its way north and west to Bothell and Seattle, or south to Redmond.

Hot-air ballooning is a popular attraction in Woodinville; contact **Over the Rainbow Balloon Flights** (425/861-8611, www.letsgoballooning.com) for details.

Camping can be found at **Lake Pleasant RV Park** (24025 Bothell-Everett Hwy., 425/483-9436, year-round), offering lakeside RV pads and campsites. You can also park an RV at **Twin Cedars RV Park** (17826 Hwy. 99, 425/742-5540 or 800/878-9304).

ACCOMMODATIONS

Willows Lodge (425/424-3900 or 877/424-3930, www.willowslodge.com) is a trendy hotel directly across the parking lot from the Herbfarm and Barking Frog restaurants, and just a short walk from the Chateau Ste. Michelle and Columbia wineries. The 88 guest rooms ($220–290) and suites ($350–750) are nicely appointed and include all the amenities well-heeled business travelers want, including fine linens, private patios or decks, fridges, robes, and high-speed Internet lines. A spa here is open to the public as well, offering massage, facials, and much more.

Also of note is **SpringHill Suites by Marriott** (3850 Monte Villa Pkwy., 425/398-9700 or 888/287-9400, www.springhillsuites.com, $99–109 s or d), with an indoor pool, hot tub, fitness room, and suites containing microwaves and fridges.

FOOD

Woodinville

Just up the road from Chateau Ste. Michelle

Winery, Redhook Brewery, and Columbia Winery is the **Herbfarm** (206/784-2222, www.theherbfarm.com, by reservation), one of the Northwest's most famous restaurants. The setting is Victorian (to excess), and meals are an elaborate nine-course affair that includes paired wines. This isn't a place for those with threadbare wallets; prix fixe menus are a shocking $189–195 per person. The Herbfarm books up fast, months ahead of time. Fortunately, you can get on the waiting list, as there are often cancellations. Many herbs used at the restaurant are grown at a one-acre farm just down the road.

A few steps from Herbfarm is **Barking Frog** (part of the luxurious Willows Lodge, 425/424-2999, 6 A.M.–2:30 P.M. and 5–10 P.M. daily, $35), another high-end gourmet restaurant with such specialties as roasted venison and grilled beef tenderloin. The wine selection is impressive and the dining room cozy at this artistic bistro.

Not every Woodinville eatery is so spendy. **Forecasters Public House** at Redhook Ale Brewery appeals to more plebeian tastes, as does **Texas Smoke House Bar-B-Q** (14455 Woodinville-Redmond Rd., 425/486-1957, 11 A.M.–9 P.M. Mon.–Sat., noon–9 P.M. Sun., $15), a great spot for those who love ribs, slow-roasted chicken, or just the enormous spuds. It's inexpensive and tasty.

Chan's Place (14203 NE Woodinville Duvall Rd., 425/483-2223, 11:15 A.M.–9:15 P.M. Sun.–Thurs., 11:15 A.M.–10:15 P.M. Fri.–Sat., $12), is a little Chinese restaurant with surprisingly good food. **Italianissimo** (17650 140th Ave. NE, 425/485-6888, www.italianissimoristorante.com, 11 A.M.–9:30 P.M. Mon.–Thurs., 11 A.M.–10 Fri., 5–10 P.M. Sat., 5–9:30 Sun., $20) is a delightful place where the pasta is homemade and veal is the house specialty. Vegetarians love the eggplant parmigiana.

Out in Maltby (approximately five miles northeast of Woodinville on Highway 522) is **Maltby Café** (425/483-3123, 7 A.M.–3 P.M. daily, $10), where the outstanding breakfasts and lunches are well worth the drive.

Bothell

The **Main St. Alehouse & Eatery** (10111 Main St., 425/485-2972, 11 A.M.–10 P.M. Mon.–Thurs. and Sat., 11 A.M.–11 P.M. Fri., closed Sun., $13) is a good place to enjoy local microbrews (14 on tap) and tasty fare in a family-friendly setting. Thursday night usually features ribs.

Also of note are **Stella Mia** (23718 Bothell-Everett Hwy., 425/488-1486, 11:30 A.M.–2 P.M. daily and 5–9 P.M. Sun.–Thurs., 5–10 P.M. Fri.–Sat., $15) for Italian meals, **Sushi Zen** (13206 Bothell-Everett Hwy., Mill Creek, 425/357-1611, 11:30 A.M.–2 P.M. Mon.–Sat. and 5–10 P.M. Mon.–Sat., 5–9 P.M. Sun., $22) for very good sushi, and **Acapulco Fresh Mexican Grill** (6016 NE Bothell Way, Kenmore, 425/482-0334, 11 A.M.–9 P.M. Mon.–Sat., 11 A.M.–8:30 P.M. Sun., $9) for ultra-fresh South-of-the-border favorites.

Get produce at the **Country Village Farmers Market** (238th and Bothell-Everett Hwy., 425/483-0660, 10 A.M.–3 P.M. Fri.).

INFORMATION

Get local information from the **Woodinville Chamber of Commerce** inside the old city hall (13205 N.E. 175th St., 425/481-8300, www.woodinvillechamber.org, 9 A.M.–5 P.M. Mon.–Fri.) or at Bothell's **Northshore Chamber of Commerce** (18414 103rd Ave. NE, 425/486-1245, www.northshorecc.org, 8 A.M.–5 P.M. Mon.–Fri.).

GETTING THERE AND AROUND

Metro Transit (800/542-7876, http://transit.metrokc.gov) has daily bus service between Seattle and the neighborhoods of Woodinville and Bothell. Once in Bothell you can travel to Lynnwood, Edmonds, or Everett on **Community Transit** (800/562-1375, www.commtrans.org).

Shuttle Express (800/487-7433, www.shuttleexpress.com) provides frequent direct service from Bothell to Sea-Tac Airport.

Kenmore Air (206/486-1257 or 800/543-9595, www.kenmoreair.com) has daily floatplane flights from the nearby town of Kenmore on the north end of Lake Washington to Victoria, B.C., and the San Juan Islands.

NORTH PUGET SOUND

Outdoor enthusiasts can find a whole lot to do once they break the Seattle northern city limits. The Puget Sound region in this direction is awash in marine parks, dramatic beaches, scenic drives, colorful flower fields, and quiet marina towns. Pedal the rolling hills of historic Ebey's Landing on Whidbey Island or cast a fly on one of Deception Pass State Parks' lakes. Slip on some flippers and a scuba tank and immerse yourself in the Edmonds Water Park or pedal along the trails at Japanese Gulch in Mukilteo. Whatever your predilections, there's plenty to get the ol' ticker pounding while enjoying the scenery along the way.

And if it's something a little calmer that really sets your heart aflutter, no worries: Try window shopping antique towns like La Conner or Snohomish. Lay a picnic blanket under the Peace Arch at the Canadian border. Or tour the giant jumbo-jet production line in Everett. Any way you shake it, the northern reaches of the Sound have got enough afternoon excursions to keep you busy for a long time.

© ERICKA CHICKOWSKI

HIGHLIGHTS

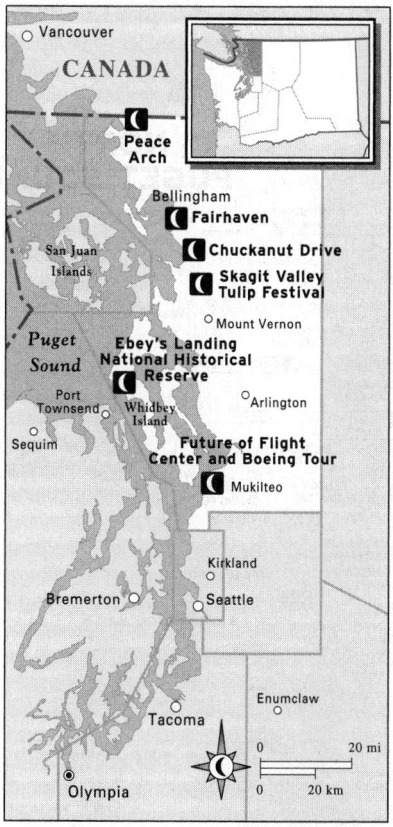

Ebey's Landing National Historical Reserve: Tour the undulating agrarian hillsides, the pebbly beaches, and the blast-from-the-past seaport of Coupeville at this historic treasure (page 135).

Future of Flight Center and Boeing Tour: Come see the engineers and assembly line crew at work on the next generation of jumbo jets on this landmark tour (page 144).

Skagit Valley Tulip Festival: During the month of April, the valley erupts into a rainbow quilt of color (page 156).

Chuckanut Drive: The nicest back-road tour in all of the Puget Sound, this one tracks along marshland, bluff sides, and wooded parkland (page 164).

Fairhaven: This is Bellingham's storied historic district, home to boutique shopping and scads of cute restaurants (page 166).

Peace Arch: The giant white arch marks the entrance to Canada and symbolizes the friendly relations of American and Canadian people (page 179).

LOOK FOR TO FIND RECOMMENDED SIGHTS, ACTIVITIES, DINING, AND LODGING.

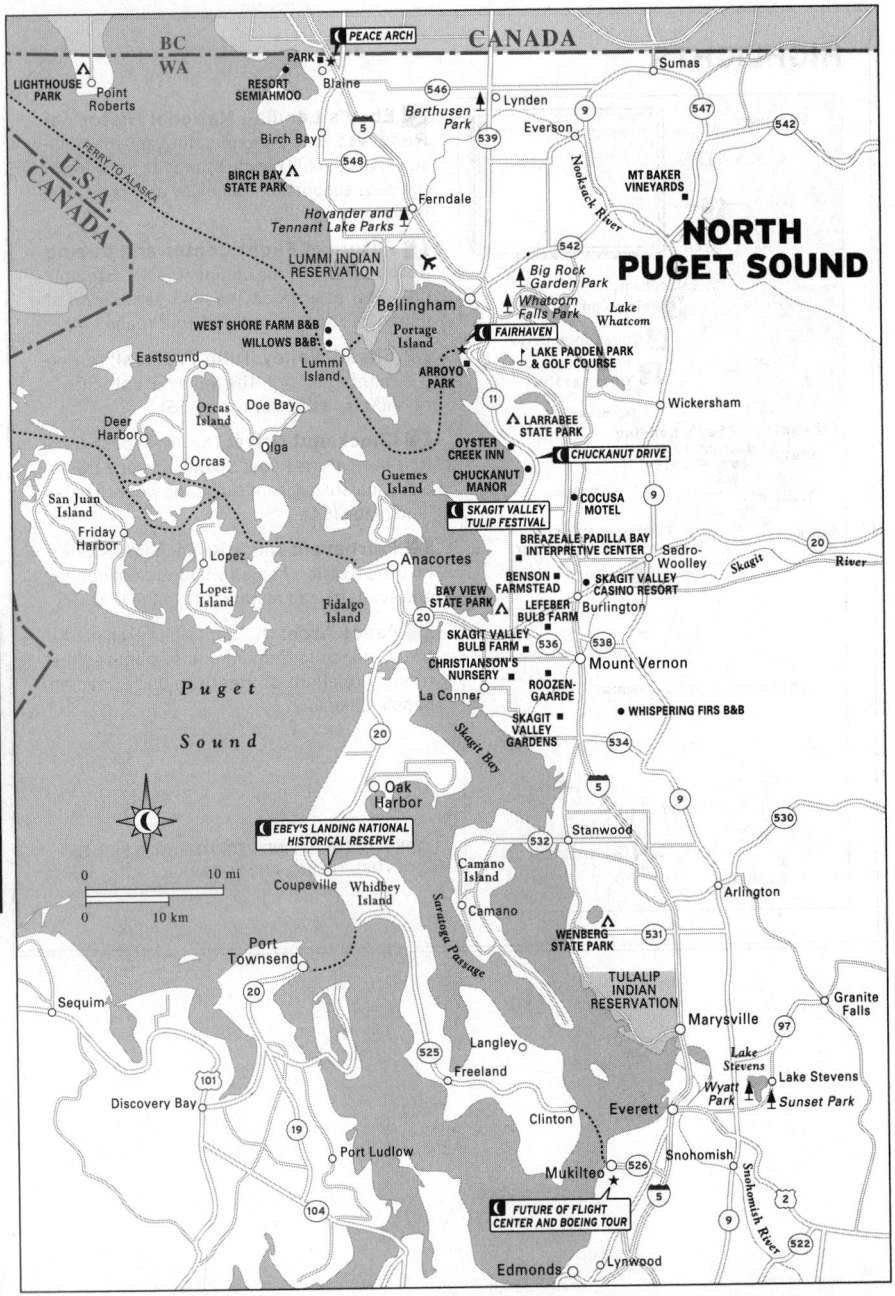
NORTH PUGET SOUND
CANADA
BC
WA
PEACE ARCH
PARK
LIGHTHOUSE PARK
Point Roberts
RESORT SEMIAHMOO
Blaine
Sumas
Lynden
Berthusen Park
Everson
Birch Bay
BIRCH BAY STATE PARK
FERRY TO ALASKA
U.S.A.
CANADA
Ferndale
Hovander and Tennant Lake Parks
Nooksack River
MT BAKER VINEYARDS
LUMMI INDIAN RESERVATION
Big Rock Garden Park
Whatcom Falls Park
Lake Whatcom
Bellingham
Portage Island
FAIRHAVEN
WEST SHORE FARM B&B
WILLOWS B&B
Eastsound
Lummi Island
LAKE PADDEN PARK & GOLF COURSE
ARROYO PARK
Wickersham
Orcas Island
Doe Bay
Deer Harbor
Olga
Orcas
LARRABEE STATE PARK
OYSTER CREEK INN
CHUCKANUT DRIVE
Guemes Island
CHUCKANUT MANOR
COCUSA MOTEL
San Juan Island
SKAGIT VALLEY TULIP FESTIVAL
Friday Harbor
BREAZEALE-PADILLA BAY INTERPRETIVE CENTER
Sedro-Woolley
Skagit River
Lopez
Anacortes
BENSON FARMSTEAD
SKAGIT VALLEY CASINO RESORT
Lopez Island
Fidalgo Island
BAY VIEW STATE PARK
LEFEBER BULB FARM
Burlington
SKAGIT VALLEY BULB FARM
CHRISTIANSON'S NURSERY
Mount Vernon
Puget Sound
La Conner
ROOZEN-GAARDE
WHISPERING FIRS B&B
SKAGIT VALLEY GARDENS
Skagit Bay
Oak Harbor
EBEY'S LANDING NATIONAL HISTORICAL RESERVE
Stanwood
Camano Island
Coupeville
Whidbey Island
Arlington
Camano
Saratoga Passage
WENBERG STATE PARK
Port Townsend
TULALIP INDIAN RESERVATION
Sequim
Granite Falls
Marysville
Langley
Lake Stevens
Freeland
Wyatt Park
Lake Stevens
Sunset Park
Discovery Bay
Everett
Clinton
Port Ludlow
Snohomish
Mukilteo
Snohomish River
FUTURE OF FLIGHT CENTER AND BOEING TOUR
Edmonds
Lynnwood
0 10 mi
0 10 km

Edmonds and Mukilteo

Motor north along I-5 from Seattle and you'll soon stumble along two waterfront communities ripe for afternoon strolls, window shopping, and leisurely dinners.

First comes Edmonds, a pleasant little town whose core is centered on a scenic marina and fishing pier. Art galleries, antique shops, and friendly little bistros line the well-tended, pedestrian-friendly streets here. The biggest draw, though, isn't by the water—it's *in* the water. Just offshore from the ferry terminal and Brackett's Landing lies Edmonds Underwater Park, one of the most popular dive sites in the sound.

One town north of Edmonds, Mukilteo (muck-il-TEE-o) offers another idyllic shoreline spot to circle the wagons. The highlight here is a postcard-perfect lighthouse set on a scenic little state park with windswept vistas of Whidbey Island in the distance. Mukilteo was known for its ideal location long before the first Anglos settled there in 1858—the name comes from a Native American term for "good meeting place." The town is the signing place of the infamous Point Elliot Treaty, in which 22 Native American tribes were tricked into handing over their land to white settlers.

SIGHTS

Edmonds Waterfront

A good way to see Edmonds is to begin with a stroll on the half-mile-long **Sunset Avenue** with its Victorian homes and views of Puget Sound and the Olympic Mountains. If the tide is out you can walk back along the beach.

The marine sanctuary at **Olympic Beach** (200 W. Dayton St.) is an excellent place to take youngsters to look at tidal creatures and shellfish when the tide is low. From Memorial Day through Labor Day come on the weekends to the **visitors center** (425/775-1344) to talk with docents about local marinelife and see the tanks with native species swimming around. Also on premises is the lighted **Edmonds Fishing Pier,** which runs 950 feet over the Sound. Try your hand at fishing or just watch anglers cast for salmon and bottom fish and jig for squid.

Walkers and joggers like the boardwalk that runs 0.25 mile along the Port of Edmonds marina. The marina is home to 1,000 boats, including the largest charter fishing fleet on Puget Sound. It is only a short walk down to the small **Edmonds Marina Beach Park** (498 Admiral Way). This is a perfect place to fly kites, cook a dinner over a beach fire, and watch ferries crossing the sound into the sunset.

The prized park of Edmonds, **Brackett's Landing Park** envelops the ferry dock downtown. Here you can see picnicking families mingle with wet-suited diving enthusiasts gearing up to slip into the water to tour the 27-acre **Edmonds Underwater Park,** located just offshore.

Mukilteo Lighthouse Park

Adjacent to the ferry terminal, Mukilteo Lighthouse Park is home to the scenic **Mukilteo Lighthouse** (425/355-9602, www.parks.wa.gov). Built in 1905, this red-and-white beauty is still functional and, along with its restored outbuildings, is open for tours noon–5 P.M. Saturday and Sunday April–September, for a token $1 donation.

The park also has a popular beach for sunbathing, launching boats, and casting lines from shore into the bountiful Possession Sound. Because of consistent winds, the park is also a favorite with kite flyers and windsurfers. The water around here is treacherous, though, so it isn't recommended for casual swimmers.

Museums

Behind the Rosehill Community Center at the corner of 3rd Street and Lincoln Avenue, the tiny **Mukilteo Historical Museum** (425/355-2514, 1–3 P.M. Sat. Oct.–Mar., free) houses photos, artifacts, and rotating exhibits.

The **Edmonds Historical Museum** (118 5th Ave. N, 425/774-0900, 1–4 P.M. Wed.–Sun., free) has a working shingle mill model, historical

© ERICKA CHICKOWSKI

Mukilteo Lighthouse

photos, a marine room, model trains, and other displays depicting Edmonds's past.

ENTERTAINMENT AND EVENTS

On the third weekend of June, the **Edmonds Art Festival** (425/771-6412) includes a juried art show, artists in action, arts and crafts booths, and live music. The **Taste of Edmonds Festival** (425/670-9112) on the second weekend of August is a popular street fair with ethnic foods, a carnival, music, and beer garden.

Held at the base of the city's pride and joy, the mid-August **Mukilteo Lighthouse Festival** (www.mukilteofestival.org) features a pancake breakfast, parade, salmon barbecue, fishing derby, arts and crafts display, and country music and dancing.

SHOPPING

Lynnwood

East of Mukilteo, the strip-mall town of Lynnwood is barely worth a stop—unless you're in a shopping mood. Enormous **Alderwood Mall** (3000 184th St. SW, www.alderwoodmall.com, 10 A.M.–9:30 P.M. Mon.–Thurs., 10 A.M.–10 P.M. Fri.–Sat., 11 A.M.–7 P.M. Sun.) on the east side of Lynnwood hosts The Bon Marché, Nordstrom, JC Penney, Sears, Lamonts, and many smaller stores; the mall is surrounded by smaller shopping plazas. More cheesy developments, discount megamarts, car dealers, condos, fast-food joints, cheap motels, and strip malls line busy Highway 99.

Edmonds Antiques and Galleries

Edmonds has several large antique and collectibles stores, including the **Waterfront Antique Mall** (190 Sunset Ave. S, 425/670-0770, 10 A.M.–6 P.M. Mon.–Sat., noon–6 P.M. Sun.) inside an antique Safeway building, which offers a good mix of art deco, mid-century, and Victorian pieces.

Edmonds has a vibrant art scene, with numerous galleries popping up within downtown. One of the best is **Gallery North** (508 Main St., 425/779-0946, www.gallery-north.com) an artists' cooperative that has been going strong for over 40 years.

Get a good overview of the local gallery scene each third Thursday of the month during the **Edmonds Art Walk,** which focuses on a rotating list of participants. For a list of activities and a map, visit www.edmondswa.com/Events/ArtWalk/.

Rick Steves' Europe Through the Backdoor

Rick Steves' Europe Through the Backdoor (130 4th Ave., 425/771-8303, www.ricksteves.com) is headquarters for this surprisingly large operation directed by the well-known travel author (and star of his own PBS television show). The staff sets up guided tours of Europe, and the center is a great stop for anyone planning a trip to the Continent. In addition to a large travel library, the center puts on free travel workshops twice a week in the summer, along with free Saturday lectures.

For additional travel tips, drop by **The Savvy Traveler** (112 5th Ave. S, 425/744-

6076 or 877/225-1994, www.savvytraveleredmonds.com, 10 A.M.–6 P.M. Mon.–Sat., noon–5 P.M. Sun.). In addition to a wide choice of guidebooks, it sells all sorts of travel paraphernalia and offers free travel seminars once or twice a month.

SPORTS AND RECREATION

Gear up in Lynnwood, which has an **REI** (4200 194th St. SW, 425/774-1300, www.rei.com) with all sorts of outdoor gear.

Diving

Edmonds is home to one of the premier diving sites within the Seattle metropolitan area. Just offshore from Brackett's Landing and the ferry terminal lies the very first underwater park ever established in Washington, **Edmonds Underwater Park.** The artificial reef was formed in 1935 when municipal leaders sank a 300-foot DeLion dry dock to act as a breakwater. Since then the marine environment has claimed the DeLion, as it has with the other ships and debris dropped into the watery depths in order to build up the reef.

Today, divers can explore the underwater, rope-lined "streets" that have been developed over the years to help them navigate the park. Observant divers should be able to find dozens of species of fish, crustaceans, and marine vegetation that thrive here.

You can fill your tanks, rent diving equipment, learn to dive, or find a dive buddy at **Underwater Sports** (264 Railroad Ave., 425/771-6322), two blocks south across the street from the Amtrak depot.

Walking and Running

Just two blocks from downtown is the **Edmonds Marsh,** a haven for wildlife of all kinds. It's an amazing little piece of the natural world where blackbirds, herons, ducks, and crows feed in an enclave hidden from the suburban development that surrounds it. A boardwalk overlooks the marsh and provides an excellent path for walkers and joggers.

The popular **Interurban Trail** is an 11-mile paved path that follows an old railroad route across Lynnwood and continues north all the way to Everett. Or get the locals to give you a tour—visit the shoe store **Running in Motion** (610 Main St., Ste. B, 425/774-0637) at 8:30 A.M. Sunday to join its free weekly runs around town.

Mountain Biking

Spin your way through the miles of single-track carved throughout the greenery within **Japanese Gulch** in Mukilteo. This forested slice of private land rests on a ravine and is accessible from Mukilteo Boulevard. Park in the lot at **Centennial Park** (1126 5th St.) and cross the street to ride. The park offers a nice square of grass to sit on during a leisurely post-ride picnic.

Golf

Harbour Pointe Golf Course (11817 Harbour Pointe Blvd., 425/355-6060 or 800/233-3128, greens fees $62, carts $14), a challenging, water-dependent set of links so well-tended it seems as if the groundskeepers use grooming shears instead of lawnmowers.

If you just want a quick golf fix, **Ballinger Lake Golf Course** (23000 Lakeview Dr., Mountlake Terrace, 425/774-4940, www.ballingerlakegolf.com, $17) is a well-maintained nine-hole municipal course not far from Mukilteo and Edmonds. The pretty water of Ballinger Lake plays a part in two holes.

Camping

Road-trippin' RV owners looking for a place to park their rigs close to Seattle's sights might consider **Twin Cedars RV Park** (17826 Hwy. 99, Lynnwood, 425/742-5540 or 800/878-9304).

ACCOMMODATIONS

Under $100

There might not be much to see in nearby Lynnwood, but it is a good halfway point when you're looking for an affordable base of operations for exploration into Seattle and Snohomish County.

There are a number of chain hotels clustered right near the I-5/I-405 junction and between

Highway 99 and I-5 east of Edmonds, but for a consistently affordable option, consider **Hotel International** (5621 196th St. SW, 800/626-5750 or 425/771-1777, $70 s, $90 d), an independent hotel with tidy and spacious rooms, an indoor spa, and very gracious staffers.

Of course, if you're headed to Edmonds or Mukilteo for the charm of the neighborhood, then a friendly bed-and-breakfast is probably more your speed. Mukilteo offers two B&Bs that won't break the bank. Two miles north of downtown Edmonds, **Maple Tree B&B** (18313 Olympic View Dr., 425/774-8420, $90 d) rests atop a bluff facing the sound and the Olympics beyond. Soak up the view from the solarium, and once the sun goes down, check out the constellations from the telescope set up there. The single guest room has a private bath, and a light breakfast is served. And the centrally located **Dayton House B&B** (522 Dayton, 425/778-3611, $95 d) is a private upstairs apartment with a view deck, within walking distance of Brackett's Landing and the ferry terminal.

$100-150

If those two small establishments are booked, or if you're looking for a full-service hotel in Edmonds proper, then you'll want to stay at **Edmonds Harbor Inn** (130 W. Dayton St., 425/771-5021 or 800/441-8033, www.nwcountryinns.com/harbor, $119–139 s or d). The decor is modern, a light breakfast is included, and guests pay just $5 extra for access to an excellent health club with lap pool and track right next door. Suites with jetted tubs, fireplaces, and kitchenettes are available for $189.

Mukilteo also offers a pair of bed-and-breakfasts at moderate rates. Most remarkable is **Hogland House** (917 Webster St., 425/742-7639, www.hoglandhouse.com, $115–125 d), a Craftsman bungalow home built in 1906. The home has been in the innkeeper's family for over 60 years; she'll treat you to local lore as well as a country breakfast.

The smaller **By the Bay B&B** (821 4th St., 425/347-4997, www.bythebay.net, $80–110 d) has a guest room in the main house and a private cottage for families on its property. Breakfast is a simple continental spread, and guests are encouraged to enjoy the lovingly tended English garden on the property.

$150-200

Mukilteo's major hotel is the posh **Silver Cloud Inn** (425/423-8600 or 800/311-1461, www.scinns.com, $159–189 d) right on the downtown waterfront adjacent to the ferry dock. Many of the rooms have stunning views of the water and passing ferries to Whidbey Island. Complimentary Wi-Fi is provided, as is a continental breakfast and a local shuttle. Luxurious rooms with private hot tubs and fireplaces are $219–289.

FOOD

Mukilteo

Enjoy an espresso and pastry in the flower-filled courtyard at **Whidbey's Coffee Co.** (619 4th St., 425/348-4825, 7 A.M.–5 P.M. daily, $5). Hidden away at the top of the hill overlooking the ferry, this is a great place to escape the traffic on a sunny morning.

Mukilteo has one of the Ivar's chain of seafood restaurants, but you're better off heading uphill to **Arnie's** (714 2nd St., 425/355-2181, 11:30 A.M.–9 P.M. Sun.–Thurs., 11:30 A.M.–10 P.M. Fri.–Sat., $20) for water views from two levels. Enjoy very good lunches and dinners of salmon and other seafood, along with chicken, steaks, and a Sunday champagne brunch.

Legend has it that back in the 1920s Al Capone used to distill whiskey and smuggle it out to his docks from a tunnel underneath the big brick mansion that now hosts **Charles at Smuggler's Cove** (8310 53rd Ave. W., 425/347-2700, www.charlesatsmugglerscove.com, 11 A.M.–2 P.M. Tues.–Fri. and 5–10 P.M. Tues.–Sat., reservations recommended, $25). He'd probably find the restaurant sufficiently classy to impress his rich gangster buddies — this cozy and authentic French restaurant is a birthdays-and-anniversaries sort of place. You're likely to rub elbows with Boeing execs wining and dining clients as you look over the

© KAY SCHELLER/HOGLAND HOUSE

Hogland House

vistas of Possession Sound from the window and sup on superb continental fare.

Edmonds

For a heartier breakfast, **Pancake Haus** (530 5th Ave. S., 425/771-2545, 6 A.M.–3 P.M. Mon.–Fri., 6 A.M.–2 P.M. Sat.–Sun., $9) in Edmonds has got the lock on the best breakfast award for the area. This 30-year-old legend is the Wonka of pancakes, with every imaginable ingredient including fruits, chocolate, and even bacon.

Arnie's has a twin location in Edmonds (300 Admiral Way, 425/771-6533, 11:30 A.M.–9 P.M. Sun.–Thurs., 11:30 A.M.–10 P.M. Fri.–Sat., $20), just two blocks south of the ferry terminal. The bar here is a perfect perch to settle in and watch the sun set over the ferries.

Chanterelle (316 Main St., 425/774-0650, www.chanterellewa.com, 8 A.M.–3 P.M. and 5–9 P.M. Mon.–Sat., 8 A.M.–1 P.M. Sun. and , $16) is a popular downtown bistro and espresso place, with three dependably tasty meals served daily.

INFORMATION AND SERVICES

The friendly folks at the log cabin **Edmonds Visitors Bureau** (120 5th Ave. N, 425/776-6711, www.edmondswa.com, 9 A.M.–4 P.M. Mon.–Fri., 11 A.M.–3 P.M. Sat. in summer, 9 A.M.–4 P.M. Mon.–Fri. in winter) will be happy to provide you with maps and current information.

The **South Snohomish County Chamber of Commerce,** (3400 188th St. SW, 425/774-0507, www.sscchamber.org 8 A.M.–5 P.M.Mon.–Thurs., 8 A.M.–4 P.M. Fri. year-round) has local information.

Contact the city of **Lynnwood** (425/775-1971, www.ci.lynnwood.wa.us) for additional details on the area.

GETTING THERE AND AROUND

By Ferry

Both Edmonds and Mukilteo are known as gateways in the Washington State Ferry system. Edmonds is the departure point to Kingston on the Kitsap Peninsula, which connects to the

Olympic Peninsula. Meanwhile, Mukilteo is the busiest ferry terminal in the state, with service to Whidbey Island.

The **Washington State Ferry** (206/464-6400 or 888/808-7977, 800/843-3779 for automated information, www.wsdot.wa.gov/ferries) crossing from Edmonds to Kingston takes 30 minutes and leaves about every 40 minutes during the day. Summertime fares are $14.45 one-way for car and driver, $6.70 for passengers or walk-ons.

WSF has service between Mukilteo and the town of Clinton on the south end of Whidbey Island every half hour 5 A.M.–2 A.M. The 20-minute crossing costs $3.95 round-trip for passengers or walk-ons, $1 extra for bikes, and $8.60 one-way for car and driver. You only pay on the westbound leg of the trip (leaving Mukilteo). Busiest times are during the weekday commute periods, Saturday morning (after 9 A.M. when going to Whidbey), and late in the afternoon on Sunday.

By Train

From Edmonds Station (210 Railroad Ave.), catch a connection on **Amtrak's Cascades** route from Oregon to Vancouver, British Columbia. Ride to Seattle to connect to the eastbound Empire Builder to Spokane and Chicago, and the southbound Coast Starlight with stops all the way down to San Diego. For information on Amtrak, visit www.amtrak.com or call 425/778-3213 or 800/872-7245.

Amtrak does not service **Mukilteo Station** (920 1st St.), but the stop does offer connections on the commuter Sound Transit **Sounder** line to Seattle, as does Edmonds Station. Sounder runs three times on weekdays southbound in the morning and three times northbound in the evening. The ride takes just under 50 minutes from Mukilteo and just over 30 minutes from Edmonds. Fares are $4 from Mukilteo and $3.50 from Edmonds.

By Bus

Community Transit (425/778-2185 or 800/562-1375; www.commtrans.org) covers nearly all of Snohomish County, with service south to Seattle and east as far as Snohomish and Darrington.

Whidbey Island

The longest island in the lower 48 states—New York's Long Island was declared a peninsula by a U.S. Supreme Court ruling in 1985—Whidbey Island encompasses 208 square miles in its 45-mile length, no spot of which is more than five miles from the water. The island is a favorite place for a Sunday-afternoon drive, with Deception Pass State Park the primary "stop and gawk" spot along the way.

Also popular are the quaint towns of Coupeville and Langley, along with the quiet shoreline and picturesque agricultural land of Ebey's Landing National Historical Reserve. The largest metropolitan center, Oak Harbor, is home to Whidbey Naval Air Station.

History

When the first European explorers reached Whidbey Island, they found it one of the most densely populated places in the Northwest. The original inhabitants, the Salish tribe, depended upon the rich resources of both the sea and the land and used fire to keep the prairies open. The prairies in southern Whidbey attracted settlers in the 1850s, who took advantage of the Homestead Act to carve out farms.

Credit for the 1792 "discovery" of Whidbey Island goes to Joseph Whidbey, master of George Vancouver's flagship, the HMS *Discovery*. Whidbey explored the island in a small vessel, although he wasn't the first one there; while exploring the island's west side,

Whidbey stumbled upon the rotted remains of another ship, too weather-beaten to identify.

Exploring the Island

Whidbey is a perfect destination for a day trip or a weekend outing, with lots to explore and a wide variety of places to stay. The island is also a great place for cyclists, with many miles of quiet back roads; get maps from the Langley South Whidbey Chamber of Commerce Visitor and Information Center (try saying that one fast). One nice aspect of Whidbey is that the charm of its picturesque towns of Langley and Coupeville is natural, a result of their history, not a theme created to attract tourism.

For a fast day tour, take the Mukilteo–Clinton ferry to the south end of the island, followed by a leisurely drive up the island, with stops in each town and park. To really see Whidbey, you'll need more than a hurried day trip. Take the time to explore the many natural areas and historic sites, camping out in one of the excellent state parks or staying in a local B&B. Be warned, however, that lodging rates are high in most local B&Bs, typically $85 d and up (to over $300 d) with breakfast. Motels and hotels are limited, but a few places (primarily in Oak Harbor) have rooms for under $65 d. Reservations are highly recommended for summer weekends. If you're on a budget, your best bet is to camp out. Contact **Island County Visitor Information** (888/747-7777, www.whidbey.net) for information and brochures on Whidbey. Another helpful site is the online **Whidbey Island Visitor's Guide** at www.visitwhidbey.com.

Getting There

To drive onto Whidbey Island, you've got only one option: the Deception Pass Bridge at the island's north end. To get there, go west on Highway 20 from I-5. Access to the south end of Whidbey is a relaxing **Washington State Ferry** (206/464-6400 or 888/808-7977, www.wsdot.wa.gov/ferries) ride from Mukilteo or Port Townsend.

The Mukilteo ferry leaves for Clinton about every half hour 5 A.M.–1 A.M., and the 20-minute crossing costs $2.70 round-trip for passengers or walk-ons, $1 extra for bikes, and $6.25 one-way for car and driver. You only pay on the westbound leg of the trip, so if you drive down Whidbey via the Deception Pass Bridge, your ride is free. Busiest times are during the weekday commute periods, Saturday morning (after 9 A.M. when going to the island), and late afternoon Sunday. Sunday evenings after 7 P.M. are quieter, so just enjoy the island and let folks in a hurry wait in the traffic jams while you sit on a beach or in a café.

From the Olympic Peninsula, board the ferry in Port Townsend to arrive at the Keystone landing next to Fort Casey State Park approximately 30 minutes later. These ferries operate about every 45 minutes 7 A.M.–10 P.M. in the summer, and one-way fares are $2 for passengers ($0.35 extra one-way for bikes), and $8.75 for car and driver. Be ready for a two-hour wait during peak times on summer weekends.

Getting Around

South Whidbey Island was seemingly designed for biking. The rolling hills, clean air, and beautiful weather are inspiring enough, but occasional whale and eagle sightings add to the pleasure. **Island Transit** (360/678-7771 or 800/240-8747, www.islandtransit.org) is a free bus system that offers Mon.–Sat. service all across Whidbey Island, from Clinton on the south to Deception Pass on the north. All buses have bike racks.

CLINTON AND LANGLEY

The southern gateway to Whidbey Island, Clinton rests on a bluff overlooking the ferries that chug across Possession Sound to unload at the docks here. You'll pass through it in a blink on your journey northward to Langley, a charming little town best enjoyed without a watch or a cell phone. Langley lies along the waters of Saratoga Passage, with views of Camano Island and the North Cascades on a good day. It is a getaway dream town, with boutiques, bed-and-breakfast inns, and galleries galore.

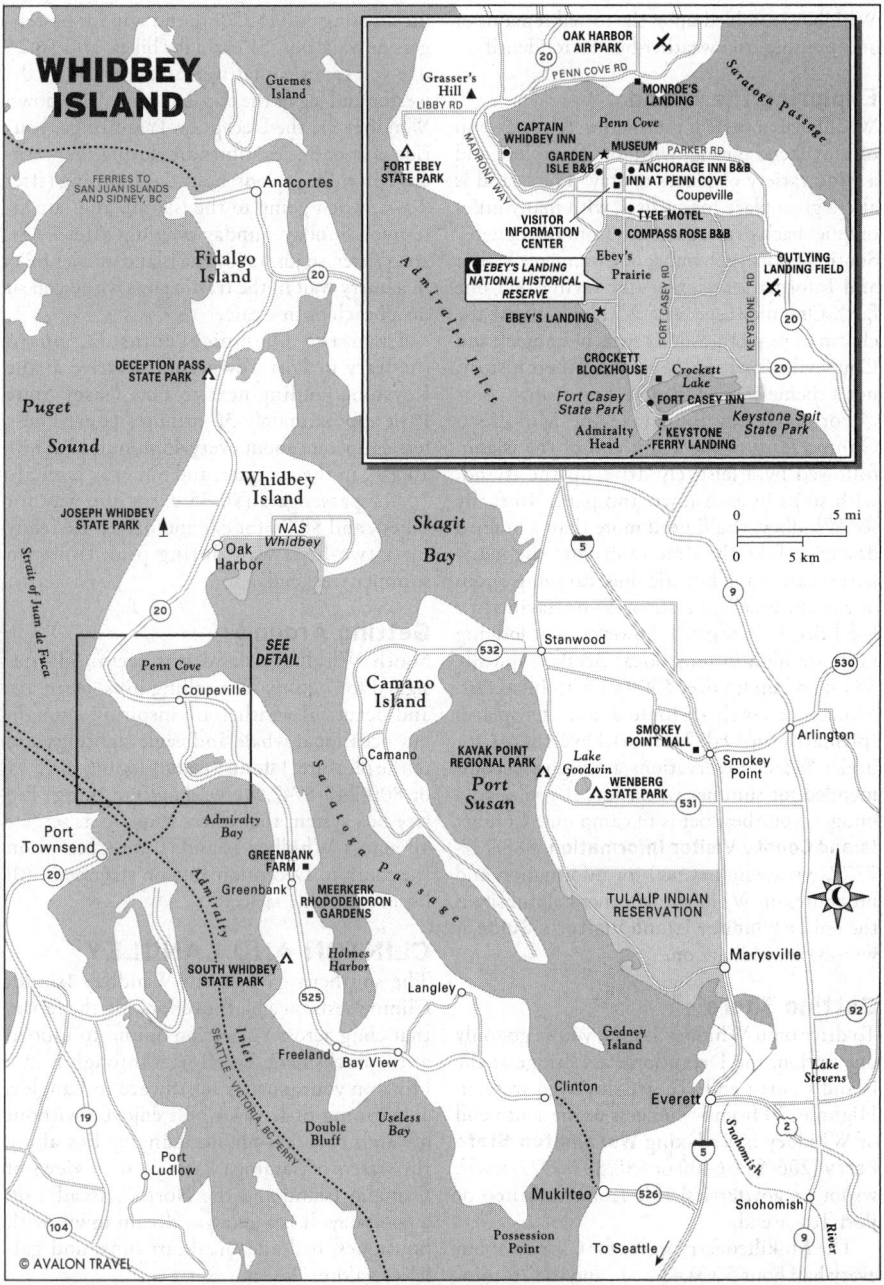
WHIDBEY ISLAND
Guemes Island
FERRIES TO SAN JUAN ISLANDS AND SIDNEY, BC
Anacortes
Fidalgo Island
DECEPTION PASS STATE PARK
Puget Sound
Whidbey Island
JOSEPH WHIDBEY STATE PARK
NAS Whidbey
Oak Harbor
Skagit Bay
Strait of Juan de Fuca
SEE DETAIL
Penn Cove
Coupeville
Camano Island
Camano
KAYAK POINT REGIONAL PARK
Lake Goodwin
WENBERG STATE PARK
Port Susan
SMOKEY POINT MALL
Smokey Point
Arlington
Stanwood
Admiralty Bay
Port Townsend
GREENBANK FARM
Greenbank
MEERKERK RHODODENDRON GARDENS
Saratoga Passage
Admiralty Inlet
TULALIP INDIAN RESERVATION
Marysville
SOUTH WHIDBEY STATE PARK
Holmes Harbor
Langley
Gedney Island
Freeland
Bay View
SEATTLE-VICTORIA, BC FERRY
Clinton
Everett
Lake Stevens
Double Bluff
Useless Bay
Port Ludlow
Mukilteo
Snohomish
Snohomish River
Possession Point
To Seattle
0 5 mi
0 5 km
OAK HARBOR AIR PARK
PENN COVE RD
MONROE'S LANDING
Grasser's Hill
LIBBY RD
Penn Cove
CAPTAIN WHIDBEY INN
MUSEUM
PARKER RD
GARDEN ISLE B&B
ANCHORAGE INN B&B
INN AT PENN COVE
Coupeville
FORT EBEY STATE PARK
MADRONA WAY
VISITOR INFORMATION CENTER
TYEE MOTEL
COMPASS ROSE B&B
EBEY'S LANDING NATIONAL HISTORICAL RESERVE
Ebey's Prairie
OUTLYING LANDING FIELD
EBEY'S LANDING
FORT CASEY RD
KEYSTONE RD
CROCKETT BLOCKHOUSE
Crockett Lake
Fort Casey State Park
FORT CASEY INN
Keystone Spit State Park
Admiralty Head
KEYSTONE FERRY LANDING
© AVALON TRAVEL

Sights

DOWNTOWN LANGLEY

The main attraction in Langley is simply the charismatic town itself, perched right above Puget Sound. A favorite downtown spot for photos is the life-size bronze ***Boy and Dog*** by local sculptor Georgia Gerber. The 160-foot fishing pier offers great views and a chance to test your fishing pole, and the beach here is a popular place for picnicking and swimming. **South Whidbey Historical Museum** (312 2nd St., 360/730-3367, 1–4 P.M. Sat.–Sun.) has local memorabilia in a century-old building.

If your kids are getting restless window shopping, take a quick break at the **wooden castle,** located in the community park a mile west of town on Maxwelton Road.

WHIDBEY ISLAND WINERY

Stop for a picnic overlooking the vineyard and apple orchard at Whidbey Island Winery (5237 S. Langley Rd., 360/221-2040, www.whidbeyislandwinery.com, noon–5 P.M. Thurs.–Sun.), a family-run vintner. The tasting room here offers sips of creative rhubarb wines and vintages fermented from estate-grown Madeline Angevine grapes.

Entertainment and Events

The **Whidbey Island Center for the Arts** (565 Camano Ave., 360/221-8268 or 800/638-7631, www.whidbey.net/wica) features concerts and plays throughout the year. The historic **Clyde Theatre** (1st St., 360/221-5525, www.theclyde.net, $6) is the only place to watch first-run movies on the south end of Whidbey Island.

In late February, several thousand people converge on town to search out the culprit in the annual **Langley Mystery Weekend.** Langley's popular **Choochokam Festival of the Arts** (360/221-7494) is held the second weekend of July with a juried arts festival, food, crafts, music, and dancing. Don't miss Langley's **Island County Fair** (360/221-4677, www.islandweb.org/fair), a four-day event in late August that includes a logging show, carnival, parade, music, and 4-H exhibits.

© ERICKA CHICKOWSKI

Langley village on Whidbey Island

Shopping

Tiny Langley is home to numerous art galleries. The two best, **Museo Piccolo Gallery** (215 1st St., 360/221-7737, 11 A.M.–5 P.M. daily) and **Karlson/Gray** (302 1st St., 360/221-2978, www.karlsongraygallery.com, 10 A.M.–5 P.M. daily) have unusual and highly creative works. Also of note is **Lowry-James Fine Antiques** (101 Anthes, 360/221-0477, www.lowryjames.com, 10 A.M.–5 P.M. Wed.–Mon., closed Tues.) with a fine collection of natural history engravings and lithographs. Langley's galleries open for evening **Art Walks** on the first Saturday of each month.

Moonraker Books (209 1st St., 360/221-6962, 10:30 A.M.–5:30 P.M. Mon.–Sat., 11 A.M.–5 P.M. Sun.) carries a fine selection of regional titles. **North Star Trading Co.** (101 1st St., 360/221-1202 or 800/446-9276, www.sheepskingoods.com, 10:30 A.M.–5:30 P.M. daily in summer, 11 A.M.–4 P.M. Thurs.–Mon., closed Tues.–Wed. in winter) produces ultra-soft sheepskin slippers and hats.

Sports and Recreation

Driving or biking around Clinton's rural, wooded back roads provides fresh air and great views. Take Deer Lake Road (watch the signs—the road takes 90-degree turns without notice) to **Deer Lake Park** for swimming, boating, and fishing in a secluded, wooded area. From Highway 525, go left on Maxwelton Road, and stay on it all the way to Maxwelton Beach in **Dave Mackie County Park,** where you'll find the island's best Dungeness crabbing, along with shallow water for swimming.

Possession Beach County Park covers just two acres at the southern tip of Whidbey Island; it is a popular fishing site and a fine place to enjoy the views.

LANGLEY FOUNDED BY GANGLY TEEN

Langley is probably the only Washington town founded by a teenager. In 1880, an ambitious 15-year-old German immigrant, Jacob Anthes, settled here. Because he was too young to file for a homestead, Anthes spent $100 to buy 120 acres of land, adding to his holdings with a 160-acre homestead claim when he reached 21. He later built a store and post office and teamed up with Judge J. W. Langley to plot the new town.

Accommodations

Spontaneous travelers can stop by the Langley Chamber of Commerce visitors center (208 Anthes Ave.) to see photos of each place. Each night after 5 P.M., vacancies are posted in the front window.

UNDER $100

Some of the most affordable south Whidbey digs short of a tent site are at **Langley Motel** (526-B Camano Ave., 360/221-6070, $95–125 d). This little establishment was designed by the architect-owner and features four mid-century retro-style rooms.

Another budget option is **Inverness Inn** (2479 E. Hwy. 525, 360/321-5521, www.whidbey.net/info, $100 for up to four) is a little motel with six duplex cottages with kitchenettes.

$100-150

The rambling **Ashingdon Manor B&B Inn** (5023 Langley Rd., 360/221-2334 or 800/442-4942, www.ashingdonmanor.com, $129–179 s or d) is one of the more distinctive local places, with a 14-acre country location, six guest rooms with private baths (three with fireplaces), a grand piano, and a lovely pond and patio. The rate includes a gourmet breakfast (one of the owners is a chef).

Located on pastureland overlooking Sunlight Beach, **The Farmhouse** (2740 E. Sunshine Ln., 360/321-6288 or 888/888-7022, www.farmhousebb.com, $129–179 d) has four suites, all with fireplaces, private baths (two with jetted tubs), outside entrances and decks, and kitchens. The refrigerators are stocked for a full breakfast, and guests have access to an outdoor hot tub.

Soak up the views across Saratoga Passage at **Eagles Nest Inn** (4680 E. Saratoga Rd., 360/221-5331, www.eaglesnestinn.com, $125–175 d), a unique four-story octagonal home tucked into a wooded lot that adjoins the Saratoga Woods Preserve trail system. After a hike, relax in the hot tub or enjoy the private decks and grand piano.

Families who may find a trip to a bed-and-breakfast too expensive or nerve-wracking have got an option in **Sweetwater Cottage** (6111 S. Cultus Bay Rd., 360/341-1604, www.whidbey.com/sweetwater, $150 s or d), a secluded two-bedroom cottage with a kitchen, woodstove, and sauna on 22 forested acres. You can even bring along your furry family—horses and other pets are allowed here.

$150-200

The **Primrose Path Cottage** (3191 E. Harbor Rd., 360/730-3722 or 800/333-4724, www.primrosepath.net, $179 d, $20 per extra person up to six people) is another private family-friendly space. This charming 1928 two-bedroom cottage in the woods has a path to a private beach and a relaxing hot tub.

All of the rooms at **Country Cottage of Langley B&B** (215 6th St., 360/221-8709 or 800/713-3860, www.acountrycottage.com) have water views and private decks; two of them even have hot tubs. The breakfasts here are the stuff of legends—innkeepers use local produce to create gourmet fare.

For downtown lodging at its best, stay at **Garden Path Inn** (111 1st St., 360/221-5121, www.gardenpathsuites.com, $140–200), where the two attractive suites include a continental breakfast.

$200-250

Langley's largest lodging option is the modern **Saratoga Inn** (201 Cascade Ave., 360/221-5801 or 800/698-2910, www.foursisters.com, $185–245 s or d, $315 suite), right in town. This 15-room place offers the privacy of a hotel but adds a hot buffet breakfast. The spacious rooms are attractively appointed, and all include gas fireplaces.

Boating fans can take port at **Boatyard Inn** (200 Wharf St., 360/221-5120, www.boatyardinn.com). You can hear the rigging pinging against the masts at the public marina right next door to this architecturally distinctive inn, which pays homage to the old canneries of the Puget Sound with its sloping corrugated roofs and colorful siding. It has 10 modern beachfront studio ($195 d) or loft units ($250 for up to four) with kitchens, fireplaces, and decks.

OVER $250

The luxurious **Inn at Langley** (400 1st St., 360/221-3033, www.innatlangley.com) has rooms ($275–295 d), suites ($395 d), a cottage ($495 d), and full apartments ($595), each with its own private patio overlooking Saratoga Passage, a whirlpool tub, fireplace, and continental breakfast. A two-night minimum applies on weekends. Also here is the Essencia Spa, with massage, aromatherapy, body masks, and more.

Three cottages—**Dove House, Chauntecleer House,** and **The Potting Shed**—(360/221-5494 or 800/637-4436, www.dovehouse.com, $250–325 d, $25 per extra person) are located on six acres of gardens and ponds overlooking Saratoga Passage. All have private hot tubs and fireplaces.

Those looking for a homey spot convenient to the ferry terminal can cozy up in **Sunset Cottage** (360/579-2770, www.whidbeynet.net/beach, $275 d). This kid-friendly cottage features a king-size bed, full kitchen, and patio. It sits along sandy Maxwelton Beach, a good place to spot eagles.

Food

It's almost a challenge to get a bad meal in this town!

Cafe Langley (113 1st St., 360/221-3090, 11:30 A.M.–2:30 P.M. and 5–8 P.M. Mon.–Thurs., 11:30 A.M.–3 P.M. Fri.–Sun. and 5–9 P.M. Fri.–Sat., 5–8:30 P.M. Sun., $17) has a huge local following who come for great Greek and Middle Eastern dishes.

Less fancy, but noteworthy nonetheless, is **Village Pizzeria** (108 1st St., 360/221-3363, 11:30 A.M.–9 P.M. daily, $15). It serves up delicious, thin-crust, New York–style pies that taste best when enjoyed at the outdoor tables with great views of the water.

Located atop a hill a 10-minute walk from downtown, **China City** (510 Cascade Ave., 360/331-8899, 11 A.M.–8:30 P.M. Mon.–Thurs., 11 A.M.–9 P.M. Fri.–Sun., $10) serves excellent Chinese meals in an upscale setting. Big windows and a small patio offer striking 180-degree views of Saratoga Passage and the Cascades, while tall evergreen trees accent the yard. Prices are reasonable and the atmosphere is relaxed. There's even dancing to DJ tunes on Saturday night.

Martini Bakery (360/221-3525, 8 A.M.–4 P.M. Wed.–Sun.) bakes out-of-this-world breads and sweets. And the **South Whidbey Tilth Farmers Market** (Hwy. 525 at Thompson Rd., 360/579-1871, 10 A.M.–2 P.M. Sat. and 4–7 P.M. Wed. mid-May–Oct.) offers all-organic fruits and vegetables, plus

© ERICKA CHICKOWSKI

Stop for a cone before driving over the bridge.

flowers, baked goods, and seafood. The hours are the same for a second version, the **Bayview Farmers Market** (Bayview Rd. at Hwy. 525, 360/221-6903). The Wednesday Bayview Farmers Market is only open July–September and includes nonorganic items.

Information and Services

Clinton doesn't have a chamber of commerce, but you can find some information at www.whidbeynet.net/clinton.

Langley South Whidbey Chamber of Commerce (208 Anthes Ave., 360/221-6765, www.whidbey.com/Langley) is open 10 A.M.–5 P.M. daily all year.

The **Langley Library** (360/221-4383, www.sno-isle.org) is located at 104 2nd Street.

Getting There and Around

The state ferry (206/464-6400 or 888/808-7977, 800/843-3779 for automated information, www.wsdot.wa.gov/ferries) departs Clinton for Mukilteo approximately every half hour throughout the day.

Island Transit (360/321-6688 or 800/240-8747, www.islandtransit.org) offers free bus service Mon.–Sat. throughout Whidbey Island. From the ferry terminal in Clinton, you can catch Route 1 for service to Freeland, Greenbank, Coupeville, and Oak Harbor via Highway 20. Or catch Route 7 with service to Langley and Freeland.

FREELAND AND GREENBANK

Freeland was founded in 1900 by a utopian group of socialists. They formed a cooperative, the Free Land Association, and each contributed $10 toward five acres of land; the balance was to be paid off through cooperative labor. Their experiment didn't last long, but the name stuck. Today it is an unassuming little town with a few quiet parks ideal for picnics on the way to the ferry terminal or Oak Harbor.

Also worth a stop is the pinprick-small "town" of Greenbank. The turn-of-the-20th-century general store, restaurant, and post office are easy to miss—but you can't miss the big red barn marking Whidbey Island Greenbank Farm, an icon for the entire island.

Sights and Recreation

FREELAND PARKS

Find a small, sunny picnic area and a boat launch at **Freeland Park** on Holmes Harbor, about two streets over from "downtown" Freeland—just look for the water. The beach is popular with clammers. **Double Bluff Beach Park,** three miles south of Freeland, is an interesting place to explore and a good place to find big chunks of soft coal that eroded from the cliff. Do not try to climb these unstable bluffs; a number of people have been injured trying to do so.

WHIDBEY ISLAND GREENBANK FARM

At one point the Whidbey Island Greenbank Farm (360/678-7700, www.greenbankfarm.com) used to be the largest loganberry farm in the world. After the owners closed it down in 1996, local citizens organized to keep the area from being turned into a housing development and persuaded the county to purchase it in 1997.

Today, new loganberry vines have been planted, and the farm's gift shop (10 A.M.–5 P.M. daily in summer, noon–4 P.M. Mon.–Wed. and 11 A.M.–5 P.M. Thurs.–Sun. the rest of the year) sells loganberry wine (produced elsewhere), along with grape and fruit wines from small local wineries. A **farmers market** takes place here 11 A.M.–3 P.M. Sunday May–mid-October. The third weekend of July brings the **Loganberry Festival,** featuring a pie-eating contest, arts and crafts, live music, and food stands.

SOUTH WHIDBEY STATE PARK

Easily the island's most underrated park, South Whidbey State Park (360/331-4559, www.parks.wa.gov) on Smuggler's Cove Road (halfway between Greenbank and Freeland) has outstanding hiking and picnicking, campsites, and striking Olympic views. As of the printing of this book, the narrow, sandy beach is closed due to bluff erosion—there's no telling when it will reopen.

As a solace, wander through the park's 85 acres of old-growth Douglas fir and red cedar, which protect resident black-tailed deer, foxes, raccoons, rabbits, bald eagles, ospreys, and pileated woodpeckers. Be sure to hike **Wilbert Trail,** a 1.5-mile path that circles through these ancient forests; it starts directly across from the park entrance.

You can also camp at South Whidbey State Park ($17 for tents, or $23 for RVs with hookups, open late Feb.–October). Make reservations ($7 extra) at 888/226-7688 or www.parks.wa.gov. If these campsites are full, **Mutiny Bay Resort** in Freeland (5856 S. Mutiny Bay Rd., 360/331-4500) also has RV hookups and tent spaces.

MEERKERK RHODODENDRON GARDENS

The delightful Meerkerk Rhododendron Gardens (360/678-1912, www.meerkerkgardens.org, 9 A.M.–4 P.M. daily, adults $8, children under 16 free) boast more than 1,500 varieties of rhododendron species and hybrids on a 53-acre site just south of Greenbank off Resort Road. Begun by Max and Anne Meerkerk in the 1960s, the gardens are now maintained by the Seattle Rhododendron Society and are a major tourist attraction. Peak season for "rhodies" is in late April and early May.

Accommodations

UNDER $100

Families traveling with Fido and not a lot of dough will sleep soundly at the simple **Harbour Inn Motel** (1606 E. Main St., 360/331-6900, www.harbourinnmotel.com, $84–99 s or d). This pet-friendly motel with outdoor corridors has 20 rooms, some with kitchenettes, and serves a generous continental breakfast on weekends and holidays.

Situated on five secluded acres, **The Yoga Lodge** (3475 Christie Rd., 360/678-2120, www.yogalodge.com) is a peaceful place to spend a night surrounded by gardens and trees. Those with allergies will breathe easier knowing this place caters to those with chemical sensitivities, cleaning only with natural products. There are three quiet guest rooms here with a shared bathroom, and rates include a continental breakfast and wood-fired sauna. Guests can join in mid-week yoga lessons ($15 per person) or private lessons on weekends ($70 for two).

$100-150

Watch the goats and llamas graze the pastures at **Bay Breeze B&B Cottages** (5660 S. Double Bluff Rd., 360/321-4277 or 888/547-4179, www.baybreezecottages.co, $139–149 d), a delightful retreat that sits next door to a flower farm and less than 1.5 miles from Double Bluff beach. Each cottage comes with its own bath, indoor hot tub, fireplace, and kitchenette.

Another beachfront guesthouse possibility is **Bush Point Wharf** (229 E. Main St., 360/331-0405 or 800/460-7219, www.whidbey.com/bushpoint), which has two guest suites ($115 s or d) and a three-bedroom penthouse ($195 d), all with private baths, a deck, and hot tub.

$150-200

Set amid 25 wooded acres, **Guest House Log Cottages** (3366 S. Hwy. 525, 360/678-3115, www.whidbey.net/logcottages) is a quiet, kid-free retreat that mingles four-star amenities with the down-home style of cedar cabins. Accommodations include a modern log home ($325 d) with fireplace, indoor hot tub under a glass ceiling, and king bed, plus five cottages ($165–235 d) with fireplaces, kitchens, and jetted tubs. All have access to the outdoor pool, hot tub, and small exercise room, along with make-it-yourself breakfasts.

Those bringing wee ones may prefer **Smugglers Cove Haven B&B** (3258 Smugglers Cove Rd., 360/678-7100 or 800/772-7055, www.smugglerscove.com, $125–175 s or d), which has three private units, each with a woodstove, kitchen, and make-it-yourself breakfast.

OVER $250

For the ultimate in luxury, stay at **Cliff House B&B** (727 Windmill Dr., 360/331-1566, www.cliffhouse.net) where the stunning modern home ($495 d) sits atop a cliff over Admiralty Inlet and has a hot tub, king-size bed, stone fireplace, and gourmet kitchen. A light breakfast is in the fridge. Also on the 13 acres of wooded land is a cottage with equally grand vistas for $175 d. There is a two-night minimum stay at either place.

Food

Likely the best restaurant on the entire island, **Gordon's on Blueberry Hill** (5438 Woodard Ave., Freeland, 360/331-7515, $19) is roundly lauded for the Northwest cuisine it serves within a bustling ranch-style house in Freeland. The owner-chef here mixes local ingredients such as mussels and homegrown herbs with flavors of Asia and Europe. Try unique dishes such as tandoori-style game hens ($19) or butternut squash ravioli in Sambuca cream sauce ($19).

Freeland Café (1642 E. Main St., 360/331-9945, www.whidbey.com/freelandcafe, 6 A.M.–9 P.M. daily, $10) is an old-time establishment with breakfast served anytime; it's very popular with the locals when they've got a hankering for a burger.

For a slice of warm pie à la mode, nobody beats those baked up at **Whidbey Pies Cafe** (765 Wonn Rd., 10 A.M.–5 P.M. daily May–Sept., 11 A.M.–4 P.M. Mon.–Fri., 10 A.M.–5 P.M. Sat.–Sun. Oct.–Apr.) at Greenbank Farm, which features the farm's renowned loganberries.

Practicalities

Freeland Chamber of Commerce (1640 Main St., 360/331-1980, www.islandweb.org/freeland) is open 11 A.M.–3 P.M. Tuesday–Saturday. The **Freeland Library** (360/331-7323, www.sno-isle.org) is located at 5495 Harbor Avenue.

Ride **Island Transit** (360/321-6688 or 800/240-8747, www.islandtransit.org, free) to Freeland and Greenbank from Clinton on Route 1 and from Langley to Freeland on Route 5.

COUPEVILLE

The second oldest town in Washington, the "Port of Sea Captains" was founded and laid out in 1852 by Capt. Thomas Coupe, the first man to sail through Deception Pass. The protected harbor at Penn Cove was a perfect site for the village that became Coupeville, and timber from Whidbey was shipped from here to San Francisco to feed the building boom created by the gold rush.

Today, modern businesses operate from Victorian-era buildings amidst the nation's largest historical preservation district. Downtown has an immaculate cluster of false-fronted shops and restaurants right on the harbor and a long wharf that was once used to ship local produce and logs to the mainland. This is a cat-friendly town; perhaps half the downtown businesses have one inside.

Sights

EBEY'S LANDING NATIONAL HISTORICAL RESERVE

With its bucolic farmland, densely wooded ridges, and steep shoreline bluffs, Ebey's Landing has the most striking coastal view on Whidbey. No wonder parts of the 1999 movie *Snow Falling on Cedars* were filmed here.

Unfurling over 25 square miles of rich farmland, this was the first designated national historical reserve in America. The rolling hills and whispering winds of the sound are the main attraction here, easily enjoyed by car or bike over the quiet ribbons of scenic blacktop that run through the reserve.

Much of the land in Ebey's Landing is privately owned—in fact, the reserve's boundaries encircle the entire historic town of Coupeville—but there are a trio of scenic state parks perfect for throwing down a picnic blanket or going for a nature walk.

Among them is the tiny **Ebey's Landing State Park,** the site where island pioneer Isaac Ebey landed his boat to gain access to the nearby fertile land that he homesteaded in 1850. Because this is the thinnest point in the island, Ebey's Landing later became a popular beach for locals to land in order cross overland to the eastern shores of Whidbey at Penn Cove. There is still an 1858 ferry house that serviced these travelers standing at the site.

In Coupeville you'll find one of the original Whidbey Island fortifications: The **Alexander Blockhouse,** built in 1855, stands outside the museum, along with a shelter housing two turn-of-the-20th-century Native American racing canoes. Historical Reserve headquarters are upstairs from the museum (360/678-6084, www.nps.gov/ebla). Also out front are attractive gardens with herbs and drought-tolerant plants. Additional blockhouses can be found at the Sunnyside Cemetery, just south of town, and near Crockett Lake.

FORT CASEY STATE PARK

Once a part of the Iron Triangle that guarded the entrance to the Puget Sound and the Bremerton Naval Shipyard, Fort Casey has long since seen the retirement and meltdown of the 10-inch disappearing carriage guns that stood sentinel there during the turn of the 20th century.

Nowadays it is home to a state park (12901 Hwy. 20, 360/679-7391, www.parks.wa.gov) that not only gives a glimpse into Army life back in the day but also offers spectacular Olympic views along two miles of beach, as well as prime picnic grounds and hiking trails.

Much of the fort is open for public viewing, including ammunition bunkers, observation towers, and underground storage facilities (bring your flashlight). Military buffs will especially get a kick out of two carriage guns brought in from an old fort in the Philippines during the 1960s to replace the originals.

Be sure to visit the **Admiralty Point Lighthouse Interpretive Center** (11 A.M.–5 P.M. Wed.–Sun. June–Sept., with reduced hours the rest of the year) where you can learn more about coast artillery and the 1890 defense post. The lighthouse itself has not been used since 1927, but you can climb to the top for a wonderful view of Puget Sound and the Olympic Mountains.

A small and crowded campground (360/678-4519, www.parks.wa.gov, $22 for tents, $27 for RVs with hookups) at Fort Casey is open year-round and has showers.

These exposed sites are right on the water next to the busy ferry terminal. No reservations are accepted, so get here early to be assured of a site on summer weekends.

FORT EBEY STATE PARK

Located southwest of Coupeville on Admiralty Inlet, Fort Ebey State Park (360/678-4636, www.parks.wa.gov) has campsites (standard $17, RV hookups $23), a large picnic area, three miles of beach, and two miles of hiking trails within its 644 acres. The fort was constructed during World War II, though its gun batteries were never needed.

The concrete platforms remain, along with cavernous bunkers, but the big guns have long since been removed. Due to its location in the Olympic rain shadow, the park is one of the few places in western Washington where cactus can be found; it also has stands of second-growth forests and great views across the Strait of Juan de Fuca.

PENN COVE MUSSELS

Right in the midst of the cozy bed-and-breakfasts, antique shops, and small-town splendor of Whidbey Island lies one of the oldest and largest mussel farms in the United States. The Stillaguamish and Skagit Rivers bring the area a nutrient-rich outflow, and the additional sunshine provided by the Olympic rain shadow makes sure the plankton on which these mussels feed is especially nourishing. The result is a fat, sweet mussel that tastes just as wonderful in a creamy white-wine sauce as it does with just a few drops of butter and a sprig of basil. Penn Cove Shellfish has won multiple awards for quality and taste and is one of the few seafood brands to which connoisseurs are strongly loyal.

ISLAND COUNTY HISTORICAL MUSEUM

The Island County Historical Society Museum (Alexander and Front Sts., 360/678-3310, 10 A.M.–5 P.M. Wed.–Mon. May–Sept., 11 A.M.–4 P.M. Fri.–Mon. the rest of the year, $2 adults, $1.50 seniors, students, and military personnel, $4.25 families, free for kids under 6) has pioneer relics, oddities such as a shadow box with flowers made from human hair, and interesting newsreels from the 1930s on the Indian Water Festival. Out front is a garden with drought-tolerant native plants and herbs.

While at the museum, pick up its brochure describing a walking tour of the town's beautiful Victorian buildings. It lists some 40 buildings in Coupeville of historical significance and tells the family histories of many owners.

Events

Lots of events take place in tiny Coupeville, starting with the **Penn Cove Mussel Festival** the first weekend of March, with scavenger hunts, arts and crafts, and mussel cooking competitions. The **Penn Cove Water Festival** in early May includes canoe races, arts and crafts, kayak events, and entertainment. The **Coupeville Arts and Crafts Festival** on the second weekend in August features a juried art show that attracts participants from across the Northwest, plus arts and crafts exhibits, food, music, and entertainment.

On Sundays in July and August, **Concerts on the Cove** (360/678-4684) are held in the Town Park pavilion, featuring a wide variety of music. The **Coupeville Farmers Market** (8th and Main Sts., 360/678-6757) is held 10 A.M.–2 P.M. Saturday April–mid-October.

If you're here the second weekend in October, don't miss the **Harvest Festival,** with music, food booths, a giant pumpkin contest, scarecrows, an art and antique auction, and flea market. On the first Saturday of December, the **Greening of Coupeville** is a popular craft bazaar and tree-lighting festival. A number of historical homes are open for this event and also for a **Home Tour** on the first Saturday in August (360/678-3310).

Sports and Recreation

SCENIC DRIVES

Head northwest from Coupeville along Madrona Way to take a ride underneath the curvy road's namesake, the Pacific madrona (a.k.a. madrona) trees, whose distinctive red bark and leathery green leaves line the route. Quite a few summer cottages and cozy homes can be found here, along with the one-of-a-kind Captain Whidbey Inn. Offshore are dozens of floating pens where mussels grow on lines hanging in Penn Cove. On the northwest corner of Penn Cove, Highway 20 passes scenic **Grasser's Hill,** where hedgerows alternate with open farmland. Development restrictions prevent this open country from becoming a mass of condos. Just north of here are the historic San de Fuca schoolhouse and Whidbey Inn.

Another scenic route crawls along Hill Road, two miles south of Coupeville. Follow it through the second-growth stand of Douglas fir trees. It emerges on a high bluff overlooking Admiralty Inlet before dropping to the shoreline at tiny Ebey's Landing State Park.

WATER SPORTS

Anglers, divers, and pleasure boaters will find the area around Coupeville an ideal place to get their craft out into Puget Sound. There are two boat ramps at Fort Casey State Park and a boat launch, small marina and fuel dock at the Coupeville Wharf along Penn Cove.

Rent sea kayaks and inflatable boats (summers only) from **Whidbey Water Works** (360/678-9301, www.whidbeywaterworks.com), located at the Captain Whidbey Inn. Kayak rentals may also be available at the wharf in downtown Coupeville.

Just offshore from Fort Casey State Park is the **Keystone Jetty underwater park,** a marine reserve that gives divers the opportunity to explore a forest of kelp and come face to face with lingcod, crab, and sculpin, among other critters. The park is particularly popular for its abundant population of waving plumose anemones.

The closest place for scuba divers to get air fills, rent equipment, and schedule chartered dives is in Oak Harbor, at **Whidbey Island Dive Center** (1020 N.E. 7th Ave., #1, 360/675-1112, www.whidbeydive.com, 10 A.M.–5 P.M. Mon.–Tues., 9 A.M.–6 P.M. Wed–Sat., 10 A.M.–4 P.M. Sun.).

One of the major draws within Fort Ebey State Park is **Lake Pondilla.** Formed by a glacial sinkhole, this is a delight for bass fishermen and swimmers. Follow the signs from the north parking lot at the park for a two-block hike to the lake.

HIKING

From the small parking area at the water's edge at Ebey's Landing State Park, hike the 1.5-mile trail along the bluff above **Parego Lagoon** for a view of the coastline, Olympics, and the Strait of Juan de Fuca that shouldn't be missed. If you hit the seasons right, the lagoon may be teeming with migratory birds, so bring some binoculars. Return along the beach, or continue northward to Fort Ebey State Park (three miles from Ebey's Landing). Along the way, keep your eyes open for gem-quality stones such as agate, jasper, black and green jade, plus quartz and petrified wood.

Another trail leads 1.4 miles from Ebey's Landing to **Sunnyside Cemetery,** where you can look north to snowcapped Mt. Baker and south to Mt. Rainier on a clear day. The cemetery is also accessible from Cook Road. The **Davis Blockhouse,** used to defend against Tlingit and Haida attacks, stands at the edge of the cemetery; it was moved here in 1915.

From the north parking lot at Fort Ebey, follow trails that lead south along the bluffs down to the beach. After consulting a tide chart and taking a bit of care, adventurous folks can continue all the way to Fort Casey State Park, eight miles away.

CAMPING

In addition to the campgrounds at Fort Ebey and Fort Casey State Parks, you could try **Rhododendron Park** a Department of Natural Resources–managed park two miles east of Coupeville on Highway 20. It's easy to miss; look for the small blue camping sign on the highway. Here you'll find eight free in-the-woods campsites (with water) in a second-growth stand of Douglas fir trees, with an understory that includes blooming rhododendrons each April and May.

Accommodations

Coupeville is blessed with many historic buildings, several of which have been turned into delightful B&Bs and inns. Unfortunately, they are priced accordingly and equally likely to be full on summer weekends. Be sure to make advance reservations. A useful website with links to local lodging places is www.cometocoupeville.com.

UNDER $100

Tyee Motel (405 S. Main St., 360/678-6616, $70–80 s or d) has nine basic rooms. **Coupeville Inn** (200 N.W. Coveland St., 360/678-6668 or 800/247-6162, www.coupevilleinn.com, $95–145 s or d) has standard motel rooms with waterside views of Penn Cove.

Anchorage Inn B&B (807 N. Main St., 360/678-5581 or 877/230-1313, www.anchorage-inn.com, $89–149 s or d) offers five guest rooms with private baths in a large and luxurious Victorian-style inn with striking red gables.

$100-150

One of the most striking local places is **Compass Rose B&B** (508 S. Main St., 360/678-5318 or 800/237-3881, www.compassrosebandb.com, $115 s or d), a Queen Anne Victorian home built in 1890 and packed with antiques. Two guest rooms share a bath. Friendly owners, too.

Garden Isle Guest Cottages B&B (207 N.W. Coveland St., 360/678-5641 or 877/881-1203, www.gardenislecottages.com, $130–140 d) features two cottages with kitchens and a continental breakfast. One cottage has a gas fireplace, and both share an outside hot tub.

The Inn at Penn Cove B&B (702 N. Main, 360/678-8000 or 800/688-2683, www.whidbey.net/penncove, $129–149 d) spreads across two lovingly restored Victorian homes built in 1887 and 1891. Inside each are three guest rooms with private or shared baths and fireplaces. Kids are accepted with advance notice.

$150-200

Captain Whidbey Inn (2072 W. Captain Whidbey Inn Rd., 360/678-4097 or 800/366-4097, www.captainwhidbey.com) has European-style rooms with shared baths ($94–165 d) and suites ($171 d) inside this classic two-story inn built in 1907 from madrona logs. Also here are modern cabins and cottages ($193–230 d). The madrona-draped grounds face Penn Cove. Even if you aren't staying here, be sure to stop and take in the scenery or sip a drink in the bar. The lodge also operates a 52-foot wooden ketch, the ***Cutty Sark,*** with regularly scheduled sailing trips.

Right next to Fort Casey State Park, **Fort Casey Inn** (360/678-5050 or 866/661-6604, www.fortcaseyinn.com) consists of 10 restored Georgian revival homes that served as officers' quarters during World War I. These large two-story homes are divided into two duplex units each, with full kitchens and private baths. The basements were built to be used as bomb shelters in case of attack, and some still have the original steel-shuttered windows. These duplexes rent for $165–175 for up to four people. One motel-style unit is also available for $85 s or d.

Food

The townies on Whidbey like to take their squeezes out on dates to **Christopher's** (23 NW Front St., 360/678-5480, www.christophersonwhidbey.com, 11:30 A.M.–2 P.M. Mon.–Fri., noon–2:30 P.M. Sat. and 5–9 P.M. daily, $18). They don't come for the view—there isn't one—or trendy decor. The main attraction here is the food. The chef simmers art on the stove, with creations such as raspberry barbecued salmon ($19.50) and bacon-wrapped pork tenderloin with smoked cheddar gratin ($17.95).

Get dependably good pub grub—including

fish and chips, Reubens, and mussel chowder—at **Toby's Tavern** (8 NW Front St., 360/678-4222, 11 A.M.–10 P.M. daily, $10). The 1884 red building *is* a bar, so no kids allowed.

The Oystercatcher (901 Grace St., 360/678-0683, www.oystercatcherwhidbey.com, 5–9 P.M. Wed.–Sun., closed Mon.–Tues., entrées $25) is a delightful little out-of-the-way place behind the *Coupeville Examiner* newspaper office. The limited menu changes frequently but always includes shellfish hors d'oeuvres.

You can also get a mussel appetizer and a drink and enjoy the quiet ambience in the dining room at **Captain Whidbey Inn** (2072 W. Captain Whidbey Inn Rd., 360/678-4097 or 800/366-4097, www.captainwhidbey.com, 5–9 P.M. daily), which offers unparalleled views of Penn Cove Reservations required; dinner entrées run $18–25.

Information and Services

Coupeville lacks a visitors center, but the museum has local brochures, or you can get them from the **Central Whidbey Chamber of Commerce** (360/678-5434, www.centralwhidbeychamber.com). The **Coupeville Library** (360/678-2911, www.sno-isle.org) is located at 788 N.W. Alexander Street.

Coupeville Arts Center (360/678-3396, www.coupevillearts.org) teaches a wide range of first-rate workshops throughout the year, from photography to watercolor to fiber arts. For books, head to **The Kingfisher** (360/678-3252) on Front Street.

Getting There and Around

Island Transit, (360/678-7771, or 800/240-8747, www.islandtransit.org) has free bus service Mon.–Sat. throughout Whidbey. **Whidbey Scenic Flights** (360/678-8384) offers airplane flights over the island.

OAK HARBOR

Settled first by sea captains, then the Irish, and finally by immigrants from Holland, Oak Harbor takes its name from the many ancient Garry oak trees that grew here; those remaining are protected by law. The arrival of the military during World War II transformed this town, making it a busy place.

The city's historic downtown faces the water and retains a bit of local character. But the Highway 20 arterial comes as a shock if you've just driven in from genteel Coupeville and Langley; this commercial area is filled with strip malls and suburban flotsam. The convenience kind of makes up for it—Oak Harbor is the cheapest place to pick up gas and groceries on the island and there are number of affordable motels here.

Sights

The **Whidbey Island Naval Air Station** (360/279-1080 or www.naswi.navy.mil) just outside Oak Harbor is home to electronic warfare squadrons of EA-6B carrier-based jets, EA-6B Prowlers, and EP-3E surveillance planes. Watch planes landing from the CPO Club (open to the public) on Ault Field Road along the north border of the base. The National Park Service has developed an ecotour driving/biking map for a portion of the base; get a brochure from the Oak Harbor Visitor Center. Be aware that a valid ID is required to get on the base.

Entertainment and Events

Whidbey Playhouse, (730 S.E. Midway Blvd., 360/679-2237 or 800/606-7529, www.whidbeyplayhouse.com) has plays throughout the year.

For something completely different, **Blue Fox Drive-In Theatre** (1403 Monroe Landing Rd., 360/675-5667 www.bluefoxdrivein.com) is one of the last outdoor movie theaters in Washington.

The last weekend in April, Oak Harbor's Dutch roots appear as it hosts **Holland Happening**—a downtown street festival, parade, international dance festival, Dutch dinner, and tulip show in Holland Gardens. The **4th of July** includes a parade and fireworks, followed in mid-July by **Whidbey Island Race Week** (360/675-6399, www.whidbey.net/raceweek), one of the top 20 yachting regattas in the world. In early December, the **Christmas Boat Parade** departs from Oak Harbor, proceeding around Penn Cove to the Coupeville Wharf and back.

Sports and Recreation

City Beach Park (360/679-5551), at the end of Beeksma Drive, has a sandy beach with piles of driftwood, sheltered picnic tables, swimming and wading pools, a gazebo, tennis and baseball facilities, campsites along the lagoon, and a Dutch-style windmill. There's a nice view of the peaceful and protected harbor from here, and a great kiddie playground. Look for ducks along the shore. Tent camping costs $8 and RVs $15 with full hookups; no reservations.

Camping is also available at beautiful **Deception Pass State Park,** nine miles north, for $14–20. Other options are **Quinn's Deception Pass Campground** (5050 N. Hwy. 20, 360/675-9597) or nearby **Sunrise Resort at Deception Pass** (550 W. Cornet Bay Rd., 360/675-6575). And there's always the local Wal-Mart (1250 SW Erie St.) lot, which becomes an unofficial RV park each summer.

Smith Park at Midway Boulevard has a fine collection of old Garry oak trees and a large erratic boulder left behind by the last ice age.

Joseph Whidbey State Park (www.parks.wa.gov) just south of the Naval Air Station on Swantown Road, is largely undeveloped, with picnic tables and a few trails. The real attraction here is a long and scenic beach, one of the finest on the island.

The hip-roofed **Neil Barn** (100 E. Whidbey Ave.) is owned by the city parks department and used as a roller-skating rink.

The city is home to the 18-hole **Gallery Golf Course** (Crosby Rd., 360/257-2295).

Rent kayaks from **Adventure Marine** (at the marina, 360/675-9395).

Accommodations

It might not be as scenic as Whidbey's more idyllic towns, but Oak Harbor can be just the right post on which budgeting families can hitch for the night. Lodging options are less expensive and the town has an abundance of fast-food joints and grocery stores.

Among the cheapest is **Queen Ann Motel** (450 S.E. Pioneer Way, 360/675-2209, $59–79 d). Interiors are plain painted cinderblock and are worn, but the rooms have kitchenettes with stove, microwave, and fridge. The property has a heated indoor pool and an outdoor picnic area with a barbecue.

Kitchenette units are more expensive at **Auld Holland Inn** (33575 Hwy. 20, 360/675-2288 or 800/228-0148, $59–149 d) but worth the extra couple of bucks, as they are a bit more charming and clean. This Dutch-style motel has a whirling windmill outside and old country furnishings with floral linens within. The property is flush with amenities, including an outdoor pool and hot tub, a sauna, tennis court, exercise room, and lawn games.

Though slightly more expensive than the motel competition, **Coachman Inn** (35959 Hwy. 20, 360/675-0727 or 800/635-0043, www.thecoachmaninn.com, $105–209 d) is a good option to keep on the summertime short list. The well-tended rooms range from basic units to suites and even a townhouse apartment. There's an outdoor pool and exercise room, and continental breakfast is included.

Nicest of the bunch is **Best Western Harbor Plaza** (33175 Hwy. 20, 360/679-4567 or 800/927-5478, www.bestwesternwashingon.com, $149–169 d), which kids love for the deluxe breakfast's do-it-yourself waffle maker and the fresh popcorn and cookies served in the afternoon. Rack rates here are some of the priciest in Oak Harbor, but you're also more likely to get a deep discount online for this place than any other accommodations in Oak Harbor. The property has an outdoor pool, hot tub, and fitness center.

Food

As might be expected given the strong military presence in Oak Harbor, most eating places fall in the traditional American food groups: McDonald's, pizza joints, and steakhouses.

The best among these types of establishments is **Flyers** (32295 Hwy. 20, 360/675-5858, www.eatatflyers.com, 11:30 A.M.–9 P.M.

daily, $15), a kid-friendly brewery restaurant with a book-length menu that goes far beyond the typical fried-meal-in-a-basket pub grub. Flyers makes 10 different salads, quality prime rib and steaks, seafood, and even lamb shanks. This boisterous place is definitely meant to satisfy big parties with different tastes.

For Cantonese and Szechuan meals, stop by **China Harbor Restaurant** (630 SE Pioneer Way, 360/679-1557, 11 A.M.–midnight daily, $9). Another dependable standby in town is **Zorba's** (841 SE Pioneer Way, 360/279-8322, 11 A.M.–9 P.M. Mon.–Sat., $13), a delightful Greek restaurant where you'll find staples like gyros and some Italian dishes, along with more traditional entrées like moussaka. It gets very busy (and loud) most evenings.

If you intend on touring the island for the day, stop by **Bayleaf** (720 S.E. Pioneer Way, Ste. 1-B, 360/675-6600, www.bayleaf.us, 11 A.M.–6 P.M. Tues.–Fri., 10 A.M.–5 P.M. Sat., noon–4 P.M. Sun.) first for some picnic provisions. This little store is a foodie's delight, serving up fresh artisan cheeses, gourmet cured meats, olives, fresh rustic breads, fancy crackers, and a good selection of wine to pair with it all.

The **Oak Harbor Public Market** (360/675-0472) is held 3–7 P.M. Thursday June–September next to the visitors center. Head to **Safeway** (8075 80th St. NW, 360/679-3011) for the best selection of groceries on the island.

Information

The **Oak Harbor Visitor Center** (32630 Hwy. 20, 360/675-3535, www.oakharborchamber.org) is open 9 A.M.–5 P.M. Monday–Friday all year, plus 10 A.M.–4 P.M. Saturday in the summer. The **Oak Harbor Library** (360/675-5115, www.sno-isle.org) is located at 1000 S.E. Regatta Drive.

Getting There and Around

Catch **Island Transit** (360/321-6688 or 800/240-8747, www.islandtransit.org, free) Route 1 in Oak Harbor bound for parts south and Clinton. Route 5 snakes north all the way off the island to Mount Vernon.

Ride on **Airporter Shuttle** (360/380-8800 or 800/235-5247, www.airporter.com) between Oak Harbor and Sea-Tac Airport.

DECEPTION PASS STATE PARK

Washington's most popular state park, Deception Pass is best known for the spectacular green bridge that spans the narrow waterway that flows between Fidalgo and Whidbey Islands. When Capt. George Vancouver first sighted this waterway in 1792, he called it Port Gardner. When he realized the inlet was actually a tidal passage between two islands, he renamed it Deception Pass, a name that took on greater significance from the swirling and tricky waters here that warded sailors off until 1852, when Capt. Thomas Coupe sailed a fully rigged three-masted vessel through the narrow entrance.

Nine miles north of Oak Harbor on Highway 20, the 3,600-acre park covers ground on either end of the bridge and offers facilities that rival those of some national parks: swimming and fishing at two lakes, four miles of shoreline, 28 miles of hiking trails, fresh and saltwater fishing, boating, picnicking, rowboat rentals, boat launches, viewpoints, an environmental learning center, and several hundred campsites.

Sights

Completed in 1935, **Deception Pass Bridge,** a steel cantilever-truss beauty built by the Civilian Conservation Corps (CCC), which also built many other park structures. The bridge towers 182 feet above the water. It's estimated that each year more than three million people stop at the bridge to peer over the edge at the turbulent water and whirlpools far below, or to enjoy the sunset vistas. The best view of this architectural marvel, though, is from below. Check out the trusses from their underbelly at the south end of the bridge. The beach below is accessible by taking the road to the North Beach picnic area.

Bowman Bay is just north of the bridge on the west side of the highway and has campsites, a boat launch, and a fishing pier. Also

THE MAIDEN OF DECEPTION PASS

The Samish Tribe told the story of the beautiful Maiden of Deception Pass, Ko-Kwal-Alwoot. She was gathering shellfish along the beach when the sea spirit saw her and was at once enamored; as he took her hand, Ko-Kwal-Alwoot became terrified, but the sea spirit reassured her, saying he only wished to gaze upon her loveliness. She returned often, listening to the sea spirit's declarations of love.

One day a young man came from the sea to ask Ko-Kwal-Alwoot's father for permission to marry her. Her father, suspecting that living underwater would be hazardous to his daughter's health, refused, despite the sea spirit's claim that Ko-Kwal-Alwoot would have eternal life. Miffed, the sea spirit brought drought and famine to the old man's people until he agreed to give his daughter away. There was one condition: that she return once every year so the old man could be sure she was properly cared for. The agreement was made, and the people watched as Ko-Kwal-Alwoot walked into the water until only her hair, floating in the current, was visible. The famine and drought ended at once.

Ko-Kwal-Alwoot kept her promise for the next four years, returning to visit her people, but every time she came she was covered with more and more barnacles and seemed eager to return to the sea. On her last visit her people told her she need not return unless she wanted to; since that time, she's provided abundant shellfish and clean spring water in that area. Legend has it that her hair can be seen floating to and fro with the tide in Deception Pass.

Today this Samish legend is inscribed on a story pole on Fidalgo Island. To get there, follow Highway 20 to Fidalgo Island, go west at Pass Lake, following the signs for Bowman Bay and Rosario Beach, and hike the trail toward Rosario Head.

here is the **CCC Interpretive Center** (Thurs.–Mon. summers only), inside one of the attractive stone structures built by the young men of CCC.

Rosario Beach, just north of Bowman Bay, features a delightful picnic ground with CCC-built stone shelters. The **Maiden of Deception Pass** totem pole here commemorates the tale of a Samish girl who became the bride of the water spirit.

Sports and Recreation

WATER SPORTS

Only electric motors, canoes, or rowboats are allowed on the park's lakes. The most visible of the two is **Pass Lake,** around which Highway 20 curves. This is a fly-fisher's delight, and on any given weekend you're likely to see plenty of anglers looping their lines overhead as they bob in float-tubes. The fishery is delicate here, so there's only catch-and-release angling allowed. You can observe beaver dams, muskrats, and mink in the marshes on the south side of shallow **Cranberry Lake,** which also hosts a seasonal concession stand. There's good fishing for trout here, and the warm water makes it a favorite swimming hole. The waters around the pass are also a magnet for anglers, with good saltwater fishing for lingcod, salmon, smelt, and bottom fish. One of the best holes for some leisurely shore fishing is **Hoypus Point,** at the end of Coronet Bay Road.

Anglers and pleasure boaters can get their craft in the water at the one-lane launch at Bowman Bay. But be aware that the tricky waters of the pass still require skill to navigate, even today—at peak tide the current can reach up to 8 knots.

This warning is especially important for kayakers—don't even think about crossing the pass by paddle unless you have years of experience. Instead, stick to the calmer waters along the rest of the park's shorelines, which can provide hours of exploration and a chance to find seals, porpoise, and other marinelife along the way. **Anacortes Kayak Tours** (800/992-1801, May.–Oct., $35 adults, $25 children) caters to first-time paddlers and

© ERICKA CHICKOWSKI

Deception Pass offers two excellent freshwater fishing lakes.

those without their own boats during its 1.5-hour guided trips within Bowman Bay.

If you are set on riding through the pass but you don't have the boat or the maritime skills, then hop aboard ***The Island Whaler,*** an open-deck jet catamaran run by Deception Pass Tours (360/914-0096 or 888/909-8687, www.deceptionpasstours.com, $21 adults, $19 children), which runs hourly boat tours from April through October. Tickets are sold at a concession in the parking lot on the south end of the bridge. Directions to the dock are given after you buy.

If you get your kicks below water rather than over it, then bring your dive gear out to Rosario Beach. Just offshore is an underwater park that stretches all the way to Northwest Island.

HIKING

A delightful and scenic trail leads down from the southwest side of the bridge to a rocky beach strewn with bleached driftwood.

A 15-minute hike to the highest point on the island, 400-foot **Goose Rock,** provides views of the San Juan Islands, Mt. Baker, Victoria, and Fidalgo Island, and possibly bald eagles soaring overhead. The trail starts at the south end of the bridge, heading east from either side of the highway; take the wide trail as it follows the pass, then take one of the unmarked spur trails uphill to the top. A half-mile hiking trail circles Rosario Head, the wooded point of land that juts into Rosario Bay (technically part of the 75-acre Sharpe County Park). The shoreline is a fine place to explore tidepools.

Other hiking trails lead throughout the park, ranging from short nature paths to unimproved trails for experienced hikers only.

CAMPING

With 178 campsites, **Deception Pass State Park** (360/675-2417) offers some of the finest camping in this part of Washington, with tall Douglas fir trees and a gorgeous lakeside setting. Unfortunately, the park's popularity means that you'll be accompanied by a multitude of fellow visitors. The primary campground along Cranberry Lake has year-round sites, and a second campground (open summers only) is just north of the bridge at Bowman Bay. The cost for both is $14 for tents, $20 for RVs, or $6 for bikes, including hot showers and disposal stations. Make reservations ($7 extra) at 888/226-7688 or www.parks.wa.gov. Head to the park's outdoor amphitheater on weekend evenings in the summer for natural history lectures and slide shows.

Everett

Flanked by craggy mountains to the east and sweeping vistas of Whidbey Island to the west, Everett is a convenient stopover for those in search of recreational escape. Highway 2 begins its eastward march to Stevens Pass and Wenatchee here, and the Snohomish River curves north on the edge of town and creates a maze of islands and sloughs before emptying into Puget Sound.

Though the town is in the process of gentrification by commuters slogging through traffic to Seattle each day, it is at heart a blue collar community. The neighborhoods here are filled with sailors serving at nearby Naval Station Everett, lineworkers laboring at the town's Boeing factory, and even some bastions of Everett's oldest trade working away at the local lumberyards and paper mill.

Visitors will find South Everett a forgettable tangle of strip malls, chain restaurants, and used car lots, but venture north and you'll be rewarded with a small but pleasant downtown enclave of restored brick buildings and well-tended historic homes.

© ERICKA CHICKOWSKI

a view over the Everett waterfront

SIGHTS

Future of Flight Center and Boeing Tour

Aviation buffs can get a close-up look at how Boeing puts together its giant 747, 767, 777, and future 787 jets at its gargantuan Everett factory plant. Big planes need a big building—this structure is the largest building by volume in the world. The facility is so huge, in fact, that you'll sometimes see workers riding on one of the bicycles the company keeps to get them around in a hurry.

The tour begins at the slick Future of Flight Center (8415 Paine Field Blvd., 425/438-8100 or 800/464-1476, www.futureofflight.org, $15 adults, $8 children under 15), where kids and kids-at-heart flock to the 727 flight deck to imagine they're at the controls. Visitors will also encounter narrated videos on Boeing innovations of the past and the near future, flight simulators, and a 200-yard runway with the nose of a 727 about to take off.

Then it is on to the assembly line tour, a 90-minute walk through the building and onto an observation deck that overlooks shiny airplanes under construction.

For security reasons, visitors are not allowed to bring cameras, cell phones, purses, or other personal items on the tour. Babies and toddlers

BOEING STATS

Boeing has grown from the tiny company formed by William E. Boeing in a Seattle barn into the second-largest aerospace and defense contractor in the world. While it is no longer headquartered in Washington, Boeing is still a major employer here.

EVERETT ASSEMBLY BUILDING FACTS

- The building is the largest in the world in terms of volume, enclosing 472 million cubic feet of space.
- The site covers 1,025 acres.
- Boeing owns a 33,000-square-foot rail-terminal building next to the factory.
- Up to 15 railcars deliver parts to the assembly building per day.
- Overhead cranes in the building reach to 90 feet in height and move along 31 miles of crane rail.
- 25,000 employees work three shifts at the site.

are also banned from the tour and there is no daycare on premises, so plan accordingly. Tours begin on the hour starting at 9 A.M., with the last tour departing at 3 P.M.

Jetty Island

Families flock to Jetty Island (425/257-8300, www.everettwa.org) as regularly as the waterfowl and sea mammals. This two-mile stretch of sand is a happy byproduct of dredging done at the nearby mouth of the Snohomish River.

The island is an ideal spot to strike out with binoculars dangling from your neck and a picnic basket from your arms. Don't forget a bathing suit—the shallow water nearby warms up to 70°F by August. A free passenger ferry (425/257-8300, www.everettwa.org) departs Marina Park for Jetty Island every half hour from July to mid-September.

Downtown Everett

In its early years, Everett was home to some of the timber industry's most successful entrepreneurs. These lumber barons built elaborate mansions in the north end of town on Grand and Rucker Avenues, many of which still stand.

They surround a small but well-restored commercial district around the vicinity of Hewitt Avenue from Broadway west to Grand Avenue. If you tour down Grand Avenue, be sure to stop at the grassy strip that is **Grand Avenue Park.** With your back to the stately homes in this neighborhood, you will get a panoramic view of Port Gardner and **Everett Marina,** the Puget Sound's second largest. That will whet your appetite for another great viewpoint at American Legion Park less than two miles away—simply head north on Grand Avenue and veer right to **Alverson Boulevard** when the road forks. You can't miss the grassy banks of the park sitting on the bluff.

Museums and Art

Paine Field is home to the **Museum of Flight Restoration Center** (425/745-5150, www.museumofflight.org, 9 A.M.–5 P.M. Tues.–Sat., $2 donation), where aircraft are restored for this outstanding Seattle museum. The center is located in Building C-72. Get here from the Boeing Tour Center by returning to Highway 526 eastbound and taking the first exit (Airport Road). Head south on Airport Road for a mile, and turn right onto 100th Street SW. Building C-72 is on the right side.

The **Everett Center for the Arts** (1507 Wall St., 425/257-8380, www.artscouncilofsnoco.org, 10 A.M.–5 P.M. Mon.–Fri., 11 A.M.–3 P.M. Sat.), in the historic Monte Cristo Hotel, exhibits works of regional artists and includes a permanent collection of Dale Chihuly glass.

The **Imagine Children's Museum** (1502 Wall St., 425/258-1006, www.imagineCM.org, 10 A.M.–4 P.M. Tues., Wed., and Sat., 10 A.M.–5:30 P.M. Thurs.–Fri., 11 A.M.–5 P.M. Sun., $7) has fun children's exhibits, including a rooftop playground, art studio, and great make-believe settings like a bank, train, and café.

ENTERTAINMENT AND EVENTS

Nightlife

Check the Friday edition of the ***The Herald*** for the weekly music scene, or get the same at www.heraldnet.com. The sprawling **Club Broadway** (1611 Everett Ave., 425/259-2756, www.clubbroadway.com) has five dance floors, with music on Friday and Saturday nights for all tastes: top-40 discs in one room, a rhythm and blues room, plus a sports bar with pool tables, darts, karaoke, and classic rock bands. The Big Apple Casino here allows off-track betting, blackjack ($100 limit), and pull tabs.

Get your fill of twang and twirls at **McCabe's American Music Café** (3120 Hewitt Ave., 425/252-3082), which plays country music and offers dance lessons. Meanwhile, **Alligator Soul** (2013 Hewitt Ave., 425/259-6311) cranks the blues on Friday and Saturday nights.

Spectator Sports and Concerts

The 10,000-seat Comcast Arena at Everett Events Center is the largest concert venue in the North Sound region. The arena regularly hosts top-billed stars such as Rod Stewart, Lynyrd Skynyrd, and Bette Midler. It is also the home rink for the **Everett Silvertips** (www.everettsilvertips.com), a major junior hockey team playing in the Western Hockey League. When the puck isn't on the ice, this is also a favorite stopover for big-name ice-skating shows like *Disney on Ice*.

The Seattle Mariners' Class-A farm team, the **Everett Aquasox** (3802 Broadway, 425/258-3673, www.aquasox.com), plays at Everett Memorial Stadium from mid-June to Labor Day. The games offer great family fun.

The Arts

Theatrical performances are held throughout the year in the new showpiece **Performing Arts Center** (2710 Wetmore Ave., 425/257-8600). The theater features touring musicals, plays, concerts, and regional performing arts groups, and also houses the fine **Arts Council Gift Gallery.** The remodeled **Historic Everett Theatre** (2911 Colby Ave., 425/258-6766, www.everetttheatre.org) is home to movies, concerts, and live theater productions throughout the year.

The **Everett Symphony** (425/257-8382, www.everettsymphony.org) performs at the Everett Civic Auditorium October through June. The **Port Gardner Bay Chamber Music Society,** (360/658-1129, www.everettchorale.org) performs at the historic Hartley Mansion (2300 Rucker Ave.) during the winter months. For something less formal, the **Music in the Parks** program (425/257-8300) brings live music to local parks on Sunday and Tuesday afternoons in July and August.

Festivals and Events

Held on the first weekend in June, **Salty Sea Days** (425/339-1113, www.saltyseadays.org) features a parade, Navy ship tours, hydroplane races, an arts show, live music, and outrigger canoe races. Return in August for two days of blues music at **Blues by the Bay** (425/339-1113, www.bluesbythebay.com).

A summer-long recreational event from July to September sponsored by the parks department, **Jetty Island Days** (425/257-8300) includes free ferry rides to the island from Marina Village, guided nature walks, sailing and rowing regattas, concerts, and campfire programs, as well as picnicking, beachcombing, and bird-watching on a saltwater beach.

SHOPPING

The area's largest shopping center is **Everett Mall** (www.everettmall.com), with over 140 small shops, as well as giant department stores Macy's and Sears. Everett Mall Way and intersecting Evergreen Way are also a mecca for discount shoppers, with enough strip malls to keep granny shopping for days. Along the bay at **Everett Marina Village** is an 1890s-style waterfront marketplace with restaurants, gift shops, and clothing stores, to name a few.

The **Everett Public Market** (2804 Grand Ave.) has more than 100 antique dealers, plus fresh fish and produce, and Sisters Restaurant.

For discount shopping, it's hard to beat

Evergreen Way (Highway 99), where all the big stores can be found, complete with acres of paved parking spaces. It's not the most attractive area, but it serves a purpose. A surprising number of thrift stores cluster around Evergreen at 52nd Street, including Value Village, St. Vincent de Paul's, Salvation Army, and Children's Hospital Thrift Store.

SPORTS AND RECREATION

Water Sports

The **Everett Marina** (1720 W Marine View Dr., 425/259-6001, www.portofeverett.com) is the second largest in Puget Sound, with three large guest docks with water and electricity hookups, along with shower, laundry, and restroom facilities. Reservations for moorage ($0.55 per foot per night in winter, $0.75 per foot per night in summer) are accepted during the summer between Memorial Day and Labor Day and on a first-come, first-serve basis the rest of the year. There are also pump-out and dump facilities, a fuel dock, and several restaurants on premises. Guests can stay up to six hours at no charge.

Skippers looking to get their craft into the waters of the Puget Sound should go a couple blocks away to the **10th Street Boat Launch** (10th St. and Marine View Dr., 425/259-6001, 4 A.M.–11 P.M. daily Apr.–Sept., 6 A.M.–7 P.M. daily Oct.–Mar., $5 per launch).

If you're without a boat, **Sail Express** (1724 W. Marine View Dr., www.sailexpress.com) rents sail boats and offers sailing lessons out of the marina. Also operating out of the marina is **Northwest Fishing Charters** (206/949-0221, http://nwfishingcharters.com), which offers a standard seven-hour fishing trip for $170 per person, as well as private charters aboard its 28' boats.

In the summer, you can rent canoes, rowboats, sailboats, and paddleboats from **Everett Parks and Recreation Department** at Silver Lake (425/257-8300, www.ci.everett.wa.us). This is also a great place to swim and sunbathe in the summertime—a lifeguard is on duty between late June and Labor Day

Golf

Perched on a hill overlooking the Everett waterfront, **American Legion Memorial Course** (144 W. Marine View Dr., 425/259-4653, $30) offers up some primo views of Puget Sound. The grounds are fairly decent for municipal links and the price. Everett's other muni, the **Walter E. Hall Golf Course** (1226 W. Casino Rd., 425/353-4653, $26) is a gentle course that presents the opportunity for a round with the family in a lightly-wooded setting.

Running and Biking

The paved 11-mile-long **Interurban Trail** connects Lynnwood with Everett and is very popular with cyclists and in-line skaters. Also check out the 1.6-mile **Lowell Riverfront Trail** located just off Lenora Street. Get local park information at 425/388-6600 or www.co.snohomish.wa.us/parks.

Camping

There are no nearby public parks with campgrounds, but **Lakeside RV Park** (12321 Hwy. 99 S, 425/347-2970 or 800/468-7275, $34) is on a three-acre lake with all hookups and facilities.

ACCOMMODATIONS

Under $100

There are a bevy of discount hotels and motels in the northern and southern outskirts of town. Particularly beware many of the cut-rate offerings on North Broadway Avenue. Some of these joints are a health inspector's worst nightmare and attract a live-in crowd of questionable character. If you are absolutely desperate for a cheap overnight spot, **Welcome Motor Inn** (1205 N. Broadway Ave., 425/252-8828 or 800/252-5512) has threadbare rooms for $49–72 s or $59–79 d, some with kitchenettes. Nonsmoking rooms still smell smoky here.

A better budget bet is on the south end of town at **Sunrise Motor Inn** (8421 Evergreen Way/Hwy. 99, 425/347-1100 or 888/222-2112, $54–66 s or d), with a continental breakfast.

$100-150

It is worth it to jump up a price bracket. For not much more than a motel, you can stay comfortably at **Gaylord House B&B** (3301 Grand Ave., 425/339-9153 or 888/507-7177, www.gaylordhouse.com, $100–135 s or d), a 1910 Craftsman home in a quietly elegant neighborhood near downtown. The inn has five luxurious guest rooms with antiques, private baths, and gourmet breakfasts. Kids are accepted, and a four-course high tea ($15) is available to guests and the general public by reservation, as are dinners by special request.

At the scenic Everett Marina, **The Inn at Port Gardner** (1700 W. Marine View Dr., 425/252-6779 or 888/252-6779, www.innatportgardner.com, $109–189 d, $235 d for a deluxe suite) has the best hotel view in town. The cannery-style lodge is a good-looking specimen, though the furniture is a bit cheap for the image the exterior and lobby present. But the cleanliness of the rooms, the cheerfulness of the staff, and the dockside location make up for the shortcomings. If you are traveling on business, be sure to tell staffers as much—there is a generous mid-week discount to road warriors.

If you prefer the predictability of chain hotels, your top pick should be the **Holiday Inn Downtown Everett** (3105 Pine St., 877/863-4780, www.holidayinn.com, $126 d). Just a stone's throw from the Everett Transit Center and downtown, and conveniently located right off the freeway, this airy tower hotel has clean and updated rooms, along with a pool, spa, and fitness center. Rooms face away from the freeway for a quiet night's sleep, and morning brings a breakfast buffet smorgasbord that is the envy of other establishments' measly continental offerings.

FOOD

Cafés

Start the day at **The Sisters Restaurant** (2804 Grand Ave., 425/252-0480, 7 A.M.–4 P.M. Mon.–Fri., $8), a friendly place with great breakfast specials and espresso coffees. Lunches include great soups (especially the chilled tomato and avocado), salads, veggie burgers, and homemade ice cream.

If you're down on the marina, find lunchtime panini sandwiches and other tasty light meals at **Meyer's Café** (1700 W. Marine View Dr., 425/259-3875, 6:30 A.M.–4 P.M. Mon.–Thurs., 6:30 A.M.–6 P.M. Fri.–Sat., 7:30 A.M.–4 P.M. Sun., $7).

Steak and Seafood

Everett Marina Village has a couple of popular seafood restaurants with views to match the food. **Anthony's HomePort** (1726 W. Marine View Dr., 425/252-3333, www.anthonys.com, 11 A.M.–3 P.M. Mon.–Sat. and 4:30–9:30 Mon.–Thurs., 4:30–10:30 Fri.–Sat., 3–9:30 P.M. Sun., brunch 10 A.M.–2 P.M. Sun., $30) has fresh Northwest and imported seafood flown in fresh daily, plus tasty fish and chips for a simpler meal. **Anthony's Woodfire Grill** (1726 W. Marine View Dr., 425/258-4000, www.anthonys.com, 11:30 A.M.–3:30 P.M. Wed.–Sun., and 4–9:30 P.M. Mon.–Tues., 3:30–9:30 P.M. Wed.–Thurs. and Sun., 3:30–10:30 Fri.–Sat., $16) serves steak, prime rib, pasta, and seafood.

Alligator Soul (2013 Hewitt Ave., 425/259-6311, www.thealligatorsoul.com, 11 A.M.–9 P.M. Mon.–Sat., closed Sun., $11) is a fun place with heaping helpings of old-South and Cajun favorites, including seafood gumbo and smoked ribs.

In fact located on Silver Lake, **Emory's on Silver Lake** (11830 19th Ave. SE, 425/337-7772, www.emorys.com, 11:30 A.M.–3 P.M. Mon.–Fri. and 4–9 P.M. Mon.–Thurs., 4–10 P.M. Fri.–Sat., 4–8:30 P.M. Sun., brunch 10 A.M.–3 P.M. Sun., $20) is a pleasant, upscale place for seafood and steak.

International

For waterfront views while you enjoy your pasta or pizza, head to **Lombardi's Cucina** (1620 W. Marine View Dr., 425/252-1886, www.lombardiscucina.com, 11:30 A.M.–9:30 P.M. daily, $15), a favorite lunchtime hangout for the suit-and-tie crowd and a very pleasant spot to take a date for late afternoon drinks and appetizers.

Another very good pasta and pizza spot is **Gianni's Ristorante Italiano** (5030 Evergreen Way, 425/252-2435, www.giannisitialian.com, 11 A.M.–10 P.M. Mon.–Thurs., 11 A.M.–midnight Fri.–Sat., 3–9 P.M. Sun., $15), a relic of the Rat Pack days.

Spice of Thai (607 Everett Mall Way SE, 425/290-7900, 11 A.M.–9 P.M. Sun.–Thurs., 11 A.M.–10 P.M. Fri.–Sat., $9) is one of those unexpected gems. Located in a strip mall, this small restaurant cranks out great curries, Thai eggplant, and other specialties for inexpensive prices.

Pub Grub

Sporty's Beef & Brew (6503 Evergreen Way, 425/347-1733, 11 A.M.–11 P.M. daily, $8) serves burgers and beer and attracts sports fans with its large-screen televisions. Two other restaurants offer full-menu dining in a brewpub environment. Right on the main Colby strip downtown, **Flying Pig Brewing Co.** (2929 Colby Ave., 425/339-1393, 11 A.M.–8 P.M. Sun.–Thurs., 11 A.M.–midnight Fri.–Sat., $12) prepares the better menu of the two. By day, servers bring out pub classics like pulled pork and French dip sandwiches and big burgers. But at night, the chefs really roll up their sleeves to serve gourmet dishes such as seafood cioppino, crab cakes, and rib eye with green peppercorn butter.

For beer and atmosphere, **Scuttlebutt Brewing Co.** (on the waterfront at 1524 W. Marine View Dr., 425/257-9316, 11 A.M.–8 P.M. Mon.–Thurs., 11 A.M.–9 P.M. Fri.–Sat., closed Sun.,$10) wins the prize. Situated at Everett Marina, Scuttlebutt brews up consistent award-winning ales that run the rainbow from light blonds to deep porters. The good brews are a magnet for locals during after-work hours.

Bakeries and Markets

On a cold Northwest day, there's nothing more inviting than the warm smell of earthy breads and European pastries that greets you upon entering the door at **Pavé Specialty Bakery** (2613 Colby Ave., 425/252-0250, www.pavebakery.com, 7 A.M.–5 P.M. Mon.–Fri., 7 A.M.–3 P.M. Sat., closed Sun.). Be sure to pair your baked goodies with a bowl of the homemade soup simmered up each day here.

The **Everett Farmers Market** (425/347-2790) takes place at Port Gardner Landing in the marina on 11 A.M.–4 P.M. Sunday June–September.

INFORMATION AND SERVICES

For maps and brochures, stop by the **Snohomish County Visitor Information Center** (101 128th St. SE, 425/348-5802 or 888/338-0976, www.snohomish.org, 9 A.M.–5 P.M. daily, extended summer hours) just off I-5 exit 186.

The **Everett Public Library's** (2702 Hoyt Ave., 425/257-8005, www.epls.org) Northwest Room houses many historical sources from the area. The library only allows cardholders access to its Internet computers, but free Wi-Fi is available for those with laptops.

GETTING THERE AND AROUND

The impressive **Everett Station** is the biggest multimodal station serving Snohomish County. Settled at the junction of Pacific Avenue and Smith Avenue, this is a major hub for local buses, Amtrak trains, and Sounder commuter trains.

By Bus

Everett Transit (425/257-8803, www.everettwa.org/transit) buses provide transportation within the city and to the Mukilteo ferry dock. Route 7 connects downtown to South Everett via Colby Avenue and Evergreen Way, Route 2 connects North Everett and downtown to Boeing facilities, and Route 23 offers service between Everett Station and Mukilteo. Fares are $0.50.

To get out of town, use **Community Transit** (425/778-2185 or 800/562-1375, www.commtrans.org). From Everett station, this service goes south to Lynnwood Transit Station near Edmonds and north to Arlington and Smokey Point via Routes 200, 201, and 202. Also from downtown, Routes 270, 271, and 275 service cities east, including Snohomish, Monroe, and Gold Bar. Service north to Granite Falls and Lake Stevens can be found on Route 280. Commuter service is available on Routes 510 and 513 to Seattle and 532 and 535 to Bellevue. Fares are $1.25 within Snohomish County and $3 to King County destinations.

For long-haul service along the I-5 corridor, **Greyhound** (800/231-2222, www.greyhound.com) is the best bet, linking Everett to Bellingham; Olympia; Vancouver, Washington; and other points south.

Travelers from Spokane or Boise may want to consider the **Northwestern Trailways** (800/366-3830, www.nwadv.com/northw) line running across the mountains over Stevens Pass on Highway 2. Roundtrip fares to Spokane are about $75.

If you're flying into Sea-Tac airport, **Shuttle Express,** (425/981-7000 or 800/487-7433, www.shuttleexpress.com) has door-to-door van service between Sea-Tac and Everett; reservations are required.

By Train

Each weekday Sound Transit's commuter train the **Sounder** (206/398-5000, www.soundtransit.org) runs three times in the morning from Everett to Seattle, with stops at Mukilteo Station and Edmonds Station along the way, and three routes back again in the evening. The ride takes about one hour and costs $4.50 each way.

Amtrak trains serve the area from Everett Station (425/258-2458 or 800/872-7245, www.amtrak.com). The *Empire Builder* heads south to Seattle and east to Spokane and Chicago. The *Cascades* provides daily train connections between Portland, Oregon, and Vancouver, B.C., via Mount Vernon and Bellingham.

Northern Snohomish County

Driving north from Everett on I-5, visitors will encounter a mixture of suburbs, outlet malls, sprawling developments and some slower-paced rural enclaves that point to the logging and agricultural roots of Snohomish County. While towns such as Marysville, Arlington, and Lake Stevens are hardly tourism magnets, Snohomish County does have a few noteworthy destinations and plenty of pretty country roads ready for a leisurely drive.

Coastal Camano Island has a pair of stunning state parks and cabins galore for a relaxing getaway without actually having to get away. Tulalip Casino on the outskirts of Marysville is one of the finest gambling resorts in the state. And southwest of Everett off Highway 2, the charming antique village of Snohomish provides a prime opportunity for window shopping and daydreaming about the good old days.

SIGHTS

Historic Snohomish

The attractive downtown in the charming town of Snohomish has a classic small-town feel and a real sense of the past. Settled in 1859 along the banks of the Snohomish and Pilchuck Rivers, Snohomish maintains a collection of eclectic historic homes and brick commercial buildings that host some of the best antique shops in the state. At the heart of it all is the **Blackman Historic Museum** (118 Ave. B, 360/568-5235, noon–4 P.M. Fri.–Sun. summers only, $2 adults, $1 seniors or children), an 1878 mansion built by a lumberman as a proud display of his cedar shingles. Today it's filled with area artifacts and Victorian furniture.

For more history, head to the **Old Snohomish Village Museum** (2nd and Pine Sts. next to Rite Aid Pharmacy, 360/568-5235, noon–4 P.M. Wed.–Sun., Memorial Day–Labor Day, $2 for adults, $1 for children or seniors). Here are six historic structures and a tiny replicated graveyard.

Camano Island State Park

Located 14 miles southwest from Stanwood, this state park (www.parks.wa.gov, open year-round) covers 134 acres along Saratoga Passage.

The picnic tables on the park's west side provide striking views of Whidbey Island and the Olympics. Hiking trails, including a half-mile interpretive loop, wind through 600-year-old Douglas firs with possible sightings of bald eagles, deer, raccoon, and opossum. Other activities here include fishing from the Point Lowell boat launch and sunbathing along the cliff-backed beaches. The park's two camping areas have tent sites ($13, no hookups) and coin-operated showers.

Other Parks

In addition to nature trails, a duck pond, and a petting zoo (360/659-8581, 10 A.M.–6 P.M. daily mid-May–mid-August), the 50-acre **Jennings Nature Park** (6915 Armar Rd., 360/659-3005) is home to the Gehl House Historical Museum.

Mother Nature's Window (100th St. NE and 55th Ave. NE in Marysville) is a private second-growth forest with an outdoor amphitheater and various carved objects.

Enjoy a picnic lunch at **Twin Rivers Park** along the North Fork of the Stillaguamish River, just east of Arlington.

Lundeen Park covers eight acres of shoreline just west of town, with a roped-off swimming beach, playground, picnic tables, and grand views across the water to the Cascade Range.

Another Snohomish County park—**Wyatt Park**—occupies the west shore of Lake Stevens with a dock, boat launch for anglers and waterskiers, picnic area, plus a sandy beach for sunbathing and swimming.

ENTERTAINMENT AND EVENTS

Pilchuck Glass School

The Pilchuck Glass School (360/445-3111, www.pilchuck.com) east of Stanwood was begun in 1971 by Dale Chihuly, one of the world masters in the creation of glass sculptures. The school occupies a 64-acre wooded campus where both students and faculty live during their intensive May–September sessions. Today Pilchuck has 25 teachers and attracts artists from all over the world. Public tours are given only during an early August open house. The school also puts on an immensely popular annual auction, held in Seattle in October.

Gambling

Operated by the Tulalip Tribes, **Tulalip Casino** (off I-5 at exit 199, 360/651-1111 or 888/272-1111, www.tulalipcasino.com) offers slots, keno, blackjack, craps, roulette, baccarat, and poker. This massive casino is the closest it comes to Vegas in Washington and gamblers will enjoy the on-site spa, hotel, and free valet parking when they come here for a good time.

Arlington Events

Arlington's airport is the third largest general aviation facility in Puget Sound and calls itself the world's largest ultralight airport. On the second weekend of July, it is home to the **Northwest Experimental Aircraft Association Fly-In** (360/435-5857, www.nweaa.org), America's third biggest fly-in. It includes experimental planes, military aircraft, hot-air balloons, and an air show.

The weekends around the 4th of July bring **Arlington Festival** (www.ci.arlington.wa.us), the town's annual celebration, with parades, an auto show, triathlon, and rubber duck race.

Harvest Events

The third week in June brings the **Strawberry Festival** (360/659-766, www.marysvillestrawberryfestival.com), the town's tribute to one of its major crops. This is the area's biggest summer event, with parades, a carnival, car show, art and food booths, and adult trike races.

Starting in late September, several local farms create amazingly intricate **corn mazes** and open their **pumpkin patches** for family fun and frolics in the fields. Get a brochure showing the locations from the chamber of commerce. The best corn maze is created by **The Farm** (7301 Rivershore Rd., 425/334-4124).

Snohomish Events

The town's biggest event is **Kla Ha Ya Days** (360/568-7076, www.klahayadays.com) on the third week of July. Kla Ha Ya is Snohomish for Welcome; activities include a carnival, parade, frog jump, arts and crafts, and entertainment.

The **Snohomish Classic Car and Hot Rod Display** (360/568-2526, http://cityofsnohomish.com) is the last Sunday of September. Over 700 cars and trucks line the streets of downtown Snohomish.

SHOPPING

Snohomish Antiques

With more than 15 local dealers in vintage goods, Snohomish is justified in calling itself the "Antique Capital of the Northwest." Antique shops of all sorts line First Street, including ones specializing in old toys, Victorian furnishings, realistic models of sailing ships, Persian rugs, and clocks. The biggest of all is **Star Center Antique Mall** (829 2nd St.), where 200 dealers have small booths, covering such specialties as marbles, Chinese scrolls, or historic newspapers. Bibliophiles also must stop by **Upper Case Books** (121 Glen Ave., 360/568-5987), which has a trove of thousands of used, out-of-print, and rare books.

Tulalip Outlets

Cozied right up to the Tulalip Casino, **Seattle Premium Outlets** (10600 Quil Ceda Blvd., 360/654-3000, 10 A.M.–9 P.M. Mon.–Sat., 10 A.M.–7 P.M. Sun.) is the nicest outlet center in Western Washington, with over a hundred primo shops such as Coach, Burberry, Calvin Klein, and Ralph Lauren taking up residence in this outdoor shopping complex.

SPORTS AND RECREATION

Cycling

The enormously popular **Centennial Trail** follows an old railway route, connecting Snohomish with Lake Stevens, eight miles north. This paved trail is a great spot for biking, in-line skating, or running.

Scenic Flights and Balloon Rides

Get a glimpse of the rich farmlands, verdant forests and towering peaks of Snohomish County from up above. Hop aboard a basket and watch the envelope fill with hot air aboard the colorful balloons launched by **Airial Balloon Company** (360/485-3658, www.airialballoon.com). Or take a more conventional ride aboard a plane on one of the scenic flights offered by **Snohomish Flying Service** (360/568-1541, www.snohomishflying.com).

Golf

Nearby is the 18-hole **Kayak Point Golf Course** (360/652-9676 or 800/562-3094, www.golfkayak.com, $42), considered one of Washington's finest public courses.

Camping

Twelve miles north of Marysville, **Wenberg State Park** (360/652-7417 or 888/226-7688, www.parks.wa.gov) on Lake Goodwin has a very popular swimming beach, fishing for rainbow and cutthroat trout, waterskiing, a concession stand for fishing supplies and snacks, plus campsites ($9–14 for tents; $20 with hookups) on 46 acres. Open year-round. Get here early on summer weekends to find a space, or pay $7 extra to make reservations.

Covering 650 acres, **Kayak Point County Park** (425/388-6600, www.co.snohomish.wa.us/parks), approximately 15 miles west of Marysville on Marine View Drive, is home to a popular swimming beach, picnic area, and boat launch. Camp here year-round for $12 tents or $17 RVs. Yurts are available for $35. No showers, and the restrooms are closed in the winter months.

Year-round camping ($12 for tents; $17 for hookups) is available at **River Meadows County Park** (360/435-3441, www.co.snohomish.wa.us/parks) several miles east of town on the South Fork of the Stillaguamish River. Drive east on Highway 530 for 0.75 mile, turn right onto Arlington Heights, and continue two miles. Turn right on Jordan Road, and drive another three miles to the park. River Meadows Park offers enjoyable hiking trails, picnic grounds, and a mile of river shoreline for fishing. The surrounding area is filled with farms with all sorts of contented critters, from long-haired Scottish cattle to Peruvian horses. Lots of horses are pastured around here, and Byle's Tit Farm (hey, I don't name these places) makes a great place to pose for a comical photo.

Park RVs at **Smokey Point RV Park** (17019 28th Dr. NE, 360/652-7300 or 800/662-7275), **Mystic Mountain** (29909 Oso Loop Rd., 360/435-5888) or **Camp Ki RV Resort** (2904 Lakewood Rd., 360/652-0619).

Or motor to the Stanwood Fairgrounds (360/445-2806), where the **Stanwood-Camano Community Fair** is held in late July and early August. More RV parking can be had at **Cedar Grove Resort & Campground** (16529 Lake Goodwin Rd., 360/652-7083), south of town along Lake Goodwin, and **Lake Goodwin Resort** (4726 176th St. NW, 800/242-8169).

Scenic Drives

For a delightful country drive, head southeast from Stanwood on the road to the tiny burg called **Silvana.** Along the way, you'll wind along wooded Prestliens Bluff, overlooking big dairy farms, haystacks, and aging barns.

ACCOMMODATIONS

Under $100

There are a number of cheap motor inns along the I-5 corridor between Marysville and Mount Vernon. I found the best one in Arlington, off exit 206. The **Smokey Point Motor Inn** (17329 Smokey Point Dr., 360/659-8561, $69 s or $79 d) doesn't look like much from the outside, and the rooms probably haven't been updated in decades, but they are the absolute cleanest budget units along this stretch.

The best deals in this area are away from the freeways at Camano Island's two state parks. **Camano Island State Park** ($43 for up to 5) rents rustic cabins in the woods that sleep five. These truly are roughing-it set-ups, as there are no kitchens; bathrooms and pay-showers are shared with campers. Outside each cabin is a covered porch, pedestal grill, fire ring, and picnic table.

One of Washington's newest state parks, ☾ **Cama Beach State Park** was a fishing resort built in the 1930s. The views are spectacular from the waterfront cedar cabins and bungalows lined up on the beach here. Standard cabins sleep five and come with refrigerator, sink, microwave, and a coffee pot. Showers are shared. Waterfront cabins go for $45 per night, while second row cabins rent for $27. The deluxe bungalows also sleep five and have similar amenities, with the addition of small private baths and a separate bedroom. They rent for $56 nightly.

All of the cabins at the two Camano Island parks lack linen service, so you'll need to bring along sheets and blankets, as well as kitchen implements.

$100-150

The comfortable **Inn at Snohomish** (323 2nd St., 360/568-2208 or 800/548-9993, www.snohomishinn.com) has standard motel rooms for $122 s or d, and ones with whirlpool tubs for $142 d.

Countryman B&B (119 Cedar, Snohomish, 360/568-9622 or 800/700-9622, www.countrymanbandb.com, $95–115 d with continental breakfast or $105–125 d with full breakfast) has three rooms with private baths on the second floor of an 1896 Queen Anne Victorian home. Kids are welcome.

Snohomish Grand Valley View B&B (8816 E. Lowell Larimer Rd., 360/668-7096, $95–125 s or d with full breakfast) is a two-story Victorian farmhouse built in 1880. The two guest rooms (private baths) are furnished with antiques. Kids are allowed.

Cadyville Carriage House (304 Avenue A, 360/568-5390, www.cadyvillecarriage.com, $105) is an apartment-style unit that sleeps four. Amenities include a full kitchen stocked for a make-it-yourself breakfast, and a hot tub in the garden.

The **Inn at Barnum Point B&B** (464 S. Barnum Rd., Camano Island, 360/387-2256 or 800/910-2256, www.innatbarnumpoint.com, $125–225 s or d, including full breakfast) has three spacious guest rooms with private baths in a modern Cape Cod–style home on a bluff overlooking the water. This is a fine place for a quiet and romantic getaway. Kids accepted.

Hawthorn Inn and Suites (16710 Smokey Point Blvd., at I-5 exit 206, 360/658-7868 or 800/527-1133, www.hawthorn.com, $99–149 s or d) is the newest lodging in town. All rooms include microwaves and fridges, and access to the indoor pool, hot tub, fitness center, and hot breakfast buffet.

$150-200

Nearly a century old, the lovingly remodeled **Camano Island Inn B&B** (1054 S.W. Camano Dr., 360/387-0783 or 888/718-0783, www.camanoislandinn.com, $120–195 s or d) has six waterfront guest rooms with private baths, a wraparound deck, and full breakfasts. Guests can rent kayaks to paddle along Saratoga Passage, and kids are welcome.

The brand new digs at **Tulalip Resort Casino and Spa** (10200 Quil Ceda Boulevard, 888/272-1111, www.tulalipresort.com, $180–210 d) are the swankiest in Snohomish County, featuring decor with bold palettes, plush linens, walk-in showers, and huge HD TVs. The suites ($310 and up) are over the top, many with jetted tubs, fireplaces, and even pool tables. The entire hotel is set up for reliable free wireless Internet.

FOOD

Snohomish

For coffee or a light snack, head to **Rivers Edge Café** (1011 1st St., 360/568-5835, 7 A.M.–11 P.M. Sun.–Thurs., 7 A.M.–midnight Fri.–Sat., $13), a comfortable place with tasty breakfasts and a historic setting. **Cabbage Patch Restaurant** (111 Ave. A, 360/568-9091, 10 A.M.–10 P.M. Mon.–Fri., 8 A.M.–10 P.M. Sat.–Sun., $12) sells sandwiches, salads, pasta, beef, seafood, and homemade desserts in an old house.

Collector's Choice Restaurant (118 Glen Ave., 360/568-1277, 7 A.M.–9 P.M. Sun.–Thurs., 7 A.M.–10 P.M. Fri.–Sat., $15) in the Star Center Antique Mall serves a diverse menu of pasta, meats, and seafood. Also of note is **Oxford Saloon & Eatery** (913 1st St., 360/568-3845, 11 A.M.–midnight Mon.–Thurs., 11 A.M.–2 A.M. Fri.–Sat., 11 A.M.–9 P.M. Sun., $10), with pub grub and live music. Built in 1889, it is supposedly haunted by a former policeman who was killed while breaking up a knife fight in its earliest years. **Mardini's** (1001 1st St., 360/568-8080, 11 A.M.–10 P.M. Mon.–Sat., 8 A.M.–10 P.M. Sun., $16) serves well-prepared pasta, seafood, chicken, and steaks in a romantic setting.

Fred's Rivertown Alehouse (1114 1st St., 360/568-5820, 11 A.M.–10 P.M. Sun.–Thurs., 10:30 A.M.–11 P.M. Fri.–Sat., entrées $8–17) is a friendly pub with more than 30 beers on draft and dozens of malt scotches. The menu includes such treats as Thai chicken wraps, Caesar salads, and halibut and chips.

Get fresh fruits and veggies, baked goods, and crafts, at the **Snohomish Farmers Market** (425/347-2790), held downtown 5 P.M. to sunset Thursday mid-May through September.

Snohomish is also home to **Quilceda Creek Vintners** (5226 Old Machias Rd., 360/568-2389), a small family-run operation producing just 1,500 cases per year of highly regarded cabernet sauvignon. Open by appointment.

Marysville and Arlington

In business for over 70 years, Marysville's **Village Restaurant** (220 Ash St., 360/659-2305, 6 A.M.–10 P.M. Sun.–Thurs., 6 A.M.–midnight Fri.–Sat., $10) is famous for its "mile-high" meringue pies and other all-American fare.

The best place to eat in Marysville is **Fanny's Restaurant** (505 Cedar St., 360/653-8164, $10), where the diverse and eclectic menu includes international and vegetarian dishes.

Over in Arlington, **La Hacienda** (210 W. Division, Arlington, 360/435-9433, 11 A.M.–10 P.M. Sun.–Thurs., 11 A.M.–11 P.M. Fri.–Sat., $12) serves authentic Mexican cooking. The weekends are bustling here, as the locals crowd to the large bar for karaoke and a few bottles of Corona and Dos Equis.

From mid-June to mid-July, you can purchase fresh raspberries and strawberries from

Sno-Co Berry Pak (4th St. and Cedar Ave., Marysville); most of the packing is for wholesale customers.

Stanwood and Camano Island

Head on down to **The Chatter Box** (9819 270th St. NW, 360/629-0600, www.thechatterboxrestaurant.com, 11 A.M.–9 P.M. Tues.–Sat., noon–8 P.M. Sun., closed Mon., $12) to find one of the most creative and tasty restaurants in the area. Housed in a cute little farmhouse with an airy interior accented by light hardwood floors and pale peach walls, you'd think this place would be the type of place to stick to strictly down-home country cookin'—but you'd be wrong. The menu is Asian fusion, with cuisine elements from Thailand, India, and Malasia. If you're saddled with a picky eater, there are burgers here, too. If you've got a sweet tooth, be sure to try a Thai tea or a Malaysian coffee.

For more conventional fare, eat at **Jimmy's Pizza and Pasta** (9819 Hwy. 532, 360/629-6565, www.jimmyspizza.com), which serves surprisingly good pies compared to most small-town pizzerias.

Get fresh produce at the **Schuh Farms** (9828 Hwy. 532, 360/653-9056, 9 A.M.–6 P.M. daily Apr.–Dec.).

INFORMATION

The **Snohomish Chamber of Commerce** (127 Ave. A, 360/568-2526, www.ci.snohomish.wa.us, 9 A.M.–5 P.M. Mon.–Fri.) is located in the Firehouse Center. Unfortunately, it's closed on weekends. Pick up a self-guided tour brochure for the town's elegant Victorian-era homes (part of the Snohomish National Historic District), or see inside them during the annual **Historic Homes Tour** on the third Sunday of September.

The **Camano Island Visitor Center** (360/629-7136, www.whidbey.net/camano, staffed in the summer only) is visible as you come onto the island.

GETTING AROUND

Community Transit (360/778-2185 or 800/562-1375, www.commtrans.org) has daily bus service throughout Snohomish County and on to Seattle.

Airporter Shuttle (360/380-8800 or 800/235-5247, www.airporter.com) offers direct service between Sea-Tac Airport and Snohomish County's major towns.

Island Transit (360/387-7433 or 800/240-8747, www.islandtransit.org) is a free bus system that offers weekday service around Camano Island.

Skagit Valley and Mount Vernon

The rich bottomland of the Skagit (SKAJ-et) Valley near Mount Vernon produces peas, potatoes, cabbage, cauliflower, broccoli, cucumbers, strawberries, raspberries, spinach, corn, vegetable seeds, and the area's best-known crops: daffodils, tulips, and irises. More than half the world's cabbage and spinach seeds are grown in the valley.

With a fast-growing population of more than 26,000, the city of Mount Vernon is largest in the county, and in spring is certainly among the prettiest: tulips and daffodils are *everywhere,* from fields to yards to gas stations. The attractive downtown features brick-fronted buildings, planters filled with flowers, and a prosperous mixture of stores.

SIGHTS

Farms

A handful of farms invite the public to stroll through their display gardens and order bulbs for fall delivery. Owned by the Washington Bulb Co., **RoozenGaarde** (15867 Beaver March Rd., 360/424-8531 or 800/732-3266, www.tulips.com) offers retail and mail-order bulb sales, fresh-cut flowers, and a gift shop; it's open daily March–May, and Mon.–Sat. the rest of the year. The Dutch-style windmill is a local landmark.

Skagit Valley Gardens (18923 Johnson Rd., just off I-5, 360/424-6760) has additional floral displays in both spring and fall. **LeFeber Bulb Company** (15379 Highway 536, 360/424-6234 or 800/524-3181, www.lefeberbulb.com) also sells bulbs, gifts, and fresh-cut flowers from its big shop. A small **Museum on Bulb History** is on the premises, with agricultural displays during the Tulip Festival.

La Conner Flats Display Garden (15920 Best Rd., 360/466-3190) has an assortment of flowers (primarily roses) in bloom March–September. **The Gardens at La Conner Flats** restaurant serves delicious lunches and high tea (reservations required) 11 A.M.–4 P.M. Tues.–Saturday. Next door, **Christianson's Nursery** (15806 Best Rd., 360/466-3821) features the 600 varieties of roses, plus rhododendrons, azaleas, dogwoods, and other flowering plants.

The **Skagit Display Gardens** (16650 Hwy. 536, www.mtvernon.wsu.edu, cover 10 acres at a Washington State University research station north of Mt. Vernon. Included are native Washington plants, fruit trees (including antique apple varieties), roses, and more.

Edgewater Park

Sitting on the banks of the Skagit River near the center of Mount Vernon, Edgewater Park is a perfect slice of greenery to bring the family and a picnic basket after touring the flower fields. Wide-open lawns invite the kids to enjoy a spontaneous game of tag, and a playground on the premises provides another good way to burn off pent-up energy after having behaved so well during the tulip tour.

ENTERTAINMENT AND EVENTS

Lincoln Theatre

Historic Lincoln Theatre (712 S. 1st St., 360/336-2858 or 877/754-6284, www.lincolntheatre.org) is the place for films, plays, and musical productions throughout the year. The original Wurlitzer organ—used for silent films and vaudeville shows in the 1920s—still works.

© ERICKA CHICKOWSKI

Skagit Valley Tulip Festival

Skagit Valley Tulip Festival

With its rich loamy soil and mild weather, the Skagit Valley is Washington's primary bulb-growing region and home to Washington Bulb Co., the largest producer of bulbs in America. From late March through April, more than 2,000 acres of the valley are carpeted with flowering daffodils, tulips, irises, and lilies; more than 40 million bulbs are produced annually. The first commercial tulips were test-planted here in 1908, but commercial success did not come until after World War II, when Dutch immigrants brought their bulb-growing skills to the valley.

The 17-day countywide Tulip Festival (360/428-5959, www.tulipfestival.org), held annually in early April, corresponds with the blooming of the tulip and daffodil fields and includes bus tours, Skagit River trips, bike rides, street fairs, foot races, llama exhibits, antique shows, a salmon bake, volleyball tournaments, and art shows. Tour buses dump hundreds of sightseers on the area, and many more drive up from Seattle to photograph the colorful fields. Daily shuttle buses help alleviate some of the congestion, but with several hundred thousand visitors, it still gets crazy, especially on weekends between 11 A.M. and 4 P.M. After mid-January, get maps of the floral fields from the Mount Vernon Chamber of Commerce Office. Or, just head west from Mount Vernon toward La Conner; most of the fields are in an area bounded on the north by Memorial Highway 536, on the west by La Conner-Whitney Road, on the south by Chilberg Road, and on the east by the Skagit River. Crops are rotated to preserve the soil and to keep insect pests down, so last season's field of yellow daffodils may be home to a crop of flowering broccoli this year—more nutritious, but not nearly as photogenic.

Fuji sponsors an official photo platform at **Tulip Town** (15002 Bradshaw Rd., 360/424-8152) along with music, art, pony rides, kite flying, espresso coffee, cut flowers, and refreshments.

In Mount Vernon itself, the Tulip Festival action centers on a downtown **Street Fair** that includes more than 200 art and craft vendors, plus live entertainment and food.

Other Events

Berry Dairy Days (360/757-0994) on the third weekend of July celebrates Burlington's agricultural roots, with a big parade, carnival, arts and crafts, classic car show, music, and plenty of strawberry shortcake.

In early July, the **Highland Games & Scottish Fair** (360/416-4934, www.celticarts.org) comes to Mt. Vernon, with a parade, dancing, competitions, food, fireworks, and enough bagpipe music to drive you batty.

The second weekend of August brings the **Skagit County Fair** (360/336-9453, www.skagitcounty.net) to the fairgrounds on the southwest side of Mount Vernon off Blackburn Road. Fair activities include live entertainment, agricultural exhibits, food, and lots more.

SHOPPING

Browse through the shops in downtown Mount Vernon, particularly 1st Street's bakeries, gift and clothing stores, and cafés. You'll also discover four different bookstores here, including spacious **Scott's Bookstore** (120 N. 1st St., 360/336-6181 or 800/532-2665, www.scottsbookstore.com), a great place to linger while paging through the merchandise.

If you prefer to shop in a mall, Mount Vernon and Burlington have several to choose from, including **Cascade Mall** (www.shopcascademall.com), with Sears, JCPenney, Macy's, plus dozens of others, along with **Prime Outlets Burlington** (234 Fashion Way, 360/757-3549) with more than 50 outlet stores.

SPORTS AND RECREATION

Skagit Speedway

The speed-through-it town of Burlington is home to Skagit Speedway (360/568-2529, www.skagitspeedway.com), with auto racing between mid-April and late September.

Cycling

With its nice, flat roads and breathtaking views of Mount Baker and the Cascades, the farm country of Skagit Valley is a great place to bicycle. When the flowers are blooming, the scenery gets even better, but the traffic can be a real bear on weekends during the Tulip Festival. During these times those normally quiet back roads are crowded with cars, buses, and cyclists, not to mention tractors and other farm equipment.

If you've left your wheels at home, stop by **Skagit Cycles** (1704 S. Burlington Blvd., Burlington, 360/757-7910, 10 A.M.–6:30 P.M. Mon.–Sat. to pick up a rental. The shop offers a variety of bikes for $30–60 a day. This is also a good stop to pick up spare tubes and other accessories.

Hiking

Located in the Padilla Bay National Estuarine Research Reserve, the **Breazeale Interpretive Center** (360/428-1558, 10 A.M.–5 P.M. Wed.–Sun., free) has natural history and marine displays, hands-on exhibits for kids, and a range of programs. Borrow a trail guide from the center for a 0.75-mile nature hike through the upland cedar forest and fields, where you might see bald eagles, herons, ducks, or geese. Find it just north of Bay View State Park on Bay View-Edison Road.

Catch peekaboo views of the Olympics, San Juan Islands, and Skagit Valley farmland along the trails at **Little Mountain Park.** The highlight of the 490-acre park is the summit observation area, which offers an unobstructed panorama view from the 927-feet above the valley floor. To get there, follow Blackburn Road to Little Mountain Road.

Camping

Eight miles west of Burlington on Padilla Bay, **Bay View State Park** (360/757-0227, www.parks.wa.gov) has year-round campsites for $13 ($19 for RVs) across Bay View-Edison Road from the waterfront. Make reservations ($7 extra) at 888/226-7688 or online.

Additional campsites can be found at **Skagit County Fairgrounds** (360/336-9453), on the corner of Hazel and Virginia in Mount Vernon.

Private RV parks include **Burlington KOA** (646 N. Green Rd., 360/724-5511 or 800/562-9154, www.koa.com), **Riverbend Park** (305 W. Stewart Rd., 360/428-4044), and **Mt. Vernon RV Park** (1229 Memorial Hwy., 360/428-8787 or 800/385-9895).

ACCOMMODATIONS

Local motels and B&Bs fill up fast for the Tulip Festival. Be sure to make reservations at least a month ahead if you plan to visit at that time. Also note that nearby La Conner is another good sleepover spot from which to tour Mount Vernon and the flower fields.

There's no better way to experience the full country experience than in an authentic farmhouse bed-and-breakfast. One of the best in the area is **Benson Farmstead B&B** (360/757-0578 or 800/685-7239, www.bbhost.com/bensonbnb), a beautifully restored 1914 home set in the fields of Bow, just three miles northwest of Burlington. The innkeepers are the grandchildren of the Norwegian pioneers who built the house. They've restored it, filled it with lots of Scandinavian curios and complete the ambience by serving up a fresh Scandinavian farm breakfast each morning. The house itself has three guest rooms with private baths ($99–150 d). Also on the property is the Garden Suite Cottage ($125 d), a deluxe suite with kitchenette in the first floor of a restored well tower. Finally, there is the humongous Barn Cottage out back. The cottage is a restored granary outfitted with a kitchenette, living room, and TV and sleeps up to eight guests for $135, though breakfast is not included in this rate.

Snuggled in the midst of 250 wooded acres three miles south of Mount Vernon, **Whispering Firs B&B** (360/428-1990 or 800/428-1992, www.whisperingfirs.com, $75–110 d) is a large, modern home with shaded seclusion. Four guest rooms have private baths, and a hot tub sits on the deck. Kids are welcome.

There are several chain motels close to the I-5 corridor, but for a cheaper stay with similar quality rooms, give **Tulip Inn** (2200 Freeway Dr. in Mount Vernon, 360/428-5969 or 800/599-5969, www.tulipinn.net, $79 s or $85 d) a try. Rooms are clean, if a bit worn, and the rate includes free wireless Internet and a modest continental breakfast each morning.

If the Tulip is booked, there are a couple of other independent motels that are satisfactory for a short stay, including the **Hillside Motel** (2300 Bonnie View Rd. in Mount Vernon, 360/445-3252, $59 s or $63 d), which has rooms with kitchenettes, and **Cocusa Motel** (370 W. Rio Vista in Burlington, 360/757-6044 or 800/628-2257, $79 s or $90 d), which has an outdoor pool.

For a step up in quality and better amenities such as an indoor pool, spa, fitness center, and business center, then go for the Fairfield Inn and Suites (9384 Old Hwy 99 N., Burlington, 360/757-2717, $129–139 d) in Burlington. The Fairfield offers newer digs and close proximity to the Burlington outlets and chain restaurants.

FOOD

Cafés and Diners

There's no doubt that you'll find the most creative meal in town at the oddball **Chuck**

Wagon Drive-In (800 N. 4th St., 360/336-2732, 11 A.M.–9 P.M. Sun.–Thurs., 11 A.M.–9:30 P.M. Fri.–Sat.). This is a burger lover's mecca, with weird concoctions such as peanut-butter burgers and hash-brown burgers on its extensive menu, along with a history of making strange custom burgers for the adventurous. The place isn't just a gimmick, either; even plain old cheeseburgers are tasty here.

Wear flannel if you want to fit in at the locals-only **Mr T's Family Café** (503 W. Fir St., 360/428-8808, 6 A.M.–2 P.M. Mon.–Sat., 8 A.M.–2 P.M. Sun.). This down-home diner is a favorite among the area farmers, loggers, and truck drivers who come for the rib-sticking biscuits and gravy, enough to keep the heartiest appetites happy.

And to satisfy the sweet tooth, stop by **Big Scoop Sundae Palace** (327 E. College Way, 360/424-3558, 11 A.M.–10 P.M. Sun.–Thurs., 11 A.M.–11 P.M. Fri.–Sat.). Festooned with a candy-stripe red roof and circus lights around the windows, this place is exactly as advertised—a fun, old-school ice cream parlor scooping up share-worthy sundaes, shakes, and root beer floats. If you insist on actually eating a meal before your dessert, it conveniently serves burgers, hot dogs, and other diner fare.

Steak and Seafood

Max Dale's Restaurant (2030 Riverside Dr., 360/424-7171, www.maxdales.com, 11 A.M.–9:30 P.M. Mon.–Fri., 4–9:30 P.M. Sat.–Sun., $22) serves fine steak, seafood, and prime rib, with entertainment and dancing on weekends.

You can also get all-American steak and seafood at **Gentleman Gene's** (1400 Parker Way, 360/424-4363, 10:30 A.M.–9 P.M. Sun.–Thurs., 10:30 A.M.–11 P.M. Fri.–Sat., $13). The pub has over a hundred beers.

International

Pacioni's Pizzeria (606 S. 1st St., 360/336-3314, 11 A.M.–3 P.M. and 5–9 P.M. Tues.–Sat., closed Sun.–Mon.) bakes outstanding thin-crust, crunchy pizzas with tasty toppings, along with calzones and paninis.

Another noteworthy eatery is **Mexico Café** (1320 Memorial Hwy., 360/424-1977, 11 A.M.–10 P.M. Mon.–Thurs., 11 A.M.–11 P.M. Fri.–Sat., 10:30 A.M.–10 P.M. Sun.), which offers tasty south-of-the-border fare, including scrumptious *chile verde* dishes and great margaritas.

Pub Grub

Skagit River Brewing Co. (404 S. 3rd St., 360/336-2884, www.skagitbrew.com, 11 A.M.–10 P.M. Mon.–Thurs., 11 A.M.–11 P.M. Fri.–Sat., 11 A.M.–9 P.M. Sun., $15) has fresh-brewed beer on tap and pub grub on the menu, plus jazz, blues, or world-beat bands most Saturday nights.

Markets

Skagit Valley Food Co-op (202 S. 1st. St., 360/336-3886, www.skagitfoodcoop.com, 8 A.M.–9 P.M. Mon.–Sat., 9 A.M.–8 P.M. Sun.) has a wide selection of bulk foods, locally baked bread, wine and beer, fresh produce, and an all-natural deli (Deli Next Door) for a takeout lunch or dinner. This is the best and most nutritious quick meal deal in town.

Another place for fresh produce (and flowers, of course) is the **Mount Vernon-Skagit Valley Farmers Market** (360/292-2648) held in downtown Mount Vernon 9 A.M.–1 P.M. Saturday June–September. Also try the **Burlington Farmers Market** (Cherry and Victoria Sts., 360/755-9717, 3–7 P.M. Friday May–Sept.).

At other times, stop by Burlington's **Country Farms Produce Market** (101 Orange Ave., 360/755-0488) for fresh locally grown fruits and vegetables.

INFORMATION

For maps, brochures, and festival information, contact the **Mount Vernon Chamber of Commerce** (117 N. 1st St., 360/428-8547, www.mountvernonchamber.com. 8:30 A.M.–5 P.M. Mon.–Fri., 9 A.M.–4 P.M. Sat., 10 A.M.–4 P.M. Sun. in the summer, closed Sun. in winter).

GETTING THERE AND AROUND

Skagit Transit (360/757-4433, www.skat.org, $0.75 per ride or $1.50 for day pass) offers daily bus service throughout Skagit Country, including Mt. Vernon and Burlington. Of particular note is Route 615, which runs from Skagit Station (105 E. Kincaid St.) through farmlands and to La Conner. The station is also the landing point for a weekday express connector from Everett Station ($2) and a Monday–Saturday express route from Bellingham ($0.75).

Amtrak (800/872-7245, www.amtrak.com) provides daily train connections from Mount Vernon north to Vancouver, B.C., and south to Seattle on the Cascades train.

Airporter Shuttle (360/380-8800 or 800/235-5247, www.airporter.com) has connections to Sea-Tac Airport. **Greyhound** (360/336-5111 or 800/231-2222, www.greyhound.com) has long-haul bus service from the Mount Vernon terminal at 1101 S. 2nd Street.

Skagit Eagle Air (360/757-1036 or 800/542-7600, www.skagiteagleair.com) takes you on flightseeing tours over the tulip fields from Skagit Regional Airport.

Festival Transportation

During the festival, the ***Victoria Clipper*** (360/448-5000 or 800/888-2535, www.victoriaclipper.com) offers a special 12-hour voyage to La Conner from Seattle's Pier 69. This includes the cruise and a guided bus tour of the tulip fields for $44 adults, with discounts for kids and advance reservations.

On weekdays during the festival, **Tulip Transit** buses (360/678-4211) depart from Burlington on two- to four-hour tours of the valley's flower fields ($10 adults, $5 seniors, $3 kids, free for children under 3). On weekends, the buses transport you around the fields for $3. The weekend versions aren't guided tours, but the buses are frequent enough to cover the area easily. Get details at 360/428-5959 or www.skat.org.

La Conner

The oldest town in Skagit County, La Conner saw the arrival of its first white settlers shortly after the Civil War. They built dikes to tame the annual floods on the Skagit River and planted crops in the fertile soil, which proved some of the most productive in the world. The town grew up along Swinomish Channel, the protected saltwater slough that separates the mainland from Fidalgo Island and linked area fishermen to the Puget Sound. In 1876, John Conner purchased a trading post and named the site after his wife, Louisa A. Conner (L. A. Conner eventually became La Conner).

Today La Conner is home to only 850 people but is one of Washington's most loved destinations. The operative term here is cute, with more frills and lace than a Victoria's Secret catalog. More than 160 local buildings in La Conner are on the National Register of Historic Places. Its galleries, gift shops, restaurants, museums, and 19th-century homes make for enjoyable exploring, and the bright-orange **Rainbow Bridge** across Swinomish Channel is a good spot for photographers to get a shot of the La Conner waterfront with a Mt. Baker backdrop.

SIGHTS

Housed in an award-winning building in the center of town, the outstanding **Museum of Northwest Art** (121 S. 1st St., 360/466-4446, www.museumofnwart.org, 10 A.M.–5 P.M. Tues.–Sun., $3 adults, free for kids under 13) features paintings and sculptures by regional artists. This is the only museum to exclusively showcase Northwest art, and it includes a permanent collection of works upstairs. Downstairs are contemporary art exhibits, including a room on glassmaking.

Skagit County Historical Museum (501

4th St., 360/466-3365, 11 A.M.–5 P.M. Tues.–Sun., $2 adults, $1 seniors and kids ages 6–12, free for under 5, $5 for families) sits high on a hill, with a panoramic view from the observation deck across the fields and farms of Skagit Valley. Inside are pioneer artifacts from the days of mining, logging, and fishing, along with historical photos, horse-drawn carriages, baskets, and even a moonshine still from the 1930s. Watch the video for a taste of local history, or stop by the gift shop for books and crafts. Hours are extended during the Tulip Festival.

Constructed in 1891, the majestic **Gaches Mansion** at 2nd and Calhoun was restored after a 1973 fire gutted the structure. The first floor contains turn-of-the-20th-century furnishings, while the upstairs houses the **La Conner Quilt Museum** (360/466-4288, 11 A.M.–5 P.M. Wed.–Sat., noon–5 P.M. Sun., $3 adults, free for kids under 12), with changing exhibits and a small gift shop that sells locally made quilts. It is one of 10 such museums in the country. Just around the corner from the Gaches Mansion at 2nd and Commercial, you'll find an 1869 log cabin that was moved here from the Skagit River. Nearby are the old brick city hall from 1886 and historic **Maple Hall,** used for theatrical and music performances.

The little **Fireman's Museum** on 1st Street contains a horse-drawn handpump that was used to put out fires in San Francisco following the 1906 earthquake. It was later used by the La Conner Fire Department; peek in the window to see it.

Pioneer Park is a quiet riverside place for a picnic beneath tall Douglas fir trees next to Rainbow Bridge. No camping is permitted. The state-owned **Skagit Wildlife Recreation Area,** a refuge south of La Conner on Fir Island, is a good place to look for wintering snow geese and trumpeter swans.

ENTERTAINMENT AND EVENTS

Head to La Conner on the **4th of July** for a big fireworks display over Swinomish Channel. In August, the **Vintage and Classic Boat Show** sails into town. The season winds down with the **Art's Alive!** celebration in early November, featuring demonstrations by painters, jewelers, potters, and others, and the **Christmas Boats Parade** up the Swinomish Channel each December. Find out more about these events at www.laconnerchamber.org.

SHOPPING

The most fun way to shop in La Conner is to simply meander through downtown, stopping for lunch or a beer and heading out again. Art galleries, gift shops (specializing in everything from olives to old fishing tackle), antique dealers, espresso places, and restaurants line 1st and Morris Streets. Most of these sell tourist claptrap, but there are several notable exceptions.

The Stall (712 1st St., 360/466-3162, 10 A.M.–5 P.M. daily) sells unusual folk art imports from all over the globe. Also worth a look is **Organic Matters** (707 S. 1st St., 360/466-4012 or 800/843-9069, www.organic- matters.com, 10 A.M.–5 P.M. Mon. –Sat., 11 A.M.–5 P.M. Sun.), selling organic cotton clothing and allergy-free wool bedding. The **Wood Merchant** (709 S. 1st St., 360/466-4741, 10 A.M.–5 P.M. daily) has gorgeous wooden furniture, cases, games, and other delights. **The Next Chapter Books** (721 S. 1st St., 360/466-2665, www.nextchapter.com, 9 A.M.–5 P.M. daily) sells books and espresso from its little shop on the east end of 1st Street.

SPORTS AND RECREATION

Boating

The Swinomish Channel is a peaceful body of water for paddling or rowing, though no local places rent boats. You'll have to venture to Anacortes for that; one of the more popular places there is **Island Outfitters** (2515 Commercial Ave.), which rents boats, paddles, and gear and runs guided excursions. Fishing and whale-watching charters also run out of Anacortes.

Those with their own boats can find short-term, first-come, first-serve moorage along the city-front Swinomish at floats located at the ends of Benton, Calhoun, and Washington

© ERICKA CHICKOWSKI

La Conner offers blocks and blocks of cute shops.

Streets. Rates are $0.50 per foot per day, payable via self-serve drop box.

Camping

Bay View State Park (360/757-0227, www.parks.wa.gov), eight miles north of La Conner, has year-round campsites for $13 ($19 for RVs). Make reservations ($7 extra) at 888/226-7688 or online.

Head south to Fir Island for **Blakes RV Park & Marina** (1171-A Rawlins Rd., 360/445-6533).

ACCOMMODATIONS

La Conner is blessed with a number of delightful inns and historic B&Bs. Find links to most of these at the chamber of commerce website, www.laconnerchamber.com.

$100-150

The distinctive cedar-shingled exterior of **La Conner Country Inn** (107 S. 2nd St., 360/466-3101 or 888/466-4113, www.laconnerlodging.com, $149 d) belies the somewhat cheaply furnished rooms here. The two-bedroom units with gas fireplaces are clean, but overpriced compared to other offerings in the area. However, this is one of the larger lodging establishments in town, and the rooms can do in a pinch during the tulip festival and high season when other places are booked.

Window shoppers can't beat the location at **Hotel Planter** (715 1st St., 360/466-4710 or 800/488-5409, www.hotelplanter.com, $109–159 d), which sits in a 1907 building right smack in the middle of bustling 1st Street. The rooms are quaintly decorated to pay homage to the building's history, and there's a hot tub and gazebo in the garden courtyard. This establishment offers a reprieve for many adults, as it doesn't allow young children.

Right on the edge of town adjacent to open farm country, **The Heron in La Conner** (117 Maple Ave., 360/466-4626 or 877/883-8899, www.theheron.com, $109–141 d) is a Victorian-style country inn with 11 guest rooms, a backyard hot tub, an on-site day spa, and a gourmet breakfast buffet. All rooms come with private baths, Egyptian cotton linens, flat-screen TVs, and wireless Internet.

There are also three suites ($199) with fireplaces and one with a Jacuzzi tub for those rainy days when you'd like to stay in.

$150-200

Wild Iris Inn (121 Maple Ave., 360/466-1400 or 800/477-1400, www.wildiris.com) is a luxurious place with seven guest rooms ($129–169 d), plus 12 view suites ($199 d) with jetted tubs, gas fireplaces, and outside decks. All guests can use the outdoor hot tub and are served a buffet breakfast. No kids under 12.

Esteps' Residence in La Conner (1st St., 360/466-2116, www.estep-properties.com, $150–175 d) offers four condo properties scattered about town. Each property has its unique charms, including kitchens, hot tubs, and views.

$200-250

La Conner Channel Lodge (205 N. 1st St., 360/466-1500 or 888/466-4113, www.laconnerlodging.com, $189–359 d) is a modern waterfront hotel with gas fireplaces, small balconies, hot tubs, and a continental breakfast.

Skagit Bay Hideaway (17430 Goldenview, 360/466-2262 or 888/466-2262, www.skagitbay.com, $229 d with a two-night minimum) is a well-appointed contemporary home across the Rainbow Bridge with a rooftop hot tub and a breakfast basket each morning.

FOOD

Cafés

Start your day at **Calico Cupboard Café and Bakery** (720 S. 1st St., 360/466-4451) for great homemade country breakfasts, plus pastries and healthy lunches and dinners. Arrive early to avoid a lengthy wait on summer weekends.

Set in the historic building that once housed the Tillinghast Seed Company, the appropriately named **Seeds A Bistro and Bar** (623 Morris St., 360/466-3280, www.seedsbistro.com, 11 A.M.–9 P.M. daily) serves dishes that emphasize farm fresh veggies and meats, just off the boat fish and shellfish, and scrumptious homemade breads.

© ERICKA CHICKOWSKI

Nell Thorn Restaurant and Pub in La Conner

Pub Grub

Based out of the La Conner Country Inn, **Nell Thorn Restaurant and Pub** (702 S. 1st St., 360/466-9932, www.nellthorn.com, 10:30 A.M.–9 P.M. Sun.–Thurs., 10:30 A.M.–10 P.M. Fri.–Sat., $18) sits perched on a hill overlooking the Swinomish in a whimsically weathered cedar-shingled building. The menu mixes comfortable pub food such as burgers with more sophisticated salad, pasta, seafood, and steak dishes.

La Conner Brewing Co. (117 S. 1st. St., 360/466-1415, www.laconnerbrew.com, 11:30 A.M.–9 P.M. daily, $11) is a lively and noisy place with five kinds of brewed-on-the-premises beer, plus tasty wood-fired pizzas, quesadillas (one with mangos), soups, and salads. The pub is entirely nonsmoking, and the outside patio is perfect for warm summer evenings.

Palmer's at the Lighthouse (512 South 1st St., 360/466-3147, 11:30 A.M.–9 P.M. Sun.–Thurs., 11:30 A.M.–9:30 P.M. Fri.–Sat., $11–20) is a popular waterside restaurant with a menu that stars fresh seafood and prime rib (from organically fed cattle). Fish and chips are always a favorite, and there's a separate bar menu.

Just down the street is **La Conner Seafood and Prime Rib House** (614 1st St., 360/466-4014, www.laconnerseafood.com, 11:30 A.M.–8 P.M. Sun.–Thurs., 11:30 A.M.–9 P.M. Fri.–Sat., $25), with waterfront dining and a diverse menu.

Kerstin's (505 S. 1st, 360/466-9111, noon–2 P.M. Wed.–Sun. and 5 –9 P.M. daily) is a delightful place for Northwest meals of pasta, lamb, chicken, steaks, or seafood, but it also has vegetarian entrées. Lunches are your best bet if you're on a budget; dinner entrées cost $18–29.

Markets

In the summer, be sure to stop at the **Hedlin's Farm Fruit Stand** (12275 Valley Rd., 360/466-3622, 10 A.M.–6 P.M. daily May–Oct.) on the east edge of town for fresh corn, tomatoes, peas, honey, strawberries, and other produce from its nearby farm.

INFORMATION

For local information, visit the **La Conner Chamber of Commerce** (4th and Morris, 360/466-4778 or 888/642-9284, www.laconnerchamber.com, 10 A.M.–4 P.M. Mon.–Fri., 11 A.M.–4 P.M. Sat.–Sun. year-round).

GETTING THERE AND AROUND

Skagit Transit (360/757-4433, www.skat.org) offers daily bus service from Mount Vernon to La Conner on Route 615. **Airporter Shuttle** (360/380-8800 or 800/235-5247, www.airporter.com) provides service between Sea-Tac Airport and La Conner.

Burlington to Bellingham

CHUCKANUT DRIVE

Heading north up the coast from the Skagit Valley, you enter one of the most scenic stretches of highway in the state—Chuckanut Drive. This 11-mile portion of Highway 11 was the first route designated a scenic drive by the state. Built as part of the now-extinct Pacific Highway, it leaves I-5 just north of Burlington and heads straight as a cue stick across the black, flat soil of the Skagit Valley. The tiny towns of **Bow** and **Edison** have begun attracting artists, and several studios are open for weekend visits.

A short distance north of Bow, the highway runs head-on into the mountains that hover over Puget Sound; it's here that the fun begins. The road doesn't have a straight stretch for seven miles as it swoops and swerves along the face of the cliff, with grand views across to Anacortes, Guemes Island, and, farther north, the San Juan and Lummi Islands. With no shoulder, a narrow strip of pavement, and tight corners, it's a bit dicey for bikes (especially on weekends when traffic is heaviest), but the views are stunning.

For more information on Chuckanut Drive, see the **Chuckanut Merchants' Association** (www.chuckanutdrive.com).

Entertainment

Skagit Valley Casino Resort (just off I-5 at Exit 236 near Bow, 360/724-7777 or 877/275-2448, www.svcasinoresort.com) is the biggest thing going in the area. Inside are slots, blackjack, craps, roulette, keno, and more ways to suck your wallet dry. The resort also has a luxury hotel ($109–119 s or d), three restaurants, and live music nightly.

Sports and Recreation

Seven miles south of Bellingham on Chuckanut Drive, **Larrabee State Park** (360/676-2093) was the state's first, created in 1923 when Charles Xavier Larrabee's family donated 20 acres in his honor. The park contains a popular campground with tent ($14) and RV ($20) sites, plus coin-operated showers. It's open year-round. Make reservations ($7 extra) at 888/226-7688 or www.parks.wa.gov. Now covering more than 2,500 acres of mountainous land, the park borders Samish Bay, with a boat launch, a sandy beach for sunning, and tidepools for marine explorations.

Nine miles of hiking trails include the southern end of the **Interurban Trail,** connecting the park with Bellingham. Other trails lead to scenic Fragrance and Lost Lakes for trout fishing, and to dramatic vistas from the 1,941-foot summit of **Chuckanut Mountain** (also accessible via a gravel road).

Continue north from Larrabee State Park to **Teddy Bear Cove,** located at the foot of the cliff just before you enter the Fairhaven District. For many years it was an unofficial nude beach, but the county purchased the land and started fining the au naturel crowd $125 per infraction in 1997. The prudes strike again.

Accommodations

Chuckanut Manor (360/766-6191, www.chuckanutmanor.com) has a two-room suite over the restaurant with a spa and private deck. Nearby is a cottage with a hot tub, antique furnishings, a private deck, and kitchen. Both of these are $150 d including continental breakfast.

Alice Bay B&B (982 Scott Rd. on Sammish Island just west of Edison, 360/766-6396 or 800/652-0223, www.alicebay.com, $155 s or d) has a two-story unit where you can soak in the hot tub on the deck overlooking Alice Bay, take the rowboat out, or walk the private beach; rates include a full breakfast. Kids are welcome.

Samish Point by the Bay (447 Samish Point Rd., 360/766-6610 or 800/916-6161, www.samishpoint.com, $185 s or d for the entire place) has four guest rooms with private baths in a secluded Cape Cod cottage facing Samish Bay. Outside, you'll find a hot tub and extensive gardens. There is a two-night minimum. The kitchen is stocked for a make-your-own breakfast.

Food

Rhododendron Café (5521 Chuckanut Dr., Bow, 360/766-6667, www.rhodycafe.com, 11:30 A.M.–9 P.M. Wed.–Fri., 9 A.M.–9 P.M. Sat.–Sun., closed Thanksgiving until the last Friday in January), at the Bow-Edison intersection, serves good food and is populated on weekends by bicyclists and weekend-drive aficionados, particularly during the morning hours when brunch is served.

As you drive north from Bow on Chuckanut Drive, you'll pass several good places to eat. Overlooking Sammish Bay and the San Juans, **Chuckanut Manor Restaurant and B&B** (302 Chuckanut Dr., 360/766-6191, www.chuckanutmanor.com, 11:30 A.M.–9 P.M. Tues.–Thurs., 11:30 A.M.–10 P.M. Fri.–Sat., 10:30 A.M.–9 P.M. Sun., closed Mon.), at the southernmost end of the drive, specializes in fresh seafood and continental dishes, a Friday night smorgasbord, and a Sunday champagne brunch. The bar has the best and usually quietest seats in the house and serves 26 different single malt scotches. The oyster stew here is to die for.

The oyster-sized **Oyster Bar** (240 Chuckanut Dr., 360/766-6185, www.theoysterbaronchuckanutdrive.com, 11:30 A.M.–10 P.M. daily) is a cozy and romantic place clinging to the side of the mountain. The entire west-facing wall is windowed, offering superb sunset views of the San Juan Islands. This is arguably one of the best places in the state to sup on fresh oysters on a half shell—the house-made jicama relish served as a side brings these slippery treats to a new level.

If you'd prefer to make up your own seafood smorgasboard, stop by the shoreline digs at **Taylor Shellfish Farm** (2182 Chuckanut Dr., Bow, 360/766-6002, www.taylorshellfish.com, 9 A.M.–6 P.M. daily Apr.–Sept., 9 A.M.–5 P.M. daily Oct.–Mar.) for locally raised fresh oysters, clams, scallops, mussels, and Dungeness crabs (cooked while you wait).

Bellingham

Throw a hiking boot down any one of Bellingham's commercial thoroughfares and you're just as likely to land it in front of an outdoor sporting goods shop as you are in front of some passerby who, just for a second, might think "Hey, that isn't mine, is it?"

Yep, this is a town that is bonkers for bikes, skis, kayaks, and any other means of conveyance that will get them out into the pristine water, trails and slopes that surround their neighborhoods.

The town is a microcosm of all the best that Western Washington has to offer, with beautifully restored historic buildings, extraordinary museums, and quirky boutiques and creative cafés.

It is also the last major outpost for Canada-bound travelers looking to cross at Blaine or Sumas and hearty travelers planning to take the rugged Alaska Marine Highway ferry.

SIGHTS

Fairhaven

Fairhaven Historic District is considerably more sedate today than its original incarnation. You can see its old buildings and

© ERICKA CHICKOWSKI

Bellingham's Fairhaven Historic District

FAIRHAVEN'S ROWDY DAYS

The boomtown of Fairhaven grew to prominence in the late 1880s, when rumors circulated that it would be the western terminus for the Great Northern Railroad. At its peak, the town hummed with 35 hotels and boardinghouses, seven saloons, an opera house, and 11 real estate offices. Despite the large number of hotels, many men were forced to sleep in tents along the beach.

The selection of Tacoma as the Great Northern's terminus sent Fairhaven into a tailspin, but the arrival of a smaller line – the Fairhaven and Southern Railroad – brought service from Skagit Valley. Men working on the railroad would follow the tracks back to 9th Street for an evening's entertainment; rowdy bars and hotels such as Miss Reno's provided much more than just a bed for their patrons – Fairhaven had quite a hot reputation. One unidentified man romanced himself into a state of exhaustion and dropped dead while walking up 9th Street. Another, John Moore, had a few too many at the Gilt Edge Saloon and decided to sleep it off on the tracks – poor John never heard the 2:30 A.M. train pulling into town.

In 1903, the cluster of four towns – Whatcom, Sehome, Bellingham, and Fairhaven – was consolidated to form Bellingham, but only after a long battle between the two main rivals, Fairhaven and Whatcom; residents of each demanded that theirs be the new town's name.

Victorian homes in a walking tour. Maps are available from the visitors bureau (904 Potter St., 360/671-3990) and various Fairhaven shops and restaurants.

Western Washington University

This 189-acre campus has five colleges and two schools for 12,000 students. It began as the State Normal School in 1893, and became a full-fledged university in 1977. The campus is also known for its 22 sculptures in the **Outdoor Sculpture Garden.** Contact the Admissions office (360/650-3861, www.wwu.edu) for campus tours. **Viking Union** includes a bookstore, deli and other food options, a post office, and information desk.

Overlooking Bellingham Bay and accessible via a footpath from the university, the **Sehome Hill Arboretum** provides splendid views of the San Juans and Mt. Baker, plus 70 acres of tall Douglas firs, wildflowers, and bigleaf maples preserved in their natural state. The 3.5 miles of paved trails provide views of Bellingham and the San Juans, along with Mt. Baker.

Museums

Located on a high bluff overlooking Bellingham Bay, the outstanding **Whatcom Museum of History and Art** (121 Prospect St., 360/676-6981, www.whatcommuseum.org, noon–5 P.M. Tues.–Sun., free) is housed in old city hall, an ornate redbrick building capped by a four-corner cupola and a tall clock tower. Built in 1892 as the New Whatcom City Hall, it remained in use until 1939. Today, the museum has grown to include the old city hall, along with three nearby structures.

The main building contains historical displays, changing exhibits, Victorian clothing, woodworking tools, toys, and contemporary art. Also here is a small gift shop with unusual items from around the globe.

Two nearby structures house separate collections that are also part of the Whatcom Museum "campus." The **Arco Exhibits Building** (206 Prospect St., same hours as Whatcom) across the street houses changing fine-art and historical exhibits. The **Children's Museum** (227 Prospect St., 360/733-8769, noon–5 P.M. Sun., Tues., and Wed., 10 A.M.–5 P.M. Thurs.–Sat., $2.50) has many participatory exhibits for kids of all ages, including an infant/toddler exploration center and puppet theater.

Make it a point to visit **Mindport** (111 Grand Ave., 360/647-5614, www.mindport.org, 10 A.M.–5 P.M. Wed.–Sat., noon–4 P.M. Sun., $2 for adults, $1 for kids), a creative center that will amuse, fascinate, and educate both

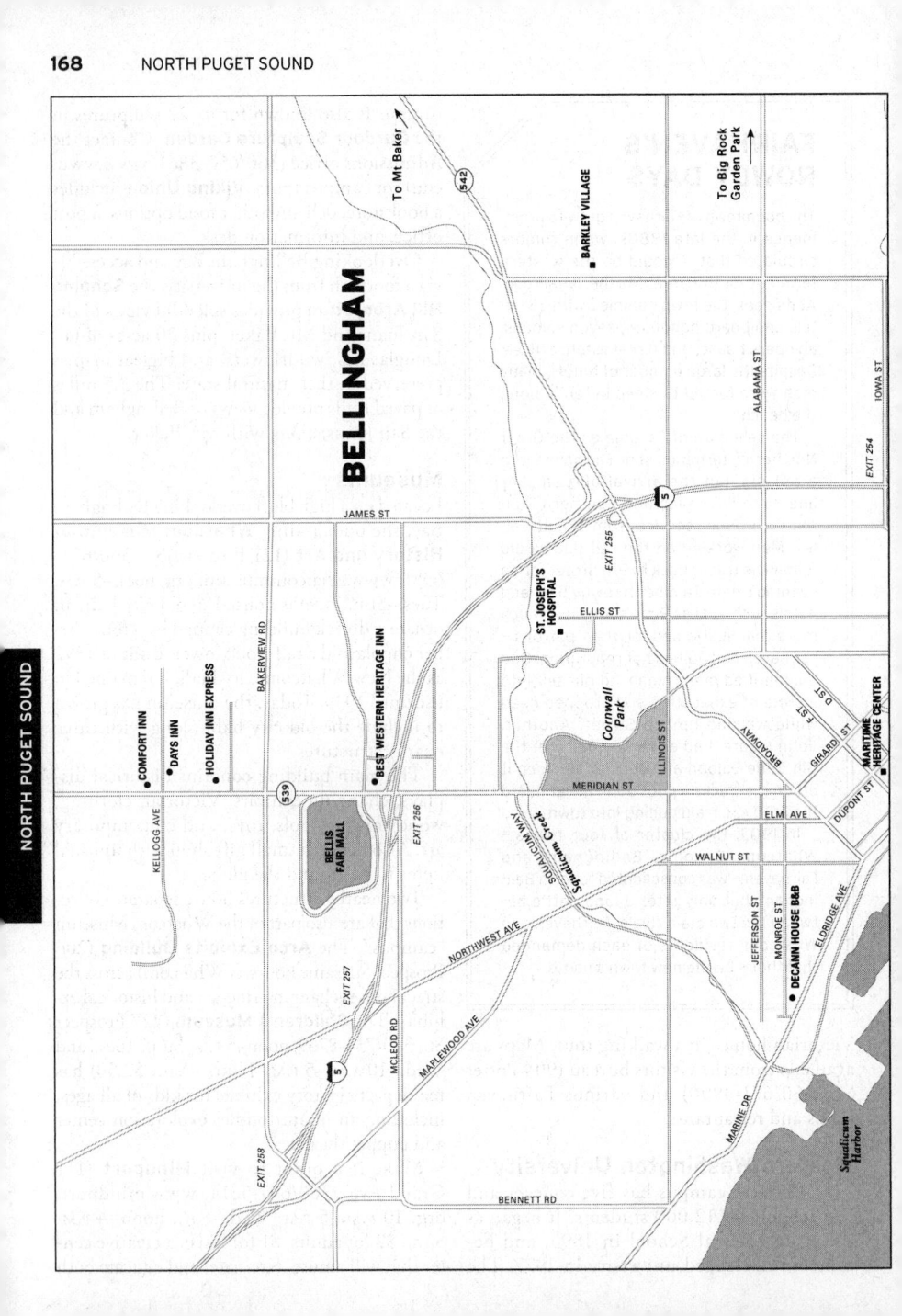
BELLINGHAM
To Mt Baker
To Big Rock Garden Park
BARKLEY VILLAGE
542
ALABAMA ST
IOWA ST
EXIT 254
5
JAMES ST
EXIT 255
ST. JOSEPH'S HOSPITAL
ELLIS ST
Cornwall Park
ILLINOIS ST
BROADWAY
F ST
D ST
GIRARD ST
MARITIME HERITAGE CENTER
DUPONT ST
MERIDIAN ST
ELM AVE
WALNUT ST
JEFFERSON ST
MONROE ST
DECANN HOUSE B&B
ELDRIDGE AVE
MARINE DR
Squalicum Harbor
Squalicum Creek
SQUALICUM WAY
NORTHWEST AVE
MAPLEWOOD AVE
MCLEOD RD
BENNETT RD
EXIT 256
EXIT 257
EXIT 258
BELLIS FAIR MALL
539
BEST WESTERN HERITAGE INN
BAKERVIEW RD
HOLIDAY INN EXPRESS
DAYS INN
COMFORT INN
KELLOGG AVE

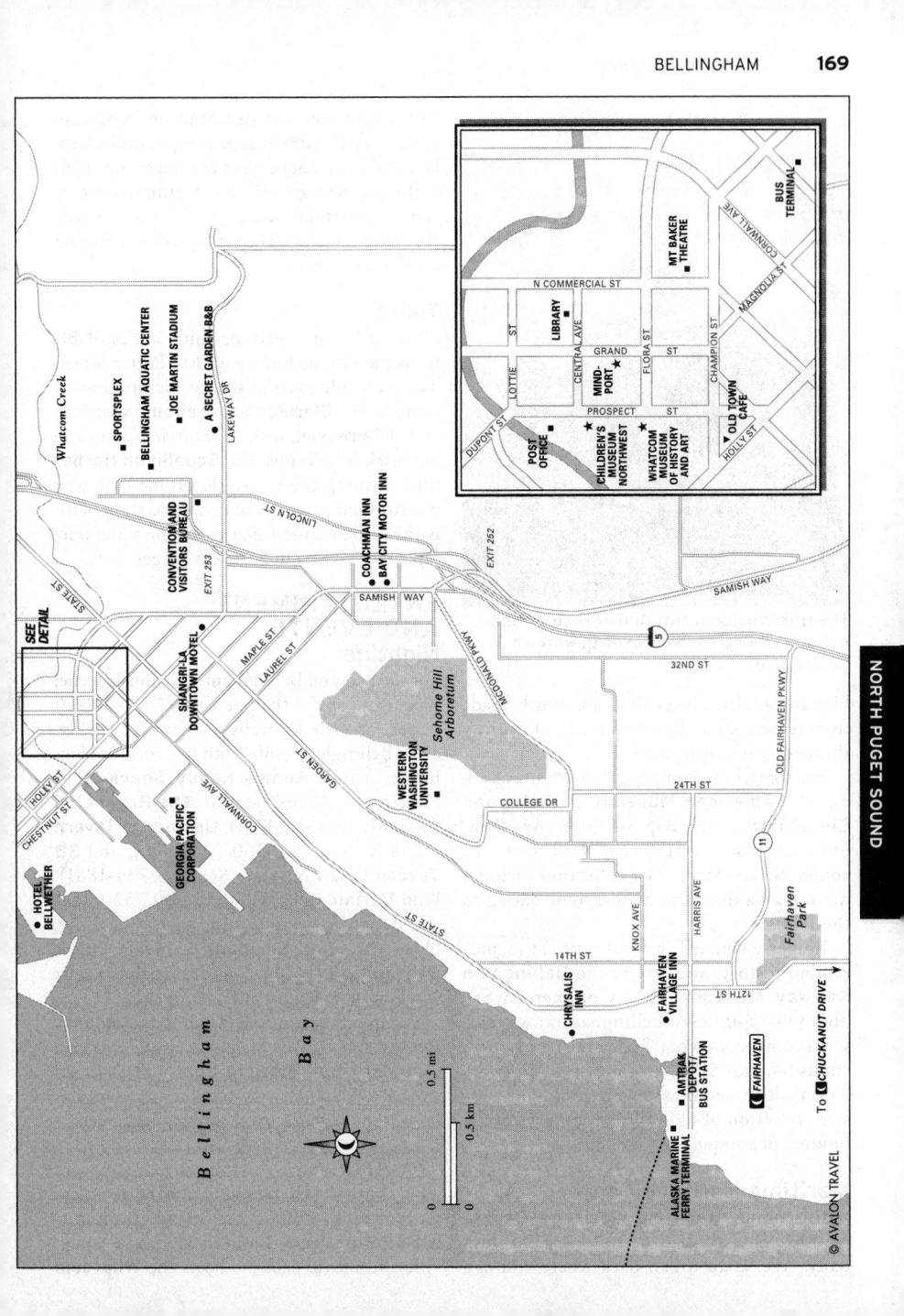
Bellingham Bay
Whatcom Creek
SPORTSPLEX
BELLINGHAM AQUATIC CENTER
JOE MARTIN STADIUM
A SECRET GARDEN B&B
LAKEWAY DR
CONVENTION AND VISITORS BUREAU
EXIT 253
LINCOLN ST
COACHMAN INN
BAY CITY MOTOR INN
SAMISH WAY
EXIT 252
SAMISH WAY
SEE DETAIL
STATE ST
SHANGRI-LA DOWNTOWN MOTEL
MAPLE ST
LAUREL ST
MCDONALD PKWY
Sehome Hill Arboretum
WESTERN WASHINGTON UNIVERSITY
GARDEN ST
HOLLY ST
CHESTNUT ST
CORNWALL AVE
GEORGIA PACIFIC CORPORATION
HOTEL BELLWETHER
COLLEGE DR
32ND ST
24TH ST
OLD FAIRHAVEN PKWY
KNOX AVE
HARRIS AVE
14TH ST
12TH ST
CHRYSALIS INN
FAIRHAVEN VILLAGE INN
Fairhaven Park
AMTRAK
AMTRAK BUS STATION
FAIRHAVEN
To CHUCKANUT DRIVE
ALASKA MARINE FERRY TERMINAL
0 0.5 mi
0 0.5 km
N COMMERCIAL ST
LIBRARY
MT BAKER THEATRE
BUS TERMINAL
CORNWALL AVE
MAGNOLIA ST
DUPONT ST
LOTTIE ST
CENTRAL AVE
GRAND ST
FLORA ST
CHAMPION ST
PROSPECT ST
HOLLY ST
POST OFFICE
CHILDREN'S MUSEUM NORTHWEST
MIND-PORT
WHATCOM MUSEUM OF HISTORY AND ART
OLD TOWN CAFE
© AVALON TRAVEL

© ERICKA CHICKOWSKI

The free Whatcom Museum of History and Art stands impressively over downtown Bellingham.

kids and adults. The exhibits are mostly made from reused old junk, with a touch of whimsy thrown in. It's great fun.

For something completely different, check out the **American Museum of Radio and Electricity** (1312 Bay St., 360/734-4168, www.amre.us, noon–5 P.M. Wed.–Sat., $5 adults, $2 children). The collection includes more than a thousand radios, some dating to the 1940s.

Immerse yourself in local railroad memorabilia, history, and lore at the **Bellingham Railway Museum** (1320 Commercial St., 360/393-7540, www.bellinghamrailwaymuseum.com, noon–5 P.M. Tues. and Thurs.–Sat., adults $4, kids $1) in downtown Bellingham. This little museum has a particularly impressive collection of old railroad lanterns and a number of antique scale models.

Maritime Heritage Center

Bellingham's **Maritime Heritage Center** (1600 C St., 360/676-6806, 9 A.M. to dusk daily, free) is an urban park where you can fish for salmon and steelhead on Whatcom Creek, watch salmon spawning in mid-October, and learn about hatchery operation. Kids will enjoy the marinelife touch tank where they can pet intertidal creatures. It's located inside the Harbor Center Mall at Squalicum Harbor off Roeder Avenue.

Tours

Maps of historic walking tours are available from the visitors bureau at 904 Potter Street. These include tours of stately Victorian mansions in the **Eldridge** and **Sehome** districts, and of **Fairhaven,** with its 1880s mansions and old brick storefronts. The **Squalicum Harbor** tour is along the two-mile promenade past pleasure and commercial boats and ships. This is the second-largest marina in the state; only Shilshole Marina in Seattle is bigger.

ENTERTAINMENT AND EVENTS

Nightlife

For the latest on Bellingham's live music scene, pick up a copy of the free *Every Other Weekly* paper, or visit its website, www.eoweekly.com. Bellingham clubs with live rock or blues music include **Anna's Kaddy Shack** (1114 Harris Ave., 360/671-6745), **The Royal** (208 E. Holly, 360/738-3701), **Up and Up Tavern** (1234 N. State St., 360/733-9739), and **3B Tavern** (1226 N. State St., 360/734-1881). **Wild Buffalo** (208 W. Holly, 360/752-0848) is a delightful casual joint with rockabilly, blues, and more. **Elephant & Castle Pub & Restaurant** (360/671-4545) at Bellis Fair Mall has comedy on Sunday nights.

For live jazz on weekends, drop by **Calumet Restaurant** (113 E. Magnolia, 360/733-3331). **Boundary Bay Brewing Co.** (1107 Railroad Ave., 360/647-5593, www.bbaybrewery.com) also hosts jazz and blues sets several nights a week.

The Arts

The historic **Mt. Baker Theatre** (106 N. Commercial, 360/733-5793, www.mountbakertheatre.com)—built in 1927 as a vaudeville and movie palace—hosts the **Whatcom**

Symphony Orchestra (360/734-6080, www.whatcomsymphony.com) plus many other musical and theatrical performances. The two-week-long **Bellingham Festival of Music** each August brings world-class classical and jazz musicians to town, and the **Brown Bag Music Series** (360/676-6985) features concerts on the public library lawn each Friday mid-June through August.

Staffed and performed entirely by local volunteers, the **Bellingham Theatre Guild** (1600 H St., 360/733-1811, www.bellinghamtheatreguild.com) produces five plays a year from fall to spring in the old Congregational Church building. More plays are presented in the **Theatre Arts** (360/650-6146) series at Western Washington University.

Events

Bellingham's **Ski to Sea Race** (360/734-1330, www.skitosea.org), held Memorial Day weekend, tests the physical endurance and athletic skills of its participants over an 85-mile course that includes cross-country and downhill skiing, running, bicycling, canoeing down the Nooksack River, mountain biking, and finally kayaking across Bellingham Bay to the finish in the Fairhaven District. In existence for almost 30 years, the race is the highlight of a weeklong festival that includes parades, a street fair with crafts, live music and dancing, food, and a beer garden on Sunday after the race.

All summer long the city puts on free **Concerts in the Parks** at Boulevard Park (Saturday evenings) and Elizabeth Park (Thursday evenings), plus Friday children's concerts at on the Bellingham Library lawn. All are free.

There's a big **4th of July** fireworks show over Bellingham Harbor each summer. Every August, Western Washington University is the home of the two-week **Bellingham Festival of Music** (360/676-5997, www.bellinghamfestival.org). You'll hear outstanding classical and jazz performances. Around the same time, the **Bellingham Chalk Art Festival** (360/676-8548) attracts a wide range of talent, from kids to serious artists. Great fun as everyone gets to draw on the city's sidewalks and not get arrested.

Like many other Puget Sound cities, Bellingham sponsors a Christmas **Lighted Boat Parade** (360/733-7390) in Bellingham Bay in mid-December.

SHOPPING

Downtown Galleries

Bellingham has a diverse arts community, with a number of fine galleries. **Allied Arts of Whatcom County** (1418 Cornwall Ave., 360/676-8548, www.alliedarts.org) has a large gallery. During the first two weekends of November, local artists' studios are open to the public. Get the full story at www.studiotour.net or call 360/734-9472 for details. In Barkley Village, **Hamann's Gallery** (2940 New Market, 360/733-8898) displays original artwork, etchings, and limited-edition prints. The **Blue Horse Gallery** (301 W. Holly St., 360/671-2305) has high-quality works from 20 regional artists. A few blocks away is **Pacific Marine Gallery** (700 W. Holly St., 360/738-8535, www.pacificmarineexchange.com), where all the pieces reflect the marine environment.

Located behind the visitors bureau office, **Jody Bergsma Gallery** (1344 King St., 800/237-4762, www.bergsma.com) shows works of this prolific artist. See her brother's work at **Mark Bergsma Photographer Gallery** (1306 Commercial St., 360/671-6818), including multi-panel landscape photographs.

Fairhaven Shops

The Fairhaven District is Bellingham's most enjoyable place to stroll and shop. Several interesting shops and galleries can be found in the district. **Good Earth Pottery** (1000 Harris Ave., 360/671-3998, 11 A.M.–6 P.M. Mon.–Sat., noon–5 P.M. Sun.) has fine ceramics; the cooperatively owned **Artwood** (1000 Harris Ave., 360/647-1628, www.pacificws.com/artwood, 10 A.M.–6 P.M. Mon.–Sat., 10 A.M.–5 P.M. Sun.) sells handcrafted woodworking; and **Gallery West** (1300 12th St., 360/734-8414, 10 A.M.–6 P.M. daily) offers paintings, sculpture, pottery, weavings, and jewelry.

Brenthaven (200 W. Holly, 360/752-5537 or 888/212-5301, www.brenthaven.com, 10 A.M.–6 P.M. Mon.–Fri.) sews and sells high-quality day packs, shoulder bags, and soft luggage.

One of the most popular places in Fairhaven, or in all of Bellingham for that matter, is **Village Books** (1210 11th St., 360/671-2626 or 800/392-2665, www.villagebooks.com, 10 A.M.–9 P.M. Mon.–Sat., 11 A.M.–7 P.M. Sun.) and its companion, **Colophon Café,** sharing space on both floors. Village Books usually has Sunday book readings. Another bookselling alternative is **Eclipse Bookstore** (915 Harris Ave., 360/647-8165), which offers an array of used titles.

Bellis Fair Mall

Massive **Bellis Fair Mall** (I-5 exit 256B), has over 150 shops (including Sears, JCPenney, Macy's, Kohl's, and Target), a food court, and a six-plex theater. Keep going out Meridian Street to enjoy the frenzy of shopping even more; here you'll find all the big discount chain stores, fast-food joints, motels, and hundreds of British Columbia license plates.

Antiques

Whatcom County has a number of antique shops and malls. In Bellingham proper, check out several along West Holly Street, particularly **Old Town Antique Mall** (427 W. Holly St., 360/647-1073, 10 A.M.–6 P.M. Mon.–Sat., noon–5 P.M. Sun.), which features a wide selection of collectibles from 40 dealers. Downstairs, at the same address, **Aladdin's Lamb Antique Mall** (427 W. Holly St., 360/647-0066, 10 A.M.–6 P.M. Mon.–Sat., noon–5 P.M. Sun.) sells jewelry, glassware, toys, and radios.

SPORTS AND RECREATION

Parks

Whatcom County has one of the best collections of city- and county-owned parks in the state. In Bellingham alone there are more than 35 places that qualify as parks, including green belt areas, fitness areas, and trails. These parks range from less than half an acre to over a thousand acres. Details at 360/733-2900 or www.co.whatcom.wa.us/parks.

Beautiful **Samish Park** (I-5 exit 246 south of Bellingham, 360/733-2362) is a 39-acre county park along Lake Samish with swimming, fishing, boating, picnicking, hiking, and a children's play area. Rent canoes, kayaks, hydrobikes, paddleboats, or rowboats.

Whatcom Falls Park (1401 Electric Ave.) near Lake Whatcom has hiking trails, tennis courts, a playground, a picnic area, and a state fish hatchery on 241 acres.

With 12 acres on the lake itself, **Bloedel Donovan Park** (2214 Electric Ave.) has a swimming beach, boat launch, playground, and picnic area.

Lake Padden Park (4882 Samish Way) has over 1,000 acres of hiking and horse trails, a golf course, picnic areas, and a playground, plus swimming, fishing, and nonmotorized boating on the lake.

Thirty-eight acres of practically untouched canyon wilderness is yours for the hiking at **Arroyo Park** on Old Samish Road, with nature and horse trails and creek fishing.

Overlooking Lake Whatcom, **Big Rock Garden Park** (2900 Sylvan St.) includes a hundred varieties of rhododendron and azaleas, along with dozens of Japanese maples. Surrounded by suburban sprawl, this is an oasis of tranquility, with forests and outdoor sculptures.

Climbing

Bellingham is home to the **American Alpine Institute** (1515 12th St., 360/671-1505, www.aai.cc), the nation's preeminent center for mountaineering education. The school's staff is made up of accomplished mountain climbers and educators who teach courses from the basics to advanced monthlong programs. Classes are taught all over the world, with beginning mountaineering courses in the North Cascades. AAI also rents outdoor equipment.

Learn to rock climb indoors at **Leading Edge Rock Gymnastics** (1409 Fraser St., 360/733-6969).

Water Sports and Tours

In the summer months you can swim at **Lake Padden Park** (4882 Samish Way, 360/676-6985), **Lake Samish** (673 N. Lake Samish Dr., 360/733-2362), and **Bloedel Donovan Park** (2214 Electric Ave., 360/676-6985).

Sail the San Juans (360/671-5852 or 800/729-3207, www.stsj.com) offers six-day fully crewed charters around the islands, departing from Bellingham. The visitors bureau has a complete listing of other sailing and fishing charter operators, and cruises.

Moondance Sea Kayaking Adventures (360/738-7664, www.moondancekayak.com) offers guided sea kayak tours from Bellingham. You can rent sea kayaks, rowboats, and sailboats in summer from **Bellingham Bay Community Boating Center** (501 Harris Ave., 360/647-2469, www.sailpaddlerow.com), near the Bellingham Cruise Terminal. **Bellingham Boat Rentals** (3034 Silvern Lane, 360/676-1363) has canoes and pedal boats for rent on Lake Whatcom and is open May through August.

Orca whale-watching trips are becoming increasingly popular from Bellingham, and a number of companies offer these day trips. One of the best is **Island Mariner Cruises** (5 Harbor Esplanade, 360/734-8866 or 877/734-8866, www.orcawatch.com, $55 for adults, $45 for seniors, or $35 for kids under 16) run by the always-entertaining "Captain Trivia." Also popular are his 2.5-hour narrated historical harbor cruises for $15 per person. These are offered on Thursday evenings mid-June to mid-August. Tours depart from the boat harbor in town. **San Juan Island Shuttle Express** (360/671-1137 or 888/373-8522, www.orcawhales.com) also offers three-hour whale-watching cruises from Bellingham for $65 for adults, or $55 for students.

The ***Snow Goose*** (360/733-9078 or 888/877-1770) is a 65-foot fully equipped research vessel operated by two local marine biologists. They offer a range of trips, from one day to five days. On all of these you'll get a first-hand look at marinelife and how researchers work in Puget Sound. In the summer months they operate along Alaska's Inside Passage.

SKI TO SEA

The Bellingham region offers enough opportunity to keep outdoor lovers busy for years. No event highlights the joys of the area's recreational bliss more than **Ski to Sea** (www.skitosea.com), the mother of all adventure races. This whopping seven-sport relay attracts teams of athletes from all over the world, who start atop Mount Baker and rush to the shores of Bellingham Bay over snow, water, trail, and road.

The race begins with cross-country skiing, then moves on to downhill skiing. Those are followed by running, road cycling, and canoeing. Then it is the mountain bikers' turn, followed by a sea kayak finish. All told, the grueling race can take anywhere from 5.5 to over 8 hours to complete, all followed with a rockin' party in Fairhaven to celebrate everyone's efforts.

Hiking

Stop by the visitors bureau for descriptions of more than 20 hiking trails in and around Bellingham, including trails in Whatcom Falls Park and Sehome Hill Arboretum. Another 2.6 miles of paths circle Lake Padden Park.

The **Interurban Trail** is a six-mile path that follows a former railroad bed from Old Fairhaven Parkway south to Larrabee State Park. It is a great place for a jog or bike ride.

Camping

The closest public campsites ($14 for tents, $20 for RVs) are seven miles south of Bellingham at **Larrabee State Park** (360/676-2093), with a boat launch and sandy beach. Additional camping can be found 14 miles north in **Birch Bay State Park** (5105 Helwig Rd., 360/371-2800), with year-round tent sites ($14) and RV hookups ($20) in the trees. Make reservations ($7 extra) for either of these parks at 888/226-7688, www.parks.wa.gov.

Private RV parks include **Sudden Valley Resort** on Lake Whatcom (2145 Lake Whatcom Blvd., 360/734-6430); and

Bellingham RV Park (3939 Bennett Dr., 360/752-1224 or 888/372-1224).

Other Recreation

Strap on some skates and glide the rink at **Sportsplex** (1225 Civic Field Way, 360/733-9999, $5), which offers year-round skating at its indoor facilities.

Tee off at the pastoral **Shuksan Golf Club** (1500 Axton Rd., 360/398-8888, www.shuksangolf.com, $25), a pretty and affordable course with ample elevation changes set by the gurgling Ten Mile Creek. You'll catch glimpses of the namesake Shuksan Mountain as you walk the course.

Rent bikes, skis, and snowboards from **Fairhaven Bike & Mountain Sport** (1103 11th St., 360/733-4433).

ACCOMMODATIONS

Under $100

Surprisingly, for a town with so many college students, hippies, and vagabonding ski bums, there's no hostel in Bellingham proper. Travel 20 miles north to stay in a pleasant hostel in the quiet Birch Bay.

For cheap accommodations in town, North Samish Way near the university is the major motel thoroughfare. The quality is unpredictable and the neighborhood is a little spotty, so be wary of snapping up a super cheap rate over the phone at a motel you haven't vetted. One of the best values is at the **Coachman Inn** (120 N. Samish Way, 360/671-9000 or 800/962-6641, $60 s or d). The exterior here looks a bit worn, but inside the rooms are updated and clean. Plus it has an outdoor pool, hot tub, and sauna.

Another clean and safe establishment is **Bay City Motor Inn** (116 N. Samish Way, 360/676-0332 or 800/538-8204, $75 s or $85–95 d). The rooms are accessible only via indoor corridor, and there's a fitness center, billiard table, laundry facility, and free continental breakfast in the morning. Spend a little extra coin and rent one of three whirlpool-tub suites for $125 d.

Or just go for the bed and breakfast option. The imminently affordable **DeCann House B&B** (2610 Eldridge Ave., 360/734-9172, www.decannhouse.com, $90–110 d) lets two guest rooms with private baths. This 1902 charmer is adorned with stained glass, etchings, family heirlooms, and fine views of the San Juan Islands. Unwind with a cue stick or book in hand in the English-style library. This alluring room makes you wish for a smoking jacket and glass of brandy with its dark wood, floor-to-ceiling bookshelves and classic billiard table. Kids are accepted here by prior arrangement.

$100-150

Near Bellis Fair Mall there are numerous big chain hotels to choose between. I particularly enjoyed staying at the **Best Western Heritage Inn** (151 E. McLeod Rd., 360/647-1912 or 800/528-1234, www.bestwestern.com/heritageinnbellingham, $129 s or $139 d), a reasonably priced hotel complex with New England colonial-style buildings and interiors. The grounds are well tended, and there's an outdoor pool, hot tub, fitness center, airport shuttle service, and complimentary breakfast. The rooms sport super comfy mattresses, new linens, and big flat-screen TVs. The only downside to some rooms can be the traffic drone—ask for a room facing away from the freeway.

Or get out of town and stay at **Anderson Creek Lodge** (5602 Mission Rd., 360/966-0598, www.andersoncreek.com, $120–160). Llamas graze in the pasture on this 55-acre property 10 miles northeast of Bellingham. Rooms in the lodge have king-size beds, private baths, and access to a hot tub.

$150-200

The Victorian Italianate-style **Fairhaven Village Inn** (1200 10th St., 360/733-1311 or 877/733-1100, www.fairhavenvillageinn.com, $179–219 d) blends well with its historic Fairhaven neighbors. This distinctive boutique hotel is one of the best in Bellingham, with large rooms, luxe furnishings, bathrobes, free continental breakfast and free Wi-Fi. The best rooms come equipped with gas fireplaces; the two-room suite ($289) comes with a large dining table and jetted tub. Some rooms are also pet friendly.

A large Craftsman home high on a hill overlooking Lake Whatcom **South Bay B&B** (4095 S. Bay Dr., 360/595-2086 or 877/595-2086, www.southbaybb.com, $149–245 d) is a quiet retreat featuring five guest rooms with whirlpool tubs, fireplaces, and private patios; rates include a big gourmet breakfast. This is a great romantic getaway.

$200-250

The **Hotel Bellwether** (1 Bellwether Way, 360/392-3100 or 877/411-1200, www.hotelbellwether.com, $202–264 d) offers Bellingham's most indulgent (and expensive) lodging, with a waterfront location, spacious rooms, balconies, Italian furnishings, gas fireplaces, and marble baths with jetted tubs. There are also a few splurge-worthy suites available. Regular suites with separate living areas run for $499. And honeymooners looking for a room to remember can book a spot in the distinctive three-level lighthouse suite for $699—ask about the lighthouse package, which includes champagne and caviar, plus a three-course dinner served by your own private butler. No matter which room you choose, pampered pooches are welcome. A lavish breakfast buffet is available for an extra $11.95.

The luxurious rooms at the waterfront **Chrysalis Inn and Spa at the Pier** (804 10th St., 360/756-1005 or 888/808-0005, www.thechrysalisinn.com, $199–209 s or d) are beautifully appointed, with such amenities as king-size beds, down comforters, CD players, fireplaces, fridges, high-speed Internet access, plus a substantial buffet breakfast. Suites ($299 d) also include whirlpool tubs, wet bars, and bay vistas. Fino Restaurant is on the main floor.

Above Lake Whatcom and surrounded by tall evergreens is a very private cottage at **Schnauzer Crossing** (4421 Lakeway Dr., 360/734-2808 or 800/562-2808, www.schnauzercrossing.com, $250 d). The wraparound deck overlooks the lake and the brand new interior sports a kitchenette and wet bar, gas fireplace, king-size bed, and Jacuzzi tub.

© ERICKA CHICKOWSKI

Hotel Bellwether

FOOD

Bellingham has an amazing variety of creative eating establishments. Head to Fairhaven and just walk around to see what looks interesting, or check out the places below.

Cafés and Delis

A particular favorite among health-conscious foodies looking for organic grub is **Old Town Café** (316 W. Holly St., 360/671-4431, 6:30 A.M.–3 P.M. Mon.–Sat., 8 A.M.–2 P.M. Sun., $8), where the waitress is likely to have a nose ring and the queue of customers is out the door on a weekend morning. The atmosphere is laid-back and noisy. Another popular downtown place is **Daisy Cafe** (114 W. Magnolia St., 360/733-8996, www.thedaisycafe.com, 7:30 A.M.–2 P.M. daily, $8) with a diverse breakfast and Sunday brunch menu. It's a favorite of the suit-and-tie crowd.

A completely different dining experience can be found at **The Little Cheerful Café** (113 E. Holly St., 360/738-8824, 7 A.M.–2 P.M. daily, $8). The setting is casual and the breakfasts are always great (especially the hash browns), with ample portions. Be prepared to wait if you get here after 10 A.M. on weekends.

Swan Café (1059 N. State St., 360/734-8158, 7 A.M.–9 P.M. daily, $6), inside the Community Food Co-Op, serves hearty salads and sandwiches. This is a fine place for an inexpensive downtown lunch.

If you're in Fairhaven and want great sandwiches, bagels, quiche, or just a scoop of ice cream, drop by **Colophon Café** inside Village Books (1210 11th St., 360/647-0092, www.colophoncafe.com, 9 A.M.–10 P.M. daily, $10). Be sure to give the unique African peanut soup a go—this rich, velvety concoction has a complex meaty flavor and a little bit of a spicy kick. Colophon is also great for Paul Bunyan–size slices of carrot cake. Get here early at lunch or be ready to wait.

If you aren't looking for the gourmet variety burger, **Boomer's Drive In** (310 N. Samish Way, 360/647-2666, 11 A.M.–10 P.M. Sun.–Thurs., 11 A.M.–11 P.M. Fri.–Sat., $5) has the best around.

Steak and Seafood

Cliff House Restaurant (331 N. State St., 360/734-8660, www.bellinghamcliffhouse.com, 4:30–9:30 P.M. daily, $30) is famous for its whiskey crab soup, oyster bar, fresh seafood, and Angus beef. This is an old favorite with a big deck facing Bellingham Bay for alfresco dining.

The fair-weather favorite **Fairhaven Fish and Chips** (1020 Harris Ave., 360/733-5021, 11 A.M.–7 P.M. Mon.–Sat., noon–5 P.M. Sun.) is easy to find — just look for the red double-decker bus surrounded by patio umbrellas and tables. Step up to the bus window to order a basket of golden crispy deliciousness, plus clam chowder, Italian sodas, and ice cream.

Harborside Bistro (1 Bellwether Way, 360/392-3100 or 877/411-1200, www.hotelbellweather.com, 7 A.M.–9 P.M. daily, $25) is a charming place for fresh seafood and hormone-free beef. It's right on the water at the luxurious Hotel Bellwether. A few steps away on the marina is **Anthony's HomePort** (25 Bellwether Way, 360/647-5588, www.anthonys.com, 11:30 A.M.–9:30 P.M. Sun.–Thurs., 11:30 A.M.–10:30 P.M. Fri.–Sat., $30), part of a Northwest chain of upscale seafood restaurants.

Dirty Dan Harris' (1211 11th St., 360/676-1011, www.dirtydanharris.com, 5–9:30 P.M. Sun.–Thurs., 5–10 P.M. Fri.–Sat., $24) in the Fairhaven District serves prime rib, steaks, and fresh seafood dinners in an 1800s-style saloon. It's named for Daniel Jefferson Harris, a feisty eccentric best known for his bathing habits—or lack thereof—who platted the town's streets, built a dock, and sold lots to the thousands of folks who rolled into Fairhaven in 1883. He made a small fortune in the process.

Italian and Pizza

D'Anna's Café Italiano (1319 N. State St., 360/714-0188, www.dannascafeitaliano.com, $13) is a fine little bistro specializing in homemade pasta, ravioli, and sausage. The chicken parmesan is the best around. **Pastazza** (2945 Newmarket Pl. #101, 360/714-1168, www.pastazza.com, 11 A.M.–9 P.M. Mon.–Thurs.,

11 A.M.–10 P.M. Fri., noon–10 P.M. Sat., noon–9 P.M. Sun., $15) is an excellent place for homemade pastas and wonderful desserts.

For pizza, **Rudy's Pizzeria** (1230 N. State St., 360/647-7547, 11 A.M.–11 P.M. Mon.–Wed., 11 A.M.–midnight Thurs.–Fri., noon–midnight Sat., 4 –10 P.M. Sun., $15) is popular with the college set and big families. Choose between a range of gourmet toppings, plus several types of crusts and sauces.

Other International

Fairhaven's **Dos Padres** (1111 Harris Ave., 360/733-9900, 11 A.M.–9 P.M. Sun.–Thurs., 11 A.M.–9:30 P.M. Fri.–Sat., $10) has an extensive menu of Mexican dishes with a Southwest twist. It's locally famous for margaritas and nachos. Come here for lunch, when prices are lower. Another very good Mexican restaurant—with more traditional fare—is **El Gitano** (1125 Sunset Dr., 360/714-1065, www.elgitano.com, 11 A.M.–10 P.M. Sun.–Thurs., 11 A.M.–11 P.M. Fri.–Sat., $13). Some of the area's best Southwestern-style meals can be found at **Pepper Sisters** (1055 N. State St., 360/671-3414). This place is highly recommended.

Cafe Akroterii (1219 Cornwall Ave., 360/676-5554, 11 A.M.–10 P.M. Mon.–Sat., 4 P.M.–9 P.M. Sun., $14) is a fine little place for Greek food downtown.

India Grill (1215 Cornwall Ave., 360/714-0314, www.indiagrill.us, 11 A.M.–3 P.M. and 4–9 P.M. daily, $11) is *the* place for Indian food, including tandoori and vegetarian specials.

Several local places have good Thai food; two of the best are **Busara Siamese Cuisine** (324 36th St., Sehome Village Mall, 360/734-8088, 11:30 A.M.–9:30 P.M. daily, $11) and **Thai House Restaurant** (187 Telegraph Rd., 360/734-5111, www.bellinghamthaihouse.com, 11 A.M.–9 P.M. daily, $9).

Oriento Restaurant (2500 Meridian St., 360/733-3322, 11 A.M.–8:30 P.M. Mon.–Sat., noon–8:30 P.M. Sun., $9) has a big Chinese menu that includes Mandarin, Szechuan, and Cantonese favorites along with vegetarian specials. **Little Tokyo** (Barkley Village, 360/752-2222, lunch 11 A.M.–3 P.M. daily, dinner 4:30 P.M.–9 P.M. Mon.–Thurs., 4:30 P.M.–10 P.M. Fri.–Sat., 4–9 P.M. Sun., $15) is a casual sushi bar and Japanese restaurant; it's considered the best in town. Penny pinchers should try to go on Wednesdays between 5 P.M. and 7 P.M., when the place plates $1 sushi.

Pub Grub

Boundary Bay Brewery & Bistro (1107 Railroad Ave., 360/647-5593, www.bbaybrewery.com, 11 A.M.–11 P.M. daily, $10) features seven beers on tap and a limited pub menu. The big doors open up on sunny days.

Markets and Bakeries

Bellingham's **Community Food Co-Op** (1059 N. State St., 360/734-8158, www.communityfoodcoop.com) is a spacious natural foods market, and home to the Swan Café. **Haggen Foods** has three large gourmet markets (210 36th St., 2814 Meridian St., and Barkley Village, www.haggen.com), with fine delis offering Chinese food, pizza by the slice, sandwiches, and a salad bar. They're a good deal for fast meals.

Find European-style breads, plus sandwiches and soups at **Avenue Bread Co.** (1313 Railroad Ave., 360/676-9274, 7 A.M.–4:30 P.M. Mon.–Sat., 9 A.M.–4 P.M. Sun.). For French pastries, meander into **La Vie En Rose French Bakery** (111 W. Holly St., 360/715-1839, www.laviebakery.com, 7:30 A.M.–5:30 P.M. Mon.–Fri., 8 A.M.–4 P.M. Sat., closed Sun.).

The **Bellingham Farmers Market** (360/647-2060, www.bellinghamfarmers.org, 10 A.M.–3 P.M., Sat.–Sun., early April–October) is held in the parking lot at Chestnut Street and Railroad Avenue. Across town at 11th and McKenzie, the **Fairhaven Farmers Market** (360/647-2060) takes place 3–7 P.M. Wednesday June–September.

INFORMATION

For maps, brochures, and general information, contact the **Bellingham and Whatcom County Convention and Visitors Bureau** (904 Potter St. at exit 253 off I-5, 360/671-3990 or 800/487-2032 (recording), www.bellingham.org, 8:30 A.M.–5:30 P.M. daily). An information booth at the Bellingham Cruise Terminal (where the Alaska ferry docks) is staffed Tuesday, Thursday, and Friday in the summer, and brochure racks are located inside the Bellis Fair Mall.

GETTING THERE AND AROUND

By Car

Downtown Bellingham makes up for its relatively small size with odd street intersections that send you off in the opposite direction you intended. It's as if someone laid out a grid, and then took the central (downtown) section and twisted it 45 degrees. Newcomers are guaranteed to get lost at least once.

By Ferry

The **Bellingham Cruise Terminal,** located three blocks downhill from Fairhaven, is where you can catch ferries to the San Juans, Victoria, and Alaska. The terminal has reservation and ticketing booths for the **Alaska Marine Highway** (360/676-8445 or 800/642-0066, www.state.ak.us/ferry), which provides passenger and vehicle ferry service to Southeast Alaska destinations. Alaska ferries depart on Friday year-round, plus Tuesday in summer. The ticket office inside the terminal is open weekdays. Also here are a gift shop, storage lockers, and a fine little seafood café.

Victoria-San Juan Cruises (355 Harris Ave., 360/738-8099 or 800/443-4552, www.whales.com) has all-day cruises from Bellingham to Victoria and back, with time around the San Juan Islands. You'll sail aboard the *Victoria Star II,* a 100-passenger boat. The cost—including a seafood dinner—is $89 for adults, $84 for seniors, or $45 for kids. Tours are offered late May to mid-October.

Also inside the ferry terminal is the **San Juan Island Commuter** (360/734-8180 or 888/734-8180, www.islandcommuter.com, $35 adults, $18 kids, $5 bikes, $20 kayaks), which has daily seasonal service (mid-May through September) to Rosario Resort on Orcas Island or Friday Harbor on San Juan Island;. It operates two boats along the route and also has whale-watching trips out of Friday Harbor.

San Juan Island Shuttle Express (360/671-1137 or 888/373-8522, www.orcawhales.com, $33 adults, $29 seniors, $27 students round-trip, $5 bikes) operates a passenger ferry connecting Bellingham with Orcas, Lopez, and San Juan Islands. Add a whale-watching trip out of Friday Harbor on San Juan Island for $25 more. The ferry runs daily late May–September. A second Shuttle Express boat also offers three-hour whale-watching cruises from Bellingham for $65 adults, $55 students.

By Train

Amtrak (800/872-7245, www.amtrak.com) provides daily train connections on its modern Cascades train north to Vancouver, B.C., and south to Mount Vernon, Everett, Edmonds, and Seattle. It stops at the Fairhaven depot, just a short walk from the ferry terminal.

By Air

Allegiant Air (702/505-8888, www.allegiantair.com), **Horizon Air** (800/547-9308, www.horizonair.com), and **United Express** (800/241-6522, www.ual.com) all operate flights out of Bellingham International Airport (www.portofbellingham.com/airport) to Seattle. Many Canadians use this airport because they can get more convenient flights to some U.S. destinations, cheaper tickets, and the parking—$7 a day—is a big savings, too. **San Juan Airlines** (360/671-8463 or 800/874-4434, www.sanjuanairlines.com) has scheduled service to the San Juan Islands, plus charter flights and flightseeing trips.

If you're flying into Sea-Tac Airport and can't make good connections, **Airporter Shuttle** (360/380-8800 or 866/235-5247, www.airporter.com) runs daily van service to Bellingham. Similarly, **Quick Shuttle** (604/940-4428 or 800/665-2122, www.quickcoach.com) runs service to Vancouver, British Columbia.

By Bus

Locally, **Whatcom Transit** (360/676-7433, www.ridewta.com) provides bus service Monday–Saturday to Bellingham, Ferndale, Lynden, Blaine, and the Lummi Reservation. **Greyhound** (360/733-5251 or 800/231-2222, www.greyhound.com) has nationwide bus connections from the Amtrak depot in Fairhaven.

North to Canada

Many road-weary travelers heading up to the Canadian border tend to let the scenery blur by along I-5 once they pass the outskirts of Bellingham, but there are a number of worthwhile stops along the way.

Just north of Bellingham, the little hamlet of Ferndale is home to one of the best collections of historic log buildings in the state and is a darned fine spot for a piece of pie and a cup of coffee.

Along the waterfront, Birch Bay's moon-shaped waters have drawn families from both sides of the border for generations to enjoy its warm waters come summertime. Similarly, Lummi Island and Semiahmoo Spit also offer a shoreside respite and a chance to walk quiet beaches, ply the waters for fish, and soak in the sunsets.

For a more terrestrial treat, little Lynden's shady streets and spinning windmills present travelers a taste of old world Holland. Set amid the idyllic dairy fields and ruby red barns along Highway 539, this small town also offers visitors a chance to peek in at one of the best history museums they've never heard of.

All roads eventually lead to Blaine, the largest Canadian border crossing in the northwest. Before hopping in line, be sure to pull off at Peace Arch Park to walk the greens and take a gander at the white arch standing proudly as a testament to the long-lasting friendship between two countries.

SIGHTS

Peace Arch

The 40-acre **Peace Arch State Park** at the Canadian border has beautifully landscaped grounds and gardens surrounding the Peace Arch, a symbol of friendship between the U.S. and Canada that stands with one "foot" in each country. The park was constructed in 1921 by American and Canadian volunteers and funded by Washington and British Columbia schoolchildren, who contributed from $0.01 to $0.10 each for the project. Pieces of the *Mayflower* and the Hudson's Bay Company steamer *Beaver* are included in the monument.

A path lined with rhododendrons, dahlias, and azaleas leads from the arch greens to a picnic area and playground. Get to the Peace Arch by heading north on 2nd Street into the parking lot; customs officers from both nations don't like folks stopping at the border crossing to enter the park.

Semiahmoo Spit

Head out the 1.5-mile-long Semiahmoo Spit to **Semiahmoo County Park** (360/371-5513), where you'll find restored salmon cannery buildings, a gift shop and art gallery, and a museum (noon–4 P.M. Fri.–Mon. June–Aug. only) that depicts early fishing and cannery operations. The park itself is open daily year-round. The Raven-Salmon Woman Totem Pole stands outside. A paved bike path parallels the road along Semiahmoo Spit.

The **M.V. *Plover*** was built in 1944 as a ferry for cannery workers at Semiahmoo. Today the 32-foot boat has been lovingly restored and serves as a passenger and bike ferry (360/332-5742, donation requested). It operates between the harbor at Blaine and the Inn at Semiahmoo noon–8 P.M. Friday–Saturday and 10 A.M.–6 P.M. Sunday summers only, departing on the hour from Blaine and on the half hour from Semiahmoo.

Lummi Island

Lummi Island is geographically the northernmost blip on the San Juan archipelago, but because the eight-minute ferry ride here originates so far north of Anacortes, it is regarded as a haven of its own.

Lummi is a quiet island, home primarily to artists, weekenders, and a community of Native Americans on the 13,000-acre Lummi Reservation here.

Most of the island is private property with no public access, but you can ride the roads to a few public places around the island. Most notable among them is a checkerboard of land preserved by the Lummi Island Heritage Trust (360/758-7997). Largest among them is **The Otto Farm,** a 120-acre property that includes a 70-acre wildlife preserve located on Sunrise Road, between South Nugent Road and Seacrest Drive.

Readily accessible public beaches are scant on the island, with most only accessible by boat. The best bet for the boatless is a stretch of shoreline just north of the ferry terminal. Go north on Nugent Road until you reach a viewing platform and descend the adjacent stairs.

Many of the Lummi who live on the reserve still fish the waters in the style of their ancestors. Stroll the western shore along Legoe Bay to see them line up two by two in their small barks, spreading specialized reef-nets between them to trap salmon as they migrate by the island to their spawning grounds in British Columbia's Fraser River.

Historic Ferndale

Sitting on the northwest side of the Nooksack River, Ferndale is a quiet little Main Street town whose major highlight is a pair of historic parks that have preserved a little slice of Whatcom County's past.

Located two blocks south of Main on 1st Avenue, **Pioneer Park** contains a dozen hand-hewn cedar log buildings that date back to the late 19th century, moved here and preserved since the 1930s. Inside, visitors can check out exhibits that range from aged photos to an old Linotype machine. Tours of the buildings are available 11:30 A.M.–4:30 P.M. Tues.–Sun. mid-May to mid-September and cost $2.

Head south from town on Hovander Drive and Neilsen Road to **Hovander Homestead Park** (360/384-344, www.co.whatcom.wa.us/parks), where you'll find a restored century-old Victorian home and farm on the Nooksack River, a big red barn, milk house, children's petting zoo, flower gardens (including 30 varieties of dahlias), fruit orchard, hayfields, and antique farm equipment. Bring your picnic basket for a lunch along the river. Now a National Historic site, the park is open daily, but the homestead is open only on summer weekends. Admission is $3 per car. Tours are available in the summer noon to 4:30 P.M. Thursday through Sunday.

Birch Bay State Park

Birch Bay's featured attraction is its beach, and one of the best places to enjoy it is the 193-acre **Birch Bay State Park** (360/371-2800, www.parks.wa.gov) at the west end of Helwig Road. This park follows two miles of shoreline along the bay, with campsites in the trees. The beach is a favorite place for swimming, kite flying, windsurfing, clamming, and volleyball. Other facilities include an underwater park, fishing (though there's no boat launch), a picnic area, and the half-mile Terrell Marsh nature trail through an estuary that is home to beavers, opossums, muskrats, and great blue herons.

Lynden

Most of Lynden's early settlers were dairy farmers from the Netherlands, and the town now plays up that heritage to attract tourists. The town has become a favorite stopping place for tourists from British Columbia (three miles north) heading to Bellingham (12 miles away) via Highway 539. Many downtown buildings have been outfitted with Dutch false fronts. Front Street, the main drag, is dominated by a four-story, 72-foot-tall windmill that is part of the Dutch Village Mall, which also has a 150-foot indoor "canal" with colorful koi fish, a theater, and shops along a simulated Dutch cobblestone street. Many of these are cloyingly sweet, with places selling fudge, books, cards, kitchenware, knickknacks, and heart-shaped doormats.

The Dutch theme includes provincial flags flapping in the breeze, Dutch food and gifts (yes, wooden shoes) sold in stores, and costumed clerks on special holidays such as Holland Days during the first weekend in May. Residents in costumes sweep the already-immaculate streets—just like in Holland.

Lynden is home to one of the finest small museums in Washington, the **Lynden Pioneer Museum** (217 W. Front St., 360/354-3675, www.lyndenpioneermuseum.com, 10 A.M.–5 P.M. Mon.–Sat., 1:30–5 P.M. Sun. summers, 10 A.M.–4 P.M. Mon.–Sat. the rest of the year, $3 adults, $2 seniors and students, $1 ages 5–14, free for kids under 5, free to all on Sunday). On the main floor is a re-created turn-of-the-20th-century Lynden town and a collection of artifacts. The basement is a must-see, centering on 40 or so buggies, wagons, sleighs, carts, and other horse-drawn vehicles, plus antique tractors and farm machinery, and a big antique car and truck collection.

EVENTS

Ferndale

Ferndale has several of the county's best festivals. The **Scottish Highland Games** (360/647-8500, www.bellinghamhighland.org) take place on the first Saturday in June, with bagpipe music, Highland dancing, dog trials, Celtic music, and the caber toss. Then comes the **Whatcom County Old Settlers Picnic** (360/384-1866) at Pioneer Park on the last weekend of July. More than an old-timers picnic, this century-old festival includes country music, dancing, and parades.

In early August the **Civil War Re-enactment** takes place at Hovander Homestead and includes staged battles between the Blue and Gray armies. The first weekend in December brings **Olde Fashioned Christmas at Pioneer Park** (360/384-3693). People dressed in turn-of-the-20th-century costumes take you through the cabins to experience the sounds, sights, and smells of Christmases gone-by, including horse-drawn wagon rides.

Birch Bay and Blaine

Birch Bay Discovery Days (360/371-2070) is the main summer event, with a "clampetition" clamming contest, parade, golf tournament, and arts and crafts show. It's held in mid-July. The Birch Bay area also has monthly **sandcastle contests** all summer. For something different, come here on January 1 for the annual **Polar Bear Swim** (360/371-7800) with other hardy fools.

The annual **Hands Across the Border Peace Arch Celebration,** held the second Sunday in June, brings together veterans and Boy and Girl Scouts from the U.S. and Canada to celebrate friendly relations. After ceremonially transferring the flags, the gathering turns into a big merit-badge swap for the scouts. Another summertime attraction is Blaine's **4th of July** fireworks show. Return on the first Friday of December for the **Christmas Lighting Ceremony,** when Santa visits the Peace Arch.

Lummi Island

The **Lummi Stommish Water Festival** in mid-June is held on the Lummi Reservation and features competitive war-canoe races over a five-mile course, with up to 11 people in a canoe. Other activities include arts and crafts sales, dancing, and a salmon bake. For details, call the tribal office at 360/734-8180.

Lynden

Holland Days (360/354-5885), held the first weekend of May, brings wooden shoe races, Klompen dancing, and costumed Lyndenites scrubbing down Front Street.

Mid-August brings the largest event: more than 240,000 people come to the **Northwest Washington Fair** (360/354-4111 or 800/992-8499, www.nwwafair.com), with farm animal exhibits, carnival rides, a tractor pull, demolition derby, and musical entertainers.

The **Harvest Festival** in mid-October brings rows of scarecrows, hayrides, a huge maze made from bales of hay, and other fun activities. The **Dutch Sinterklaas Celebration** in early December is a Christmas parade with lighted farm equipment, antique vehicles, horses, and floats, plus Sinterklaas (Santa Claus) atop a white horse. The Christmas season also features **Lynden in Lights,** with animated light displays all over downtown.

SHOPPING

Good Thunder Arts (2307 Tuttle Ln., 360/758-7121) has handcrafted pottery, sculptures, and other artwork.

The **Peace Arch Factory Outlets** are just off I-5 at exit 270, six miles south of the border. Here you'll find 30 outlet stores open daily, including Levi's, Carters, Mikasa, Bass—all the usual suspects.

SPORTS AND RECREATION

Golf

One of the area's premier set of links, **Semiahmoo Golf and Country Club** (9565 Semiahmoo Pkwy., 360/371-7015 or 800/231-4425, www.semiahmoo.com, $80) is the featured attraction at the sprawling Semiahmoo Resort, with two championship courses—one of which was designed by Arnold Palmer and both of which are regularly voted Washington's finest.

In Lynden, **Homestead Golf & Country Club** (360/354-1196 or 800/354-1196, www.homesteadfarmsgolf.com, $65) maintains an elaborate 18-hole championship course where one hole sits on an island. There's also a putting course, gourmet restaurant, and an impressive fitness center. All are open to the public.

Horseback Riding

Peace Arch Equestrian Center (360/366-4049, www.peacearchequestrian.net) has horse and pony rides near the outlet shops in Blaine.

Hiking

Take a walk around a bog and displays at **Tennant Lake Interpretive Center** (at the end of Nielsen Rd. just south of the turnoff to Hovander Homestead, 360/384-3444). This 720-acre park is an interpretive center for Tennant Lake, with a system of trails, a half-mile boardwalk through the marsh, and an observation tower. One of the park's highlights is the wheelchair-accessible **Fragrance Garden,** designed so people who are visually impaired—and anyone else—can experience more than 60 varieties of plants by scent.

The state-operated **Lake Terrell Wildlife Area** (four miles west of Ferndale, 360/384-4723) covers 1,500 acres and has picnic areas, trails, fishing, and three boat launches.

Camping

The **Washington Department of Natural Resources** (www.wa.gov/dnr, free) maintains a small and primitive kayak-accessible campground on the east side near the south end of the island. This is the only place to camp on Lummi Island.

Public tent ($17) and RV ($23) sites are just a few miles northwest of Ferndale at **Birch Bay State Park** (5105 Helwig Rd.). Make reservations ($7 extra) at 888/226-7688 or www.parks.wa.gov. The privately run **Cedars RV Resort** (6335 Portal Way, 360/384-2622) has full hookups and a large heated outdoor pool. **Mountain View Mobile Home Park** (6006 Portal Way, 360/384-2860) or **Nor West RV Park** (1627 Main St., 360/384-5038) also provide RV spaces.

Other places to park RVs include **Ball Bay View RV Park** (7387 Jackson Rd., 360/371-0334), **Beachside RV Park** (7630 Birch Bay Dr., 360/371-5962 or 800/596-9586), **Richmond Resort** (8086 Birch Bay Dr., 360/371-226), and **Seabreeze RV Park** (4700 Alderson Rd., 360/371-5603).

Lovers of old-growth stands should pitch a tent at the shady campsites offered at **Berthusen Park** (8837 Berthusen Rd., 360/354-2424, $12 tents, $17 RVs), which once was a sliver of a 19th-century homestead owned by a pioneer with the foresight to leave about 20 acres of virgin forest untouched when he developed the land. Additional RV hookups are available at **Lynden KOA** (three miles east of Lynden, 360/354-4772 or 800/562-4779, www.koa.com), and **Hidden Village RV Park** (7062 Guide Meridian Rd., 360/398-1041 or 800/843-8606).

Other Recreation

Kids of all ages love **Birch Bay Water Slides** (4874 Birch Bay-Lynden Rd., 360/371-7500, www.birchbaywaterslides.com, daily mid-May

BORDERING ON FRIENDLINESS

East of Blaine is one of the more vivid statements about the relationship between the United States and Canada. As you drive east toward Sumas and Lynden, you can turn north off the main road and follow it until it makes a sharp right turn to the east again. Here you will notice two, two-lane blacktop highways running east and west, side by side, with a ditch separating them. That ditch is the international boundary between Canada and America for more than 3,000 miles, the longest unprotected boundary in the world. When the boundary goes through forests, a swath is kept cleared by crews from both countries.

to Labor Day, $12 ages 6 and up, $8 ages 3–5 and seniors, free for tots). The park has a 60-foot "hydrocliff," four giant water slides, lots of other kiddie slides, plus a volleyball court and hot tub for oldsters.

Pioneer Valley Railroad (4620 Birch Bay-Lynden Rd., 360/371-7700) has miniature train rides and go-karts in the summer.

Renaissance Adventure Guides (866/424-8433, www.raguides.com) leads sea-kayaking trips from Lummi Island, from half-day local paddles to three-day trips through the San Juan Islands.

ACCOMMODATIONS

Under $100

At the bottom of the price category in Birch Bay, but not in popularity or friendliness, is the 49-bed **Birch Bay AYH-Hostel** (467 Gemini St., Birch Bay, 360/371-2180, www.birchbay.net). Dorm beds are $14 per person for hostel members or $17 per person for others. Couples stay in one of four private rooms for the same rate, and families ($7 for kids ages 7–18, free for younger kids) stay in two adjacent rooms that share a bath. A full kitchen is on the premises. Reservations are advised if you're arriving in the summer. The hostel is closed 10 A.M.–5 P.M. daily, and October–April.

For a bit more privacy, **Driftwood Inn Motel** (7394 Birch Bay Dr., Blaine, 360/371-2620 or 800/833-2666, www.driftwoodinnmotel.com) offers studio units ($80 d), rustic cottages and suites with kitchenettes ($99 for up to four), and condo units ($130–190 for eight), all with access to the outdoor pool and canoe rentals.

Border-hoppers looking for a cheap night's stay will find a number of options in Blaine, including **Anchor Inn Motel** (250 Cedar St., Blaine, 360/332-5539, $59 d, $71 d with kitchenette). Like other places in town, the rooms have older furnishings, but these are clean and well maintained. The owner is fluent in French, Farsi, Afghani, and, of course, English. Another alternative is **Motel International** (758 Peace Portal Dr., Blaine, 360/332-8222, $57 s or $81 d). All rooms have fridges here, and many come with decent views of the harbor.

Lodging on Lummi Island is limited. The most affordable choice among a handful of places is **West Shore Farm B&B** (2781 West Shore Dr., Lummi Island, 360/758-2600, $80 s or $90 d). The farm is a 21-acre spread with sweeping Georgia Strait views and private beach access. You'll stay in one of two guest rooms with king-size beds and private baths within a handcrafted octagonal home here. Rates include a full breakfast, and the friendly owners welcome kids here.

The town of Lynden is similarly quiet, with only a few options. Spend a night in a windmill at the **Dutch Village Inn** (655 Front St., Lynden, 360/354-4440, $79 s or $89 d), where six hotel rooms (three are in the windmill and two have hot tubs) feature Dutch furnishings, antiques, and a coupon for breakfast at a nearby café.

Near the little town of **Everson,** southeast of Lynden, **Kale House B&B** (201 Kale St., 360/966-7027 or 800/225-2165, www.bbonline.com/wa/kale, $95 d) is a comfortable house in the country and a great home base for those who want to be central to the border, Bellingham, and Mt. Baker. This early-20th-century home features a downstairs bedroom and upstairs suite, both with private baths. No children are permitted.

$100-150

Birch Bay is full of condo rentals for those who want a little more space to kick off their shoes. **Cabana Club Condos** (7503 Birch Bay Dr., 360/371-2511 or 206/481-6975) has a range of units, from one-bedroom condos that sleep four for $110 daily or $605 weekly, up to two-bedroom and loft units that sleep eight and cost $145 daily or $775 weekly. All have fireplaces and kitchens, as well as access to an outdoor pool, hot tub, and sauna.

Birch Bay Get Away (4973 Cottonwood Court, 877/627-2229, www.birchbaygetaway.com, $135–225 d) has one-, two-, and three-bedroom cottages.

Located on the west side of Lummi Island, ☾ **The Willows Inn B&B** (2579 W. Shore Dr., Lummi Island, 360/758-2620, www.willows-inn.com,) is a standout option in the area. Willows has four rooms in the inn ($125 d), a honeymoon cottage ($155 d), and a guest house ($290 for up to six people). All include a three-course breakfast, private baths, a hot tub, and tranquility, as no kids are allowed here. The honeymoon cottage provides additional privacy and a magnificent view of the San Juans.

$150-200

Those looking to experience a bit of luxury in Lynden should look no farther than **Homestead Farms Golf Resort** (115 E. Homestead Blvd., 360/354-1196 or 800/354-1196, www.homesteadfarmsgolf.com, $149–169 d), an ideal sanctuary for duffers and scratch golfers alike. The resort offers reasonably priced links-side lodging in cabanas, lodge condos, and hotel units, as well as a fitness center and indoor pool facility.

$200-250

Located at the end of a long sand spit guarding Blaine's Drayton Harbor, ☾ **Semiahmoo Resort** (9565 Semiahmoo Pkwy., 360/371-2000 or 800/770-7992, www.semiahmoo.com) is Washington's largest destination resort. The Inn at Semiahmoo is a part of a massive 800-acre development with facilities such as a 300-slip marina, athletic club, indoor/outdoor pool, hot tub, racquetball and tennis courts, full European spa, a movie theater, two championship golf courses (including one designed by Arnold Palmer), restaurants, lounges, and plenty of Puget Sound beachfront. Rates range widely, depending upon the room and amenities, from $189 d for a standard room up to $399 d for an executive suite with fireplace. Package rates are also available.

FOOD

Ferndale

Popular with locals are **Cedar's Café** (2038 Main St., 360/384-1848) and **Ferndale Bakery** (5686 3rd Ave., 360/384-1554). The best carnivorous meals can be found at **Pacific Prime Rib** (2254 Douglas Rd., 360/384-5111), where the menu also includes pasta, seafood, and steaks. Another favorite is **Chihuahua Family Mexican Restaurant** (3rd Ave. and Vista Dr., 360/384-5820).

Finally, those hoping to picnic at Pioneer Park should stop by **Haggen Foods** (1815 Main St., 360/380-6353, www.haggen.com) for deli items and express Chinese food takeout.

Birch Bay and Blaine

The restaurant options in Birch Bay and Blaine are limited; locals head across the border to White Rock for the best regional cooking. In Birch Bay, procure sandwiches, pizza, and sweets from the summer-only **C Shop** (Alderson Rd. at Birch Bay Dr., Birch Bay, 360/371-2070).

Otherwise, jaunt over to Blaine for some simple eats. Get breakfasts from **Cafe International** (758 Peace Portal Dr., 360/332-6035), a diner-cum-small-time casino with poker and blackjack tables.

The most popular local restaurant is **Harbor Café** (295 Marine Dr., 360/332-5176), a Blaine hangout where you'll find oyster stew, clam chowder, and ample servings of cod fish and chips.

For espresso and pastries, head to **Blackberry House** (321 H St., 360/332-9342).

The best Blaine burgers are at **Nicki's Restaurant** (1700 Peace Portal Dr., 360/332-7779). **Conto's Pizza** (825 Peace Portal Dr., 360/332-3222) is good for pizza and pasta.

Out on the end of Semiahmoo Spit, the Semiahmoo Resort (360/371-2000 or 800/770-7992, www.semiahmoo.com) has a formal restaurant, **Stars,** featuring expensive Northwest cuisine and a popular Sunday brunch, plus the less fancy **Packers Lounge,** with delicious fish and chips.

La Bonne Maison (1830 Peace Portal Dr., 360/332-6178) is a nice French restaurant with surprisingly reasonable entrées. Reservations are required. Many more restaurants—including Thai and Greek eateries—can be found in the pretty town of White Rock, just across the border.

Lummi Island

Just south of the ferry dock, the **Islander Store** (360/758-2190, 6 A.M.–10:30 P.M. daily) sells beer, pop, ice cream, and other necessities of life. North of the dock is **Beachstore Café** (360/758-2233, 11 A.M.–9 P.M. Mon.–Fri., 9 A.M.–9 P.M. Sat.–Sun.) with an eclectic choice of meals (including Sunday brunch in the summer), along with fresh baked breads and pastries.

Fresh crab, shrimp, and scallops are available at **Leo's Live Seafoods** (Legoe Bay Rd., 360/758-7318).

Lynden

You'll find more Dutch specialties and country-style dinners at **Dutch Mothers Restaurant** (405 Front St., 360/354-2174).

The always-busy **Lynden Dutch Bakery** (360/354-3911) is a wonderful place for enormous sandwiches and pastries, including excellent Dutch apple pie.

Get good steaks and other mesquite-grilled meats in nearby Everson at **Black Forest Steakhouse** (203 W. Main St., 360/966-2855, www.blackforesteverson).

Located at the golf resort of the same name, **Homestead Farms Restaurant and Pub** (115 E. Homestead Blvd., 360/354-1196 or 800/354-1196, www.homesteadfarmsgolf.com) offers upscale dining three meals a day, with vistas of Mt. Baker from the deck.

Watch as cheesemakers work their craft at **Appel Farms** (6797 W. Pole Ln., 360/312-1431, www.appel-farms.com), making a variety of traditional cheeses, including Dutch-style gouda, a European yogurtlike cheese called quark, and Indian paneer.

INFORMATION AND SERVICES

Find information about Blaine and surrounding towns at the **Blaine Visitor Information Center** (215 Marine Dr., 360/332-4544 or 800/624-3555, 9 A.M.–5 P.M. daily April–Oct., 9 A.M.–4 P.M. Thurs.–Tues. the rest of the year). Across the street is a killer whale sculpture that is popular with kids.

Check your email at **Portal Café** (43 Peace Portal Dr., 360/332-7274).

GETTING THERE AND AROUND

Whatcom Transit (360/676-7433, www.ridewta.com) provides bus service Monday–Saturday to Bellingham, Lynden, Blaine, and the rest of Whatcom County.

The **Lynden Transit Station** is on the corner of Guide Meridian Road (Highway 539) and Front Street; it also has racks with local brochures.

Airporter Shuttle (360/380-8800 or 800/235-5247, www.airporter.com) runs direct bus service between Blaine and Sea-Tac Airport.

Lummi Island Access

From I-5, go west on Slater Road to Haxton Way on the Lummi Reservation and follow it to the ferry landing. The county-owned **ferry** (360/676-6692, $2 round-trip for cars, $1 passengers and drivers, free for kids, $0.50 bikes) makes eight-minute trips back and forth from Gooseberry Point on the mainland to Lummi Island every hour on the hour from 7 A.M. to midnight (more frequently during the commute period).

Because Lummi is nearly all in private hands, access is limited. You can ride bikes or cars on the island's roads, but the undeveloped mountainous southern end of the island is off-limits. The only readily accessible public beach is just north of the ferry dock.

SOUTH PUGET SOUND

Snugged up between the heights of the Olympic Mountains to the east and the Cascade range to the west, the stunning terrain of the Puget Sound region defines the character of much of Western Washington. When the sun shines, the Puget Sound region is one of the most beautiful in the country—snowcapped peaks stand sentinel over glistening water and evergreen canopies.

This is the most populous center of the state, with Seattle smack dab in the middle of the eastern shores of the sound and dozens of towns and cities radiating north and south, all rich with histories of logging, railroads, mining, and agriculture, and many filled with historic brick buildings and Victorian homes that illustrate their past.

Visitors will encounter a breathtaking diversity in ecology along the inlets and isles of the sound, from wetlands and marshes on the banks of the waters to verdant farmlands and wooded hills at the foothills of the nearby mountain ranges. The moderate climate and constant drizzle of the region cultivates a lush display of greenery in the region. In spite of the explosion of growth that has hit the region in recent decades, locals have respected the gift of such beautiful environs by maintaining an impressive network of county, state, and municipal parks that give residents and visitors the opportunity to explore the region by foot, paddle, pedal, saddle, sail, and ski.

The south sound is dominated by Olympia and Tacoma. The capital of Washington, Olympia draws travelers with tours of the capitol dome and its surrounding gardens and stately buildings. Tacoma, meanwhile, offers some of the best museums in the region,

© ERICKA CHICKOWSKI

HIGHLIGHTS

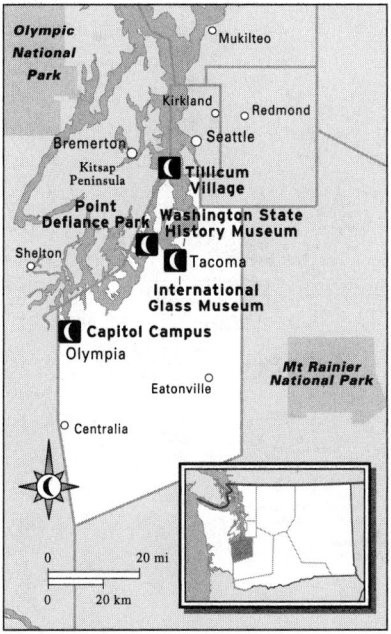

Capitol Campus: Grand halls, historic buildings, and lovely gardens all sit on the central grounds for the state's government (page 189).

International Glass Museum: Built with the help of Tacoma resident and glass-making superstar Dale Chihuly, this museum highlights the creative medium of glass (page 200).

Washington State History Museum: Bar none, this is the best history museum in the state, highlighting the unique stories that make up Washington's heritage (page 202).

Point Defiance Park: The sprawling waterfront grounds here are home to a well-regarded zoo, several historical museums, and innumerable spots to lay a blanket and picnic basket (page 203).

Tillicum Village: Watch a traditional tribal dance, enjoy a salmon feast and explore the recreated Native American village on Blake Island (page 232).

LOOK FOR TO FIND RECOMMENDED SIGHTS, ACTIVITIES, DINING, AND LODGING.

including the world famous International Museum of Glass and the nearby Bridge of Glass, with creations blown by hometown scion Dale Chihuly.

To the North, Everett is home to Boeing's largest airplane factory, which is open for tours starting from its state-of-the-art Future of Flight Center. And even closer to the Canadian border, Bellingham is an outdoor playground full of forests, lakes and bays studded with the highest concentration of parks in the region.

PLANNING YOUR TIME

Without a doubt, the best time to visit the Puget Sound is mid-July to mid-August, when you are most likely to experience the bliss of blue skies and mountain views. Much of the rest of the year is dominated by seemingly ceaseless gray and drizzly weather, infrequently interrupted by a few days of glorious sunshine here and there.

If a little bit of cloud cover doesn't bother you, though, this is the mildest region of the state. The rain doesn't often pour, thunder and lightning are an anomaly, and it rarely snows. So live like the locals—throw on a raincoat and don't let a little mist get in the way of your fun.

Just about all of the cities and towns in this chapter are easy day trips from Seattle if taken individually. For a more thorough tour of the region, including all of the museums and historic sights of Olympia and Tacoma and the recreational opportunities in the north sound, visitors should consider padding their schedule with a week or more on top of their Seattle itinerary.

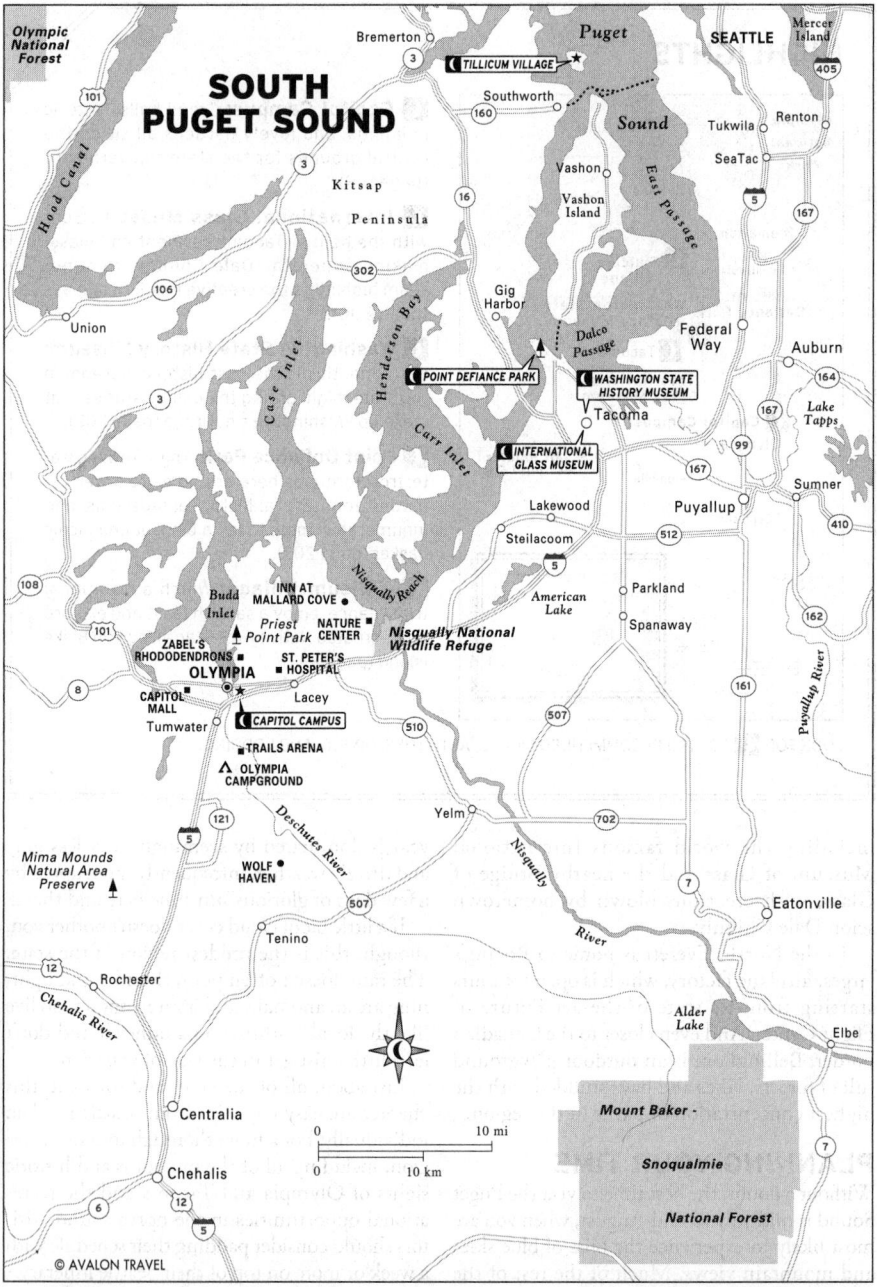
SOUTH PUGET SOUND
Olympic National Forest
Hood Canal
Bremerton
TILLICUM VILLAGE
Puget Sound
SEATTLE
Mercer Island
Southworth
Tukwila
Renton
SeaTac
Vashon
Vashon Island
East Passage
Kitsap Peninsula
Union
Case Inlet
Henderson Bay
Gig Harbor
Dalco Passage
Federal Way
Auburn
POINT DEFIANCE PARK
WASHINGTON STATE HISTORY MUSEUM
Tacoma
Lake Tapps
Carr Inlet
INTERNATIONAL GLASS MUSEUM
Sumner
Lakewood
Puyallup
Steilacoom
Nisqually Reach
American Lake
Parkland
Spanaway
Budd Inlet
INN AT MALLARD COVE
Priest Point Park
NATURE CENTER
Nisqually National Wildlife Refuge
ZABEL'S RHODODENDRONS
ST. PETER'S HOSPITAL
OLYMPIA
CAPITOL MALL
Lacey
Tumwater
CAPITOL CAMPUS
TRAILS ARENA
OLYMPIA CAMPGROUND
Puyallup River
Deschutes River
Yelm
Nisqually River
Mima Mounds Natural Area Preserve
WOLF HAVEN
Eatonville
Tenino
Rochester
Chehalis River
Alder Lake
Elbe
Centralia
Chehalis
Mount Baker - Snoqualmie National Forest
0 10 mi
0 10 km
© AVALON TRAVEL

Olympia

The southernmost finger of the Puget Sound points to Olympia, almost a geographic exclamation point. Here sits the state capital, home to the Governor's Mansion and the Washington Capitol Campus. The sprawling lawns, sunken gardens, and stately buildings on campus sit along the reflective Capitol Lake and are an excellent place to have lunch after exploring the whispery halls and rotundas of the Capitol.

In spite of its political significance, this is a town that doesn't take itself too seriously. Take the quirky Evergreen State College, for instance. This Olympia institution works on a free-spirited model that's dumped traditional letter grades and whose mascot is a mollusk. The fun vibe seeps into all aspects of the culture here, where creative cuisine and funky art galleries can be found in spades.

Visitors will also find Olympia an ideal outpost for exploration of the rural and natural surroundings that fringe its outermost borders. Along the Puget Sound, one can find marshy wildlife reserves. To the south lay lonely country roads passing Christmas tree farms, cow pastures, and sleepy hamlets like Tenino, where folks still send the kids off to swim in the old sandstone quarry. Just south of the city, one can stumble upon the mysterious Mima Mounds in the prairies that unfold near Capitol Forest.

Olympia also marks the last exit along I-5 before venturing on toward the forested path to the Olympic Peninsula and the US 101 loop.

SIGHTS

Capitol Campus

Clearly the highlight of the city—and one of the most visited attractions in the state—the landscaped grounds and majestic buildings of Olympia's Capitol Campus make it one of the country's most beautiful state capitols. Located between 11th and 14th Avenues off Capitol Way, the campus consists of 55 acres of greenery. These include an arboretum, a sunken rose garden, a replica of Denmark's Tivoli fountain, a number of historical buildings dating back

OLYMPIA OYSTERS

These tiny and sweet-tasting oysters – approximately the size of a silver dollar – were found at one time all the way from San Francisco Bay to Alaska, but overfishing, pollution, and parasites blighted the population. Today, Olympia oysters survive only in the southernmost reaches of Puget Sound in beds within Big Skookum, Little Skookum, Oyster, and Mud Bays. In the mid-1920s the average annual harvest peaked at about 48,000 bushels, but it went into a tailspin due to overharvesting and toxic wastewater from a Shelton pulp mill. The oyster population dwindled still further in the 1930s, when the importation of Japanese oysters began. These oysters brought with them two pests: the Japanese oyster drill and the Japanese flatworm, harmful only to smaller oysters like the Olympia. Although the pulp mill closed in 1957, it has taken 40 years for the water quality to improve enough to support the oysters again. Biologists are optimistic now that within a few years the southern Puget Sound population will be approaching original levels.

To see how Olympia oysters are raised, visit the largest and oldest producer (in business since 1876), **Olympia Oyster Co.,** (S.E. 1042 Bloomfield Rd., 360/426-3354, www.olympiaoyster.com). The plant is located halfway between Olympia and Shelton along Totten Inlet. **Taylor United, Inc.** (www.taylorshellfishfarms.com) – the biggest producer of clams in the nation – grows and harvests shellfish from more than 3,000 acres of tidelands around the southern Puget Sound. Visit its oyster sheds and clam hatchery at S.E. 130 Lynch Rd., three miles south of Shelton. The shop sells fresh clams and oysters; call 360/432-3300 to arrange a tour.

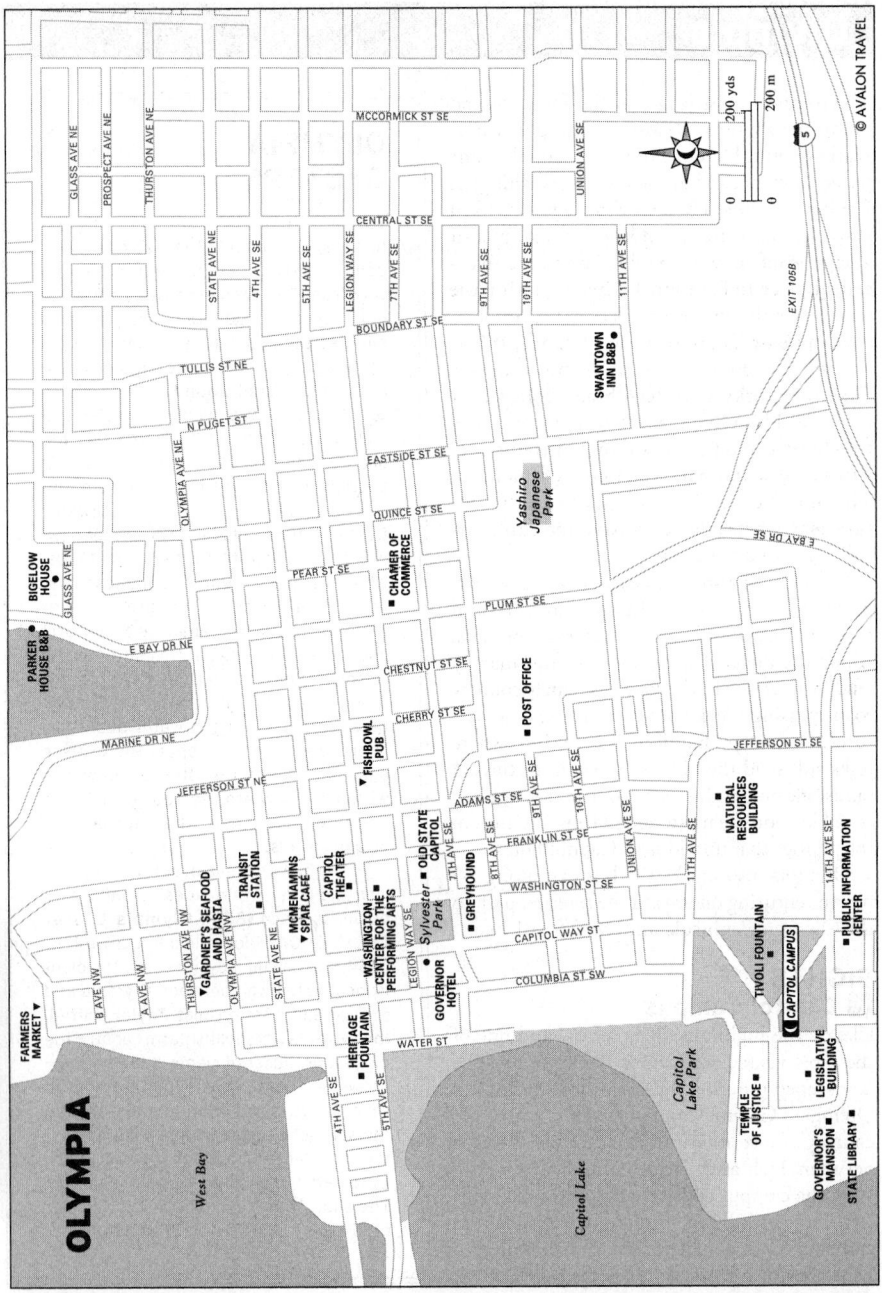
OLYMPIA
West Bay
Capitol Lake
Capitol Lake Park
FARMERS MARKET
BIGELOW HOUSE
PARKER HOUSE B&B
GARDNER'S SEAFOOD AND PASTA
TRANSIT STATION
MCMENAMINS SPAR CAFE
CAPITOL THEATER
WASHINGTON CENTER FOR THE PERFORMING ARTS
HERITAGE FOUNTAIN
GOVERNOR HOTEL
Sylvester Park
OLD STATE CAPITOL
GREYHOUND
FISHBOWL PUB
CHAMER OF COMMERCE
POST OFFICE
Yashiro Japanese Park
SWANTOWN INN B&B
NATURAL RESOURCES BUILDING
TIVOLI FOUNTAIN
CAPITOL CAMPUS
PUBLIC INFORMATION CENTER
TEMPLE OF JUSTICE
LEGISLATIVE BUILDING
GOVERNOR'S MANSION
STATE LIBRARY
EXIT 105B
200 yds
200 m
© AVALON TRAVEL

to the early 1900s, and memorials to veterans from World War I, World War II, Korea, and Vietnam. Come here in the spring to see the Japanese cherry trees in full bloom.

The best place to start is the **Public Information Center** (14th and Capital Way, 360/586-3460, www.ga.wa.gov/visitor, 8 A.M.–5 P.M. Mon.–Fri. all year, and 10 A.M.–4 P.M. Sat.–Sun. from Memorial Day to Labor Day). Here you can get maps of the campus, brochures, postcards, and tour information, plus a metered parking space. All of the on-street parking is leased, so either park in one of the visitor lots or follow the signs from I-5 exit 105A to the free shuttle bus.

LEGISLATIVE BUILDING

The imposing Legislative Building is hard to miss. Built to resemble the U.S. Capitol, its 287-foot dome was completed in 1928. The building remains the fifth-largest masonry domed building in the world. The central rotunda is the central attraction, with a 25-foot-long Tiffany chandelier suspended overhead (this was the last major piece created by Comfort Tiffany), enormous bronze doors, busts of George Washington and Martin Luther King Jr., Belgian marble steps, and gargoyle-capped draperies. Enter the Senate and House of Representatives gallery chambers from the fourth floor. Come here between early January and early March on even-numbered years, or early January to mid-April on odd-numbered years, to see the legislature in session. The capitol is open daily, with free 45-minute tours (360/586-3460, www.ga.wa.gov/capitol, tours hourly 10 A.M.–P.M.).

GOVERNOR'S MANSION

The Georgian-style redbrick Governor's Mansion (360/586-8687, www.ga.wa.gov.com) is the oldest building on the campus, dating back to 1908. Inside is a fine collection of antique furniture, including pieces by Duncan Phyfe.

STATE LIBRARY AND SUPREME COURT

In addition to state and federal publications, the State Library, on the south side of the Capitol, houses a collection of murals, mosaics, paintings, and sculpture by Northwest artists. It's a nice place to sit inside on a rainy day (a common occurrence in Olympia).

The Temple of Justice (8 A.M.–5 P.M. Mon.–Fri.) is not a sequel to *Indiana Jones and the Temple of Doom,* though it may mean doom for certain individuals. Instead, this is where the State Supreme Court meets. It is open year-round for self-guided tours. Also inside is the Washington State Law Library.

Historic Sights

A few blocks off the campus, the **Washington State Capital Museum** (211 W. 21st Ave., 360/753-2580, www.wshs.org, 10 A.M.–4 P.M. Tues.–Fri., noon–4 P.M. Sat.–Sun., $2 adults, $1.75 seniors, $1 kids, free for under age six) houses permanent exhibits that include a marvelous collection of baskets, and a hands-on Native American house with smoked salmon hanging from overhead racks. See lots more on the political and cultural history of Washington, including pioneer settlements and the early history of Northwest publishing, plus rotating exhibits, lectures, and programs. The building itself was built in 1920 as a 32-room California mission–style mansion for banker C. J. Lord. After his death, it was deeded to the state as a museum.

Also just off campus, at Legion Way and Franklin Street, the **Old State Capitol Building** (360/725-6025, 8 A.M.–5 P.M. Mon.–Fri.) was constructed in 1891 as the Thurston County Courthouse and served as the state capitol from 1903 to 1928. Today the flamboyant turreted building—complete with gargoyles—houses the State Department of Public Instruction. The Old Capitol is open for self-guided tours and has historical exhibits in the hallways.

Pick up self-guided tour brochures describing Olympia's historic neighborhoods from the chamber of commerce office. The gingerbread-decorated **Bigelow House** (Glass Ave. and East Bay Dr., 360/753-1215, 1–3 P.M. Sat.–Sun., $3 adults, $1 kids) overlooks Budd Inlet and is one of the oldest frame buildings in Washington. It was built in 1854 by Daniel and Ann Bigelow and is still owned by their descendants.

Other Museums

Olympia's **Hands On Children's Museum** (108 Franklin NE, 360/956-0818, www.hocm.org, 10 A.M.–5 P.M. Tues.–Sat., noon–5 P.M. Sun., $3.50) has kid exhibits—including a chance to explore the ocean floor—and is a fun space for play.

City Parks

With the Legislative Building so close to its shoreline, Capitol Lake acts as Olympia's unofficial reflecting pool. Enjoy the glassy waters from the lawns at Heritage Park, a grassy end stop on the lake just below the Capitol's hill. The park shows off with cherry blossoms in April, and swimming, sunbathing, sailing, hiking, biking, and picnicking the rest of the year. Each fall, the nearby Capitol Lake fish ladder is used by hundreds of king salmon returning home to spawn in the Deschutes River.

Across the street, jets of water shoot up, to the delight of bathing-suited kids at **Heritage Fountain** (6th Ave. and Water St.). The fountain is open daily except for Wednesdays, when it is closed for maintenance.

Washington's state flower is displayed in force at **Zabel's Rhododendrons** (2432 N. Bethel St., 360/357-6977), a four-acre park where 1,200 rhodies and azaleas are yours to behold from early May through Memorial Day. No pets or picnicking.

Named for city founder Edmund Sylvester, downtown's **Sylvester Park** (7th Ave. and Capitol Way) hosts concerts in the gazebo in July and August on Friday at noon, and on Wednesday evenings. Directly behind the park is the Old Capitol Building.

The **Yashiro Japanese Garden** (Plum St., 360/753-8380, 10 A.M. to dusk daily, free) near Union Avenue was built in cooperation with Olympia's sister city of Yashiro, Japan. This small and peaceful park has a main gate built without nails, a garden lantern of cut granite, a bamboo grove, and an 18-foot pagoda. The central feature is a pond and waterfall.

© ERICKA CHICKOWSKI

The Heritage Fountain is a favorite place to romp in the water.

Boat lovers can take a stroll at **Percival Landing Park** (222 Columbia St. NW), a waterside retreat with grassy lawns, lots of outdoor art, and a short boardwalk facing the Olympia harbor. Climb the **Percival Landing Tower** (open daylight hours only) at the north end of the Budd Inlett boardwalk for a panoramic view of the yacht-filled harbor with the Capitol behind, the Olympic Mountains, and freighters loading logs for Asian markets.

One of the finest nature parks within in city limits, **Priest Point Park** (dawn–dusk daily) sits less than two miles away from downtown but is worlds apart in habitat. The wooded park hugs Ellis Cove along Budd Inlet with a mile of natural and quiet saltwater shoreline.

Nisqually National Wildlife Refuge

Birders will have a ball at Nisqually National Wildlife Refuge (360/753-9467, http://nisqually.fws.gov, dusk–dawn daily, $3), a massive nature preserve that protects one of the largest surviving estuaries in the state. Over 300 species of wildlife find sanctuary here, but the real stars of the show are the birds.

Bring binoculars and a field guide and set up in one of the hidden photo blinds scattered on the trails here to spot some blue herons, bald eagles, red-tailed hawks, and more. Aim for a spring or fall visit to observe more than 20,000 geese and ducks as they fly their migratory pattern.

The visitors center here is an excellent place for estuarine information, but if you find yourself looking for more, then travel 10 minutes over to the **Nisqually Reach Nature Center** (4949 D'Milluhr Rd. NE at Luhr Beach, 360/459-0387, noon–4 P.M. Wed., Sat., Sun., free), a nature center that lies adjacent to the refuge but is sometimes overlooked because of its out-of-the-way location off the northwest corner of the estuary.

Tumwater Historic District

The 15-acre privately owned **Tumwater Falls Park** (330 Schmidt Pl. SW, Tumwater, 360/943-2550, www.olytumfoundation.org, free) is the site of the first American settlement in the Puget Sound region, founded in 1845. Situated within the Nationally Registered Tumwater Historic District, this is the site of the Schmidt house, a restored 1910 home built by the founder of the defunct but long-running Olympia Brewing Company. The neatly landscaped grounds include picnic areas, a boat launch into the Deschutes River, hiking trails, and lots of hungry ducks. You may see king salmon heading up the fish ladders late August–October; they spawn in nearby tanks.

Nearby, the **Henderson House Museum** (602 Deschutes Way, 360/754-4163, hours vary, $2 adults, $1 children) has photographic exhibits depicting life along the Deschutes River during the late 1800s and recent photos of Tumwater's people and events.

Also within the historic district is Tumwater's oldest home, **Crosby House** (adjacent to Tumwater Falls Park at Deschutes Way and Grant St., 360/943-9884, tours 12:30–2:30 P.M. Thursday, donation suggested). It was built in 1860 by Bing Crosby's grandfather, Capt. Nathaniel Crosby III, who came around the Horn to the Oregon Territory in 1847 and inspired the whole Crosby clan to follow him out West.

Wolf Haven

This 80-acre wolf refuge (3111 Offutt Lake Rd., 360/264-4695, www.wolfhaven.org, 10 A.M.–3 P.M. Mon. and Wed.–Sat., noon–3 P.M. Sun. Apr.–Sept., Sat.–Sun. only Nov.–Jan. and Mar., closed Feb., $8 adults, $6 seniors, $7 ages 3–12) is home to dozens of wolves that were taken in for a variety of reasons; some were no longer needed by researchers, some were mistreated or unwanted by zoos and refuges, and others were family "pets" who grew predictably wild. The sanctuary offers hourly guided tours and "howl-ins" on Fridays and Saturdays (6:30–9:30 P.M., $15 adults, $12 children) during the summer. Wolf Haven is at north of Tenino just off Old Highway 99.

Millersylvania State Park

Millersylvania State Park (12245 Tilley Rd S., 360/753-1519) is an 842-acre wooded park with impressive stone picnic shelters and bathhouses constructed between 1933 and 1939 by the Civilian Conservation Corps. Other facilities include two swimming beaches and an environmental learning center for school groups. Enjoy fishing for rainbow trout and boating on Deep Lake.

Tenino City Park

From downtown Olympia, follow Capitol Boulevard S onto Old Highway 99 to Tenino, a quiet old town with stone-fronted buildings lining the main street. These stones came from Tenino's sandstone quarry, now a popular swimming hole at Tenino City Park. The name Tenino (ten-NINE-oh) has a handful of possible origins, from the Native American name for a fork or junction, to the more colorful Engine Number 1090 (ten-nine-oh) that ran on the Kalama–Tacoma railroad line in the 1870s.

Mima Mounds

Eight miles south of Tumwater is the **Mima Mounds Interpretive Area** (Waddell Creek Rd. S.W., 360/753-2449, dawn–dusk daily) a registered national landmark with nature walks, an interpretive center, and picnic area. These grass-covered mounds, ranging in height up to eight feet, are also scattered throughout southern Thurston County, parts of China, and Alaska. They're often referred to as "mysterious" because no one really knows how they got there; theoretical origins range from glaciers to giant gophers, although the latter theory comes mainly from the same folks who brought you the "jackalope." Native Americans burned these areas to keep them open and productive, but today Douglas fir trees are gradually spreading across the hilly mounds.

ENTERTAINMENT AND EVENTS

Nightlife

Olympia has an active music scene. The **Capitol Theater** (206 E. 5th, 360/754-5378) is the biggest alternative-rock venue. Other downtown bars with music include **Fishbowl Pub & Café** (515 Jefferson St. SE, 360/943-3650) and **The Spar** (114 4th Ave., 360/786-1823). Gay-friendly **Thekla** (116 E. 5th Ave., 360/352-1855) is a popular dance club.

Coffeehouses

Get your buzz on at any number of Olympia's coffeehouses, which often attract the younger Evergreen State College set.

Batdorf and Bronson Roaster (513 Capitol Way S, 360/786-6717, www.batdorf.com) next to the Farmers Market, sells freshly roasted-on-the-premises coffee beans. Watch the roasting through the windows.

Get fresh bagels and espresso from **Otto's** (111 Washington NE, 360/352-8640) located just a few doors down from **Crazee Espresso Co.** (124 4th Ave. E, 360/754-8187, www.crazee.com), a place to meet the hip Olympia set over a tempting dessert.

Performing Arts

Olympia's **Washington Center for the Performing Arts** (512 Washington St. SE, 360/753-8586, www.washingtoncenter.org) is a state-of-the-art facility with hundreds of activities throughout the year—from ballet to rock concerts. Both the **Olympia Symphony Orchestra** (360/753-0074, www.olympiasymphony.com) and the **Masterworks Choral Ensemble** (360/491-3305, www.mce.org) perform here.

Capitol Playhouse '24 (360/754-5378, www.capitalplayhouse.com), located in the historic Capitol Theatre (206 E. 5th Ave.), produces plays from December to May as well as a summer **Shakespeare Festival** consisting of three plays performed June–August. The Capitol Theater also hosts a film festival in November.

Olympia Little Theater (1925 Miller Ave. NE, 360/786-9484, www.olympialittletheater.org) is the place for light comedies.

Gambling

The **Lucky Eagle Casino** (360/273-2000 or 800/720-1788, www.luckyeagle.com) sits on the **Chehalis Indian Reservation** between Rochester and Oakville and has blackjack, craps, roulette, keno, and other gambling. Also here are a restaurant and lounges with live music and comedy.

Red Wind Casino (12819 Yelm Hwy., 360/456-3328) has gambling action daily and cheap breakfast specials after a long night.

Events

Don't miss the **Olympia Arts Walk** on the third weekend of April, with performances, literary and art events, and tours of local galleries. Many downtown businesses—even furniture stores—open their windows for budding artists. The unique and whimsical **Procession of the Species** (360/753-8380 or www.olywa.net/procession) is the main event, with magically bizarre creatures and plants of every shape and form. A second Arts Walk (sans procession) takes place in April.

The **Wooden Boat Festival** (360/357-3370) held in mid-May at Percival Landing, includes a regatta and wooden boats open for public viewing. In mid-June, Evergreen State College's **Super Saturday** (360/866-6000) features hundreds of arts and crafts booths, food, and entertainment for all ages.

The city's biggest summer festival is **Lakefair** (360/943-7344, www.lakefair.org), held the third weekend of July. Activities include a twilight parade, fireworks, a carnival, food and craft vendors, and crowning of the Lakefair queen. From mid-July through August, Sylvester Park has **Music in the Park** events at noon on Wednesdays.

The fourth weekend in July brings all kinds of commotion to quiet Tenino with the **Oregon Trail Days,** including a parade, arts and crafts, entertainment, and a muzzleloading camp. The **Lighter than Air Hot Air Balloon Festival** takes place in Yelm in mid-July.

The **Thurston County Fair** (360/786-5453, www.co.thurston.wa.us/fair) held the first full weekend in August at the County Fairgrounds in Lacey, is a five-day festival with entertainment, food, and booths.

At the end of August, the **Shakespeare Festival/Renaissance Faire** at Sylvester Park brings out costumed performers of all types; performances of Shakespeare's classics are presented in the nearby Capitol Theater. **Harbor Days Festival** (360/754-4567) at Percival Landing is highlighted by a regatta and vintage tugboat races on Labor Day weekend. December brings the **Parade of Lighted Ships** (360/357-6767), put on by the Olympia Yacht Club, and **Winterfest in Historic Tenino** features wagon rides, living history demonstrations, a gingerbread house competition, a quilt contest, and 1880s arts and crafts.

SHOPPING

Downtown Olympia has a number of art galleries and boutiques on 4th and 5th Avenues. Two good ones are **State of the Arts Gallery** (500 Washington St., 360/705-0317, www.stateofthearts.com) and **Artists' Co-Op Gallery** (610 Columbia St. SW, 360/357-6920).

Given that this is a government/college town, you'd expect to find good bookstores in Olympia. Biggest is **Orca Books** (509 4th Ave. E, 360/352-0123, www.orcabooks.com, 10 A.M.–9 P.M. Mon.–Sat., 11 A.M.–6 P.M. Sun.) open late most nights for browsers. **Going Places** (515 Washington SE, 360/357-6860) has travel books, maps, and outdoor recreation guides.

Capital Mall (9th Ave. SW and Black Lake Blvd.) is the area's largest shopping center with nearly 100 shops and restaurants. Just up Black Lake Boulevard is another shopping plaza, Capital Village, with grocery, drug, and hardware stores, plus a sprinkling of fast-food restaurants. **Shipwreck Beads** (2727 Westmoor Court SW, 360/754-2323, www.shipwreck-beads.com) claims to have the world's largest selection of beads for sale, numbering in the billions.

SPORTS AND RECREATION

Capitol Forest

From Mima Mounds, continue north on Waddell Creek Road to Capitol Forest, a multiuse working forest (look out for logging trucks) in the Black Hills. The hills received their name when early Anglo settlers found the entire area had been charred by a forest fire. Free primitive campsites are available for tents and RVs at nine locations within the forest; many miles of hiking and horseback riding trails are clustered at the south end of the forest, while fat-tire bikes may roll along those in the north end.

Tolmie State Park

Tolmie State Park (five miles from exit 111, www.parks.wa.gov) has 1,800 feet of waterfront on Nisqually Reach with swimming, fishing, 3.5 miles of hiking trails, and an underwater park with an artificial reef created by the intentional sinking of three wooden barges. Open for day use only, the park also provides an outdoor shower for swimmers and divers near the lower restroom.

Running and Biking

Along Henderson Boulevard at **Olympia Watershed Park** (six miles north of Olympia on Boston Harbor Rd.), there is a two-mile hiking trail through woods, marsh, and streams.

Go to **Priest Point Park** to explore the three-mile loop that circles Ellis Cove through marsh and wooded land.

A six-mile paved cycling and walking trail leads from Martin Way in town north to Woodard Bay along an old railroad track. At Woodard Bay, the Dept. of Natural Resources has purchased 190 acres of land, managed as the **Woodard Bay Natural Resources Area.**

The **McLane Creek Nature Trail** (360/902-1234 or 800/527-3305 for directions) is a mile-long route that circles a beaver pond and meadow. To get a panoramic view of the area, follow the marked dirt road from Waddell Creek Road to 2,658-foot Capitol Peak, the highest point in the Black Hills.

Running parallel to Highway 507, the 7.5-mile **Yelm-Tenino Trail** is a rails-to-trails route that cuts through forest, pastures, wetlands, and creeks. This paved route is open to walkers, runners, and bikers. You can find a trailhead in Yelm behind the city hall (105 Yelm Ave. W), in Rainier between Centre and Minnesota Streets and in Tenino in the Tenino City Park on Washington Avenue.

Golf

The 18-hole **Merriwood Golf Course** (4550 Meriwood Dr., 360/412-0495, $42-477 for 18 holes) is considered one of the finest in the Puget Sound area.

Open to the public, the 18-hole **Tumwater Valley Golf Course** (4611 Tumwater Valley Dr. SE, 360/943-9500) has a driving range, pro shop, and lessons.

Water Sports

Deep Lake Resort (360/352-7388) has cabins and RV sites along the shore of the lake, plus a swimming beach with floats, miniature golf, rowboats, and canoes.

Tenino's swimming pool is an abandoned sandstone quarry open mid-June to early September.

Rent canoes to float the peaceful Black River from **Black River Canoe Trips** (360/273-6369, www.ool.com/blackriver) in Littlerock (west of I-5).

Climbing

Practice your rock-climbing skills at **Capital City Climbing Gym** (215 7th Ave. SW, 360/705-1585).

Off-Road Driving

Motocross fans and four-wheelers may want to try out the 150-acre **ORV Sports Park** (16 miles west of Olympia off Hwy. 8, 360/495-3243). Campsites and showers are also available here.

Camping

The closest public camping can be found at **Millersylvania State Park** (12 miles south of Olympia off I-5 at exit 95, 360/753-1519, www.parks.wa.gov). Tent ($14) and RV ($20) sites are available year-round. Make reservations ($7 extra) at 888/226-7688 or online.

Approximately 20 miles southwest of Olympia, **Capitol Forest** (www.wa.gov/dnr) has an abundance of primitive campsites (free; no water). Contact the Deptartment of Natural Resources at 360/902-1234 or 800/527-3305 for details and a map.

Olympia has an abundance of private tent and RV camping facilities, including several just a few miles from the center of town. Best among them is **Olympia Campground** (1441 83rd Ave. SW, 360/943-8778, www.olympiacampground.com), set on 10 acres of lightly wooded grounds. There are a ton of amenities, including a convenience store, a gas station, an ATM, a laundry room, a heated outdoor pool, and a game room with free Wi-Fi.

ACCOMMODATIONS

Olympia

You can't beat the **Governor Hotel's** (621 S. Capitol Way, 360/352-7700, www.olywagov.com, $99–109 d) location—it's cozied up next to the capitol campus closer than a lobbyist on voting days. It is right downtown with views of Sylvester Park and Capitol Lake. The building exterior is a bit drab, but the rooms inside are cheery enough and the list of amenities is pretty long for the rates you pay. The place has an outdoor pool, a hot tub, sauna, and exercise room.

Also right in town, **Swantown Inn** (1431 11th Ave. SE, 360/753-9123, www.swantowninn.com, $99–179 s or d) gets a few extra bonus points for style. This bed-and-breakfast is set in an 1893 Victorian mansion with four guest rooms and private baths. This little charmer is a secret weapon for tired adults in search of refuge—munchkins under 12 aren't allowed to tread over the threshold here. Full three-course breakfasts are served each morning, and the inn has an on-site day spa up in the attic that offers two-hour treatments for $99.

In the dining room at **Inn at Mallard Cove** (5025 Meridian Rd. NE, 360/491-9795, www.theinnatmallardcove.com, $150–185 s or d), you have an unobstructed view of the Puget Sound and fresh breakfasts made from organic ingredients grown on-site. This waterfront English Tudor Home is nuzzled by forests and gardens. All three guest rooms come equipped with private baths, fireplaces, and terraces. Get a closer look at the Olympic Mountain views from a complimentary kayak, or if it rains, curl up with a tome next to the floor-to-ceiling bookshelves in the library here.

Vicinity of Olympia

Olympia and the bedroom communities of Tumwater and Lacey are chock full of chain motel options, particularly clustered around the I-5 corridor.

Those in town looking for a place to get comfy during an extended stay might do well to look into **Tumwater Inn & Suites** (5895 Capitol Blvd. SW, Tumwater, 360/943-8391, www.tumwaterinnsuites.com, $59–77 d). This extended-stay place caters to government workers in town for the legislative session and has a four-night minimum, with discounted weekly and monthly rates available.

Not far from Olympia in the small town of Rainier, **7C's Guest Ranch B&B** (11123 128th St. SE, Rainier, 360/446-7957, $75–100 d) is an excellent choice for penny-pinching B&B enthusiasts. This small establishment is set in a ranch home with three guest rooms on 10 sprawling acres. The honeymoon suite has its own big bathroom. Guests are welcome to take advantage of the hot tub and gazebo outside. A full farm breakfast is served, and kids are welcome.

Olympia's newest hotel destination is **Great Wolf Lodge** (20500 Old Highway 99 SW, Grand Mound, 360/273-7718, $319–529 for four) a combination resort and water park that packs enough fun on its grounds to keep a family happy for a whole weekend. This enormous indoor facility has six slides, a six-story tube ride, three pools, a giant treehouse water fort, and more than 100 lifeguards to look after the kiddies. For mom and dad, there's a 12-room spa on premises. In short, this is the perfect in-town cure for the rainy season blues. The spacious rooms are pricey, but all rooms are suites, and the rates are typically for four people and include two-day passes to the water park for each guest. Many rooms can accommodate up to eight, with an extra charge of $30 per person beyond four.

FOOD

Olympia has many wonderful restaurants, cafés, and coffeehouses filling the downtown core. Walk a few blocks and you're bound to find a place that appeals.

Cafés and Diners

McMenamins Spar Café & Bar (114 4th Ave. E, 360/357-6444, 7 A.M.–midnight Mon.–Sat., 7 A.M.–11 P.M. Sun.) is a family place serving solid all-American breakfasts, lunches, and dinners. In business since the 1930s, the Spar has a decor to match: Classic Northwest logging photos line the walls.

For an all-natural breakfast, lunch, or dinner, try the **Urban Onion** (360/943-9242, 11 A.M.–9 P.M. Sun.–Thurs. 11 A.M.–10 P.M. Fri.–Sat. in summer, 7 A.M.–9 P.M. Sun.–Thurs., 8 A.M.–10 P.M. Fri.–Sat. the rest of the year) at the corner of Legion and Washington, with wholesome cuisine that includes salads, soups, sandwiches, Mexican meals, and vegetarian specials. Try the open-face shrimp-and-cheese haystacks at lunch, or the *huevos rancheros* for breakfast.

The **Mason Jar** (478 Cleveland Ave. SE, 360/754-7776, 9 A.M.–4 P.M. Mon.–Fri. only) is a favorite Tumwater lunch spot with homemade soups, freshly baked breads, and sandwiches.

Get some of the best pastries in southern Puget Sound at **Wagner's European Bakery & Café** (1013 Capitol Way S, 360/357-7268, 7 A.M.–6 P.M. Mon.–Sat., 8 A.M.–5 P.M. Sun.) where they also serve soups, salads, and sandwiches for lunch, as well as light breakfasts. Be prepared for a line of state workers on weekdays at lunchtime.

Steak and Seafood

Waterfront and view restaurants aren't as common in Olympia as in other Puget Sound cities, but they do exist. At Percival Landing, **Dockside Bistro** (501 N. Columbia St., 360/956-1928, http://docksidebistro.com, 11:30 A.M.–9:30 P.M. Tues.–Fri., 10 A.M.–9:30 P.M. Sat.–Sun.) offers a quiet little nook to enjoy the marina and a plate of Northwest flavors and wine.

Budd Bay Café (525 Columbia St. NW, 360/357-6963, 6:30 A.M.–8:30 P.M. Mon.–Sat., 9:30 A.M.–8:30 P.M. Sun., entrées $20) at Percival Landing is open for all meals and has a popular Sunday brunch buffet, with outdoor dining in summer featuring a marina view. This is a good place to sample famous Olympia oysters on the half shell.

Get Olympia oysters, geoduck clams, and other perfectly prepared seafood at **Gardner's Seafood and Pasta** (111 W. Thurston St., 360/786-8466, 5–9 P.M. Tues.–Sat., closed Sun.). Reservations are advised.

Asian

Saigon Rendez-Vous (117 5th Ave. W, 360/352-1989, 11 A.M.–9 P.M. Mon.–Fri., noon–8 P.M. Sat.–Sun.)is one of the best local Asian restaurants, with Vietnamese and Chinese menus and vegetarian specialties.

Get quick and reasonable meals at either location of **Happy Teriyaki:** downtown (530 Capitol Way S, 360/705-8000, 11 A.M.–9 P.M. Mon.–Sat., closed Sun.) and over in West Olympia (2915 Harrison Ave. NW, 360/786-8866, 11 A.M.–9 P.M. Mon.–Sat., closed Sun.). Two good Thai places are **Thai Garden Restaurant** (270 Capitol Mall, 360/786-1959) and **Thai Pavilion** (303 E. 4th Ave., 360/943-9093).

GOOEY DUCKS

Traveling through Western Washington, you're bound to stop and wonder, what exactly is a gooey duck? It's neither waterfowl nor a caramel-laden confection – it is the proper pronunciation of **geoduck,** a gigantic clam weighing up to three pounds. Named after the Nisqually word for "dig deep," these enormous bivalves have been known to live up to 160 years and burrow between two and 360 feet beneath the subtidal mud. In many Asian countries, the geoduck is a delicacy, and an earnest search of Washington's Chinese, Japanese, and Korean restaurants is bound to turn up some geoduck on the menu. In addition to being the mascot of Evergreen State College, this slimy fellow is thought by some to be a powerful aphrodisiac.

Italian

Casa Mia (716 Plum St., 360/459-0440, 11:30 A.M.–10 P.M. Mon.–Fri., 11:30 A.M.–11 P.M. Sat.–Sun.) is another good Italian restaurant.

Meconi's Italian Subs (5225 Lacey Blvd. SE, 360/459-0213, 10 A.M.–8 P.M. Mon.–Fri., 10 A.M.–7 P.M. Sat., closed Sun.) is the best and most authentic sub shop in the Olympia area—very popular with state workers.

Pub Grub

Fishbowl Pub & Café (515 Jefferson St. SE, 360/943-6480) offers a surprising contrast to Olympia's better-known brew. Located downtown, this small brewery and pub produces seven different beers, all with such fishy names as Trout Stout and Fish Tale Ale. Get a pizza or sandwich from the café and enjoy it in this friendly lounge-around place. It's highly recommended.

Good pizzas are also at **Brewery City Pizza** (4354 Martin Way, Lacey, 360/491-6630, 11 A.M.–10 P.M. Sun.–Thurs., 11 A.M.–11 P.M. Fri.–Sat.).

Markets and Bakeries

Located in a big building on the north end of Capitol Way, the very popular **Olympia Farmers Market** (360/352-9096, www.farmers-market.org, 10 A.M.–3 P.M. Thurs.–Sun. April–Oct., Sat.–Sun. only Nov.–Dec.) is Washington's second largest after Pike Place Market. In addition to the expected fresh fruits and veggies, you'll discover all sorts of handcrafted items, plants, meats, seafood, baked goods, and wonderful ethnic foods. The market has festivals throughout the summer.

For natural foods at other times, visit the **Olympia Food Co-op** (921 Rogers NW, 360/754-7666, and 3111 Pacific Ave. SE, 360/956-3870, 8 A.M.–9 P.M. daily). Get fresh-squeezed apple cider, take-and-bake apple pies, eggs, honey, and more at **Lattin's Country Cider Mill** (9402 Rich Rd. SE, 360/491-7328, 9 A.M.–5:30 P.M. Mon.–Sat., 9 A.M.–4 P.M. Sun.). They are located just south of the Amtrak station in East Olympia.

More healthy food at **J-Vee Health Foods & Café** (3720 Pacific Ave. SE, 360/491-1930, 9:30 A.M.–6 P.M. Mon.–Thurs., 9:30 A.M.–6:30 P.M. Fri., 10 A.M.–6 P.M. Sat., closed Sun.), a longtime natural foods store.

San Francisco Street Bakery (1320 San Francisco St. NE, 360/753-8553, 6:30 A.M.–7 P.M. daily) bakes wonderful earthy breads (using organic grains), plus pastries and bagels.

Vicinity of Olympia

In front of the Olympia Brewery and overlooking Tumwater Falls, **Falls Terrace Restaurant** (106 Deschutes Way, Tumwater, 360/943-7830, www.fallsterrace.com, 11 A.M.–8:30 P.M. Mon.–Thurs., 11 A.M.–9 P.M. Fri., 11:30 A.M.–9 P.M. Sat., 11:30 A.M.–8 P.M. Sun.) has moderately priced dinners that feature chicken, steak, seafood, and veal. They also offer a Sunday brunch. The lounge features an outside deck, a favorite place to drop by for a drink. Reservations highly are recommended.

INFORMATION AND SERVICES

For maps and general information stop by the **Olympia/Thurston County Chamber of Commerce** (521 Legion Way SE, 360/357-3362, www.olympiachamber.com, 9 A.M.–5 P.M. Mon.–Fri. year-round). At the Capitol Campus, head to the **Public Information Center** (360/586-3460, 8 A.M.–5 P.M. daily). The headquarters office for **Olympic National Forest** (1835 Black Lake Blvd. SW, 360/956-2300, www.fs.fed.us/r6/olympic) is in Olympia.

GETTING THERE

Trains and Planes

Amtrak (800/872-7245, www.amtrak.com) serves Olympia along its north–south **Coast Starlight** route from Seattle to Los Angeles. The Amtrak station is in east Olympia at 6600 Yelm Highway.

There are no scheduled passenger flights to Olympia; take a van to Sea-Tac instead. **Capital Aeroporter** (360/754-7113 or 800/962-3579, www.capair.com) and **Centralia-SeaTac Airport Express** (360/786-0636 or 800/773-9490) both serve Olympia and surrounding bedroom communities.

By Bus

Intercity Transit (360/786-1881 or 800/287-6348, www.intercitytransit.com) has daily service to Olympia, Tumwater, and most of Thurston County. All buses have bike racks. The Olympia Transit Center is on State Street between Franklin and Washington Streets.

Greyhound (Capitol and 7th, 800/231-2222, www.greyhound.com) connects Olympia to Seattle, Tacoma, Portland, and other cities along the north–south I-5 corridor.

Tacoma

Washington's third-largest city is a community actively reinventing itself. Once a drab paper-mill town 30 miles south of Seattle, Tacoma is becoming a vibrant, charming metropolis with clean air, a University of Washington campus, and an eye on the future.

Most of the smelly mills have closed, and Tacoma's downtown is enjoying an urban renaissance that includes the presence of the Washington State History Museum, the International Museum of Glass, and the Tacoma Art Museum, all under the backdrop of majestic Mount Rainier.

Along with this fresh crop of visual wonders, old warehouses are becoming artists' lofts, a thriving theater district has been created, and a downtown plaza occupies the fountain-flowing, stroller-friendly heart of the city. Add to this a diverse 700-acre city park with a world-class zoo, a rambling public market, top-quality hotels and waterfront restaurants, and a spruced up shoreline.

SIGHTS

International Glass Museum

Tacoma's artistic gem, the 75,000-square-foot International Glass Museum (1801 Dock St., 253/572-931, www.museumofglass.org, 10 A.M.–5 P.M. Mon.–Sat., noon–5 P.M. Sun. Memorial Day–Labor Day, closed Mon.–Tues. Labor Day–Memorial Day, $10 adult, $8 senior, $4 child) in downtown Tacoma, covers two acres along the waterfront, encompassing galleries and exhibition spaces, an enormous hot shop studio where you can watch artisans blow and cast glass, a theater for multimedia presentations, museum shop, and café. A highlight is the **Chihuly Bridge of Glass,** a 500-foot-long pedestrian bridge created by native son Dale Chihuly. The bridge takes you through a tunnel of brilliant light and color and crosses I-705, connecting the Glass Museum with the History Museum. Adjacent to the Glass Museum is another large glass sculpture called Water Forest that is the

© ERICKA CHICKOWSKI

International Glass Museum

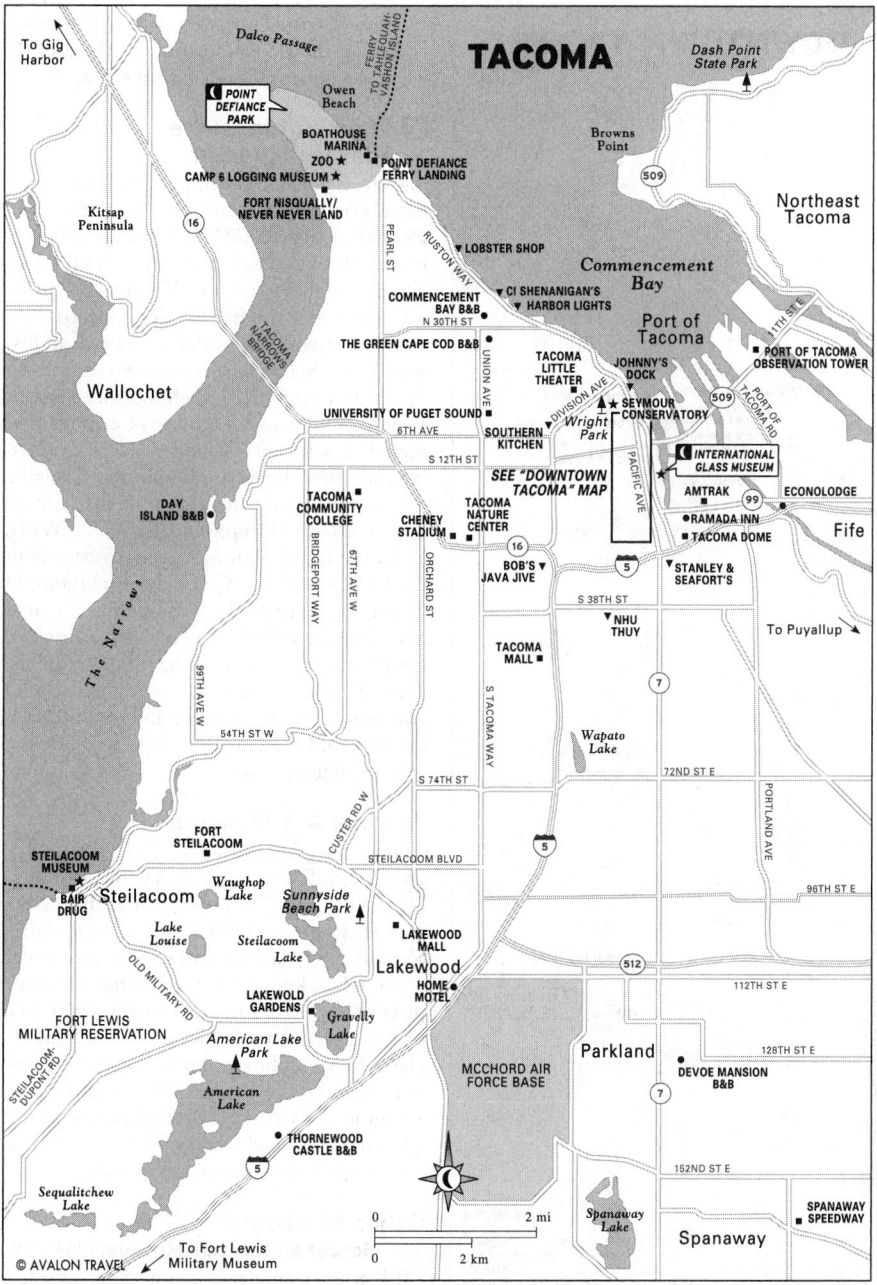
TACOMA
To Gig Harbor
Dalco Passage
FERRY TO TAHLEQUAH: VASHON ISLAND
Dash Point State Park
POINT DEFIANCE PARK
Owen Beach
BOATHOUSE MARINA
ZOO
CAMP 6 LOGGING MUSEUM
POINT DEFIANCE FERRY LANDING
Browns Point
509
Northeast Tacoma
Kitsap Peninsula
16
FORT NISQUALLY/ NEVER NEVER LAND
PEARL ST
RUSTON WAY
LOBSTER SHOP
Commencement Bay
CI SHENANIGAN'S
HARBOR LIGHTS
COMMENCEMENT BAY B&B
N 30TH ST
Port of Tacoma
11TH ST E
TACOMA NARROWS BRIDGE
THE GREEN CAPE COD B&B
UNION AVE
TACOMA LITTLE THEATER
JOHNNY'S DOCK
PORT OF TACOMA OBSERVATION TOWER
Wallochet
DIVISION AVE
SEYMOUR CONSERVATORY
PORT OF TACOMA RD
UNIVERSITY OF PUGET SOUND
6TH AVE
SOUTHERN KITCHEN
Wright Park
S 12TH ST
SEE "DOWNTOWN TACOMA" MAP
PACIFIC AVE
INTERNATIONAL GLASS MUSEUM
AMTRAK
99
ECONOLODGE
DAY ISLAND B&B
TACOMA COMMUNITY COLLEGE
CHENEY STADIUM
TACOMA NATURE CENTER
RAMADA INN
TACOMA DOME
Fife
BRIDGEPORT WAY
67TH AVE W
ORCHARD ST
BOB'S JAVA JIVE
5
STANLEY & SEAFORT'S
S 38TH ST
NHU THUY
To Puyallup
The Narrows
TACOMA MALL
7
99TH AVE W
54TH ST W
S TACOMA WAY
Wapato Lake
S 74TH ST
72ND ST E
CUSTER RD W
PORTLAND AVE
FORT STEILACOOM
STEILACOOM MUSEUM
STEILACOOM BLVD
BAIR DRUG
Steilacoom
Waughop Lake
Sunnyside Beach Park
96TH ST E
Lake Louise
Steilacoom Lake
LAKEWOOD MALL
Lakewood
512
OLD MILITARY RD
HOME MOTEL
112TH ST E
LAKEWOLD GARDENS
Gravelly Lake
FORT LEWIS MILITARY RESERVATION
American Lake Park
Parkland
128TH ST E
DEVOE MANSION B&B
STEILACOOM-DUPONT RD
MCCHORD AIR FORCE BASE
American Lake
THORNEWOOD CASTLE B&B
152ND ST E
Sequalitchew Lake
0 2 mi
0 2 km
Spanaway Lake
SPANAWAY SPEEDWAY
Spanaway
© AVALON TRAVEL
To Fort Lewis Military Museum

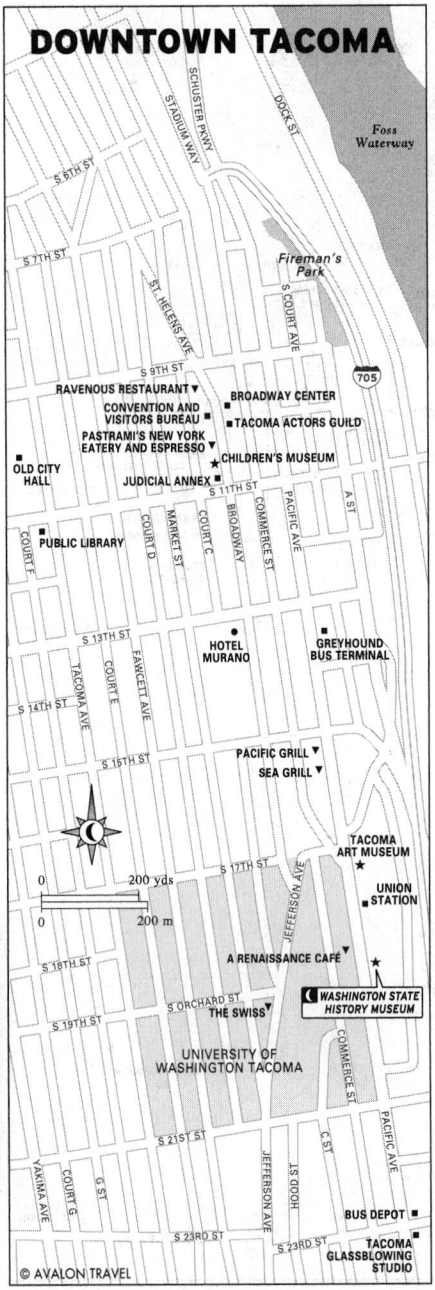

creation of artist Howard Ben Tré. Admission is free on the third Thursday of the month, when the museum is open until 8 P.M.

Washington State History Museum

Tacoma is home to the impressive Washington State History Museum (1911 Pacific Ave., 253/593-2830 or 888/238-4373, www.wshs.org/wshm, 10 A.M.–4 P.M. Mon.–Sat., until 8 P.M. Thurs., noon–5 P.M. Sun., $7 adults, $6.50 seniors, $5 ages 6–18, free for kids under 6). This 100,000-square-foot building sits next to historic Union Station and repeats its rounded design in a series of three gracefully vaulted arches. Visitors walk through a maze of exhibits that include a Salish plank house and Native basket collection, dioramas of mining and logging towns, exhibits on the arrival of the railroad and the effect of Depression and World War II, and a theater with an educational video about the Columbia River. Given the importance of high-tech industries in Washington, it comes as no surprise to find lots of interactive displays. Upstairs are galleries with temporary exhibits. The museum is joined to the restored Union Station by a scenic courtyard and amphitheater, a fine place for a lunch break. Also inside is a café and museum store.

Tacoma Art Museum

The Tacoma Art Museum (1701 Pacific Ave., 253/272-4258, www.tacomaartmuseum.org, 10 A.M.–5 P.M. Tues.–Wed. and Fri.–Sat., 10 A.M. to 8 P.M. Thurs., noon–5 P.M. Sun., $5 adults, $4 students and seniors, free under age 6) is best known for its paintings and other pieces from 19th- and 20th-century artists, plus its permanent exhibitions of Dale Chihuly glass. New exhibits come to the museum almost monthly, and there are frequent lectures and other activities, plus a museum shop with gifts, art books, and jewelry. There is no charge on the third Thursday of the month.

Other Museums

The **Pioneer Motorcycle Museum** (253/779-2401 or www.pioneercyclemuseum.com) is a

FULL OF HOT AIR

It only takes about five minutes to see that Tacoma is a town crazy about its glass art. You can thank Dale Chihuly for that. Born in Tacoma in 1941, this world-renowned glassmaker has made a name for himself through his wild and colorful pieces that often feature twisted tentacles and tendrils, uniquely patterned orbs, and a riot of colors. He helped found the Pilchuck Glass School in the 1970s and brought a whole new level of notoriety to the American glass art scene, which had never before been taken seriously compared to the masters in Murano, Italy, and other European enclaves.

Chihuly has been instrumental in the Tacoma downtown revitalization, helping to draw the International Glass Museum to town and donating thousands of unique pieces for his Bridge of Glass, which links the museum to Pacific Avenue. He's donated some of his best glass to the Tacoma Art Museum, and you can also find his work in businesses and restaurants around town. Legend has it that his trademark pieces over the bar at The Swiss got there during his younger days, before he became a superstar who could afford a regular round of beers.

private collection of historic Harley Davidson, Indian, Excelsior, Thor, and Anderson motorcycles, some of which date to 1908. A large restoration workshop is also on the premises.

Over many years, the owner of Pierce County Refuse Co.—Harold E. LeMay—amassed the world's largest private collection of automobiles. Classic car fans should definitely stop at the **Harold E. LeMay Museum** (325 152nd St. E, www.lemaymuseum.org, 10 A.M.–5 P.M. Tues.–Sat., adults $15, children $5). This is the largest collection of vintage automobiles, trucks, and motorcycles in the world, with well over 2,300 rare and vintage cars. In addition to the Chevrolets, Fords, Cadillacs, Packards, and Hudsons, the collection includes Deusenbergs, Cords, and even a 1920 Pierce Arrow.

The **Children's Museum of Tacoma** (936 Broadway, 253/627-6031, www.childrenoftacoma.org, 10 A.M.–5 P.M. Tues.–Sat., $3 adults, $4 ages 2–12, and free for tots) is a fun and educational place for kids, with changing exhibits.

Point Defiance Park

Almost 700 acres of gardens, forests, footpaths, and shady picnic areas jutting out into Puget Sound at the tip of the narrow Point Defiance peninsula make up Tacoma's Point Defiance Park. It reminds visitors of the best metropolitan parks in America, but once you've seen it, the cliff setting with its views and thick forest will make most other similar parks seem modest. This is an amazing place, with an array of attractions to please almost anyone. Originally set aside as a military reservation, the park was given to the city of Tacoma in 1888 for use as a public park.

ZOO AND AQUARIUM

The biggest attraction at park is the excellent Point Defiance Zoo and Aquarium (253/591-5335 or 253/591-5337, www.pdza.org, 10 A.M.–7 P.M. daily Memorial Day–Labor Day, 10 A.M.–4 P.M. daily the rest of the year, $7.25 adults, $5.25 seniors, $4.50 ages 4–13, and free for kids under 4), home of beluga whales, polar bears, sharks, walruses, red wolves, and elephants. The real draws here are the ocean exhibits. You'll discover a tropical reef filled with brilliantly colored fish, a huge cold-water aquarium with fish, jellyfish, eels, and other critters from the Puget Sound area, and the main event: a large tank where you can come face to face with more than 30 sharks, reaching up to 10 feet long. (Get here on Sunday and Thursday at 11 A.M. to watch the feeding frenzy.) Fascinating displays describe the lives of sharks, stingrays, and skates, and you will even get to see shark egg cases with living embryos. The Rocky Shores exhibit includes tufted puffins, harbor seals, Pacific walruses, beluga whales, and playful sea otters. Another favorite attraction is the polar bear area, which features them swimming in a deep pool; you can watch from behind a thick glass wall. The zoo has cafés and gift shops. In August and September, the Friday evening **Zoosounds concerts** are fun for the whole family. In December, come in the evening to see the twinkling **Zoolights.**

GARDENS

Point Defiance Park is home to several beautifully maintained gardens. The **Japanese Garden** features a pagoda built in 1914, plus pools, a waterfall, and immaculate landscaping. A **Rhododendron Garden** covers almost five acres and is especially striking in the spring when the 115 varieties of rhododendrons bloom. The **Rose Garden** contains a rustic gazebo and some 1,500 rose bushes that flower June through September. Other featured gardens at Point Defiance are the **Iris Garden,** the **Dahlia Trial Garden** (best time to see these is August), and the **Northwest Native Garden,** with plants from all six biotic zones in the Northwest.

FORT NISQUALLY

Once part of Hudson's Bay trading post located on the Nisqually delta near present-day Fort Lewis, the buildings of Fort Nisqually Historic Site (253/591-5339, www.fortnisqually.org, 11 A.M.–6 P.M. daily Memorial Day–Labor Day, with varying hours Wed.–Sun. the rest of the year, $3 adults, $2 ages 13–17 and seniors, $1 ages 5–13, and free for younger kids) were moved to Point Defiance and restored in the 1930s. The half dozen log buildings are still well cared for today, and volunteers in period garb frequently offer living history demonstrations.

Check out the working blacksmith shop, where you can learn how tools and hardware were fabricated for trade. Also on the grounds is a storehouse built in 1851 that is considered the oldest standing building in Washington. Come here in May to celebrate Queen Victoria's birthday, in August for a mountain man encampment, or in October for a candlelight tour.

CAMP 6 LOGGING MUSEUM

Camp 6 (253/752-0047, www.camp-6-museum.org, 10 A.M.–5 P.M. Wed.–Sun., closed Nov.–Jan., free) is a reconstructed logging camp with steam equipment from the late 1800s and early 1900s, when most Northwest logging was done from railroads. Featured attractions (everything still runs) include a 90-ton logging locomotive specially built to handle steep grades and sharp curves, a steam-powered 1887 Dolbeer Donkey engine used to yard logs, and other logging equipment from the heyday of timber harvesting in the Northwest. Also here are loggers' bunkhouses, including turn-of-the-20th-century bunkhouses on rails that could be moved as the trees were cut. The bunkhouses contain photos and artifacts from life in the logging camps.

Kids love the 1929 steam-powered **P.D.Q. & K. Railroad,** which includes log cars, cabooses, speeders, and other railcars. It offers rides on weekend afternoons for a small charge April–September. There's also a special **Santa Train** the first three weekends of December.

Other Parks

Lakewold Gardens (12317 Gravelly Lake Dr., 253/584-4106 or 888/858-4106, www.lakewold.org, 10 A.M.–4 P.M. Thurs.–Mon., noon–8 P.M. Friday April–Sept., 10 A.M.–3 P.M. Fri.–Sun. Oct.–Mar., $5 adults, $3 seniors, military, and kids under 12) is a 10-acre collection of rare plants, including blue poppies from Tibet. The gardens feature one of the largest collections of rhododendrons and Japanese maples in the Northwest and were designed by noted landscape architect Thomas Church. A lovely Georgian-style brick home on this country estate is also open to the public.

For a view of the action at the Port of Tacoma, head to the **observation tower** just off East 11th Street, where signs describe the port's history. Continue north on Marine View Drive toward **Browns Point Lighthouse Park** (201 Tulalip St. NE, 253/927-1042, www.tacomaparks.com), a sunny spot for picnicking, ship-watching, or launching your own boat. Here you've got a great view of downtown Tacoma and Point Defiance, Vashon and Maury Islands, the Olympics, and of course, the Sound. The lighthouse is open on weekends and contains an exhibit on the building of a Coast Guard boat.

Historic Sights

DOWNTOWN TACOMA

Completed in 1911, Tacoma's copper-domed **Union Station** (Pacific Ave., 8 A.M.–5 P.M. Mon.–Fri., closed weekends, free) was designed by the same firm that built New York's Grand Central Station and has a similar sense of grandeur. The depot originally served as the terminus of the Northern Pacific's rail line and was later used by the Great Northern and Union Pacific railroads before falling into disuse. A massive restoration in 1989 transformed the distinctively domed building into a federal courthouse for all of western Washington. Today, the works of the renowned Tacoma-born glass artist Dale Chihuly fills its magnificent central space. An 18-foot cobalt-blue chandelier hangs from the high center, and many other pieces provide bright accents.

Old City Hall (S. 7th St. and Pacific Ave.) is another distinctive downtown building, patterned after an Italian town hall. Its dominant feature is a tall freestanding clock tower. Built in 1905, it is now used for commercial offices. A campus of the **University of Washington** spreads through 22 restored historic downtown buildings.

STADIUM DISTRICT

One of Tacoma's most striking historic neighborhoods is the Stadium District, located near **Stadium High School** on Tacoma Avenue. Built on the top of a hill in the style of a French chateau, this extraordinary high school was begun in 1891 and intended to be a grand seven-story railroad hotel. The depression of 1893 left it vacant for several years, until it was transformed into a high school in 1906. Next door is the Stadium Bowl, the West Coast's first stadium, and the site of visits by Presidents Theodore Roosevelt, Warren Harding, and Franklin Delano Roosevelt, along with such sports legends as Babe Ruth and Jack Dempsey. More than 100 turn-of-the-20th-century mansions and stately homes can be found in the area around the stadium, including several of the city's best B&Bs. Be sure to see the **Rust Mansion** (1001 N. I St.), a Classical Revival structure built in 1905.

Wright Park (S. 3rd and G Sts.) is a shady place with gardens, paved paths, stone lions, lawn bowling greens, and a delightful surprise: the **W. W. Seymour Botanical Conservatory** (253/591-5330, www.tacomaparks.com, 10 A.M.–4:30 P.M. Tues.–Sun., $5 donation). Built in 1908 and on the National Register of Historic Places, this Victorian-style conservatory—one of just three on the West Coast—hosts a bright array of tropical plants and cacti beneath 12,000 panes of glass. This is a great place to visit on a rainy winter day (or any time, for that matter). The Conservatory shop has botanical gifts and a display of carnivorous plants.

One of Tacoma's most original museums is the **Karpeles Manuscript Library Museum** (407 S. G St., 253/383-2575, www.rain.org/~karpeles, 10 A.M.–4 P.M. Tues.–Sun., free). Located in an old Carnegie Library across from Wright Park, the museum displays rotating exhibits of rare and unique documents from all over the world, from D-Day defense plans signed by Adolf Hitler to letters written by Charles Manson.

STEILACOOM

The **Steilacoom Town Hall and Museum** (253/584-4133, www.steilacoom.org/museum, 1–4 P.M. Tues.–Sun. March–Oct., 1–4 P.M. Fri.–Sun. Nov.–Dec. and Feb., closed Jan., free) focuses on the town's pioneer period. Pick up the *Guide to Historic Steilacoom* here for a walking tour. It is located downstairs in the white New England–style Town Hall on Main and Lafayette.

Housed in a 100-year-old Congregational Church building, **Steilacoom Tribal Cultural Center and Museum** (1515 Lafayette St., 253/584-6308, 10 A.M.–4 P.M. Tues.–Sat. year-round, $2 adults, $1 seniors and kids, children under 6 free, $6 families) documents the history of the Steilacoom tribe with exhibits that feature the prehistory of the Tacoma Basin, historical artifacts, and contemporary artistry. The Steilacoom were one of the eight Washington tribes that were never allotted a reservation. The gift shop sells native crafts, and the snack bar serves light breakfasts and lunches.

East from the town of Steilacoom is **Fort Steilacoom** (253/584-2368), right next to the massive Western State Hospital mental institution. Four small frame houses remain from this fort, established in 1849. One of the buildings has an interpretive center and small museum open for summertime tours 1–4 P.M. on Saturday.

Military History Sights

With two military bases surrounding the greater Tacoma region, there's a fairly decent chance you'll run across a few soldiers or airmen while wandering about town. Military buffs can bone up on their history at museums offered by each base.

Take exit 120 from I-5, 16 miles south of Tacoma, to the **Fort Lewis Military Museum** (253/967-7206, noon–4 P.M. Wed.–Sun., free) located in a 1918 Swiss-style building originally used as a Salvation Army center. The museum emphasizes Northwest military history, including displays of the dress uniforms from various eras, the history of the I Corps, and such oddities as Gen. Norman Schwartzkopf's Jeep (he was base commander here in the early 1980s). Obtain a pass at the visitors office on the east side of the freeway near the main gate.

Another military collection is the **McChord Air Museum** (253/982-2485, noon–4 P.M. Tues.–Sun., closed holidays, free), one mile east on exit 125. The museum contains several aircraft, flying gear, uniforms, and other Air Force memorabilia from the 1930s through the 1960s. However, you'll need an Air Force buddy to get you in—visitors aren't allowed in unescorted.

ENTERTAINMENT AND EVENTS

Nightlife

One of the primary beneficiaries of Tacoma's rebirth as a haven of hip is the bar and club scene. For an exhaustive listing, pick up the free *Tacoma Weekly* (www.tacomaweekly.com) or *Tacoma Reporter* (www.tacoma.net) newspapers in racks around town.

The clubs are in an almost constant state of change; two guaranteed winners are **The Loft** (2106 Pacific Ave., 253/404-0540 or 888/550-5838, www.loftlive.com, 9–2 A.M. Wed.–Sat.) and **The Swiss** (1904 S. Jefferson, 253/572-2821, www.theswisspub.com).

Country music fans should head to **Baldy's Roadhouse** (2501 Milton Way E, 253/927-9943) or **McCabes** (2611 Pacific Ave., 253/272-5403).

Kellys Restaurant (1101 Tacoma, 253/627-6425) and **Jazzbones** (2803 6th Ave., 253/396-9169, www.jazzbones.com) are the main jazz venues.

A neighborhood favorite is **Bob's Java Jive** (2102 S. Tacoma Way, 253/475-9843) a coffee-pot-shaped bar on S. Tacoma Way with a neon-decorated handle and spout. Inside is a jukebox with classics from the 1960s and all-American meals. Built in 1927, this place is a classic inside and out.

The **Ale House Pub & Eatery** (2122 Mildred West, 253/565-9367) has one of the largest selections of draft beer in the state, with an incredible 63 different beers on tap. The menu is reasonably priced and good (especially the ribs), and the big-screen TV is popular for sporting events.

Spectator Sports and Concerts

Tacoma rocks the Puget Sound with some of the biggest concerts of the region inside the **Tacoma Dome** (253/572-3663, www.tacomadome.org.), a distinctive blue bastion of the early 1980s that remains one of the largest wood-domed structures in the world. This is where you come to see U2 or the Stones throw their mega tours or watch monster trucks crush little subcompacts into lunch-pail sized cubes.

The Pacific Coast Baseball League is represented by the **Tacoma Rainiers,** a AAA farm club for the Oakland A's that plays at Cheney Stadium (2525 Bantz Blvd., 253/752-7707, www.tacomarainiers.com), off Highway 16.

One of nearby Spanaway's main summertime attractions is the **Spanaway Speedway** (159th and 22nd Ave. E, 253/537-7551, www.spanawayspeedway.com), which holds races on Wednesday, Friday, and Saturday nights and Sunday afternoons between March and October.

The Arts

Tacoma's **Broadway Center for the Performing Arts** (www.broadwaycenter.org) contains a trio of outstanding theaters downtown near the intersection of 9th and Broadway Streets. Newest is the state-of-the art **Theater on the Square,** a 302-seat theater that is home to the nationally acclaimed **Tacoma Actors Guild** (253/272-2145), which performs through the winter season. An adjacent spot of green contains **waterfall park,** a fine place on a hot summer day. Also nearby are bronze performance masks representing various cultures.

In two lovingly restored 1918 buildings, the **Pantages Theater** and **Rialto Theater** (253/591-5894 for both) offer a taste of Tacoma's glory days in the Broadway district. Pantages is a large and ornate vaudeville palace where there's always something going on—plays, acrobats, and concerts. Get tickets early because many events sell out. The beaux arts–style Rialto is used for films, symphonies, lectures, and touring troupes. Also check the 1,650-seat **Temple Theatre** (47 St. Helens, 253/272-2042) for more theatrical events, including Broadway plays, comedy shows, and concerts. Built in 1926, the Temple is one of the grandest halls in the Northwest.

In existence for more than 75 years, the **Tacoma Little Theater** (210 N. I St., 253/272-2281, www.tacomalittletheatre.com) in the Stadium District, claims to be the oldest theater to stage continuous performances west of the Mississippi.

The **Tacoma Philharmonic** (253/272-0809, www.tacomaphilharmonic.org) plays at the Pantages Theater five times a year. The **Tacoma Symphony** (253/756-3396) brings in several guest artists each year; enjoy classical music in the theater and free pops in the parks during the summer. **Tacoma Musical Playhouse** (253/565-6867, www.tmp.org) features mystery dinners and other musicals all year. The **Tacoma Youth Symphony** (253/627-2792, www.tacomayouthsymphony.org) has 250 school musicians performing several concerts each year. The **Tacoma Master Chorale** (253/565-6867) performs a series of Christmas and folk concerts each winter.

BalleTacoma offers several performances each year, including the annual *Nutcracker* (253/272-9631) for more information. The **Tacoma Opera** (253/627-7789, www.tacomaopera.com) has English-language performances at the Pantages Theater. Call the **Arts Hotline** (253/383-9000) for upcoming events around Tacoma.

Gambling

If gambling fits your idea of fun, head to **Emerald Queen Casino** (2102 Alexander Ave., 888/831-7655, www.emeraldqueen.com) a New Orleans-style riverboat, with blackjack, roulette, craps, poker, and more. This is also a major music venue that is a favorite of past-their-prime blockbuster bands making a comeback.

Festivals and Events

Kick the year off in a nonalcoholic way at Tacoma's **First Night** (253/591-7205) celebration, with all sorts of events: theater, gallery openings, live music, comedy, mimes, and more. Activities start at noon on December 31. For three days in mid-February, **Wintergrass** (253/428-8056, www.wintergrass.com) is the largest indoor bluegrass festival in the world, with 30 bands on five stages around Tacoma.

The **Daffodil Festival** in mid-April features a parade of floral floats through downtown Tacoma, a marine parade with daffodil-decorated boats, plus live entertainment and other events.

Tacoma's big **Freedom Fair** (253/756-9808, www.freedomfair.com) on the 4th of July includes arts and cultural events, and live entertainment along the waterfront. A huge fireworks display is the feature when dusk arrives, but the main attraction is the air show—one of the largest in the nation—featuring both civilian and military aircraft over Commencement Bay. The **Taste of Tacoma** (www.tasteoftacoma.com) takes place at the same time, with dozens of local restaurants providing food, two concert stages with live music and entertainment, and a beer garden.

Several weekend **Salmon Bakes** (253/756-7336) are held July through September at Owen Beach in Point Defiance Park. The zoo in Point Defiance Park has periodic summertime concerts—**Zoo Sounds** (253/591-5358, www.pdza.org)—and a holiday **Zoolights** for additional seasonal fun.

The **Steilacoom 4th of July** includes a parade and street fair with food vendors, art booths, and live entertainment. Other events include a popular **Salmon Bake** on the last Sunday in July, a town-wide annual garage sale on a Saturday in August, the **Apple Squeeze Festival** in early October, and a **Spaghetti Feed** (253/584-4133) in February.

SHOPPING

Freighthouse Square (25th and East D, a block north of Tacoma Dome, 253/305-0678) is Tacoma's version of Pike Place Market, though it isn't nearly as successful. More than 70 small shops and restaurants can be found inside the turn-of-the-20th-century Milwaukee/St. Paul Railroad freighthouse. You can get everything from pet supplies to clothes to good food here. It's worth a look if you're in town, and a couple of the ethnic cafés are quite good. A great place to explore for used books is not far away, the **Tacoma Book Center** (324 E. 26th St., 253/572-8248).

Downtown Tacoma has more than 20 fine art galleries, along with several antique shops along **Antique Row** on Broadway between 7th and 9th Streets in downtown Tacoma.

One of the most enjoyable browsing sections in Tacoma is a mostly upscale cluster of shops and boutiques called the **Proctor District** along the 2700 block of N. Proctor. Some of the more interesting ones include the **Proctor District Antique Mall** with more than 40 dealers, and the **Pacific Northwest Shop,** which stocks only goods produced in the region.

All the major national and regional stores can be found at local shopping malls, including the biggest, **Tacoma Mall** (www.tacoma-mall.com) with 135 stores.

SPORTS AND RECREATION

Glassblowing

If you're digging all of the cool glass art around town and want to see if you have the chops to compete with Chihuly, take a walk to the end of Museum Row and enroll in a class at **Tacoma Glassblowing Studio** (114 S. 23rd St., 253/383-3499, $225 for two-day course) The teachers patiently explain the process of blowing glass, from heating the raw material to blowing to shaping and more. Your first time around it might feel like helping Dad build a treehouse—there's a lot of hand-holding early on for safety reasons—but the teachers are really friendly and you get to see the advanced artists making some cool stuff.

Point Defiance Park Natural Areas

Much of Port Defiance Park's wild nature remains from the early years, visible from a myriad of hiking paths (no bikes on unpaved trails) and a loop road that passes all the main sights. This loop road, **Five-Mile Drive,** winds through the park, offering a popular jogging, cycling, and driving route with viewpoints and picnic stops along the way. The outer loop is closed Saturday mornings (till 1 P.M.) to cars, giving joggers, cyclists, and in-line skaters free rein.

Owen Beach on Commencement Bay offers summer sun or a pleasant shoreline stroll any time of year. Rent a boat with a small motor at the Point Defiance **Boathouse Marina** (253/591-5325). The water off the point is popular with anglers, particularly during salmon season. Get fishing tackle at the shop here, or stop for a meal at the popular Boathouse Grill Restaurant next door. The state ferry to Vashon Island docks here as well. Point Defiance Park (253/305-1000, www.tacomaparks.com) is open every day from sunrise to 30 minutes past sunset.

© ERICKA CHICKOWSKI

An advanced glassblower crafts a piece at Tacoma Glassblowing Studio.

Spa

Those looking to relax after a long day of walking museum row can take a break at **Savi Day Spa** (1320 Broadway, 253/627-2000, www.savidayspa.com), a plush retreat based out of the Hotel Murano that offers full body massages ($120 for 90 min.), hot stone massages ($110 for 60 min.), and a number of foot and hand treatments on its menu of services.

Outdoor Equipment

For outdoor gear, head to **Backpackers Supply & Outlet** (5206 S. Tacoma Way, 253/472-4402), where you can also rent all sorts of outdoor supplies, including kayaks and canoes. This is the place to find out about **Tahoma Outdoor Pursuits** (253/474-8155, www.tahomaoutdoorpursuits.com), a group that offers classes and tours in kayaking, canoeing, rock climbing, mountaineering, and other recreation.

Walking and Biking

Lakewood Park (on Steilacoom Blvd.) has a trail that circles Waughop Lake. Drive down Dresdon Lane, then park by the barns to get to the trailhead.

A two-mile cycling and jogging path runs along Ruston Way, good for a breezy post-lunch or -dinner walk all the way down to Point Defiance, or just to the waterfront at **Commencement Park** or **Marine Park** along the way.

Tucked away where you'd least expect it is the **Tacoma Nature Center** (1919 S. Tyler St., 253/591-6439, www.tacomaparks.com). The 54 acres of marshland and evergreens are just a stone's throw from busy 19th Street, but this is a fine place to watch ducks and other birds. There are two miles of self-guiding nature trails. Trails are open 8 A.M.–dark daily; the interpretive center (8 A.M.–5 P.M. Mon.–Fri., 10 A.M.–4 P.M. Sat.–Sun. year-round, donations) is filled with hands-on exhibits.

Water Sports and Swimming

Public swimming beaches can be found at **Titlow Park** (just south of Narrows Bridge) and **Wapato Lake Park** (S. 72nd St. and Sheridan Ave.), where a lifeguard is present in the summer. **American Lake Park,** south of Tacoma near Fort Lewis, also has swimming.

There are two parks with fishing piers on Commencement Bay. Also known as Sundial Park for the giant stone timepiece there, **Commencement Park** is the quieter of the two. **Marine Park** has more amenities, with a long narrow strip of shoreline with open grassy areas, picnic tables, a fishing pier, bait shop, and snack stand. Fishing for dinner may not be such a smart idea, however, since Commencement Bay is one of Puget Sound's "hot spots," where the bottom fish and even salmon have shown unhealthy levels of toxins.

Golf

Local public golf courses include **Allenmore Golf Course** (2125 S. Cedar, 253/627-7211), **Meadow Park Golf Course** (7108 Lakewood Dr. W, 253/473-3033), **North Shore Golf & Country Club** (4101 North Shore Blvd. NE, 253/927-1375 or 800/447-1375), **Brookdale Golf Course** (1802 Brookdale Rd. E, 253/537-4400), **Classic Country Club** (4908 208th St. E in Spanaway, 253/847-4440) and **Ft. Steilacoom Golf Course** (8202 87th Ave. SW, 253/588-0613).

Camping

Camping is not allowed at Point Defiance Park, but head north to the city of Federal Way for **Dash Point State Park,** with year-round sites for both tents ($14) and RVs ($20). More campsites are located at **Kopachuck State Park,** 12 miles northwest of Tacoma, and **Penrose Point State Park,** approximately 20 miles west of Tacoma on the Key Peninsula. Get information at 360/902-8844. Make reservations ($7 extra) at 888/226-7688, www.parks.wa.gov.

Local RV parks include **Karwan Village** (2621 84th St., Tacoma, 253/582-1197) and **Majestic Manor RV Park** (7022 River Rd. E, 253/845-3144 or 800/348-3144).

ACCOMMODATIONS

The **Tacoma-Pierce County Convention and Visitor Bureau's** website (www.tpctourism.org) has links to many regional motels, hotels, and B&Bs and is a good place to start your lodging search.

Under $100

Many of the Tacoma area's motels are strung along Pacific Highway just off I-5, many in neighboring towns of Fife and Lakewood. **Econolodge Tacoma** (3100 Pacific Hwy. E, Fife, 253/922-9520 or 800/982-3781, $58 s or $64 d) has an outdoor pool for those toasty Tacoma summer days, plus a free continental breakfast. Pet owners can bring Fluffy with them for $10 more per night. In Lakewood, **Home Motel** (11621 Pacific Hwy. SW, Lakewood, 253/584-1717) rents singles for $55 and doubles for $59.

In Tacoma proper, **Tacoma Central Motel** (1220 Puyallup Ave., 253/272-7720, $55 s, $65 d) is a modest yet pleasant lodge with kitchenettes.

$100-150

For a just a few extra greenbacks, get a big jump in quality over the average motel offerings around Tacoma at **Guesthouse International of Fife** (5805 Pacific Hwy. E, Fife, 253/922-2500 or 800/422-3051, www.guesthousefife.com, $109 s or $119 d). This completely renovated building has well-lit rooms with quality linens and mattresses. The facility offers a fitness center, pool table, spa, complimentary hot breakfast, and free wireless Internet. There are also a spate of suite options, including a Jacuzzi suite ($165), an apartment with full kitchen ($189), and a spacious turret suite ($225) with huge windows, kitchen, and Jacuzzi.

The Green Cape Cod B&B (2711 N. Warner, 253/752-1977, www.greencapecod.com, $135–165 d) is a cozy 1929 Cape Cod antique-furnished home in north Tacoma where three guest rooms have private baths.

Built in 1911 and on the National Register of Historic Places, the elegant Colonial-style **DeVoe Mansion B&B** (208 E. 133rd St., 253/539-3991 or 888/539-3991, www.devoemansion.com, $125–155 d) is situated on 1.5 acres. The mansion was the home of Emma

DeVoe, a turn-of-the-20th-century suffragette whose efforts gave Washington women the right to vote. The four guest rooms have antiques and private baths. Guests can soak in the garden hot tub.

$150-200

In the Stadium District, **Villa B&B** (705 N. 5th St., 253/572-1157, www.villabb.com, $135–235 d) is a grand Mediterranean-style mansion built in 1925. The Villa features four large guest rooms, verandas, and gardens. In addition to a big breakfast each morning, Villa also provides snacks, pop, and water at no extra cost.

An 1889 Queen Anne Victorian in the historic Stadium District, **Chinaberry Hill B&B** (302 N. Tacoma Ave., 253/272-1282, www.chinaberryhill.com, $149–245 d) is one of the finest B&Bs in Tacoma. The home has a wraparound front porch, period furnishings, stained glass windows, and a separate carriage house for families or couples looking for privacy. Five guest rooms have private baths, and suites contain whirlpool tubs.

$200-250

Tacoma's landmark hotel is one of the nicest in all of Puget Sound—including downtown Seattle. The one-of-a-kind **Hotel Murano** (1320 Broadway Plaza, 253/238-8000, www.hotelmuranotacoma.com, $189–229 d, suites $249–469) pays homage to Tacoma's glassblowing scene in a big way. Named for the famous Italian glassmaking town, Murano will impress you right away with the enormous glass Viking boats crafted by Vibeke Skov, which are suspended from the lobby ceiling and reflect light differently throughout the day. From there it just gets better. There are pieces from all of the biggest glassmaking names around the world, including hometown hero Dale Chihuly, scattered through the lobby and posh lobby bar, the upstairs bistro, and the rest of the public nooks here. Most exciting are the individual pieces facing each elevator exit on every guest floor at this 21-floor tower. These glass pieces were specially commissioned for the hotel, and along each hallway there is an interpretive display honoring each artist's vision for the work and pictures showing the making of the piece. The rooms themselves are hardly a footnote to the story—they are stylishly decorated with modern furnishing, über-comfy beds, and sumptuous linens. The service is top notch, without the pretension that would probably surround such a hotel if it were in Seattle.

Every second Tuesday of the month, the hotel opens for a tour led by docents from the Museum of Glass. Held at 2 P.M., the tour takes you through the public spaces, meeting rooms, and guest floors, which normally are not open to the public. The tour costs $5, proceeds to the Museum of Glass.

Over $250

There's nothing else in Washington like **Thornewood Castle B&B** (8601 N. Thorne Lane SW, 253/584-4393, www.thornewoodcastle.com, $358–597 d, no kids allowed), a magnificent 1910 Tudor mansion on American Lake southwest of Tacoma, with a half-acre sunken English garden. Inside this 27,000-square-foot mansion you'll find 16th-century stained glass and other ornate furnishings. Five guest rooms have private baths. The Stephen King made-for-TV movie *Rose Red* was filmed here in 2000 for ABC.

FOOD

Cafés and Grills

Bair Drug and Hardware (1617 Lafayette, 253/588-9668, 7 A.M.–6 P.M. Mon.–Tues., 7 A.M.–9 P.M. Wed.–Sun.) is an 1895 shop with a sampling of historic items on display and a 1906 soda fountain where you can still get a soda or sundae, along with something you wouldn't find in 1906—espresso coffees. Great baked goods and pies here as well.

Start out at **Knapps Restaurant** (2707 N. Proctor St., 253/759-9009, 6 A.M.–9 P.M. Sun.–Thurs., 6 A.M.–10 P.M. Fri.–Sat.) in the Proctor District, where you'll find the best breakfasts in Tacoma, from pancakes to eggs Benedict.

Located in north Tacoma near Point Defiance Park, the **Antique Sandwich**

Company (5102 N. Pearl, 253/752-4069, 7 A.M.–7:30 P.M. daily) seems a throwback to the early 1970s. The atmosphere is earthy; the menu includes good soups, clam chowder, salads, espresso, and sweets. Come back in the evening for live acoustic or folk groups. Another terrific lunch spot is **Pastrami's New York Eatery and Espresso** (950 Broadway, 253/779-0645), which gets crowded at lunchtime.

Fife City Bar & Grill (3025 Pacific Hwy. E, 253/922-9555, www.restaurant.com/fifecitybarandgrill, 11 A.M.–9 P.M. Mon.–Thurs., 8 A.M.–9 P.M. Fri.–Sun.) gets kudos from Tacoma locals for its highly creative meals at surprisingly low prices. The menu includes a wide selection of lunch and dinner choices.

Primo Grill (601 S. Pine St., 253/383-7000, 11 A.M.–9:30 P.M. Mon.–Thurs., 11 A.M.–10:30 P.M. Fri., 5–10:30 P.M. Sat., 4:30–10:30 P.M. Sun.) has a wood-burning grill in an architecturally tasty setting. Another place to fill yourself is **Southern Kitchen** (1716 6th Ave., 253/627-4282, 8 A.M.–8 P.M. Mon.–Thurs., 8 A.M.–9 P.M. Fri.–Sat., 8 A.M.–7 P.M. Sun.) where the menu of home-cooked meals includes catfish, pork chops, collard greens, barbecued ribs, and sweet potato pie. This is a longtime Tacoma favorite.

Steak and Seafood

Located right on the water, **Harbor Lights** (2761 Ruston Way, 253/752-8600, 11 A.M.–9 P.M. Mon.–Sat., noon–9 P.M. Sun.) is a Tacoma tradition, with giant steaks, four-pound buckets of clams, tasty fish and chips, and moderate prices. It's also good for drinks.

Johnny's Ocean Fish Co. (2201 Ruston Way, 253/383-4571) in Old Town right alongside the fishing pier is a friendly market with fresh and smoked seafood of all kinds. It's a good place to pick up fish recipes, too—this is the home of the Johnny's Seasoning line of spices, which you can find at just about any grocery store around the nation.

If you want a sweeping Sound view, try the old-time **Cliff House** (6300 Marine View Dr. at Browns Point, 253/927-0400 or 800/961-0401, www.cliffhouserestaurant.com, upstairs 5–9:30 P.M. weekends, downstairs 11:30 A.M.–11 P.M. daily). The steak and seafood are very good, and the downstairs lounge offers the same view and a sandwich menu.

© JOE MCMAHON/THE LOBSTER SHOP DASH POINT

Lobster Shop Dash Point

View the glittering lights of downtown Tacoma and the port from above I-5 at **Stanley and Seafort's Steak, Chop, and Fish House** (115 E. 34th, 253/473-730, www.r-u-i.com, 4–9:30 P.M. Mon.–Thurs., 4–10:30 P.M. Fri.–Sat., 3:30–9 P.M. Sun.). This is Tacoma's culinary institution, a no-brainer stop for locals on anniversaries, birthdays, and proms. It is one of those dependably good places with fine meats, seafood, and desserts.

C. I. Shenanigan's (3017 Ruston Way, 253/752-8811, 11 A.M.–10 P.M. Mon.–Thurs., 11 A.M.–11 P.M. Fri.–Sat., 9:30 A.M.–10 P.M. Sun.) is a spiffy waterside restaurant with outdoor seating, a seafood menu, and long waits on weekends. Reservations are advised.

The **Lobster Shop Dash Point** (6912 Soundview Dr. NE, 253/927-1513, www.

lobstershop.com, 4:30–9 P.M. Sun.–Thurs., 4:30–10 P.M. Fri.–Sat.), sister to the Lobster Shop South across the bay (4015 Ruston Way. 206/759-2165, 11:30 A.M.–2:30 P.M. and 4:30–9:30 P.M. Mon.–Thurs., 11:30 A.M.–2:30 P.M. and 4:30–10:30 P.M. Fri., 4:30–10:30 P.M. Sat., 9:30 A.M.–1:30 P.M. and 4:30–9:30 P.M. Sun.) is the original, more rustic version, where the steaks, seafood, and wine list are reliably good. There are great waterside views, and reservations are advised. Lobster Shop South is open for lunch and dinner, and it serves a substantial Sunday brunch.

Asian

Throw a brick along 38th Avenue and chances are good it'll plunk down into a bowl of pho noodles. This is the epicenter of Tacoma's thriving Vietnamese community and is *the* place to go in the South Sound for fresh spring rolls, vermicelli noodle dishes, and, of course, pho. Do yourself a favor and go directly to **Nhu Thuy** (758 S 38th St., 253/474-3992, 9 A.M.–9 P.M. daily) to experience the best pho among all of these little mom-and-pop establishments. A close second is **Vien Dong Vietnamese** (3801 S. Yakima Ave., 253/472-6668, 9 A.M.–9 P.M. Mon.–Sat., 9 A.M.–8 P.M. Sun.).

For ultra-fresh Japanese sushi, head downtown to **Fujiya** (1125 Court C, 253/627-5319, 11 A.M.–2 P.M. Mon.–Fri. and 5:30–9:30 P.M. Mon.–Sat., closed Sun.).

If you've just had a full day at Point Defiance and you've got to satisfy the little ones with Americanized Asian dishes, venture over to **Imperial Dragon** (6805 6th Ave., 253/565-5477, 11 A.M.–9:30 P.M. Sun.–Thurs., 11 A.M.–10:30 P.M. Fri.–Sat.), where you can find a compromise between traditional Chinese fare and kid-friendly sweet-and-sour dishes.

Italian

Rock Pasta (1920 Jefferson Ave., 253/272-1221, 11 A.M.–midnight Sun.–Thurs., 11:30 A.M.–1 A.M. Fri.–Sat.) is the place to go for gourmet wood-fired pizzas and pasta and a big choice of microbrews. Another excellent pizza place—one reader called it the best he ever tasted—is **Cloverleaf Pizzas** (6430 6th Ave., 253/565-1111, 5–10 P.M. Mon.–Fri., 11:30 A.M.–10 P.M. Sat.–Sun.).

Ravenous Restaurant (785 Broadway, 253/572-6374, 11:30 A.M.–2 P.M. Mon–Fri. and 5:30–9 P.M. Wed.–Sat.) is a little downtown bistro that makes flavorful Italian and Northwest cuisine. It's popular with the business-lunch crowd.

Mexican

The city's best Mexican dishes are served at **Moctezuma's** (4102 S. 56th St., 253/474-5593, 11 A.M.–10 P.M. Sun.–Thurs., 11 A.M.–11 P.M. Fri.–Sat.).

Pub Grub

The Swiss (1904 S. Jefferson, 253/572-2821, www.theswisspub.com, 11 A.M.–10 P.M. daily) is a friendly pub with 37 beers on tap, splendid Chihuly glass art, and surprisingly good sandwiches and pasta. The back room has pool and darts, plus live music on weekends. Drop by on the third Sunday of the month for a brunch with live polka tunes.

Harmon Pub and Brewery (1938 Pacific Ave., 253/383-2739, www.harmonbrew.com, 11 A.M.–11 P.M. Mon.–Thurs., 11 A.M.–midnight Fri.–Sat., 11 A.M.–9:30 P.M. Sun.) is a big, bustling place with brewed-on-the-premises ales and porter, and good pub grub such as fish and chips, burgers, pizza, and pasta.

Located in a turn-of-the-20th-century firehouse, **Engine House No. 9** (611 N. Pine, 253/272-3435) stocks nearly 50 local and imported beers and features a pub menu of pizza, tacos, soups, and salads.

Established in 1913, **Spar Tavern** (2121 N. 30th, 253/627-8215) has great pub grub: burgers, sandwiches, chili, and homemade soups, but it is a bar, so no kids are allowed.

Katie Downs Tavern (3211 Ruston Way, 253/756-0771) sits on a pier and attracts a good-sized crowd with a big selection of beer and wine, deep-dish pizza, a jeans-and-sneakers atmosphere, and outdoor seating in the summer; over age 21 only.

Markets and Bakeries

The **Tacoma Farmers Market** (253/272-7077, www.tacomafarmersmarket.com) comes to 9th and Broadway (Antique Row) runs 10 A.M.–3 P.M. Thursday June through mid-October. Stock up on fresh fruits and vegetables, along with arts and crafts. Another farmers market is held in Proctor (4001 N. 26th St., 253/223-4655, 9 A.M.–2 P.M. Sat. June–early Sept.).

Out in the Proctor District, the **Queen Anne Thriftway** (2420 N. Proctor, 253/761-3663) is a great gourmet grocery store with imported and specialty foods and a fine deli.

INFORMATION AND SERVICES

For information on Tacoma and the surrounding area, head to **Tacoma-Pierce County Convention and Visitor Bureau** (1001 Pacific Ave., Suite 400, entrance is on 10th St., 253/627-2836 or 800/272-2662, www.tpctourism.org, 8:30 A.M.–5 P.M. Mon.–Fri. year-round). A second visitors center is inside the State History Museum (1911 Pacific Ave.).

The main **Tacoma Public Library** (1102 Tacoma Ave. S, 253/591-5666, www.tpl.lib.wa.us) features an amazing stained-glass dome ceiling upstairs in the Northwest Room. Tacoma's main **post office** (1102 S. A St., 253/471-6122,) has a small museum with a mail sleigh and other philatelic memorabilia, along with historic stamps.

GETTING THERE AND AROUND

By Bus

Pierce Transit (253/581-8000 or 800/562-8109, www.ptbus.pierce.wa.us) has daily service to Puyallup, Gig Harbor, Lakewood, Steilacoom, Spanaway, Fife, Buckley, and every other town in Pierce country, along with commuter service to Seattle and Olympia. The bus station is located at 1319 Pacific Avenue. The **Tacoma Link** (www.soundtransit.org) connects downtown with the transit hub at the Tacoma Dome Station. The trains run every 10 minutes, Monday through Saturday, and every 10 to 20 minutes on Sunday.

Greyhound (253/383-4621 or 800/231-2222, www.greyhound.com) runs service along the I-5 corridor, connecting Tacoma with Portland, Seattle, and Vancouver. **Northwestern Trailways** (800/366-6975, www.nwadv.com/northw) also connects Tacoma with Seattle and Everett.

By Train

Amtrak (800/872-7245, www.amtrak.com) serves Tacoma from its passenger station at 1001 Puyallup Ave., between the tide flat area and I-5 in the eastern part of the city. The Coast Starlight train provides four-times-a-day service to the Puget Sound area from Portland, San Francisco, and Los Angeles.

GALLOPING GERTIE

One of the most familiar few minutes of film footage to ever come out of the Northwest is the stunning collapse of the Tacoma Narrows Bridge in 1940. Open for a mere five months at the time of its fall, the bridge had been affectionately named "Galloping Gertie" for the undulating motion that motorists could feel as they drove over the 2,800-foot span. On November 7, 1940, the relatively moderate 40-mph winds had an unexpected effect on the bridge, causing the steel-and-concrete structure to twist and flap like a flag. The movement became more severe until the bridge finally collapsed, the dramatic moment caught on film by a local camera shop owner. Thankfully, nobody was hurt, although an elderly cocker spaniel named Tubby, trapped in a car that had just been abandoned by its owner, fell to his death in the roiling waters below. Today, two bridges carry traffic across Highway 16 between Tacoma and the Kitsap Peninsula, one built in 1950 and the other in 2007. The new bridges are sometimes referred to as "Sturdy Gertie."

By Ferry

The **Washington State Ferry** (425/355-7308 or 888/808-7977, 800/843-3779 for automated information, www.wsdot.wa.gov/ferries system) is a heavily used method of everyday transportation around the Puget Sound region. From Tacoma, however, it can only get you to Tahlequah on Vashon Island. Ferries depart from Point Defiance; summer fares are $2.90 round-trip for passengers and walk-ons, $13 round-trip for car and driver. Fares are collected only on the way to Vashon, not when you return.

Seattle-Tacoma International Airport

If you're flying into Tacoma, you'll arrive at the Seattle-Tacoma International Airport (better known as Sea-Tac). As the name suggests, it's about halfway between Seattle and Tacoma. **Capital Aeroporter** (800/962-3579, www.capair.com) offers door-to-airport service to Tacoma.

Kitsap Peninsula

The Kitsap Peninsula is an appendage to the Olympic Peninsula; in fact, visitors and locals alike sometimes confuse the two, thinking that anything west of Seattle must be the Olympic Peninsula. Not true: The Kitsap is separated from the Olympic Peninsula by Hood Canal.

The Kitsap is readily accessible by ferry from Seattle and Edmonds, and by the Tacoma Narrows Bridge from Tacoma. Its many back roads are favorite cycling destinations. Bainbridge Island is especially popular because of the easy access, diverse country, lack of traffic, and abundance of fine cafés and B&Bs. For a helpful map of recommended bike routes—plus all sorts of other local information—contact the **Kitsap Peninsula Visitor & Convention Bureau** (Port Gamble, 360/297-8200 or 800/416-5616 www.visitkitsap.com).

BREMERTON

The blue-collar city of Bremerton—the largest settlement on Kitsap Peninsula—offers sweeping views of both the Cascades and the Olympics and a waterfront crowded with decommissioned Navy ships. The run-down city center resembles a dying Massachusetts mill town; many of the businesses have fled to suburban strip malls or to the booming patches of real estate around Belfair and Silverdale. The city does, however, have several interesting historical sights, including famous battleships and a naval museum, as well as good restaurants and inexpensive housing. And in the coming years the city has committed to revitalizing its waterfront—so keep your eyes open for new improvements.

Sights

The destroyer USS ***Turner Joy*** was one of the ships involved in the Gulf of Tonkin Incident in 1964 that led to the escalation of the Vietnam War. During the shelling of Chu Lai later that year, one of its guns jammed and an ensuing explosion killed three men. The destroyer was decommissioned in 1982 and opened to the public in 1988 for self-guided tours. If you haven't been aboard a Navy ship before, a tour of the USS *Turner Joy* (300 Washington Beach Ave., 360/792-2457, www.ussturnerjoy.org, 10 A.M.–5 P.M. daily mid-May–Sept., 10 A.M.–3:30 P.M. Fri.–Sun. Oct.–mid-May, $10 adults, $8 seniors, $6 ages 5–12) will be an education, with its tight sleeping quarters and an impressive array of weaponry.

A number of other mothballed Navy ships—including the USS *New Jersey* and the USS *Oriskany*—sit at anchor in varying states of disrepair. They aren't open to the public, but **Kitsap Harbor Tours** (360/876-1260, $9 adults, $8 seniors, $6 ages 5–12) offers 45-minute boat tours around the ships several times a day mid-May through September, and on weekends in October. Get tickets on the boardwalk at the *Turner Joy*.

ANCHORS AWEIGH

With all the water around it and the deep harbor at its doorstep, Bremerton is an ideal location for the **Puget Sound Naval Shipyard,** the city's economic mainstay since 1891. Today the facility is where nuclear ships and subs are overhauled and deactivated. It is the second-largest industrial employer in Washington (after Boeing), with 9,200 civilian workers and over 10,000 military personnel. Other nearby military facilities include the Naval Hospital and Naval Supply Center in Bremerton, the Naval Undersea Warfare Center in Keyport, and the Naval Submarine Base in Bangor.

Naval history buffs will also enjoy the excellent **Bremerton Naval Museum** (130 Washington Ave., 360/479-7447, 10 A.M.–5 P.M. Tues.–Sat., 1–5 P.M. Sun., donations accepted), which displays American and Japanese naval artifacts, highly detailed models of the USS *Nimitz* and other Navy ships, and naval memorabilia of all types.

The **Kitsap County Historical Museum** (280 4th St., 360/479-6226, www.waynes.net/kchsm, 10 A.M.–5 P.M. Tues.–Sun., donations accepted) shows historical items from the Bremerton area.

Entertainment and Events

THE ARTS

The **Bremerton Symphony Orchestra** (360/373-1722) performs concerts throughout the winter season. **Bremerton Community Theatre** (599 Lebo Blvd., 360/373-5152) puts on comedy, drama, and musical theater performances. Free **Concerts on the Boardwalk** take place on Friday evenings mid-July to mid-August.

Two notable fine art galleries are **Collective Visions** (331 Pacific Ave., 360/377-8327, 10 A.M.–5 P.M. Tues.–Sat.) and **Amy Burnett Gallery** (412 Pacific Ave., 360/373-3187, 10 A.M.–5 P.M. Tues.–Sat.). The latter is said to be the largest art gallery in the Northwest.

EVENTS

The third weekend of May brings an **Armed Forces Festival and Parade** (360/479-3579), the largest celebration of its type in the nation. In late August the **Kitsap County Fair and Rodeo** (360/692-3655) comes to the Kitsap County Fairgrounds five miles north of Bremerton. Highlighted by a PRCA rodeo, the fair also includes a carnival, circus, and other entertainment. Join the late August end-of-summer party at the **Blackberry Festival** on the boardwalk, with arts and crafts, food, music, a classic car show, and fun run.

Sports and Recreation

Three miles northeast of downtown Bremerton on Highway 306, **Illahee State Park** (3540 NE Bahia Vista Dr., 360/478-6460, www.parks.wa.gov) has campsites on 75 acres, with swimming beaches, a short but steep hiking trail, a boat launch, and a pier for fishing and lolling in the sun. Illahee State Park also has camping ($17 tents, $23 RV hookups) and showers year-round. Campers can also find showers at the Bremerton marina.

Hikers will enjoy the two-mile trek to the summit of 1,700-foot **Green Mountain** for spectacular views of Kitsap Peninsula, Puget Sound, and the Seattle skyline. From downtown, take Seabeck Highway Northwest for two miles, turn left (west) on Holly Road, then take a left onto Tahuyeh Road for 1.25 miles to Gold Creek Road. Turn left onto Gold Creek and follow it for 1.5 miles to the trailhead on the left, before Gold Creek Bridge. Be sure to wear proper footwear since the trail is rocky and often wet.

Swim at **Wildcat Lake** (9205 Holly Rd. NW), where a seasonal lifeguard is on duty. Also here are bathhouses, picnic areas, and a playground.

Accommodations

Bremerton has low-cost motels in spades, but do your homework ahead of time, as some of these places can be a little sketchy.

No need for worries at the **Flagship Inn** (4320 Kitsap Way, 360/479-6566 or 800/447-9396, www.flagship-inn.com, $69 s, $75–85 d), though. This place is a nice waterfront motel with gorgeous views and patios to enjoy them. Rooms are updated and clean and there's a heated outdoor pool on premises. As an added bonus, continental breakfast is served each morning.

Families may prefer getting a little breathing room at **Oyster Bay Inn** (4412 Kitsap Way, 360/377-5510 or 800/393-3862, www.oysterbayinn.com, $94–119 s, $84–179 d), which offers more multi-room suite options and even rents out a small chalet. There's a restaurant and lounge on premises, plus an exercise room and its own private stretch of waterfront.

You'll enjoy easy ferry access and modern rooms at **Hampton Inn and Suites** (150 Washington Ave., 360/405-0200, www.hamptoninn.com, $139–169 d), pretty much the nicest hotel in town. The marina-front hotel offers comfy beds and sparkling clean facilities that include a fitness center with an indoor lap pool, business center with free printing, wireless Internet, and valet parking.

Situated on a six-acre wooded site along Puget Sound, **Illahee Manor B&B** (6680 Illahee Rd. NE, 360/698-7555 or 800/693-6680, www.illaheemanor.com, $130–220 d) offers the coziest stay in Bremerton. The six suites have private baths, most with fireplaces and whirlpool baths. The eclectically furnished and comfortable house was built in 1929. A full breakfast is served, and families can stay in the beach house.

Food

Get nachos, fresh seafood, steaks, pasta, sandwiches, or salads over the water at the **Boat Shed** (101 Shore Dr., 360/377-2600, 11 A.M.–9 P.M. daily).

Enjoy gourmet French fries served up Euro-style in little paper cones and with creative dipping sauces at **Fritz European Fry House** (94 Washington Ave., 360/479-1088, www.fritzfryhouse.com, 11 A.M.–8 P.M. Mon.–Thurs., 11 A.M.–10 P.M. Fri.–Sat., 12:30–6 P.M. Sun.), which also serves a nice selection of imported beers.

The best Italian food served this side of the Sound is masterfully plated at **La Fermata** (2204 E 11th St., 360/373-5927, 5–10 P.M. Tues.–Sat.), a romantic restaurant that specializes in Northern Italian dishes.

Enjoy a cup of joe and a breakfast burrito in the morning or a pop and a sandwich later in the day at the psychedelic **Hi-Lo's 15th St. Café** (2720 15th St., 360/373-7833, www.hilos15thstreetcafe.com, 7 A.M.–8 P.M. Tues.–Fri., 8 A.M.–3 P.M. Sat.–Sun., closed Sun.), a hippie-dippy place that has a pretty neat collection of old thermoses and lunch pails that are sure to take several generations of diners back to their childhoods for a moment.

Information

The folks at the **Bremerton Area Chamber of Commerce** (301 Pacific Ave., 360/479-3579, 9 A.M.–5 P.M. Mon.–Fri. year-round, www.bremertonchamber.org) can answer most of your questions. They also have an information booth next to the ferry terminal.

Getting There

From the Seattle waterfront you can take a 60-minute trip to Bremerton on the **Washington State Ferries** (360/842-2345, 888/808-7977, or 800/843-3779 for automated information, www.wsdot.wa.gov/ferries, one-way $14.45 car and driver, $6.25 motorcycle and driver, $6.70 extra passengers and walkers, $6.25 extra kayaks, $1 extra bikes). Ferries depart about every 70 minutes for Bremerton. A passenger-only ferry (same rates) sails from Seattle five times a day and makes the run in 50 minutes. You'll probably end up paying $4–8 if you want to park anywhere near downtown because so many folks from the Kitsap Peninsula park here and ride the ferry to Seattle.

Kitsap Transit Ferry (360/876-2300, $1.50 one-way) also offers 10-minute ferry rides across the Sinclair Inlet between Bremerton and Port Orchard for foot traffic and bikes only. It's a seven-mile drive around the head of Sinclair Inlet to Port Orchard if you drive there instead.

Kitsap Harbor Tours (360/876-1260) offers tours of the mothball fleet along with tours to Blake Island on summer weekends.

Kitsap Transit (360/373-2877 or 800/501-7433, www.kitsaptransit.org) has daily bus service throughout the peninsula and meets all state ferries. All buses have bike racks. **Bremerton-Kitsap Airporter** (360/876-1737 or 800/562-7948, www.kitsapairporter.com) offers shuttle buses to Sea-Tac Airport.

PORT ORCHARD

Across the Sinclair Inlet from Bremerton, Port Orchard—the Kitsap County seat—shows a split personality. The prosperous waterfront section faces the marina with covered walkways, colorful murals, antique shops, and cozy cafés. This contrasts sharply with the standard Wal-Mart and fast-food section sprawling outward on the south end. Port Orchard still keeps a small fishing fleet, and boat sheds fill the harbor, but it is primarily a bedroom community for Seattle and Tacoma, and for Bremerton military workers.

Port Orchard was named for H. M. Orchard, the clerk on Captain Vancouver's 1792 expedition who first discovered this bay. The town was founded in 1886 and became the county seat seven years later.

Sights

From downtown, head two blocks uphill on Sidney Avenue to the **Sidney Art Gallery and Museum** (202 Sidney Ave., 360/876-3693, www.sidneymuseumandarts, 11 A.M.–4 P.M. Mon.–Sat., 1–4 P.M. Sun.). The lower floor contains a gallery with imaginative paintings and ceramic pieces; upstairs is a small but well-presented collection of historical displays representing various turn-of-the-20th-century shops and industries.

Housed in a 1913 pioneer log home, the quaint **Log Cabin Museum** (416 Sidney Ave., 11 A.M.–4 P.M. Sat., 1–5 P.M. Sun., free) has exhibits of local history.

© KITSAP PENINSULA VISITOR & CONVENTION BUREAU/JEAN BOYLE

Port Orchard marina

Entertainment and Events

The **Bay Street Playhouse** (820 Bay St., 360/876-6610) is home to the Performing Arts Guild of South Kitsap, a group that puts on plays, musicals, and children's shows throughout the year.

Port Orchard's most peculiar event is the **Seagull Calling Contest,** held on the Saturday before Easter. Contestants in goofy costumes attempt to see who can call in the most gulls. The **Fathoms O' Fun Carnival**—Port Orchard's premier summer festival and one of the state's oldest—is held from the last Saturday in June through the 4th of July. Highlights include a big parade, carnival, fun run, fireworks, and various contests. Then comes the **Chris Craft Rendezvous,** which attracts more than a hundred vintage boats in mid-July. The **Peninsula Jazz Festival** (360/846-1979) is a two-day event at the end of July. **The Cruz** comes to Port Orchard on the first Sunday of August, and Bay Street is closed off to display more than 1,000 custom cars and hot rods, plus juried arts and crafts, food booths, live music, dancing, and games.

Shopping

Cute is the operative term at Port Orchard's many antique, craft, and gift shops, which generally cater to an audience that appreciates lots of lace, schlock, and sickly sweet smells. Try the **Victorian Rose Tea Room** (1130 Bethel Ave., 360/876-5695, 9 A.M.–5 P.M. Mon.–Fri., 8 A.M.–4 P.M. Sat.–Sun.) to see for yourself. It's a favorite of the doll-and-teddy-bear crowd. Fans of kitchy old stuff should swing by the largest antique emporium in town, the **Olde Central Antique Mall** (801 Bay St., 360/895-1902, 10 A.M.–5:30 P.M. Mon.–Sat., 11 A.M.–5 P.M. Sun.).

Sports and Recreation

Follow Beach Drive from Port Orchard for a scenic approach to **Manchester State Park** (360/871-4065 or 888/226-7688, www.parks.wa.gov), six miles away at the entrance to Sinclair Inlet. The park's 111 acres include campsites ($17 tent, $24 RV hookups, $7 extra reservation fee), hiking and interpretive trails, plus swimming, fishing, and scuba diving in Rich Passage. The main attractions here are various century-old military structures, built to protect the Bremerton Naval Shipyard from attack. These include a brick warehouse once used to store underwater mines (now it's an oversized picnic shelter) and a control center where the mines could be set off remotely if enemy warships intruded. Fortunately, the mines were never deployed, and the fort was abandoned and turned into a state park. The park is open from late April to early September.

For another camping option, park RVs in the trees at the city-owned **Orchard RV Park** (Bethel Rd. at Lund Ave., no hookups, free for 5 days) southwest of town, a quarter mile south of the Safeway.

The 200-acre **South Kitsap Community Park** (Jackson Rd. and Lund Rd.), two miles southwest of downtown, has hiking trails and a picnic area, plus kiddie steam trains (11 A.M.–4 P.M. daily June–mid-Sept., free). Swim or boat at **Long Lake County Park** (Lake Valley Rd. SE), approximately four miles south of Port Orchard.

Two 18-hole golf courses in the vicinity are **Horseshoe Lake Golf Course** (15932 Sidney Rd. SW, 360/857-3326) and **McCormick Woods Golf Course** (5155 McCormick Woods Dr. SW, 360/895-0130, www.mccormickwoodsgolf.com). The latter is considered one of the finest in the Northwest.

Accommodations

There are more hotel options in Bremerton, but Port Orchard does offer some decent hotel rooms at the **Comfort Inn** (1121 Bay St., 360/895-2666 or 800/465-4329, $99–119 d) that have microwaves and mini-fridges included. The more expensive ones even come with Jacuzzi tubs. The property has an outdoor spa and an extensive continental breakfast that includes make-your-own waffles.

There are a number of cozy bed-and-breakfasts scattered about town, including the stunning **Ladley's View Park Bed and Breakfast**

Resort (7382 View Park Rd., 866/871-0900, http://ladleysbb.com, $200–250 d, no kids allowed), tucked away on a 20-acre gated property that includes a nine-hole golf course, lighted tennis courts, a trout pond, gardens, and woodland trails—all included with the room rate. Also on the property are saunas, spas, and a fitness center. The rooms are huge, and unlike many B&Bs, this one serves breakfast at your leisure rather than at a fixed time at the crack of dawn.

Another lovely option for the budget-minded traveler is **Reflections B&B** (3878 Reflection Lane E, 360/871-5582, $65–110 d), a large two-story home with four guest rooms, a hot tub, and gazebo. Rooms offer views of Port Orchard Passage, and a full breakfast is served. Couples will enjoy the silence—no kids are allowed at this place.

Families touring with older kids can check into **Little Clam Bay Bed and Breakfast** (7801 E Jessica Way, 360/871-0619, www.littleclambay.com, $160 d), a private little cottage only about a mile away from Manchester State Park. The second bedroom with twin beds is rented out for only $35 more per person and kids over 12 are welcome. The master bedroom has a large tub meant for two and there's a fireplace in the living room, plus a deck looking out over Little Clam Bay. On top of breakfast, the innkeepers serve late evening snacks each day.

Food

Right in front of the ferry dock, **Amy's on the Bay** (833 Bay St., 360/876-1445, 11:30 A.M.–10 P.M. daily) whips up great, super-fresh seafood and pours local wines and microbrews to wash down your meal.

Myhre's Restaurant (739 Bay St., 360/876-4634, 6:30–8 P.M. Sun.–Thurs., 6:30–9 P.M. Fri.–Sat.) offers marina views while you taste the reasonably priced steaks, prime rib, and fresh seafood.

For ethnic eats, head to the popular **Puerto Vallarta** (Bethel Rd. and Lund Ave., 360/876-0788, 11 A.M.–10 P.M. Mon.–Thurs., 11 A.M.–11 P.M. Fri.–Sat., 10 A.M.–11 P.M. Sun.), serving up Mexican favorites.

Bay Street Ale House (807 Bay St., 360/876-8030, 3–11 P.M. Mon.–Fri., 3 P.M.–midnight Sat., 3–10 P.M. Sun.) has 16 beers on tap, distinctive pizzas, and other pub meals, all in a smoke-free environment.

The **Port Orchard Farmers Market** (253/857-2657) takes place behind Peninsula Feed Store on Bay Street 9 A.M.–3 P.M. Saturday May–October. This is one of the largest markets in the state and features more than 100 vendors offering homegrown fruits and veggies, homemade crafts, and ethnic foods. A winter market takes place at the community center.

Information

Get information at **Port Orchard Chamber of Commerce** (839 Bay St., 360/876-3505 or 800/982-8139, www.portorchard.com, 10 A.M.–5 P.M. Mon.–Fri., 10 A.M.–2 P.M. Sat.). Be sure to stop here to check out the beautifully crafted seven-foot-long wooden model of the *Virginia V.*

Getting There

Catch the **Washington State Ferry** (360/842-2345 or 888/808-7977, 800/843-3779 for automated information, www.wsdot.wa.gov/ferries, $18.50 one-way car and driver, $8 motorcycle and driver, $4.30 extra passengers and walkers, $8 extra kayaks, $1 extra bikes) from the Fauntleroy dock in West Seattle for the 35-minute ride to Southworth on the southeast side of the Kitsap Peninsula near Port Orchard. You can also catch a ferry from Southworth to Vashon Island every 90 minutes (one-way from Southworth $14.80 car and driver, $6.40 motorcycle and driver, $4.30 extra passengers and walkers, $8 passenger with kayak, $1 extra bikes, one-way from Vashon free).

Kitsap Transit Ferry (360/876-2300, $1.50 one-way) also offers 10-minute ferry rides across the Sinclair Inlet between Bremerton and Port Orchard for foot traffic and bikes only. Should you choose to go by car instead, it's a seven-mile drive around the head of Sinclair Inlet to Bremerton.

Kitsap Transit (360/377-2877 or 800/501-

7433, www.kitsaptransit.org, $1.50 one-way) provides daily bus service throughout the Kitsap Peninsula and Bainbridge Island and meets all Southworth ferries. **Bremerton-Kitsap Airporter** (360/876-1737 or 800/562-7948, www.kitsapairporter.com) offers shuttle buses to Sea-Tac Airport.

SEABECK

The small town of Seabeck occupies a point of land west of Silverdale on the east shore of Hood Canal, with dramatic panoramic views of the Olympic Mountains. It has a marina and a few restaurants and grocers, and it is a favorite of anglers. The oldest outdoor theater in the Northwest, **Mountaineers' Forest Theater** (206/284-6310, www.foresttheater.com) holds productions near Seabeck late May through June. The amphitheater's terraced log seats are beautifully backdropped by rhododendrons, Douglas firs, and hemlocks; be prepared for a 0.3-mile hike from your car to the theater.

Scenic Beach State Park

Scenic Beach State Park has forested campsites (360/830-5079 or 888/226-7688, www.parks.wa.gov, $17 tent, no RV hookups, $7 extra reservation fee), salmon fishing, oyster gathering in season, and Olympic Mountain views on Hood Canal. The 88-acre park is particularly pleasant when the spring rhododendrons are in bloom. The park is open for day use year-round, but the campground is only open from late April to late September.

Accommodations

Once the private residence of Colonel Julian Willcox and built in 1936, the 10,000-square-foot waterfront **Willcox House** (2390 Tekiu Rd. NW, 360/830-4492 or 800/725-9477, www.willcoxhouse.com, $169–259 d, no kids), on the Hood Canal south of Seabeck, was described as "the grand entertainment capital of the Canal region." Every room is angled to capture a water view, and the house is filled with marble and copper fireplaces and luxurious period furnishings. Outdoors, a 300-foot pier can accommodate guests' boats. Clark Gable once stayed in the room that now bears his name.

KEYPORT

Keyport is home to the top-secret **Naval Undersea Warfare Center,** a place that sounds like something out of a James Bond film. This is where much of America's torpedo research is conducted, gaining it the moniker "Torpedo Town." Just west of Keyport in Bangor is the **Naval Submarine Base,** where the fleet of eight Trident nuclear submarines is headquartered, and where some 1,600 nuclear warheads are stored—more than in France, China, and Great Britain combined! The base is also home to 5,000 military personnel.

Naval Undersea Museum

For visitors, this marvelous museum (610 Dowell St., 360/396-4148, 10 A.M.–4 P.M. daily June–Sept., 10 A.M.–4 P.M. Wed.–Mon. Oct.–May, free) offers a less-secretive look at the world of undersea warfare. One of the most fascinating museums in Washington, it houses exhibits on the history of undersea warfare and exploration, from scale models of Navy subs to underwater archaeology to mines. A large globe details the mountainous floor beneath the oceans. Some of the most interesting items are the torpedoes—including such oddities as a 19th-century wind-up torpedo and a World War II Japanese version with space for a kamikaze human driver—plus a half-scale model of an undersea rescue vehicle that appeared in the movie *The Hunt for Red October.* Out front is the blimplike Trieste II, which reached the bottom of the Marianas Trench—the deepest point on earth—in 1960. The bulk of this cumbersome, 88-ton sub was filled with aviation fuel; the two men were suspended below it in a tiny chamber.

POULSBO

The quaint town of Poulsbo occupies the head of Liberty Bay and could pass for a tourist village on the coast of Maine. The main street is crowded with antique shops, cafés, galleries, high-quality craft boutiques, a chocolate shop,

© KITSAP PENINSULA VISITOR & CONVENTION BUREAU/JEAN BOYLE

Poulsbo marina on the Kitsap Peninsula

and a wonderful quilt shop. Sailboats bob in the busy marina just a few feet away, and old-fashioned lamps brighten the evening sky. Locals jokingly call the town "Viking Junction," and it doesn't take much to see that Poulsbo loves to play up its Norwegian heritage.

History

Credit for the establishment of Poulsbo goes to Jorgen Eliason, a Norwegian who rowed across the sound from Seattle in 1883 and was reminded of the mountains, fjords, and valleys of his homeland. His relatives quickly followed, scratching out a farm at the head of Dogfish Bay. Other Norwegians arrived, and for many years more than half the residents were from Norway; anyone speaking English was likely an outsider. In 1886, Ivar Moe named the town Paulsbo—Norwegian for Paul's Place—but the postmaster general couldn't read his handwriting and listed it instead as Poulsbo. Over the years, Poulsbo survived on logging, farming, and fishing. A fleet of Bering Sea schooners sailed north to Alaska each summer and back home in the fall with cargo holds filled with salted cod. The town's insularity was broken by the arrival of World War II, as military personnel moved in to protect the vital naval base at Bremerton. (A long anti-submarine net was stretched across Port Orchard Bay.)

In the early 1960s, Poulsbo was a complacent community in need of an attraction, so it went to the University of Washington for ideas. A survey showed strong support for a "Little Norway" theme, and the concept quickly took hold, just in time for the 1962 World's Fair in Seattle. Scandinavian architecture and festivals perpetuate the culture of "Little Norway's" first immigrants; many of the downtown buildings have Scandinavian decor and sell some Scandinavian products. And, yes, there is a **Sons of Norway Hall** on Front Street in Poulsbo. Unfortunately, Poulsbo has developed something of a schizophrenic personality, its quaint old downtown contrasting with the strip of RV dealers, real estate offices, and fast-food places up the hill.

Sights

Get friendly with sea cucumbers, starfish, sea anemones, and barnacles in the saltwater touch-tank or watch a jellyfish flotilla at the fascinating **Marine Science Center** (18743 Front St. NE, 360/598-4460, www.poulsbomsc.org, 11 A.M.–5 P.M. daily, donations only). Also on-site is a huge gray whale skeleton and lots of information about other Puget Sound sea creatures and problems facing the ocean.

Stroll down the 600-foot shoreside boardwalk that connects **Liberty Bay Park** to the small arboretum at **American Legion Park.** Both parks have picnic areas, restrooms, and water access. Head uphill to the corner of 4th Avenue and Lincoln Road for the **Fordefjord Lutheran Church,** built in 1908.

Entertainment and Events

Poulsbo's calendar is packed with events celebrating the town's Scandinavian roots. The **Viking Fest** in mid-May celebrates Poulsbo's Norwegian heritage with a parade, arts and crafts show, pancake breakfast, food booths, and fun run. The **Scandia Midsommarfest** in June brings Scandinavian food, music, Norwegian folk dancers, and dancing around the midsummer pole for a solstice celebration. On the third Saturday of October, the First Lutheran Church puts on a **Traditional Lutefisk Dinner,** with Swedish meatballs for the wimps. The holiday season brings the **Yule Fest** in late November or early December, featuring Norwegian folk dancers, lighting of the Yule log, and a guest appearance by Santa Claus by boat. A **Lighted Boat Parade** follows in mid-December.

Sports and Recreation

SEA KAYAKING

Poulsbo's **Olympic Outdoor Center** (18791 Front St., 360/697-6095, www.olympicoutdoorcenter.com) is a great place to learn sea kayaking and white-water kayaking. Classes include the basics, special classes for kids, kayak rescue courses and roll clinics, and comprehensive four-day sea kayak courses. The center also leads sea kayak trips and sells and rents kayaks if you want to head out on your own.

CAMPGROUNDS

Enjoy the wide-open grassy lawns and long shoreline at **Kitsap Memorial State Park** (360/779-3205, www.parks.wa.gov, $17 tents, $24 RV water/electric and dump privileges), about six miles north of downtown on Highway 3. There are ample picnic facilities, including rentable shelters with electricity and fire pits, as well as showers on-site.

A couple miles south of town, **Eagle Tree RV Park** (16280 Hwy. 305 NE, 360/598-5988, www.eagletreerv.com, $32 full hookups) offers RV owners another good option when the state park's sites fill up.

Accommodations

Be sure to make reservations well ahead for summer weekends; some rooms are booked up a year in advance.

The family-friendly property at **Poulsbo Inn** (18680 Hwy. 305, 360/779-3921 or 800/597-5151, www.poulsboinn.com, $104–125 d) includes an outdoor pool, hot tub, and playground. There's also a fitness center and free high-speed Internet. Not only does this property offer complimentary continental breakfast each day, it also serves soup in the winter Tuesday–Thursday. Rooms are tastefully decorated and up-to-date.

Murphy House B&B (425 N.E. Hostmark, 360/779-1600 or 800/779-1606, www.murphyhousebnb.com, $109–169 d, no kids), offers in-town lodging, with five comfortable guest rooms, private baths, and a full breakfast.

Farther away is **Foxbridge B&B** (30680 Hwy. 3 NE, 360/598-5599, www.foxbridge.com, $115 d, no kids), located a half mile from the Hood Canal floating bridge. This two-story home sits on five wooded acres with a panoramic view. Several rooms come with private baths, and a decadent three-course breakfast is served each morning. There is also a complimentary bike available for light use.

Overlooking Liberty Bay about two miles away from downtown, the one-bedroom **Liberty Place Guest House** (360/779-4943, www.libertybayguesthouse.com, $125 d) affords guests a lot of privacy, plus a full kitchen and a deck.

Food

Despite its small size, Poulsbo has one of the best collections of eating places on the Kitsap. **Poulsbohemian Coffeehouse** (19003 Front St., 360/779-9199, 7 A.M.–5 P.M. Mon.–Fri., 8 A.M.–5 P.M. Sat.–Sun.) is a friendly and funky gathering place, with espresso, giant chocolate chip cookies, cozy couches and chairs, art on the walls, and ongoing arts events of all sorts. Great water views, too.

Get delicious lunches at **Liberty Bay Bakery and Café** (18996 Front St., 360/779-2828, 4:30 A.M.–5:30 P.M. daily).

Perhaps the best known Poulsbo food is Poulsbo Bread, originally baked at **Sluys Poulsbo Bakery** (18924 Front St. NE, 360/779-2798, 4:30 A.M.–6:30 P.M. daily). The Poulsbo bread sold in grocery stores is now made elsewhere, but Sluys still bakes excellent pastries, Norwegian lefse, and coarse-grained European breads.

That's a Some Italian Ristorante (18881 Front St. NE, 360/779-2266, 11 A.M.–8 P.M. Mon.–Thurs., 11 A.M.–9 P.M. Fri.–Sat., 11:30 A.M.–8 P.M. Sun.) has the traditional red-checked tablecloths, but the Italian food and pizzas have West Coast influences, including an Anaheim chili penne.

Casa Luna (18830 Front St. NE, 360/779-7676, 11 A.M.–9 P.M. daily) is one of the more distinctive Mexican-inspired restaurants in the Puget Sound area. The menu isn't the same old mashed beans and colored rice. Everything is made to order in the open kitchen and packed with flavor.

Aroydy Thai Cuisine (225 Lindvig Way NW, 360/779-4888, 11 A.M.–2 P.M. Tues.–Fri. and 5–8 P.M. Tues.–Sun.) is just north of town in the basement of a small shopping mall, but the food is authentic and exceptional.

Molly Ward Gardens (27462 Big Valley Rd., 360/779-4471, 11 A.M.–2 P.M. and 6–9 P.M. Wed.–Sat., 10:30 A.M.–1:30 P.M. and 6–9 P.M. Sun., closed Mon.–Tues.) is Poulsbo's splurge place, emphasizing fine Northwest seafood, along with fresh salads and herbs from its beautiful gardens. The menu changes seasonally.

Information and Services

For information, visit the **Greater Poulsbo Chamber of Commerce** (19131 8th Ave. NE, 360/779-4848, www.kitsapedc.org, 9 A.M.–5 P.M. Mon.–Fri.). If you're downtown, drop by the small visitors center inside Poulsbohemian Coffeehouse, open daily. Pick up a brochure detailing a walking tour of Poulsbo's historic buildings at either place.

Getting There

Kitsap Transit (360/377-2877 or 800/501-7433, www.kitsaptransit.org) provides daily bus service around the peninsula. **Bremerton-Kitsap Airporter** (360/876-1737 or 800/562-7948, www.kitsapairporter.com) offers shuttle buses to Sea-Tac Airport.

GIG HARBOR

Just across the Narrows Bridge from Tacoma, Gig Harbor is one of the finest and most scenic on Puget Sound. The pictorial village and its namesake harbor is postcard-perfect, with hundreds of sailing and fishing boats, tall pine trees, and a circle of seaside houses, all against the backdrop of Mt. Rainier.

The town was named by Lieutenant Charles Wilkes, who in 1848 sent out a survey crew in a captain's gig, which sought shelter in the protected waters of the harbor during a fierce storm. Ever since then this has been a place for sailors. Boatbuilding was an important part of Gig Harbor's history; hundreds of purse seiners, gillnetters, tenders, yachts, and other vessels were constructed here over the decades. And today those protected waters still do well to keep many commercial fishing and pleasure craft safe.

You don't need sealegs to enjoy the town, though. On land there are upscale shops, galleries, good restaurants, and at least one noteworthy tavern.

Sights

HARBOR HISTORY MUSEUM

The brand new Harbor History Museum (4218 Harborview Dr., 253/858-6722, www.gigharbormuseum.org, 10 A.M.–4 P.M. Tues.–Sat.) at the downtown waterfront offers a collection of exhibits on fishing and boatbuilding, plus local artifacts and more than 2,500 historical photos.

KOPACHUCK STATE PARK

You'd never expect so much solitude so close to a major city. Just 12 miles northwest of Tacoma off Highway 16 and seven miles northwest of Gig Harbor (follow the signs), Kopachuck (253/265-3606, www.parks.wa.gov, tents $17) has a campground (no RV hookups) and picnic areas. This 103-acre park is shaded by tall pines and has a beach for swimming, clamming, and fishing. It is one of Puget Sound's most beautiful parks, and even includes the small (5.5 acres) Cutts Island, a marine park only a short distance offshore with mooring buoys. Scuba divers come here to explore an underwater park with a sunken barge. Kopachuck's campground is open from late April to early October. Make reservations ($7 extra) at 888/226-7688 or www.parks.wa.gov.

Entertainment and Events

Gig Harbor's **Paradise Theater** (253/851-7529) has productions in Celebrations Meadow during the summer months and at Burton Park Theater on winter weekends. Celebrations Meadow is on the left side of Peacock Hill Avenue, about a half mile up from Harborview; the Burton Park Theater is at the extreme north end of 38th Avenue NW.

Tides Tavern (2925 Harborview Dr., 253/858-3982) has live rock or blues bands on the weekends.

Gig Harbor events include the **Maritime Gig** (253/851-6865) on the first weekend of June. The **Gig Harbor Art Festival** (www.ghkp-culturalarts.org) on the third weekend in July features a parade, kids' fest, art fair, fun run, live music, and a salmon dinner. Gig Harbor's **Lighted Boat Parade** (253/851-1807) on the second Saturday of December is another enjoyable event.

Shopping

Downtown Gig Harbor is strung out along the water, with shops and restaurants luring browsers. Head to the head of the harbor for a number of galleries, including **Ebb Tide Gallery of Gifts** (7809 Pioneer Way, 253/851-5293, www.ebbtidegalleryofgifts.com, 10 A.M.–5 P.M. daily), a cooperative gallery with the works of local artists, and **Gallery Row** (3102 Harborview Dr., 253/851-6020, www.gigharborgalleryrow.com, 10 A.M.–5 P.M. Mon.–Sat., noon–5 P.M. Sun.), a working art gallery featuring 15 local artists and offering lessons and commissions.

Sports and Recreation

Rent powerboats, skippered sailboats, sea kayaks, pedal boats, and other on-the-water vessels from **Rent-a-Boat & Charters** (8829 N. Harborview Dr., 253/858-7341). **Gig Harbor Kayak Center** (8809 N. Harborview Dr., 253/851-7987 or 888/429-2548, www.clearlight.com/kayak) has sea-kayak rentals and tours.

Purdy Spit, located at the head of Henderson Bay (the upper end of Carr Inlet), is bisected by Highway 302 and is a favorite place to beachcomb, dig for clams, and windsurf.

In addition to Kopachuck State Park, camping is available at the private **Gig Harbor RV Resort** (9515 Burnham Dr., 253/858-8138 or 888/226-7688), which has RV sites for $37 and tent sites $20.

Accommodations

UNDER $100

The pleasant grounds at the pet-friendly **Westwynd Motel** (6703 144th St. NW, 253/857-4047 or 800/468-9963, www.westwyndmotel.com, $69–105 d) are a cut above most mom-and-pop motels. There's a pleasant lawn lined with flower beds, a quiet picnic area, and a playground for the kiddies. Westwynd rents motel units, as well as apartments and suites with kitchens. Rooms are Spartan with plain IKEA-type furnishings, but are quite clean.

Twelve miles north of Gig Harbor on Glen Cove at the beautiful **Olde Glencove Hotel** (9418 Glencove Rd., 253/884-2835, www.glencovehotel.com, $75–95 s or d), built in 1897 and now on the National Register of Historic

Places, this waterside retreat has been restored and transformed into a family-friendly bed-and-breakfast. Inside are four guest rooms with shared or private baths.

Out in the rolling pastures of the tiny hamlet of **Olalla, Childs' House Bed and Breakfast** (8331 S.E. Willock Rd., 253/857-4252, www.childshouse.com, $85–100 d) is a good base for cyclists to rest their heads—this comfortable country home is only a block away from the rolling strip of pavement of Banner Road. The five-acre grounds are surrounded by a pleasant garden and forest. The innkeeper strives to serve local seasonal ingredients in her daily breakfast spread.

$150-200

The best digs right in Gig Harbor are at **The Maritime Inn** ($169–198 d), a 15-room boutique hotel across the street from the marina and within walking distance of shops and restaurants in the village. Rooms are beautifully appointed, with plush linens, gas fireplaces, flat-screen monitors, and a soothing neutral palette of beiges, browns, and seafoam green accents. Some rooms have jetted tubs and water views. Complimentary wireless Internet and continental breakfast are included in the room rate.

If you prefer a place with a pool and a hot tub, **Best Western Wesley Inn** (6575 Kimball Dr., 253/858-9690 or 888/462-0002, www.wesleyinn.com, $159–189 d) is another attractive hotel within easy striking distance of Gig Harbor attractions, though not with walking distance. Rooms are stylishly decorated and breakfast is complimentary.

If a spot near the harbor is not essential, **The Inn at Gig Harbor** (3211 56th St. NW, 253/858-1111 or 800/795-9980, www.innatgigharbor.com, $154 s or $164 d) is another good possibility. This large Craftsman-style hotel has a full spate of amenities, including a day spa, a well-regarded gourmet restaurant, a fitness center, an outdoor hot tub, and complimentary wireless Internet and continental breakfast. It offers a full spectrum of suites ($159–210 s or d) with amenities such as fireplaces, jetted tubs, wet bars, and kitchenettes.

$200-250

Westbay Guest Cottage (253/265-3033 or 800/420-3033, www.westbaycottage.com, $145–250 d, sleeps four) is a beautiful waterfront home on Wollochet Bay with a deck, boat dock, and porch facing the water. This is not a B&B, but it does have a full kitchen and hot tub.

Food

Gig Harbor's most acclaimed venue for victuals and vino is the hip bistro **Brix 25** (7707 Pioneer Way, 253/858-6626, www.harborbrix.com, 4:30–9:30 P.M. Mon.–Thurs., 4:30–11 P.M. Fri.–Sat., 4:30–9 P.M. Sun.). Creative and sumptuous dishes such as piccata-style trout ($25) and duck in onion demi glace ($29) are paired with an unparalleled wine list that exclusively features Washington and Oregon wines. Washington Wine Commission named Brix as the Wine Restaurant of the Year in 2008, and it is no wonder. There are over 25 wines that can be ordered by the glass or by a petite two-ounce serving to create your own wine flight.

Let your nose lead you to **Susanne's Bakery & Deli** (3411 Harborview Dr., 253/853-6220, www.susannesbakery.com, 7 A.M.–5 P.M. Tues.–Sun., closed Mon.). In the morning, pair up the freshly baked pastries and sweets with an espresso or latte. Come lunchtime, pick up a sandwich served on fresh baked bread.

Arrive by car or by boat at the bustling **Tides Tavern** (2925 Harborview, 253/858-3982). This classic dive joint has a small harborside deck to enjoy the views while munching on a burger and a beer. Besides burgers, the Tides offers pizza, sandwiches, and the best local fish and chips, plus live music on weekends.

For something a little fancier served under the sun, **The Green Turtle** (2905 Harborview Dr., 253/851-3167, 11 A.M.–2 P.M. Tues.–Fri. and 4:30–9 P.M. Tues.–Sun., closed Mon.) also has a harbor-facing deck. The menu ventures eastward, with distinctively creative Thai- and Chinese-inspired meals. Lunch is pretty casual here, but reservations are recommended come dinnertime.

Or you can just do the takeout thing and picnic at Gig Harbor City Park. Pick up fiery hot Chinese food at **Harbor Monsoon Restaurant** (4628 Pt. Fosdick Dr. NW, 253/858-9838, 11:30 A.M.–10 P.M. daily) or very good, from-scratch pizzas, pasta, subs, and salads from **Spiro's Pizza & Pasta** (3108 Harborview Dr., 253/851-9200, 11 A.M.–10 P.M. daily).

For the freshest local produce, baked goods, and crafts, head to the **Gig Harbor Farmers Market** (3500 Hunt St. NW, 253/884-2496, www.gigharborfarmersmarket.com) held 8:30 A.M.–2 P.M. Saturday May–mid-October.

Information and Services

The **Gig Harbor/Peninsula Area Chamber of Commerce** (3302 Harborview Dr., Suite 2, 253/851-6865, www.gigharborchamber.com, 10 A.M.–5 P.M. Mon.–Fri.) can provide you with local brochures and information.

Getting There

Pierce Transit (253/581-8000 or 800/562-8109, www.ptbus.pierce.wa.us) has daily service from Gig Harbor to Tacoma and other parts of Pierce County. The **Bremerton-Kitsap Airporter** (800/562-7948, www.kitsapairporter.com) offers shuttle bus connections to Sea-Tac Airport.

Islands and Inlets

CARR INLET

Anderson Island

Miles of roads and rural bike paths are the primary attractions to draw mainlanders to quiet Anderson Island. The restored **Johnson Farm** (9306 Otso Point Road), founded by John Johnson in 1881, has tours weekend afternoons in the summer. Also here is the pilothouse from the *Tahoma,* the island's ferry from 1943 to 1954. **Anderson Island Historical Museum** (253/884-2135) has local historical items on display. Both the farm and the museum have irregular hours, so call to get current information.

ACCOMMODATIONS

There are a handful of places to stay on the island. The kid-friendly modern log house at **The Inn at Burg's Landing B&B** (8808 Villa Beach Rd., 253/884-9185, www.burgslandingbb.com, $90–140 s or d) gives guests panoramic views of Mount Rainier and the Cascades. A covered deck with a hot tub overlooks the backyard fire pit and tree-dotted lawns leading to a private beach.

Watch herons glide over Little Vega Bay from the porch at **Anderson House on Oro Bay** (12024 Eckenstam-Johnson Rd., 253/884-4088 or 800/750-4088, www.non.com/anderson, $150 s or d, no kids). This beautifully restored 1920s Scandinavian farmhouse rests on a pasture surrounded by old-growth forests and an estuary. All four guest rooms have private baths, and a full breakfast is included.

For the more self-sufficient, **August Inn** (14117 Lyle Point Road, 253/884-4011, www.augustinn.com) rents a self-contained home that sleeps six for $249, plus two studio suites for $159 d. All three are right on the water, with private entrances and decks.

GETTING THERE AND AROUND

Pierce County operates the small **Anderson Island-Steilacoom Ferry** (253/798-7250), which leaves Steilacoom Dock about every two hours. Round-trip summer fares are $19 for car and driver, $4.70 for passengers and pedestrians. The ferry also visits tiny Ketron Island (no public facilities).

Fox Island

Fox Island is five miles southwest of Gig Harbor and is connected by a bridge over Hale Passage. Stop by the **Fox Island Historical Society and Museum** (253/549-2239, 1–4 P.M. Mon. and Sat., 11 A.M.–3 P.M. Wed., $1).

ACCOMMODATIONS

Beachside B&B (679 Kamus Dr., 253/549-2524, www.beachsidebb.com, $135 d) certainly lives up to its name. This modern take on a brick-and-wood lodge home butts right up to the beach; during high tide the water laps against the raised seawall. On sunny days, enjoy the extended continental breakfast served from the garden patio or the lounge chairs set up on the waterside lawn. Out on the water there is a buoy for boats and kayaks, and kids are welcomed at this getaway.

KEY PENINSULA

West of Gig Harbor and across Carr Inlet is another fingerlike appendage reaching into the southernmost end of Puget Sound: Key Peninsula. The peninsula has a small commercial center called **Home,** but it is essentially a haven of wooded residences and parks.

Penrose Point State Park (321 158th Ave. S., Lakebay, 253/884-2514 sprawls along two miles of shoreline just south of Home. This marine park is a favorite among pleasure craft and paddling enthusiasts, offering moorage and a boat dock. You can also explore by foot or bike on 2.5 miles of trails snaking through the park. Picnic tables and a large lawn and volleyball pit by the water make this an idyllic place for a picnic and a pickup game of soccer, Frisbee, or volleyball.

CASE INLET

This quiet inlet is a kayaker's dream waterway, perfect for a multi-day trip from campground to campground.

Hartstene Island

Jarrell Cove State Park (www.parks.wa.gov, tents $17, no RV hookups), along a small cove on the north end of Hartstene Island, has campsites and is open year-round. Get here on land by heading seven miles northeast of Shelton on Highway 3, crossing the bridge to Hartstene Island, and then following the signs another five miles to the park. The 43-acre park is primarily used by boaters and is a fun place to explore in a kayak.

Jarrell's Cove Marina (E. 220 Wilson Rd., 360/426-8823) rents short-term RV spaces with hookups ($26) May–September. The marina and grocery store are open year-round, but gas is by appointment only during non-summer months.

Stretch Point Island

You'll need a boat to get to tiny **Stretch Point State Park** (www.parks.wa.gov), 12 miles north of Shelton next to the town of Grapeview. It has no camping, showers, toilets, or drinking water, but it has one of the best sandy beaches around Puget Sound. Grapeview itself has vineyards, a country store, marina, and a sometimes-open museum.

Key Peninsula

On the other side of Key Peninsula, facing Case Inlet, is **Joemma State Park** (20001 Bay Rd. KP S, Longbranch, 253/884-1944) at Whitman Cove. This is another boating hotspot, with a calm little beach and a big dock.

VASHON ISLAND

Vashon Island is not the place to go if you're expecting a hot time on the ol' town. Cows and horses probably outnumber humans on this rock. The rural, slow-paced, homey environment is ideal for bike tours, not so much for barhopping. Vashon's residents are a mix of commuting yupsters, post-hippie artisans, retirees, and power-politics farmers.

Vashon Island was one of the many islands encountered in 1792 by Capt. George Vancouver, who, having named enough things after himself, decided to give this one to his Navy buddy, James Vashon.

Sights

FARMS AND MARKETS

Gourmet fruits and vegetables are a specialty of Vashon Island. **Wax Orchards** (22744 Wax Orchard, 206/463-9735, www.waxorchards.com) offers fresh cider and homemade fruit syrups; and **The Country Store and Farm** (Vashon Hwy. SW at S.W. 204th St.) is another place to find locally grown items.

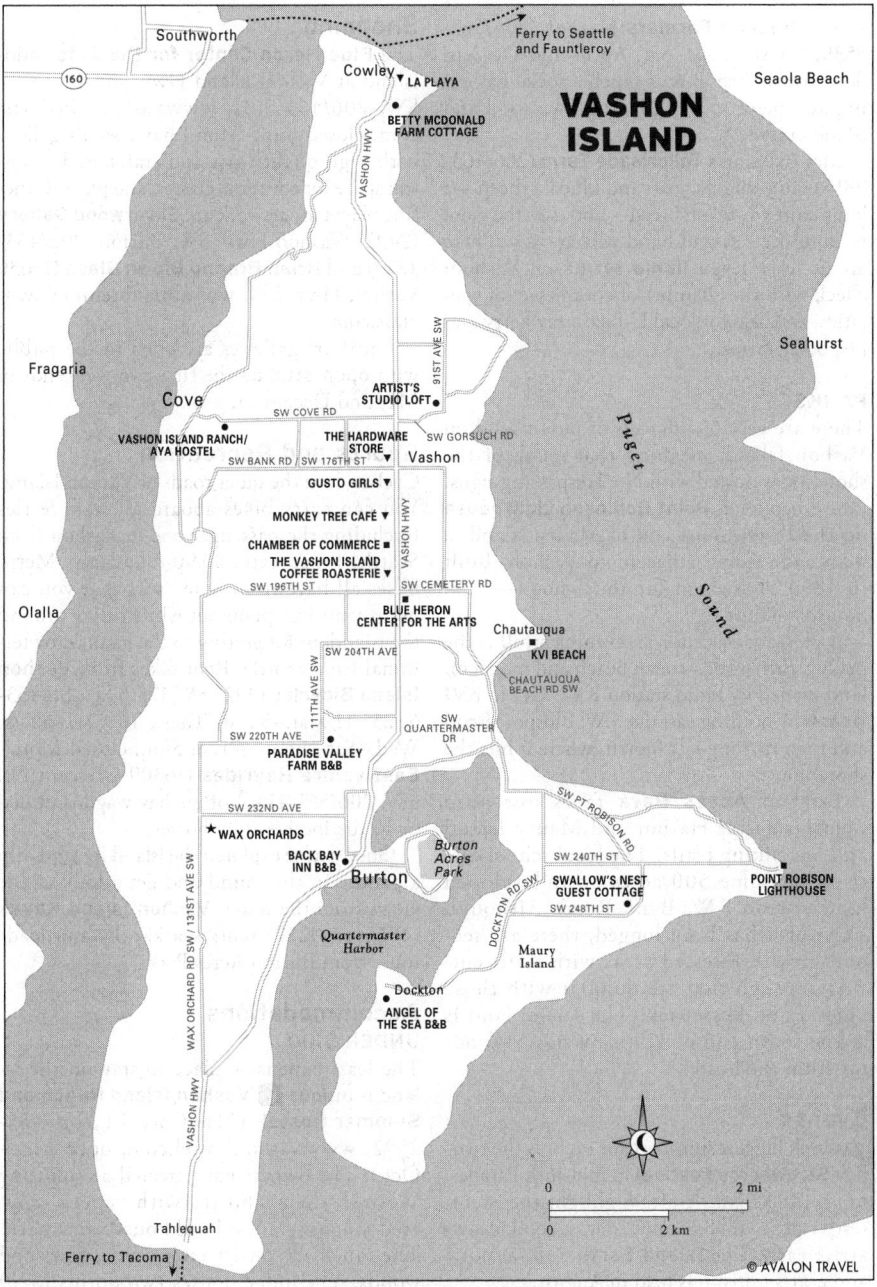
VASHON ISLAND
Southworth
Ferry to Seattle and Fauntleroy
160
Cowley
LA PLAYA
Seaola Beach
BETTY MCDONALD FARM COTTAGE
VASHON HWY
Seahurst
Fragaria
Cove
91ST AVE SW
ARTIST'S STUDIO LOFT
SW COVE RD
VASHON ISLAND RANCH/ AYA HOSTEL
THE HARDWARE STORE
SW GORSUCH RD
Vashon
SW BANK RD / SW 176TH ST
Puget
GUSTO GIRLS
MONKEY TREE CAFÉ
CHAMBER OF COMMERCE
THE VASHON ISLAND COFFEE ROASTERIE
VASHON HWY
SW 196TH ST
SW CEMETERY RD
Sound
Olalla
BLUE HERON CENTER FOR THE ARTS
Chautauqua
SW 204TH AVE
KVI BEACH
111TH AVE SW
CHAUTAUQUA BEACH RD SW
SW QUARTERMASTER DR
SW 220TH AVE
PARADISE VALLEY FARM B&B
SW PT ROBISON RD
SW 232ND AVE
WAX ORCHARDS
Burton Acres Park
BACK BAY INN B&B
Burton
SW 240TH ST
SWALLOW'S NEST GUEST COTTAGE
POINT ROBISON LIGHTHOUSE
DOCKTON RD SW
SW 248TH ST
Quartermaster Harbor
Maury Island
WAX ORCHARD RD SW / 131ST AVE SW
Dockton
ANGEL OF THE SEA B&B
VASHON HWY
0
2 mi
0
2 km
Tahlequah
Ferry to Tacoma
© AVALON TRAVEL

The **Vashon Farmers Market** (206/567-5539, 9 A.M.–2 P.M. Sat. April–mid-Oct.) in downtown Vashon is as much a social gathering as a place to buy island-grown food and island crafts.

Maury Island's **TailorMade Farm** (206/463-9816) raises angora goats and Lincoln sheep—a long-haired English breed—and uses the wool in lamb fleeces and hand-woven rugs. There are at least seven **llama farms** on Vashon; check with the chamber of commerce for specifics, and also for local U-pick strawberry and raspberry farms.

PARKS

There are very few parcels of public land on Vashon Island, meaning that much of the shoreline is posted with No Trespassing signs. One exception is **Point Robinson Lighthouse** on the easternmost end of Maury Island, a manmade island adjacent to Vashon. Built in 1893, it is open for tours noon–4 P.M. Saturday–Sunday.

A pleasant place for an evening stroll is the pebbly, driftwood-strewn beach and marsh on land owned by radio station KVI. Get to **KVI Beach** by heading east out S.W. Ellisport Road and then turning left (north) where it hits the shoreline.

Burton Acres Park faces out onto Quartermaster Harbor and Maury Island and has hiking trails. The local school district has some 500 acres of undeveloped land out on S.W. Bank Road. Although some of it has been logged, there are second-growth forested areas with trails cutting through that are popular with those afoot or on horseback. The school land is at the south end of 115th Avenue SW, not far from the hostel.

Events

Vashon's biggest summertime event is the two-day **Strawberry Festival** in mid-July. Parades, music, food, and crafts highlight the event; ferry traffic will be heavy, so it's a good idea to arrive early. The **Island Earth Fair,** a music and crafts festival, is held in August.

Shopping

The **Blue Heron Center for the Arts** (mid-island at Vashon Island Hwy. and 196th St. SW, 206/463-5131, www.vashonalliedarts.com, closed Sun.–Mon.) has a small gallery with high-quality arts and crafts, and a central space for concerts, classes, and plays. Other fine places for artwork are **Silverwood Gallery** (24927 Vashon Hwy. SW, Burton, 206/463-1722) and **Brian Brenno Blown Glass** (17630 Vashon Hwy. SW, www.brianbrennoblownglass.com).

Local art galleries are open to the public with **open studios** the first two weekends of May and December.

Sports and Recreation

Cyclists love the quiet roads of Vashon Island. You can carry bikes aboard all state ferries (including the passenger one to Vashon from Seattle) for an extra $0.90 round-trip. Metro buses all have front bike racks that you can use if your legs poop out while riding around the island, or for getting to the Fauntleroy terminal from Seattle. Rent bikes from **Vashon Island Bicycles** (9925 SW 178th St. 206/463-6225, 11 A.M.–5 P.M. Tues., 10 A.M.–6 P.M. Wed.–Sat., noon–4 P.M. Sun., closed Mon.). **Eastlyshire Hayrides** (16309 Crescent Dr. SW, 206/567-4146) offers hay wagons pulled by its distinctive Shire horses.

Once you've explored the island by land, dip a paddle in the sound and get a look at the views from the water. **Vashon Island Kayak** (206/463-9257) rents sea kayaks and leads tours from Burton Acres Park.

Accommodations

UNDER $100

The least expensive place to stay on the island is unique **Vashon Island Ranch and Summer Hostel** (12119 Cove Rd., 206/463-2592, www.vashonhostel.com, open May–Oct.). The owners have created an amusing Western-theme hostel with tepees, covered wagons, a log bunkhouse, and barn. The ranch sits on 10 acres of meadows and woods. The lodge houses two dorms ($20) and has a full kitchen. Guests can also stay in the covered wagons and teepees, or pitch their own tent, all for the same price. Guests can borrow the old one-speed bikes and rent sleeping bags or lockers. A free do-it-yourself pancake breakfast, volleyball and horseshoe games, barbecue grill, and the evening campfire provide chances to trade tales with fellow travelers. This is a very popular place for adventurous travelers from all over the globe, with 50 or so visitors on busy summer nights. The owner picks up folks at the Vashon Thriftway grocery store on weekdays or at the ferry terminal on weekends, but call ahead to make arrangements.

Run by the same folks who own the Vashon Hostel, **Lavender Duck B&B** (16503 Vashon Hwy. SW, 206/463-2592, www.vasonhostel.com, $85 s or d) is a century-old farmhouse facing Mt. Rainier. Inside are four comfortable guest rooms with private baths. Kids are welcome, and a pancake breakfast is served.

$100-150

Vashon Island has a number of delightfully romantic B&Bs and guest cottages, making this a great weekend getaway.

Families traveling with pets will feel comfortable in one of seven cottages rented out by **Swallow's Nest Guest Cottages** (6030 SW 248th St., 206/463-2646 or 800/269-6378, www.vashonislandcottages.com, $105–125 d). These private properties are scattered about the island.

Set on five acres with flower gardens and ponds, **Artist's Studio Loft** (16529 91st S.W., 206/463-2583, www.asl-bnb.com, $119–215 d, two-night minimum on weekends) has four private suites with separate entrances, a hot tub, woodstove, and a big continental breakfast.

Once the home of the well-known children's author, **Betty MacDonald Farm** (12000 99th Ave. SW, 206/567-4227 or 888/328-6753, www.bettymacdonaldfarm.com, $125–160 d) is now a tastefully romantic B&B just a few blocks from the ferry dock. The big old barn sits on six acres atop a bluff facing Mt. Rainier and has a spacious upper loft with kitchen and woodstove. A separate cottage is popular with families. The fridges are well stocked for a make-your-own breakfast.

Set within a converted country church built in 1917, the appropriately named **Angels of the Sea B&B** (Dockton Harbor, 206/463-6980 or 800/798-9249, www.angelsofthesea.com, $150 s or d) has three guest rooms with a shared or private bath. Guests are treated to live harp music during breakfast, and kids are welcome.

Food

Food options are not abundant on Vashon, but there are still a few treasures to be found. Swing by **Monkey Tree Café** (17817 Vashon Highway S.W., 206/463-4635, 8 A.M.–3 P.M. Thurs.–Tues., closed Wed.) during breakfast and lunch for truly scrumptious baked goods and flavorful vegetarian dishes that can please even the most hard-core carnivores. Bring cash and expect a leisurely meal—this casual place does a bustling business and meals are prepared from scratch.

Operating out of a converted old hardware store, the so-named restaurant **The Hardware Store** (17601 Vashon Hwy S.W., 206/463-9551, www.thsrestaurant.com, 11:30 A.M.–2:30 P.M. and 5–9:30 P.M. Wed.–Mon., closed Tues.) has a little bit for every kind of eater in search of lunch or dinner on Vashon. There are vegetarian dishes, steak, seafood, and soups and salads. The real specialties of the house are the lahvosh "pizzas," made on Armenian cracker bread. The restaurant serves a special breakfast menu 8:30 A.M.–2:30 P.M. Sunday.

The hippest (and tastiest) dinner joint on this rock is **Gusto Girls** (17629 Vashon Hwy. SW, 206/463-6626, 5–11 P.M. daily), a culinary hotspot that changes its menu to showcase fresh local ingredients. It does not accept reservations.

If you're craving a taco or you just need to grab something before heading off the island, **La Playa** (1824 Vashon Hwy., 206/567-0020, 11 A.M.–9 P.M. daily) at the north end of the ferry terminal offers the best Mexican food on the island.

Information

The **Vashon-Maury Island Chamber of Commerce** (17633 Vashon Hwy., 206/463-6217, www.vashonchamber.com) can be found in the main village of Vashon. Hours vary seasonally. Vashon Island is a local phone call from Seattle.

Getting There

Vashon is only 15 minutes by ferry from Tacoma and about the same from West Seattle. The **Washington State Ferries** (206/464-6400, 888/808-7977, or 800/843-3779 for automated information, www.wsdot.wa.gov/ferries) float auto and passenger service to both the north and south ends of Vashon Island. The return trip is always free (round-trip fare is charged on your way to the island), so you can arrive or depart from either end for the same price. There are four departure points for the island. To reach Heights Dock on the north end, you can take the half-hour passenger-only ferry from downtown Seattle's Pier 50 for $4.30 round-trip, plus an extra $1 for a bike. This ferry operates Monday–Saturday, but not on Sunday or holidays, and generally runs from 5:30 A.M. to after midnight.

By car or bus, you can take the frequent ferries from West Seattle's Fauntleroy terminal for $18.50 round-trip for car and driver. Passengers and walk-ons are $4.30 round-trip; winter fares are lower. Ferries also connect Heights Dock with the Southworth ferry terminal on the Kitsap Peninsula, and the Tahlequah dock on the south end of Vashon Island with Tacoma's Point Defiance ferry terminal. Both of these ferry runs have the same rate schedule as from Fauntleroy.

Getting Around

The main town of Vashon is five miles from the ferry landing. **Metro Transit** (206/553-3000 or 800/542-7876, http://transit.metrokc.gov, $1.75) operates route 118 Monday–Saturday, between both ferry terminals, through Vashon, and onto Maury Island. Route 116 offers direct service to and from downtown Seattle Monday–Friday.

Karma Kab (206/463-1765) runs taxi service on Vashon. **Island Air** (206/567-4697, www.island-air.com) sends off flightseeing trips over Puget Sound from Vashon Municipal Airport.

BLAKE ISLAND

Accessible only by boat, Blake Island has 476 acres of state park land with year-round camping ($10); sandy beaches for swimming, sunbathing, and clamming; fishing and scuba diving; a 0.75-mile loop nature trail; and 12 miles of other hiking trails. To reach the island from the Kitsap, rent a boat from Manchester Boatworks in Port Orchard, or check with local chambers of commerce for charter operators.

Kitsap Harbor Tours (360/876-1260) offers tours to Blake Island from Bremerton on Friday and Saturday evenings May–October.

Tillicum Village

Blake Island's main attraction is Tillicum Village (206/933-8600, www.tillicumvillage.com). This village can be visited as part of a full-day trip (daily May–Sept., $80 adults, $73 seniors, $30 kids, free for under age 4) offered by Argosy Cruises that includes a salmon bake in the cedar longhouse, traditional Native American dance performances, crafts, nature trails, Native American artifacts, and a gift shop. The cruise, dinner, and dance performances are all available separately for a lesser price.

BAINBRIDGE ISLAND

Just a 35-minute ferry ride from downtown Seattle, Bainbridge Island offers a comfortable escape from the hordes, a place where yupster commuters retreat to rural waterside homes and retirees enjoy a peaceful escape from the workaday world. Over 20,000 folks call Bainbridge home today, and more move here every week.

History

When Vancouver sailed through Puget Sound in 1792, he didn't realize that Bainbridge Island was an island. Then in 1841 Charles

N. Wilkes found Agate Pass, the waterway separating the island from the Kitsap Peninsula. Wilkes named the island for Capt. William Bainbridge, a Naval hero from the USS *Constitution*. Within 15 years of its charting, Bainbridge Island was home to one of Puget Sound's greatest lumber mills, and soon thereafter its ports were world renowned. Port Blakely had the biggest sawmill in the world, employing more than 1,000 men, and the shipyard there built the largest sternwheeler at that time in the Pacific Northwest, the *Julia*.

Today the four- by 12-mile island is almost entirely privately owned by politicians, doctors, artists, many stockbrokers, a few fishermen, and a lot of ordinary folks, including 70 percent who commute by ferry to Seattle-area jobs. Although the entire island is officially incorporated, there is only one real town: **Winslow,** located along Eagle Harbor where the ferry docks. Winslow is a genuine—albeit gentrified—town with Volvos crawling the streets, yachts in the marina, and classical music in the cafés. Several other small settlements are scattered around Bainbridge, including Lynwood Center and Island Center.

If you're arriving by ferry from Seattle, you'll find Winslow an easy place to explore by foot. Start on the shoreline footpath that heads west from the ferry to **Eagle Harbor Waterfront Park,** a fine place for a sunny-day picnic. If you're arriving by car, parking can be a real problem on weekends, and no on-street overnight parking is allowed.

Sights

BAINBRIDGE ISLAND HISTORICAL MUSEUM

The history of former mill towns Port Madison and Port Blakely is preserved in exhibits and displays at the Bainbridge Island Historical Museum (215 Ericksen Ave. NE, 206/842-2773, www.bainbridgehistory.org, 1–4 P.M. Wed.–Mon., 10 A.M.–4 P.M. Sat. in summer, $2.50 adults, $1.50 students and seniors, $5 family, kids under 5 free) in Strawberry Hill Park. The building itself offers a blast from the past; it's a charming little red schoolhouse.

PARKS AND GARDENS

Fay-Bainbridge State Park (206/842-3931, www.parks.wa.gov) covers a mere 17 acres but it offers some of the finest over-the-water vistas of the Cascades and the twinkling lights of Seattle. It is a delightful place to escape the city. Fay-Bainbridge also offers campsites in the trees ($19 for tents; $27 for RVs), plus hot showers and beach access with scuba diving and boating facilities at the island's northeast end. This is the closest public campground to Seattle—just a ferry ride and short drive or bus ride away—so it is very popular in the summer months. The park's open for day use year-round but only open to camping mid-April to mid-October.

Located six miles from the Winslow ferry terminal at the island's south end, **Fort Ward State Park** (www.parks.wa.gov) has 137 acres for day-use picnicking, bird-watching, boating, and scuba diving on a mile-long beach. There's no camping, but a one-mile path loops through the park. Like many of the state parks surrounding Puget Sound, this one began as a military fort. Established in 1891 to protect the Bremerton Naval Yard, it and Fort Manchester (now Manchester State Park) faced each other across Rich Passage. Underwater nets were placed offshore during World War II to snag any Japanese subs that might stray into these waters—but none did.

The 150-acre **Bloedel Reserve** (7571 N.E. Dolphin Dr., 206/842-7631, www.bloedelreserve.org, 10 A.M.–4 P.M. Wed.–Sun., $12 adults, $8 seniors, $6 kids, free for children under 5) contains many native plants from Washington, a bog, pond, Japanese garden, moss garden, and spacious lawns, plus the old Bloedel home, now used as a visitors center. The reserve is especially popular in the spring when the rhododendrons are in bloom, but the 15,000 cyclamen plants are also an attraction. Get here by heading six miles west from Winslow on Highway 305, then following the signs another mile to the entrance. Reservations are necessary because they only 200 people per day are admitted.

On the west side of the island, **Bainbridge**

Gardens (9415 Miller Rd. NE, 206/842-5888, www.bainbridgegardens.com) is a historic nursery with unusual trees, theme gardens, and a nature trail. The café has cuisine from a wood-fired oven and espresso.

WINERIES

One-quarter mile from the ferry terminal, **Bainbridge Island Vineyards and Winery** (682 Hwy. 305, Winslow, 206/842-9463) is the only place to buy this family-operated winery's limited-run wines, made from grapes grown on the island. The outdoor picnic area is a refreshing spot for a lunch break, and the antique wine glass collection is worth a gander. Tours and tastings are held noon–5 P.M. Wednesday–Sunday.

Rich Passage Winery (7869 N.E. Day Rd. W, 206/842-8199) is also a small family operation, producing pinot noir, chardonnay, and fumé blanc wines. The winery is generally open for tastings each day, but call ahead to be sure someone is there.

Events

In February, Puget Sound's cycling season kicks off with the popular **Chilly Hilly** bicycle marathon. More than 4,000 riders pedal around Bainbridge. The **4th of July** brings a two-day street fair and parade to Winslow. There are no fireworks, but Bainbridge offers a fine view of Seattle's fireworks show. **Concerts in the Park** take place at Waterfront Park in Winslow on Wednesday evenings in July and August, and an **Outdoor Music Festival** brings more performers to Waterfront Park in August.

Shopping

Downtown Winslow is jammed with gift and import shops, including several inside Winslow Green, the little strip mall in town. Two fine bookshops are in the center of town. One of them, **Eagle Harbor Books** (157 Winslow Way E., 206/842-5332, www.eagleharborbooks.com, 9 A.M.–7 P.M. Mon.–Wed. and Fri., 9 A.M.–9 P.M. Thurs., 9 A.M.–6 P.M. Sat., 10 A.M.–6 P.M. Sun.) has new titles, plus an espresso café in the back. Also downtown is **Bainbridge Arts and Crafts** (151 Winslow Way E., 206/842-3132, www.bainbridgeartscrafts.org, 10 A.M.–6 P.M. Mon.–Sat., 11 A.M.–5 P.M. Sun.), an excellent nonprofit gallery with local works.

Sports and Recreation

Pick up a map of hiking trails on Bainbridge from the chamber of commerce office. The largest parcel of public land—280 acres—contains second-growth forests managed by the Department of Natural Resources. Called **Grand Forest,** it's near the center of the island off Mandus Oldon Road and has two miles of paths. **Manzanita Park** is a 120-acre parcel with a two-mile hiking and equestrian trail through woods and wetlands. The park is on Day Road on the northwest side of the island.

Back of Beyond (181 Winslow Way, 206/842-9229, 10 A.M.–6 P.M. daily Apr.–Oct., open Tues.–Sun. Oct.–Mar., closed Mon., boathouse open until dusk) has sea kayak, canoe, sailboat, and rowboat rentals and tours from the Winslow waterfront.

For adventure under the water, try **Exotic Aquatics** (100 Madison Ave. N, 206/842-1980, exoticaquaticsscuba.com), which offers guided scuba dives in nearby waters.

Take advantage of the island's many back roads, as well as those on Kitsap Peninsula, on the saddle of a rented bike from **Classic Cycle** (310 Winslow Way E, 206/842-9191). If you've got your own ride but you need some supplies or a quick repair, **B. I. Cycle Rentals** (195 Winslow Way, 206/842-6413) is the best performance bike shop in the area.

Accommodations

There are dozens of little B&Bs tucked away in the residential areas of Bainbridge, but if you prefer a hotel, **Island Country Inn** (920 Hildebrand Lane NE, 206/842-6861 or 800/842-8429, $79–149 s or d) has nicely updated deluxe guest rooms and suites. The property has an outdoor pool and hot tub, plus continental breakfast in the mornings.

One of the better B&B deals on the island, **The Captain's House** (234 Parfitt Way NE,

206/842-3557, $75–100 d) is a century-old home overlooking Eagle Harbor with rowboats, tennis courts, and an old-fashioned porch swing. The two guest rooms have private baths.

Perched on five secluded acres next to Manzanita Creek is **Waterfall Gardens B&B** (7269 Bergman Rd., 206/842-1434, www.waterfall-gardens.com, $145–230 d), a gorgeous property with an impeccably maintained garden. The more expensive rooms have kitchens and private hot tubs.

Our Country Haus B&B (13718 Ellingsen Rd. NE, 206/842-8425, $150 d) is a private carriage house on two acres with gardens and pond, private bath, and kitchen. A continental breakfast is served.

Willow Brook Farm Cottage (12600 Miller Rd., 206/842-8034, www.willowbrookfarm.com, $165 s or d) is a private 1920s-era cottage on a 25-acre working organic farm. The cottage has a complete kitchen, separate living and sleeping rooms, and a hot tub on the deck.

For a taste of the Far East in the Northwest, check out **Fuurin-Oka Futon & Breakfast** (12580 Vista Dr. NE, 206/842-4916, www.futonandbreakfast.com, $169 s or d) a traditional Japanese house and garden, complete with sliding shoji screens, green tea, and private *ofuro,* or Japanese bath.

One of the swankiest sleeping spots on the island, **Ashton Woods Retreat** (5515 Tolo Rd. NE, 206/780-0100, www.ashtonwoodsretreat.com, $275 d, $40 pet fee) sits on a secluded 10-acre wooded plot complete with quiet gardens and walking trails. Guests can borrow bikes from the property or just hoof it on two feet to the trails of Grand Forest. Enjoy the exercise with your pup—this is a very dog-friendly property. The rooms are extremely well appointed and private for a B&B-type property. Fresh-baked continental breakfast is brought to your door each morning rather than served at a communal table.

Food

Streamliner Diner (397 Winslow Way, 206/842-8595, 7:30 A.M.–2:30 P.M. daily and 5–10 P.M. Tues.–Sat.) is famous for its hearty breakfasts that include wonderful home fries and omelettes. It's popular with both locals and tourists, so be ready for a wait most mornings. For something lighter, get fresh baked goods and espresso coffees at **Bainbridge Bakers** (140 Winslow Way W, 206/842-1822, 6 A.M.–6 P.M. Mon.–Sat., 6 A.M.–5 P.M. Sun.) or head to the historic brick building that houses **Pegasus Coffee House and Gallery** (131 Parfitt Way, 206/842-6725, 7 A.M.–6 P.M. Mon.–Thurs., 7 A.M.–9:30 P.M. Fri.–Sun.). This is a fun place to enjoy a relaxing light lunch and espresso. There's live music on Saturday nights.

Harbour Public House (231 Parfitt Way SW, 206/842-0969, 11 A.M.–midnight daily) has tasty on-the-water eats, including fish and chips and burgers, plus a dozen microbrewed beers.

Noted for serving some of the best Southwestern food in the Northwest is the **San Carlos Restaurant** (279 Madison N, 206/842-1999 5–9 P.M. daily, plus Fri. lunch 11 A.M.–2 P.M.), two blocks from the Winslow ferry terminal.

For Thai cooking, head to **Sawatdy Thai Cuisine** (8780 Fletcher Bay Rd., Island Center, 206/780-2429, 11:30 A.M.–1:30 P.M. Tues.–Fri. and 5–8 P.M. daily).

Winslow's **Town & Country Thriftway** (343 Winslow Way, 206/842-3848) is a big gourmet grocery with a fine wine cellar (in the cellar, of course). The **Bainbridge Farmers Market** comes to the municipal parking lot (Madison Ave. and Winslow Way, 206/855-1500, 9 A.M.–1 P.M. Sat. mid-Apr.–Oct.) with flowers, organic fruits and vegetables, handicrafts, and ethnic foods.

Information and Services

The **Bainbridge Island Chamber of Commerce Visitor Center** (590 Winslow Way E, 206/842-3700, www.bainbridgechamber.com, 9 A.M.–5 P.M. Mon.–Fri., 10 A.M.–3 P.M. Sat.) is at the top of the hill as you exit the ferry. You can also get info at the kiosk at the ferry terminal (10 A.M.–6 P.M. daily May–Oct., 10 A.M.–6 P.M. Sat.–Sun. Nov.–Apr.).

Getting There

The **Washington State Ferry** ($14.45 one-way car and driver, $6.25 motorcycle and driver, $6.70 extra passengers and walkers, $6.25 extra kayaks, $1 extra bikes) provides service between downtown Seattle and Winslow on Bainbridge Island every 50 minutes throughout the day. The crossing takes 35 minutes. The Seattle–Bainbridge route is the busiest ferry run in Washington—over six million riders each year. Be ready for long delays—especially in the summer—if you're traveling on Friday evenings from Seattle to Bainbridge, and on Sunday evenings back to Seattle. Avoid the wait by leaving your car behind and taking the bus.

Kitsap Transit (206/373-2877 or 800/501-7433, www.kitsaptransit.org) provides daily service around Bainbridge Island and the Kitsap Peninsula and meets all state ferries in Winslow. All buses have bike racks.

Tours of Bainbridge and surrounding areas are offered by **Taxis & Tours** (206/842-7660, $35 per hour, two hours minimum).

Puyallup Valley to White River Valley

Puyallup (pyoo-AL-up) sits less than a dozen miles southeast of Tacoma in the scenic, nearly level Puyallup Valley. The scenery is dramatic in Puyallup in the springtime, when Mount Rainier decides to peek out from under the clouds. This town's agricultural pace is an antidote to traffic jams and fast-paced living. It is home to the most beloved fair in the Puget Sound; together with its neighbor, Sumner, Puyallup prides itself on its historic buildings and homes and the bucolic sights that surround them.

Best of all, Puyallup is hardly in the middle of nowhere: Head north on Highway 167 toward the White River Valley to find more lodging choices, fast-food options, and entertainment venues in the bedroom communities of Auburn and Kent.

SIGHTS

Historic Sights

Furnished in 1890s style, the 17-room **Ezra Meeker Mansion** (312 Spring St., 253/848-1770, www.meekermansion.com, tours 1–4 P.M. Wed.–Sun. Mar.–mid-Dec. $4 adults, $3 teens and seniors, $2 children under 12, half price on Thurs.) was built by the city's founder and first mayor. The original stained-glass pieces, ceiling artwork, six inlaid fireplaces, and a grand staircase offer a glimpse into the lives of the elite of this time. As a hugely successful hop grower and broker, Meeker earned the moniker "Hop King of the World" and was for a time the richest man in the Pacific Northwest; he once earned more than $500,000 in a single year. The double whammy of the financial panic of 1890 and an infestation of hop lice nearly drove him into bankruptcy. Meeker lived through a fast-changing era: He drove a team of oxen over the Oregon Trail, later rode the route in a train, drove it in an automobile, and flew over it in an airplane. His fascination with the Oregon Trail led to the erection of markers along the route and the preservation of the historic trail.

Over in Sumner, the **Ryan House Museum** (1228 Main St., Sumner, 253/863-8936, 1–4 P.M. Sat.–Sun.) showcases a Victorian farmhouse from 1875, with tall backyard trees and regional history displays. Named for the first mayor of Sumner, who lived here for many years, the home is open April–October and December only.

Auburn's **White River Valley Historical Museum** (918 H St. SE, 253/939-2783, www.wrvmuseum.org, 1:30–4:30 P.M. Thurs.–Sun. year-round, free) has artifacts from the early days in the valley, including old photos, a one-room schoolhouse, country store, and farm machinery. Ask here for directions to the majestic **Neely Mansion,** built in 1894.

VanLierop Bulb Farms

Two miles east of Puyallup, VanLierop Bulb Farms (13407 80th St. E, 253/848-7272 or 877/666-8377) was created by Simon VanLierop, a Dutch immigrant from a family with a long history of bulb growing. VanLierop helped establish the bulb industry in the Puyallup area in the 1930s, and the farm is still a family operation, now producing more than 20,000 bulbs each year. Each spring these fields glow with the colors of 150 different varieties of crocus, daffodils, hyacinths, tulips, and other flowers. You can have them shipped or take them with you. The flower shop is open 9 A.M.–5 P.M. daily mid-September to mid-November and 9 A.M. to 6 P.M. daily mid-January to early June. Best time to see the flowers in bloom is mid-March to mid-April.

ENTERTAINMENT AND EVENTS

Entertainment

Located on the north side of Auburn, **Emerald Downs** (253/288-7000 or 888/931-8400, www.emeralddowns.com) is the Seattle area's thoroughbred horse racing center, with races April–September.

The **Auburn Avenue Dinner Theater** (10 Auburn Ave., 253/833-5678) has fun musical productions and plays. It's Washington's oldest and largest dinner theater.

Gamblers can try their luck at blackjack, craps, roulette, or poker at **Muckleshoot Indian Casino** (2402 Auburn Way S, 253/939-7484 or 800/804-4944, www.casino-fun.com). This is one of the largest casinos in the Puget Sound; it also services visitors with two restaurants and a lounge that is popular with the locals on the weekends.

Also popular are auto and motorcycle racing at **Seattle International Raceway** (31001 144th Ave. SE, Kent, 253/631-1550).

Events

Puyallup is famous as the home of the **Puyallup Fair** (Meridian St. and 9th Ave. SW, 253/841-5045, www.thefair.com), officially known as the Western Washington Fair. One of the nation's 10 largest, the fair runs for 17 days in September (starting the Friday after Labor Day) and attracts a crowd of more than 1.2 million fairgoers to its top-flight concerts, livestock displays, a PRCA rodeo, carnival rides, and refreshments. Don't miss the justly famous raspberry scones.

The **Spring Fair and Daffodil Festival** (253/627-6176, www.daffodilfestival.net) is another of Puyallup's well-known attractions. Sponsored by the region's bulb farms, and in existence since 1934, it's a two-week series of events throughout Pierce County; the Grand Floral Parade (the third-largest parade of flowers in the nation) heads through Puyallup, Tacoma, Sumner, and Orting.

A big summer event is the outdoor production of ***Jesus of Nazareth*** in Puyallup's open-air amphitheater (14422 S Meridian, 253/848-3411), performed at 8 P.M. every Friday and Saturday from the third weekend in July through Labor Day. In this, one of seven major passion plays in the country, the cast of hundreds is assisted by horses, cows, sheep, pigeons, and a donkey.

SHOPPING

Shoppers head to the enormous **SuperMall of the Great Northwest** (1101 SuperMall Way, www.supermall.com, 10 A.M.–9 P.M. Mon.–Sat., 11 A.M.–6 P.M. Sun.), with over 140 outlet and "rack" stores located just off Highway 167 at 15th Street Southwest.

Also, **South Hill Mall** (3500 S. Meridian, 10 A.M.–9 P.M. Mon.–Sat., 10 A.M.–6 P.M. Sun.) has over 150 stores at the intersection of Highway 512 and South Meridian.

RECREATION

Camping

Puyallup RV parks include **Majestic Mobile Manor** (7022 River Rd., 253/845-3144) and **River Road Motor Home Court** (7824 River Rd. E, 253/848-7155).

Park RVs or pitch a tent in Kent at **Seattle-Tacoma KOA Kampground** (5801 S. 212th St., 253/872-8652 or 800/562-1892, www.koa.com). This is one of the few RV parks in the Seattle area.

ACCOMMODATIONS

Puyallup

Those searching for a simple room to hang their hat after a night at the fairgrounds would do well to check into **Northwest Motor Inn** (1409 S. Meridian, 253/841-2600 or 800/845-9490, $59 s or $65 d). This tidy little motel has an outdoor hot tub and is only a few minutes' walk to the fair.

Standing behind a white picket fence and two giant evergreens, **Hedman House** (502 9th St S.W., 253/848-2248, www.hedmanhouse.com, $110 d) is also within walking distance of the fairgrounds. Relax on the porch swing or in front of the living room fire in the evening; come breakfast time you'll be treated to a sit-down breakfast in the country-themed dining room. The two rooms in the house share a bath, but for $25 extra you can reserve one room for a private stay. There's also a fenced-in backyard with a large deck and hot tub.

On the edge of town, **Tayberry Victorian Cottage B&B** (7406 80th St. E, 253/848-4594, $105–125 s or d) is a modern Victorian-style home with a wraparound porch and hot tub with a view of the valley. All three guest rooms are equipped with TVs and VCRs, and private baths featuring clawfoot tubs and bathrobes. Two-course full breakfasts are served each morning, and the inn caters to special dietary needs.

Best Western Park Plaza (9620 S. Hill Place E, 253/848-1500 or 800/238-7234, www.bestwestern.com, $154–204 d) has the nicest hotel rooms in town, plus an outdoor pool and hot tub, in-room hot tubs, exercise facility, and continental breakfast.

Kent and Auburn

Up north between the I-5 and Highway 167 corridors, Kent and Auburn are teeming with every shape and size of chain hotel and motel. Their proximity to Sea-Tac makes them a convenient stopover when flying in or out of the region.

You can find a relatively cheap night's sleep at **Days Inn** (22420 84th Ave., Kent, 253/872-5525 or 800/443-7777, $89 s or $99 d), which often offers discounted rates online. Amenities include a hot tub, continental breakfast, wireless Internet, and a desktop computer available for use 24 hours a day. This is also one of the few area hotels that still has smoking and nonsmoking rooms.

For a few extra dollars, though, **Best Western Plaza by the Green** (24415 Russell Rd., 253/854-8767 or 800/835-3338, $119 s or d) is a better value. The hotel is situated on the 8th green of the Riverbed Golf Course, so be sure to ask for a room with a view. Guests are welcome to relax in the sauna, hot tub, and exercise room. Continental breakfast is complimentary, as is the airport shuttle.

For a homier stay, try **Victorian Gardens Bed and Breakfast** (9621 S. 200th St., Kent, 888/850-1776, www.victoriangardensbandb.com, $135–155 d). This 1888 home is surrounded by an award-winning garden, lush green lawns, and a backyard pool. Sticking to the Victorian theme, three of the rooms are all floral and lace, but for those who prefer a more understated look, the Tuxedo Room is an elegantly masculine choice with rich purple-and-gray furnishings. All come equipped with private bath, refrigerator, TV, and wireless Internet.

FOOD

Puyallup

The deep, dark accent woods of the furnishing and decor at **Hungry Goose Bistro** (1618 E Main St., Puyallup, 253/845-5747, www.hgbistro.com, 5–9:30 P.M. Tues.–Sat.) set the tone for a classy meal supping on Nuevo Bistro–style fare. Inventive entrées such as apple bacon–wrapped scallops drizzled with plum port reduction ($18) and sweet Georgia pecan chicken ($13) light up the menu. On Saturday and Sunday, the Goose pulls out all the stops with a special brunch menu served 8 A.M.–3 P.M.

Another favorite Puyallup eatery is **Mama Stortini's** (3207 E. Main St., 253/845-7569, www.mamastortinis.com, 11:30 A.M.–9 P.M. Sun.–Thurs., 11:30 A.M.–10 P.M. Fri., noon–10 P.M. Sat.), a lively spot that focuses on

Northwest cooking fused with French and Italian flavors.

For more traditional Italian fare—and the best local pizzas—try **Casa Mia** (505 N. Meridian, 253/770-0400, 11 A.M.–10 P.M. Sun.–Thurs., 11 A.M.–11 P.M. Fri.–Sat.).

Taste German wines at **Baron Manfred Vierthaler Winery** (253/863-1633), a Bavarian-style hilltop chalet just east of Sumner on Highway 410. The wine-tasting room is open 11 A.M.–10 P.M. Tuesday–Sunday; be sure to try the port and dessert wines. The adjoining restaurant serves traditional German-Bavarian dishes and has a dining room overlooking the Puyallup Valley.

The popular **Puyallup Farmers Market** (253/845-6755, 9 A.M.–2 P.M. Sat. May–Labor Day) features fresh local produce. The market is held downtown next to Pioneer Park. At other times, head out River Road to find the produce stands, or stop by the chamber of commerce for a list of local places.

Kent and Auburn

There's not a lot of standout cuisine farther north in Auburn and Kent, with both towns mostly dominated by chain restaurants and drive-throughs. But if you are in the neighborhood on a summer Saturday, be sure to stop by the large, open-air **Kent Farmers Market** (206 Railroad Ave., 253/813-69769 A.M.–4 P.M. Sat., 10 A.M.–3 P.M. Sun. June–Sept.).

INFORMATION

The **Puyallup Area Chamber of Commerce** (41 7 E. Pioneer, 253/845-6755, www.eastpiercechamber.com, 9 A.M.–5 P.M.Mon.–Fri.) is open year-round.

Get local information from the **Auburn Area Chamber of Commerce** (108 S. Division St., 253/833-0700, www.auburnareawa.org, 9 A.M.–5 P.M. Mon.–Fri.). There is also a **Kent Chamber of Commerce** (524 W. Meeker St., 253/854-1770, www.kentchamber.com).

GETTING THERE

Pierce Transit (253/581-8000 or 800/562-8109, www.ptbus.pierce.wa.us, has daily service to Tacoma and other parts of Pierce County, along with Seattle and Olympia. **Capital Aeroporter** (253/754-7113 or 800/962-3579, www.capair.com) operates shuttle vans between Puyallup and Sea-Tac Airport.

Metro Transit (253/553-3000 or 800/542-7876, http://transit.metrokc.gov) has bus service to Auburn, Kent, and the rest of King County.

Sea-Tac Corridor

The southern end of King County encompasses several rapidly growing suburbs and industrial areas, with Sea-Tac Airport as a central focal point. A maze of highways, shopping malls, and towns fill the American dream of escaping from the cities. Unfortunately, this escape has transformed rich farmland into yet more development. This part of Washington has little to offer the traveler, other than cheap lodging and food, though each town has something of interest.

SIGHTS

Wild Waves

Federal Way is best known 'round the Sound for its amusement and water park, Wild Waves (36201 Enchanted Pkwy. S., 253/661-8000, www.wildwaves.com, $35 adult, $30 child, hours vary, open May–Sept.). This enterprise is a nice summer destination to keep the whole family amused. The water park offers 400 feet of white-water rapids on its Raging River Ride, four giant water slides, a "beach" with artificial five-foot waves for bodysurfing, and scaled-down versions of the adult attractions for the kiddies. All the water is heated, so don't worry about the weather. The dry side of the park has 16 rides (including a 1906 carousel), bumper boats, a free-flight bird aviary, pony rides, children's museum, petting zoo, and other attractions.

Parks and Gardens

The Rhododendron Species Foundation Garden (Weyerhaeuser Way, 253/661-9377, www.rhodygarden.org, 10 A.M.–4 P.M. Fri.–Wed. March–May, 11 A.M.–4 P.M. Sat.–Wed. the rest of the year, $3.50 adults, $2.50 students and seniors, free for kids under 12) displays over 2,100 varieties of wild rhododendrons from around the world in a 24-acre garden. This is the world's largest collection in one garden, and something is in bloom March–September. The garden is operated by the nonprofit Rhododendron Species Foundation, which also offers workshops, classes, and tours for members.

Just south of the Rhododendron Garden is **Pacific Rim Bonsai Collection** (253/924-5206, www.weyerhaeuser.com/bonsai, free), operated by the Weyerhaeuser Corporation; corporate headquarters is just up the way. The collection contains more than 90 bonsai trees, some more than 500 years old. Go 0.75 mile east from exit 142A, then a half mile north on Weyerhaeuser Way. (By the way, the correct pronunciation for bonsai—Japanese for a tree in a pot—is bone-sigh.) Hours are the same as the rhododendron garden. Lectures on growing bonsai trees are held April–September throughout the year.

Two miles south of Des Moines on Marine View Drive South, **Saltwater State Park** (253/661-4956, www.parks.wa.gov) is one of the most popular summer spots around. The sandy beach is very popular for swimming, scuba diving, and sea kayaking, and a two-mile path loops through the forest. Also here are picnic tables and a refreshment stand. Showers are available. Unfortunately, the park is in the flight path of Sea-Tac and planes land or take off over the park, so don't expect peace and quiet.

Dash Point State Park (5700 SW Dash Point Rd.) is in Federal Way, five miles northeast of downtown Tacoma on Puget Sound, on Highway 509, a.k.a. Dash Point Road. On Sound side of the park there's a beach (the water here is warm enough for swimming—or at least wading—in summer), picnic tables, and trails that lead to the water.

Rocker's Remains

The simple grave of **James M. "Jimi" Hendrix** can be found in Greenwood Memorial Park, located east of town on N.E. 3rd at Monroe. Find the ground-level grave marker by heading toward the sundial and then turning right. Born in Seattle in 1942, Hendrix died in 1970 from a drug-related suffocation. Hundreds of people of all ages still make the pilgrimage to his grave each year, leaving behind tokens of all sorts, from flowers to pinwheels. Be sure to stop by the office near the cemetery entrance to sign the guest book and read comments from visitors who arrive from around the globe. Seattle's Experience Music Project has much more on this rock legend.

ENTERTAINMENT AND EVENTS

In Federal Way, the **Red, White & Blues Festival** gets down with the blues on the 4th of July, and **Family Fest** brings family fun in late August.

Tukwila has popular **Tukwila Days** each July, while nearby Burien (pop. 32,000, just west of the airport) is home to the **Strawberry Festival** each June, along with a fun **4th of July Parade.** SeaTac's Angle Lake Park features a **Music in the Park** series in the summer. For live music, weekend dancing, and a casino, head to **Pete's Flying Aces** (14101 Pacific Hwy. S, 206/248-1224).

IKEA Renton River Days in late July or early August is the main local event, with parades, live music, games, food and craft vendors, and more. Each December Ivar's Acres of Clams puts up an amusing set of colorful **Clam Lights** at Coulon Beach Park.

SHOPPING

Malls

Southcenter Mall, located south of the intersection of I-5 with I-405 in Tukwila (pop. 17,000). Major department stores here are Macy's, Nordstrom, JCPenney, and Sears (the company's "flagship store"), plus 150 other stores.

The **Commons at Federal Way** (S. 320th

St., www.tcafw.com) has over 100 stores including Macy's and Sears. Also in Federal Way is an **REI** (2565 S. Gateway Center Plaza, 253/941-4994, www.rei.com), with camping and backpacking supplies galore.

Downtown Renton

For a surprisingly complete selection of Western garb, be sure to tie up at the state's largest cowboy shop, **Renton Western Wear** (724 S. 3rd, 425/255-3922 or 800/886-3922, www.rentonww.com). Antique lovers will have fun wandering through the downtown antique shops along Wells Avenue South near 3rd.

SPORTS AND RECREATION

On the northern edge of Federal Way, also on the Sound, is the community of **Des Moines.** The city marina is one of the largest in the area. Nearby is a 670-foot fishing pier that provides great views of the mountains for anglers and strollers. To the north of the pier is the **Des Moines Beach Park,** a 20-acre park with Des Moines Creek, to which salmon return each year.

Several public swimming pools are in the area, but the star attraction is the **Weyerhaeuser King County Aquatic Center** (650 S.W. Campus Dr., 253/927-5173), constructed to host the 1990 Goodwill Games and used for other national swimming meets. You don't have to be a hotshot to swim here, or to try out the diving boards.

The **North Shore Golf & Country Club** (4101 North Shore Blvd. NE, 253/927-1375 or 800/447-1375, www.northshoregc.com) is an 18-hole public course.

Camping

Campers and RVers will enjoy the amenities at **Aqua Barn Ranch** (15227 Renton-Maple Valley Hwy., 425/255-4618). The RV sites come with an indoor pool, a big-screen TV, and movies. **Riverbend RV Park** (17410 Maple Valley, 425/255-2613) has adults-only tent sites on 12 acres.

The wooded camping area on the east side of **Dash Point State Park** (5700 SW Dash Point Rd., 253/233-03221) has primitive sites ($12), tent sites ($17) and RV sites ($23). The park is open year-round. Make reservations ($7 extra) at 888/226-7688 or www.parks.wa.gov.

During the summer between late April and early September, **Saltwater State Park** (25205 8th Pl. S., Des Moines, 253/661-4956, www.parks.wa.gov) also runs a small campground for tent campers ($17). There are no reservations, so get here early on the weekends.

ACCOMMODATIONS

SeaTac and Burien

The hotel alley along Highway 99 near the airport in the town of SeaTac was once a notoriously dirty and sketchy neighborhood, but over the last five years or so the area has really spiffed itself up. Older hotels have been remodeled and decrepit motels torn down in favor of newer establishments. As a result, there are fewer places that remain under $100 per night, but those that do are typically cleaner and safer than what used to be offered in this pool.

One of the best deals in the area is at ☾ **Sea-Tac Crest Motor Inn** (18845 International Blvd., 206/433-0999 or 800/554-0300, www.seataccrest.com, $69 s or $79 d), two blocks south of the airport. This is a friendly mom-and-pop operation that caters to no-nonsense travelers. Rooms are accessible only by indoor corridor, with 24-hour front desk and security. Beds are reasonably comfortable and the units are spic and span—no need to wear socks in the room here. Coffee and muffins are served in the morning, there's free shuttle service to the airport (dial #20 from airport courtesy phones) and seven days of free parking are included with one night's stay.

For something a little slower-paced, but still convenient to the airport, ☾ **Three Tree Point Bed & Breakfast** (17026 33rd Ave. SW, 206/669-7646 or 888/369-7696, www.3pointbnb.com) rests in the little town of Burien, about 10 minutes southwest of SeaTac. This waterfront inn rests by a little point jutting out into the Puget Sound. There are two light and airy units here. First there's a deluxe suite ($150 d) with living room, dining room, separate bedroom, and laundry room. And then there's a cottage ($190) with bedroom and master bath, a beautiful kitchen with gas stove and oven, a living room with fireplace, and a laundry room. Both units come with a porch and some amazing water views. A gourmet breakfast is delivered to your kitchen each morning.

If you've got an early morning flight to catch, **Best Western Airport Executel** (20717 International Blvd., 206/878-3300, $119 s or d) is one of the best budget chain hotels on the International Boulevard strip. Rooms are very clean, furnishings are new, and access is only by indoor corridor. Get work done in the business center and then relax in the indoor pool, hot tub, and steam room. There's also a fitness center and a restaurant on-site. Wireless Internet is free, and a hot breakfast is served each morning starting in the wee hours at 5 A.M. The hotel runs a free shuttle to the airport.

Federal Way

Another clean and comfortable option is to motor south on Highway 99 down to the **Days Inn** (34827 Pacific Hwy. S, 253/838-3164, $82) in Federal Way. Beds are comfy and the building is very well kept. Though it is just off busy Highway 99, soundproofing is good so light sleepers should be able to rest soundly. Rate includes free continental breakfast. There's no pool, but the Federal Way Aquatic Center is just around the corner.

Renton

Situated right next to the greenery of Cedar River Park, **Silver Cloud at Renton** (1850 Maple Valley Hwy., 425/226-7600 or 800/205-6936, $104 s or $114) is a quiet and pleasant alternative to the SeaTac pack of motels. Several miles of trails are just outside the door here, and the facilities include an exercise room, hot tub, and rooms with kitchenettes. Rooms are tidy, and wireless Internet is included.

Also here is **Clarion of Renton** (3700 E. Valley Rd., 425/251-9591 or 800/578-7878, $119 s or $129 d), which offers a free airport shuttle, has a hot tub, and serves continental breakfast each morning.

FOOD

SeaTac and Burien

SeaTac eats are mostly dominated by fast-food chains, but there are a few charmingly quirky independent establishments scattered along Highway 99.

Anxuyen Bakery (2823 S 200th St., 206/878-4087) is a convenient hole-in-the-wall donut and pastry shop to stop at before dumping a rental car at one of the off-site car lots along this stretch and catching the shuttle for a morning flight. Everything is made fresh in the morning, including great French bread, and there's even an espresso machine—though it was broken the last time I visited. That's OK, though, because the drip coffee is decent and cheap. If you stop by at lunch, try one of the Vietnamese-style sandwiches for $1.75.

Kitty-corner from it is **Herfy's Burgers and Teriyaki** (19840 Pacific Hwy. S, 206/870-1500, 10:30–9 P.M. Mon.–Fri., 11 A.M.–9 P.M. Sat., 11 A.M.–8 P.M. Sun.), a super clean little mom-and-pop eatery. Don't be scared off by the weathered sign outside. Inside has white tablecloths, immaculate hardwood floors, and a sort of shorthand Asian decor. Burgers are big and come with stadium crinkle-cut fries ($3.99). Pair one up with one of numerous flavors of thick, hand-dipped shakes, such as peanut butter and blueberry. The menu is huge, with a sizable teriyaki and noodle section.

You can also get the real deal in diner food at **Dave's Diner & Brews** (2825 S 188th St., 206/277-7196, 6 A.M.–10 P.M. daily), just about a block away from the airport. Get a big plate of chicken-fried steak swimming in flavorful gravy, with a side of real mashed potatoes, veggies, and a roll for under $10. Air travelers take note: Dave's also does lunch boxes to go for $8.59.

The **SeaTac Farmers Market** (4424 S. 188th, 206/248-9346) takes place 10 A.M.–3 P.M. Saturday June–August.

Federal Way

Redondo, just west of Federal Way on Puget Sound, has a fishing pier, boat launch, and one of the area's best restaurants: **Salty's at Redondo** (28201 Redondo Beach Dr. S,

253/946-0636, www.saltys.com/seattle_south). Primarily a seafood restaurant, Salty's has one of the best sunset views around, and you can drink or dine outdoors on the pier in the summer months.

A good place for a light meal is **Lolli's Broiler & Pub** (32925 1st Ave. S, 253/838-5929), a restaurant/tavern that serves huge burgers and good sandwiches, along with an extensive selection of beers on tap—32 at last count.

Renton

Rainier Avenue is Renton's major commercial byway, lined with big chain restaurants. The best comestibles on this strip are found at **Royal Orchid Thai Cuisine** (104 Rainier Ave. S, 425/271-4219, 11 A.M.–10 P.M. daily), which serves authentic Southeast Asian fare with a smile. The dining room is full of real orchids. Try one of the complex curry dishes.

Right across from the downtown train station, **Whistle Stop Ale House** (340 Burnett Ave. S, 425/277-3039, 11 A.M.–10 P.M. daily) is a friendly little bar and eatery with microbrews on tap and good sandwiches. You can also get good Italian food at **Armondo's Café Italiano** (919 South 3rd St., 425/255-5001, 11 A.M.–9 P.M. Mon.–Thurs., 11 A.M.–10 P.M. Fri., 4–10 P.M. Sat., 4–9 P.M. Sun.).

INFORMATION

For a handful of local brochures, drop by **Southwest King County Chamber of Commerce** (16400 Southcenter Pkwy., Ste. 210, 206/575-1633 800/638-8613, www.swkcc.org).

The **Renton Chamber of Commerce** (300 Rainier N, 425/226-4560, www.renton-chamber.com) is open 8:30 A.M.–5 P.M. Monday–Friday. Behind it on the Boeing Field tarmac, you'll see new Boeing 737s and 757s in the finishing stages before delivery.

GETTING THERE AND AROUND

By Air

Seattle's airport is 12 miles south of town and midway between Seattle and Tacoma, hence the name, **Sea-Tac International Airport** (206/431-4444 or 800/544-1965, www.portseattle.org). All the major domestic, and many international, airlines fly into Sea-Tac. Foreign travelers can change money at the Thomas Cook booth in the main terminal.

Storage lockers are scattered around the airport, but you'll need to pass through security before you reach them. Another option is **Ken's Baggage and Frozen Food Storage** (206/433-5333, 5:30 A.M.–12:30 A.M. daily), located near the baggage claim area.

Also near the baggage claim is a volunteer-staffed **Visitor Information Booth** (9:30 A.M.–7:30 P.M. daily in the summer, brochures available at other times), along with car rentals counters and kiosks with information on Metro buses, shuttle buses, and limo services. The airport website has updates on airport parking, weather and traffic conditions, ground transportation, and other services.

Sound Flight (425/255-6500 or 800/825-0722, www.soundflight.com) at the **Boeing Field Airport** offers flightseeing tours over Seattle, Mt. Rainier, the San Juan Islands, and north to Vancouver Island, plus scheduled service to the San Juan Islands, the Gulf Islands, Victoria, and other destinations on Vancouver Island. **Northwest Seaplanes** (425/277-1590 or 800/690-0086, www.nwseaplanes.com) also flies scheduled service to the San Juans, British Columbia, and Alaska from Boeing Field.

By Bus and Van

Metro Transit (253/447-4800 or 800/542-7876 http://transit.metrokc.gov) provides bus service to Seattle and other parts of King County. **Pierce Transit** (253/581-8000 or 800/562-8109, www.ptbus.pierce.wa.us) operates service to Tacoma and other parts of Pierce County, along with Seattle and Olympia.

Renton Urban Shuttle (425/277-5555) has free bus service around town. **Shuttle Express** (206/622-1424 or 800/942-7433, www.shuttleexpress.com) has van service to Sea-Tac Airport.

SAN JUAN ISLANDS

Scattered like emerald nuggets in the sapphire that is the Puget Sound, the San Juan Islands offers travelers a glimpse into the secret life they might have if they threw caution to the wind, quit their jobs, and gave up Starbucks and mall shopping for life.

Step aboard one of the state's trademark green-and-white ferries in Anacortes and glide over to one of the chain's four largest islands—Orcas, Lopez, Shaw, or San Juan—to find pastoral land grazed by livestock, winding country roads, and not a chain store or restaurant in sight. Peer over the shoreline to scan for orcas spyhopping and lobtailing in nearby waterways. Look overhead to spot bald eagles circling over lakes and glades hidden within island interiors.

While the thread of natural beauty unites these most popular San Juan Islands, each has its own unique personality and individual flair. Lopez Island attracts low-key people who care less than most about an extravagant lifestyle, people who are comfortable alone or in a small community. The island is quiet, rural, and a cyclist's paradise. San Juan Island contains the biggest town, Friday Harbor, with impressive dining, lodging, and recreation possibilities, including whale-watching and sea kayaking. San Juan is also rich in history, and home to San Juan Island National Historical Park, where a war nearly erupted over a pig. Orcas Island is the most rugged and beautiful of the San Juans, with the tallest mountains, best camping, and a relaxed atmosphere that attracts a lot of artists, writers, and free spirits. Shaw, the quietest island,

© ERICKA CHICKOWSKI

HIGHLIGHTS

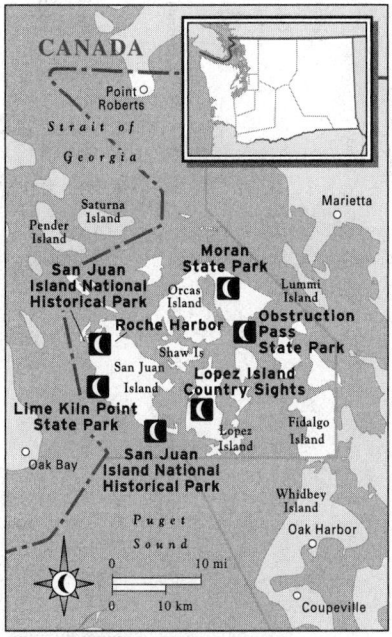

LOOK FOR ☾ TO FIND RECOMMENDED SIGHTS, ACTIVITIES, DINING, AND LODGING.

☾ **San Juan Island National Historical Park:** Explore the American and British Camps of this two-site park that is preserved in remembrance of an international standoff started over a pig (page 256).

☾ **Roche Harbor:** Situated on the north side of the San Juan Island, this is a classic little seaport resort community with historic roots (page 258).

☾ **Lime Kiln Point State Park:** Also known as Whale Watch Park, this is the best land-based spot on all of the islands to spot orcas (page 259).

☾ **Moran State Park:** The main attraction on Orcas Island, this massive park offers the best camping in the Puget Sound, pristine freshwater lakes, a tumbling waterfall, and the highest peak in all of the islands (page 270).

☾ **Obstruction Pass State Park:** Hidden away on Orcas Island, this remote little park offers a short hike down to a solitary beach filled with skipping stones and driftwood (page 272).

☾ **Lopez Island Country Sights:** Cycle the rural roads of Lopez and stop off to pick berries, watch cows munch the fields, and sip on organic wine (page 281).

is known for its residents' hands-off approach. Visitors are welcomed here but not catered to, so the only lodging here is available under the great blue yonder at the island's small campgrounds. This is the place to get away from it all—including swarming tourists.

Wedged between Washington mainland and Vancouver Island, the San Juan archipelago is more than just these four islands. The chain is made up of 786 islands at low tide and more than 172 named islands. Those with a boat can widen their base of explorations by paddle, sail, or motor to discover a kaleidoscope of tidepools, rocky shorelines, and hidden campgrounds enough to satisfy even the most pressing case of wanderlust.

To get to any of these islands by car, you'll pass through the mainland town of Anacortes, a charming port city that definitely merits a stop for a night or two.

PLANNING YOUR TIME

No matter what the season, chances are you will catch more sunshine in the San Juans than anywhere else in the Puget Sound. Shielded by the Olympic and Vancouver Island mountains, the San Juans see less than 25 annual inches of rain, with the sun shining an average of 247 days a year.

The islands are immensely popular in the summer, particularly during the peak season of July and August when it is sunny and moderate—

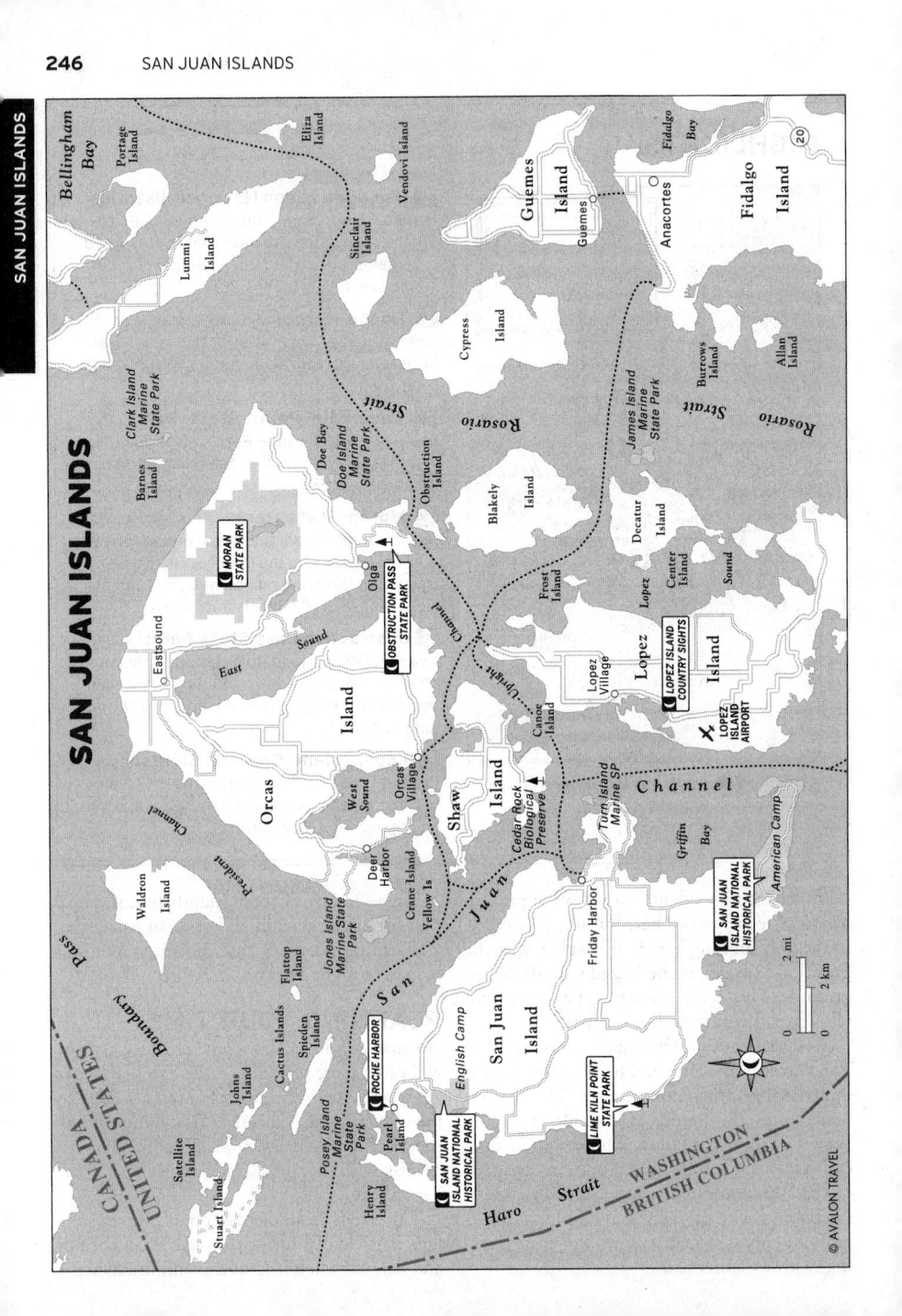
SAN JUAN ISLANDS
CANADA
UNITED STATES
Bellingham Bay
Portage Island
Eliza Island
Lummi Island
Vendovi Island
Sinclair Island
Clark Island Marine State Park
Barnes Island
Doe Bay
Doe Island Marine State Park
Obstruction Island
Cypress Island
Blakely Island
Guemes Island
Guemes
Anacortes
Fidalgo Bay
Fidalgo Island
Burrows Island
Allan Island
James Island Marine State Park
Decatur Island
Center Island
Frost Island
Lopez Village
Lopez
Lopez Island
Canoe Island
Orcas Island
Eastsound
East Sound
Orcas Village
West Sound
Deer Harbor
Crane Island
Yellow Is
Shaw Island
Cedar Rock Biological Preserve
Turn Island Marine SP
Friday Harbor
Griffin Bay
American Camp
San Juan Island
English Camp
Waldron Island
Jones Island Marine State Park
Flattop Island
Spieden Island
Cactus Islands
Johns Island
Satellite Island
Stuart Island
Posey Island Marine State Park
Pearl Island
Henry Island
Boundary Pass
Presidents Channel
San Juan Channel
Obstruction Pass Channel
Rosario Strait
Haro Strait
WASHINGTON
BRITISH COLUMBIA
MORAN STATE PARK
OBSTRUCTION PASS STATE PARK
LOPEZ ISLAND COUNTRY SIGHTS
LOPEZ ISLAND AIRPORT
SAN JUAN ISLAND NATIONAL HISTORICAL PARK
ROCHE HARBOR
LIME KILN POINT STATE PARK
0 2 mi
0 2 km
© AVALON TRAVEL

with temperatures rarely exceeding 85°F. If you plan a visit at these times, there may well be no room in the inn, and not a lot of mangers available either. Save yourself a lot of headaches by making reservations far in advance, even if you plan on camping. At the older and more established B&Bs this means calling at least four months ahead of time for a midsummer weekend reservation. If you're looking for space on Memorial Day, the 4th of July, or Labor Day, make reservations up to a year in advance. Also plan on staying at least two nights, as most places on the islands require a minimum stay in the summer and sometimes year-round.

For the locals, September and October are the nicest months of the year: The tourists are gone, the weather is still warm and dry, with highs in the 60s and lows in the 40s or 50s, and the salmon are running. In the winter you'll find fewer fellow travelers and lower lodging rates (often 30 percent less), but the weather won't be quite as inviting and things won't be as green. December is the wettest month, with 4.5 inches of rain on the average and temperatures in the low 40s. It rarely snows in the San Juans, and when it does it lasts but a few days. Still, winter holidays (especially Christmas to New Year's) are likely to be booked well in advance.

For maps and other information before you arrive, contact the San Juan Islands Visitor Information Service, (360/468-3663 or 888/468-3701, www.guidetosanjuans.com) and request *Your Guide to the San Juan Islands,* packed with up-to-date information.

GETTING THERE

By Ferry

If you can only take one ride aboard a **Washington State Ferry** (206/464-6400, www.wsdot.wa.gov/ferries), the trip from Anacortes to the San Juans should be the one. When the ferry pulls away from the Anacortes dock, it is almost like departing on a cruise ship. The scenery is so beautiful that even amateur photographers can get spectacular sunset-over-the-islands shots. In the summer, ferries leave Anacortes at least a dozen times a day 4:30 A.M.–12:20 A.M., stopping at Lopez, Shaw, Orcas, and Friday Harbor, in that order; it takes roughly two hours from Anacortes to Friday Harbor. Not every ferry stops on each island, but nearly all of them stop at Friday Harbor on San Juan Island. Ferries between Anacortes and Sidney, B.C., run twice a day in the summer and once a day the rest of the year. (Vehicle reservations are *required* for service between the San Juans and Sidney.) The ferries have food and booze onboard, and a duty-free shop can be found on ferries heading to British Columbia. For more information, call 360/293-8166 in Anacortes, 206/464-6400 in Seattle, 888/808-7977 statewide or 604/381-1551 in Victoria. Call 800/843-3779 for automated information.

During the peak summer season, it's wise to arrive at least two hours early on weekends, or an hour early on weekdays. On holiday weekends you may find yourself in line for up to five hours! Parking is available at the Anacortes ferry terminal if you're heading over on foot or by bike. Both San Juan and Orcas Islands have excellent bus services, so you really don't need a car there anyway. The terminal usually has information on current campsite availability at the San Juans parks (meaning they often say none are available) to help in planning where to stay that night. Avoid the crowds by traveling midweek, early morning, late evening (except Friday evenings), or better yet, by foot, kayak, or bike.

The ferry system operates on a first-come, first-served basis, with reservations available only for the routes from Anacortes to Sidney, B.C., and from Orcas Island or San Juan Island to Sidney. No reservations are accepted for travel to the San Juans—just get in line and wait like everyone else. In Anacortes, tune your radio to **AM 1340** for broadcasts of current ferry status, including any backups or other problems.

Peak season fares to Friday Harbor, the last American stop, are $11.85 for passengers, $46.15 for car and driver. Bikes are $4 extra, and kayaks cost $8.10 more. Car-and-driver fares to the other islands from Anacortes are a few dollars less. Interisland ferries are free for passengers and bikes, and $20.85 for cars and drivers. Cash, credit cards, in-state checks, and travelers checks are accepted. Most of these rates are lower in the off-season.

Ferry travelers are only charged in the westbound direction; eastbound travel within the San Juans or from the islands to Anacortes is free. (The only exception to this is for travelers leaving from Sidney, B.C.) If you're planning to visit all the islands, save money by heading straight to Friday Harbor, and then working your way back through the others at no additional charge.

If you're driving around the islands, be sure to fill your tank in Anacortes before getting on the ferry. Because of the cost of shipping fuel here (and because they can get away with it), gas stations on the islands charge at least 30 percent more for gas than on the mainland.

Once a day, a ferry continues on from Orcas and Friday Harbor to Sidney, B.C.; fares are $11 for passengers or $41 for car and driver.

The passenger-only ***Victoria Clipper*** (206/448-5000 or 800/888-2535, www.victoriaclipper.com) has high-speed catamaran day trips between Seattle and San Juan Island ($75 for adults, $37.50 for kids round-trip).

The **San Juan Island Commuter** (360/734-8180 or 888/734-8180, www.islandcommuter.com) is a popular way to reach the islands. Its passenger-only boats depart from Bellingham on daily cruises to the San Juans mid-May through September, less frequently the rest of the year. Round-trip adult fares from Bellingham are $59 to either Rosario Resort on Orcas Island or Friday Harbor on San Juan Island. Kids pay $39, bikes are an extra $5, and kayaks cost $20. The company operates two boats along the route, as well as whale-watching trips out of Friday Harbor.

San Juan Island Shuttle Express (360/671-1137 or 888/373-8522, www.orcawhales.com, $59 adults, $49 seniors, $39 students, $5 bikes) operates a passenger ferry connecting Bellingham with Orcas, Lopez, and San Juan Islands. The ferry runs daily late May–September. You can add a whale-watching trip from Friday Harbor for $30.

Puget Sound Express (360/385-5288, www.pugetsoundexpress.com, $68 round-trip, bikes and kayaks $10 extra) provides passenger-only service between Port Townsend and Friday Harbor. The boat leaves Port Townsend daily April–October and stays in Friday Harbor long enough for a quick three-hour visit, or you can overnight there and return to Port Townsend later.

By Air

Kenmore Air (206/486-1257 or 800/543-9595, www.kenmoreair.com) has scheduled floatplane flights from Lake Union in Seattle and Lake Washington in Kenmore to Friday Harbor and Roche Harbor on San Juan Island, to Lopez Islander and Fisherman Bay on Lopez Island, and to Rosario Resort and West Sound on Orcas Island. Peak fares are approximately $263 one-way. A 24-pound baggage weight limit is in effect for these flights, with excess baggage charged at $1/pound. Kenmore Air also offers charter service to other destinations in the San Juans and flightseeing trips.

San Juan Airlines (360/293-4691 or 800/874-4434, www.sanjuanairlines.com) has daily wheeled-plane flights from Anacortes and Bellingham to most of the San Juan Islands. Typically tickets cost $53–68 one-way. Also available are charters from Seattle's Boeing field starting at $375. San Juan Airlines also offers flightseeing trips over the San Juans from Bellingham for about $175 for a half-hour flight on a five-seat aircraft.

Another option is **Sound Flight** (425/255-6500 or 800/825-0722, www.soundflight.net), which provides regular floatplane service between Renton and the San Juans mid-June–mid-September. Most flights cost around $149 one-way.

Northwest Seaplanes (425/277-1590 or 800/690-0086, www.nwseaplanes.com) also flies out of Renton, with floatplane charter service to Lopez Island, Rosario Resort, West Sound, Friday Harbor, and Roche Harbor.

The cost to charter a six-passenger aircraft is $800 one-way.

Rose Air (503/675-7673, www. roseair.com) offers charter flights between Portland International Airport and the San Juan Islands. Charters start at $364 one-way for a three-seat flight.

Island Air (360/378-2376 or 888/378-2376, www.sanjuan-islandair.com) has charter flights and flightseeing trips from San Juan Island Airport. Fares vary, with a three-person flight from Seattle's Boeing Field to Friday Harbor starting at $275 one-way.

Anacortes

Many visitors know Anacortes (ah-nah-KOR-tez) only as the jumping-off point for the San Juan Islands, but this city of 15,000 is far more than a ferry dock on the tip of Fidalgo Island. It is one of the more pleasant cities of its size in the Puget Sound basin and has a casual, end-of-the-road atmosphere.

Although it's hard to believe, Anacortes is legally on Fidalgo Island; Swinomish Slough cuts a sluggish, narrow swath from the La Conner area around the hills known as Fidalgo Head. The slough is kept open for boaters and is spanned by a beautiful arc of a bridge.

© ERICKA CHICKOWSKI

downtown Anacortes

SIGHTS

Museums and Historic Buildings

The **Anacortes Museum** (1305 8th St., 360/293-1915, www.anacorteshistory museum.org, 1–5 P.M. Thurs.–Mon., donation) has local historical exhibits, photographs, and period furniture. Get another taste of the past in a walk around Anacortes to see almost 50 (mostly small) **historic murals** on local buildings. The visitors center has descriptions of each, including the mural of Anna Curtis across the street from the center.

Other remnants of earlier days are scattered throughout town, including the historic sternwheeler ***W. T. Preston***—now a National Historic Landmark—on display at 7th Street and R Avenue next to the marina (360/293-1916, 11 A.M.–5 P.M. Sat.–Sun., $2 adults, $1 kids and seniors, free for kids under 8). The *Preston* operated as a snagboat for the U.S. Army Corps of Engineers from 1914 till she it finally retired in the 1970s and given to the city of Anacortes; it was the last sternwheeler operating on Puget Sound. The *Preston* kept the waterways clear of debris by towing off snags, logs, and stumps that piled up against bridge supports. The boat underwent a $2 million restoration in 2001 and reopened to the public the following year. Right next to the *Preston* is the 1911 Burlington Northern Railroad Depot at 7th and R, now home to the Depot Arts Center, plus the Anacortes Farmers Market on summer Saturdays.

Causland Park covers a city block at 8th

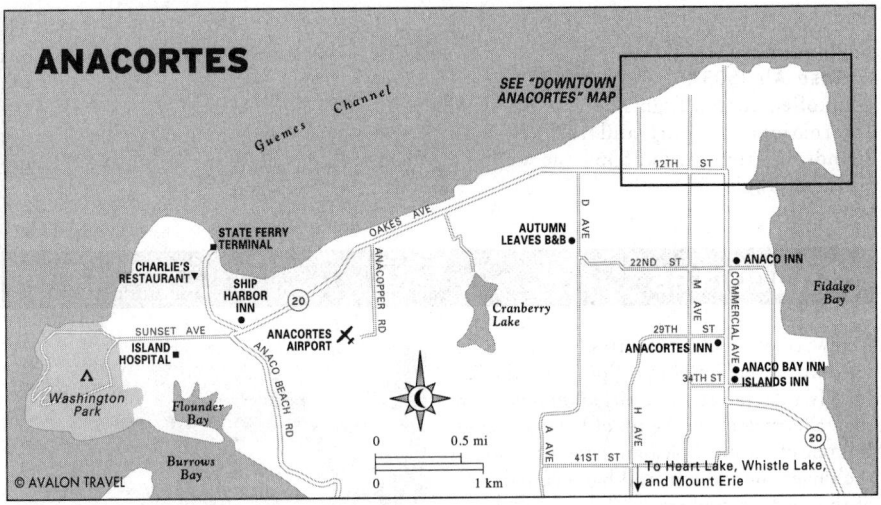

Street and N Avenue; its colorful and playfully ornate mosaic walls and gazebo were built in 1920 with stones from area islands. Also here is a small amphitheater. Nearby are a number of 1890s homes and buildings, many restored to their original splendor. The home owned and built by Amos and Anna Curtis Bowman in 1891 stands at 1815 8th Street; at 807 4th Street, an architect's office is now housed in what was probably the finest bordello in the county in the 1890s. The little church at 5th and R was built by its Presbyterian congregation in 1889; still in use is the Episcopal Church at 7th and M, built in 1896.

Viewpoints

Five miles south of downtown Anacortes, 1,270-foot **Mt. Erie** is the tallest "mountain" on Fidalgo Island. The steep and winding road leads 1.5 miles to a partially wooded summit, where four short trails lead to dizzying views of the Olympics, Mt. Baker, Mt. Rainier, and Puget Sound. Don't miss the two lower overlooks, located a quarter mile downhill from the summit. Get to Mt. Erie by following Heart Lake Road south from town, past Heart Lake to the signed turnoff at Mount Erie Road. Trails lead from various points along Mount Erie Road into other parts of Anacortes Community Forest Lands.

For an impressive, low-elevation viewpoint of the Cascades and Skagit Valley, visit **Cap Sante Park** on the city's east side, following 4th Street to West Avenue. Scramble up the boulders for a better look at Mt. Baker, the San Juans, and the Anacortes refineries that turn Alaskan oil into gasoline. Not far away, a short trail leads to **Rotary Park** next to Cap Sante Marina, where you'll find picnic tables overlooking the busy harbor.

Washington Park

Three miles west of downtown Anacortes, Washington Park is a strikingly beautiful picnic spot with 200 waterfront acres on Rosario Strait affording views of the San Juans and Olympics. Walk, bike, or drive the 2.3-mile paved scenic loop, and pull into one of many waterfront picnic areas. Other facilities include a popular boat launch, several miles of hiking trails offering views of the San Juans and the Olympics, a playground, and crowded campsites. The original park acreage was donated by one of Fidalgo Island's earliest pioneers, Tonjes Havekost, who said, "Make my cemetery a park for everybody." His grave stands on

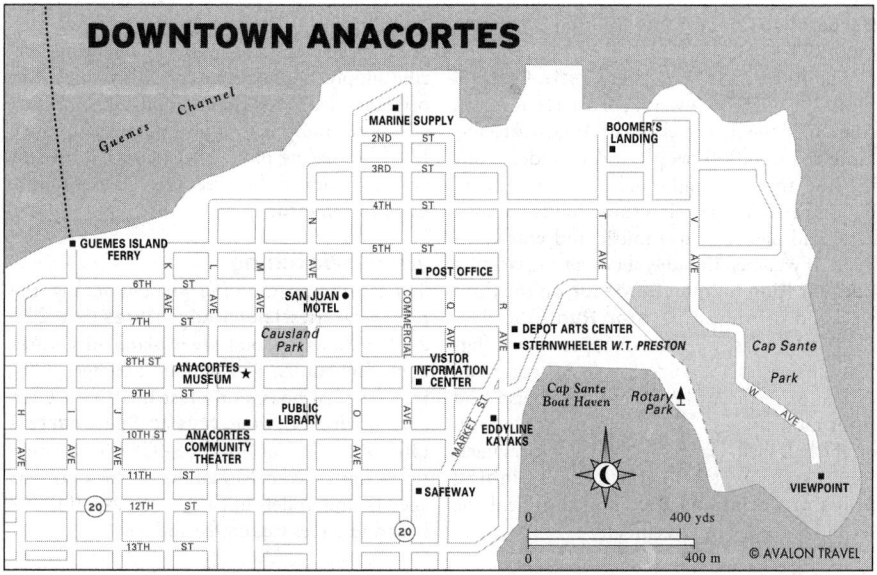

the southern edge of the park, overlooking Burrows Channel. Additional acreage was bought by the Anacortes Women's Club in 1922 with proceeds from the sale of lemon pies—they paid just $2,500 for 75 beachfront acres.

ENTERTAINMENT AND EVENTS

Nightlife

Find live music on Friday and Saturday nights at three downtown bars, all of which share an $8 cover charge: **Rockfish Grill & Anacortes Brewery** (320 Commercial Ave., 360/293-3666, www.anacortesrockfish.com), **Brown Lantern Ale House** (412 Commercial Ave., 360/293-2544, www.brownlantern.com), and **Watertown Pub** (314 Commercial Ave., 360/293-3587).

The Arts

Depot Arts Center (7th St. and R Ave., 360/293-3663) houses a gallery that showcases local artists. It's adjacent to the historic *W. T. Preston* ship. Anacortes also has a number of forgettable downtown galleries.

The **Anacortes Community Theatre** (10th St. and M Ave., 360/293-6829) stages plays and musicals, plus annual Christmas performances. The **Vela Luka Croatian Dancers** (www.velaluka.org) is a local group that performs all over the world. This is the most obvious example of Anacortes' strong Croatian community; it's claimed that a quarter of local residents are of Croatian descent.

Meet regional authors during book and poetry readings at the excellent **Watermark Book Co.** (612 Commercial Ave., 360/293-4277 or 800/291-4277).

Festivals and Events

The **Anacortes Waterfront Festival,** (www.anacortes.org) held at Cap Sante Boat Haven the weekend before Memorial Day each May, celebrates the city's maritime heritage with a food court and beer garden, craft booths, farmers and seafood markets, boat show and regatta, and art show.

Anacortes, like every other town in America, has a parade and fireworks on the **4th of July.** The last weekend in July brings the self-explanatory **An-O-Chords Annual**

Barbershop Concert and Salmon Barbecue (360/293-1282).

The **Anacortes Arts and Crafts Festival** (360/293-6211, www.anacortesarts festival.com), held the first weekend of August, attracts more than 50,000 people and includes a juried fine-art show, high-quality arts and crafts booths, a children's fair, ethnic foods, antique cars, and plenty of live music and entertainment. If you miss this one, shoot for the **World's Largest King Salmon Barbecue** on the third weekend of August. **Oyster Run** (360/757-1515) on the last weekend of September brings more than 6,000 motorcyclists to Anacortes; it's a great place for leather lovers. You'll also find stunt motorcyclists, a beer garden, and oysters on the half shell. Catch the holiday spirit, Puget-sound style: Watch for the annual **Lighted Ships of Christmas Boat Parade,** held the second Saturday in December.

Gambling

Swinomish Northern Lights Casino & Bingo (360/293-2691 or 800/877-7529, www.swinomishcasino.com) has gambling—including bingo, craps, roulette, blackjack, poker, and Sic Bo—at its casino just across the Highway 20 bridge on Fidalgo Island. A gift shop here sells native arts and crafts, the cabaret has live music, and the restaurant features a seafood and prime rib buffet.

SPORTS AND RECREATION

Boating

Anacortes is home to the largest concentrations of bareboat charters in North America; get a list from the visitors center (360/293-3832, www.anacortes.org). The sea kayak manufacturer Eddyline has a factory in nearby Burlington. Learn about kayaking at the **Eddyline Watersports Center** (1019 Q Ave., 360/299-2300 or 866/445-7506, www.eddyline.com) along the Anacortes marina. You can take boats out for a test paddle, rent a kayak, try on the high-tech clothing, or join classes or tours.

Founded in 1913, **Marine Supply & Hardware Co.** (2nd St. and Commercial Ave., 360/293-3014, www.marinesupplyhardware.com) is the oldest continuously operating marine supply store west of the Mississippi. The original oiled wood floors and oak cabinets are still here, along with a potpourri of supplies. It's a fascinating place to visit, with a friendly cat. Right across the street is the large **Dakota Creek Shipyard.**

Whale-Watching

Two local companies offer whale-watching trips from Anacortes. **Island Adventures** (360/293-2428 or 800/465-4604, www.island-adventures.com, $69 adults, $64 seniors, $49 ages 3–17, free for tots) boasts of a fast boat with guaranteed whale viewing. **Mystic Sea Charters** (360/466-3042 or 800/308-9387, www.mysticseacharters.com, $79 adults, $69 seniors, $49 ages 17 and under) has a comfortable 100-foot boat and serves free coffee and tea.

Hiking

Stop by the Anacortes visitors center for a guide to trails within the 2,200-acre **Anacortes Community Forest Lands** around Mt. Erie and Cranberry, Whistle, and Heart Lakes. More than 25 miles of trails are here, with mileage, elevation, and highlights. Many of these paths can be linked into loop hikes for folks of varying physical ability.

The 3.5-mile **Whistle Lake Shore Loop** circles this small body of water, offering water views, lots of birdlife, and old-growth stands of Douglas fir and cedar. An easy and almost-level path is the **Erie View Trail,** which departs from Heart Lake Road and follows a seasonal creek to a fine view of Mt. Erie a mile out.

From the trailhead at the intersection of Mount Erie and Heart Lake Roads, hike the half-mile **Pine Ridge Loop Trail** for more views of Mt. Erie and Sugarloaf. This moderately difficult hike takes from one to two hours. Another short hike is the 1.6-mile **Sugarloaf Trail,** starting on Ray Auld Drive six miles from its intersection with Heart Lake Road. Follow the trail from the marshy trailhead straight up, ignoring side trails, to views to the west of Port Townsend, the San Juan

Islands, and the Strait of Juan de Fuca, and north to Bellingham.

The Cranberry Lake area also has a number of hiking paths, including the mile-long **John M. Morrison Loop Trail,** which starts at the end of 29th Street. This easy loop hike provides bluff-top views of Cranberry Lake and old-growth Douglas fir forests, where some trees are seven feet wide.

Camping

Three miles west of Anacortes, the city-run **Washington Park** (360/293-1918, $12 tents, $15 RVs) has crowded campsites in the woods, with showers and boat launches. No reservations are accepted. Two popular state parks with campsites are within 20 miles of Anacortes: Deception Pass State Park near Oak Harbor and Bay View State Park near Mount Vernon.

Park RVs at **Fidalgo Bay Resort** (1107 Fidalgo Bay Rd., 360/293-5353 or 800/727-5478, www.fidalgobay.com), **Lighthouse RV Park** (1900 Skyline Way, 360/293-3344), or **Pioneer Trails Campground** (527 Miller Rd., 360/293-5355 or 888/777-5355, www.pioneer-trails.com). Pioneer Trails even has covered wagons for family camping.

Other Recreation

Pioneer Trails Campground (527 Miller Rd., 360/293-5355 or 888/777-5355, www.pioneer-trails.com) has horseback riding, camping, and other family adventures.

Similk Beach Golf Course (360/293-3444) has a nine-hole course with Puget Sound vistas.

Swim at the public **Fidalgo Pool and Fitness Center** (1603 22nd St., 360/293-0673, www.fidalgo.net/~pool).

ACCOMMODATIONS

Anacortes is natural place to rest your head before or after a long haul on the ferries across the San Juans. It is also an excellent base camp for families and young travelers sticking to a budget—rooms are significantly less expensive than on San Juan, Orcas, or Lopez, and all the islands are within easy reach for a day trip. Make reservations far ahead for the summer months; some places fill up by March for the peak season in July and August.

Under $100

Lake Campbell Motel (1377 Hwy. 20, 360/293-5314, $55–105 s or d) is four miles south of Anacortes along Lake Campbell. This is a good family place with microwaves and fridges in all the rooms; the more expensive ones contain full kitchens.

San Juan Motel (1103 6th St., 360/293-5105 or 800/533-8009, $55 s or $61 d, kitchenettes $65 s or $74 d) is a centrally located, clean place.

Anacortes Inn (3006 Commercial Ave., 360/293-3153 or 800/327-7976, www.anacortesinn.com, $90 s or d, suites $93–128) has rooms with fridges and microwaves, plus a seasonal outdoor pool.

Islands Inn (3401 Commercial Ave., 360/293-4644 or 866/331-3328, www.islandsinn.com, $79–89 d) has 36 comfortable motel rooms and suites ($140 d) with fireplaces, wet bars, and jetted tubs. An outdoor pool and hot tub are on the premises, and La Petite Restaurant offers gourmet dining, plus a complimentary Dutch breakfast. The owner is from Amsterdam.

$100-150

Anaco Inn (905 20th St., 360/293-8833 or 888/293-8833, www.anacoinn.com) is a well-kept, newer place where standard rooms are $89 s or d, those with jetted tubs and kitchens cost $104–139 d, and apartment units run $149 d. A hot tub is available, and a full breakfast is included.

With large rooms, an outdoor pool, hot tub, and continental breakfast, **Fidalgo Country Inn** (1250 Hwy. 20, 360/293-3494 or 800/244-4179, www.nwcountryinns.com, $109 d) is located on the outskirts of town, convenient for those who would like to visit both Anacortes and La Conner. Larger suites with kitchenette, fireplace, and jetted tub are available for $159 d.

Anyone heading out to the San Juans by ferry should consider the homey **Ship Harbor Inn** (5316 Ferry Terminal Rd., 360/293-5177 or 800/852-8568 (U.S.) or 800/235-8568 (Canada), www.shipharborinn.com), located near the ferry terminal. It is quiet and peaceful, with clean rooms ($109 d), cottages ($129 d) with kitchenettes and fireplaces, and a several hot tub suites ($159–179 d). There's even a petting zoo with miniature horses, goats, and a donkey. This place is recommended.

$150-200

Autumn Leaves B&B (2301 21st St., 360/293-4920, www.autumn-leaves.com, $155–175 d,) is a contemporary home with three romantic guest rooms furnished with French antiques. Rates include a gourmet breakfast. No kids under 12 are allowed.

FOOD

Cafés and Delis

Start your day at **Calico Cupboard Café & Bakery** (901 Commercial Ave., 360/293-7315, 7:30 A.M.–3 P.M. daily) for great homemade country breakfasts and healthy lunches. Save room for dessert: The fudge pecan pie and apple dumplings are legendary. Get there early on weekends, or be ready for a wait.

Let your nose lead you to **La Vie en Rose French Bakery** (418 Commercial Ave., 360/299-9546, www.laviebakery.com, 7:30 A.M.–5:30 P.M. Mon.–Fri., 8 A.M.–5:30 P.M. Sat., closed Sun. except in July and Aug. when open 10 A.M.–4 P.M.) which bakes warm French pastries and breads, while stirring up delicious soups and sandwiches for lunch. If you're heading out on the ferry, have them put together a box lunch special.

For food with a side of sass, stop by **Gere-a-Deli** (502 Commercial Ave., 360/293-7383, www.gere-a-deli.com, 7 A.M.–4 P.M. Mon.–Sat., closed Sun.). This funky little eatery offers cleverly named (and tasty) sandwiches, salads, soups, and homemade desserts. Munch away while enjoying the antique signs and advertisements lining the walls here.

Seafood

Over at the ferry terminal, **Charlie's Restaurant** (360/293-7377, 11:30 A.M.–8:30 P.M. daily) is the most convenient place to stop for a drink while you're waiting for your ship to come in. The dining room has moderately priced seafood, plus steaks and pasta.

If your palate seeks something a bit more sophisticated and you have a bit more time to spare, try **Randy's Pier 61** (209 T Ave., 360/293-5108, 11:30 A.M.–9 P.M. daily, $22), on the waterfront, is a fine seafood restaurant with vistas of Guemes Channel. The Sunday brunch is a favorite of locals.

Contemporary

One might not expect it in the ho-hum hamlet of Anacortes, but there are actually two hip restaurants in town that could easily compete with most of the fashionable restaurants in Seattle.

Better of the two is **Adrift** (510 Commercial Ave., 360/588-0653, www.adrift-restaurant.com, 8 A.M.–10 P.M. Mon.–Sat., closed Sun.). Driftwood furniture and local art accent the interior here, fostering an inviting dining place with a cozy nautical theme that celebrates Anacortes' roots. The menu relies on fresh greens, seafood, poultry, and steaks, cooked up with a bit of international flair. On the seasonal dinner menu you're as likely to find Cuban pork sandwiches or Vietnamese chicken burgers as cioppino or steak. Adrift also serves hearty breakfasts and fresh lunches.

The trendy digs at **Star Bar Café** (416 Commercial Ave., 360/299-2120, www.Starbaranacortes.com, 5–9:30 P.M. Tues.–Sat., lounge opens at 3 P.M.) serve as the mood enhancer for the seasonal salads, fresh seafood, and world fusion cuisine.

Pub Grub

You won't go wrong with a lunch or dinner at **Rockfish Grill & Anacortes Brewery** (320 Commercial Ave., 360/588-1720, www.anacortesrockfish.com, 11:30 A.M.–10 P.M. Sun.–Thurs., 11:30 A.M.–midnight Fri.–Sat., $15). Choices include seafood, pastas, wood-fired pizzas, and fresh ales from the on-the-premises brewery. Just down the street is **Brown Lantern Ale House** (412 Commercial Ave., 360/293-2544, www.brownlantern.com, 11 A.M.–9 P.M. Sun.–Wed., 11 A.M.–10 P.M. Thurs.–Sat., $10), where the burgers and halibut fish and chips are noteworthy and the classic pool table sees plenty of action.

Markets

Get groceries at the big **Food Pavilion** store (1519 Commercial Ave., 360/588-8181). Get smoked salmon and other treats from **Seabear Smokehouse** (30th St. and T Ave., 360/293-4661 or 800/645-3474, www.seabear.com). There are free tours daily in the summer, plus a mail-order catalog.

The **Anacortes Farmers Market** (7th St. and R Ave., 360/293-9404) takes place 9 A.M.–2 P.M. Saturday from mid-May to mid-October.

INFORMATION AND SERVICES

For maps, brochures, and up-to-date information, drop by the **Anacortes Visitor Information Center** (819 Commercial Ave., 360/293-3832, www.anacortes.org, 9 A.M.–5 P.M. daily May to mid-Sept., 9 A.M.–5 P.M. Mon.–Fri., 10 A.M.–3 P.M. Sat., noon–3 P.M. Sun. the rest of the year). Across the street is a mural of Anna Curtis, for whom the town was named. The *Anacortes American* newspaper's website, www.goanacortes.com, is another useful place for local information and links.

GETTING THERE AND AROUND

By Ferry

To reach the San Juan Islands or British Columbia via **Washington State Ferry** (206/464-6400, www.wsdot.wa.gov/ferries), you have no choice but to leave from Anacortes. Be prepared for a lengthy wait on summer weekends. Avoid the waits by leaving your car in the lot at the terminal ($25 for three days) and walking aboard; there's always space for walk-on passengers. A free park-and-ride lot is located at March Point eight miles east of here, and a shuttle bus transports you to the ferry terminal.

Island Transport Ferry System (360/293-6060) is a fast catamaran that delivers people, kayaks, and camping gear anywhere on the San Juans at an hourly rate. It's useful for families and small groups looking to get off the main ferry routes quickly.

By Air

Departing from Anacortes Airport, **San Juan Airlines** (360/293-4691 or 800/874-4434, www.sanjuanairlines.com) offers commuter flights year-round to all three major islands.

By Bus

Skagit Transit (360/299-2424, www.skat.org) has daily bus connections from Anacortes to Mt. Vernon, La Conner, and other parts of Skagit County. **Airporter Shuttle** (360/380-8800 or 800/235-5247, www.airporter.com) offers daily shuttles between Anacortes and Sea-Tac Airport.

San Juan Island

The largest island in the archipelago, San Juan Island is about 20 miles long and seven miles wide, covering 55 square miles. Picturesque Friday Harbor sits along the west side, its marina protected by Brown Island. Acting as the county seat, Friday Harbor is the only incorporated town in the islands and is the commercial center of the San Juans. It is a U.S. Customs port of entry, as is Roche Harbor on the other side of the island.

SIGHTS

San Juan Island National Historical Park

In one of the stranger pieces of history, the killing of a pig by an American settler nearly set off a war between the U.S. and Britain; see the sidebar *The Pig War* for details on this bizarre incident. Fortunately, conflict was averted and the San Juan Islands were eventually declared American territory.

The sites where the American and British forces were based during the peaceful standoff are now part of the San Juan Island National Historical Park (headquarters on Spring St. in **Friday Harbor,** 360/378-2240, www.nps.gov/sajh, 8:30 A.M.–5 P.M. daily Memorial Day through Labor Day, 8:30 A.M.–4:30 P.M. Mon.–Fri. the rest of the year). Summertime activities include guided historical walks at 11:30 A.M. Thursday–Sunday and living history exhibitions 12:30–3:30 P.M. on Saturday. The office houses a small exhibit about the Pig War. The park itself is in two sections on different ends of the island: American Camp and English Camp. Both sites have picnic areas and beach access for day use only, with no campgrounds. The grounds are open year-round.

AMERICAN CAMP

Located on the southeast corner of San Juan Island, American Camp sits on a windswept

© ERICKA CHICKOWSKI

visiting with the alpacas at Krystal Acres Farm

THE PIG WAR

San Juan Island on the northern edge of the Puget Sound is the site of one of the weirdest international incidents in American history. Two nations, confirmed adversaries, squared off for armed confrontation on this tiny island in 1859. Sloops of war sailed into harbor and positioned their guns. Camps were built and battle lines were drawn. Soldiers drilled in the rain and prepared for battle. Their cause? A British pig that couldn't be kept from eating American potatoes.

As Americans moved west along the Oregon Trail and settled in Washington, the British started to get cagey about the new residents in the area. The existing law of the land had called for joint occupation by Americans and British, a right that the Hudson's Bay Company had taken full advantage of, conducting trapping and trading operations throughout the Northwest. This arrangement had outlived its usefulness, however, and both sides met in 1849 to thresh out a more permanent solution. The resulting Oregon Treaty set a boundary formalizing U.S. and British land claims. Unfortunately, ambiguity in the wording of the treaty left it unclear who exactly owned San Juan Island. Both sides claimed sovereignty, and Hudson's Bay built a large sheep ranch here, while 25 or so Americans also settled in to farming the opposite side of the island.

This uneasy peace was soon to be disturbed by a pig in Her Majesty's service. The pig, which belonged to the Hudson's Bay Company, was fond of straying into American settler Lyman Cutlar's farm and sampling his crops. Numerous petitions to the company brought no solution, and in June of 1859, a frustrated Cutlar shot and killed the pig. This outrage led to both sides pleading for military intervention; in short order, both sides got their wish. An armed standoff ensued, although few probably imagined that this drizzly cold war would ultimately last 12 years. British Royal Marines established a base at English Camp on the northern shore of the island, while the Americans fortified the southern tip, known as American Camp. Each force's orders were the same: Return fire if fired upon, but do not initiate attack.

Tensions waxed and waned as Americans were distracted by the Civil War and troubles elsewhere. During this time, it's said that both sides enjoyed fairly cordial relations, visiting each other's camps and playing against one another in sporting events. If any other livestock got out of line during this period, it went unrecorded. Finally in 1872, the dispute was submitted for arbitration to Germany's Kaiser Wilhelm I, who ruled in favor of the Americans. The British withdrew soon afterward, pigs and all, just barely having prevented what might have been one of the silliest wars in history.

grassy peninsula six miles from Friday Harbor. This is a wonderful place on a sunny summer afternoon, with both the Cascades and Olympics in view. It's also a satisfyingly lonely place to explore on a rainy winter day.

Two buildings remain at American Camp—an officers' quarters and a laundresses' quarters—along with a defensive fortification (redoubt) constructed by Henry M. Roberts of *Roberts' Rules of Order* fame. A long white picket fence circles the grounds, and a trail leads downhill past the old Hudson's Bay Company Farm site on Grandma's Cove. Other nature trails take off to Mt. Finlayson (hardly a mountain at just 290 feet) and through the forests along **Jackle's Lagoon,** or you can explore driftwood-jammed **South Beach,** a wonderful place for a sunset walk on the sandy shores. This is the longest public beach on the island. The park is also home to thousands of rabbits whose ancestors were brought to the islands as a food source, but the inevitable happened and they keep multiplying. Birders come to American Camp to see the only nesting **Eurasian skylarks** in the United States; they were introduced to Vancouver Island early in the 1900s and a small number ended up here.

The **American Camp Visitor Center** is

open 8 A.M.–5 P.M. daily in the summer, and 8:30 A.M.–4:30 P.M. Thurs.–Sun. in winter. It houses historical exhibits.

At the tip of the peninsula is **Cattle Point Interpretive Area,** where you'll find a picnic shelter in an old powerhouse, and trails to a nearby lighthouse and beach.

ENGLISH CAMP

Ten miles from Friday Harbor on the northwest side of the island, English Camp (also known as British Camp) includes a restored hospital, a picturesque reconstructed blockhouse right on the water's edge, a commissary, an impressive formal garden, and a small white barracks. The blockhouse and barracks are open 8:30 A.M.–4:30 P.M. daily in the summer, closed the rest of the year. The location is a beautiful one, with protected waters on both sides of Bell Point—a sharp contrast to American Camp—and spreading maple trees overhead. The mile-long **Mt. Young Trail** leads from English Camp to the old British cemetery where six Royal Marines are buried, and then up through second-growth forests to 650-foot Mt. Young with fine vistas of the archipelago from the top. An almost-level nature path heads a mile out to the tip of **Bell Point.**

Museums

The Whale Museum (62 1st St. N in Friday Harbor, 360/378-4710 or 800/946-7227, www.whalemuseum.org, 10 A.M.–5 P.M. daily, $6 adults, $5 seniors, $3 ages 5–18 and students, free for kids under 5) has whale and porpoise displays including the genealogy of Puget Sound orcas and full skeletons of a baby gray whale, plus adult killer and minke whales. Watch a fine video on orcas, examine whale fetuses, and learn about snoring whales, echolocation, and how they mate. You can also "adopt" one of the 80 or so local orcas. There's also a gift shop in the museum with games, T-shirts, and jewelry. If you spot a whale anywhere around the San Juans, swimming or stranded, call the museum's 24-hour **Whale Hotline** at 800/562-8832. The museum posts hotline reports on its website.

The small, privately run **Pig War Museum** (Tucker and Guard Sts., 360/378-6495, 1–6 P.M. Wed.–Sat. Memorial Day through Labor Day, $5 adults, $4 seniors, $3 students, free for kids under 5). The museum is a bit odd and the exhibits are clearly done on a budget.

San Juan Historical Museum (405 Price St., Friday Harbor, 360/378-3949, www.sjmuseum.org, 10 A.M.–4 P.M. Thurs.–Sat. and 1–4 P.M. Sun. May–Sept., 1–4 P.M. Sat. in October, March, and April, closed the rest of the year, $2 adults, $1 ages 6–18, free for kids under 5). Housed in an 1890s farmhouse, the museum includes fascinating antiques, old photos, and historical artifacts, plus old farm equipment outside. Also on the property are the first county jail, a log cabin, and other historic buildings.

Krystal Acres Farm

If you're out for a cruise or a bike ride through the middle of the island, be sure to take a break at Krystal Acres Farm (152 Blazing Tree Rd., 360/378-6125, www.krystalacres.com), an alpaca ranch with lovely grounds and lightly bleating beauties grazing the pastures. Step inside to check out the woolen wares made from alpaca fur, which makes for some of the softest scarves and sweaters on the planet.

Roche Harbor

Located on the north end of San Juan Island, Roche Harbor (360/378-2155 or 800/451-8910, www.rocheharbor.com) is a delicious step into the past. In 1886, John S. McMillin established the Roche Harbor Lime & Cement Co., mining lime deposits from 13 hillside quarries and processing the lime in brick-lined kilns along the shore. By the 1890s this was the largest lime works west of the Mississippi and required 4,000 acres of forest just to keep the kilns running. McMillin built a company town for his employees, had warehouses that extended hundreds of feet into the bay, and operated a general store on the wharf. His **Hotel de Haro** began as a log bunkhouse but later grew into the distinctive three-story

THE LIME WORKS OF SAN JUAN ISLAND

Mention a trip to the San Juan Islands and thoughts come to mind of whale-watching, shopping, leisurely bike rides, or just relaxing by the water. And while San Juan Island has always been a bit of a resort town, in the distant past, it was also a home of industry. Take a walk around the grounds of the historic Hotel De Haro in Roche Harbor, and you absolutely cannot miss the lime works. These high-reaching ovens were once used to heat limestone until calcium oxide was formed, a process called calcining. The calcium oxide, or quicklime, was critical for whitewash, mortar, and plaster. By the 1930s, most of the pure limestone deposits had been depleted; that, coupled with diminishing demand, ended lime's 60-year dominance on the island forever. Today, you can still visit the lime works at the Hotel de Haro, or look out for orcas from another former hub of industry, Lime Kiln Park.

wood structure of today. McMillin's home is now a waterside restaurant, facing the protected harbor filled with sailboats.

Take some time to explore the area around the hotel (now on the National Register of Historic Places) and the little New England–style **Our Lady of Good Voyage Chapel,** built in 1892, and the only privately owned Catholic church in the nation. The bizarre family **mausoleum** (named "Afterglow Vista," no less) is approximately a mile from the hotel. Located north of the cottages and a quarter-mile hike up a dirt side road, the mausoleum's centerpiece is a stone temple packed with Masonic symbols and containing the family's ashes in chairs around a limestone table. There's even a broken column symbolizing the "unfinished state" of life, but the planned bronze dome was never added to this once-grandiose mausoleum. Pick up a brochure describing the mausoleum inside Hotel de Haro.

Wescott Bay Sculpture Park

As you approach Roche Harbor, it is pretty hard to miss the Wescott Bay Sculpture Park (across from the Roche Harbor Airstrip on Roche Harbor Road, dawn to dusk daily, free). This unique outdoor museum and promenade displays over 100 unique pieces of art on a 19-acre natural preserve. Art often changes with the seasons, featuring work in wood, ceramic, metal, glass, and stone. Nature lovers will also appreciate the interpretive displays scattered across the trails, which cross over freshwater and saltwater wetlands, forests, and meadows. The park is open rain or shine, with free umbrellas for use at the entrance gatehouse.

Lime Kiln Point State Park

A good spot to watch for whales is from Lime Kiln Point State Park (www.parks.wa.gov.) along Haro Strait on the island's west side; it's the only park in the country dedicated exclusively to whale-watching. Sit here long enough on a summer day (it may be quite a while) and you're likely to see killer whales (orcas), and possibly minke and pilot whales, Dall's porpoises, or harbor porpoises. Rangers are usually at the park in the summer and fall and can answer your questions. The small white lighthouse was built in 1914 and has a foghorn that announces its presence frequently. Researchers use the lighthouse to watch for whales and to determine if boats are affecting their behavior. If there aren't any whales to watch, you can just take in the vistas that stretch to Victoria. No camping is available at the park.

Bald eagles live on the island year-round; look for them between Eagle Cove and Cattle Point on the island's east side.

ENTERTAINMENT AND EVENTS

Nightlife

China Pearl (51 Spring St., 360/378-5551) has music and dancing on weekends. **Bella Luna** (175 1st St., 360/378-4118) serves up

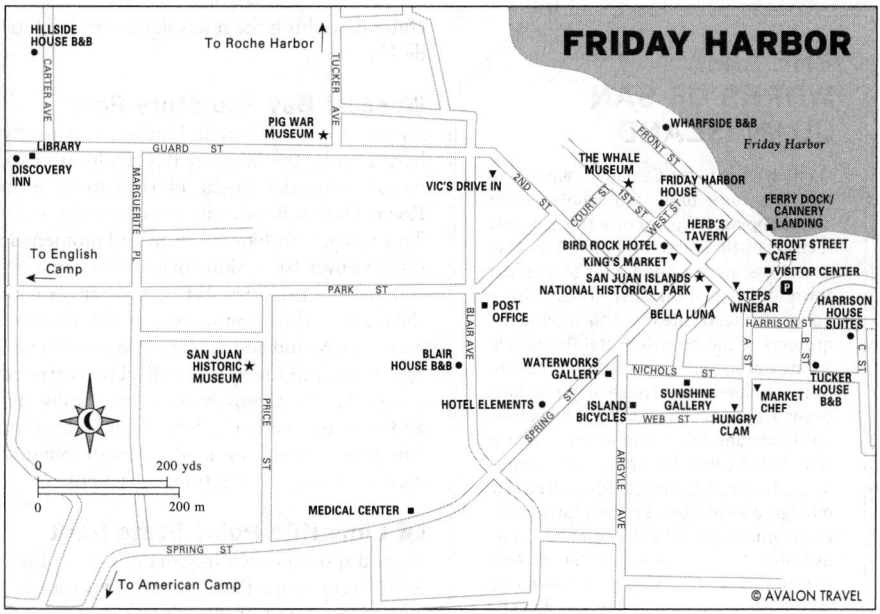

jazz dinner tunes on Sunday and Wednesday evenings. Come summertime, **Front St. Ale House** offers a full slate of live music on the weekends. The bar also hosts a quiz night at 7 P.M. Thursday throughout the year.

For a friendly game of pool and some chit-chat with the locals, pop into **Herb's Tavern** (80 1st St., 360/378-7076).

The Arts

THEATER

The impressive **San Juan Community Theatre & Arts Center** (100 2nd St., 360/378-3211, www.sanjuanarts.org) is the center for local performing arts, with year-round musical programs and plays. Watch first-run films at **Royal Theatre** (209 Spring St., 360/378-4455).

GALLERIES

Friday Harbor is home to several excellent art galleries, including **Waterworks Gallery** (315 Argyle, 360/378-3060, www.waterworksgallery.com, 10 A.M.–6 P.M. Mon.–Sat., 11 A.M.–4 P.M. Sun.), a large, contemporary gallery with impressive paintings, prints, watercolors, and sculpture by island and international artists. **Sunshine Gallery** (85 Nichols St., 360/378-5819, 10:30 A.M.–5:30 P.M. Wed.–Mon., closed Tues.) is a cooperatively run place selling quality local artwork. **The Garuda & I** (60 1st St., 360/378-3733, www.thegarudaandi.com, 10 A.M.–5:30 P.M. Mon.–Sat., 11 A.M.–3 P.M. Sun.) is a unique gallery with ethnic artifacts, beautiful jewelry, and a large cage filled with chirping zebra finches. Also of note is **Rainshadow Arts Gallery** (20 1st St. N, 360/378-0988, www.rainshadow-arts.com) with photography, prints, and other works of art. **Island Studios** (270 Spring St., 360/378-6550, www.island-studios.com) features work from more than 90 local artists, including paintings, stained glass, jewelry, pottery, and more.

Festivals and Events

In mid-May, the **Return of the Orcas Festival** (360/378-5240) brings kayak races, art booths, children's games, and music to Roche Harbor. A popular **Summer Arts Fair** on the third weekend of July includes art exhibits, food booths, and live music.

The **4th of July** brings a variety of fun events, including a parade, pig barbecue contests with celebrity judges, a 10K race, music, dancing, and evening fireworks over Friday Harbor. (The best local 4th of July fireworks, however, are over at Roche Harbor Village.)

The four-day **San Juan County Fair** (360/378-4310, www.sanjuancountyfair.org) in mid-August features a sheep-to-shawl race, chicken and rabbit races, music, livestock judging, and, of course, carnival rides. Each **Memorial Day,** Friday Harbor has a popular parade with speeches. **Oktoberfest** comes to the fairgrounds in early October, with polka music and dancing, along with German beer and food.

Wine-Tasting

San Juan Vineyards (360/378-9463 or 888/983-9463, www.sanjuanvineyards.com) is housed in a century-old schoolhouse three miles out Roche Harbor Road. It produces a limited bottling of wines from the vineyard here, but most of its wine comes from eastern Washington grapes. Stop by for wine-tasting noon–6 P.M. daily.

There are no vineyards at **The Island Wine Company** (next to the ferry dock in Friday Harbor, 360/378-3229 or 800/248-9463, www.sanjuancellars.com, 10 A.M.–6 P.M. daily), but you can sample wines made from eastern Washington grapes and bottled under its San Juan Cellars label.

One of the best places to swirl a few glasses of vino under your nose is **Steps Winebar** (140 A 1st St., Friday Harbor, 360/370-5959, www.stepswinebarandcafe.com). This elegant restaurant and bar offers some of the best selections of wine on any of the islands, and expert staff are on hand to offer great pairing suggestions for the restaurant's creative menu. Check ahead for special seasonal dinners with selected wine pairings.

SHOPPING

Bookstores

Friday Harbor has three good places to buy new books: **Boardwalk Books** (upstairs from Front St. Café, 360/378-2787, 9 A.M.–7 P.M. daily), **Griffin Bay Bookstore** (40 1st St., 360/378-5511, 9 A.M.–9 P.M. daily in summer, 9 A.M.–6 P.M. daily in winter), and the largest place in town, **Harbor Bookstore** (upstairs in Cannery Landing, 360/378-7222, 9 A.M.–7 P.M. daily in summer, 9 A.M.–5 P.M. daily in winter). Because I'm partial to well-loved books, my favorite bookstore on the island is **Serendipity Books** (at the top of the ferry lanes, 360/378-2665, 10 A.M.–5:30 P.M. daily), which offers used titles at good prices. The selection is fantastic, and titles are well organized.

SPORTS AND RECREATION

Bike and Moped Rentals

Although many folks bike around San Juan Island, it isn't as bike-friendly as slower-paced Lopez. Be ready for narrow roads and speeding cars.

Rent mountain bikes ($9 per hour, $36 per day), road bikes ($12 per hour, $48 per day) or even tandems ($18 per hour, $72 per day) to cruise around San Juan Island from **Island Bicycles** (380 Argyle St., 360/378-4941, www.islandbicycles.com).

Susie's Moped and Car Rentals (360/378-5244 or 800/532-0087, www.susiesmopeds.com, 9 A.M.–6 P.M. daily mid-Mar.–mid-Oct., $130-$150 per day) rents motor scooters in the summer from its two shops: one at the top of the ferry lanes in Friday Harbor and the other at the resort entrance in Roche Harbor.

Sea Kayaking

One of the best ways to soak up the sights of San Juan Island is to haul out of Friday Harbor or Roche Harbor in a sea kayak and paddle along the shoreline. Doing so can give you a good vantage point to check out the lighthouses, madronas, and neat rocky outcroppings of the coast. It can also put you in prime position to look for whales, particularly along their favorite stretch of waterway, Haro Strait, which passes along the west edge of the island.

Those with little to no experience paddling should definitely consider a guided tour, as currents and tides can be tricky in these parts. **Crystal Seas Kayaking** (360/378-7899 or 877/732-7877, www.crystalseas.com) offers a six- to nine-mile round-trip out of Snug Harbor resort for $89, which includes free transport from Friday Harbor. If you'd like to see the island washed aglow in the sunset, check out the sunset kayak trip offered by **Discover Sea Kayak** (360/378-2559 www.discoverseakayak.com), which leaves out of Friday Harbor and lasts about four hours. Discover also offers a longer day trip for the same price and full moon trips for $69. Another well-respected outfit is **San Juan Safaris** (360/378-1323 or 800/450-6858, www.sanjuansafaris.com), which offers three-hour tours out of Friday Harbor or Roche Harbor for $69. It also features five-hour Orca search tours out of either harbor for $85.

If you prefer to do it yourself without a guide, you can rent a sit-on-top kayak from San Juan Safaris from Roche Harbor, but you'll be limited to the protected waters around Roche Harbor and British Camp. The cost is $90 per day for a single and $108 per day for a double.

For a bit more freedom and better equipment, check out **San Juan Kayak Expeditions** (360/378-4436, www.sanjuankayak.com), which offers fiberglass kayaks for rent and advice on where to go and what to watch for while on the water. Cost is $90 for single-day rentals and $80 per day for multi-day rentals. This outfit also offers expeditions led by experienced guides.

Whale-Watching

Whale-watching has become a big business on the San Juans, particularly during June and July. Expect to pay around $50 for a three-hour trip.

The Puget Sound's resident pods of orca whales love the San Juans about as much as the tourists do. Their prime salmon hunting grounds are right around San Juan Island on Haro Strait, and it would be a shame to take a trip to the island without trying to spot these black-and-white beauties as they swim through their natural habitat. There are dozens of whale-watch tours and charters available. The best ones will provide a knowledgeable biologist or naturalist as a guide and should operate by the Whale Watch Operators Association Northwest guidelines, namely keeping at least 100 yards distance between the boat and the whales. Most services charge around $69 for a four-hour tour. One highly regarded service is **Maya's Whale Watch Charters** (360/378-7996, www.mayaswhalewatchbiz.com), run by the lovable Captain Jim Maya, a funny and knowledgeable guy whose clients rave about his tours.

If you've always wondered what whales sound like when they're talking to each other,

KILLER ANTICS

When you go out whale-watching in the San Juans or are hanging around Lime Kiln State Park, see if you can spot some orcas fooling around. These spirited creatures come above the water level quite frequently. Here's a guide to some of their favorite moves:

- **Spyhop:** That's when they peek out of the water with their head perpendicular to the waterline.
- **Breach:** Anytime an orca breaks the surface of the water, that's called breaching. If you're ever lucky enough to see one jump completely out of the water, count your blessings. Called a full breach, this is a rarity.
- **Lobtail:** This is when the whale sticks its tail completely out of the water, waving it like a fan.
- **Fin Slap:** Scientists don't quite know why they do it, but orcas frequently like to slap the water with their pectoral and dorsal fins.

climb aboard the *Odyssey,* a whale ship outfitted with a special underwater hydrophone to pick up the whales' chattering. Run by the folks at **San Juan Excursions** (800/809-4253, www.watchwhales.com,), the *Odyssey* takes off from Friday Harbor for four-hour whale-watching trips. This outfit also distinguishes itself with a whale-sighting guarantee—if you don't spot an orca, the next trip is on them. **San Juan Safaris** (360/378-1323 or 800/450-6858, www.sanjuansafaris.com) is another recommended company that also offers hydrophones, but it operates smaller boats with a more intimate guide experience.

Boat Charters, Sailing, and Fishing

As the forests of masts and rigging in Friday Harbor and Roche Harbor can attest, sailing and cruising is the preferred pastime on San Juan Island. If you don't have a boat of your own, there are a number of charter and cruise companies available to take you out on the water in style.

If you're looking to splurge, **Caramel Cruises** (360/378-9816 or 888/875-1774) offers three-hour afternoon sails aboard a 37-foot Hunter Legend sailboat for $384 per couple. Sunset sails, dinner cruises, and multi-day sails are also available.

Another fun (and more affordable) option for history buffs are the dinner cruises run by **Scamper Charters** (360/370-5133 or 877/314-3532, www.scampercharters.com) aboard the lovingly maintained 1920 wooden yacht *Scamper.* If you want more time to check the boat out, it is also available to charter for $100 per hour with a four-hour minimum.

For fishing and other boat charters from Friday Harbor, contact **Trophy Charters** (360/378-2110, www.fishthesanjuans.com) or **Buffalo Works** (360/378-4612).

Additional fishing charters—and day trips to Victoria—are available at **Roche Harbor Marina** (360/378-2155 or 800/451-8910, www.rocheharbor.com), the largest marina in the San Juans and a U.S. Customs port of entry for boaters coming in from Canada. Facilities here include permanent and guest moorage, showers and laundry, a store, restaurant, bar, and full-service resort. Motorboats, canoes, kayaks, and paddleboats are available for rent.

Diving

Locals claim that the San Juans offer the finest cold-water diving on earth, noting that Jacques Cousteau called them his second-favorite place to dive. When clear, one can glimpse a thriving ecosystem teeming with fish, amenomes, coral, starfish, octopi, and more. Let **Naknek Charters** (Spring St. Landing in Friday Harbor, 360/378-2772 or 800/303-8386, www.divesanjuan.com) show you around. This charter company offers dive trips off of its 45-foot boat, training, equipment, and scuba tank filling.

Camping

Pitch a tent at the 12-acre **San Juan County Park** (along West Side Rd., 360/378-8420, www.co.san-juan.wa.us/parks, $28–39), a mile north of Lime Kiln State Park. The 1998 film *Practical Magic* was filmed here. Because this is the only public campground on the island, you'll need to make advance reservations for the summer. Call 360/378-1842 for reservations ($8 fee) between six days and three months ahead of time. You may find space on a summer weekday, but weekends are usually fully reserved, especially in August. The park has a boat ramp and drinking water but no RV hookups.

Park that RV or pitch a tent at the spacious **Lakedale Resort** (2627 Roche Harbor Rd., 360/378-2350 or 800/617-2267, www.lakedale.com), which offers a good compromise to families divided between the nature enthusiasts and lovers of creature comforts. The platform canvas cabins at Lakedale offer a camplike setting without the necessity of sleeping on the hard ground. Equipped with queen-size beds and sleeper sofas, these luxury campsites go for $139 for two adults and two kids. This rate includes a continental breakfast served up at the nearby canvas Longhouse each morning.

Lakedale also offers traditional tent sites

($20–42) and RV sites ($57) on the property, plus boat, fishing equipment, and bike rentals to better explore the 82-acre property and its surrounding lakes. It's located near the center of the island, 4.5 miles from Friday Harbor, and is open mid-March to mid-October.

More campsites are available at **Snug Harbor Marina Resort** (1997 Mitchell Bay Rd., 360/378-4762, www.snugresort.com, $25) where you'll also find rentals of skiffs, fishing tackle, and crab pots. A small store has supplies and dive tank refills.

Coin-operated showers are available at the **Friday Harbor Marina** and **Roche Harbor Marina.**

Other Sports and Recreation

The **San Juan Golf & Country Club** (2261 Golf Course Rd., 360/378-2254, www.sanjuangolf.com, $24 Mar.–May, $28 Jun.–Oct.) is a nine-hole public course. Golf fanatics who don't care about cold weather might want to give the course a go November–February, when they can play unlimited holes for $15 during the week and $20 on weekends.

Fitness devotees might want to take advantage of one-day memberships at **San Juan Fitness and Athletic Club** (435 Argyle Ave., 360/378-4449, www.sanjuanislandfitness.com, 6 A.M.–8 P.M. Mon.–Fri., 9 A.M.–2 P.M. Sat., 11 A.M.–4 P.M. Sun.) For $17.77 you'll have access to the entire facility including racquetball, handball, and squash courts, classes and strength-training equipment, a sauna, steam room, hot tub, and juice bar.

ACCOMMODATIONS

During the summer it's a good idea to make reservations several months ahead of time to be assured of a bed, particularly on weekends. **San Juan Central Reservations** (360/378-8773 or 888/999-8773, www.vacationsanjuanisland.com) is a fine source for up-to-date lodging information. It makes reservations for dozens of local B&Bs, inns, resorts, and vacation homes.

Call the **Bed & Breakfast Association of San Juan Island** hotline (360/378-3030, www.san-juan-island.net) for availability at 25 or so of the finest local B&Bs; its website has links to B&B homepages.

Under $100

The only hostel on San Juan Island, **Wayfarers Rest** (35 Malcolm St., www.rockisland.com/~wayfarersrest) is in a comfortable home with a full kitchen just a short walk from downtown Friday Harbor. The 10-bed hostel has dorm room beds for $30 per person and private double rooms for $70. Kids are welcome.

Another cheap alternative in Friday Harbor is **Orca Inn** (700 Mullis St., 360/378-2724 or 877/541-6722, $84–99 d). Rooms are dated, but acceptably clean for the type of crowd that will spend most of their time out on the water anyway.

Go inland for one of the best deals on the island. **States Inn B&B** (360/378-6240, www.statesinn.com, $99–169 d) is a country home on a working ranch with sheep, chickens, and alpacas seven miles northwest of Friday Harbor. This welcoming bed-and-breakfast serves up fresh cookies in the afternoon and distinguishes itself as one of the only B&Bs on the island to offer several rooms for under $100 during peak summer months. All guest rooms have private baths. The inn caters to families and also offers a four-person cottage for $249 and a three-room suite for four for $229.

$100-150

Sitting right on the edge of Friday Harbor, the rooms at **Discovery Inn** (1016 Guard St., 360/378-2000 or 800/822-4753, www.discovery-inn.com, $129 d, $149 with kitchenette) aren't much to sing about, but the grounds do have attractive gardens, a cedar sauna, hot tub, and sundecks.

Out in the open fields near American Camp, **Olympic Lights B&B** (360/378-3186 or 888/211-6195, www.olympiclights.com, $145–155 s or d) offers a slice of solitude and serenity to its guests. This 1895 Victorian farmhouse has four guest rooms with private baths and is surrounded by pleasant grounds that showcase amazing views of the Olympic Mountains in the distance.

$150-200

A spacious contemporary home with seven guest rooms and private baths, **Hillside House B&B** (365 Carter Ave., Friday Harbor, 360/378-4730 or 800/232-4730, www.hillsidehouse.com, $125–275 d) is notable for its full-flight aviary and fine harbor views. The home sits on an acre of wooded land just a half mile from town.

A mile west of Friday Harbor, **Trumpeter Inn B&B** (318 Trumpeter Way, Friday Harbor, 360/378-3884 or 800/826-7926, www.trumpeterinn.com, $155–195 s or d) is set on five acres of pastoral land, complete with a tranquil pond. The showcase of the property is the lovingly tended garden featuring several varieties of lavender and a well-placed hot tub from which to soak it all in. The five guest rooms in this contemporary home have private baths, and the rate includes a sumptuous breakfast.

For a real waterfront room, **Wharfside B&B** (360/378-5661 or 800/899-3030, www.slowseason.com, $179 d) has two small staterooms aboard the gracious 60-foot sailing vessel *Jacquelyn,* docked at the Friday Harbor Marina. If you have the opportunity, splurge a little for the two-night cruise package. For $468 you'll get two nights and a morning cruise to nearby Seal Rock.

Those looking to stay closer to Roche Harbor and British Camp can consider **Wildwood Manor** (5335 Roche Harbor Rd., 360/378-3447 or 877/298-1144, www.wildwoodmanor.com, $199–265 d), a B&B in a large Queen Anne–style home atop a knoll above Roche Harbor, with a view across the water to British Columbia. The lavish modern home is surrounded by 11 acres of forests, and each of the four rooms follows the Victorian theme.

The sleek, modern interior of **Bird Rock Hotel** (35 1st St., 800/352-2632, www.birdrockhotel.com) contrasts nicely with the historic exterior of one of downtown Friday Harbor's oldest buildings. Dark woods and clean lines dominate the furnishings, which are highlighted with comfy pillow-top beds and big flat-screen TV monitors. A light breakfast can be brought directly to your room each morning or served in the downstairs salon, which is where you can also pick up the scrumptious cookies and lemonade served each afternoon. The smallest rooms with shared bathrooms go for $117–147 s or d, while standard rooms are $167–187 s or d. The superior suites are $217–287.

The charming **Hotel De Haro** (248 Reuben Memorial Dr., Roche Harbor, 360/378-2155) was built in 1886 and fronts a gracious formal garden and the harbor. The hotel's downstairs lobby is worth a look even if you aren't staying here, with historic photos and a big fireplace. Rates at the hotel start at $129 s or d for an old-fashioned room (bath down the hall and no TV) that faces the harbor, up to the presidential suite ($159 s or d) with its own fireplace and private bath. This one really is a presidential suite—Theodore Roosevelt slept here.

$200-250

Snug Harbor Resort (1997 Mitchell Bay Rd., 360/378-4762, www.snugresort.com) is a cozy resort along Mitchell Bay on the west side of the island. Choose from a variety of waterfront cabins for $169–229 d. Boat and kayak rentals are available, along with guided kayak trips and whale-watching trips.

I consider **Hotel Elements** (410 Spring St., Friday Harbor, 360/378-4000, www.hotelelements.com, $197–237 d) a very nice motel rather than a hotel per se. When rates are high in the summer, this place may seem a tad overpriced, but relative to the rest of the island it is pretty much on par and the maintenance and cleaning staff does an excellent job. Once you consider the indoor pool, hot tub, sauna, and fitness studio at this centrally located property, it is a decent value. The property also has a two-bedroom house on premises available for $387 per night.

Over $250

One of my favorite spots on the island is set by three small lakes near the center of San Juan

Island. **Lakedale Resort** (360/378-2350 or 800/617-2267, www.lakedale.com) features a number of accommodation options, starting with the well-appointed but still down-to-earth rooms in its lakeside lodge, which go for $249 d in high season. The resort also has six attractive two-bedroom lakeside log cabins with full kitchens and shared bath houses. Rates are $339 d (plus $35 per extra adult). Larger families and groups may also appreciate the three-bedroom Lake House ($439 for four), which features a greatroom with a fireplace, three bathrooms with Jacuzzi tubs, and a huge deck. Resort amenities include a hot tub, continental breakfast basket, rowboats, canoes, and paddleboats.

Right on the harborfront, **Friday Harbor House** (130 West St., 360/378-8455, www.fridayharborhouse.com) is a contemporary place with stylish rooms and suites for $250–360 s or d. All have fireplaces, whirlpool tubs, fridges, windows facing the harbor, and a continental breakfast. A two-night minimum is in effect on summer weekends.

One of the nicest bed-and-breakfast options in Friday Harbor is offered by sister properties **Harrison House Suites B&B** (235 C St., Friday Harbor, 360/378-5587 or 800/407-7933, www.harrisonhousesuites.com) and **Tucker House B&B** (260 B St., Friday Harbor, 360/378-2783 or 800/965-0123, www.tuckerhouse.com). Set side by side within easy walking distance of the ferry, these two establishments shine come morning, when the resident innkeepers serve up a dazzling multi-course meal sure to wow even the most experienced B&B veteran. Harrison House features five well-appointed suites (one is 1,600 square feet) for $185–375 and has hot tubs available for all guests. Tucker House offers a more traditional B&B experience in the rooms within its 1898 Victorian house ($125–225 s or d). It also has three cottages ($130–175 d) with private baths and woodstoves. Guests can use the hot tub, and kids are welcome in the cottages. Both Harrison House and Tucker House are pet-friendly.

Located on the west side of the island, **Highland Inn** (directions provided with reservation, 360/378-9450 or 888/400-9850, www.highlandinn.com) offers some of the finest lodging in the area, with two luxurious suites ($275 d), each with a king-size bed, steam showers, jetted tubs, and fireplace. A covered porch runs the length of the house, providing knock-your-socks-off views across Haro Strait; it's a great place to watch for orca whales, and a hot tub is on the grounds.

The classic 19th-century **Roche Harbor Village** (360/378-2155 or 800/451-8910, www.rocheharbor.com) at beautiful Roche Harbor offers a wide range of lodging options. Employees of the Roche Harbor Lime Company once occupied the rustic cottages, and all cottages have two bedrooms and full kitchens for $579–609 s or d. Also available are a number of condos, starting at $235 for one-bedroom units up to $350 for three-bedroom condos. The modern condos seem glaringly out of place in this historic and scenic place.

For the most luxurious Roche Harbor accommodations, book one of the four McMillan Suites located in an old harborside home. Each of these features a wraparound covered deck, king-size bed, gas fireplace, ceiling fans, clawfoot tubs and radiant heated floors in the bath, and tasteful furnishings. These cost $395 s or d and are a great splurge.

FOOD

San Juan Island has a wide range of restaurants and eateries, including some real gems. Unless otherwise noted, all the restaurants listed below are located in the town of Friday Harbor.

Cafés and Diners

Front Street Café (101 Spring St., 360/378-2245, 7 A.M.–4 P.M. daily) is a good breakfast hangout place, with a fun atmosphere, espresso and pastries, and a ferry-side location. The dependable lunches include homemade soups, salads, sandwiches, and more. **Angie's Cannery House Restaurant** (174 N. 1st St., 360/378-2500) is another good destination for lunchtime sandwiches and soups.

THE SAN JUAN FOOD CHAIN

Folks who live in the San Juan Islands year-round are a special breed. Tough and self-reliant, locals take a great deal of rightly deserved pride in their unique home. Coming to visit the islands makes it clear that getting there from more populous areas can be tricky, and shipping in supplies is expensive. Combine these challenges with the islands' fertile farmland and agrarian roots and it is easy to see how locally sourced food has become a point of pride around here. Island farmers grow berries and produce, raise livestock, and pick their eggs fresh from the henhouse each day. And don't forget that fresh Puget Sound seafood!

The local agricultural community has gone so far as to create the **Islands Certified Local** program to recognize those hospitality industry businesses in the community that support the locavore cause. If you're into the freshest food, look for restaurants and bed-and-breakfasts with this seal of approval and consider the fresh, delicious, and locally sourced food just one more of the many benefits of your ferry ride to the San Juans.

© ERICKA CHICKOWSKI

Serve yourself at Westcott Bay Seafood Farm.

An old standby, **Blue Dolphin Café** (185 1st St., 360/378-6116, 5 A.M.–2 P.M. daily) is just a block and a half from the ferry. The big breakfast menu is the main draw, with all the usuals, including eggs Benedict, omelettes, and hash browns for reasonable prices.

Another simple place near the ferry terminal is **Hungry Clam** (130 1st St., 360/378-3474, 11 A.M.–7 P.M. daily), where you will find cheap and very good fish and chips served in a basket, plus clam chowder, burgers, and grilled chicken sandwiches.

No place in Friday Harbor serves healthier, heartier lunches than **The Market Chef** (225 A St., 360/378-4546, 10 A.M.–6 P.M. Mon.–Fri. in summer, 10 A.M.–4 P.M. Mon.–Fri. in winter), a deli and bistro that offer up scrumptious sandwiches on house-made breads, inventive salads, and soothing soups, all made with organic and local ingredients.

San Juan Coffee Roasting Company (18 Cannery Landing, 360/378-4443 or 800/624-4119, www.rockisland.com/~sjcoffee, 9 A.M.–6:30 P.M. daily Apr.–Labor Day, 9:30 A.M.–5:30 P.M. Labor Day–Nov., 10 A.M.–5 P.M. Nov.–Mar.) specializes in full and dark roasted coffees, sold by the cup or pound.

If you're in search of a great all-American burger, fries, and shake, head to **Vic's Drive-In** (25 2nd St., 360/378-2120, 7 A.M.–7 P.M. Mon.–Fri., 7 A.M.–2 P.M. Sat., closed Sun.)

Lime Kiln Café (360/378-2155 or 800/451-8910, www.rocheharbor.com, 7 A.M.–9 P.M. daily in summer, 7 A.M.–2 P.M. in winter) offers quick meals out of Roche Harbor Resort. Though the fish-and-chips and burger fare here is forgettable and overpriced, it is the cheapest at the resort.

Steak and Seafood

Duck Soup Inn, five miles north of Friday Harbor on Roche Harbor Rd. (360/378-4878, 5–10 P.M. daily summer only, $30), specializes in superbly done local seafood, along with a constantly changing and eclectic menu with an international flavor. The country setting adds to the relaxed and romantic atmosphere. This is where locals go for a celebration night.

The Place Next to the Ferry Café (360/378-8707, 4:30–9 P.M. daily in summer, 5–8 P.M. Tues.–Sat. in winter) gets the nod from locals who come here for a creative, seafood-rich menu and a semi-casual atmosphere. The menu changes periodically, and as might be surmised from the name, this restaurant has a great location—on the marina adjacent to the ferry dock.

A mile east of Roche Harbor, **Westcott Bay Seafood Farm** (4071 Westcott Dr., 360/378-6388, www.westcottbay.com, 10 A.M.–5 P.M. Mon.–Sat., 11 A.M.–5 P.M. Sun., closed in winter) supplies local restaurants with gourmet oysters and clams; get them at the source for the freshest available. The farm also features several days each summer when you can pick your own oysters; these are timed around the lowest tides.

Friday Harbor House's **Harbor View Restaurant** (130 West St., 360/378-8455, www.fridayharborhouse.com, 5:30–8 P.M. Thurs.–Sun., plus Wednesday in the summer months, closed Mon.–Tues., entrées $28–34) is one of the finest local dining establishments, with a menu that changes weekly, depending upon what is fresh.

Roche Harbor Resort's nicest fare can be found at the second-story **McMillan's Dining Room** (248 Reuben Memorial Drive, 360/378-5757, 5 P.M.–10 P.M. daily, $30). This swanky little pad is outfitted with a player piano and great views of the marina. It serves up fine steaks, mouthwatering pasta, and fresh seafood. Call for reservations at McMillan's, especially during the summer months.

International

Bella Luna (175 1st St., 360/378-4118) serves pasta and pizzas, along with veal parmesan, prime rib, and other specialties.

Mi Casita (4–8:30 P.M. Mon.–Sat.) is a good bet. Pork lovers should definitely give the house specialty carnitas a try.

Finally, if you get a hankering for some sweet-and-sour chicken, **China Pearl** (51 Spring St., 360/378-5551) serves an Americanized Chinese menu. For really authentic Asian fare, swing by **Golden Triangle** (140 1st St., 360/378-3560), a casual eatery that serves pad Thai, spring rolls, and other Thai staples.

Pub Grub

One of the most popular eating establishments on San Juan Island is **Friday's Crabhouse** (65 Front St., 360/378-8801, www.fridayscrabhouse.com, open at 11:30 A.M. daily, closing hours vary) directly across from the ferry. Open summers only, this is the place for finger-lickin' fish and chips, shrimp cocktail, or grilled crab cakes, along with fajitas, burgers, and veggie burgers—most for under $10. Service is fast, making this a great last-minute stop while waiting for your ship to come in. The dining is alfresco.

The **Front St. Ale House** (1 Front St., 360/378-2337, 11 A.M.–midnight Mon.–Thurs., 11 A.M.–1 A.M. Fri.–Sat., 11 A.M.–11 P.M. Sun.) sits next door to San Juan Brewing Company, and its ales are all on tap here. The huge menu includes burgers, fish and chips, pasta, steak, and other crowd-pleasing favorites. It's very popular for lunch and dinner.

If you're looking for a leisurely lunch or a dinner cocktail in Roche Harbor, try **Madrona Bar & Grill** (360/378-2155 or 800/451-8910, www.rocheharbor.com, 11 A.M.–10 P.M. daily in summer, 4–10 P.M. daily in winter) for waterside patio dining.

Markets

The **San Juan Farmers Market** (360/378-6301, is held 10 A.M.–1 P.M. on summer Saturdays at the county courthouse parking lot, with lots of organic fruits, vegetables, berries, and flowers.

The island's largest grocer is **King's Market** (160 Spring St., 360/378-4505), with fresh meats and fish, a fine deli, fishing tackle, and sportswear.

INFORMATION AND SERVICES

The **San Juan Island Chamber of Commerce Visitor Center** is upstairs behind Front St. Ale House (1 Front St., 360/378-5240, www.sanjuanisland.org). Hours are 9 A.M.–2 P.M. Tues.–Fri. and 10 A.M.–1 P.M. Sat., with longer summer hours when volunteer staff are available.

Check your email free at the **San Juan Island Library** (1010 Guard St., 360/378-2798, www.sanjuan.lib.wa.us), or pay to do so at **The Menu Bar** (435 Argyle Ave., 360/378-1987, www.interisland.net/menubar) or **Madelyn's Bagel Bakery** (A St., 360/378-4545), above the ferry parking area.

Store luggage in the coin-operated **lockers** opposite the ferry terminal next to Friday's Crab House. **Sail-In Laundromat** is just behind here, or you can do your own laundry at **Sunshine Coin-Op Laundry** (210 Nichols St., 360/378-9755).

GETTING AROUND

Warning: Friday Harbor has a big parking problem in the summer, and the city *strictly* enforces a two-hour downtown parking limit. Get back to your car three minutes late and you'll probably have a ticket pasted on the windshield.

The **Washington State Ferry** (206/464-6400, www.wsdot.wa.gov/ferries) stops right in Friday Harbor on San Juan Island. In the summer, ferries leave Anacortes at least a dozen times a day 4:30 A.M.–12:20 A.M.; nearly all of them stop at Friday Harbor. See *Getting There* at the beginning of this chapter for details on ferry service (including private ferries) and scheduled flights to San Juan Island.

By Bus

You don't need a car on San Juan Island. **San Juan Transit & Tours** (360/378-8887 or 800/887-8387, www.sanjuantransit.com) operates shuttle buses between Friday Harbor and Roche Harbor, with stops at Lakedale, Lime Kiln State Park, San Juan County Park, Mitchell Bay, and English Bay. Unfortunately, they do not run to the south end of the island (American Camp). Buses operate May–September, and service is daily in summer and weekends only until mid-May. The cost is a reasonable $5 one-way, $10 round-trip, or $15 for an all-day pass, and buses can carry bikes and luggage. The office is next to the Friday Harbor ferry in the Cannery Landing Building.

By Car and Taxi

M&W Auto Rentals (360/378-2886 or 800/323-6037, www.sanjuanauto.com/rental, $50–70 per day) offers a range of vehicles for rent, including two- and four-door sedans, convertibles, SUVs, and large passenger vans.

Susie's Moped and Car Rentals (360/378-5244 or 800/532-0087, www.susiesmopeds.com.) also rents tiny Geo Trackers from its shop at the top of the ferry lanes in Friday Harbor, in addition to bikes and mopeds.

Call **Bob's Taxi & Tours** (360/378-6777 or 877/482-9426) for local rides year-round. Friday Harbor to Roche Harbor is around $22 for two people.

Orcas Island

Known as "The Gem of the San Juans," Orcas Island is considered the chain's most beautiful island. It is definitely the hilliest—drive, hike, or bike to the top of 2,409-foot Mt. Constitution for a panoramic view from Vancouver, B.C., to Mt. Rainier. Orcas' most prominent mansion, Moran Mansion at Rosario Resort, regularly graces the pages of national travel magazines. The island—named by a Spanish explorer in 1792 for the viceroy of Mexico, not for the orca whales common in neighboring waters—is home to 3,500 people, half of whom seem to now operate real estate offices.

© ERICKA CHICKOWSKI

clamming Orcas Island

Towns

The ferry docks at the cluster of cafés and gift shops called **Orcas Village,** located on the south end of this horseshoe-shaped island. The tiny settlement of **West Sound** is eight miles northwest of the ferry landing and has a large marina, along with a couple of stores. Approximately four miles west of here is another little gathering place, **Deer Harbor,** with a handful of resorts and B&Bs, a couple of restaurants, charter sailboats, and kayak rentals. It's appropriately named for the many black-tailed deer in the area and throughout the San Juans. The town of **Eastsound** sits at the head of Orca's horseshoe shape. This is the primary village on the island, and *the* place to go for groceries, gas, and a wide choice of gift shops, cafés, and galleries. It also probably has more lounging cats per shop than any other town in Washington!

SIGHTS

Moran State Park

Near Eastsound, 5,252-acre Moran State Park (360/376-2326 or www.parks.wa.gov) is most popular for its steep, paved road to the 2,409-foot summit of **Mt. Constitution,** where you'll discover a 52-foot stone observation tower constructed by the Civilian Conservation Corps in 1936. This is the highest point on the San Juans and offers a commanding view in all directions, from Mt. Rainier to British Columbia. If you've ridden to the top by bike, it's an exciting ride back down. Another popular attraction is **Cascade Falls,** where Cascade Creek drops into a deep pool 100 feet below. A quarter-mile path leads to the falls, and you can continue uphill to two less-impressive waterfalls.

The park has more than 30 miles of other hiking trails, from easy nature loops to remote and rugged out-of-the-way hikes. Get a park map for details on all of these. A four-mile loop trail circles Mountain Lake, offering a chance to see black-tailed deer, particularly in the morning and early evening. You can climb to the summit of Mt. Constitution from Mountain Lake on a 3.7-mile path, or save your legs by catching a ride to the top and hiking downhill instead.

Moran State Park has several lakes that are popular for fishing, nonmotorized boating, and swimming in the cold water. Rent rowboats

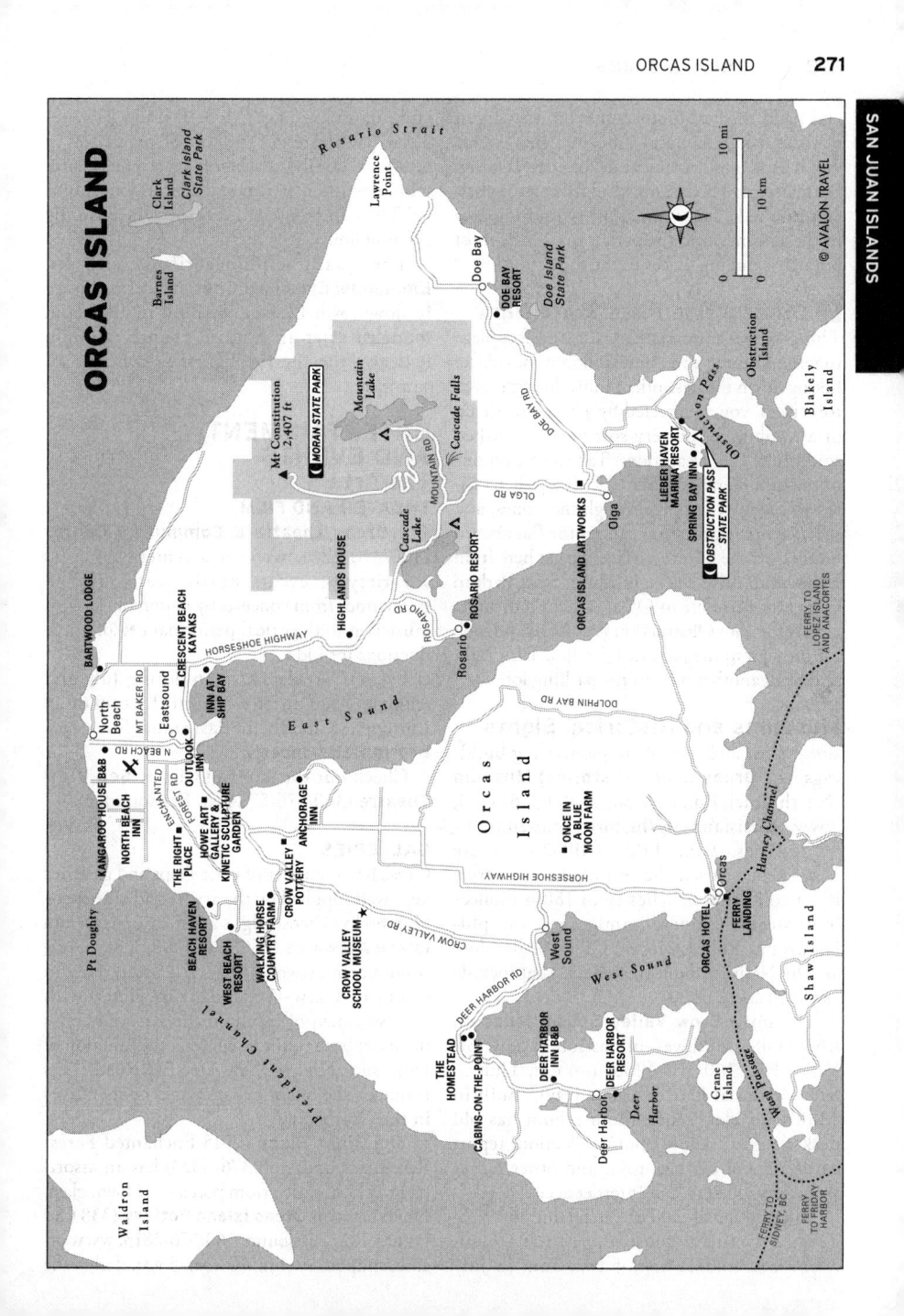
ORCAS ISLAND
Rosario Strait
Clark Island
Clark Island State Park
Barnes Island
Lawrence Point
Doe Bay
DOE BAY RESORT
Doe Island State Park
Mt Constitution 2,407 ft
MORAN STATE PARK
Mountain Lake
Cascade Falls
DOE BAY RD
MOUNTAIN RD
Cascade Lake
OLGA RD
ROSARIO RD
ROSARIO RESORT
Rosario
HIGHLANDS HOUSE
ORCAS ISLAND ARTWORKS
Olga
LIEBER HAVEN MARINA RESORT
SPRING BAY INN
OBSTRUCTION PASS STATE PARK
Obstruction Pass
Obstruction Island
Blakely Island
© AVALON TRAVEL
10 mi
10 km
0
0
BARTWOOD LODGE
North Beach
MT BAKER RD
Eastsound
CRESCENT BEACH KAYAKS
HORSESHOE HIGHWAY
INN AT SHIP BAY
East Sound
KANGAROO HOUSE B&B
NORTH BEACH INN
N BEACH RD
ENCHANTED FOREST RD
OUTLOOK INN
THE RIGHT PLACE
HOWE ART GALLERY & KINETIC SCULPTURE GARDEN
ANCHORAGE INN
Pt Doughty
BEACH HAVEN RESORT
WEST BEACH RESORT
WALKING HORSE COUNTRY FARM
CROW VALLEY POTTERY
President Channel
Waldron Island
CROW VALLEY SCHOOL MUSEUM
CROW VALLEY RD
Orcas Island
ONCE IN A BLUE MOON FARM
DOLPHIN BAY RD
HORSESHOE HIGHWAY
West Sound
DEER HARBOR RD
THE HOMESTEAD
CABINS-ON-THE-POINT
DEER HARBOR INN B&B
DEER HARBOR RESORT
Deer Harbor
Deer Harbor
West Sound
ORCAS HOTEL
Orcas
FERRY LANDING
Harney Channel
Crane Island
Shaw Island
Weeks Passage
FERRY TO LOPEZ ISLAND AND ANACORTES
FERRY TO SIDNEY, BC
FERRY TO FRIDAY HARBOR

and paddleboats (summers only) at the largest of these, Mountain and Cascade Lakes, where you'll find good trout and kokanee fishing. Both also have boat ramps and fishing supplies. Cascade Lake has a roped-off swimming area in the summer, and the park is one of the most popular camping places in the state.

Obstruction Pass State Park

This postage-stamp state park is a perfect place to teach a young child how to skip stones. After hiking down the network of trails through madrona trees, you are greeted by a beach made up of a rainbow of buttery-soft pebbles washed smooth by the ocean tides. Take a seat on one of the innumerable bleached drift logs here, listen to the waves ripple through the stones, and see how many times you can get the flat ones to bounce off the water's surface. To get here from Eastsound, drive through Moran State Park to Olga and turn left to Olga. After a half mile, turn right onto Obstruction Pass Road and look for the sign to the park in 1.5 miles. Turn right and head another mile to the parking lot.

Museums and Historical Sights

Located in a cluster of six pioneer log buildings, the **Orcas Island Historical Museum** (North Beach Rd., Eastsound, 360/376-4849, www.orcasisland.org/historicalmuseum, 1–4 P.M. Tues.–Sun. (Fridays till 7 P.M.) late May–Sept., closed the rest of the year, free) has a collection of relics from 1880s pioneer homesteads, Chinese immigrants, and philanthropist Robert Moran. Of particular note are the Native American artifacts that include carvings and baskets.

The small **Crow Valley School Museum** (three miles southwest of Eastsound on Crow Valley Rd., 360/376-4260, 1–4 P.M. Thurs.–Sat. Memorial Day to Labor Day),. Built in 1888, this classic one-room school has old desks, a great school photo collection, report cards, school clothes, toys, and other pieces from a bygone era. No Internet access here!

The Funhouse (30 Pea Patch Lane 360/376-7177, www.thefunhouse.org, 10 A.M.–6 P.M. Mon.–Sat. and 11 A.M.–5 P.M. Sun. in July and August, 3–6 P.M. Mon.–Fri. and 10 A.M.–3 P.M. Sat. the rest of the year, $5 per person or $20 for a family) is a hands-on science center with more than 50 fun and educational exhibits. The Fun House also has special teens-only evening hours.

The quaint and beautifully situated **Emmanuel Episcopal Church** faces the water in downtown Eastsound. Built in 1886 and modeled after an English country church, it is also the site for Thursday concerts all summer.

ENTERTAINMENT AND EVENTS

The Arts

THEATER AND FILM

The **Orcas Theatre & Community Center** (360/376-2281, www.orcascenter.org) hosts a variety of events nearly year-round in Eastsound, from concerts by nationally known musicians to theatrical performances and productions for kids.

Every Thursday at noon during July and August, head to the beautiful Emmanuel Episcopal Church in Eastsound for a free **Brown Bag Concert.**

Check out the latest movies at **Sea View Theatre** (360/376-5724) in Eastsound.

GALLERIES

Orcas has a number of craft shops and galleries kept well supplied by the artists and craftspeople who live there. Olga's artist co-op is **Orcas Island Artworks** (360/376-4408, www.orcasisland.com/artworks, 10 A.M.–6 P.M. daily in summer, 10 A.M.–5 P.M. daily in winter) with an assortment of locally made arts and crafts in an old barn (built in 1936) at the junction of Horseshoe Highway and Doe Bay Road. This is one of the oldest artist-owned cooperatives in the Northwest.

The Right Place (2915 Enchanted Forest Rd., Eastsound, 360/376-4023) has an assortment of local crafts, from pottery to blown glass. Not far away is **Orcas Island Pottery** (338 Old Pottery Rd., Eastsound, 360/376-2813, www.orcasislandpottery.com, 10 A.M.–5 P.M. daily), the oldest pottery studio in the Northwest. **Crow Valley Pottery** (2274 Orcas Rd., Eastsound, 360/376-4260, www.crowvalley.com) is housed in an 1866 log cabin between Orcas Landing and Eastsound, and features the works of more than 50 artists, with pottery, paintings, jewelry, and other locally produced pieces. The cabin is only open between Memorial Day and mid-September, 10 A.M.–5 P.M. daily, but you can catch the artwork 10 A.M.–5 P.M. daily at the Crow Valley Pottery store at 296 Main Street in Eastsound.

For something completely different, head west from Eastsound on Horseshoe Highway and look for the bizarre and playful welded metal mobiles hanging along the road. Follow the signs up Two Hills Road to reach **Howe Art Gallery & Kinetic Sculpture Garden** (360/376-2945, www.howeart.net, 10 A.M.–5 P.M. daily in summer, winter by appointment), where more of these large kinetic sculptures fill the grounds and a gallery. Don't miss this place!

Festivals and Events

Eastsound—like nearly every small town in the U.S.—has a fun parade on the **4th of July,** followed by boat races, music, and fireworks.

The first weekend of August brings a popular **Orcas Island Fly-In** (www.orcasisland.org/flyin) that features many antique planes. It's followed on the second Saturday of August by the **Library Fair** (360/376-4985, www.orcaslibrary.org), a big arts and crafts fair and book sale. Late August and early September is the time for the always-sold-out **Orcas Island Chamber Music Festival** (360/376-6636, www.sanjuanweb.com/orcaschambermusic).

SHOPPING

Bookstores

Darvill's Bookstore (296 Main St., Eastsound, 360/376-2135, 9:30 A.M.–6 P.M. Mon.–Sat., 9:30 A.M.–5 P.M. Sun.) has a big selection of books on the San Juans; its adjacent **Rare Print Shop** (360/376-2351) sells prints from the 18th and 19th centuries, plus limited-edition prints by contemporary Northwest artists.

SPORTS AND RECREATION

Bike Rentals

With its steep terrain and long roads, Orcas Island is definitely the toughest of the islands to get around on bike. However, it can be pretty fun if you're up for the challenge. In Eastsound you can pick up a rental steed from **Wildlife Cycles** (350 N Beach Rd., 360/376-4708, www.wildlifecycles.com, 10 A.M.–6 P.M. Mon.–Fri., 10:15 A.M.–4:45 P.M. Sat.–Sun., winter hours vary so call ahead, $30 per day). If you prefer to rent a bike at the ferry and take the long haul into Eastsound or other remote parts of the island, **Dolphin Bay Bicycles** (360/376-4157, www.rockisland.com/~dolphin) is right at the ferry landing and rents bikes for $30 per day.

Sea Kayaking

Orcas Island is as crazy for kayaks as the rest of the San Juans, and there are many spots along the shoreline to launch a great adventure on the water. If you're planning on launching your own kayak, be forewarned that you may be subject to a launching fee ($5 at Deer Harbor) if you aren't on public lands.

Pick up last-minute supplies at **Shearwater Adventures** (360/376-4699, www.shearwaterkayaks.com) in Eastsound, which sells kayak and camping gear, plus a slew of natural history books to learn about the areas you'll be paddling around. Shearwater is also one of the best-regarded tour companies, offering daily paddles from Rosario Resort, Deer Harbor Resort, and Doe Bay Resort starting at $60 for three hours.

For a unique paddling adventure, try your hand at the reins of the hand-built, traditional Aleutian–style kayaks used by **Osprey Tours** (360/376-3677 or 800/529-2567, www.ospreytours.com). The tours leave from Bartwood Lodge on the north end of the island and can range from one hour ($50) to a full six-hour day ($150). Box lunches can be purchased for longer tours.

Finally, you can just go it alone and rent single or double kayaks in Eastsound from **Crescent Beach Kayaks** (239 Crescent Beach

© ERICKA CHICKOWSKI

The best sights in the San Juans are seen with paddle in hand.

Drive, Eastsound, 360/376-2464, www.crescentbeachkayaks.com, 9 A.M.–6 P.M. daily, $50 per person half day or $18 per person per hour) or at Obstruction Pass from **Lieber Haven Marina Resort** (360/376-2472, www.lieberhaven.com, 8 A.M.–8 P.M. daily, $10–35 per hour).

Whale-Watching

Due to its closer proximity to Haro Strait, San Juan Island is better suited for heading out on an orca adventure than Orcas Island. However, if you won't be on San Juan, you can still find a couple of quality companies heading out from Orcas.

One of the most comfortable rides is aboard the 50-foot cruising yacht run by **Orcas Island Eclipse Charters** (360/376-4663 or 800/376-6566, www.orcasislandwhales.com) in Orcas Landing. Eclipse guides Dan and Denise Wilks are contributors to the Center for Whale Research and they even played bit roles in the movie *Free Willy II.*

Another excellent option is **Deer Harbor Charters** (360/376-5989 or 800/544-5758, www.deerharborcharters.com) in Deer Harbor, the longest-running whale-watching business on the island. The smaller vessels used by this company run on biodiesel to make as low an environmental impact as possible on the whales.

Boat Charters and Rentals

Like San Juan Island, Orcas is a good departure point to motor or sail the outer islands in the San Juan archipelago. Based out of Rosario Resort, **Orcas Island Sailing** offers a good value with its charter sails on its small day sailboats. For $220–260, its captains will take your group out for three to four hours and teach you to sail; extend the trip to all day for $410. You can also feel the wind whip up the sails (and your hair) aboard the **Northwest Classic Daysails** (360/376-5581, www.classicdaysails.com) sailing sloop, *Aura.* A three-hour sail for two is just $140.

If you prefer to motor out on your own, **Orcas Boat Rentals** (360/376-7616, www.orcasboats.com) rents runabout motorboats at Deer Harbor Marina for $250–275 per day.

Camping

Orcas Island's finest camping is at **Moran State Park,** with more than 150 campsites in four different campgrounds along Cascade and Mountain Lakes, plus a separate bike-in area ($12). Tent sites are $21–25, with showers provided. There are no RV hookups, though they do have a disposal station. Due to the park's popularity, reservations are required in the summer months. All sites are pre-assigned, so check in at the pay station across from Cascade Lake when you arrive. Make reservations ($7 extra) at 888/226-7688 or www.parks.wa.gov. The campground is open year-round.

Obstruction Pass State Park is a tiny place with a boat ramp, a beach, and nine free walk-in campsites a half mile from the road. No reservations or potable water. The park is located at the end of Obstruction Pass Rd., 2.5 miles southeast of Olga.

Doe Bay Resort (near Olga, 360/376-2291, www.doebay.com) has tent sites (no RVs) for

$25; the hippie resort's features include community bathrooms and showers, kayak tours, yoga and massage, and a café.

Camp in comfort at the **West Beach Resort** (three miles west of Eastsound, 360/376-2240 or 877/937-8224, www.westbeachresort.com) in one of its canvas platform tents. The spacious tents each have a queen-size bed, a futon, and a small writing desk, plus a private picnic table, barbecue, and fire pit outside. West Beach also offers tent campsites ($27–33) and RV hookups ($33–38) along a scenic beach. Also here is a marina with boat rentals, sea-kayak tours, fishing and scuba supplies, and groceries.

Other Recreation

Walking Horse Country Farm (360/376-5306 or 877/376-9423, www.walkinghorse farm.com) leads guided trail rides on its distinctive Tennessee walking horses, as well as carriage rides. The **Orcas Island Country Golf Club** (Orcas Rd. southwest of Eastsound, 360/376-4400, www.orcasisland.com/golf) is a nine-hole public course.

Gnat's Nature Hikes (360/376-6629) guides hikes within Moran State Park or to one of the outer island marine parks; these start at $25 per person for a 3.5-hour hike. **Tortas and Hare Excursions** (360/376-2464) offers historic tours of Orcas Island.

Orcas Athletics (100 A St., Eastsound, 360/376-6361, www.bellacorporate.com) is a full athletic club with racquetball court, swimming pool, saunas, hot tub, and more. Nonmembers can work out here for a $15 fee.

The Seattle YMCA's **Camp Orkila** (206/382-5001, www.seattleymca.org) has an excellent day camp all summer long for school-age children.

ACCOMMODATIONS

Anyone planning to stay on Orcas in the summer—particularly on weekends—should make reservations several months ahead of time to be assured of a space. Call the Orcas Island Chamber of Commerce **lodging hotline** (360/376-8888 or 888/376-8888) for availability. It's updated on a daily basis in the summer.

© ERICKA CHICKOWSKI

The views from atop Mount Constitution are the best on the island.

Its website, www.orcasisland.org, has links to quite a few local places, but a better bet is www.orcasisle.com, where you'll find comprehensive links to local B&Bs, cabins, and resorts.

Under $100

During the summer it is nigh impossible to find a hotel or bed-and-breakfast willing to put you up for under $100 per night, and even in the winter it is no small feat. The cheapest lodging *sans* tent that you'll find on Orcas Island is at the hostel at **Doe Bay Resort** (360/376-2291, www.doebay.com, dorm beds $35–50), a funky, hippie enclave with a laid-back mix of characters eager to chat with solo adventurers and penny-pinching travelers. Save on gas and hassles by taking the resort's shuttle from the ferry for $12 round-trip; call in advance for a ride. There are two private couples' rooms in the hostel building for $75–100.

$100-150

One of the best lodging deals on the island can be had by those who prepare in advance. The

Camp Moran Vacation House (360/902-8600, www.parks.wa.gov/vacation houses, $117) inside beautiful Moran State Park is one of a handful of vacation homes rented out by the state parks department. This spacious two-bedroom rental sleeps 10, and its large kitchen comes fully equipped. All you need to bring is bed linens and firewood for the fire ring in the private yard outside. The word is out about this super deal, though, so check with the parks department a year in advance to lock up your dates.

Couples seeking solitude on the beach need look no further than **Beach Haven Resort** (684 Beach Haven Rd., 360/376-2288 or 888/422-2825, www.beach-haven.com), which has private little cabins right on the beach for $135 per night. For a special treat, its Stargazer's Cottage with a skylight above the bed, a jetted tub, and a private beach cabana is just five bucks more per night. Beach Haven can also be family friendly, offering two-, three- and four-bedroom cabins for $165–310 nightly. The property has a playground, horseshoe pit, and ping-pong table on-site.

Spread out across 33-acres along Otter Cove, **Doe Bay Resort** (360/376-2291, www.doebay.com) is a legendary institution on the island dating back to the 1970s. The resort attracts a free-spirited and artistic-minded bunch, who come to relax in the property's soaking tubs and sauna, stretch their minds and bodies at the on-site yoga studio, and unwind with a cup of tea in the community lounge and library.

Though it continues to stay true to its down-to-earth roots, Doe Bay Resort has undergone a bit of a renaissance over the past several years, with many of its cabins getting a much-needed face-lift in the process. Full bathroom and kitchen cabins range $170–260 per night, while woodstove cabins with community bathrooms and showers run $100–125 nightly. Between May and October, the resort also rents out yurts for $110 per night.

The resort has a small store with limited supplies, plus sea kayaking tours ($45 for three hours), a massage therapist on call, and a café featuring organic veggies grown on the property.

Deer Harbor Inn (360/376-4110 or 877/377-4110, www.deerharborinn.com) is a contemporary log lodge surrounded by an apple orchard near Deer Harbor, eight miles west of the ferry dock. The eight small guest rooms ($139 d) in the main lodge contain log furniture and private baths. Four private cottages ($229–385 d) have fireplaces and a two-night minimum in summer. All rates include a continental breakfast (in a picnic basket) and access to the hot tub. Kids are accepted in the cottages. Deer Harbor Inn is also home to a fine dining restaurant, housed in a farmhouse built in 1915.

$150-200

Located on the southeast corner of Orcas Island near Olga, **Lieber Haven Marina Resort** (360/376-2472, www.lieberhavenresort.com) offers charming and affordable beachfront lodging in cottages, apartments, studios, and rooms, most of which contain full kitchens. Rates are $135–165 for up to four people. This is a great family place to relax and take in the harbor scene. Kayaks and motorboats are available for rent at the protected marina, along with sailing trips, whale-watching, and fishing charters. The property also offers free Wi-Fi access.

For classic lodging, stay at beautiful **Orcas Hotel** (360/376-4300 or 888/672-2792, www.orcashotel.com), a 12-room century-old Victorian inn overlooking the ferry landing in Orcas,. Rates are $89–114 d for modest rooms with shared baths, or $138–208 d for those with private baths. The nicest of these is a suite with a private deck and hot tub. For ease of access, the location can't be beat; just get off the ferry and you're at your hotel. The hotel is a popular place for weddings and family gatherings, though it isn't exactly quiet, being so close to the ferry traffic.

On the north end of the island, **Bartwood Lodge** (178 Fossil Bay Dr., 360/376-2242 or 866/666-2242, www.orcasisland.com/bartwood, $159–239 d) is a beachfront lodge with 16 private rooms. Amenities include a tennis court, boat launch, and private moorage for guests. Kids are welcome. Bartwood is home to one of the finest restaurants in the San Juans, Sean Paul's.

The Inn at Ship Bay (326 Olga Rd., 360/376-5886 or 877/276-7296, www.innatshipbay.com), just east of Eastsound, features 10 state rooms ($195 s or d) and an executive suite ($250 s or d), all with king-size beds, private balconies with water views, gas fireplaces, and fridges. Rates include a big continental breakfast, and a fine restaurant (Ship Bay Oyster House) is also on the premises. There's a two-night minimum stay in the summer, and kids are accepted.

North Beach Inn in Eastsound (360/376-2660, www.northbeachinn.com, $135 s or d, $17 extra person) has beachfront cottages on a beautiful private beach. The cabins contain kitchens and fireplaces. Two bedroom and larger cabins are or $210–250 for four people. Kids are welcome, as are pets with an extra fee of $10 per pet per day. The inn is closed December to mid-February. Reserve far ahead for this popular place.

Outlook Inn (171 Main St., 360/376-2200 or 888/688-5665, www.outlookinn.com) is a beautifully restored 1888 hotel right in Eastsound with its own private beach. Classic economy rooms with shared baths and no TVs are available in the historic hotel for $84 s or d. Standard rooms in the hotel with private baths and TVs are $140 s or d, and a newer building contains deluxe suites with king-size beds, whirlpool tubs, and mini-bars for $245 s or d.

The kangaroo is long gone, but the name remains at The **Kangaroo House** (just north of Eastsound Village, 360/376-2175 or 888/371-2175, www.kangaroohouse.com, $150–190 s or d), an attractive 1907 home outfitted with a big fireplace, period furnishings, decks, and a garden hot tub. Bought in the 1930s by a sea captain, Harold Ferris, the house picked up its name when he brought a young female kangaroo on one of his Australian voyages. Nowadays you'll only see the innkeepers bouncing around the house—during morning time, that is, when a truly memorable multi-course breakfast is served. Bird-watchers will appreciate the many species that come to the feeders in the surrounding yard. The five guest rooms have private or shared baths. Families are welcome, and the whole inn can be rented for $850.

$200-250

Rosario Resort & Spa (1400 Rosario Rd., 360/376-2222 or 800/562-8820, www.rosarioresort.com) is a famous and historic getaway five miles south of Eastsound, and the largest resort on the islands. It's well worth a look even if you can't afford to stay here. The perfect island setting and delightful amenities make it a very popular outdoor wedding location. The resort is housed in an early 1900s mansion that once belonged to shipbuilder and Seattle mayor Robert Moran. Moran wasn't blessed with musical talent, so he played the 1,972-pipe organ like a player piano and none of his guests were the wiser; organ concerts are still held frequently. The historic building—on the National Register of Historic Places—has been beautifully restored, offering fine dining, an indoor pool, hot tub, sauna, fitness facility, and massage (extra fee). Rooms cost $199–319 d, and suites are $239–599 d. These vary greatly in size, amenities, and the age of the furnishings, but most are a disappointment, particularly given the beauty of the main building. You'll find nicer rooms for less elsewhere on the island.

Over $250

Cabins-on-the-Point (2101 Deer Harbor Rd., Eastsound, 360/376-4114, www.islandcabins.com, $195–450 s or d) has six romantic cabins—popular with honeymooners—with woodstoves and full kitchens. Two of them include access to the hot tub, and all guests will enjoy the private beach. The poshest among them is **Highlands House,** a large two-bedroom house with a fireplace, open kitchen, hot tub on the deck, and impressive water vistas.

Once in a Blue Moon Farm (412 Eastman Rd., Eastsound, 360/376-7035, www.onceinabluemoonfarm.com) sits on a peaceful 35-acre farm estate with panoramic water and mountain views. This is one of the few places that allow visitors to bring along their pets (with advance notice); a kennel is adjacent to each unit. The owners have their own menagerie of animals that includes goats, llamas, horses, ducks, and chickens, plus an old orchard with apple, plum, cherry, and pear trees. Two rental apartments are available in a house on the farm: a three-bedroom unit (sleeps nine comfortably) with a large deck, fireplace, two baths, and kitchen for $250 d up to $450 for nine, and an attractive two-bedroom unit that includes a kitchen, woodstove, bath, and covered patio for $200 d or $245 for four people. Larger groups may want to rent the entire five-bedroom house.

Sitting right along the shoreline next door to Obstruction Pass State Park, **Spring Bay Inn B&B** (360/376-5531, www.springbayinn.com, $240–280 s or d) has five guest rooms with waterfront views, private baths, and fireplaces. The largest also features a hot tub with a water view. This kid-friendly inn sits on 60 acres with a network of trails that hook up into Obstruction Pass trails for further exploration. Rates include not only brunch but a way to work up your appetite beforehand—free kayak tours are guided each morning by the owners, both retired park rangers.

Located on three acres of waterfront property along West Sound, **The Homestead** (360/376-5284, www.homesteadorcas.com) began life as a hay barn, but it has been transformed into a delightful home with large windows facing the water. This is a primo rental for families and groups to spread out and kick back. It has a large living room with a wood-burning stove, a seaside deck with gas barbecue, a large hot tub, full kitchen and bath, and modern furnishings. The cost is $400 per night for four people and includes the use of a kayak and rowboat moored on the dock out back.

FOOD

The "big city" on Orcas—Eastsound—has the best choice of food on the island, though you'll find a scattering of fine restaurants and cafés elsewhere.

Eastsound Area

Get quick Asian-influenced takeout fare—including hot and sour soup, teriyaki chicken, and spring roll wraps—at **The Kitchen** (249 Prune Alley, 360/376-6958, 11 A.M.–7 P.M. Mon.–Sat. in summer, 11 A.M.–4 P.M. Mon.–Sat. in winter, closed Sun. year-round, $13). Another good spot for finger food is **The Lower Tavern** (Langell St. at Orcas Rd., 360/376-4848, 11 A.M.–10 P.M. Mon.–Sat., 11 A.M.–9 P.M. Sun., $12), where the tasty bar meals include the best fish and chips in town, along with burgers and soups. The television has sports on most afternoons, making this a good rainy day retreat.

For Mexican meals, **Bilbo's Festivo** (360/376-4728, 11:30 A.M.–3 P.M. and 5 P.M.–9:30 P.M. daily, $28) is a local legend. It has distinctive handcrafted furniture and large servings of tasty Mexican/Southwest favorites, mesquite-grilled meats, seafood, and fresh-fruit margaritas. Crab enchiladas are especially good, and the chips and salsa are house-made. Outside dining is available in the courtyard. The setting is fun and friendly, but meals are surprisingly expensive; it's easy for two people to drop $60 with drinks. Bilbo's stays crowded even in the winter months, so reservations are advised.

Get pizzas by the slice or pie at **Portofino Pizzeria** (A St., 360/376-2085, www.portofinopizzeria.com, 11:30 A.M.–8:30 P.M. Mon.–Sat., 4 P.M.–8:30 P.M. Sun., $18). The deep-dish pizza is your best bet. This is a fine place to take kids and offers a view across Eastsound from the second-floor deck.

Enjoy the great outdoors on a sunny summer day by sliding into one of the picnic tables set in the garden courtyard at **Sunflower Café** (Prune Alley at A St., 360/376-2335, 7:30 A.M.–3:30 P.M. daily, $9). Housed in a cute little cottage right on the main drag, this acclaimed eatery serves up healthy and hearty breakfasts and fresh deli foods for lunch.

Inn at Ship Bay Restaurant (326 Olga Rd., 360/376-5886, www.innatshipbay.com, $22), just east of Eastsound, is the best place to taste fresh oysters in the San Juans. This

© ERICKA CHICKOWSKI

Eastsound is the place to go for a quick bite to eat.

spacious old farmhouse overlooking Ship Bay attracts both visitors and locals for a variety of fresh-from-the-sea daily specials; try the Pacific rim hot pot: salmon, rockfish, and mussels in a hot and sour broth with udon noodles. The appetizer list always includes fresh oysters from Buck Bay, prepared in a multitude of ways.

Set inside the historic Outlook Inn **New Leaf Café** (171 Main St., 360/376-2200 or 888/688-5665, www.outlookinn.com, call for reservations, $22) has a great view of East Sound and is conveniently located right in the hubbub of town. The New Leaf menu focuses on free-range meats and seafood, offering smaller-size dishes à la carte to encourage family-style eating.

Enjoy excellent Northwest cuisine at the acclaimed **Christina's** (located on Main St. upstairs and directly behind the gas station, 360/376-4904, www.christinas.net, reservations 5–9 P.M. daily, $30). The menu changes daily, and there's a patio out back overlooking the sound. Christina's has been here for more than two decades, so you know it's doing something right. Diners will appreciate the cozy atmosphere, attention to detail, and excellent service. It's a great special-occasion spot, and children are welcome. Stop by 4–6:30 P.M. for lighter and more reasonably priced meals off the bar menu.

The West End

When you step off the ferry at Orcas, the grand old Orcas Hotel faces you. Inside is **Octavia's Bistro** (360/376-4300 or 888/672-2792, www.orcashotel.com, $14–24) with such offerings as filet of beef, peppercorn-crusted salmon, or chicken piccata. Unfortunately, service can be slow and you will probably find better meals elsewhere.

Housed in a farmhouse built in 1915, **The Restaurant at Deer Harbor Inn** (360/376-4110 or 877/377-4110, www.deerharborinn.com, $20–38) is a spacious and comfortable place with outstanding meals. It's a bit off the beaten path if you're staying near Eastsound, but worth the drive. You can get something as simple as freshly baked bread and homemade soups, or choose a full dinner from the blackboard listing daily specials. There's always grilled seafood and a vegetarian entrée.

The East End

Cafe Olga, inside the Orcas Island Artworks building near Olga, has inexpensive and delicious home-style lunches. The food covers a broad spectrum: sandwiches (including a great roasted eggplant and hummus version), vegetarian dishes, quiche, pasta, ethnic dishes, espresso, and its justly famous blackberry pie. Guaranteed to please, and the out-of-the-way location keeps the crowds at bay. You also won't want to miss the adjacent cooperative gallery.

The Mansion Room (five miles south of Eastsound, 360/376-2222 or 800/562-8820, www.rosarioresort.com, $18–24) at Rosario Resort & Spa, has spectacular views and romantic dining, plus a popular Friday night seafood buffet and Saturday prime rib buffet. Reservations are required.

More casual fare is offered at Rosario Resort's **Cascade Bar & Grill,** which serves a lineup of seafood and chips, burgers, hot dogs, and other summertime favorites. The grill is connected with a small market, open 7 A.M.–9 P.M. daily.

Markets

For groceries, film, and other essentials, stop by the **Island Market** (360/376-6000) in downtown Eastsound. This is the largest grocery store in the islands, with an in-store bakery and deli.

The **Orcas Island Farmers Market** (Eastsound's Village Square, www.orcasonline.com/farmersmarket, 10 A.M.–3 P.M. Sat. Apr.–Oct.) sells local produce, flowers, crafts, and clothing. More fresh organic produce is available on Wednesday near the ferry landing in Orcas Village.

Homegrown Market (Eastsound, 360/376-2009) has natural foods and a deli with daily specials and salads, plus fresh crab and salmon in season. The same folks also run the small **Orcas Market** (360/376-8860) at the ferry dock.

INFORMATION AND SERVICES

The **Orcas Island Chamber of Commerce** (360/376-2273, www.orcasisland.org) has a kiosk at Moran State Park that is open 9:30 A.M.–1:30 P.M. Mon.–Fri. June–Labor Day. You can also pick up brochures inside the **Orcas Online** building (254 N. Beach Rd., Eastsound, 360/376-4124, www.orcasonline.com), where you can check your email ($10/hour). Check email for free at the attractive and modern **Orcas Island Library** (500 Rose St., Eastsound, 360/376-4985, www.orcaslibrary.org). **Orcasisle.com** (www.orcasisle.com) is a helpful Web source with comprehensive links to local businesses.

Airport Center Self-Service Laundry (360/376-2478) is located at the southwest end of the airport and just north of Eastsound.

GETTING AROUND

The **Washington State Ferry** (206/464-6400, www.wsdot.wa.gov/ferries) docks at Orcas Landing on the south end of the island. See *Getting There* at the beginning of this chapter for details on ferry service and flights to Orcas Island. **Magic Air Tours** (360/376-2733 or 800/376-1929, www.magicair.com, $299 for two passengers) offers scenic biplane tours from Eastsound Airport.

By Car and Taxi

Rent cars at the Orcas ferry landing from **Orcas Moped** (360/376-5266, www.sanjuanauto.com/rental, $60 per day) or at the Eastsound Airport from **San Juan Airlines** (360/293-4691 or 800/874-4434, www.sanjuanairlines.com, $50–70 per day).

Local taxis are operated by **Orcas Island Taxi** (360/376-8294). Typical fare for two between the ferry landing and Eastsound is $27.

By Bus

Public bus service is available June through September from **Orcas Island Shuttle** (360/376-7433, www.orcasislandshuttle.com, $6 one-way, $12 all day pass). The buses circle the island five times a day and are equipped to handle bikes ($1 extra). This shuttle service also offers group charters and tours of the island by reservation starting at $50 per hour.

Lopez Island

Because of its gently rolling hills and lack of traffic, Lopez is very popular with cyclists; views of the surrounding islands and mountains to the east and west poke out from every turn. Despite being one of the largest San Juan Islands, Lopez is probably the friendliest. Waving to passing cars and bicycles is a time-honored local custom, and failure to wave will label you a tourist as surely as a camera around your neck and rubber thongs.

The business center for the island is **Lopez Village,** where you'll find a scattering of cafés, shops, a museum, stores, and especially real estate offices—which should tell you something about the island's newfound popularity. A few more businesses can be found along pretty Fisherman Bay—filled with sailboats and other craft—but the rest of the island is essentially undeveloped. Note that many local businesses shut down for the winter.

SIGHTS

Historic Sights

Lopez Historical Museum (Weeks Rd., Lopez Village, 360/468-2049, http://lopezmuseum.org, noon–4 P.M. Wed.–Sun. during July and Aug., noon–4 P.M. Fri.–Sun. in May, June, and Sept., closed the rest of the year) contains local flotsam and jetsam: the first car driven on the island, old farm equipment, and historical photos. Outside, find a reef net boat and an aging tractor.

A couple of other buildings are worth a gander on the island. The **Lopez Library** is housed in a bright red-and-white 19th-century schoolhouse just east of Lopez Village. **Lopez Island Community Church** in Lopez Village was built in 1904 and is notable for its steeple that splits into four cupolas. **Center Church,** built in 1887, is a simple white wood structure surrounded by a picket fence and next to a hilltop cemetery. The church is home to both Catholics and Lutherans (what would Martin Luther think of this?) and is approximately two miles south of Lopez Village on Fisherman Bay Road.

Country Sights

Lopez's main attraction is its rural, pastoral countryside. The long stretches of hills, pastures, orchards, and woods might just as well be New England. Cows and sheep are a common sight, including some exotic long-haired breeds at **Cape St. Mary Ranch** on the southeast end of the island. Also of interest are the bright fields of daffodils, tulips, lilies, gladiolus, and delphiniums at **Madrona Farms** (near the intersection of Richardson and Davis Bay Roads, 360/468-3441). For a complete list of nearly 50 Lopez farms, pick up the *Farm Products* brochure at the museum, or find details at www.lopezclt.org.

Lopez Island Vineyards (Fisherman Bay Rd., 360/468-3644, www.lopezislandvineyards.com, noon–5 P.M. Wed.–Sat. in summer, noon–5 P.M. Fri.–Sat. fall and spring, closed Christmas–March) is a small, family winery that grows organic grapes and produces wines from these, along with grapes from eastern Washington.

Bucolic Lopez Island is a delightful place to explore, but unfortunately, many of the beaches are privately owned and closed to the public—check for signage before traipsing to the shoreline.

Parks

On the east side of the island, the 130-acre **Spencer Spit State Park** (360/468-2251, www.parks.wa.gov) has a mile-long beach for good year-round clamming, beachcombing, hiking, and picnicking. Also here are seasonal campsites, mooring buoys, and an RV disposal station. A brackish lagoon frequently has ducks and shorebirds, and black-tailed deer are a common sight in the evening.

Additional campsites and a boat launch are available at **Odlin County Park** (360/468-2496, www.co.san-juan.wa.us/parks) at the north end of the island, just a mile from the ferry landing. A two-mile-long sandy beach and numerous hiking trails add to the allure.

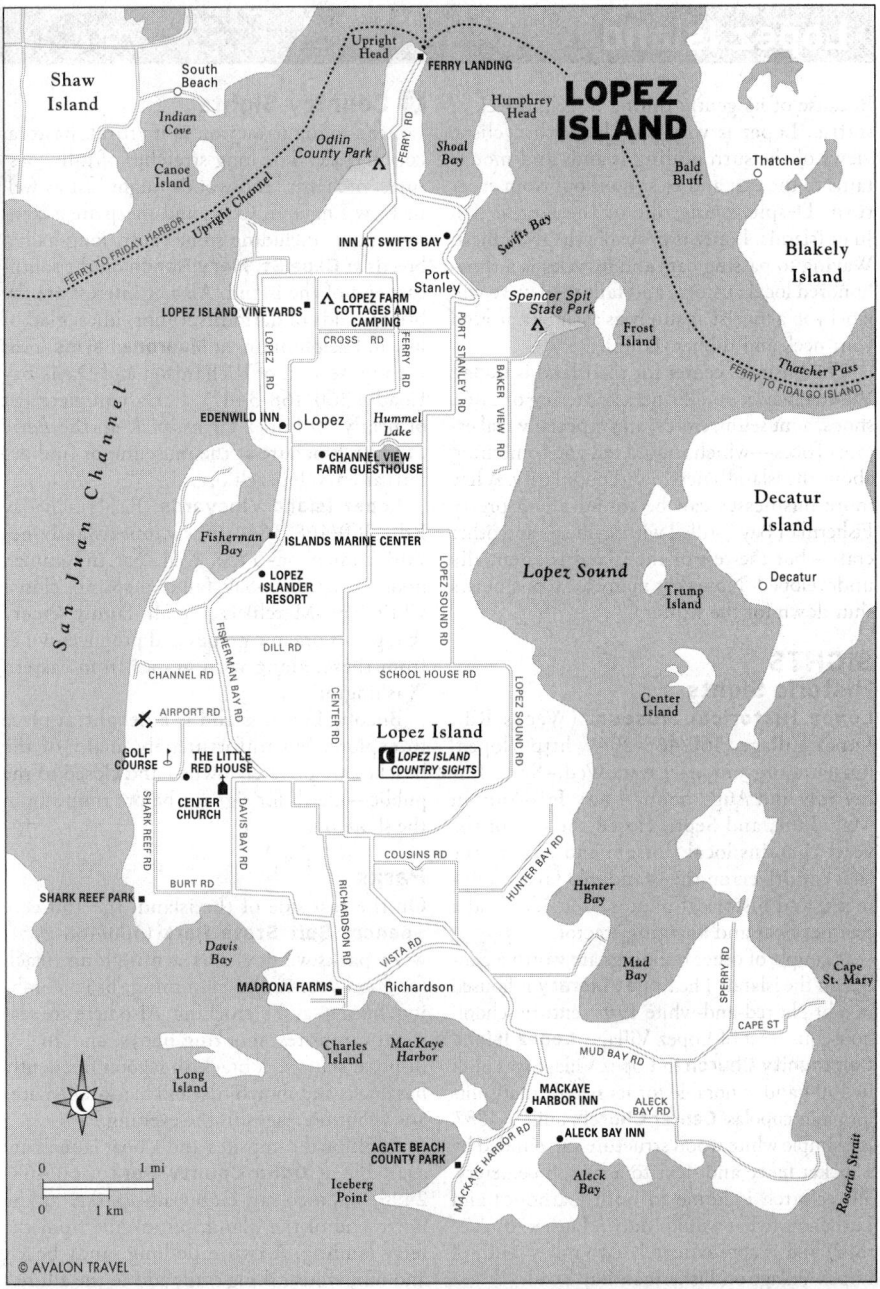
LOPEZ ISLAND
Shaw Island
South Beach
Indian Cove
Canoe Island
Upright Head
FERRY LANDING
Humphrey Head
Odlin County Park
FERRY RD
Shoal Bay
Bald Bluff
Thatcher
Upright Channel
FERRY TO FRIDAY HARBOR
INN AT SWIFTS BAY
Swifts Bay
Blakely Island
Port Stanley
LOPEZ ISLAND VINEYARDS
LOPEZ FARM COTTAGES AND CAMPING
Spencer Spit State Park
Frost Island
CROSS RD
LOPEZ RD
FERRY RD
PORT STANLEY RD
BAKER VIEW RD
Thatcher Pass
FERRY TO FIDALGO ISLAND
EDENWILD INN
Lopez
Hummel Lake
CHANNEL VIEW FARM GUESTHOUSE
San Juan Channel
Decatur Island
Fisherman Bay
ISLANDS MARINE CENTER
LOPEZ ISLANDER RESORT
Lopez Sound
Trump Island
Decatur
LOPEZ SOUND RD
FISHERMAN BAY RD
DILL RD
CHANNEL RD
SCHOOL HOUSE RD
Center Island
AIRPORT RD
CENTER RD
Lopez Island
LOPEZ ISLAND COUNTRY SIGHTS
GOLF COURSE
THE LITTLE RED HOUSE
CENTER CHURCH
SHARK REEF RD
DAVIS BAY RD
COUSINS RD
HUNTER BAY RD
BURT RD
SHARK REEF PARK
RICHARDSON RD
Hunter Bay
Davis Bay
VISTA RD
Mud Bay
SPERRY RD
Cape St. Mary
MADRONA FARMS
Richardson
CAPE ST
Charles Island
MacKaye Harbor
MUD BAY RD
Long Island
MACKAYE HARBOR INN
ALECK BAY RD
ALECK BAY INN
AGATE BEACH COUNTY PARK
MACKAYE HARBOR RD
Iceberg Point
Aleck Bay
Rosario Strait
0 1 mi
0 1 km
© AVALON TRAVEL

Very few of Lopez's beaches are open to the public. One exceptional exception is **Agate Beach,** located on the south end of the island at the end of MacKaye Harbor Road. This little park provides access to a beach filled with colorful wave-rounded stones. Another fine small park is **Shark Reef Recreation Area,** located at the south end of Shark Reef Road on the southwest side of the island. An easy half-mile path takes you through one of the few old-growth stands of trees left on Lopez to the rocky coastline. This is a good place to look for harbor seals, sea lions, and bald eagles.

EVENTS

The big event in Lopez Village is the **4th of July,** with a parade, fun run, barbecue, and fireworks. In addition to being loads of fun, the event funds the public shower facilities in the heart of Lopez Village.

Also of note is the **Tour de Lopez** (360/468-4664, www.lopezisland.com/tourdelopez.htm), a noncompetitive bike tour of the island held each April. Riders choose from routes of 10–26 miles and are treated to lunch in the village once they've pushed their last pedal.

SHOPPING

Don't miss **Chimera Gallery** (360/468-3265, www.chimeragallery.com) in Lopez Village, a cooperatively run gallery with unusual blown-glass pieces, sweaters, pottery, and jewelry. Also of interest in the Village is **Gallery 10 Fine Art** (360/468-4910, www.gallery10.com).

Get books from **Islehaven Books** (Lopez Village, 360/468-2132, www.islehaven.com). Owner Phyllis Potter is a great source for book recommendations and information on the island.

SPORTS AND RECREATION

Biking

A favorite local activity is pedaling the 30-mile loop around Lopez Island. Once you get beyond the steep initial climb from the ferry dock, the rest of the island consists of gently rolling hills, perfect conditions for families.

© ERICKA CHICKOWSKI

searching the tidepools at Shark Reef Recreation Area

Mountain bike rentals and tours are available from **Lopez Bicycle Works** (360/468-2847, www.lopezbicycleworks.com, 10 A.M.–5 P.M. daily Sept.–May, 10 A.M.–6 P.M. daily Jun.–Aug.), along Fisherman Bay just south of Lopez Village, both of which will deliver rental bikes to you at the ferry terminal or your lodging place for a small fee. Be sure to call ahead, as the owners are sometimes not in the shop during posted hours. **Cycle San Juans** (360/468-3251) guides bike tours around Lopez.

Water Sports

Lopez Kayaks (360/468-2847, www.lopezkayaks.com, $25 per day single, $40 per day double) has sea-kayak rentals and tours from Fisherman Bay; inquire at Lopez Bicycle Works on Fisherman Bay Road. Staff can deliver the kayak to you anywhere on the island. **MacKaye Harbor Inn** (MacKaye Harbor Rd., 360/468-2253 or 888/314-6140, www.mackayeharborinn.com, $25 per day) also rents kayaks May–December.

Harmony Charters (360/468-3310, www.interisland.net/countess) has a luxurious 63-foot classic motor yacht available for $375 per person per day including meals and crew. **Kismet Sailing Charters** (360/468-2435, www.rockisland.com/~sailkismet) has a 36-foot sailing yacht available.

Golf

Lopez Island Golf Club (589 Airport Rd., 360/468-2679, $18) is a nine-hole course open to the public when no member events are scheduled.

Camping

Camping is available at three comfortable places on Lopez, but none of these have RV hookups, and the two public campgrounds do not have showers. Coin-operated showers are available at the public restrooms near Lopez Village Market and at the Islands Marine Center along Fisherman Bay.

Odlin County Park (360/468-2496, www.co.san-juan.wa.us/parks $5–15 for walk-in or bike-in sites, $19–22 for car-accessible sites), just a mile south of the ferry landing, has year-round waterfront campsites. No RV hookups or showers, but the park does have a boat ramp, a long sandy beach, and hiking trails. Call 360/378-1842 for summertime reservations ($5 fee, available up to three months ahead).

Spencer Spit State Park (360/468-2251, www.parks.wa.gov, closed Nov.–Feb.), five miles from the ferry landing on the east end of Baker View Road, has primitive ($12) and regular ($17–23) campsites, plus two Adirondack-style shelters ($25). No showers or RV hookups. A delightful sandy spit is a short walk from the campground. It fills early on summer weekends, so make reservations in advance ($7 extra) by calling 888/226-7688.

Lopez Farm Cottages and Tent Camping (Fisherman Bay Rd., 360/468-3555 or 800/440-3556, www.lopezfarmcottages.com, $36 d) has 10 nicely designed walk-in campsites in the woods with hammocks and Adirondack chairs, plus a central building for cooking and showers. Other amenities include

© ERICKA CHICKOWSKI

Spencer Spit State Park

barbecues, a fireplace, croquet, and badminton. These tent sites are perfect for couples; no children under 14 or RVs allowed. Open June–October only.

ACCOMMODATIONS

During the summer it's a good idea to make reservations a month or more ahead of time, particularly on weekends. Many of the resorts, inns, and cottages offer weekly rates.

$100-150

Located along Fisherman Bay, **Lopez Islander Resort** (2864 Fisherman Bay Rd., 360/468-2233 or 800/736-3434, www.lopezislander.com) offers both motel-style units ($100–140 s or d) and three-bedroom suites with full kitchens ($250–260 for up to five people). Also here are an outdoor pool, hot tub, and marina.

Located a mile south of the ferry, the **Inn at Swifts Bay** (360/468-3636, www.swiftsbay.com) is a beautiful Tudor-style home with two guest rooms ($95–110 s or d) that share a bath, plus three suites ($155–185 s or d) with private baths. A wonderful gourmet breakfast is served, and guests will appreciate the private beach, hot tub, and sauna at this romantic getaway.

Closer into town, **Channel View Farm Guesthouse** (360/468-4415, www.channelviewfarm.com, $135 s or d) is a quaint, family-friendly cottage with a full kitchen and bath. The glass conservatory is great on a rainy day, and it's within walking distance of Lopez Village.

For the perfect home away from home right in the village, check into the ☾ **Garden Cottages** (360/468-4889, www.interisland.net/cc/, $150 s or d). These two comfy little guesthouses each come equipped with a full kitchen, woodstove, queen-size bed, deck, and a washer and dryer for cleaning up after kayaking and biking the day away. On warm summer nights you can open the windows to take advantage of the Puget Sound breezes blowing through and wake up to the gurgling of the fountain in the lovingly maintained garden.

Relax and enjoy the spectacular views of Jasper Bay from the gazebo at **Blue Fjord Cabins** (360/468-2749 or 888/633-0401, www.interisland.net/bluefjord, $130–150 d). This quiet property has two chalet-style cabins with full kitchens in a secluded wooded setting. There is a minimum stay of two to three nights, depending on the time of year.

$150-200

Surrounded by floral gardens, **Edenwild Inn B&B** (360/468-3238 or 800/606-0662, www.edenwildinn.com) is a contemporary Victorian-style inn right in Lopez Village. This is an ideal retreat for weary parents, as no kids under 12 are allowed. The eight rooms all have private baths and range $110–170 s or d.

For delightful in-the-country lodging, stay at ☾ **Lopez Farm Cottages and Tent Camping** (360/468-3555 or 800/440-3556, www.lopezfarmcottages.com, $150 d) on Fisherman Bay Road. The four immaculate and modern cottages come with kitchenettes, fireplaces, a continental breakfast brought to your door the previous evening, and an outdoor hot tub. Guests walk in the last 100 yards or so to preserve the quiet ambience. Also here is a larger and more luxurious cottage with king-size bed and private hot tub for $175 d. You can drive up to this one, and it is wheelchair-accessible. The adjacent pasture has several friendly sheep.

If you're looking to stay on the secluded south end of Lopez, rest your head in the stately 1904 farmhouse at **MacKaye Harbor Inn** (360/468-2253 or 888/314-6140, www.mackayeharborinn.com). The four rooms ($155–185 s or d) have shared or private baths, and the suite ($215 d) features a fireplace, private deck, antique furnishings, and private bath. All are just a stone's throw from the water, where you can rent kayaks to explore protected MacKaye Harbor. Children are accepted with advance reservations, and guests can borrow a bike to explore the island.

FOOD

One of Lopez Island's best traits is its laid-back atmosphere. Unfortunately, this means that store and restaurant hours are pretty fluid, varying greatly depending on the seasons and the whims of the owners. Restaurants that close altogether during low season are noted; call ahead to find out when the others will be open.

Love Dog Café (Lopez Village, 360/468-2150, $15) serves fresh fish, steaks, and sandwiches year-round. The café is open for three meals a day and has a few tables on the patio.

Holly B's Bakery (360/468-2133, open Apr.–late Nov., $4) in Lopez Village is *the* place to go for great breads, cookies, scones, and cinnamon rolls. Next door is **Caffe La Bohemé** (360/468-2294, $4), where you can sip espresso at tables out front. **Isabel's Espresso** (Lopez Village, 360/468-4114, $4) is a hip hangout with a large outdoor deck that attracts locals; it sometimes has live music, too.

Lopez Island Pharmacy (Village Rd. in Lopez Village, 360/468-2616, www.lopezislandpharmacy.com, $6) has an old-fashioned soda fountain that fills with locals at lunchtime. **South End Café** (1176 Rural Route 2, 360/468-3198) bakes good pizzas.

The **Bay Café** (Lopez Village, 360/468-3700, www.bay-cafe.com, $25) is Lopez Island's four-star restaurant, with Northwest cuisine that includes seafood and grilled meats. Open only for dinner. Reservations are essential at this very popular place with a deck facing Fisherman Bay.

Not as expensive, but still very good is **Bucky's Lopez Island Grill** (Lopez Village, 360/468-2595, closed Oct.–Mar., $10). Bucky's has the best burgers in town as well as great fish and chips, barbecued ribs, salads, and chicken.

The **Galley Restaurant and Lounge** (360/468-2713, $12) on Fisherman Bay is a friendly locals' joint best known for its enormous omelettes, prime rib, abalone, and rooftop dining.

Get groceries from **Village Market** (360/468-2266) in Lopez Village. It is closed on Sunday, so stock up ahead of time or eat in a restaurant. The **Lopez Island Farmers Market** in Lopez Village is open 10 A.M.–2 P.M. Saturday mid-May to early September. Stop by for fresh garden produce and flowers, along with arts and crafts.

© ERICKA CHICKOWSKI

Bay Café on Lopez Island

INFORMATION

Contact the **Lopez Island Chamber of Commerce** (360/468-3800, www.lopezisland.com) for local information, or pick up a free *Map and Guide of Lopez Island* from the museum or local real estate offices. Check your email at the **Lopez Library** (360/468-2265) near Lopez Village, and wash laundry at **Keep it Clean** (Fisherman Bay Rd., a mile north of Lopez Village, 360/468-3466).

GETTING AROUND

The **Washington State Ferry** (206/464-6400, www.wsdot.wa.gov/ferries) docks at the north end of Lopez Island, approximately four miles from Lopez Village. See *Getting There* at the beginning of this chapter for details on ferry service (including private ferries) and flights to Lopez Island. There is no bus service on Lopez, but **A Lopez Cab Courier** (360/468-2227) has taxi service and rental cars.

Other Islands

In addition to the three main islands, the San Juans contain a myriad of smaller ones, including some islets that only appear at low tide. Shaw Island is served by the ferry system but has limited services. Of the remaining islands, only Blakely Island has a store and marina. The rest are either marine state parks, part of the San Juan Islands National Wildlife Preserve, or private property.

Getting There and Around

The state ferry does not stray beyond the four most popular islands (San Juan, Orcas, Lopez, and Shaw), and access to the others is generally by private boat or floatplane.

SHAW ISLAND

The least visited of the ferry-served islands, Shaw (pop. 200) is primarily residential and remains essentially undeveloped, with second-growth forests covering most of the land. No trespassing signs limit access to all but a few beaches. You won't find any B&Bs, cottage industries, or bike rental places on the island, but for campers and day-trippers seeking solitude this can make for the perfect getaway.

By law, the **Little Portion Store** (360/468-2288) at the ferry landing is the only business allowed. The store itself sells groceries, along with beer, wine, and chocolate for decadence. You can learn more about Shaw on the Shaw Island Association's website: www.shawislanders.org.

© ERICKA CHICKOWSKI

Washington State Ferries offer a vital link to island explorers.

Sights and Camping

Shaw Island Historical Museum (360/468-4068) is housed in a small log cabin at the intersection of Blind Bay and Hoffman Cove Roads. It's open 2–4 P.M. Tuesday, 10 A.M.–noon Thursday, and 2–4 P.M. Saturday (the same hours as the adjacent library). Out front is a reef-netting fishing boat similar to those still used to fish for salmon in the San Juans. Across the way is the **Little Red Schoolhouse,** an old one-room grade school on the National Register of Historic Places.

South Beach County Park (a.k.a. Shaw Island County Park, www.co.san-juan.wa.us/parks), two miles south of the ferry landing, has a dozen in-the-trees campsites ($10–12), a picnic area, boat launch, and limited drinking water. There are no showers. There are no other camping or lodging options on Shaw, so advance reservations (360/378-1842; $5 fee) are recommended on summer weekends. The 65-acre park is best known for its long beach, where you'll often find sand dollars. The campground is open year-round.

The University of Washington's **Cedar Rock Biological Preserve** is a quiet, off-the-beaten-path place on the south end of Hoffman Cove Road. A trail leads through fields, woods, and past small coves.

ISLAND STATE PARKS

A number of the smaller islands in the San Juan archipelago are preserved as marine state parks and largely undeveloped. Access is by private boat or sea kayak. The parks have primitive campsites, no drinking water (bring plenty with you), and no garbage collection. Sea kayaks are a popular island-hopping mode of transportation, but since some of the smaller islands are several miles out, be careful not to overestimate your ability. Sailboats and motorboats can tie up at mooring buoys in these marine parks for a fee, typically $0.50 per foot per day.

The parks listed below all have camping and are easily reachable by kayak. In addition, many other islets are open to day use, but islands within the San Juan Islands National Wildlife Refuge are off-limits to protect nesting birds and other animals. For information on the marine parks and the wildlife refuge, talk with folks at Lime Kiln State Park on San Juan Island (360/378-2044, www.parks.wa.gov).

Sucia Island State Park

Covering 564 acres, Sucia Island State Park is the largest and most popular marine state park, and with good reason. The U-shaped park sits three miles north of Orcas Island and contains numerous protected anchorages, 50 mooring buoys, 55 primitive campsites ($10), and six miles of trails. The shoreline has delightful sandy beaches for sunbathing, exploring, clamming, and crabbing, plus bizarre water-carved sandstone formations. Offshore, you can scuba dive on sunken wrecks. Don't expect to be the only visitor on Sucia Island; on a summer weekend the waters around the island are jam-packed with U.S. and Canadian vessels of all description. The island is about 2.5 miles away from Orcas, perhaps putting it out of the reach of some beginning paddlers. Hire a guide if you are unsure of your abilities.

Outer Island Expeditions (360/376-3711, www.outerislandx.com) offers a once-daily ferry to Sucia from Orcas Island for $45 round-trip per person, plus $10 for a mountain bike or camping gear and $20 for a small kayak.

Blind Island State Park

This three-acre grassy island just north of Shaw Island in Blind Bay is a great place to watch the ferries pass by. The tiny park has mooring buoys and four primitive campsites ($10).

Doe Island State Park

Located just southeast of Orcas Island, Doe Island has five primitive campsites ($10) on a small, secluded island with a rocky shoreline. There are no mooring buoys, but it is just a short kayak paddle from the hot tubs at Doe Bay Village Resort.

James Island State Park

Less than a half mile east of Decatur Island and just four miles from the Anacortes ferry terminal, James Island has 13 primitive campsites ($10) on a small, cliff-faced, forested island with sunny beaches on the Rosario Strait. The island also has short hiking trails, mooring buoys, and a dock.

Jones Island State Park

One of the most used of the San Juan state marine parks, this 188-acre island is just a mile west of Orcas Island near Deer Harbor. The park has 10 primitive campsites ($10), seven mooring buoys, and a public dock. Hiking trails cross the island, passing places where a 1990 storm knocked down magnificent old-growth trees.

Turn Island State Park

Turn Island, just a quarter mile from San Juan's east shore and within easy kayaking distance of Friday Harbor, is a very popular place for picnickers and campers. It features 10 primitive campsites ($10), three mooring buoys, two beaches, and three miles of wooded hiking trails.

Posey Island State Park

This pinprick of an island covers just one acre and is located a quarter mile north of San Juan Island's Roche Harbor. Shallow waters and a single primitive campsite ($10) make this a favorite spot for folks on kayaks and canoes in search of their own little island.

PRIVATE ISLANDS

The rest of the San Juan Islands are home to a few hundred individuals. Some islands have only a single home, others a few dozen residences occupied seasonally. None have more than 80 or so people. Privacy is closely guarded on most of these islands, and visitors are not appreciated.

As the state ferry heads west from Anacortes to the San Juans, it threads its way between two privately owned islands, **Blakely** and **Decatur.** Blakely Island has a public marina with a store, post office, fuel, laundry, and showers on the north end, but the rest of the island is private and off-limits.

Waldron Island, northwest of Orcas, is nearly all private land, and much of the island is flat and marshy, though the south end rises to 600 feet at Disney Mountain. Over 400 acres along Cowlitz Bay and Disney Mountain are lands managed by the Nature Conservancy (www.tnc-washington.org) and San Juan Preservation Trust (www.sjpt.org), with public access for day use only.

OLYMPIC PENINSULA AND THE COAST

Washington's Olympic Peninsula juts up like a thumb hitchhiking a ride from Canada. This diverse 6,500-square-mile landmass ranges from remote rocky beaches to subalpine meadows, from majestic glacier-faced mountains to spooky rainforests. One of the most remarkable parts of the state, the peninsula has a rugged and wild beauty that embodies the spirit of the Evergreen State as much as any place in Washington. The beating heart of the peninsula is Olympic National Park, an unspoiled forest rich with old growth trees, wildlife, and awe-inspiring vistas. Beyond the park, the peninsula lives by the chainsaw, with lumber still providing paychecks for local residents. Tree farms abound, many with signs indicating when they were last cut and when the next round of logging will take place. The large trucks hauling massive cut logs are a common sight.

© WASHINGTON STATE TOURISM

HIGHLIGHTS

Dosewallips State Park: Hike, swim, fish, or clam at this recreational centerpiece where the Dosewallips River meets the Hood Canal (page 301).

Fort Worden State Park: Explore underground bunkers, an airship balloon hangar, and even a marine science center in this park on the northeast corner of the Olympic Peninsula (page 308).

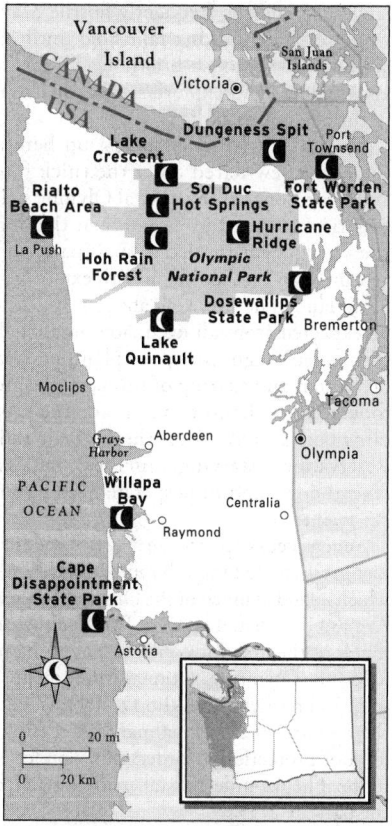

Dungeness Spit: Walk the longest naturally occurring sand spit in the United States all the way to the end and reward yourself with a tour of the historic lighthouse (page 316).

Hurricane Ridge: Peer over at Canada, Seattle, and even Mount Hood atop this amazing viewpoint. In the summer, the wildflowers abound here (page 324).

Lake Crescent: Explore the vividly colored lake by boat, or just take a hike by the shore (page 332).

Sol Duc Hot Springs: Nothing beats a post-hike soak in Washington's most famous hot springs (page 334).

Rialto Beach Area: The towering sea stacks dotted with evergreens, the enormous blanched driftwood logs, and the thundering surf all make for a dramatic visit to this stretch of shoreline (page 341).

Hoh Rain Forest: Who says rainforests are only in South America? Bring a slicker and enjoy the magnificently mossy trees and shrouds of ferns covering this forest (page 342).

Lake Quinault: Take a hike through the old-growth forest that surrounds this showcase of the Quinault Valley (page 345).

Cape Disappointment State Park: Sitting at the mouth of the Columbia River, this is the most impressive of all the state parks, offering museums, beaches, wooded trails, lighthouses, and military history galore (page 366).

Willapa Bay: Hunt for oysters, kayak the flats, and explore the islands at one of the nation's most pristine estuaries (page 369).

LOOK FOR TO FIND RECOMMENDED SIGHTS, ACTIVITIES, DINING, AND LODGING.

Olympic National Park

Hard-core hikers and campers who think they've seen it all will never forget the wonder of the Olympic National Park, even after just one visit. The deep, damp rain forests, the frosted mountaintops, the aquamarine rivers have a fantastical allure, seeming to leap from the pages of storybooks. Auto roads barely penetrate the park, but more than 600 miles of hiking trails meander through, crossing and connecting the park's virgin forest core, its matchless beaches, and its alpine peaks.

Olympic National Park is probably most famous for the lush rain forests that carpet the western flanks of the mountains. The best known and most visited is Hoh Rain Forest, but the others—Quinault and Queets—are fascinating, too, and visitors are more likely to have a more personal experience. Soaking up the ample rainfall, enormous spruce, cedar, fir, and hemlock trees covered with moss and lichen tower over the traveler, forcing a certain degree of perspective on life. The crystal-clear rivers and streams, the thick scent of fertility, and the tickle of mist on your eyelashes give this forest an unforgettable feeling of enchantment.

The diversity of climate and geography in Olympic National Park's 908,720 acres of wilderness is one of many reasons it was among the 100 parks named a World Heritage Park by the United Nations in 1981. The largest old-growth coniferous forest in the Lower 48 states, the park is home to 200 species of birds and 70 species of mammals, including Roosevelt elk, black bear, deer, bald eagles, and Olympic marmots. Today Olympic National Park sees over four million visitors a year. Despite its popularity, the park's size and hard-to-reach interior mean it's not hard to find peaceful solitude on the many lakes and trails.

HISTORY

American Indian tribes once sparsely inhabited the land now known as the Olympic Peninsula; evidence of their presence here dates back thousands of years. Coastal tribes lived off of the once-abundant salmon or hunted the Pacific gray whale, a tradition still practiced by treaty right by the Makah Tribe today. Starting in the 16th century, the region attracted the attention first of the Spanish, then the English, and finally, Americans. Due to the unforgiving landscape and the frequently hostile Makah, white settlement didn't take hold until 1851, although the Spanish briefly held a fort here and trappers and explorers plied their trades in the area much earlier.

Coastal settlements sprang up here and there, but few dared enter the thick forests and steep slopes of the central Olympics. This situation changed in 1889 when the *Seattle Press* newspaper funded a small party of adventurers and tasked them with exploring the hinterland. The trip went about as well as can be expected from an excursion organized by the media. Plagued by poor planning, a brutal winter, and a string of mishaps, the group took six months to travel across the mountains before arriving on the Quinalt Indian Reservation—starving, minus two mules and several dogs, and in desperate need of medical attention.

Seven years after the *Press* expedition, Congress created the Olympic Forest Reserve, which included much of the Olympic Peninsula. In 1909 President Theodore Roosevelt set aside much of the area for conservation by naming it Mount Olympus National Monument, and in 1938 President Franklin D. Roosevelt made the monument a national park, increasing the level of protection afforded this wonder even more. The 62-mile coastal strip was added to the park in 1953.

The peninsula itself has a long history of boom-and-bust cycles. Cities on the northern coast jockeyed over the right to collect customs charges from incoming shipping, while other towns rose up overnight in anticipation of the transcontinental railroad.

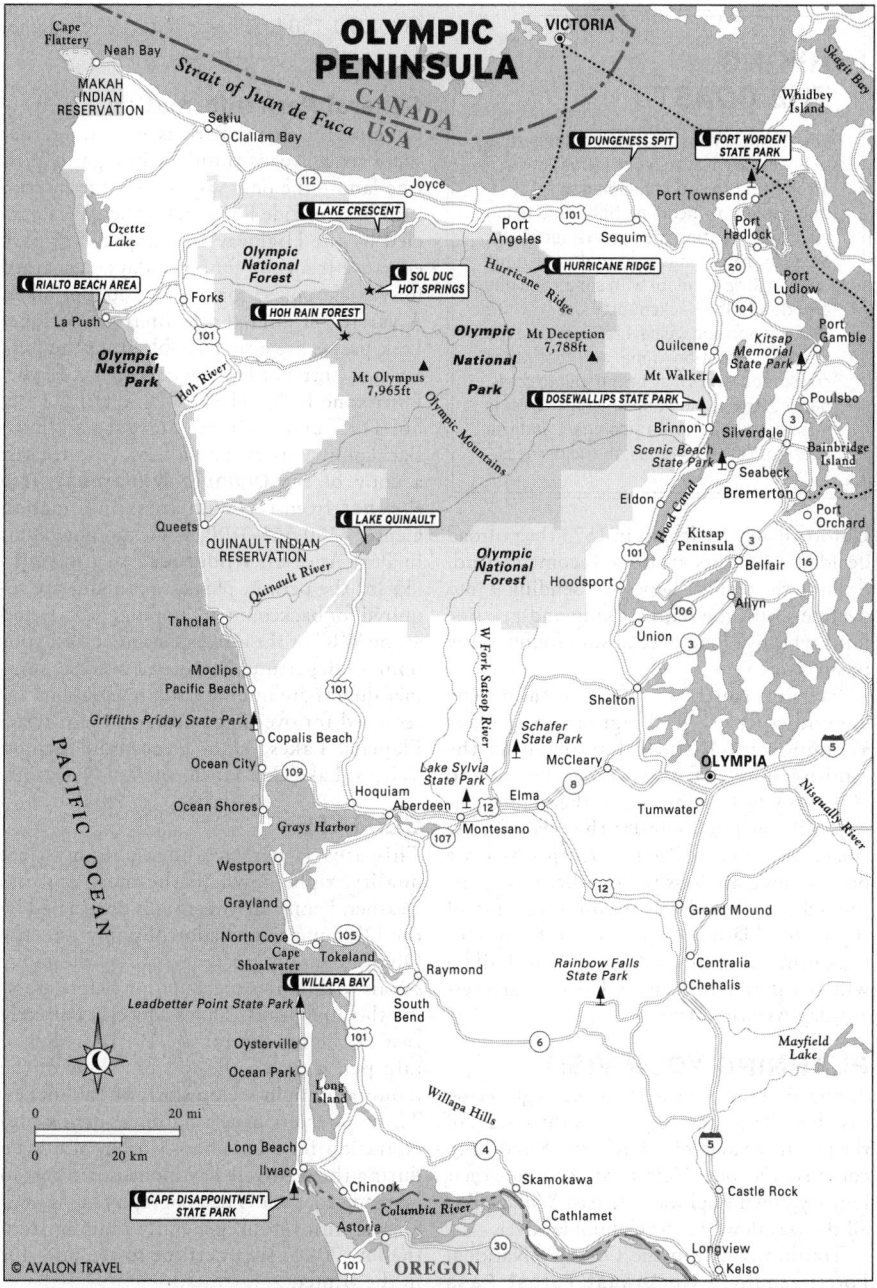
OLYMPIC PENINSULA
VICTORIA
Cape Flattery
Neah Bay
MAKAH INDIAN RESERVATION
Strait of Juan de Fuca
CANADA
USA
Sekiu
Clallam Bay
Whidbey Island
Skagit Bay
DUNGENESS SPIT
FORT WORDEN STATE PARK
Joyce
Port Townsend
LAKE CRESCENT
Port Angeles
Sequim
Port Hadlock
Ozette Lake
Olympic National Forest
SOL DUC HOT SPRINGS
HURRICANE RIDGE
Hurricane Ridge
Port Ludlow
RIALTO BEACH AREA
Forks
La Push
HOH RAIN FOREST
Olympic National Park
Hoh River
Mt Deception 7,788ft
Quilcene
Kitsap Memorial State Park
Port Gamble
Mt Olympus 7,965ft
Olympic Mountains
Mt Walker
DOSEWALLIPS STATE PARK
Poulsbo
Brinnon
Silverdale
Scenic Beach State Park
Bainbridge Island
Seabeck
Bremerton
Eldon
Hood Canal
Port Orchard
Queets
LAKE QUINAULT
QUINAULT INDIAN RESERVATION
Quinault River
Kitsap Peninsula
Belfair
Hoodsport
Allyn
Taholah
Union
W Fork Satsop River
Moclips
Pacific Beach
Shelton
Griffiths Priday State Park
Copalis Beach
Schafer State Park
McCleary
OLYMPIA
Ocean City
Lake Sylvia State Park
Hoquiam
Aberdeen
Elma
Tumwater
Nisqually River
Ocean Shores
Grays Harbor
Montesano
PACIFIC OCEAN
Westport
Grayland
Grand Mound
North Cove
Cape Shoalwater
Tokeland
Raymond
Rainbow Falls State Park
Centralia
Chehalis
WILLAPA BAY
Leadbetter Point State Park
South Bend
Oysterville
Mayfield Lake
Ocean Park
Long Island
Willapa Hills
0 20 mi
0 20 km
Long Beach
Ilwaco
Skamokawa
Castle Rock
CAPE DISAPPOINTMENT STATE PARK
Chinook
Columbia River
Cathlamet
Astoria
Longview
Kelso
OREGON
© AVALON TRAVEL

HIKING THE COAST

The Olympic coastline can be dangerous to hikers. Two "watch out" situations are attempting to round headlands and getting caught by incoming tides, and being struck by floating logs in the surf. Park Service offices have a helpful *Olympic Coastal Strip* handout with a map and dos and don'ts for backcountry users. Note that the Hoh and Quillayute Rivers are too deep to ford at any time, and that other creeks and rivers may be difficult to cross, particularly at high tide or when runoff is strong. Always take a tide chart and use caution. This is, after all, the wilderness.

Unfortunately for locals, in 1873 the railroad decided to end its route in Tacoma instead, dashing the region's hopes and sending it into decline. Still, the hardworking and genuine folks who live here have always found a way to survive.

Farther south at the mouth of the Columbia River, Washington's coast holds an important historical position as the landing point of Meriwether Lewis and William Clark at the end of their transcontinental journey in 1805; they had finally "reached the great Pacific Ocean which we been so long anxious to See." Because game proved scarce and the Washington side of the Columbia lacked protection from winter storms, they crossed the river to build a winter camp called Fort Clatsop near present-day Astoria, Oregon.

PLANNING YOUR VISIT

A ringed network of roads makes sightseeing easy here. Highway 101 follows three sides of the peninsula and joins Highways 8 and 12 to complete the loop. Visitors can continue their journey down Highway 101 past Willapa Bay all the way down to the Columbia River.

Trailheads within the Olympic National Forest require a **Northwest Forest Pass** (800/270-7504, www.fs.fed.us/r6/feedemo, $30 annual, $5 daily).

General Park Information

Olympic National Park is unique in that there are no roads running through its pristine land—the only way to visit the interior is to hike or ride horseback. The park is circled by the Highway 101 loop. A $15 park entrance fee, good for seven days, is charged for vehicles, or $5 for those on foot or bikes. A variety of annual and lifetime National Park passes are also available from the park service. Entrance fees are collected at Elwha, Hurricane Ridge/Heart O' the Hills, Hoh, Sol Duc, and Staircase entrance stations. Backcountry users should be sure to request a copy of the ***Olympic Wilderness Trip Planner*** from the Wilderness Information Center (360/565-3100, www.nps.gov/olym) in Port Angeles. **Wilderness use permits** ($5 for the permit, plus $2 pp/night) are required for backcountry camping; pick one up at the WIC or the ranger station nearest your point of departure. Because of overuse, summer quotas are in effect and reservations are required for overnight hikes in the Ozette, Flapjack Lakes, Hoh, Grand and Badger Valleys, Lake Constance, and Sol Duc areas.

CLIMATE

This area is has an undeniable mystical quality, right down to the most unusual weather. Peninsular weather is dominated by the Olympic rain shadow. Simply put, the Olympic mountain range causes the moist sea air to dump its precipitation before crossing the high peaks. That's why cities directly east of the mountains see 10–17 inches of rain per year, but the western slope of the mountain might see upwards of 160 inches! Three-quarters of the national park's precipitation falls October–March, and even during the relatively dry months, it's best to be ready for rain. The geography helps keep temperatures mild, generally ranging from the low 70s in summertime to the mid-40s in the winter.

Hood Canal and Vicinity

The Kitsap Peninsula is separated from the Olympic Peninsula by the Hood Canal, a 1.5-mile-wide, 65-mile-long channel of saltwater. Highway 101 follows the west side of the "Canal Zone," providing a delicious tidewater drive through second-growth forests with countless vistas of the waterway from every possible angle. The road hugs the canal, tucking in and out of various inlets along the way. Much of the route between Quilcene and Union is minimally developed, and scattered resort estates dot the shoreline. Several places sell freshly shucked oysters along the way. At the southwest corner of Hood Canal, the waterway makes a sharp bend, angling northward and nearly turning the Kitsap Peninsula into an island. South from this elbow is the largest town in the area, Shelton, and at the head of the canal is the fast-growing region around Belfair.

In addition to the glorious vistas along Hood Canal, you'll discover camping and hiking at two state parks and on nearby Olympic National Forest and Olympic National Park lands, plus outstanding scuba diving and fishing. Lake Cushman is a popular fishing and summer recreation spot, just east of the Staircase entrance to Olympic National Park, and the dam at the lake's southeast end produces some of Tacoma's electricity.

History

Like many other features in Washington, Hood Canal received its name from Capt. George Vancouver during his 1792 exploration of Puget Sound. He called it "Hood's Channel," after a British naval hero, Lord Hood, but a printer's error in Vancouver's report changed the word channel to canal. Hood Canal is *not* a canal, but actually a long, glacially carved fjord. The waters of Hood Canal are more susceptible to pollution than other parts of Puget Sound because of limited tidal flushing. Rapid

© ERICKA CHICKOWSKI

Hood Canal

development around the southern end of Hood Canal has led to increasing concerns over water pollution, and several beaches have been closed to shellfish gathering in recent years.

HOOD CANAL BRIDGE

Hood Canal is spanned at only one point along its entire length, by the 6,471-foot-long **Hood Canal Floating Bridge** that connects the Kitsap and Olympic Peninsulas near Port Gamble. The world's third-longest floating bridge (the longest over tidewater) was opened in 1961 and served the peninsulas well until February 13, 1979, when a violent storm with 100-mph gales broke off and sank nearly a mile of the western portion of the bridge. In a remarkable feat of driving, a trucker in his 18-wheeler backed the semi at almost full throttle off the bridge when it began to sink. To prevent another sinking, the center span of the rebuilt bridge is now opened when wind conditions are severe. You can cast a line for salmon or bottom fish from the fishing pontoon; there's a special anglers' parking lot at the Kitsap end of the bridge. Keep your eyes open for submarines; the Navy's Trident fleet often passes through en route to or from the Bangor submarine base. Just north of the bridge, **Salsbury Point County Park** has a boat launch and camping.

SHELTON

The peaceful blue-collar town of Shelton (pop. 9,000) occupies the head of Oakland Bay on the southwest toe of Puget Sound. It is both the Mason County seat and the only incorporated city in the county. Put on your plaid shirt and baseball cap to blend in. It's easy to see the importance of timber here: a sprawling yellow Simpson Timber Co. lumber and plywood mill dominates the town, and the surrounding land is filled with tree farms in varying stages of regrowth. Rayonier Research Center, where the chemistry and manufacture of pulp is studied, is also here, as is a maximum-security state prison. Downtown has wide streets and a friendly atmosphere, but up the hill you'll find homogenized America, with a McDonald's, Wal-Mart, and Super 8 Motel.

© KITSAP PENINSULA VISITOR & CONVENTION BUREAU/JEAN BOYLE

The Hood Canal Bridge is the longest floating bridge over saltwater.

Mason County is one of the nation's largest Christmas tree–producing areas; every year, over two million trees are shipped worldwide. Originally named Sheltonville, the town was founded in 1855 by David Shelton. Forestry and oystering were, and still are, the primary industries here, beginning in 1878 when the first shipment of highly prized Olympia oysters left Kamilche.

Sights

The **Mason County Historical Museum** (5th St. and Railroad Ave., 360/426-1020, noon–5 P.M. Tues.–Fri., noon–4 P.M. Sat., donations accepted), in the old library building, emphasizes the importance of logging in Shelton's history with displays on railroad logging, historical photos, and artifacts.

"Tollie," the locomotive in downtown Shelton between 2nd and 3rd on Railroad Ave., is a 96-ton Shay logging engine that saw most of the country in its heyday. Behind it sits a red caboose housing the visitors center. Downtown Shelton has a number of antique shops scattered along Railroad Avenue.

The **Bronze Works** (50 W. Fredson Rd., 360/427-3857 or 888/821-0372, www.nwwebessentials.com/bronzeworks, 8 A.M.–5 P.M. Mon.–Fri., 10 A.M.–6 P.M. Sat.) is a critical part of the Kimberly T. Gallery and Sculpture Garden. Located four miles south of town on Highway 101, this is the only bronze foundry in Washington. Visitors can tour the facility and view finished pieces in the gallery; bronze is poured most Thursdays. Classes and workshops are available.

Tour the Department of Wildlife's **Shelton Trout Hatchery** (Eells Hill Rd., approximately eight miles north of Shelton, 360/426-3669, 8 A.M.–5 P.M. daily). Continue up the road, turning right at the sign marking Denny Ahl Seed Orchard, and cross over the 440-foot-high **Steel Arch Bridge** that spans the Skokomish Gorge.

Entertainment and Events

Little Creek Casino (91 W. Hwy. 108, 360/427-7711 or 800/667-7711, www.littlecreek-casino.com, 9 A.M.–4 A.M. Sun.–Thurs., 9 A.M.–5 A.M. Fri.–Sat.) deals blackjack, craps, and roulette and hosts frequent no-limit Hold éEm tournaments. Try the inexpensive buffet dining or the surprisingly good café.

Early June's **Mason County Forest Festival** (www.masoncountyforestfestival.com) includes parades, a carnival, musical entertainment, arts and crafts, and logging competition in such events as the Two-Man Double Buck, Speed Climb, Ax Throw, and the ever-popular Jack and Jill.

Mason County Fair (www.masoncountyfair.com) is held the last weekend in July at the fairgrounds. Highlights include live entertainment and traditional county fair favorites such as 4-H exhibits and cake and preserve competitions.

Come back in September for The West Coast Oyster Shucking Championship and Seafood Festival, a.k.a. **OysterFest** (www.oysterfest.org). The main event is high-speed oyster shucking, and those shells will fly. Surrounding the competition are two days of wine-tasting, an oyster cook-off, food booths, art and boating exhibits, dancers, bands, and magicians.

The holiday season brings Santa to Shelton during the annual **Christmas Parade and Bazaar** (www.sheltonchamber.org), held the first weekend in December with a parade by land and by sea.

Sports and Recreation

Play a quick round of golf at **Lake Limerick Country Club** (790 E. Saint Andrews Dr., 360/426-6290, www.lakelimerick.com) a fir tree–lined nine-hole course playable year-round.

Cyclists can check out a relatively level nine miles of forested single-track just north of Shelton. The Lower South Fork Skokomish Trail can be reached by taking Highway 101 north of town, turning west on Skokomish Valley Road, taking Road 23 to the Brown Creek Campground and then following Forest Service Road 2394 for a bumpy quarter mile.

Shelton is a good place to enjoy some of

Mason County's better hunting. Deer, elk, grouse, turkey, goose, and duck are all legal within season. Or, if you've got the guts, come out and take down a fearsome bear. Regulations are many and can be found at the Washington Department of Fish and Wildlife (360/902-2464, www.wdfw.wa.gov).

You'll need a boat to get to tiny **Stretch Point State Park** (12 miles north of Shelton next to the town of Grapeview, www.parks.wa.gov), which has no camping, showers, toilets, or drinking water but has one of the best sandy beaches around Puget Sound. Grapeview itself has vineyards, a country store, marina, and a sometimes-open museum.

Accommodations

When it comes to chain motels in Shelton, **Super 8 Motel** (2943 N. View Cir., 360/426-1654 or 800/843-1991, www.super8.com, $55 s or $65 d) is it. The rooms aren't a disaster, but they aren't all that comfy either. Most guests—even non-gamblers—would be better served heading into Hoodsport or splurging a little and checking in to the ☾ Little Creek Casino Resort (91 W. Highway 108, 360/427-7711, www.little-creek-casino.com, $145–275 d), which offers very nice rooms for reasonable rates. There's a spa on-site, plus an indoor pool and the ever-popular buffet restaurant.

Food

A good place to start the day is **Pine Tree Restaurant** (102 S. 1st, 360/426-2604, 5 A.M.–8 P.M. daily) a family place with big breakfasts served all day, plus seafood and steak for dinner.

Owned by Taylor United and managed by Xinh Dwelley—a talented Vietnamese chef and former oyster-shucking champ—☾ **Xinh's Clam & Oyster House** (221 W. Railroad Ave., 360/427-8709, 5–9 P.M. Tues.–Sat.) delivers such treats as hot and spicy seafood soup, oysters sautéed in black bean sauce, and grilled halibut.

If tasty affordable food beats out elegance as your chief concern, try **Suzan's Grill** (1927 Olympic Hwy. N, 360/432-8939, www.suzansgrill.com, 8 A.M.–3 P.M. Sun.–Thurs., Fri.–Sat. 8 A.M.–9 P.M.). This family-owned eatery trumpets "Nothing from Cans at Suzan's."

You can wallow in nostalgia and a big beefy burger at the same time at the local **A&W Family Restaurant** (1729 Olympic Hwy N., 360/426-2002). The drive-in still offers its namesake root beer and classic curbside service.

Get produce at the **Shelton Farmers Market** (3rd St. between Cedar and Franklin, 360/427-8260, 9 A.M.–2 P.M. Sat. mid-May to late-Sept).

Information and Services

For maps and festival information, contact the **Shelton-Mason County Chamber of Commerce** (in the caboose on Railroad Ave., 360/426-2021 or 800/576-2021, www.shelton-chamber.org. 9 A.M.–6 P.M. Mon.–Fri., 9 A.M.–3 P.M. Sat.–Sun. June–Sept., 10 A.M.–5 P.M. Mon.–Fri. Oct.–May.).

Mason General Hospital (901 Mountain View Dr., 360/426-3102) is the nearest emergency room to Shelton. Hurt pets can be taken to Haigh Veterinary Hospital (81 S.E. Walker Park Rd., 360/426-1840) or Shelton Veterinary Hospital (104 E. J St., 360/426-2616).

Getting There

Mason County Transit (360/427-5033 or 800/374-3747) has free bus service throughout the county. All buses are kitted-out with bike racks. **Olympic Air** (360/426-1477, www.olyair.com, $250 per hour) offers scenic flights over the area.

UNION

The scattered settlement of Union occupies land near the "elbow" where Hood Inlet angles abruptly to the northeast. Summer and weekend homes crowd the highway, struggling to find their place among the relics of the past, such as the very picturesque **Dalby Waterwheel,** built in 1923 and still able to generate electricity if the need arose. A few miles west is the **Skokomish Indian Reservation,** near the intersection of Highways 101 and 106.

You can tell you're on the reservation by all the fireworks stands that line the highway. The tribal center houses a small museum with arts and crafts.

Sights and Recreation

Twanoh State Park (seven miles east of Union on Hwy. 106, 360/902-8608, www.parks.wa.gov) is a very popular spot for picnicking beneath tall trees, and swimming and water-skiing on relatively warm Hood Canal. The 182-acre park also has several miles of hiking trails along scenic Twanoh Creek, sturdy CCC-constructed structures from the 1930s, a tennis court, a concession stand with snacks and groceries, bathhouses, and camping in tent ($19) and RV ($26) sites with coin-operated showers.

The Skokomish Tribe operates the **Lucky Dog Casino** (19330 N. US Hwy. 101, 360/877-5656, 9 A.M.–midnight Sun.–Thurs., 9 A.M.–2 A.M. Fri.–Sat.), a smoke-free house featuring slots, blackjack, Pai Gow, and an amateur Texas Hold éEm league with free tournaments.

Practicalities

The guest rooms at Union's elegant ☾ **Alderbrook Resort and Spa** (7101 E. Hwy. 106, 360/898-2200 or 800/622-9370, www.alderbrookinn.com, $190–420 s or d) are simply but beautifully decorated, many augmented by views of the Olympic mountains. Its spa offers traditional services plus unique treatments such as ancient Hawaiian lomilomi massage. The downstairs Restaurant at Alderbrook showcases local seafood, and the bar serves beer, wine, and cocktails.

Robin Hood Village (6780 E. Hwy. 106, 360/898-2163, $85–155 d) has seven cottages with hot tubs and kitchenettes. The smaller, older ones fit two people cozily, while the newer, larger ones are ideal for two couples. Also on-site is the **Robin Hood Pub** (6791 E. Hwy. 106, 360/898-4400, 5–9 P.M. Wed.–Sun.), which serves a full range of meals from a $12 burger and fries up to a $40 tenderloin. Great desserts, too. **Union Country Store** (5130 E. Hwy. 106, 360/898-2641) has a small deli.

Mason County Transit (360/427-5033 or 800/374-3747) provides free bus service throughout the county.

HOODSPORT AREA

The town of Hoodsport is the largest along the west side of Hood Canal and can provide most of your travel needs. This is the place to get Forest Service and Park Service information and to stock up on food before heading north. Hoodsport's lodgings cater to scuba divers, particularly small groups who come to explore the amazingly diverse creatures in the deep, clear waters just offshore. The lack of strong currents and minor tidal fluctuations help make this a good place for beginning divers. Visibility is best in the winter—to 50 feet—when fewer plankton are in the water. Other people come to water ski, sail, windsurf, or to catch shrimp, fish, and crabs. The **Hood Canal Hatchery** is right in town.

Five miles north from Hoodsport is the village of **Lilliwaup,** with a general store and motel, an RV park, and a pair of restaurants. The little burg of **Potlatch** is two miles south of Hoodsport on Highway 101.

Potlatch State Park

Enjoy camping, diving, clamming, crabbing, and fishing in Hood Canal at Potlatch State Park (three miles south of Hoodsport on Hwy. 101, 360/877-6947, www.parks.wa.gov). Have a picnic on the water, or explore the underwater park with scuba gear. The park is named for the feasts held by many Northwestern Indians, in which the exchanging of gifts was the primary focus. The campground ($17 for tents, $23 for RVs) is open year-round.

Hoodsport Winery

A small, family-run operation, Hoodsport Winery (23501 Hwy. 101, 360/877-9894 or 800/580-9894, www.hoodsport.com) produces wine from Puget Sound fruits and berries and is especially known for its rhubarb wine. It also has varietal grape wines, including a surprising cabernet sauvignon. The tasting room is open 10 A.M.–6 P.M. daily.

Entertainment and Events

The main summer event is **Celebrate Hoodsport Days,** with a street fair, food, kids' parade, and fireworks on the first full weekend of July.

August brings the annual **Hood Canal Salmon Derby** (360/790-6589, www.sschapterpsa.com/Derby_Page.htm), where $25 and some angling luck can win a $1,000 prize. Kids' events and a barbecue are all part of the fun.

Sports and Recreation

Rent dive gear, get air refills, and take classes from **Hood Sport 'N Dive** (24080 N. Hwy. 101, a mile north of Hoodsport, 360/877-6818, www.hoodsportndive.com) or **Mike's Dive Center** (38470 N. Hwy. 101, Lilliwaup, 360/877-5324, www.mikesbeachresort.com). Both places also rent dive kayaks and sea kayaks.

Practicalities

Glen-Ayr Canal Resort (25381 N. U.S. Hwy. 101, 360/877-9522 or 866/877-9522, www.glenayr.com), 1.5 miles north of Hoodsport, is the most elaborate and diverse local resort, with motel rooms for $85–95 s or d. The one-bedroom suites start at $150. A hot tub, recreation room, and marina round out the amenities here. Or park at one of 38 RV sites with full hookups for $33 per day.

Sunrise Motel and Resort (24520 Hwy. 100 on the north side of Hoodsport, 360/877-5301, www.hctc.com/~sunrise) is a favorite of scuba divers and has rooms for $59–69 d. A package including a dorm bed for two nights and three days and including free air tank refills is $60 per person. RV sites are $30 per night, and pets cost an extra $10.

The **Waterfront Resort** (in Potlatch, 360/877-9422, motel $99 s or d, cabin $138–179 up to 6) offers quite nice shore-view rooms, plus manufactured home–style cabins with kitchens. The resort also rents spaces to RV campers ($38–43 full hookups).

You can't visit the Hood Canal without feasting on some oysters. In Hoodsport, the place to do it is **The Tides** (27061 N. U.S. Hwy. 101, 360/877-8921), a family diner that serves up shellfish and smiles. Try the panfried oysters, its best dish.

Information and Services

Stop by the **Hood Canal Ranger Station** (360/877-5254, 8 A.M.–4:30 P.M. Mon.–Fri. year-round, plus 8 A.M.–4:30 P.M. Sat.–Sun. mid-May to mid-Sept.) in Hoodsport for Olympic National Forest and Olympic National Park information.

Mason General Hospital (901 Mountain View Dr., 360/426-3102) is the nearest emergency room to Hoodsport. Sick pets can be taken to Haigh Veterinary Hospital (81 S.E. Walker Park Rd., 360/426-1840) or Shelton Veterinary Hospital (104 E. J St., 360/426-2616) in nearby Shelton.

Getting There

Mason County Transit (360/427-5033 or 800/374-3747) has free bus service along Hood Canal and throughout the county.

LAKE CUSHMAN AREA

Lake Cushman was a popular resort area at the turn of the 20th century, offering fishing, hiking, and hunting. By the 1920s, the two lakeside resorts had shut down and the city of Tacoma built a dam on the Skokomish River. When completed, the dam increased the lake's size tenfold to 4,000 acres. Though private summer homes are springing up around the lake, the area still has a decidedly remote feel, thanks in part to its protected neighbor, Olympic National Park, about 10 miles up the road.

Sights and Recreation

A once-upon-a-time state park, **Camp Cushman** (7211 N. Lake Cushman Rd., 360/877-6770, $5 day-use fee) is now managed by a private company. This 500-acre plot of rugged forest, pristine shoreline, and shaded picnic areas draws in recreational enthusiasts of all stripes. Anglers love to vie for cutthroat, kokanee, and rainbow trout in the lake. Divers come to explore the sunken forest and an old resort that was here before the dam was built. Hikers enjoy the four miles of hiking trails, leading from lake's edge to deep woods. Others come to swim, water ski, and, in winter, cross-country ski.

Camp Cushman makes for a good base camp to explore the area. Follow Lake Cushman Rd. to a T intersection at road's end; go left and follow the lake's edge to 70-foot **Cushman Falls,** near the lake's northwest end, about 11 miles from Hoodsport. Or, turn right at the T, then turn left in another 1.5 miles onto Big Creek Road 2419 for six miles to **Big Creek Viewpoint** for a sweeping view to the east.

The **Mt. Ellinor Trail** leaves Road 2419 at the five-mile point; the trail heads up one mile for a view over Lake Cushman. Hiking trails lead into Olympic National Park from Staircase Trailhead at the head of Lake Cushman, providing a range of hiking options. The **Flapjacks Lake** area is accessed by hiking up the North Fork Skokomish Trail, and then turning up the four-mile side route to the lake. For longer hikes, you can continue up the North Fork Trail, which connects to others, providing a number of lengthy loop-trip options. A steep and challenging three-mile trail switchbacks from the campground to **Wagonwheel Lake,** gaining over 3,200 feet en route.

Golfers can enjoy the summer sunshine at the nine-hole, par 35 **Lake Cushman Golf Course** (210 West Fairway Dr, 360/877-5505, greens fees $31–33), four miles west of Hoodsport.

Practicalities

Cushman Lake Resort (4621 N. Lake Cushman Rd., 800/588-9630, www.lakecushman.com) has rustic cabins ($55–135 d) with kitchens and baths; canoe, personal watercraft, and boat rentals; a convenience store, plus tent and RV sites.

Camp in one of the two campgrounds at **Camp Cushman** (7211 N. Lake Cushman Rd., 360/877-6770, $20 tents, $26 RVs with hookups), with loads of nearby recreation opportunities.

The Forest Service's **Big Creek Campground** (877/444-6777, www.recreation.gov, $10, open May–Sept.) is nine miles up Highway 119. The road ends after a total of 16 miles at **Staircase Campground** (www.nps.gov/olym, $12, no reservations), just west of the lake below the Staircase Rapids of the North Fork of the Skokomish River. This beautiful Olympic National Park site has year-round camping surrounded by old growth forest. Chose a riverside site for the ultimate nighttime lullaby.

ELDON TO BRINNON

Not much to Eldon—just a café, gas station, shellfish farms, and a diver's resort. The Hamma Hamma River enters Hood Canal here, and a paved road leads to two Forest Service campgrounds on the edge of Olympic National Park. In the winter, bald eagles gather along the banks of the Hamma Hamma to feed on spawning salmon. Brinnon isn't much bigger than Eldon, but this stretch of Hood Canal has a number of interesting attractions.

Sights

DOSEWALLIPS STATE PARK

A half mile south of Brinnon on Highway 101, Dosewallips State Park covers 425 acres at the base of the Olympic Mountains, offering both fresh- and saltwater activities where the Hood Canal comes together with the Dosewallips River. Enjoy camping ($17 for tents, $23 for RV hookups) and fishing for salmon and steelhead in the river. Clams are sometimes available here in season—check with the Washington Department of Fish and Wildlife (360/902-2700, www.wdwa.wa.gov). Six miles of hiking trails provide access to the forested west end of Dosewallips.

Two miles south of Brinnon, **Pleasant Harbor State Park** has a protected dock adjacent to a private marina, but no camping, boat launch, or swimming facilities.

HAMMA HAMMA RECREATION AREA

Hamma Hamma Road begins two miles north of Eldon and continues to the edge of the Mt. Skokomish Wilderness. **Hamma**

Hamma Campground (877/444-6777, www.recreation.gov, $10, May–mid-Nov.) is six miles up the road and can accommodate tents and trailers up to 22 feet in length. Continue another two miles to **Lena Creek Campground** (877/444-6777, www.recreation.gov, $10, year-round), which provides access to miles of hiking. **Lena Lake Campground** is a free walk-in campground at this pretty lake, a three-mile trek from the Lena Creek Campground. Expect a compost toilet and no potable water at this fairly primitive site. Built by the CCC in the 1930s, the historic **Hamma Hamma Cabin** (360/877-5254, $40) is available for groups up to six. This rustic abode has no running water.

Webb Lookout is a popular high spot, although it offers no Olympic views, just a broad shot of the canal. Take Hamma Hamma Road and turn right on a logging road at about 2.5 miles and follow the signs. Park along the road and hike the half-mile trail to the lookout.

MOUNT SKOKOMISH WILDERNESS

Covering a little more than 13,000 acres, the Mt. Skokomish Wilderness occupies steep terrain bordering the western edge of Olympic National Park. The **Putvin Trail** starts from Forest Road 25, approximately four miles beyond Lena Creek Campground on Hamma Hamma Road, and climbs steeply, rising more than 3,700 feet in less than four miles. The trail ends at rock-rimmed Lake of the Angels, just inside the park boundary. The Mt. Skokomish Wilderness is managed by Olympic National Forest (360/877-5254). Wilderness permits are not required.

DOSEWALLIPS RECREATION AREA

Scenic Dosewallips Road (Forest Road 2610) heads west from Brinnon, following the Dosewallips River into the heart of the Olympics and ending 15 miles later at Dosewallips Campground within Olympic National Park. Sadly, though, the road is washed out at mile 9.2 and may remain so for some time due to environmental concerns. Look for elk along the way. Approximately three miles up is **Rocky Brook Falls.** The turnoff isn't marked, but look for the bridge and small hydro plant on the right side. It's a short walk to the 80-foot falls, but use care since water levels can change quickly.

The Forest Service's **Elkhorn Campground** (free, open May–Sept.) features sites right along the river approximately three-quarters of a mile past the washout on Dosewallips Road. Vault toilets are the rule here. **Dosewallips Falls** cascades over enormous boulders just inside the Olympic National Park boundary, about four miles past Elkhorn along the road-turned-trail. Just another mile farther is the National Park Service's **Dosewallips Campground** (www.nps.gov/olym, free, no reservations), a primitive site with no water and pit toilets. A trailhead here provides access to the park backcountry via the West Fork and Main Fork Dosewallips trails. The site is not to be confused with the easier-access Dosewallips State Park.

DUCKABUSH RECREATION AREA

Duckabush Road (Road 2519) heads west from Highway 101 four miles south of Brinnon, providing access to both the Brothers Wilderness and Olympic National Park. Four miles up Duckabush Road is the rustic **Interrorem Ranger Cabin,** built in 1907 as headquarters for Olympic National Forest. Today the Forest Service rents this historic four-person cabin for $30; call 360/877-5254 for details. Two short trails—the **Interrorem Nature Trail** and **Ranger Hole Trail**—provide access to the densely forested country near the cabin. Another mile up Duckabush Road is **Collins Campground** ($10, May–Sept.). Continue a short distance up Duckabush Road to Forest Road 2530, and follow it 1.3 miles. From here, **Marhut Falls Trail** climbs 0.75 mile to this picturesque waterfall.

BROTHERS WILDERNESS

This 16,682-acre wilderness lies within Olympic National Forest and occupies a blip of land on the eastern flank of Olympic National Park. Wilderness permits are not required in the Brothers Wilderness. Only a few developed trails exist in the wilderness; the primary one is the **Duckabush River Trail,** which begins a mile up from the Collins Campground in Duckabush Recreation Area. The trail climbs six miles to the park boundary, with a view from Big Hump rock. Once inside the park, you can connect to a maze of other routes through the high country. From Lena Lake Campground on Hamma Hamma Road, a hiking trail leads uphill to Lena Lake on the edge of the wilderness, and then on to **Upper Lena Lake** inside Olympic National Park. This is a perfect overnight backcountry trip.

OTHER SIGHTS

In Brinnon, **Whitney Gardens & Nursery** (306264 Hwy. 101, 360/796-4411, www.whitneygardens.com, 9 A.M.–dusk daily, $1 admission, $2 for a guided tour) has seven acres of display gardens that include more than 3,000 rhododendrons, azaleas, and other flowering plants. It is especially stunning from mid-May to mid-June, but you'll find something in bloom all summer.

Learn how oysters, mussels, and clams are raised at Brinnon's **Point Whitney Shellfish Lab** (1000 Point Whitney Rd., 360/796-4601), run by the Washington Department of Fisheries.

In Eldon, the **Seafood Store** (38546 N. U.S. Hwy. 101, 360/877-5811 or 888/877-5844, www.hamahamaoysters.com) sells fresh shucked, smoked, shell, and even pickled oysters! Tours of the facility are welcomed.

Events

Brinnon's **Hood Canal ShrimpFest** (360/796-4886) over Memorial Day Weekend includes an art fair, street dance, boat show, farmers market, and shrimp cooking contests. Bring along your decorated belt sander to participate in the zany Belt Sander Race.

Recreation

A number of public campgrounds are described under *Sights*. In addition to these, the Forest Service's **Seal Rock Campground** ($12, open May–Sept.) is just north of Brinnon and features saltwater-facing sites with great clam harvesting, as well as piped water and flush toilets. **Cove RV Park** (303075 U.S. Hwy. 101, 360/796-4723, $27 nightly, $170 weekly) has RV hookups, plus bathrooms and showers. It is located three miles north of Brinnon.

Accommodations

Mike's Beach Resort (38470 Hwy. 101, Lilliwaup, 360/877-5324 or 800/231-5324, www.mikesbeachresort.com, $20 per person hostel, $70–130 d) is a fun and friendly place with a variety of accommodations, including dorm beds in a hostel with a full kitchen, cabins, and even Airstream RVs for rent. Tent spaces ($25) and RV hookups ($30) are also available, and pets are welcome throughout the resort. The main attraction here is the boat launch and dive facility; divers can fill tanks at the air station here, and for a fee even non-guests can launch boats or access the water from Mike's beach. There's great scuba diving at an artificial reef just offshore; ask about the eight-foot octopus.

Bayshore Motel (31503 Hwy. 101, 360/796-4220 or 800/488-4230, $55 s or d) has large and comfortable rooms.

Houseboats for Two (360/796-3440 or 800/966-5942, www.houseboats4two.com, $195–240 d) rents private one-bed houseboats afloat on Pleasant Harbor near Brinnon. The accommodations are luxurious and include a hot tub, fireplace, and pool. This is a favorite honeymoon spot.

Elk Meadows B&B (3485 Dosewallips Rd., 360/796-4886, www.elkmeadowswa.com, $95 d, no kids under 14) is a big ranch-style home three miles up Dosewallips Road in the heart of elk country. Two guest suites have private baths, and a full breakfast is served each morning.

Food

Brinnon's **Half Way House Restaurant** (41 Brinnon Lane at Hwy. 101, 360/796-4715, 7 A.M.–8 P.M. Sun.–Thurs., 7 A.M.–9 P.M. Fri.–Sat.) has a gourmet chef and reasonable prices on seafood, steak, burgers, and lighter fare.

This is also the place to go for a homemade breakfast. The **Geoduck Tavern** (307103 U.S. Hwy. 101, Brinnon, 360/796-4430, kitchen open 4–8 P.M. Tues.–Thurs., 11 A.M.–9 P.M. Fri.–Sat.) is a great place to soak up the local vibe. It serves up burgers and sometimes there's live music on weekends.

Getting There

Jefferson Transit (360/345-4777 or 800/833-6388, www.jeffersontransit.com) has bus service connecting Brinnon with Port Townsend, Sequim, and Poulsbo. **Mason Transit** (360/427-5033 or 800/374-3747) has free bus service south to Shelton and other parts of Mason County.

QUILCENE AREA

Tiny Quilcene has a rough-at-the-edges country feeling reminiscent of Northern California. The compact town has simple homes and trailers, piles of split wood in the yards, and smoke curling from the chimneys. Chainsaw carving is considered high art, and the surrounding cutover landscape looks like a bad haircut.

Sights

BUCKHORN WILDERNESS

Covering 44,258 acres, the Buckhorn Wilderness occupies barren ridges and peaks topping 7,000 feet within Olympic National Forest and bordering on the extensive wilderness within Olympic National Park. The **Mt. Townsend Trail** begins from Forest Road 2760 off Road 27, northwest of Quilcene. This six-mile route climbs to the top of 6,280-foot Mt. Townsend, providing incredible vistas in all directions. **Big Quilcene Trail** starts at the three-sided shelter 10 miles up Forest Road 2750 from Quilcene and follows the Big Quilcene River into the high country before switchbacking to the summit of Marmot Pass at 6,000 feet. From here, you can continue into Olympic National Park via the Constance Pass Trail. The Big Quilcene is famous for the multitudes of rhododendrons that bloom here in early summer. Contact the Hood Canal Ranger District (360/765-2200) for more information on the Buckhorn Wilderness.

MOUNT WALKER

The most popular viewpoint along Hood Canal is 2,804-foot **Mt. Walker,** five miles south of Quilcene. A narrow gravel road leads to the summit, or you can hike up via a two-mile path through tall Douglas fir forests and a lush understory of huckleberry and rhododendron. The trail (or road) emerges onto a ridge with panoramic views of Seattle, Mt. Rainier, and the Cascades to the east, and the Olympics to the northwest. Bring a lunch to enjoy at the summit picnic area.

OTHER SIGHTS

Two miles south is the **Quilcene National Fish Hatchery** (360/765-3334, open daily, hours vary). The **Quilcene Historical Museum** (360/765-4848, noon–5 P.M. Fri.–Mon. late Apr.–late Sept.) houses a historic kitchen, old logging and farming tools, and a millinery exhibit.

Events

The **Olympic Music Festival** (360/732-4800, www.olympicmusicfestival.org) is a summertime concert series held weekends late June to early September in a century-old barn located 10 miles west of Hood Canal Bridge, off Highway 104. Donkeys wander the grounds as patrons sit on hay bales in the barn listening to chamber music or enjoy picnics outside with mountain (and cow) vistas. The Philadelphia String Quartet and guest artists perform these "Concerts in the Barn" 0.25 mile south of Highway 104 on Center Road.

Recreation

The Forest Service's very popular **Falls View Campground** (877/444-6777, www.recreation.gov,$10; open May–Sept.) is 3.5 miles south of Quilcene and offers 14 RV sites without hookups and 16 tent sites. The half-mile **Falls View Canyon Trail** drops down to the Big Quilcene River from the campground. Additional campsites can be found at **Lake Leland Park** (six miles north of Quilcene, $12, open Apr.–Oct.), a small county facility that has a boat ramp for small boats and a dock, plus a short nature trail.

Accommodations and Food

Enjoy the wooded scenery at Quilcene's **Mount Walker Inn** (360/765-3410, www.mountwalkerinn.com, $65–95 s or d), a humble little place with rooms featuring kitchenettes. No telephones in rooms, but pets and kids are welcome.

Prime rib, roast beef, and seafood (including ultra-fresh local oysters) distinguish the **Timber House** restaurant (295534 U.S. Hwy. 101, 360/765-3500, 11 A.M.–9 P.M. Mon.–Fri., 9 A.M.–9 P.M. Sat.–Sun.), a half mile south of Quilcene.

Information

The Olympic National Forest **Quilcene Office of the Hood Canal Ranger District** (295142 Hwy. 101, 360/765-2200) has maps and information on local camping and hiking options on both Forest Service and National Park lands.

Port Townsend

Standing on the northern tip of Quimper Peninsula—a point off the northeast corner of the Olympic Peninsula—Port Townsend (pop. 9,000) is best known for its many excellent Victorian homes. Sandwiched between the perpetually snow-covered Olympic Mountains and the ship-filled Strait of Juan de Fuca, Port Townsend is a working town with much to see and explore. Many folks consider it one of the most interesting and beautiful towns in Washington.

History

Port Townsend is the main port of entry to Puget Sound and the first town site on the Olympic Peninsula. As such, the city has hosted consulates from Chile, Sweden, Norway, Germany, France, Great Britain, and the kingdom of Hawaii. The hopes that the port city would be the end point for the Union Pacific's transcontinental railroad fueled a huge late-1800s building boom, resulting in the grand Victorian mansions still in evidence today. A period of financial depression followed, and many of the mansions were abandoned and converted into rooming houses and apartments, left to wait forlornly for the rescue that would eventually save a small percentage of these historical beauties.

Over the years, military bases and a pulp and paper mill restored Port Townsend's economic stability. The "far-out" location attracted a hippie crowd in the 1970s, leaving an indelible mark on the city's culture. Today tourism, fed by a gorgeous setting with breathtaking views over Admiralty Inlet and the nearby Olympic Mountains, accounts for much of Port Townsend's prosperity. Many of the remaining Victorian mansions have been transformed into lavish B&Bs, and several galleries, shops, and gourmet restaurants have sprung up to serve visitors from near and far. Today the citizens of Port Townsend are a blend of blue-collar millworkers, generally harmless tree-huggers, and wealthy newcomers and retirees.

SIGHTS

Port Townsend's main attractions are its historic late 19th-century homes and businesses, along with impressive Fort Worden State Park. Downtown's main boulevard, Water St., consists of stout brick buildings filled with fine galleries, restaurants, and shops selling antiques, books, clothing, wines, and gifts.

One of the more distinctive town sights is the **Haller Fountain,** which features a bronze, scantily clad maiden emerging from a shell that is supported by water-spraying cherubs and fish. Theodore N. Haller donated the fountain to the city "in memory of early pioneers."

Port Townsend is still very much a seafaring town. Its Port Hudson Harbor is jammed with yachts, and quite a few boatbuilding businesses are based nearby. Of particular note is the **Northwest School of Wooden**

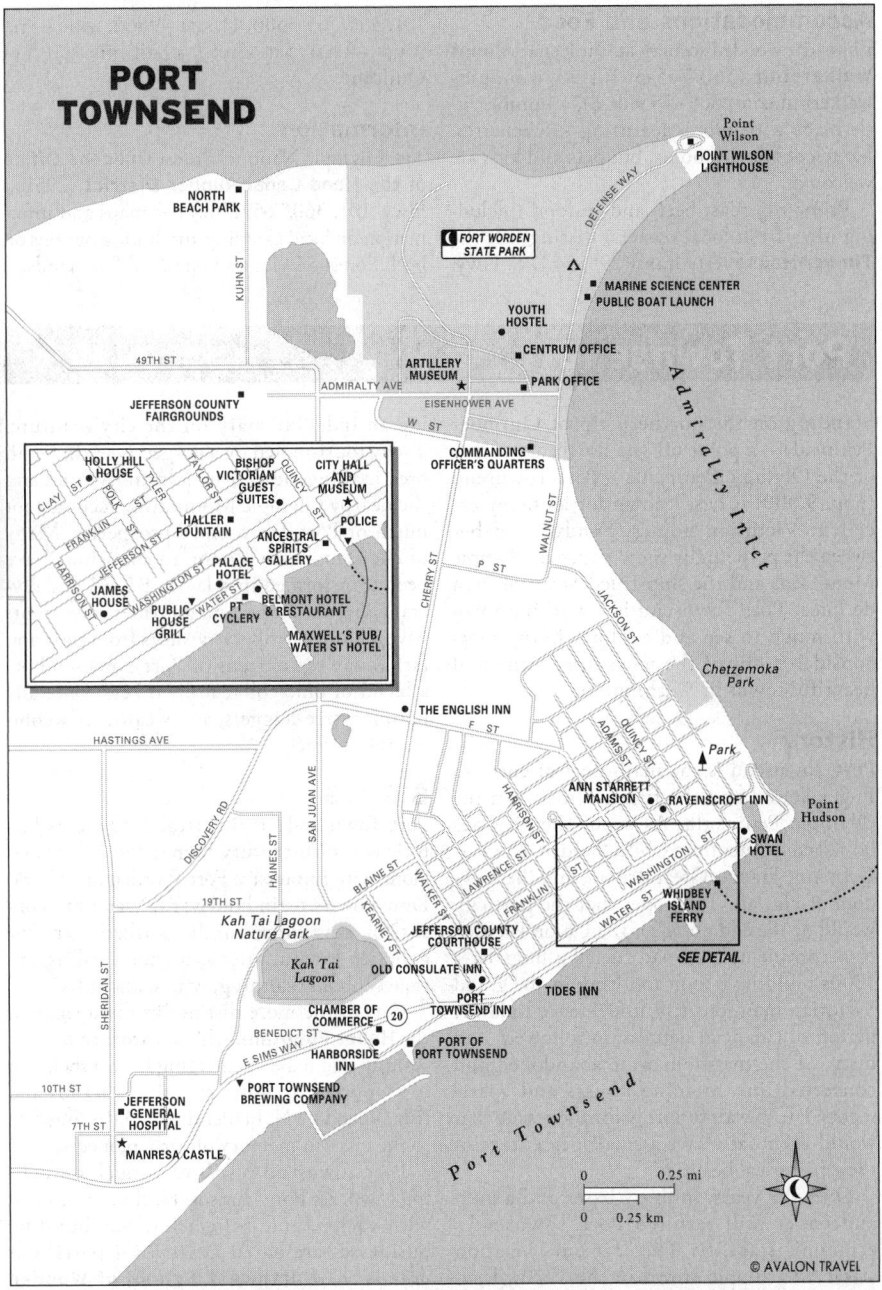
PORT TOWNSEND
Point Wilson
POINT WILSON LIGHTHOUSE
DEFENSE WAY
NORTH BEACH PARK
KUHN ST
FORT WORDEN STATE PARK
MARINE SCIENCE CENTER
PUBLIC BOAT LAUNCH
YOUTH HOSTEL
CENTRUM OFFICE
49TH ST
ARTILLERY MUSEUM
ADMIRALTY AVE
PARK OFFICE
Admiralty Inlet
JEFFERSON COUNTY FAIRGROUNDS
EISENHOWER AVE
W ST
COMMANDING OFFICER'S QUARTERS
HOLLY HILL HOUSE
CLAY ST
TYLER ST
TAYLOR ST
BISHOP VICTORIAN GUEST SUITES
QUINCY ST
CITY HALL AND MUSEUM
POLK ST
HALLER FOUNTAIN
POLICE
FRANKLIN ST
ANCESTRAL SPIRITS GALLERY
JEFFERSON ST
WALNUT ST
HARRISON ST
PALACE HOTEL
WASHINGTON ST
P ST
JAMES HOUSE
WATER ST
PUBLIC HOUSE GRILL
PT CYCLERY
BELMONT HOTEL & RESTAURANT
CHERRY ST
MAXWELL'S PUB/ WATER ST HOTEL
JACKSON ST
Chetzemoka Park
THE ENGLISH INN
F ST
HASTINGS AVE
QUINCY ST
ADAMS ST
Park
HARRISON ST
ANN STARRETT MANSION
RAVENSCROFT INN
Point Hudson
DISCOVERY RD
SAN JUAN AVE
HAINES ST
SWAN HOTEL
WASHINGTON ST
BLAINE ST
WALKER ST
LAWRENCE ST
FRANKLIN ST
WHIDBEY ISLAND FERRY
WATER ST
19TH ST
KEARNEY ST
Kah Tai Lagoon Nature Park
JEFFERSON COUNTY COURTHOUSE
SEE DETAIL
Kah Tai Lagoon
OLD CONSULATE INN
SHERIDAN ST
TIDES INN
PORT TOWNSEND INN
CHAMBER OF COMMERCE
20
BENEDICT ST
PORT OF PORT TOWNSEND
E SIMS WAY
HARBORSIDE INN
10TH ST
PORT TOWNSEND BREWING COMPANY
JEFFERSON GENERAL HOSPITAL
7TH ST
MANRESA CASTLE
Port Townsend
0 0.25 mi
0 0.25 km
© AVALON TRAVEL

Boatbuilding (42 N. Water St., 360/385-4948, www.nwboatschool.org, 10 A.M.–4 P.M. Mon.–Fri.), where several-day classes and six- and nine-month programs develop skills through intensive classes and hands-on projects. The facility is also open for self-guided tours.

Historic Tours

Stop by the chamber of commerce (2437 E. Sims Way, 360/385-2722, www.ptchamber.org) to pick up a tour map of historic downtown and other parts of Port Townsend. Guided tours of the waterfront, saloons, and historic homes are available by appointment from **Kathy Hill Step On Tours** (360/385-4356, $10).

Historic Home Tours are held the third weekend in September; owners of private Victorian residences open their doors to the public. Call the visitor information center for tickets (360/437-4065, $16).

Uptown

A second section of historic Port Townsend, "Uptown," covers a block or so of Lawrence Street near Taylor Street. This is where you're more likely to meet people who actually live in town. It was created as a turn-of-the-20th-century shopping district for the genteel ladies living in the hilltop mansions, a place to avoid the bawdy waterfront shopping district ("the most wicked city north of San Francisco" in the 1880s). Today, Uptown's mansions are elaborate B&Bs and offbeat stores. You'll discover great views across Admiralty Inlet from a tiny park at Monroe and Clay Streets.

Museums

Housed in the city's 1891 City Hall Complex, **Jefferson County Historical Society Museum** (210 Madison St., 360/385-1003, www.jchsmuseum.org, 11 A.M.–4 P.M. daily, $4 adults, or $1 children 3–12), this excellent museum rambles over three floors of boat exhibits and models, intricate baskets, button and bottle collections, a Victorian bedroom, and even two buffalo-horn and bearskin chairs from an old photo studio. Downstairs is the old city jail, in use until the 1940s.

There's also a small museum inside the lobby of the **post office** (1322 Washington St.). During the 1880s, this imposing stone building served as the Customs House, the port of entry for all international traffic into Puget Sound.

Another building of interest is the **Jefferson County Courthouse,** standing high on a hill at Jefferson and Walker Streets. Built in 1892, this redbrick building is one of Washington's oldest courthouses and is notable for the 100-foot-tall clock tower that serves as a beacon to mariners.

Rothschild House

The Rothschild House (Franklin and Taylor St., 11 A.M.–4 P.M. daily Apr.–Oct., 10 A.M.–5 P.M. Sat.–Sun. Nov., closed Dec.–Mar., $4 adults, $1 children 3–12) was built in 1868 by D. C. H. Rothschild, a Port Townsend merchant and a distant relative of Germany's famous Rothschild banking family. This restrained Victorian still has much of the original furniture, wallpaper, and carpeting, and it is surrounded by herb and flower gardens.

Manresa Castle

The Manresa Castle (651 Cleveland St., 360/385-5750 or 800/732-1281, www.manresacastle.com, free) is an 1892 mansion variously owned by a tycoon, the Jesuit Order, and a hotelier. Originally, Manresa had only one bathroom per floor, but when the film *An Officer and a Gentleman* was filmed, the Hollywood crew ran out of rooms at other hotels and motels. Their contracts called for a bathroom for each room, so the studio made a deal with Manresa's owner: It advanced him money against the rent, and it was used to build the 43 bathrooms of today. A restaurant and lounge are on the premises, and an attractive rose and rhododendron garden provides a quiet place to enjoy the vista of Port Townsend and Admiralty Inlet.

Ann Starrett Mansion

Easily the most opulent Victorian structure in Port Townsend, the Ann Starrett Mansion (744 Clay St., 360/385-3205 or 800/321-0644, www.starrettmansion.com, noon–3 P.M. daily, $2 adults, kids under 12 free) is a National Historic Landmark and a favorite B&B. Take a tour or stay here to enjoy the luxury up close. The rooms are furnished with period antiques and offer outstanding views. Dormer windows in the dome admit light that illuminates a different red ruby stone for each season of the year.

Old Fort Townsend State Park

Old Fort Townsend State Park (4 mi. south of town, 360/385-3595) has campsites and seven miles of hiking trails through tall firs, sloping down to a 150-foot cliff along Port Townsend Bay. The 377-acre park is open mid-April to mid-September only. A fort was established here in 1856 to guard against possible American Indian attacks. The fort was used during World War II as an enemy munitions defusing station. In 1958 it was turned over to the State Parks Commission. A short self-guided historical walk starts at the display board near the park entrance.

☾ Fort Worden State Park

Capping Point Wilson, Fort Worden, along with Fort Flagler on Marrowstone Island and Fort Casey on Whidbey Island, served as the "Iron Triangle" of forts protecting the entrance to Puget Sound. Fort Worden's guns were never fired in battle, and advances in military technology made them obsolete almost as soon as they were in place. After the army left in 1953, Fort Worden served as a state detention center before becoming a state park in 1973. If the place seems familiar, it may be because much of the movie *An Officer and a Gentleman* was filmed here.

Many of the fort's buildings remain, the highlight being the **Commanding Officer's House** (10 A.M.–5 P.M. daily June–Aug., noon–4 P.M. Sat.–Sun. Mar.–May and Sept.–Oct., one weekend per month Nov.–Feb., $2 adults, $1 kids 6–12, free for kids under 6) containing period Victorian furnishings. One of the old barracks buildings now houses the **Coast Artillery Museum** (360/385-0373, 10 A.M.–5 P.M. daily July–Aug., 11 A.M.–4 P.M. daily the rest of the year, $2 adults, $1 kids 6–12, free for kids under 6), where you'll learn how the enormous gun batteries out on the coastal bluffs worked.

Don't miss the photo op provided by the 1917 **Point Wilson Lighthouse.** No public tours of the building are offered, but the beach here makes for wonderful sunup or sundown strolls, with dramatic Mt. Baker seeming to rise directly across the water.

Contemporary facilities include a campground, boat launch, tennis courts, underwater scuba-diving park, rhododendron garden, hiking trails, and a hostel. Also visit the **Port Townsend Marine Science Center** (360/385-5582, www.ptmsc.org, hours and days vary by exhibit, $5 adults, $3 kids 6–17, free for kids under 6, discounts Nov.–Mar.) offering intimate, hands-on relationships with local sea creatures, beach walks, and evening slide shows and lectures.

ENTERTAINMENT AND EVENTS

Live Music

The Public House Grill & Ales (1038 Water St., 360/385-9708, www.thepublichouse.com, 11 A.M.–11 P.M. daily) has live music on in-season weekends, and good pub food, especially for lunch. **Ajax Café** (21 N. Water St., Port Hadlock, 360/385-3450, www.ajaxcafe.com, 5–9 P.M. Tues.–Sun.) also has live music most weekend nights.

Theater

Rose Theatre (385 Taylor St., 360/385-1089, www.rosetheatre.com) is a refurbished and reinvigorated old-time movie house, now showing concerts, plays, and the occasional art-house movie. The **Key City Public Theatre** puts on plays and musicals throughout the year at the Key City Playhouse (419 Washington St.,

360/385-7396, www.keycitypublictheatre.org). The **Port Townsend Community Orchestra** (360/732-6898, www.porttownsendorchestra.org) gives four free performances between October and May.

Events

Port Townsend's calendar is jam-packed with activities, many of which are sponsored by the nonprofit **Centrum Foundation** (360/385-3102 or 800/733-3608, www.centrum.org). These include events such as performances by jazz, bluegrass, blues, and classical musicians; folk dance festivals; plays; seminars; and readings by well-known authors. For a schedule of upcoming events, contact the Centrum Foundation.

Held the third week in May, the **Rhododendron Festival** (www.rhodyfestival.org) features a big Saturday parade, dances, antique and art shows, a carnival, rhododendron displays, and the pomp and circumstance of choosing rhododendron royalty.

The summertime music season kicks off with the **Festival of American Fiddle Tunes** (360/385-3102 x127, www.centrum.org) at the end of June, followed by mid-July's **Jazz Port Townsend,** which blends directly into the **Port Townsend Blues Festival** (360/385-3102 X127, www.centrum.org).

The second weekend in August is reserved for the **Jefferson County Fair,** (www.jeffcofairgrounds.com), the old-fashioned kind with livestock shows, 4-H displays, and a mud race. A particular highlight of the year's calendar is the **Wooden Boat Festival** (www.woodenboat.org) in early September, full of music, regattas, boat tours, and exhibitions.

Early October brings the fairly strange **Kinetic Sculpture Race** (www.ptkineticrace.org) to Port Townsend; costumed characters pilot human-powered mechanical sculptures over land *and water* in a race to the finish.

If you're in town on the first Saturday in December, you'll be able to join the fun as Santa arrives by ferry, and people gather to sing carols on Water Street and watch the **tree lighting ceremony** (360/385-7911).

SHOPPING

Water Street houses numerous art galleries, antique shops, cafés, trendy gift shops, and an import toy store. **Ancestral Spirits Gallery** (921 Washington St., 360/385-0078, www.ancestralspirits.com, 10 A.M.–6 P.M. Sun.–Fri., 10 A.M.–8 P.M. Sat.) features an impressive blend of modern and traditional Native American art, masks, and jewelry. **Earthenworks Gallery** (1002 Water St., 360/385-0328, www.earthenworksgallery.com, 10 A.M.–5:30 P.M. daily) sells high quality, creative works—especially ceramics. **Gallery Walks** are held the first Saturday of each month, 5:30–8 P.M. March–Dec., during which galleries hang new works, serve refreshments, and often have artists on hand. Walks are self-guided, so just show up downtown and go for a walk!

FairWinds Winery (1984 Hastings Ave. W., 360/385-6899, www.fairwindswinery.com, noon–5 P.M. daily Memorial Day–Labor Day) is a tiny family operation producing mainstream varietals as well as some unique offerings such as Aligote and its award-winning Fireweed Mead.

RECREATION

City Parks

Chetzemoka Park on Admiralty Inlet at Jackson and Roosevelt Streets is a small, shady park with eight flower gardens, picnicking, a bandstand, and beach access. Bird-watchers may be interested in **Kah Tai Lagoon Nature Park** (12th St. near Sims Way), which encompasses 85 acres of wetlands, grasslands, and woodlands, explorable through 2.5 miles of trails.

Water Sports

PT Outdoors (Flagship Landing on Water St., 360/379-3608, www.ptoutdoors.com) has kayak lessons, rentals, and tours. A kayak with paddles and life vest will run you $45 for a half day's use. The 133-foot, 1913 schooner *Adventuress* (360/379-0438, www.soundexp.org) sails on voyages of all lengths throughout the summer and fall. Rates range from a

$40 day cruise up to $400 for a three-night San Juans cruise. The ship allows no smoking nor alcohol, and all meals are vegetarian. **Brisa Charters** (360/376-3264, www.olympus.net/brisa_charters, $75 per person) offers day and sunset sails about the 45-foot Lapworth sloop, the *Annie Too.*

South of Port Townsend, **Anderson Lake State Park** (Anderson Lake Rd. and Hwy. 20) is an isolated lake surrounded by trees. No camping or swimming, but it's a popular place to fish for cutthroat and rainbow trout, although toxic algae blooms in the lake have limited its use in the last few years.

Camping

Fort Worden State Park (360/385-4730, www.parks.wa.gov, $33–38 full hookups, $19–21 tent, $7 extra reservation fee) has 50 year-round beachside campsites and another 30 near the conference area. All of these sites accommodate RVs with full hookups. A mere five primitive tent sites are available, as are coin-op showers.

Four miles south of town, **Old Fort Townsend State Park** (360/385-3595, www.parks.wa.gov, $17) has shady campsites under tall firs along Port Townsend Bay. It also has showers. The campground is open for camping mid-April to mid-September only.

RVers can park at the private **Point Hudson Resort** on the beach (360/385-2828 or 800/826-3854, $35 full hookups) or the campground adjacent to the **Jefferson County Fairgrounds** (4907 Landes St., 360/385-1013, www.jeffcofairgrounds.com/camping.htm, $20).

Other Recreation

PT Outdoors (Flagship Landing on Water St., 360/379-3608, www.ptoutdoors.com) rents basic cruising bikes for $15 per half day or $25 for the full day. For mountain, touring, and tandem bikes rental, check **P.T. Cyclery** (252 Tyler St., 360/385-6470, www.ptcyclery.com) The store has created several maps of great mountain-bike rides in the area, for bikers looking for places to hit the trails. You can also rent bikes, sea kayaks, and camping gear from **Sport Townsend** (1044 Water St., 360/379-9711, www.sporttownsend.com)

Peninsula Sportsman (360/379-0906, www.peninsulasportsman.com) outfits and guides a wide variety of family or individual expeditions, from salmon, trout, or halibut fishing to trophy hunting for sea ducks.

Port Townsend Athletic Club (229 Monroe St., 360/385-6560) has exercise and weight rooms, racquetball courts, yoga and cardio classes, and a sauna and hot tub.

Local golf courses include the public eighteen-hole **Discovery Bay Golf Club** (7401 Cape George Rd., 360/385-0704, www.discobaygolf.com, $28 weekdays, $32 weekends). The **Port Townsend Golf Club** (1948 Blaine St., 360/385-4547, www.porttownsendgolf.com, $16 nine holes, $23 eighteen holes) is a municipal par-35, said to be the driest course on the Olympic Peninsula.

ACCOMMODATIONS

Port Townsend has some of the most exquisite lodging choices in the state, most notably the myriad old Victorian homes that have been turned into bed-and-breakfasts, along with a dozen or so motels and hotels, and an equal number of cabins and guesthouses. The city is a popular destination, and reservations are advised, especially in the summer and on weekends. The chamber of commerce (360/385-2722, www.ptchamber.org) tracks local accommodations and can tell you where rooms are available.

Under $100

Enjoy daily all-you-can-eat pancake breakfasts at the uniquely placed **Olympic Port Townsend AYH Hostel** (360/385-0655, www.hiayh.org, $17 dorm beds, $45 couples' rooms), located in a former barracks building at Fort Worden. Reservations are strongly advised in summer months, especially for the couples' rooms. The hostel is open year-round, but guests must be out 9:30 A.M.–5 P.M.

For a bit of a step up—and more privacy—try **Port Townsend Inn** (2020 E. Washington

St., 360/385-2211 or 800/216-4985, www.porttownsendinn.com, $68 s or d). The normal rooms are pretty standard hotel fare with unremarkable furniture, but the grassy grounds are nice and there's an indoor pool and hot tub on the premises. Splurgers can upgrade to a whirlpool-bath suite ($168 d) with wet bar.

Built in 1885, the **Belmont Hotel and Restaurant** (925 Water St., 360/385-3007, www.thebelmontpt.com, $79–129 s or d), was once host to sailors, ship captains, and gamblers. The ornately decorated Italianate-style inn right in the heart of downtown offers guests a chance to savor the past.

The Waterstreet Hotel (635 Water St., 360/385-5467 or 800/735-9810, www.waterstreethotelporttownsend.com, $50–160 s or d) is on the second and third floors of the 1889 N. D. Hill Building, with Water Street Brewing and Ale House on the first level. Suites with private decks overlooking the bay are available.

Built in 1889, the **Palace Hotel** (1004 Water St., 360/385-0773 or 800/962-0741, www.palacehotelpt.com,$59–159 s or d), once the "Palace of Sweets" brothel, is a beautifully restored boutique hotel with antique furnishings, high ceilings, and old-world charm. Rooms come decorated with antique furnishings and high ceilings, some with shared and some with private baths. Continental breakfast is served daily.

$100-150

For a piece of Hollywood history, stay at **Tides Inn** (1807 Water St., 360/385-0595 or 800/822-8696, www.tides-inn.com, $68–269 s or d), where parts of the 1982 film *An Officer and a Gentleman* were filmed. Some rooms have private decks and hot tubs and some have kitchenettes; a newlywed suite is also available.

Harborside Inn (330 Benedict St., 360/385-7909 or 800/942-5960, www.harborside-inn.com, $90–160 s or d) is a 63-room waterfront motel with large rooms (each with a microwave, fridge, a private patio, and a striking view), an outdoor pool, hot tub, and continental breakfast.

A charming, three-tier wedding-cake Victorian house at the end of Water St. near Admiralty Inlet is home to **The Swan Hotel** (222 Monroe St., 360/385-1718 or 800/776-1718, www.theswanhotel.com). The property offers romantic little studio cottages ($160 d), suites ($99–145 d), and one penthouse unit ($275–400 d). The lodging is friendly to kids and dogs, even both at the same time.

Six miles west of Port Townsend on a bluff overlooking Discovery Bay is **Bay Cottages** (4346 S. Discovery Rd., 360/385-2035, www.baycottagegetaway.com, $85–150 s or d). The property's two cottages each include full kitchen, feather beds, and fresh flowers. Kids are welcome.

Holly Hill House (611 Polk St., 360/385-5619 or 800/435-1454, www.hollyhillhouse.com, $108–190 s or d), built in 1872, has been beautifully renovated to provide five guest rooms, each with a private bath. The parlor showcases the owner's collection of military aviation artwork and WWII memorabilia. The home is surrounded by tall holly and elm trees.

Standing on a hill, with a garden, gazebo, and outdoor hot tub on the patio, **The English Inn** (9718 F St., 360/385-5302 or 800/254-5302, www.english-inn.com, $99–135 s or d) is a lush, tastefully decorated inn. All five guest rooms have British themes and small private baths.

$150-200

One of Port Townsend's most remarkable bed-and-breakfast inns sits inside **Manresa Castle** (651 Cleveland St., 360/385-5750 or 800/732-1281, www.manresacastle.com, $109–229 s or d), a unique 1892 castle-hotel with antique furnishings and bay views. Each room is unique, with one-of-a-kind antique furnishings and lavish linens. A spacious tower room set within the castle's turret is a favorite among honeymooners.

Explore the private English gardens and then settle into the comfortable rooms at **Bishop Victorian Guest Suites** (714 Washington St., 360/385-6122 or 800/824-4738, www.bishopvictorian.com, $135–225 s or d). Rooms feature period decorations, Victorian lighting, fireplaces, and kitchenettes. A continental breakfast is included.

Ann Starrett Mansion (744 Clay St., 360/385-3205 or 800/321-0644, www.starrettmansion.com) has nine rooms ($115–175 s or d) in the 1889 mansion and two in a separate cottage ($179–225 s or d). A gourmet breakfast is served.

Stay in a lovely turreted Queen Anne at **The Old Consulate Inn** (313 Walker St., 360/385-6753 or 800/300-6753, www.oldconsulateinn.com, $99–210 s or d), overlooking Port Townsend from atop a high bluff. Once the office of the German Consul, this 1889 beauty has fireplaces in two parlors, a large billiard and game room, and playable grand piano and antique organ. A gazebo encloses the hot tub. Eight guest rooms all have private baths. A gourmet breakfast is served.

Three short blocks from downtown, the elegant **Ravenscroft Inn** (533 Quincy St., 360/385-2784 or 800/782-2691, www.ravenscroftinn.com, $109–210 s or d) features wide verandas with sound and mountain views in a custom-built B&B. The eight guest rooms have private baths, and two suites have fireplaces and tubs. Elegant gourmet breakfasts will get you out of bed, guaranteed.

James House (1238 Washington St., 360/385-1238 or 800/385-1238, www.jameshouse.com, $145–210 s or d) is known for the dizzyingly elegant decor of its antique-laden guest rooms. Most offer commanding views of the town, as well as private baths and a relaxing garden that looks out on the water. There's also a secluded bungalow with two beds ($250 d).

$200-250

An interesting alternative lodging—especially for families and groups—is one of the former officers' homes in **Fort Worden State Park** (360/344-4400). The 32 houses have mostly been refitted with Victorian-style furnishings and modern conveniences. These cozy homes sleep 7–14 guests. Rates begin at $104 per night for a one-bedroom apartment unit and go up to $375 for an 11-bedroom barracks. Because of their popularity—especially during summer festivals—reservations for these houses should be made far in advance.

FOOD

Cafés and Diners

The Wild Coho (1044 Lawrence St., 360/379-1030, www.thewildcoho.com, 5–10 P.M. Thurs.–Sun.) is an Uptown eatery serving an eclectic breakfast, lunch, and dinner menu of vegetarian specials, black-bean chili, frittatas, and fruit blasts.

Salal Café (634 Water St., 360/385-6532, 7 A.M.–2 P.M. daily) has a lovely sundeck and a wide variety of fresh breakfast and lunch options. Come here to enjoy the homemade jams and famous potatoes and salsa.

Lehani's (221 Taylor, 360/385-3961, 7 A.M.–6 P.M. daily) is another downtown spot for morning coffee and baked goods, delicious chocolate treats, and quick lunches.

Stop by **Sea J's Café** (2501 Washington St., 360/385-6312, 6 A.M.–8 P.M. Mon.–Sat., 7 A.M.–8 P.M. Sun.) for the best fish and chips in town.

Great sub sandwiches to go can be found at **Jordini's** (924 Washington St., 360/385-2037, 11 A.M.–7 P.M. daily).

Contemporary Northwest

Sandwiched between a launderette and a Radio Shack store, **T's Restaurant** (2330 Washington St., 360/385-0700, www.ts-restaurant.com, 4–10 P.M. Wed.–Mon., closed Tues., entrées $20–31) is a big surprise. Step inside to find an elegant atmosphere and Italian-inspired Northwest seafood and meats.

Fountain Café (920 Washington St., 360/385-1364, 11:30 A.M.–3 P.M. and 5–9 P.M. daily) serves wide-ranging gourmet dishes full of local ingredients and fresh seafood in its small but charming backstreet location. It's a popular place, so be ready to wait for a table on summer weekends.

Silverwater Café (Washington and Taylor Streets, 360/385-6448, 5–9 P.M. daily, entrées $10–15) is well known for fresh and reasonably priced pasta, meat, and seafood served in a bright and airy space.

International

Lanza's Ristorante/Pizzeria (1020 Lawrence St., 360/379-1900, 5–9 P.M. daily) in Uptown has several kinds of excellent pizzas, plus outstanding home-cookin' in the form of antipasto and pastas. A simpler but nevertheless tasty choice is to get a slice of pie and a Coke at **Waterfront Pizza** (951 Water St., 360/385-6629, 11 A.M.–8 P.M. daily). It's the perfect place to try a sourdough-crust pizza if you've never had one before.

Ichikawa and Sushi Bar (1208 Water St., 360/379-4000, 11 A.M.–1:30 P.M. and 5–9 P.M. Tues.–Sat., closed Sun.–Mon.) serves up sushi, sashimi, and robata-yaki, as well as grilled and alder-smoked seafood, chicken, and steaks.

Pub Grub

Port Townsend Brewing Company (330 10th St., 360/385-9967, www.porttownsendbrewing.com) brews a variety of quality beers, including a pale ale, stout, IPA, and a bitter. You can check out the different flavors in the tasting room.

For the full sit-down brewpub experience, check out **Waterstreet** (126 Quincy St., 360/379-6438, noon–10 P.M. daily) with very tasty pub food like steamed mussels, oyster shooters, hearty burgers and grilled sandwiches, plus several home-brewed beers to wash them down.

Markets

Located in Uptown, **Aldrich's Grocery** (940 Lawrence St., 360/385-0500, 7 A.M.–9 P.M. daily) has all the staples, but you'll also find gourmet specialties and a big wine selection. The deli here (Sally's) makes fantastic baked goods and the best soups around.

Find fresh fish and other seafood at **Key City Fish Co.** (307 10th St., 360/379-5516 or 800/617-3474, www.keycityfish.com, 9 A.M.–6 P.M. Mon.–Sat., closed Sun.), right next to the ferry terminal. They'll pack your fish in ice to take home aboard the ferry.

Get baked goods, organic produce, crafts, and flowers at the **Port Townsend Farmers Market** (360/379-5054) held downtown 8:30 A.M.–1 P.M. Saturday May–October and in Uptown 3:30–6 P.M. Wednesday May–August.

INFORMATION AND SERVICES

For local information and a ton of brochures, head to the **Port Townsend Chamber of Commerce Tourist Information Center** (2437 E. Sims Way, 360/385-2722 or 888/365-6978, 9 A.M.–5 P.M. Mon.–Fri., 10 A.M.–4 P.M. Sat., and 11 A.M.–4 P.M. Sun.). For general tourist information about the town, look up www.ptguide.com on the Web.

Port Townsend Public Library (1220 Lawrence St., 360/385-3181) is one of the many Carnegie Libraries built early in this century.

The local emergency room is at Jefferson Healthcare Emergency (834 Sheridan St., 360/385-5600). Sick pets can find help at Chimacum Valley Veterinary Hospital in nearby Port Haddock (820 Chimacum Rd., 360/385-4488).

GETTING THERE

By Car and Bus

Parking can be a nightmare on summer weekends; avoid the hassles (and parking tickets) by parking at the Park & Ride (Haines Pl. and 12th St.); stop on the south side of town and hop aboard a **Jefferson Transit** (360/385-4777 or 800/773-7788, www.jeffersontransit.com) bus, serving Port Townsend and Jefferson County.

By Ferry

Port Townsend is served directly by the **Washington State Ferry** (206/842-2345 or 888/808-7977, 800/843-3779 for automated information, www.wsdot.wa.gov/ferries/) from Keystone on the southwest side of Whidbey Island. The ferries depart about every 50 minutes, and in summer cost $2.60 one-way for passengers and walk-ons, $11.15 one-way for car and driver, $0.50 extra for bikes.

P.S. Express (360/385-5288, www.pugetsoundexpress.com, $78 round-trip, bikes and kayaks $12 extra) provides passenger-only service between Port Townsend and Friday Harbor on San Juan Island. The boat leaves Port Townsend daily April–October and takes you through Admiralty Inlet and the Strait of Juan de Fuca, where you're likely to see seals, sea otters, and orcas. The boat stays in Friday Harbor long enough for a quick three-hour visit, or you can overnight there and return to Port Townsend later.

By Air

Goodwin Aviation (360/531-1727) offers charter service to Sea-Tac Airport, Victoria, the San Juan Islands, and other Northwest destinations.

Oak Bay Area

Those who chose to motor up to Port Townsend from the Kitsap Peninsula or the rest of the Hood Canal area would do well to take the slow route up along the gentle waters of Oak Bay on Oak Bay Road. The stretch from the Hood Canal Bridge all the way to Port Townsend will have you pass little villages such as Port Ludlow, Port Hadlock, and Irondale, as well as the pastoral Marrowstone Island. Each of these has a cluster of businesses and a number of fascinating historic homes, including **Hadlock Manor** on Curtiss Street in Hadlock, built in the 1890s by a Swedish sea captain.

SIGHTS

Shine Tidelands State Park

Shine Tidelands State Park (www.parks.wa.gov) occupies a 13-acre spot at the north end of the Hood Canal Bridge and is popular with sea kayakers and windsurfers. No camping is allowed.

Fort Flagler State Park

Marrowstone Island's biggest attraction is Fort Flagler State Park, at the island's northern tip. Surrounded by water on three sides, the park is perfect for boating, picnicking, crabbing, and fishing. Wooded hiking trails and camping at beach sites are also available in this 783-acre park. Since it is in the Olympic rain shadow, the park gets lots of sun and only 17 inches of rain per year.

Fort Flagler joined with Fort Worden and Whidbey's Fort Casey to guard the narrow Admiralty Inlet against hostile incursions into Puget Sound. Built in the late 1890s, the fort served as a training center during the two World Wars. The massive gun emplacements were, thankfully, never needed for anything but gunnery practice. The fort was closed in 1955 and later became a state park. Today, nine gun batteries remain. From these, you can watch the ships, barges, sailboats, and fishing vessels cruise past; it's pretty easy to see why a fort was built on this strategic bottleneck.

Fort Flagler's spacious green parade grounds are bordered by barracks and gracious old officers' quarters. Several trails cut through wooded sections of the park. The **Marrowstone Point Lighthouse** (closed to the public) stands on the northeast edge of the fort, with massive Mt. Baker creating an attractive photographic backdrop.

Other Marrowstone Island Sights

Quiet Marrowstone Island is off the beaten path but offers wooded country, attractive summer homes, and a fascinating historic fort. The only real business on the island is **Nordland General Store,** which rents sea kayaks.

Upper Oak Bay Jefferson County Park on the southwest corner of Marrowstone Island has fine views east across Puget Sound. Summer-only camping is available, but no hookups or showers.

Tiny, boat-friendly **Mystery Bay State Park** (www.parks.wa.gov), just north of

COASTAL DEFENSE FORTS

A trip down the Pacific Coast of Washington is bound to reveal an interesting piece of the state's military heritage. Nestled among the bluffs and sandy beaches is a series of concrete bunkers that once protected the shore against enemy assault. The network runs along the entire coast, especially focused at the mouth of the Puget Sound and the Columbia River delta. These massive guns never drew a bead on a hostile force, but the picturesque ruins now make a great spot for a picnic.

In the North Puget Sound, the military history buff can check out what was once known as the **Iron Triangle,** the zone formed by Fort Casey, Fort Flagler, and Fort Warden, meant to protect the Puget Sound's cities as well as the strategically important Bremerton shipyard. What are now **Fort Casey State Park** on Whidbey Island, **Fort Flagler State Park** on Marrowstone Island, and **Fort Warden State Park** near Port Townsend all make for excellent historical hikes, and the elevated views of Admiralty Inlet are stunners at each park. The true artillery fan should focus on Fort Casey with its two salvaged 10-inch disappearing carriage guns and two three-inch AA emplacements.

Fort Ebey, on the eastern shore of Whidbey Island near Coupeville, has a gorgeous view, and the grassy field makes an excellent rest stop for a Whidbey Island bike ride. It's not as impressive from a historical perspective – it only housed two six-inch guns, and today nothing is left but earthworks and concrete. Likewise for Camp Hayden near Port Angeles, now part of the Salt Creek Recreation Area: Once home to a 16-inch naval cannon and a six-inch disappearing carriage gun as well as 150 soldiers, today nothing is left but a damp concrete bunker, some rusting metal, and one heck of a nice campground.

Guarding the strategic chokepoint at the entrance to the Columbia River is **Fort Canby,** an outpost established in 1852. This battery was used sporadically for training up until 1947. None of the six-inch long-range guns remain today, but the mossy concrete structures at what is now Cape Disappointment State Park are fascinating to roam.

Nearby **Fort Columbia** is one of the few intact defense emplacements along the coast, meaning that virtually all barracks, officers' quarters, and battery buildings are still there and available for exploration. Two decommissioned six-inch guns are also viewable at this site, although they were purchased from Canada in 1994, obviously not part of the fort's original armament.

Nordland, has a picnic area, beach, pier, boat moorage, and protected waters for small boats, along with striking Olympic views, but no camping.

PRACTICALITIES

Port Ludlow

The Inn at Port Ludlow (1 Heron Rd., 360/437-2222 or 800/732-1239, www.portludlowresort.com, $109 d–$599 for 8) dominates Port Ludlow. Port Ludlow offers the utmost in luxury: large heated outdoor and indoor pools, hot tub, saunas, squash and tennis courts, paved bike paths, three nine-hole golf courses, and 300-slip marina on Port Ludlow Bay complete with rental sailboats. A wide variety of rooms are available, from standard rooms to four-bedroom suites that sleep eight.

Harbormaster Restaurant in the Resort at Port Ludlow (1 Heron Rd., 360/437-7400, 7:30 A.M.–2 P.M. Sun.–Wed., 7:30 A.M.–10 P.M. Thurs.–Sat.) serves breakfast, lunch, and dinner, with entertainment most nights in the lounge. The outside deck is a favorite place for a romantic evening meal.

The **Port Ludlow Farmers Market** (360/437-0882) comes to town 9 A.M.–2 P.M. Fridays May–early September.

Port Hadlock

A 1911 plant built to distill alcohol from sawdust has found new life as the swanky **Inn at**

Port Hadlock (310 Hadlock Bay Rd., 360/385-7030 or 800/785-7030, www.innatporthadlock.com). Just east of Port Hadlock on the way to Indian and Marrowstone Islands, this most unusual lodge and restaurant counts an in-house art gallery among its amenities. Hotel rooms go for $189–299 d. The reasonable steak and seafood restaurant provides fine harbor views and has a popular Sunday brunch.

Ferino's Pizzeria (846 Ness Corner Rd., 360/385-0840, 11:30 A.M.–8 P.M. Mon.–Thurs., 11:30 A.M.–9 P.M. Fri.–Sat., 3–8 P.M. Sun.) bakes outstanding gourmet pizzas and sells them by the slice. Also in Port Hadlock is **Ajax Café** (271 Water St., 360/385-3450, 11 A.M.–9 P.M. daily) with the best steaks in the area, plus a variety of creative Northwest seafood and chicken dishes. There is live music on weekends.

Chimacum Café (9253 Rhody Dr., Chimacum, 360/732-4631, 6 A.M.–9 P.M. daily in summer, 6 A.M.–8 P.M. daily rest of year) another locals' favorite, makes all-American steaks, chicken, burgers, and chocolate malts.

Marrowstone Island

The Ecologic Place (10 Beach Dr., 360/385-3077 or 800/871-3077, www.ecologicplace.com, $85–160 d) in Nordland has 11 rustic cabins with Oak Bay and Olympic views. Each comes with complete kitchen and bath facilities, plus a woodstove. There's a two-night minimum; no pets allowed.

The best bet on Marrowstone is at **Fort Flagler State Park** (360/902-8600 or 888/226-7688, www.parks.wa.gov). Three of the fort's old buildings are rented out as vacation homes ($105–170) and the campground ($14 tents, $20 full hookups, $7 extra reservation fee, late Feb.–Oct.) accommodates tenters and RV campers. Coin-operated showers are available.

INFORMATION

Stop at the **Olympic Peninsula Gateway Visitor Information Center** (Hwy. 104 and Beaver Valley Rd., Port Ludlow, 360/437-0120, 9 A.M.–4 P.M. daily in summer) for local information and brochures.

GETTING THERE

Jefferson Transit (360/385-4777 or 800/773-7788, www.jeffersontransit.com) serves all of Jefferson County, with connections to Port Angeles via Clallam Transit or the Kitsap Peninsula via Kitsap Transit.

Sequim

As storms pass over the Olympic Peninsula, they split in two; one part clings to the Olympics and the other is blown along by the strait's air currents, bypassing Sequim (pronounced SKWIM) like an island in the stream. The result is Sequim's famous "blue hole"—a miraculous gap in the sky of cerulean cloudlessness. The 17 inches of rain that fall here are less than fall on Los Angeles, and a typical year has 299 days of sun. The pleasant climate has transformed this former farming and mill town into a booming retirement community, with more than 25,000 people spread across the surrounding Dungeness Valley.

SIGHTS

Museum and Arts Center

One block north of Highway 101 lies the Museum and Arts Center (175 W. Cedar St., 360/683-8110, www.sequimmuseum.org, 9 A.M.–4 P.M. Mon.–Sat., 1–4 P.M. Sun., donation requested). Built to store the 12,000-year-old tusks, bones, and artifacts unearthed at Sequim's famous Manis Mastodon Site, the museum has branched out to include several antique cedar bark baskets, pioneer farming displays, and timber exhibits.

Dungeness Spit

The word Dungeness (meaning sandy cape)

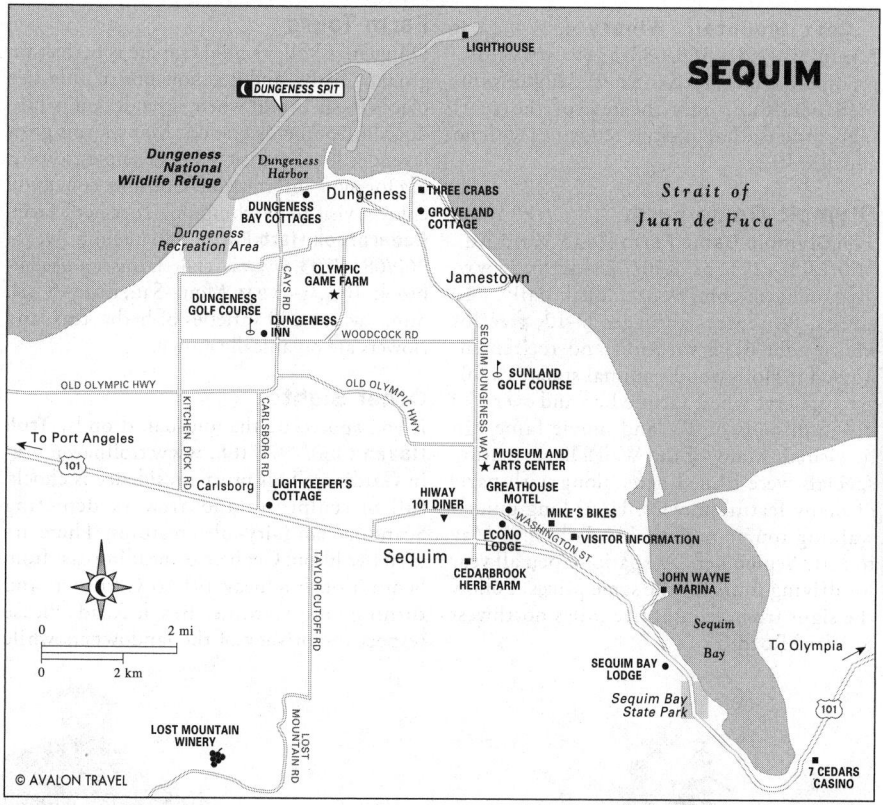

is a fitting description for this 5.5-mile-long stretch of sand that creates Dungeness Bay. The **Dungeness National Wildlife Refuge** (Voice of America Rd., 360/457-8451, www.fws.gov/washingtonmaritime/dungeness, $3 per group) provides habitat for 250 species of birds on the nation's longest natural sand spit. As many as 30,000 birds rest at this saltwater lagoon during their migratory journeys.

Built in 1857, the **New Dungeness Lighthouse** at the tip of the spit is managed by volunteers and offers tours, but you'll have to hike a total of 10 miles round-trip to see it. It's a good idea to check the tide charts before starting out. For an overview of the area, hike the half-mile trail from the parking lot to a bluff overlooking Dungeness Bay. Clamming, fishing, and canoeing are permitted in this protected wildlife refuge, but no camping, dogs, firearms, or fires. The spit is closed to horses on weekends and holidays April 15–October 15.

Wineries

Two local wineries produce wines from eastern Washington grapes. **Olympic Cellars** (255410 Hwy. 101, 360/452-0160, www.olympiccellars.com, 9:30 A.M.–5:30 P.M. daily) is housed in a century-old cedar barn along Highway 101 just west of Sequim. The three women who run the place, known collectively as "The Olympic Women in Wine," produce wines under their Working Girl, La Dolce Vida, and Dungeness labels.

Lost Mountain Winery (3174 Lost Mountain Rd., 360/683-5229, www.lostmountain.com, 11 A.M.–5 P.M. daily in summer, Sat.–Sun. only the rest of the year) makes robust, Italian-style red wines with no added sulfites.

Olympic Game Farm

The **Olympic Game Farm** (1423 Ward Rd., 360/683-4295 or 800/778-4295, www.olygamefarm.com, 9 A.M.–dusk daily, $10 adults, $8 seniors and ages 6–12, free for kids under 6), a vacation and retirement home for Hollywood's animal stars, is a 90-acre preserve where Gentle Ben and over 200 other animals of TV and movie fame can be visited. Many of the Walt Disney nature specials were filmed here, along with parts of many feature movies. Hour-long guided walking tours are available daily mid-May to early September. The park is open all year for driving tours for the same prices. Follow the signs from Sequim five miles northwest to Ward Road.

Farm Tours

Dungeness Valley's mild climate is perfect for growing herbs, and it is now one of only two places in the world where lavender oil is produced (the other is France). Many farms grow lavender locally; visit www.lavendergrowers.org for more information. Gourmet cooks will enjoy a visit to Washington's first herb farm, **Cedarbrook Herb Farm** (986 Sequim Ave. S, 360/683-7733, www.lavenderfarms.com/cedarbrook, 10 A.M.–5 P.M. Mon.–Sat., noon–5 P.M. Sun.), where 200 varieties of herbs, teas, and flowers are organically grown.

Other Sights

If you appreciate the unusual, drop by **Troll Haven** (360/797-7168, www.trollhaven.org) in Gardiner. This private residence is chock-full of sculptures and artwork depicting Scandinavian fairy-tale creatures. There are even live bison! Get here by heading east from Sequim on Highway 101 to Gardiner, and turning onto Gardiner Beach Road. Please respect the privacy of the landowners while

© ERICKA CHICKOWSKI

Lavender farms scatter the country roads in Sequim.

viewing the art from a distance, or call in advance to request a tour.

John Wayne loved the Northwest because he could visit the area and not be hounded by autograph seekers, and he especially loved the Strait of Juan de Fuca. The Duke liked it so much he bought land on Sequim Bay and donated it for a marina. The **John Wayne Marina** has 422 slips, a landscaped park and picnic area, and a bronze statue of the Duke as he appeared in the 1949 flick *She Wore A Yellow Ribbon*. Rent boats here at **The Bosun's Locker** (360/683-6521, www.portofpa.com/marinas/john-wayne-marina.html, 9 A.M.–6 P.M. daily). Bosun's also sells John Wayne souvenirs.

The enormous **7 Cedars Casino** (270756 Hwy. 101, 360/683-7777 or 800/458-2597, www.7cedars casino.com), near Blyn at the head of Sequim Bay, has bingo, blackjack, craps, keno, poker, and roulette; it is run by the Jamestown S'Klallam Tribe. Inside, several restaurants serve a variety of cuisines from regional favorites to hot dogs and fries. Also here is **Northwest Native Expressions Gallery** (360/681-4640, 9 A.M.–5 P.M. daily), with masks, paintings, jewelry, and weaving.

The artist's co-op **Blue Whole Gallery** (129 W. Washington St., 360/681-6033, bluewholegallery.com, 10 A.M.–5 P.M. Mon.–Sat., 11 A.M.–3 P.M. Sun.) features pieces by local artists.

EVENTS

Maybe a festival celebrating ditch-digging doesn't excite you. But the **Sequim Irrigation Festival** (www.irrigationfestival.com) is the longest-running festival in Washington State, so it must have something going for it! Parades, art and flower shows, a carnival, fireworks, logging show, and a one-of-a-kind chainsaw carving contest (second largest in America!) commemorate the annual event, held on the first full week of May each year.

In July, the **Celebrate Lavender Festival** (877/681-3035, www.lavenderfestival.com) features tours of local lavender farms, speakers, and an open-air market offering food, music, and demonstrations.

SPORTS AND RECREATION

Camping

Dungeness Recreation Area (554 Voice of America West, 360/683-5847), a 216-acre Clallam County park at the base of the refuge, has camping February–October ($18) with showers, beach access, and a picnic area. **Sequim Bay State Park** (just east of Sequim on Hwy. 101, 888/226-7688, www.parks.wa.gov, $19 tent, $24 full hookups, $7 extra reservation fee) offers wooded tent sites, RV hookup sites, a boat launch, scuba diving, hiking, tennis courts, and superb views of Sequim Bay.

The Forest Service offers campgrounds in the mountains 11 miles south of Sequim via Forest Roads 2909 and 2958 at **Dungeness Forks Campground** ($10, open late May–early Sept.). This well-water and vault-toilet hideaway has 10 sites close to hiking and fishing. Trailers and motor homes might have a tough time on the road. Contact the Quilcene Ranger Station (360/765-3368) for details.

Sequim's best RV park is **Rainbow's End RV Park** (261831 Hwy. 101, 360/683-3863, $34 daily, $193 weekly), where you can catch rainbow and golden trout in the property's stocked fishing pond. This pet-friendly park offers a fenced off-leash area, laundry and shower facilities, and free wireless Internet. There's a creek bordering the property and plenty of views of the mountains.

Other Recreation

Recreation in the Sequim area focuses on the protected waters inside the inner harbor of Dungeness Bay, a favorite place for windsurfers and sea kayakers. The six-mile path to the lighthouse on Dungeness Spit is a very popular place for a seaside walk or horseback ride. **Dungeness Kayaking** (360/681-4190, $90 per person, minimum of two) leads beginners on sea kayak trips around the bay.

Mountain bike rentals and tours of the nearby foothills are available from **Mike's Bikes** (551 W. Washington St., 360/681-3868, www.mikes-bikes.net, 10 A.M.–6 P.M. Mon.–Fri., 10 A.M.–5 P.M. Sat., closed Sun.).

One superb full-day ride near Sequim is up Forest Road 2860, which winds up the side of the Dungeness River Valley (with spectacular views) to a junction with the end of the Lower Dungeness Trail. The 11-mile single-track descent to Gold Creek is one of the best on the Olympic Peninsula, if not the entire state. Get there by car via Palo Alto Road, which leaves Highway 101 three miles east of Sequim, following signs to Forest Road 28. The lazy can arrange for a lift up the dirt road, but the downhill ride just isn't quite as satisfying that way.

The **Sequim Aquatic Recreation Center** (610 N. 5th Ave., 360/683-3344, www.sarc-fitness.com) has two swimming pools, a gym, racquetball courts, exercise equipment, and a sauna.

Northwest golfers will be in heaven in Sequim, where it is possible to play a round just about any month of the year. There are several championship courses within city limits, but the best is unquestionably the par-72 **Dungeness Golf Course** (north of Carlsborg on Woodcock Rd., 360/683-6344, www.dungenessgolf.com, greens fees $34–39 for 18 holes in summer), which keeps greens pristine and poses some good challenges with its well-positioned bunkers. It's also got a pretty decent 19th hole: the Dungeness Inn Restaurant.

ACCOMMODATIONS

The Sequim Chamber of Commerce's website (www.visitsun.com) has links to most local motels and B&Bs in the area.

Under $100

Greathouse Motel (740 E. Washington St./Hwy. 101 E, 360/683-7272 or 800/475-7272, $45–79 s or d) includes a continental breakfast in the nightly rates. **Sequim West Inn** (740 W. Washington St., 360/683-4144 or 800/528-4527, www.sequimwestinn.com, $52–99 s or d) has rooms with microwaves and fridges.

Similarly, **Econo Lodge** (801 E. Washington St., 360/683-7113 or 800/488-7113, $79 s or $85 d) offers rooms with microwaves and fridges, plus a continental breakfast.

$100-150

Privacy seekers will love the **Lightkeeper's Cottage** (206 Carlsborg Rd., 360/681-2055, $125 d), a self-contained one-bedroom cottage with a full kitchen on a secluded, quiet property just west of Sequim.

Sequim Bay Lodge (1788 Hwy. 101 E, 360/683-0691 or 800/622-0691, www.sequimbaylodge.com, $90–150 s or d), three miles east of town, has an outdoor pool and hot tub.

Dungeness Bay Cottages (140 Marine Dr., 360/683-3013 or 888/683-3013, www.dungenessbay.com, $120–170 d) is five miles north of town along the bay and has five cottages with full kitchens on a private beach.

East of Sequim, find **Sunset Marine Resort** (40 Buzzard Ridge Rd., Blyn, 360/681-4166, www.sunsetmarineresort.com, $125–215 d), where generally pet-friendly six-person cabins with kitchens are spread over cliffs and grassy shorelines.

Groveland Cottage (4861 Sequim-Dungeness Way, 360/683-3565 or 800/879-8859, www.grovelandcottage.com, $110–155 s or d) is a century-old house with a large lawn and pond five miles north of Sequim. Inside are five whimsical guest rooms with private or shared baths.

$150-200

Located across from the marina, **Sequim Bay Resort** (2634 West Sequim Bay Rd., 360/681-3853, www.sequimbayresort.com, $130–200 s or d) offers waterfront views from its lightly wooded property. The grounds are scattered with seaside cabins—some with kitchenettes—and campsites.

Just north of the main town are the **Juan de Fuca Cottages** (182 Marine Dr., 360/683-4433 or 866/683-4433, www.juandefuca.com, $155–305 s or d), six fully equipped housekeeping cottages perched on a 50-foot cliff overlooking Dungeness Spit. A hot tub is available. There is a two-night minimum on weekends.

Flower fans won't want to miss the gardens at **BJ's Garden Café B&B** (397 Monterra Dr., Port Angeles, six miles north of Sequim, 360/452-2322 or 800/880-1332, www.bjgarden.com, $160–240), a Victorian-style B&B

with award-winning greenery that's been featured in national magazines such as *Country Garden*. Each of the five guest rooms comes with fireplaces; some have jetted tubs.

$200-250

Colette's B&B (339 Finn Hall Rd., 360/457-9197, www.colettes.com, $195–395 s or d) is a luxurious 10-acre seaside estate with flower gardens, whirlpool baths, king-size beds, fireplaces, and gourmet breakfasts.

FOOD

Start out the day at **Oak Table Café** (292 W. Bell, 360/683-2179, 7 A.M.–3 P.M. daily) where the breakfasts are filling and delicious (try the wonderful soufflé-style baked apple pancakes).

Housed in a historic white church, **Jean's Deli** (134 S. 2nd Ave., 360/683-6727, 7 A.M.–3 P.M. Mon.–Fri. year-round, also 10:30 A.M.–3 P.M. Sat. in summer) is the best lunch spot in town, with delightful pastries, sandwiches, and espresso.

The Three Crabs (Three Crabs Rd., 360/683-4264, 11:30 A.M.–7 P.M. Sun.–Thurs., 11:30 A.M.–8 P.M. Fri.–Sat.) has served Dungeness crab and other local seafood specialties for nearly 30 years at its waterfront location. It also has a retail seafood market. The crabs are well prepared, but the rest of the rather pricey menu isn't noteworthy.

Another place for fast and well-prepared lunches is **Hiway 101 Diner** (392 W. Washington St., 360/683-3388, 6 A.M.–8 P.M. Mon.–Thurs., 6 A.M.–9 P.M. Fri.–Sat., 7 A.M.–8 P.M. Sun.) a "fabulous fifties" family diner with the biggest local burgers. It's also popular for breakfast.

The **Dungeness Inn** (491-A Woodcock Rd., 360/683-3331, 4–9 P.M. Mon.–Fri., 9 A.M.–9 P.M. Sat.–Sun.) overlooking the Dungeness Golf Course, specializes in prime rib, steak, and seafood. **Tarcisio's** (609 W. Washington St., 360/683-5809, 7 A.M.–8 P.M. Sun.–Thurs., 7 A.M.–9 P.M. Fri.–Sat.) is the place to go for from-scratch pizzas.

Fans of Mexican food will enjoy two local eateries: **Las Palomas** (1085 E. Washington, 360/681-3842, 11 A.M.–9 P.M. daily) and **El Cazador** (531 W. Washington, 360/683-4788, 11 A.M.–9 P.M. Sun.–Thurs., 11 A.M.–10 P.M. Fri.–Sat.). The latter has a pleasant outside deck.

The **Sequim Open Aire Market** (2nd and Cedar, 360/683-9523) takes place 9 A.M.–3 P.M. Saturday late May to mid-October.

INFORMATION

For maps, brochures, and lots of local information drop by the helpful **Sequim-Dungeness Valley Chamber of Commerce Visitor Information Center** (1192 E. Washington St., 360/683-6690 or 800/737-8462, www.visitsun.com, 9 A.M.–5 P.M. daily).

GETTING THERE

Clallam Transit (360/452-4511 or 800/858-3747, www.clallamtransit.com) connects Sequim with Port Angeles, Forks, and Neah Bay. **Jefferson Transit** (360/385-4777, www.jeffersontransit.com) has transportation east to Port Townsend and Poulsbo.

Olympic Bus Lines (360/417-0700 or 800/457-4492, www.olympicbuslines.com, $49 one-way) has a daily shuttle to Sea-Tac Airport.

Port Angeles

Port Angeles is the largest city on the northern Olympic Peninsula and the gateway to many of its pleasures. Its busy harbor, protected by the strong sandy arm of Ediz Hook, is visited daily by logging ships, fishing boats, and the Victoria ferry MV *Coho*. The view from the Port Angeles city pier is breathtaking: Rocky Hurricane Ridge, made more ominous by a wispy cloud cover, seems to rise straight out of the turbulent waters of the Strait of Juan de Fuca. Because of its location as an entry point to both Vancouver Island (via the ferry) and to nearby Olympic National Park, Port Angeles bustles during the summer.

History

The original inhabitants along the northern shore of the Olympic Peninsula—members of the S'Klallam, Hoh, Quinault, Quileute, and Makah tribes—lived off the bounty of the land and waters, establishing fishing camps along the sandy beaches. Although the area was mapped by Spain in the late 18th century, whites did not permanently settle here until 1857. The town did not truly blossom until 1862, when a customs inspector named Victor Smith decided that Port Angeles should take over customs duties from already-established Port Townsend. This did not sit well with the residents of Port Townsend, but the dispatch of a warship to their harbor helped bring them around to the idea. That same year, President Abraham Lincoln named large sections of Port Angeles and Ediz Hook military reservations. The township of Port Angeles was thusly laid out by the federal government. The Board of Trade was moved to call it the "second National City"— second, that is, to Washington DC.

Like many seaside locations, Port Angeles once struggled with being so close to the tideline. In 1914, a massive engineering project sought to raise the level of local streets using walls and pilings, leaving many former first-stories beneath the level of the new sidewalk. The resulting "underground" is still visible in places around town.

Summer anchorage of parts of the U.S. Navy's Pacific Fleet through the 1920s and '30s helped sustain the local economy in those tough times. Long a major lumber and fishing town, Port Angeles became more reliant on tourism after the 1997 closing of the big Rayonier pulp mill and the declining salmon runs. Port Angelinos hope that feeding, sheltering, and entertaining many of the three million visitors that visit the Olympic National Park each year will help to pick up the slack.

SIGHTS

Municipal Pier and Marine Laboratory

The best part of Port Angeles—outside of its proximity to Olympic National Park—is clearly the city pier. An observation tower at pier's end provides 360-degree views of the city, harbor, and majestic Olympic mountains, while a sandy beach with picnic area is available for day use. Also located on the pier near the *Coho* ferry dock, the **Arthur D. Feiro Marine Laboratory** (360/417-6254, www.olypen.com/feirolab, noon–4 P.M. Sat.–Sun. year-round, 10 A.M.–8 P.M. daily in summer, $3 adults, $2 seniors, $1 for kids ages 3–17, and free for under age 2), operated by Peninsula College, has hands-on displays and exhibits of the area's sealife, with volunteers to answer questions. More than 80 species are here, including sea slugs, eels, octopuses, starfish, and sea urchins.

Waterfront Trail

Stop by the downtown visitors center for a walking-tour brochure that leads you through the historical sights of Port Angeles. The city's Waterfront Trail is a delightful six-mile paved path that follows the downtown shoreline and continues out to the Coast Guard base on **Ediz Hook**—a 3.5-mile-long natural sand spit protecting the Northwest's deepest harbor.

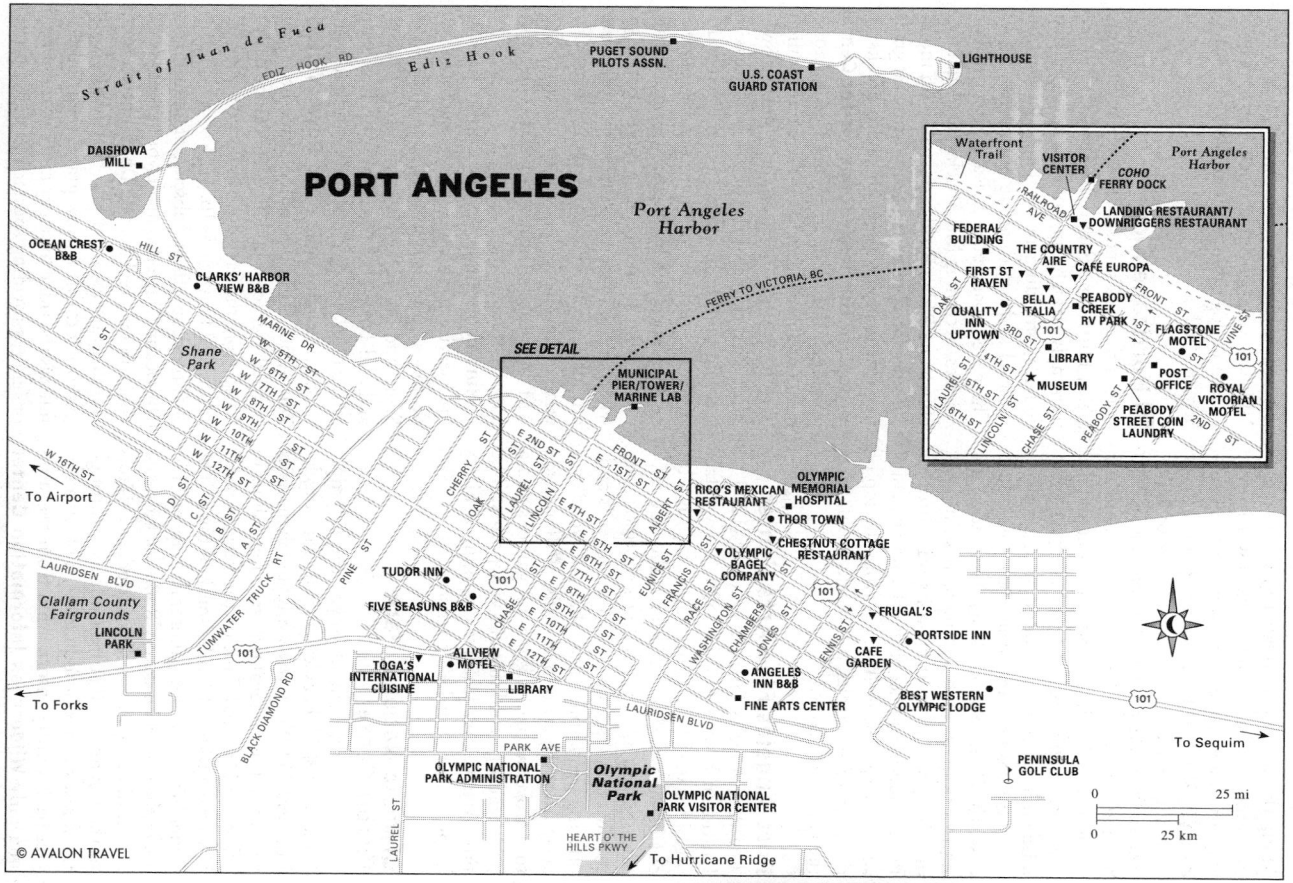
PORT ANGELES
Strait of Juan de Fuca
Ediz Hook
EDIZ HOOK RD
PUGET SOUND PILOTS ASSN.
U.S. COAST GUARD STATION
LIGHTHOUSE
DAISHOWA MILL
Port Angeles Harbor
OCEAN CREST B&B
HILL ST
CLARKS' HARBOR VIEW B&B
FERRY TO VICTORIA, BC
MARINE DR
Shane Park
SEE DETAIL
MUNICIPAL PIER/TOWER/ MARINE LAB
W 16TH ST
To Airport
LAURIDSEN BLVD
Clallam County Fairgrounds
LINCOLN PARK
TUMWATER TRUCK RT
TUDOR INN
FIVE SEASUNS B&B
TOGA'S INTERNATIONAL CUISINE
ALLVIEW MOTEL
LIBRARY
To Forks
BLACK DIAMOND RD
PARK AVE
OLYMPIC NATIONAL PARK ADMINISTRATION
Olympic National Park
OLYMPIC NATIONAL PARK VISITOR CENTER
HEART O' THE HILLS PKWY
To Hurricane Ridge
LAURIDSEN BLVD
RICO'S MEXICAN RESTAURANT
OLYMPIC MEMORIAL HOSPITAL
THOR TOWN
CHESTNUT COTTAGE RESTAURANT
OLYMPIC BAGEL COMPANY
FRUGAL'S
PORTSIDE INN
CAFE GARDEN
ANGELES INN B&B
FINE ARTS CENTER
BEST WESTERN OLYMPIC LODGE
PENINSULA GOLF CLUB
To Sequim
0 25 mi
0 25 km
© AVALON TRAVEL
Waterfront Trail
VISITOR CENTER
COHO FERRY DOCK
Port Angeles Harbor
RAILROAD AVE
LANDING RESTAURANT/ DOWNRIGGERS RESTAURANT
FEDERAL BUILDING
THE COUNTRY AIRE
CAFE EUROPA
FIRST ST HAVEN
BELLA ITALIA
PEABODY CREEK RV PARK
QUALITY INN UPTOWN
FRONT ST
FLAGSTONE MOTEL
LIBRARY
MUSEUM
POST OFFICE
ROYAL VICTORIAN MOTEL
PEABODY STREET COIN LAUNDRY

Along the way you're treated to views across to Vancouver Island and back toward town with the snowcapped Olympics in the background. Watch as freighters are guided in, or take out your own boat for fishing or sightseeing. Picnicking and beachcombing are also popular activities. The U.S. Coast Guard Air Station occupies the far end of the spit and has the cutter *Active* docked at the city pier when it isn't out on rescue missions or drug searches. Located a short distance from the Coast Guard base, the Puget Sound Pilots Association assigns a pilot to each commercial ship passing this point to steer it on its way through Puget Sound. Another place offering fine vistas across to Vancouver Island is from the top of the Laurel Street stairs, two blocks uphill from the *Coho* ferry dock.

Port Angeles Fine Arts Center

The Port Angeles Fine Arts Center (1203 E. Lauridsen Blvd., 360/417-4590, www.pafac.org, 11 A.M.–5 P.M. Thurs.–Sun., free) is a bit out of the way, but well worth the side trip. Located on a hill, the building's enormous picture windows face north to Vancouver Island, offering panoramic vistas that pull your eyes away from the art on the walls. Walk outside to discover a small forest with gardens and a path leading to additional viewpoints. The Fine Arts Center features changing exhibits by prominent Northwest artists.

Olympic National Park Visitor Center

Located a mile out of town, the Olympic National Park Visitor Center (3002 Mt. Angeles Rd., 360/452-0330, www.nps.gov/olym, daily year-round) is an ideal first stop for visitors to Olympic National Park or the very popular Hurricane Ridge, 17 miles south of town. The center includes a large panoramic map, exhibits about the park, a Discovery Room for kids, and a 12-minute slide show that introduces visitors to the Olympics. Nature trails lead through the forest to park headquarters, a block away. Get backcountry information from the summer-only **Wilderness Information Center** (directly behind the visitors center, 360/565-3100, www.nps.gov/olym/wic). Also here is the Beaumont log cabin, built in 1887 and moved here in 1962.

Hurricane Ridge

One of the park's most scenic and most visited areas, Hurricane Ridge rises over 5,200 feet seemingly straight up from the Strait of Juan de Fuca, providing an awesome contrast from sea level and breathtaking 360-degree views. The paved road starts at Race Street in Port Angeles, becoming Mt. Angeles Road and then Hurricane Ridge Road as it snakes up mountainsides for 17 miles at an easy 7 percent grade; frequent turnouts allow for photo breaks. At the top, the **Hurricane Ridge Visitor Center** provides a must-stop location to peer across a meadow-and-mountain landscape that might have been imported straight from the Swiss Alps. This is one of the park's best areas for spotting wildlife; black-tailed deer often bound across the parking lot, marmots are found in nearby slopes, and black bears are occasionally visible from a distance. The ridge's name isn't without basis in fact: the first lodge at the summit lost its roof in a strong winter blast. The weather can change quickly up here; tune in to AM 530 in Port Angeles for weather and other park information.

Hurricane Ridge Visitor Center provides food service, a gift shop, winter ski rentals, and ski-tow service. It is usually open daily May–Sept., and on weekends only during October and mid-December through April. Park naturalists offer summertime walks and talks plus wintertime snowshoe treks. **Royal Victoria Tours,** 360/417-8006, offers three-hour (very hurried) bus tours up Hurricane Ridge daily at 1 P.M. from the ferry dock in Port Angeles; $21 adult, $12 kids age 5–16.

If the drop-offs and absence of guardrails on Hurricane Ridge Rd. made your palms sweat, you're in for a real treat on **Obstruction Point Road.** Starting from the Hurricane Ridge parking lot, this narrow gravel road (no RVs) follows the ridge for eight miles without a rail or fence, providing spectacular views for the

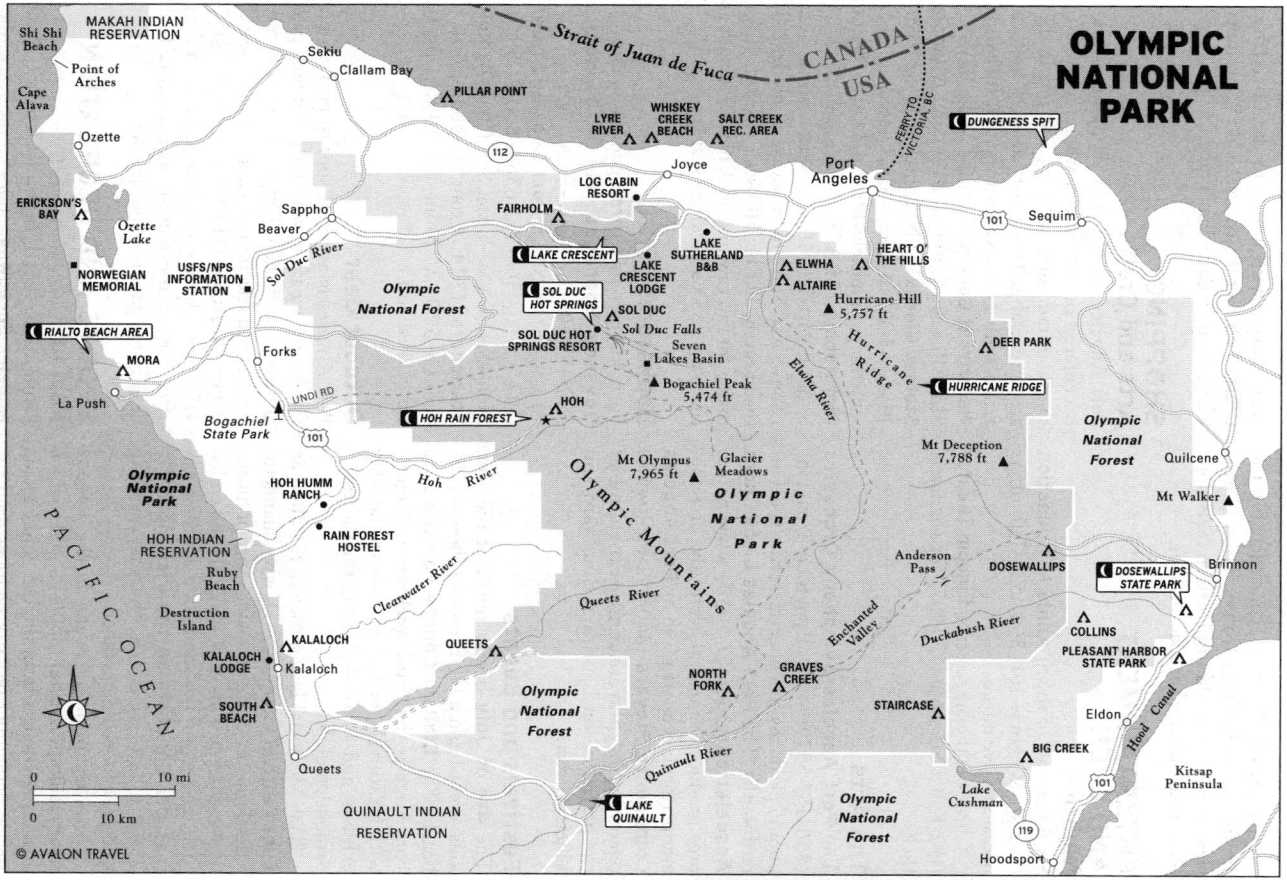
OLYMPIC NATIONAL PARK
Strait of Juan de Fuca
CANADA
USA
FERRY TO VICTORIA, BC
MAKAH INDIAN RESERVATION
Shi Shi Beach
Point of Arches
Cape Alava
Ozette
Sekiu
Clallam Bay
PILLAR POINT
LYRE RIVER
WHISKEY CREEK BEACH
SALT CREEK REC. AREA
DUNGENESS SPIT
Port Angeles
Joyce
LOG CABIN RESORT
ERICKSON'S BAY
Ozette Lake
Sappho
Beaver
FAIRHOLM
Sequim
NORWEGIAN MEMORIAL
USFS/NPS INFORMATION STATION
Sol Duc River
LAKE CRESCENT
LAKE CRESCENT LODGE
LAKE SUTHERLAND B&B
ELWHA
HEART O' THE HILLS
ALTAIRE
Hurricane Hill 5,757 ft
Olympic National Forest
SOL DUC HOT SPRINGS
SOL DUC
SOL DUC HOT SPRINGS RESORT
Sol Duc Falls
Seven Lakes Basin
DEER PARK
RIALTO BEACH AREA
MORA
Forks
Hurricane Ridge
HURRICANE RIDGE
Elwha River
La Push
UNDI RD
Bogachiel Peak 5,474 ft
Bogachiel State Park
HOH RAIN FOREST
HOH
Olympic National Forest
Quilcene
Mt Deception 7,788 ft
Mt Walker
Olympic National Park
HOH HUMM RANCH
Hoh River
Mt Olympus 7,965 ft
Glacier Meadows
Olympic Mountains
Olympic National Park
RAIN FOREST HOSTEL
HOH INDIAN RESERVATION
Ruby Beach
Destruction Island
PACIFIC OCEAN
Clearwater River
Anderson Pass
DOSEWALLIPS
DOSEWALLIPS STATE PARK
Brinnon
Queets River
Enchanted Valley
Duckabush River
COLLINS
PLEASANT HARBOR STATE PARK
KALALOCH
KALALOCH LODGE
Kalaloch
QUEETS
NORTH FORK
GRAVES CREEK
SOUTH BEACH
Olympic National Forest
STAIRCASE
Eldon
Hood Canal
BIG CREEK
Queets
Quinault River
Kitsap Peninsula
Lake Cushman
LAKE QUINAULT
QUINAULT INDIAN RESERVATION
Olympic National Forest
Hoodsport
0 10 mi
0 10 km
© AVALON TRAVEL

strong-hearted. The road, constructed in the 1930s by the Civilian Conservation Corps, went as far as it could until a steep talus slope prohibited any further road-making.

ENTERTAINMENT AND EVENTS

Nightlife

Six miles west of town, **Annie M's Junction** (242701 W. Hwy. 101, 360/452-9880) offers occasional live music.

Check out the big screen at **Lincoln Theater** (132 E. 1st St., 360/457-7997) for the latest flicks.

The Arts

The **Port Angeles Symphony Orchestra** (360/457-5579, www.olypen.com/pasymphony) performs six concerts during the winter months. The **Port Angeles Light Opera Association** (360/457-5630, www.paloa.org) produces a musical each July. Live theater performances are given by **Port Angeles Community Players** (360/452-665, www.pacommunityplayers.com) year-round at the playhouse on Lauridsen Boulevard and Liberty Street.

Festivals and Events

The **4th of July** brings music at the pier, kids' events, and a big fireworks show off the beach. The **Clallam County Fair** comes to Port Angeles the third weekend of August, with a carnival, rodeo, horse shows, farming exhibits, and a crowd-pleasing smash-'em-up demolition derby.

Each Memorial Day weekend, the **Juan de Fuca Festival** (360/457-5411, www.juandefucafestival.com) features a wide range of music, dance, comedy, kids' activities, arts and crafts, food, and more. For something a bit less formal, free **Concerts on the Pier** (360/452-2363) take place every Thursday evening mid-June to mid-September.

Another popular event is the **Forest Storytelling Festival** (360/417-5031), which attracts tale-tellers from the U.S. and Canada in late September or early October. End the year in style with a visit to the **Christmas Crafts Fair** on the first weekend of December, where local artisans display their works.

SHOPPING

Arts and Crafts

Port Angeles's downtown shopping district is centered on 1st Street, where you'll find shops, restaurants, galleries, and movie theaters. Several galleries carry artwork by local artists with Northwestern themes, including **Waterfront Gallery** (Landing Mall, 360/452-8165, 10 A.M.–5:30 P.M. daily) and **Olympic Stained Glass** (112 N. Laurel, 360/457-1090, 10 A.M.–5:30 P.M. Mon.–Sat., closed Sun.). For something completely different, head to **Pacific Rim Hobby** (124-A W. 1st St., 360/457-0794 or 800/994-6229, 10 A.M.–6 P.M. Mon.–Sat., noon–5 P.M. Sun.) for a voyage to model railroad heaven. The big HO-scale railroad village makes for fun gawking; look for such details as the giant insect attacking villagers.

Bookstores

Port Angeles has three good bookstores: **Odyssey Bookshop** (114 W. Front St., 360/457-1045, 9 A.M.–7 P.M. Mon.–Sat., 10 A.M.–5 P.M. Sun.), **Port Book and News** (104 E. 1st, 360/452-6367, 8 A.M.–8 P.M. Mon.–Sat., 8 A.M.–5 P.M. Sun.) and **Olympic Stationers** (122 E. Front St., 360/457-6111, 8:30 A.M.5:30 P.M. Mon.–Fri., 10 A.M.–3 P.M. Sat., closed Sun.).

Outdoor Gear

Port Angeles is an ideal spot to gear up before venturing afield within the national park and the rest of the Olympic National Forest. Find a good selection of outdoor gear for sale at **Browns Outdoor** (112 W Front St., 360/457-4150, www.brownsoutdoor.com), including often forgotten essentials such as stove fuel, dehydrated goodies, and the like.

SPORTS AND RECREATION

Racing

From early April to mid-October, **Port Angeles Speedway,** 360/452-4666, six miles east of Port Angeles on Hwy. 101, has stock- and hobby-car races on Saturday nights.

Winter Sports

Between late December and late March, Hurricane Ridge is a popular winter destination for cross-country and downhill skiers, snowboarders, and tubers. A small **ski area** (360/452-0330) has two rope tows and a Poma lift. It's open on weekends and during the Christmas–New Year's holiday. Ski rentals, including cross-country and Telemark packages, are also available, along with ski lessons. Backcountry skiers will discover a wealth of open country at Hurricane Ridge—check avalanche conditions before heading out.

Park Service naturalists (360/452-0330) offer guided snowshoe walks on weekends and other times in the winter. Snowshoes are provided ($2 donation suggested). The visitors center—where you can warm up—and cafeteria are open winter weekends. The road to the top is open 9 A.M.–dusk Sat.–Mon. and is closed overnight or during storms. Entrance fees are charged on weekends. Call ahead (360/452-0329) for current road and weather conditions, and always come prepared for the worst. No overnight parking at the summit.

Swimming

Swim at the **William Shore Memorial Pool** (225 E. 5th St., 360/457-4595. For lake swimming, head a dozen miles west of town to **Lake Sutherland,** where the water gets quite warm by late summer.

Bike and Kayak Rentals

Rent mountain and road bikes along with kayaks from **Sound Bikes and Kayaks** (120 E. Front St., 360/457-1240, www.soundbikeskayaks.com, 10 A.M.–6 P.M. Mon.–Sat., closed Sun.). Bikes are $9 for the first hour, $5 per additional hour, or $30 for the day. **Beckett's Bike Shop** (117 W. 1st. St., 360/452-0842, www.beckettsbikeshop.com, 10 A.M.–5 P.M. Mon.–Sat., closed Sun.) has a great selection of bikes and parts and organizes weekly group rides.

Hiking

A number of trails begin at Hurricane Ridge, including 1.5-mile **Hurricane Hill Trail,** a paved walk to the top of 5,757-foot Hurricane Hill that passes picnic areas, marmot colonies, and spectacular vistas. A longer hike, the **Klahanee Ridge Trail,** follows the ridge's summit for four miles after leaving the paved trail near the marmot colonies. It continues downhill to Heart O' the Hills Campground, or you can return back to Hurricane Ridge.

In addition to these, visitors to Hurricane Ridge will find three other short paved trails through the flower-filled meadows with views of the Olympics. Longer paths lead downhill to the Elwha Valley and along the Little River. From Obstruction Peak, additional trails provide access into the heart of the Olympics.

Camping

No camping or overnight lodging is available at Hurricane Ridge, but several options are nearby. **Heart O' the Hills Campground** (five miles south of Port Angeles on Hurricane Ridge Rd., $12) has year-round camping, with campfire programs are offered July through Labor Day. Located at an elevation of 5,400 feet, **Deer Park Campground** ($8, mid-June to late September) sits at the end of a narrow 18-mile gravel road on the eastern edge of the park. No RVs are permitted, and it is not accessible from the Hurricane Ridge area.

Near the airport, **Lincoln Park's** (W. Lauridsen Blvd. and Bean Rd.) authentic pioneer cabins and a longhouse accompany tennis courts, baseball diamond, campsites ($8 tent and RV, no hookups), nature trails, picnic area, and children's fishing pond at this 144-acre park. Campers can use the showers at the local swimming pool (225 E. 5th St.) or the boat harbor.

RV owners hoping to catch a ferry to Victoria may find **Peabody Creek RV Park** (127 S. Lincoln, 360/457-7092 or 800/392-2361, $27 with full hookups) convenient. This very basic park isn't much more than a parking lot with utilities, but it is right next to the docks.

For a few more amenities, try **Conestoga**

Quarters RV Park (40 Sieberts Creek Rd., 360/452-4637 or 800/808-4637, $25 with full hookups), which—in spite of cramped spaces—offers an off-leash area for dogs, showers, laundry facilities, free Wi-Fi, and a clubhouse. Also in town, **Crescent Beach RV** (2860 Crescent Beach Rd., 360/928-3344 or 866/690-3344, $40 with full hookups) is another pet-friendly private campground that offers access to a long, sandy beach, along with coin-op showers and laundry, plus a convenience store.

ACCOMMODATIONS

Because of the popularity of Port Angeles in the summer months, it's a good idea to make reservations ahead of your visit. Stop by the visitors center to check the board for availability at local motels, B&Bs, and RV parks, or to use its phone to make reservations. The chamber of commerce website (www.cityofpa.com) has links to most local lodging places. Many of these offer free transport from the airport or ferry terminal upon request.

Under $100

The best deal in Port Angeles can be found at **Thor Town** (316 N. Race St., 360/452-0931, www.thortown.com, $14 dorm bed, $30 d private room), a free-spirited hostel set in a red barn-style farmhouse. Guests can make use of laundry facilities and the full kitchen, with the choice of buying food here or hopping on one of the hostel's rental bikes and picking up grub at the grocery store. This hostel has no lockout hours during the day.

Another value-minded option is **All-View Motel** (214 E. Lauridsen Blvd., 360/457-7779, www.allviewmotel.com, $49–99 d), a frayed-at-the-edges mom-and-pop motel that makes a decent overnighter. Kitchenettes are available in some units.

Flagstone Motel (415 E. 1st St., 360/457-9494 or 888/304-3465, www.flagstonemotel.net, $49 s or $69 d) is a centrally located motel with an indoor pool and sauna; continental breakfast is included.

Perched on a hilltop, rooms at the **Quality Inn Uptown** (101 E. 2nd St., 360/457-9434 or 800/858-3812, $85–96 s or d) all have lots of light streaming through the floor-to-ceiling windows, with peekaboo views of the harbor and mountains. Rooms are pretty worn, but the hot breakfast, friendly staff, and reasonable rates balance this out a bit. Plus, the property is dog friendly.

The three-story **Portside Inn** (1510 E. Front St., 360/452-4015 or 877/438-8588, www.portsideinn.com, $49–89 d) has fairly standard motel rooms, plus an outdoor pool and hot tub.

$100-150

A small family hotel on a hill right in downtown, **Port Angeles Inn** (111 E. 2nd St., 360/452-9285 or 800/421-0706, www.portangelesinn.com, $59–175 s or d) has comfortable rooms, many with panoramic views over the harbor.

Also with impressive views of the mountains and water is **Best Western Olympic Lodge** (140 Del Guzzi Dr., 360/452-2993 or 800/600-2993, www.portangeleshotelmotel.com, $116–197 s or d), with spacious rooms and continental breakfast. The hotel has an outdoor pool, hot tub, exercise room, and free airport and ferry shuttles.

Ocean Crest B&B (402 S. M St., 360/452-4832 or 877/413-2169, www.oceancrestbnb.com, $75–95 s or d), a mile west of Port Angeles looking down on the waterfront, has three tasteful bedrooms with private baths and free transportation to and from the ferry. Kids are accepted.

Tudor Inn B&B (1108 S. Oak, 360/452-3138, www.tudorinn.com, $125–160 s or d, discount for active-duty U.S. armed forces) is a 1910 half-timbered English Tudor home with five pretty guest rooms featuring crown molding; one has a canopied bed. Mountain and water views come at no additional charge. Most rooms have private baths.

The Five SeaSuns B&B (1006 S. Lincoln, 360/452-8248, www.seasuns.com, $90–165 s or d) is a grand 1926 Dutch Colonial home on spacious grounds. Inside are five guest rooms, shared or private baths, and period furnishings.

$150-200

Inn at Rooster Hill B&B (112 Reservoir Rd., 360/452-4933, www.innatroosterhill.com, $149–189 s or d) is a five-bedroom country house in the foothills of mountains outside of town.

$200-250

Located halfway between Port Angeles and Sequim, **Domaine Madeleine** (146 Wildflower Ln., 360/457-4174, www.domaine-madeleine.com, $195–310 s or d) is an elegant waterfront estate overlooking the Strait of Juan de Fuca. The four guest rooms and a separate cottage (perfect for honeymooners) are luxuriously appointed, and a multicourse epicurean breakfast starts your day. The innkeepers speak French in addition to English.

FOOD

Because of its location as a jumping-off point for Olympic National Park and Vancouver Island, Port Angeles is packed with high-quality eateries of all persuasions.

Cafés and Diners

The acclaimed **First Street Haven** (1st and Laurel, 360/457-0352, 7 A.M.–4 P.M. daily, 8 A.M.–2 P.M. Sun.) serves hearty breakfasts, along with reasonable sandwiches, quiche, pastas, and salads for lunch. The location is tiny, but the food is hard to beat and on Sundays you can gorge on breakfast all day long. The same owners run the equally popular **Chestnut Cottage Restaurant** (929 E Front St., 360/452-8344, 7 A.M.–3 P.M. daily) featuring creative egg dishes for breakfast, plus salads, pastas, fajitas, and burgers for lunch. The setting is cozy and friendly.

Another fine breakfast and lunch spot is **Cafe Garden** (1506 E. 1st St., 360/457-4611, 6:30 A.M.–2:30 P.M. daily) where the menu covers the spectrum from Belgium waffles for breakfast to Asian stir-fries and deli sandwiches for lunch.

Good breakfasts, along with the best local fish and chips, can be found at **Landing Restaurant** (115 E. Railroad Ave., 360/457-6768, 7 A.M.–9 P.M. daily).

Get the best burgers and fries anywhere around at **Frugals** (1520 E. Front St., 360/452-4320, 10:30 A.M.–10 P.M. Sun.–Thurs., 10:30 A.M.–11 P.M. Fri.–Sat.). There's no seating—just drive up or walk up to order.

Steak and Seafood

A popular steak and seafood restaurant overlooking the water is **Downriggers Restaurant** (115 E. Railroad, 360/452-2700, 11:30 A.M.–9 P.M. Sun.–Thurs., 11:30 A.M.–9:30 P.M. Fri.–Sat.). **The Bushwacker Restaurant** (1527 E. 1st, 360/457-4113, 4:30–9 P.M. daily) specializes in fresh seafood and prime rib and also has a good salad bar. Open for dinner only.

International

For tasty, reasonably priced, and authentic south-of-the-border meals, visit **Rico's Mexican Restaurant** (636 E. Front St., 360/452-3928, 11 A.M.–9:30 P.M. daily), with an extensive menu and daily specials. Housed in a cozy Victorian-era home, **Toga's International Cuisine** (122 W. Lauridsen Blvd., 360/452-1952) specializes in upscale German and Hungarian dinners, but also includes Northwest seafood. This place is very nice, but expensive.

Four miles east of Port Angeles, **C'est Si Bon** (23 Cedar Park Dr., 360/452-8888, 5–9 P.M. Tues.–Sun., closed Mon., entrées $20–25) prepares delicious local seafood with a French accent. The Olympics and rose garden views add to the luxurious ambiance.

Located downstairs from an organic grocery, **Bella Italia** (117B E. 1st St., 360/457-5442, 4–10 P.M. Mon.–Sat., 4–8:45 P.M. Sun.) blends traditional Italian cooking with a natural foods sensibility. The result is easily Port Angeles' finest Italian restaurant, with great desserts, too.

Bakeries

Pick up the freshest bagel on the peninsula with loads of cream cheese or filled up sandwich style at **Olympic Bagel Company** (802

E 1st St., 360/452-9100, www.olympicbagel.com, 6 A.M.–4 P.M. Mon.–Sat., 7 A.M.–3 P.M. Sun., winter hours may vary), which serves lots of breakfast and lunch items, plus Tully's coffee.

Markets

Get the freshest local fare at **Port Angeles Farmers Market** (360/683-4642, 9 A.M.–3:30 P.M. Sat.) held year-round near the corner of 8th and Chase Streets. **Sunny Farms Country Store** (360/683-8003) has a large produce stand located halfway between Port Angeles and Sequim. Also sold here: everything from hanging plants to homemade pizzas.

The Country Aire (117 E. 1st St., 360/452-7175, 9 A.M.–7 P.M. Mon.–Sat., 11 A.M.–4 P.M. Sun.) has a big selection of natural and organic foods. For the freshest local seafood—along with canned and smoked specialties—stop by **Hegg & Hegg** (801 Marine Dr., 360/457-3344, 9 A.M.–6 P.M. Mon.–Sat., 10 A.M.–5 P.M. Sun.). They also have a small gift shop in the Landing Mall, where the ferry docks (360/457-3733).

INFORMATION AND SERVICES

For maps, brochures, and more local information, contact the **Port Angeles Chamber of Commerce Visitor Center** (121 E. Railroad Ave., 360/452-2363, www.cityofpa.com, 8 A.M.–9 P.M. daily Memorial Day–mid-Sept., 10 A.M.–4 P.M. daily the rest of the year).

Just a few steps away is the **Port Angeles-Victoria Tourist Bureau** (360/452-1223, 7 A.M.–5 P.M. daily). Here the focus is on travel, motel, and B&B reservations for southwest British Columbia—particularly nearby Vancouver Island—but they can also make motel reservations for Port Angeles. Tons of British Columbia maps and brochures are free for the taking. Both the chamber of commerce and the tourist bureau are exceptionally helpful. Another source of information is the **North Olympic Peninsula Visitor and Convention Bureau** (338 W. 1st. St., 360/452-8552, www.olympus.net).

The **Olympic National Park Visitor Center** (3002 Mt. Angeles Rd., 360/452-0330) can give you sightseeing, hiking, camping, and other park information.

Campers and backpackers will appreciate **Peabody Street Coin Laundry** (212 S. Peabody, 24 hours daily) after getting back to nature in Olympic National Park. **The Spa** (511 E. 1st St., 360/452-3257 or 800/869-7177) has been around since 1928, with Finnish-style steam rooms, massage, herbal body wraps, and a juice bar and tearoom. (The hostel is also here.)

GETTING THERE AND AROUND

By Ferry

Port Angeles is a major transit point for travelers heading to or from Victoria, B.C., just 18 miles away across the Strait of Juan de Fuca. The MV ***Coho*** (360/457-4491, www.cohoferry.com, $47.50 one-way for car and driver, $12.50 for passengers, $6.25 for kids 5–11, free under age 5, and $17.75 for bicycle and rider) sails on a 90-minute run between Port Angeles and Victoria four times daily in summer (mid-May through October), and twice daily the rest of the year. For specific departure times, contact the Black Ball ferry terminal at the foot of Laurel Street in Port Angeles. Vehicle space is at a premium on summer weekends and no reservations are accepted; get there very early to be assured of passage. Another option is to park your car in one of the lots near the ferry terminal ($10/day) and take the *Victoria Express* over. The *Coho* is out of service for maintenance from early January to early March.

The ***Victoria Express*** (360/452-8088 or 800/633-1589, www.victoriaexpress.com, $12.50 one-way, $5 bicycles and kayaks), a passenger-only ferry, makes the same run in an hour, two or three times a day from late May to early October. The ferry departs the Landing Mall terminal in Port Angeles. Advance reservations are advised July–Labor Day.

By Air

Horizon Airlines (800/547-9308) provides daily commuter service to Victoria, B.C., and to Sea-Tac Airport from Fairchild International Airport on the city's west side. **Harbor Air** (800/359-3220) also flies to Sea-Tac.

Rite Bros. Aviation (360/452-6226) offers flightseeing and charter flights over the Olympics from Port Angeles.

By Bus

Public bus service now extends throughout the Olympic Peninsula, making it possible to reach all the towns for a minimal fare on any of the four different public transit systems. **Clallam Transit** (360/452-4511 or 800/858-3747, www.clallamtransit.com) provides Monday–Saturday service around the Olympic Peninsula to Forks, Neah Bay, La Push, and Olympic National Park's Sol Duc Hot Springs and Lake Crescent. The buses have bike racks. They also connect with **Jefferson Transit** (360/385-4777 or 800/773-7788, www.jeffersontransit.com) in Sequim for Port Townsend and other Jefferson County points, and with **Grays Harbor Transit** in Queets for points to the south.

Olympic Bus Lines (360/417-0700 or 800/457-4492, www.olympicbuslines.com) offers van service connecting Port Angeles with Seattle and Sea-Tac Airport.

Port Angeles to Sol Duc

ELWHA RIVER VALLEY

Take Olympic Hot Springs Road south from Highway 101 just west of Port Angeles into the Elwha River watershed, best known for a bulwark project currently underway to demolish two dams and restore the river to its former pristine state. This river valley offers some of the closest remote hiking, camping, and rafting to Port Angeles.

Sports and Recreation

RIVER RAFTING

With Class II white-water conditions, The Elwha River is a popular destination for riverrunners of all experience levels. Check with the Park Service for current flow conditions and precautions if you decide to run it yourself. **Olympic Raft and Guide Service** (360/452-1443, www.northolympic.com/olympicraft) leads scenic two-hour trips down the Elwha River ($49 adults, $39 kids), plus sea kayaking in Lake Crescent, Lake Aldwell, and Freshwater Bay.

HIKING

Nearly everyone in Washington knows of Sol Duc Hot Springs, but less well known are **Olympic Hot Springs,** located at the end of Boulder Creek Rd., off Elwha River Road. The springs were once the site of a large resort, but today they are essentially undeveloped. A 2.5-mile trail leads to shallow rock-lined pools, where the water varies from lukewarm to 138°F. The Park Service discourages bathing and prohibits nudity (but that doesn't stop many folks from bathing au naturel).

Take the Elwha River Trail for two miles to **Humes Ranch,** built in 1889 by Grant Humes, who made his living leading wilderness expeditions and by hunting and trapping game. Today his cabin is on the National Register of Historic Places.

When a day hike is not enough, a number of hiking trails head into the backcountry from the Elwha area, and a variety of short and long hikes are available, including an across-the-park route that follows the Elwha Trail to Low Divide and then drops down to Quinault Lake on the North Quinault Trail, a distance of 44 miles.

For a north–south 44-mile trek, start at Lake Mills near Elwha on the **Elwha River Trail.** The trail runs 27.5 miles until it links up at Low Divide with the **North Fork Trail,** which follows the North Fork Quinault River until you reach the North Fork Ranger Station near Lake Quinault. You'll be hiking the route of James Halbold Christie, leader of the *Seattle*

Press expedition across the then-unexplored Olympic Peninsula. It took Christie and his party six months and one black bear to complete the route in 1890; it should take you only four days and a packful of gorp.

CAMPING

Pitch your tent at the Elwha and Altaire campgrounds ($12) along the road north of Lake Mills (created by Glines Canyon Dam).

Accommodations

Situated in a country home overlooking the Elwha River valley, **Elwha Ranch B&B** (360/457-6540, www.elwharanch.com, $140–150 d) has two guest rooms with private baths, a deck, and full breakfasts. The property features a private log cabin ($165) for those seeking a bit more seclusion.

LAKE CRESCENT

According to Native American legend, Mount Storm King once became so fed up with the fighting between the Clallams and Quileutes that he broke a rock off his head and threw it down at the warring tribes. The scientific view of the Lake Crescent's origin isn't much different; it's attributed to ancient landslides that divided a glacial lake into two large sections (Lake Crescent and Lake Sutherland), sending water from Lake Crescent out the Lyre River. However you look at it, Lake Crescent is an azure jewel set amid the emerald forests.

Sights and Recreation

Today, freshwater Lake Crescent, 624 feet deep and 8.5 miles long, is famous for its Beardslee trout, a subspecies that is large (some are in the 12–14 pound range) and a hard fighter when hooked. Swimming, boating, camping, picnicking, and, of course, fishing are popular lake activities. The lake has an impressive mountain-rimmed setting. The Park Service's **Storm King Ranger Station** (360/928-3380) is staffed during the summer months.

The nonprofit **Olympic Park Institute**

© WASHINGTON STATE TOURISM/JIM POTH

Lake Crescent on Olympic Peninsula, near Port Angeles

(360/928-3720 or 800/775-3720, www.yni.org/opi) offers excellent hands-on field seminars covering such diverse topics as Makah basketry, ecology of the forest canopy, and wolf biology. Seminars last 2–5 days and some may be taken for college credit. They also have an Elderhostel. Headquarters for the institute is the historic Rosemary Inn, near Lake Crescent Lodge. Students stay in nearby cabins, and meals are served family style at the inn.

HIKING

From the ranger station, follow the **Marymere Falls Trail** 0.75 mile for a spectacular view of this 90-foot falls. Not a lot of water, but it's quite impressive nevertheless. Return via the Crescent Lake Lodge Trail for a two-mile loop hike.

The **Mt. Storm King Trail** splits off from the Marymere Trail and climbs more than 3,000 feet in a bit over a mile, with fine views across the lake. The path ends before the summit, and the Park Service recommends against continuing to the top due to hazardous conditions.

A four-mile hike starting at Lyre River Road or North Shore Road at opposite ends of Lake Crescent, the **Spruce Railroad Trail** follows the tracks of the 1918 Spruce Railroad, built to supply spruce for World War I aircraft. The war was over before the railroad was completed, however, and the spruce was no longer needed. Two tunnels (closed) and depressions from the railroad ties remain. Besides a taste of local history, the almost-level hike provides a view of Lake Crescent.

CAMPING

Fairholm Campground ($12; open year-round), on the west end of Lake Crescent, has summertime naturalist programs on some evenings. The Forest Service's **Klahowya Campground** (nine miles west of Lake Crescent on Hwy. 101, $12) opens sites May to mid-October.

Park RVs along Lake Sutherland at **Shadow Mt. RV Park** (360/928-3043).

Fairholm General Store (360/928-3020) on the west end of Lake Crescent, is open April–September, and has tent sites and RV hookups, plus motorboats, rowboats, and canoes for rent. It also serves meals in the café; eat alfresco on a deck overlooking the lake.

Accommodations

The lake has two concession-operated lodges around its perimeter. Built in 1916, **Lake Crescent Lodge** (360/928-3211, www.olypen.com/lakecrescentlodge, $99–158 d lodge, $180–231 cottages, Apr.–Oct. only) is a cozy place with a comfortable feeling from decades of guests, including President Franklin D. Roosevelt, who stayed here in 1937. Sit on the porch for incredible views of the mountains and Lake Crescent, or lounge in front of the big fireplace on a cool evening. The lodge has all sorts of accommodations, including lodge rooms (bath down the hall), cottages (some with fireplaces), and modern motel units. The lodge has a restaurant and gift shop, and rents rowboats.

Rent out motel rooms, rustic cabins, or waterfront A-frame chalets at **Log Cabin Resort** (three miles from Hwy. 101 on E. Beach Rd., 360/928-3325, www.logcabinresort.net, $89–145 d, Apr.–Oct. only) at the northeast end of the lake. There are also camping cabins ($55) available for those with simple tastes. Many of the buildings have stood here since the 1920s. In addition to accommodations, the resort also has meals, a gift shop, grocery store, RV and tent sites, and rowboat, paddleboat, canoe, and kayak rentals.

East of Lake Crescent is the smaller Lake Sutherland, a popular place to swim. **Lake Sutherland Lodge B&B** (360/928-2111 or 888/231-1444, $65–90 s or d) is a modern log home with a covered deck facing the lake. The four guest rooms have private or shared baths, and a full breakfast is served.

SOL DUC

The wild and free Sol Duc River Valley offers hikers a chance to go deep into the mystical Olympic forests, experience soothing hot springs, and take a gander at one of the prettiest waterfalls on the peninsula.

Recreation

SOL DUC HOT SPRINGS

About 30 miles west of Port Angeles and 12 miles south of Highway 101, is Sol Duc (SOLE duck) hot springs (9 A.M.–9 P.M. daily mid-May through Aug., till 8 P.M. in Sept., 9 A.M.–8 P.M. Sat.–Sun. Apr.–mid-May, and Oct., $10 adults, $6.50 two hours or less before closing, $7.50 seniors). Bask in the 99–105°F mineral water piped into three large outdoor pools. A fourth freshwater pool is also on the site. Massage is also available.

FISHING

Sol Duc is legendary for its steelhead fishing in winter, plus year-round chinook and king salmon fisheries. Avoid the hassle of schlepping your own gear and schedule a trip with **Piscatorial Pursuits** (800/347-4232, www.piscatorialpursuits.com, $300 per person per day), which provides guidance based on years of reading the river, a boat, and all the tackle necessary to land one for the record books. The guide even cleans the fish for you.

HIKING

Several trails head up the Sol Duc Valley. A favorite is the one-mile **Sol Duc River Trail,** which passes through enormous western hemlocks and Douglas firs to Sol Duc Falls, one of the state's best-known waterfalls. A footbridge crosses the deep gorge cut by the river. From here, you can climb another three miles (one-way) to **Deer Lake,** bordered by trees. For variety, return to the campground from Sol Duc Falls on the **Lovers Lane Trail,** a three-mile path along the south side of the river.

A fine loop trip for backpackers (wilderness permit required) is to head up the Sol Duc River Trail to Seven Lakes Basin, then uphill to the summit of Bogachiel Peak and back out for a round-trip of 22 miles.

Practicalities

The springs were long known to the native peoples who first lived here, and white settlers were attracted to the area as a place of healing. By 1912, the area had an elegant hotel, theater, bowling alley, a 100-bed sanitorium, plus immaculately landscaped grounds with a golf course, tennis courts, and croquet grounds. A fire, begun by a defective flue, brought this to a crashing halt four years later. As the hotel burned to the ground, a short circuit caused the player organ to begin playing Beethoven's "Funeral March."

Today's **Sol Duc Hot Springs Resort** (360/327-3583, www.northolympic.com/sol-duc, $141–172 d, mid-May–Sept. only) isn't quite so lavish, but it does have a restaurant, grocery store, and gift shop, plus cabins (some with kitchenettes). A two-night minimum applies on holidays.

Outdoor lovers may prefer to pitch a tent at the Park Service's **Sol Duc Campground** ($12), open all year, but sometimes closed in the winter months due to flooding. Between July and Labor Day, park naturalists offer evening programs in the amphitheater some evenings.

Partway between Sol Duc and Forks, **Bear Creek Motel** (15 miles northeast of Forks in the town of Beaver, 360/327-3660, www.hungrybearcafemotel.com, $50–85 d, $20 RV, $7 tent) makes a good stop for Olympic loop adventurers who just can't bear to drive past another mile marker. The **Hungry Bear Café** (5 A.M.–8 P.M. daily) here also makes a handy mealtime pitstop.

STRAIT OF JUAN DE FUCA

Highway 112 offers one of the most dramatic shoreline drives in Washington; the narrow road winds along cliff faces and past extraordinary views. The area is windswept and remote—the only radio stations to be found are from Canada—and the ocean is up close and personal much of the drive. At the end of the road, 72 miles from Port Angeles, Neah Bay sits on the 44-square-mile **Makah Indian Reservation** in virtual isolation, at the northwesternmost point of the contiguous United States. Anyone who has spent time in a remote Alaskan village will feel right at home in Neah Bay.

Sights

SALT CREEK COUNTY PARK

The scenic and diverse grounds at Salt Creek County Park (three miles east of Joyce off Hwy. 112, 360/928-3441) is an open secret among Washingtonians. This is, hands down, the nicest municipal park on the peninsula. Situated three miles east of the village of Joyce, this was the site of Fort Hayden during World War II, and the concrete gun emplacements are still explorable, though the 45-foot-long guns are long gone. The fort sits on a bluffside, with grassy lawns and picnic areas adjoining campsites. A path down to the rocky beach offers lots of tidepools during low tide. Farther up the bluff are several miles worth of trails.

OTHER PARKS

The beaches beyond Slip Point Lighthouse, on the east end of Clallam Bay, are great for beachcombing and exploring the tidepools, and the area east of here is famous for its marine fossils. County parks in the Clallam Bay area are **Clallam Bay Spit,** a 33-acre waterfront park for day use only, and **Pillar Point County Park** (360/963-2301), just east of Clallam Bay. Pillar Point is a four-acre park with a boat launch.

MAKAH MUSEUM

In 1970, tidal erosion unearthed old Ozette homes that had been destroyed by a mud slide some 500 years earlier. The slide entombed and preserved the material, and 11 years of excavations by archaeologists from Washington State University unearthed one of the richest finds in North America. Find thousands of these artifacts at the Makah Museum (Hwy. 112 & Bay View Ave., 360/645-2711, www.makah.com, 10 A.M.–5 P.M. daily Memorial Day–September 15; closed the rest of the year, $5 adults, $4 seniors and students) at Neah Bay. This is the finest collection of Northwest Coast Native American artifacts from pre-contact times, with an extraordinary range of material, including beautifully carved seal clubs, spears, bentwood boxes, combs, paddles, bows and arrows, clothing, woven baskets, whale bones, and much more. Not on display—it is too fragile—but visible in photos is an intricate plaid blanket woven from woodpecker feathers, dog hair, cattail fluff, and cedar bark. A re-created 15th-century longhouse is the museum's centerpiece, showing how the people lived in the abundance of the land. Outside, a modern longhouse is sometimes used for basketry and carving demonstrations.

An hour-long video about Neah Bay and the archaeological dig is shown at 11 A.M. and 2 P.M. daily. The small gift shop sells local baskets and beadwork. You can also obtain local information here.

Events

Makah Days is the town's big annual festival, celebrating the day the reservation first raised the American flag in 1913. Held on the weekend closest to August 26, the three-day festival is highlighted by dances, a parade, fireworks show, salmon bake, canoe races, and bone games (Native American gambling). Also popular is the **Chito Beach Bluegrass Jamboree** in mid-June.

Sports and Recreation

CAPE FLATTERY

The **Cape Loop Road** provides an interesting drive or mountain bike ride to the tip of Cape Flattery. The narrow dirt road is not for RVs. Pick up a route map at the museum, or head west from town to the Makah Tribal Center, and then turn right to the cape (left will take you to Hobuck Beach and a fish hatchery). About eight miles from town, you'll come to one of the few unlogged areas remaining on the cape, and the new **Cape Flattery Trail.** This fine boardwalk path leads downhill 0.75 mile to the rocky shoreline, with views of Tatoosh Island and **Cape Flattery Lighthouse,** built in 1858. Most folks return to Neah Bay the same way they came out, but mountain bikers and four-wheelers will enjoy the very rough road that leads back eastward around the cape to Neah Bay, passing a small waterfall with sculpted pools large enough to sit in on a warm summer day, and several miles later a dump that has to be one of the worst in the state of Washington (but a good place to look for ravens and eagles). The total length of this loop is approximately 16 miles.

POINT OF ARCHES AND SHI SHI BEACH

Near the north park boundary, Point of Arches is a testimony to the relentless power of the Pacific where, with a force of two tons per square inch, the ocean carved giant arches out of ancient rock. The Arches, legendary children of Destruction Island and Tatoosh Island, were pushed from Mother Tatoosh's canoe when she deserted her husband because, she said, "You'd probably grow up just like your father!" The bluffs above neighboring Shi Shi (shy-shy) Beach provide a vantage point for watching the spring and fall gray whale migrations; the best viewing season is March–May. This stretch of coastline features some of the finest beaches and tidepools anywhere on the Washington coast; you might even find remains of a shipwreck still visible.

OZETTE LAKE AREA

Located in the northwest corner of the coastal strip, eight-mile-long Lake Ozette is the third-largest natural lake in Washington. A 21-mile paved road heads southwest from Sekiu, ending at the **Ozette Ranger Station** on the north end of the lake (360/963-2725, open daily in summer, no set hours in winter). This area has one of the most popular overnight hikes along the Olympic coast, and summer weekends attract outdoor enthusiasts. Parking costs $2 per day.

Two trails head to the coast from the ranger station. One leads southwest to **Sand Point,** three miles away; the other goes three miles northwest to **Cape Alva**—the westernmost point in the Lower 48. By hiking the beach connecting the two, you can create a triangular loop trip of 9.3 miles. You can also continue south on the beach for 2.3 miles to the **Norwegian Memorial,** a tribute to the victims of a 1903 shipwreck. There is much to explore in the Cape Alva area: fascinating tidepools, cannonball shaped rocks, an anchor from one of the ships that ran aground here, and even an occasional Japanese glass ball. This is probably the best place to see wildlife in Olympic National Park, with bald eagles in the air, deer along the beach, sea lions and seals in the water, and migrating gray whales in fall and spring. This area contains the largest population of sea otters in the Lower 48; look for them in the kelp beds off Sand Point. The Wedding Rocks area between Cape Alva and Sand Point is well known for its petroglyphs, carved by the original inhabitants of this land at an unknown time. Pick up a handout describing the petroglyphs from the ranger station.

Practicalities

ALONG HIGHWAY 112

Right on the river and only a few steps from the Strait of Juan de Fuca, **Lyre River Recreation Area** offers free primitive campsites year-round. The best camping choice on the entire Strait, though, is at **Salt Creek County Park** (three miles east of Joyce off Hwy. 112, 360/928-3441, $24 full hookups, $18 tent), a gorgeous park that accommodates tent campers and RVers alike and is surrounded by trails, an old fort, and loads of tidepools to explore.

Farther along the route in Sekiu, **Curley's Resort** (360/963-2281 or 800/542-9680, www.curleysresort.com, $48–100 s or d) has nice motel units and cabins with kitchenettes, as well as RV hookups, boat and kayak rentals, a dive shop, and even whale-watching trips through its **Puffin Charters** service.

Also of note is **Winter Summer Inn B&B** (360/963-2264, www.northolympic.com/winters, 75–115 d), with decks overlooking the Clallam River and full breakfasts. The B&B has two rooms with private baths, as well as a separate studio apartment that doesn't include the breakfast.

NEAH BAY

Neah Bay lodging can leave much to be desired. The "resorts" are mostly shoestring operations dependent upon fishermen and hunters who don't mind ancient furnishings and marginally clean rooms. The nicest in-town motel is **The Cape Motel** (360/645-2250, $55–85 d) with rooms including kitchenettes. RV ($24) and tent spaces ($15) are available in summer only.

Washburn's General Store (360/645-2211, 9 A.M.–7 P.M. Mon.–Sat., 9 A.M.–6 P.M. Sun.) sells groceries and has a deli with fresh sandwiches and espresso (this is Washington, after all), plus a small gift shop selling jewelry, baskets, carvings, and knitted items. **Raven's Corner Gifts & Indian Arts** sells local crafts and T-shirts with Makah designs.

Get seafood and burgers at **Warm House Restaurant** (1471 Bay View Ave., 360/645-2924, breakfast and dinner only).

OZETTE LAKE

The Lost Resort (360/963-2899 or 800/950-2899, www.lostresort.net, $50 cabin, $15 campsite) has a general store, deli, camping supplies, showers, and private campsites next to the lake.

Because of overcrowding and resource damage, the Park Service has instituted a **quota system** for overnight hiking in the Ozette area between May 1 and September 30. (There are no restrictions on day use, however.) Make reservations at the Wilderness Information Center in Port Angeles (360/565-3100, www.nps.gov/olym/wic). If you don't have a permit, you might try arriving early to grab one of the 18 campsites accessible by car, but if those are gone, you'll have to drive all the way back to a private campground in Sekiu. The busiest times are weekends in July and August.

The small **Ozette Campground** has camping ($16) year-round, but get here early to be sure of a space (no reservations). The lake is a popular place for boats, canoes, and kayaks, but winds can create treacherous wave action at times. The free **Erickson's Bay** boat-in campground is halfway down the lake on the west side. There is good fishing for largemouth bass, cutthroat trout, kokanee, and other fish here.

Getting There

Clallam Transit (360/452-4511 or 800/858-3747, www.clallamtransit.com) provides daily bus service to Neah Bay and throughout the northern Olympic Peninsula.

Olympic Coast and Hoh Rain Forest

When the highway emerges on the coastline south of Forks, you will quickly become aware that the northern half of Washington's coastline is a picture of how the Pacific coast looks in brochures and calendar photos: pristine beaches, pounding waves, trees sculpted by relentless sea breezes.

Washington's rocky and essentially undeveloped Olympic coast is truly a national gem, and in 1994 it was declared the **Olympic Coast National Marine Sanctuary,** a designation that helps protect the shore and ocean from development. The coast contains rich fishing grounds; more species of whales, dolphins, and porpoises than anywhere on earth; some of the largest seabird colonies in the Lower 48; and an unparalleled beauty that attracts painters, photographers, and anyone with a sense of wonder. The shore is dotted with cliff-rimmed beaches and forested hills.

Farther inland, you'll encounter a different kind of spectacle—one of mossy trees, gurgling streams, and misty forests. These are the most famous woods in America, the Hoh Rain Forest. Bring your raincoat and a sense of adventure, and prepare to meander.

FORKS

The westernmost incorporated city in the Lower 48, Forks is the economic center and logging capital of the western Olympic Peninsula—a big handle for this town of 3,400 with one main drag. For travelers, the town's big selling point is its proximity to the west side of Olympic National Park and Pacific coast beaches. Also nearby is a modern

© ERICKA CHICKOWSKI

moss-draped trees at Hoh Rain Forest

University of Washington natural resources research facility.

Sights

TIMBER MUSEUM

The **Forks Timber Museum** (360/374-9663, 10 A.M.–4 P.M. daily mid-Apr.–Oct., free) has historical exhibits that include a steam donkey, a logging camp bunkhouse, old logging equipment, and various pioneer implements. The real surprise is a large 150-year-old canoe that was discovered by loggers in 1990. Out front is a memorial to loggers killed in the woods and a replica of a fire lookout tower.

BOGACHIEL STATE PARK

Six miles south of Forks on Highway 101, Bogachiel (Native American for Muddy Waters) State Park encompasses 123 acres on the usually clear Bogachiel River. Enjoy the short nature trail through a rain forest, or swim, paddle, or fish in the river—famous for its summer and winter steelhead, salmon, and trout. The park has campsites (360/374-6356, www.parks.wa.gov, $13 for tents, $19 for RV hookups) and is open year-round.

Events

Forks' **4th of July** is actually a three-day festival of fun that includes an art show, pancake breakfast, parades, a loggers show, frog jump, demolition derby, dancing, and fireworks.

Sports and Recreation

Right on the opposite side of the highway from the park entrance is Undi Road, which leads east five miles (the last two are gravel) to the **Bogachiel River Trailhead.** The trail follows the lush, infrequently visited rainforest valley of the Bogachiel River east for two miles through national forest land until reaching the edge of Olympic National Park, where the trail continues all the way up to Seven Lakes Basin (27 miles) or Sol Duc Hot Springs (27 miles). The lower section of trail in the rain forest is a lovely place for a day hike. Mountain bikers are allowed on the trail as far as the edge of the national park, but it's a pretty soggy ride.

FORKS FOR *TWILIGHT* FANS

"City of Forks," a notice in Forks reads, "Population: 3175 Vampires: 8.5." It might seem out of place in this out-of-the-way logging community on the remote Olympic Peninsula. But for those in the know this is just one more sign that this obscure little town has been bitten by *Twilight* fever.

Seemingly overnight, Forks has been overrun with fans of the teenage vampire book series penned by Stephanie Meyer and adapted into a major motion picture released in 2008. Even though Meyer never even visited the town before using it as the setting for her books, the good-natured folks of Fork have had fun with the fame. All around town you'll find *Twilight* t-shirts for sale, signs welcoming fans, menu specials, and even custom-decorated motel rooms. Sightseers will find a red pickup similar to the one driven by the heroine, Bella, parked out front of the visitor's center, and the folks there have teamed up with the local chamber of commerce to offer a special *Twilight* tour of Forks. Included on the tour is a stop in front of Forks High School, where camera crews shot scenes for the movie. For more information, visit www.forkswa.com/HomeofTwilighttheBook.

CAMPING

Camp at **Bogachiel State Park,** four miles south on Highway 101 (360/374-6356, www.parks.wa.gov, year-round $13 for tents, $19 for RV hookups), or at the Park Service's **Mora Campground** (open year-round, $10), 14 miles west of Forks, which offers summertime naturalist programs and nature walks. Dispersed camping (pullouts off the road) is allowed on Forest Service lands throughout Olympic National Forest.

Park RVs at **Forks 101 RV Park** (901 S. Forks Ave., 360/374-5073 or 800/962-9964). Camp for free at Rayonier's **Tumbling Rapids Park** (11 miles northeast of Forks along Hwy. 101, 360/374-6565).

Accommodations

Forks has the most lodging options on the west side of the 101 loop, though some of the motels can leave a little to be desired. The best bet for multi-day stays is to opt for a B&B.

The decor reminds you of a neglected granny's house—faux wood paneling, flowery bedsheets, and spent-looking furniture at **Bagby's Town Motel** (1080 S. Forks Ave., 360/374-6231 or 800/742-2429, www.bagbystownmotel.com, $58–64 d), but the owners are friendly, the gardens outside are pretty, and it is comfortable enough to suffice for a cheap night's stopover while making the Olympic loop.

If you've got the dough, though, upgrade yourself to the **Olympic Suites** (800 Olympic Dr., 1.5 miles north of Forks, 360/374-5400 or 800/262-3433, www.olympicgetaways.com/olympicsuites, $79–119 d) down the road. Here you'll find updated one- and two-bedroom suites with kitchens and free wireless Internet on a nicely wooded property. Pet owners will also find rooms here that accept Rover.

Another very clean motel choice is the **Pacific Inn Motel** (352 S. Forks Ave., 360/374-9400, www.pacificinnmotel.com, $58–89 and up), a basic but newish property that remains well-tended and cares for you with a friendly staff. There aren't a ton of amenities, but you will find coin-op laundry facilities and free coffee and tea in the lobby.

The best choices in town are the bed-and-breakfasts. There are a number of off-the-beaten-path properties ideal for those looking to feel close to the natural surroundings around the town. For example, the **Fisherman's Widow B&B** (31 Huckleberry Lane, 360/374-5693, www.northolympic.com/fw, $125–135 d) is a comfy lodgelike home sitting right on the banks of the Sol Duc river, a favorite among anglers and kayakers who can head right out the back door for their daily adventures. The rooms are spacious and can accommodate up to five people, so adventuring groups can save some cash by sharing.

Also a favorite among anglers, especially fly-fishing fans, is **Brightwater House B&B** (360/374-5453 www.brightwaterhouse.com, $125 d), also on the Sol Duc and which boasts a "liberal" cancellation policy that allows anglers to change their plans when the river conditions change. The common River Room offers great views through its floor-to-ceiling windows.

Historic architecture buffs will best enjoy **Miller Tree Inn** (654 E. Division, 360/374-6806, www.millertreeinn.com, $110–195 d), a family- and pet-friendly inn that rests inside a well-cared-for 1914 homestead. The downstairs common rooms are especially homey, with rich wood paneling and a living room fireplace. Outside there's a back deck with a large hot tub overlooking the attractive grounds. You can also expect a full farmhouse breakfast.

Food

Meet the loggers over coffee and donuts at **The Coffee Shop** (314 Forks Ave. S, 360/374-6769, 5 A.M.–8 P.M. daily), with friendly waitresses and dependably good food three meals a day.

The In Place (320 S. Forks Ave., 360/374-4004, 6 A.M.–9 P.M. daily) is a good lunch spot, with deli sandwiches and great mushroom bacon burgers. They also serve pasta, steak, and seafood dinners.

A mile north of Forks at the La Push road junction on Highway 101, the **Smoke House Restaurant** (360/374-6258, 11 A.M.–9 P.M. Mon.–Fri., noon–9 P.M. Sat.–Sun.) is open daily for lunch and dinner with wonderful prime rib and a full menu of other all-American faves.

Pacific Pizza (870 Forks Ave. S, 360/374-2626, 11 A.M.–9 P.M. Sun.–Thurs., 11 A.M.–10 P.M. Fri.–Sat.) has the best local pizzas and pasta.

The **Forks Farmers Market** (360/374-6623, 10 A.M.–2 P.M. Fri.–Sat. May–mid-Oct.) takes place next to Sully's Drive-In at the north end of town.

Information and Services

Get local information on the south end of town at the helpful **Forks Chamber of Commerce Visitor Center** (1411 S. Forks Ave., 360/374-2531 or 800/443-6757, www.forkswa.com, 9 A.M.–5 P.M. daily in summer, 10 A.M.–4 P.M. daily rest of the year).

The **Olympic National Forest and Park Recreation Information Office** (551 Forks Ave. N, 360/374-7566, 8:30 A.M.–12:30 P.M. and 1:30–5:30 P.M. daily in summer, 8:30 A.M.–12:30 P.M. and 1:30–5:30 P.M. Mon.–Fri. the rest of the year) is housed in the transportation building. Stop here for recreation information, maps, and handouts, and to take a look at the big 3-D model of the Olympic Peninsula.

Getting There

Local buses all stop at the transportation building (521 N. Forks Ave.) in Forks. **Clallam Transit** (360/452-4511 or 800/858-3747, www.clallamtransit.com) provides daily service north to Port Angeles and Neah Bay, and west to La Push. Catch the free **West Jefferson Transit** (800/436-3950, www.jeffersontransit.com) bus, south from Forks to Kalaloch, Queets, and Lake Quinault. At Lake Quinault, join the Grays Harbor Transit system for points south and east.

LA PUSH AREA

A 14-mile road heads west from Forks through the Bogachiel/Quillayute River Valley. Nearly all this land has been logged at least once, so be prepared for typical Olympic Peninsula clear-cut vistas. The road ends at La Push, a small village bordering the Pacific Ocean on the south side of the Quillayute River, and the center of the **Quileute Indian Reservation.** The name La Push was derived from the French (*la bouche,* meaning mouth), a reference to the river mouth here. It is an attractive little town with a fantastic beach for surfing and kayaking in the summer or watching storm waves in the winter. Locals have a small fleet of fishing and crabbing boats, a seafood plant, a fish hatchery, and a resort offering simple shoreside accommodations and camping.

Sights

The main attraction at La Push is simply the setting: James Island and other rocky points sit just offshore, and waves break against First Beach. The small **Quileute Tribe Museum** (8 A.M.–3 P.M. Mon.–Thurs., 2–4 P.M. Fri.) housed in the Tribal Center office, has a few artifacts. Ask here for local folks who sell beadwork and other handicrafts, and about ocean and river tours in traditional cedar canoes.

Mora Road branches off from La Push Road three miles east of La Push and provides access to **Rialto Beach** within Olympic National Park. It's pretty easy to tell you've entered public land; instead of clear-cuts, you'll find tall old-growth trees. Mora Campground is here, and the beach is a favorite picnicking area and starting point for hikers heading north along the wild Olympic coast. The town of La Push is just across the wide river mouth to the south.

RIALTO BEACH AREA

This is one of the most popular entry points for the coastal strip of Olympic National Park. Rialto Beach is on the north side of the Quillayute River, just west of the Mora campground and ranger station. The 1.5-mile beach is popular with folks out for a stroll or day hike, but continue northward and the crowds thin out as the country becomes a jumble of sea stacks—remnants of the ancient coast. Hole in the Wall is one of the most interesting of these. This treacherous stretch of shore has claimed many lives, as memorials to Chilean and Norwegian sailors attest. The 21 long and remote miles between Rialto Beach and the Ozette Ranger Station feature abundant wildlife—including bald eagles, harbor seals, shorebirds, and migrating whales at different times of the year. The resident raccoons are here year-round, so hang your food in a hard-sided container!

A popular day hike from the La Push area is **Second Beach,** an easy 0.75-mile trail that starts just south of La Push, followed by 1.5 miles of beach, tidepools, and sea stacks, including a pointed one called the Quillayute Needle. You can camp at a couple of points under the trees, making this some of the most accessible beach camping in the state.

Park at Third Beach, just south of the Second Beach trailhead, for a challenging hike all the way down to **Oil City,** 17 miles away on the north side of the Hoh River. Be sure to carry a tide chart. Oil City neither has oil nor is it a city. Three different exploration parties came here in search of oil—attracted by crude seeping from the ground just north of here. During the 1930s, 11 exploratory wells were drilled and a town was platted, but there simply wasn't enough oil to justify development. A part-paved, part-gravel road leads 11 miles from Highway 101 to the Oil City trailhead.

Clallam Transit (360/452-4511 or 800/858-3747) provides daily bus service to La Push from Port Angeles and Forks. Hikers can catch the bus as far as the turnoff to Rialto Beach and walk or hitch the final three miles.

Events

The unannounced **Surf Frolic Festival** in January attracts surfers and kayakers, but the big event is **Quileute Days** in mid-July, with a tug-of-war, bone games, a fish bake, canoe races, and fireworks.

Recreation

CAMPING

Olympic National Park's **Mora Campground** (open year-round, $10) is a pretty in-the-trees place to pitch a tent. Check with the ranger station here for summertime naturalist programs and nature walks.

RV owners can pull their rigs into **Lonesome Creek RV Park** (360/374-4338, $30–35 full hookups), which offers many sites with ocean views. RVers can also park at nearby **Three Rivers Resort** (360/374-5300, www.northolympic.com/threerivers, $18 with full hookups).

Accommodations

The obvious pick in La Push for lodging, **Quileute Oceanside Resort** (320 Ocean Dr., 360/374-5267, www.quileutenation.com, $45–240 s or d,) offers a range of options, everything from bare-bones camper cabins and simple motel rooms on up to duplex units and brand new cabins facing the breathtaking seastacks.

It is activities central at **Three Rivers Resort** (360/374-5300, www.northolympic.com/threerivers, $59–69 up to 4), which offers guided fishing trips, horseback rides, and float trips at the intersection of La Push and Mora Roads (halfway between Forks and La Push). This pet-friendly establishment is also a good spot to bring Spot.

Manitou Lodge (360/374-6295, www.manitoulodge.com, $139–179 d) is a modern country lodge on 10 acres of forested land off Mora Road. Seven luxurious guest rooms with private baths are $85–125 s or d, including a full breakfast. Also on the property are two cedar-shingle camping cabins ($65–99 d) available spring through fall only. Book up to six months ahead for summer weekends. A gift shop here sells quality baskets, woodcarvings, and beadwork.

Olson's Resort (3243 Mora Rd., 360/374-3142, $80) has space for up to five in a cozy and quiet cabin with a kitchen, just 2.5 miles from Rialto Beach.

Food

There are no restaurants in La Push, but you can get locally famous burgers plus soups and sandwiches east of town at **Three Rivers Resort** (360/374-5300, 11 A.M.–9 P.M.).

Information

The Olympic National Park's **Mora Ranger Station** (360/374-5460) next to the Mora Campground is usually staffed daily June–August, but the rest of the year it's catch-as-catch-can. Stop by for a tide chart and information on hiking along the coast. Rangers offer daily beach walks and short guided hikes, and summer campfire programs on Friday–Sunday nights at the amphitheater.

Getting There

Clallam Transit (360/452-4511 or 800/858-3747, www.clallamtransit.com) provides daily bus service to La Push and other parts of the Olympic Peninsula, transporting you south as far as Lake Quinault, and north to Port Angeles and Neah Bay.

HOH RIVER VALLEY

Heading south from Forks on Highway 101, you pass through the heart of the Olympics and get a taste of the economic importance of logging and how it has changed the landscape. Despite reductions in the amount of timber cut in recent years on Forest Service lands, you're bound to meet a constant parade of trucks laden with logs from private land and reservations.

Hoh Rain Forest

One of Olympic National Park's most famous sights is also one of its most remote. Fourteen miles south of Forks is the turnoff to the world-famous Hoh Rain Forest, located at the end of the paved 19 mile Upper Hoh Road. The road follows the Hoh river through a beautiful valley with a mix of second-growth stands and DNR clear-cuts. Once you enter the park, old-growth stands dominate. The **Hoh Rain Forest Visitor Center** (360/374-6925, 9 A.M.–7 P.M. daily July–Aug., 9 A.M.–4 P.M. daily the rest of the year) offers interpretive exhibits and summertime guided walks and campfire programs. Stop by for brochures, information, books, and educational exhibits on the life of the forest and the climate. It rains a *lot* here; 140 inches of rain per year keep this forest perpetually green and damp under towering conifers over 200 feet tall and up to 10 feet wide. The driest months are July and August.

Two short interpretive trails lead through the lush spikemoss-draped forests behind the visitors center. Lacy ferns carpet the forest floor, and some even survive in the tops of the bigleaf and vine maples. A paved wheelchair-accessible mini-trail is directly behind the center, and the **Hall of Mosses Trail** offers an easy 0.75-mile loop.

Shopping

Five miles up the Hoh Rain Forest Road is **Peak 6 Adventure Store** (360/374-5254, 9:30 A.M.–5:30 P.M. daily) selling all sorts of camping and climbing gear and clothes. The owners are friendly and knowledgeable about local trails, and prices are reasonable.

Sports and Recreation

HIKING

Spruce Nature Trail covers a 1.25-mile loop that crosses a crystalline spring-fed creek and then touches on the muddy, glacially fed Hoh River. More adventurous folks can head out the **Hoh River Trail,** an 18-mile path that ends at Blue Glacier and is used to climb Mt. Olympus. Hikers heading into the wilderness need to pick up permits at the visitors center or the Wilderness Information Center in Port Angeles.

CLIMBING

Climbing the glacier-clad 7,965-foot **Mt. Olympus** is a 44-mile round-trip trek. From the Hoh Ranger Station—the closest and most popular departure point—hike 12 flat miles along the Hoh River Trail, then another five steep ones to the Olympus base camp, Glacier Meadows. Crossing Blue Glacier and the Snow Dome requires rope, an ice ax, crampons, and mountaineering skills; a hard hat is advised because of rock falls near the summit. The eight-mile climb from Glacier Meadows to the summit takes about 10 hours. The best months for climbing are late June through early September, the driest months in the park; prior to that time mud and washouts may slow you down.

Inexperienced climbers and those unfamiliar with the area might be wise to hire a guide to accompany them up to the top. National park guide service contracts change year by year, but one company is a perennial fave: **Mountain Madness** (3018 SW Charlestown St., Seattle, 206/937-8389) runs four-day treks to the top of Olympus meant for beginners on up.

CAMPGROUNDS

The Park Service's ☾ **Hoh Rain Forest Campground,** 19 miles east from Highway 101 at the end of the road, is open year-round with in-the-trees camping for $10. The visitors center has evening naturalist programs in the summer.

The Department of Natural Resources has five small, free, year-round campgrounds near the Hoh River: **Hoh Oxbow Campground** (near milepost 176), **Cottonwood Campground** (two miles west on Oil City Rd.), **Willoughby Creek Campground** (3.5 miles east on Hoh Rain Forest Rd.), **Minnie Peterson Campground** (4.5 miles east on Hoh Rain Forest Rd.), and **South Fork Hoh Campground** (6.5 miles east on Hoh Mainline Rd.). Willoughby Creek is right on the river but has just three sites.

Accommodations

Budget travelers will want to check out the quirky **Rain Forest Hostel** (23 miles south of Forks on Hwy. 101, 360/374-2270, $10 pp, $5 kids). The hostel is out in the sticks and has two dorm rooms with bunk beds, a family room, and a trailer outside for couples. It's closed 10 A.M.–5 P.M., lights out at 11 P.M., and no booze is allowed. Guests are asked to do 15 minutes of chores in the evening or morning before departure. Those without vehicles can catch the West Jefferson Transit bus.

Bring your own bedding to the rustic roadside cabins at **Hoh River Resort** (15 miles south of Forks on Hwy. 101, 360/374-5566, $65 s or d), a quiet property perfect for families and others who may not feel like camping in rain forest country. Tent ($17) and RV ($25) spaces are also here.

Animal lovers will fall head over hoofs for the ☾ **Hoh Humm Ranch** (20 miles south of Forks on Hwy. 101, 360/374-5337, www.olypen.com/hohhumm, $35 s or d), where innkeepers raise a zoo's worth of critters: llamas, strange breeds of cattle, goats, sheep, ducks, geese, rhea birds, and Asian Sika deer. Stay in one of five guest rooms with shared bathrooms at a steal of a rate.

Food

Be sure to bring food if you plan to spend the whole day at the Hoh, as dining options are very limited. Your only option is at the park entrance, where you'll find **Hard Rain Cafe**

(5763 Upper Hoh Rd., 360/374-9288, 9 A.M.–7 P.M. daily), a quiet little mercantile and burger stand that's good for lunches and quick bites on the way in or out of the park.

RUBY BEACH TO KALALOCH

The southern end of Olympic National Park's coastal strip is the most accessible, with Highway 101 running right along the bluff for more than a dozen miles. Short trails lead down to the water at half a dozen points, and at the southern end one finds the town (of sorts) called Kalaloch, with a comfortable lodge, two Park Service campgrounds, and other facilities. Beach camping is not allowed along this stretch of the coast.

Ruby Beach Area

Highway 101 rejoins the coast at Ruby Beach, just south of the mouth of the Hoh River. A very popular trail leads down to beautiful sandy shoreline dotted with red pebbles (garnets, not rubies), with piles of driftwood and the flat top of **Destruction Island** several miles offshore. The island is capped by a 94-foot lighthouse.

The tiny, 400-acre **Hoh Indian Reservation** is a couple miles north of Ruby Beach at the mouth of the Hoh River. A three-mile road leads to the tribal center building (360/374-6582). Stop here to ask about locally made cedar bark baskets, but be ready to pay upward of $200. The village is a trashed, badly littered place, but the ocean views are impressive. On the north side of the river is the area called Oil City, accessible via a partly gravel 11-mile road off Highway 101.

South of Ruby Beach, the highway cruises along the bluff, with five more trails dropping to shoreline beaches, creatively named Beach 1, Beach 2, Beach 3, and so on. A massive western red cedar tree stands just off the highway near Beach 6.

Kalaloch

The bluff and beach called Kalaloch has a campground, gas station/country store, and the **Kalaloch Lodge** (360/962-2271 or 866/525-2562), operated as a park concessionaire. The lodge consists of three different types of facilities: the 1950s-era main lodge ($164 d), cabins of various types ($181–300), and the Seacrest House Motel ($164–186). There are no TVs in the rooms, but the sitting room has one for those who can't miss their soaps. Some of the cabins have kitchens and offer waterside views. Make reservations far ahead for the nicest rooms or the bluff cabins; some places are reserved 11 months ahead of time for July and August. The lodge also has a café, gift shop, and lounge.

Across from the lodge is the Park Service's **Kalaloch Visitor Information Center** (360/962-2283, daily June–Sept., with variable hours the rest of the year) where you'll find natural history books, maps, pamphlets, and tide charts for beach walking.

The National Park Service's **Kalaloch Campground** ($12; open year-round) sits on a bluff overlooking the beach. During the summer, attend campfire programs or join a tidepool walk at Beach 4. The primitive **South Beach Campground** ($8, open summers only) is on the southern edge of the park three miles south of Kalaloch. These are the only two campgrounds on the dozen miles of Pacific shoreline between Queets and the Hoh Reservation.

Queets and Quinault

QUEETS RIVER AREA

South of Kalaloch, Highway 101 crosses the **Quinault Indian Reservation,** where you get to see what clear-cuts really look like. A narrow corridor of Olympic National Park extends along the Queets River, protecting a strip of old-growth timber bordered by cut-over DNR and private lands. The gravel Queets River Road (well marked) follows the river eastward from Highway 101, ending 14 miles later at **Queets Campground.** This free, primitive campground has no running water, but it is open year-round. A seasonal ranger station is also here. The **Queets Loop Trail** departs the campground for an easy three-mile walk through second-growth forests and fields where elk are often seen. Another route, the **Queets Trail,** is more challenging. It requires the fording of Queets River near the campground—wait till late summer or fall for this hike, and use caution—and then continues along the river for 15 miles, passing through magnificent old-growth stands of Sitka spruce. Not for beginners, but an impressive hike.

Olympic Raft & Kayak (360/452-1443 or 888/452-1443, www.raftandkayak.com) leads relaxing float trips down the Queets River each spring.

The Quinault Reservation beaches, from just south of Queets almost to Moclips, have been closed to the public since 1969. However, you can arrange for an escorted tour of Point Grenville or Cape Elizabeth, two good bird-watching spots, by calling 360/276-8211.

The Department of Natural Resources has additional free campsites approximately 14 miles up Hoh-Clearwater Mainline Road. The turnoff is at milepost 147 on Highway 101 (three miles west of the Queets River Rd. turnoff).

LAKE QUINAULT

Surrounded by steep mountains and dense rainforest, Lake Quinault is bordered on the

© ERICKA CHICKOWSKI

Lake Quinault Resort

northwest by Olympic National Park and on the southeast by Olympic National Forest; the lake itself and land to the southeast are part of the Quinault Reservation and subject to Quinault regulations. Located at the southwestern edge of Olympic National Park, Lake Quinault is a hub of outdoor activity during the summer months. This very scenic tree-rimmed lake is surrounded by cozy lodges, and level hiking trails provide a chance for even total couch potatoes to get a taste of the rainforest that once covered vast stretches of the Olympic Peninsula.

The Quinault Rain Forest is one of three major rain forests that survive on the Peninsula; here the annual average rainfall is 167 inches, resulting in enormous trees, lush vegetation, and moss-carpeted buildings. If you arrive in the rainy winter months, bring your heavy rain gear and rubber boots, not just a nylon poncho and running shoes. If you're prepared, a hike in the rain provides a great chance to see this soggy and verdant place at its truest. July and August are the driest months, but even then it rains an average of three inches. Typical Decembers see 22 inches of precipitation.

Sports and Recreation

DAY HIKING

The Quinault area is a hiker's paradise, with trails for all abilities snaking through a diversity of terrain. The 10-mile **Quinault National Recreation Trail System,** accessible from Willaby and Falls Creek Campgrounds and Lake Quinault Lodge, provides several loop trail hiking opportunities along the lakeshore and into the rain forest. Easier still is the half-mile **Quinault Rain Forest Nature Trail,** where informative signs explain the natural features. A good hike for those traveling with small children begins at North Fork Campground, following the Three Lakes Trail for the first mile to **Irely Lake.** The half-mile **Maple Glade Rain Forest Trail** begins at the Park Service's Quinault Visitor Center on North Fork Road.

Another easy jaunt is the **Graves Creek Nature Trail,** a one-mile loop that begins at the Graves Creek Campground on the South Shore Road. From the same starting point, the **Enchanted Valley Trail** takes you through a wonderful rainforest along the South Fork of the Quinault River. Day hikers often go as far as Pony Bridge, 2.5 miles each way, but more ambitious folks can continue to Dosewallips, a one-way distance of 28 miles.

BACKCOUNTRY HIKING

You'll find two across-the-park hikes that begin or end in the Quinault area, one heading northeast over to Dosewallips, and the other heading north over Low Divide to the Lake Elwha area.

The 11,961-acre **Colonel Bob Wilderness** borders the South Shore Road just east of Quinault Lake and has a couple of popular backcountry paths. For an overnight hike, the seven-mile (each way) **Colonel Bob Trail** provides views of Mt. Olympus, Quinault Valley, and the Pacific Ocean from its 4,492-foot summit and passes through impressive rainforests. Drive past Lake Quinault on South Shore Road until you see the trailhead on the right. The two-mile **Fletcher Canyon Trail** doesn't get a lot of use, but it's a fine chance to see virgin timber and a pretty waterfall. The trail starts from South Shore Road just before it enters the park. Access to the wilderness from the south side is via Forest Road 2204, northeast from the town of Humptulips. If you enter from this remote area, be sure to visit the beautiful Campbell Tree Campground (free) and to check out the **West Fork Humptulips River Trail** that departs from the campground.

A 21-mile loop begins near the North Fork Campground, heads up the **Three Lakes Trail** for seven miles to three shallow alpine lakes, and then turns down the **Elip Creek Trail** for four miles before catching the **North Fork Trail** back through dense rainforests to your starting point. An added advantage of this loop is the chance to see the world's largest Alaska cedar, located just off the trail approximately a mile east of Three Lakes.

CAMPING

Choose from seven different public campgrounds in the Lake Quinault area. The Forest Service maintains three campgrounds on the south shore of Lake Quinault: **Falls Creek** (open late May–mid-Sept., $14); **Gatton Creek** (no water, open late May–mid-Sept., $11); and **Willaby** (open mid-April–mid-Nov., $14). Willaby is the nicest of these and has a boat ramp. Olympic National Park campgrounds are more scattered, and all three are open year-round. **July Creek** ($10) is a walk-in campground on the north shore of the lake. **Graves Creek** ($10) is near the end of the South Shore Road, 15 miles from the Highway 101 turnoff. The free **North Fork Campground** is at the end of the North Shore Road. It does not have running water and is not recommended for RVs.

Check out **Rain Forest Village Resort** (516 S. Shore Rd., 360/288-2535 or 800/255-6936, $25 with water and electric hookups) for serene lakefront RV sites. The property is the only campground by the lake with showers on premises, and it also sports a restaurant and general store. Another RV option is **Quinault River Inn** (360/288-2237, $21–25), which is convenient to the gas station and restaurants of Amanda Park.

Accommodations

The rambling **Lake Quinault Lodge** (345 S. Shore Rd., 360/288-2900 or 800/562-6672, www.visitlakequinalt.com, $143–300 d) sits in a magnificent throne of grassy lawns and lakeside shores near the shroud of Quinault's old-growth forests. This is how a lodge should look, with a darkly regal lobby interior and a big central fireplace surrounded by comfortable couches and tables. There are activities galore, with an indoor pool and sauna, lodge-led tours of the Quinault area, and seasonal boat rentals on the property. Inside the rooms, though, the lodge shows its wear as a "classic" lodge with tight quarters and less than luxury furniture that may make some guests feel taken aback by the premium prices. Visitors who go into a stay with the understanding that the premium is for the location and the history will likely come away much more satisfied than those expecting a four-star resort experience.

Those looking to get a bit more bang for their buck will feel more comfortable in the fireplace cabins offered at **Rain Forest Resort Village** (360/288-2535 or 800/255-6936, www.rainforestresort.com, $149–199 d), just a short way up South Shore Road. This nice little property also sits on the waterfront with its own banked lawns. Cabins are a bit rustic, but updated and roomier than lodge rooms. The resort also has some run-down motel rooms ($95–105 d) that will do in a pinch for those who won't spend much time there. There's also a good restaurant and lounge, a general store, laundry, RV hookups, and canoe rentals on-site. Whether you stay there or not, be sure to wander on the grounds and spot the world's largest Sitka spruce. This thousand-year-old behemoth is more than 19 feet in diameter and 191 feet tall.

For the absolute nicest place in Quinault, you'll have to travel to the other side of the lake. This is the quieter, less-developed side and home to **Lake Quinault Resort** (314 N. Shore Rd., 360/288-2362 or 800/650-2362, www.lakequinalt.com, $169–199 d), which rents out sparkling clean and very updated townhouse and kitchenette units facing the lake. Units all line up along a picturesque deck overlooking the property's lawn and the lake. This is a primo spot to watch the winds whip up the water in winter or sailboats lazily float by in summer. Across the road, a trail leads to the world's largest western red cedar—63 feet in circumference and 159 feet tall.

Between north and south sides of the road in the little town of Amanda Park, **Quinault River Inn** (8 River Dr., 360/288-2714, $105 d) offers clean and comfortable rooms convenient to the highway and to all of Lake Quinault's destinations. This is a favorite spot of anglers, who enjoy access to launch boats on the Quinault River, which flows behind the property. But new owners have given this place quite a face-lift, so it is nicer than many peninsula motels catering to the fishing and hunting crowd.

Food

Get groceries at the **Mercantile** (352 S. Shore Rd., 360/288-2620, hours vary—call ahead) across the road from Quinault Lodge. The snack bar sells pizzas, burgers, milk shakes, espresso, and sandwiches. Quite good meals are available at **Quinault Lodge** (360/288-2571, entrées $14–20) and just up the road at **Rain Forest Resort** (360/288-2535). The tiny village of Amanda Park on the west end of the lake along Highway 101 has a fine old country store with narrow aisles and sloping wooden floors.

Information and Services

The Forest Service's **Quinault Ranger District Office** (360/288-2525, 8 A.M.–4:30 P.M. daily in summer, Mon.–Fri. the rest of the year), next door to Quinault Lodge on the south side of the lake, gives out informative handouts and offer guided nature walks and talks at the lodge in the summer.

Or stop by the Olympic National Park **Quinault River Ranger Station** (5.5 miles up North Fork Rd., 9 A.M.–5 P.M. daily June–Labor Day, intermittently the rest of the year) for brochures, maps, and information on the park. The area around the station is a good place to see Roosevelt elk, especially in early summer and after September.

In Amanda Park along Highway 101 you'll find the essentials: a motel, library, church, school, general store, gas station, post office, café, and liquor store.

Getting There

A road circles Lake Quinault, with side routes up both the East and North Fork of the Quinault River for a total of 31 scenic miles. While most of the road is paved, the upper few miles are gravel. This makes a great bike ride. One of the nicest sections is up South Shore Road, which passes scenic **Merriman Falls** and continues through towering old-growth forests to Graves Creek Campground.

West Jefferson Transit (800/436-3950, www.jeffersontransit.com) provides free daily bus service between Forks and Amanda Park. Continue southward from Lake Quinault on **Grays Harbor Transit** (360/532-2770 or 800/562-9730, www.ghtransit.com) to Moclips, Ocean Shores, and Aberdeen.

North Beach

Grays Harbor—one of just three deepwater ports on the West Coast—forms the southern border to the Olympic Peninsula. The northwestern part of the bay and the Pacific Coast north to the Quinault Reservation is commonly called North Beach. Towns included in this 22-mile long stretch of beachfront are Moclips, Pacific Beach, Copalis Beach, Ocean City, and Ocean Shores.

Some commercial development has occurred along this stretch, but the only significant development is Ocean Shores. This resort/residential complex was developed as a summer resort area in the 1960s and '70s and has never become as popular as its developers expected, in part because of the overcast, damp, windy weather, and in part because it lacks the offshore rugged beauty of, say, Cannon Beach, Oregon. Still, it is one of the most popular resort areas on the Washington coast.

MOCLIPS TO OCEAN CITY

Two small settlements—Moclips and Pacific Beach—occupy the northern end of the North Beach region, with a handful of stores, lodging places, and cafés. The drive from Moclips south to Ocean Shores marks the transition from the timber-dominated lands of the Olympic Peninsula to beachside resorts. Between Moclips and Copalis Beach, Highway 109 winds along the crest of a steep bluff, with dramatic views of the coastline. From Copalis Beach southward to Ocean Shores, the country is far less interesting and the highway straightens out on the nearly level land. The broad sandy beaches are backed by grassy dunes and fronted by summer and retirement homes. The entire 22 miles of beach between Moclips and Ocean Shores is open to the public, with various vehicle entry points along the way.

The pocket-sized town of Copalis Beach has a cluster of older buildings on the Copalis River, along with RV parks, motels, and gift shops. Ocean City, three miles farther south, is a bit larger, consisting mostly of simple homes set in the trees.

Sights

Crane your neck upward to get a load of the kites afluttering at one of the most popular shoreline parks on the North Shore stretch, **Pacific Beach State Park** (49 2nd St.). Plunked down right in the middle of Pacific Beach's cute village atmosphere, the park offers beach lovers a meandering sandy reach adorned with sea-oat covered dunes. The camping facilities draw in lots of RVing families, making this a great spot for folks looking to get the little ones to socialize.

Just west of Copalis Beach, **Griffiths-Priday State Park** (www.parks.wa.gov) is a quieter day-use facility at the mouth of the Copalis River. This is a birder's delight, as the Copalis Spit here is one of three snowy plover breeding grounds on the Washington coast. Visitors must be mindful, because this endangered species is very sensitive to human intrusion. To protect the plovers, large areas of the beach north of the park entrance are closed to the public—from the high-tide mark to the dunes—between mid-March and late August. The restricted areas are marked on the map at the park entrance. A boardwalk leads to the beach, where you can dig for razor clams below the tide line.

The **Anderson Cabin** (360/289-3842) on the east side of the highway, is open in the summer. Built of beach logs in the 1920s, the cabin contains period furnishings and a display on local author Norah Berg.

Copalis Beach and Ocean City are "Home of the Razor Clam." The State Department of Fisheries sponsors clam-digging clinics (360/249-4628, www.parks.wa.gov) and beach walks throughout the summer at Ocean City State Park to prepare you for the short, intense razor clam season.

Events

The **Chief Taholah Day Celebration** in early July includes arts and crafts, a powwow, salmon bake, canoe races, a parade, and games on the reservation. The **Kelper's Parade & Shake Rat Olympics** is Pacific Beach's festival, featuring two parades on Labor Day weekend. It's followed in mid-September by a **Sandcastle Sculpture Contest** open to everyone.

Ocean City sponsors the area's big 4th of July **Fire O'er the Water** fireworks and picnic, with live music and arts and crafts. In early August, Copalis Beach comes alive with **Copalis Days,** featuring a car parade, street dancing, and food booths. Head to Copalis Beach in mid-September for a popular **Sandsculpture Contest** with contestants of all levels of ability.

Sports and Recreation

CAMPING

The 10-acre **Pacific Beach State Park** (49 2nd St., 360/276-4297 or 888/226-7688, www.parks.wa.gov, $17 for tents, $22 for RVs with hookups, $7 extra reservation fee) in Pacific Beach offers beachfront campsites that put visitors in prime position for early morning beachcombing, kite flying, and sunset watching. The park is open for camping late February to October, and on weekends and holidays the rest of the year.

Ocean City State Park has year-round camping (888/226-7688, www.parks.wa.gov, $14 for tents, $20 for RV hookups, $7 extra for reservations) near the intersection of Highways 109 and 115. Showers are available here.

Copalis has the best selection of RV parks among all for North Shore cities. Settled on the Copalis River near Griffiths-Priday State Park, **Driftwood Acres** (3209 Hwy. 109, 360/289-3484, www.driftwoodacres.com, $30 tent and RV) offers water and electric RV hookups, along with some very nice and private tent sites in the woods. The site has hot showers to clean up after beach play and nature walks. Plus, the free bundle of firewood is a nice touch.

Active families will dig the recreation room at **Riverside RV Park** (6 Condra Rd., Copalis Beach, 360/289-2111, www.riversidervresort.net, $21 full hookup, $16 tent), which includes darts, billiards, and other games. Plus, outside you'll find horseshoe pits, shuffleboard, a playground, and a hot tub. This park is also right next to the Copalis River, so you don't have to wander far in the morning to start fishing; once done, clean up your catch at the clam- and fish-cleaning station. There are showers on-site, plus a convenience store.

Practicalities

You'll find the most dining, lodging, and convenience options in the Moclips and Pacific Beach area. The most RV camping choices fall in Copalis Beach.

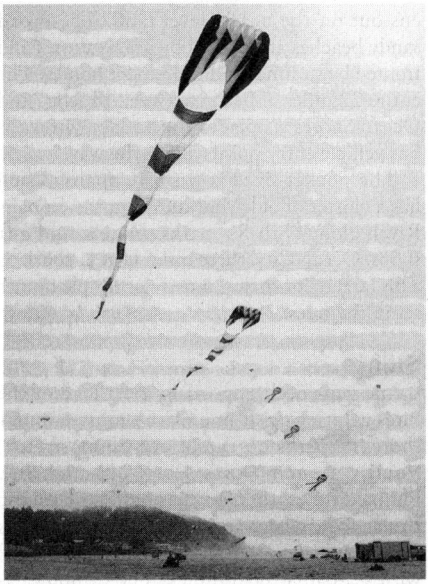

© ERICKA CHICKOWSKI

Kites fly aloft at Pacific Beach State Park.

MOCLIPS AND PACIFIC BEACH

Watch the sunset from the veranda at **Moonstone Beach Motel** (4849 Pacific Ave., Moclips, 360/276-4346, www.moonstonemoclips.com, $99–125 for 4), a simple beachfront property with large kitchenette units that can capably handle families.

The nicest resort in the area is unquestionably **Ocean Crest Resort** (Moclips, 360/276-4465, or 800/684-8439, $79–209), set on a wooded bluff over Moclips Beach. There's an indoor pool, sauna, hot tub, and exercise rooms, plus the best restaurant in town. The rooms are not luxurious, but they are the best-maintained units north of Ocean Shores. You'll get fireplaces and full kitchens with the pricier rooms. Be sure to reserve far in advance, as this place is not a secret.

Within easy walking distance of Pacific Beach State Park, **Pacific Beach Inn** (12 1st St. S., 360/276-4433, www.pbinn.com, $79–129) provides clean, well-maintained rooms, many with kitchenettes. Furniture is comfy, and many rooms have oceanfront views.

For ocean-view dining, try the excellent **Ocean Crest Restaurant** (360/276-4465, 8:30 A.M.–2:30 P.M. and 5–9 P.M. daily) at the Ocean Crest Resort in Moclips. The varied dinner menu features Northwest specialties, steak, and seafood, with weekend entertainment in the lounge. They've got good breakfasts, too. Be sure to ask for a window seat—the views are amazing.

If you rent a unit with a kitchen, pick up supplies at **D and K Grocery** (58 Main St., Pacific Beach, 360/276-4400)

COPALIS BEACH AND OCEAN CITY

Beachwood Resort (3009 Hwy. 109, Copalis Beach, 360/289-2177, $75 s or d) is a summertime pick among families who like the outdoor pool, hot tub, and sauna facilities. Also on premises is a game room and playground for the kiddies. Beach access is pretty limited, though.

Choose among everything from simple motel rooms to full two-bedroom apartments at **North Beach Motel** (2601 Hwy. 109, Ocean City, 360/289-4116 or 800/640-8053,

$45–100 s or d), a bare-bones property perfect for those just lookin' for a roof over their heads and a place to stash their stuff.

Check out **Pacific Sands Resort** (2687 Hwy. 109, Ocean City, 360/289-3588, http://pacific-sands.net, $76 d, $87 up to 4) for a bit more in the amenities department. The property has an outdoor pool, volleyball net, barbecues, a horse corral, and a koi pond. Plus it is dog friendly. Pick between motel rooms with kitchenettes or cabins with full kitchens and fireplaces.

There aren't a whole lot of dining options in Copalis Beach or Ocean City—drive north to Moclips or, better yet, south into Ocean Shores for grub.

Information

Gather information at the **Washington Coast Chamber of Commerce** (2616 Hwy. 109, Ocean City, 360/289-4552 or 800/286-4552, www.washingtoncoastchamber.org, 11 A.M.–5 P.M. Thurs.–Mon. in summer, 11 A.M.–5 P.M. Mon. and Thurs.–Sat., 10 A.M.–2 P.M. Sun. the rest of the year).

Getting There

Grays Harbor Transit (360/532-2770 or 800/562-9730, www.ghtransit.com) has daily service throughout the county, including Moclips to Ocean Shores.

It may not be on your map, but Moclips is connected to Highway 101 by the 20-mile-long Moclips-Quinault Road. Once a rutted and bumpy gravel road, this stretch was recently paved and makes a great shortcut between Quinault and the beaches.

OCEAN SHORES

The summer-home/retirement community of Ocean Shores occupies the six-mile dune-covered peninsula at the north side of the entrance to Grays Harbor. It's an odd place out here, so far from other developments, with a big gate

© ERICKA CHICKOWSKI

Ocean Shores is a favorite among sandcastle "contractors."

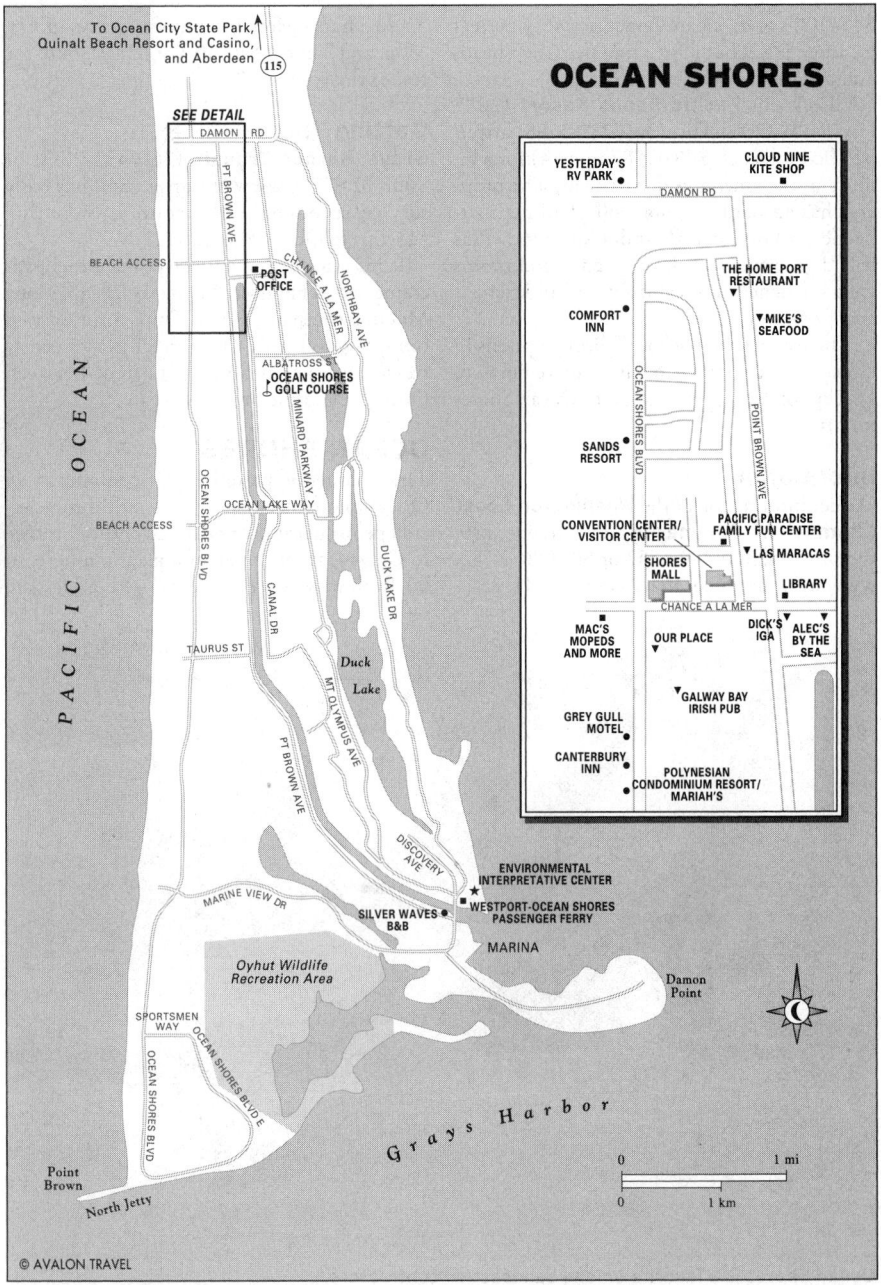

© AVALON TRAVEL

that welcomes visitors, businesses strewn along a wide main drag, and homes on a network of 23 miles of canals. Some of these homes are elaborate contemporary structures, other lots simply have a concrete pad to park an RV, and many more feature For Sale signs. Many of the working folks live in trailer parks in nearby Ocean City. Two main roads head down the peninsula: the four-lane Ocean Shores Boulevard near the shore, and the bumpy Point Brown Avenue in the center. The latter follows the canals to the marina area. There are no trees on the east side of the peninsula, just low sand dunes.

More than three million visitors come to Ocean Shores annually to play on the beach, fly kites, play miniature golf, and ride bumper cars, bikes, mopeds, and go-karts.

Sights

The **Ocean Shores Environmental Interpretative Center** (five miles south of town center at the marina, 360/289-4617, 10 A.M.–4 P.M. Thurs.–Mon. Memorial Day–Labor Day only) features saltwater and freshwater aquariums and displays on the history of the area, how the peninsula was formed, and how it continues to grow as sand is added each year. Other exhibits detail the animals of the area, and you can watch natural history slide shows.

A pair of wildlife reserves on the southern end of the peninsula offer outstanding **bird-watching**—more than 200 species have been recorded. **Damon Point** (a.k.a. Protection Island) is an important breeding area for the rare snowy plover (this is their northernmost nesting area) and semipalmated plovers (their southernmost nesting area). This is the only place in the world where both species coexist as breeding birds. Parts of the 300-acre preserve are closed March–September to protect the plovers, but the wet sands in the tidal zone are open to fishing and walking. The 682-acre **Oyhut Wildlife Recreation Area** (sometimes spelled Oyehut) at the south end of the peninsula is another good place for bird-watching, with trails through the marshy landscape.

Also on the south end of the peninsula, **North Jetty** reaches a mile out into the Pacific and is a great place to fish, watch storm waves, or enjoy the sunset.

Two miles north of Ocean Shores on Highway 115, **Ocean City State Park** (360/289-3553, www.parks.wa.gov) has campsites close to the town's restaurants and shops. Open year-round, the park has camping in the trees, picnicking, two little ponds for bird-watching, and a path leading through the dunes to the beach. There is no vehicle access here, but there are six access points in Ocean Shores—just head south along Ocean Shores Boulevard and look for the turnoffs. Signs are posted with beach driving regulations and safety warnings. Pedestrians have the right-of-way; cars must yield. Drive only on the higher hard sand, not in the water, on the clam beds, or in the dunes, and observe a 25-mph speed limit. If you get stuck, put boards or other hard, flat material under your tires and pull out slowly. Be sure to hose down your car after driving on the beach, since salt spray can lead to rust.

With all that ocean out there, it's easy to overlook Ocean Shores' six-mile-long **Duck Lake,** but it's a haven for small boats, canoes, anglers (trout, bass, and crappie are all here), swimmers, and water-skiers. You can launch your boat from City Park, at Albatross and Chance à la Mer, or Chinook Park Boat Launch on Duck Lake Drive. At the south end, the lake connects with a maze of canals that lead past housing developments. Pick up a map before heading out, since these channels can be confusing.

Events

Ocean Shores hosts an annual **Beachcombers Fun Fair** at the convention center in early March. See displays of glass floats and driftwood art, and sample the fresh seafood. Ocean Shores' annual **Festival of Colors,** held each May, is family fun with a sandcastle contest, arts and crafts bazaar, and kite festival. The **International Kite Challenge** competition is held out on the beach in the first week of June.

In late July, the leather-jacket crowd rolls into Ocean Shores for the **Harley Owners Group Sun & Surf Run,** an event that attracts 2,000 bikes and riders. The **Dixieland Jazz Festival** in early November features acts from all over the Northwest at the convention center and around town.

Shopping

Ocean Shores' **Shores Mall** has bike and moped rentals, a kite shop, bank, clothing store, and state liquor store on Chance à la Mer, just before the beach. In Homeport Plaza on Point Brown Avenue, Ocean Shores' **Gallery Marjuli** (360/289-2858) is open daily with art and gifts created by Northwest artists. **Tide Creations Gift Shop** (Pt. Brown Ave., 360/289-2550) near the marina has thousands of items, from kites and windsocks to fudge.

Sports and Recreation

Beachcombing is a favorite activity on the six miles of sandy beach along Ocean Shores, as is digging for razor clams in season (generally in March and October). Check with the chamber of commerce for the regulations and where to buy a license.

Rent boats and canoes from **Summer Sails** (360/289-2884) located on the canal at the south end of Point Brown Avenue. Rent mopeds and bicycles at three different places in town: **Mac's Mopeds and More** (798 Ocean Shores Blvd., 360/289-9304), **O. W. W. Inc.** (Shores Mall on Chance à la Mer, 360/289-3830), and **This & That** (748 Ocean Shores Blvd., 360/289-0919).

Ride horseback along the shore on steeds provided by **Chenois Creek Horse Rentals** (360/533-5591). Or, for a unique equine experience, try out the "horse camp" run by **Nan-Sea Stables** (360/289-0194, $60). Adults and kids are all welcome at Nan-Sea's ranch, where you'll learn to care for horses, to properly muck a stall, and take a trail ride during this four-hour long camp.

Ocean Shores is a great place for kite flying, with strong offshore winds much of the year. If you didn't bring your own, head to one of several local kite shops, including **Cutting Edge Kites** (676 Ocean Shores Blvd. NW, 360/289-0667, www.cuttingedgekites.com, 10 A.M.–6 P.M. Mon.–Fri., 9 A.M.–6 P.M. Sat., 9 A.M.–5 P.M. Sun.) and **Cloud Nine Kite Shop** (380 Hwy. 115, 360/289-4424, 10 A.M.–6 P.M. Mon.–Fri., 9 A.M.–8 P.M. Sat., 9 A.M.–7 P.M. Sun.).

At Canal and Albatross in Ocean Shores, **Ocean Shores Golf Course** (360/289-3357) is an 18-hole championship course open to the public.

Pacific Paradise Family Fun Center (767 Minard Ave., 360/289-9537, 11 A.M.–6 P.M. Mon.–Tues. and Thurs.–Fri., 10 A.M.–6 P.M. Sat.–Sun., closed Wed., closed Dec. 1–Dec. 26) has miniature golf, an entertainment center, bumper boats, and more fun options for kids.

CAMPING

One of the only sites in town is **Yesterday's RV Park** (512 Damon Rd., 360/289-9227, $16 tent, $25 full hookup), which offers sites for RVs and tents right on the beach. All sites have fire rings, and there are showers on premises.

Accommodations

Ocean Shores has more than two dozen motels, along with dozens more private home rentals. Note that many places have a two-night minimum on weekends and July–August, and a three-night minimum on holidays. On holidays, the chamber of commerce (360/289-0226 or 800/762-3224, www.oceanshores.org) keeps track of room availability.

UNDER $100

Silver Waves B&B (982 Point Brown Ave. SE, 360/289-2490 or 888/257-0894, $85–130 s or d) has two decks facing the Grand Canal. Four guest rooms and a separate family-friendly cabin all have private baths and a breakfast buffet.

$100-150

Canterbury Inn (643 Ocean Shores Blvd. NW, 360/289-3317 or 800/562-6678, www.canterburyinn.com, $126–150 d) has studios with kitchenettes, along with one- and two-bedroom suites with full kitchens and fireplaces ($204–258 d). The beachfront complex, which has many privately owned units, has a large indoor pool and hot tub. There is a two-night minimum.

$150-200

With its gray-shingled roof in the shape of a stylized gull with its wings spread, the **Grey Gull Motel** (651 Ocean Shores Blvd. SW, 360/289-3381 or 800/562-9712, www.thegreygull.com, $130–195 d) appears (from the appropriate angle) in imminent danger of flying away. The hotel has modern, spacious efficiencies, one- and two-bedroom suites, as well as penthouses ($350 d). There is a two-night minimum on summer weekends. Amenities include a sauna and outdoor pool.

Don't let the brand fool you: The **Comfort Inn** (829 Ocean Shores Blvd., 360/289-9000 or 866/289-9003, $159–279 d) in Ocean Shores is nicer than you'd think—this is a large, upscale place on the beach, with spacious, modern rooms and attentive service. The property includes a pool, fitness center, business center, and continental breakfast.

Situated north of Ocean Shores on land purchased by the Quinalt tribe, **Quinalt Beach Resort and Casino** (78 Hwy. 115, 360/289-9466 or 888/461-2214, www.quinaltbchresort.com, $179 d, $349–549 suites) offers the area's most spacious and comfortable rooms, most with ocean-facing views. Service is very good, and the hotel has a full-service spa with sauna and massage service, walkways out over the dunes to the beach, a nice restaurant, and a café. Plus, of course, there's a full casino.

Polynesian Condominium Resort (615 Ocean Shores Blvd. NW, 360/289-3361 or 800/562-4836, www.thepolynesian.com, $129–229 d) caters to families with its indoor pool, game room, sauna, and hot tub. Choose among hotel rooms, kitchenette efficiencies, or full suites with kitchens and fireplaces. There's a two-night minimum in the summer.

Food

Our Place (676 Ocean Shores Blvd. NW, 360/289-8763, 6 A.M.–2 P.M. daily) is a tiny eatery with inexpensive but filling breakfasts and all-American lunches.

The Home Port Restaurant (857 Pt. Brown Ave., 360/289-2600, 8 A.M.–9 P.M. Sun.–Thurs., 8 A.M.–10 P.M. Fri.–Sat.) serves three meals, including good breakfasts and specialties such as salmon, Dungeness crab, and steak and lobster dinners.

Find very good south-of-the-border meals at **Las Maracas Mexican Restaurant** (729 Point Brown Ave. NW, 360/289-2054, 11:30 A.M.–9 P.M. daily).

Mariah's (615 Ocean Shores Blvd. N.W., 360/289-3315, 4–9 P.M. daily) at the Polynesian Resort is the most upscale local restaurant, with seafood, steak, and pasta, along with a weekend breakfast buffet. The lounge has live music Friday and Saturday evenings.

Alec's by the Sea (131 E Chance à la Mer NE, 360/289-4026, 10 A.M.–8 P.M. Sun.–Thurs., 10 A.M.–9 P.M. Fri.–Sat.) next to Dick's IGA, has low prices and a big menu that includes burgers, fresh clams, salads, steaks, pasta, seafood, and chicken.

Galway Bay Irish Pub (676 Ocean Shores Blvd., 360/289-2300, 11 A.M.–10 P.M. daily) makes great clam chowder.

Mike's Seafood (830 Point Brown Ave. NE, 360/289-0532, 10 A.M.–8 P.M. Mon.–Sat., 11 A.M.–7 P.M. Sun.) sells fresh-cooked crab from a roadside stand.

Get homemade ice cream, fudge, and chocolates from **Murphy's Candy and Ice Cream** (in the Shores Mall, 360/289-0927, 9 A.M.–9 P.M. daily in summer, noon–8 P.M. Mon.–Tues. and Thurs.–Fri., 10 A.M.–8 P.M. Sat., 10 A.M.–6 P.M. Sun.)

Information

Get information from the helpful folks at **Ocean Shores Chamber of Commerce Visitor Information Center** (120B W. Chance à la Mer, 360/289-2451 or 800/762-3224, www.oceanshores.org, 9 A.M.–5 P.M. Mon.–Fri., 10 A.M.–4 P.M. Sat.–Sun.)

Getting There

Grays Harbor Transit (360/532-2770 or

800/562-9730, www.ghtransit.com) has daily bus service throughout the county, connecting Ocean Shores with Aberdeen, Lake Quinault, and Olympia. Ocean Shores has an airport, but no commercial service.

The **Westport-Ocean Shores Passenger Ferry** *El Matador* (360/289-0414, $10 round-trip, free for kids under 4) is a 74-foot passenger boat with service to Westport. Gray whales are often seen along the way. The ferry leaves six times a day and takes 20–40 minutes, with daily service mid-June to Labor Day, and weekends-only service mid-April through mid-June and in September. There is no service the rest of the year. The boat leaves from the marina; get tickets at the Marina Store.

Grays Harbor and Vicinity

Discovered in 1792 by Capt. Robert Gray, an American en route to China to trade sea otter pelts for tea, Grays Harbor is presided over by Aberdeen and Hoquiam (HO-qwee-um). Grays Harbor has long been a major center for the timber industry, and the surrounding country bears witness to this. Heading toward Aberdeen and Hoquiam from any direction leads you through mile after mile of tree farms, with second- or third-growth forests interspersed with newly logged hillsides.

ABERDEEN AND HOQUIAM

Sitting on the easterly tip of Grays Harbor, these twin cities are separated only by the Hoquiam River. Primarily working-class mill towns, they offer weary peninsula and coast travelers a good opportunity to gas up, fill up, and catch some zzz's before hitting the road again. If you stop, be sure to check out the historical sights around town, particularly the Grays Harbor Seaport.

Sights

GRAYS HARBOR HISTORICAL SEAPORT

Captain Gray's discovery of the harbor in the 18th century was only the beginning of what was to become the area's love affair with the sea. The calm waters of the harbor and the ready supply of timber made Aberdeen an ideal shipbuilding headquarters from its early beginnings in the 19th century. Between 1887 and 1920 her port saw off some 130 new ships.

Today the Grays Harbor Historical Seaport (813 West Heron St., Aberdeen, 360/532-8611, www.historicalseaport.org) highlights the rich maritime heritage of the region, acting as host to two magnificent tall ships. The first, ***Lady Washington,*** is a full-scale replica of one of the ships in Gray's discovery fleet. This fluttering spectacle of spindly masts and oiled decks carries the honor of sailing as Washington State's Official Ship and is typically in the historical seaport at least two months out of the year along with her companion ship, the ***Hawaiian Chieftain,*** a steel-hulled, topsail ketch. (The rest of the year they are featured in maritime and tall-ship festivals up and down the West Coast). While in port, *Lady* is open for tours (10 A.M.–1 P.M. daily, $3 adults, $2 seniors and students, $1 children) and offers outstanding three-hour sailing trips most afternoons and weekend evenings ($55 adults, $45 children). The crew is entirely in costume. Schedules change year by year, so be sure to check the Seaport website for up-to-date information.

You might also ask about volunteering aboard the *Lady.* This is not for everyone—simple food, cramped quarters, limited water, and lots of hard work—but at least you aren't subjected to floggings or surgery without anesthesia. No grog either. This is an incredible chance to learn about sailing the old-fashioned way.

MANSIONS AND MUSEUMS

In 1897, lumber baron Robert Lytle built **Hoquiam's Castle** (515 Chenault Ave., Hoquiam, 360/533-2005, 10 A.M.–5 P.M. daily in the summer, 11 A.M.–5 P.M. Sat.–Sun. the rest of the year, closed in Dec., $4 adults, $1 kids), a stunning maroon-and-white, three-story spectacle that's been restored to its original luster, with the original oak woodwork. It's completely furnished in turn-of-the-20th-century antiques, Tiffany-style lamps, and cut-crystal chandeliers. Half-hour tours are offered throughout the day. The hillside mansion overlooks town and has a distinctive monkey-puzzle tree outside.

Another wealthy lumber magnate, Alex Polson, once owned the largest logging operation in the world, Polson Logging Company (now a part of Rayonier). In 1923 he funded the building of a home for his son and daughter-in-law on property adjoining his own house. This 26-room **Polson Museum** (1611 Riverside Ave., 360/533-5862, www.polsonmuseum.org, 11 A.M.–4 P.M. Wed.–Sat., noon–4 P.M. Sun. Apr. 1–Dec. 23, noon–4 P.M. Sat.–Sun. Dec. 27–Mar. 31, $10 families, $4 adults, $2 students) is now named in his honor. Alex Polson's own home was razed after his death in 1939; his widow didn't want anyone else to live in it. The site of their home is now a small park with a rose garden, historic logging equipment, and a blacksmith shop. The museum houses all sorts of memorabilia: a magnificent old grandfather clock, a fun model railroad, a model of an old logging camp, a two-man chainsaw, and even an old boxing bag.

The **Aberdeen Museum of History** (117 E. 3rd St., 360/533-1976, 10 A.M.–5 P.M. Tues.–Sun., free) displays exhibits of local history, including a century-old kitchen and bedroom, pioneer church, blacksmith shop, four antique fire trucks, a dugout canoe, thousands of pro-union buttons, and a short video about the great fire of 1903 that destroyed 140 buildings. There's lots of offbeat what-was-that-used-for stuff here.

WILDLIFE REFUGE

Due west of Hoquiam off Highway 109, **Grays Harbor National Wildlife Refuge** (360/753-9467, http://graysharbor.fws.gov) is a 500-acre wetland in the northeast corner of Grays Harbor Estuary. This is one of the most important staging areas for shorebirds in North America, attracting up to a million birds each spring. The two dozen shorebird species that visit the basin include the western sandpiper, dunlin, short- and long-billed dowitcher, and red knot; other birds seen here are the peregrine falcon, northern harrier, and red-tailed hawk. A one-mile path leads to the viewing areas, but bring your boots since it's often muddy. The best viewing time is one hour before and one hour after high tide.

Entertainment and Events

The **Driftwood Players,** a community theatrical company, puts on several plays a year at Driftwood Playhouse (120 E. 3rd in Aberdeen, 360/538-1213).

Kick the year off with a fun time at Aberdeen's **Dixieland Jazz Festival,** held on Presidents' Day weekend in mid-February. The **Grays Harbor Shorebird Festival** in late April—the peak of the migration—includes bird-watching field trips and workshops. In early May, the city's **Grays Harbor Discovery Days Celebration** attracts longboats from throughout the Northwest for rowing and sailing races.

Hoquiam's **Loggers Playday,** held the second weekend in September, is an opportunity for sedentary executives to see what real work is all about. After kicking off the event with a parade and salmon barbecue, loggers compete in ax-throwing, log-chopping, and tree-climbing events. Evening brings a big fireworks show.

Sports and Recreation

At E. 9th and N. I Streets, Aberdeen's **Samuel Benn Park** has rose and rhododendron gardens, tennis courts, a playground, and picnic facilities. **Lake Aberdeen** at the east entrance to town has swimming and nonmotorized boating and play equipment. For an indoor pool, head to the **Hoquiam Aquatic Center** (717 K St., 360/533-3474).

CAMPING

Campsites are available at **Lake Sylvia State Park** (360/249-3621, www.parks.wa.gov, open late Mar.–Sept., $9–14 for tents, no hookups) near Montesano, approximately 12 miles east of Aberdeen.

Situated near 20 acres of heavily wooded wilderness, near a creek with catchable crawdads, **Arctic Park** (893 Hwy. 101, Aberdeen, 360/533-4470, http://users.techline.com/articrv/, $22 with full hookups, $10 tents) offers an unusual amount of privacy over the typical corral-type RV park, with vegetation separating many sites. The owners grow a garden with veggies and berries that guests are welcome to pick, and the property includes showers, a volleyball court, and a convenience store. Nearby there's 1.5 miles of trails that run through the forest.

Accommodations

The twin cities of Aberdeen and Hoquiam are less vacation destinations and more convenient stopovers on the way to other points on the peninsula and coast such as Ocean Shores, Lake Quinault, and Kalaloch. Many of the hotels and motels are on the shabbier side of rundown, but there are a few exceptions.

One acceptable choice is the **Guest House Inn and Suites** (701 East Heron St., Aberdeen, 360/537-7460, www.guesthouseintl.com), a clean place that has the only motel pool in town. Guests are invited to munch on a simple continental breakfast each morning.

There are also a couple of very nice bed-and-breakfasts in town. Most impressive among them is the gorgeous **Hoquiam's Castle B&B** (515 Chenault, 360/533-2005 or 877/542-2785, www.hoquiamscastle.com, $145–195 s or d), which features rooms with four-poster beds, claw-footed tubs, and more dainty linens than you can shake a stick at. Breakfast in the morning is an elaborate affair that should sate even the hungriest hikers before heading out into the woods.

Check out some amazing panoramas of the harbor at the colonial revival-style **A Harbor View B&B** (113 W. 11th St., 360/533-7996, www.aharborview.com, $149–225 s or d, no kids under 12). Sitting high on a hill, this bed-and-breakfast offers five bedrooms furnished in Victorian period pieces and colorful quilts. All rooms include private baths, TVs, and wireless Internet.

Food

In business since 1945, **Duffy's** is the local family restaurant, featuring a varied, inexpensive-to-moderate seafood and steak menu and great blackberry pies. Try this local favorite at two locations, one in Aberdeen (1605 Simpson Ave., 360/532-3842, 6 A.M.–10 P.M. Sun.–Thurs., 6 A.M.–11 P.M. Fri.–Sat.) and one in Hoquiam (825 Simpson Ave., 360/532-1519, 11 A.M.–10 P.M. Tues.–Sat., 11 A.M.–9 P.M. Sun.–Mon.).

Aberdeen's **Breakwater Seafood** (306 S. F St., 360/532-5693, 9:30 A.M.–7 P.M. Mon.–Sat., 11 A.M.–6 P.M. Sun.) is a seafood market/restaurant with good chowder and fresh fish and chips to eat in or take out.

Reservations are recommended for dinner at **Mallard's** (118 E. Wishkah, 360/532-0731, 5–7:30 P.M. Tues.–Sat.), a small place with good quality European-style cuisine prepared by a Danish chef, with daily specialties.

The atmosphere is elegant but not stuffy at **Bridge's** (112 N. G St., Aberdeen, 360/532-6563, 11 A.M.–9 P.M. Mon.–Sat., 4–9 P.M. Sun.), which serves prime rib, steak, and seafood dinners, including razor clams. It is open for lunch and dinner daily plus Sunday brunch.

Billy's Bar & Grill (322 E. Heron, Aberdeen, 360/533-7144, 8 A.M.–10 P.M. Mon.–Sat.) is a restored saloon that serves delicious and reasonably priced steaks, seafood, and burgers.

Decent Italian food and the best local pizzas are at **Casa Mia Pizza** (2936 Simpson Ave., Hoquiam, 360/533-2010, 11 A.M.–midnight Mon.–Thurs., 11 A.M.–1 A.M. Fri.–Sat., 11 A.M.–10 P.M. Sun.).

The **Hoquiam-Grays Harbor Farmers Market** (360/538-9747, 9 A.M.–6 P.M. Tues. and Thurs.–Sat. year-round) takes place at Hoquiam's Levee Park, on the river on Highway 101 North.

Information

The **Grays Harbor Chamber of Commerce and Visitor Center** (506 Duffy St., Aberdeen,

360/532-1924 or 800/321-1924, 9 A.M.–5 P.M. daily) is a good place to find out about the twin cities of Aberdeen and Hoquiam, along with other county towns.

Getting There

Aberdeen and Hoquiam are well served by **Grays Harbor Transit** (360/532-2770 or 800/562-9730, www.ghtransit.com). Buses take you throughout the county seven days a week, including Lake Quinault, Westport, Ocean Shores, and even east to Olympia. **Pacific Transit System** (360/875-9418 or 800/875-9418) provides bus service southward to Raymond, Long Beach, and Astoria, Oregon.

MONTESANO TO OLYMPIA

Zipping up Highway 12 and then Highway 8 on the way to Olympia, this southern link in the Olympic loop is dotted by a few little burgs, including the cozy town of Montesano, which occupies the juncture of the Chehalis, Satsop, and Wynoochee Rivers. The town is home to tidy brick buildings and the hilltop Grays Harbor County Courthouse, built in 1910 of marble and granite. Not far away is the nation's first tree farm, established by Weyerhaeuser in 1941; along Highway 8 you'll whiz by other little hamlets such as Elma and McCleary.

Sights and Recreation

About a mile north of Montesano off Highway 12, **Lake Sylvia State Park** (360/249-3621, www.parks.wa.gov, open late March–Sept.) encompasses 233 acres around this narrow but scenic reservoir. The lake was created by a dam built in 1909 to supply water and power and is a popular place to swim, canoe, or fish. Two miles of trails circle the lake and connect with two more miles of trail in adjacent Chapin Collins Memorial Forest. Be sure to check out the four-foot wooden ball, carved by loggers from a spruce log and used for log rolling until it became waterlogged and sank. The ball was rediscovered in 1974 when the lake level was lowered and is now on display.

Chehalis Valley Historical Museum (703 W. Pioneer Ave., 360/249-5800, noon–4 P.M. Sat.–Sun., free) houses historical logging equipment and century-old photos in what was originally a 1906 church.

Vance Creek County Park, just west of Elma, has nature trails, jogging paths, and swimming in two small lakes. McCleary's **Carnell House Museum** (314 2nd St., noon–4 P.M. Sat.–Sun. Memorial Day–Labor Day only) displays historic photos and a collection of farming, logging, and household equipment from the past.

Festivals and Events

The **Festival of Lights** in December includes a big lighted parade that features everything from logging trucks to cement mixers.

Elma is home to the county fairgrounds, where you can take in an indoor pro rodeo in late March, horse racing in late July, the old-fashioned **Grays Harbor County Fair** in mid-August, and Saturday night auto racing April–September. The **McCleary Bear Festival** in mid-July offers two parades, entertainment, arts and crafts, and food booths. In mid-September, Elma has a **Wild Blackberry Festival** with a pie contest, car show, arts and crafts, and parade.

Practicalities

MONTESANO

Abel House B&B (117 Fleet St. S, 360/249-6002 or 800/235-2235, www.abelhouse.com, $100–130 d) is a historic 1908 home with five guest rooms, Tiffany chandeliers, and attractive grounds. A full breakfast is served.

Lake Sylvia State Park (360/249-3621, www.parks.wa.gov, $9–14) has wooded campsites with no hookups along the shore and is open late March–September. **Lake Wynoochee,** approximately 35 miles north of Montesano, is a popular summertime fishing, hiking, and swimming area within Olympic National Forest. Pitch a tent at **Coho Campground** (353 S. Shore Rd., $10) and hike the scenic 12-mile Wynoochee Lake Shore Trail.

For breakfasts and lunches, the small **Savory Faire** (135 S. Main St., 360/249-3701, www.savoryfaire.com, 10:30 A.M.–3:30 P.M. Mon.–Fri., plus 5:30–8:30 P.M. Fri.) is hard to beat, with a menu that includes omelettes, from-scratch soups, fresh salads, and sandwiches, plus fresh-baked breads, pastries, and espresso to go. Also try **Bee Hive Restaurant** (Main and Pioneer, 360/249-4131, 6 A.M.–8:45 P.M. Mon.–Thurs., 6 A.M.–10 P.M. Fri.–Sat., 7 A.M.–8:45 P.M. Sun.) for all-American meals and homemade pies.

ELMA

The **Grays Harbor Hostel** (6 Ginny Ln., Elma, 360/482-3119, www.ghostel.com, $18 s shared bath, $35 s or d private bath) is a sprawling ranch house situated on eight acres of land. The spotless facilities include an outdoor hot tub, two common rooms, a kitchen, and storage rooms. Blankets and pillows are available, and there's even an 18-hole disc golf course. Open all year, but closed 9 A.M.–5 P.M. daily. Tent space is available for cyclists.

Follow the signs for 12 miles north of Elma to **Schafer State Park** (www.parks.wa.gov, open Apr.–Sept. only, $13 for tents, $19 for RVs) on the Satsop River. Originally a park for Schafer Logging Company employees, today it has public campsites, riverside picnic areas, and a fine collection of mossy trees. There is good fishing for steelhead (late winter) and sea-run cutthroat (summers) in the East Fork of the Satsop River.

MCCLEARY

Built in 1912 and on the National Register of Historic Places, the three-story **Old McCleary Hotel** (42 Summit Rd., McCleary, 360/495-3678, $55–65 s or d) was originally the home of Henry McCleary, for whom the town is named. Today it is owned by Penny Challstedt, who has kept the place as something of a museum, with the original furniture, brass beds, unusual toilets, dark paneling, and Victorian wallpaper. Don't expect a TV or fax machine here. The owner also serves family-style meals, but these are mainly for wedding receptions.

Information

Get local information from the **Elma Chamber of Commerce** (360/482-3055). It is located inside Image Flowers and Fine Chocolates (117 N. 3rd St.).

Getting There

Grays Harbor Transit (360/532-2770 or 800/562-9730, www.ghtransit.com) has daily bus service throughout the county, including Lake Quinault, Westport, Ocean Shores, and east to Olympia.

WESTPORT

Westport, the principal South Beach city, once called itself "The Salmon Capital of the World," and charter services and commercial fishing and crabbing boats still line the waterfront. This is one of the most active ports in Washington, and chain-smoking fishermen drive beat-up old pickups through town. The town also has a crab cannery and several seafood markets, plus the expected waterfront shops offering kitschy gifts, saltwater taffy, and kites. Ragged-at-the-edges Westport is quite unlike its upscale cross-bay twin, Ocean Shores.

Sights

MARITIME MUSEUM

In Westport, the **Westport Maritime Museum** (2201 Westhaven Dr., 360/268-0078, westportwa.com/museum, 10 A.M.–4 P.M. daily June–Sept., noon–4 P.M. Wed.–Sun. Oct.–May, $3 adults, $1 kids) is housed in a magnificent old Coast Guard station built in 1939. Capped by six gables and a watchtower with a widow's walk, the building was used until 1974, when newer quarters were completed just down the road. Inside are photographs of the early Aberdeen–Westport plank road, cranberry and logging industry exhibits, and Coast Guard memorabilia. Out front in glass cases are gray whale, minke whale, sea lion, and porpoise skeletons. Also on the grounds is a building housing the massive lens from the Destruction Island Lighthouse. Built in 1888, it was replaced in 1995 by an automated light. On weekends March–May, the museum offers talks about whales and whale-watching; also check out the interesting video on fish trapping.

PARKS AND BEACHES

Head to the 0.75-mile **South Jetty** at the end of State Park Access Road for a chance to fish, look for birds and marine mammals, or watch the winter storms roll in. Use care on the slippery rocks. The road passes Half Moon Bay, popular with scuba divers. A tall **observation tower** on the east end of Nettie Rose Drive in town provides a fine vantage point to view freighter activity, scenery, sunsets, or an occasional whale, and a lower **ramp tower** on the east end of Nettie Rose looks into the marina. In front of this is a small memorial to fishermen lost at sea.

Entertainment and Events

Westport's **World Class Crab Races & Feed** in mid-April is not a good time to be a crab; the races are followed by a big crab feed. Live music is also featured. The **Blessing of the Fleet,** held annually in May, includes a memorial service for people lost at sea and demonstrations of Coast Guard sea-air rescues. Held in early July, the two-day **Kite Festival** has contests for the youngest and oldest kite flyers, best crash event, longest train of kites, and more. Mid-July has the **Longboard Classic Surf Festival,** attracting top longboard surfers from throughout the Northwest. In August, an **International Nautical Chainsaw Carving Contest** (no, it is not done underwater), and the **Brady's Oyster Feed** both come early in the month.

A very popular event—it's been going on for more than 50 years—is the **Westport Seafood Festival** on Labor Day weekend. Taste salmon, oysters, crab, and all sorts of other fresh-from-the-sea foods, with musical accompaniment.

Sports and Recreation

Open for day use only, **Westhaven State Park** (Hwy. 105 just north of Westport, www.parks.wa.gov) is popular with rockhounds, beachcombers, and divers. Surfers and sea kayakers find some of the most consistent waves in Washington. The jetty was built here to increase the velocity of the seagoing water, collected from six rivers flowing into Grays Harbor. Prior to the construction of the jetty, deposits of sediment mandated annual channel dredging. The jetty worked—the channel hasn't required dredging since 1942.

Westport Light State Park (www.parks.wa.gov), about a mile south of Westhaven off Highway 105 (continue straight when 105 goes left), is another day-use park good for kite flying, rockhounding, and fishing for ocean perch, but no camping. A paved, mile-long **Dune Interpretive Trail** wanders through the dunes, providing several observation platforms that overlook the water. There's vehicular beach access here, but the sand is considerably softer than at other drivable beaches; be careful if you don't have four-wheel drive. Check with the park for regulations on beach driving, since some sections are closed part or all of the year. The classic **lighthouse** inside the park—the tallest on the West Coast—was built in 1898 and is visible from an observation platform on Ocean Avenue. The building is closed to the public, but tours may be offered by the museum. The lighthouse originally stood much closer to the water, but the accretion of sand has pushed the beachfront seaward.

On Highway 105, two miles south of Westport, **Twin Harbors State Park** (www.parks.wa.gov) has campsites, a 0.75-mile sand dune nature trail, picnic areas, and a playground. This is one of the most popular oceanside campgrounds, especially when razor clam harvesting is allowed (usually March and October). Twin Harbors is open for day use all year.

FISHING AND CLAMMING

Even the casual visitor to Westport will see that this is a major sport and commercial fishing port. The harbor is packed with vessels of all dimensions, and charter operators line the marina. You don't have to charter a boat to go fishing; the whole stretch from Westport to North Cove is popular for surf fishing.

The rock jetty near Westhaven State Park is a good spot for catching salmon, rockfish, lingcod, surf perch, and crabs. In September and October, a coho salmon run returns to the marina area (the young are raised in pens here, so this is "home"). Clamming is seasonal and requires a license; see the chamber of commerce for a copy of the regulations. The 1,000-foot-long **Westport Fishing Pier,** off the end of Float 20 at the Westport Marina, is another landlubber fishing option.

Offshore rocks and reefs are feeding grounds for salmon, bottom fish, halibut, and even albacore tuna; take a charter boat to find the best spots, not to mention having your fish cleaned and ready to cook by the time you get back to shore. The charter services all charge about the same amount, so when you call for reservations be sure to check whether the price includes bait and tackle, cleaning, and sales tax, to see if your "bargain" is really a good deal. Note, however, that most departures are at the frightfully early hour of 6 A.M., with a return around 3:30 P.M. Be sure to take along your seasickness pills. Some companies also offer overnight trips that head far offshore in search of tuna. Wander along Westhaven Drive to check out the various charter companies, or get a listing of boats from the visitors center. Expect to pay around $125 per person for halibut charters, $375 for tuna, or $60–75 pp for coho salmon or bottom fishing.

WHALE-WATCHING

Many of the local fishing charter operators provide whale-watching trips March–May, when the gray whales are heading north from their winter quarters off Baja California. Get a list of operators from the visitors center. Expect to pay $20–30 for a three-hour trip. You may also spot whales from the jetty or from the Westport viewing towers. The passenger ferry to Ocean Shores is an inexpensive way to watch for the whales that periodically wander into Grays Harbor. The Maritime Museum offers weekend whale-watching seminars, films, and workshops in season.

SURFING

Surfers can check out the waves at Westhaven State Park, one of the most popular surfing beaches in the state. The man-made jetty here has developed the most consistent point break in Washington, making it well worth braving the icy waters when it is firing. Rent surfboards and wetsuits from the **Surf Shop** (207 Montesano St., 360/268-0992).

KITE FLYING

Cutting Edge Kites (2549 Westhaven Dr., 360/268-0877) has kites and windsocks of every description.

CAMPING

Camp at the very popular **Twin Harbors State Park** (two miles south of town, 888/226-7688, www.parks.wa.gov, $17 tent, $21 full hookups, $7 extra reservation fee). Some campsites are just steps away from the beach, and showers are available. The campground is open late February–October.

Westport is jam-packed with RV parks catering to the fishing crowd. Perhaps the most laden with amenities, **American Sunset Resort** (360/268-0207 or 800/569-2267, www.americansunsetrv.com, $29 full hookups, $19 tent) offers a heated outdoor pool, horseshoe pits and playgrounds, showers, and laundry facilities, plus free Wi-Fi. The property is pet friendly, offers plenty of space for larger rigs, and sports a convenience store and a special area for tent campers. It even rents out two permanent trailers parked at the property.

Accommodations

Most Westport accommodations are straightforward, down-to-earth affairs. Many have kitchenettes, but only a few offer hot tubs or pools. As one owner told me in her broken English, "no pool—big giant ocean out there!" Contact the chamber of commerce (360/268-9422 or 800/345-6223 www.westportgraylandchamber.org) for a list of rental homes in the Westport area.

Most of the rooms at **Alaskan Motel** (708 N. 1st St., 360/268-9133 or 866/591-4154, www.westportwa.com/alaskan, $60–82 s or d) are simple kitchenette units, though there are some newer guest cottages with enclosed decks ($140–165 d).

A three-story building in the boat basin, **Coho Motel** (2501 N. Nyhus, 360/268-0111 or 800/572-0177) has rooms for $49–54 s or d, and third-floor suites for $68 d. The owners also manage a popular charter fishing operation.

An unpretentious, one-story motel with a gazebo for fresh fish barbecues, **Mariners Cove Inn** (303 Ocean Ave., 360/268-0531 or 877/332-0090, www.marinerscoveinn.com, $59–74 s or d) has clean, modern hotel rooms.

It might fool you at first glance, but **Chateau Westport Motel** (710 Hancock, 360/268-9101 or 800/255-9101, www.chateauwestport.com, $111–124 d, suites $217–383) is actually pretty nice inside. The rooms are comfortable and well equipped, many with balconies and ocean views. The hotel has an indoor heated pool and hot tub. Facilities also include a horseshoe pit and playground, plus free Wi-Fi. As an added bonus, the free continental breakfast starts at the dark hour of 4:30 A.M. for those headed out on fishing trips.

There might not be a pool, but fun-lovin' families will appreciate the go-kart track right on the property at **Breakers Motel** (971 Montesano St., 360/268-0848, www.westportwa.com/breakers, $94–140 d). The motel offers standard rooms and kitchenette units, as well as newer hot-tub suites ($210–230).

Built in 1898 and surrounded by tall evergreens, **Glenacres Inn B&B** (222 N. Montesano St., 360/268-9391 or 800/996-3048, $80–135 d) is the most interesting place to stay in Westport. The B&B has eight guest rooms with private baths, and guests are treated to a full breakfast. A gazebo encloses the hot tub.

Food

Because of the early morning departure of fishing charters, several local cafés are already open when the clock strikes five in the morning. Another recommended lunch place with a salad bar and good seafood is **Barbara's by the Sea** (2323 Westhaven Dr., 360/268-1329, 8 A.M.–6 P.M. Mon.–Thurs., 8 A.M.–8 P.M. Fri.–Sat.) across from the marina. **Las Maracas Mexican Restaurant** (202 W. Ocean Ave., 360/268-6272, 11 A.M.–8 P.M. daily) makes good enchiladas, tostadas, and chimichangas.

You'll find a "surf and turf" menu that includes oysters, halibut, and prawns, along with steaks and pasta, at **King's LeDomaine** (105 Wilson St., 360/268-2556, 7 A.M.–9 P.M. daily).

Buy freshly shucked oysters to go from **Brady's Oysters** (3714 Oyster Place E, 360/268-0077, 9 A.M.–6 P.M. daily). This company was the first to grow oysters on suspended lines, a method that many claim produces a more delicately flavored oyster. You can often buy ultra-fresh fish from commercial fishermen at the marina, and fresh-cooked crab at **Merino's Seafood** (301 E. Harbor St., 360/268-5324, 10 A.M.–6 P.M. daily in summer, 10 A.M.–4 P.M. Sat.–Sun. in winter).

Information

Find maps, brochures, and festival and tour information at the **Westport-Grayland Chamber of Commerce Visitors Center** (2985 N. Montesano St., 360/268-9422 or 800/345-6223, www.westportgrayland-chamber.org, 9 A.M.–5 P.M. Mon.–Fri. year-round, plus 10 A.M.–3 P.M. Sat.–Sun. May–Sept.).

Getting There

Grays Harbor Transit (360/532-2770 or 800/562-9730, www.ghtransit.com) provides daily bus service throughout the county, including Grayland, Aberdeen, Lake Quinault, Ocean Shores, and even to Olympia.

The **Westport-Ocean Shores Passenger Ferry,** *El Matador* (360/268-0047) is a passenger ferry that runs between Ocean Shores and Westport for $8 round-trip (free for kids under 5). The ferry leaves six times a day, with daily service mid-June–Labor Day, and weekend-only service early May–mid-June and in September. There's no service the rest of the year. The ferry departs from Float 10 at the Westport marina.

CRANBERRY COAST

The section of coastline between Westport and North Cove is known as both South Beach and the Cranberry Coast—the former because it is the southern entrance to Grays Harbor, the latter because of the bogs east near Grayland that produce much of the state's cranberry crop. The area is especially popular for sportfishing but also offers long beaches, good surfing, and reasonably priced lodging. The beaches are favorites of post-storm beachcombers who still turn up an occasional glass ball from old Japanese fishing floats.

Sights and Recreation

The crimson crush of cranberry bogs is this quiet region's biggest claim to fame. Visitors can get a roadside tour of the local crop along the aptly named Cranberry Road, as well as Larkin and Turkey Roads. If the tour sparks your interest and you plan on driving farther south, be sure to check out the Cranberry Museum on the Long Beach Peninsula.

A mile south of Grayland on Highway 105, **Grayland Beach State Park** (off Midway Beach Rd., 888/226-7688, www.parks.wa.gov) has 7,450 feet of ocean frontage, 200 acres for picnicking and camping, and a self-guided nature trail through huckleberry, Sitka spruce, and lodgepole pine. This is a popular place to dig for clams. Grayland Beach also has 60 campsites, all with shower access and hookups for $20 ($7 extra for reservations), and is open year-round.

Park RVs at the well-maintained **Kenanna RV Park** (2959 S. Hwy. 105, 360/267-3515 or 800/867-3515, www.kenannarv.com, $25 full hookups, $15 tent)

Entertainment and Events

The third weekend of March, Grayland-area artists display their driftwood and shell creations at the town's **Beachcombers Driftwood Show.** The **4th of July** means a big fireworks display over Booming Bay, and a fun run, arts and crafts, and food booths in Grayland. Early October brings the **Cranberry Harvest Festival** with bog tours, a cranberry cook-off, parade, and dancing.

For some day-to-day excitement, try your luck at **Shoalwater Bay Bingo and Casino** (at the Hwy. 105 turnoff to Tokeland, 360/267-2048 or 888/332-2048, www.shoalwaterbay-casino.com).

Accommodations

Check into **Grayland Motel & Cottages** (2013 Hwy. 105, 360/267-2395 or 800/292-0845, westportwa.com/graylandmotel, $55–93 s or d) and you'll be able to walk out your door to the beach. This family- and pet-friendly facility has a play area for kids and dogs. It also offers complimentary clam guns and shovels to its guests, plus a sink outside to clean them once you catch them.

CRANBERRIES

Introduced to Washington in 1883, Cranberries grow on perennial vines in acidic peat bogs and were named by imaginative pilgrims for its flowers that resemble the head and bill of a crane. Today the state produces 16,000 tons of cranberries annually, 4 percent of the nation's total output. Nearly all of the 130 cranberry farms in the state are family-run operations averaging just 11 acres each. They typically sell the crop to Ocean Spray Cranberries, a farmers' cooperative best known for its juice cocktails. It runs two plants in southeast Washington: at Grayland on the "Cranberry Coast" and in Long Beach.

The traditional way to harvest cranberries has been to flood the fields, causing the berries to float to the surface for harvesting. This is still done on some bogs, but most in Washington use dry-harvesting equipment that combs the vines to pull the berries, thanks largely to the Grayland farmer who invented its design.

The most interesting times to visit the cranberry bogs are in mid-June, the peak blooming season, or mid-October, to see the harvest.

© WASHINGTON STATE TOURISM/LEVY SHECKLER

scenic drive along the Cranberry Coast Scenic Byway

WASHAWAY BEACH

The town of North Cove occupies the northern edge of the entrance to Willapa Harbor; it was once considerably larger. Over the years, the sea has been winning the war with the land, pulling a lighthouse, lifesaving station, canneries, homes, hotels, and schools over the retreating cliff. The shore is now more than two miles back from its position a century ago, a rate unparalleled elsewhere on the Pacific Coast. Although the rate of erosion has slowed, there's often something ready to go over the edge at the aptly named Washaway Beach.

Or try **Grayland B&B** (1678 Hwy. 105, 360/267-6026, $110 s or d) for a homier atmosphere. The proprietors let out two bedrooms with a shared bath in a two-story home built in the 1930s.

A focal point in Tokeland is the wonderfully old-fashioned **Tokeland Hotel** (Kindred Rd. and Hotel Rd., 360/267-7006, www.tokelandhotel.com, $55 s, $65 d). Built as a home in 1885, it became an inn in 1899 and is now on the National Register. The hotel and town are named for Chief Toke, whose daughter married a worker at the lifesaving station here. Together they built a home that was later turned into the Tokeland Hotel. Now on the National Register of Historic Places, it's said to be the oldest resort hotel in Washington, and the spacious front lawn, brick fireplace, and jigsaw puzzles provide an air of relaxation. The restored hotel has upstairs rooms with bath down the hall; reserve several weeks ahead for summer weekend stays. The restaurant, in an open dining room overlooking Willapa Bay, serves three meals a day, specializing in reasonably priced seafood ($10–15 entrées).

Food

Both Grayland and Tokeland are pretty quiet settlements. It makes for nice little getaways, but the drawback is there aren't a whole lot of restaurant options. Most days of the week you can nosh on the comestibles served up at **Mutineer Restaurant** (2120 Hwy. 105, Grayland, 360/267-2077, 8 A.M.–8 P.M. Thurs.–Mon.), which serves all three meals. If you stop by for lunch or dinner, be sure to try some clam chowder.

For those serious about their seafood, head to **Nelson Crab, Inc.** (3088 Kindred Ave., Tokeland, 360/267-2911, 9 A.M.–5 P.M. daily) for fresh-cooked crab and other seafood for picnics and cookouts.

Information

The small **Cranberry Coast Chamber of Commerce** (2190 Hwy. 105, 360/267-2003 or 800/473-6018, www.cranberrycoast.com) is next to Grandma's Treasure Chest store.

The **Shoalwater Bay Tribe** has a small reservation and tribal offices at Tokeland (Willapa Bay was originally called Shoalwater Bay).

Getting There

Grays Harbor Transit (360/532-2770 or 800/562-9730, www.ghtransit.com) provides daily bus service throughout the county, including Westport, Aberdeen, Lake Quinault, and Ocean Shores.

Long Beach Peninsula

The Long Beach Peninsula is a 28-mile-long strip of sand and fun off the southwestern corner of Washington. Locals call it the "World's Longest Beach," though you're bound to hear disagreement from folks in Australia and New Zealand. Be that as it may, this is one *very* long stretch of sand, and a favorite getaway for folks from Seattle and Portland.

Ask most Puget Sounders who frequent the Long Beach Peninsula what they think about it, and you'll probably get the same protective response Washingtonians have about their state when talking to Californians and North Dakotans: they love it and don't want it to change. The towns on this peninsula have a lived-in look to them, and many of the houses are so sand-peppered and rain-washed that they look as though a designer talked everyone into the weathered-home look. The peninsula is the kind of place where you'll find rubber boots and heavy rain gear on almost every porch—it rains over 70 inches a year here, so be ready to get wet even in the summer—and somewhere in every house is a glass float from a Japanese fishing net and a piece of driftwood.

The central tourist and commercial town on the island, Long Beach has the only walkable downtown area on the coast, with little shops and the typical souvenir joints—like a *real* beach town. At the north end of the peninsula, things are drastically different, with beautifully restored century-old homes in Oysterville, and an isolated natural area at Leadbetter Point.

SIGHTS

Cape Disappointment State Park

Ignore the name—Cape Disappointment State Park (360/642-3078, www.parks.wa.gov) is anything but a letdown. Arguably the most scenic state park in Washington, this 1,882-acre recreational retreat offers dramatic vistas

Cape Disappointment on Washington's southern coast

© WASHINGTON STATE TOURISM/JIM POTH

across the mouth of the Columbia River, old-growth forests, incredible fishing, century-old military fortifications, historic lighthouses, and an impressive museum dedicated to Lewis and Clark.

This is the spot where Meriwether Lewis and William Clark stood in November of 1805, finally having "reached the great Pacific Ocean which we been so long anxious to See." Because game proved scarce and this side of the Columbia lacked protection from winter storms, they crossed the river to build a winter camp called Fort Clatsop near present-day Astoria, Oregon. The fascinating museum at **Lewis and Clark Interpretive Center** (360/642-3029, 10 A.M.–5 P.M. daily) honors the famous duo and is one of the must-see places on Long Beach Peninsula. The interpretive center has enormous windows with expansive views of Cape Disappointment Lighthouse, the Columbia River, and the mighty Pacific.

You can see the mouth of the Columbia by turning right at the concession area and driving to the road's end; park here and walk through the sand to the lookout atop North Jetty. **Cape Disappointment Lighthouse** is the Northwest's oldest, built in 1856; follow the quarter-mile trail from the interpretive center or a steep quarter-mile path from the Coast Guard Station.

The commanding presence and strategic location of Cape Disappointment made it a vital fort location for the new Oregon Territory. The initial cannons arrived in 1862, and **Fort Canby** went on to protect the mouth of Columbia for 95 years. Many of the old bunkers and gun emplacements remain, making for interesting explorations.

WHAT A LETDOWN

Located at Washington's southernmost point, **Cape Disappointment** earned its name in 1788 from British fur trader John Meares, who was searching for the fabled Northwest Passage. He had heard tales of an enormous river near here from a Spaniard, Bruno Heceta, who had written about it in 1775. Meares failed to find the river (which he hoped would lead to the Passage). The mighty river is surprisingly easy to miss from the sea – Captain George Vancouver also sailed past. The river wasn't officially "discovered" until 1792, when American Capt. Robert Gray sailed his *Columbia Rediviva* into the treacherous river mouth.

Ilwaco

Historic Ilwaco (ill-WOK-o) is a charter, sports, and commercial fishing town on the south end of the Long Beach Peninsula, with docks on protected Baker Bay. The town was named for a Chinook leader, Chief Elowahka Jim. Walk around town to find five murals on the sides of local businesses, and some wonderful old buildings. Ilwaco's old Fire Station No. 1 on Lake Street contains the "Mankiller," an 1846 hand pumper that was the first fire-fighting apparatus of its kind in Washington Territory. You can view the Mankiller through a window when the building isn't open. Just north of Ilwaco is a pullout along scenic Black Lake; paddleboats are available for rent here in the summer (360/642-3003).

Visit the excellent **Ilwaco Heritage Museum** (115 S.E. Lake St., 360/642-3446, 9 A.M.–5 P.M. Mon.–Sat., noon–4 P.M. Sun. in summer, 9 A.M.–4 P.M. Mon.–Sat. fall–spring) for a look into Pacific Coast history via models, Native American exhibits, and photographs of early settlers' fishing, oystering, and logging methods, along with Cape Disappointment shipwrecks and rescues. Of particular interest is a detailed scale model of the Columbia River estuary, and a display on the *Sector* ($3 adults, $2.50 seniors, $1 children under 12), a 26-foot boat that Gérard D'Aboville rowed from Japan to Ilwaco in 1991.

Washington State Parks conducts tours (360/642-3078, $1) of historic **Colbert House** at the corner of Spruce and Quaker Streets daily in the summer.

Long Beach

Long Beach makes up the commercial core of the peninsula, with all the typical beachfront services, including kitschy gift shops, fish-and-chips takeouts, real estate offices, kite stores, saltwater taffy shops, strip malls, RV parks, motels, and bumper boat, go-kart, and miniature golf amusement parks. Not everything is tacky, but don't come here expecting a classy, romantic experience; this is a family fun-for-all place. In the summer Long Beach hums with traffic and the ringing of cash registers; in winter it slows to a quieter pace but is still popular as a weekend getaway.

Several fine murals grace the sides of buildings in Long Beach. One of the peninsula's most photographed local spots is the **"World's Longest Beach" arch** that rises over Bolsted Street as you head toward the ocean. An elevated and wheelchair-accessible **boardwalk** takes off from here and continues a half mile south to 10th Street; it's a great place for romantic sunset strolls. The gravel **Dune Trail** extends for two miles across the dunes, from 17th Street S to 16th Street N, and is popular with cyclists and hikers.

WORLD KITE MUSEUM

Befitting its beachside location, Long Beach is home to the World Kite Museum and Hall of Fame (3rd St. NW and Pacific Hwy., 360/642-4020, www.worldkitemuseum.com, 11 A.M.–5 P.M. daily May.–Sept., 11 A.M.–5 P.M. Fri.–Mon. Oct.–Apr., $5 adults, $4 seniors, $3 children). Inside, you'll learn the history of kites and how they were used during wartime and in developing airplanes. Also here are kites from around the globe, a re-created Japanese kite artist workshop, and a gift shop. The museum offers kite-making workshops the first Saturday of the month May–August.

CRANBERRY ATTRACTIONS

Around 600 acres of cranberries are grown in the Long Beach Peninsula area, and you're bound to see them growing along Highway 101 as you approach the peninsula. Cranberries were originally called "crane berries" by early settlers who thought the blossoms resembled cranes' heads. Ocean Spray Cranberries, Inc. has a processing plant on Sandridge Road in Long Beach, and a second one in Westport. **Anna Lena's Pantry** (111 Balstad Ave., Long Beach, 360/642-8948 or 800/272-6237, 10 A.M.–5 P.M. Mon.–Thurs., 10 A.M.–5:30 P.M. Fri.–Sat., 10 A.M.–4 P.M. Sun.) sells locally made cranberry products.

About a mile northeast of Long Beach is the **Cranberry Museum & Gift Shop** (Pioneer Rd., 360/642-5553, 10 A.M.–5 P.M. Fri.–Sun. May–mid-Dec., free). Operated jointly by the University of Washington and the Pacific Coast Cranberry Research Foundation, the museum shows old and new ways of growing and harvesting cranberries. Visitors can walk the adjacent 10-acre demonstration cranberry bog at any time to learn about this unique crop. Try to time your visit for June, the peak bloom season, or October, to see the harvest.

"CLARK WUZ HERE"

The first Easterners to arrive in Long Beach were the **Lewis and Clark** party, who traveled through this area of sand dunes and pine trees in late 1805, stopping long enough for William Clark to carve his initials on a tree; it's the westernmost point reached by the expedition.

Walking along the Discovery Trail from Ilwaco to Long Beach, you can find a 20-foot bronze statue of a windswept tree memorializing that pine on which Clark cut his mark. Visitors can also check out a life-size bronze statue of the explorers in downtown Long Beach.

Ocean Park

Once the Pacific Highway (a.k.a. Hwy. 103) exits the north end of hectic Long Beach, you are suddenly in an almost flat landscape of lodgepole pine trees and scattered summer and retirement homes. You can't see the ocean or Willapa Bay from here, but there are access points all along the way, including at Klipsan Beach. After 11 miles of this, the highway widens into Ocean Park (pop. 1,400), a place considerably more sedate than Long Beach, but nevertheless a popular summer retreat. The **Wreckage,** on the south side of 256th just west of Highway 103, is a unique house constructed in 1912 from logs salvaged after a storm broke apart a raft of logs being towed off the coast. It's on the National Register of Historic Places.

Loomis Lake State Park (south of Klipsan Beach) has picnic tables on the ocean, not the lake; the real Loomis Lake is about a quarter mile north. No camping is allowed here.

Willapa Bay

No matter which way you shuck it, the truth is that the Willapa Bay towns of Nahcotta and Oysterville are quite literally defined by the slurpy sweet meat of the mollusk of love. The latter's name says it all, while the former's namesake is Chief Nahcati, the Native leader who first clued the white man into the oystery bounty of the bay.

The oyster beds are closed to the public, but interpretive signs next to the Nahcotta's Willapa Bay Field Station explain local ecology and the lives of shellfish. **Willapa Bay Interpretive Center** (south side of the Port of Peninsula breakwater, Nahcotta, 360/665-4547, www.opwa.com/interp, 10 A.M.–3 P.M. Fri.–Sun. late May–mid-Oct.) displays exhibits on the oyster industry and the natural history of Willapa Bay.

You can purchase fresh oysters and other seafood in Nahcotta at **Wiegart Brothers Oyster Co., Bendiksen's East Point Seafood Co.,** or the smaller **Hilton's Coast Oyster Company.** Or stop at **Oysterville Sea Farms** (360/665-6585, www.oysterville.net) for fresh or smoked oysters and clams.

A number of homes constructed during the town of Oysterville's heyday have been restored and are now part of the **Oysterville National Historic District.** For a self-guided walking tour map, visit the beautiful white-and-red **Oysterville Baptist Church,** built in 1892.

RISE AND FALL OF OYSTERVILLE

Following the discovery of gold in California, San Franciscans had both gold and a yen to spend it on good food, especially fresh oysters. With oysters selling for up to $50 a plate, the demand led men to search far and wide for new sources. In 1854, Chief Nahcati (the source of the name Nahcotta) showed R. H. Espy and I. A. Clark the rich oyster beds of Willapa Bay. Sensing profit potential, they quickly built the new town of Oysterville on the site, and within a scant few months another 500 boomers had arrived.

The rowdy town grew to become the county seat within two years, and even had a college for a brief period, before overharvesting and winter freezes made the oysters scarce in the late 1880s. With the loss of oysters and the money and jobs they attracted, Oysterville's economy collapsed, and county voters decided to move the Pacific County seat to the logging town of South Bend. Oysterville claimed railroad workers in South Bend had stuffed the ballot box and sued to overturn the vote.

A bitter legal battle ensued that threatened to keep the matter tied up in the courts for years, so a group of South Bend men decided to force the issue. On a Sunday morning in February of 1893, some 85 men crossed to Oysterville abroad two steamships. They first stopped for liquid reinforcement at a local saloon. Then, finding most everyone in church, the mob proceeded to plunder the county courthouse, stealing (or legally removing, depending upon who is telling the story) all the records and furniture. After returning to South Bend with the booty, they sent a bill to Oysterville for services rendered in the process of moving the county records! The county seat has been in South Bend ever since, but the bill was never paid.

On Sunday afternoons in summer the church comes alive with vespers programs featuring an ecumenical mix of secular and religious music.

ENTERTAINMENT AND EVENTS

Nightlife

Every Saturday all summer long, you'll find free concerts in Long Beach's downtown gazebo. Seaview's **Sou'wester Lodge** (360/642-2542) often has concerts, lectures, or poetry on Saturday nights. During the summer and fall, **Nick's West** (1700 Pacific Ave. S, 360/642-5100) has country or rock bands on the weekends.

Festivals and Events

In April, come to Long Beach for the **Ragtime Rhodie Dixieland Jazz Festival.** Then comes Ocean Park's **Garlic Festival,** held the third weekend of June, which features garlic shucking and garlic eating contests, plus all sorts of garlicky meals. Bring a couple of bottles of Listerine along. Long Beach hosts the annual 4th of July **Fireworks on the Beach,** and Ocean Park has a popular **Street Fair** the same weekend. Then comes **Sandsations Sand Sculptures** at the end of the month.

The year's biggest event, the **Washington State International Kite Festival** (www.kitefestival.com) lasts the entire third week of August and draws well over 200,000 spectators and participants. This is the largest kite festival in the western hemisphere, and every day brings a different contest, ending with Sunday's grand finale in which the sky teems with upwards of 4,000 kites of all sorts. The world record for keeping a kite aloft (over 180 hours) was set here in 1982.

Ocean Park hosts an enormously popular classic car show, the **Rod Run to the End of the World,** on the second weekend of September that ends with a 15-mile-long parade. The annual **Cranberrian Fair,** held in Ilwaco in mid-October, celebrates more than a century of coastal cranberry farming. Bog tours give you the chance to see the flooded fields with thousands of floating berries awaiting harvest. It's followed the third weekend of October by **Water Music Festival** with chamber music concerts all over the peninsula.

SHOPPING

It may be campy, but you definitely don't want to miss **Marsh's Free Museum** (409 S. Pacific Ave., 360/642-2188, www.marshfreemuseum.com), a huge souvenir shop in downtown Long Beach. Inside is a delightful collection of the tasteless and bizarre, much of it from old amusement parks, traveling shows, and attics. You'll find an impressive collection of glass fishing balls, the world's largest frying pan, a vampire bat skeleton, an old bottle with a human tapeworm, a gruesome photo of a 1920 triple hanging, and a two-headed calf. Drop a nickel for a flapper-era peep show, pay a dime to test your passion factor on the "throne of love," or search the jam-packed shelves for a stupid postcard, goofy T-shirt, cheap trinket, or bright seashell. Oh, and you won't want to miss "Jake the Alligator Man," stuck in a back corner inside a glass aquarium; he once starred in that arbiter of tabloid discernment, the *Weekly World News.* If you like kitsch, you'll rate this as Washington's finest gift shop! Out front of Marsh's is a small climbing wall ($5 per climb).

The Long Beach Peninsula is one of the best places in Washington for kite flying. Pick up kites, string, supplies and advice at **Above it All Kites** (312 Pacific Blvd. S, Long Beach, 360/642-3541, www.aboveitallkites.com, daily 9 A.M.–5 P.M.).

Wiegardt Studio Gallery (2607 Bay Ave., 360/665-5976, www.ericwiegardt.com, 11 A.M.–4 P.M. Mon.–Fri., 11 A.M.–5 P.M. Sat. July–Aug., 11 A.M.–4 P.M. Fri., 11 A.M.–5 P.M. Sat. Sept.–June) contains the watercolor works of Eric Wiegardt, one of several respected local artists. Wiegart runs numerous art workshops throughout the year, so be sure to check the website for the schedule during your trip.

Shoalwater Cove Gallery (1401 Bay Ave., 360/665-4382, www.shoalwatercove.com, 11 A.M.–5 P.M. daily spring–fall, winter hours vary) has beautifully detailed pastels by Marie Powell.

SPORTS AND RECREATION

Cape Disappointment State Park

North Head Lighthouse was built in 1898 and stands above Dead Man's Hollow, named for the sailors of the ill-fated *Vandelia,* which sank here in 1853. The lighthouse is no longer used; today marine lanterns shine out instead from North Head. The lighthouse is a short walk through the trees from the upper parking lot, or a two-mile hike from McKenzie Head (just west of the campground). Lighthouse tours (360/642-3078, $1) are given daily during the summer. To the south are the dunes and driftwood piles of **Benson Beach** (no vehicles allowed), with Long Beach pointing its finger northward. **West Wind Trail** leads a mile north from the lighthouse through the old-growth forests to Beards Hollow. From there you can continue along the beach all the way to the town of Long Beach, four miles away.

North Head is a favorite place to watch for migrating **gray whales** heading north March–May or south late December–early February. It's also an awe-inspiring place during winter storms when waves pound hard against the rocks below.

Tiny **Waikiki Beach** is a favorite local spot for picnics and swimming in the summer (no lifeguard is present). The beach received its name when a Hawaiian sailor's body washed ashore here after his ship was wrecked in a failed attempt to cross the Columbia River bar in 1811. You can follow a trail uphill from Waikiki to the Lewis and Clark Interpretive Center, and then on to Cape Disappointment Lighthouse.

For a taste of old-growth forests, take the 1.5-mile **Coastal Forest Trail** that begins at the boat ramp along Baker Bay. This is a very enjoyable loop hike.

Cape Disappointment (888/226-7688, www.parks.wa.gov) is one of the most popular places to camp in Washington, welcoming tent ($22)and RV ($31 with full hookups) campers, plus groups of four or less seeking shelter in its permanent yurts ($50 up to six). If you need to clean up, there are coin-operated showers on premises. The campground—within a few yards of beautiful Benson Beach—is open all year.

Leadbetter Point State Park

The northern tip of Long Beach Peninsula is capped by two publicly owned natural areas, Leadbetter Point State Park, and a portion of the Willapa National Wildlife Refuge. Leadbetter has a 1.5-mile trail through the evergreen forest, connecting both parking lots. From the north lot, you can enter Willapa and walk through stunted lodgepole pine forests to beachgrass-covered sand dunes along the Pacific Ocean, or head down to the shore of Willapa Bay for a beach walk. The northern end of Willapa National Wildlife Refuge is closed to all entry April–August to protect the threatened snowy plover that nests on the dunes here. This area is also a very important sanctuary for waterfowl, particularly during spring and fall migrations. Bird-watchers will see thousands (and sometimes hundreds of thousands) of black brant, Canada geese, dunlin, plovers, sandpipers, and other birds in the marshes and beaches during these times. No fires or camping are allowed.

Long Beach

Long Beach is best known for its delightful beach, a favorite of kite enthusiasts. If you don't own a kite, several local shops sell them for all levels of flying ability.

Contrary to expectations, the 28 miles of sandy beach on Long Beach Peninsula are not safe for swimming. Not only are there dangerous undertows and riptides, but rogue waves can occur, and there are no lifeguards. Every year waders or swimmers get trapped in these bitterly cold waters; sometimes the accidents end in tragedy. Locals and visitors looking for a chance to swim generally head to Waikiki Beach, or to local motel swimming pools. Dunes Bible Camp in Ocean Park (360/665-5542, $3) has a large indoor pool open to the public for.

Fishing and Boating

Ilwaco is home to the peninsula's fishing fleet. Some of the more popular excursion companies include **Sea Breeze Charters** (185 Howerton Way SE, 360/642-2300, www.seabreezecharters.net) and **Pacific Salmon Charters** (191

Howerton Way, 360/642-3466, www.pacificsalmoncharters.com), both of which lead deep-sea fishing trips off the coast for rockfish, flounder, sole, lingcod, salmon, and sometimes albacore tuna. They also lead river trips for those in hope of hooking salmon and the Columbia River's mighty sturgeon.

Or stay on shore to fish: More than 230 ships were wrecked or sunk on the Columbia bar before jetties were constructed to control the sand. The longest of these is North Jetty at Cape Disappointment State Park, which reaches a half mile out from the end of the cape and is a popular place to fish for salmon, rock cod, perch, and sea bass.

Stop by the visitors center for a complete listing of local charter operators, along with information on razor clam seasons and harvesting. Clamming is a popular pastime on the sandy stretches of Long Beach. All it takes is a bucket and a shovel, but clam guns can help the success rate. Most people have the best luck about an hour before low tide. Check the Washington State Department of Fish and Wildlife's website (www.wdfw.wa.gov) for information on clamming and fishing seasons and to buy licenses. You can also pick up licenses at **Pioneer Market** (2006 N. Pacific Hwy. 103, Long Beach, 360/642-4004). For fishing supplies, visit **Ed's Bait and Tackle** (207 2nd Ave. SW, Ilwaco, 360/642-2248).

Other Recreation

Rent mopeds, bikes and surreys from **Long Beach Moped** (Sid Snyder Dr., just west of the stoplight at Pacific Hwy. 103, 360/289-3830, 9 A.M.–dark daily Memorial Day–mid-Sept., 9 A.M.–dark Fri.–Sun. the rest of the year).

Horse enthusiasts can rent horses for guided beach rides from **Skipper's Equestrian Center** (S Blvd. and 10th St., 360/642-3676, $25 per hour) or **Back Country Wilderness Outfitters** (10th St. S, Long Beach, 360/642-2576, www.backcountryoutfit.com, $20 per hour).

Two local golf courses are open to the public: **Peninsula Golf Course** (Long Beach, 360/642-2828) and **Surfside Golf Course** (north of Ocean Park, 360/665-4148).

Camping

Great camping for tents or RVs can be had at Cape Disappointment, and RVers will find more than 20 different parking lot/campgrounds along the Long Beach Peninsula. Get a complete listing at the visitors center, or just drive along Pacific Highway until one looks acceptable. For unbeatable oceanfront access, **Andersen's RV Park** (1400 138th St., Long Beach, 360/642-2231 or 800/645-6795, www.andersensrv.com, $45 oceanfront with full hookups, $35 regular full hookups) is the way to go. This dog-friendly park is just a few yards from the sand and surf—grab a fishing pole and tromp through the dune trail to spend the day fishing. There's even a fish- and clam-cleaning station on the property. Facilities also include hot showers and wireless Internet. There are no open fire pits, to preserve the dune grasses, but guests can rent enclosed fire containers ($6/day). Another well-maintained and friendly option, **Driftwood RV Park** (1512 N. Pacific Hwy., 360/642-2711 or 888/567-1902, www.driftwood-rvpark.com, $36 with full hookups) offers grassy sites with lots of space to unwind. Rent a clam gun here to take out to the beach and then use the clam- and fish-cleaning station on premises.

ACCOMMODATIONS

Lodging can be hard to come by on summer weekends, especially during the big festivals. Many rooms are booked a year ahead for Memorial Day weekend, the International Kite Festival in August, and Labor Day weekend. It's a good idea to reserve two to four weeks ahead for other summer weekends. The visitors bureau (360/642-2400 or 800/451-2542, www.funbeach.com) tries to keep track of which accommodations have space. It also has a listing of several dozen vacation houses and cabins available for longer periods of time.

Ilwaco

In Ilwaco, **Heidi's Inn** (126 Spruce St., 360/642-2387 or 800/576-1032, $79–99 s or d) is a tidy, simple little motel that accepts pets.

Owned by the same folks who run the

Shelburne Inn in Seaview, **China Beach Retreat** (222 Capt. Robert Grey Dr., Ilwaco, 360/642-5660 or 360/642-2442, www.chinabeachretreat.com, $215–245) is a lovely 1907 house set amidst an orchard near the mouth of Columbia River. The house is beautifully decorated.

One of the most distinctive local lodging places is at Cape Disappointment State Park, where you can rent one of three historic three-bedroom **Lighthouse Keeper's Residences** (360/642-3078). The head lighthouse keeper's residence ($377) offers the best views of the lighthouse and the mouth of the Columbia, and assistant lighthouse keepers' residences ($267) are nearby. All homes sleep six and feature fully-equipped kitchens and living rooms with TVs and DVD players.

Long Beach

Equipped with a hot tub, sauna, and a small fitness center, **Our Place at the Beach** (1309 S. Ocean Beach Blvd., Long Beach, 360/642-3793 or 800/538-5107, www.willapabay.org/~opat, $52–67 d) has 23 rooms, many with ocean views, each with a fridge. Two larger cabins are also available.

Just across the street from the beach in town, **Anthony's Cabins** (1310 Pacific Hwy. N, Long Beach, 360/642-2802 or 888/787-2754, www.anthonyshomecourt.com, $79–125 s or d) offers studio and one-bedroom units with kitchens in a 1930s-era house.

About a mile north of downtown, **The Breakers** (Hwy. 103 and 26th St., 360/642-4414 or 800/219-9833, www.breakerslongbeach.com, $119–139 s or d) offers pretty standard motel rooms, plus spacious one or two-bedroom suites with kitchens ($179–278) for up to four. Amenities include an indoor pool, sauna, and hot tub.

For a bit more privacy, try **Boardwalk Cottages** (800 S. Boulevard St., Long Beach, 360/642-2305 or 800/569-3804, www.boardwalkcottages.com, $89–139) with its one- and two-bedroom cottages, many with kitchenettes and decks.

Anchorage Cottages (2209 N. Boulevard St., Long Beach, 360/642-2351 or 800/642-2351, www.theanchoragecottages.com, $80–128) provides beachside units with either one or two bedrooms, most with fireplaces, as well as more spacious two-bedroom cottages with fireplaces. All units have fully equipped kitchens.

There are also several B&Bs right in town. Set within a contemporary home, **A Rendezvous Place Bed and Breakfast** (1610 California Ave. S, Long Beach, 360/642-8877 or 866/642-8877, www.rendezvousplace.com, $129–169 d, suite $219) is one of the rare bed-and-breakfasts that doesn't have so many antiques that you feel like you're in a mausoleum or fear you're going to break something expensive. Rooms are comfy and nicely decorated, and outside there is a hot tub and deck overlooking the private backyard.

Another option is **Boreas B&B** (607 N. Boulevard St., 360/642-8069 or 888/642-8069, www.boreasinn.com, $160–179 s or d), a quiet and cozy 1920s beachfront home with airy and light-colored interiors and an enclosed sundeck with a hot tub. The four guest rooms have shared or private baths. The proprietors also rent out a family- and pet-friendly cottage next door.

Seaview

If you're looking for standard motel accommodations, there are plenty of places along the peninsula, including the immaculately maintained **Coho Motel** (3701 Pacific Hwy., Seaview, 360/642-2531 or 800/681-8153, $45–80 s or d), which provides simple motel rooms with kitchenettes available.

But if you want a friendly place with a funky sense of nostalgia, character, and charm, look no farther than Seaview's **Sou'wester Lodge** (38th Pl., 360/642-2542, www.souwesterlodge.com). Here, literary owners Leonard and Miriam Atkins have created a rustic and offbeat haven for those who appreciate simple comforts. The accommodations include "Bed and Make Your Own Damn Breakfast" rooms in the stately three-story lodge ($119–199 d) built in 1892 as a summer estate by Henry Winslow Corbett, a wealthy timber baron, banker, and U.S. senator from Oregon. Outside are weathered beach cottages ($129–139 d) furnished in "early Salvation Army" decor, and even a hodgepodge of 1950s-era trailers ($69–179 d). Tent and RV space are also available. Artists and writers often "book in" for months at a time, relaxing in this cozy and informal lodge. On many Saturday nights, the sitting room comes to life with lectures, concerts, or poetry. You're likely to find everything from chamber music to discussions on Sufism.

The oldest continuously used lodging in Washington, Seaview's acclaimed **Shelburne Inn** (4415 Pacific Way, 360/642-2442 or 800/466-1896, www.shelburneinn.com, $139–199 d) sits within an elegant 1896 Victorian building. The inn is packed with tasteful antiques, stained-glass windows (from an old English church), and original artwork. TVs would be jarring in such a quaint little place, so don't expect to tune in during your stay. A full country breakfast is included; for many, it's the highlight of their stay. The inn is, however, located just a few feet from busy Pacific Highway, and roadside rooms can be quite noisy. Also beware of the ghost who is rumored to wander the third floor some nights.

Ocean Park

Next to a small pond frequented by ducks and the occasional blue heron is **Shakti Cove Cottages** (1204 253rd Pl., Ocean Park, 360/665-4000, www.shakticove.com, $80–90 d) with 10 cabins nestled in a grove of trees.

Covered in sea-salt-weathered clapboard, **Klipsan Beach Cottages** (22617 Pacific Hwy., Ocean Park, 360/665-4888, www.klipsanbeachcottages.com, $130 d, $155 for 4, $215 for 6) are comfortable older cottages with kitchens and ocean views. This is a quaint place with a lovely meadow on one side and a row of tall pine trees on the other, 200 yards from the beach.

The modern Victorian-style **Caswell's on the Bay B&B** (25204 Sandridge Rd., Ocean Park, 360/665-6535, www.caswellsinn.com, $160–210) offers friendly and comfortable accommodations facing Willapa Bay. This is a quiet and relaxing place on a three-acre spread. Five guest rooms are furnished with antiques and private baths.

FOOD

Long Beach

In downtown Long Beach, **Cottage Bakery** (118 S. Pacific Ave., 360/642-4441, 4 A.M.–6 P.M. daily) has cabinets filled with sticky-sweet old-fashioned pastries. It's a favorite place for a coffee and dessert while watching the people stroll by.

Dooger's Seafood & Grill (900 Pacific Ave. S, Long Beach, 360/642-4224, daily 11 A.M.–9 P.M.) is a bit formulaic, but it is one of the best seafood restaurants in town, with brags about its sourdough bowls full of homemade clam chowder, fish and chips, pan fried oysters, and salads with fresh bay shrimp.

The kiddies will appreciate the pirate-themed **Castaways Seafood Grill** (208 Pacific Ave S, 360/642-4745, www.castawaysseafoodgrille.com), a lively seafood eatery with loads of golden-fried fishies, plus burgers, sandwiches, and salads.

Corral Drive-In (2506 Pacific Ave N, 360/642-2774, 11 A.M.–7 P.M. Mon.–Fri., 11 A.M.–8 P.M. Sat.–Sun.) is another very family-friendly joint. This place is known 'round Washington as the home of the pie-tin sized Tsunami burger—a beast of a sandwich that can literally feed six people. Get the napkins ready, because it sure is messy!

For beef Philly-style, saunter over to **Surfer Sands** (1113 Pacific Ave S, Long Beach, 360/642-7873, 10 A.M.–5 P.M. Sat.–Thurs., 10 A.M.–7 P.M. Fri.), a roadside stand that specializes in ooey-gooey cheese steaks. Summer brings variable extended hours—call ahead.

Seaview

Two Seaview restaurants vie for the breakfast crowds. **Laurie's Homestead Breakfast House** (4214 Pacific Hwy., 360/642-7171, 6:30 A.M.–1 P.M. daily) has a seven-page breakfast menu and very good food. Across the street is **Cheri Walker's 42nd St. Café** (360/642-2323, 8 A.M.–2 P.M. Thurs.–Mon., 9 A.M.–2 P.M. Tues. and 4:30–8:30 P.M. Sun.–Thurs., 4:30–9 P.M. Fri.–Saturday) with traditional American breakfasts, lunches, and dinners. The restaurant features iron-skillet fried chicken, pot roast, steaks, and seafood, with homemade bread and jam, all served in heaping helpings.

Chico's Pizza (Hwy. 103, right near Sid's Market, Seaview, 360/642-3207) makes tasty pizzas and pastas.

Seaview is also home to one of the peninsula's finest dining options, **The Depot** (38th & L, Seaview, 360/642-7880). Cozied up inside of a restored train station, this creative café plates inventive dishes like grilled wild boar on mashed fava beans and house-made cannelloni stuffed with fresh crab and saffron béchamel sauce.

Ocean Park

The Dunes Restaurant (1507 Bay Ave., Ocean Park, 360/665-6677, 7 A.M.–8 P.M. Sun.–Thurs., 7 A.M.–9 P.M. Fri.–Sat.) serves fresh fish, clam chowder, and Saturday night prime rib. Another good spot to nibble on seafood is **Pilot House Restaurant and Lounge** (1201 West Bay Ave., 360/665-3800, 6:30 A.M.–8 P.M. Sun.–Thurs., 6:30 A.M.–9 P.M. Fri.–Sat.), which serves steaks and pastas along with an ocean view. This is also a convenient spot for country-style breakfasts. In the same building above Pilot House, **Luigi's** (1201 Bay Ave., 360/665-3174, 5–8 P.M. Sun.–Thurs., 4–8 P.M. Fri.–Sat.) bakes up pizza and other Italian classics in a casual setting.

INFORMATION AND SERVICES

Long Beach is the place to go to do your laundry, buy groceries, or get your car washed. Get information at the **Long Beach Peninsula Visitors Bureau** (at the junction of Hwys. 101 and 103, 360/642-2400 or 800/451-2542, www.funbeach.com, 9 A.M.–5 P.M. Mon.–Sat. and 9 A.M.–4 P.M. Sun. in summer, 9 A.M.–4 P.M. Mon.–Sat. fall–spring). Call **Long Beach Info-Line** (800/835-8846) for a recording of current activities, festivals, fun things to do, B&Bs, and more.

The two local **public libraries** are in Ilwaco (158 1st Ave. N, 360/642-3908) and in Ocean Park (1308 256th Pl., 360/665-4184).

GETTING THERE AND AROUND

Getting Around

The Long Beach Peninsula is divided by two parallel main roads: Highway 103, going through the commercial centers on the ocean side, and Sandridge Road, passing the largely residential sections on the bay side. The roads intersect at Oysterville, where only one road continues to Leadbetter Point.

Pacific Transit System (360/642-9418 or 800/642-9418, Mon.–Sat.) has countywide bus service, and dial-a-ride service in certain areas. The system connects with Grays Harbor Transit buses in Aberdeen, and also crosses the bridge to Astoria, Oregon. There is no Greyhound service to the area, and the nearest airport with commercial service is in Astoria. For taxi service, call **Limo Cab** (360/642-4047).

Beach Driving

Approximately 15 miles of Long Beach are open to driving during the summer, but stay on the hard-packed sand, away from the car-eating soft sand and rich clam beds along the water's edge. The sand dunes are off-limits to all vehicles. The maximum speed is 25 mph, and it *is* enforced. If you decide to drive the beach, be sure to wash the salt spray off your car immediately to prevent later rust problems. Check at the visitors center for a current description of areas open to beach driving.

APPROACHING LONG BEACH

From Raymond

Highway 101 continues south from Aberdeen to mill-town Raymond past a patchwork of Weyerhaeuser tree farms and clear-cuts. The winding road can be a traffic nightmare of logging trucks, pokey RVs, and too-few passing lanes. The cops are often out in force here, so don't even think about going over the speed limit.

Continuing south, Washington's coastline wraps around Willapa Bay, the 25-mile-long inlet protected by the Long Beach Peninsula. It is believed to be the cleanest and least developed estuary on the West Coast of the Lower 48 states. Locals posit that these waters produce the best-tasting oysters in the nation (a claim disputed by folks in Grays Harbor and Shelton). Highways 105 and 101 skirt Willapa's scenic marshy shoreline, and tree farms carpet the surrounding hills. This is timber country. A handful of small settlements—notably Raymond and South Bend—offer accommodations and meals.

SIGHTS AND RECREATION

Hikers and cyclists will enjoy the 3.5-mile **Rails to Trails** paved path that follows the river from Raymond to South Bend. Along the way, look for the historic *Krestine,* a majestic, 100-foot sailing ship that plied the North Sea waters for many years.

Follow the signs up the hill to the **Pacific County Courthouse,** built in 1910 and covered by an immense, multicolored stained-glass dome over mosaic-tile flooring. This "gilded palace of reckless extravagance" as it was called, was built at the then-extravagant cost of $132,000, but not everything is as it appears: the marble columns are actually concrete painted to look like marble. A county jail inmate painted the columns and created the decorative panels inside. The courthouse's parklike grounds—complete with a stocked duck pond—offer views of Weyerhaeuser-shaved hills and the town below.

The biggest obstacle to visiting **Long Island** in Willapa Bay is also its biggest asset. This rugged, old-forest-covered island is accessible only by private boat. The muddy tide flats and rich salt grass marshes ringing the island are important resting and feeding areas for migratory waterfowl, and the entire rock is encompassed by the **Willapa National Wildlife Refuge.**

If you can find a means to putt or row out there, you'll have the opportunity to take a stroll through a 0.75-mile trail that meanders through an ancient grove of enormous cedars carpeted with lush mosses.

You don't have to get out to the island to enjoy the wildlife, however; there are numerous turnouts along Highways 105 and 101 where you can pull off and watch herds of elk or black-tailed deer.

Boaters can reach the island from launch areas at refuge headquarters (nine miles west of Naselle and 12 miles north of Ilwaco at 3888 Hwy. 101, 360/484-3482). Before heading to the island, get a map and more information from refuge headquarters. The island has five primitive campgrounds that often fill up on summer weekends (bring your own water, no reservations), but getting there can be tough due to tidal fluctuations—during low tide, you can practically walk out to it.

EVENTS

South Bend's Memorial Day weekend **Oyster Stampede** (360/875-5608) includes oyster shucking and eating contests, wine-tasting, art shows, plus country music and dancing.

RECREATION

Camp along the bay at **Bruceport County Park** (five miles northeast of South Bend on Hwy. 101, 360/875-6611, $10–13 tent, $21 full hookups). Camping and great views across the bay are available nearby at **Bush Pioneer County Park** (2nd and Park, Bay Center, open summers only). Year-round, tenters and RV campers can find respite at **Bay Center KOA** (360/875-6344 or 800/562-7810, $31–36 full hookups, $23 tent), which has showers on-site, plus a playground and a trail to the bay.

PRACTICALITIES

The Russell House B&B (902 E. Water St., 360/875-5608 or 888/484-6907, www.russell-housebb.com, $75–145 s or d) is a beautiful antique-filled Victorian mansion with views of Willapa Bay. The four guest rooms have private or shared baths, a full breakfast is served, and kids are accepted.

If your tummy starts grumbling in Raymond, make it a point to park in front of **Slater's Diner** (124 N. 7th St., 360/942-5109, 11 A.M.–8 P.M. Sun.–Thurs., 11 A.M.–9 P.M. Fri.–Sat.). Fill up on lots of good, ol'-fashioned home cooking and maybe even spot The King in street clothes—one of its staffers moonlights as an Elvis impersonator.

The Boondocks Restaurant (1015 W. Robert Bush Dr., 360/875-5155 or 800/875-5158) is *the* place to eat in South Bend. The specialty, not surprisingly, is oysters, and for breakfast (served anytime) you'll get "hangtown fry," fresh pan-fried Willapa oysters. Also featured are seafood quiche, pastas, veal, and fresh fish.

INFORMATION

Get information about Raymond and South Bend at the **Raymond Chamber of Commerce** (415 Commercial St., 360/942-5419, http://visit.willapabay.org, 11 A.M.–9 P.M. daily).

From Oregon

Most tourists heading from I-5 in Longview and Kelso choose to rumble along the lower Columbia River from the southern Oregon side in order to reach the Long Beach Peninsula. The route along Highway 30 is faster, and it allows visitors to stop off in the unique outpost of **Astoria, Oregon** before heading over the 4.4-mile Astoria-Megler Bridge, the longest continuous-truss span bridge on the continent.

For specifics about Astoria, check out ***Moon Oregon*** by Elizabeth and Mark Morris. While in Oregon, historical enthusiasts shouldn't miss **Fort Clatsop,** the winter encampment site of the Lewis and Clark expedition, where a reconstructed fort features buckskin-clad park rangers and demonstrations all summer long.

SIGHTS

Just a couple of miles west of the Astoria-Megler Bridge on Highway 101, **Fort Columbia State Park** (360/642-3028, www.parks.wa.gov, 10 A.M.–5 P.M. daily Apr.–Sept.) is a National Historic Site built in the late 1890s. It, along with Fort Canby and Fort Stephens in Oregon, formed a triad of military bases guarding the mouth of the Columbia. Fort Columbia remained in use through World War II but never engaged in battle. It still has 30 of the original buildings, along with various concrete batteries and two rapid-firing six-inch guns that face out over the mouth of the Columbia. A couple of delightful trails wind through the steep country along the river and an interpretive center in the enlisted men's barracks features two floors' worth of history. History buffs should also make time for the old **Commander's House,** furnished with period pieces.

PRACTICALITIES

Travelers can rent one of two historic guesthouses at Fort Columbia State Park (two miles west of Astoria-Megler Bridge, 360/642-3078, www.parks.wa.gov/fortcolumbia). The first is **Scarborough House** ($268), a restored fort building with accommodations to sleep up to 12 people in four bedrooms, with a full kitchen. The house is named for Captain James Scarborough, who first built a cabin on the land where the fort now stands. Also available is **Steward's House** ($165), a quaint and historic two-bedroom home that sleeps four and has an excellent view of the Columbia River.

This stretch of 101's claim to gastronomic fame is the **Sanctuary Restaurant** (794 Hwy. 101, Chinook, 360/777-8380, www.sanctuaryrestaurant.com, noon–5 P.M. Fri.–Sun.). Housed in a century-old church, the restaurant features fresh seafood and Scandinavian specialties prepared in unusual ways. The desserts are a special treat.

INFORMATION

Pick up information about the lower Columbia River and nearby Long Beach Peninsula at the **Megler Visitor Information Center** (a mile east of the Astoria Bridge on Hwy. 401, 360/777-8388, 9 A.M.–5 P.M. daily May–Sept., 11 A.M.–4 P.M. Fri., 9 A.M.–4 P.M. Sat., 10 A.M.–4 P.M. Sun. Oct.–Nov. and Mar.–Apr., closed Dec.–Feb.), overlooking the river at Megler Cove.

Along Ocean Beach Highway

On the Washington side of the Columbia River, Highway 4 hugs the riverbank for long stretches. This is the road less traveled. Tall cottonwood trees line the riverbanks; high rocky cliffs and Douglas fir trees line the slopes above the highway. As you drive west, the lower Columbia is marked by a series of islands, many little more than sandbars with a fringe of willows and grass. The road banks away from the river at Skamokawa, where it heads toward the sinuous Grays River, which cuts a wide swath, with bucolic farms and fields on both sides and timber country climbing the hillsides.

SIGHTS

The first town you'll encounter after Longview is the little burg of Cathlamet. Stop to visit the small **Wahkiakum Museum** (360/795-3954, 11 A.M.–4 P.M. Tues.–Sun. June–Sept., 1–4 P.M. Thurs.–Sun. Oct.–May, $5 adults, $1 kids), which contains photos and exhibits on early logging practices. Next door is Strong Park and Waterfront Trail. In the park is an unusual geared steam locomotive that hauled logs up steep grades from 1923 to 1958.

Just south of town lies the only populated island in the lower Columbia. Settled by dairy farmers from Switzerland and Scandinavian fishermen, Puget Island offers 27 miles of quiet country roads on rolling hills ideal for a Sunday afternoon drive or bike ride. It is connected to the Washington side by a bridge across the narrow channel, and to Oregon by a small ferry, the *Wahkiakum* ($3 cars, $0.50 passengers, 5 A.M.–10 P.M. daily).

Just west of Cathlamet is the 4,400-acre **Julia Butler Hansen National Wildlife Refuge** (360/795-3915, www.r1.fws.gov), established in 1972 to protect the few remaining Columbian white-tailed deer around the lower reaches of the river. Brooks Slough Road and Steamboat Slough Road circle the refuge, offering a chance to see the small deer sharing grazing rights with dairy cattle and numerous birds, including bald eagles. To protect the deer from disturbance, hiking is prohibited, but you may see them from a blind located at a highway pullout.

Skamokawa's most notable building is **Redmen Hall,** located on a steep bluff overlooking the creek and river. The 1894 schoolhouse was taken over by the Redmen, a fraternal organization that died out in the 1950s. The restored hall is now the **River Life Interpretive Center** (1394 W. Hwy. 4, 360/795-3007, noon–4 P.M. Wed.–Sat., 1–4 P.M. Sun.), featuring historical photos, artifacts, and regional displays. Be sure to stop here and climb the belfry for extraordinary views over the Columbia River estuary.

Follow the signs from Rosburg to the only covered bridge in Washington still in use. The 158-foot-long **Grays River Covered Bridge,** on the National Register, was built in 1905 and covered five years later. The bridge was carefully restored in 1989 and is now a National Historic Landmark. A **Grays River Covered Bridge Festival** is held at the local Grange each August, and includes a parade, crafts booths, music, and a logging contest.

SPORTS AND RECREATION

The best spot to enjoy the recreational opportunities offered by the lower Columbia is in Skamokawa with its quiet estuaries, sloughs and inlets. Launch motorized craft from **Skamokawa Vista Park** (360/795-8605) or wade in at the park's sandy swimming beach (no lifeguard). This is also good place to watch ships crossing the treacherous Columbia River Bar; the busiest time is an hour before or an hour after low tide. When conditions are rough, you'll see enormous swells and waves breaking over these sandbars.

Things are much calmer and more serene along the protected waters of Steamboat Slough, a favorite paddling spot of the guides who lead kayak tours run by **Skamokawa Center** (www.skamokawapaddle.com, $70 one-day tour). The center also offers independent paddlers the chance to rent their own canoes ($40 for two hrs.) or kayaks ($20 two hrs.). Cyclists can also pick up cheap bike rentals ($12 per day) to tour the quiet country roads of Skamokawa, Cathlamet, and Puget Island.

Pitch a tent or pull up small campers halfway

between Longview and Cathlamet at **County Line Park** (2076 E. Hwy. 4, Cathlamet, 360/577-3030, $10 with electric hookups), set right on the river. There are grassy banks for picnicking and plenty of spots to settle down and plunk a line into the water.

Paddlers, RV enthusiasts, tenters, and even those who don't like roughing it too much can find a comfy camping option at the waterfront **Skamokawa Vista Park** (13 Vista Park Rd., 360/795-8605). The park offers simple tent sites ($16), RV hookups ($23), and even yurts ($36–46). Be sure to make a reservation for RV spots and yurts, as this is a popular spot.

Approximately two miles east of Naselle along Highway 4 is the pocket-sized **Salmon Creek Park** in a clump of old-growth forest. Camp here for free under the big trees along Salmon Creek.

PRACTICALITIES

Head into Cathlamet for a solid roof over your head. **Bradley House Inn** (61 Main St., Cathlamet, 360/795-3030, $79–99 d) is set literally on Main Street, offering a small-town America brand of hospitality in a 1907 Eastlake-style home. This former lumber baron mansion offers views of the town, the river, and Puget Island.

You can extend your stay on Puget Island by checking into **Redfern Farm B&B** (277 Cross Dike Rd., 360/849-4108, $55–65 s or d.) where the two guest rooms have a private bath and hot tub. A full breakfast is served, and children are not permitted.

Farther along the route, restored **Skamokawa Inn** (1391 W. Hwy. 4, Skamokawa, 360/795-8300 or 888/920-2777) is the unofficial town square. You'll find a general store, post office, and café at the inn, along with a recreation center that rents kayaks and runs water trail tours. Lodging in the inn ($80 s or $90–95 d) includes a full breakfast. Bring big groups this way—also on the property are apartment and suite rentals sleeping four to 20 ($145–400).

Longview and Kelso Vicinity

The twin blue-collar cities of Longview and Kelso are sandwiched between I-5 and the Columbia River, approximately 40 miles north of Portland. With a long history in fishing and timber, this freeway stopover is a portal to the Long Beach Peninsula 70 miles to the east. It is also a gateway to Mount St. Helens and Portland, Oregon.

SIGHTS

Longview's early planning is revealed by the beautiful **Lake Sacajawea Park,** a 110-acre greenbelt that bisects the city along Nichols Boulevard with a string of serene lakes surrounded by grassy hillsides, shady trees, and a gravel jogging/cycling path.

R. A. Long Park (a.k.a. Civic Center) is a grassy green in the city's core, at the intersection of Olympia and Washington Ways. Surrounding the green are many of the city's oldest buildings, including the wonderful redbrick **Public Library** donated by the town's founder and finished in 1926.

Just up Olympia Way from the Civic Center, the **Nutty Narrows** (600 Louisiana St.) is the world's only sky bridge for squirrels. Builder and developer Amos J. Peters built it in 1963 to save the critters as they attempted to cross the busy street. Peters is honored for his effort with a many-times-greater-than-life-size squirrel sculpture between the library and sky bridge.

Visit the Cowlitz County Historical Museum (405 Allen St., Kelso, 360/577-3119, www.co.cowlitz.wa.us/museum, 9 A.M.–5 P.M. Tues.–Sat., 1–5 P.M. Sun.) to see well-presented Chinook and Cowlitz artifacts, a cabin from 1884, historic photos from the heyday of logging, and changing exhibits.

© WASHINGTON STATE TOURISM/LEVY SHECKLER

Lake Sacajawea

ENTERTAINMENT AND EVENTS

The **Columbia Theatre** (1231 Vandercook Way, 360/423-1011), a legacy from the prosperous 1920s, hosts local theater and dance groups as well as national acts. The **Southwest Washington Symphony** (360/425-5346) gives performances there November–April. During July and August, music lovers head to Lake Sacajawea for free Sunday **concerts in the park** featuring everything from tuba fests to country-western bands.

In late June, the **Cowlitz River Canoe Race** is a fast 14-mile river run that starts in Castle Rock and pulls out at Kelso. The Independence Day **Go 4th Celebration** is said to be one of the largest in the country, with a parade, logging show, rubber-duck race, concession stands, and a big fireworks show. In mid-July, the **Summer Arts Festival** attracts artisans from throughout the Lower Columbia. Held at the fairgrounds in late July or early August, the **Cowlitz County Fair** (360/577-3121) has exhibits and entertainment, including the PRCA Thunder Mountain Rodeo. In late August, the **Unique Tin Weekend** features old cars, street cruising, and dancing at the fairgrounds.

On the last Sunday of August, the **Three Rivers Air Show** attracts stunt pilots, hang gliders, hot-air balloons, military aircraft, and private planes of all types. The **Kelso Highlander Festival,** held the second weekend of September each year, features a parade, wine festival, art show, rubber-duck race, Scottish bagpipe music, dancing, and food at Tam O'Shanter Park.

SHOPPING

Pick up clothes and other essentials at the sprawling **Three Rivers Mall** (just off I-5 at Longview/Kelso exit 39, 351 Three Rivers Dr. #116, 360/577-5218, www.threeriversmall.com, 10 A.M.–9 P.M. Mon.–Sat., 11 A.M.–6 P.M. Sun.), home of big retailers such as Macy's, JCPenney, Sears, and scores of smaller specialty shops.

Stop by **Broadway Gallery** (1418 Commerce Ave., 360/577-0544, 10 A.M.–5:30 P.M. Mon.–Sat.) to see an outstanding collection of southwestern Washington art produced by more than 30 area artists, including jewelry, pottery, watercolors, weaving, baskets, sculpture, and more.

SPORTS AND RECREATION

Play a round of golf at **Mint Valley** (4002 Pennsylvania, Longview, 360/577-3395, www.mint-valley.com).

If you have a canoe, the Cowlitz River from Castle Rock to Longview is a scenic 16-mile float. The current can be strong and sandbars are visible at low water, but there are no major obstructions along the way.

Windsurfers flock to the Columbia River west and south of Longview, where wind conditions are often perfect for intermediate-level boarders.

Campers will enjoy the lush green lawns and breezy deciduous trees scattered around the pleasant **Brookhollow RV Park** (2506 Allen St., 360/577-6474 or 800/867-0453, www.brookhollow.com, $30 d full hookup, $1 extra for kids and pets), which offers campsites and RV hookups in the heart of Kelso. The closest public camping spaces are at Lewis and Clark State Park, near Winlock.

ACCOMMODATIONS

Built in 1923, **Monticello Hotel** (1405 17th Ave., Longview, 360/425-9900, $60 d) is a redbrick Italianate beauty that still stands as Longview's most elegant structure. The well-appointed luxury suites ($200–250 d) are some of the nicest in the area, and the modest regular rooms in the hotel's adjoining annex are comfortable and reasonable choices for budget travelers. The location can't be beat, as the building faces R. A. Long Park from 17th Avenue.

Sitting on 26 acres outside of town, **Rutherglen Mansion B&B** (420 Rutherglen Rd., 360/425-5816, www.rutherglenmansion.com, $95–125 d) offers three daintily decorated rooms under its English Colonial eaves. Each comes with private bath and fireplace. The hostess serves a full breakfast each morning and spreads a gluttonous Sunday brunch. The restaurant downstairs also serves dinners nightly except Sunday.

Super 8 Motel (250 Kelso Dr., 360/423-8880 or 800/800-8000, www.super8.com, $69 s, $79 d) offers some of the best budget rooms in the area, along with with an indoor pool. **Comfort Inn** (440 Three Rivers Dr., 360/425-4600 or 800/228-5150, $79–109 s or d) is another good chain hotel. The property has an outdoor pool and continental breakfast, plus free Wi-Fi.

For a more personal touch at budget prices, check one of two friendly mom-and-pop motels in town. The **Town House Motel** (744 Washington Way, 360/423-7200, www.townhousemo.com, $50 s, $65 d) offers tidy rooms that include microwaves, fridges, and free high-speed Internet. The property has an outdoor heated pool, and continental breakfast is served each morning.

There's no pool at **Hudson Manor Inn** (1616 Hudson, Longview, 360/425-1100, www.hudsonmanorinn.com, $60 s, $80 d), but the rooms are a little more nicely decorated and also include fridges and microwaves. Hudson has free wireless Internet, plus a free business center and complimentary continental breakfast. The owners here are especially kind.

FOOD

Big breakfast lovers should make haste to give some meaning to the name at **Stuffy's Restaurant** (418 Long Ave., 360/423-6356, 6 A.M.–9 P.M. Mon.–Fri., 7 A.M.–9 P.M. Sat.–Sun.), which features an extensive menu, friendly family service, and enormous servings.

Or nosh on hearty sandwiches and soups, as well as cold smoothies at **Old Creekside Deli** (1323 Commerce Ave., 360/423-7225, 10 A.M.–4 P.M. Mon.–Fri., 11 A.M.–4 P.M. Sat., closed Sun.). Pick up a book at the **Benevolent Bookworm** across the street and plunk yourself down at a courtyard table to read.

Henri's Restaurant (4545 Ocean Beach Hwy., 360/425-7970, 11 A.M.–10 P.M. Sun.–Thurs., 7 A.M.–10 P.M. Fri.–Sat.) is a popular spot for the "power-lunch" business crowd. Specializing in moderately priced salmon or steak dinners and an impressive wine collection, it's open weekdays for lunch, Mon.–Sat. for dinner.

Located in—of all places—the bowling alley, **Hilander Restaurant** (1509 Allen St., 360/423-1500, 6 A.M.–midnight daily) is a real surprise. This locals' favorite serves great strawberry waffles and big omelettes for breakfast, a salad bar, homemade soups, and tasty halibut fish and chips.

Yan's Chinese Restaurant (300 Long Ave. W, 360/425-3815, 11 A.M.–10 P.M. daily) has reasonable prices and serves up ample portions.

The **Cowlitz Community Farmers Market** (7th and Washington, 360/425-1297, 8 A.M.–1 P.M. Tues. and Sat. April–Oct.) has fruit, flowers, fresh vegetables, honey, bedding plants, berries, and more.

INFORMATION

For information on either Longview or Kelso, contact the **River Cities Chamber of Commerce** (1563 Olympia Way, 360/423-8400, www.rivercitieschamber.com, 9 A.M.–5 P.M. Mon.–Fri.).

The **Kelso Visitors' Center** (just east of the I-5 entrance ramp at 105 Minor Rd., 360/577-8058, 9 A.M.–5 P.M. daily May–Oct., Wed.–Sun. only Nov.–Apr.) provides local information and a small exhibit for those who may have missed the *real* Mount St. Helens visitors centers closer to the mountain. This one has a 15-foot model of the volcano and Toutle River valley, plus photos and exhibits of the 1980 eruption.

GETTING THERE

Community Urban Bus Service (254 Oregon Way, 360/577-3399) provides local service in the Kelso-Longview area Monday–Saturday.

Getaway Express (360/636-5656, $70 one-way) operates shuttle van service between Longview/Kelso and Portland International Airport.

Amtrak (501 S 1st Ave., Kelso, 800/872-7245, www.amtrak.com) trains head north from Kelso to Centralia, Olympia, Tacoma, Seattle, and points beyond, and south to Vancouver, Portland, and California. Service is four times a day. Catch a **Greyhound** (360/423-7380 or 800/231-2222, www.greyhound.com) at the train station (501 S. 1st. Ave.) in Kelso.

COLUMBIA GORGE AND WINE COUNTRY

Follow the course of the mighty Columbia River from Vancouver eastward and you'll experience a parade of photogenic panoramas. From the sheer basalt cliffs diving into the river's depths along the Columbia Gorge to the windswept wheat hillocks of Walla Walla to the shady apple orchards of Yakima and Wenatchee, the region is the stuff of postcards.

It's not just a feast for the eyes, either: This is Washington wine country. Resting at the same latitude as the famed French wine chateaus of Bordeaux and Burgundy, central Washington's distinct landscapes are bound together in the pursuit of perfecting reds and whites. Over the last decade, the state has seen an explosion in wineries—from slightly over 100 in 1997 to more than 500 now. Most of those new growers and winemakers have set up shop in central Washington, home of seven of the eight official wine appellations in Washington.

A day's drive can put you in position to walk the rows at scenic vineyards and chat up winemakers in their cozy tasting rooms. Wine country vagabonds will also find artisan cheeses, freshly picked fruits, and other culinary delights dished up in the hidden countryside cafés and bistros that have sprung up from the region's viticultural boom. And you needn't worry about the scale after your gastronomic excess: The region offers plenty of outdoor activities that will make a four-course meal and a bottle of wine seem well justified by day's end.

Cyclists can spin on serpentine bands of blacktop winding through the country past historic

© ERICKA CHICKOWSKI

HIGHLIGHTS

Vancouver National Historic Reserve: History buffs will be in heaven here, exploring a reconstructed Hudson's Bay Company fort, turn-of-the-20th-century barracks, and a historic airfield (page 388).

Beacon Rock State Park: Lewis and Clark spotted this gigantic volcanic rock on their journey west. Climb to the top of the rock for the best view of the Gorge (page 397).

Maryhill Museum of Art: Dubbed "Castle Nowhere," this remote museum is remarkable for its collections of Rodin sculptures and chess sets (page 407).

Ellensburg Rodeo: One of the most famous cattle ropin' roundups in the country circles the wagons in Ellensburg every Labor Day weekend (page 445).

Ohme Gardens: A green oasis sitting high above the hard-scrabbled dry land east of Wenatchee, this garden sanctuary features rock terraces, alpine vegetation, soothing waterfalls and quiet ponds (page 449).

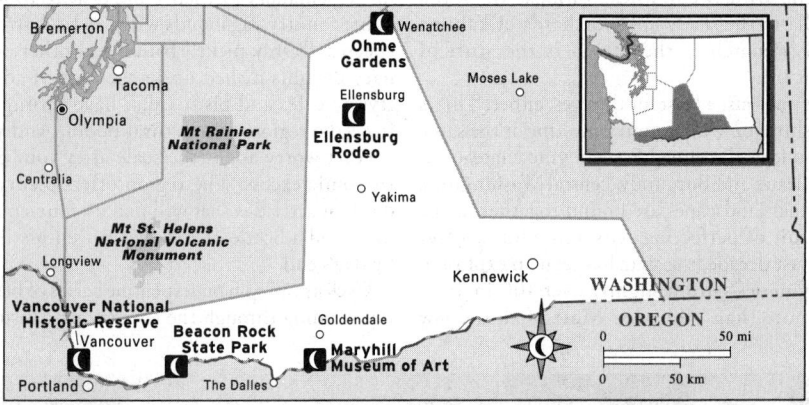

LOOK FOR TO FIND RECOMMENDED SIGHTS, ACTIVITIES, DINING, AND LODGING.

train depots and scenically dilapidated barns. Hikers and equestrians can scramble through rugged multiuse trails in ponderosa stands, desert wildflowers, and sylvan canyons. And watersports lovers will be in heaven—temperatures soar on the dry eastern side of the Cascades, making the prospect of a good drenching more than appealing. Experience the wind-whipped excitement of kitesurfing or sailboarding the Columbia River. Or enjoy a lazy afternoon tubing or fly-fishing its tributaries.

So slip on your driving gloves and prepare to hit the road. Even the most remote outposts along the Gorge and the rest of central Washington's country roads are well worth the trip.

HISTORY

In 1792, American trading captain Robert Gray discovered the great Columbia River on his journey to become the first American to sail around the world. Gray claimed the river and its huge drainage area for the United States, naming the river after his ship, the *Columbia Rediviva* (Columbus Lives Again). After Gray's discovery, Vancouver sent William Broughton out to explore the upriver territory for England; Broughton asserted that Gray hadn't found the

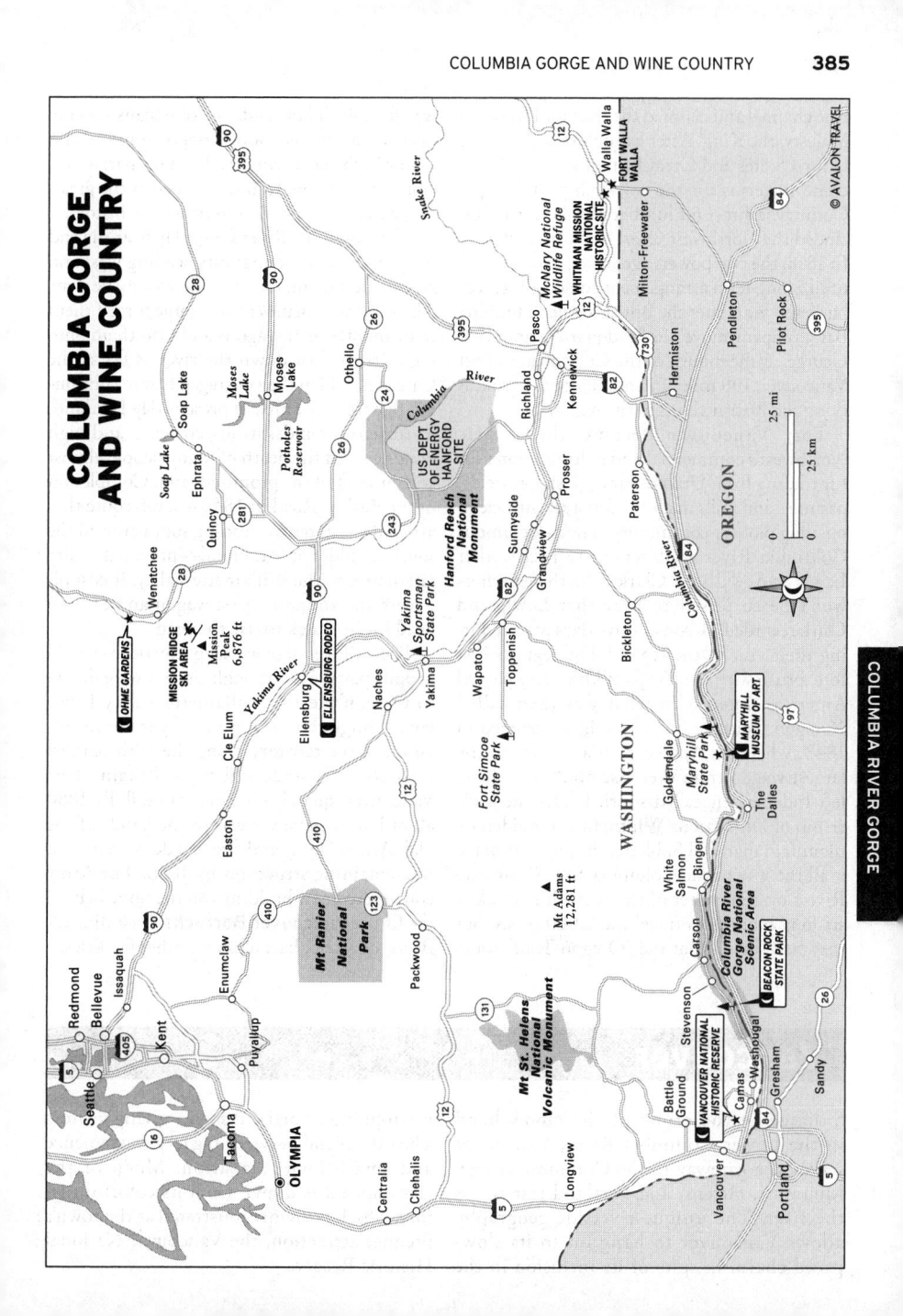
COLUMBIA GORGE AND WINE COUNTRY
Redmond
Bellevue
Issaquah
Seattle
Kent
Puyallup
Tacoma
OLYMPIA
Enumclaw
Easton
Cle Elum
Wenatchee
OHME GARDENS
MISSION RIDGE SKI AREA
Mission Peak 6,876 ft
Yakima River
Ellensburg
ELLENSBURG RODEO
Quincy
Ephrata
Soap Lake
Moses Lake
Potholes Reservoir
Mt Rainier National Park
Packwood
Centralia
Chehalis
Mt St. Helens National Volcanic Monument
Longview
Naches
Yakima
Yakima Sportsman State Park
Wapato
Toppenish
Fort Simcoe State Park
Mt Adams 12,281 ft
Sunnyside
Grandview
Prosser
Hanford Reach National Monument
US DEPT OF ENERGY HANFORD SITE
Columbia River
Othello
Richland
Pasco
Kennewick
Snake River
McNary National Wildlife Refuge
WHITMAN MISSION NATIONAL HISTORIC SITE
Walla Walla
FORT WALLA WALLA
Milton-Freewater
Hermiston
Pendleton
Pilot Rock
Paterson
Bickleton
Goldendale
Maryhill State Park
MARYHILL MUSEUM OF ART
The Dalles
WASHINGTON
OREGON
Columbia River
White Salmon
Bingen
Carson
Stevenson
Columbia River Gorge National Scenic Area
BEACON ROCK STATE PARK
Washougal
Gresham
Sandy
Battle Ground
VANCOUVER NATIONAL HISTORIC RESERVE
Camas
Vancouver
Portland
0 25 mi
0 25 km
© AVALON TRAVEL

true channel and claimed the river for His Royal Majesty, the King. After Broughton's claim, the United States and Great Britain were unable to come to terms on the ownership of Oregon Country, a fur- and lumber-rich land that included the Northwest Coast of North America. In 1818, the two powers agreed to share the land until a long-term arrangement could be reached, but seven years later the British-owned Hudson's Bay Company moved its headquarters from Fort George, at the mouth of the Columbia, to Fort Vancouver, 100 miles inland, in hopes of solidifying the British claim to the region.

Fort Vancouver became the Pacific Northwest's commercial and cultural center for fur trading from Utah to Hawaii; shops, fields, pastures, and mills made the fort a self-sufficient, bustling pioneer community. The most famous Columbia River explorers were Meriwether Lewis and William Clark. Northwesterners won't be surprised to hear that Lewis and Clark recorded 31 consecutive days of rain during their visit to the region! The region's historic brush with the Corps of Discovery piqued American interest in what was then called "Oregon Country." The floodgates opened in 1843, when the Applegate Wagon Train, the largest wagon train ever assembled anywhere, left Independence, Missouri. Under the leadership of Dr. Marcus Whitman and guided by mountain man Bill Sublette, the pioneers made it all the way to the Columbia and Willamette Rivers by September of that year. It had taken six long months to travel the 2,000 miles, but they had shown that the "Oregon Trail" route was feasible. Thousands of Americans seeking open vistas and economic opportunity would follow in the next two decades. The march west along the Oregon Trail is regarded as the greatest peacetime migration in America's history.

The Columbia River Gorge lay near the end of the journey for emigrants heading west and posed the last major obstacle along the way. The narrow confines of the gorge forced them to dismantle their wagons and load them onto log rafts to float down the river as far as the Cascades, which they portaged before continuing by raft to the area of present-day Portland. Treacherous rapids, strong currents, and high winds caused the death of many people almost within sight of the promised land. Completion of the Barlow Road in 1846—a toll route that avoided the gorge by heading south around the south shoulder of Mt. Hood—provided a safer alternative to the Willamette Valley. It cost pioneers an exorbitant $5 a wagon and $0.10 a head for livestock to use the road.

These droves of pioneering Americans would happily pay the fee, though, as they were drawn to Oregon's fertile Willamette Valley farmland, a migration that eventually led to the division of the territory along the 49th parallel in 1846—a boundary that put Britain's Fort Vancouver squarely on American soil. By 1860 all of Fort Vancouver was in the hands of the U.S. Army. Decay and fire had destroyed all of the remaining structures by 1866. The Army constructed new buildings on the slope behind the fort at **Vancouver Barracks,** including officers' quarters, barracks and other facilities.

Vancouver

Situated in the crook of the elbow bend in the Lower Columbia River, Vancouver serves as a gateway to the Columbia Gorge, Mount St. Helens, and Portland just across the river. The unique riverside geography allows Vancouver to hang on to its slow-paced charm in spite of its inclusion in the metropolitan Portland scene, giving visitors a healthy blend between big city convenience and small-town relaxation. Much of the city's appeal is drawn from its colorful history, which is vividly illustrated at the town's premier attraction, the Vancouver National Historic Reserve.

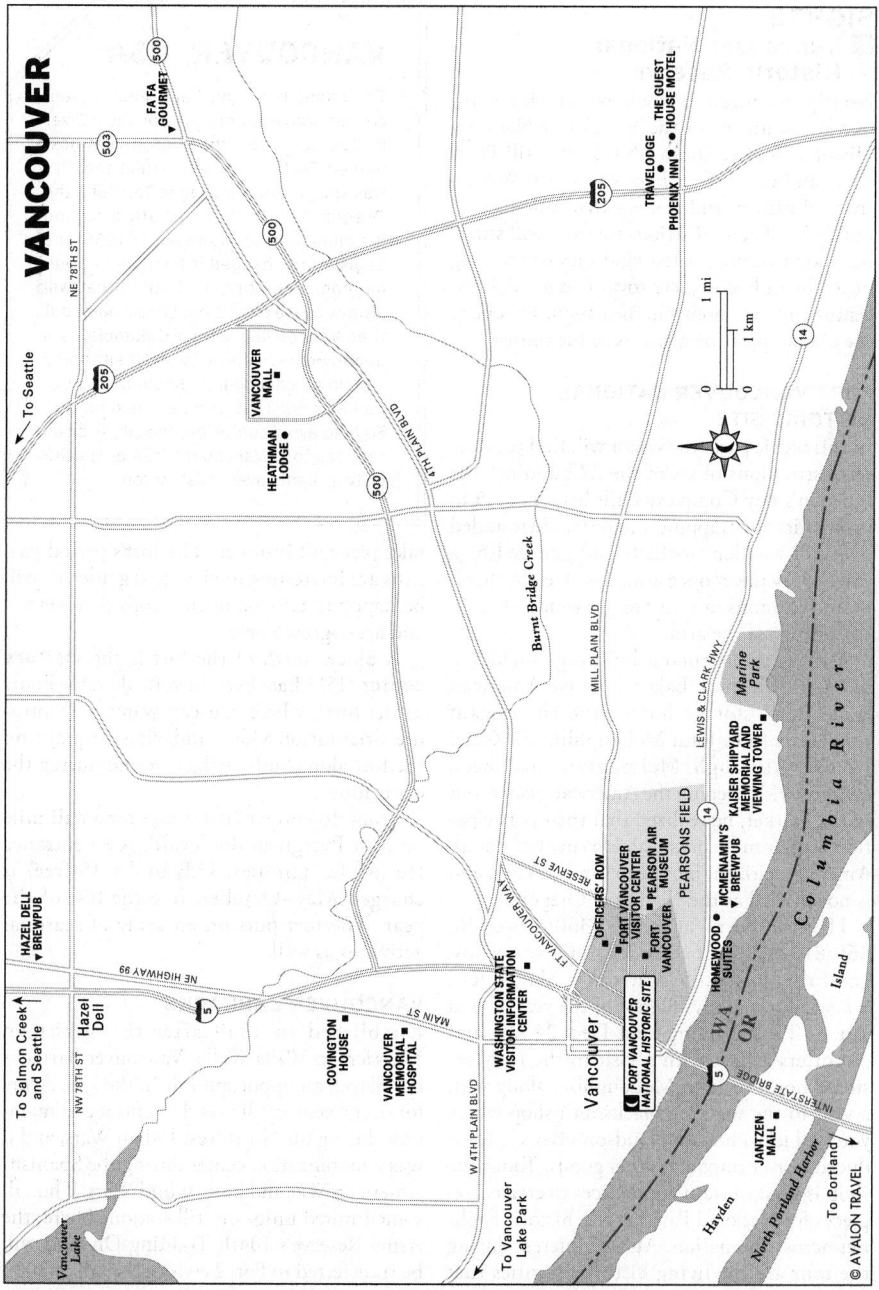
VANCOUVER
To Seattle
NE 78TH ST
FA FA GOURMET
THE GUEST HOUSE MOTEL
TRAVELODGE
PHOENIX INN
VANCOUVER MALL
HEATHMAN LODGE
47TH PLAIN BLVD
Burnt Bridge Creek
MILL PLAIN BLVD
LEWIS & CLARK HWY
Marine Park
Columbia River
KAISER SHIPYARD MEMORIAL AND VIEWING TOWER
PEARSONS FIELD
MCMENAMIN'S BREWPUB
HOMEWOOD SUITES
OFFICERS' ROW
FORT VANCOUVER VISITOR CENTER
PEARSON AIR MUSEUM
FORT VANCOUVER
FORT VANCOUVER NATIONAL HISTORIC SITE
RESERVE ST
FT VANCOUVER WAY
WASHINGTON STATE VISITOR INFORMATION CENTER
Vancouver
WA
OR
INTERSTATE BRIDGE
Island
JANTZEN MALL
Hayden
North Portland Harbor
To Portland
To Vancouver Lake Park
W 4TH PLAIN BLVD
MAIN ST
COVINGTON HOUSE
VANCOUVER MEMORIAL HOSPITAL
NE HIGHWAY 99
NW 78TH ST
Hazel Dell
HAZEL DELL BREWPUB
To Salmon Creek and Seattle
Vancouver Lake
0 1 mi
0 1 km
© AVALON TRAVEL

SIGHTS

Vancouver National Historic Reserve

No trip to Vancouver would be complete without an excursion to the Vancouver National Historic Reserve (from I-5 take E. Mill Plain Blvd. and turn left at Fort Vancouver Way), a trove of history and scenery that unfolds over hundreds of acres. Curious travelers will stumble upon a reconstructed Hudson's Bay trading post, the only complete row of restored 19th-century officers' homes in the nation, and one of the oldest operating airfields in the country.

FORT VANCOUVER NATIONAL HISTORIC SITE

In this scenic park, the visitor will find accurate reconstructions of six of the 27 buildings the Hudson's Bay Company built here in 1845 to protect its fur-trapping interests. Surrounded by a tall wooden stockade and guarded by a three-story tower once armed with eight three-pound cannons, it's easy to get wrapped up in the history of the area.

Other reconstructed buildings include a blacksmith's shop, bakery, Native American trade shop, storage house, and the elegant residence of Dr. John McLoughlin, the Chief Factor. Although McLoughlin had been charged with keeping the American traders out of the market, he realized that their participation was far more practical. He later became an American citizen, moved to Oregon City, and is now hailed as the "Father of Oregon."

Historic Fort Vancouver (360/816-6230, 360/816-6200 for recorded info, www.nps.gov/fova, 9 A.M.–5 P.M. daily Mar.–Oct., 9 A.M.–4 P.M. daily the rest of the year, closed Jan. 1, Thanksgiving, and Dec. 24, 25, and 31) offers a tour with a visit to the fully restored home of John McLoughlin, along with a visit to the working blacksmith shop where you will learn how the Hudson's Bay Co. produced beaver traps and other goods. Today the shop is used to train apprentices to create iron pieces for National Park Service historic facilities across the nation. Also of interest during the tour are the living history activities that take place all summer. The fort's period gardens are interesting to view, and gardeners will be happy to tell you of the crops that were—and are—grown here.

A block north of the fort is the **visitors center** (1511 East Evergreen Blvd., same hours as the fort), where you can watch a 15-minute orientation video and view displays on the fort along with artifacts found during the excavations.

From downtown, drive east for a half mile on East Evergreen Boulevard. A $3 entrance fee ($5 for families, kids under 15 free) is charged May–October, free the rest of the year. The fort puts on an array of seasonal activities as well.

VANCOUVER BARRACKS

Established in 1849 after the Whitman Massacre in Walla Walla, Vancouver Barracks has played an important role in the U.S. Army for over a century. It was the central command post during the Northwest Indian Wars, and it was a mobilization center during the Spanish-American War and both World Wars. Though some limited units are still stationed here, the Army Reserve's 104th Training Division will be transferred to Fort Lewis in the fall of 2009

VANCOUVER, USA

The name, honoring Capt. George Vancouver, who explored the Columbia River in 1792, came from the Hudson's Bay post named Fort Vancouver. While the city was still part of the Oregon Territory, the Oregon Territorial Legislature named it Columbia City. However, in 1855, the Legislature changed it back to its original name, creating a situation that will always cause confusion. Locals point out that Vancouver, British Columbia, is a Johnny-come-lately city and if any name should be changed, it should be the Canadian one. That prospect is doubtful. To help avoid confusion, the city is often referred to as Vancouver, USA or specifically as Vancouver, Washington.

and the Army will transfer several World War I–era barracks to the city for public use. Take a stroll down the sun-speckled, tree-lined Barnes Street and McClellan and Hatheway Roads to get a close look at the picturesque brick structures built around the turn of the 20th century.

OFFICERS' ROW

The only complete row of restored Army officers' homes in the nation is at Vancouver's Officers' Row National Historic District. The homes occupy one side of a tree-shaded street and are now used by local businesses; opposite is spacious **Central Park**—a favorite place for locals to relax on a sunny day. Find here an old Army cemetery with the graves of around 1,400 soldiers, including four Medal of Honor recipients.

The two most famous buildings on Officers' Row are houses named for General George C. Marshall and President Ulysses S. Grant. The **Marshall House** (1313 Officers' Row, 360/693-3103, 9 A.M.–5 P.M. Mon.–Fri., and 11 A.M.–6 P.M. Sat.–Sun. if no weddings are scheduled) is open for free tours and has videotapes describing the fort and Officers' Row. The building is very popular for weddings and other events, so it is often closed to the public on weekends. Named for the man who authored the famous post-WWII Marshall Plan, it was George C. Marshall's home during his time as commanding officer at Vancouver Barracks 1936–1938.

Built in 1849, **The Grant House** is the oldest remaining building on Officer's Row. This stately home was built as the commanding officer's residence and is now home to The Restaurant at Historic Reserve (360/906-1101). While President Grant never actually lived in the house, he was a frequent visitor during his time as the post's quartermaster in the 1850s.

PEARSON AIRFIELD

Ever wanted to strap into a genuine flight simulator? The **Pearson Air Museum** (1115 E. 5th St., 360/694-7026, www.pearsonairmuseum.org, 10 A.M.–5 P.M. Wed.–Sat., 11 A.M.–4 P.M. Sun. in summer, open Wed.–Sat. only the rest of the year, $8 adults, $5 seniors and active duty military with ID, $3 ages 6–12, free for kids under age 6) offers you the chance. The museum also displays dozens of aircraft and memorabilia from all periods in aviation history. The adjacent Pearson Airfield is one of the oldest operating fields in the nation; its first landing was a dirigible that floated over from Portland in 1905, and the first plane arrived seven years later. This was also where the Russian transpolar flight ended in 1937.

Parks

Marine Park occupies the site of the Kaiser Shipyards, where "Rosie the Riveter" hurriedly constructed more than 140 ships during World War II before the facilities were decommissioned and dismantled. Today you can climb a three-story riverside tower next to Kaiser Center for dramatic views of Vancouver and Portland. Also in the park is the new **Water Resources Education Center** (4600 S.E. Columbia Way, 360/696-8478, 9 A.M.–5 P.M. Mon.–Sat., free). The center houses hands-on exhibits, a video theater, and a 350-gallon aquarium filled with Columbia River creatures. Not far away is the **Chkalov Monument,** commemorating the Soviet transpolar flight of 1937, when three Russian aviators were the first to cross over the north pole and into America.

Old Apple Tree Park, along the river just east of I-5, honors what is believed to be the oldest apple tree in the Northwest. The tree was planted in 1826 and still bears small green apples each summer.

Shady **Esther Short Park** (W. 6th and Esther) contains the historic Slocum House Theater, along with a Victorian rose garden, playground, and a monument to pioneer women. The site is a popular one for festivals and concerts throughout the summer.

Ridgefield National Wildlife Refuge

About half an hour north of Vancouver, nature lovers will have ample opportunity to explore fields, woodlands, and wetlands at **Ridgefield**

National Wildlife Refuge (360/887-4106), which fans over 5,150 acres around the marshy lower Columbia River. Bring your binoculars in winter, when up to 10,000 geese and 40,000 ducks land here. Hiking and fishing are permitted—the two-mile **Oaks to Wetlands Wildlife Trail** is popular with all ages. Parts of the refuge are closed October–mid-April.

Other Sights

The **Clark County Historical Museum** (1511 Main St., 360/993-5679, http://cchmuseum.org, 11 A.M.–4 P.M. Tues.–Sat., $4 adults, $3 students and seniors, $2 children 6–18, $10 for a family of four, free for historical society members and children under 5) hosts a changing lineup of exhibits related to Clark County History.

Be sure to drive by the **St. James Church** (12th and Washington Sts.). Built in 1885, this was the first Gothic Revival-style church in Washington and is home to the state's longest-standing Catholic congregation.

ENTERTAINMENT AND EVENTS

Nightlife

Enjoy the Columbia River view from **Beaches Restaurant & Bar** (1919 S.E. Columbia River Dr., 360/699-1592, www.beachesrestaurantandbar.com, 11 A.M.–9 P.M. Sun.–Mon., 11 A.M.–10 P.M. Tues.–Sat., bar open until 2 A.M.), a fun place with tasty appetizers, a diverse menu, and a hopping bar. Also facing the river is **Who-Song and Larry's Cantina** (111 E. Columbia Way, 360/695-1198, 11 A.M.–10 P.M. Sun.–Thurs., 11 A.M.–11 P.M. Fri.–Sat., bar open until 2 A.M.), where the singing waiters are a local phenomenon.

Wine connoisseurs should make a beeline to **Salut! Wine Company** (16020 S.E. Mill Plain Blvd., Ste. 105, 360/891-5505, www.salutwine.com) on Fridays 5–8 P.M. This well-stocked shop buzzes during these times as the locals flock to partake in the weekly tastings. Salut! also offers special events periodically on Saturday and Thursday, including Introduction to Wine classes that can make a perfect start to a tour of the wineries of central Washington. Call ahead for details, as some events are by reservation only.

The Arts

Tired of living in Portland's shadow, proud Vancouverites have worked hard to establish a lively arts and entertainment scene of their own. Skip the bridge, and check out some of these local venues.

Listed on the National Register of Historic Homes, the 60-seat **Slocum House Theater** (360/696-2497, www.slocumhouse.com) was built in 1867. The theater stages productions year-round.

Music lovers need not venture south to enjoy a quality performance. The unique **Vancouver Symphony Orchestra** (360/735-7278, www.vancouversymphony.org) attracts talented local musicians and a roster of traveling professionals to its full season of classical performances. Its venue, Skyview Concert Hall (1300 NW 139th St.), is wonderfully intimate and acoustically striking. The season runs September–May annually.

The city's well-attended **Six to Sunset** (360/619-1111, www.cityofvancouver.us, free) concert series in central Esther Short Park sets out to offer something for everyone. These weekly summertime concerts range from orchestral music to Beatles cover bands to contemporary rock. Food vendors and blanket seating complete the town carnival atmosphere.

Festivals

Don't miss the annual Vancouver Rodeo (360/896-6654, www.vancouverrodeo.com), a four-day benefit show taking place around the 4th of July. Look for bull-riding, dances, and even pony rides for the little 'uns. Also in July, the annual **Fort Vancouver Brigade Encampment** fills the fort with trappers and traders dressed in 1840 period costumes. There are tepees, baking and cooking demonstrations, tomahawk throwing, and other demonstrations.

On the first Saturday in October, the locals get together to venerate their nearly-two-century-old apple tree at the sensibly-named **Old Apple Tree Festival** (360/619-1108, free). The festival focuses on environmental and historical preservation, and the Urban Forestry Commission is on hand to give away free cuttings from the legendary tree itself. In early October, don't miss the very popular **Fort Vancouver Candlelight Tours** with interpreters dressed in 1840s period clothing.

The **Christmas Ship Parade** (www.christmasships.org) is another favorite event, with decorated vessels plying the Columbia and Willamette Rivers on the second and third weeks of December. You'll also find Officers' Row decorated with traditional evergreens for the holidays, plus concerts and carriage rides to get you in the spirit of the holidays.

SHOPPING

The two-level **Westfield Mall a.k.a Vancouver Mall** (8700 N.E. Vancouver Mall Dr., 360/892-6255) has over 115 shops, restaurants, and services, including JCPenney, Macy's, Nordstrom, Sears, and Old Navy. It is hard to miss at the junction of Interstate 205 and Highway 500.

SPORTS AND RECREATION

The 14-foot-wide, paved **Columbia River Waterfront Trail** follows the shore eastward for 3.5 miles from downtown to Tidewater Cove. It's a wonderful place for a sunset stroll or bike ride. Find trailheads at Wintler Community Park, Marine Park, Waterfront Park or downtown Vancouver.

Vancouver Lake Park (6801 NW Lower River Rd., 360/487-7100, daily 7 A.M.–dusk daily, $2 cars, free for pedestrians and bikes), three miles west of downtown, is a local hot spot for both sailboarders and anglers. The nearly 300-acre strip of land offers picnicking, swimming, and fishing, plus grassy and shady areas. It is also home to one of the largest great blue heron rookeries in the region, and bald eagles can be found roosting in the trees during the winter months.

A 2.5-mile hiking trail connects Vancouver Lake park with **Frenchman's Bar Park** (9612 N.W. Lower River Rd., 360/619-1123, 7 A.M.–dusk daily) along the Columbia River, where there is a public beach for swimming, fishing access, and a very popular sand pit with eight volleyball courts set up in the summer.

There are no lifeguards at either park, which is why most families prefer **Salmon Creek Park** (off N.W. 117th St., 360/696-8171), a small lake with trained professionals on the lookout during the summer months.

Camping

The closest public campgrounds are **Paradise Point State Park** (360/263-2350), 16 miles north on I-5 near Woodland, and **Battle Ground Lake State Park** (360/687-4621), 20 miles northeast of town in Battle Ground. Campsites are reservable May through September by calling 888/226-7688 or visiting www.parks.wa.gov.

Private parks in the area include **Vancouver RV Park** (7603 N.E. 13th Ave., 360/695-1158, $22–38) and **99 RV Park** (1913 N.E. Leichner Rd., 360/573-0351, $20–29) in Salmon Creek.

ACCOMMODATIONS

While comfy lodging is plentiful on the Washington side of the river, dozens of motels and a hostel are also available in Portland, Oregon.

Under $100

Right in downtown Vancouver, near I-5, there is an **Econolodge** (601 Broadway, 360/693-3668, $70 s or $80 d) with standard motel rooms with fridges and microwaves. Whirlpool-bath rooms are also available.

For the touch of home that only a B&B can offer, try the **Briar Rose Inn** (314 W. 11th St., 360/694-5710, $75 d), a lovely 1908 Craftsman in the center of downtown. The four rooms, two of which have private baths, have wireless Internet and the unbeatable "Grandma's house" feel of antique sumptuousness.

There are two Shilo Inn locations in the metropolitan Vancouver area. Pass up the one downtown on East 13th; it is ho-hum at best. Instead, visit **Shilo Inn & Suites Salmon**

Creek (13206 N.E. Hwy. 99, 360/573-0511, www.shiloinns.com, $79–89 s or d) in Hazel Dell. It may not look special from the outside, but walk through the door and you'll see it is a class above most chains. The interiors are brand new and immaculate at this well-tended hotel. The property has a pool, spa, and sauna. Beds are comfortable and rooms have fridges and microwaves. There's also free Wi-Fi, continental breakfasts, and cookies during the day.

$100-150

Convenient to downtown and the fort district, **Red Lion Vancouver at the Quay** (100 Columbia St., 360/694-8341 or 800/733-5466, www.redlion.com, $100 s or $110 d) sits right at the base of the I-5 Interstate Bridge next to a 1.8-mile riverfront trail. Ask for a room with a view of the river to watch the lights of Portland twinkle over the Columbia. The furnishings and bathroom fixtures are a bit tired, but the rooms are clean and the linens are new. There's an outdoor pool, fitness center, business center, and a restaurant and lounge on premises. The hotel also offers free wireless Internet and a free Portland airport shuttle to its guests. Plus, it is pet friendly.

East of downtown, just off of I-205, is **Phoenix Inn** (12712 S.E. 2nd Circle, 360/891-9777 or 888/988-8100, www.phoenixinnsuites.com, $129 s or $134 d) with 98 mini-suites. A free continental breakfast buffet is included, along with an indoor pool and hot tub.

$150-200

Residence Inn by Marriott (8005 N.E. Parkway Dr., Orchards, 360/253-4800 or 800/331-3131, www.residenceinn.com, $159 s or $189 d) has apartment-style rooms with kitchens and fireplaces, plus an outdoor pool, hot tub, and airport shuttle.

The **Heathman Lodge** (7801 N.E. Greenwood Dr., 360/254-3100 or 888/475-3100, www.heathmanlodge.com, $119–159 s or d) is not affiliated with the über-luxurious Heathman Hotel across the Columbia in Portland, but it is one of the nicest hotels in Vancouver. It features spacious rooms and rustic lodge-style touches like wood beams, leather lampshades, and handcrafted furniture, as well as modern comforts like an indoor pool and complete exercise facility.

Homewood Suites by Hilton Hotel (701 S.E. Columbia Shores Blvd., 360/750-1100 or 800/225-5466, www.homewood-suites.com, $169 s or d) is a luxurious business hotel right on the Columbia River with kitchen suites.

$200-250

The Frank Lloyd Wright-esque **Bridge View Bed and Breakfast** (11734 S.E. Evergreen Hwy., 360/609-1381, www.bridgeviewbandb.com) was custom designed to pleasingly complement the aesthetics of the Glen Jackson Bridge under which it stands. The giant great room features a curving bank of floor-to-ceiling windows that presents views of this larger-than-life bridge and the Columbia River. The interior is also a compilation of luxe modern furnishings with shared amenities like a full kitchen, dining room, and living room with large-screen HD TV and Surround Sound. About 10 minutes east of downtown, the house has an upstairs master suite ($210) with a whirlpool tub, walk-in shower, and double-sink bathroom, plus a separate office with built-in cabinet desk. Downstairs are two standard rooms ($80) with double bed in each.

FOOD

It's a fact that many Vancouver locals cross the bridge into Portland for the bonanza of restaurants the big city offers. But for the smaller-town feel and the personal attention that comes with it, save the travel time and explore the local treats Vancouver has available.

Cafés

One place wins hands-down on the Vancouver breakfast front: **Dulin's Village Café** (1905 Main St., 360/737-9907, 7 A.M.–3 P.M. daily), with great home fries, omelettes, and whole-wheat pancakes. It's also popular at lunch with the downtown crowd.

Travelers can relax with an espresso and croissant at **Java House** (210 W. Evergreen Blvd.,

6 A.M.–5 P.M. Mon.–Fri., 8 A.M.–2 P.M. Sat., closed Sun., 360/737-2925) or **Paradise Café** (1304 Main St., 360/696-1612, 7 A.M.–5 P.M. Mon.–Fri., 8 A.M.–4 P.M. Sat., closed Sun.). Paradise also has a deli with fresh sandwiches.

Tommy O's Aloha Café (210 W. Evergreen Blvd., 360/694-5107, 6 A.M.–9 P.M. Sun.–Thurs., 8 A.M.–9:30 P.M. Fri.–Sat.), at the Vancouver Market Place, has interesting and healthy lunches like stir-fry with tofu, teriyaki burgers, and spicy chicken or beef bento, as well as soups and sandwiches.

If you can handle the suited throngs that line up at **Rosemary Cafe** (1003 Main St., Vancouver, 360/737-7611) during workday lunch hour, your patience will be rewarded. This homey café in downtown Vancouver slaps together some of the best sandwiches the city has to offer. My fave is the super grilled cheese sandwich with multiple types of cheeses on parmesan artisan bread. Rosemary also mixes remarkably fresh salads and homemade soups—I haven't tried it, but I heard the lady next to me raving about the beer cheese soup.

Contemporary Northwest

Enjoy stylish lunches and dinners in an elegant, historic setting at **The Restaurant at Historic Reserve at the Grant House** (1101 Officers' Row, 360/906-1101, www.restauranthr.com, entrées $22). Pick from a menu of glazed, grilled, and baked seafood, chops, and chickens. The restaurant also throws open the doors on Sunday mornings to serve a special brunch menu.

Lose yourself in the food amidst the din and clatter of quiet conversation and wine glasses at **1220 Main Restaurant & Bar** (1220 Main St., Ste. 100, 360/448-2020, www.1220main.com, 11 A.M.–10 P.M. Sun.–Thurs., 11 A.M.–11 P.M. Fri., 4–11 P.M. Sat.). With comfortable booths and a flair for making Northwest ingredients such as salmon and farm-fresh veggies dance in your mouth, this intimate eatery has established itself as one of Vancouver's finest. Reservations are recommended, especially Thursday–Saturday, when live musicians serenade diners.

Seafood

On the banks of the Columbia, **Joe's Crab Shack** (101 E. Columbia Way, 360/693-9211, 10 A.M.–10 P.M. Sun.–Thurs., 10 A.M.–11 P.M. Fri.–Sat.) makes up a mess of large and delectable portions of seafood.

Italian and Pizza

Try **Bortolami's Pizzaria** (9901 N.E. 7th Ave., 360/574-2598, 11:30 A.M.–8 P.M. Sun.–Mon., 11:30 A.M.–9 P.M. Tues.–Thurs., 11:30 A.M.–10 P.M. Fri.–Sat.) for gourmet pies and a good selections of microbrews on tap. Or mosey over to **Little Italy's Trattoria** (901 Washington St., 360/737-2363, 11 A.M.–9 P.M. Sun.–Thurs., 11 A.M.–10 P.M. Fri.–Sat.), which not only has good pizzas, but also a satisfying selection of Italian pasta and lasagna.

There's nothing like a perfectly crafted plate of from-scratch pasta to bring out the flavors of a locally made merlot. **Cafe Al Dente Italian Restaurant and Wine Bar** (907 Main St., 360/696-3463, www.cafealdente.net, 11 A.M.–9 P.M. Tues.–Sat.) offers the ideal combination of delectable homemade pastas and sauces with winning wine pairings for a blissful culinary experience.

Other International

For an authentic taste of Asia, try **Thai Orchid Restaurant** (1004 Washington St., 360/695-7786, 11:30 A.M.–9:30 P.M. Mon.–Fri., noon–9:30 P.M. Sat.–Sun.), serving Thai curries, noodles, and desserts, or **Fa Fa Gourmet Restaurant** (11712 N.E. 4th Plain Blvd., 360/260-1378, 11:30 A.M.–9:30 P.M. Mon.–Thurs., noon–9:30 P.M. Fri.–Sat.) for Chinese cuisine.

Hidden House is named for its builder, Lowell M. Hidden, and not for any difficulty you'll have finding it. **The Touch of Athens at Hidden House** (100 W. 13th St., 360/695-6198, 11 A.M.–2 P.M. and 5–9 P.M. Mon.–Thurs., 5–10 P.M. Fri.–Sat.) offers traditional Greek foods and atmosphere, complete with belly dancing and accordion music on weekend evenings.

Pub Grub and Burgers

Hazel Dell Brew Pub (8513 N.E. Hwy. 99, 360/576-0996) serves pub meals, including fish and chips, burgers, and pasta in a lively, noisy setting to accompany its 14 different brewed-on-the-premises beers. And the setting of **McMenamins of the Columbia Brew Pub** (1801 S.E. Columbia River Dr., 360/254-3950, www.mcmenamins.com, 11 A.M.–midnight Sun.–Wed., 11 A.M.–1 A.M. Thurs.–Sat.) is sublime, sidled up to the river on Hidden Way just east of Marine Park.

The sporting set is always at home at **Out of Bounds** (14415 S.E. Mill Plain Blvd., 360/253-4789, 11 A.M.–1:30 A.M. daily), chowing down on traditional sports-bar fare like wings, burgers, and beer.

You'll find pretty much the best fast-food burgers in the state, if not all of the Pacific Northwest at **Burgerville USA** (www.burgerville.com)—yes, Seattleites, even better than Dick's. The flagship store (360/694-4971, 7 A.M.–10 P.M. daily) is at 7401 East Mill Plain Boulevard, where the first Burgerville opened in 1961 and let loose the goodness. But I find the coolest location is the ☾ **second shop Burgerville ever opened** (307 E. Mill Plain Blvd. 360/693-8801, 7 A.M.–10 P.M. Mon.–Sat., 8 A.M.–10 P.M. Sun.); it's the only one that has been left as a walk-up stand, as it originally was built in the early 1960s. All of the food at any Burgerville is cooked with fresh ingredients, with a special focus on seasonal, local ingredients like thick-cut sweet Walla Walla onions for the fried rings and tart Northwest blackberries in the shakes and lemonade. The chain has a commitment to environmental sustainability and a policy of paying fair wages, so you're likely to be greeted with a smiling face when you step up to the counter.

Markets

The **Vancouver Farmers Market** (5th and Ester Sts., 360/737-8298, 9 A.M.–3 P.M. Sat.–Sun. April–Oct.) takes place downtown. It's a great place to look for local produce, herbs, arts and crafts, baked goods, and entertainment.

INFORMATION AND SERVICES

For maps or other information, visit the **Washington State Visitor Information Center** (750 Anderson St., 360/750-1553, 8 A.M.–5 P.M. Mon.–Fri., 8:30 A.M.–5 P.M. Sat.–Sun.) located in the O. O. Howard House of Vancouver Historic Reserve. Also helpful is the **Greater Vancouver Chamber of Commerce** (404 E. 15th St., 360/694-2588 or 800/377-7084, www.vancouverusa.com), reachable by taking a left off the I-5 Mill Plain exit 1D.

The **Gifford Pinchot National Forest Supervisor's Office** (10600 N.E. 51st Circle, Orchards, 360/891-5000, 360/891-5009 for recorded recreation information, 8 A.M.–5 P.M. Mon.–Fri.) is in Vancouver. Stop by for details on Mount St. Helens and other nearby outdoor attractions. By the way, Pinchot (PINCH-oh) is named for Gifford Pinchot, director of the U.S. Forest Service under President Theodore Roosevelt.

Emergency medical services are provided by **Legacy Salmon Creek Hospital** at (2211 N.E. 139th St., 360/487-1000). Pet medical care is available at **VCA East Mill Plain Animal Hospital** (9705 East Mill Plain Blvd., 360/892-0032).

GETTING THERE AND AROUND

The local transit system is **C-TRAN** (360/695-0123, www.c-tran.com, $1.30–2.35 per ride, $3 all-day pass, $3 express ride to Portland), which provides daily service throughout Clark County, as well as to downtown Portland.

For cross-country trips, contact **Greyhound** (613 Main St., 360/696-0186 or 800/231-2222, www.greyhound.com).

Amtrak (360/694-7307 or 800/872-7245, www.amtrak.com) trains stop at a classic early-1900s depot at the foot of West 11th Street, with daily connections north and south on the Coast Starlight, and eastward up the Columbia River aboard the Empire Builder.

For air service, head south across the Columbia River to **Portland International Airport** (7000 NE Airport Way, Portland,

OR, 877/739-4636, www.flypdx.com), second only in the Pacific Northwest to Sea-Tac International Airport. The airport is serviced by all the major domestic and international airline carriers and is a major hub for Alaska Airlines and Horizon Airlines, which offer dozens of flights to Seattle, Spokane, and other nearby Northwest destinations.

The main parking lot is $24 per day or $3 per hour here, with long-term economy parking for $8 per day. Dozens of shuttle and van carriers service Vancouver from here, including **Blue Start Transportation Group** (800/247-2272, www.bluestarbus.com, $24–32), which offers door-to-door shuttle service.

Pearson Air Field (VUO, within Vancouver National Historic Reserve) provides services to private pilots.

The Columbia Gorge

This stretch of the Columbia River is treasured by residents of both Washington and Oregon. No matter the season, no matter the weather conditions, the Gorge is always beautiful. You can choose your pace: I-84 roars along the Oregon side of the Gorge at river level, blasting through the rocky hills through a number of tunnels. On the Washington side, things are a little more relaxed. A cross between country road and highway gently follows the contours of the land and the bends of the river. On the western stretch, the Lewis and Clark Highway (Hwy. 14) winds through maple and Douglas fir forests punctuated by stunning vistas into the river valley far below.

The scenery along the route blends the green forested hills of the western section into the dry basaltic and barren hills of the eastern half.

© ERICKA CHICKOWSKI

kiteboarding the Columbia River

In a distance of just 40 miles—from Cascade Locks to The Dalles—average annual rainfall changes by 40 inches! The gorge has its own climate, and temperature extremes on the east side range from zero or less in winter to 110°F of dry heat in summer. It isn't unusual to descend into the Gorge and into a gale because this narrow gap is the only place weather systems can push through the towering mountains. Sometimes in the winter a sudden arctic blast comes down the Gorge to create an ice storm, which, around these parts, they call a "silver thaw."

The gorge between Highway 97 and I-5 is heavily traveled on both sides of the river, but the area from Highway 97 at Maryhill Museum east to Paterson is the less so, so expect fewer services. The description below follows the river up from Vancouver to McNary Dam, where the highway heads away from the river and north to the Tri-Cities area.

STURGEON

The Columbia River basin is home to an ancient monster – several thousand, in fact. The white sturgeon is the country's largest freshwater game fish, and it just happens to love the depths below any of the Columbia's dams. Measuring up to 18 feet in length and weighing up to 1,500 pounds, these prehistoric behemoths are often chased by both commercial and recreational fishermen. Check current regulations before wetting a line, and before preheating the oven, bear in mind that these bottom-feeders have plenty of time to soak up toxins over their 100-plus-year lifespan.

Information

In 1986, President Ronald Reagan signed into law a measure that established the **Columbia River Gorge National Scenic Area,** encompassing 292,000 acres on both sides of the river from Washougal to Maryhill. The national scenic area is managed jointly by the U.S. Forest Service, the states of Washington and Oregon, and six local counties across both states. Headquarters for the scenic area are in Hood River, Oregon; call 541/386-2333 for details.

A $5 National Forest Recreation Day Pass is required for parking at all Forest Service trailheads in the scenic area. Or pick up an annual Northwest Forest Pass ($30) that is valid for most national forest trailheads in Washington and Oregon. Get one from most local sporting-goods stores, any Forest Service office (800/270-7504), or at www.fs.fed.us/passespermits.

Getting There and Around

BY CAR

While the trip along Highway 14 does offer some beautiful Gorge scenery, by the time you arrive at Maryhill Museum you may feel that Columbia River trek is a bit longer than it looks on the map. This is truly a remote part of the state, so stock up on soft drinks, chips, and other necessities first.

Also keep your eyes peeled for speed limit signs. The now-you-see-'em-now-you-don't towns that you'll whiz by require slower speeds within their sometimes hard-to-gauge boundaries, creating speed traps that are zealously checked by local cops.

SCENIC CRUISES

Take a cruise on the Columbia, with views of steep basalt cliffs and stops at Cascade Locks, Bonneville Dam, and Stevenson, aboard the triple-decked sternwheeler ***Columbia Gorge*** (503/224-3900, www.portlandspirit.com). The cruise boards at Marine Park at Cascade Locks in the heart of the Scenic Area and ranges $20–90 depending on the length of the trip as well as several dining options.

BY TRAIN

Amtrak (800/872-7245, www.amtrak.com) has service up the Columbia Gorge, departing from Portland or Vancouver and stopping at Bingen/White Salmon and Wishram before continuing to Pasco, Spokane, and points east.

BY BUS

Bus service to these parts is close to nonexistent. Vancouver's **C-TRAN** (360/695-0123, www.c-tran.com) will get you as far east as Camas and Washougal. Cross over to the Oregon side for Greyhound bus service along I-84.

CAMAS AND WASHOUGAL AREA

While the sight and scent of the enormous Georgia-Pacific paper mill seem to dominate Camas, Camas and neighboring Washougal are attractive small towns right along the Columbia, with big trees lining the main route.

Sights and Recreation

The **Two Rivers Heritage Museum** (Front and 16th Streets, 360/835-8742, 11 A.M.–3 P.M. Tues.–Sat., $3 adults, $2 seniors, $1 ages 6–18) in Washougal has local historical artifacts and photos. A lovely walking path along the Columbia River levee leaves from Steamboat Landing Park in Washougal.

The **Rocket City Neon Museum** (1554 N.E. 3rd Ave., Camas, 360/571-5885) is one of the more unusual museums in Washington, with hundreds of neon signs, some more than 50 years old.

On Highway 14 between Washougal and North Bonneville, the **Cape Horn Viewpoint** (milepost 25) provides a good spot for photographing the dramatic west entrance to the Gorge and for viewing massive Beacon Rock. For a short and scenic side trip, take Cape Horn Drive downhill to the river, through overhanging maples and Douglas fir trees.

Washougal's claim to fame is the **Pendleton Woolen Mill** (17th and A Sts., 503/226-4801 or 800/568-2480, www.pendleton-usa.com), in operation since 1912 and still producing its acclaimed woolen products. The mill gives guided tours by appointment. An outlet store here sells seconds and overstocked items.

Camas has a summer-only outdoor **swimming pool** (120 N.E. 17th, 360/834-2382).

Events

Camas Days (360/834-2472), held annually on the fourth weekend of July, includes a parade, wine and microbrew street, live entertainment, craft and food booths, and of course, the bathtub races, which are not to be missed.

Accommodations and Food

For the most basic of accommodations, consider staying at the **Rama Inn** (544 6th St., Washougal, 360/835-8591, $55 s or $65 d), which has an outdoor pool on premises.

The stately colonial Greek-revival **Fairgate Inn** (2213 N.W. 23rd Ave, Camas, 360/834-0861, $125–175 d) makes an attractive alternative to more humble lodgings. All eight of the elegant rooms come complete with private bath, fireplace, high-speed Internet, and a full breakfast served in the dining room.

Information

Get answers to your questions at the **Camas-Washougal Chamber of Commerce** (422 N.E. 4th Ave., Camas, 360/834-2472, www.cwchamber.com, 9 A.M.–5 P.M. Mon.–Fri.).

BEACON ROCK STATE PARK

Beacon Rock State Park (509/427-8265, www.parks.wa.gov) is 35 miles east of Vancouver on Highway 14, and just west of the little town of North Bonneville. You can't miss it; the centerpiece of the park is an 848-foot-high ancient volcano core believed to be the largest such monolith in North America. Lewis and Clark named it when they traversed the Gorge in 1805.

Hike the steep one-mile trail to the pinnacle for spectacular views of the Gorge; the trail boasts a 15 percent grade, but handrails make the hiking both easier and safer. This and other trails provide 14 miles of hiking in the park. Advanced climbers only may attempt to climb on the south side of the rock, but it is closed part of the year to protect nesting hawks; register at the trailhead. The main part of the park is north of the highway, and old roads are perfect for mountain biking and horseback riding. A four-mile trail switchbacks to the 1,200-foot summit of **Hamilton Mountain,** passing the very scenic Rodney Falls. Anglers can

© WASHINGTON STATE TOURISM/JIM POTH

Beacon Rock

launch their boats from the boat ramp to catch Columbia River white sturgeon, and campers can stay in the densely forested sites (no RV hookups) for $19, $10 for an extra vehicle. The campground is open April–October. A smaller state park campground below the noisy railroad tracks along the river is open all year, but there are no showers. Campers can take showers at the nearby private Beacon Rock RV Park (360/427-8473).

BONNEVILLE DAM AREA

Bonneville Dam snakes across the Columbia in three sections, connecting the shorelines and Bradford and Cascades Islands. This was the site of the famous Columbia River Cascades that made travel down the river so treacherous for Oregon Trail emigrants. An Army base, **Fort Cascades,** was constructed on the Washington side of the Cascades in the early 1850s and remained in use until 1861. Today, Fort Cascades Historic Site has an interesting 1.5-mile loop path with interpretive signs describing the area's rich history.

Bonneville Dam

The original Bonneville dam and power plant were built here between 1933 and 1937; a second plant was added on the Washington shore in 1981. Together they produce over a million kilowatts of power that feed into the grid for the Northwest and California.

Visit the **Bonneville Second Powerhouse** visitors center (509/427-4281, 9 A.M.–5 P.M. daily, closed major holidays), on the Washington side of the Bonneville Dam, to see the inner workings of the powerhouse (including a peek inside a spinning turbine) and informative displays. You'll feel dwarfed by the enormity of the river, dam, and surrounding hills. Windows offer a chance to watch coho, sockeye, and king salmon, along with steelhead, shad, lamprey, and other fish as they head upstream each summer and fall.

Cross **The Bridge of the Gods** ($1 toll for autos) into Oregon and visit the original **Bonneville Lock and Dam** (541/374-8820), a popular tourist spot with continuous presentations, exhibits, and fish viewing.

STEVENSON

The small town of Stevenson (pop. 1,360) has been the governmental seat for Skamania County since 1893, but it is only now starting to come into its own. An enjoyable museum, one of the fanciest lodges in Washington, and hordes of summertime windsurfers and kiteboarders give life to the awesome natural surroundings. **Rock Creek Park** (Rock Creek Dr. and Rock Creek Park Rd.) on the west side of town provides an excellent place for beginner sailboarders and kitesurfers to practice their art.

Columbia Gorge Interpretive Center

Located a mile west of Stevenson, this award-winning museum (990 S.W. Rock Creek Dr., 800/991-2338, www.columbiagorge.org, 10 A.M.–5 P.M. daily, closed Thanksgiving, Christmas, and New Year's Day, $7 adults, $6 seniors and students, $5 ages 6–12, free for kids under 6) looks across Rock Creek Cove to the

© WASHINGTON STATE TOURISM/LEVY SHECKLER

The Columbia Gorge Interpretive Center is a showcase for the area's diversity.

mighty Columbia River. Highlights include an enormous simulated basalt cliff, with its crevices filled by Native American and pioneer artifacts, a 37-foot-high fish wheel, a restored Corliss steam engine, and Native American artifacts. Another section introduces you to the spiritual side of the Columbia Gorge. The museum also is home to *objets d'art* and furniture once belonging to Russian mystic Baron Eugene Fersen, along with the world's largest collection of rosaries. Special exhibits change frequently, and a museum store features the works of local artisans.

Events

The **4th of July** brings the usual fireworks, picnics, and concessions to Skamania County; the best way to see the fireworks is aboard the sternwheeler *Columbia Gorge* (503/224-3900, www.portlandspirit.com), which offers a special tour. In late July, the **Columbia Gorge Bluegrass Festival** (800/989-9178, www.columbiagorgebluegrass.net) brings foot-stompin' music, contests, dances, and plenty of food all day long at the Rock Creek Fairgrounds in Stevenson. The annual **Skamania County Fair and Timber Carnival** (509/427-3979), held in August, offers entertainment, a parade, timber contests, exhibits, and food. The Fair prides itself on being one of the last original free fairs.

Sports and Recreation

Rent sailboards, kayaks, canoes, snowshoes, climbing gear, and mountain bikes from **Waterwalker** (509/427-2727). This popular store also offers sailboard lessons most summer afternoons.

To leave the planning and equipping to the pros and spend more time out in the wild, try **Martin's Hike and Bike** (877/290-8687, www.martinshikeandbike.com). Package tours for individuals, families, and groups get you out to waterfalls or wildflowers with a minimum of fuss, either on foot or by bike. Check online for currently scheduled trips with pickup service in North Bonneville, Stevenson, and elsewhere.

Park RVs at **Lewis & Clark RV Park** (509/427-5982, $20 nightly) in North

THE BRIDGE OF THE GODS

The Klickitat, Yakima, and Warm Springs people of the Pacific Northwest all share a legend describing the creation and destruction of a massive stone bridge spanning the Columbia River between Skamania County and Cascade Locks, Oregon. According to the Klickitat version, two great chiefs, Klickitat and Wy'East were given rich new lands by the Great Spirit, their respective lands separated by the Columbia. As a symbol of peace, the Great Spirit built an enormous bridge across the river, connecting the two territories. Unfortunately, the two groups took to fighting, and in the ensuing chaos, the enormous bridge was destroyed. It's believed that the legend refers to a historical event – roughly 500 years ago, a powerful landslide was said to have blocked the Columbia river until the water flow eroded all but a slender bridge that crossed the river. Eventually, that bridge collapsed, but the rocks from the bridge have come to form the Columbia Rapids. Today, the modern steel-and-concrete Bridge of the Gods spans the river close to where the legendary bridge was thought to have been. In order to cross, you no longer have to contend with Loo-Wit, the appointed guardian of the bridge, but you will have to pay a buck in tolls.

Bonneville, which offers well-spaced campsites on its grassy and tree-shaded property.

Accommodations

The finest luxury resort in the Gorge, **Skamania Lodge** (1131 S.W. Skamania Lodge Dr., 509/427-7700 or 800/221-7117, www.skamania.com, $209–289 d) is a huge property sporting an indoor pool, sauna, hot tubs, fitness center, tennis courts, 18-hole golf course, hiking trails, and convention facilities. The lodge has a classic feeling. Its tall windows face the Columbia River and an enormous river rock fireplace heats up the lobby. Rooms come in various sizes and have views of the mountain or the river. Pet rooms are available for an additional fee. Inside is a small Forest Service **information center and bookshop** (509/427-2528, 9 A.M.–5 P.M. daily). It also hosts guest speakers each spring and fall.

If those rates are a little rich for your blood, **Columbia Gorge Riverside** (509/427-5650, www.cgriversidelodge.com, $79–199 d) offers a cozy atmosphere in its modern, well-appointed log cabins along the Columbia River near Stevenson. It has no phones or TVs, but each has a kitchen, back deck, and access to the hot tub.

Food

Joe's El Rio (193 Hwy. 14, 509/427-4479, 4–9 P.M. daily) has authentic Mexican cuisine to eat in or carry out.

Skamania Lodge serves gourmet Northwest cuisine three meals a day in an elaborate and busy setting. Be ready to drop $40 or more per person for dinner and be sure to get reservations, especially on summer weekends. The Sunday brunch is especially popular.

Information

The **Stevenson Chamber of Commerce and Visitor Information Center** (167 N.W. 2nd, 800/989-9178, www.skamania.org, 8 A.M.–5 P.M. daily in summer, Mon.–Fri. only in winter) is the place to go for the scoop on Stevenson.

CARSON AREA

Just a few miles east of Stevenson is the little town of Carson, known for its hot springs and as an entry point into Gifford Pinchot National Forest. The drive north from Carson to the east side of Mount St. Helens offers photographic and recreational opportunities aplenty.

Sights

Historic **Carson Hot Springs Resort** (509/427-8292 or 800/607-3678, www.carsonhotspringresort.com) has been drawing visitors to its 126°F natural mineral baths since 1876. The St. Martin Hotel was built in 1897 and cabins were added in the 1920s. Hot mineral baths and wraps ($20), and one-hour massages ($60) are available and still the chief draw.

The **Big Lava Bed Geologic Area** encompasses 12,500 acres of lava beds, the eerie remains of an ancient volcano. The steep walls of the tree-covered crater rise 800 feet on the north end of the area, sheltering a meadow deep inside. When exploring the lava beds, be sure to bring plenty of water and keep track of your wanderings, since there are no marked trails to follow. It's even rumored to be haunted. Get here by heading north up Cook-Underwood Road from the town of Cook, eight miles east of Carson on Highway 14. It turns into South Prairie Road (Forest Road 66) after several miles and continues to the lava beds, approximately 14 miles up. The road follows the east side of the lava for the next 10 miles or so.

Events

For a walk far on the wild side, plan your trip to catch Carson's **Bigfoot Daze** festival, held on the last weekend of August every year. The wacky festival features talks and panels on the legendary beast plus a costume contest, sasquatch yell contest, and a chili cook-off.

Sports and Recreation

Several day hikes await the adventurous, including the Bob Kuse Memorial Trail, leading to the 1,000-foot summit of **Wind Mountain,** a three-mile hike that provides dramatic views over the Columbia Gorge and a peek at historical Indian vision-quest sites. The trailhead is a mile up Wind Mountain Road on the east side. Be on the lookout for rattlesnakes during the summer months!

For a good view of the area's peaks, take a short hike to the top of **Little Huckleberry Mountain,** best hiked mid-July to October. Take Forest Service Road 66 (along the east edge of the lava bed) to the 49 trailhead; climb the steep grade for 2.5 miles to the summit and a refreshing berry break. The trail is open to hikers, equestrians, and mountain bikers.

A $5 National Forest Recreation Day Pass is required for parking at all Forest Service trailheads in the scenic area. Or pick up an annual Northwest Forest Pass ($30) that is valid for most national forest trailheads in Washington and Oregon. Get one from most local sporting-goods stores, any Forest Service office (800/270-7504), or at www.fs.fed.us/passespermits.

Several Forest Service campgrounds are north of Carson off Wind River Road. Closest is **Panther Creek Campground** (open mid-May–mid-Nov.) nine miles up Wind River Road, and 1.5 miles up Forest Service Road 6517. This tranquil campground is on a stream and has water spigots and toilet facilities. **Beaver Campground** (mid-Apr.–Oct.) is 12 miles up Wind River Road and offers easy RV parking, fishing, and hiking. A shaded, lightly used respite, **Paradise Creek Campground** (mid-May–mid-Nov.) is 21 miles up Wind River Road, and another six miles on Forest Road 30. All three of these campgrounds range $17–34; make reservations ($9 extra) at 518/885-3639 or 877/444-6777.

Big Cedars County Park (north of Willard on Oklahoma Rd.) has 28 primitive campsites available; there are 23 more at **Home Valley County Park** (509/427-9478), along with a coin-operated shower. RVers can park at **Carson Hot Springs Resort** (509/427-8292).

Accommodations and Food

Service is known to be a bit iffy, and even the recently renovated rooms are a bit creaky at **Carson Hot Springs Resort** (509/427-8292 or 800/607-3678, www.carsonhotspringresort.com). But the hotel rooms ($80 d) and basic cabins ($60 d) at this historic hot springs are a convenient stopover for those seeking a soak in the soothing spring water. Reserve early if you plan to stay on a weekend. The restaurant serves three meals a day, none of which is likely to wow you.

For something a little nicer, **Carson Ridge Private Cabins** (509/427-7777, $210–235 s or d) redefines "roughing it" with whirlpool tubs, plush robes, and a DVD library. Each unit has a private porch with its own charming log-swing for relaxing and taking in the scenery. Wake up to a view overlooking the mountains and enjoy the full, hot breakfast served daily.

WHITE SALMON AND BINGEN

Continuing eastward from Carson and Home Valley, the highway passes the trailhead (Forest Pass required for parking) for **Dog Mountain Trail,** a rugged, switchback-filled, 3.5-mile climb to the summit of this 2,900-foot peak.

This is a good chance to stretch your legs and enjoy wildflower-filled meadows in spring. Beyond the trailhead, the Lewis and Clark Highway cuts through five short tunnels and the landscape begins to open up, with fewer trees and broader vistas. At Cook-Underwood Road, you'll encounter **Little White Salmon/Willard National Fish Hatchery** (13 miles east of Stevenson) and the **Spring Creek National Fish Hatchery** (two miles west of the Hood River Bridge). Both are free to visit and open 7:30 A.M.–4 P.M. daily. Their goal is the reestablishment of a self-sustaining coho salmon fishery in the Wenatchee River Basin.

The German-themed speed-trap known as Bingen (pop. 700) straddles Highway 14; its bigger twin, White Salmon (pop. 2,330), is just 1.5 miles up the hill. Bingen has a big SDS Lumber Company sawmill, which produces 8.5 megawatts of electricity per hour with its surplus steam alone. White Salmon, meanwhile, has several Bavarian-style buildings and a 14-bell **glockenspiel** mounted above its city hall. The only one of its kind on the west coast, it chimes hourly 8 A.M.–8 P.M. and plays music on holidays. East of these two towns, the road continues along the river's edge and through the tiny village of **Lyle.**

Sights

A well-preserved 1911 church provides the home of The **Gorge Heritage Museum** (202 E. Humbolt, Bingen, 509/493-3228, 11:30 A.M.–4:30 P.M. Thurs.–Sun. late May–Sept.). The collection includes local pioneer relics, Native American artifacts, and historic photos.

WINERIES

Wineries around this stretch of Highway 14 fall within the Columbia River Gorge (www.columbiagorgewine.com) bi-state viticultural appellation. Standing as they are on the wetter side of the mountains, the vineyards here tend to produce more delicate wines than the rest of Central Washington. The region also makes for a change of scenery compared to the rest of Washington wine country, with vineyards surrounded by more trees and vegetation than wheat fields and sagebrush.

Set on a hill overlooking Mt. Hood and the Gorge, **Wind River Cellars** (196 Spring Creek Rd., Husum, 509/493-2324, www.windrivercellars.com, 10 A.M.–6 P.M. daily, closed Dec. 15–Jan. 1, $5 tasting fee is waived if you purchase a bottle) is located off Highway 141 in Husum. Try the estate-grown white riesling in the tasting room, which is set within the winery's lovely cottage with sloping eaves and cedar deck.

Check out the all-natural winemaking process at **Klickitat Canyon Winery** (6 Lyle-Snowden Rd., Lyle, 509/365-2900, www.columbiagorgewinery.com), which prides itself on its from-the-earth methods. The wines here are fermented using only the yeast on the grapes—winemakers don't add any bi-sulfites and 100 percent of its grapes come from the Columbia Gorge, making its vintages a true reflection of the region's terroir. Klickitat offers tours and barrel room tastings noon–6 P.M. Saturday–Sunday.

Plan ahead and call **Gorge Crest Winery** (509/493-2026, www.gorgecrest.com) to schedule a tasting appointment in its modern but comfortable big red barn winery center. The grounds are gorgeous—a favorite for weddings.

Sports and Recreation

RIVER RAFTING

Between Klickitat Gorge and the White Salmon River, the area has enough thrills and spills for the hardest-core river rat. Here, you can find runs anywhere from class III up through the experts-only class IV rapids, along with an experienced pro to guide you through. The best rafting tends to run from May to June. Expect one-day trips to cost around $100, depending on your choice of runs.

All Rivers Adventures (800/743-5628, www.alladventuresrafting.com) provides full-service river guidance and even owns a private ranch available for barbecues and volleyball after your run. **Blue Sky Outfitters** (800/228-7238, www.blueskyoutfitters.com) guides one-day and overnight trips. **Wildwater River Tours** (800/522-9453, www.wildwater-river.com) takes a wide variety of trips and even offers guide training, if white water truly gets in your blood.

OTHER SPORTS AND RECREATION

North Western Lake Riding Stables (509/493-4965, www.nwstables.com) has horseback rides near White Salmon ranging $40–160 per person. Rides can be had between 8 A.M. and sunset, weather permitting. Cross the river to Oregon to pick up a rental bike at **Discovery Bikes** (116 Oak St., Hood River, Oregon, 541/386-4820, $20–55 per day), which keeps a huge corral of mountain bikes, road bikes, and kiddie bikes with training wheels on hand for visitors.

Events

White Salmon's **Spring Festival** (509/365-4565, www.whitesalmonspringfestival.com) on the third weekend of May in Rheingarten Park includes a parade, food, entertainment, and a chili cook-off. Or, for some autumnal fun, pay a visit to Bingen's **Huckleberry Fest** (509/637-0411, www.huckleberryfest.com) on the second weekend of September. The parade and talent show play second fiddle to the main attraction: the huckleberry products. If it can be made with huckleberries, you can try it here.

Accommodations

Built in 1860, **Joslyn House B&B** (706 W. Steuben, 509/493-4888, www.joslynhouse.com, $86–107 s or d) has seven antique-filled guest rooms with shared baths, plus an outdoor hot tub. A full breakfast is served, and kids are welcome. It is popular during the winter months for visitors eager to ski nearby Mt. Hood Meadows.

Another cozy inn with a long history is **Inn of the White Salmon** (172 W Jewett Blvd., 509/493-2335 or 800/972-5226, www.innofthewhitesalmon.com, $90 s or $106–135 d) in White Salmon. This homey hideaway features charming decor, wireless Internet, a fireplace, hot tub, and delicious gourmet breakfasts. Most rooms have private baths, but if you're looking for a bargain ask about the eight-bed hostel room ($25 per person).

For a break from the norm, the **Columbia River Gorge Hostel** (Humboldt and Cedar Streets, 509/493-3363, www.bingenschool.com) might be just your style. This restored 1938 schoolhouse offers 48 hostel beds ($19 pp) and six private rooms ($49 d). This place is a big hit with visiting windsurfers and rock climbers—so much so that windsurfing rentals and lessons are offered on-site and one of the Inn's amenities is a private climbing wall. A weight room, indoor basketball court, and kitchen area are among the hostel amenities. The Inn is home to memorabilia from the old school days. Reservations are recommended in midsummer.

Food

Those craving a hearty breakfast can count on satisfaction at **Big River Diner** (740 E. Steuben St., Bingen, 509/493-1414, 8 A.M.–8 P.M. daily), which serves ample portions of old favorites like biscuits and gravy, pancakes, and eggs.

For something homier, **Inn of the White Salmon** (509/493-2335) pulls out its dining chairs to nonguests who'd like to partake in its locally famous country breakfasts ($10). Phone ahead for reservations.

Road-trippin' families toting little ones should consider unloading the minivan at **Solstice Wood Fire Café** (415 W. Steuben St., Bingen, 509/493-4006, www.solsticewoodfirecafe.com, 11:30 A.M.–2 P.M. and 5–8 P.M. Mon.–Thurs., 11:30 A.M.–2 P.M. and 5–9 P.M. Fri., 11:30 A.M.–9 P.M. Sat., 11:30 A.M.–8 P.M. Sun.). This kid-friendly restaurant has a special play area and a chalkboard for the kids to unload a little of that pent-up road trip energy. The food's delish, too, with a menu full of wood-fired pizzas, sandwiches, and salads. The pizzas range from plain for picky eaters to inventive, such as the combo with chicken, potatoes, and sweet peppers. This is one of the few eateries in the gorge open on Monday.

If you're craving a really good burger, drive up Highway 141 about 10 minutes to **Hooba's** (820 Hwy. 141, Husum, 509/493-4440, www.killerburgers.com, entrées $10) at the Husum golf course. This quirky establishment makes up thick, fresh patties served on ciabatta, along with other choices like tilapia fish tacos with pineapple salsa. The carefree owner doesn't post hours—it's simply open for lunch and dinner Thursday through Sunday.

Information and Services

Get regional information from the **Mt. Adams Chamber of Commerce** (509/493-3630, business.gorge.net/mtadamschamber, 8 A.M.–5 P.M. daily June–Sept., Mon.–Fri. only the rest of the year) next to the toll bridge just west of Bingen.

Emergency medical services are provided by **Skyline Hospital** (211 Skyline Dr., 509/493-1101) in White Salmon. Pets can go to **Alpine Veterinary Hospital** (208 Lincoln Dr., 509/493-3908) in Bingen.

Getting There

The Bingen **Amtrak** (509/248-1146 or 800/872-7245, www.amtrak.com) station is located at 800 Northwest 6th Street. Service is daily, heading west to Vancouver and Portland, and east to Wishram, Pasco, Spokane, and all the way to Chicago.

THE DALLES AREA

A transformation begins east of the Lyle area as the country opens up into rolling dry hills of grass and rock. In this desolate place the rumble of long freight trains and the sounds of tugs pushing barges upriver mingle with those of nature to create a hauntingly resounding symphony.

The Dalles Dam

"The Dalles" is from the French (La Grand Dalle de la Columbia, meaning flagstone), a reference to the basaltic rocks lining the narrows. In the pre-dam days, this was the most dangerous point in the river for early navigators who approached a virtual staircase of rapids called Celiclo Falls. Most Oregon Trail travelers opted to portage around the rapids at The Dalles. For centuries the falls were a major fishing spot for Native Americans who caught salmon as they headed upstream to spawn. When Lewis and Clark visited this area in 1805, they reported a village of 21 large wooden houses and called the place a "great emporium . . . where all the neighboring nations assemble."

The dam at The Dalles was completed in 1957 and the half-mile-long powerhouse now produces some 1.8 million kilowatts of power. Some salmon still make it up this far, and Native American fishing platforms can occasionally be found on both sides of the river. At the time of this writing, there is no public access to the dam owing to Homeland Security directives.

At one time, you could camp for free in undeveloped **Spearfish Park** on the Washington side of the Dalles Bridge, but rampant drug use and a homeless invasion has lead to a crackdown by the Army Corps of Engineers. For a quick night's stay in your camper, instead visit **Columbia Hills RV Park** (111 Highway 197, 509/767-2277, $20), which has camping spaces just north of the bridge. There's also a convenience store and gas station on-site.

Horsethief Lake State Park

Located two miles east of Highway 197 on Highway 14, Horsethief Lake State Park has good trout and bass fishing from your boat or one of the park's rentals, with two boat launches—one on the lake, one on the river. Nearby is 500-foot-high Horsethief Butte, a favorite of rock climbers. The park is surrounded by some of the oldest petroglyphs and pictographs in the Northwest. The campground at Horsethief (509/767-1159, open April–Oct.) has four standard sites ($17), eight partial

WINDSURFING

Because the Columbia is the only major break in the Cascade Range, it acts as an 80-mile-long wind tunnel. The wind blowing through the Columbia Gorge provides some of the best windsurfing and kiteboarding conditions in the nation. In 1991, a windsurfer set the national speed record, 47.4 miles per hour, here. This place isn't for beginners: Gusty winds, large waves, a strong current, and frigid water make the Gorge challenging for even experienced sailors, and the constant parade of tugs and barges adds more hazards. Winds average 16 mph between March and mid-October, but most surfers and boarders prefer to come in July and August when the water is warmer and the current is slower.

The most protected waters in the Gorge are at Vancouver Lake near Vancouver, and at Horsethief Lake near the Dalles bridge, but here strong winds may make it difficult for the beginner to return to the upwind launch area. A good place to learn is The Dalles Riverfront Park, just across the river in Oregon, where you can take lessons and rent equipment in a relatively protected location. Board rentals are also available in Stevenson and Bingen, Washington, and Hood River, Oregon. If you just want to watch, the best place is near the Spring Creek Fish Hatchery three miles west of Bingen, where you may see upwards of 300 boarders on a windy August day.

Several good places for intermediate-level boarders are near Stevenson, Home Valley, Bingen, and Avery Park (east of Horsethief Lake). Avery Park is especially good because it has a long, straight stretch of river that gets nicely formed waves.

Expert-level conditions can be found at Swell City, four miles west of the Bingen Marina; the Fish Hatchery, 3.5 miles west of White Salmon; Doug's Beach, 2.5 miles east of Lyle; Maryhill State Park, where the river is less than a half mile wide; and the east end of the river near Roosevelt Park. Experts head to The Wall, 1.5 miles east of Maryhill State Park.

For general information on the sport, contact the Columbia Gorge Windsurfing Association (541/386-9225, www.cgwa.net) in Hood River, Oregon. The Gorge Cup (541/386-6561, www.gorgecup.com) has windsurfing contests throughout the summer.

More than 50 sites provide access on both sides of the Columbia River; check with local shops for details. For up-to-date wind conditions, listen to radio stations 104.5 FM and 105.5 FM, or check with windsurfing shops in Hood River, Oregon – the center of the windsurfing universe. On the Web, head to www.windance.com for live Gorge "windcams" and weather updates. Showers are available at the Lyle Merc store or the Bingen School Inn.

utility sites ($23), six primitive sites ($12), a dump station, and a restroom.

Doug's Beach State Park

This tiny park is a staging area for the throngs of windsurfers who come here all summer long to play on the Columbia River. This is not a place for beginners since the swells can reach six to eight feet at times. There's no water or camping, but it does have outhouses. The park is located 2.5 miles east of the town of Lyle along Highway 14, and seven miles west of Horsethief Lake State Park. Park hours are 6:30 A.M.–dusk in summer and 8 A.M.–dusk in winter.

Getting There

Amtrak (800/872-7245, www.amtrak.com) trains stop at the little settlement of Wishram, nine miles east of the Dalles dam. Service is daily, heading west to Bingen, Vancouver, and Portland, and east to Pasco, Spokane, and continuing all the way to Chicago.

GOLDENDALE AREA

Highway 97 heads north from the Columbia to the little town of Goldendale (pop. 3,700), 10 miles away, passing scores of cows, happily munching away or taking it easy along the route. The horizon is dominated by the snow-capped summits of Mt. Hood to the south and Mt. Adams, Mount St. Helens, and Mt. Rainier to the west. North of Goldendale, Highway 97 climbs through ponderosa pine forests as it reaches 3,107-foot **Satus Pass,** before descending into the scenic and lonely Yakama Reservation, and finally the town of Toppenish in Yakima Valley, 50 miles away. Goldendale began when the first farmers and loggers settled here in 1879 and has grown slowly over the decades since.

Sights and Recreation

Goldendale's 20-room **Presby Mansion** (127 W. Broadway, 509/773-4303, 10 A.M.–4 P.M. Mon.–Thurs., 9 A.M.–5 P.M. Fri.–Sun. mid-Apr.–mid-Oct., $4.50 adults, $1 ages 6–12, free for children under age 6) is the home of **Klickitat County Historical Museum.** Built in 1902, this magnificent white-clapboard mansion is filled with pioneer furnishings, historic photos, farm equipment, and other artifacts. Be sure to check out the annual Christmas lighting party on the first Sunday of December.

Head a mile north of town and uphill through open ponderosa pine forests to **Goldendale Observatory State Park** (509/773-3141, www.parks.wa.gov), where you'll find one of the nation's largest telescopes open to public viewing as well as several smaller portable telescopes. Take a tour and enjoy free audiovisual programs, displays, and demonstrations 2–5 P.M. and 8–midnight Wed.–Sun. April–September, 2–5 P.M. and 7–10 P.M. Friday–Sunday in winter.

Camp at **Brooks Memorial State Park** (509/773-4611, www.parks.wa.gov), 15 miles north of Goldendale on Highway 97. Tent ($19) and full-utility RV ($27) sites on 700 forested acres are available year-round. Enjoy the nine miles of hiking trails through cool coniferous forests and good trout fishing in the Klickitat River. The park has great cross-country skiing in winter, too.

Events

G'day Goldendale Community Days (509/773-3677) in early July features arts and crafts, ethnic food, a flea market, antique auction, beer garden, and parade. If the antique auction doesn't get your adrenaline pumping quite enough, check out Goldendale's annual **4th of July Demolition Derby and Motocross Race** (509/250-0206) at the Klickitat County Fairgrounds. The **Klickitat County Fair and Rodeo** (509/773-3900) is another thrill-ride held over Labor Day weekend, including a carnival, parade, and chute after chute of angry bulls! This is one little town that knows how to do "extreme."

Accommodations

Lodging options are few and far between in this area. The best choice in town is **Quality Inn** (808 E. Simcoe Dr., 509/773-5881 or 800/358-5881, $89 s or $99 d), which sports a seasonal outdoor pool, continental breakfast, and clean motel units. The price is a little over the top, mostly because they know they've gotcha.

A cheaper alternative is the **Ponderosa Motel** (775 E. Broadway St., 509/773-5842, $60 s or $70 d), which is not quite as nice as the Quality Inn, but makes up for it with friendly and attentive service.

Out in the pine country north of Goldendale, **Pine Springs Resort** (2471 Hwy. 97, 509/773-4434, www.pinespringsresort.net) is a neighborly retreat offering small cabins ($89), RV hookups ($22) and tent camping ($13). The social center of the place is a cozy snack bar with a rustic pine counter and stools and a big-screen TV. Also on premises is a game room, laundry room, grocery store, and gift shop. Dogs are welcome, and rates include free wireless Internet access.

Food

Tucked away into a restored Folk Victorian cottage on a quiet downtown Goldendale street, **The Glass Onion** (604 S. Columbus Ave., 509/773-4928, www.theglassonionrestaurant.com, 11 A.M.–4 P.M. Wed., 11 A.M.–9 P.M. Thurs.–Sat.) is a secret little treasure that foodies will want to take a detour to visit while rambling the vineyards of the Gorge. The seasonal menu is short, but every dish is an artfully plated symphony of flavors, such as the from-scratch pea soup and the grilled pork tenderloin served with ratatouille. Don't skip a salad with that entrée—they are as fresh as it gets. Check out the fine art photos displayed on the walls while waiting for your dishes—they're taken by the chef's wife, a professional photographer.

For more day-to-day fare, **Gee's Family Restaurant** (118 E Main St., Goldendale, 509/773-6999, 10:30 A.M.–9:30 P.M. Mon.–Sat., 11:30 A.M.–8:30 P.M. Sun.) has decent Americanized Chinese dishes. Interestingly enough, it also grills up Goldendale's best burgers. These suckers are big enough for a couple of lumberjacks to split.

Sodbuster's Restaurant (1040 E. Broadway, Goldendale, 509/773-6160, 6 A.M.–9 P.M. Mon.–Sat., 6 A.M.–8 P.M. Sun.) is also a reliable choice with its versatile diner menu. It's got the best breakfast fare in town.

Information and Services

For local information, stop by **Goldendale Chamber of Commerce** (903 E. Broadway, 509/773-3400, www.goldendalechamber.org, 9 A.M.–3 P.M. daily June–Sept., Mon.–Fri. only the rest of the year).

Emergency medical services are provided by **Klickitat Valley Hospital** (310 S. Roosevelt, 509/773-4022), while ailing pets can find succor at **Mid-Columbia Veterinary Clinic** (417 E. Broadway, 509/773-4363).

MARYHILL

Named after the daughter of businessman Sam Hill, the little settlement of Maryhill now boasts just 38 permanent residents. Hill dreamed that his town would one day become a thriving Quaker settlement, a wish that never materialized. The railroad man and campaigner for good roads left his mark nevertheless.

Although many of his original town buildings burned, Hill's mansion and the scale replica he built of Stonehenge as a war memorial still stand as a symbol of his hopes. The dusty intersection of Highways 14 and 97 may be remote, but it offers the wandering traveler some unique sights and some wonderful wines to add to the mystique of this place.

Sights

MARYHILL MUSEUM OF ART

You'd be hard-pressed to find a collection more wonderfully eclectic than that of the Maryhill Museum of Art (35 Maryhill Museum Dr., 509/773-3733, www.maryhillmuseum.org, 9 A.M.–5 P.M. daily Mar. 15–Nov. 15, closed the rest of the year, $7 adults, $6 seniors, $2 ages 6–16, free for kids under 6). The beautiful 1914 concrete-and-steel home was originally built as a mansion for Sam Hill but now houses exhibits ranging from an extensive selection of Auguste Rodin sculpture to hundreds of international chess sets to a full gallery of memorabilia related to Queen Marie of Romania, a close friend of Sam Hill's. Along with the surprisingly large permanent collection, Maryhill attracts top-notch traveling exhibits as well. Be sure to enjoy a moment on the patio watching the peacocks roam the grounds while enjoying the Columbia River vistas that brought Sam Hill here.

WINERIES

Overlooking the depths of the Gorge, **Cascade Cliffs Winery** (8866 Hwy. 14, 509/767-1100, www.cascadecliffs.com, 10 A.M.–6 P.M. daily) produces some deliciously obscure red wines. The winery has the distinction of bringing the first Washington-grown Barbera wine to market and is one of the few Washington wineries to produce Nebbiolo. The exposed-beam warehouse tasting room (11 A.M.–5 P.M. Fri.–Sun. Apr.–Nov.) gives visitors the opportunity to sample wines.

The real centerpiece of the Gorge's winery scene, **Maryhill Winery** (9774 Highway 14, Goldendale, 877/627-9445, www.maryhillwinery.com, 10 A.M.–6 P.M. daily) sits next door to the museum on a terraced cliff over Maryhill State Park's lush vegetation. Its comfortable tasting room and patio afford the most breathtaking scenery at any winery in the state. Much of the vineyard sits on a level below the tasting room terrace, its rows seemingly

CASTLE NOWHERE

The Northwest has no Hearst Castles or Winchester Mystery Houses, no Death Valley Scotties. In that favorite tourist category of eccentric mansions, the Northwest offers only the **Maryhill Museum of Art,** a place whose evolution from barren hillside to empty palatial home to museum took 26 years.

The museum – jokingly called "Castle Nowhere" – stands in isolated splendor on a bleak, sagebrush-strewn section of desert along the Columbia River, 100 miles east of Portland and Vancouver and 60 miles south of Yakima. This was just the setting that Seattle attorney and entrepreneur Sam Hill wanted when he was searching for a homesite early in the 20th century. Forced to be the primary breadwinner for his family at age 10, Hill grew up fast. He later went to the finest schools before becoming an attorney and gaining a strong reputation for his lawsuits against the Great Northern Railway, run by James J. Hill (no relation). James Hill was so impressed that he put Sam Hill on his payroll, so as to have him as an ally rather than an adversary. Sam would later marry the railway magnate's daughter, Mary Hill. Although many of his later ventures failed, he went on to form the "Good Roads" program and was a major force behind the creation of the Columbia River Highway, the coastal highway (101), and what would become today's Interstate 5.

MARYHILL

Hill's most extravagant venture was an attempt to establish a utopian Quaker town "where the rain of the west and the sunshine of the east meet." He purchased 7,000 acres of treeless terrain on the north side of the Columbia River south of Goldendale, and in 1914 began building his concrete palace, which was to be the farm's centerpiece. He named the spread Maryhill, after his wife, daughter, and mother-in-law, all three named Mary Hill. Hill attempted to interest Quakers – who shared his pacifist philosophy – to invest in his community. He built them a meeting hall and a few other facilities as enticement, but the Quakers declined; they wanted no part of that sun- and wind-blasted countryside. His wife, too, refused to live in this godforsaken place, taking the children and returning to Minnesota. All of

extending to the very lip of the Gorge. The panoramic view of the vineyard, the Gorge, and Mt. Hood in the background make for unbelievable sunsets. The patio is pleasant when the wind doesn't whip up too much, and the tasting room itself is an elegant affair with a river-rock fireplace and an enormous 12-foot-high oak and inlaid mirror bar built during the turn of the 20th century. Also on the premises right next to the winery arbor and tasting room is the brand new, 4,000-seat Maryhill Winery Amphitheater, which draws summertime shows such as B. B. King and Crosby, Stills and Nash.

OTHER SIGHTS

Three miles east of Maryhill is another unexpected attraction. On a hilltop surrounded by open grass and sage sits a poured-concrete **replica of England's Stonehenge** (7 A.M.–10 P.M. daily) but with all the monoliths neatly aligned. Built by Sam Hill, an ardent Quaker and pacifist, the array is a monument to Klickitat county's 13 men who lost their lives in World War I. It is meant to illustrate the needless human sacrifice of war and is believed to be the nation's first World War I memorial. The ashes of Sam Hill himself are in an urn just down the slope from Stonehenge.

Just down the hill from the Stonehenge replica are fruit orchards surrounding the small settlement of Maryhill, with its New England–style white church and old steam engine. The **Maryhill Fruit Stand** and **Gunkel Orchards** sell some of the finest peaches, apricots, cherries, and other fresh fruits that you'll ever taste.

the buildings constructed for the utopian town were destroyed in a fire in 1958.

About three miles upriver from the museum, just east of Highway 97, Hill built a concrete replica of England's Stonehenge, as it might have looked when intact, and dedicated it to the Klickitat County soldiers who died in World War I. Hill also built the Peace Arch that marks the U.S./Canadian border at Blaine, Washington.

The WWI years saw the mansion incomplete and bereft of inhabitants. After the war, President Herbert Hoover appointed Hill to a commission to help with Europe's reconstruction. There he met the three women who were responsible for Maryhill becoming a museum: Loie Fuller, a modern-dance pioneer at the Folies Bergère; Alma Spreckels, of a prominent California sugar family; and Queen Marie of Romania, whose country Hill aided during the recovery period.

Fuller was particularly enthusiastic about the project and introduced Hill to members of the Parisian artistic community. Hill soon bought a large Auguste Rodin collection of sculptures and drawings.

When the 1926 dedication of the still-unfinished museum neared, Queen Marie agreed to come to New York and cross America by train to attend the ceremonies – the first visit of any European royalty to this country. She brought along a large collection of furniture, jewelry, clothing, and religious objects to be donated to the museum. Today her collection is one of the museum's largest.

Hill died in 1931 and was interred just below the Stonehenge monument, overlooking the river. At the time of Hill's death, the museum still wasn't complete. Alma Spreckels took over the project, donating many pieces from her extensive art collection and seeing to it that the museum was finished and opened in 1940. On that occasion *Time* magazine called it "the loneliest museum in the world."

Sam Hill's original 7,000-acre spread remains intact, though most of the land is leased to ranchers and farmers. Adjoining the Stonehenge monument is the Maryhill State Park, featuring a swimming area, boat launch into the Columbia, picnic areas, and 50 overnight campsites with restrooms and hot showers.

Sports and Recreation

Maryhill State Park (509/773-5007) is five miles east of the Maryhill Museum and right along the Columbia River near the intersection of Highways 14 and 97. Maryhill State Park offers Columbia River waterfront access for boating, windsurfing, and fishing. A $7 fee grants you all-day access to one of two boat launches and a nearby dock. Once you dry off, you can also unwind taking a stroll and looking for waterfowl along 1.1 miles of trails here. The park is open for day use 6:30 A.M.–dusk in summer and 8 A.M.–dusk the rest of the year. You can also camp here year-round, in 50 full-utility RV campsites ($24), 20 standard tent sites ($17), and showers. Make reservations ($7 extra) at 888/226-7688 or www.parks.wa.gov. A **Travel Information Center** here has Columbia Gorge and Washington state information seasonally.

You can also camp or park RVs along the river at **Peach Beach Campark** (509/773-4698).

EAST TO TRI-CITIES

The stretch of Highway 14 between Maryhill and McNary Dam is some of the most sparsely populated country in Washington. Dry grassy hills provide grazing land for cattle, and a few scattered old farmsteads are slowly returning to the land. The land is bisected by tall power lines marching like misshapen insects over the landscape. There's not much traffic here, so tune in to the Spanish-language radio station, KDNA (FM 91.9) for music. Two bucolic settlements—**Roosevelt** and **Paterson**—are the only signs of human life on this side of the Columbia.

© WASHINGTON STATE TRAVEL/LEVY SHECKLER

The Maryhill Museum of Art features an extensive art collection.

John Day Lock and Dam

The John Day Lock and Dam, 24 miles upriver from The Dalles and six miles east of Stonehenge, gave birth to Lake Umatilla and produces enough electricity for two cities the size of Seattle. Here you'll find one of the largest single-lift locks in the world, hefting vessels 113 feet. At the dam on Oregon's I-84, enjoy the fish-viewing room, visitors' gallery, and Giles French Park, which has a boat launch, a picnic area, and fishing.

A good portion of the power generated is used in the enormous Columbia Aluminum Corporation plant that stretches for two-thirds of a mile next to the dam. Camp for free at undeveloped **Cliffs Park,** approximately three miles off the highway on John Day Road.

Bickleton

For a pleasant side trip, drive north from Roosevelt to the farming town of Bickleton, with a friendly café on one side of the street and a tavern on the other. Bickleton has the unique distinction of being the **bluebird capital of the world;** houses for the little guys are everywhere. The bluebird housing project started in the 1960s when Jess and Elva Brinkerhoff built one, then another and another, and soon it was a community project. When the birds leave for the winter, the 700 houses are taken down, cleaned, and painted if they need it. Spring is the best time to view the bluebirds, but you're likely to see them all summer long.

In Cleveland Pioneer Park, four miles west of town, is a delightful old **carousel** with 24 wooden horses and a musical calliope. Built at the turn of the 20th century, the carousel has been here since 1928 and is a rare type that moves around a track. The horses are locked away in a secret location with the exception of a two-day period each summer: during the **Alder Creek Pioneer Picnic and Rodeo** in mid-June. This is the oldest rodeo in the state of Washington and also a cheap thrill at only $7.

For another piece of history, visit **Bluebird Inn** (121 E. Market St., 509/896-2273), said to be Washington's oldest tavern. Built in 1892, it has a classic century-old Brunswick pool table

© ERICKA CHICKOWSKI

Stonehenge replica at Maryhill

with leather pockets (still in use), along with other local artifacts.

The **Whoop-N-Holler Ranch Museum** (East Rd. between Bickleton and Roosevelt, 509/896-2344, 10 A.M.–4 P.M. Apr.–Sept., $3) contains a lifetime of collecting by Lawrence and Ada Whitmore. Two large buildings are filled with antique cars, as well as local historical items and family heirlooms that tell the interesting story of the Whitmore family. This is one of the largest collections of antique and classic cars in the state.

Wineries

Get lost in the sweet desolation of the Horse Heaven Hills viticultural region. Call ahead and make an appointment with **Destiny Ridge Vineyard** (509/786-3497), estate vineyard of Prosser-based Alexandria Nicole Cellars and a major grower for dozens of other wineries. Take in the sweeping views of the Columbia River as winemakers take you on a 2.5-hour tour ($35) of the vineyards followed by a barrel room tasting with light hors d'oeuvres. The vineyard also recently began a "glam-camp" program. Cozy up in a 14- by 17-foot platform tent equipped with electricity and water. Campers will be serviced with food to fire up a barbecue dinner and a breakfast in the vineyards for a one-of-a-kind getaway. Call for pricing.

Also here in the hills of the state's most remote region, **Columbia Crest** Winery (Hwy. 221, Columbia Crest Dr., Paterson, 509/875-2061, www.columbia-crest.com, 10 A.M.–4:30 P.M. daily) is perched just north of Paterson with its own commanding view across the Columbia River and adjacent vineyards. Founded in 1962, and now one of Washington's largest wine producers, Columbia Crest operates much of the winery below ground, making it easier to maintain cool temperatures throughout the year.

Crow Butte State Park

Located at the site of one of many camps used by the Lewis and Clark Expedition, this 1,312-acre park sits along a lonesome stretch of highway halfway between the little towns of Roosevelt and Paterson. It offers boating, swimming, fishing, and waterskiing, with tent ($19) and RV sites ($24) and coin-operated showers. The campground is open daily late March to late October, plus winter weekends. Make reservations ($7 extra) at 888/226-7688 or www.parks.wa.gov. Crow Butte State Park covers half of an island created when the John Day Dam backed up the river to form Lake Umatilla; the other half is within **Umatilla National Wildlife Refuge** (509/546-8300, http://midcolumbiariver.fws.gov/Umatillapage.htm), which straddles both sides of the Columbia. A 0.75-mile trail leads to the top of Crow Butte (671 feet), with views across the Columbia to Mt. Hood when the weather permits; keep your eyes open for rattlesnakes. The Umatilla National Wildlife Refuge has an overlook a few miles east of Crow Butte where you can peer across the river below while browsing a brochure describing the refuge and its abundant waterfowl.

McNary Dam

By the time you reach the McNary Dam area, the land has opened into an brushy desert of sage and grass broken only by center-pivot irrigation systems. The Columbia River's McNary Lock and Dam, 30 miles south of Pasco in Umatilla, Oregon, creates 61-mile-long Lake Wallula, which reaches up past the Tri-Cities to Ice Harbor Dam.

The **McNary National Wildlife Refuge,** next to McNary Dam, has a mile-long hiking trail popular with bird-watchers. Area species include hawks, golden and bald eagles, and prairie falcons.

Information and Services

This is God's country; the combined population of Roosevelt and Paterson is a minuscule 301. As a result, services are extremely limited. If you're coming from the west and your gas tank isn't full, be sure to take the 30-minute side trip up to Goldendale to fill up. From the west or north, gas up in the Tri-Cities or Prosser. Failing to do so could wreck a trip, leaving you stranded for hours in the hot sun.

If you're starving, Roosevelt has a very basic roadhouse establishment, **M&T Bar & Grill** (215 Roosevelt Ave., Roosevelt, 509/384-9440). Paterson has no restaurant, but it does have the small **Paterson Store** (48201 Paterson Ave., 509/875-2741) with basic provisions.

Tri-Cities

The sun-scorched confluence of the Snake and Columbia Rivers marks the end of a straight-shot journey along Highway 14 and the Columbia Gorge. Here you'll find an industrious trio of cities—Kennewick, Pasco, and Richland—at the rivers' junction. The Tri-Cities are book-ended by the Yakima and Walla Walla Valleys, surrounded by bountiful fields of potatoes, grains, fruits, and veggies, much of which is exported to Pacific Rim countries.

So how does a collection of agricultural towns grow into a metropolitan area with more than 120,000 people? The answer lies north of Richland at Hanford Site, birthplace of the Manhattan Project and home to the decommissioned nuclear munitions plant whose cleanup has funneled more than $12 billion into the local economy. Lucky visitors can get an up-close look at selected portions of Hanford site during limited tours offered by the Department of Energy.

SIGHTS

Hanford Site

In a cloak of secrecy that not even the workers who built it could see through, Hanford's Plant B reactor was the birthplace of the atomic age. This was the first large-scale plutonium production reactor ever to be built, creating a supply chain of radioactive materials that made it possible to create the first atomic bomb and Fat Man, the bomb that was dropped over Nagasaki, Japan, contributing to the end of World War II.

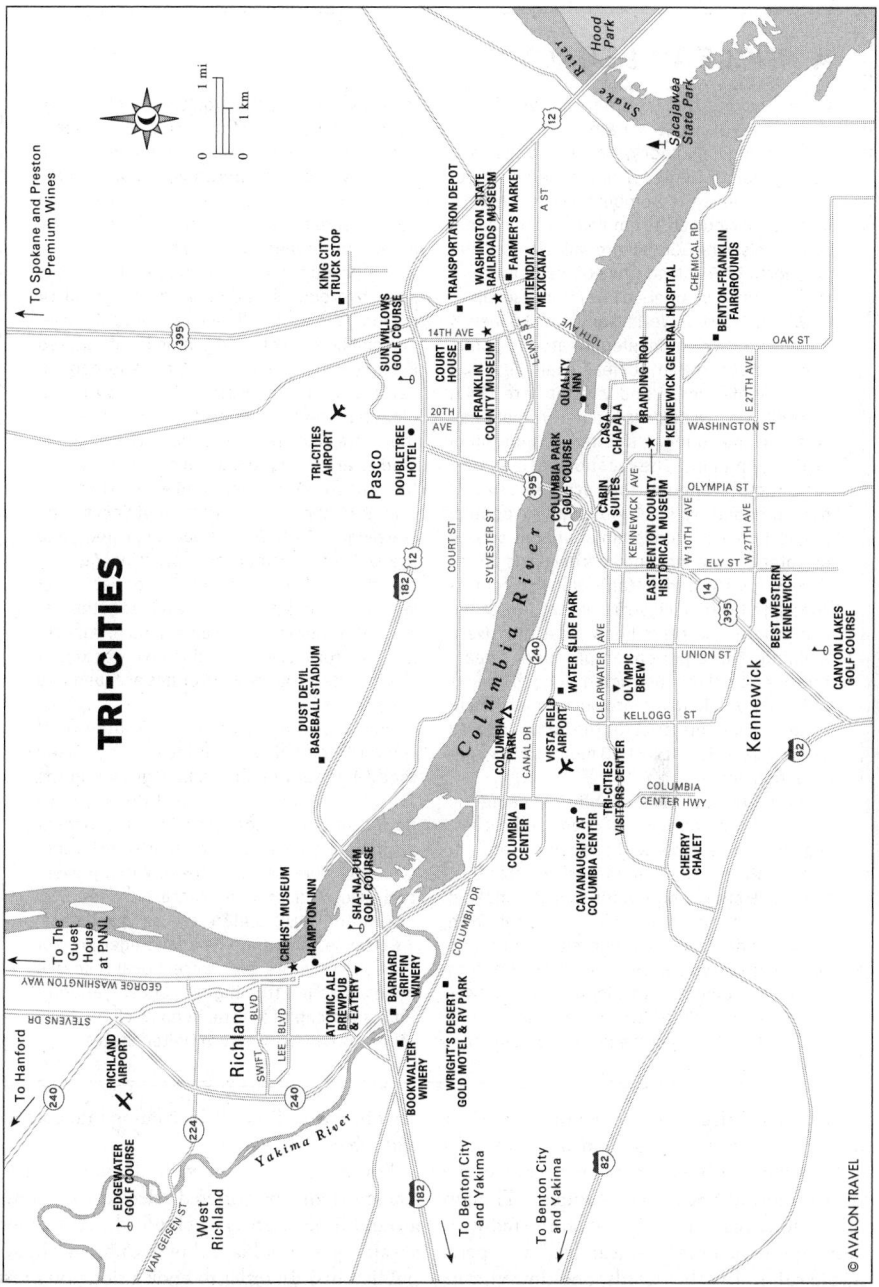

COLUMBIA RIVER GORGE

A NUCLEAR LEGACY

Cruise around the Tri-Cities and you'll find Atomic Ale Brewpub & Eatery, Atomic Body Shop, Atomic Laundry, Atomic Foods, and Atomic Health Center. The local high school team's name is the Bombers, with an atomic mushroom cloud as its emblem. There's a reason for this – the 560-square-mile Hanford Site just north of Richland, the source of much of the plutonium in America's nuclear arsenal.

With the start of World War II, the U.S. began a frenzied race to develop an atomic bomb. The first controlled nuclear chain reaction experiments were conducted in late 1942, and within a few months the government had selected the Hanford site for its plutonium production plant. The location seemed perfect: remote enough that accidents would not immediately kill thousands of people, but still near railroads, an abundant source of water for cooling, and hydroelectric power for energy. The entire Manhattan Project was conducted with such secrecy that few of the construction workers knew what they were building. Three plutonium production reactors were quickly constructed along the banks of the Columbia River, providing the concentrated nuclear material for the bomb dropped on Nagasaki, Japan, just 28 months after construction began.

During the Cold War, Hanford became the center of fuel fabrication, chemical processing, and nuclear waste management and research. Production began to slow after this, and by 1971 only one plant was still making plutonium for nuclear weapons. It shut down in 1988, and a plutonium-uranium extraction plant was closed two years later. The Hanford Site is still home to a Washington Public Power Supply System (WPPSS) nuclear plant.

After the closing of the last plutonium reactor, the environmental problems that had been shrouded in secrecy for more than 45 years began to surface. The worst damage is from the early years of operation, when the hazards were not as well understood, and when the pressure to build nuclear bombs as quickly as possible meant lax safety measures.

The production of plutonium 239 creates many byproducts, and Hanford left behind 54 million gallons of radioactive chemical waste. The highly concentrated contaminants, stored in leaky underground tanks, have spread underground into the water table. Airborne radioactive iodine collected on plants, where they were eaten by people and cattle. Ongoing studies are trying to determine the effects on these people and others who were exposed.

In 1994, the U.S. Department of Energy, the Washington State Department of Ecology, and the U.S. Environmental Protection Agency began the full-scale cleanup. The easiest problems at Hanford have been resolved in the last few years, but real problems remain, particularly the toxic stew of radioactive waste that sits in underground tanks or has escaped into the ground.

One surprising effect of the shutdown of Hanford and subsequent cleanup has been that it has spawned economic growth in the Tri-Cities. Billions of federal dollars have flowed into the region, providing employment for thousands of engineers, spill experts, construction workers, and others. With an eventual price tag of somewhere between $30 billion and $100 billion, the environmental cleanup has proven to be a far bigger project than the reactors ever were. Local research needs have led to a higher concentration of Ph.D.s per capita in little Kennewick than any other town in the western United States!

Since being decommissioned in 1968, Plant B has been meticulously scrubbed as a part of a decades-long, $1 billion-per-year cleanup of the entire Hanford Site nuclear complex. Though this historic reactor is still contaminated with radiation, none of it is "smearable," as experts would call it. In other words, one-time visitors can't be harmed simply by coming into contact with objects there.

For several years now the Department of Energy (DoE) has offered selected road tours around limited areas of Hanford that include a walking tour of Plant B (www5.hanford.gov/publictours). In order to book a slot, you must be an adult U.S. citizen who can plan well in advance. Online bookings fill up extremely quickly once the DoE announces the tour schedule. The only way to snag a free ticket is to regularly check the website. Plant B's availability may soon be opening up, though. In 2008 the building was placed on the National Registry of Historic Places, and DoE officials are currently working on plans to open the reactor to more public visits.

In spite of Hanford's toxic legacy, in a remarkable twist of fate it was also single-handedly responsible for preserving the last free-flowing, nontidal stretch of the "River of the West." The 51-square-mile buffer needed to protect outsiders from Hanford and vice versa during World War II and the Cold War is now protected as **Hanford Reach National Monument,** an amazing preserve that helps sustain healthy runs of chinook salmon and offers safe haven for deer, coyotes, bobcats, white pelicans, and other flora and fauna. For more information, contact the USFWS Monument/Refuge headquarters at 509/371-1801 or www.hanford.gov/doe/culres.

Museums

The **Columbia River Exhibition of History, Science, and Technology** (95 Lee Blvd., Richland, 509/943-900, www.crehst.org, 10 A.M.–5 P.M. Mon.–Sat., noon–5 P.M. Sun., $3.50 adults, $2.75 seniors, $2.50 children) best illustrates the Tri-Cities' split personality with agricultural and natural displays on one side, and nuclear exhibits on the other. Try out a "hot cell" manipulator arm or check out the scale models of the reactors, samples of radioactive waste containment tanks, and a Geiger counter to check your radiation level.

Just a few steps from CREHST, **Three Rivers Children's Museum** (650 George Washington Way, 509/946-5437, www.owt.com/trcm, 10 A.M.–5 P.M. Mon.–Sat., noon–5 P.M. Sun., $2.50) offers fun, hands-on exhibits that are a bit more accessible to the kiddies.

Kennewick's **East Benton County Historical Museum** (205 Keewaydin Dr., 509/582-7704, www.owt.com/ebchs, noon–4 P.M. Tues.–Sat., $2 adults, $0.50 seniors and kids) and Pasco's **Franklin County Museum** (305 N. 4th Ave., 509/547-3714, noon–4 P.M. Tues.–Sat., donation requested) display a hodgepodge of pioneer relics, old Indian artifacts, and agricultural objects.

The **Washington State Railroads Historical Society Museum** (122 N. Tacoma Ave., 509/543-4159, www.cbvcp.com/wsrhs, 9 A.M.–3 P.M. Sat., donation requested) sits across from the dilapidated old Pasco train station as a testament to its better days, with its railroad memorabilia inside and display of antique locomotives and railcars outside.

City Parks

Columbia Park (509/783-3711, www.ci.kennewick.wa.us, open year-round) forms a 609-acre border along the south shore of the Columbia River (Lake Wallula) in Kennewick, with four boat ramps for fishing and waterskiing, an 18-hole golf course, tennis courts, a picnic area, nature trails, and campsites ($7) and RV spaces ($11). One of the main attractions is a six-mile paved path that's a favorite of cyclists, in-line skaters, joggers, and lovers out for a riverside stroll. Two other popular spots are the **Columbia Park Family Fishing Pond** and **Playground of Dreams.** The pond was built by a consortium of community groups, and the playground was constructed in five days with help from over 5,000 volunteers.

Lake Sacajawea

Nine miles east of Pasco on the Snake River, **Ice Harbor Lock and Dam** is the first of four dams on the Lower Snake, with one of the highest single-lift locks in the world, rising 103 feet. Take a self-guided tour, watch the fish climb the ladders, or stop by the visitors center (9 A.M.–5 P.M. daily Apr.–Oct.).

The dam creates Lake Sacajawea, accessible for fishing, waterskiing, or swimming at **Levey Park** on the Pasco-Kahlotus Road on the lake's west side, and Charbonneau and Fishhook Parks on the east side. **Charbonneau Park** (14 miles northeast of Pasco, 509/547-7783,

© WASHINGTON STATE TOURISM/LEVY SHECKLER

Columbia Park, Tri-Cities area

Apr.–Oct., $18–22) and **Fishhook Park** (off Highway 124, May–mid-Sept., $14–22) have campsites with water, fire rings, and showers. Make reservations for both these Army Corps of Engineers campgrounds at 518/885-3639, 877/444-6777, or www.reserveusa.com.

Lake Wallula

Five miles east of Kennewick off Finley Road, **Two Rivers County Park** is open daily for boating, swimming, and picnicking along the Columbia River/Lake Wallula.

The U.S. Army Corps of Engineers operates **Hood Park** (four miles southeast of Pasco, 877/444-6777, May–mid-Sept., $18–20), just east of Pasco for boating, swimming, and picnicking. You can also camp here, on the Snake River near its confluence with the Columbia. Make reservations at 518/885-3639, 877/444-6777, or www.reserveusa.com.

Sacajawea State Park

Two miles east of Pasco off Highway 12, Sacajawea State Park (509/545-2361, www.parks.wa.gov, 6:30 A.M.–dusk Wed.–Sun. April–Sept.) sits at the confluence of the Snake and Columbia Rivers at the site where Lewis and Clark camped in 1805 on their way to the Pacific Ocean. You can fish, water-ski, or picnic here; there is no camping. An **interpretive center** (1–5 P.M. Fri.–Tues.) contains exhibits on Sacajawea—the Shoshone woman who acted as interpreter for the Lewis and Clark party—plus information about the expedition, videos, and Native American artifacts.

Juniper Dunes Wilderness

This 7,140-acre parcel of BLM wilderness (509/536-1200) is 16 miles northeast of Pasco on Pasco-Kahlotus Road. It contains the six largest remaining western juniper groves in Washington, along with sand dunes that top 120 feet high and are up to 1,200 feet long. Access is only through private land, so you'll need to get the permission of local ranchers to reach the dunes, and you may need a 4WD vehicle for the last several miles of road. There are no trails or drinking water, and summer temperatures often exceed 100°F, so come prepared.

KENNEWICK MAN

In 1996, a college student stumbled upon a skull along the Columbia's riverbank near the Tri-Cities that set off a firestorm of legal battles with long-standing ramifications. This was no murder mystery: The skull and the full skeleton that went with it were found to be 9,200 years old. Dubbed **Kennewick Man,** this ancient human was thought to have features that could possibly link him to Asian or European peoples.

The problem was, some people didn't think scientists had the right to study him. Local Native American tribes wanted the bones reburied. The case took eight years to settle, until in 2004 the courts decided in favor of the scientists unless the tribes could prove a significant cultural relationship with the remains.

The best time to visit is in the spring and fall, when temperatures are more moderate.

Wineries

Most of the best wine-tasting around the Tri-Cities can be found to the east in the Yakima Valley and to the west in Walla Walla valley. However, travelers on a tight schedule can still find enough wineries close by to fill up a pleasant afternoon.

The parklike grounds at **Preston Premium Wines** (509/545-1990, www.prestonwines.com, 10 A.M.–5:30 P.M. daily) are perfect for a picnic. The second-story deck off the tasting room overlooks the vineyards and a grassy area lined with birch trees and flower beds. Take a stroll and enjoy the antique tractors and shady gazebo. The tasting room sells a selection of gourmet goodies to get that picnic started on the right foot.

Ask the expert staff at **Bookwalter Winery** (710 S. Windmill Rd., Richland, 509/627-5000, www.bookwalterwines.com, 10 A.M.–8 P.M. Mon.–Tues., 10 A.M.–11 P.M. Wed.–Sat., 10 A.M.–6 P.M. Sun.) for help pairing tasting wines with the artisan cheeses and meats offered in its first-rate tasting room. Slide into a stool at the tasting bar or set up shop in the garden patio. In the evening hours you'll be serenaded by the live music acts that play here. If you go to Bookwalter, be sure to make time to also stop in at **Barnard Griffin Winery** (878 Tulip Lane, Richland, 509/627-0266, www.barnardgriffin.com, 10 A.M.–5 P.M. daily).

ENTERTAINMENT AND EVENTS

Nightlife

The **Coast Tri-Cities Hotel at Columbia Center** (1101 N. Columbia Center Blvd., Kennewick, 509/783-0611 or 800/325-4000) hosts lively karaoke nights on Friday, Saturday, and Sunday. **Branding Iron** (109 W. Kennewick Ave., 509/586-9292, 4 P.M.–1:30 A.M. Wed.–Sat.) plays live country and other types of music and opens up its big dance floor Thursday–Saturday and hosts karaoke on Wednesday.

The Arts

For those of classical taste, enjoy events staged by the **Mid-Columbia Symphony** (509/943-6602, www.midcolumbiasymphony.org), in existence for more than 50 years. The **Mid-Columbia Regional Ballet** (1405 Goethals, Richland, 509/946-1531) and **Columbia Basin College Performing Arts** (509/547-0511) also offer scheduled performances.

Events

The festival season kicks into high gear with the **Cinco de Mayo** Mexican festivities in Pasco. The **Columbia Valley Wineries Barrel Tasting** in early June is a favorite introduction to local wineries.

Richland's **Sunfest** is a summer-long series of weekend activities that feature international food, music, and dancing. Sunfest events include the **Tri-Cities Children's Festival** in mid-June, **Ye Merrie Greenwood Renaissance Faire** in late June, and the **Sidewalk Art Show** in late July—southeast Washington's largest arts and crafts show.

The Tri-Cities' biggest event is the annual

Unlimited hydroplane races on the Columbia River, the highlight of the late-July **Columbia Cup** (509/547-2203, www.columbiacup.com). Originally called the "Atomic Cup," the races have been going on for more than three decades. The action centers on Columbia Park in Kennewick, but you can also watch from the Pasco side if you don't mind the sun in your face; get to the park early on Friday or Saturday to take a pit tour before the races. A talent show, parade, and military aerial demonstrations round out the **Tri-Cities Water Follies** week.

Kennewick hosts the **Benton Franklin Fair and Rodeo** (1500 S. Oak St., 509/586-9211, www.bffairrodeo.com) every August, with top entertainers performing at the fairgrounds. More music, arts, food, and dancing is at the **Fiery Foods Festival** on the weekend after Labor Day. November brings the **Tri-Cities Wine Festival** to Kennewick, featuring 60 different wineries. December's big event is the **Christmas Lights Boat Parade,** when decorated boats cruise up and down the Columbia.

SHOPPING

Columbia Center in Kennewick (509/783-2108, 10 A.M.–9 P.M. Mon.–Sat., 11 A.M.–7 P.M. Sun.) is the Tri-Cities' largest shopping mall, with 100 stores including Macy's, Sears, and JCPenney. For something a bit less hectic, head to **Pasco Village Marketplace,** on the corner of 4th and Lewis in Pasco, where various shops sell arts and crafts, clothing, gourmet food, imported textiles, jewelry, and antiques.

SPORTS AND RECREATION

Cycling

The Sacajawea Heritage Trail is a 22-mile contiguous path linking Tri-Cities' parks. Kennewick's **Columbia Park** has a popular six-mile paved, nearly level path, and Richland's Riverfront Trail offers a shady seven-mile option for biking or in-line skating. Rent bikes from **Kennewick Schwinn** (3101 W. Clearwater Ave., Kennewick, 509/735-8525).

Swimming and Boating

Take your swimsuit to **Oasis Waterworks** (6321 W. Canal Dr., Kennewick, 509/735-8442, daily in summer) and try its 10 water slides, a "rolling rapids river ride," 5,000-square-foot swimming pool, shaded picnic area, 100-person hot tub, and more.

Rent pontoon boats at **Columbia Park Marina** (1776 Columbia Dr. SE, Richland, 509/783-1649).

Racing

The favorite local racing events are the hydroplane races during the Columbia Cup (509/547-2203, www.columbiacup.com).

Watch auto racing on Saturday nights in the summer at **Tri-City Raceway** (two miles west of West Richland, 509/967-3851, www.tricityraceway.com), called the fastest half-mile track west of the Mississippi.

At Kennewick's Benton-Franklin Fairgrounds, **Sundowns Horseracing Track** (E. 10th Ave., 509/582-5434) hosts quarter-horse racing in the spring and fall.

Golf

Golfers will find nine 18-hole public courses in the Tri-Cities area, including Pasco's **Sun Willows Golf Course** (2335 N. 20th, 509/545-3440, www.sunwillowsgolfcourse.com), **Columbia Point Golf Course** (225 Columbia Pt. Dr., Richland, 509/946-0710, www.cybergolf.com/columbiapoint), **Canyon Lakes Golf Course** (3700 Canyon Lakes Dr., 509/582-3736, www.canyonlakesgolfcourse.com), **Meadow Springs Country Club Golf Course** (700 Country Club Place, Richland, 509/627-2234), **Tri-Cities Country Club** (314 N. Underwood, 509/783-6014), **West Richland Municipal Golf Course** (4000 Fallon Dr., 509/967-2165), and Richland's **Horn Rapids Golf Course and Championship Putting Course** (509/375-4714, www.cybergolf.com/hornrapids).

Spectator Sports

The Tri-Cities are home to two professional teams. The **Tri-City Dust Devils** (509/374-2757, www.dustdevilsbaseball.com), a Colorado

Rockies "A" team, play at Pasco Stadium (6200 Burden), while the **Tri-City Americans** (509/783-9999, www.amshockey.com) smack the puck in the Western Hockey League.

Camping

Campers will enjoy many local state and Army Corps of Engineers parks, detailed under *Sights* in this chapter. Another area option for camping is **Columbia Park** (two miles west of Kennewick on Hwy. 240, 509/783-3711, www.ci.kennewick.wa.us).

Private RV parks in the Tri-Cities area include **Columbia Mobile Village** (4901 W. Clearwater Ave., Kennewick, 509/783-3314), **Desert Gold RV Park** (611 Columbia Dr. SE, Richland, 509/627-1000), **Green Tree RV Park** (2200 N. 4th, Pasco, 509/547-6220), **Maxey's Mobile Home Park** (3708 W. Clearwater Ave., Kennewick, 509/783-6411 or 800/722-5762), and **Trailer City Park** (7120 W. Bonnie Ave., Kennewick, 509/783-2513).

ACCOMMODATIONS

It's a good idea to book your lodging well ahead, especially during July when the hydroplane races attract throngs of visitors from across the Northwest. To get a jump, contact the chamber of commerce (800/254-5824, www.visittri-cities.com) for links to local lodging.

Under $100

Travelers on a shoestring budget will surely appreciate the facilities of **The Guest House at PNNL** (620 Battelle Boulevard, Richland, 509/943-0400, www.pnl.gov/guesthouse), a somewhat under-the-radar establishment run by the Pacific Northwest National Research Laboratory to provide lodging for visiting scientists and government workers. The unique 81-room inn offers utilitarian units reminiscent of college dorm facilities that are cleaner and better equipped than most motels running at this rate. All guests can take advantage of the grounds' courtyard, exercise room, and coin-operated laundry machines. There are several room types to choose among. A standard dorm ($35 s) comes with a single twin bed and private bath. These are clustered in groups of six to eight rooms with shared living room, dining room, and fully equipped kitchen. Queen studios ($75 s or $85 d) are larger private set-ups with microwave, fridge, and coffeemaker—bring your own utensils. The one-bedroom apartments ($80 s or $90 d) have a separate bedroom with desk, a living room with hide-a-bed, and a fully equipped kitchen.

If government-style quarters aren't your thing, then try **Wright's Desert Gold Motel & RV Park** (611 Columbia Park Trail in Richland, 509/627-1000 or 800/788-4653, $42 s or $47 d). This simple and clean motel park has an outdoor pool, hot tub, and game room.

Quality Inn (7901 W. Quinault Ave., Kennewick, 509/735-6100 or 800/205-6938, www.scinns.com, $84–94 s or d) is a slight step up. These are standard chain motel rooms, on an amenity-filled property that includes two pools, a fitness center, business center, and extended continental breakfast.

Situated in a suburban neighborhood, **Cabin Suites** (115 N. Yelm St., Kennewick, 509/374-3966 or 509/866-374-3966, $75–95 s or d) isn't a real cabin per se, but all three rooms are gussied up with rough-hewn log bed frames and plaid flannel linens. This is a private B&B, as the innkeepers don't live on-site, only coming in the morning to serve breakfast. For maximum seclusion, the whole house can be rented for $195.

$100-150

All three of the Tri-Cities are full of reasonably priced chains. One of the best values is **Hampton Inn** (486 Bradley Blvd., 509/943-4400, www.hampton-inn.com, $109 s or $114 d) in Richland. This snappily decorated establishment faces the Columbia River, offering dock facilities for boaters and a pretty view for the rest of us. Do yourself a favor and plunk down an extra $20 for a room with a view. The property has a fitness center and a hot tub and offers a continental breakfast and a complimentary airport shuttle.

Another good bet is **Best Western**

Kennewick (4001 W. 27th Ave., Kennewick, 509/586-1332 or 800/528-1234, www.bestwestern.com, $85–130 d), a clean and friendly property with a raft of amenities. There's an indoor pool, hot tub, sauna, and fitness center, plus a business center. Pets are welcome, and there's room outside to walk them. The hotel serves a hot breakfast buffet with French toast, biscuits and gravy, sausage, bacon, and more. Come evening time, staff sets out warm cookies. Suites with whirlpool bath and fireplace are available for $170.

Relax to the sound of a gurgling fountain waterfall on the shady and secluded patio at **Cherry Chalet** (8101 West 10th, Kennewick, 509/783-6406, $110 d). This modest suburban-style home is cloistered on a 20-acre cherry orchard that's close enough to Kennewick to offer easy access to restaurants and activities.

FOOD

Mexican

Because of the large number of agricultural workers from Mexico and other points south, the Tri-Cities have an abundance of Mexican restaurants. The finest of these is probably **Casa Chapala #1** (107 E. Columbia Dr., Kennewick, 509/582-7848) with authentic Mexican food and ultra-fresh tortillas. They also have restaurants in Pasco and Richland.

The big Mexican grocery store is **Mitiendita Mexicana** (106 10th Ave., Pasco), with the popular **Panaderia la Reyna** bakery right next door. An even bigger Mexican bakery is **Panaderia Colima** (4th Ave.); if you don't speak Spanish you may be the only one here who doesn't.

Other International

Emerald of Siam (1314 Jadwin Ave., Richland, 509/946-9328, 11:30 A.M.–2 P.M. Mon.–Fri. and 5–9 P.M. daily) creates authentic and delicious Thai food and has an inexpensive lunch buffet weekdays ($8) and a popular dinner buffet on Friday and Saturday ($14). **Bangkok Restaurant** (8300 Gage Blvd., Kennewick, 509/735-7631, 11 A.M.–2 P.M. and 5–9 P.M. Mon.–Fri., 11 A.M.–3 P.M. and 5–9 P.M. Sat., closed Sun.) is also popular for Thai cooking.

Mandarin House (1035 Lee Blvd., Richland, 509/943-6843, 11 A.M.–2 P.M. and 4–9 P.M. Mon.–Fri., 4–9:30 P.M. Sat., closed Sun.) has the best local Chinese food.

Located in a cozy old railroad dining car, **Monterosso's Italian Restaurant** (1026 Lee Blvd., Richland, 509/946-4525, 5–9 P.M. Mon.–Thurs., 5–10 P.M. Fri.–Sat.) simmers and stews classic Italian cuisine and nightly seafood specials. Reservations are recommended.

Steaks and Brew

Olympic Brew (5011 W. Clearwater Ave., Kennewick, 509/735-2138, 11:30 A.M.–8 P.M. Sun.–Thurs., 11:30 A.M.–9 P.M. Fri.–Sat.) is a popular lunch emporium with sandwiches, quiche, and other fare.

For seafood, steak, prime rib, and pasta with outside riverside seating, head to **Cedars Pier 1** (7 Clover Island, next to the Quality Inn, 509/582-2143, 5–9 P.M. Sun.–Thurs., 5–10 P.M. Fri.–Sat.).

Probably because Yakima Valley and Columbia Basin lead the nation in hops production, the Tri-Cities have become a center of microbrewed beer. **Atomic Ale Brewpub & Eatery** (1015 Lee Blvd., Richland, 509/946-5465, 11 A.M.–10 P.M. Mon.–Thurs., 11 A.M.–11 P.M. Fri.–Sat., 11 A.M.–8 P.M. Sun.) is the oldest of the lot (from way back in 1997). Its beers include the appropriately named Plutonium Porter, Atomic Amber, and Half-Life Hefeweisen. The menu centers on distinctive pizzas cooked in a wood-fired oven, though they also have steaks, seafood, and bratwurst. There's live music every Monday evening, and no smoking.

Kimos at Rattlesnake Mountain Brewing Company (1250 Columbia Center Blvd., Richland, 509/783-5747, www.rattlesnake-brew.com, 3–11 P.M. Mon.–Thurs., 11 A.M.–1 A.M. Fri., 9 A.M.–1 A.M. Sat., 9 A.M.–10 P.M. Sun.) is one of the nicer local places and also features outside dining along the Columbia River with a wide-ranging and reasonably priced menu. Items on the menu worth attention are the Oriental wasabi chicken salad and Rattlesnake Buffalo wings. Don't miss the Honey Red Ale!

Markets

Visit the **Pasco Farmers Market** (4th Ave. and Columbia St., 509/545-0738, 8 A.M.–noon Wed. and Sat. May–Nov. for local produce, sausages, fresh breads, and arts and crafts. This is the largest open-air farmers market in Washington. Don't miss the tiny powdered donuts. The **Kennewick Farmers Market** (corner of Kennewick Ave. and Benton St., 509/586-3101, 8 A.M.–noon Wed. and Sat. June–Oct.) is held on Flag Plaza. The **West End Farmer's Market** (509/967-0521, Sat. May–Oct.) is at Flat Top Park in West Richland.

Adam's Place Country Gourmet (910 E. Game Farm Rd., Pasco, 509/582-8564, 10 A.M.–6 P.M. Mon.–Fri., 10 A.M.–2 P.M. Sat., closed Sun.) is located in an apple orchard and makes all sorts of sweet confections, even chocolate-covered pizzas.

Country Mercantile (232 Crestloch Rd., 10 miles north of Pasco, 509/545-2192, 7 A.M.–8 P.M. daily) has a produce market and ice-cream parlor, along with "agricultural entertainment" that includes a seasonal cornfield maze, petting zoo, and pumpkin patch. It's great fun for families.

INFORMATION

Pick up all the current maps and information you need from the **Tri-Cities Visitor and Convention Bureau** (509/735-8486 or 800/254-5824, www.visittri-cities.com, 8 A.M.–5 P.M. Mon.–Fri.), housed in the Vista Airport building at the end of Grandridge Boulevard in Kennewick.

GETTING THERE AND AROUND

By Bus and Train

Public transportation comes together at the **Transportation Depot** (535 N. 1st Ave.) in Pasco. Here you can catch a local bus from **Ben Franklin Transit** (509/735-5100, www.bft.org, $1, $2.75 all day pass) for service to the three cities and the airport Monday–Saturday. **Greyhound** (509/547-3151 or 800/231-2222, www.greyhound.com) also stops here, as does **Amtrak** (509/545-1554, 800/872-7245, www.amtrak.com), whose Empire Builder train provides daily service east to Spokane, Minneapolis, and Chicago, and west to Portland.

By Air

Departing from the Tri-Cities Airport in Pasco—the oldest airport west of the Mississippi—are **Horizon Air** (509/547-6352 or 800/547-9808), **Delta Air Lines** (800/221-1212, www.delta.com), and **United Express** (800/241-6522, www.ual.com).

Bergstrom Aircraft (509/547-6271) offers flightseeing trips out of the Richland airport over the Tri-Cities area for $99 for up to three people on a Cesna 172.

Tours

Columbia River Journeys (509/734-9941 or 888/486-9119, www.columbiariverjourneys.com) runs jetboat trips to Hanford Reach. As you cruise up the river, you'll see heron rookeries, curious coyotes, huge salmon beds, and the surreal Hanford reactors along the horizon.

Walla Walla

As you drive toward Walla Walla from the east, Highway 12 takes you past mile after mile of gently rolling wheat growing out of the rich chocolate-brown soil. It's enough to make Midwest farmers drool. The strip-cropped patterns of plowed and fallow land look like cresting waves, with the Blue Mountains bordering the southeast horizon.

If you arrive in the pretty town of Walla Walla on a hot summer day, you'll probably wonder, at least momentarily, if you took a wrong turn somewhere and drove to New England. Walla Walla (30,000 people, plus another 7,000 in neighboring College Place) is an oasis in arid eastern Washington. Here, trees have been cultivated for decades and offer

© ERICKA CHICKOWSKI

downtown Walla Walla

much-needed shade and visual relief from the sameness of the eastern Washington landscape. Walla Walla University, Whitman College, and Walla Walla Community College supply a strong youthful influence, while the big Washington State Penitentiary supplies the most jobs. This includes inmate work—they really do stamp license plates here.

Geography and Climate

Walla Walla has four distinct seasons, with an average of four days over 100°F in summer, two winter days below zero, and about 20 inches of snow. There are nearly 300 sunny days most years. The Walla Walla Valley also enjoys a variety of elevation that much of eastern Washington lacks; the western end of town lies at 300 feet above sea level, while the Blue Mountain foothills to the east rise to 3,000 feet. The valley enjoys a long growing season, with wheat, potatoes, asparagus, peas, alfalfa, grapes, and the famous Walla Walla sweet onions as the big money crops. Livestock and dairy products are also significant parts of the economy.

History

The Lewis and Clark party passed through the Native American hunting grounds here in 1805, but the first permanent white settlement wasn't until some time later. Dr. Marcus Whitman, a doctor and Presbyterian missionary arrived in 1836 and established a settlement he called Waiilatpu. The Cayuse, suffering from measles that Whitman could not cure and resentful of Whitman and his party's aggressive conversion techniques, massacred 15 of the settlers in 1847, including Whitman and his wife. This put a bit of a damper on local white settlement until the Treaty of 1855 reopened the region to American migration.

In 1856, Col. Edward Steptoe built **Fort Walla Walla** at Mill Creek to keep the peace. The surrounding town was later named Walla Walla, meaning "Many Waters" in the Cayuse tongue. In 1859, the city was named the county seat and has since witnessed many booms and busts, from a minor gold rush in neighboring Idaho to disastrous fires that razed the entire town to the renaissance in the local wine industry that has made the town well known today.

SIGHTS

Museums

Walla Walla has a surprising number of historic places to explore. Step back in time with a visit to the **Fort Walla Walla Museum Complex** (Dalles Military & Myra Road, 509/525-7703, www.fortwallawallamuseum.org, 10 A.M.–5 P.M. Tues.–Sun. Apr.–Oct., $7 adults, $6 seniors and students, $3 ages 6–12, free for younger kids). This excellent museum features 15 original and re-created pioneer buildings. A 19th-century cemetery containing the bodies of both Native Americans and cavalry soldiers borders the property. A short nature trail and campground is nearby.

Visit the **Kirkman House** (214 N. Colville, 509/529-4373, www.kirkmanhousemuseum.org, 10 A.M.–4 P.M. Wed.–Sat., 1–4 P.M. Sun., $3 adults, $2 students and seniors), a red-brick mansion built in 1880 by entrepreneur William Kirkman. The ornate Italianate-style structure features a widow's walk and figurehead keystones and is on the National Register of Historic Places.

Kids will be nearly overcome with wonder and delight at the **Children's Museum of Walla Walla** (77 Wainwright Place, 509/526-7529, www.cmwallawalla.org, 10 A.M.–5 P.M. Thurs.–Sun., $4). The tykes can jump around on stage in costume along with life-size puppets at the Enchanted Theater. The Bug Patch Party Room is full of flowers and various kinds of insects. Kids can pretend to shop at the Wee Walla Walla Harvest Market, and visit a make-believe doctor's office, Mexican restaurant, or Construction Junction. Check the website for special events planned throughout the year.

Walking Tour

Pick up a brochure from the chamber of commerce for a walking tour of the historic downtown area. Some of the sights you'll pass are the 1917 **Liberty Theatre,** built on the site of the original Army fort at W. Main and Colville, and the **Dacres Hotel,** built in 1899 at W. Main and 4th. The **Reynolds-Day Building,** on Main between 1st and 2nd, was constructed in 1874. Washington's first State Constitutional Convention was held here in 1878. It's hard to miss the 10-story **Marcus Whitman Hotel,** built in 1928 at 2nd and W. Rose, the brick centerpiece of downtown. The **Baker Boyer Bank** is the oldest bank in Washington and one of the few independent banks left in the state. Its seven-story home office at the corner of Main and 2nd Streets was built in 1910 and was the town's first "skyscraper."

Colleges

Walla Walla University (204 South College Ave., www.wallawalla.edu) is located east of town. The quiet campus of this Seventh-day Adventist school educates some 1,600 students and is particularly strong in business and engineering. Founded in 1859, **Whitman University** (www.whitman.edu) was the first higher education center in the West and is home to 1,300 students. The campus is just west of downtown Walla Walla. The tall clock tower, built in 1900, is on the National Register of Historic Places. Walla Walla is also home to 2,200-student **Walla Walla Community College** (500 Tausick Way, 509/522-2500, www.wwcc.edu).

Big Trees and Parks

Walla Walla is famous for its tall, stately trees, a heritage from pioneer settlers who wanted a reminder of their eastern homes. A booklet, available at the chamber of commerce, describes some of the largest of these, including the 25 different individual trees among the biggest in Washington. One of the trees, a 21-foot-in-circumference catalpa on the Whitman College campus, is the largest in America. The 47-acre **Pioneer Park** (Alder St. and Division St.) contains many more state-record trees. This well-kept city park was originally a cow pasture but now includes—in addition to marvelous forested areas—an aviary, rose garden, duck pond, swimming pool, gazebo, brass cannon, and picnic tables. The design for Pioneer Park came from John C. Olmstead, creator of New York's Central Park. **Fort Walla Walla Park** is home to more tall trees, along with the Fort Walla Walla Museum. **Mountain View Cemetery** (on S. 2nd Ave. near Abbott Rd.) dates back to 1853 and is considered one of the most attractive in the state.

Farm Tours

West from Walla Walla lies farming country with a Midwestern look; this could just as well be Nebraska. Far to the southeast lie rolling tree-covered hills that rise into the Blue Mountains. A blanket of snow covers the summits till late summer.

Take a dip in a sea of purple at the **Blue Mountain Lavender Farm** (345 Short Rd., 509/529-3276, www.bluemountainlavender.com) in nearby Lowden. Owned by a French-American family, the farm was inspired by nostalgia for the extensive lavender fields in the south of France. An on-site gift shop sells dozens of luxurious items made from the local crop. Call ahead for tours.

Whitman Mission

You can get the whole story of Marcus and Narcissa Whitman's pioneer mission on the Oregon Trail at the **Whitman Mission National Historic Site** (28 Whitman Mission Road, 509/529-2761), seven miles west of Walla Walla on Highway 12. None of the original buildings remain, but you can walk self-guided trails to the mission site, grave, monument, and locations of the first house, blacksmith shop, and gristmill. Cultural demonstrations—including adobe brick making, beadwork, moccasin making, and butter churning—take place on summer weekends.

Maintained by the National Park Service, the visitors center here (8 A.M.–6 P.M. daily mid-June–Labor Day, 8 A.M.–4:30 P.M. daily the rest of the year, closed Thanksgiving, Christmas, and New Year's, $3 adults, $5 for a family arriving in one car, free for kids under 16) contains a diorama of the Whitman mission, plus artifacts found here and an informative exhibit about the Cayuse tribe and the sad end to the Whitmans' work.

The grounds are open till dusk year-round. Be sure to walk up the hill to the Whitman Memorial, a 27-foot-tall obelisk overlooking this lonely place. Come here on a late fall day with the clouds overhead, the brown grass at your feet, great blue herons on the shore of the pond, and a chilly west wind to really appreciate the peaceful wildness that both the Cayuse and the Whitmans loved. A restored section of the Oregon Trail (used until 1844) passes right through the Whitman Mission site.

Wallula

The tiny settlement of Wallula stands along the east shore of Lake Wallula, the Columbia River reservoir created by McNary Dam. Look for **Two Sisters,** twin basalt pillars that the Cayuse legends said were two sisters who had been turned to stone by that trickster, Coyote. A plaque in Wallula commemorates one of the earliest garrisons in the Northwest. In 1818, the Northwest Fur Company established **Fort Nez Percé** at the junction of the Walla Walla and Columbia Rivers. The fort soon became a center for fur trade in the region. Fearing Native American attacks, the company built two strong outer walls and armed the men heavily; it was soon being called the "Gibraltar of the Columbia." In 1821, the British-owned Hudson's Bay Company took over the business, later renaming it Fort Walla Walla. The fear of attacks intensified, and in 1856 the company abandoned the fort rather than risking capture. The fort's commander ordered his men to dump the black powder and shot balls into the Columbia River to keep them out of Cayuse hands. Shortly after his men abandoned the fort, American Indian warriors burned it to the ground.

Two years later a new Fort Walla Walla rose, this time as a U.S. Army military garrison farther up the river. This fort would eventually become the center around which the city of Walla Walla grew. The original fort site later grew into the town of Wallula, but in the late 1940s, construction began on the McNary Dam downstream along the Columbia River. After its completion, the old town and fort site were inundated, and the town's residents moved to higher ground.

Grape Power

Walla Walla Valley is one of Washington state's eight official viticultural appellations and is best known for cabernet sauvignon, merlot, riesling, and chardonnay grapes. There are dozens of wineries in and around town. As you head close to city limits from the west, you'll encounter the very attractive **Three Rivers Winery** (5641 West Highway 12, 509/526-9463, www.threeriverswinery.com). The tasting room and winery building sit on a bank overlooking the vineyard and a large grassy area with a small three-hole pitch-and-putt course. The building itself is an impressive combination of river rock, pitched roofs, and warm-red exposed wooden beams. Inside there's a river rock bar and fireplace to keep you cozy while tasting. Try the estate-grown gewürztraminer; it is superb.

Visit **Woodward Canyon Winery** (11920 W. Hwy. 12, 509/525-4129, www.woodwardcanyon.com, 10 A.M.–5 P.M. Mon.–Sat.,

ICE WINE

For some Washington vintners, the glimpse of a crystalline frost over ripe grape clusters is a beautiful sight. In these parts, such a picture portends the prospect of ice wine, an intensely flavorful and sweet concoction that can only be produced when the stars align just so to give wineries the chance to create it.

Ice wine is pressed from grapes that have frozen while still on the vine. In order to make this happen, vineyards must take a gamble. They'll reserve a selection of grapes past harvest time, protecting them from hungry birds and other critters with nets, and hope that the frost falls before the grapes go bad. If the weather doesn't cooperate, the vine's precious cargo is lost.

If it does, the grapes must be picked immediately so they can be squeezed while still frozen. When a grape freezes on the vine, it's only the water in the fruit that seizes up. The sugars and solids in the grape remain unfrozen. So when it is pressed, that fruit yields only a fraction of the liquid a normal grape would, but it is a highly concentrated juice.

Ice wine is prized not only for its smoothness and flavor, but also for its rarity. Because it is produced so infrequently and because the grapes yield much less ice wine than normal wine, expect to pay a premium. But if you have the means, do give it a try. It is the smoothest dessert wine you'll ever sip.

noon–5 P.M. Sun.), about 10 miles west of town in Lowden, for a taste of top-quality chardonnay and cabernet sauvignon. The $5 tasting fee is refundable with any purchase. **L'Ecole No. 41 Winery** (509/525-0940,www.lecole.com, 11 A.M.–4 P.M. daily), also in Lowden, specializes in semillon and merlot wines. The tasting room is an old schoolhouse—relax by doodling on the chalkboard as you sip. Tasting fees are a refundable $5.

Other notable Walla Walla wineries include the largest local winery, **Waterbrook Winery** (31 E. Main St., 509/522-1262, www.waterbrook.com, 10:30 A.M.–6:30 P.M. daily), as well as **Canoe Ridge Vineyard** (1102 West Cherry St., 509/527-0885, www.canoeridgevineyard.com, 11 A.M.–4 P.M. daily Oct.–Apr., 11 A.M.–5 P.M. daily May–Sept., closed major holidays and Dec. 24–Jan. 1) and **Patrick M. Paul Vineyards** (1554 School Ave., 509/526-0676, www.pmpvineyards.com, 1–4 P.M. Sat.–Sun.).

ENTERTAINMENT AND EVENTS

The Arts

The **Walla Walla Symphony Orchestra** (26 E. Main, 509/529-8020, www.wwsymphony.com) has been performing since 1907 and is the oldest continuously performing symphony in the West. Its season runs October–May, with the special Mares 'n' Music performance falling in June.

Founded in 1944, the **Walla Walla Little Theatre** (1130 E. Sumach, 509/529-3683,,www.ltww.org) is a community theater that produces four plays each season. **Harper Joy Theatre** at Whitman University (345 Boyer, 509/527-5180) also stages several student productions each year, and the local community college puts on **Outdoor Summer Musical** productions at Fort Walla Walla amphitheater each July.

Art buffs will want to visit the **Clyde and Mary Harris Gallery** (509/527-2600) at Walla Walla College, focusing on faculty, student, and regional shows. Other galleries include the **Sheehan Gallery** (509/527-5249, www.whitman.edu/sheehan) at Whitman College, home of the Davis Collection of Asian Art. The **Carnegie Art Center** (109 S. Palouse, 509/525-4270, www.carnegieart.com, 11 A.M.–4:30 P.M. Tues.–Sat., free) sits on the site of the historic 1855 Great Indian Council. Once a public library, the 1904 building is home to a pottery studio and a changing gallery of largely regional artwork.

Events and Festivals

A popular event with photographers is the **Walla Walla Balloon Stampede** held in mid-May. The Northwest's signature hot-air balloon rally stages concerts, arts and crafts displays, and plenty of food to go along with the racing fun. A big **4th of July** at Pioneer Park is followed by the **Walla Walla Sweet Onion Harvest Festival** a week later. Labor Day weekend's **Walla Walla Frontier Days Fair & Rodeo** (509/527-3247) brings ropin', wrasslin', racin', and ridin' to the Walla Walla County Fairgrounds. In mid-September, the **Fall Harvest and Community Festival** at Fort Walla Walla Museum provides a chance to learn about pioneer life.

SPORTS AND RECREATION

Cycling

Enjoy the bike path from Cambridge Drive to Rooks Park, or from 9th and Dalles Military Road to Myra Road. For a more adventurous ride, head out scenic Old Milton Highway south of town. It's especially pretty in the fall.

Fishing

Walla Walla is a fly fisher's paradise, giving you the drop on unsuspecting trout, smallmouth bass, and the mighty steelhead. **Stone Creek Fly Fishers** (509/520-7039, http://stonecreek-flyfishers.com) teaches introductory classes for beginners, including special classes for women and children. Guide service is also available.

Swimming

Outdoor summer-only swimming pools (509/527-1099) include one in Jefferson Park (9th Ave. and Malcolm St.) and a 50-meter pool on Rees Avenue at Sumach Street.

Golf

Veteran's Memorial Golf Course (201 E. Rees Ave., 509/527-4507, http://vetsgolf.com), off Highway 12, is an 18-hole course open to the public. Greens fees are $29 for 18 holes or $16.75 for just the front nine.

Camping

For information on hiking and camping in the Blue Mountains of Umatilla National Forest, visit the **Walla Walla Ranger Station** (1415 W. Rose St., 509/522-6290, www.fs.fed.us/r6/uma).

RVs can park and dump at **Four Seasons RV Resort** (1440 Dalles Military Rd., 509/529-6072, $28 per night or $168 for seven days), a privately run campground.

Tent campers can pitch at **Lewis and Clark Trail State Park** (509/337-6457), 26 miles northeast of Walla Walla. Standard tent sites large enough to fit RVs are available April 1–September 15. Primitive sites are open year-round. No reservations are accepted at this park.

ACCOMMODATIONS

Under $100

Colonial Motel (2279 E. Isaacs, 509/529-1220, www.colonial-motel.com, $59 s or $79 d) is a rare local-family-owned motel with a nice view and a running waterfall on-site.

$100-150

Prepare to relax hard-core when you check in to one of the three rooms at the **Inn At Blackberry Creek** (1126 Pleasant St., 509/522-5233, www.innatblackberrycreek.com, $142–188 d) Cozy rooms pay homage to artists Cézanne, Monet, and Renoir. The Inn is well located for visiting shops and historic sites.

For splendid semi-private downtown digs, check in at **The Wine Country Inn** (915 Alvarado Terrace, 509/386-3592, www.wallawallawinecountry.net, $150 d). The simply and tastefully appointed rooms offer wireless Internet access, 1930s flair, and private baths. Be sure to take advantage of the knowledge of the innkeepers, both of whom are long-time residents of the area.

$150-200

Green Gables Inn B&B (922 Bonsella, 509/525-5501 or 888/525-5501, www.greengablesinn.com, $154–192 s or d) is located in a beautiful 1909 Craftsman mansion along a tree-lined street. The five guest rooms all have private baths, and each has a theme based on L. M. Montogomery's *Anne of Green Gables.* A full gourmet breakfast is served.

The elegant **Marcus Whitman Hotel and Conference Center** (6 W. Rose St., 509/525-2200 or 866/826-9422, www.marcuswhitmanhotel.com, $169–194 s or d) first opened in 1927. After a major renovation, the 127-room hotel is once again Walla Walla's premier lodging choice, with 22 suites also available.

The **Fat Duck Inn** (527 Catherine, 509/526-3825 or 888/526-871, http://fatduckinn.com, $165–185 d) is a smartly decorated Craftsman cottage offering four suites and a gourmet breakfast. Amenities include a complimentary wine hour, with tastings of local vintages and the option of enjoying a delicious dinner right in its dining room for an additional charge. Well-behaved dogs are welcomed with prior arrangements.

$200-250

Take your pick when you stay at the **Walla Walla Inns** (123 East Main St., 509/301-1181 or 877/301-1181, www.wallawallainns.com, $115–325 s or d): Stay in one of the six rooms at its historic downtown property or at the more tranquil hilltop Vineyard property. Children of all ages are welcomed here. The Inn pulls out all the stops for canine companions, too. A $100 nonrefundable pet fee gets you toys, treats, furniture, and even a crate, so your tail-wagger can pack light.

A unique lodging experience (unless you could be considered "livestock") is provided by the **Inn at Abeja** (2014 Mill Creek Rd., 509/522-1234, www.abeja.net, $235–285 d). The original outbuildings of this 100-year-old farm have been converted into tony, light-filled guest cottages and suites. The 35-acre vineyard property is the picture of country comfort. You can be proud to tell your friends you slept in a chicken coop. Reservations for popular local and winery events are filled by lottery.

Complimentary telescopes supplement the stellar accommodations at Touchet's **Cameo Heights Mansion** (1072 Oasis Road, 509/394-0211, $179–249 d). The suites, a few of which have private entrances, are decorated after a variety of European, Mediterranean, and Asian styles. The rich breakfast might just convince you to stick around for the gourmet nighttime offerings, including an optional private four-course fondue feast.

Over $250

Check out the little Craftsman hideaway called **Many Waters Guest House** (709 Washington St., 206/323-7800, http://manywatersguesthouse.com, $270–360 depending on how many bedrooms you need). Soft beds, a fenced backyard with jumbo gas grill, and the fact that you don't have to share the house with guests not in your party make this an incredible pick for small groups or families.

FOOD

Cafés and Diners

Start your day at **Clarette's Restaurant** (15 S. Touchet, 509/529-3430, 6 A.M.–8 P.M. daily) for the best home-style breakfasts in Walla Walla. For lunch, try **Merchants Ltd.** (21 E. Main, 509/525-0900) is a great deli with a lunch buffet that includes homemade soups, fresh salads, and baked goods. Unfortunately, the staff lacks a certain warmth. Also of note for lunch is **Cookie Tree Bakery & Café** (23 S. Spokane, 509/522-4826, 6 A.M.–2:30 P.M. Mon.–Fri.), with homemade breads and pastries. **Blue Mountain Tavern and Casino** (2025 E. Isaacs Ave., 509/525-9941) serves excellent sandwiches for lunch and shows big-screen TV sports at night. No kids are allowed here.

Although Walla Walla has all the standard fast-food eateries (out on Wilbur and Isaacs), you'd do far better visiting **The Ice Burg** (616 W. Birch, 509/529-1793, 11:30–10 P.M. Sun.–Thurs., 11:30 A.M.–11 P.M. Fri.–Sat.). This popular drive-in makes great hamburgers and wonderful banana shakes.

Contemporary Northwest

For a more stylish meal out, try **26 Brix** (207 W. Main St., 509/526-4075, www.twentysixbrix.com, 5–9 P.M. Thurs.–Mon., 9 A.M.–2 P.M. Sun.), the "it" eatery in downtown Walla Walla. Serving breakfast and brunch on weekends and dinner the rest of the week, the French-inspired menu focuses on local ingredients and changes seasonally.

ONION POWER

Although wheat is the most important crop in the Walla Walla area, onions are the town's claim to fame. The famous Walla Walla sweet onions were developed from Spanish and Italian varieties first brought here in the late 19th century. Their sweetness is illusory: these mild-flavored, juicy, large onions actually have almost no sugar, but they have only half the sulfur of other onions. And it's the sulfur that gives onions their strong bite and causes tears.

If you've got a kitchen and a barbecue in your hotel unit, grab a bag of sweets while in Walla Walla and wow your travel companions with the following recipe.

GRILLED AND ROASTED WALLA WALLA SWEETS WITH PINE NUT BUTTER

4 medium Walla Walla sweet onions, peeled and cut in half from top to bottom
1 Tablespoon olive oil
½ cup pine nuts, toasted
3 ounces unsalted butter, softened
½ teaspoon lemon zest
½ teaspoon chopped fresh rosemary
¼ teaspoon freshly ground black pepper
¼ teaspoon salt, or to taste
⅓ cup freshly grated Parmesan cheese
2 Tablespoons toasted pine nuts, lemon wedges, and rosemary sprigs for garnish

1. Toast the pine nuts in a 350°F oven for 6 to 7 minutes, or until golden brown. Cool. Caution: pine nuts burn easily.

2. Preheat the oven to 375°F and prep an outdoor grill. Brush onions with oil and place cut side down on the preheated grill. Once grill marks form, put onions on a cookie sheet and cook in oven for another 25 minutes, or until tender. Barbecue step can be replaced by broiling – just be sure to let the oven cool once you are ready to finish cooking.

3. While onions are cooking, take roasted pine nuts and pulse them in a food processor until finely ground. Then put butter, lemon zest, rosemary, black pepper, and salt in the bowl and process until smooth. If you're traveling, you'll need to improvise: Place pine nuts in a zip-top bag and crush finely with a frying pan. Place in a bowl and mix with the rest of the ingredients.

4. Spread pine nut butter over the cooked onions and put back in oven until butter is melted.

5. Serve warm, with grated parmesan and a few extra pine nuts sprinkled over them.

Recipe courtesy of the Walla Walla Sweet Onion Marketing Committee and Chef Tom Douglas, who serves this dish at Dahlia Lounge in Seattle.

© ERICKA CHICKOWSKI

Pick up a bag of Walla Walla sweets while you're in town.

International

The Walla Walla area has a rich Italian heritage, best illustrated by the sweet Walla Walla onion—developed by an Italian transplant to the area—and the tasty pasta houses in town. A good example is **T. Maccarone's** (4 S. Colville St., 509/522-4776, www.tmaccarones.com, 11 A.M.–2 P.M. and 4–9 P.M. Mon.–Fri., 9 A.M.–2 P.M. and 4–9 P.M. Sat.–Sun.), a trendy place downtown that puts its own twist on traditional Italian fare. This is the best place in town to pair a Walla Walla red wine with antipasto.

The food isn't as good at **Lorenzo's** (1415 Plaza Way, 509/529-6333, 11 A.M.–9 P.M. daily), but it has a fun atmosphere and works well for starving students and money-minding families. It offers an all-you-can-eat buffet 11 A.M.–2:30 P.M. ($7.49) and 5–8 P.M. daily ($9.49). Kids 12 and under eat for $0.59 per year of age.

Looking for Mexican meals and great margaritas? Head to **El Sombrero's** (428 Ash St, 509/525-2598) for big portions and a bunch of big hats. **La Casita** (315 S. 9th Ave., 509/522-4941) has noteworthy pico de gallo and can accommodate large groups. The **China Buffet** (1618 Plaza Way, 509/526-7797, 11 A.M.–9:30 P.M. daily) specializes in feed-trough-style Chinese food.

Pub Grub

Mill Creek Brewpub (11 S. Palouse St., 509/522-2440, 11 A.M.–8:30 P.M. Mon.–Thurs., 8:30 A.M.–9:30 P.M. Fri.–Sat., noon–8 P.M. Sun.) is a fun place with fresh-brewed beer on tap and pub grub from the kitchen.

Bakeries and Markets

Although Walla Walla has the big chain markets, one grocer is noteworthy: **Andy's Market** (1117 S. College Ave., 509/529-1003, closed Sat.) out in College Place. Because of the Seventh-day Adventist college nearby, this large market is almost entirely vegetarian. You'll find a few frozen meat items (but no pork), lots of frozen and canned "vegemeat" products, bulk foods, and plenty of gluten-free foods.

Not far away is **Rodger's Bakery** (166 N. College Ave., 509/522-2738) with breads, bagels, breadsticks, and hot soups. **John's Wheatland Bakery** (1828 E. Isaacs, 509/522-2253) is another excellent bake shop that uses fresh local ingredients.

INFORMATION

For local information, contact the **Walla Walla Chamber of Commerce** (29 E. Sumach, 509/525-0850 or 877/998-4748, www.wwvchamber.com, 8:30 A.M.–5 P.M. Mon.–Fri. all year, plus 9 A.M.–4 P.M. Sat.–Sun. in the summer).

GETTING THERE AND AROUND

Valley Transit (509/525-9140, www.valleytransit.com) serves the Walla Walla/College Place area Monday–Saturday. The **Greyhound** depot is at 315 N. 2nd, 509/525-9313 or 800/231-2222, www.grey hound.com.

Walla Walla Regional Airport is at 310 A. Street and provides passenger terminals for **Horizon Air** (509/526-4876 or 800/547-9308, www.horizonair.com) service to Seattle and Portland. Blue Ridge Aircraft services is the local FBO. Info is available at 509/529-4243.

Yakima Valley

Yakima (YAK-a-ma) is one of the largest cities in Central Washington and the commercial hub for the Yakima Valley. The population includes a rapidly growing Latino community that now represents more than half of the Yakima County population.

Much of the remaining Yakima Valley blends together superbly with an identity of much more recent vintage. Naturally, we're referring to Washington's wine country, a string of vintners, many of whom have gained some degree of national or international renown, situated along the Yakima River. Here, Interstate 82 cuts across the north side of the valley, with the older Highway 22 following a parallel route on the south side. Several small towns dot the route between Yakima and the Tri-Cities; the largest are Zillah, Granger, Sunnyside, Grandview, and Prosser.

The Yakima Valley's volcanic soil is hard to beat, supporting tons of apples, winter pears, fruit trees, hops, and mint.

History

The resident Native Americans fiercely opposed permanent white settlement here until the end of the 1855–1857 Indian War. With the Native Americans' resettlement on the Yakama Reservation complete in 1858, pioneer ranchers and their herds moved in to this sun-scorched region. The 1860s brought modern irrigation to the region, and soon after, John W. Beck planted a small apple and pear orchard. Since then, the Yakima Valley has taken root and grown into one of the agricultural centers of the United States.

SIGHTS

Historic Yakima

The North Front Street Historical District boasts some of Yakima's oldest buildings, including the 1898 Lund Building, which once housed a saloon and brothel (now the Greystone Restaurant) directly across from the Northern Pacific Railroad depot.

Three miles northwest of Yakima on Highway 12 you'll find the mysterious **Indian Painted Rocks,** a state historical site. Although the pictographs were partially destroyed by an early irrigation flume, some remain at Naches Highway and Powerhouse Road. The cliffs nearby are popular with local rock climbers.

The **Ahtanum Mission,** east of Yakima along Ahtanum Creek, was built in 1852 by Catholic priests. Though it burned down during the Yakama Indian wars of the 1850s, the church was rebuilt in 1869 and is still used. You can visit the mission and surrounding park for a small fee.

Toppenish

As one local jokester puts it, "People come to Toppenish just to watch the paint dry." This whistle-stop Western town 18 miles southeast of Yakima is best known for the colorful and brilliantly crafted murals splashed on its historic brick buildings that tell the story of Toppenish. The biggest draw is on the first Saturday in June, when bleachers are set up and folks watch as 12–16 artists complete a **"Mural-in-a-Day."**

Visit the chamber of commerce (11 S. Toppenish Ave., 509/865-3262, www.toppenish.net, 10 A.M.–4 P.M. Mon.–Sat. Apr.–Oct.) to pick up a map of the 80-plus wall-art pieces, or hop aboard one of the wagon rides offered by **Toppenish Mural Tours** (509/967-8995, $12 adults, $5 kids, 10 A.M.–1 P.M. Mon.–Sat.) that leave from the depot area on one-hour tours May–September.

The town is also home to two interesting museums. The **American Hop Museum** (22 S. B St., 509/865-4677, www.americanhopmuseum.org, 10 A.M.–4 P.M. Wed.–Sat., 11 A.M.–4 P.M. Sun. May–Sept., closed Mon.–Tues., $3 adults, $2 students, free for children under 5) is the only one of its kind, shining a bright spotlight on the underappreciated hops, a vital bittering ingredient in the production of beer and ale and a huge local cash-crop.

And the once-bustling 1911 railroad depot near town square is home to **Northern Pacific Railway Museum** (10 S. Asotin Ave., 509/865-1911, 10 A.M.–4 P.M. Tues.–Sat. and noon to 4 P.M. Sun. May–Oct., $3 adults, $2 kids and seniors). Explore rail and steam artifacts and a restored telegraph office here.

Museums

Start your visit to Yakima at the large **Yakima Valley Museum** (2105 Tieton Dr., 509/248-0747, www.yakimavalleymuseum.org, 10 A.M.–5 P.M. Mon.–Sat. and 11 A.M.–5 P.M. Sun., $5 adults, $3 students and seniors, $12 families, free for under age 5). Easily one of the best large museums in Washington, it boasts an extraordinary collection of Yakama Native American artifacts and one of the finest collections of horse-drawn vehicles west of the Mississippi. The Oregon Trail and local fruit tree industry exhibits are absolutely stellar.

If rusty old things are "your thing," drop by the **Central Washington Agricultural Museum** (4508 Main St., 509/457-8735, www.centralwaagmuseum.org), displaying early Yakima Valley farm equipment on 15 acres in Fulbright Park. The collection is spread throughout more than a dozen buildings, all arranged around a working windmill. A Burlington-Northern boxcar houses railroad memorabilia, and the Magness Room is a special treat, packed with more than 3,000 antique hand tools. Feel free to drive across the grounds and stop at the buildings that pique your interest. The main collection and Magness Room are open 9 A.M.–3 P.M. Tuesday, 9 A.M.–5 P.M. Wednesday–Saturday, 1–4 P.M. SUNDAY APRIL–OCTOBER, 9 a.m.–3 P.M. Tuesday, 9 A.M.–1 P.M. Thursday–Sunday November–March. A popular Threshing Bee is held here each August.

The impressive **Yakama Cultural Heritage Center** (100 Spiel-yi Loop, 509/865-2800, www.yakamamuseum.com, 8 A.M.–5 P.M. daily, $5 adults, $3 seniors and children 11–18, $1 children under 10, $12 family of four, free for enrolled Yakama members) on the Yakama Reservation features a museum that tells the story of the Yakama Nation from its beginnings to the present, a library specializing in Native American books, a theater that presents first-run movies and stage productions, a restaurant, and an RV park.

The museum's library contains the collection of 10,000 books from **Nipo Stongheart,** an honorary Yakama tribesman, who began his show-business career with Buffalo Bill's Wild West Show at the age of 11 and went on to star in many Hollywood Westerns.

YAKAMA RESERVATION

Toppenish is the capital of the Yakama Indian Nation and the commercial center for the 1.37 million-acre Yakama Reservation (509/865-5121). (The tribal council decided in 1994 that the correct spelling for their tribe is Yakama, rather than Yakima; it is formally known as the Confederated Tribes and Bands of the Yakama Nation.) The reservation is home to approximately 5,000 Native people from 14 different tribes and bands, along with another 20,000 non-Indians. The Yakamas run several businesses including a furniture factory, a juice bottler, orchards, ranches, a casino, and a sawmill. The westernmost edge of the reservation includes land within the Mt. Adams Wilderness, and a permit is required for camping, fishing, or hunting.

Fort Simcoe State Park

Head 27 miles west from Toppenish through the heart of the Yakama Reservation to peaceful Fort Simcoe State Park (509/874-2372, www.parks.wa.gov, 6:30 A.M.–dusk daily April–Oct., free). The drive takes you through fields of grapes and hops, past fast-growing Heritage College, past Native American burial grounds with decorated gravesites, to the fort.

Fort Simcoe was erected by the Army in 1856 to help keep peace between Indians and white settlers. Two blockhouses and a barracks have been reconstructed, and five of the original buildings have been restored and furnished. Tour the buildings and the brick interpretive center (9:30 A.M.–4:30 P.M. Wed.–Sun.) with artifacts and old photos, then enjoy a picnic lunch on the parklike grounds. No overnight camping is permitted at Fort Simcoe.

Other Parks

More than 250 species of birds live in the marshy **Toppenish National Wildlife Refuge** (five miles south on Hwy. 97, then south a half mile on Pump House Road, 509/865-2405). The interpretive center and nature trail will get you started and up-to-date on current regulations. Winter and spring are the ideal seasons for spotting raptors and other feathered friends.

The **Yakima Area Arboretum** (1401 Arboretum Drive, 509/248-7337, www.ahtrees.org, dawn–dusk daily) is a peaceful 46-acre park with a Japanese garden and bird sanctuary, plus over 2,000 specimens of native and exotic woody plants near I-90 and Nob Hill Boulevard.

Across the Yakima River from Union Gap, bird-watchers will want to visit the **Hazel Wolf Bird Sanctuary** at the Wenas Creek Campground in the Wenas Valley, five miles west of Selah on Wean Road. Over 100 species of birds have been sighted in the 40-acre sanctuary.

Wineries

Yakima Valley is one of the premier wine-growing regions in the entire state, covering two distinct viticultural appellations, Yakima Valley and Rattlesnake Hills. Stop at local visitors centers for a map of more than two dozen local wineries, or request a copy from the **Yakima Valley Wine Growers Association** (800/258-7270, www.yakimavalleywine.com).

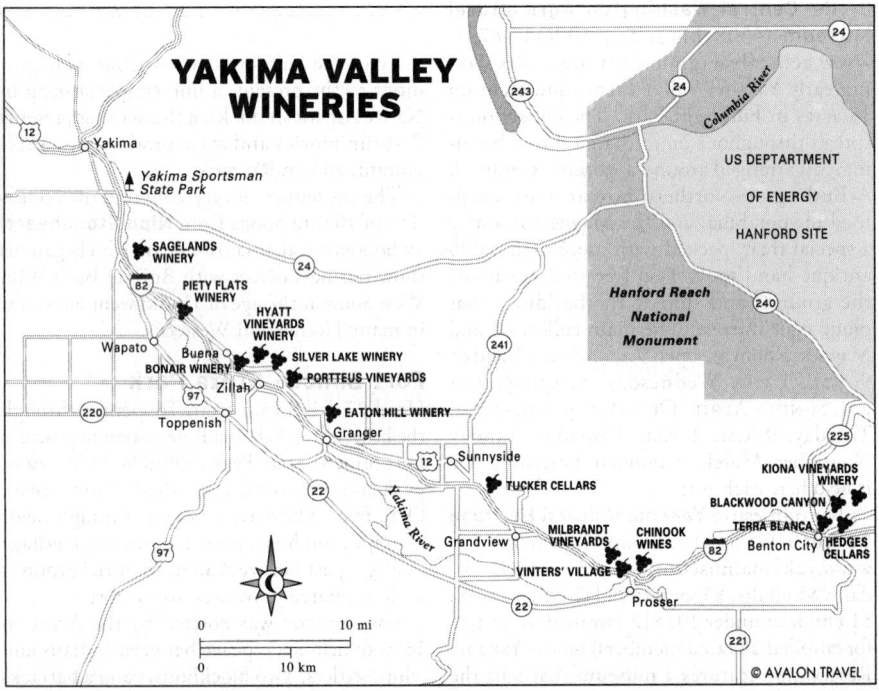

UPPER YAKIMA VALLEY

No need to truck deep into the valley for a charming vineyard experience. Keep close to the city and visit **The Tasting Room Yakima** (250 Ehler Rd., 509/966-0686) out near Cowiche Canyon. Here you'll encounter a small turn-of-the-20th-century farmhouse that acts as a cooperative tasting room to three boutique wineries. Outside, there is a verdant lawn and a patio for picnicking, a well-tended garden, and a small chicken coop. All of this is adjacent to a small nine-acre biodynamic vineyard and over 80 more acres of sage land open to hiking.

RATTLESNAKE HILLS

You'll get a stunner of a view of the Yakima Valley and the looming, majestic Mt. Adams from **Sagelands Vineyard's** (71 Gangl Road, Wapato, 509/877-2112, www.sagelandsvineyard.com) hilltop location. Be sure to check out the stonework and beautifully carved doors at the lodge-style tasting room. Try the merlot and cabernet sauvignon during tasting hours (10 A.M.–5 P.M. Mar.–Oct., noon–5 P.M. Nov.–Feb.), or schedule a winery tour to get a closer look at the operation.

The pleasantly fragrant vineyard grounds at **Bonair Winery** (500 S. Bonair Rd., Zillah, 509/829-6027, www.bonairwine.com, 10 A.M.–5 P.M. daily) also present great views of the mountain and of nearby orchards. Stop by the shady pond to give Bonair's resident Aussie shepherd dog a scritch behind the ears before heading into the new pale-yellow French chateau tasting room. You'll be greeted with a smile by the friendly owners, who have the gift of gab. Call ahead to arrange a guided vineyard or winery tour ($10).

Sit on a bench near a giant wine barrel to sip a glass and survey the surroundings at the **Hyatt Vineyards Winery** (2020 Gilbert Rd., Zillah, 509/829-6333, www.hyattvineyards.com, 11 A.M.–5 P.M. daily April–Oct., 11 A.M.–4:30 P.M. daily Nov.–Dec. and Feb.–Mar., closed Jan.). An immaculate lawn, colorful rose garden, and a giant windmill sit directly outside the tasting room patio. Surrounding them

WINE COUNTRY TOURS

Washington's wine country is filled to the brim with fantastic vineyards and wineries, but the true connoisseur will need to put some miles on the odometer in order to get a good survey of the scene. One of the safest and most relaxing ways to enjoy wine country is to hitch a ride aboard a tour. These tours start from the region they focus on, unless otherwise noted.

YAKIMA VALLEY, TRI-CITIES, WALLA WALLA

Sacco Tours (509/783-7060, www.saccotours.com, $300 for a six-hour tour for up to four poeple) runs small group tours aboard shuttle vans through wineries in your choice of Yakima Valley, the Tri-Cities, or Walla Walla.

A+ Pacific Limousine (509/438-9625, www.limo01.com, $69-79 per person) runs scheduled tours Wednesday, Saturday, and Sunday that head out to six Tri-Cities wineries and stop for lunch at Alexandria Nicole Cellars. Lunch and snacks are included.

Blue Stocking Tours (509/522-4717, www.bluestockingtours.com, $430 for a six-hour trip for up to four people) wanders the wineries of Walla Walla, treating guests to a boxed lunch along the way.

COLUMBIA RIVER GORGE

Swirl Tours (541/399-6676, www.swirlwineclub.com, $250 for a six-hour trip for two) start in Portland and cover Columbia River Gorge wineries on both the Washington and Oregon sides.

WENATCHEE

BonVivant Wine Tours (206/437-1298, www.bonvivanttours.com, $79 per person) offers a laundry list of wine tours throughout the state, including tours in Wenatchee and Leavenworth. Pickups can be arranged in Wenatchee or Seattle ($50 more per person).

are acres of orderly vineyard rows just waiting to be photographed.

The historic McDonald Mercantile building houses **Piety Flats Winery** (11 A.M.–5 P.M. Fri.–Sun., closed Dec.–Feb.). Surrounded by a lawn and picnic table shaded by young walnut trees, this 1911 country store building nostalgically offers bric-a-brac, candies, and gourmet foods to go along with the wine tastings.

The mezzanine tasting room at **Silver Lake Winery** (1500 Vintage Rd., Zillah, 509/829-6235, 11 A.M.–4 P.M. Thurs.–Mon. Dec.–Mar., 10 A.M.–5 P.M. daily Apr.–Nov.) affords a nice vineyard view and windows into the winery's distilling operation. The patio and porch are especially pretty in the fall when the leaves begin to turn. Silver Lake also offers barbecue dinners on Saturdays.

You'll wind through gravel roads hugged by grapevine to get to the barrel room tasting bar at **Portteus Vineyards** (5201 Highland Dr., Zillah, 509/829-6970, www.portteus.com, noon–5 P.M. daily in summer, call for winter hours). Don't let the warehouse-like atmosphere scare you away—the winemakers here produce some prized reds.

LOWER VALLEY AND PROSSER

Once a part of a vast fruit and vegetable empire, the cannery building that holds **Eaton Hill Winery** (530 Gurley Rd., Granger, 509/854-2220, 10 A.M.–5 P.M. daily) dates back to the early 1900s. See for yourself how barrels have replaced cans in this historic structure while you take a sip or two of the winery's award-winning gewürztraminer.

Tucker Cellars (70 Ray Rd., Sunnyside, 509/837-8701, www.tuckercellars.com) throws open the doors to its 10,000-square-foot facility and 50-acre vineyards for tours every day (10 A.M.–5 P.M. in summer, 10 A.M.–4 P.M. in winter). Once you've worked up an appetite, head to the on-site market to pick up a host of gourmet food grown, cooked, or canned by the Tucker family. Favorite treats include fresh fruit and produce, pickled asparagus spears, and home-popped white cloud corn.

Hugged by its own small vineyard and a stand of plum and cherry trees, the boutique **Chinook Wines** (220 Wittkopf Ln. off of Wine Country Rd., Prosser, 509/786-2725, www.chinookwines.com, noon–5 P.M. Sat.–Sun.) lies inside renovated farm buildings. Get a peek inside the winery and the barrel room before heading into the farmhouse tasting room. The personable owners happily welcome people to wander the grounds and spread out blankets and baskets in the shady garden picnic area. Be sure to bring some food that will pair well with the specialty sauvignon blanc.

© ERICKA CHICKOWSKI

If you can't make time for a valley wine tour, at least stop in for a tasting at one of downtown Yakima's wine rooms.

The town of Prosser is a good place to survey the Yakima Valley wine scene without having to drive all over the countryside. In addition to the tasting rooms and wine bars scattered over town, Prosser is also home to the unique **Vinters' Village complex,** a hub of 12 distinct wineries and **The Winemakers' Loft** (357 Port St., 509/786-2705, www.thewinemakersloft.com, 11 A.M.–6 P.M. daily), a new winery "incubator" that helps upstart winemakers experiment and launch their own brands. Some of the highlights among the Vinters' Village dozen include **Milbrandt Vineyards** (508 Cabernet Ct., 509/788-0030), which serves a varied tapas and salad menu to go with its vintages, and **Thurston Wolfe Winery** (588 Cabernet Ct., 509/945-4292, 11 A.M.–5 P.M. Thurs.–Sun.), known best for its full-bodied zinfandel, syrah, and sangiovese.

Also at the village is the funky **Airfield Estates** (560 Merlot Dr., 509/643-1282, www.airfieldwines.com, 11 A.M.–5 P.M. Sun.–Thurs., 10 A.M.–5 P.M. Fri.–Sat.), a lively winery whose decor plays off of its vineyard history—the vines were all planted around an old World War II airbase. The winery was built to resemble an old military hanger, including a 40-foot water tower that acts as a VIP tasting room and wine library for the facilities. Big band music pipes inside when you step into the gorgeous building and get a look through the giant picture windows that frame the barrel room. Airfield is open one hour later on summer Saturdays.

While you're in town, be sure to also drop in on **Desert Wind Winery** (2258 Wine Country Rd., Prosser, 509/786-2505), a handsome new winery that eschews the typical chateau motif. The buildings are made up like an old New Mexico adobe hut, with eclectic Southwest decor to match within the luxury tasting room. The property is also home to a four-room bed-and-breakfast and a sumptuous fine-dining establishment.

Benton City

The quiet small town of Benton City provides a sharp contrast to the bustling Tri-Cities, just a few miles to the east. Stop here to enjoy the lush valley with vineyards and fruit trees.

Melt into the comfy leather chairs inside the tasting room at **Kiona Vineyards Winery** (44612 N. Sunset NE, Benton City, 509/588-6716, noon–5 P.M. daily) The modern decor is accented by fine art photography taken by a Tri-Cities local. Step outside on the patio and lawn for a nice view of Red Mountain.

The facilities at **Blackwood Canyon** (509/588-6249, 10 A.M.–6 P.M. daily, $10 standard, $25 reserve) are nothing to get excited about, but that would detract from the wine anyway. The winery sits at the end of a rough gravel road in the middle of the vineyards, and the tasting room is just a counter in the warehouse. The real star of the show is the eccentric winemaker, a believer in old-method, small-batch fermentation processes that produce, hands down, the best wines in Yakima valley. If you have the time, he'll take you through several hours of tasting, even bringing out bits of food he's prepared to pair with his masterpieces. The chardonnays, cabernets, and late-harvest wines are quite distinctive.

If you crave better atmosphere, then head to the beautiful French chateau tasting room at **Hedges Cellars** (53511 N. Sunset Rd., Benton City, 509/588-3155 or 800/859-9463, www.hedgescellar.com, noon–4 P.M. Fri.–Sun. Mar.–Nov.). The attractive high-ceilinged room is accented with a one-of-a-kind bar crafted locally and a big stone fireplace.

Tour through the cool, dark wine storage caves at **Terra Blanca** (34715 N. DeMoss Rd., Benton City, 509/588-6082, www.terrablanca.com, 11 A.M.–6 P.M. daily) on Red Mountain. The $15 tour (noon and 3 P.M. Sat.–Sun.) allows you to walk the caves, the fermentation bays, the barrel room, and the vineyard, followed up with a chance to taste the fruit of all the labor.

ENTERTAINMENT AND EVENTS

Music

The **Yakima Valley Community Band** (www.yakimacommunityband.org) has free concerts on Wednesdays and Thursdays throughout the summer, as well as a spring program. Summer concerts are held in one of several parks and create perfect picnic opportunities. The **Yakima Symphony Orchestra** (509/248-1414, www.yakimasymphony.org) performs a diverse season of music at the Capitol Theater October–April.

A new hub of Yakima's performance community, **The Seasons Performance Hall** (101 N Naches Ave., 509/453-1888) has some of the best acoustics east of the Cascades. This grand old building was converted from an old Seventh-day Adventist church and now draws quality jazz, classical, Latin, and world-beat musicians.

The historic **Capitol Theater** (19 S. 3rd St., 509/853-2787, www.capitoltheatre.org) is a beautifully restored 1920 theater, now hosting a full schedule of musical, theatrical, and Broadway productions.

Racing

The **Yakima Speedway** (1600 Pacific Ave., 509/248-0647, www.yakimaspeedway.us) hosts auto racing every Saturday night April to early October, ranging from Super Stocks to Youth Hornets. If that doesn't completely get your motor running, take part in the annual **Vintiques Northwest Nationals** (www.vintiques.com) car show and Rod Run held in late July and early August. You're bound to see some of the Northwest's finest mechanical muscle right here, plus a parts-oriented swap-meet, drag racing events, food, camping, and a carnival atmosphere.

Events

CENTRAL WASHINGTON STATE FAIR

The most popular local event is the **Central Washington State Fair** (1301 S. Fair Ave., 509/248-7160, www.fairfun.com) held in late September, which features a PRCA championship rodeo, carnival, nationally recognized musical talent, nitro-fueled demolition derby, and agricultural displays. It attracts well over 300,000 visitors each year. The **Antique Power Show** (509/457-8735) on the third weekend of August features an old-time threshing bee and working displays of farm equipment at the Central Washington Agricultural Museum.

OTHER EVENTS

In mid-February, visit the valley for a **Celebration of Chocolates and Red Wine,** during which the various wineries provide chocolate sweets to match their reds. The biggest annual wine event is the **Yakima Valley Spring Barrel Tasting** (800/258-7270) in late April, when the wineries pour samples of their new releases straight from the barrel and offer tours, hors d'oeuvres, and educational exhibits. All 25 wineries are open 10 A.M.–5 P.M. during this three-day event.

Dog lovers will enjoy Prosser's **National Championship Chukar Field Trials** on the last weekend in March. It attracts English pointers and shorthairs from all over the country.

The early-June **Mural-in-a-Day** (509/865-3262) program pits than two dozen artists against the dramatic goal of completing a wall-sized mural in just one day. This fun demonstration coincides with an arts and crafts and food fair.

Treaty Days and the All-Indian Rodeo and Pow Wow in nearby White Swan is held in early June to celebrate the signing of the Treaty of 1855. The rodeo features the Yakama Nation in a pow wow and parade.

Fort Simcoe (509/874-2372) puts on a great show in June also, complete with living history presentations, traditional tribal dance, a flag-raising ceremony, military re-enactors, antique car shows, and best of all, free cake!

The 4th of July weekend brings a frenzy of activity to Toppenish: the **Pow Wow & Rodeo** (509/865-5566) is an event with something for everyone—a carnival, nightly rodeos, dancing, fireworks, a Wild West parade featuring cowboys, cowgirls, and Yakama in full regalia, an antique power show, and arts and crafts booths.

The **Prosser Wine & Food Fair** (800/408-1517) on the second Saturday of August is the largest outdoor wine and food show in the state, attracting thousands of people for a chance to sample wine, beer, and food. The event usually sells out, so order advance tickets. It's only open to people over age 21.

In September, the Yakima Valley girds up to go ga-ga for the great **Grandview Grape Stomp.** (114 Grandridge, 509/882-2100). In the town's grandest gala of the year, groups of three grapple to gouge grapes as in times gone by and gain some Grandview glory. And a trophy. A fee of $30 gains you general admission and covers family activities galore.

The **Prosser Balloon Rally and Harvest Festival** on the third weekend of September attracts balloon enthusiasts for morning launches, nighttime lighted balloons, and arts and crafts exhibits.

Late into the season, November brings **Tribal Jam** (509/865-2800, $25), a showplace for some of the country's best American Indian musicians and singers. The show is held at the Heritage Theater at the Cultural Heritage Center.

The season starts to winds down with **Thanksgiving in Yakima Valley Wine Country,** featuring food and wine-tasting at most local wineries. This is a fine way to taste a variety of gourmet foods and to get recipe ideas.

In early December, the **Country Christmas Lighted Farm Implement Parade** features bulb-bedecked tractors, farm machinery, and horse-drawn carriages and wagons in one of the premier lighted parades in the northwest. Call the Sunnyside Chamber of Commerce (509/837-5939) for details.

SHOPPING

Yakima's biggest shopping center is the **Valley Mall** (2529 Main St., 509/453-8233, www.shopatvalleymall.net) just south of town in Union Gap. It's complete with Macy's, Sears, 85 specialty shops, and a 225-seat food court.

At Yakima Avenue and North 1st, a trainful of 22 old railroad cars and pseudo-Victorian buildings house the **Track 29 Shopping Mall** with gift shops and eateries. Many more places—including the largest collection of antique pedal cars on the West Coast—can be found in antique shops inside the adjacent **Yesterday's Village.**

Several downtown art galleries offer high-quality works, including **Simon Edwards Gallery** (811 W. Yakima Ave., 509/453-7723).

Toppenish is rife with antique stores, craft shops, and gift shops. **The Amish Connection** (509/865-5300) has handcrafted Amish furniture, dolls, quilts, and other items. A few doors away is **Kraff's** (509/865-3000), the largest retailer of Pendleton blankets in the United States. **Roses Native Designs** (212 W. 1st Ave., 509/865-9325) offers local Native American art and crafts. For authentic Native American arts and crafts, visit the gift shop at Yakama Nation Cultural Heritage Center.

SPORTS AND RECREATION

Spectator Sports

Yakima County Stadium (1220 Pacific Ave., 509/452-1450) is home to the **Yakima Bears** (509/457-5151, www.yakimabears.com), a short-season class-A affiliate of the Arizona Diamondbacks. Games are affordable and the team offers several promotions throughout the June–September schedule. The **Yakima Reds** (509/453-2086, www.yakimareds.com) play some exciting soccer under the UDL Premier Development League at **Marquette Stadium** (5400 West Chestnut Ave.). General admission tickets are $6 and the season runs May–August.

Scenic Drives

Driving on I-82 between Ellensburg and Yakima, you'll realize that Central Washington isn't the flat, boring terrain you might have heard about. As the road snakes up treeless ridges over 2,000 feet high, the far-off brown hills look as if they're covered with soft velvet; up close, it resolves into sagebrush, scrub, and grass. Along the way, you'll cross the **Fred Redmon Memorial Bridge,** the largest single concrete span bridge in North America. Pull into the rest stop at the south end of the bridge for a stunner of a view of the icy summits of Mt. Adams and Mt. Rainier in the distance.

The **Jacob Durr Wagon Road** (a.k.a. Wenas Road) is not recommended for vehicles without four-wheel drive. It was once the only route linking Yakima and Ellensburg; today, it's surely the most scenic, climbing over Umtanum Ridge for a 360-degree view of the Cascades and Yakima Valley. Drive north from Selah on N. Wenas Avenue, which becomes Wenas Road, the old Durr Wagon Road. The more standard route northward (I-90) also offers excellent vistas from the **Manatash Ridge Viewpoint** into the lush Kittitas Valley, with the Wenatchee Mountains rising behind the town of Ellensburg.

Water Sports

Yakima is home to four outdoor public pools open in the summer. Best among them is the one at **Franklin Park** (21st Avenue and Tieton Drive), which sports a slippery spiral water slide. The grassy hills at this park are also a local hot spot for sledding in the winter.

At **Eschbach Park** (4811 South Naches Rd., 509/574-2435, www.co.yakimacounty.us), five miles past the fish hatchery on the Old Naches Highway, rent a tube or kayak and take a lazy float down the Naches River. The day-use, 168-acre county park offers boating, swimming, picnicking, and play areas.

Many locals also float, water ski, or fish (trophy-sized rainbows for catch-and-release fishing only) in the beautiful 27-mile **Yakima River Canyon** (509/665-2100) between Ellensburg and Yakima owned by the private Nature Conservancy. The river is paralleled by State Highway 821, with several boat ramps and picnic sites along the route and is home to the greatest concentration of nesting raptors in the state.

Before you head out to swish your rod around, pick up a few flies and nymphs from **Gary's Fly Shoppe** (423 West Yakima Ave., Yakima, 509/457-3474, www.garysflyshoppe.com), whose helpful staff can point you in the right direction if you know what you're doing or sign you up for one of their guided excursions if you don't.

Cycling

The Yakima Valley farming country makes for great back-roads cycling, with a multitude of possible loop trips. Get a map of local cycling routes from the visitors center. Unfortunately, there are absolutely no bicycle rental shops in the Yakima Valley, Tri-Cities, or Walla Walla Valley areas. Pick up a rental on the way. If you are headed over via I-90, stop off at **Cle Elum Bike and Board** (316 W. 1st St., 509/674-4567). Or try one of the numerous rental shops in the Gorge if you are coming in from parts south.

If you need some supplies or want to buy a new ride, **Jake's Bike Shop** (507 W. Nob Hill Blvd., 509/469-9602) is a friendly local bike store that does right by its customers.

Golf

Yakima has five public golf courses. The **Apple Tree Resort** (8804 Occidental, 509/966-5877, www.appletreeresort.com, $50 nonresidents) features a signature par 3 17th hole—a tricky forced carry on to an apple-shaped island. **Suntides** (231 Pence, 509/966-9065, $25) offers a par-70 course. The city-owned, executive-length **Fisher Park Golf Course** (823 S. 40th Ave., 509/575-6075) can be a nice, quick indulgence at $9.25 for nine holes. You can even rent clubs here. The **Westwood West Golf Course** (6408 Tieton Dr., 509/966-0890) is another executive course with a driving range. Nine holes will run you $28.

Hiking

The **Yakima River Greenway** encompasses 3,600 acres east of the city, connecting Selah, Yakima, and Union Gap along a 10-mile paved biking and walking path.

Cowiche Canyon is a scenic and remote rocky canyon just a few minutes west of Naches. The abandoned railroad line ribbons along and across Cowiche Creek, passing distinctive rock formations, with some that resemble the Easter Island faces. The canyon is managed by Cowiche Canyon Conservancy (509/966-8608;www.cowichecanyon.org), which produces a brochure on the three-mile trail. To continue your journey, follow the out-and-back Uplands Trail spur off of the main trail. You can follow that about 1.5 miles to a shady grove of birch trees before returning.

Camping

About a mile east of town off I-82, an oasis of green awaits at **Yakima Sportsman State Park.** Year-round, kids can fish the pond, stocked with bluegill, trout, catfish, and carp. Adults can try their luck on the nearby Yakima River. Tent sites run $19 and RV sites are $26. ADA sites are available, as are coin-operated showers. Be sure to tackle the miles of hiking trails while you're here. Make reservations ($7 extra) at 888/226-7688, www.parks.wa.gov.

Wenas Creek Campground is home to the Hazel Wolf Bird Sanctuary in the Wenas

Valley. Camping here is primitive—we mean it! There is no fresh water available and you can expect to dig your own trenches.

Stagecoach RV Park (16201 N. Wenas Rd., 509/697-9650, www.stagecoachrv.com, $20 daily or $120 weekly) is in nearby Selah; there are no tent spaces here. Generators are not permitted. **Trailer Inns** (1610 N. 1st St., 509/452-9561 or 800/659-4784, www.trailerinnsrv.com) charges $20–38 depending on length of trailer and camping space selected.

The **Yakama Nation Resort RV Park,** next to the Cultural Heritage Center (280 Buster Rd., 509/865-2000 or 800/874-3087, www.winesnw.com/YakNtnRVListing.htm) has 125 parking spaces for RVs ($26), plus 14 very popular tepees ($30, sleeps five), a tent-camping area ($16), outdoor pool, hot tub, two saunas, exercise room, and other facilities.

ACCOMMODATIONS

Most of Yakima's in-town motels can be found along the Highway 97 corridor through town (1st Street). Several cheaper places on the south end of Union Gap are not included but may be acceptable if the need is strong.

Under $100

Cruise into town on Highway 82, cross the Yakima River, and take 1st to find the **Days Inn** (1504 N. 1st St., 509/248-3393 or 800/248-3360, $70 s or $75 d). Also affordable (and pet-friendly) is **Howard Johnson Plaza** (9 N. 9th St., 509/452-6511, $75 s or $95 d).

For valley accommodations, **Best Western Lincoln Inn** (515 S. Elm St., Toppenish, 509/865-7444 or 800/222-3161, www.bestwestern.com, $80s or $90 d) is the best choice in Toppenish, with its indoor pool, hot tub, exercise room, fridges, microwaves, and continental breakfast.

Farther east, **Sunnyside Inn B&B** (804 E. Edison, Sunnyside, 509/221-4195 or 800/221-4195, www.sunnysideinn.com, $89–99 d) is situated in the 1919 Fordyce house and has thirteen spacious rooms with private baths, eight of which feature whirlpool tubs. A hearty country breakfast is served, and kids are accepted.

Also in Sunnyside, **Country Inn and Suites** (408 Yakima Valley Hwy., Sunnyside, 509/837-7878 or 800/578-7878, $55 s or $66 d) has a heated outdoor pool, hot tub, and continental breakfast.

When you drive into Prosser, you can't miss **The Barn Motor Inn** (490 Wine Country Rd., 509/786-2121, $50 s or $55 d). Just like the name tells you, this motel is fashioned like a big red country barn. Rates are pretty good for the level of cleanliness and comfort offered by the rooms here. There's a pool and a restaurant on-site. You can also park RVs in the trailer facility around back ($17.50).

$100-150

Quality Inn Comfort Suites (I-82 and Valley Mall Blvd., 509/249-1900 or 800/228-5150, www.choicehotels.com, $129 s or $140 d) looks out over islands in the Yakima River. This all-suites motel has an indoor pool, hot tub, exercise room, continental breakfast, and free wireless Internet.

Holiday Inn Express (1001 E. A St., 509/249-1000 or 800/315-2621, www.hiexpress.com, $140 s or d) features an indoor pool, hot tub, fitness room, and continental breakfast. An extra $20 will warm the staff toward the idea of your pet staying the night with you.

A classic Queen Anne Victorian built in 1889, **A Touch of Europe B&B** (220 N. 16th Ave., 509/454-9775,888/438-7073, www.winesnw.com/toucheuropeb&b, $123–136 s or d) serves candlelit European breakfasts (included in rate), high tea ($30), and lavish five- to seven-course dinners ($50) in its elegant dining room. The German- and English-speaking owners provide an acre of shady grounds and three well-appointed guest rooms in a relaxing adults-only environment.

At the **Birchfield Manor B&B** (2018 Birchfield Rd., 509/452-1960 or 800/375-3420, www.birchfieldmanor.com, $119–220 d), guests may sample from a wine cellar amply stocked with local vintages. The biggest local B&B, Birchfield plumps the pillows for guests in four luxurious rooms in the 1910 main house and four adjacent, newer cottages. All rooms have private baths with whirlpool tubs, and some are equipped with gas fireplaces and private decks. The parklike grounds contain a swimming pool. Breakfasts are memorable, and dinners in the restaurant here are some of the finest around (Thurs.–Sat., $27–38 for full dinners). Ask about the golf packages in partnership with the Apple Tree Resort.

Orchard Inn B&B (1207 Pecks Canyon Dr., 509/966-1283, www.orchardinnbb.com, $109–129 d) is a lovely contemporary home tucked away in an orchard of cherry trees. The three guest rooms have private baths, private entrances, and the use of outdoor gazebos. A full, slow-food breakfast is served. The friendly bilingual (German and English) owners welcome kids and well-behaved dogs on approval.

$150-200

Feed a horse an apple grown right outside your door at **Cherry Wood Bed and Breakfast** (3271 Roza Dr., Zillah, 509/829-3500, www.cherrywoodbandb.com, $145–165 d), a fun little gem hidden away on a working farm in Zillah. This quirky inn offers a spate of different lodging options. First there are very comfortable and well-appointed rooms within the farmhouse, available year-round. Then there are the luxury teepee and themed retro trailers that open up in the warm summer months. Everyone sups on the welcoming innkeeper's gourmet breakfasts inside the main house dining room, and many guests stick around for her guided horseback winery tours ($150), offered by appointment.

Over in Grandview, you'll be pampered from the get-go when you set your suitcases down at **Cozy Rose Inn B&B** (1220 Forsell Rd., 509/882-4669, www.cozyroseinn.com, $189 d). Lush tapestries, soft bedding, and smartly painted designer rooms await you here. All suites come with whirlpool tub and big-screen TV, and each has individual amenities including fireplaces, fridges, and private entrances. For maximum romance, breakfast can be delivered to your door and a special dinner can be arranged with the innkeeper.

Over $250

Dust off your fancy cowboy hat and tuck yourself in the luxurious rooms at the Southwest-style **Desert Wind Winery Inn** (2258 Wine Country Rd., Prosser, 509/786-7277, www.desertwindwinery.com, $250–300 d). The concert-hall-sized suites all come equipped with gas kiva fireplaces, large-screen TVs with Bose sound and DVD players, and balconies overlooking the winery courtyard and the Yakima River.

FOOD

Yakima

CAFÉS AND DINERS

One of the top-10 most visited drive-ins in the country, **Miner's Drive-In** (2415 S. 1st St., 509/457-8194, 8:30 A.M.–4 A.M. daily) is a Yakima institution. The loyal customers line up for the flying-saucer sized burgers and golden onion rings. Miner's also serves a book-length list of milk shake flavors. Freshness is the key here—you'll see the phrase "Nothing is cooked until you order it!" plastered on signs in the store.

Looking for just the cure for a wine-induced hangover? Head to the local greasy spoon, **Mel's Diner** (314 N. 1st St., 509/248-5382, open 24 hours) and get yourself a big ol' breakfast with a fresh cup or three of coffee served up by waitresses who'll call you "hon."

Also of note is **Jack's Sports Bar** (432 S. 48th Ave., 509/966-4340), a fun place with burgers, sandwiches, and a big-screen TV, open till 1:45 A.M. on the weekends.

CONTEMPORARY NORTHWEST

One of Yakima's finest supper spots, **Birchfield Manor** (two miles east of the city on Birchfield Rd., 509/452-1960 or 800/375-3420, dinner Thurs.–Sat.) seats diners in a restored 1910 farmhouse. Formal dinners are complemented by a vast selection of Yakima Valley wines. The innovative cuisine changes seasonally, but there is always a perfect filet mignon. Reservations are essential.

In the historic district, **The Greystone Restaurant** (5 N. Front St., 509/248-9801, entrées $30) aspires to be a fine dining establishment on par with big city cousins over in Seattle, and it certainly does have some strong points. The towering ceilings with antique molding and the ruggedly elegant exposed stonework certainly make for a dramatic dining room, and the food is delicious. Where it is seriously lacking, however, is in the service and presentation departments. When I arrived on a quiet evening I was seated at a table with a dirty tablecloth. Even after that was sorted out, service was dreadfully slow. Your best bet is to bring some lively companions to pass the time, sit in the lounge, and order a bottle of wine with some scrumptious light appetizers.

Then head across the street to **The Depot Restaurant and Lounge** (32 N. Front St., 509/949-4233, 11:30 A.M.–10 P.M. daily, entrées $20), in Yakima's old 1910 Pacific Northern Railroad station, which has an equally exciting dining room and none of the pretense. The depot is beautifully restored, and you'll likely spend parts of dinner looking upward, mouth agape, at the molding and scrollwork in the domed ceiling. The chef dishes out mouthwatering plates of seafood, chops, and fresh salads at extremely reasonable prices.

MEXICAN

Yakima is one of the rare places in Washington where you can find really, truly authentic Mexican restaurants, which serve the large community of Hispanic farm workers in the valley.

One of the best spots in town is at **Los Hernandez** (3706 Main St., Union Gap, 509/457-6003, 11 A.M.–6 P.M. Tues.–Fri., 10 A.M.–7 P.M. Sat., 11 A.M.–6 P.M. Sun., closed Mon.), which serves homemade tamales better than you can get even in Southern California. You'll regularly see folks load up coolers full of them to take home. If you go in springtime, be on the lookout for the inventive asparagus tamales. They may sound strange, but they sure are delicious.

Santiago's Gourmet Restaurant (111 E. Yakima Ave., 509/453-1644, 11:30 A.M.–2 P.M. and 5–9 P.M. Mon.–Fri., 5–10 P.M. Sat., closed Sun.) is a lively and popular Mexican restaurant with all the standards and excellent daily specials.

El Pastor (315 W. Walnut, 509/453-5159, 11 A.M.–8 P.M. Mon.–Fri., noon–8 P.M. Sat.) is a small place with inexpensive and delicious Mexican dishes. Find lots more *tortillerias* and *panaderías* on South 1st Street heading toward Union Gap.

OTHER INTERNATIONAL

For gourmet Italian food and Northwest specialties, visit **Gasparetti's** (1013 N. 1st St., 509/248-0628, 11 A.M.–midnight daily). The pastas are all freshly made, and desserts are a real treat. Interestingly enough, it is also well known for its onion rings. You really can't do wrong giving them a try.

Let the chef win you over at **Keoki's Oriental Restaurant** (2107 W. Lincoln Ave., 509/453-2401, 11 A.M.–2 P.M. and 4–10 P.M. daily), where the cooking takes place at your table. The teriyaki steak is always a pleaser.

MARKETS

Finding food out in the winery back roads can be a hit-or-miss affair. Load up on picnic supplies in town before you head out to ensure a happy and fulfilling wine excursion. **Deep Sea Deli** (9th and Summitview, 509/248-1484, 9 A.M.–6 P.M. Mon.–Sat., closed Sun.) stocks specialty cheese, meats, and crackers. It also smokes its own salmon right on the property. Or leave the lunch packing up to **Buhrmaster Baking Co. and Restaurant** (1 West Yakima Ave. #30, Track 29, 509/469-9973, 8 A.M.–8 P.M. Mon.–Fri., 11 A.M.–8 P.M. Sat., closed Sun.), which prepares box lunches to go for wine tourists.

Pulse Foods (4315 Main St., Union Gap, 509/452-5386) has delicious artisan breads and health foods.

Fresh fruit, vegetable stands, and U-pick places can be found throughout the Yakima Valley. From Yakima, the easiest way to find them is to take Highway 97 and exit off Lateral A Road. Head down south and let the signs guide you. The farm roads are ruler-straight, so it is pretty much impossible to get lost.

One sure winner is **Barrett Orchards** (1209 Pecks Canyon Rd., 509/966-1275, www.treeripened.com), where you can pick cherries, pears, apples, peaches, or whatever is in season. Or let them do the work and buy from its farm store. It's also fun to just head down Highways 97 and 22 until something looks interesting—hand-painted signs are as numerous as the fruit they advertise.

Valley Eats

TOPPENISH

Toppenish's strong Hispanic culture is evidenced in the plethora of Mexican restaurants, clothing stores, and Se Habla Español signs. **Taqueria Mexicana** (105½ S. Alder St., 509/865-7116) has the best south-of-the-border meals in town.

Also near Toppenish, the **Yakama Nation Cultural Center** (100 Spiel-yi Loop, 509/865-2800) has a popular restaurant with a large salad bar, salmon, buffalo, and fry bread. The Sunday brunch is very popular.

You'll discover the best burgers around, along with floats, shakes, and cold drinks, at the old-fashioned soda fountain in **Gibbons Pharmacy** (117 S. Toppenish Ave., 509/865-2722).

ZILLAH

In business since 1950, **El Ranchito** (just south of Zillah, 509/829-5880) is fast Mexican food at its meaty best, with no pretense. Order at the counter and wait for your order to arrive on a paper plate. Satisfaction guaranteed, but get here early—it closes at 7 P.M. most nights.

Another popular, long-running Zillah restaurant is **Squeeze Inn** (611 1st Ave., 509/829-6226), where the breakfasts bring out the coffee klatch crowd, and the dinners of steak, prime rib, and seafood attract folks from all over the valley. Squeeze Inn has been owned by the same family since 1932.

SUNNYSIDE AND GRANDVIEW

Sunnyside's big Darigold cheese factory is one of the largest cheese plants in the nation. **Darigold Dairy Fair** (400 Alexander Rd., 509/837-4321) has self-guided tours, fun exhibits (including flying cows), and videos, plus fresh ice cream, cheeses, sandwiches, and gifts.

Snipes Mountain Brewing Inc. (905 Yakima Valley Hwy., Sunnyside, 509/837-2739, 10 A.M.–10 P.M. Sun.–Thurs., 11 A.M.–11 P.M. Fri.–Sat.) is hard to miss. It's the huge log-and-lodgepole building near the center of town, with a brewery behind glass and a diverse menu that includes everything from wood-fired pizzas to seafood satay. It's very popular, with a lively atmosphere and tasty grub.

PROSSER

The Barn Inn and Restaurant (490 Wine Country Rd., 509/786-2121) on the west end of town is one of the best local restaurants for all-American steak and seafood platters; munch the great appetizers while watching sports on the big-screen TV. Another local favorite is **The Blue Goose** (306 7th St., 509/786-1774), which features a menu that includes prime rib, pastas, and seafood. Come here for breakfast omelettes.

More refined palates will prefer the comestibles at **Picazo 717** (717 6th St., 509/786-1116, www.picazo717.com) an arty, modern tapas and wine bar that serves food that will make you want to sing. Try the daring shellfish cakes ($10) with shrimp, crab, and scallops drizzled with a poblano remoulade. Or bring a friend and order the paella for two ($34). The well-educated staff is ready to offer the perfect wine pairing from the jam-packed cellar.

The **Prosser Farmers Market** (509/786-3600, 8 A.M.–12:30 P.M. Sat. June–Sept.) takes place in the city park.

INFORMATION AND SERVICES

For maps, brochures, and current festival information, contact the **Yakima Valley Visitors and Convention Bureau** (10 N. 8th St., 509/575-3010 or 800/221-0751, www.visityakima.com, 8 A.M.–5 P.M. Mon.–Fri. all year, plus 9 A.M.–5 P.M. Sat. and 10 A.M.–4 P.M. Sun. May–Oct.).

Emergency medical service is provided by **Yakima Valley Memorial Hospital** (2811 Tieton Dr., 509/575-8000) in the city. Emergency medical care is also available at the 63-bed **Toppenish Community Hospital** (502 West 4th Ave., 509/865-3105) which, along with high-tech care, also provides a Native American Spiritual Care Center featuring facilities for performing healing rituals and ceremonies. **Sunnyside Community Hospital** (10th & Tacoma, 509/837-1500) runs a 24-hour ER.

Sick pets are welcomed at **Pet Emergency Service** (510 W Chestnut Ave., 509/452-4138) in Yakima or at the **Wapato Toppenish Veterinary Clinic** (Hwy. 97 and Branch Rd., 509/865-3435).

GETTING THERE AND AROUND

By Air

The **Yakima Air Terminal-McAllister Field** (2300 West Washington Ave., 509/575-6149) is the largest airport in the area. **Horizon Airlines** (800/252-7522, www.alaskaair.com) provides daily passenger service to and from Sea-Tac airport. **Noland-Decoto Flying Service** (509/248-1370) and the McCormick Air Center (509/248-1680) are full-service Fixed Base Operators.

Several rental car agencies have desks here as well.

By Bus

Yakima Transit (509/575-6175, www.ci.yakima.wa.us/services/transit/) serves the Yakima area, including the municipal airport, with Monday–Saturday service.

For local tours, contact **Accent! Tours** (509/575-3949 or 800/735-0428, www.accenttours.com).

To get out of town or across the country, hop aboard **Greyhound** (509/457-5131 or 800/231-2222, www.greyhound.com) from its Yakima station (602 East Yakima Ave.). Greyhound also stops in Toppenish (at the Branding Iron, 509/865-3773) and Sunnyside (13th St. and Hwy. 12, 509/837-5344).

Ellensburg

One of Washington's best-known Western-style towns, Ellensburg is famous for its Labor Day weekend rodeo that attracts thousands of spectators and top rodeo talent from across the country. Surprisingly enough, the town itself has more the look of a quiet college town than an old-school Western movie set. At its heart is Central Washington University, one of the state's first, established in 1891. The western roots of Ellensburg are better illustrated in the ranches and mining outposts that radiate around the town.

Situated as it is just over Snoqualmie Pass along I-90, Ellensburg has long been a popular overnight spot for Puget Sound concert-goers attending events at the Gorge Amphitheater in George. Increasingly, though, as the number of wineries grows within central Washington, the town is fast becoming known as the gateway to wine country.

SIGHTS

Museums

The **Kittitas County Historical Museum** (E. 3rd and Pine Streets, 509/925-3778, $1) has Native American artifacts and displays of pioneer tools, photographs of early Ellensburg, and an impressive collection of petrified wood and gemstones. Open Tuesday–Saturday; hours vary.

The **Clymer Museum** (416 N. Pearl, 509/962-6416, www.clymermuseum.com, 10 A.M.–5 P.M. Mon.–Fri., noon–5 P.M. Sat.–Sun., donations accepted) honors John Ford Clymer, who was born in Ellensburg in 1907 and went on to fame for his nature illustrations and carefully researched paintings of the Old West, published in the *Saturday Evening Post.* At the museum, you can watch a video on Clymer's life and view dozens of his cover art

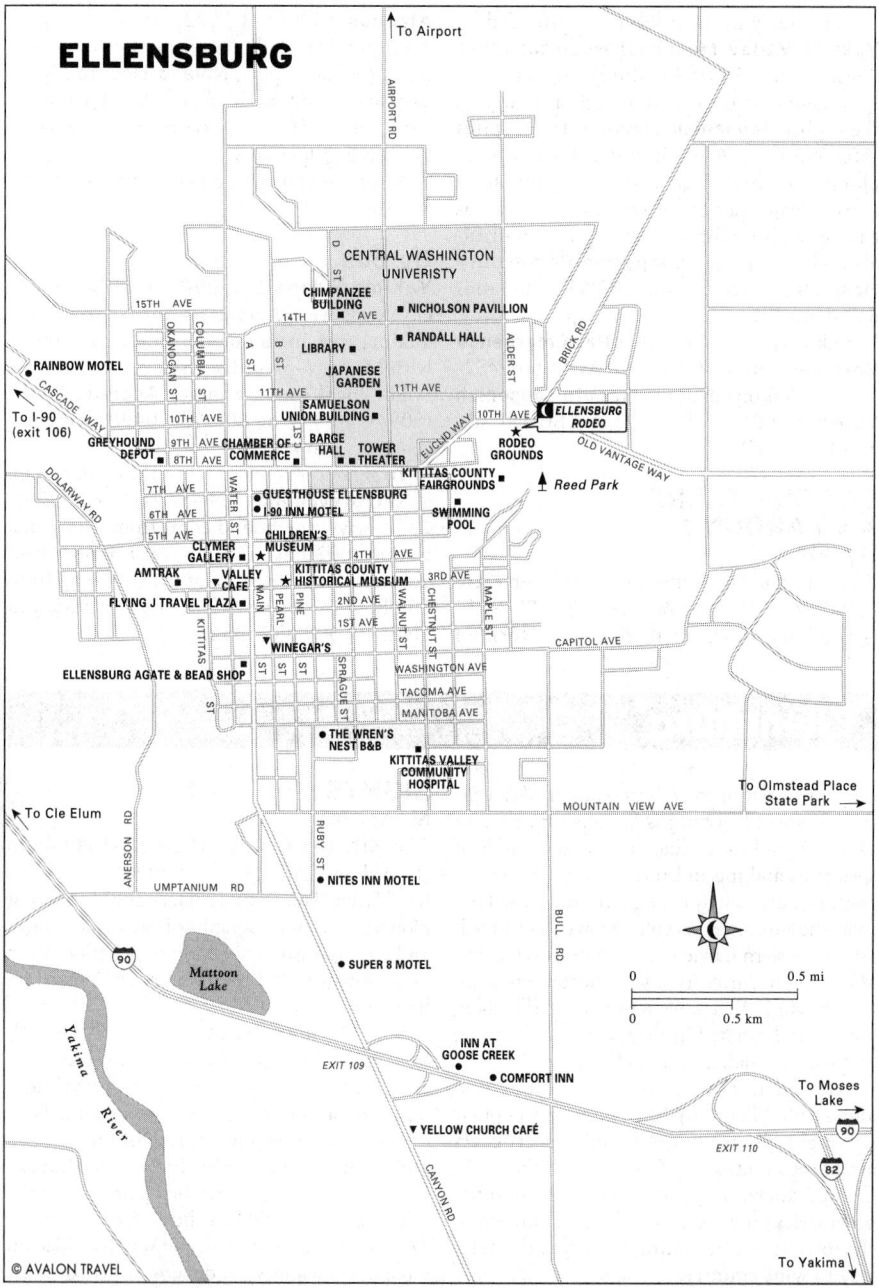
ELLENSBURG
To Airport
AIRPORT RD
CENTRAL WASHINGTON UNIVERISTY
D ST
CHIMPANZEE BUILDING
NICHOLSON PAVILLION
15TH AVE
14TH AVE
RANDALL HALL
ALDER ST
BRICK RD
LIBRARY
RAINBOW MOTEL
OKANOGAN ST
COLUMBIA ST
A ST
B ST
JAPANESE GARDEN
CASCADE WAY
11TH AVE
11TH AVE
To I-90 (exit 106)
10TH AVE
SAMUELSON UNION BUILDING
10TH AVE
ELLENSBURG RODEO
GREYHOUND DEPOT
9TH AVE
8TH AVE
CHAMBER OF COMMERCE
C ST
BARGE HALL
TOWER THEATER
EUCLID WAY
RODEO GROUNDS
OLD VANTAGE WAY
DOLARWAY RD
KITTITAS COUNTY FAIRGROUNDS
Reed Park
7TH AVE
WATER ST
GUESTHOUSE ELLENSBURG
I-90 INN MOTEL
SWIMMING POOL
6TH AVE
5TH AVE
CHILDREN'S MUSEUM
CLYMER GALLERY
4TH AVE
AMTRAK
VALLEY CAFE
KITTITAS COUNTY HISTORICAL MUSEUM
3RD AVE
MAIN ST
PEARL ST
PINE ST
WALNUT ST
CHESTNUT ST
MAPLE ST
FLYING J TRAVEL PLAZA
2ND AVE
1ST AVE
KITTITAS ST
WINEGAR'S
CAPITOL AVE
ELLENSBURG AGATE & BEAD SHOP
SPRAGUE ST
WASHINGTON AVE
TACOMA AVE
MANITOBA AVE
THE WREN'S NEST B&B
KITTITAS VALLEY COMMUNITY HOSPITAL
To Olmstead Place State Park
To Cle Elum
MOUNTAIN VIEW AVE
ANERSON RD
RUBY ST
UMPTANIUM RD
NITES INN MOTEL
BULL RD
90
Mattoon Lake
SUPER 8 MOTEL
0 0.5 mi
0 0.5 km
Yakima River
INN AT GOOSE CREEK
EXIT 109
COMFORT INN
To Moses Lake
YELLOW CHURCH CAFÉ
EXIT 110
82
CANYON RD
© AVALON TRAVEL
To Yakima

designs, along with a number of his Western paintings. A separate gallery here exhibits changing displays of contemporary artwork, and a gift shop has local crafts and books.

Historic Buildings

Pick up a map at the chamber of commerce for a self-guided tour of 31 Victorian-era buildings, most located within a five-block area between 6th and 3rd Avenues and Main and Pearl Streets. These "painted ladies" make up the backbone of Ellensburg's storied historical district and currently house apartments, shops, and galleries.

Thorp Grist Mill (11640 N. Thorp Hwy., Thorp, 509/964-9640, www.thorp.org, 11 A.M.–3 P.M. Thurs.–Sun. late May–Sept.), in the town of Thorp (eight miles northwest of Ellensburg), is a restored 1883 flour mill with the Northwest's most complete display of historic milling equipment. The mill was used to grind flour and cornmeal until 1946 and is now a National Historic Landmark. An interpretive slide show is provided.

Offbeat Sights

On a park bench on 4th and Pearl sits a friendly ***Ellensburg Bull,*** complete with discreetly placed cowboy hat. It was created by noted sculptor Richard Beyer. An amusing gunslinger sculpture by Dan Klennerd guards the corner of 5th and Pearl. Also in town is **Dick & Jane's Spot** (101 N. Pearl, www.reflectorart.com) an art-site boasting 10,000 bottle caps and thousands of reflectors among its one-of-a-kind decorative elements. It is a private yard, so please be respectful.

Central Washington University

Founded in 1891, the 350-acre Central Washington University campus (400 E. University Way, www.cw.edu) makes for a nice sunny stroll. For tours of the campus, call the Admissions Office at 509/963-1262. A **Japanese Garden** near the center of campus is open year-round and contains interesting Japanese lanterns and grounds landscaped with dozens of types of plants, including cherry trees donated by the Japanese Consulate General. The **Sarah Spurgeon Art Gallery** (509/963-2665, www.cwu.edu/~art) exhibits student and professional alumni art on a rotating basis, as well as offering talks on occasion.

CWU's **Chimpanzee & Human Communication Institute** (509/963-2244, www.cwu.edu/~cwuchci) houses the research project geared toward training chimpanzees to use American Sign Language to communicate with humans and each other. Visitors can attend fascinating two-hour-long **Chimposiums** ($10 adults, $7.50 students) on Saturday mornings and Sunday afternoons. Reservations are recommended, and attendees must be over the age of 16.

Parks

Four miles southeast of Ellensburg on Ferguson Road, see one of the first Kittitas Valley farms at **Olmstead Place State Park** (509/925-1943, www.parks.wa.gov, dawn–dusk daily Memorial Day to Labor Day, by appointment the rest of the year). Here, you'll find a working pioneer farm, Tours are available noon–4 P.M. Saturday–Sunday.

Irene Rinehart Riverfront Park, on the Yakima River off Umptanum Road, is a welcome relief from the relentless summer sunshine. You can cool your toes in the swift green river, hike, play some volleyball on nice sandy courts, or grill up some bratwurst. **Reed Park** at the end of Craig Avenue has a small shaded green for reading and relaxing, plus superb views of the county below and the snow-covered Stuart Range to the northwest.

ENTERTAINMENT AND EVENTS

Ellensburg Rodeo

Labor Day weekend's Ellensburg Rodeo (509/962-7639 or 800/426-5340, www.ellensburgrodeo.com) is one of the top rodeos in the nation, attracting cowboys from all over with prize money of more than $250,000. The rodeo has been around since 1923 and features calf roping, wild horse races, cliff races, Brahma bull riding, and wild cow milking during this

ELLENSBURG BLUE AGATE

Formed millennia ago and deposited in the glacier till surrounding the Ellensburg mountainsides, the rare and beautiful Ellensburg Blue Agate has captivated local people for only a blink of an eye compared to the length of its existence.

Also known simply as **E-blue,** this precious gem comes in a range of colors from sky blue to a deep purplish color, though prized above all is a vibrant cornflower blue. According to local legend Native American tribes valued these blue stones for their beauty, so much so that only tribal chiefs were allowed to wear them.

The first white man to pluck them from the agate beds was Ellensburg's first mayor, Austin Mires, who in 1905 sent them to Seattle to be set into rings. But it wasn't until 1913 that they drew widespread attention. In that year, jeweler J. N. O. Thomson had the local Native Americans show him where to find E-blue and started promoting them heavily. His marketing paid off – for several decades tourists came up to Ellensburg just to root around the soil for E-blue. The famed New York jeweler Tiffany & Co. even used the gem in some of its jewelry.

This popularity was the gem's undoing, however – by 1940 or so the most productive agate beds were depleted. Today it is a difficult prospect getting your hands on this scarce rock. Most of the existing beds are on private land, and even those who do get a chance to scour them consider a single small find pretty good for a whole day's work.

four-day event. It's held in conjunction with the carnival, parade, exhibits, and top-notch country entertainment of the **Kittitas County Fair** at the fairgrounds at the east end of 6th Avenue. Rodeo tickets include admission to the fair; order up to a year in advance. Nearly all the tickets are gone for the weekend events by early August.

Other Events

Visit the **Ellensburg National Art Show and Auction** (509/962-2934) the third weekend in May. More than 200 artists display their works. The highlight for many is the "Quick Draw," when about a dozen artists each create a work of art in 45 minutes.

The **Whisky Dick Triathlon** (509/925-3137 or 888/925-2204, www.whiskydick.com/race) subjects entrants to a one-mile swim in the 60°F Columbia River and a 28-mile bike leg climbing 1,900 feet in the first 12 miles. At least the 10K running leg is on level ground!

Held the second weekend following Labor Day at Olmstead Place State Park, the **Threshing Bee** (509/925-3137) gives city slickers an opportunity to see blacksmithing, plowing, and steam and gas threshing. A big country breakfast is served in the morning, and an antique tractor pull contest is a highlight.

SHOPPING

Be on the lookout for the beautiful "Ellensburg Blue" agate, sold at local jewelry stores uncut or finished and fashioned into earrings, necklaces, and rings. **Ellensburg Agate & Bead Shop** (201 S. Main St., 509/925-4998, 9 A.M.–5 P.M. Mon.–Sat., until 6 P.M. in summer) is one of the most well known, and a friend to rock hounds looking for advice and equipment to help them scour the region for a bit of blue to bring home. Also popular are **Art of Jewelry** (709 South Main St.) and **Kim Khap Gems and Jewelry** (108 N. Main St.).

There are dozens of other cute boutiques and galleries around these jewelry shops on the main parallel parkways of Pearl and Main (just a block apart). **Gallery One** (408½ N. Pearl, 509/925-2670) features works by some of the best regional artists upstairs in the grand 1889 G. R. Stewart Building. And the quirky **Dancing Ewe Yarns & Teas** (109 E 3rd Ave., Ste. 1, 509/962-5648, www.dancingewe-yarns.com) is a knitter's delight.

SPORTS AND RECREATION

Iron Horse Trail

The Ellensburg area has an abundance of enjoyable backcountry roads for bike and (of course) horseback riding, along with more strenuous trips into the Cascades to the west. The best among them is Iron Horse Trail, alternately known as John Wayne Trail, which stretches 110 miles across the state. The trail runs parallel to the Yakima River, with several trailheads in and around Ellensburg.

Mountain High Sports (105 E. 4th Ave., 509/925-2626) rents mountain bikes, in-line skates, tents, climbing shoes, skis, backpacks, and other outdoor gear.

For horseback rides, contact **Happy Trails Horse Adventures** (Eaton, 509/925-9428, www.happytrailsateastonwa.com). They offer horseback rides along of almost any length, all of them at least partially on the Iron Horse. Prices range from $90 for a three-hour ride to $165 for an overnighter, and, yes, food is included. In the fall and winter, the ranch offers old-fashioned hayrides and sleigh rides, sure to put a smile on the face and some red on the cheeks.

The 0.75-mile **Altapes Creek Trail** leads from the red barn to the Seaton Cabin Schoolhouse, originally located farther away in a meadow. The park also offers some relaxing seasonal fishing in the Coleman Creek.

Water Sports

The **Yakima River** is a favorite place for tubing during the summer, and a great place to cool off when temperatures top 100°F. Much of the 40-mile stretch between Cle Elum and Roza Dam is a relaxing float, but you need to watch for dangerous logs in the water. For specific put-in points and hazardous areas, check with the chamber of commerce visitors center. The most popular run is the 15 miles from Teanaway Bridge (below Cle Elum) to the diversion dam; it generally takes five to six hours.

Rent rafts and kayaks in Thorp, or schedule a guided tour at **Rill Adventures** (509/964-2520, www.rillsonline.com). Try its magical Full Moon Floats on the "Yak" with snacks and light beverages ($40).

The river is also a productive fly-fishing hole for beautiful, fat rainbow trout, and few can get you outfitted more thoroughly than the delightfully named **Worley-Bugger Fly Co.** (306 S. Main St. #3, 888/950-3474, www.worleybuggerflyco.com). The experienced guides offer full-day and half-day tours starting at $300.

Swim at the **Ellensburg City Pool** (815 E. 6th Ave., 509/962-7211, $4.50 adults, $2.30 seniors, $2.30 kids 17 and under for nonresidents), where you'll also find a sauna, fitness center, and hot tub.

Other Recreation

Rockhounds know that Kittitas County is the only place on earth you'll find the "Ellensburg Blue" agate. Most finds are made on private or leased land northwest of Ellensburg, making it a difficult prospect for rock hunters as most owners won't allow you on their land. Fortunately, you can still try your luck at the **Rock N Tomahawk Ranch** (2590 Upper Green Canyon Rd., 509/962-2403, $5). The owners here will give you a brief orientation about finding Ellensburg blue and then set you loose on their 160-acre spread to see what you can find. If you want to scour public lands, you can check Dry Creek on Highway 97, or Horse Canyon Road. Here are the rules: no digging—surface hunting only; respect property lines and fences; and don't bother the cows. If you come up empty-handed, Ellensburg stores sell the uncut stones, as well as jewelry.

Winter visitors to the Ellensburg area can watch around 750 elk at the feeding station in Watt Canyon, 15 miles west of town. The elk are fed hay by the Washington Department of Wildlife. Get here by heading west on I-90 to exit 101, then across the freeway and uphill a quarter mile. Turn right on Old Thorp Cemetery Road and follow it to Watt Canyon Road, where you turn left and continue a mile to the elk-feeding site.

Camping

The nearest public campground is 27 miles east at Wanapum State Recreation Area in the Columbia Basin. Closer to Ellensburg,

RV spaces are available at the **Kittitas Valley Event Center** (800/426-5340) during the summer months. More camping and RV spaces are available at **E&J Resort,** operated in cooperation with Days Inn (901 Berry Rd., 509/933-1500 or 888/889-9870, $30, continental breakfast $3 extra) and **Yakima River RV Park** (791 Ringer Loop, 509/925-4734, www.yakimarv.com). Rates are variable, based on the amount of electricity desired, ranging from $20 per night for no power up to $30 for 50 amps. The park is set up on a working ranch with three stalls available to guests traveling with horses. Guests can fly fish for free on the property.

ACCOMMODATIONS

Lodging can be dicey during the Ellensburg Rodeo in early September, the Western Art show in May, and Gorge Concerts on summer weekends. The Ellensburg Chamber of Commerce (509/925-3137 or 888/925-2204, www.ellensburg-chamber.com) keeps track of which lodgings have space. Reservations should be made far in advance for these times—before mid-January for the rodeo. Also be forewarned that during the rodeo, rates may be considerably higher than those listed here.

Fans of Craftsman-style architecture will love **The Wren's Nest Bed & Breakfast** (300 E. Manitoba Ave., 509/925-9061, www.wrensnest.com, $90–110 d), a 1912 home that has been restored inside and out to spec with the clean style of the movement—everything except, of course, the two lions sitting on the stone porch railings, which are charming in their own right. Inside the woodwork is deliciously golden and nutty, cut in simple lines to let the medium speak for itself.

The **Inn at Goose Creek** (1720 Canyon Rd., 509/962-8030 or 800/533-0822, $119 s or d) is different. Very different. The 10 rooms all have different motifs, ranging from a room in which it's Christmas all year long, to the All-Star Sports Fan room, complete with basketball hoop table. Each room includes a fridge and whirlpool tub, and a continental breakfast is served.

A favorite among parents visiting their kids at CWU, **GuestHouse Ellensburg** (606 N. Main St., 509/962-3706 or 888/699-0123, $135 d) is an easy four-block walk from campus and close to the shops of the historic downtown. The Victorian home situates guests in one of two suites done up with the best of the old and the new: English antiques and big flat-screen TVs. Wine lovers will be pleased to find Ellensburg WineWorks operating beneath them on the first floor.

Rainbow Motel (1025 Cascade Way, 509/933-7100$57–105 s or d) has standard rooms; kitchenettes are also available. **I-90 Inn Motel** (1390 Dolarway Rd., exit 106 off I-90, 509/925-9844, $62 s or $72 d) has lakeside rooms with continental breakfast; pets are welcome. **Nites Inn Motel** (1200 S. Ruby, 509/962-9600, $62–65 d, pets $8 extra) has parklike grounds and microwaves and fridges in all rooms.

Super 8 Motel (1500 Canyon Rd., 509/962-6888 or 800/800-8000, www.super8.com, $81 s or $94 d) has an indoor pool and hot tub. **Quality Inn** (1700 Canyon Rd., 509/925-9801 or 800/321-8791, $95 s or $99 d) has an indoor pool, sauna, and hot tubs. The **Comfort Inn** (1722 Canyon Rd., 509/925-7037 or 800/221-2222, www.hotelchoice.com, $104 s or d) features an indoor pool, hot tub, and continental breakfast.

FOOD

The Valley Café (103 W. 3rd Ave., 509/925-3050, 11 A.M.–9 P.M. daily) is a European-style bistro where you won't go wrong any meal of the day. Dinner highlights include Ellensburg lamb, seafood, chicken, or pasta. The attractive brick building was built in the 1930s.

Grant's Pizza Place (716 E. 8th Ave., 509/925-9855, 11 A.M.–10 P.M. daily) has quick food: pizzas, nachos, chicken hot wings, and a salad bar.

Built in 1923 as a German Lutheran sanctum, **Yellow Church Café's** (111 South Pearl St., 509/933-2233, www.yellowchurchcafe.com, 11 A.M.–9 P.M. Mon.–Fri., 8:30 A.M.–9 P.M. Sat.–Sun.) waitresses float in with a heavenly spread of healthy lunches and dinners daily.

Housed in a 1920s gas station, **D&M Drive-Thru** (408 S. Main, 509/962-6333, 5:30 A.M.–10 P.M. daily) is a great place to get an espresso and a muffin without having to get out of your car.

Ellensburg's hot summer days and Winegar's silky ice creams are made for each other. **Winegar's** is an institution in the valley, with two locations in town, one near the rodeo arena (1013 E. University Way, 509/933-1823, 6 A.M.–10 P.M. daily) and the other downtown (608 N. Main St., 509/933-1821, 6 A.M.–6 P.M. Mon.–Fri., 7 A.M.–6 P.M. Sat., 8 A.M.–5 P.M. Sun.). There are a stableful of inventive flavors, but the very best have its delicious maple flavoring. Winegar's also serves a damn fine cup of espresso—the debate rages in town as to whether it beats the joe poured at D&M.

The **Kittitas County Farmers Market** (on 4th St. between Pearl and Pine, 509/925-1776, www.kcfarmersmarket.com, 9 A.M.–1 P.M. Sat. May–Oct.) brings fresh produce, baked goods, and arts and crafts. The annual schedule usually includes performances by musicians and dance troupes.

If Ellensburg is a gateway to wine country, then **Ellensburg Wine Works** (606 N. Main St., 509/962-8463, noon–7 P.M. Tues.–Sat.) is your ticket puncher. This quaint emporium of all things vinous is tucked away in the bottom floor of a charming bed-and-breakfast. The owners pride themselves on their eclectic and sometimes obscure selection of local wines. Taste their hand-picked vintages all day on Friday and Saturday.

INFORMATION

The **Ellensburg Chamber of Commerce** (801 S. Ruby St., 509/925-2002 or 888/925-2204, www.ellensburg-chamber.com) is open 8 A.M.–5 P.M. Monday–Friday and 10 A.M.–2 P.M. Saturday year-round.

GETTING THERE AND AROUND

Kittitas County Connector (509/933-2287) has bus service in Ellensburg, and to Thorp, Cle Elum, Roslyn, and Vantage. Call **Rodeo Town Taxi** (407 N Walnut St., 509/929-4222) for local cab rides. **Greyhound** (1512 Hwy. 97, 509/925-1177 or 800/231-2222, www.greyhound.com) can get you out of town from its depot in Ellensburg.

The nearest commercial airport is in Yakima.

Those looking for a cheap and convenient place to gas up and catch up on email via Wi-Fi should take I-90 exit to stop at **Flying J Travel Plaza** (2300 Canyon Rd.).

Wenatchee

Set on the northern reaches of the Columbia just east of the North Cascades, Wenatchee is a thriving place with an abundance of shops, museums, and restaurants, plus a fun riverside path and many great places to explore nearby. The name Wenatchee comes from a Native American term meaning "water flowing out." Philip Miller was Wenatchee's pioneer apple grower and one of the first white settlers. In 1872, Miller took squatter's rights on a parcel of land in the Wenatchee Valley and planted a handful of apple seedlings that eventually grew to make Wenatchee what it is today.

Wenatchee gets over 300 sunny days and only 10–15 inches of rain per year. The warm, sunny days, cool nights, and volcanic ash soil combine to provide ideal conditions for apples, pears, cherries, peaches, and other fruits in the mountain valleys, while the irrigated flatlands to the east are ideal for vineyards.

SIGHTS

Ohme Gardens

Once the private joy of the Ohme family, these highly acclaimed gardens (junction of Highways 2 and 97, 509/662-5785,

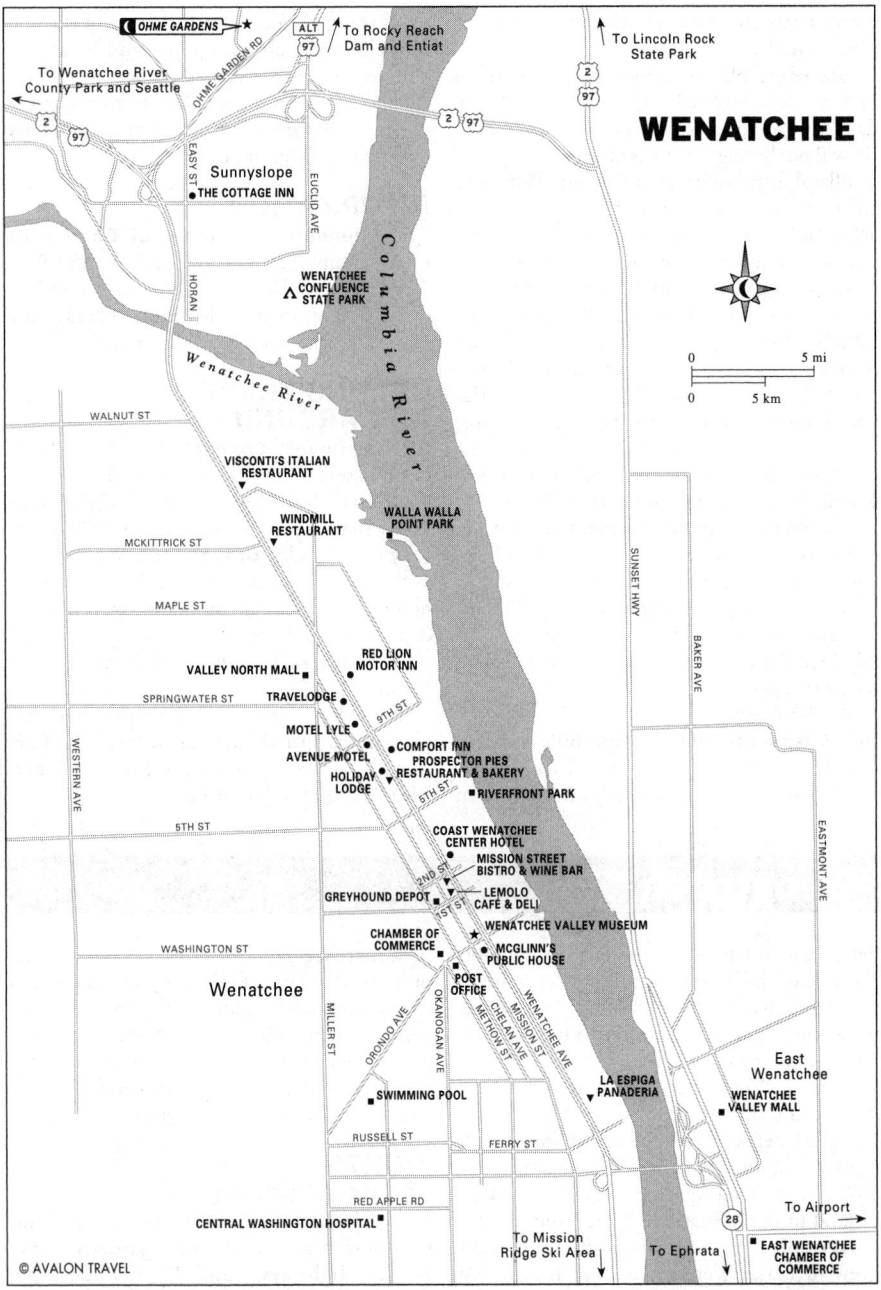
WENATCHEE
OHME GARDENS
OHME GARDEN RD
ALT 97
To Rocky Reach Dam and Entiat
To Lincoln Rock State Park
To Wenatchee River County Park and Seattle
2
97
Sunnyslope
THE COTTAGE INN
EASY ST
EUCLID AVE
HORAN
WENATCHEE CONFLUENCE STATE PARK
Columbia River
Wenatchee River
0 5 mi
0 5 km
WALNUT ST
VISCONTI'S ITALIAN RESTAURANT
WINDMILL RESTAURANT
WALLA WALLA POINT PARK
MCKITTRICK ST
MAPLE ST
SUNSET HWY
BAKER AVE
RED LION MOTOR INN
VALLEY NORTH MALL
SPRINGWATER ST
TRAVELODGE
9TH ST
MOTEL LYLE
COMFORT INN
AVENUE MOTEL
PROSPECTOR PIES RESTAURANT & BAKERY
HOLIDAY LODGE
5TH ST
RIVERFRONT PARK
WESTERN AVE
5TH ST
COAST WENATCHEE CENTER HOTEL
MISSION STREET BISTRO & WINE BAR
2ND ST
GREYHOUND DEPOT
LEMOLO CAFÉ & DELI
1ST ST
WENATCHEE VALLEY MUSEUM
CHAMBER OF COMMERCE
WASHINGTON ST
MCGLINN'S PUBLIC HOUSE
POST OFFICE
Wenatchee
MILLER ST
ORONDO AVE
OKANOGAN AVE
CHELAN AVE
METHOW ST
MISSION ST
WENATCHEE AVE
EASTMONT AVE
East Wenatchee
LA ESPIGA PANADERIA
SWIMMING POOL
WENATCHEE VALLEY MALL
RUSSELL ST
FERRY ST
RED APPLE RD
CENTRAL WASHINGTON HOSPITAL
To Airport
28
To Mission Ridge Ski Area
To Ephrata
EAST WENATCHEE CHAMBER OF COMMERCE
© AVALON TRAVEL

© WASHINGTON STATE TOURISM/LEVY SCHECKLER

Ohme Gardens features a huge variety of plants and a view of the Wenatchee Valley.

www.ohmegardens.com, 9 A.M.–7 P.M. daily Apr. 15–Oct. 15, 9 A.M.–6 P.M. daily the rest of the year, $7 adults, $3.50 ages 7–17, free for kids under 7) just north of Wenatchee were purchased by the state in 1991. Now covering nine acres, the gardens resemble natural alpine scenery: Evergreens, grass, ponds, and waterfalls blend with the existing rock—a cool reprieve from the scorching Wenatchee sunshine. A lookout from the gardens' highest point provides broad views of the valley, Cascades, and Columbia River. Steep drop-offs in some sections make this a hazardous place for toddlers. Please leave your pets at home.

Rocky Reach Dam

If you're not already all dammed-out, take a stretch break at Rocky Reach Dam (509/663-8121, www.chelanpud.org, 8 A.M.–6 P.M. daily Memorial Day–Labor Day, 8 A.M.–4 P.M. daily in the spring and fall, closed Jan.–mid-Feb.), one of the more unusual and interesting visitor attractions in Washington. The 4,800-foot-long dam and nicely landscaped surroundings offer boating, fishing, picnicking, a museum, interpretive center, and viewable fish ladder.

Museums

Wenatchee Valley Museum and Cultural Center (127 S. Mission St., 509/664-3340, www.wenatcheewa.gov, 10 A.M.–4 P.M. Tues.–Sat., closed Sun.–Mon. and holidays, $5 adults, $4 seniors and students, $1 ages 6–12, free for kids under 5) is one of the most charming museums in the state, housing a surprisingly large collection spread over two floors and two connected buildings. The museum explores Wenatchee history from its earliest Native American residents through the pioneer days and up to art and miniatures of more recent vintage. Upstairs, you'll discover an impressive model railroad that chugs through a Cascades mountain setting. While here, pick up a walking tour brochure describing Wenatchee's historic downtown buildings.

Apples

To get out under the orchards and see the area's prized crop in all its deliciousness, try a tour

TAKE A BITE OUT OF WENATCHEE

Washington Apples are famous throughout the world for their diversity and crispness. The city of Wenatchee calls itself "The Apple Capital of the World." Dating back to 1872, this, the county seat of Chelan County, has been obsessed with apples. Apples are plastered across store signs, churches, sports teams, to say nothing of the thousands of trees bearing the genuine article.

- **Braeburn** – This crisp, juicy, red apple is a transplant from New Zealand. They start coming to market in mid-October.
- **Cameo** – A great cooking apple and a Washington state discovery, the cameo resists browning and works great in salads.
- **Fuji** – These reddish-pink apples store well and taste sweet. They grow in Washington between late September and early November.
- **Gala** – Red dappled with yellow, the gala is small but perfect for snacking. Look for them in early fall.
- **Gingergold** – A rare treat, the gingergold is a transplant from the east coast and grows just a few short weeks at the end of summer.
- **Golden Delicious** – Great for cooking or eating raw, the golden delicious is just the ticket for perfect cider.
- **Granny Smith** – The firm, slightly sour apple appears in mid-October and makes a bang-up pie. Try slicing these green gems and sprinkling them with a tiny bit of salt.
- **Jonagold** – These delicious, bright red apples are perfect for dessert. Enjoy them in the fall, since they are not available year-round in stores.
- **Pink Lady** – This blushing beauty is delightfully sweet and nuanced. A newer favorite, this apple is available from fall through early spring.
- **Rome** – These apples can taste a little mealy when eaten fresh but are absolutely ideal for cooking. Look for them from fall through early winter.
- **Red Delicious** – Who isn't familiar with the Red Delicious? This firm, succulent apple is number one for a reason. Tasty and with undeniable eye-appeal, the Red Delicious tastes best when icy cold.

from **Washington Apple Country** (866/459-9614, www.appleorchardtours.com, $24–59), which offers everything from orchard hay rides and "u-pick" tours to specialty dining tours that blend orchard and vineyard visits.

The **Washington State Apple Commission Visitor Center** (2900 Euclid Ave., 509/663-9600 or 509/662-3090 (weekends), www.bestapples.com/about/about_interpretivecenter.shtml, 8 A.M.–5 P.M. Mon.–Fri., 9 A.M.–5 P.M. Sat., 10 A.M.–4 P.M. Sun. May–Dec., 8 A.M.–5 P.M. Mon.–Fri. the rest of the year) has a video and displays about the apple industry, along with apples and apple juice samples.

Waterville

Approximately 25 miles northeast of Wenatchee is the small farming town of Waterville (pop. 1,100) with wide streets and classic American homes. It is the county seat for Douglas County and the town with the highest elevation in all of Washington. The 10-mile drive from Orondo (on the banks of the Columbia) gains 2,000 feet in elevation, climbing up a steep canyon before emerging onto the flat farming plateau around Waterville. Several beautiful old buildings remain here, including the **Douglas County Courthouse,** the 1916 **St. Joseph's Catholic Church,** and the classy three-story **Waterville Historic Hotel** (509/745-8695 or 888/509-8180, www.watervillehotel.com, $42–89 s or $49–95 d). Built in 1903, the hotel has been lovingly restored to its authentic beauty and is now on the National Register of Historic

Places. Inside are original and other antique furnishings. Rooms have private or shared baths, including some deluxe suites.

Waterville is also home to the **Douglas County Historical Museum** (509/745-8435, 11 A.M.–5 P.M. Tues.–Sun. May 20 to mid-Oct., admission by donation), where the collection includes a 73-pound meteorite, a two-headed calf, and the old Winthrop post office. Ask here about tours of nearby wheat farms.

Local events include **Waterville Days** in mid-July, and the **North Central Washington Fair** in late August. A large outdoor pool is in the city park. **Badger Mountain** (509/745-8273), six miles south of Waterville, is a small area with three rope tows and a 1,500-foot drop—a family place for downhill and cross-country skiing and snowboarding.

Link Transit (800/851-5465, www.linktransit.com) has free bus service from Waterville to the rest of Douglas and Chelan counties.

ENTERTAINMENT AND EVENTS

Bars and Coffeehouses

On many Friday and Saturday nights **Caffé Mela** (17 N. Wenatchee Ave., 509/888-0374, www.caffemela.com, 7 A.M.–7 P.M. Mon.–Fri., 8 A.M.–7 P.M. Sat.) hosts a parade of talented locals on its intimate stage, keeping the doors open until at least 10 P.M. Some nights are free, while there's a cover on others; visit the website for a schedule. Mela is a fun, airy space when the lights are off and stage isn't set up. Vibrant local art hangs from the walls, and resident artists pour out their own brand of beauty right into your cup—expect to see deliciously creamy patterns of flowers, leaves, and other coffee art adorning your latte.

Prepare to be serenaded *en Espanol* at **Grizzly's Lounge** (1225 N. Wenatchee Ave., 509/663-0711, 4–11 P.M. Sun.–Thurs., 4 P.M.–1:30 A.M. Fri.–Sat.), which hosts an array of musicians on Friday nights, focusing especially on Spanish music.

A DJ spins rock and pop music most nights at the **Wenatchee Roaster & Ale House** (201 N. Wenatchee Ave., 509/662-1234). Situated inside the Wenatchee Center Hotel, the Roaster is a lively place to take a date for a late-night bite to eat in the lounge, where the kitchen is open until midnight. Music plays 9 P.M.–12:30 A.M. Tuesday–Thursday and 9 P.M.–1:30 A.M. Friday–Saturday.

For a casual game of pool and a bit of flirty conversation, head over to **Willie's Sports Bar** (921 Valley Mall Pkwy., 509/884-7917) in East Wenatchee. Outfitted with big-screen TVs and big pitchers of brew, this is a bustling spot for the just-turned-21 set.

Or for a classier evening, sip and swirl local vintages at the mood-lit lounge in **Shakti's** (218 N Mission St., 509/662-3321, 4:30–8:30 P.M. daily), which also serves a mean martini and lots of inventive appetizers.

The Arts

Wenatchee is home to a thriving performing arts scene that seems to support many more performances than one would expect from a town of its size. The focal point of this community is the 550-seat **Pacific Arts Center Wenatchee** (123 N. Wenatchee Ave., www.pacwen.org), an up-to-date facility that hosts traveling performances from troupes such as the Moscow ballet, the Seattle Symphony string quartet, and the Seattle Opera Young Artists program.

Complementing the PAC is the **Music Theatre of Wenatchee** (233 N. Wenatchee Ave., 509/662-7814, www.mtow.org), where local performers run regular musical theater shows throughout the year.

Perhaps the most unique venue in town is the **Press Room Theatre** (14 N. Mission, 509/670-8233), a cozy little performance hall built in the old printing press room the local *Wenatchee World* left empty after building new print facilities. The building proved an extremely apt theatre venue due to the acoustic panels installed during the press days to dampen printing noise and prevent it from bothering workers in the rest of the building. Press Room Theatre is home to the local **Mission Creek Players** (www.ncwtheater.com), which also puts on performances at the

Music Theatre. This is also home to cabaret-style improv comedy acts on Friday nights at 8 P.M. Admission costs $5.

Events

Ridge to River Relay (509/662-8799, www.r2r.org) consists of six different competitions, with teams competing over a 35-mile course that includes cross-country and downhill skiing, running, cycling, and canoeing. It attracts 2,000 participants each year and is held in April. There is also a Junior Ridge to River event.

The self-proclaimed "Apple Capital of the World" is the only proper place to hold the annual **Apple Blossom Festival** (509/662-3616, www.appleblossom.org), which blooms in the beginning of May. Truly a grand event, the culmination is the Apple Blossom Parade, complete with elaborate floats and an honorary king and queen. Other festivities include carnivals, a charity auction, pancake breakfasts, arts and crafts fair, and lots more.

The **Wenatchee Youth Circus** (509/662-0722, www.wenatcheeyouthcircus.com), is commonly called "The Biggest Little Circus in the World." Local youth train throughout the year in such skills as trapeze, juggling, high wire, and clowning. Come summer, they take their show on the road to venues throughout Washington. The circus is regarded as one of the absolute top nonprofessional circus troupes in the country.

SHOPPING

The Wenatchee area has several big malls, including **Wenatchee Valley Mall** (511 Valley Mall Parkway, 509/884-6645, www.wenatcheevalleymall.com) in East Wenatchee. Downtown has a wide selection of boutiques, including a number of fine-art galleries and a quilt shop. **Victorian Village** (611 S. Mission) consists of a row of small shops and restaurants, ranging from nail salons to pizza parlors. And for the strictly functional, head up Wenatchee Avenue to find all the big chains such as Wal-Mart.

SPORTS AND RECREATION

Spectator Sports

The new **Town Toyota Center** (1300 Walla Walla Ave., 509/667-7847, www.towntoyotacenter.com) is open for ice skating, NAHL hockey, and arena events.

Racing fans have plenty to get their hearts pounding at the **Wenatchee Valley Super Oval** (3385 Fancher Field Rd., 509/884-8592, www.wvso.com) on Fancher Heights above East Wenatchee. The April–September schedule features stock cars, sprints, monster trucks, and even a bus race! Leave your video equipment at home, as it is strictly prohibited.

Apple Capital Recreation Loop

The Apple Capital Recreation Loop Trail is more than 13 miles of paved trail perfect for a stroll, bike ride, run, or skate session. During the winter months, you may even find cross-country skiers getting in shape here.

For $18 a day, you can rent a bike to cruise the loop trail from **The Second Wind Bicycle and Nordic Shop** (85 N.E. 9th St., 509/884-0821) in East Wenatchee. Come winter you can also pick up a pair of cross-country skis for $20 per day.

Several parks provide restroom facilities, picnic grounds, and play areas along the loop. The trail follows both sides of the Columbia River, connecting parks such as **Wenatchee Confluence State Park,** where you can swim in a roped off area in the summer and **Riverfront Park** (509/661-4551), with an ice rink and mini-railroad available for special events. Near where the Columbia and Wenatchee Rivers meet, **Walla Walla Point Park** (509/661-4551) also has a swimming beach and provides areas for soccer, softball, swimming, tennis, volleyball, and horseshoes. There is even a handicapped-accessible fishing pier.

On the south end, the trail crosses the river on a footbridge to East Wenatchee. One path heads north through Porter's Pond Nature Area and back over the Odabashian Bridge, and a second continues south to tiny **View Point Park,** a great place to watch sunsets. Two miles farther south is **Rock Island Hydro Park,** another riverside park with paths, a boat ramp, and a swimming area.

Skiing

Just 12 miles from Wenatchee, **Mission Ridge Ski Area** (7500 Mission Ridge Rd., 509/626-5208, www.missionridge.com, lift tickets run $50 adults, $32 seniors, $44 ages 13–17, $30 ages 7–12, $9 kids age 6 and under) is the area's largest slope and Washington's east-side secret, with drier powder and more sun than other Cascade ski areas. It has 36 runs (plus a snowboard half-pipe) spread across 2,000 acres and a base elevation of 4,570 feet. At the base, you'll find a restaurant, lounge, ski and snowboard rental shop, ski school, and child-care facility. Mission Ridge is generally open Thanksgiving to early April. Night skiing is $15 for all ages. A SkiLink bus (509/663-6543, www.linktransit.com, $3 round-trip) operates from Wenatchee, Leavenworth, or Chelan. Your skis are safely stowed in racks attached to the side of the bus.

Golf

Golfers will enjoy playing at three local courses. The par-69 **Three Lakes Golf Club** (W. Malaga Rd. off the Wenatchee-Malaga Hwy., 509/663-5448) offers views of the river and mountains. Peak greens fees are $43, which includes cart rental.

The Jack Frei–designed **Desert Canyon Golf Resort** (1201 Desert Canyon Boulevard, 800/258-4173, www.desertcanyon.com), north of E. Wenatchee in nearby Orondo, opened in 1993 and provides a full restaurant, a sports bar, and an outdoor snack shop. Greens fees are $89 in summer, $69 in spring and fall.

Rock Island Golf Course (509/884-2806, $22) is a nine-hole, par-36 course in Rock Island that's perfect for a quick morning outing.

Other Sports and Recreation

BlueSky Outfitters (800/228-7238,www.blueskyoutfitters.com) offers half-day ($74), full-day ($92), and overnight ($249) rafting trips on the Wenatchee River, considered one of the top 10 rafting runs in the United States. Trips put in at Riverside Park.

Skaters can shred one of Washington's best skateboard parks, **Pioneer Skate Park** (220 Fuller St., dawn–10 P.M. daily) The park is lit at night. Safety equipment is strongly recommended.

If you can't wait to get wet, check out **Riverside Recreation** (509/670-6457, www.riversiderecreation.net) to rent personal watercraft or full-sized boats for some river fun. Tow and launch yourself or opt for their delivery service. Jet Skis are $200 for six hours while a 20-foot Openbow will run you around $330 per day.

If you prefer your locomotion drier and four-legged, take a horseback trail ride at the **Lake Wenatchee State Park Riding Stable** (Lake Wenatchee State Park, 509/763-3647, May–Sept.). Guided rides run from $23 for a two-mile ride up to $130 for a full-day ride.

Camping

Wenatchee Confluence State Park (509/664-6373, open year-round) sits at the juncture of the Wenatchee and Columbia Rivers, just north of town, and has a pedestrian bridge across the Wenatchee River to marshes on the south side. Tent sites are $17, and RV hookups cost $24. Neatniks should bring some change, as there are coin-operated showers on-site. Make reservations for Wenatchee-area state parks ($7 extra) at 888/226-7688 or www.parks.wa.gov.

Six miles west of Wenatchee on Highway 2, **Wenatchee River County Park** (509/662-2525, Apr.–Sept.) has playgrounds, picnic areas, and camping for tents ($19) and RVs ($29).

Some say that the geologic feature across the river from **Lincoln Rock State Park** (509/884-8702, www.parks.wa.gov, mid-Mar.–Oct.) looks like old Abe's profile. The park is seven miles north of East Wenatchee on Highway 2 and sports a day-use area that has a swimming beach on the Columbia River, boat moorage, and tennis courts. The park has tent sites ($17) and full-hookup RV spaces ($24). Interpretive programs are offered at the amphitheater on summer evenings.

ACCOMMODATIONS

The Wenatchee Area Chamber of Commerce (509/662-2116 or 800/572-7753, www.wenatchee.org) keeps track of room availability and can transfer you to local motels and B&Bs that are chamber members. Many of the motels offer ski package deals in the winter.

Under $100

Out on bustling Wenatchee Avenue, you'll find a number of affordable lodging choices. Try **Lyles Motel** (924 N. Wenatchee Ave., 509/663-5155, $55 s and $65 d). **Holiday Lodge** (610 N. Wenatchee Ave., 509/663-8167 or 800/722-0852, $50 s or $65 d) is one of the best deals in town, with an outdoor pool, hot tub, and sauna. **Avenue Motel** (720 N. Wenatchee Ave., 509/663-7161 or 800/733-8981, www.avenuemotel.com, $55 s or $65 d) also includes an outdoor pool, hot tub, and kitchenettes.

A cozy inn along the big bend of the Columbia is **Travelodge** (1004 N. Wenatchee Ave., 509/662-8165 or 800/578-7878, www.travelodge.com, $80 s or $90 d), with an outdoor pool, hot tub, and sauna. Similarly priced is **Econolodge** (232 N. Wenatchee Ave., 509/663-7121 or 800/561-8856, $64 s or $75 d).

Rimrock Inn B&B (1354 Pitcher Canyon Rd., 509/664-5113 or 888/664-5113, www.rimrockinn.com, $80 d) has quiet accommodations three miles south of Wenatchee. The three guest rooms have private baths, there's a hot tub, and a full breakfast is served; no young kids are allowed.

$100-150

Set on a peaceful 10-acre riverside spread, **Warm Springs Inn** (1611 Love Lane, 509/662-8365 or 800/543-3645, www.warmspringsinn.com, $105–140 s or d) is a sprawling 1917 ivy-covered mansion. The three guest rooms and suite all have private baths and full breakfasts. This is a very popular wedding venue.

Comfort Inn (815 N. Wenatchee Ave., 509/662-1700 or 800/228-5150, www.comfortinn.com, $109 s or $119 d) comes with an indoor pool, exercise room, and continental breakfast.

Red Lion Hotel (1225 N. Wenatchee Ave., 509/663-0711 or 800/547-8010, www.redlion.com, $135–155 s or d) is a notch up in both price and amenities (outdoor pool and hot tub).

For a deluxe stay, try the **Coast Wenatchee Center Hotel** (201 N. Wenatchee Ave., 509/662-1234 or 800/426-0670, www.wenatcheecenter.com, $130–165 s or d). This hotel has a great view of the river and mountains, and the Wenatchee Roaster and Ale House is conveniently located on the 9th floor. Ask about special golf or romance packages.

FOOD

Cafés

Start the day with delicious breakfasts and espresso at **Wild Huckleberry Bakery & Breakfast House** (302 S. Mission, 509/663-1013, 8 A.M.–2 P.M. Sun.–Mon., 7 A.M.–3 P.M. and 5–9 P.M. Tues.–Sat.). Also popular for breakfast is **Prospector Pies Restaurant & Bakery** (731 N. Wenatchee Ave., 509/662-1118, 7 A.M.–10 P.M. Sun.–Thurs., 7 A.M.–11 P.M. Fri.–Sat.). Wrap your mouth around a rich Mexican pastry at **La Espiga Panaderia** (818 S. Wenatchee Ave., 509/664-7254, 8 A.M.–9 P.M. daily).

Once a sporting-goods store, **McGlinn's Public House** (111 Orondo, 509/663-9073, www.mcglinns.com, 11 A.M.–10 P.M. Mon.–Thurs., 11 A.M.–10:30 P.M. Fri.–Sat., 11 A.M.–9 P.M. Sun.) is an intriguing tavern and eatery in an old brick-walled building adorned with baseball caps and mitts. It has plenty of microbrews on tap, plus burgers, salads, and wood-fired pizzas for a light dinner.

Excellent lunches and dinners are also at **Lemolo Café & Deli** (114 N. Wenatchee Ave., 509/664-6576, 10 A.M.–4 P.M. daily). They offer deli sandwiches, soups, salads, and distinctive stone-oven pizzas. The place gets packed at lunch.

Steak

Warm wood paneling, cozy booths, and red vinyl and stainless steel stools at the counter pay homage to the roadhouse past of **The Windmill** (1501 N. Wenatchee Ave., 509/665-9529, www.thewindmillrestaurant.com, 5–9 P.M. daily). The bootleg liquor and crazy times of the early 1930s are long gone, however, replaced by Wenatchee's nicest steakhouse. Thick, juicy cuts of beef are accompanied by home-cooked sides prepared from scratch. Leave a few bites on your dinner plate to justify one of the rich dessert pies. In the summer, the signature berry cream cheese pie is not to be missed. The restaurant's name comes from the twirling windmill built into this lovely brick-and-shingle building.

International

Woo someone special with the house specialty crepes at the candlelit **Mission Street Bistro & Wine Bar** (202 N Mission St., 509/665-2406, www.missionstreetbistro.com, 9 A.M.–10 P.M. Mon.–Sat., 11 A.M.–3 P.M. Sun.). These tantalizing creations are enough to put a food lover into a reverie, served with a wide array of fillings and paired with any number of local wines from Mission's amply stocked cellar. At **The Wine Bin** (10 A.M.–7 P.M. Mon.–Fri., 10 A.M.–5 P.M. Sat., closed Sun.) next door, Mission's proprietors sell the necessary ingredients for continuing a romantic evening at home: over 400 different wines, artisan cheeses, fine chocolates, and elegant stemware.

Visconti's Italian Restaurant (1737 N. Wenatchee, 509/662-5013, 11 A.M.–9:30 P.M. Mon.–Fri., 5–10 P.M. Sat.–Sun.) serves quite good Northern Italian food in a white-linen setting. Prices are fairly reasonable. Another Italian eatery in East Wenatchee is **Garlini's Italian Restaurant** (810 Valley Mall Pkwy. E, 509/884-1707, 11 A.M.–9 P.M. Mon.–Fri., 4–9 P.M. Sat.–Sun.).

Get authentic Mexican meals at **El Abuelo** (601 S. Mission, 509/662-7331, 11 A.M.–10 P.M. daily) or a couple of blocks away at **La Fuente's** (816 S. Mission, 509/664-1910, 11 A.M.–10 P.M. daily). Another option is to stop by one of the taco trucks arrayed around town for affordable and meaty tacos.

Wok-About Grill (110 N. Wenatchee Ave., 509/662-1154, 11 A.M.–9 P.M. Mon.–Sat. in summer, 11 A.M.–8 P.M. Mon.–Thurs., 11 A.M.–9 P.M. Fri.–Sat. in winter, closed Sun.) has a Mongolian barbecue with a big grill in the center of the room and quick service. This is a great place to fill your belly on a budget.

Burgers and Pizza

Chomp into one of the thick, juicy hamburgers at **EZ's Burger Deluxe** (1950 N. Wenatchee Ave., 509/663-1957, 10:30 A.M.–10 P.M. daily), but don't forget to leave room for the house specialty—the olive oil and garlic fries are a rich and pungent dish of goodness not to be missed.

Or head to **Bob's Classic Bar & Grill** (110 2nd St., 509/663-3954, 6 A.M.–10 P.M. Sun.–Tues., 6 A.M.–midnight Wed.–Sat.), where you can sidle up to the counter and enjoy burgers served in a flashy 1950s decor.

The Cottage Inn (134 Easy St., 509/663-4435, www.cottageinn.com, 4:30–9 P.M. Sun.–Thurs., 4–9 P.M. Fri.–Sat.) has been serving chicken, steak, and seafood for dinner only at this location since 1940.

For the best local pizzas—made with a distinctively spicy sauce—head to one of two **Abby's Legendary Pizza** locations, one in Wenatchee proper (5th and Western, 509/662-2226) or the other in East Wenatchee (702 Grant Rd., 509/884-7211). Both locations are open 11:30 A.M.–10 P.M. Monday–Thursday, 10:30 A.M.–11 P.M. Friday–Saturday, closed on Sunday.

Markets

The Wenatchee area is filled with fruit stands selling fresh apples, apricots, cherries, peaches, and pears in season. **Stemilt Growers** is a large local apple, cherry, and pear grower with tours and a retail shop (3615 Hwy. 97 Alt., 509/663-7848, www.stemilt.com).

The **Wenatchee Valley Farmers Market** (509/668-0497, www.wenatcheefarmersmarket.com, 9 A.M.–1 P.M. Fri. June–Sept.) takes place in Riverside Park. Other Wenatchee farmers markets take place on Columbia Street (Sat. May–Oct.), at Methow Park (Thurs. July–Oct.), and at Leavenworth Lions Club Park (Tues. June–Oct.).

INFORMATION AND SERVICES

For maps, brochures, or specific information on the Wenatchee area, contact the **Wenatchee Valley Convention and Visitor Center** (25 N. Wenatchee Ave., 509/6633723 or 800/5727753, www.wenatcheevalley.org) and the **Wenatchee Area Chamber of Commerce** (300 S Columbia St., 509/662-2116, www.wenatchee.org, 8:30 A.M.–5 P.M. Mon.–Fri.).

Get camping and hiking information from the **Wenatchee National Forest** headquarters (215 Melody Lane, junction of Highways 2 and 97, 509/662-4335, www.fs.fed.us/r6/wenatchee).

Emergency medical services can be obtained at **Central Washington Hospital** (1201 S. Miller St., 509/662-1511) or **Wenatchee Emergency Physicians** (1300 Fuller St., 509/665-6163).

Hurt animal companions are cheerfully healed at the **Animal Hospital of Wenatchee** (10 N. Chelan Ave., 509/663-8845).

GETTING THERE

By Air

Pangborn Memorial Airport (1 Pangborn Ave., 509/884-2924, www.pangbornairport.com) serves the region's aeronautical needs. **Horizon Air** (800/547-9308, www.horizonair.com) operates a number of flights between Pangborn Field and Seattle.

Wings of Wenatchee (3764 Airport Way, 509/886-0233, www.wowgofly.com) offers charter and flightseeing trips out of Pangborn. An affordable 30-minute zoom over the area runs $89 for up to three people, with every additional hour costing $160. Longer flights are flown in a slightly bigger plane, costing $224 per hour for up to three passengers. Charter rates are comparable, with custom service all over the Northwest.

By Bus and Train

Columbia Station (at Wenatchee and Kittitas) is Wenatchee's downtown transportation center. Amtrak trains, Link buses, and Northwest Trailways all stop here, providing convenient connections for travelers.

Link (509/662-1155 or 800/851-5465, www.linktransit.com) has bus service throughout Chelan and Douglas counties, including Wenatchee, Chelan, Leavenworth, and to Mission Ridge Ski Area. The buses also carry bicycles. **Northwestern Trailways** (800/366-3830, www.northwesterntrailways.com) offers bus service east to Spokane and west to Everett and Seattle.

Amtrak's (800/872-7245, www.amtrak.com) Empire Builder train serves Wenatchee, with daily service east to Spokane and Chicago, and west to Seattle.

NORTH CASCADES

The Cascade Range is Washington's great divide. In addition to creating almost opposite climates on either side of the state, the mountains also serve as a political and psychological barrier between east and west, resulting in what seems like two states within one. Many historians have said the founding fathers erred in creating the state, and that they should have drawn the state border along the crest of the Cascades. Perhaps—but that would have robbed the state of much of its cultural and geographical richness.

The two halves of the state are different not only in appearance but also in other, less-obvious ways. Speaking very generally, western Washington is urban-oriented, with an emphasis on commerce and manufacturing, while eastern Washington is mainly rural and agricultural.

Crossing the Cascade passes in winter—an adventure many Washingtonians prefer to forgo—is an experience that thousands of avid skiers tolerate to reach the slopes. They simply learn to live with the snow tire and chain requirements, snow-packed and icy roads, and occasional pass closures.

In summer, the Cascades take on a more benign image and become a popular destination for all manner of travelers, who have a wide variety of places and experiences from which to choose. Millions of acres have been set aside for recreation. The North Cascades and Mount Rainier National Parks, Mount St. Helens National Volcanic Monument, the areas around Mt. Baker and Mt. Adams, along with numerous wilderness areas and wildlife refuges—all

© WASHINGTON STATE TOURISM/LEVY SHECKLER

HIGHLIGHTS

Heather Meadows Area: One of the North Cascades' best year-round recreational destinations, this serene spot at the base of Mount Baker is equally beautiful blanketed with snow or flowers (page 465).

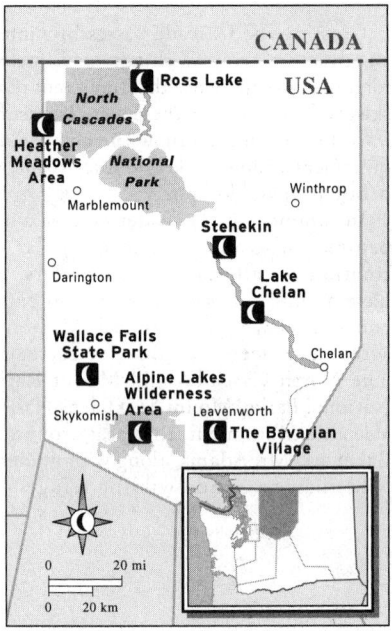

Ross Lake: Get a bird's-eye view of this massive reservoir from the trails that summit nearby peaks, or see it from water level on a motorboat or canoe (page 487).

Lake Chelan: This is the state's longest lake and a favorite summertime destination for travelers looking to splash around and then dry out under central Washington's hot summer sun (page 504).

Stehekin: Reachable only by boat, this little mountain hamlet is a hub for hikers exploring deep into the Cascades National Park, Lake Chelan-Sawtooth Wilderness, or Glacier Peak Wilderness (page 511).

The Bavarian Village: Cozied up under mountainsides that look strikingly similar to the Alps, Leavenworth dresses up as a delightfully campy Bavarian town (page 518).

Alpine Lakes Wilderness Area: Crystalline lakes, craggy mountaintops, and emerald meadows await the hearty adventurer willing to trek into this pristine wilderness (page 527).

Wallace Falls State Park: You can see this white gush of water from Highway 2, but don't just zoom by. The trails that take you up close are well worth the effort (page 532).

LOOK FOR TO FIND RECOMMENDED SIGHTS, ACTIVITIES, DINING, AND LODGING.

constitute the backbone of Washington's outdoor recreation.

This lengthy chapter roughly follows the Cascade Range from Mt. Baker at the north all the way to the Mt. Adams area near the state's southern border, following the main highways over the passes, and visiting the sights, backcountry trails, and settlements en route.

GEOLOGY AND CLIMATE

The Cascade Range is about 25 million years old, but the range's volcanoes in Washington—Adams, St. Helens, Rainier, Glacier Peak, and Baker—plus another 15 or so in Oregon and California, are less than a million years old. Although none can be declared totally dead, only two have erupted in this century: Northern California's Mt. Lassen in 1914, and Mount St. Helens in 1980. Not long before Mount St. Helens came to life in such a violent manner, Mt. Baker began heating up and sent out clouds of steam and melted some of its glaciers, but Mount St. Helens stole the show in 1980.

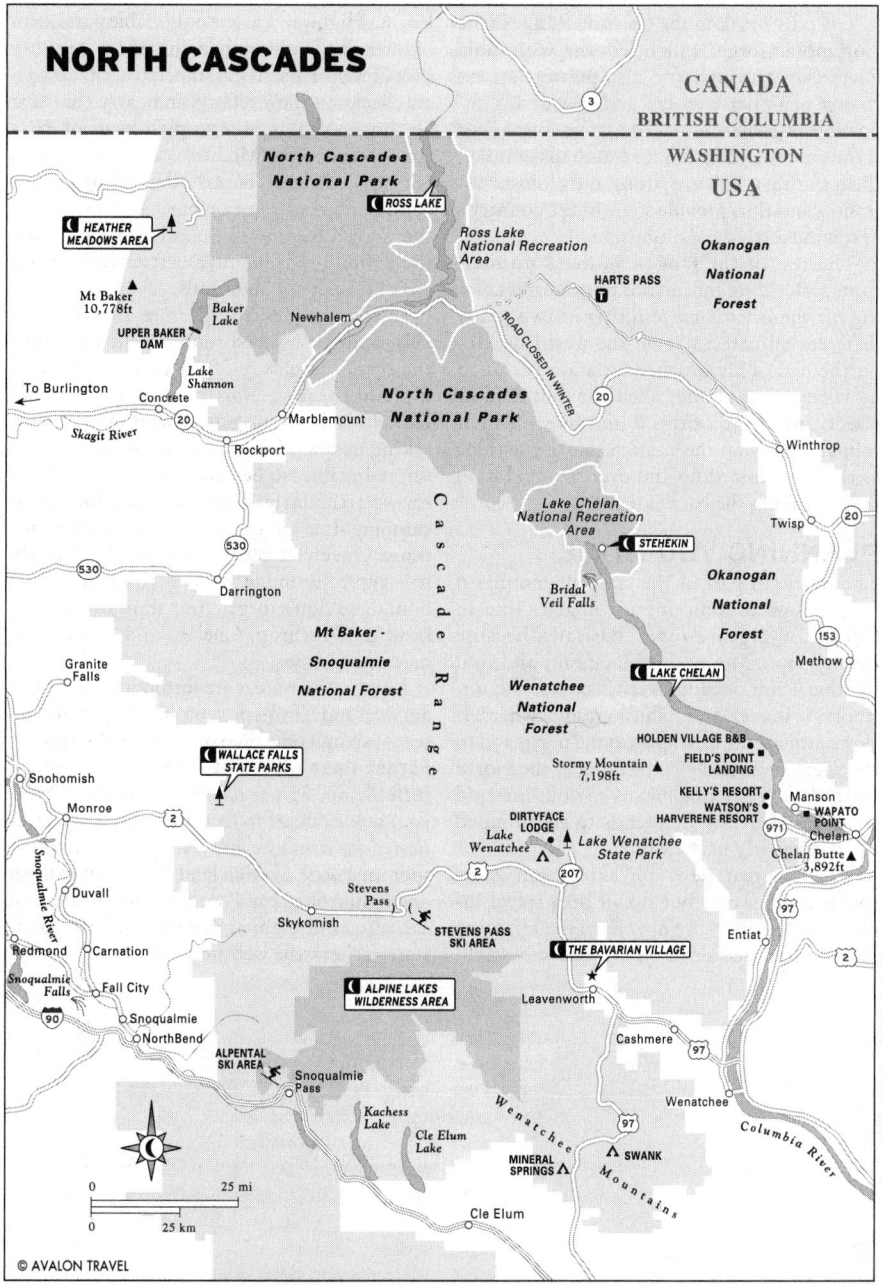
NORTH CASCADES
CANADA
BRITISH COLUMBIA
WASHINGTON
USA
North Cascades National Park
ROSS LAKE
HEATHER MEADOWS AREA
Ross Lake National Recreation Area
Okanogan National Forest
HARTS PASS
Mt Baker 10,778ft
Baker Lake
UPPER BAKER DAM
Newhalem
ROAD CLOSED IN WINTER
Lake Shannon
To Burlington
Concrete
Skagit River
Marblemount
Rockport
North Cascades National Park
Winthrop
Lake Chelan National Recreation Area
Twisp
STEHEKIN
Bridal Veil Falls
Okanogan National Forest
Darrington
Cascade Range
Mt Baker - Snoqualmie National Forest
Granite Falls
Methow
LAKE CHELAN
Wenatchee National Forest
HOLDEN VILLAGE B&B
FIELD'S POINT LANDING
WALLACE FALLS STATE PARKS
Stormy Mountain 7,198ft
Snohomish
KELLY'S RESORT
WATSON'S HARVERENE RESORT
Manson
WAPATO POINT
Monroe
DIRTYFACE LODGE
Lake Wenatchee
Lake Wenatchee State Park
Chelan
Chelan Butte 3,892ft
Snoqualmie River
Duvall
Stevens Pass
Skykomish
STEVENS PASS SKI AREA
Entiat
Redmond
Carnation
THE BAVARIAN VILLAGE
Snoqualmie Falls
Fall City
ALPINE LAKES WILDERNESS AREA
Leavenworth
Snoqualmie
NorthBend
Cashmere
ALPENTAL SKI AREA
Snoqualmie Pass
Wenatchee
Kachess Lake
Cle Elum Lake
Wenatchee Mountains
Columbia River
SWANK
MINERAL SPRINGS
Cle Elum
0 25 mi
0 25 km
© AVALON TRAVEL

The only break in the Cascade Range is the Columbia Gorge, which lets the Columbia River flow through and also permits an exchange of air between east and west that is impossible elsewhere along the range. Because it is the only such corridor for hundreds of miles, the resulting winds are strong and almost constant—and thus provide some of the country's best windsurfing conditions.

The rest of the range continues uninterrupted, shielding the interior from storms coming off the ocean and resulting in two vastly different climates: wet on the west side, dry on the east. This weather variation is caused by what is commonly called the rain shadow effect: Incoming storms dump most of their rain and snow on the western side of the ridge as the air is forced up and over the mountain range, leaving the back side drier.

PLANNING YOUR TIME

The northern part of the Cascade mountain range is what some meteorologists like to call a "convergence zone." Basically, because the Olympic Mountains block rain and foul weather from passing over its peaks, the unstable air that creates it must go somewhere. It flows around the Olympics to the north and to the south, eventually converging at the North Cascades. What this means to you, intrepid visitor, is that this area tends to get dumped on, particularly in the winter.

This is great news for skiers and snow sports enthusiasts, but it can be a travel inconvenience. By November or so the Highway 20 pass is closed until springtime snowmelt, leaving Highway 2 as the only viable pass north of Interstate 90. Even then, things can be tricky over Stevens Pass, so it is imperative that travelers check out snow reports and carry chains at all times. Also, be sure to plan loads of extra time to get to the Methow Valley, which can take up to six hours of travel depending on pass conditions. And you can forget about traveling the rugged Mountain Loop Highway during these months, as its interior stretches are impassable once the snow falls.

In the summer, things open up considerably, and the favored route east is definitely the scenic Highway 20. It twists and turns directly through North Cascades National Park, by wild rivers, glacier lakes, and breathtaking passes. However, these mountains are unpredictable, so be sure to bring lots of layers—particularly if you plan on hiking or camping. It is not unusual to see summertime snow. Once you get over the passes, though, it is typically much warmer than the Puget Sound, so don't forget your shorts when you head to Winthrop, Chelan, and other summer destinations.

Most of these areas are surrounded by Forest Service land. If you plan on enjoying trails and scenic areas, come prepared with a **Northwest Forest Pass** (800/270-7504, www.fs.fed.us/r6/feedemo, $5 per day, $30 annual). This is your golden ticket to recreational fun—it is required at virtually every trailhead and parking spot on Forest Service land here. You can get one online or at any Forest Service office. You can also find them at certain sporting goods store—check the website for details.

Mount Baker and Vicinity

Mount Baker, the northernmost of the Cascade volcanoes, towers dramatically over the surrounding hills. At 10,778 feet, it is bathed in glaciers and snowfields and serves as a scenic backdrop for Bellingham and Vancouver, British Columbia. Besides improving the scenery, the Mt. Baker area offers up a wealth of recreational activities, from skiing to hiking to white-water rafting. Much of this land lies within the Mt. Baker Wilderness and National Recreation Area. Bordering them to the east is North Cascades National Park, another favorite of those who love the outdoors.

The Natural World

The four "life zones" on the mountain, from sea-level forest to alpine meadows, have a wide variety of wildlife, including coyotes, black bears, black-tailed deer, porcupines, elk, marmots, and mountain goats. Forest birds include grouse, gray jays, ptarmigan, and a large winter population of bald eagles on the Skagit (rhymes with gadget) and Nooksack Rivers. All five species of Pacific salmon spawn in the rivers, and the insect population is well represented by three of its least popular members: the mosquito, black fly, and no-see-um.

History

Discovered in 1792 by Captain Vancouver's first mate, Joseph Baker, Mt. Baker had been known for centuries to local Native Americans as Koma Kulshan (Broken One), a reference to an early eruption that blew out part of its summit. Like other Cascade volcanoes, Baker is asleep, but not dead. In 1843 it awoke from its slumber, spewing vast amounts of smoke and ash for the next 16 years and causing a major forest fire on the east shore of Baker Lake. The mountain lay dormant from 1884 to 1975, when it again began to release steam, leading seismologists to believe it would erupt, but it was upstaged in a grand manner in 1980 by Mount St. Helens. Since that time, the mountain continues to vent steam periodically, with small clouds frequently visible over the summit. There is little evidence of a return to life—but this could change at any time.

Mt. Baker has been a source for year-round recreation since 1868, when librarian-turned-mountaineer Edmund Coleman and his party climbed to the summit after two failed attempts. Either poor planners or extremely conscious of pack weight, the entire climbing party shared one plate and spoon and ate only bacon, bread, and tea during the 10-day ascent. By 1911, the mountain had become an integral part of the Mt. Baker marathon, a 118-mile round-trip between Bellingham and the summit using any mode of transportation in addition to at least 24 miles on foot. The marathons were discontinued two years later, after one competitor fell into a crevasse, though he lived to tell about it. More recently the race has been revived as the 85-mile **Ski to Sea Marathon,** where teams begin by skiing down Mt. Baker, and relays of bike riders, paddlers in canoes, and runners complete the course to Puget Sound.

SIGHTS

Mt. Baker Highway

Highway 542 is the primary access road to Mt. Baker, a 62-mile drive from Bellingham, through the little towns of **Nugents Corner, Deming, Kendall, Maple Falls,** and **Glacier,** and then all the way to the end of the road at Heather Meadows. Not much to these settlements, but you may want to stop by for the **Deming Logging Show** in mid-June and the **Everson-Nooksack Summer Festival** on the second weekend in July.

The Nooksack Tribe runs **Nooksack River Casino** (5048 Mt. Baker Hwy., Deming, 360/592-5472, www.nooksackcasino.com), where you can try your hand at blackjack, craps, roulette, poker, and keno.

Mount Baker Vineyards (between Deming and Nugents Corner on Hwy. 542, 360/592-2300, daily 11 A.M.–5 P.M.) offers tours and

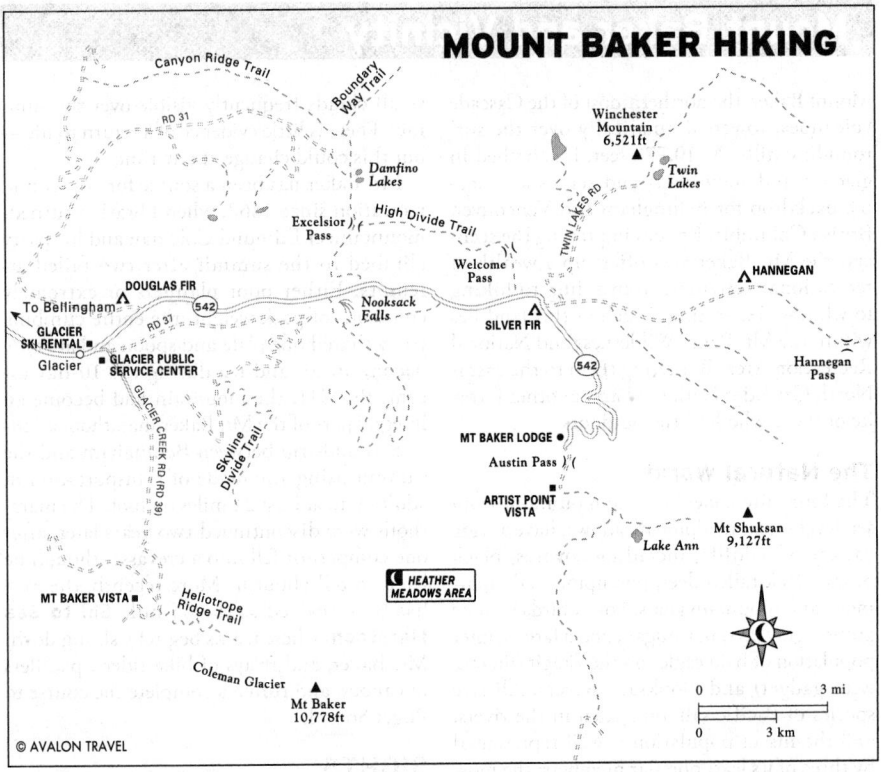

tastings. The vineyard grows several unusual varieties of grapes, including Madeline Angevine and Müller–Thurgau. The cooperative gallery **Cloudy Mountain Pottery** (five miles north of Kendall, 360/988-8645) displays pottery by local artisans.

Nooksack Valley

Highway 542 climbs along the beautiful Nooksack River Valley, gently at first, then in a series of steep switchbacks as you approach the terminus near the mountain. The road enters Mt. Baker-Snoqualmie National Forest just east of Glacier, where you'll find the Glacier Public Service Center, along with a handful of businesses. East from here to the end, the road is officially a National Forest Scenic Byway. Enjoy the finest views of Mt. Baker at the end of paved Glacier Creek Road (Forest Road 39), which begins just east of Glacier and heads south for seven miles to a parking lot and trailhead at an elevation of almost 2,900 feet.

East of Glacier, the highway cruises through a wonderful stand of 700-year-old Douglas firs. Seven miles east of Glacier is the turnoff to impressive **Nooksack Falls** (one mile away along a gravel side road), a thundering cataract. As you wend your way eastward from here, you'll find periodic views down the valley. Around mileage marker 44 is a good-sized patch of impressive old-growth forest right along the highway, easily accessible with a brief hike. The road passes columnar volcanic rock just below the **Mt. Baker Ski Area,** where you can purchase snacks on summer weekends or full meals in the winter, and then circles famous **Picture Lake.** Join the crowd for a photo of Mt. Shuksan rising behind the mirrored waters of this small lake. It's one of Kodak's favorite places in America.

Heather Meadows Area

The highway ends at 5,200-foot **Artist Point** in Austin Pass, 23 miles east of Glacier, and the only alpine area in the North Cascades accessible by car. The surrounding area—Heather Meadows—delivers incredible vistas, enjoyable picnic sites, and a multitude of hiking trails to explore in late summer. The stone-walled **Heather Meadows Visitor Center** (10 A.M.–4:30 P.M. daily July–September), built by the CCC in 1940, offers local information.

Heather Meadows, stuck between Mt. Baker and Mt. Shuksan, has been drawing tourists since the first lodge was built here in 1927 (it burned to the ground four years later). The lakes, meadows, and rock formations surrounded by snowcapped peaks were the setting for Clark Gable's *Call of the Wild* and Robert DeNiro's *The Deer Hunter.*

The road to Picture Lake is kept plowed all winter, but the last five miles from here to Artist Point close with the first snows—generally mid- to late October—and usually don't open till late July. Because of the short season, the months of August and September are busy beyond belief, especially on weekends. Try to visit on a weekday instead.

SPORTS AND RECREATION

River Rafting

The Nooksack River emerges from Nooksack Glacier, high up Mt. Shuksan, and drops over Nooksack Falls before entering a wild gorge. After four miles of class II–III white water, the silt-laden waters emerge into the lower river delta, providing fine views of Mt. Baker and the chance to observe bald eagles and other wildlife. Several rafting companies offer eight-mile white-water trips down the Nooksack from Glacier to Deming June–August, including **River Recreation** (800/464-5899, www.riverrecreation.com, $78–88), which gives participants the option to ride in a raft with the rest of the group or in an individual inflatable

© ERICKA CHICKOWSKI

black bear at Heather Meadows Area

kayak. Whichever you pick, you'll be treated to a buffet lunch at the end of the trip.

A more leisurely summertime float—extremely popular with inner tubers and families—is the South Fork of the Nooksack River from Acme to Van Zandt.

Hiking

More than 200 miles of hiking trails meander through the Mt. Baker district, and, fortunately for hikers, all of them are closed to motorized vehicles. The variety of trails is great: both backpackers and one-milers alike can find striking scenery within their reach. Wilderness permits are not needed for hiking within the Mt. Baker Wilderness, but be sure to get one at the Glacier Public Service Center if you will be entering North Cascades National Park from the Mt. Baker area.

One of the most popular local day hikes is the 3.5-mile round-trip **Heliotrope Ridge Trail** to the edge of **Coleman Glacier,** the starting point for Mt. Baker summit climbs.

An easy four-mile round-trip hike leaves from the end of Twin Lakes Road off Mt. Baker Highway to a lookout atop **Winchester Mountain,** with excellent views of Mt. Baker, Mt. Shuksan, and the North Cascades.

Popular with equestrians and hikers alike is the six-mile round-trip **Skyline Divide** trail, beginning 13 miles up Road 37 and providing ample Baker views and wildflower meadows.

LOOP TRIPS

Only a few loop trails are suitable for overnight trips; most Mt. Baker trails are walk-in, walk-out propositions. Still, the scenery here is good enough to see twice. One loop trip, perhaps too short for the more robust, starts across from Nooksack Falls, seven miles east of Glacier, for a 4.5-mile hike to **Excelsior Pass,** gaining a tortuous 3,800 feet en route. It then follows the **High Divide Trail** for four miles, with spectacular views of Baker and Shuksan, and returns to Road 3060 via **Welcome Pass** for 1.8 miles. The descent is via 67 demented switchbacks. Sections of this loop make popular, albeit difficult, day hikes. To stretch it out, travel north for three miles past the Excelsior Pass/High Divide junction to **Damfino Lakes** and Forest Road 31.

The **Copper Ridge-Chilliwack Loop Trail** is an extremely popular 35-mile trek into Mount Baker Wilderness and North Cascades National Park that begins from the Hannegan Campground at the east end of Forest Road 32. The first four miles are gentle, but after that the trail climbs abruptly to **Hannegan Pass,** then back down to a fork at the entrance to North Cascades National Park. The right fork continues east over Whatcom Pass and eventually to Ross Lake. Take the left fork instead, and climb along the spine of **Copper Ridge,** with vistas across the top of the Cascades. From here, the trail drops into Indian Creek, where you join the Chilliwack Trail for the return trip along Chilliwack River. A cable car provides a crossing over the river. This trail is best hiked from late July through September. Wilderness permits are required for this hike; get them at the Glacier Public Service Center.

HEATHER MEADOWS HIKES

The Heather Meadows area is an immensely popular late-summer hiking area. Access is easy, since the Mt. Baker Highway (Highway 542) ends at 4,700-foot Austin Pass, with trails branching out in all directions for all levels of ability. Easiest is the **Artist Ridge Trail,** a mile-long loop with interpretive signs and views all the way to Mt. Rainier on clear days. The first 200 feet are wheelchair-accessible. Another easy path, **Fire and Ice Trail,** is paved to an overlook above Bagley Lakes.

Starting at Austin Pass near the end of Mt. Baker Highway, the four-mile one-way hike to **Lake Ann,** one of the Cascades' most beautiful high-country lakes, is a popular route with day hikers and the major approach trail to 9,127-foot Mt. Shuksan. Lake Ann Trail is often covered by snow till late summer.

From the end of Highway 542 at Artist Point, follow the steep 2.5-mile trail up lava cliffs to the appropriately named, flat-topped **Table Mountain.** Enjoy incredible views of Mt. Baker and Mt. Shuksan from here.

The 5.5-mile **Chain Lakes Trail** begins at the end of the road, traverses Table Mountain, and passes a series of alpine lakes. Beyond this, the trail climbs over Herrmann Saddle, enters the Bagley Lakes basin, and ends near the Mt. Baker Ski Area. For a return loop, take the **Wild Goose Trail** back to Artist Point.

Climbing

Mount Baker offers one of the most challenging and rewarding climbs in the cascades. This one is not for beginners, so don't attempt to climb Mt. Baker without previous alpine climbing experience. The trail begins from Road 39 off Mt. Baker Highway and gains 1,500 feet along the way. **Mountain Madness** (206/937-8389 or 800/328-5925, www.mountainmadness.com) leads technical climbs of Mt. Baker and nearby peaks.

Skiing

It might be out of the way, but ski-bums flock to **Mt. Baker Ski Area** (56 miles east of Bellingham on Mt. Baker Hwy., tickets 360/734-6771, ski report 360/671-0211 or 206/634-0200, www.mtbakerskiarea.com, $43 adult, $38 senior, $33 children, $32–43 ski rentals) for its premium powder. The geography and elevation of the ski area enables it to run the longest seasons in the state, typically keeping the lifts running from early November through April. Eight chairlifts (two of these are quads) put 1,500 vertical feet of slope underski, from machine-groomed intermediate runs to open powder bowls. Other facilities include a big day lodge, child care, ski school, rentals, restaurant, and bar.

Cross-country and backcountry skiers will find plenty of trails to keep them happy in the area around Mt. Baker. For rentals, contact **Glacier Ski Shop** (9999 Mt. Baker Hwy., 360/599-1943, $25–35 Nordic, $30–40 alpine), which offers both Nordic and alpine skis by the day.

Camping

Camp at one of three Forest Service campgrounds in the Mt. Baker area. **Douglas Fir Campground** (two miles east of Glacier on Mt. Baker Hwy., 518/885-3639 or 877/444-6777, www.recreation.gov, mid-May to mid-Sept., $16–18, $9 extra reservation fee), is situated in a beautiful old-growth forest along the Nooksack River and is open all winter. **Silver Fir Campground** (13 miles east of Glacier, 518/885-3639 or 877/444-6777, www.recreation.gov, mid-May to mid-Sept., $16–18, $9 extra reservation fee) is along the Nooksack with great mountain views. **Hannegan Campground** (17 miles east of Glacier and right next to the Mount Baker Wilderness on Forest Road 32, mid-May to mid-Sept.) is a primitive campground with no running water and no fees.

The 411-acre **Silver Lake County Park** (three miles north of Maple Falls, 360/599-2776, $22 electricity, $17 no hookups) has a beautiful day lodge/information center, year-round camping and RV hookups, showers,

BACK IN THE DAY . . .

Mt. Baker has been a source for year-round recreation since 1868, when librarian-turned-mountaineer Edmund Coleman and his party climbed to the summit after two failed attempts. Either poor planners or extremely conscious of pack weight, the entire climbing party shared one plate and spoon and ate only bacon, bread, and tea during the 10-day ascent. By 1911, the mountain had become an integral part of the Mt. Baker marathon, a 118-mile round-trip between Bellingham and the summit using any mode of transportation in addition to at least 24 miles on foot. The marathons were discontinued two years later, after one competitor fell into a crevasse, though he lived to tell about it. More recently the race has been revived as the 85-mile **Ski to Sea Marathon,** where teams begin by skiing down Mt. Baker, and relays of bike riders, paddlers in canoes, and runners complete the course to Puget Sound.

swimming, plus boat rentals. **Hutchinson Creek Campground** (Mosquito Creek Rd. near Acme) has free camping, but no water. More free camping is at **Nooksack City Park** (Nooksack Ave. and Madison St.). Dispersed camping is free on Forest Service land below milepost 52; just find a good off-the-road place to camp. Campers and hikers can take **showers** at the Texaco mini mart near the intersection of Highways 9 and 542.

ACCOMMODATIONS

Accommodations near Mt. Baker are mostly in the form of cabins, B&Bs, and condos; the closest are in the town of Glacier, 15 miles below Mt. Baker Ski Area. Note that many places require a two-night minimum on weekends and have higher rates around Christmas and New Year's. Call well ahead for weekend reservations during the ski season.

One of the best sources of options is the well-rounded reservation service offered by **Mt. Baker Lodging** (360/599-2453 or 800/709-7669, www.mtbakerlodging.com), which offers dozens of chalets, cabins and condos along the Mount Baker Highway.

Set within a modern chalet just a half mile west of Glacier, **Mt. Baker B&B** (9447 Mt. Baker Hwy., Glacier, 360/599-2299, www.mtbakerbedandbreakfast.com, $80–110) serves full breakfasts and offers a steaming hot tub perfect to soothe the old bones after a day of hiking or skiing.

The log cabin **Glacier Guest Suite** (8040 Mt. Baker Hwy., 360/599-2927, www.mtbaker.com, $105 s or d) overlooks Nooksack River Valley with views of Mt. Baker and the 100-acre farmstead it sits on. The cabin comes with a kitchenette and fireplace, and a continental breakfast is served each morning.

Situated between the whooshing serenity of Glacier and Gallup Creeks, **Glacier Creek Lodge** (10036 Mt. Baker Hwy., Glacier, 360/599-2991 or 800/719-1414, www.glaciercreeklodge.com, $60–85 d, $135–165 up to 4) offers both motel and cabin digs, from cozier couple rooms to spacious units including kitchens and fireplaces. They even have a barrier-free cabin available for outdoor lovers with disabilities. All guests are also granted access to an outdoor hot tub.

The Logs at Canyon Creek (9002 Mt. Baker Hwy., 360/599-2711, $125 s or d, $250–300 up to 8) has five cozy cabins with fireplaces, kitchens, and a swimming pool along the Nooksack River. **The Guest House** (5723 Schornbush Rd., Deming, 360/592-2343, $50 d) is a quaint a country cottage with kitchenette.

FOOD

North Fork Brewery (6186 Mt. Baker Hwy., Deming, 360/599-2337, www.northforkbrewery.com) has brewed-on-the-premises beer and a menu centered on hand-thrown pizzas. If you love fresh homemade pasta, don't miss **Milano's** (9990 Mt. Baker Hwy., Glacier, 360/599-2863, Mon.–Thurs. 10 A.M.–8 P.M., Fri.–Sun. 10 A.M.–9 P.M.). The prices are reasonable, and the atmosphere is friendly and lighthearted. Milano's also has a deli for lunchtime sandwiches, and Tuesday night pizzas.

Take your pick of creative dishes with international flair at **Graham's Restaurant** (9989 Mt. Baker Hwy., Deming, 360/599-1964, daily noon–9:30 P.M.), an unassuming little roadside eatery with loads of scrumptious dishes, including fish tacos and juicy steaks. The spectacularly carved wooden bar here is a favorite spot for skiers to order up a pint of brew after a long day on Baker's slopes.

Fidalgo Bay Roasting Company sells espresso drinks, teas, and snacks out of a converted trailer just west of town.

INFORMATION

Located in a stone building built by the CCC in 1938, **Glacier Public Service Center** (34 mi. east of Bellingham on Mt. Baker Hwy., 360/599-2714, mid-Jun. to mid-Sept. daily 8:30 A.M.–4:30 P.M., call for hours rest of year) is the place to go for information on Mt. Baker and surrounding areas. Rangers here also issue backcountry permits and have summertime interpretive talks and walks.

Heather Meadows Visitor Center (at the end of Mt. Baker Hwy., July–Sept. daily 10 A.M.–5 P.M.) offers a variety of interpretive activities on late summer weekends. You can also pick up maps and information at the **Mt. Baker Ranger District** (810 Hwy. 20, Sedro-Woolley, 360/856-5700, www.fs.fed.us/r6/mbs) offices.

The Mountain Loop: Granite Falls to Darrington

The scenic Mountain Loop Highway, one of the state's most popular weekend drives, connects Granite Falls to Darrington via a 55 mile long road. From Granite Falls, the road is paved for the first 22 miles as it follows the South Fork of the Stillaguamish River to its headwaters at Barlow Pass, entering the Mt. Baker-Snoqualmie National Forest near Verlot. Numerous campgrounds and hiking trails offer diversions along the way, and access to three fabulous swaths of wild mountain country: Boulder River Wilderness, Henry M. Jackson Wilderness, and Glacier Peak Wilderness. North of Barlow Pass, the road turns to gravel and becomes narrow and winding as it drops along the Sauk River. It remains gravel for 14 miles; the last seven miles to Darrington are paved. West of Darrington, the Mountain Loop Road passes through a wide valley bisected by the North Fork of the Stillaguamish River and filled with hay piles, beehives, horses, sheep, chickens, hogs, big red barns, cut-your-own Christmas tree farms, lumber mills, clear-cuts, and regenerating stands of trees. Openings provide glimpses of the snowy peaks that cap the Cascade Range.

History

Parts of today's Mountain Loop Highway overlay trails that were used for centuries by the Native Americans who first inhabited these lands. The 1889 discovery of gold and silver in the Monte Cristo area led to a mad rush of miners and others attempting to get rich quick. To transport the (assumed) mineral wealth, a railroad was constructed from Monte Cristo over Barlow Pass, down the canyon created by the South Fork of the Stillaguamish River, through the new town of Granite Falls, and on to Everett, where the ore would be refined. Funded by an East Coast syndicate with financial backing from John D. Rockefeller, the railroad was poorly designed and subject to repeated flooding. These floods, combined with a financial depression in the 1890s, forced the mine owners to sell out to Rockefeller in 1899, and even he was compelled to give up when the ore petered out a few years later.

With cessation of mining, the Monte Cristo area began attracting tourists, and the trains turned to offering weekend excursions into the mountains. Business flourished in the 1920s, and hotels were added in Silverton and near Big Four Mountain to cater to the wealthy—the latter even featured a nine-hole golf course. All this came to a screeching halt following the stock market crash of 1929. The railroad shut down in 1936, and the old railroad grade became an automobile road. Two years later, the CCC began construction of a narrow mountain route north from Barlow Pass to Darrington, completing the final link in today's Mountain Loop Highway.

Weather

The Darrington area is an anomaly in the Cascades. Whereas the Seattle area receives 30–40 inches of rain per year, Darrington gets an average of 80 inches, while Monte Cristo gets over 140 inches, creating a dense rainforest much like those of the Olympics. The low elevation here means questionable snowfall, though cross-country skiing and snowmobiling are popular area activities.

It is imperative to carry adequate clothing while hiking in this part of the Cascades, even if you're out on a short hike. The weather changes rapidly sometimes, and nearly every

along the Mountain Loop Highway

summer someone dies of hypothermia a short distance from his or her car.

The highway and logging roads are popular snowmobile routes in winter, but that portion of the road over 2,361-foot Barlow Pass is blocked by snow beyond Elliot Creek on the north side and Deer Creek on the south side from mid-November to mid-April.

HIKING

More than 300 miles of trails lie within the Darrington Ranger District. Many of these are maintained by volunteers, so do your part to keep them clean. Parking-area theft is a major problem in this isolated area, so don't assume your valuables are safe in the trunk. Leave them at home or carry them with you. Report all thefts to a ranger station or the county sheriff. The following hiking trails are listed in a roughly northeastward progression from Verlot to Darrington along the Mountain Loop Highway.

Mount Pilchuck State Park

The 5,324-foot Mt. Pilchuck (6.9 mi. up FS Rd. 42, www.parks.wa.gov) offers a challenging day hike, with dramatic 360-degree views of the Cascades and Puget Sound from the summit. Get to the trailhead by heading a mile east of Verlot Public Service Center and turning onto Forest Road 42. Follow it seven miles uphill to the park entrance at an abandoned ski area. Allow five hours for the six-mile round-trip hike, and be prepared for a 2,300-foot gain in elevation and some boulder hopping at the end; the hike is best in late summer. Drinking water is scarce along the trail, so take plenty with you. Mountain climbers practice their techniques on the rugged northeast side of Mt. Pilchuck; be sure to sign the climbers' register at the Verlot Public Service Center before doing so.

Other Verlot Area Hikes

The subalpine forests and meadows are as much the attractions as the clear mountain lake on the four-mile round-trip hike to **Heather Lake.** To reach the trailhead, take Forest Road 42 for 1.5 miles, then hike up an old logging road before reaching the forest and then open meadows. Allow three hours; elevation gain is 1,100 feet. Because of its easy access, Heather Lake is a very popular day-hiking spot on summer weekends.

Late spring is a good time to hike the 2.7 miles to **Lake 22** (trail No. 702), a scenic alpine lake whose ho-hum name doesn't do it justice. When you get to the lake you're likely to be greeted by waterfalls and mini avalanches crashing off the cliff walls butting up to the lake (but safely away from the trail). The trail starts two miles east of the Verlot Ranger Station, passing through an old-growth western red cedar forest on the way to the mountain lake. Allow four hours for the 1,400-foot elevation gain; no camping is allowed in the area.

Boulder River Wilderness

Established in 1984, the 49,000-acre Boulder River Wilderness occupies the low range of mountains between Verlot and Darrington. A handful of trails provide access to the wilderness from various sides, but travel off these paths can be a challenge in this rugged and oft-brushy terrain. The main attraction is Three Fingers, a 6,850-foot peak offering outstanding alpine vistas.

The 6.7-mile one-way trail to **Tin Pan Gap** and **Three Fingers Mountain** is a popular overnight hike. From Verlot, go west on Mountain Loop Highway for four miles, then head north on Forest Road 41, following it 18 miles to the trailhead at Tupso Pass. The trail climbs through dense forest for 2.5 miles to four-acre Saddle Lake; continue for another 2.3 miles through meadows to Goat Flat, an oft-crowded camping spot. Use only a campstove; fire rings leave near-permanent scars in these fragile meadows. The trail reaches Tin Pan Gap after about six miles; from here, the hike becomes a technical climb (not for the inexperienced) over Three Fingers Glacier and a scramble to the top of Three Fingers Mountain and the old fire lookout.

Ice Cave

The **Big Four Ice Cave** (trail No. 723) is a favorite two-mile round-trip hike, starting 26 miles from Granite Falls at the Big Four Picnic Area. The hike begins on boardwalks over a beaver-created marsh, then heads through a dense forest and across the South Fork of the Stillaguamish River to the ice caves and a view of 6,135-foot Big Four Mountain. The caves—created when water channels under a small glacier—are generally exposed in late July and are visible through October. Admire them from afar; the caves are very dangerous to enter because tons of ice may separate from the ceiling at any time, as happened in the summer of 1993 when the roof caved in on a young man but, miraculously, didn't kill him. In winter and spring the snowfield is susceptible to avalanches.

Be aware that this area was badly hit by 2006 storms, and the main bridge leading to the ice caves was blown out. The Forest Service expects to rebuild in time for the 2009 hiking season, but be sure to call ahead for details.

Mount Forgotten Meadows

A full-day hike to an alpine meadow starts 26 miles from Granite Falls and heads up 6,005-foot **Mt. Forgotten** for an eight-mile round-trip hike. Take the Mountain Loop Highway 15 miles east from the Verlot Public Service Center, then go north on Perry Creek Road (No. 4063) for a mile to the Perry Creek trailhead. The trail climbs past **Perry Creek Falls** at about two miles, heading through an old-growth forest for another 1.7 miles to the first meadow. Allow seven hours to reach the meadows at 5,200 feet, an elevation gain of 3,100 feet. The trail continues through meadows to Mt. Forgotten's climbing route (for experienced alpine climbers only).

Monte Cristo Area

The magnificent alpine-topped 103,591-acre **Henry M. Jackson Wilderness Area** is accessible from several trailheads on the eastern end of the Mountain Loop. The most popular hiking paths here center on the fascinating old mining town of Monte Cristo. In the 1890s, gold and silver strikes lured 2,000 people to this boomtown, but the ore turned out to be of poor quality, and within 20 years Monte Cristo had become a ghost town. The fireplace and foundation of the Big Four Inn—a luxurious century-old resort that burned to the ground in 1949—stand as mute reminders of the town's earlier glory. During the Depression, the railroad to Monte Cristo was replaced by the Mountain Loop Highway. Today, the town site and abandoned mines around Monte Cristo remain privately owned.

Get here by driving 20 miles east from Verlot to Barlow Pass, where the four-mile side road to Monte Cristo begins. Floods in 1980 and 1990 left it impassable to cars, but it remains a popular place for mountain bikers and hikers in the summer, and cross-country skiers and snowmobilers in the winter. Check at the Forest Service offices in Darrington or Verlot for current road and bridge conditions. The Forest Service's free **Monte Cristo Campground** offers a pleasant overnight spot near the ghost town.

Glacier Basin Trail (No. 719) is a popular two-mile hiking route from Monte Cristo into nearby high country. The trail follows an old railroad grade for the first half mile, then climbs steeply past Glacier Falls, around Mystery Hill, and into gorgeous Glacier Basin, gaining 1,300 feet in elevation. The route passes all sorts of rusting mining equipment, pieces of the cable tramway, and old mine shafts on the way. Bring your stove, since no campfires are allowed in the high country, and avoid camping on the fragile meadow areas. Good campsites can be found at Ray's Knoll and Mystery Ridge.

Another very steep hike (trail No. 708, 4.4 miles one-way) climbs over **Poodle Dog Pass** from Monte Cristo. This trail leaves from the town site, ascends to Silver Lake, and then on to an open ridge offering panoramic views of the surrounding mountains.

Glacier Peak Wilderness

Covering 576,865 acres—35 miles long by 20 miles wide—massive Glacier Peak Wilderness is one of Washington's largest stretches of wilderness landscape. Its dominant geologic feature, Glacier Peak, is the fourth-highest mountain in the state, reaching 10,541 feet. A dormant volcano, Glacier Peak last erupted some 12,000 years ago; today its summit is almost encircled by glaciers. In the Glacier Peak Wilderness, you're likely to see deer, blue grouse, and marmots, plus an occasional lynx, mountain goat, and cougar. Deep snow buries much of the wilderness high country till late June, and some trails are not free of snow until mid-July.

More than 450 miles of backcountry trails provide diverse hiking opportunities in the wilderness, with access from all sides, including the Marblemount, plus the Lake Chelan, Stehekin, and Entiat River areas. The western side of the wilderness reaches almost to the Mountain Loop Highway, with access via several Forest Service spur roads. The ultimate hiking experience, the **Pacific Crest Trail,** cuts right through the heart of Glacier Peak Wilderness, following the ridges for 60 miles of ascending and descending paths.

Once the most popular path in the Glacier Peak Wilderness, **White Chuck Trail** (No. 643) was badly damaged when the river rerouted itself during a 2003 storm that ravaged many parts of the North Cascades. The storm completely consumed the popular Kennedy Hot Springs along the trail, and Forest Service rangers and volunteers are just now clearing the trail again for use. Call Verlot Public Service center (360/691-7791) for the most up-to-date info on this trail, which acts as a major junction with the Pacific Crest Trail and other side trails in the Wilderness.

Mountaineers heading up the glaciers of Glacier Peak often use White Chuck Trail to reach the base of the mountain, scrambling to the timberline and following the Sitkum Glacier to the summit. Consult a North Cascades climbing guidebook for a detailed description of the route and be sure to call Verlot for avalanche information in the spring.

The Pacific Crest Trail is accessible from the west side at various points off the Mountain Loop Highway. One of the best of these is the

North Fork Sauk Trail (No. 649), an 8.4-mile path offering a gentle riverside route through a magnificent old-growth cedar forest, before relentlessly switchbacking upward to the Pacific Crest Trail, gaining 3,900 feet en route. An excellent loop hike (26 miles round-trip) is to continue south on the PCT to its junction with the **Pilot Ridge Trail** (No. 652), and then follow that trail back downhill past alpine lakes to its junction with the North Fork Sauk Trail. The Pilot Ridge Trail offers hikers vistas of Glacier Peak and Mt. Rainier, but be sure to carry plenty of water, since portions of this loop hike lack water sources. Get to the North Fork Sauk trailhead by driving east from the Verlot Public Service Center for 27 miles (or south from Darrington for 20 miles) and turning east onto Sloan Creek Road 49 near the Bedal Campground. The trailhead is located 6.6 miles up, where the road crosses Sloan Creek.

Darrington Area Trails

Several short paths provide fun day hikes in the Darrington area. **Old Sauk Trail** (No. 728) is an easy three-mile stroll that departs from Clear Creek Campground, four miles south of Darrington. The trail parallels the Sauk River, passing riverside alder stands and moss-covered cedar stumps. Salmon and steelhead spawn in Murphy Creek at the southern end of the Old Sauk Trail.

A three-mile path, **Beaver Lake Trail** (No. 629), starts across from White Chuck Campground, 10 miles south of Darrington. The trail sits atop an old railroad grade and crosses beaver ponds where you're likely to see ducks and herons. It continues through a beautiful stand of old-growth cedar trees at the upper end before looping back to the Mountain Loop Highway. Both of these are also good for mountain bikes.

Another hike through virgin timber is the **Boulder River Trail** (No. 734). Get here by heading 8.2 miles west from Darrington, turn south onto French Creek Road 2010, branch right after a mile, and then follow it another 2.8 miles to the trailhead. In addition to thick old-growth forests, this four-mile trail passes a delightful series of Boulder River waterfalls and cascades.

OTHER RECREATION

River Rafting

The **Sauk River,** a National Wild and Scenic River that rises in the Henry M. Jackson Wilderness and joins the Skagit River near Rockport, offers a combination of fast and complex rapids, fantastic mountain scenery, and plenty of wildlife. **Orion Expeditions** (800/553-7466, http://orionexp.com, $75–90) runs trips that start 10 miles upriver and end in Darrington, with lots of class III–IV white water along the way. The primary season is May to mid-August. Orion provides lunch after the trip.

The **Suiattle River** (soo-AT-ul) starts in the Glacier Peak Wilderness and meets the Sauk River north of Darrington. This is a good whitewater river for families and folks starting out, with great mountain scenery and lots of small rapids along the 13 miles of river. Because of its glacial origins, the Suiattle has a milky, silt-laden appearance and braided channels. The main season for river-running is June to early September. Both **Blue Sky Outfitters** (800/228-7238, www.blueskyoutfitters.com) and **North Cascades River Expeditions** (800/634-8433, www.riverexpeditions.com) send rafts down the Suiattle, with lunch served after.

Experienced, do-it-yourself river runners can also enjoy the challenges of the Sauk and Suiattle Rivers on their own. The Suiattle is the tamer of the two, rated class II–III from Boundary Bridge to the Sauk River; it's not navigable within the national forest due to logjams, hidden stumps, and debris. Put in at Boundary bridge. The Sauk River ranges from class I to V; from the White Chuck launch area to Clear Creek it's a IV or V, with difficult rapids through narrow passages. From Bedal to White Chuck, the river is classified as a class III–IV, and below Clear Creek it ranges from class I to III. North of Darrington, the river is considerably calmer and is popular for canoeing.

Canoeing and Fishing

The Darrington District boasts a large number of small lakes, some of which provide excellent fishing. Check at the ranger station or public service center for a list of lakes and suggestions on the best ones for boating, fishing, or paddling.

Paddlers and rafters will enjoy exploring six-acre **Coal Lake,** a subalpine lake at 3,600 feet elevation. Go east on the Mountain Loop Highway for 15 miles from the Verlot Public Service Center, then go north on Coal Lake Road 4060 for 4.5 miles to the trailhead. Carry your boat about 50 feet to the lake, where you'll find a limited number of campsites that fill up quickly.

Another lake with easy canoe and raft access is five-acre **Canyon Lake.** From the Verlot Public Service Center, drive four miles on the Mountain Loop Highway to Road 41; turn right, continuing for two miles to Green Mt. Road 4110. Turn right again (heading east now), driving almost 1.4 miles to Road 4111; follow this road for 10.75 miles to the trailhead on the left side of the road. Carry your boat along the 50-foot trail to Canyon Lake, surrounded by trees and a few campsites; fair fishing can be found here.

Cross-Country Skiing

Skiers and snowshoers can count on solitude when exploring the Darrington District; most roads aren't plowed and snowfall is unpredictable at this low elevation. Any existing snow here is often wet and difficult to ski through. Still determined? Take these routes as suggestions; if the roads themselves aren't snow-covered, keep driving along the route until you come to some that are.

From Highway 530 on the way to Darrington, go south on **French Creek Road 2010** to the snow line, and then ski uphill from there. The road takes you through dense forest and switchbacks for great views and a fast downhill trip back. Or, from the Darrington Ranger Station, drive north on Highway 530 for 6.5 miles to **Suiattle River Road 26;** follow it till you hit snow, and then ski up the road and along the river. Enjoy fine views of Glacier Peak along the way.

On the Granite Falls side, the **Big Four** area is very popular with skiers, snowshoers, snowmobilers, and winter hikers; take the Mountain Loop Highway 23 miles from Granite Falls to the end of the maintained road at Deer Creek Road 4052. Ski two miles from the parking area to Big Four Picnic Area, following the South Fork of the Stillaguamish River; continue another mile to the snowfield near the Big Four Ice Cave. The avalanche danger here is severe; don't travel beyond the edge of the clearing—it's the force of avalanches that created and maintains that clearing! Allow 3–5 hours round-trip; this route is suitable for beginning skiers.

A more challenging route is the **Deer Creek/Kelcema Lake Ski Route,** which follows Deer Creek Road uphill to Kelcema Lake, a distance of 4.6 miles, with an elevation gain of 1,600 feet. Allow 5–7 hours for the round-trip, and avoid it during periods of high avalanche danger. Get here by heading 12 miles east from the Verlot Public Service Center to the end of snow plowing and the start of the ski route. No snowmobiles are allowed here.

Another popular cross-country ski route (for advanced skiers only) begins at the Deer Creek parking area and continues 11 miles to the old mining town of Monte Cristo, gaining 1,275 feet in elevation en route. This is best done as an overnight trip due to its length; be sure to check on avalanche conditions before heading out.

Camping

The Forest Service operates 16 campgrounds (518/885-3639 or 877/444-6777, www.recreation.gov, generally open Memorial Day to mid-September, $8–14, $9 extra reservation fee) along the Mountain Loop. Free dispersed camping is allowed on Forest Service lands away from the developed campgrounds.

From Granite Falls, neighboring **Turlo** and **Verlot** campgrounds are near the Verlot Service Center, while **Gold Basin Campground** is 2.4 miles east of the service center. Gold Basin also features an amphitheater where Saturday night campfire programs are presented in the summer. Across the road is a short, wheelchair-accessible interpretive trail. Continuing on from Verlot, other campsites include **Boardman Creek Campground** (open all year), six miles east; and **Red Bridge Campground,** seven miles east.

From Darrington, Forest Service campsites include **Clear Creek Campground,** four miles south, and **Bedal Campground,** 18 miles south, both open year-round. A mile east of Bedal Campground on Forest Road 49 is a quarter-mile path to the base of spectacular **North Fork Sauk Falls,** where the river plunges 45 feet.

From Darrington via Suiattle River Road No. 26, **Buck Creek Campground,** 22 miles northeast of town, features a quiet riverside setting in an old-growth forest. **Sulphur Creek Campground,** 28 miles from Darrington (near the end of Suiattle River Rd.), is just a mile away from the Glacier Peak Wilderness and is open year-round. A short trail leads from the campground along Sulphur Creek to colorful pools containing rather odoriferous hydrogen sulfide gas. See *Darrington* for other camping options.

INFORMATION

Get detailed camping, hiking, and historical information at the Mt. Baker-Snoqualmie National Forest's **Verlot Public Service Center** (11 miles east of Granite Falls, 360/691-7791, June–Labor Day daily 8 A.M.–4:30 P.M., plus Thurs.–Mon. 8 A.M.–4:30 P.M. in the spring and fall, closed in winter). The buildings at Verlot were built by the CCC between 1933 and 1942. The **Darrington Ranger District** (1405 Emmens St., Darrington, 360/436-1155, www.fs.fed.us/r6/mbs, Mon.–Fri. 8 A.M.–4:30 P.M.) is another good source of local info.

GRANITE FALLS

Granite Falls sits at the southwest end of the Mountain Loop Highway with Pilchuck Mountain offering a dramatic backdrop. The town began in 1889 as construction headquarters for the railroad route to the mines at Monte Cristo and grew up as a way station and center for logging and farming in the area. Because of its location at the base of the Cascades, the town provides a jumping-off point for hikers, campers, cross-country skiers, and snowmobilers exploring the Mt. Baker-Snoqualmie National Forest.

Sights

The **Granite Falls Museum** (109 E. Union St., 360/691-2603, www.gfhistory.org, 1–4 P.M. Sun. in summer, closed in winter) houses local memorabilia; check out the cross section from an enormous 1,200-year-old Douglas fir tree in the front.

Just east of town is the **Granite Falls Fish Ladder,** the world's longest vertical baffle fish ladder when it was built in 1954. Stop here to marvel at the raging South Fork of the Stillaguamish River as it roils over the falls (actually more of a giant rapids) for which the town was named. Salmon swim up a 240-foot tunnel dug through the granite.

Accommodations and Food

Step out onto the deck at **The Country Cedar Inn** (5732 Robe Menzel Rd., 360/691-3830, www.countrycedarinn.com, $99–149 d) and get a close-up view of Mt. Pilchuck and Three Fingers. Nestled in the foothills of the Snohomish Cascades, this quiet bed-and-breakfast is set within a beautiful cedar-sided home built with lumber milled from trees cut right on the forested five-acre property. All rooms come with private bathrooms; in addition to a home-style breakfast each morning, guests are treated to homemade cookies in the afternoon and sometimes dessert in the evening. There is also an option to order a four-course dinner in the evening.

Walk down the main drag to find several places with standard fare, including **Ike's Diner** (101 W Stanley St., 360/691-6636, Mon.–Fri. 8 A.M.–8 P.M., Sat.–Sun. 8 A.M.–7 P.M.) where the Formica-and-burger atmosphere is straight from the 1950s. It has good chicken burgers and fries, and even a decent teriyaki.

The **Granite Falls Farmers Marketplace** (360/691-6173) comes to town noon–4 P.M. Sunday late June–September.

Information and Transportation

Pick up a handful of local brochures at **Granite Falls Town Hall** (360/691-6441). Local events include the **Show 'N Shine Festival** on the first weekend of August and **Railroad Days** on the first weekend of October.

Community Transit (425/353-7433 or 800/562-1375, www.commtrans.org) offers daily bus service throughout Snohomish County.

DARRINGTON

Darrington, in the foothills of the Cascades northeast of Everett, was home to the Sauk and Suiattle tribes until white miners in search of gold and silver arrived in the late 1800s and early 1900s. Though some deposits were found, the real money in this area was in logging. Swedish, Irish, Welsh, and Norwegian loggers, plus a very large group from North Carolina, Georgia, and Tennessee, founded a community that still reflects its ethnic origins, especially the North Carolinians, who take great pride in their Tarheel heritage and mountain music.

Darrington, backdropped to the southwest by the 6,563-foot summit of Whitehorse Mountain, is located in a low pass separating the Sauk River from the North Fork of the Stillaguamish River. A collection of old buildings occupies the streets. Prominent among these is the **Trafton School,** a two-story white clapboard structure built in 1907. The town has a run-down feel, as if it were just waiting to be discovered by the next wave of out-migrating Seattleites in search of a peaceful place to escape the city life. With a setting like this, that shouldn't take long.

Events

The last weekend in June brings the **Timber Bowl Rodeo** to the rodeo grounds four miles west of town. Darrington's three-day **Bluegrass Festival and Street Fair** in mid-July is one of the most popular musical events in the Puget Sound Basin, in part because the area has developed some of the best bluegrass musicians outside Kentucky and Tennessee.

Camping

The closest Forest Service campground is the **Clear Creek Campground** (four miles south of town on Forest Rd. 20, 518/885-3639 or 877/444-6777, www.recreation.gov, $12, $9 extra reservation fee). **Squire Creek County Park** (four miles west of Darrington on Hwy. 530, 360/435-3441, $15) offers year-round camping amid old-growth Douglas fir and cedar trees. The park is also home to the largest cottonwood tree in Washington.

Sauk River County Park (seven miles north of Darrington on Sauk Valley Rd., free) has more campsites. There is no drinking water.

Accommodations

Darrington Motor Inn (1100 Seaman St., 360/436-1776, $59 s or d) is an attractive, small motel with rooms offering mountain views.

Food

Situated in a red-roofed diner with mountain views, **Glacier Peak Café** (1215 Hwy. 530 NE, 360/436-0602) is an ideal spot to sip on a cup of joe over some eggs before a hike or gulp down some soda with a salmon burger afterward.

For something a bit speedier, stop at the **Whitehorse Store** (five miles west of Darrington on Hwy. 530) for old-fashioned ice-cream cones.

Information and Transportation

For up-to-date information on trail conditions, campgrounds, fishing, and other outdoor activities, contact the **Darrington Ranger Station** (0.5 mile north of town, 360/436-1155, www.fs.fed.us/r6/mbs). Across the street from the Darrington Ranger Station is **Nels Bruseth Memorial Garden,** with several Sauk cedar canoes on display.

Community Transit (425/353-7433 or 800/562-1375, www.commtrans.org) offers daily service throughout Snohomish County.

North Cascades Highway

The North Cascades Highway—State Highway 20—begins in the Skagit River Valley, and follows this drainage to 5,477-foot Washington Pass, before descending into Methow Valley on the east side of the Cascade Range. Along the way, the road passes several small towns—Sedro-Woolley, Concrete, Rockport, and Marblemount—but after this you enter North Cascades National Park and Okanogan National Forest lands. This is magnificent mountain country, with numerous pullouts for viewing the striking scenery and a multitude of recreation options—campgrounds, visitors centers, and access to many other hiking paths, including the Pacific Crest Trail. Because of this, Highway 20 is one of the most popular and scenic drives in Washington. But don't plan on just driving through; bring your hiking boots, map, and a flexible schedule to really experience the North Cascades. Highway 20 is also a popular cycling route in the summer months, providing an official Bikecentennial route across rural America from Anacortes, Washington, to Bangor, Maine. This description of the North Cascades Highway starts on the eastern end at Sedro-Woolley and follows the road over the mountains into the Methow Valley.

History

The earliest white men to explore the North Cascades were Alexander Ross and his party, who crossed today's southern park boundary at Cascade Pass in 1814. In 1859, Henry Custer, working as an assistant of reconnaissance for the International Boundary Commission, traversed the region and commented: "Nowhere do the mountain masses and peaks present such strange, fantastic, dauntless and startling outlines as here.... [It] must be seen, it cannot be described." From 1880 to 1910, prospectors struck gold, platinum, lead, and zinc, but mountain travel was too difficult to justify the modest return.

On the west side of the mountains, the potential of the Skagit River wasn't harnessed until 1924, when the first of three dams was built by Seattle City Light. This rugged area was preserved as the North Cascades National Park Service Complex in 1968, incorporating the Ross Lake and Lake Chelan National Recreation Areas that were created as buffers to the park.

The North Cascades Scenic Highway (Highway 20) was originally commissioned in 1893, when state legislators set aside $20,000 for the completion of the Cascade Wagon Route. Over the decades that followed, sections of the road were gradually completed, and by 1968—the year the national park was established—a rough dirt road crossed the summit. The highway finally opened in 1972, some 79 years after the first shovel of dirt had been dug.

Climate

Summer weather on the west side of the North Cascades is cooler and wetter than the eastern portion, which is protected by the rain-shadow effect. The east side of the range gets quite hot in the summer and is usually dry. One of the major attractions of the Methow Valley for Puget Sounders is the usually sunny weather, the cold Colorado-style winters, and the hot, dry summers that make a perfect antidote to the damp, often overcast Puget Sound weather.

Driving Highway 20

No gas stations, restaurants, or other facilities (except restrooms at Washington Pass) are found along the 75 miles of Highway 20 between Ross Dam and Mazama, so fill up when you leave I-5 (Sedro-Woolley is cheapest if you get lots of miles per tank). No bus service goes along this route either; the closest you'll get is Mount Vernon on the west and Pateros and Okanogan on the east.

The middle section of Highway 20 closes for the winter after the first major snowfall because of avalanche danger. It is usually

© ERICKA CHICKOWSKI

along the North Cascades Highway

gated in late November and doesn't open again until late April, sometimes nearly June, depending on the amount of snow. In mid-winter, snow depths can exceed 15 feet at the summit. Parts of the highway remain open to snowmobile traffic from Colonial Creek Campground on the west side to Early Winters Campground near Mazama. Lower-elevation hiking trails, such as those along Ross Lake, are generally accessible from April through mid-October; at higher elevations, trails are usually snow-free from mid-July through September.

Cascade Loop Trips

Highway 20 joins Highway 153 at Twisp, Highway 97 near Pateros, and Highway 2 near Wenatchee to form the northwest portion of the "Cascade Loop." This 400-mile scenic drive winds through the North Cascades, past Lake Chelan, through Leavenworth on its approach to Stevens Pass, and returns to western Washington and Whidbey Island. You'll find free *Cascade Loop* booklets at visitors centers along the way, or ask the Cascade Loop Association (509/662-3888, www.cascadeloop.com) in Wenatchee for a copy.

A similar promotional highway route is called the North Cascades Loop. It follows the same route over Highway 20, continues on to the twin towns of Omak and Okanogan, turns north on Highway 97, and goes across into British Columbia's Okanagan (note that Canada and the U.S. spell the word differently), then heads west on the Trans-Canada Highway to the Vancouver area. Look for free *International Loop* booklets at visitors centers.

SEDRO-WOOLLEY

The riverside town of Sedro-Woolley is a town in transition. The decline of the logging industry in recent years has hit hard, forcing the town to look elsewhere for an economic base. It remains a commercial center for the farmlands that surround it, while becoming an outfitting town for adventurers on their way east into North Cascades National Park. This odd amalgam is reflected in two downtown buildings. One is home to a gun association (the U.S. Practical Shooting Association);

the other houses an organic foods company (Cascadian Farm).

History

Settlement of land at the mouth of the Skagit River began as early as 1863, but a huge natural logjam prevented any upriver development until it was dynamited apart in 1879. After this, sternwheelers could move up and down the river, opening the country to mining and logging. Five years later, Mortimer Cook opened a general store in a riverside town he named "Bug"—for the mosquitoes that tormented him in the summer. Cook later succumbed to local pressure and changed the name to Sedro, a corruption of *cedra,* the Spanish word for the cedar trees that once covered this area. About the same time, P. A. Woolley built a sawmill a few miles away that became the economic basis of a small but thriving community. The towns were so close together it was difficult to determine their borders, so in 1898 they agreed to join forces while retaining both names. Hence the only hyphenated town name in Washington, and one of just two in America.

After a pair of devastating fires early in the last century, the town was rebuilt using bricks. As a major logging settlement, Sedro-Woolley attracted many of its residents from North Carolina, a heritage that is still evident today. By the early 1900s, the town was home to 17 lumber mills, a steel foundry, and a big state hospital. Very little of these remain. An effort is now under way to re-create Sedro-Woolley's 1920s-era downtown with old-style lamps and restored brick buildings.

Sights

Sedro-Woolley Museum (727 Murdock St., 360/855-2390, http://sedrowoolleymuseum.homestead.com, Wed.–Thurs. noon–4 P.M., Sat. 9 A.M.–4 P.M., Sun. 1:30–4:30 P.M.) contains local memorabilia and old logging and farming equipment. While here, pick up a walking tour of historic sights around town, including a steam donkey from 1913. Seven of the historic logging pictures by famed documentary photographer Darius Kinsey have been turned into murals on downtown buildings.

NORTH CASCADES INSTITUTE

The nonprofit North Cascades Institute (2105 Hwy. 20, Sedro-Woolley, 360/856-5700, ext. 209, www.ncascades.org/nci) offers a wide spectrum of classes, lectures, kayak trips, whale-watching cruises, bird-watching safaris, photography training, and even poetry workshops. Many of the trips are exceptionally good deals; for example, a three-day hiking trip guided by wildlife biologists or professional photographers costs only $185. You'll find something going almost all the time between April and December.

North from Sedro-Woolley

Highway 9 north from Sedro-Woolley leads through quiet Nooksack Valley with its aging dairy barns, big bales of hay, and comfortable homesteads. A series of podunk towns form wide spots in the road: **Wickersham, Acme, Clipper, Van Zandt, Deming, Nugents Corner,** and **Nooksack.** A favorite tubing float trip is down the warm South Fork of the Nooksack River from Saxon to Van Zandt. On hot August weekends several thousand folks join in the fun, creating traffic congestion and conflicts with spawning salmon.

Everybody stops at the century-old **Everybody's Store** (5465 Potter Rd., Van Zandt, 360/592-2297, daily 8 A.M.–8 P.M.) where the shelves are filled with all manner of supplies: delicious baked goods, ice-cream cones, wool caps, 40 kinds of cheese, Indonesian batiks, and organic produce from the backyard garden. The deli here makes great sandwiches.

Woolly Prairie Buffalo Co. (360/856-0310 or 800/524-7660, Mon.–Fri. 8 A.M.–5:30 P.M., Sat. 8 A.M.–noon, closed Sun.) just north of

Sedro-Woolley, offers summertime hay rides where you can learn about bison.

Events

In mid-May the town carves out a niche for itself with **Woodfest,** a celebration of woodcarving and woodworking from inelegant chain-saw art to intricately carved works. The 4th of July brings the weeklong **Loggerodeo** to Sedro-Woolley—an annual event for more than 65 years—with logging contests, parades, a rodeo, street dance, bed race, carnival, vintage car show, crafts fair, and big fireworks display. **Founders' Day** in mid-September includes a pancake breakfast, animal parade, and children's games.

Accommodations and Campgrounds

Three Rivers Motel (210 Ball St., 360/855-2626 or 800/221-5122, $99–159 s or d) has comfortable lodging including an outdoor pool, hot tub, and continental breakfast. **Skagit Motel** (1977 Hwy. 20, 360/856-6001, $50 s or $54 d) is another option.

Riverfront RV Park (McDonald Ave., 360/855-1661, $15 water and electric hookups, $10 tent, $15 extra reservation fee) has tent and RV sites on the banks of the Skagit River.

Food

Get authentic Greek food at **Rhodes Pizza & Pasta** (108 W. Moore St., 360/855-2313, Sun.–Thurs. noon–10 P.M., Fri.–Sat. 4–11 P.M.).

Hal's Drive-In (321 State St., 360/855-0868, 11 A.M.–8 P.M. daily) is a longtime favorite, with burgers, shakes, corn dogs, and onion rings. **Esteban's Restaurant** (360/855-1387, Tues.–Sat. 11 A.M.–10 P.M., Sun.–Mon. 11 A.M.–9 P.M.) offers a variety of Mexican specialties like enchiladas and burritos served in huge portions.

Information and Transportation

On Highway 20, just west of Sedro-Woolley, you'll find the **Mt. Baker Ranger Station/ North Cascades National Park Service Complex** (810 Hwy. 20, 360/856-5700, www.fs.fed.us/r6/mbs, summer Sun.–Thurs. 8 A.M.–4:30 P.M., Fri. 8 A.M.–6 P.M., winter Mon.–Fri. 8 A.M.–4:30 P.M.) with a North Cascades relief map, books and brochures for sale, and information on road conditions.

The **Sedro-Woolley Chamber of Commerce** (714-B Metcalf, 360/855-1841 or 888/225-8365, www.sedro-woolley.com, Mon.–Fri. 9:30 A.M.–5 P.M., and Sat. 9:30 A.M.–1 P.M.) also has visitors' info.

Skagit Transit (360/757-4443, www.skat.org, $0.50) buses connect Sedro-Woolley with other towns in Skagit County.

BAKER LAKE

Nine-mile-long Baker Lake was created by the Upper Dam on the Baker River; the Lower Baker Dam created Lake Shannon, just off Highway 20 near Concrete. Baker Lake is very popular with campers, swimmers, motor boaters, and water-skiers, despite the enormous stumps that lurk just below the water's surface. To get there, take Baker Lake-Grandy Lake Road north from Highway 20. Get to 100-foot-high **Rainbow Falls** by driving 20 miles out Baker Lake Road, and then another five miles up Forest Road 1130. The name comes from the rainbow that appears at the base on sunny days.

Rasar State Park

Settled on a quiet 128-acre site along the Skagit River, Rasar State Park (just off Hwy. 20 along Cape Horn Road, Concrete, www.parks.wa.gov, $17 for tents or $21 for Rvs, no reservations) is a great place for a riverside picnic, and bald eagles are visible early in the year. Several trails lead through the tall second-growth forests, and year-round camping is available.

Sports and Recreation

HIKING

The easiest hike in the area is the half-mile, wheelchair-accessible **Shadow of the Sentinels Trail** that winds through an old-growth Douglas fir stand. It begins a mile beyond the Koma Kulshan guard station.

An excellent, gentle rainforest hike is up

the **Baker River.** To reach the trailhead for this six-mile round-trip hike, drive north on Baker Lake-Grandy Lake Road for 14 miles to the Komo Kulshan Guard Station. Follow the Forest Service road for 11.5 miles, then left a mile, then right on the first side road for half a mile to the start of Trail 606. This level, low-elevation trail affords views of glaciers and beaver ponds on the way to Sulphur Creek, the turnaround point. Because of its low elevation, the trail is snow-free from early spring to late fall.

Another Baker Lake hike takes you to **Park Butte,** a 5,450-foot summit with incredible views of Mt. Baker glaciers. This summer-only trek is seven miles round-trip, but with an elevation gain of over 2,200 feet it'll take a good part of the day to complete. Go north for 12.5 miles on Baker Lake-Grandy Lake Road, then turn left on Loomis-Nooksack Road 12 for 3.5 miles, then turn right onto Road 13 for five miles to the road's end. The trail is west of the road, crossing Sulphur Creek before the switchbacks begin.

CAMPING

Six miles past the Forest Service's Koma Kulshan Guard Station on the west shore, **Baker Lake Resort** (888/711-3033, $75 for 4–6) has a dozen rustic cabins with full kitchens, camping and RV sites, boat rentals, a store, and restaurant. There's a two-night minimum on weekends, and the resort is open only from mid-April through October.

Puget Sound Energy maintains the **Kulshan Campground** (near Upper Baker Dam on Baker Lake Rd., $10 summer, free during shoulder season). Free camping (no running water) is available at **Grandy Lake County Park** (four miles northeast of Hwy. 20 on Baker Lake Hwy.). Keep driving up Baker Lake Road to take your pick from a spate of Forest Service campgrounds (518/885-3639 or 877/444-6777, www.recreation.gov, $9 extra reservation fee), including **Horseshoe Cove** ($16), **Panorama Point** ($14), **Shannon Creek** ($14–16), **Boulder Creek** ($14), and **Park Creek** ($12). There is no drinking water at Boulder Creek or Park Creek. A boat-in or hike-in campground at **Maple Grove** is also available.

CONCRETE

East from Sedro-Woolley, Highway 20 skirts the Skagit River, climbing easily toward the first Cascade foothills. The landscape is farms, fields, and forests, with the serrated summit of Sauk Mountain to the east. Clear-cut hillsides, second- (or third-) growth forests, and closed lumber mills offer contrasting versions of the logging heritage.

The fading town of Concrete was home for many years to the largest cement plant in the state, and the source for cement used in building Grand Coulee Dam, as well as the Ross and Diablo dams. Although environmental regulations closed the outdated, dusty plant in 1968, the prosaic town name remains. (It could have been worse; the town's original name was Cement City.) The town burned several times in the early part of the last century and was finally rebuilt, using concrete, of course. The 5,537-foot summit of Sauk Mountain rises straight behind Main Street. Today, the rundown town limps along on a mix of tourism and timber. All that remains of the cement industry are the aging silos on the west end of town, a scattering of other buildings, and the quarry near Lake Shannon.

There aren't a lot of in-town attractions; your best bet is to pick a Main Street bench and sit with the locals a spell. Of minor interest is Superior Street, with its unique under-the-high-school access to the airport. Eagles are visible along the Skagit River in winter, and elk herds can be seen just west of town in winter and spring.

Camp Seven Logger's Museum (Railroad Ave., 360/853-7185, open weekends in summer, $2) is a small private collection of logging-era flotsam and jetsam.

Just east of town is the **Henry Thompson Bridge** over the Baker River. When completed in 1918, it was the longest single-span cement bridge in the world. A quarter mile east of this is the **Puget Sound Energy Visitors Center.**

Check out the unusual fish elevator nearby, used to help get returning salmon around the Baker Dam; see the salmon here between June and December. **Sauk Mountain Pottery,** three miles east of Concrete, is worth a visit for wood-fired stoneware and porcelain.

Events

The **Upper Skagit Bald Eagle Festival** celebrates the hundreds of eagles that gather along the Skagit River in late January. Festivities include music, an arts and crafts show, and naturalist presentations in Concrete, Marblemount, and Rockport. Other local events include the **Concrete Fly-In** on the third weekend in May, attracting pilots from around the Northwest; the **River Raft Challenge Race,** held the fourth Saturday in July; and **Good Olde Days,** on the third weekend in August.

Accommodations and Food

Located just west of town, **North Cascade Inn** (44618 Hwy. 20, 360/853-8870, www.cascademountainlodge.com, $99–119 s or d) looks like a typical roadside motel, but inside the furnishings are more reminiscent of a quiet bed-and-breakfast with unique furniture and quilts. It also offers microwaves, fridges, and coffeemakers, though there are no phones. Spring for the king rooms to get a flat-screen TV and DVD player.

Eagles Nest Motel (46346 Hwy. 20, 360/853-8662, $45 s or $50 d) offers simple motel rooms and also has space for tents and RVs.

Five miles west of Concrete, **Cascade Mountain Inn B&B** (360/826-4333, www.cascade-mtn-inn.com, $240 s or d) offers a cozy stay. Most of the five guest rooms have views of Sauk Mountain, and each has a private bath. Full breakfast is included, and kids are not permitted.

Located on the 700-acre working cattle ranch, **Ovenell's Heritage Inn B&B** (4442 Concrete Sauk Valley Rd., 360/853-8494, www.ovnells-inn.com, $135–160 s or d) sits inside a 1915 ranch house with. A full breakfast is served. The inn also rents a guesthouse with full kitchen, and new cabins with kitchens that sleep four.

Visit Concrete's **Saturday Market,** where produce, crafts, baked goods, and art are offered for sale 9 A.M.–4 P.M. every Saturday mid-May through August.

Information and Transportation

The **Concrete Chamber of Commerce** office (360/853-8400, www.concrete-wa.com, open weekdays) is right off Highway 20 in the Community Center. Catch the **Sockeye Express** trolley here ($3) for a 45-minute historical tour of town on weekends and holidays in the summer. **Skagit Transit** (360/757-4433, www.skat.org) offers free daily bus service throughout the county, from Anacortes to Concrete.

ROCKPORT AND MARBLEMOUNT

There isn't much to the tiny settlement called Rockport, but two pleasant parks offer a break from the highway, and bald eagles congregate along the Skagit River here. Entering Marblemount from the west, signs warn Last Gas for 69 Miles and, more importantly, Last Tavern for 89 Miles. The little town is a good place to stock up on these—and other—essentials, and to get information and backcountry permits for North Cascades National Park.

Sights

The **Bald Eagle Interpretive Center** (360/853-7614, Fri.–Sat. 10 A.M.–4 P.M. and Sunday noon–4 P.M.) is inside the fire hall in Rockport.

The pretty country settlement of Marblemount is surrounded by open fields and bigleaf maple trees (brilliant yellow in the fall) and is split by two rivers: the Skagit and the Cascade. Among the bigleaf maples is quaint **Wildwood Chapel,** covering barely enough space for a minister and the couple to be married. The chapel was built here in 1977 and has been used for weddings and countless I-was-there photos.

The **Marblemount Fish Hatchery** (a mile

EAGLE EYE

The Skagit River is one of the best places in the Lower 48 to watch wintering bald eagles, with over 300 birds stopping by on their journey south from Alaska and Canada. Just east of Rockport, the Nature Conservancy's 1,500-acre **Skagit River Bald Eagle Natural Area** (206/343-4344, www.skagiteagle.org) is a haven for these birds; they arrive in October and feast on Skagit River salmon through March. Eagles are visible from Highway 20 pullouts all along the Skagit River Valley, but the best way to see them is on a scenic float trip down the river. You're likely to see at least 50 of these majestic birds perched in trees along the nine-mile float from Marblemount to Rockport. To protect the eagles, this stretch of the river is voluntarily closed to all boats 5 A.M.–11 A.M. late December–February.

southeast of town on Fish Hatchery Rd.) rears and releases thousands of king, silver, and chum salmon each year.

Shopping

Rockport Country Store (50502 Hwy. 20, 360/853-8531) has something you don't see every day, a "self-kicking machine." Great for masochists. **Cascadian Farm Roadside Stand** (55749 Hwy. 20, 360/853-8173, May–Oct.) sells organic strawberries, blueberries, and raspberries, along with sweet corn and other produce from the cooperative's gardens. They also offer homemade ice cream, espresso, and wonderful fresh berry shortcakes.

Sports and Recreation

ROCKPORT STATE PARK

As you drive east from Concrete on Highway 20, there are few old-growth trees remaining on private land anywhere in the area, and it isn't till you reach Rockport State Park (Albert St. and Hwy. 20), about 10 miles east of Baker Lake, that you realize what has been lost. Covering 457 acres, the park has five miles of wooded hiking trails, Skagit River steelhead fishing, and camping ($14) at tent sites (those with Adirondack shelters and RV sites are $20) beneath incredible 250-foot high old-growth Douglas fir trees. The campground is open mid-April through October and has showers but takes no reservations. The paved and wheelchair-accessible **Skagit View Trail** leads right down to the riverbank, providing a great place to look for bald eagles in the winter.

Immediately west of the park is the start of **Sauk Mountain Road,** a 7.5-mile gravel road that takes you to a trailhead most of the way up this 5,537-foot peak. A steep, switchback-filled trail begins at the parking lot, climbing another 1.5 miles to the summit, where you're treated to views of the northern Cascades and the Skagit and Sauk River Valleys.

FLOAT TRIPS

A number of companies offer scenic bald eagle float trips December–February, when the population is at a peak. The river is so gentle that wet suits are not necessary; just wear warm winter clothing. One well-regarded outfitter, **Pacific Northwest Float Trips** (360/757-1201, www.pacificnwfloattrips.com) offers two trip choices on the Skagit. The long version runs four hours and includes lunch at the end of the line ($77), while the mini trip floats for about two hours ($45).

Nature lovers apprehensive about the cold and discomfort may also want to look into **Ackerlund's Guide Service** (360/848-1848, www.ackerlunds.com, $65), which offers its guests propane-heated boats and comfy seats on its four-hour floats.

RIVER RAFTING

In the summer, you can float eight miles of the upper Skagit River through North Cascades National Park, where the water is a bit rougher, but nothing over class III. It's a good beginning river for white-water enthusiasts and a perfect run to take the little ones—kids ages six and up are welcome. Try **Alpine Adventures** (800/723-8386, www.alpineadventures.com, $79) or **Orion Expeditions** (800/553-7466, http://orionexp.com, $85). Both firms offer experienced guides—Orion is a little pricier because it serves a buffet lunch after the trip.

CAMPING

Right on Highway 20 is **Wilderness Village RV Park** (57588 Hwy. 20, 360/873-2571, $11 tent, $18 full hookups) offering tent and RV sites. The public launderette here has **showers.**

Howard Miller Steelhead Park (52804 Rockport Park Rd., 360/853-8808, $14 tent, $20 full hookups or Adirondack shelters) is a small county park with big grassy lawns right along the river. In the park you'll find Chief Campbell's old dugout canoe and a log cabin built in the early 1880s. The old **Rockport Ferry** last used in 1961, sits along the river.

There are also a few camping options attached to local lodges and motels.

Accommodations and Food

Halfway between Rockport and Marblemount is **Totem Trails Motel** (57627 Hwy. 20 Rockport, 360/873-4535, www.totemtrail.com, $50 s), a basic one-story motel good for quick overnight stays. There are no fridges in the rooms, but there is a shared refrigerator on-site.

Buffalo Run Inn (360/873-4311, www.buffaloruninn.com, $49–109) presents the best lodging options around Marblemount. It was built in 1889 as a roadhouse for workers attempting to build a road over the mountains. The road they began was not completed until the 1972 opening of Highway 20. After years of service as a restaurant, the building was renovated into a well-appointed inn a few years ago. The name comes from the fantastic restaurant across the street, **Buffalo Run Restaurant** (360/873-2461,11-9), whose specialty is anything made with buffalo meat. The owners run a buffalo ranch a few miles out of town and they make the best meals in the area using their own stock. The home-baked breads, berry pies, hearty soups, and fresh-from-the-garden organic greens are special treats.

Hide away in a quiet little cabin at **Grace Haven** (three miles west of Marblemount, 360/873-4106, http://gracehavenretreat.com, $105 s or d). This quiet property offers clean, traditional cabins, fully furnished and including full kitchens and a charcoal grill out back. After a day of hiking, chill out with a game of badminton or horseshoes and then relax by the fire pit on the property.

Three miles west of Marblemount, **Clark's Skagit River Cabins** (58468 Clark Cabin Rd., 360/873-2250 or 800/273-2606, www.northcascades.com, $79–129 s or d, $15 tents, $25 full hookups) offers a variety of rustic cabins, space for tents and RVs, plus showers on-site for campers. Visitors also have the option to stay in a bed-and-breakfast-style room at the property's **Brookhaven Lodge** ($99 s or $109 d). Also here is **The Eatery Restaurant** (7 A.M.–9 P.M.) with all-American meals. Be sure to check out the curious hand-sewn flag made in 1890. Rabbit lovers will have a hopping time here; dozens of bunnies are all over the big green grounds.

Information

Follow the signs to the National Park Service's **Wilderness Information Center in Marblemount** (milepost 105.3 on Hwy. 20, 360/854-7245 Sun.–Thurs. 7 A.M.–6 P.M., and Fri.–Sat. 7 A.M.–8 P.M. in July and August, with reduced hours in June and the first half of September, call ahead). Get **backcountry permits** here for the park. Because there are no advance reservations, weekend campers arrive early to get permits for the most popular sites, especially Cascade Pass, Hidden Lake, Monogram Lake, Ross Lake, and Thornton Lakes. If you're willing to accept alternate destinations, you should be able to get into the backcountry under most circumstances. Behind the Wilderness Office is a greenhouse used to grow plants to revegetate damaged backcountry areas.

NEWHALEM AND EASTWARD

Heading east from Marblemount, Highway 20 enters North Cascades National Park after five miles, then passes Goodell Creek and Newhalem Campgrounds, the turnoff to North Cascades Visitor Center, and **Skagit General Store** in Newhalem.

The little settlement of Newhalem is a quiet company town with only one focus, producing electricity for Seattle at nearby Gorge, Diablo, and Ross dams. The parklike grounds are surrounded by trim clapboard homes occupied by employees of Seattle City Light. In the town park find **Old Number Six,** a 1928 Baldwin steam locomotive that hauled passengers and supplies to the Skagit River dams; today it's a favorite of kids. The small **Seattle City Light Visitor Center** here makes a good restroom stop.

East of Newhalem, Highway 20 begins a serious climb into the forested Cascades, and quickly passes a chain of three dams and reservoirs—Gorge, Diablo, and Ross—that constitute the centerpiece of Ross Lake National Recreation Area (a part of North Cascades National Park). Tours of Diablo Dam and Lake are a popular attraction here. Be sure to stop at the Forge Creek Falls overlook near milepost 123 for views of the creek plunging into the gorge below. Colonial Creek Campground is along the highway near Diablo Lake, and a mile east is an overlook where you can peer down on the emerald green lake waters and across to the jagged summits of Pyramid Peak and Colonial Peak.

Continuing eastward, the highway climbs along Granite Creek before topping two passes—4,855-foot Rainy Pass and 5,447-foot Washington Pass. A short paved trail leads from Washington Pass to over-the-highway viewpoints of 7,720-foot Liberty Bell—the symbol of the North Cascades Highway—and Early Winters Spires. Beyond this, the highway spirals downward to Methow Valley and the town of Winthrop, 30 miles to the east and 3,600 feet lower.

NORTH CASCADES NATIONAL PARK

The half-million-acre North Cascades National Park is one of the wildest in the Lower 48, and an outdoors lover's paradise. It has 318 glaciers—more than half of the total number outside Alaska. Few roads spoil this pristine wilderness, where rugged peaks, mountain lakes, and waterfalls greet the determined backcountry hiker. Nearly all of the park lies within the **Stephen Mather Wilderness,** and it is surrounded by additional wilderness buffers covering well over a million acres: Liberty Bell Primitive Area, Noisy-Diobsud Wilderness Area, Glacier Peak Wilderness Area, Pasayten Wilderness Area, and Mt. Baker Wilderness Area.

North Cascades National Park is actually a complex of three distinct units: the park itself is split into northern and southern units by Ross Lake National Recreation Area (Highway 20 passes along this corridor), while the southern end includes Lake Chelan National Recreation Area. All three sections are managed by the National Park Service, but Ross Lake National Recreation Area contains dams and power plants that are operated by Seattle City Light; these three plants supply nearly all of Seattle's electrical needs. If this isn't confusing enough, look at the maps to find that east-side portions of Mt. Baker-Snoqualmie National Forest are administered by Okanogan National Forest. To most visitors, these distinctions are of little meaning; this is all public land, and although the dams and reservoirs are certainly not natural, almost everything else is wild and undeveloped, providing fantastic opportunities for explorations afoot and afloat.

Gorge and Diablo Lakes

Two small reservoirs created by Seattle City Light dams on the upper Skagit River are Gorge Lake, covering 210 acres, and Diablo Lake, covering 910 acres; both are accessible from Highway 20. Diablo and Gorge Lakes get their emerald-green color from fine sediments in the glacial runoff.

The **Gorge Powerhouse** observation lobby (8 A.M.–4 P.M. daily May–Sept.) is accessed by a cable suspension footbridge. Continue beyond the power plant to **Ladder Creek Falls and Rock Gardens.** The colorful flower gardens were first planted here in the 1920s and

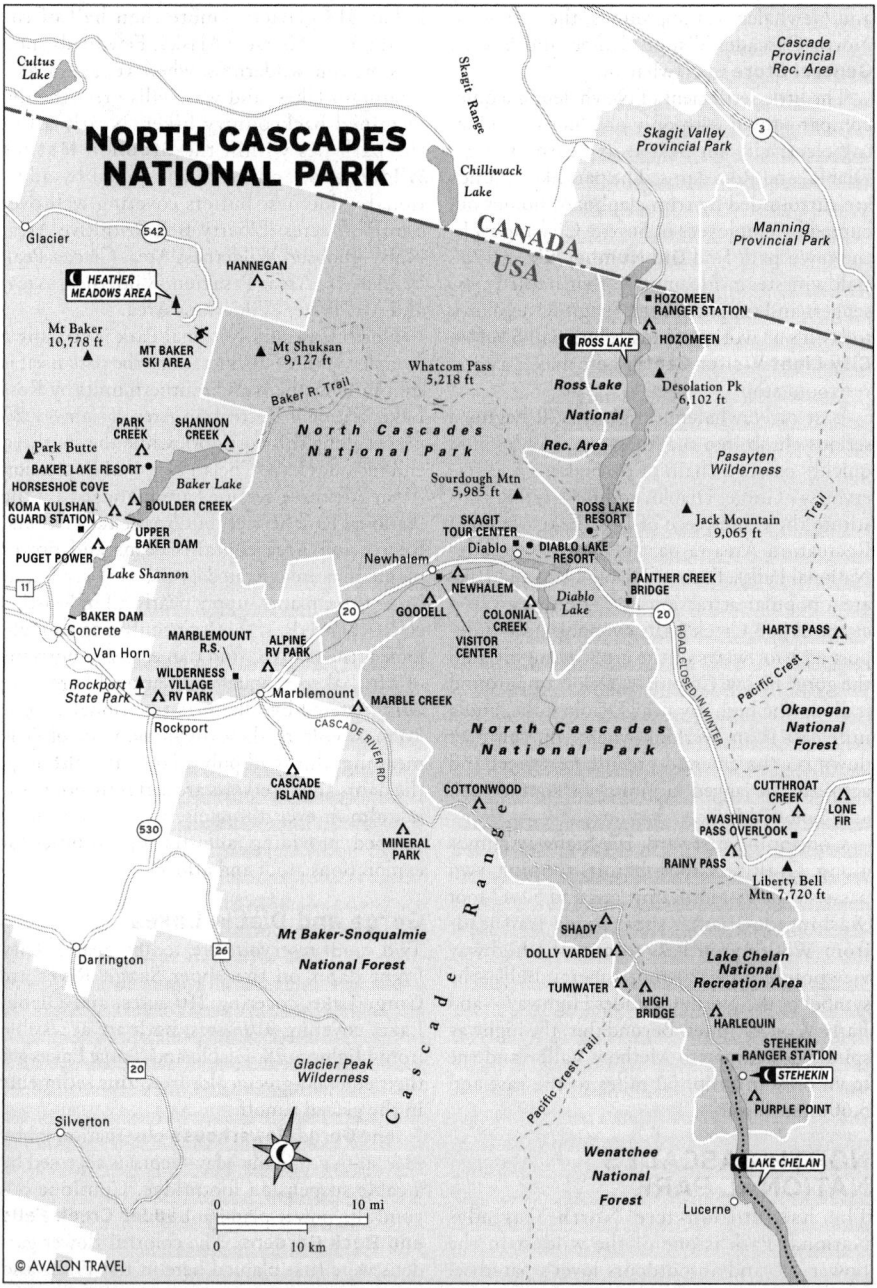
NORTH CASCADES NATIONAL PARK
Cultus Lake
Skagit Range
Cascade Provincial Rec. Area
Skagit Valley Provincial Park
Chilliwack Lake
CANADA
USA
Manning Provincial Park
Glacier
542
HEATHER MEADOWS AREA
HANNEGAN
HOZOMEEN RANGER STATION
HOZOMEEN
ROSS LAKE
Mt Baker 10,778 ft
MT BAKER SKI AREA
Mt Shuksan 9,127 ft
Whatcom Pass 5,218 ft
Baker R. Trail
Ross Lake National Rec. Area
Desolation Pk 6,102 ft
PARK CREEK
SHANNON CREEK
North Cascades National Park
Park Butte
BAKER LAKE RESORT
HORSESHOE COVE
Baker Lake
Pasayten Wilderness
Sourdough Mtn 5,985 ft
KOMA KULSHAN GUARD STATION
BOULDER CREEK
ROSS LAKE RESORT
Jack Mountain 9,065 ft
Trail
UPPER BAKER DAM
SKAGIT TOUR CENTER
Diablo
DIABLO LAKE RESORT
PUGET POWER
Newhalem
Lake Shannon
11
NEWHALEM
PANTHER CREEK BRIDGE
BAKER DAM
Concrete
GOODELL
COLONIAL CREEK
Diablo Lake
20
VISITOR CENTER
HARTS PASS
MARBLEMOUNT R.S.
ALPINE RV PARK
Van Horn
ROAD CLOSED IN WINTER
Pacific Crest
WILDERNESS VILLAGE RV PARK
Rockport State Park
Marblemount
MARBLE CREEK
Rockport
CASCADE RIVER RD
North Cascades National Park
Okanogan National Forest
CASCADE ISLAND
COTTONWOOD
CUTTHROAT CREEK
LONE FIR
530
WASHINGTON PASS OVERLOOK
MINERAL PARK
RAINY PASS
Liberty Bell Mtn 7,720 ft
Cascade Range
SHADY
Mt Baker-Snoqualmie National Forest
Darrington
26
DOLLY VARDEN
Lake Chelan National Recreation Area
TUMWATER
HIGH BRIDGE
HARLEQUIN
STEHEKIN RANGER STATION
20
Glacier Peak Wilderness
STEHEKIN
Pacific Crest Trail
PURPLE POINT
Silverton
Wenatchee National Forest
LAKE CHELAN
Lucerne
0 10 mi
0 10 km
© AVALON TRAVEL

© WASHINGTON STATE TOURISM/LEVY SHECKLER

The half-million acre North Cascades National Park is one of the most pristine national parks.

create a delightful setting for the adjacent falls. At night both are lit up.

A mile off Highway 20 is the tiny company town of **Diablo,** the home of Diablo Powerplant and the Skagit Tour Center. A half dozen free campsites (no potable water) are available at nearby **Gorge Lake Campground,** and a popular (but very steep) five-mile trail leads from here to the 5,985-foot summit of **Sourdough Mountain.** Hikers are treated to lush alpine meadows and panoramic views.

Seattle City Light Tours

Seattle City Light (206/684-3030, www.ci.seattle.wa.us/light/tours, $55 adults, $50 seniors, $45 teens, $40 kids 6–12, free for kids under 6) has been offering regularly scheduled tours of its Skagit facilities since 1928. A four-hour guided tour begins with a slide presentation at the Skagit Tour Center in Diablo, followed by a 558-foot ride up Sourdough Mountain on an antique incline railway that was used to haul supplies during the construction of the Diablo Dam. Then, enjoy a cruise across deep-green Diablo Lake and back to an all-you-can-eat dinner. Tours leave Thursday–Monday from mid-June through August, and on weekends only in September. Reservations are strongly recommended.

A 2.5-hour Diablo Lake Adventure cruise ($25 adults, $20 seniors, $12 kids 6–12, free under age 5) is also offered Saturday–Sunday from mid-June to early September, also on Fridays July–August. A fuel surcharge of $5 adults and $3 seniors (not charged for kids) is now added to each tour.

Ross Lake

The second-largest lake in the North Cascades after Lake Chelan, Ross Lake is 24 miles long and up to two miles wide, covering 12,000 acres from the Skagit River up to and beyond the Canadian border. It was created by a 540-foot-high hydroelectric dam completed in 1949 by Seattle City Light. Fortunately, efforts to enlarge the dam were thwarted in the 1980s by environmentalists and the government of British Columbia. You can see the reservoir from the Ross Lake overlook at milepost 135 on Highway 20 or area hiking trails, but the only vehicle access and motorboat launch is at the lake's north end, via a 39-mile gravel road from Canada. This means that Ross Lake is more of a canoeing and kayaking lake than other reservoirs in the Cascades. The glacier-fed waters of Ross Lake are too cold for swimming.

Although you can't drive to **Ross Lake Resort** (206/386-4437, www.rosslakeresort.com, $122–261 d, $10 extra person) you can catch the **Seattle City Light boat** ($20 round-trip) that leaves the parking lot across Diablo Dam daily at 8:30 A.M. and 3 P.M. The tug takes you to the end of Diablo Lake, where a truck ($7 round-trip) carries you on to Ross Lake. This is one of the most unusual lodging places in Washington; everything here is literally on the water, with cabins and bunkhouses built on log floats. Visitors can stay in modern cabins, rustic 1950s-era cabins, a 10-person bunkhouse, or nine-person cabins. Enjoy fantastic views up the lake to 8,300-foot Mt. Hozomeen at the Canadian border. You can rent motorboats, kayaks, or canoes here, but there are no telephones, groceries, or food service. The lodge is open mid-June through October.

Ross Lake has water-side campsites and half a dozen trailheads that provide access into adjacent North Cascades National Park. Ross Lake Resort runs a **water taxi** (206/386-4437) service to these, along with boat tours and portages from Diablo Lake for small boats and canoes. The water taxi fares are by the boatload (it can hold six), not per person, so it's best if you can coordinate your travel with other folks to save money. These water-taxi trips are a fun way to reach the backcountry, but be sure to pick up backcountry permits from the Wilderness Information Center in Marblemount before heading out to camp along Ross Lake or hike in the backcountry.

Hiking

DAY HIKES

More than 300 miles of maintained trails provide ample opportunities to explore North Cascades National Park. Short hikes—some are wheelchair-accessible—abound around Colonial Creek Campground and Newhalem; pick up flyers describing these and others at the visitors centers. Trails below 3,000 feet are generally open by mid-April or May; higher up, you may meet snow in July, so be prepared.

Some of the park's most spectacular scenery can be seen at **Cascade Pass.** Drive to the trailhead at the end of Cascade River Road, a 23-mile mostly gravel road from Marblemount. The first two miles of the seven-mile round-trip hike climb steadily through forest and meadows to the 5,400-foot pass at 3.7 miles. Allow about five hours for this hike.

BACKCOUNTRY TREKS

A free **backcountry permit** is required for all overnight trips into the park, a policy meant to reduce overcrowding and preserve the fragile alpine environment. Pick one up from the Wilderness Information Center in Marblemount or from information or ranger stations in Newhalem, Hozomeen, Sedro-Woolley, Winthrop, Twisp, Chelan, or Stehekin. Some areas fill up on summer weekends, so you may need to go with another option. The North Cascades are among the most rugged mountains in the Lower 48, so plan accordingly: lots of wool clothing, extra food, a waterproof tarp, and a flexible schedule for waiting out storms or resting feet and muscles sore from all the ups and downs.

From June to November, enjoy the 31-mile trip from the East Bank Trailhead (milepost 138) to Hozomeen along Ross Lake's **East Bank Trail.** The trailhead is on Highway 20, eight miles east of the Colonial Creek Campground at the Panther Creek bridge. The trail leads through low forest and along the lakeshore for 18 miles, at which point you have the option of continuing to Hozomeen or taking a side trip up 6,102-foot **Desolation Peak.** The round-trip up the peak is nine miles, almost straight up, with an elevation gain of 4,400 feet; you'll be rewarded with views of Mt. Baker, Mt. Shuksan, Jack Mountain, and The Pickets. To get right to the peak, skip the first 18 miles of hiking by taking the water taxi to the Desolation Peak trailhead; stay overnight

DESOLATION ANGELS

High atop the summit on Desolation Peak sits an aerie with an amazing view of the surrounding North Cascades and of Ross Lake far below. This fire lookout tower was memorialized by the lyrical ramblings of beat author Jack Kerouac, who spent a solitary summer working as a fire spotter. The alone time gave him plenty to ponder and write:

> *Those afternoons, those lazy afternoons, when I used to sit, or lie down, on Desolation Peak, sometimes on the alpine grass, hundreds of miles of snowcovered rock all around, looming Mount Hozomeen on my north, vast snowy Jack to the south, the encharmed picture of the lake below to the west and the snowy hump of Mt. Baker beyond, and to the east the rilled and ridged monstrosities humping to the Cascade Ridge, and after that first time suddenly realizing "It's me that's changed and done all this and come and gone and complained and hurt and joyed and yelled, not the Void"...*

When he finally came down from the clouds he published his thoughts (including the one above) nearly unedited in the tome *Desolation Angels*.

at Lightning Creek Campground, since you probably won't return in time to catch the boat. Beat Generation fans will want to make this pilgrimage to spend time as one of their own did: Jack Kerouac spent the summer of 1955 as a fire lookout here.

The **Pacific Crest Trail** enters the park from the south from Glacier Peak Wilderness Area, crossing Highway 20 at Rainy Pass and heading north through the Liberty Bell Roadless Area and the Pasayten Wilderness Area to the Canadian border.

If you can set up a vehicle shuttle or are willing to hitchhike, an excellent long hike begins at the Colonial Creek Campground, climbs over 6,100-foot **Park Pass** via Thunder Creek and Park Creek trails, and ends at Flat Creek Campground, a total hike of 27 miles. From here, you can catch the shuttle bus to Stehekin and then ride the *Lady of the Lake II* down Lake Chelan to the town of Chelan. An alternate ending would be to hike (or catch the shuttle bus) four miles up Stehekin Valley Road and follow **Cascade Pass Trail** over this 5,400-foot pass to the end of Cascade River Road (23 miles south of Marblemount).

If you don't mind a long uphill slog, **Easy Pass** makes a fine overnight hike. The trailhead is six miles west of Rainy Pass on Highway 20 (46 miles east of Marblemount), and the misnamed Easy Pass Trail climbs steadily for 3.7 miles to this 6,500-foot summit, where you enter North Cascades National Park. The magnificent vista includes knife-edged mountains and active glaciers. From here, you can continue deeper into the wilderness on **Fisher Creek Trail.** Easy Pass Trail is usually open from late July to late September.

Additional hiking trails leading into the park can be accessed from the Mount Baker, Baker Lake, Liberty Bell, Harts Pass, and Stehekin areas.

Pack Trips

Early Winters Outfitters (509/996-2659 or 800/737-8750, www.earlywintersoutfitting) has horse pack trips of all types throughout the northern Cascades. If you're traveling with young children, your best bet may be **Back Country Burro Treks** (509/996-3369). The outfitters will supply you with a burro for the child and will pack all of your camping equipment and meet you at a designated campsite; trips are a minimum of three days.

For a more environmentally friendly animal tour, try **Deli Llama** (360/757-4212, www.delillama.com), a delightful pack company run by a well-traveled husband and wife team who will entertain you with colorful stories over a plate of their gourmet trail food as the llamas bleat and graze nearby. The llamas carry your gear, opening up a range of backcountry possibilities for those who can't (or won't) shoulder their own backpacks.

Camping

Park Service campgrounds accessible by car on the North Cascades Highway include **Goodell Creek** (518/885-3639 or 877/444-6777, year-round, $10), **Newhalem Creek** (518/885-3639 or 877/444-6777, www.recreation.gov, mid-May to mid-October, $12, $9 extra reservation fee), and the best choice, **Colonial Creek** (518/885-3639 or 877/444-6777, mid-May to mid-October, $12). All are on a first-come, first-served basis, with no reservations. Brave the 39-mile gravel road from Canada and camp at the free **Hozomeen Campground** at the north end of Ross Lake, open mid-May through October. A handful of free campsites (no potable water) are available at **Gorge Lake Campground** (just north of Diablo on Hwy. 20). Enjoy summer naturalist activities at the Colonial Creek and Newhalem Creek campgrounds.

Along Cascade River Road, southeast of Marblemount, stay at **Marble Creek Campground** (518/885-3639 or 877/444-6777, www.recreation.gov, year-round, $8, $9 extra reservation fee). The free **Mineral Park Campground** is also open year-round. On the east side of Washington Pass, you can camp at the very popular **Lone Fir, Klipchuck,** and **Early Winters** campgrounds managed by the Forest Service.

Information

The elaborate **North Cascades Visitor Center** (milepost 120 on Hwy. 20, 206/386-4495, daily 9 A.M.–5 P.M. from April through mid-November, extended to 6 P.M. in July and August, Dec.–Mar. weekends only 9 A.M.–4:30 P.M.) is 14 miles east of Marblemount and a half mile south of Highway 20 in Newhalem. Inside are natural history exhibits, a large relief model of the region, a theater with slide shows, movies, and other presentations, and a gift shop. Ask at the center about borrowing one of the free audiotapes that describe the region's rich natural and human history. Daily naturalist walks are offered during the summer, with weekend talks in the winter months.

Immediately behind the center is a guaranteed-to-please 330-foot saunter to a view of the precipitous **Picket Range,** a barrier-free trail ideal to take in the view and to enjoy the sounds of bird calls.

GRIZZLY BEARS

The Northern Cascades of Washington is home to somewhere between 15 and 30 wild grizzly bears, making them rare but still extremely dangerous. This threatened species can weigh up to 1,800 pounds, run upwards of 30 miles per hour, and stand up to 12 feet on its hind legs. The grizzly is considered one of the most aggressive species of bear, despite its diet of mostly vegetation and carrion. These giants are uncommon, but should be treated with the greatest respect. Always look for bear warning signs at trailheads and campsites and observe all bear safety recommendations.

LIBERTY BELL ROADLESS AREA

The 141,000-acre Liberty Bell Roadless Area adjoins Highway 20 at Washington Pass and includes a long stretch of the Pacific Crest Trail, as well as some of the finest rock climbing in the Cascades. An outstanding day hike takes you past two forest-rimmed lakes and over **Maple Pass.** The trail begins right along Highway 20, from the south parking lot at Rainy Pass (30 miles west of Winthrop). An almost-level paved trail (wheelchair-accessible) leads a mile to **Rainy Lake,** with interpretive signs along the way. The cirque lake is backed by high cliffs with plummeting waterfalls. From here, you can continue up a steeper trail to Maple Pass, and then loop back past **Lake Ann** (good fishing for cutthroat trout) before returning to the parking area, a total distance of approximately six miles. No camping is allowed anywhere along this popular route.

Also popular is an easy trail to **Blue Lake** that leads two miles through subalpine meadows to the emerald waters of this mountain lake. Surrounding it is a trio of spectacular summits: Liberty Bell Mountain, Whistler Mountain, and Cutthroat Peak. The Blue Lake trailhead is a half mile west of Washington Pass.

PASAYTEN WILDERNESS

One of the largest wilderness areas in Washington, the Pasayten (pa-SAY-tin) Wilderness covers 530,000 acres of mountain country. Its northern edge is the U.S./Canadian border, while to the south it extends almost to Methow Valley. The country contains deep canyons, mountains topping 7,500 feet, and an abundance of wildlife that includes a few gray wolves and grizzly bears.

Hiking

The Pasayten Wilderness contains more than 600 miles of trails; pick up *100 Hikes in Washington's North Cascades: National Park Region* by Ira Spring and Harvey Manning (Seattle: The Mountaineers) for more information on hiking. An enjoyable short hike is the 12-mile long **Billy Goat Loop Trail.** To get here, drive nine miles north from Winthrop on West Chewuch Road, and turn left onto Eightmile Creek Road. Continue another 17 miles to the trailhead at the end of the road. The trail climbs through evergreen forests and then over Billy Goat Pass before dropping into the narrow Drake Creek Valley. From here, it circles back around the other side of Billy Goat Mountain and over Eightmile Pass before returning you to the starting point.

The trailhead for a longer loop hike (approximately 30 miles) is 20 miles west of Mazama at the second switchback above Harts Pass on the way to Slate Peak. Follow the **Buckskin Ridge Trail** (No. 498) from here through high meadows and past Silver Lake to Silver Pass and Buckskin Ridge (7,300 feet) before descending to the Pasayten River. Here you catch trail No. 478 and follow it upriver through old-growth forests to trail No. 498, which takes you back to your starting point. Check out the Green Trails maps or talk with folks at the Winthrop Forest Service office before heading up this interesting but challenging route.

Pack Trips

Several companies lead horse pack trips into the Pasayten, including **Early Winters Outfitters** (509/996-2659 or 800/737-8750, www.earlywintersoutfitting), **North Cascade Outfitters** (509/997-1015, www.cowboypoet.com), **Back Country Burro Treks** (509/996-3369), **North Cascade Safari** (509/996-2350), and **Sawtooth Outfitters** (509/923-2548). For a unique experience, **Pasayten Llama Packing** (509/996-2326, www.mtllama.com) leads llama trips into the wilderness.

Methow Valley

Scenic Methow Valley is a land of contrasts. To the west are the massive, glacially carved summits of the Cascades, with dense Douglas fir forests carpeting their lower flanks, but as you enter the valley, the forests are replaced by irrigated pastures surrounded by rounded hills covered with sage, grass, and scattered pines. Highway 20 follows the Methow River, with tall riverside cottonwoods providing a shady screen from the hot summer sun.

In recent years the Methow (MET-how) has become a haven for mountain bikers, river rafters, and cross-country skiers. There are excellent lodges and restaurants, and a comfortably relaxed country atmosphere.

The bustling town of Winthrop is the center of activity in Methow Valley, with its made-over Western theme. Thirteen miles northwest of here is minuscule Mazama (the name means mountain goat in Greek), while 11 miles south is the ranching town called Twisp. The valley is accessible from all sides during the summer, but Highway 20 closes from late November through April, depending on snowfall.

HARTS PASS AREA

After the discovery of gold and silver near Harts Pass in 1893, prospectors hurriedly built a road from Methow Valley to the mines. The precious metals petered out, but in the 1940s, fear of a Japanese invasion led the military to flatten the top of the Slate Peak and erect an early warning station, supplied in winter via dogsled. The site was later used for a Cold War radar station.

Today, a gravel road leads 19 miles from Mazama past the 2,000-foot slopes of glacially carved **Goat Wall,** and on to Harts Pass (6,197 feet), where it crosses the Pacific Crest Trail (PCT). The road splits at the pass. Turn left (south) for nine downhill miles to the ghost towns of Barron and Chancellor, once home to 2,000 miners. Turn right (north) for three steep miles to **Slate Peak Lookout.** When you park here, you're at the highest point you can drive to in Washington: 7,440 feet. A short walk leads to the lookout tower; be ready for spectacular 360-degree views of the entire Cascade Range. Harts Pass Road is steep and narrow; RVs and trailers are prohibited. It's a great, but tiring, mountain bike ride. The road is not plowed beyond Lost River in the winter. Near Harts Pass, you can camp at two free Forest Service campgrounds with gorgeous alpine settings: **Meadows** and **Harts Pass.** They are usually open mid-July to late September; there is no potable water.

This high alpine country offers some of the most popular day hiking in this part of the state. **Windy Pass Trail** begins 1.5 miles up Slate Peak Road from Harts Pass and follows the PCT for 3.5 miles to Windy Pass. The hike begins at 6,800 feet with little additional elevation gain but offers striking views of peaks and meadows all along the route. A second fun hike with little change in elevation begins at Harts Pass and proceeds along the PCT south to **Grasshopper Pass.** The round-trip distance is 11 miles, and the route follows the crest of the mountains to beautiful meadows at Grasshopper Pass. Because of the high elevation, these trails are often covered with snow until late July.

WINTHROP

Located near the junction of the Methow and Chewuch (CHEE-wuk) Rivers, Winthrop began as a mining settlement, settled into middle age as a ranching town, and has reemerged as a tourist mecca. Home to fewer than 400 year-round residents, Winthrop greets over 600,000 visitors annually. Winthrop's Main Street buildings have been remodeled with an Old West theme to reflect the town's 1890s mining boom—and to encourage hungry, tired Highway 20 drivers to stop for a meal, gas, and souvenirs. Winthrop also hosts annual festivals and rodeos that reflect the Western mood.

History

The Methow Valley was originally part of the Moses Reservation, but when members of the Moses-Columbia tribe refused to be placed on land away from their home along the Columbia River, the government opened the valley to homesteaders. The first white settlers reached the site of present-day Winthrop in the 1880s, lured by gold fever. The town itself goes back to 1891, when an easterner named Guy Waring opened Methow Trading Company. A devastating fire two years later nearly destroyed the new town and forced Waring to return East to recoup his losses and get East Coast financing. After returning, Waring incorporated the town in 1897 and named it in honor of John Winthrop, the colonial governor of Massachusetts (another version says it was for Theodore Winthrop, an early Washington settler killed in the Civil War). Waring stayed in business for almost half a century, and at one time owned every building on the main street except the town hall. One of Waring's Harvard classmates, Owen Wister, came to visit and used some of his friend's experiences in his famous novel, *The Virginian*—considered the first Western novel. (This is the Washington

© ERICKA CHICKOWSKI

The wild west of Winthrop is a favorite summer vacation spot.

version; folks in Medicine Bow, Wyoming, say the book was inspired by their townsfolk, and they seem to have a stronger point. A hero has many fathers.)

After the collapse of mining in the area, Winthrop headed toward oblivion; even the founder went bankrupt and moved back East. But then, as the North Cascades Highway was completed in the late 1960s, the citizens of Winthrop began looking for a way to pull themselves out of the doldrums. The successful transformation of nearby Leavenworth into a Bavarian-theme town inspired locals to do their own makeover into a Hollywoodesque Old West town. A local benefactor, Kathryn Wagner, widow of a sawmill owner, put up matching funds, and Leavenworth architects brought in their design expertise. By the time the first carloads of tourists crossed Washington Pass in 1972, Winthrop had covered its concrete buildings with false fronts, laid down wooden sidewalks, and added Old West signs and hitching posts. Today the shops are crowded with trendy gear, trinkets, upscale foods, books, and, of course, espresso. Warning: gas prices here are some of the highest in the state of Washington. Tank up elsewhere!

Sights

Winthrop's **Shafer Museum** (Castle Ave., 509/996-2712, Thurs.–Mon. 10 A.M.–5 P.M. late May to September, closed the rest of the year, donations appreciated) is housed in an 1897 log home (a.k.a. "The Castle") built by the town's founder, Guy Waring. Displays include pioneer farming and mining tools, bicycles, furniture, an impressive rifle collection, and other relics from the early days in the Methow Valley. Outside, you'll find a town's worth of buildings, including a general store, print shop, homestead cabin, schoolhouse, and assay office, plus old wagons, mining equipment, and aging farm implements. The 1923 Rickenbacker automobile here is one of just 80 still in existence.

Walk down Riverside (Main Street) to find all sorts of Western shops, some with authentic arts and crafts, most with junk. **White Buck Trading Co.** (509/996-3500) is named for a big white buck displayed inside. It was shot in 1953. The informal **White Buck Museum** in the rear of the store contains more stuffed critters and a collection of trivial items from the past, including—of all things—the first dial phone in Chicago. **Last Trading Post** (509/996-9833) is packed with Old West Americana, from antiques to painted cattle skulls. Downstairs is a museum of sorts, with historic flotsam and jetsam, plus various Native American artifacts.

The Forest Service's **North Cascade Smokejumper Base** (halfway between Winthrop and Twisp along Hwy. 20, 509/997-2031, www.fs.fed.us/r6/oka June–Sept. daily 9 A.M.–5 P.M.) is open for tours during the fire season. It was here in the fall of 1939 that the first experimental parachute jumps were held to determine the safety and effectiveness of reaching remote mountain forest fires from the air. The first fires were successfully attacked by smoke jumpers from this base the following summer. Today, the "birthplace of smoke jumping" has historical photos, but it is also a very active center during the peak of fire season and home to an elite group of firefighters.

The **Winthrop National Fish Hatchery** (a mile south of town, 509/996-2424, daily 8 A.M.–4 P.M.) raises 1.5 million spring chinook salmon and 750,000 trout annually in large, covered raceways.

Entertainment and Events

Three-Fingered Jack's Saloon usually has rock or R&B bands on summer weekends.

The second weekend of May marks the start of Winthrop's festival season with **49ers Days,** featuring a parade, horse-packing demonstrations, a chili cook-off, dance, and baseball tournament. This is followed by Memorial Day weekend's popular **Winthrop Rodeo Days.**

The three-day-long **Winthrop Rhythm and Blues Festival** in mid-July has quickly become a major blues event, attracting more than 5,000 fans to hear such acts as Charlie Musselwhite, B. B. King, or John Hammond. (And if you like the blues, be sure to tune in to the eclectic Methow Community Radio station, KVLR, at 106.3 FM.) The **Methow Music Festival** (888/463-8469) brings nationally known classical performers to Mazama each August.

Summer ends the way it begins, with the big **Labor Day Rodeo.** The **Antique Auto Rally** in mid-September features more than 60 old vehicles and is followed in early October by the **Methow Valley Mountain Bike Festival,** which brings over 500 participants for races, hill climbs, and group rides. Winthrop's **Octoberfest** includes a festival with vendors, dancing, and the obligatory beer garden.

The **Methow Valley Sport Trails Association** (800/682-5787, www.mvsta.com) offers a series of ski races, triathlons, and foot races throughout the year.

Sports and Recreation

MOUNTAIN BIKING

Mountain bikes can be rented from **Winthrop Mountain Sports** (509/996-2886 or 800/719-3826, www.winthropmountainsports.com).

Winthrop is a summer mecca for cyclists, with an incredible range of trails and country roads spreading through the valley and into the surrounding mountains. There are routes for every level of ability. Pick up descriptions of local routes at the Forest Service visitors center, or call the **Methow Valley Sport Trails Association** (509/996-3287 or 800/682-5787, www.mvsta.com) for information and maps to more than a hundred miles of mountain biking and hiking trails; they become cross-country ski paths in winter. A good place for bikers to access the trail system is from the Sun Mountain Lodge parking lot. Approximately seven miles of trails are wheelchair-accessible.

One good, though very challenging, ride in the national forest near Winthrop is the **Cedar Creek Trail,** which turns off Highway 20 17 miles northwest of Winthrop. The first three miles of trail are brutally steep and rocky, but past that the next four miles farther up the narrow valley are wonderful and remote. Another popular trail, not as technical as Cedar Creek, is the **Twisp River Valley Trail,** which parallels the Twisp River. For more details on these and other rides around Winthrop, pick up a copy of

Methow Valley Mountain Bike Routes, published by the Northwest Interpretive Association and the Forest Service.

RIVER RAFTING

The Methow River is a favorite of white-water enthusiasts, with many access points and a wide range of conditions, from easy float trips to class III–IV white water. Rafters generally float the river from early May till early July, when the river is running hard from spring runoff but the air is warm and dry. The sections below Winthrop grow progressively more difficult as you follow the Methow to the Columbia, 17 miles down river. Black Canyon is the pinnacle, with roller-coaster waves and wild action as the river plunges through dozens of rapids.

One of the best ways to experience the long succession of Methow River rapids is to set aside time for an overnight trip. **Orion Expeditions** (800/553-7466, http://orionexp.com, $150) operates an overnighter, taking care of all rafting equipment and all meals from lunch on day one. Guests can also request tents, though they will need to bring their own sleeping bags.

For a really incredible experience on and above the water, try the day trip Air-River package from **Alpine Adventures** (800/723-8386, www.alpineadventures.com, $299). Alpine teamed up with Kenmore Air to give guests the opportunity to fly over the North Cascades from Seattle, landing on Diablo Lake before being whisked over to the put-in on the Skagit. Enjoy a full river-rafting run on the Methow River and a buffet lunch and then hop in the float plane for your flight back to Seattle. Not only does the flight offer some amazing views, it is also a good way to avoid the hours-long drive up to the Methow.

HIKING

A multitude of hiking trails surround the Methow Valley. For horseback rides and pack trips, contact **Early Winters Outfitters** (509/996-2659 or 800/737-8750, www.earlywintersoutfitting), **Rocking Horse Ranch** (509/996-2768), **Chewack River Riding Stables** (509/996-2497), or **North Cascade Outfitters** (509/997-1015, www.cowboypoet.com).

The 578-acre **Pearrygin Lake State Park** (five miles north of Winthrop, www.parks.wa.gov) offers a sandy beach for swimming, plus fishing, camping, a boat launch, store, and boat rentals. This small spring-fed, glacially carved lake is a delightful break from the dry summer hills of sage and pine that surround it.

CLIMBING

The mountains around Methow Valley are becoming increasingly popular with rock climbers. **Mazama Mountaineering** (42 Lost River Rd., Mazama, 509/996-3802) teaches one- to seven-day classes and guides rock climbing, backcountry skiing, snowboarding, and mountain biking trips.

Winthrop Mountain Sports (509/996-2886 or 800/719-3826, www.winthropmountainsport.com) rents bikes, skis, backpacks, snowshoes, and sleeping bags.

OTHER SUMMER RECREATION

Winthrop's **Bear Creek Golf Course** (19 Bear Creek Golf Course Rd., 509/996-2284) is a nine-hole course. **Morning Glory Balloon Tours** (509/997-1700, www.balloonwinthrop.com, $195 adult, $150 kids) flies hot-air balloon rides year-round in Methow Valley.

WINTER SPORTS

In winter, when Methow Valley often has two or three feet of powdery snow on the ground and sunshine in the sky, outdoor recreation changes from hiking, biking, and river-running to cross-country skiing. The nonprofit **Methow Valley Sport Trails Association** (MVSTA, 509/996-3287 or 800/682-5787, www.mvsta.com) maintains four sets of interconnected cross-country ski trails throughout the valley. They groom 175 kilometers of trails—second longest in America—setting tracks for both classical and skate skis. Fees are $15 for one day or $35 for three days. Call for trail conditions, maps, and ski passes. The MVSTA's ski trail systems connect to several local inns and lodges, making it possible to walk outside and ski right from your door. A public warming hut is located at WolfRidge Resort, and several of the lodges welcome skiers with hot drinks. A van service (509/996-8294) provides transport to trailheads throughout the valley.

To get deeper into the backcountry, backcountry skiers may also want to consider hut-to-hut skiing opportunities on the MVSTA-maintained Rendezvous Trail system. A series of five fully equipped cabins (each cabin sleeps eight) are located 7–12 kilometers apart in the mountains north of Winthrop. Call **Rendezvous Outfitters** (509/996-8100 or 800/257-2452, $35 per person) for details. In addition to lodging, Rendezvous will also provide ski guides or on-trail gear hauling for an extra fee.

Rent skis and get cross-country lessons from **Sun Mountain Resort** (509/996-2211 or 800/572-0493), **Mazama Country Inn** (509/996-2681 or 800/843-7951), **Jack's Hut at Freestone Inn** (509/996-2752), or **Winthrop Mountain Sports** (509/996-2886 or 800/719-3826).

The nearest place for alpine skiers and snowboarders is **Loup Loup Ski Bowl** (509/826-2720, www.skitheloup.com, $38 adults, $32 young adults and seniors, $24 youth, free for kids under 6), a small family place 12 miles east of Twisp on Highway 20. Loup Loup has a new quad chairlift, two Pomas, a rope tow, and a vertical drop of 1,240 feet. Shredders will have fun on the half-pipe. Ski lessons, ski and snowboard rentals, and groomed cross-country tracks are here, along with a snack bar.

For those with the bucks, **North Cascade Heli-Skiing** (509/996-3272 or 800/494-4354, www.methow.com/~heli-ski) will take downhillers into untracked powder or provide drop-offs for backcountry telemark skiers.

Public **ice skating** ponds are available at Sun Mountain Resort and North Cascade Base Camp. Mazama Country Inn (509/996-2681 or 800/843-7951) offers hour-long **sleigh rides.** Snowmobile rentals are available from several local shops.

CAMPING

Find rest and repose by the shoreline at **Pearrygin Lake State Park** (five miles north of Winthrop, 509/996-2370 or 888/226-7688, www.parks.wa.gov, $17 tent, $23 full hookup, $7 extra reservation fee), which offers lakeside campsites mid-April through October. This is the largest lake in the area, with lots of space to fish, swim, boat and even water ski.

The Forest Service maintains a dozen campgrounds ($10) within 25 miles of Winthrop, and most other areas are open to free dispersed camping (with the exception of the Highway 20 corridor). Closest are the campgrounds up West Chewuch Road: **Falls Creek, Nice, Flat,** and **Buck Lake.** Falls Creek has the added attraction of a beautiful falls just a quarter-mile hike away, while quiet Buck Lake has ducks and cattails. Other often-full Forest Service campgrounds are west of Winthrop along Highway 20: **Early Winters, Klipchuck** (a very quiet spot), and **Lone Fir.** Most of these campgrounds are open June–September. Get more information from the Winthrop Ranger District office (509/996-2266).

RV campers can also choose to stay at **Big Twin Lake Campground** (210 Twin Lakes Rd., 509/996-2650, $27 full hookups), a private property right on the 90-acre lake offering rowboat rentals ($25 per day), fishing, and free wireless Internet.

Accommodations

Visitors should reserve well ahead for summer weekends. Many of these lodging places are just southeast of Winthrop along the Methow River. If you plan to stay at one of the cross-country ski lodges over the hectic Christmas–New Year's holiday, you'll find some places full six months in advance. Contact **Methow Valley Central Reservations** (509/996-2148 or 800/422-3048, www.mvcentralres.com, 9 A.M.–5 P.M. Mon.–Fri.) for reservations at most hotels and vacation rental cabins, guesthouses, and apartments.

UNDER $100

You'll find several hotels in town to choose from, starting with **Duck Brand Hotel**

(509/996-2192 or 800/996-2192, www.methownet.com/duck, $69–79 s or d) in downtown Winthrop over the restaurant of the same name. The six clean but simple rooms come with private baths, and most also have balconies.

The pet-friendly **Winthrop Inn** (960 Hwy. 20, 509/996-2217 or 800/444-1972, www.winthropinn.com, $75–90 s or $85–95 d) has clean and comfortable rooms with microwaves and fridges, sharing a small outdoor pool and hot tub. Munch on fresh muffins and coffee each morning while checking your email through the free wireless Internet. Winter guests and mountain bikers will be pleased to note that there's a trailhead just two blocks away.

Snow lovers should also consider a stay at **Chewack River Guest Ranch** (588 E. Chewuch Rd., 509/996-2497, $85 d, $225 up to 6), six miles north of Winthrop. Owned by avid snowmobilers, this establishment rents out snowmobiles and can also arrange guided trips. Chewack is also a great summertime retreat, particularly for horse lovers—guests can board their steeds for free here, and the property sits right next to public land with miles of trails. Choose between several lodge rooms or rent the ranch house with a full kitchen and a wood-burning stove. Finish the day off soaking in the hot tub or cooking up a dinner on the outdoor stone barbecue.

Three-quarters of a mile south of Winthrop, **Winthrop Mountain View Chalets** (509/996-2191 or 888/996-2525, www.winthropchalets.com, $55 to $95 s or d) rents out cute little cabins built for two. They come equipped with kitchenettes and decks and share access to a large hot tub.

Several cozy lodges dot the valley around Winthrop, including **Brown's Farm Inn** (Wolf Creek Rd., 509/996-2571, www.methownet.com/brownsfarm, $80–95 d, or $10 per additional guest), nestled into tranquil corner of the Methow Valley eight miles west of Winthrop. Two of the cabins have kitchenettes and sleep four, while the third has a full kitchen and sleeps up to 10. Big supporters of the local trail system, the family owners will happily show you great hiking, biking, or cross-country skiing destinations within the vicinity.

$100-150

One of the best budget spots in town is **Mt. Gardner Inn** (611 Highway 20, 509/996-2000, www.mtgardnerinn.com, $89–149 d) a little mom-and-pop place run by a friendly young couple who keep the place in tip-top shape. The furniture is new and rooms are spic and span. There are several room options, including pet-friendly rooms and more luxurious rooms with private decks, flat-screen TVs, microwaves, and refrigerators. For a bit more privacy, try the apartment-style suite ($199) that includes a full kitchen, separate bedroom, and a living room with gas fireplace and sleeper couch.

Just south of downtown Winthrop is **Hotel Rio Vista** (285 Riverside, 509/996-3535 or 800/398-0911, www.hotelriovista.com, $100–155 s or d), an Old West–style lodge with rooms overlooking the Methow River. A path leads from the hotel down to a picnic area along the river.

$150-200

Located right along the Methow River, **WolfRidge Resort** (412-B Wolf Creek Rd., 509/996-2828 or 800/237-2388, www.wolfridgeresort.com, $89–199 d) offers families plenty of fun features, including an outdoor pool, a bubbling hot tub enclosed by a gorgeous river-rock gazebo, a recreation room with a pool table, and over 60 acres of aspen- and pine-forested land to explore. Rooms are in pine cabin-style lodge buildings, ranging from studios up to two-bedroom houses with full kitchens.

Popular with cross-country skiers because of its easy access to the trail system is **Aspen Loft** (four miles east of Mazama, 509/996-2110, $140 s, $150 d), run by the folks who own Hotel Rio Vista. The cabin, tucked into a grove of aspen trees, sleeps up to six and includes a fully equipped kitchen, TV with VCR, and fireplace.

Located a half mile west of Winthrop, **River Run Inn** (509/996-2173 or 800/757-2709, www.riverrun-inn.com) is a small resort that includes private rooms ($115–140 s or d), a six-bedroom house ($450), and cabins ($175–200 for up to four people). Guests will also appreciate the indoor pool, outdoor hot tub, and riverside location. The house and cabin have full kitchens, and kitchenettes are available in some of the rooms.

North Cascades Basecamp (255 Lost River Rd., Mazama, 509/996-2334, www.ncbasecamp.com, $175 d) serves up hearty meals to all its lodge guests. In winter, rates include full room and board, while summertime comes with a hefty breakfast. Guests share bathrooms and very comfortable group areas, including a fireplace living room, a playroom for kids, library, and a hot tub. Families will also enjoy the sledding hill just outside the lodge. Groups seeking a bit more privacy can choose to rent one of Basecamp's cabins for six with a full kitchen ($185–285 up to 6), though meals aren't included with this option.

$200-250

Another recommended place is **Mazama Country Inn** (509/996-2681 or 800/843-7951, www.mazamacountryinn.com, $90–140 d in summer, $190–240 d in winter), with comfortable guest rooms in a delightful rural setting. Similar to other inns in the Methow Valley, this rustic mountain lodge offers full board in the winter months. Work up a sweat on the property's squash court, tennis court, or in the exercise room and then relax those old bones in the sauna and hot tub. Kids are accepted in the summer, but when winter comes, this is an adults-only place.

Freestone Inn and Early Winters Cabins (17798 Hwy. 20 in Mazama, 509/996-3906 or 800/639-3809, www.freestoneinn.com, $185–235 inn, $235–335 cabins) is set right on the edge of Freestone Lake. Rooms in the modern, elaborate wooden lodge include a light meal served each morning. Or rent cabins with kitchens by the day or the week. The property organizes myriad outdoor activities for guests, such as horse riding, mountain biking, backcountry skiing, fly-fishing, and more. And if you just want to relax, enjoy the fantastic views out over the lake and surrounding mountains.

OVER $250

Spring Creek Ranch (491 Twin Lakes Rd., 509/996-2495, www.springcreekwinthrop.com, $290 for 9) is a great option for families. This grand, fully equipped country home was built in 1929 and is furnished with antiques. Also here is a separate modern cabin with fireplace that sleeps four ($190). Situated on the far side of the Methow River from the town of Winthrop, the hotel has 60 acres of property inhabited by white-tailed deer, bald eagles, and other wildlife.

Atop a 5,000-foot peak with panoramic views into the North Cascades and the Methow Valley is **Sun Mountain Lodge** (nine miles southwest of Winthrop, 509/996-2211 or 800/572-0493, www.sunmountainlodge.com, $205–405 s or d), one of the premier destination resorts in Washington. Sun Mountain has almost every activity you could want, from fly-fishing lessons and children's programs to the largest string of saddle horses in the region, as well as a swimming pool, exercise room, and three hot tubs. A two-night minimum is required on weekends.

Food

Because of the town's compact size, it's easy to find a place to eat in Winthrop; just walk the two-block downtown to see what looks good. For casual dining in a cluttered and funky atmosphere, downtown's **Duck Brand Hotel & Cantina** (248 Riverside Ave., 509/996-2192, daily 7 A.M.–9 P.M.) serves outstanding, artfully presented, and moderately priced Mexican and American food. There's an outside deck for sunny days. Breakfasts are a real treat: huge piles of potatoes come with the meals, and monstrous cinnamon rolls sit temptingly on the bakery counter.

Housed in the Emporium Building, **Boulder Creek Deli** (509/996-3990, Thurs.–Tues. 10 A.M.–4 P.M., closed Wed.) makes very good sandwiches and salads for lunch.

Get a breakfast omelette or lunchtime slice

of pizza to go from **Grubstake & Co.** (509/996-2375, Tues.–Sun. 8 A.M.–3:30 P.M., closed Mon.); there's espresso here, too.

One of the most popular places on a summer afternoon is **Sheri's Sweet Shoppe** (at the downtown corner, 509/996-3834, summer daily 7:30 A.M.–9 P.M., year-round 7:30 A.M.–5 P.M.) with homemade ice cream, chocolates, and caramels. Don't leave town without trying the Moosetracks ice cream—it contains house-made chocolate-peanut butter candies that taste heavenly after a long hike.

The small **Old School House Brewery Company** (155 Riverside, 509/996-3183, www.oldschoolhousebrewery.com, Sun.–Thurs. noon–9 P.M., Fri.–Sat. noon–11 P.M., call for extended summer hours) serves up some of the best burgers in the valley and features dishes with a distinctive beer sauce simmered on-site. Enjoy burgers and brew on the riverside deck and beer garden.

For pizza, snacks, sandwiches, and ribs, mosey over to **Three-Fingered Jack's Saloon** (176 Riverside Ave., 509/996-2411, Mon.–Sat. 7 A.M.–11 P.M., Sun. 9 A.M.–5 P.M.), also downtown. This is a favorite among big groups.

Epicureans will want to hightail it to the **Sun Mountain Dining Room** (in Sun Mountain Resort, 509/996-2211 or 800/572-0493) just as the sun goes down. This is the best restaurant in the valley, with spectacular views and a superb menu that leans toward Northwest cuisine. Try the award-winning smoked duckling in plum sauce. Definitely make reservations for dinner here.

Mazama Store (50 Lost River Rd., Mazama, 509/996-2855, daily 7 A.M.–6 P.M.) is another very good place for lunch and pretty much the only gig in that little hamlet, serving sandwiches, salads, pastas, and espresso.

Information and Transportation

Local information is available at several Winthrop locales. The downtown **Chamber of Commerce Information Station** (202 Hwy. 20, 509/996-2125 or 888/463-8469, www.winthropwashington.com, mid-Apr.–Sept. daily 10 A.M.–5 P.M., call for hours the rest of the year) is the best place to get info about local inns and restaurants.

The **Methow Valley Visitors Center** (49 Hwy. 20, 509/996-4000, mid-May to mid-October daily 9 A.M.–5 P.M.) is near the can't-miss-it red barn just west of town. Get booklets on mountain biking, scenic drives, and day hikes here.

The Methow Valley has no bus service of any kind, and there is no scheduled air service. The nearest commercial airport is in Wenatchee.

TWISP AND VICINITY

The name Twisp is believed to have originated from the Native American word Twasp-tsp, an onomatopoeic sound based upon the noise made by yellow jacket wasps. Established in 1898, Twisp grew up on a diet of precious metals from the now-defunct Alder Mine, but then suffered through a string of disasters. A devastating 1924 fire destroyed all but a few of the town's buildings, and a 1948 flood rampaged through, carrying more buildings downstream. This was followed in 1968 by a bitter freeze (temperatures dropped to -48°F!) that wiped out local apple orchards.

Today Twisp is experiencing a spillover effect from nearby Winthrop. It's still a minor ranching and logging center, but the town also has a couple of interesting antique shops, a beautiful B&B, a great brewpub, and several good restaurants.

Events

The annual **Freeze Yer Buns Run** takes place in late January and features a 10K run with a Hawaiian vacation to the winner. In late June the **Twisp Show 'N' Shine** brings classic and antique cars to town.

Recreation

Twisp's summer-only outdoor **swimming pool** (509/997-5441) is on the northeast edge of town.

HIKING

To visit a working fire tower with mountain vistas in all directions, take the Alder Creek Road southwest from Twisp to Lookout Mountain. At the end of the road a trail leads 1.3 miles to **Lookout Mountain Lookout.**

Twisp River Road, west of town, provides access to the north side of the 145,667-acre **Lake Chelan-Sawtooth Wilderness,** with a dozen different paths taking off from the valley. A fine loop trip of approximately 15 miles begins just southwest of War Creek Campground on Forest Road 4420. The **Eagle Creek Trail** starts at an elevation of 3,000 feet and climbs steadily through Douglas fir forests and meadows, reaching 7,280-foot Eagle Pass after seven miles. Here it meets the **Summit Trail,** with connections to the Stehekin end of Lake Chelan or to other points in the wilderness. To continue the loop hike, follow it south a mile to **Oval Creek Trail.** This path leads back down to the trailhead, passing beautiful West Oval Lake on the way; a two-mile detour climbs to two additional cirque lakes.

CAMPGROUNDS

A half dozen Forest Service campgrounds are west of town out Twisp River Road. Closest is **War Creek Campground** (late May–early Sept., $6), 15 miles out. RV parking is available at **River Bend RV Park** (two miles north of Twisp on Hwy. 20, 509/997-3500, www.riverbendrv.com, $29 full hookups).

Accommodations

Built in 1910, the lovingly restored old **Methow Valley Inn B&B** (234 2nd E. Ave., 509/997-2253, www.methowvalleyinn.com, $99 s or d) is one of the few structures to survive the fire of 1924. It's a friendly and homey place, with seven guest rooms (four with private baths) and a full breakfast. No kids are permitted.

Other local places offer more standard accommodations. **Sportsmen Motel** (less than a mile east of Twisp on Hwy. 20, 509/997-2911, $39 s or $44 d) is a friendly small place with kitchens in most rooms. **Blue Spruce Motel** (1321 E. Methow Valley Rd., 509/997-8852, $38 s or $45 d, $50 d with kitchenettes) is just across the street from Sportsmen. **Idle-A-While Motel** in town (509/997-3222, $50 s or $58 d) has brightly painted cottages and motel rooms, including a hot tub and sauna.

Food

The tastiest restaurant in Twisp is **Tappi** (201 Glover St., 509/997-3345), which offers smoky, flavorful dishes prepared in its wood-fired ovens, fresh salads, and a fantastic wine selection. Next door is the **Confluence Art Gallery,** which displays changing exhibits of local artists. **Hometown Pizza** (509/997-2100, 11:30 A.M.–8 P.M. Mon.–Tues. and Thurs.–Sat., closed Sun. and Wed.) competes with Tappi for the title of the best pizzas in Methow Valley.

Treat your nose and your taste buds to the smell and flavor of fresh breads and pastries at **Cinnamon Twisp Bakery** (509/997-5030, 6 A.M.–3 P.M. Mon.–Sat., closed Sun.), which specializes in baked goods, organic coffees, and other healthy foods.

The unofficial town hall in Twisp is inside **Twisp River Pub** (209 E. 2nd Ave., 509/997-6822, www.methowbrewing.com, 11:30 A.M.–8:30 P.M. Wed.–Thurs., 11:30 A.M.–9 P.M. Fri.–Sat., 10 A.M.–8:30 P.M. Sun.), a lively brewhouse that features fresh cookin' and local art and hosts live music on some weekends. If you don't sip on the mighty fine brew, at least indulge in one of the decadent homemade desserts. On Sunday, guests are treated to an extended brunch.

Get organic produce at **Glover Street Market,** or come to town for Twisp's **Farmers Market** (9 A.M.–noon Sat. mid-Apr.–mid-Oct.).

Information

The **Twisp Visitor Information Center** (201 Hwy. 20 S., 509/997-2926, www.twispinfo.com, 8 A.M.–5 P.M. Mon.–Fri.) displays interesting historical school photos on its walls.

The Okanogan National Forest's **Methow Valley Ranger District** office (502 Glover St., 509/997-2131, www.fs.fed.us/r6/oka, 7:45 A.M.–4:30 P.M. Mon.–Fri.) is a good source for trail and camping information.

METHOW AND PATEROS

Scenic Drives

East of Twisp the highway splits; Highway 20 continues east to Okanogan and Omak, and Highway 153 turns south along the Methow River. Highway 20 offers a chance to cruise past old farms and ranches with aging wooden barns, horses grazing in the pastures, and hay piles draped with sky-blue tarps. The road then climbs into Ponderosa pine forests with openings of sage, before topping out in the western larch forests of Okanogan National Forest. These larch trees are especially pretty in the fall when the needles turn a vivid yellow. Near the summit of Loup Loup Pass is Loup Loup Ski Bowl.

Highway 153 is another gorgeous drive, with the cottonwood-lined Methow River bottom surrounded by ranches and rolling hills covered with sage and Ponderosa and lodgepole pines. It leads to the small towns of Methow and Pateros. There is nothing of note at Methow, but you can camp at **Lightning Pine RV Park** (331 Burma Rd., Methow, 509/923-2572, www.lightningpine.com, $24 full hookups).

Pateros

Five miles south of Methow, at the junction of Highways 97 and 153, is Pateros (pop. 600). This town has more to it, including popular Alta Lake State Park and access to the Lake Pateros (the dammed-up Columbia River). Pateros was moved here during construction of Wells Dam, just a few miles downstream on the Columbia. The surrounding country is crowded with fruit orchards and apple processing plants. For a taste, stop at **Rest Awhile Fruit Stand** (just north of town, 509/923-2256, summer daily 7 A.M.–7 P.M., spring and fall 7 A.M.–6 P.M.). In addition to fruit, they also sell fresh baked breads and pies, plus espresso coffee. You can also pick your own fruit in their orchard (one of the few places around here that lets you do this).

Pateros itself consists of a few stores and a pretty waterfront park; it's a popular place to stop and fish or play in the reservoir. Be sure to look up into the hills above town to one of the state's more unusual art installations—15,000 colorful reflectors covering two old water towers.

South to Chelan

Highway 97 south from Pateros is a busy thoroughfare paralleling the reservoir all the way to Chelan, 17 miles away. **Wells Dam** (seven miles south of Pateros, daily 8 A.M.–6 P.M.) has a vista viewpoint where you can look across the blue lake to the surrounding rocky, arid landscape of grass and sage. The dam sits in a narrow canyon, and one of the old turbines is also at the vista point, along with a rock covered by pictographs. Wells Dam visitors center also features a fish-viewing area and salmon hatchery.

Events

The popular and tasty **Apple Pie Jamboree** hits Pateros the third weekend of July and includes a parade, street dance, arts and crafts fair, and fireworks. But people really come for the big pie feed, featuring 500 volunteer-baked apple pies with homemade ice cream. The **Pateros Hydro Classic** in mid-August is another big attraction, with inboard hydroplane boats topping 150 mph.

Recreation

Right in the town of Pateros is **Peninsula Park,** a verdant green stretch along Lake Pateros. Here are picnic areas, swimming, water-skiing, RV parking, and showers. Sprinklers keep tent campers away.

Popular with the summer crowd is **Alta Lake State Park** (two miles southwest of Pateros off Hwy. 153, 509/923-2473, www.parks.wa.gov). Fish for rainbow trout, swim in the clear waters, or just enjoy the east-of-the-mountains sunshine. A mile-long trail takes you up 900 feet to a scenic plateau overlooking the Columbia River Valley. The campground has tent sites ($13) and RV hookups ($19), and is open April–October, plus weekends and holidays the rest of the year. No reservations are taken. In winter, the park is a favorite of cross-country skiers and snowmobilers.

Accommodations

Lodging is available at modern **Lake Pateros Motor Inn** (509/923-2203 or 800/444-1985, www.lakepaterosinn.com, $82 s or $102 d). The motel has an outdoor pool and dock on Lake Pateros.

Two miles from Pateros, **Alta Lake Golf Resort** (140 Alta Lake Rd., 509/923-2359, $75–95 s or d) offers the nicest rooms around, many with kitchenettes. An outdoor pool is here, along with an 18-hole golf course.

Whistlin' Pine Resort/Sawtooth Outfitters (off Hwy. 153 on the south end of Alta Lake, 509/923-2548, $112 d) is a popular resort for horseback riding and fishing. Rustic cabins ($40 d) and tent cabins ($52 for 4) are also available, as well as RV camping ($30).

Chelan and Vicinity

Lake Chelan (sha-LAN) occupies a long, glacially carved valley on the eastern edge of the Cascades. The town of Chelan sits on the southeast shore of the lake; Manson is seven miles northwest, and tiny Stehekin 55 miles away on the north shore. Stehekin is the only town on the Washington mainland that cannot be reached by road.

Lake Chelan is one of Washington's favorite summer playgrounds, offering resort accommodations, fine restaurants, water-skiing, swimming, and boating, but also delivering magnificent wilderness country just a boat ride away. Over the years the Chelan area has developed into a resort community that has managed to retain its small-town charm. It's still a genuine town with real orchardists, farmers, wilderness outfitters, and forest and park rangers standing in line with you in the grocery checkout line. Your children can meet and play with the children of residents and visitors from all over the world. Few other small towns in Washington have such a wide cross-section of people.

The vast majority of the Lake Chelan watershed is in public ownership and not open to major development, but such is not the case on the privately held portions. Here, the lake's popularity may prove its undoing. Tacky developments of all sorts are packing the shoreline between Chelan and Manson, as time-share condos, elaborate resorts, ranch-style homes, retirement villas, and summer cottages crowd up the hillsides and through the apple orchards. The first orchard in the area—at Wapato Point—is now the site of the elaborate Wapato Point Resort.

Climate

These statistics will tell you why Chelan is so popular in Puget Sound: only 24 days per year, on average, register temperatures below 32°F, and 33 days are above 90°F. Rainfall occurs less than nine days in an average year, and snow, sleet, or hail in excess of an inch falls on 31 days per year. The lake never freezes. The most telling statistic: although no official records are kept on the number of sunny days, it is roughly 300 days per year.

Apple Land

Most visitors to Lake Chelan tend to think of it in terms of recreational opportunities, but in agricultural circles, the shores of the lake are much better known for the finest apples in the world. This isn't a slogan created by the local community; Chelan apples are known all over the world for their excellent taste, long shelf life, and vivid colors.

Gross income from the apple industry is in the $100 million-per-year range, and upwards of 10,000 acres are devoted to apple orchards. Most of these are relatively small, averaging 30 acres or less. Annual production is in the range of 8 million boxes. The most popular apples are Red Delicious and Golden Delicious, followed by the reddish-yellow Galas and the pinkish-red Fujis, an apple developed in Japan.

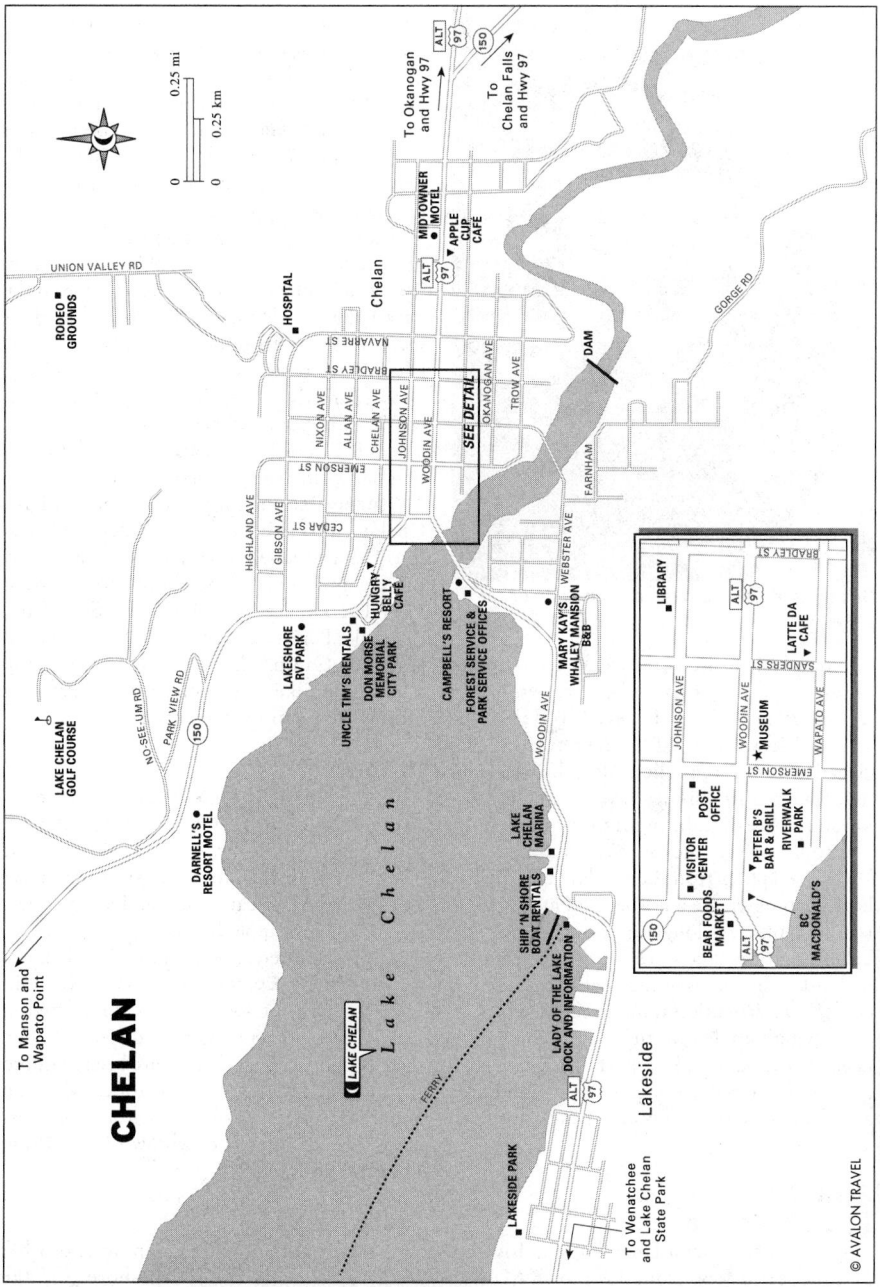

© AVALON TRAVEL

© ERICKA CHICKOWSKI

Get around Lake Chelan on the *Lady of the Lake.*

Nobody is quite sure why Chelan apples are so much better than those grown only a few miles away. Some believe it is due to the soil, which was created by the retreating glaciers that carved the valley. Also, the lake helps moderate the air temperature, keeping the valley above freezing during most of the winter, and cooling things down in the summer. This keeps the apples from being damaged by the heat, helping create a crisper and juicier apple that remains fresh longer in storage. Some also believe that the lake water used to irrigate the orchards contributes to the quality because it is colder than irrigation water used elsewhere.

Although apples are the major crop grown around the lake, some soft fruits are also grown. Scattered among the apple orchards are smaller plots of cherries, pears, apricots, and peaches.

SIGHTS

Lake Chelan

On the north shore of Lake Chelan, drive the 12-mile scenic loop from downtown Manson along the shore of Lake Chelan, up into apple orchards, and past smaller lakes in the foothills, with striking views all along the way. From Manson, drive west on Lakeshore Drive and Summit Boulevard, north on Loop Avenue and Manson Boulevard, east on Wapato Lake Road, then south on the Chelan-Manson Highway back to Manson.

Another scenic drive is on the south shore of the lake; follow Highway 97 to the **Chelan Butte Lookout** sign across the street from the Park Lake Motel. The road curves upward for seven miles, with pullouts for photos of the lake and surrounding hills, the Columbia River almost directly below, the wheat fields of eastern Washington, and acres of apple orchards. The 3,892-foot butte is also one of the state's best launching pads for hang gliders.

Stormy Mountain has views across Lake Chelan, into the North Cascades, and over into the arid wheat country. You reach it by driving up Lake Chelan's South Shore Road to its end at Twenty-Five Mile Creek State Park, then take Forest Service Road 2805 to its end at Windy Camp. The view here is wonderful; a half-mile hike to the summit of 7,198-foot Stormy Mountain is even better.

In Town

Visit the **Lake Chelan Museum** (Woodin Ave. and Emerson St., Chelan, 509/682-5644, June–Sept. daily 1–4 P.M., by appointment the rest of the year, free) to see displays of pioneer and Native American relics, and a big collection of colorful apple-box labels.

The most interesting building in Chelan is **St. Andrew's Episcopal Church** (Woodin Ave.), a charming log structure completed in 1899. The architect remains in dispute, though there is evidence that it may have been Stanford White, the designer of New York's Madison Square Garden. A carillon rings out the hours daily. Also of interest downtown is the **Ruby Theater,** built in 1913.

State Parks

Two state parks provide camping and other attractions along the south shore of Lake

LAKE CHELAN BY THE NUMBERS

The crystal clear Lake Chelan is Washington's deepest and longest lake. Carved by Ice Age glaciers that slid down surrounding mountain peaks, this fingerlike lake is 55 miles long but seldom more than two miles wide. Motor to the middle and you're likely to find your anchor chain a bit short – at its deepest point Chelan plunges down 1,486 feet. The only two deeper lakes in America are Oregon's Crater Lake (1,962 feet) and California and Nevada's Lake Tahoe (1,645 feet).

Chelan. **Lake Chelan State Park** is right on the lake, nine miles west of Chelan, with an underwater park, a boat launch, and concession stand. **Twenty-Five Mile Creek State Park** (20530 S Lakeshore Rd., www.parks.wa.gov) has a swimming pool for campers and a boat launch.

Apple Tours

Trout Blue Chelan (509/682-2591, www.chelanvalley.com) gives free tours of its huge apple warehouses and packing sheds on the road to Chelan Falls. Call ahead to schedule a tour (not offered during the hectic Sept.–Oct. harvest period). **Sunshine Fruit Market** (just west of town at the junction of Hwy. 97A and South Lakeshore, 509/682-5695) has a roadside fruit stand open every day during daylight hours in the summer.

ENTERTAINMENT AND EVENTS

The year begins with **Lake Chelan Winterfest,** featuring fireworks, a cross-country ski race, snow-sculpting contest, snowmobile events, Christmas tree bonfire, chili cook-off, and a splash in the lake for the really bold. Arts and crafts, a carnival, live music, and food fill the streets on the fourth weekend of June, for the annual **Taste of Chelan Street Fair.** See a popular PRCA rodeo and watch the crowning of the rodeo queen at **Lake Chelan Western Days,** the fourth weekend in July.

The nine-day **Lake Chelan Bach Feste** comes to town each July with concerts in the new Performing Arts Center, and in local churches and parks.

The **Apple Blossom Festival** is held the second weekend in May in Manson, with a parade, car shows, and a chicken-noodle dinner (!) at the American Legion Hall. It's been happening here for over 75 years. The third weekend of May brings a **Chinook Salmon Derby,** with $5,000 for the biggest fish. Manson's **4th of July** brings fireworks, an arts and crafts fair, a spare-rib barbecue, and a watermelon-seed-spitting contest.

SHOPPING

In addition to the restaurants and markets, Chelan and Manson have a number of interesting specialty shops. **The Harvest Tree** (109 E. Woodin Ave., 509/682-3618) offers gift baskets of apples, some with additional foods such as trail mix, Aplets, Cotlets, and honey.

Three local galleries are well worth a visit: **The Gallery at Allisons** (Manson, 509/687-3534, www.mansonvillage.com/allisons), **Sunburst Gallery** (215 E. Woodin Ave., Chelan, 509/682-8708), and **Wapato Studio and Fine Art** (108 E. Woodin Ave., Chelan, 509/682-2423). The last of these has works by the famed sculptor Rich Beyer and oils by Rod Weagant.

Out in the orchards near Manson sits **Bee's Antiques,** with a huge warehouse filled with beautifully restored (and pricey) antiques. It's one of the best-known antique stores in Washington but doesn't advertise and has an unlisted phone; ask in town for directions.

SPORTS AND RECREATION

Hiking

The entire Chelan Valley is user-friendly for walkers and runners because the heaviest vehicle traffic is limited to the main routes—Highway 97A, the Chelan-Manson Highway, and the south shore route. Several day hikes are available in the Twenty-Five Mile Creek area; for a complete description of hiking trails around the lake, stop by the Chelan District (428 W. Woodin Avenue).

If you're just out for a walk and want to enjoy the scenery, one of the nicest paths is at **Riverwalk Park.** It runs a mile along the Chelan River from the Woodin Avenue bridge to the next bridge downstream and just above the dam. The park has restrooms, a picnic area, and boat launch.

A steep but brief climb is up the cross-topped hill overlooking town, nearby apple orchards, and the lake. The path begins at the intersection of South Saunders Street and East Iowa Avenue.

Hang Gliding and Paragliding

Chelan has an international reputation as an excellent place to hang glide or paraglide. The best place for launching (or watching) is the summit of 3,892-foot Chelan Butte, where the hot winds blowing in from the Columbia River Basin give enormous lift. The flying is so good, in fact, that it isn't unusual for a hang glider to launch here and go nonstop to Spokane or into Idaho. Craft can also be launched to the west over the town and lake, with a choice of several landing sites along the lakeshore.

Find a flying partner or learn from the locals who belong to **Chelan Flyers** (www.chelanflyers.com). Newcomers to the sport can get lessons from **Sky Brothers** (612/280-9850).

Golf

The **Chelan Municipal Golf Course** (509/682-5421) has one of the most beautiful settings of any course in the region, overlooking the lake. A small executive course, **Ma-8 Golf Course** (509/687-6338) is southeast of Manson near Mill Bay Casino, and the acclaimed **Desert Canyon Resort** (509/682-2697 or 800/258-4173, www.desertcanyon.com) offers championship-style links halfway between Lake Chelan and Wenatchee.

Swimming

The lower end of Lake Chelan is lined with sandy beaches just right for swimming in the clean, cool waters. By late summer the water at the lower end of the lake is a bearable 70°F. Most public parks have popular swimming beaches, including Lake Chelan State Park, Chelan City Park, and the newer parks built by Chelan County, including Manson Bay Park, Old Mill Park, Chelan Riverwalk Park, Chelan Falls Park, and Beebe Bridge Park. Up-lake beyond Manson and Lake Chelan State Park, the beaches become fewer due to the steep terrain. Swimming is possible in the Stehekin area, but with the water seldom above 50°F, few people are found in the lake by choice. The lake never freezes.

© ERICKA CHICKOWSKI

There are plenty of hiking options near Lake Chelan.

Fishing

Lake Chelan is a very popular fishing spot, with kokanee salmon, chinook salmon, lake trout, rainbow trout, cutthroat trout, smallmouth bass, and burbot. Fish get big in these waters, with lake trout and chinook salmon averaging 6–10 pounds; a 24-pound lake trout was caught in the lake. Nearby, on the Columbia River and in mountain lakes, you will find smallmouth bass and rainbow, cutthroat, brown, and eastern brook trout, as well as other game fish. The chamber of commerce has a brochure with fishing tips for Lake Chelan. Two guide companies who operate in the area are **Mountain Dew Guide Service** (509/687-3084, www.mtdewguideservice.com) and **Darrell and Dad's Family Guide Service** (509/966-8678).

Boats and Personal Watercraft

Whatever kind of boating activity you like, you'll find it at Lake Chelan; sightseeing by boat, sailboarding, water-skiing, Jet Skiing, kayaking, canoeing, rowing, and paddleboating are all popular. You'll also see sailboards and sailboats of all sizes. You can bring your own craft or rent personal watercraft, sailboats, canoes, and water-ski boats from several local companies: **Lake Chelan Marina** (1228 W. Woodin, 509/682-2336), **Lakeland Marine Services** (3414 Wapato Lake Rd., 509/687-3504), **Reed Shoreline Corp.** (15 Hale St., Manson, 509/687-1302 or 888/558-7333), and **Ship 'n Shore Boat Rentals** (1230 W. Woodin, 509/682-5125). **Chelan Parasailing** (509/687-7245) brings this resort sport to Lake Chelan in the summer.

Play Parks

Slidewaters at Lake Chelan (102 Waterslide Dr., 509/682-5751, www.sliders.com, Memorial Day–Labor Day daily 10 A.M.–7 P.M., $17 over 4 ft. tall, $14 under 4 ft.), one of Chelan's most popular places for children, is a short walk from the downtown area. Ten water slides overlook the town and lake, plus kiddie slides, a 60-person hot tub, swimming, inner tube ride, picnic area, video arcade, gift shop, and concession stand.

Lakeshore Bumper Boats in **Don Morse Memorial City Park** (Park Rd. and Nixon, 509/793-2126, Memorial Day–Labor Day daily 10 A.M.–10 P.M.) are the floating equivalent of bumper cars—very popular with kids. Paddleboats, miniature golf, and go-carts can also be found in Don Morse Park.

Bicycling

The popularity of mountain biking has made the Lake Chelan area a particular favorite with bike riders. All sorts of scenic loop trips are possible, covering a wide diversity of terrain. Both highways that go up-lake from Chelan are popular, as are several roads with lighter traffic such as the Manson Loop, the Echo Ridge cross-country ski trails, and numerous Forest Service roads and trails open to mountain bikes. Check with the Chelan Ranger District for information and maps on roads and trails. The forest road winding out past Twenty-Five Mile Creek Campground, up a steep mountainside, is a good workout, offering fantastic views out of the upper reaches of Lake Chelan. Trails can be found branching off into the mountains from this road, which eventually comes out again at Entiat. Bikes of decent quality can be rented at **Chelan Rentals** (509/670-8467, daily 9 A.M.–5 P.M.), right at the entrance to Don Morse Park in town.

Winter Sports

The Lake Chelan Valley is a heavily skied area. In Echo Valley, 12 miles northwest of Chelan, **Echo Valley Ski Area** (509/687-3167, www.echovalley.org, mid-Dec–late-Feb. Sat.–Sun. 10 A.M.–4 P.M., $20) has day and night downhill skiing on 3,000-foot Echo Mountain, served by three rope tows and a Poma lift. Other facilities here include ice-skating and snowmobile trails. Get to Echo Valley aboard the free Link buses connecting Chelan with Manson; ski racks are on all the buses.

The **Echo Ridge** (trailhead parking on Cooper Gulch Rd., www.lakechelannordic.org, $5) area contains 27 kilometers of groomed cross-country ski trails for every level of ability. Vistas from the summit are extraordinary, encompassing Lake Chelan, the Cascades, and the Columbia River Valley. These are maintained by the Lake Chelan Nordic Ski Club and are used as mountain bike paths in the summer. Other Chelan-area Nordic ski trails include three miles of groomed runs at **Lake Chelan Golf Course** ($5), and another three miles of groomed trails plus plenty of backcountry touring at Stehekin. Get ski trail maps from the chamber of commerce.

Rent cross-country and downhill ski equipment from **Lake Chelan Sports** (137 E. Woodin Ave., 509/682-2629, www.lakechelansports.com, Mon.–Sat. 9 A.M.–6 P.M., Sun. 10 A.M.–4 P.M.).

Snowmobilers will enjoy the 125 miles of trails on both sides of Lake Chelan, accessible from three Sno-Parks. For information contact the Lake Chelan Ranger Station (509/682-2576).

Ice-skaters will find outdoor rinks at Don Morse Memorial Park in Chelan, Echo Valley Ski Area, and Roses, Wapato, and Dry Lakes in Manson.

Gambling

Located on land owned by the Colville Tribe and staffed in part by workers who commute all the way from the reservation, **Mill Bay Casino** (455 Wapato Lake Rd., 509/687-2102 or 800/648-2946, www.millbaycasino.com) is a mile southeast of Manson. Smoke-filled rooms contain folks playing blackjack, craps, keno, roulette, poker, or yanking the handles on the slot machines.

Camping

Right in town, the **City of Chelan Lakeshore RV Park** (509/682-5031, $22 full hookups) has both tent sites and RV spaces, along with showers, public swimming, and picnic areas. Rates are lower in the off-season.

Lake Chelan State Park (509/687-3710 or 888/226-7688, www.parks.wa.gov, $17 tents, $23 full hookups, $7 extra reservation fee) is 12 miles up-lake from Chelan along the south shore and offers swimming, tent sites, and RV sites. The park is open daily April–October, and on weekends and holidays the rest of the year. This is the largest and most popular park in the area, with a swimming beach, boat ramp, docks, and summertime campfire programs.

The pleasant, wooded **Twenty-Five Mile Creek State Park** (509/687-3610 or 888/226-7688, www.parks.wa.gov, open May–Sept., $17 tents, $23 full hookups, $7 extra reservation fee) park is 22 miles west of Chelan at the end of S. Lakeshore Drive, and 10 miles beyond Lake Chelan State Park. It's a favorite place for boaters who use the launch ramp here and purchase supplies at the marina store. It's also a good overnight spot for those about to catch the morning *Lady of the Lake* boat ride from Fields Point.

The Forest Service's primitive and free **Ramona Creek Campground** is just three miles uphill from Twenty-Five Mile Creek State Park, although it is often closed due to flood danger. Four miles uphill via dirt road beyond Ramona Campground is **Grouse Mountain Campground,** another primitive site on a mountain top, with no water but great views.

Tiny **Daroga State Park** (509/664-6381, www.parks.wa.gov, open late Mar.–late Oct., $14 primitive sites, $23 full hookups) is 22 miles southeast of Chelan on the east bank of the Columbia River and just off Highway 97. Be ready for towering high-voltage power lines right next to the campground. More camping is available at **Wapato Lake Campground** (509/687-6037, $17 tent, $17 with electricity) near Manson.

The shore of Lake Chelan is dotted with 14 boat-in campgrounds, accessible by private boat or from the *Lady of the Lake II.* Check with the Forest Service office (428 W. Woodin, 509/682-2576, 7:45 A.M.–4:30 P.M. Mon.–Fri. year-round, plus 7:45 A.M.–4:30 P.M. Sat.–Sun. late June–early Sept.) for specifics. Several other campgrounds are on the road system, including Antilon Lake Campground, north of Manson.

Beebe Bridge Park (509/663-8121, mid-Apr.–Oct., $20) sits along the Columbia River across from the town of Chelan Falls. It has tent and RV sites for along with showers, a swimming area, and play fields.

ACCOMMODATIONS

Make mid-summer reservations as early as possible; many of the rooms book up six months ahead of time for weekends in July and August. Winter rates are often 30 percent lower than the listed summer rates. In addition to the places listed here, the Chelan area has many private vacation homes available; the Lake Chelan Chamber of Commerce keeps a complete list, and also keeps track of motel availability in the summer.

Under $100

Many people stay at **Holden Village B&B** (509/687-9695, www.holdenvillage.org/bandbl, $20–30 per person) en route to Holden Village; the boat stops at nearby Fields Point. This quiet little pit stop is 25 miles west of Chelan, with mountain and lake vistas. It has six guest rooms with shared baths, plus a small dormitory.

Midtowner Motel (721 E. Woodin Ave., 509/682-4051, www.midtowner.com, $85–119 s or d) features rooms with kitchenettes, plus an outdoor pool, hot tub, and sauna. **Mountain View Lodge** (25 Wapato Point Pkwy., Manson, 509/687-9505 or 800/967-8105, www.mountainviewlakechelan.com, $91 s or d) also offers an outdoor pool and hot tub. Kitchenettes are available.

$100-150

Apple Country B&B (5220 Manson Blvd., Manson, 509/687-3982, www.applecountryinn.com, open May–Sept., $85–120 s or d) is a 1930 ranch house with three guest rooms that share a bath. A fourth room and a separate cottage have private baths. Guests have access to the hot tub.

Wapato Point Village Inn (Wapato Point, Manson, 509/687-2500 or 800/771-5300, www.wpvillageinn.com, $115–125 s or d) has rooms with microwaves and fridges.

$150-200

Relax in old-timey splendor at the romantic **Mary Kay's Whaley Mansion B&B** (415 3rd St., 509/682-5735 or 800/729-2408, $155–165 s or d), an elegantly restored 1911 home. It has six guest rooms with private baths.

$200-250

Watson's Harverene Resort (10 miles west of Chelan, 509/687-3720 or 800/687-3720, www.watsonsresort.com, $200–305 up to 6) is a quiet family place with beachfront cottages that share a private beach, outdoor pool, and hot tub.

Kelly's Resort (12800 South Lakeshore Rd., 509/687-3220, www.kellysresort.com, $210–225 s or d) is a friendly and quiet family resort 13 miles west of Chelan. Shoreside cottages have kitchens, fireplaces, boat moorage, and lake swimming. Choose between cottages in the woods or lakeside units.

Over $250

The longest-running and best resort on Lake Chelan, **Campbell's Resort** (104 W. Woodin Ave., 509/682-2561 or 800/553-8225, www.campbellsresort.com, $210–330 s or d, $320–450 suites) is right in town and offers 150 rooms, plus two pools, hot tubs, boat moorage, and a 1,200-foot sandy beach. Campbell's is also a popular convention facility.

Darnell's Resort Motel (901 Spader Bay Rd., 509/682-2015 or 800/967-8149, www.chelan.com/darnells, $210–446 for up to four) features luxury family accommodations with a private beach, heated pool, hot tub, sauna, exercise room, lighted tennis courts, putting greens, rowboats, bicycles, moorage, and kids' play area. A four-night minimum is required in midsummer.

FOOD

Chelan has a large number of restaurants from which to choose. They tend to change quite frequently, and new owners or chefs can dramatically improve (or worsen) the reputation, so ask around to see what's hot, or simply take a look inside to see if it looks interesting.

Cafés and Diners

Apple Cup Café (804 E. Woodin Ave., 509/682-2933, daily 6 A.M.–10 P.M.) is a family-type place with very good breakfasts—great cheese blintzes—in a Denny's-like setting. Head to **Latte Da Coffee Stop Café** (303 E. Wapato Ave., 509/682-4196, Mon.–Sat. 6 A.M.–4:30 P.M., Sun. 6 A.M.–3 P.M.) for the best local espressos, plus light breakfasts and lunches in a cozy atmosphere.

Hungry Belly Cafe (246 W. Manson Way, 509/682-8630, Sun.–Thurs. 11 A.M.–8 P.M., Fri.–Sat. 11 A.M.–9 P.M.) features stir-fry and vegetarian dishes, along with soda fountain specials for lunch or dinner.

For some solid Mexican food served up by a family from Jalisco, check out **Cantina** downtown (114 N. Emerson, 509/682-5553, daily 11 A.M.–2 P.M., 5–8:30 P.M.). Try the *enchiladas cangrejo,* done with Dungeness crab, or for more standard fare, a heaping plate of nachos or a burrito.

For the best pizzas around—including a spicy chicken garlic version—head to **Uncle Tim's Pizzaria** (76 W. Wapato Way, Manson, 509/687-3035, daily 11:30 A.M.–2 P.M. and 4–8:30 P.M.).

Steak and Seafood

Peter B's Bar & Grill (116 E. Woodin Ave., 509/682-1031, daily 10:30 A.M.–9 P.M.) sits right along the Chelan River, with a diverse menu of steaks, burgers, pastas, chicken, and seafood. Good food, reasonable prices, and a busy, convivial atmosphere.

BC MacDonald's (104 E. Woodin Ave., 509/682-1334, daily 8 A.M.–8:30 P.M.) is a noisy, happening place with an old cherry wood back bar that delivers lots of microbrews on tap. The trendy but tasty menu features gourmet burgers, fresh seafood, chicken, pastas, and homemade soups. BC's has blues and rock acts on throughout the week in summer.

Built in 1930, the **Campbell House** in Campbell's Resort (104 W. Woodin Ave., 509/682-2561, open by reservation) is the old standby, offering elegant dining and a continental menu specializing in Angus steaks and fresh seafood; prices are moderate to expensive. Reservations highly recommended in the summer. The patio is popular on summer evenings.

Markets

Golden Florins Cafe inside **Bear Foods Market** (125 E. Woodin Ave., 509/682-5535, Mon.–Sat. 10 A.M.–4 P.M., closed Sun.) doesn't look like much outside, but step inside to find a healthy café tucked into a spacious natural-foods store with a big selection of organic produce and other goods.

The **Chelan Valley Farmers Market** (Johnson St. next to the chamber of commerce office, 509/682-3243) comes to town June to mid-October on Saturday 8:30 A.M.–noon. Manson also has a **farmers market,** held Saturday mornings during the summer and early fall at the Manson Grange.

INFORMATION

For maps or other information, contact the **Lake Chelan Chamber of Commerce** (102 E. Johnson, 509/682-3503 or 800/424-3526, www.lakechelan.com, June–Aug. Mon.–Sat. 9 A.M.–6 P.M., Sunday 10 A.M.–4 P.M., daily with reduced hours in the spring and fall, Nov.–March Mon.–Fri. 9 A.M.–5 P.M., Saturday 10 A.M.–4 P.M.).

The combined Forest Service/National Park Service, **Chelan Ranger District Office** (428 W. Woodin, 509/682-2576, 7:45 A.M.–4:30 P.M. Mon.–Fri. year-round, plus 7:45 A.M.–4:30 P.M. Sat.–Sun. late June–early Sept.) dispenses information on all forms of outdoor recreation, including many places to camp, picnic, or just have a look around.

GETTING THERE AND AROUND

By Bus

Link (509/662-1155 or 800/851-5465, www.linktransit.com, Mon.–Fri., $1 to Wenatchee, $2 to Leavenworth) has bus routes covering Chelan and Douglas Counties, including the towns of Chelan, Manson, Wenatchee, and Leavenworth. You can put your skis on the bus in Chelan and ride to Wenatchee, then change to Route 40 and ski at Mission Ridge. Or put your bicycle on the special racks and ride anywhere one-way and pedal back.

No long distance bus service operates to Chelan, but you can catch the Link bus to Wenatchee for connections to Northwest Trailways and Amtrak.

By Air

Chelan Airways (509/682-5065, www.chelanairways.com) offers daily seaplane service to Stehekin, Domke Lake, and other up-lake destinations, plus sightseeing flights over Lake Chelan and Stehekin Valley. The nearest airport with air service to larger cities is in Wenatchee.

STEHEKIN

Stehekin (ste-HEE-kin) sits at the northwest end of Lake Chelan and can be reached only by boat, floatplane, or foot; thousands of visitors take the boat trip up-lake from Chelan for lunch or an overnight stay at one of Stehekin's resorts. The town is also a launching point for treks into the heart of North Cascades National Park, or beyond into Lake Chelan-Sawtooth Wilderness and Glacier Peak Wilderness.

The name Stehekin, a Native American term meaning "the way through," fits this mountain gateway well. The town began in the late 1880s when prospectors came here in search of gold and silver. They found the minerals, but not in sufficient quantity to establish a large mine, and Stehekin has never been connected to the outside world by road. Today it is home to fewer than 100 permanent residents but has all the basics, including a post office, grocery store, restaurant, and grade school. A summer-only outdoor supply shop and bakery are also in town.

Holden Village

Like Stehekin, the old copper and gold mining town of Holden is off the main road system. The *Lady of the Lake* stops at Lucerne, and a bus takes you 12 miles uphill to Holden (509/687-3644, www.holdenvillage.org, $30 per person). The mine closed in 1957, but the historic buildings remain, now run as a friendly Lutheran retreat that is especially popular with families. There are classes of all sorts, plus sessions on theology, the environment, and interpersonal issues. It's a spectacular mountain-rimmed setting, and many fine trails surround Holden, becoming ski trails in winter. You don't have to be religious or a member of any church to stay here. Guests stay in simple but comfortable lodges, and three healthy meals are included in the rate. A sauna, hot tub, pool room, bowling alley, and snack bar are also in the village. The Lake Chelan Boat Company's vessels stop here daily.

© ERICKA CHICKOWSKI

dockside at Stehekin

Sports and Recreation

The center for outdoor recreation options is the **Courtney Log Office** (150 yards past the post office along the lake). Here you can set up wagon and horseback rides, as well as week-long guided hikes, through **Cascade Corrals** (509/682-7742, www.courtneycountry.com).

Book an easy raft trip down the Stehekin River through **Stehekin Valley Ranch** (800/536-0745, $50 adults, $40 kids, $10 reservation fee), or rent mountain bikes from **Discovery Bikes** (509/686-3014, www.stehekindiscoverybikes.com, $4 per hour, $20 daily). Discovery also offers a guided ranch breakfast ride each morning ($30).

HIKING

The Stehekin area is a favorite of hikers of all levels—trails wander in all directions. The National Park Service shuttle buses make it easy to get to the trailheads or back to Stehekin. Keep your eyes open when you walk, since the area has a fair number of rattlesnakes.

A short 0.75-mile loop hike—the **Imus Creek Nature Trail**—begins behind the visitors center and climbs a nearby hill overlooking the lake. Spectacular **Rainbow Falls**—a towering cataract of water that plummets 312 feet—is just off the road amid tall western red cedar trees. Get there by walking (or catching the shuttle) 3.5 miles up the road.

Take the shuttle to High Bridge for a beautiful day hike to **Coon Lake.** The 1.2-mile trail leads uphill to this scenic lake, with excellent views of Agnes Mountain and good bird-watching. Those with more energy can continue another seven miles to the 8,122-foot summit of **McGregor Mountain,** a tortuous climb up countless switchbacks.

One of the most rewarding and family-friendly backpacking hikes to Stehekin takes a bit of advance planning. The **Lakeshore Trail** sidles along the northeast shore of the lake for some amazing views of the pristine water from piney forests and bluffs. Get *Lady of the Lake II* to drop you off 17 miles southeast of Stehekin at Prince Creek Campground and plan at least an overnight hike to get back to Stehekin.

Prince Creek Campground is a great departure point for a fine day hike up **Prince Creek Trail.** The route switchbacks through pine forests and then follows the creek into the high country around Cub Lake (a good place to camp). You'll discover dramatic vistas of the high Cascades from here. The Prince Creek Trail can also be used as part of a 38-mile loop trip that leaves Prince Creek Campground, climbs to the **Summit Trail,** and follows it along the ridge before dropping down to Stehekin. This hike features lots of ups and downs through forests and alpine meadows, and striking views of surrounding mountains. Much of the Summit Trail passes through the **Lake Chelan-Sawtooth Wilderness** with side trails leading north into the Twisp River drainage.

Additional boat-accessible hikes start from Holden Village, providing access to the Glacier Peak Wilderness. One of the most popular is the **Hart/Lyman Lakes Trail** (No. 1256). From Holden it follows Railroad Creek for 3.5 miles to Hart Lake before switchbacking up to Crown Point Falls and Lyman Lake and on to Cloudy Pass (10.5 miles), where it meets the Pacific Crest Trail. This trail gets a lot of use in midsummer so don't expect solitude, and bears can be a problem in campsites along Railroad Creek. Showers and campsites are available in Holden Village.

CAMPING

Purple Point Campground is just a third of a mile from the boat landing in Stehekin. Campers can also ride the shuttle bus from Stehekin to **Harlequin, Bullion, High Bridge, Tumwater, Dolly Varden, Shady, Bridge Creek, Park Creek,** and **Flat Creek** campgrounds along the Stehekin River. **Weaver Point Campground** is a very popular boat-access campground at the north end of the lake across from Stehekin. The old Weaver homestead here was the site where *The Courage of Lassie* was filmed in 1944, starring none other than Elizabeth Taylor (and Lassie, of course). All of these campgrounds are free; obtain a camping permit at Golden West Lodge Information Center. All boat-access campgrounds on Lake Chelan do not require a camping permit but do require a dock site pass ($5 per day or $40 for a season pass).

Accommodations

Stehekin is a wonderful place to relax and enjoy the wilderness splendor without interference from TVs or phones. As with all places in the Lake Chelan area, advance reservations are a must in the summer. **Stehekin Landing Resort** (509/682-4494, www.stehekinlanding.com, $139–185 s or d) has lodge rooms and housekeeping units. Amenities include a restaurant, bar, bike and boat rentals, a marina, gas, and groceries. During the winter, the Park Service and the resort jointly maintain 19 kilometers of free **cross-country ski trails.** Rent skis in Chelan or bring your own. The resort has snowshoes for rent.

At **Stehekin Valley Ranch** (509/682-4677 or 800/536-0745, www.courtneycountry.com, open mid-June–early Oct., $85–95 per person), nine miles up from Stehekin, your lodging, three hearty meals, and local transportation are included in the price of your cabin. Most are primitive tent cabins with no running water or electricity, and kerosene lamps for light. Showers are nearby. They also have several nicer cabins with private baths.

Several other Stehekin area houses and cabins are also available for rent by the day or week. These include **Silver Bay Inn at Stehekin** (509/682-2212 or 800/555-7781, www.silverbayinn.com), **Stehekin Log Cabin** (509/682-7742, www.courtneycountry.com), and **Flick Creek House** (888/841-3556, www.stehekinvalley.com). Call for rates, as they vary wildly by date.

Food

Stehekin Valley Ranch Restaurant (509/682-4677, June–Sept.) serves a menu that includes steaks, burgers, salad bar, and homemade desserts—all of which will taste pretty good after a week of backcountry travel or a long day in the saddle. Reservations are required. The restaurant is nine miles up the valley from Stehekin, but free transportation is provided. Two miles up from the boat dock is **Stehekin Pastry Company** (open summers only), which offers delicious baked goods, ice cream, breakfasts, and espresso. Another restaurant—open all year—is inside **Stehekin Landing Resort** (509/682-4494) just a short walk from the dock.

Information and Services

The National Park Service–run **Golden West Visitor Center** (360/856-5700, ext. 340, then ext. 14, www.nps.gov/noca, year-round Mon.–Fri. 8 A.M.–4:30 P.M., mid-May to mid-Sept. daily 8:30 A.M.–5 P.M.) in Stehekin is the place to go for information on hiking and camping in the area. Talks and evening programs are offered during the summer.

Nearby are **The House That Jack Built,** selling locally made crafts, and **McGregor Mt. Outdoor Supply.** The only public phone in the Stehekin area is next to the coin-operated laundry and shower facility, 200 yards up-lake from the Stehekin landing.

Getting There

A longtime favorite of visitors to Lake Chelan is the 55-mile voyage from Chelan or Manson to Stehekin. **Lake Chelan Boat Company** (1319 W. Woodin Ave., 509/682-2224, www.ladyofthelake.com) has been operating boats along this route for more than 65 years and runs two vessels: the 350-passenger *Lady of the Lake II* ($39), which takes four hours to reach Stehekin, and the 65-foot-long *Lady Express* ($59), which gets there in two hours. Food is available on both boats, and onboard Forest Service interpreters give talks on the human and natural history of the area. Only the *Lady Express* operates November–April, and there is no winter boat service on Tuesday and Thursday.

In addition to Chelan and Manson, the boats stop at Field's Point (accessible by car along the south shore), Lucerne (with access to Holden), and Stehekin. The *Lady II* also makes flag stops at any Forest Service campsite upon request during the summer season. Service changes through the year; pick up a copy of the schedule at visitors centers or from the Lake Chelan Boat Company at the southwest end of Chelan. A separate service provides weekly barge trips up the lake carrying vehicles, fuel, groceries, and supplies to Stehekin. Mix and match the boat schedules for day trips to Stehekin. You can also carry bikes, canoes, or kayaks aboard the boats for an extra charge.

Chelan Airways (509/682-5555, www.chelanairways.com) offers daily seaplane service to Stehekin and flightseeing over the Stehekin Valley. You may wish to fly one-way and take a boat in the other direction.

Getting Around

The National Park Service and Stehekin Adventure Company combine to offer daily van or bus transportation from the dock at Stehekin to Flat Creek, 20 miles into the mountains. This service is offered from late May through mid-October and costs $6 one-way to High Bridge, or $12 one-way to Flat Creek. Both buses carry backpacks, and the Stehekin Adventure bus also carries bikes. Contact the Park Service's Golden West Visitor Center in Stehekin for details or reservations (360/856-5700, ext. 340, then ext. 14, www.nps.gov/noca, year-round Mon.–Fri. 8 A.M.–4:30 P.M., mid-May to mid-Sept. daily 8:30 A.M.–5 P.M.) or stop by their visitors centers in Stehekin or Chelan. Reservations are not needed for the larger Stehekin Adventures buses. Passengers on both services are given a narrated tour along the way, and you can get on or off at any point along the route.

In the summer, **Stehekin Landing Resort** (509/682-4494) offers daily trips to Rainbow Falls. Its bus meets the *Lady Express* and *Lady of the Lake II* boats when they arrive in Stehekin and provides a narrated 45-minute tour ($7). They also offer bus tours ($20) that include a picnic lunch at High Bridge and a visit to Rainbow Falls and Buckner Orchard, a historic grove said to be home to the oldest strain of Common Delicious apples in the United States.

ENTIAT AREA

Heading south from Chelan on Highway 97A, the highway descends to the Columbia (or the dammed version thereof) through hills draped in sage and grass. The town of Entiat (ANN-ee-at; pop. 900) sits along Lake Entiat, that portion of the Columbia River that backs up behind massive Rocky Reach Dam 10 miles downriver. This is orchard country; stop at a local fruit stand for fresh apples, cherries, apricots, peaches, or pears in season. South of Entiat, Highway 97A hugs the shore of the lake, passing rugged rocky slopes. Orchards edge the east shoreline.

Sights and Recreation

Near the city park, the **Entiat Historical Museum** (2117 Lakeshore Dr., 509/784-1832, summers only 10 A.M.–4 P.M. Sat., 10 A.M.–2 P.M. Sun.) contains local memorabilia in an 1895 farmhouse.

A mile south of Entiat is the turnoff to Entiat River Road, which leads to **Entiat National Fish Hatchery** (509/784-1131) and eventually to the Entiat trailhead for the Glacier Peak Wilderness. Hiking trails lead up to mountain lakes above here. Also of note is **Silver Falls,** 30 miles up the road, with a campground and a 1.5-mile loop trail to this 150-foot waterfall.

Practicalities

Along the Entiat River Road, choose between seven Forest Service campgrounds (open May–Oct., $12); the closest is the free **Pine Flat Campground,** 14 miles up and located along the Mad River. Get supplies at the small store in the tiny settlement of **Ardenvoir,** nine miles up.

Camping and RV places are also available along the lake at **Entiat City Park** (509/784-1500 or 800/736-8428, open Apr.–mid-Nov., $18).

For information on the area, head to the Wenatchee National Forest **Entiat Ranger Station** (509/784-1511).

Link (509/662-1155 or 800/851-5465, www.linktransit.com) has inexpensive daily bus service throughout Chelan and Douglas Counties, including Entiat, Chelan, Wenatchee, and Leavenworth.

Cashmere

Tucked between strip-mall Wenatchee and Bavarian-mall Leavenworth, tiny Cashmere (pop. 3,000) has long featured a Colonial American theme on its buildings. Highway 2 between Leavenworth and Cashmere is lined with fruit orchards (visit in late April to enjoy the trees in bloom); the dry climate helps produce the finest D'Anjou pears in America. A half dozen fruit stands sell fresh apples, pears, cherries, apricots, peaches, plums, and berries in season. Because of this fruit production, Cashmere was a logical place to establish a business that produces a confection made from fruit juice, walnuts, and powdered sugar—the treats known as Aplets and Cotlets.

SIGHTS

Candy Town

If you have a sweet tooth, be certain to stop at **Liberty Orchards** (117 Mission St., 509/782-2191, www.libertyorchards.com, Apr.–Dec. Mon.–Fri. 8 A.M.–5:30 P.M., Sat.–Sun. 10 A.M.–4 P.M., Jan.–Mar. Mon.–Fri. 8:30 A.M.–4:30 P.M.), the home of Aplets and Cotlets. These all-natural confections are made of fruit juices (apple, grape, and apricot) and walnuts and are coated with powdered sugar and cornstarch. Tours take 15 minutes or so and end back in the gift shop, where you can sample a number of different candies and purchase gift boxes and various knickknacks.

The original sweets were developed by two Armenian immigrants, Mark Balaban and Armen Tertsagian, who had established fruit orchards in the Cashmere area. Unable to sell all the fruit they produced, they decided to mix apple juice and walnuts to make a Middle Eastern confection called locum. More than 75 years have passed, but the candy is still made in Cashmere (two million pounds a year), and the company president is a grandson of the original owners. Old standbys such as Aplets and Cotlets are still around, along with several dozen other varieties, from chocolate passion fruit to sugar-free, nut-free versions. On weekends you aren't likely to see a lot of activity in the plant during a tour, but the free samples make any stop worthwhile.

Chelan County Historical Museum

Considered one of the top pioneer villages in the country, the Chelan County Historical Museum (600 Cottage Ave., 509/782-3230, www.chelancounty.com/ccmpv.htm, Tues.–Sun. 9:30 A.M.–5 P.M., closed Nov.–March, $4 adults, $3 seniors and students, $2 ages 5–12, families for $8) has restored and furnished 20 of the oldest buildings in Chelan County to create an authentic Old West atmosphere. A blacksmith shop, railroad caboose, school, gold mine, mission building, hotel, and assay office are part of the Pioneer Village; there's also a large waterwheel that lifted water out of the Wenatchee River to irrigate the orchards. The

© WASHINGTON STATE TOURISM/ LEVY SHECKLER

The Chelan County Historical Museum has outstanding displays of Native American artifacts and natural history.

main museum building houses an extraordinary collection of Native American artifacts—baskets, prehistoric antler carvings, beaded clothing, medicines, pipes, and more—along with natural history and pioneer exhibits.

EVENTS

Celebrated the first week in July, the highlight of **Founder's Days** is the Stillman Miller Hill Climb, inspired by an early resident who claimed he could pour himself a beer in the local tavern, run up Numbers Hill, and be back before the head settled. Whether or not he actually made it is anybody's guess, but the concept was so appealing that runners are still trying it today. Other events include a parade, barbecue, arts and crafts show, and street dance.

Cashmere is also home to the **Chelan County Fair,** held the second week in September, highlighted by rodeos, musical entertainment, a carnival, and exhibits. The first weekend in October brings **Cashmere Apple Days,** featuring apple-bin races, an apple pie–baking contest, music, dancing, and staged shootouts.

RECREATION

Camping

Camping ($19) and RV spaces ($29 with full hookups, $24 with water and electricity only) with showers are available at **Wenatchee River County Park** (just west of town, 509/662-2525, open Apr.–late Oct.). This park now has free Wi-Fi and a sand volleyball court. No reservations are accepted.

ACCOMMODATIONS

Cashmere has two comfortable places. **La Toscana Bed and Breakfast** (9020 Foster Rd., 509/548-5448, $110 s or d), between Cashmere and Peshastin, offers elegantly decorated rooms in a lodge on the grounds of small winery. On a less grand scale, **Village Inn Motel** (229 Cottage Ave., 509/782-3522 or 800/793-3522, www.cashmerevillageinn.com, $69 s, $79 d) offers humble motel rooms in its two-story roadside property.

FOOD

Far from being a one-trick pony, **Brian's Bulldog Pizza** (107 Cottage Ave., 509/782-1505, www.briansbulldogpizza.com, Sun.–Thurs. 10 A.M.–8:30 P.M., Fri.–Sat. 11 A.M.–10 P.M.) has lots going for it, including a baked potato bar, lasagna, and other goodies to go along with the pizza. Tasty baked goods can be found just down the street at **Sure to Rise Bakery** (115 Cottage Ave., 509/782-2424, Tues.–Sat. 7:30 A.M.–6 P.M., closed Mon.).

GETTING THERE AND AROUND

Catch an inexpensive **Link** bus (800/851-5465, www.linktransit.com) for connections from Cashmere to other parts of Chelan and Douglas Counties, including Leavenworth, Wenatchee, and Lake Chelan.

Cascade Helitours (509/548-4759) provides scenic helicopter flights over the Cascades out of Cashmere.

Leavenworth

One of the most distinctive towns in the Pacific Northwest, Leavenworth has a scant 2,000 residents but manages to attract more than a million visitors per year.

The attraction? A fanciful Bavarian village, complete with authentic architecture, hand-carved benches, and flower-bedecked streets, all backdropped by peaks of the Cascades. Add in the female clerks in Bavarian dirndl dresses and waiters in lederhosen, and the town gets a bit hokey at times, but it is certainly unique in America. With almost 100 lodging places and dozens of restaurants and shops, it's pretty clear that people love this place.

History

Although preceded by prospectors and Hudson's Bay fur traders, the first Eastern

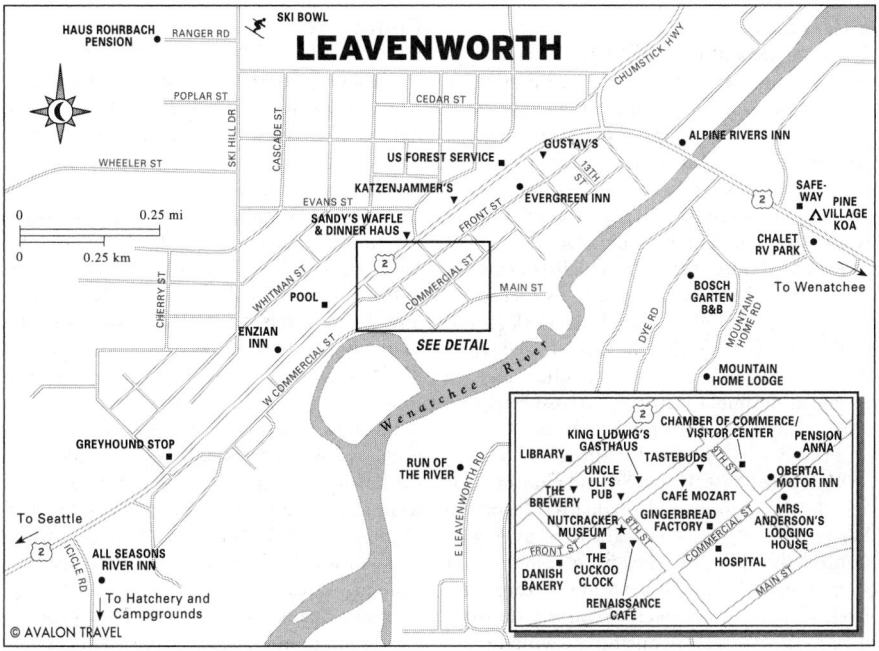

settlers in the Leavenworth area didn't arrive until the late 1880s, with the news that the Great Northern Railway planned to lay tracks through the valley. The resulting population "boom" brought Leavenworth (originally called Icicle) about 300 people by the early 1900s. They were mostly railroad men or lumberjacks employed by the Lamb-Davis Lumber Co., operators of one of the state's largest sawmills. The after-hours rowdiness of these laborers gave little Leavenworth a rather unrefined reputation that took years to live down. Even so, by the early 1920s a wave of families bought tracts of land to grow "Wenatchee Big Red" apples.

When the railroad moved its switching yard from Leavenworth to Wenatchee, and the sawmill closed its doors after logging all its waterfront land, these family-based fruit farms provided much of the town's income. But by the 1960s, it was clear that Leavenworth needed more than apples to survive. With help from the University of Washington, a committee on tourism was formed to brainstorm, and it suggested a fall festival and a major remodeling job.

Suggestions for the town's new motif ranged from a Gay '90s theme to a Western town, but with the impressive mountain backdrop, an alpine village seemed the best answer. One of the first proponents was Ted Price, owner of a Swiss Bavarian–style café in Coles Corner. (The building, now Squirrel Tree Inn, still stands 14 miles northwest of Leavenworth.) The town's renovation was financed with private funds and backed by local bankers. It quickly earned national recognition for the attention to detail, aggressive promotion, and bootstrap efforts. Many of the buildings were designed by Karl Heinz Ulbricht, who had fled East Germany in the 1950s and who insisted upon authenticity and quality construction. By the late 1960s, the Bavarian theme had taken hold; it now covers almost every commercial building in town. Tourism has transformed a going-nowhere place into a premier success story in community improvement.

SIGHTS

The Bavarian Village

Start your tour of the Bavarian Village in the heart of town, on Front Street, where there's plenty of on-street parking. Shops, restaurants, taverns, and hotels are squeezed side by side, all beautifully decorated with carved wood, flower boxes, and murals—even the automated teller machine is surrounded by a painted alpine scene.

Front Street Park (sandwiched between Hwy. 2 and the shops of Front St.) is a relaxing, sunny spot for a picnic lunch or break in the central gazebo. It's also the place to see street dances, art exhibits, and other public events, or to stop at the public restrooms. Across Highway 2 is the Chamber of Commerce Visitor Center, and the city hall/library building.

Waterfront Park (8th St. and Commercial St.) on the cottonwood-shaded banks of the Wenatchee River, has walkways over and around the river, benches for a respite from shopping, and views of the peaks surrounding Icicle Canyon. You can cross-country ski from here to the golf course during the winter.

Fish Hatchery and Interpretive Trail

The **Leavenworth National Fish Hatchery** (two miles out Icicle Rd., 509/548-7641, daily 8 A.M.–4 P.M.) cranks out some 2.5 million salmon each year. Built 1939–1940, the hatchery was the largest such facility in the world when completed. Water for the hatchery comes from Icicle Creek, the Wenatchee River, deep wells, and a half-mile tunnel from Snow Lakes in the Alpine Lakes Wilderness. Stop by to watch the steelhead trout and chinook salmon in the raceways (favorite spots for dive-bombing belted kingfishers), or step inside to see displays and educational videos. Exhibits reveal how Columbia River dams and development have devastated natural salmon and steelhead runs and how the hatchery attempts to mitigate some of the damage. The real attraction here is an "outdoor aquarium" where you can watch rainbow trout in the eye-level concrete "stream."

Icicle Creek Interpretive Trail provides a mile-long circular path from the hatchery.

© WASHINGTON STATE TOURISM/JIM POTH

The charming town of Leavenworth features Bavarian-style shops.

Pick up an informative trail brochure before heading out to see various sites along the creek, including a wildlife-viewing blind. Keep your eyes open for the resident ospreys.

Blewett Pass

Highway 97 heads south from the Leavenworth area, connecting Highway 2 with I-90. The road climbs 21 miles to 4,102-foot Blewett Pass, a popular area for hiking, skiing, and snowmobiling. **Blewett Pass Interpretive Trail** offers a three-mile loop through high-country forests. Several nearby Forest Service campgrounds (Bonanza, Tronsen, Swauk, and Mineral Springs) have campsites for $12 or less. For more adventure, take the slightly shorter but significantly steeper and more serpentine old highway over Blewett Pass.

The **Swauk Forest Discovery Trail** is an easy three-mile path at the summit of Swauk/Blewett Pass. The trail passes through both old-growth forests and clear-cuts, and educational signs are scattered along the way.

Blue Creek Road (Road 9738) leads from the Mineral Springs area west approximately seven miles to an old fire lookout on Red Top Mountain, providing vistas in all directions. This is a popular area to search for blue agates and geodes (a.k.a. thunder eggs).

Also nearby is **Mineral Springs Resort** (509/857-2361, $10 with electric hookups, $8 without), which has RV spaces and good meals. Come winter, this area is popular with snowmobilers and cross-country skiers. Sno-Parks at Swauk Campground and Pipe Creek provide skier-only access to many miles of cross-country trails. For details, contact the Forest Service's Cle Elum Ranger Station (509/674-4411).

ENTERTAINMENT AND EVENTS

The Arts

Leavenworth's **Icicle Creek Music Center** has a series of diverse musical performances, including jazz, chamber music, bluegrass, symphonies, and string quartets. These are held at Sleeping Lady Retreat and Conference Center (7375 Icicle Rd., 509/548-6347 or 800/574-2123, www.icicle.org).

The **Leavenworth Summer Theater** (509/548-7324, www.leavenworthsummertheater.org) presents very popular all-ages musical productions of such classics as *The Sound of Music, Carousel,* and *Heidi* at the Ski Hill outdoor stage.

On a less sophisticated level, accordion-playing musicians and polka-dancin' fools can be found weekend evenings at **Andreas Keller** (829 Front St., downstairs, 509/548-6000) and **King Ludwig's Gasthaus** (921 Front St., 509/548-6625).

Festivals

Leavenworth always finds something to celebrate—festivals and fairs circle the calendar. Contact the chamber of commerce (509/548-5807) for more information about all of these. January brings **Bavarian Ice Fest** and its snowshoe and cross-country ski races, dogsled pulls, a tug of war, and fireworks in mid-month. Smaller festivals fill the months until the big **Maifest,** held on Mother's Day weekend, when costumed Bavarian dancers circle the Maypole, and concerts, a parade, and Saturday night street dance are accompanied by oompah music from the bandstand and the chiming of bells from the Marlin Handbell Ringers. Another fun Maifest event is the authentic traditional Bavarian farm wedding. Maifest also marks the start of **Art in the Park,** featuring area artists every weekend May–October in Front Street Park.

Other summer festivals are **Craftfair** in early June, and two popular mid-June events, **The International Folk Dance Festival** and **Kinderfest. Leavenworth International Accordion Celebration** in early August brings concerts, workshops, and fun competition for all ages. The **Washington State Autumn Leaf Festival** takes place the last weekend of September and the first weekend of October, with a grand parade featuring dozens of marching bands. It also includes daily polka music in the gazebo, Saturday night street dances, a pancake feed, flea market, and food booths.

Christmas is Leavenworth's most festive holiday. The **Christmas Lighting Festival** is held the first and second Saturday in December, when all the Christmas lights go on simultaneously at dusk and Mr. and Mrs. Claus appear in their house in the park. Caroling, sleigh rides, concerts, and food booths add to the holiday festivities. The lights stay lit till February, so there's no need to hurry to see them.

SHOPPING

Trinket and gewgaw places are spread throughout town—shops with plastic Santas, inane T-shirts, and made-in-Taiwan Bavarian figurines—but fortunately, Leavenworth also has more than its share of distinctive, great-for-browsing places. **A Matter of Taste** (647 Front St., 509/548-6949 or 800/497-3995, www.amatteroftasteinc.com, daily 9 A.M.–9 P.M.) lets you savor all sorts of unusual treats, from "Ass Kickin' Chicken Wing Sauce" to coffee jelly. Just above its entrance is the town **glockenspiel,** with carved dancers who clog on the hour. Another "glock" lives above the entrance to **The Cuckoo Clock** (725 Front St., 509/548-4857, daily 10 A.M.–4 P.M.), with dancers coming out of the closet (so to speak) every half-hour. Inside are tall grandfather clocks priced over $5,000, weird and wacky timepieces, and more than a few Bavarian cuckoo clocks. Tromp up the stairs to wander through **Jubilee Global Gifts** (723 Front St., 509/548-3508, daily 10 A.M.–5 P.M.) with handmade gifts from all over the planet—but nothing from Germany.

A few doors down (and past the Danish Bakery, if you can make it beyond the luscious pastries without being enticed inside) is **Nusskracker Haus** (735 Front St., 509/548-7014, www.nussknackerhaus.com, daily 9:30 A.M.–5:30 P.M.), showcasing imported collectibles and hundreds of German nutcrackers. For an even more impressive collection, head upstairs to the **Nutcracker Museum** (509/548-4708 or 800/892-3989, 2–5 P.M. daily May–Oct., weekends the rest of the year, $2.50 adults, $1 ages 5–16), where over 2,000 different kinds of nutcrackers are displayed. It's enough to drive Tchaikovsky nuts.

Next comes **Der Marketplatz** (801 Front St., 509/548-7422, daily 9:30 A.M.–6 P.M.), which has an extraordinary stein collection for beer drinkers, European crystal, Hummel figurines, and even Bavarian polka CDs. Continue down the block and down the basement stairs to **Die Musik Box** (933 Front St., 509/548-6152 or 800/288-5883, www.musicboxshop.com), where 5,000 intricate music boxes from around the globe create a chorus of whimsical sounds.

SPORTS AND RECREATION

State Parks

Lake Wenatchee State Park (23 mi. N. on Hwy. 207, www.parks.wa.gov, $17 no hookups) is a popular year-round recreation area, with cross-country skiing in winter, plus swimming, fishing, and canoeing in summer. The spectacular Lake Wenatchee waterfront is set against a backdrop of majestic snow-covered peaks. Other facilities include boat rentals, weekend interpretive programs, and wooded campsites. A number of sites are plowed for winter camping. Horseback rides are available in summer from **Icicle Outfitters and Guides** (509/679-1703 or 800/497-3912).

Eight miles east of Leavenworth on Highway 2 is **Peshastin Pinnacles State Park,** where a series of sandstone spires jut out of an arid hillside, making for a rock-climbing mecca across 35 acres. Climbing difficulty generally ranges from 5.6 to 5.11, with many routes bolted. This is a great spot for beginners still learning how to lead climb with the use of bolts (sport climb). Several spots make for good bouldering (for example, the outcrop just to the right of the gate). One great bonus of climbing at Peshastin is that the weather, and hence the rock, is often dry because of its location on the east side of the mountains. Nonclimbers can stop to photograph the dramatic pinnacles, walk the short trails, or watch more daring folks. There is no camping here.

Cross-Country Skiing

Leavenworth, a popular spot with cross-country ski enthusiasts, offers 25 kilometers of groomed trails within minutes of downtown. Three ski areas are maintained by the Leavenworth Winter Sports Club with both classical and skate-skiing lanes. The most accessible of these—**Waterfront Park**—is just a block from downtown and covers eight kilometers along the Wenatchee River. These connect with the **Leavenworth Golf Course Trail. Icicle River Trail,** one mile from Leavenworth on Icicle Road, has eight kilometers of level tracks at the mouth of Icicle Canyon, through meadows and forests above the fish hatchery. **Ski Hill Trail** has a five-kilometer track, with two kilometers lighted for night skiing (till 9 P.M.) that roll over the hills adjacent to the downhill ski area. Here you get the added benefit of a lodge and weekend food service. The club often grooms trails up the last several miles of Icicle River Road, on an unplowed stretch. Trail fees are $8 per day for adults, free for kids under five. For more information, contact the **Leavenworth Winter Sports Club** (509/548-4608, www.skileavenworth.com). Rent cross-country and skate skis at **Der Sportsman** (837 Front St., 509/548-5623) or **Leavenworth Ski & Sports** (940 Hwy. 2, next to the Chevron station in the middle of town, 509/548-7864).

Lake Wenatchee State Park, 23 miles northwest of Leavenworth, has 10 kilometers of maintained free trails in the park and on surrounding land, but you'll need a Sno-Park permit (www.parks.wa.gov) to park here; pick one up in Leavenworth. Cross-country ski lessons and rentals are available nearby at **Leavenworth Outfitters** (509/763-3733 or 800/347-7934, www.thrillmakers.com) next to Parkside Grocery.

Contact the Leavenworth Ranger District office (509/548-6977) for more details about skiing options over ungroomed wilderness trails and logging roads around Blewett Pass in Wenatchee National Forest. Skiers need a Sno-Park permit to park here. The Lake Wenatchee Ranger District (509/763-3103, www.fs.fed.us/r6/wenatchee) has details on cross-country trails near the lake.

Backcountry Skiing

For overnight cross-country skiing (17 miles of ski trails), snowshoeing, and snowboarding, plus some of the finest Telemark skiing in the high Cascades, stay in rustic luxury at **Scottish Lakes Backcountry Cabins** (509/884-2000 or 800/909-9916, www.scottishlakes.com, $40 d). Eight cozy cabins come equipped with woodstoves, mattresses, propane stoves, kerosene lamps, and cooking utensils. From the parking area near Coles Corner (16 miles northwest of Leavenworth), the cabins are 8.5 miles away and 3,000 feet higher in elevation. Most folks choose to ride up and back aboard the lodging's 12-passenger Sno-Cat or snowmobile, but they will haul your gear (extra charge) if you have the energy to ski up and back yourself. The cabins are on private timber company land adjacent to 5,000-foot McCue Ridge in the Alpine Lakes Wilderness and are generally open Thanksgiving through April, plus mid-October to mid-November for fall hikers. These cabins are recommended.

Downhill Skiing

Leavenworth has its own tiny ski area, **Leavenworth Ski Hill** (509/548-5115), with two rope tows providing uphill transportation for the handful of runs. There's also a snowboard half-pipe. The ski season here is generally shorter than at the bigger areas because of the lower elevation.

Two larger ski areas are close by: **Stevens Pass,** 35 miles to the west on Highway 2, and **Mission Ridge,** 35 miles in the other direction near Wenatchee. Mission Ridge is a favorite of locals because of the dry snow and less-crowded slopes.

Other Winter Recreation

Sleigh rides are available from three local places in winter. **Red-Tail Canyon Farm** (11780 Freund Canyon Rd., 509/548-4512 or

800/678-4512, www.redtailcanyonfarm.com) has champion Belgian draft horses that pull you through scenic Red-Tail Canyon. **Eagle Creek Ranch** (509/548-7798 or 800/221-7433, www.eaglecreek.ws) offers sleigh rides over the meadows and through the woods surrounding the ranch, two miles north of town off Highway 209. **Mountain Springs Lodge** (14 miles north of Leavenworth, 509/763-2713 or 800/858-2276, www.mtsprings.com) has a similar service.

See the Cascades and the Leavenworth valley from a unique perspective aboard a dogsled from **Enchanted Mountain Tours** (509/763-2975) or **Alaska Dreamin' Sled Dog Company** (509/763-8017).

Mountain Spring Lodge (509/763-3483 or 800/858-2276, www.mtsprings.com) runs snowmobile tours out of Plain.

River Rafting

The rivers of the central Cascades support many rafting outfitters, but the Wenatchee is easily the most popular river in the state. Above Leavenworth, the Wenatchee drops through rugged Tumwater Canyon, with several class VI stretches before calming down to more manageable class III rapids below town. Leavenworth is the most common put-in point, and white-water trips cover 16–24 miles. Conditions change through the year; high spring runoff creates excellent white-water conditions from April to mid-July (and often longer). Gentler float trips begin at Lake Wenatchee and cover the stretch of easy water before the river enters Tumwater Canyon near Tumwater Campground (the take-out point). These are especially popular when flow levels drop during August and September. Inner tubers often float down slower parts of the Icicle and Wenatchee Rivers to Blackbird Island near Leavenworth's Waterfront Park. Rent inner tubes at **Leavenworth Sports Center** (940 Hwy. 2, 509/548-7864), next to the Chevron station, or rent kayaks and canoes at Lake Wenatchee from **Osprey Rafting** (800/743-6269) or **Leavenworth Outfitters** (509/763-3733 or 800/347-7934).

For half-day rafting excursions, expect to pay $50 for white-water trips or scenic float trips. Most companies include guides, wet suits, booties, meals, and shuttle bus service. Contact one of the following companies for more information, or look for their brochures in the visitors center: **All Rivers Adventures** (800/743-5628, www.allrivers.com), **Blue Sky Outfitters** (800/228-7238, www.blueskyoutfitters.com), **Leavenworth Outfitters** (800/347-7934, www.thrillmakers.com), and **Orion River Expeditions** (800/553-7466, http://orionexp.com).

Mountain Biking

Cyclists love the back roads around Leavenworth, including an almost-level seven-mile loop through Icicle Valley. A more adventurous ride climbs the dirt road up Tumwater Mountain, just north of town, and offers vistas into Tumwater Canyon and the Wenatchee Valley far below. Stop by the local Forest Service offices for descriptions of other mountain biking trails.

Rent mountain bikes from **Leavenworth Ski & Sports** (940 Hwy. 2, next to Chevron, 509/548-7864, daily 9 A.M.–6 P.M.) or **Der Sportsman** (837 Front St., 509/548-5623, daily 10 A.M.–6 P.M.).

Hiking

The Alpine Lakes Wilderness Area, one of the most popular and scenic hiking destinations in Washington, lies just a few miles west of Leavenworth. Stop by the Wenatchee National Forest's **Leavenworth Ranger District** (600 Sherbourne, 509/548-6977, www.fs.fed.us/r6/wenatchee) for a brochure on nearby day hikes and a detailed trail guide to longer treks.

The **Lake Wenatchee** area at the north end of Highway 207 has an extensive system of hiking trails. Popular with hikers and photographers is the **Dirtyface Trail,** a steep 4.5-mile one-way hike from the Lake Wenatchee Ranger Station to the Dirtyface Lookout at 6,000 feet with views of the lake and surrounding scenery. Backpackers may want to try the **Nason Ridge Trail,** a 22-mile one-way scenic trail along the length of the Nason Ridge, starting at South Shore Road off Highway 207. A number of other one-day or longer hikes start from various points along a complicated network of numbered forest roads; your best bet is to check at the ranger station for detailed maps and printed trail descriptions. This is black bear country; hikers and campers should use standard bear precautions.

The upper Chiwawa River drainage north of Lake Wenatchee is one of the most popular access points for the Glacier Peak Wilderness. Several trails take off near the end of this road, including the heavily used **Phelps Creek Trail,** which follows the creek for five miles to mountain-rimmed Spider Meadows inside the wilderness.

Equine Expeditions and Excursions

During the summer months, **Eagle Creek Ranch** (509/548-7798 or 800/221-7433, www.eaglecreek.ws, $29–40)—a 580-acre ranch surrounded by Wenatchee National Forest—offers a number of pack trips to nearby wilderness areas, along with horseback rides, wagon rides, and barbecue dinners. The same activities also take place at **Mountain Springs Lodge** (509/763-2713 or 800/858-2276, www.mtsprings.com, $25–225). **Icicle Outfitters and Guides** (509/679-1703 or 800/497-3912, www.icicleoutfitters.com, $24–130) provides guided all-day rides into the Cascades and an assortment of pack trips.

For something even easier, hop on one of the **horse-drawn carriages** (509/548-6825) that roll through Leavenworth all summer long.

Other Summer Recreation

Icicle Junction (565 Hwy. 2, 888/462-4242) is the local fun park, with miniature golf, bumper-boat rides, video games, and a miniature train.

The two local golf courses are **Leavenworth Golf Club** (Icicle Rd. along the Wenatchee River, 509/548-7267, www.leavenworthgolf.com) and **Kahler Glen Golf Course** (near Lake Wenatchee, 509/763-4025, www.kahlerglen.com).

Camping

Wenatchee National Forest campgrounds near Leavenworth are generally open May to late October and charge $8–12. Get there very early on summer weekends or all the spaces may be gone! The closest to Leavenworth is **Eightmile Campground** (eight miles up Icicle Rd.). Six more Forest Service campgrounds are within 20 miles of Leavenworth along Icicle Road.

Another very popular Forest Service tenting spot, **Tumwater Campground** is 10 miles northwest from Leavenworth along Highway 2. Farther afield (16 miles northwest) is Lake Wenatchee, where you can pitch a tent at the Forest Service's **Nason Creek** and **Glacier View** Campgrounds. Four more Forest Service campgrounds lie northwest of the lake. Other, free campsites (with a Northwest Forest Pass) can be found driving from Lake Wenatchee up Chiwawa Valley Road, past Fish Lake to where the road turns to dirt. Unimproved campsites out this way along the Chiwawa River include **Finner Creek, Riverbend,** and **Rock Creek,** among others.

Showers are available at **Oxbow Trading Post** in Cole Corner (16 miles northwest of Leavenworth). Hiker and campers can also find hot showers and washing machines at **Die Wascherei** (1317 Front St., daily 7 A.M.–9:30 P.M.).

ACCOMMODATIONS

As a favorite vacation spot in both winter and summer, Leavenworth is jam-packed with accommodations options. Because of its popularity, prices are high, and you'll have a tough time finding anything under $60 d a night. Leavenworth has no hostel, so travelers on a tight budget should consider staying in nearby Wenatchee or camping out. Prices at many motels and B&Bs rise on Friday and Saturday nights, and many places require a two-night minimum for weekends (especially festival weekends). If you're arriving on a weekend or in the peak summer or winter holiday seasons, try to book your lodging as early as possible, since rooms fill up early. Crowding is not nearly as much of a problem on weekdays, especially in the winter.

The **Leavenworth Chamber of Commerce** (509/548-5807, www.leavenworth.org) has brochures describing local lodging places and keeps a list of those with vacancies.

Under $100

At the low end, you won't go wrong at **Mrs. Anderson's Lodging House** (917 Commercial St., 509/548-6984 or 800/253-8990, www.quiltersheaven.com, $88–146 d) where nine small but comfortable rooms (one has a balcony) are available in a historic lodging house. Light breakfast is included.

Another reasonably priced lodge downtown is the **Evergreen Inn** (1117 Front St., 509/548-5515 or 800/327-7212, evergreeninn.com, $79–109 d), with continental breakfast included.

It is adults only at **Blue Grouse Lodge** (19944 Hwy. 207 near Lake Wenatchee, 800/883-2611 or 509/763-0108, www.bluegrouse.com, $95 s or d), which lets out four rooms with access to a sauna and a common room with fireplace.

$100-150

More standard motel-style accommodations can be found downtown at the **Obertal Village Motor Inn** (922 Commercial St., 509/548-5204 or 800/537-9382, www.obertal.com, $139–149 s or d). More expensive suites are available with hot tub and fireplace ($159–179).

Or stay in a rambling, three-story wooden chalet outside of town at **Haus Rohrbach Pension** (12882 Ranger Rd., 509/548-7074 or 800/548-4477, www.hausrohrbach.com, $105–130 s or d), with 10 rooms. Many rooms have decks and great views of the surrounding mountains. The owners also offer Austrian gourmet cooking classes.

The cozy, quiet **Hotel Pension Anna** (926 Commercial St., 509/548-6273 or 800/509-2662, www.pensionanna.com, $135–155 d) also offers a bit of authentic Austria flair, with furnishings imported from Europe by the owner.

AlpenRose Inn (500 Alpine Pl., 509/548-3000 or 800/582-2474, www.alpenroseinn.com, $105–170 s or d) is located in a quiet area just outside of town, near Icicle Road. Guests are offered access to an outdoor pool, hot tub, and exercise room. Some rooms have a deck and fireplace.

Autumn Pond B&B (10388 Titus Rd., 509/548-4482 or 800/222-9661, www.autumnpond.com, $129 s or d) sits along a pond on three acres of land and has a hot tub and six guest rooms with private baths.

Tumwater Mountain Bed and Breakfast (104 Center St., 800/318-2578 or 509/548-2072, www.tumwatermtn.com, $125–175) has rooms in a renovated home in a quiet neighborhood near downtown.

Vienna Woods B&B (12842 Prowell Rd., 509/548-7843 or 888/548-7843, www.innviennawoods.com, $130–160 d) is an elegant home on two wooded acres in Icicle Valley. The three large guest rooms have private baths, and kids are accepted.

The creekside lodge **Alpine Rivers Inn** (1505 Alpensee Strausse, 509/548-5875 or 800/873-3960 (U.S.) or 800/255-3151 (Canada), www.alpineriversinn.com, $109–139 d) is only about a 10-minute walk from city center's shops and restaurants. Enjoy an outdoor pool and a complimentary round of putting at Enzian Falls Championship Putting Course in the summer, or take advantage of the complimentary Nordic ski gear in the winter. Rooms include kitchenettes, and a European breakfast is served each morning.

$150-200

Head to **Enzian Inn** (590 Hwy. 2, 509/548-5269 or 800/223-8511, www.enzianinn.com, $150–265 d) for one of the most authentically furnished local places. Rooms are decorated with Bavarian crafts and furniture, and the owner even plays an alpenhorn from the top floor each morning! The hotel has large indoor and outdoor pools, hot tubs, and an exercise facility.

Bosch Garten B&B (9846 Dye Rd., 509/548-6900 or 800/535-0069, www.boschgarten.com, $149–176 d) has tall windows facing the mountains and three guest rooms with private baths. The attractive grounds include a Japanese-style garden with an enclosed hot tub.

Featherwinds Farm B&B (17033 River Rd., 509/763-2011, www.featherwinds.com, $185–195 s or d), on farmland near Lake Wenatchee, has three guest rooms with private baths. Outside, find an outdoor pool and hot tub.

All Seasons River Inn (8751 Icicle Rd., 509/548-1425 or 800/254-0555, www.allseasonsriverinn.com, $185–230 s or d) presents guests with antique-furnished rooms, some with fireplaces, in a large contemporary home. Breakfast is served on the riverfront deck. There's a two-night minimum on weekends.

Abendblume Pension (12570 Ranger Rd., 509/548-4059 or 800/669-7634, www.abendblume.com, $158–298) offers elegant rooms with fireplaces in a luxurious small inn; there's a two-night minimum. Austrian breakfast is served.

$200-250

Run of the River (9308 E. Leavenworth Rd., 509/548-7171 or 800/288-6491, www.runoftheriver.com, $220–255 d) is one of the finest local B&Bs, a luxurious log home along Icicle Creek with a flower-filled yard, outside deck, and hot tub. The six guest rooms have private baths and are decorated with knotty-pine furnishing and whimsically rustic decor. Rooms include whirlpool baths surrounded by river rock, bathrooms with rain showers, Egyptian cotton linens, and private decks with mountain views. Be sure to leave the kids behind, as this one is adults only.

Over $250

Tucked away in the hillsides, the luxurious **Mountain Springs Lodge** (19115 Chiwawa Loop Rd., 18 miles NW of Leavenworth, 509/763-2713 or 800/858-2276, www.mtsprings.com, $250–350 d) has cabins with kitchens and private hot tubs, as well as suites with fireplaces, kitchenettes, and spa tubs. There's a two-night minimum on weekends; horseback, wagon, and sleigh rides are available.

Another notable place is **Mountain Home Lodge** (three miles east and 1000 feet above Leavenworth in its own little alpine valley, 509/548-7077 or 800/414-2378, www.mthome.com, $150–360 s or d in summer, $300–530 d in winter), which offers a full breakfast, outdoor pool, hot tub, and tennis in the summer. This is particularly popular in the winter when they groom 40 miles of private cross-country trails and lay out three gourmet meals for guests each day. Guests also can take advantage of cross-country skis, snowshoes, and toboggans on the property. During the winter, guests are taken to the hotel by a private Sno-Cat. It is for adults only.

FOOD

Leavenworth village has a number of restaurants, all very Bavarian from the outside but often more diverse on the inside; even the local McDonald's features pseudo-German architecture (but no bratwurst or *leberkäse*).

Cafés and Diners

Two local places are popular for breakfast. **Sandy's Waffle & Dinner Haus** (894 Hwy. 2, 509/548-6779, daily 7 A.M.–2 P.M.) is crowded most every morning and has all the old breakfast standbys. The **Renaissance Café** (217 8th St., 509/548-6725, Sun.–Thurs. 7 A.M.–3 P.M., Fri.–Sat. 7 A.M.–8 P.M.) strays a bit, with huevos rancheros, pancakes, or omelettes, plus a lunchtime menu of salads, wraps, and salads.

Also recommended is **Uncle Uli's Pub Restaurant** (9th and Front, 509/548-7262, daily 11 A.M.–10 P.M.), where the lunch menu includes soups, salads, great sandwiches, and at least one pasta. Another decent spot for a sandwich or afternoon ice cream is **Tastebuds** (843 Front St., 509/548-7716, daily 9 A.M.–6 P.M.), which also sells German gourmet foods.

Los Camperos (200 8th St., 509/548-3314, Sun.–Thurs. 11 A.M.––9:30 P.M., Fri.–Sat. 11 A.M.–10:30 P.M.) has tasty and reasonably priced Mexican favorites. A good spot for pizzas is **Leavenworth Pizza Co.** (894 Hwy. 2, 509/548-7766, Mon.–Fri. 4–9 P.M., Sat.–Sun. 11 A.M.–9 P.M.).

Steak and Seafood

Visit **Katzenjammer's** (221 8th St., 509/548-5826, Sun.–Thurs. 4–9 P.M., Fri.–Sat. 4–10 P.M.) for a romantic evening with a dinner of Alaskan king crab or prime rib, accompanied with a trip to the salad bar. The dining room decor is reminiscent of an elegant wine cellar, and on summer evenings diners can sup alfresco on the lovely shaded patio.

Bavarian

Several eateries dish out the dense, meaty German fare one expects to find in a Bavarian village. You'll get the real thing at **Café Mozart** (829 Front St., 509/548-0600, daily 11:30 A.M.–9 P.M.) including *leberkäse,* knackwurst, and *kassler kottlets.* Be sure to order the big Bavarian-style pretzels—quite unlike the standard shopping-mall variety—with your brew. Right downstairs at the same address is the similar **Andreas Keller** (509/548-6000, 11 A.M.–8:30 P.M.).

King Ludwig's Gasthaus (921 Front St., 509/548-6625, Sun.–Thurs. 11 A.M.–8:30 P.M., Fri.–Sat. 11:30 A.M.–10 P.M.) features German and Hungarian dishes, along with more standard American faves. **Gustav's** (617 Hwy. 2, 509/548-4509, Sun.–Thurs. 11 A.M.–9 P.M., Fri.–Sat. 11 A.M.–10 P.M.) also serves Germanic fare but is best known for great hamburgers, including an Ortega Mexican burger.

Bakeries and Markets

Leavenworth's bakeshops provide something for all tastes. **The Gingerbread Factory** (828 Commercial St., 509/548-6592 or 800/296-7097, Thurs.–Mon. 8:30 A.M.–4:30 P.M.) is famous for its wonderful soft gingerbread cookies and houses; try the amusingly decorated cookies even if you aren't generally a gingerbread fan. The lunchtime deli here is a local favorite for salads, sandwiches, and espresso.

The Danish Bakery (731 Front St., 509/548-7514, daily 9 A.M.–6 P.M.) sells fresh soft pretzels and outstanding Danish pastries and cookies. Near the fish hatchery is **Homefires Bakery** (13013 Bayne Rd., 509/548-7362, Mon.–Sat. 6 A.M.–6 P.M., Sun. 6 A.M.–5 P.M.), where delicious sourdough breads, pies, and cinnamon rolls emerge from a German brick oven. Homefires is a popular stopping place for hikers and cyclists.

Monaco's Corner Store (703 Front St., 509/548-7216, Sun.–Thurs. 9 A.M.–7 P.M., Fri.–Sat. 9 A.M.–8 P.M.) offers sweets, healthy sandwiches, and espresso coffees.

Leavenworth Farmers Market (509/667-8654) takes place 9 A.M.–1 P.M. Tuesday mid-June to mid-September next to the swimming pool.

INFORMATION AND SERVICES

For maps, brochures, and additional information, stop by the **Leavenworth Chamber of Commerce Visitor Center** (220 9th St., 509/548-5807, www.leavenworth.org, Mon.–Sat. 8:30 A.M.–6 P.M., Sun. 10 A.M.–4 P.M.).

Hikers and campers can chat up the rangers at Wenatchee National Forest **Leavenworth Ranger District** (600 Sherbourne St., 509/548-4067, www.fs.fed.us/r6/Wenatchee, daily 7:45 A.M.–4:30 P.M. mid-June to mid-October, Mon.–Fri. 7:45 A.M.–4:30 P.M. the rest of the year).

The **public library** (509/548-7923) sits right across from Front Street Park and features a periodicals room with a fireplace and stunning mountain vistas.

GETTING THERE AND AROUND

The nearest commercial airport and Amtrak station are in Wenatchee, approximately 30 miles east of Leavenworth.

By Car

Driving to Leavenworth in the winter over Stevens Pass has been described as "driving through a Christmas card." Rocky, snow-covered peaks surround the highway as you approach the 4,061-foot pass; closer to Leavenworth, the Wenatchee River rushes alongside the road through high, rocky walls. The trip from Seattle is about 125 miles. From late fall to early spring, check out the

Department of Transportation's **Mountain Pass Report** (888/766-4636, www.traffic.wsdot.wa.gov/sno-info) for up-to-date info. Have your chains ready! As an alternate route, take I-90 over Snoqualmie Pass to Highway 97 north over Sauk Pass; these passes are generally drier and snow-free earlier than Stevens.

By Bus

Inexpensive local **Link** (800/851-5465, www.linktransit.com) buses connect Leavenworth with other parts of Chelan and Douglas Counties, including Lake Wenatchee, Cashmere, Wenatchee, and the popular tourist destinations of Lake Chelan and the Mission Ridge Ski Area. Buses run Monday–Saturday and can carry bikes in the summer or skis in the winter.

Northwest Trailways (800/366-6975, www.trailways.com) stops in Leavenworth at the Park & Ride near Safeway, with service east to Spokane and west to Everett.

Stevens Pass and Skykomish Valley

U.S. Highway 2 is one of the state's most beautiful drives, and the western end of a transcontinental two-lane route that runs eastward all the way to Maine. Heading west from Leavenworth, the highway enters spectacular Tumwater Canyon, with the roiling Wenatchee River—a popular rafting and kayaking waterway—as a guide into the mountains. The road eventually tops out at 4,061-foot **Stevens Pass,** named for John F. Stevens, the chief locating engineer for the Great Northern Railway that was pushed through here in 1892. (Stevens is perhaps better known as the builder of the Panama Canal.)

At Stevens Pass you'll find popular downhill and cross-country ski areas, and a jumping-off point for the **Pacific Crest Trail.** Serious backpackers can hook up with the Pacific Crest Trail and hike clear up to Canada or down to Mexico if they like—or, more likely, just a short chunk of the trail. Two wilderness areas on either side of the pass—Henry M. Jackson Wilderness and Alpine Lakes Wilderness—contain striking natural features, from glaciers and alpine meadows to dense forests intersected by clear, clean rivers. Much of the area's beauty can be seen through your car windows and from short roadside paths, but hundreds of miles of hiking trails let you experience its splendor at close range.

On the western side of the pass, Highway 2 drops quickly—2,000 feet in 14 miles—to the little town of Skykomish. As you switchback down from the summit, the Burlington Northern railroad tracks emerge from seven-mile-long **Cascade Railroad Tunnel,** one of the longest in the western hemisphere. The drive downhill takes you past rugged snow-covered peaks, plunging waterfalls, popular campgrounds, fishing holes in the Skykomish River, and nature trails to explore along the way. Finally, the grade lessens in the wide Skykomish Valley (a.k.a. "Sky Valley"), as the highway slips through a chain of small towns before emerging into the flat farmland and spreading suburbia near Monroe.

SPORTS AND RECREATION

Alpine Lakes Wilderness Area

The spectacular Alpine Lakes Wilderness covers 393,000 acres of high Cascades country, a diverse landscape ranging in elevation from 1,000-foot valleys to towering 9,000-foot mountain spires. Much of the area—hence the name—is high alpine country filled with some 700 crystalline lakes, ponds, and tarns.

Because of its proximity to Seattle, an abundance of short and long hiking possibilities, and the dramatic alpine-and-lake scenery, this is one of the most heavily used wild places in Washington. In some ways, Alpine Lakes Wilderness is being loved to death; people come to escape city life but instead find crowded backcountry sites and abused trails. Avoid the

© WASHINGTON STATE TOURISM/LEVY SHECKLER

bridge over Skykomish River along Stevens Pass Scenic Byway

crowds by coming here midweek rather than on weekends. To alleviate crowding, the Forest Service has instituted a wilderness permit system that limits the number of hikers in the Enchantment area near Leavenworth. Call the **Alpine Lakes Wilderness information hotline** (206/775-9702 or 800/627-0062) before heading out. Permits are required throughout the wilderness June 15 to October 15. In most areas of the wilderness, free, self-issued permits can be obtained at the trailheads. In the Enchantments, lottery-based permits (www.fs.fed.us/r6/wenatchee/passes/enchantments, $5 per person per day) are required for overnight camping, and they may be obtained anytime after March 1. Midsummer weekends fill up fast, so apply right on March 1 for your best chances. Day use is free in the Enchantments, but you'll need to fill out a permit at the trailhead.

Heading south from Highway 2, the **Pacific Crest Trail** climbs past the downhill ski area and Lake Susan June before reaching Josephine Lake on the wilderness boundary (4.5 miles from the highway). From here, you enter a web of trails that covers the high alpine land, opening up many loop-trip possibilities. Two fun and very popular trails (wilderness permits required) begin from the Foss River Road (Forest Road 68, two miles east of Skykomish). One of these, the **Necklace Valley Trail** (No. 1062) starts up an old narrow-gauge railroad bed before entering a tight canyon and ascending quickly to a cluster of lakes in upper Necklace Valley. The one-way length is 7.5 miles, with a gain of 3,140 feet in elevation. A second excellent short hike is to follow **West Fork Foss River Trail** to Trout Lake, and then on to a chain of half a dozen jewel-like lakes. The one-way distance is seven miles, with an elevation gain of 2,900 feet.

Many popular trails lead into the Enchantment portion of the wilderness, including the seven-mile **Snow Lake Trail,** which starts from Icicle Road out of Leavenworth. Backpackers often use Snow Lake as a base area and day hike into the rugged and spectacular **Enchantment Lakes.**

Henry M. Jackson Wilderness Area

This 103,591-acre mountain wilderness is accessible from the Stevens Pass, Skykomish, Lake Wenatchee, and Darrington areas. It was named for a longtime U.S. senator from Washington, Henry M. Jackson, who was instrumental in helping establish wilderness areas throughout the West. The glacier-carved landscape has a Swiss-Alps quality: numerous alpine lakes, prominent knife-edged ridges, and deep U-shaped valleys. Dozens of backcountry hikes are possible, and ambitious backpackers could continue on into the adjacent Glacier Peak Wilderness Area. The Pacific Crest Trail passes through the center of Henry M. Jackson Wilderness before crossing Highway 2 and continuing on southward into the Alpine Lakes Wilderness.

An interesting and scenic 18-mile loop trek can be made by following the Beckler River Road (Forest Road 65) from the town of Skykomish to Jack Pass and continuing another mile to Forest Road 63. Turn right here, and proceed to the trailhead at the end of the road. The **North Fork Trail** (No. 1051) climbs into high mountain country from here, through masses of hillside wildflowers in midsummer, eventually emerging into the alpine after five miles or so. It meets the Pacific Crest Trail at Dishpan Gap. Turn right and follow the PCT past Lake Sally and then back around 6,368-foot Skykomish Peak to the Pass Creek Trail, which will take you back to your starting point. Another option is to turn left at Dishpan Gap and follow **Bald Eagle Mountain Trail** (No. 650) back to trail No. 1050, which leads back to the road.

Contact the **Skykomish Ranger Station** (360/677-2414) for current conditions, use restrictions, and trail descriptions.

Downhill Skiing

About halfway between Skykomish and Lake Wenatchee is **Stevens Pass Ski Area** (206/812-4510, 206/634-1645 for snow conditions, www.stevenspass.com, $57 adult, $35 kids and seniors, $12 over age 70, $7 under age 6) one of the most popular Alpine ski areas with Seattleites. With a base elevation of 3,821 feet and a summit elevation of 5,845 feet, it features 10 lifts that cover 1,125 acres of beginner through expert terrain. Stevens Pass is generally open mid-November through late April, offering night skiing, ski and snowboard rentals and lessons, a ski shop, restaurant, cafeteria, and cocktail lounges. Many different ski and snowboard schools operate out of Stevens Pass; contact the ski area for a listing. A tubing and sledding area is adjacent to the ski hill.

Lodging is not available at Stevens Pass, although RVs can park in the lot (no hookups). The nearest overnight accommodations are in Skykomish (16 miles west) and Leavenworth (35 miles east).

Cross-Country Skiing

Rent cross country and skate skis at **Stevens Pass Nordic Center** (five miles east of the Stevens Pass downhill area, 360/973-2441, open Fri.–Sun. and on winter holidays, $18.50 adults, $13 youth, $15 seniors, $6.50 kids), which offers 30 kilometers of groomed trails, most of which follow closely along the noisy overhead power lines. The main route climbs uphill for 7.5 kilometers, gaining over 700 feet along the way. Once you work up an appetite, head back to the trailhead, where there's a snack bar with hot food.

River Rafting

The Skykomish River is an extremely popular rafting place during the peak snowmelt period from mid-March to mid-July. The upper portion of the "Sky" from Skykomish to Baring and the South Fork from Skykomish to Index are *not* for beginners. The famous "Boulder Drop" section is class IV+ water, and there are many other deep plunges and vertical drops of class IV. The various commercial rafting companies recommend that anyone running the upper Skykomish have previous rafting experience and be in good physical condition. Trips are available on most early summer weekends, with fewer weekday runs. Some companies restrict Skykomish rafting to those at least 16 years old.

Based in Index, **Chinook Expeditions** (800/241-3451, www.chinookexpeditions.com) runs excellent float and white-water trips, including a six-day Cascade loop trip (May–July, $865) that includes runs down the Skagit, Skykomish, Methow, and Wenatchee rivers. Chinook also offers Skykomish trips ($79) in the fall months when conditions are fast and wild. **Wave Trek** (206/793-1705 or 800/543-7971, www.wavetrek.com, $85) is an Index-based rafting and kayaking company with trips down both the main fork of the Sky, and the wild North Fork. They also teach multi-day kayaking classes for those who want to take a bigger step into river-running.

For a do-it-yourself trip, the lower Skykomish is a peaceful river to raft or kayak, with a few small, generally avoidable, rapids above Sultan. It's rated class II+ from Big Eddy State Park (a.k.a. Sky River State Scenic Park, two miles east of Gold Bar where Highway 2 crosses the river) to Sultan, and class I from Sultan to Monroe.

Waterfalls

The Highway 2 planners must have loved waterfalls: several raging falls are right along the roadside. Easternmost of these is **Deception Falls,** right along the highway approximately seven miles west of Stevens Pass. A short paved path crosses the Tye River and continues to a cascading torrent of water, but much more interesting is the half-mile nature trail that drops down along the river. Educational plaques describe the forest and river, leading to two more impressive cataracts, both backdropped by the deep green rainforest. Some of this is second-growth timber, while other parts were never logged. The lowest falls is the biggest surprise, but I'll let you discover it for yourself. **Deception Creek Trail** starts on the south side of Highway 2 and provides a delicious old-growth forest hike. The trail climbs 10 miles (gaining almost 2,500 feet along the way) to Deception Pass in the Alpine Lakes Wilderness Area, where you can join up with the Pacific Crest Trail.

About 1.5 miles farther west, **Alpine Falls** drops 50 feet into the Tye River below; park on the south side of the highway and follow the can't-miss path. **Bridal Veil Falls,** a quarter mile east of the Index junction, vary with the season; summer brings two distinctive "veils," while winter freezes the falls into a glistening sheet of ice. Scenic **Eagle Falls** on the South Fork Skykomish River is a favorite place for summertime swimmers who play in the big jade-green plunge pool. Be careful if you join in the fun, since there are more falls just downstream. The falls are 11 miles west of Skykomish and right along Highway 2.

Camping

Forest Service campgrounds provide in-the-woods lodging options in the Skykomish vicinity. **Beckler River** and **Money Creek** (518/885-3639 or 877/444-6777, www.recreation.gov, $16, $9 extra reservation fee) are open late May through September. Beckler River is two miles north of Skykomish on Forest Road 65. Money Creek is four miles west of Skykomish and right along Highway 2. Two other, more primitive places—Troublesome Creek and San Juan Campgrounds—are near Jack Pass.

GETTING THERE

Stevens Pass is often a challenge to traverse and is sometimes closed by winter storms. If you're heading up to ski at Stevens Pass or continuing east to Leavenworth or Wenatchee, be sure to check the Department of Transportation's **Mountain Pass Report** (206/368-4499 or 888/766-4636, www.traffic.wsdot.wa.gov/snoinfo). For avalanche and mountain weather information in the winter, call 206/526-6677.

Northwestern Trailways (800/366-6975, www.trailways.com) stops at Stevens Pass, with service east to Spokane and west to Everett and Seattle.

SKY VALLEY

As you head down from the Cascades into Skykomish ("Sky") Valley, several towns pop up along Highway 2, each a little larger than the last, till you reach the edge of Seattle's sprawl at fast-growing Monroe.

Skykomish

The historic railroad town of Skykomish (sky-KOH-mish; pop. 250) is primarily a resting point on the way into or out of the mountains. There's a café with respectable food, a motel and hotel, gas station, and Forest Service office, but not much else. **Sky River Inn** (333 E. River Dr., 360/677-2261 or 800/367-8194, www.skyriverinn.com, $83–145 d) offers comfy rooms right along the Skykomish River. The hotel has a grassy front yard with picnic tables, plus restful river views. This is a popular stopping point for weekend skiers in the winter, so it's a good idea to reserve ahead at those times. The historic **Cascadia Inn and Café** (210 Railroad Ave. E, 360/677-2477, www.historiccascadia.com, $60–85 d) has also long been a favorite among Stevens Pass skiers. The hotel was constructed in 1905, and the back room was popular with card-playing railroad crews. The old depot still stands next to the tracks, but Amtrak doesn't stop on its way through.

Skykomish Ranger Station (360/677-2414, daily 8 A.M.–4:30 P.M. Memorial Day to Labor Day, and Mon.–Fri. 8 A.M.–4:30 P.M. the rest of the year) offers recreation tips and topographic maps, books, and current information on trails and campgrounds.

The **Maloney-Sobieski Mountain Road** provides views of Glacier Peak and deep valleys. To get there, head east from the ranger station for a half mile, then turn left onto Foss River Road 68. Drive about 5.5 miles to the intersection of Roads 68 and 6835; go right onto 6835. When you reach the next fork, stay to the right onto 6846 until the next fork; then go left to Sobieski Mountain or right to Maloney Mountain, with spectacular views on either route.

Over Jack Pass

For a fascinating 26-mile side trip away from busy Highway 2, head up Beckler River Road, which starts a half mile east of Skykomish. The road (Forest Road 65) climbs 13 miles up—the last five are dusty gravel—along the river into Mt. Baker-Snoqualmie National Forest before switchbacking over Jack Pass and down the Galena Road. A forest lookout tower atop **Evergreen Mountain** can be reached via a 1.5-mile one-way hike from the end of Evergreen Mountain Road 6554. The road takes off to the right (east) from Beckler River Road just before you reach Jack Pass. The trail gains 1,300 feet in elevation, but on a clear day the 360-degree view includes Glacier Peak and Mt. Rainier. Regrettably, this trail is open to off-road vehicles. The lookout tower is available for rent (360/677-2414).

Privately owned Garland Hot Springs (near Jack Pass) has a few old buildings and a caretaker who shoos away stray tourists. A mile down Galena Road is primitive **San Juan Campground** ($12), with no running water. Two miles farther downhill is **Troublesome Creek Campground** (518/885-3639 or 877/444-6777, www.recreation.gov, $16, $9 extra reservation fee). Also here is **Troublesome Creek Nature Trail,** a delightful half-mile path through rainforest and canyon. Beyond the campgrounds, Galena Road parallels the North Fork Skykomish River for 10 miles—paved the entire way—ending at Highway 2 near the town of Index. You can also camp for free anywhere on Forest Service land. Just look for the side roads heading into the woods.

Index

Tiny Index (pop. 150) lies a mile off Highway 2 and just across the clear waters of the Skykomish River. This quaint old mining, logging, and quarrying camp has tidy homes, a delightful old lodge, and an almost-encircling Cascade Range backdrop that features the extremely impressive spire of Mt. Index. There are plenty of hiking, rock climbing, steelhead fishing, and mountain biking options in the area. The granite quarry (closed in the 1930s) was the source of stones for the state capitol steps in Olympia.

SIGHTS AND RECREATION

Pickett Historical Museum (505 Ave. A, 360/793-1534, Memorial Day through September Sat.–Sun. noon–3 P.M., $1 adults, free for kids) is housed in a little clapboard structure. Pick up a brochure here that indexes Index's historic buildings. Lee Pickett's extraordinary collection of photographs from the early 1900s makes up the centerpiece of the museum. He was the official photographer for the Great Northern Railway.

Directly behind town rises **Index Town Wall,** a 400-foot granite cliff that's a favorite of Seattle-area rock climbers. A steep path leads much of the way up the slope for those who aren't climbers; ask at the Bush House for directions. **Wave Trek** (360/793-1705 or 800/543-7971, www.wavetrek.com) is an Index-based company that teaches beginner-level climbing classes at the Index Wall.

For a short day hike near Index, try the one-mile one-way hike from Highway 2 just east of town to **Heybrook Lookout.** This Forest Service fire tower provides views of Mt. Index, Baring Mountain, and the Skykomish Valley. Slightly longer (2.2 miles one-way) but with little elevation gain is the **Barclay Lake Trail,** which follows the course of Barclay Creek to the lake with a nice view of Baring Mountain. To get to the trailhead, take Barclay Creek Road 6024 for four miles.

PRACTICALITIES

Index General Store (500 Ave. A, 360/793-0693, daily 8 A.M.–9 P.M. Mar.–Oct., daily 8 A.M.–8 P.M. Nov.–Feb.) is an old-time general store, selling everything from gardening supplies to espresso. Its home-baked goods are especially noteworthy.

Guests will enjoy the solitude at **A Stone's Throw Bed and Breakfast** (360/793-0100, www.acabinonthesky.com, $90 d). There's only one room available in this 1912 home, but you get the entire upper floor to yourself, including a bath and private hot tub; full breakfast is included.

A Rivers Edge Country Cottage (360/793-0392, $90 d) is a cottage with a kitchen, full breakfast, and spa in the courtyard. Kids are accepted.

Index has a popular **Easter Sunday Pancake Breakfast,** but the town's big shindig comes on **Memorial Day Weekend** with ballgames, a goofy relay fun run, and a popular spaghetti feed. Of course, the town's **4th of July** has the all-American standards: a parade, crafts fair, live music, a rubber-duck derby, and fireworks echoing off the surrounding mountains.

Community Transit (425/353-7433 or 800/562-1375, www.commtrans.org) has daily bus service to Index and other parts of Snohomish County.

Wallace Falls State Park

Located two miles northeast of Gold Bar, this 678-acre park (360/793-0420, www.parks.wa.gov, daily in the summer, Wed.–Sun. Oct.–mid-Apr.) is famous for its towering 265-foot cataract (visible from Highway 2). A half dozen gorgeously situated walk-in tent sites are available ($12; no showers), but the main attraction is the falls. Two routes lead to Wallace Falls, an easy path along an old railroad grade that's open to mountain bikes, and a steeper route (Woody Trail) that follows closer to the river. The two trails join for the last 1.5 miles, with several viewpoints along the way, including one atop the falls. The hike to the falls is six miles round-trip via Woody Trail and eight miles round-trip via the old railroad grade. Along the way, you gain almost 1,400 feet in elevation.

Startup and Gold Bar

Located in an old church, the **Parallax Gallery** (360/793-9588) in minuscule Startup has an interesting collection of fine art, ceramics, and jewelry by local artists. They also serve espresso.

The small **Gold Bar Museum** (360/793-2138) in Gold Bar is open summers Saturday–Sunday noon–3 P.M. Just west of here is the turnoff to **Skykomish State Salmon Hatchery,** a small operation of interest to anglers.

Located along Highway 2 a mile east of Monroe, the **Reptile Serpentarium** (22715-B Hwy. 2, 360/793-2000, www.reptileman.com, daily 10 A.M.–6 P.M., $6) claims to house one of the most complete collections of reptiles on the West Coast, including anacondas and black mambas. Kids get to hold 10 of the snakes.

For an interesting drive or mountain bike ride, head up Kellogg Lake Road out of Startup and follow it four miles to Sultan Basin Road. Turn right and continue uphill along Olney Creek to Spada Lake (Everett's water source; no swimming or motorboating allowed). The last part of the road is gravel and can be dusty in the summer, but the fine mountain and river vistas make this a pleasant trip.

Community Transit (425/353-7433 or 800/562-1375, www.commtrans.org) has daily bus service to Gold Bar and Startup, along with other parts of Snohomish County.

Sultan

Sultan (pop. 3,000) is home to the **Sultan Summer Shindig** the second weekend of July, with a parade, games, food booths, and arts and crafts displays. You'll also find live music at Sultan River Park on summer Sundays. The town itself doesn't have much to offer, though you may want to take a look at the tiny wayside chapel two miles west of town. The clean and friendly **Dutch Cup Motel** (819 Main St., 360/793-2215 or 800/844-0488, www.dutchcup.com, $64–88 d) is a favorite among Highway 2 travelers and Stevens Pass Skiers. Penny-pinchers can find kitchenettes in some rooms, and ski packages are available. This is also Sultan's de facto chamber of commerce headquarters.

For something different, camp north of town at **Lake Bronson Family Nudist Park** (360/793-0286, $7 tent, $15 RV with water and electric). This 320-acre resort includes a lodge, lake, sauna, hot tub, café, campsites, RV park, and more. Call for directions.

The **Sultan Farmers Market** (360/793-2565, 9 A.M.–2 P.M. Sat. May–Sept.) is held in River Park.

Community Transit (425/353-7433 or 800/562-1375, www.commtrans.org) has daily bus service to Sultan and other parts of Snohomish County.

MONROE

Located just 30 commuter-miles from Seattle and 50 weekend-miles from downhill skiing at Stevens Pass, the town of Monroe is a booming bedroom community of condos, tract houses, and more established residences. A local promotional brochure brags about the "thoughtful planning" that makes Monroe such a great place to live. But first impressions—especially if you're coming from the relatively undeveloped Cascades or the pretty town of Snohomish—are a bit different. Highway 2 through Monroe is a sickening chain of strip malls, fast-food joints, and neon signs. Despite this, there is at least one redeeming quality that attracts visitors to Monroe: the state fair.

The small **Monroe Historical Society Museum** (207 E. Main St., 360/794-7056, 11 A.M.–3 P.M. Sat. April–Labor Day) houses local memorabilia and videos from old-timers. Also of interest is the open farmland that surrounds Monroe (at least till the "thoughtful planning" spreads out more) and pleasant backcountry roads that are great for bike riding. To the south are **U-pick farms** for strawberries, raspberries, and blueberries, and farm stands offering fresh produce. Horse owners especially like the mild climate here, making Monroe a regional center for horse training and breeding.

Evergreen State Fairgrounds

On the west end of Monroe sits the enormous Evergreen State Fair (360/794-7832 or 360/794-4344) complex, which features a raceway, outdoor arena, exhibit halls, and a 3,000-seat indoor Equestrian Park—one of the finest on the West Coast. The fairgrounds are the site of major equestrian shows all year long, including the **Washington Hunter/Jumper Spring Nationals** in April, the **Pacific Northwest Quarter Horse Shows** in May and September, along with a diversity of other events: medieval tournaments in January, a big craft show in April, an antique car show in May, and a Christmas crafts fair in December.

The biggest month is August, when the calendar is packed with activities, including an **Old Time Threshing Bee** and the ever-popular **Evergreen State Fair,** the largest fair in Washington. Besides all the usual fair activities—agricultural displays, live entertainment, food and craft booths, and carnival rides—there's a fun run, parade, and all sorts of other activities. The fair lasts for 11 days, from the last full week in August through Labor Day weekend.

Also at the fairgrounds is the **Evergreen Speedway** (360/794-7711, www.evergreenspeedway.com), where you can watch NASCAR auto racing, demolition derbies (biggest of all is on the 4th of July), and other contests of bravado late March to mid-September.

Camping

The closest public campsites ($12 tents, $17 RVs) are in two county parks: **Flowing Lake Park** (10 miles north of Monroe, 360/568-2274, open year-round, no water in the winter months) and **Lake Roesiger Park** (12 miles north of Monroe, 360/568-5836, open mid-May through September). Both of these parks have popular swimming beaches, and Flowing Lake has ranger-led nature hikes, along with Saturday-night amphitheater programs in the summer.

Park RVs ($10) or pitch tents ($5) during events at **Evergreen State Fairgrounds** (360/794-4344).

Accommodations

The nicest local motel is **Best Western Baron Inn** (19233 Hwy. 2, 360/794-3111 or 800/238-7234, www.bestwesternwashington.com, $79 s or $89 d), which features an outdoor pool, hot tub, exercise room, and continental breakfast, plus free wireless Internet. Also serviceable is the **Holiday Inn** (19103 Hwy. 2, 360/863-1900, www.rogueweb.com/holidaymonroe, $89 s or $109 d) with 66 rooms and access to an indoor pool and fitness center.

Food

Although the scent of deep-fry cookers often pervades Monroe's air, several local places go beyond this greasy menu. Start the day at **Monroe Café** (19837 Hwy. 2, 360/794-6940), where breakfast is served all day. **Hitching Post Café** (107 W. Main St., 360/805-5495) is a popular family spot downtown for breakfast and lunch. **Sky River Bakery** (117 W. Main, 360/794-7434, Tues.–Fri. 7 A.M.–5 P.M., Sat. 7 A.M.–4 P.M., closed Sun.–Mon.) serves Starbucks coffee and fresh-baked goodies.

You'll find very good seafood at **Sailfish Bar & Grill** (104 N. Lewis, 360/794-4056, daily 5–10 P.M.). The same building houses the classy **Twin Rivers Brewery.** And, of course, there's always McDonald's, Burger King, Domino's, KFC, Skippers, or Taco Time if you just want to eat and escape Monroe as fast as possible.

Information

The **Monroe Chamber of Commerce** (211 E. Main St., 360/794-5488, chamber.monroe.net, Mon.–Fri. 9:30 A.M.–4 P.M.) offers brochures about the area.

Getting There

Community Transit (425/353-7433 or 800/562-1375, www.commtrans.org) has daily bus service from Monroe to other parts of Snohomish County.

SOUTH CASCADES

Washington's identity is inextricably tied to the breathtaking beauty of Washington's tallest and best-known peak, the perennially snowcapped Mt. Rainier. To the residents of Puget Sound, it is simply "The Mountain," a singular peak towering above all others in the Cascades.

A pilgrimage to its base (and for some, its summit) is a must for any Washington traveler, who will be dazzled by surrounding alpine meadows, thundering waterfalls, up-close encounters with glaciers and wildlife, and—if the mountain chooses to peek out from under the clouds—a neck-crick-inducing view of the peak that is more impressive than the postcards imply.

But Mt. Rainier isn't nearly the only natural wonder in the vast recreational playground of the South Cascades. Here too are the mountain's volcanic siblings—temperamental and denuded Mount St. Helens, and remote and wild Mt. Adams beg to be explored as well. Surrounding all of it are untouched tracts of wilderness, hiking trails galore, ski summits and cross country trails, chilly glacier lakes full of trout, and gurgling creeks meant to be paired with a pitched tent and a crackling fire.

PLANNING YOUR TIME

Recreation junkies can spend a whole summer or a lifetime wandering the trails and peaks of the South Cascades. When you've got limited time, the big visits are to Mt. Rainier and Mount St. Helens. Seattle visitors can conceivably drive by both in a single day, as they are only a couple of hours away from one another,

© ERICKA CHICKOWSKI

HIGHLIGHTS

Snoqualmie Falls: Made famous by David Lynch in his eerie 1990s classic *Twin Peaks*, this is the most easily accessible and picturesque waterfall in the state (page 538).

Roslyn: Another darling of TV fans, this quiet village is as cute in real life as it looked when it played Cicely, Alaska, in *Northern Exposure* (page 544).

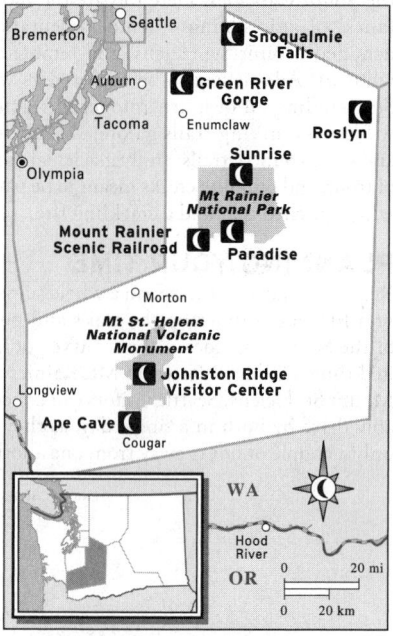

LOOK FOR TO FIND RECOMMENDED SIGHTS, ACTIVITIES, DINING, AND LODGING.

Green River Gorge: The emerald banks of this white-water retreat are bookended by two fabulous state parks (page 548).

Mount Rainier Scenic Railroad: You'll get enough snapshot opportunities to fill a photo album aboard the open-air car chugging along this line (page 551).

Paradise: The first European settlers gave the flower-filled subalpine valley beneath Rainier its heavenly name the moment they set foot there. No one's argued with their assessment ever since (page 559).

Sunrise: The highest point you can reach by automobile in the entire Mount Rainier National Park, this spot offers the most stunning views of the mountain and dozens of trails for exploration (page 561).

Johnston Ridge Visitor Center: Even nearly 30 years after Mount Saint Helens blew its top, the surrounding blast zone is an awesome sight. See the toothpick-like timbers strewn in Spirit Lake, the remnants of mudflows, and the mountain itself from a perch on this ridge (page 587).

Ape Cave: Formed when St. Helens erupted 1,900 years ago, these lava tubes were carved out when a lava flow cooled on the surface but magma continued to ooze below ground for a short time (page 588).

but most of that time would be spent in the seated position. Travelers should ideally plan a week at minimum to get out on the trails.

Ideal summertime exploration falls between snowmelt and first snowfall, usually between July and September. Visitors need to be aware of weather conditions prior to heading out. This area of the Cascades typically sees heavy snowfall from as early as October until as late as May, which can be a good or a bad thing depending on your perspective. Certain roads and attractions are closed, but others open up to a whole new dimension of recreational activity only possible when snowdrifts are present.

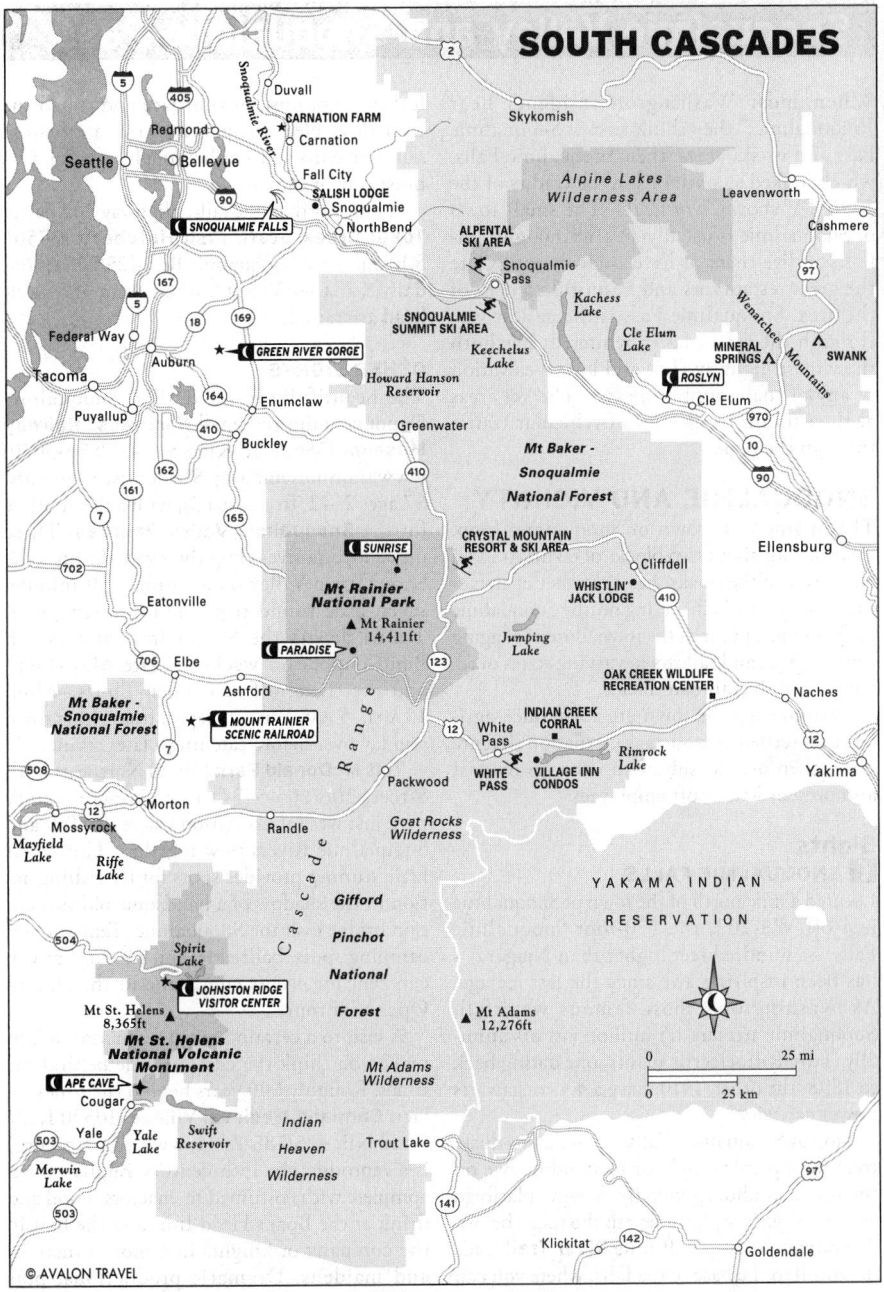
SOUTH CASCADES
Duvall
CARNATION FARM
Carnation
Snoqualmie River
Redmond
Seattle
Bellevue
Fall City
SALISH LODGE
Snoqualmie
NorthBend
SNOQUALMIE FALLS
Skykomish
Alpine Lakes Wilderness Area
Leavenworth
Cashmere
ALPENTAL SKI AREA
Snoqualmie Pass
Kachess Lake
SNOQUALMIE SUMMIT SKI AREA
Cle Elum Lake
Wenatchee Mountains
MINERAL SPRINGS
SWANK
Federal Way
Auburn
GREEN RIVER GORGE
Tacoma
Keechelus Lake
Howard Hanson Reservoir
ROSLYN
Cle Elum
Puyallup
Enumclaw
Greenwater
Buckley
Mt Baker - Snoqualmie National Forest
SUNRISE
CRYSTAL MOUNTAIN RESORT & SKI AREA
Cliffdell
Ellensburg
Eatonville
Mt Rainier National Park
WHISTLIN' JACK LODGE
Mt Rainier 14,411ft
PARADISE
Jumping Lake
Elbe
OAK CREEK WILDLIFE RECREATION CENTER
Naches
Ashford
Mt Baker - Snoqualmie National Forest
MOUNT RAINIER SCENIC RAILROAD
INDIAN CREEK CORRAL
White Pass
Rimrock Lake
WHITE PASS
VILLAGE INN CONDOS
Yakima
Packwood
Morton
Mossyrock
Randle
Goat Rocks Wilderness
Mayfield Lake
Riffe Lake
Cascade Range
YAKAMA INDIAN RESERVATION
Gifford Pinchot National Forest
Spirit Lake
JOHNSTON RIDGE VISITOR CENTER
Mt St. Helens 8,365ft
Mt St. Helens National Volcanic Monument
Mt Adams 12,276ft
Mt Adams Wilderness
APE CAVE
Cougar
Yale
Yale Lake
Swift Reservoir
Indian Heaven Wilderness
Trout Lake
Merwin Lake
Klickitat
Goldendale
0 25 mi
0 25 km
© AVALON TRAVEL

Snoqualmie Valley and Snoqualmie Pass

When most Washington residents hear "Snoqualmie," they think first of Snoqualmie Pass and its ski areas, then Snoqualmie Falls, which looked so ominous in the credits of the 1990 TV show *Twin Peaks.* The small town of Snoqualmie is usually an afterthought, unless you live there or have come to appreciate the great restaurants and beautiful scenery of the area. Snoqualmie Pass is the easiest way through the Cascades in winter: It has both the widest highway (I-5) and lowest elevation of any of the mountain passes. The ski areas at the summit bring a lot of vehicular traffic through the region.

SNOQUALMIE AND VICINITY

The quaint little town of Snoqualmie (pop. 2,000), with about two blocks of civilization on either side of the tracks, has a number of attractions worth a look, including nearby Snoqualmie Falls. As you approach the town, dozens of aging train engines and railcars in varying states of repair crowd the railroad tracks.

Surrounding the town are a few once-agricultural settlements such as Carnation that are now taken over as suburban enclaves by past and present Microsoft employees.

Sights

SNOQUALMIE FALLS

Located a mile north of the town of Snoqualmie just off WA-202, the 270-foot Snoqualmie Falls—a hundred feet higher than Niagara—has been inspiring awe since the last ice age. As Washington's most famous waterfall, Snoqualmie attracts 1.5 million visitors annually. Two hydroelectric plants, one dating back to 1898, the other, 1910, have a 4.4-megawatts power capacity.

Stop at Snoqualmie Falls (open dawn–dusk, free) for a picnic lunch, or to stand in awe on the non-acrophobic-friendly viewing platform as the noisy river plummets to the rocks below. A moderately steep half-mile **River Trail** leads downhill to the base of the falls, where you can feel the cool mist on your face and watch the river flow. Near the parking area, a gift shop sells souvenirs and a rather rough espresso. Pets must stay in the car.

A mile north of the falls, Highway 202 passes **Tokul Creek State Fish Hatchery** (37501 S.E. Fall City-Snoqualmie Rd., 425/222-5464, daily 8 A.M.–4:30 P.M.), where trout and steelhead are raised.

OTHER SIGHTS

The beautifully restored 1890 Snoqualmie Depot contains the small **Northwest Railway Museum** (38625 SE King St., 425/888-3030, www.trainmuseum.org, $10 adults, $9 seniors, $7 ages 2–12, free under 3), with a ticket office for the **Snoqualmie Valley Railroad.** These diesel locomotives chug their way through the Snoqualmie Valley on a leisurely 50-minute, seven-mile round-trip ride to North Bend. Trains depart the Snoqualmie and North Bend depots on weekends late May–Oct., and the ticket office is open Thurs.–Mon. 10 A.M.–5 P.M. You can depart from either town and lay over before catching a later train.

Tolt McDonald Park (31020 Northeast 40th Street, 206/205-5434) is a 574-acre county park just west of Carnation where the Tolt and Snoqualmie Rivers flow together. This secret little stunner provides spots for fly-fishing action in the shadow of a handsome old suspension bridge over the Snoqualmie. Tent and RV camping spots, ballfields, and a barn that you can rent for events contribute to the charm. Open year round.

A visit to a certain part of Carnation might make you think the city is a little behind the times. Roughly 600 years behind the times, in fact. **Camlann Medieval Village** (10320 Kelly Road NE, 425/788-8624, www.camlann.org) is a reproduction 15th-century English town complete with costumed re-enactors. Food and drink at the Boar's Head Inn taste the best in the company of knights in armor, minstrels, and maidens. Dramatic productions, plus

© ERICKA CHICKOWSKI

The thundering waters of Snoqualmie Falls are at their best in winter.

crafts and food, can be enjoyed year-round. Special programs are offered on Michaelmas, Yuletide, St. George's Feast, and other obscure dates throughout the year.

In the middle of this is **Remlinger Farms** (32610 N.E. 32nd in Carnation, 425/333-4135) with pick-your-own berries, pumpkins, and other produce in season.

Events and Entertainment

Set amongst towering evergreens at the foot of the falls, the **Snoqualmie Falls Forest Theater** (36800 SE David Powell Rd., 425/222-7044, www.foresttheater.org) has stage performances and barbecue dinners Fri.–Sun. in July and August. This is the only outdoor dinner theater in Washington. Tickets run around $18, and reservations are required for dinner shows.

The newly opened **Casino Snoqualmie** (37500 SE North Bend Way, www.casinosnoqualmie.com) intends to put a distinctly Northwest spin on Vegas-style gambling. The log-and-lodgepole architecture, the 24-hour espresso stand, and the forested setting make this casino as "Seattle" as a well-worn raincoat. Complete with five dining options, two entertainment stages, over 1600 slot machines, craps, roulette, blackjack, and a 17-table poker area let you have an exciting time.

Accommodations

The **Salish Lodge** (6501 Railroad Ave., 425/888-2556 or 800/826-6124, www.salishlodge.com, $299–499 s or d), atop Snoqualmie Falls, is easily the most luxurious hotel in the area, featuring a fireplace, hot tub, feather bed with goose-down comforter in every room, plus a balcony in most. Further treats include a fully equipped exercise room, sauna and steam room, hydrotherapy pools, tanning booths, massage rooms, library, and one of the finest restaurants in the area. This is a great place for a honeymoon or a getaway weekend; plunk down $849 for a particularly sweet suite.

A strange and wonderful stay is guaranteed at **Bethabara Farms Bed and Breakfast** (35909 SE 94th St., 425/888-2549, www.bethabarafarms.com, $95 s or $125 d), also known as the House in the Trees. This eclectic structure resembles not so much an inn as a stamp mill, but don't be fooled. The unusual design is brilliantly complemented by the comfortable rooms, the wide and flowery grounds, and the delicious country breakfast served each morning.

Located on five wooded acres, **Windsong Farm B&B** (515 286th Ave. SE, 425/222-4734) is a charming modern farmhouse with a single guest room. A full breakfast is served. The B&B is a favorite of bird-watchers.

The privately run **Snoqualmie River Campground** (34807 S.E. 44th Pl., 425/222-5545, www.srcghsg.com, $30 with hookups and dump privileges) in Fall City has 91 RV sites and 31 tent spaces. **Tolt MacDonald Park** (31020 NE 40th St.) just outside of town has tent sites for $18 per night, RV sites with hookups for $28 per night, or yurts for $40 per night.

Food

The **Salish Lodge Restaurant** (6501 Railroad Ave., 425/888-2556) atop Snoqualmie Falls has run continuously since 1916. The dinner menu features seafood and game entrées at around the price-point you'd expect for such lavish digs. The farm-style four-course Sunday brunch remains a regional favorite. The homey lodge atmosphere complete with overstuffed chairs surrounding a warm fire in the lounge is worth the price of admission. Reservations are required, especially if you want a window seat.

Opened in 1997 by a group of local beer connoisseurs, the **Snoqualmie Falls Brewing Company** (8032 Falls Ave., 425/831-2337, www.fallsbrew.com, Mon.–Thurs. 11 A.M.–10 P.M., Fri.–Sat. 11 A.M.–11 P.M., Sun. 11 A.M.–9 P.M.) has fast been racking up awards and loyal fans with its excellent Wildcat IPA, Copperhead Pale Ale, Snoqualmie ESB, Steam Train Porter, and several seasonal beers. Pick any and pair it with a bit of satisfying pub grub served up in the brewery's taproom.

Getting There and Around

Seattle's **Metro** (206/447-4800, $2.25 one-way) bus routes 209 and 214 serve Snoqualmie Falls, Snoqualmie, and North Bend.

NORTH BEND

Located at the foot of Mt. Si, the settlement of North Bend (pop. 4,000) is the last Snoqualmie River town before I-90 climbs into the Cascade Range. This sleepy little burg provides many people with bottled water, gas, and beef jerky before they tackle nearby trails.

Sights

The **Snoqualmie Valley Museum** (320 Bendigo Blvd. South, 425/888-3200, www.snoqualmievalleymuseum.org, Thurs.–Sun. 1–5 P.M. April–Oct., and the first two weeks of December, donation) has permanent displays of Native American artifacts and pioneer and logging history, and a small gift shop.

Shopping

Hikers with family members unappreciative of the great outdoors will thank their lucky stars for the **Factory Stores at North Bend** (461 South Fork Avenue SW, 425/888-4505, Mon.–Sat. 10 A.M.–8 P.M., Sun. 10 A.M.–5 P.M.). This sprawling collection of brand-name outlets such as Adidas, Nine West, and Van Heusen is one of the best and closest to the Seattle, and a good excuse to get the non-trekkers out to North Bend.

Sports and Recreation

MOUNT SI AND LITTLE SI

The 4,167-foot-tall Mt. Si is a classic area hike, running about eight miles round-trip. The 3,100-foot elevation gain makes the trail a popular off-season training-ground for locals, so don't come here expecting solitude. On a clear day, the views at the summit can be worth the considerable physical effort. To reach the trailhead, turn left on 432nd SE (Mt. Si Road) about a mile from the east edge of North Bend. After you cross the Middle Fork of the Snoqualmie River, go right at the first intersection, then drive 2.5 miles to the parking lot, trailhead, and picnic area. The trail is generally snow-free April to November.

An easier alternative to Mt. Si is Little Si, offering views across Snoqualmie Valley. The trail is 2.5 miles each way and offers a still-considerable 1,574-foot gain. Get to the trailhead by following North Bend Way a half mile southeast from the Forest Service Ranger Station to Mt. Si Road; then turn left and go a half mile to a bridge. Park at the gravel lot here across the bridge, and walk downhill to the signed trailhead just past the fifth house on the right.

TWIN FALLS

Just a short distance from busy I-90, at **Olallie State Park** (www.parks.wa.gov), the South Fork of the Snoqualmie River drops 300 feet over a stunning series of cataracts. The park is accessible from exit 34 (five miles east of North Bend); after exiting, turn right on Edgewick Road, and then left onto S.E. 159th St.; continue a half mile to the park. A 1.3-mile path leads to Twin Falls, and from there, you can cross a footbridge and continue uphill another 1.6 miles to a second trailhead near exit 38. Day use only, and no mountain bikes or horses allowed on the trails. Olallie State Park continues eastward along the river above Twin Falls, with several good spots for catching hatchery trout.

The 113-mile-long **Iron Horse State Park** trail (www.parks.wa.gov) also starts from Olallie State Park and follows a gentle old railroad grade over Snoqualmie Pass and all the way down to the Columbia River, 113 miles later. See *Cle Elum* for details on this popular hiking, horseback riding, biking, and ski trail.

RATTLESNAKE MOUNTAIN SCENIC AREA

Peak-baggers who don't feel up to taking on Mount Si for the day are quite fond of the 1.5-mile walk up Rattlesnake Mountain to the 2,079-foot **Rattlesnake Ledge,** with amazing views of the Snoqualmie Valley, Mount Si, and **Rattlesnake Lake** below. Munch on a lunch on the flat rock ledge or wait to head down and picnic on the lake, watching anglers spin and fly cast for the regularly stocked trout swimming in the chilly water. To get to the lake and the trailhead, take exit 32 off I-90, go south on 436th Ave. SE and drive 3.1 miles to the parking area.

CAMPGROUNDS

Pitch your tent or park your trailer at one the convenient Forest Service campgrounds in the Mount Baker-Snoqualmie National Forest. Situated along the South Fork of the Snoqualmie River, **Tinkham Campground** (exit 42 off I-90, drive east on Tinkham Road 55 for 1.5 mi., 541/338-7869, www.recreation.gov, $14–16) is a favorite among local Scout troops who'd like to get out in the woods but don't want to get *too* far from civilization. Same goes for **Denny Creek Campground** (exit 47 off I-90, take left and go under freeway then follow signs to campground 3 mi. away, 541/338-7869, www.recreation.gov, $18 tent, $24 RV), which sits in a valley under the I-90 overpass high above. Tinkham welcomes small RVs but has no hookups, and Denny Creek has electric-only hookups. Both sites are located near a bunch of great trailheads, including the Denny Creek Trail, which leads to some fun natural water slides only a mile away from the campground. Both sites also offer a couple of barrier-free campsites. Both are open May–September.

Accommodations

Lodging isn't fancy in North Bend, but the motels here do make a cheap stop for those heading west over the pass toward Seattle. **Edgewick Inn** (14600 468th Ave. SE, 425/888-9000, $75 s or $85 d) doesn't have the absolute cheapest rooms, but with easy freeway access and updated and well-kept rooms it is the best value. There is a microwave and a fridge in the lobby available for guest use.

The Roaring River at North Bend B&B (46715 S.E. 129th St., 425/888-4834 or 877/627-4647, www.theroaringriver.com, $109–175 d, no kids) offers views of the Middle Fork of the Snoqualmie River. Most of the five rooms have private entrances and baths, gas fireplaces, and decks. A warm breakfast basket is delivered to your door.

Food

George's Bakery (127 W. North Bend Way, 425/888-0632, Tues. 7 A.M.–3 P.M., Wed.–Sun.

7 A.M.–5 P.M., closed Mon.) is a favorite local gathering place that serves sweets, fresh-baked breads, sandwiches, and salads.

The standout place in North Bend is **Gaston's** (101 W. North Bend Way, 425/888-1803), with a romantic atmosphere and food that includes a variety of reasonably priced homemade pastas. Delicious desserts, too.

Information and Services

The **North Bend Ranger Station** (902 SE North Bend Way, Bldg. 1, 425/888-1421, Mon.–Fri. 8 A.M.–4:30 P.M.), a half mile east of town, has information on local trails, mountain bike routes, and campgrounds. The **Upper Snoqualmie Valley Chamber of Commerce** has a small visitors center at the North Bend Train Depot (205 E. McClellan St., 425/292-9176, www.snovalley.org), where they will be glad to provide you with maps, brochures, and other information.

Getting There and Around

Seattle's **Metro** buses (206/447-4800 or 800/542-7876) serve North Bend and surrounding communities. **Greyhound** (800/231-2222, www.greyhound.com) stops in North Bend at the corner of 219 Main Ave. S, with connections throughout the nation.

SNOQUALMIE PASS

Sports and Recreation

SKIING

Located 53 miles from downtown Seattle, and right along I-90's Snoqualmie Pass is **The Summit at Snoqualmie** (425/434-7669, www.summitatsnoqualmie.com, $35–55), Washington's oldest and largest downhill ski area. The four separate areas, **Alpental, Summit West, Summit Central,** and **Summit East,** range from beginner trails to backcountry and advanced slopes.

Snoqualmie's **Summit Nordic Center** is a cross-country playground with over 31 miles of groomed and tracked trails, and the weekends-only **Summit Tubing Area** ($12–17) rents inner tubes and offers lighted rope tows. Summit at Snoqualmie services include ski shops, equipment rentals, ski schools, day lodges, food service, child care, and bus service to the area.

© WASHINGTON STATE TOURISM/LEVY SHECKLER

The Alpine Lakes Wilderness is one of the state's finest hiking grounds.

NIGHT SKIING

More and more skiers are being attracted to nighttime at the mountain. Lower-priced lift tickets, smaller crowds, plus a major coolness factor have driven many of Washington's premier ski resorts to stay open a few hours after darkness falls. It can be a great comfort, especially when this northern-latitude state starts getting dark outside well before 5 P.M.

Most of the ski areas at **Summit at Snoqualmie** are open until 10 P.M. Tuesday through Sunday. Even the tubing park is open until 9 P.M. on Friday and Saturday.

White Pass near Mt. Rainier offers a $20 deal for night skiing, or do it in the dark for free if you bought a daytime pass.

Wenatchee's **Mission Ridge** offers a night-skiing lift pass for $15, lasting 4–9 P.M.

ALPINE LAKES WILDERNESS

Snoqualmie Pass is one of the most accessible portals into the Alpine Lakes Wilderness, which stretches between I-90 and Highway 2 at Stevens Pass and Leavenworth. You'll find a number of classic northwest treks in this southern reach of the Alpine Lakes area, including the breathtaking stretch of the Pacific Crest Trail over **Kendal Katwalk** (PCT trailhead at exit 53 westbound and 52 eastbound off I-90), an exhilarating strip of trail that clings to the granite mountainside, seemingly floating amid a colorful display of wildflowers in spring and summer. You can make it to the Katwalk and back (10.5 miles) in a long day, but many adventurous backpackers prefer to extend the trip to a 33-mile round-trip through meadows and alpine forests to the 6,700-foot pinnacle of Spectacle Point, which provides a breathtaking panorama of the northern Alpine Lakes territory. Just beware of snow—under no circumstances should you attempt to cross the precarious Katwalk when the white stuff is on the ground.

CAMPGROUNDS

RV parking is permitted at the summit parking lots, but no hookups are available.

Summertime visitors will find camping just a few miles over the pass at **Kachess Lake Campground** (exit 62, then Forest Road 49 approximately 5 miles to campground, 509/649-3744, www.reserveamerica.com, mid-May–mid-Sept., $17), which has tent sites and can accommodate RVs up to 35 feet, though there are no hookups. The blue-green lake offers swimming, boating, picnicking, and a nature trail. Its accessibility from the freeway and to the trails make this an extremely popular place to roast up s'mores, so you're taking a gamble coming here without reservations on a holiday weekend, though there are a number of sites available on a first-come, first-served basis.

Crystal Springs Campground (exit 62, then right on Forest Road 54 for 0.5 mi., 509/852-1100, mid-May–mid-Sept.) is another favorite base camp retreat for Seattleites with just a spare weekend to get outside. Smaller than Kachess, the grounds tend to be quieter and all sites are first-come, first served.

Accommodations

The **Summit Lodge at Snoqualmie Pass** (603 Hwy. 906, 425/434-6300 or 800/557-7829, www.snoqualmiesummitlodge.com, $139–259) pretty much has the corner on the lodging market up by the Snoqualmie slopes, but it doesn't let the position get too much to its head. Rooms are decent and clean and the property has an indoor pool, hot tub, sauna, and a restaurant. Though rates can be on the high side on winter weekends and holidays, discounts are frequently available at other times.

Sitting directly on the slopes, **Valley High Mountain Lodge** (425/432-1409, $450–600) is an ideal retreat for large groups and big families. This large chalet-style home sleeps a whopping 16, with a kitchen and two fireplaces to warm by once the chairlifts stop turning. Call for directions.

Food

Atop Snoqualmie Pass, **Family Pancake House** at the Summit Inn (425/434-6249, Sun.–Thurs. 6 A.M.–9 P.M., Fri.–Sat. 6 A.M.–11 P.M.) serves hearty meals in front of their enormous fireplace. Have some fluffy pancakes and coffee and let your parka dry off. Food is also available at all four ski areas in the winter.

Information

Snoqualmie Pass Visitor Center (at Snoqualmie Summit, 425/434-6111, Memorial Day–Labor Day, Thurs.–Mon. 8:30 A.M.–3:30 P.M., Jan.–Mar. Fri.–Sun. 8:30 A.M.–3:30 P.M.) has information and issues wilderness permits. This is also the meeting point for Forest Service ranger-led snowshoe hikes in the winter. Hikes are held Friday–Sunday for $10, including snowshoes and poles. The Forest Service is also experimenting with interpretive hikes in the summer. Call for the schedule.

Getting There

Although Snoqualmie Pass is generally the easiest way to traverse the Cascades, it does get snowy and sometimes closes during heavy storms. Contact the Department of Transportation for the **Mountain Pass Report** (888/766-4636, www.traffic.wsdot.wa.gov/sno-info). The website includes a webcam showing current conditions at Snoqualmie Pass.

Cle Elum and Vicinity

The towns of Cle Elum and Roslyn provide interesting side trips or starting points for hiking or horseback treks into the magnificent Cascade mountain country just to the north and west. Access is easy, with I-90 cutting down from Snoqualmie Pass along the upper Yakima River Valley, passing fields, farms, and stream-laced valleys as you descend.

CLE ELUM

Cle Elum (KLEE-ell-UM, a Native American name meaning Swift Water) was settled in 1870 by Thomas L. Gamble, but growth was slow until geologists working for the Northern Pacific Railroad discovered coal in 1884. A forest fire in the late 1880s wiped out a large part of the mining town, but additional coal veins discovered in 1889 gave Cle Elum four quite prosperous years. Today the town is a jumping-off point for hiking, fishing, and other recreational activities in the Wenatchee National Forest.

Sights

MUSEUMS

Cle Elum was the last place in America to use a manually operated switchboard, and the last to institute the touch-tone dial system. The old phone building was transformed into the **Cle Elum Historical Telephone Museum** (221 E. 1st St., 509/674-5702, noon–4 P.M. Sat.–Sun. Memorial Day–Labor Day, and by appointment the rest of the year, free). Inside this surprisingly well-done little museum are switchboard exhibits, photographs of early Cle Elum, and other memorabilia. For something different, try the "coal" candy sold here.

The spacious **Carpenter Museum** (302 W. 3rd St., 509/674-5702, noon–4 P.M. Sat.–Sun. Memorial Day–Labor Day, free) was built in 1914 by a prosperous local banker, Frank Carpenter. His granddaughter donated it, along with much of the original furnishings—including Tiffany lamps, an oak dining table with 11 leaves, and a beautifully carved rosewood chair—to the local historical society.

ROSLYN

Located almost at road's end on Highway 903, the little town of Roslyn has long been a favorite of Washingtonians. Roslyn's main attractions are its Old-West false-fronted buildings, many of which appeared in the 1990s television hit *Northern Exposure,* including the famous Roslyn Café sign. **Central Sundries** (509/649-2210) was the location of "Ruth-Anne's General Store." The **Brick Tavern,** across the street, is the oldest licensed tavern in Washington. It opened in 1889 and is famous for the 23-foot long running water spittoon that still washes away patrons' tobacco juice.

The **Roslyn Museum** (203 Pennsylvania Ave, 509/649-2776, daily 1–4 P.M.), next to the Roslyn Café, houses an interesting combination of mining equipment and *Northern Exposure* memorabilia.

Goths, geneaologists, and those with morbid temperaments are drawn to Roslyn's 26 **cemeteries**—quite a few, considering the city's population was never higher than 4,000. The wide variety of ethnic groups, religions, and fraternal brotherhoods that thrived here during the town's early coal mining days are the reason for the extreme segregation of the town's dead.

Events

Cle Elum's big event is **Pioneer Days** (509/674-5958) on the 4th of July, which features family-friendly activities such as a street fair, parade, softball and boccie ball tournaments, and fireworks.

Roslyn's **Coal Miner Days Festival** over Labor Day weekend includes coal-shoveling contests, performers, a street fair, and the coronation of King Coal. People and pets step out for October's **Paws on Parade** event, featuring a pomp-filled walk through town with local and visiting four-footed friends. **Moosefest** in mid-July is a *Northern Exposure* fan-fest, sometimes complete with a parade, dinner, theater, and live music. The town hosts many other quirky events throughout the year, such as a sled run in mid-January and March's Running Water Spittoon Race, in which tiny boats face off at the Brick for a purse of up to $200.

Sports and Recreation

IRON HORSE STATE PARK

This is Washington's most unusual state park (509/656-2230, www.parks.wa.gov), a 113-mile long trail that starts near North Bend, crosses the Cascades, and continues all the way to the Columbia River. A centerpiece of the state's rails-to-trails program, the park is open to hikers, skiers, mountain bikers, and horseback riders but closed to motorized vehicles. The trail begins at Olallie State Park (I-90 Exit 34), climbs up the west slope of the Cascades to Snoqualmie Pass, and then descends past Cle Elum and Ellensburg (there is a short gap near here) before ending near Vantage along the Columbia River. The gravel trail is gentle, with a maximum 2 percent grade. It crosses 30 substantial trestles and goes through four tunnels, including the 2.3-mile Snoqualmie Pass tunnel; bring flashlights and warm clothes. No overnight camping is allowed. Trailhead access points can be found near many I-90 exits along the way, including Olallie State Park, Snoqualmie Pass, Easton, South Cle Elum, and Thorp.

LAKE EASTON STATE PARK

About 15 miles west of Cle Elum just off I-90, Lake Easton State Park encompasses 518 forested acres on the west and north sides of Lake Easton and is a popular camping spot (if you can ignore the traffic noise). The mile-long reservoir is good for swimming, boating, trout fishing, and water-skiing. The water level changes through the year in this reservoir, and it is drained each winter to provide irrigation water for eastern Washington farms. Hiking, cross-country skiing, and snowmobiling are popular dry-land sports. Kids enjoy the big-toy playground.

OTHER SPORTS AND RECREATION

The **Cle Elum Ranger District** (west end of 2nd St., 509/674-4411, www.fs.fed.us/r6/wenatchee, Mon.–Fri. 7:45 A.M.–5 P.M. and Sat. 8 A.M.–2 P.M.) office of the Wenatchee National Forest has information on more than 750 miles of hiking trails. Stop by their office for maps, a detailed trail guidebook, and camping, cross-country skiing, and snowmobiling information.

Take Highway 903 from Cle Elum northwest to Cle Elum Lake; a number of forest roads branch off to backcountry hiking trails, including access to the south end of Alpine Lakes Wilderness Area. From the north end of the lake, take forest roads 4308 and 4312 to the Thorp Creek trailhead for a 3.1-mile hike to tiny **Thorp Lake** and **Kachess Ridge.**

A six-mile one-way hike on Trail 1307 leaves Salmon la Sac Campground and follows a ridge to an excellent view atop **Jolly Mountain.**

For horseback trips into the backcountry, contact **Three Peaks Outfitter/Guide Service** (509/674-9661,www.3peaksoutfitters.com) for day rides or multiple-day pack rides. They even provide guided fishing and hunting trips. **High Country Outfitters** (509/674-6852 or 888/235-0111, www.highcountry-outfitters.com) will bring along everything you need for an overnight pack trip, ranging $90–350 depending on the level of service you'd prefer. The area offers choice cross-country skiing at **Cabin Creek Nordic Ski Area,** a groomed "sno-park" at exit 63 off I-90, and west of Lake Easton State Park. Permits for day-use will cost you $11 and are available at any ranger station, REI store, or a variety of other retailers.

CAMPING

The camping here is heavenly, with many options to choose from. Closest to Cle Elum is 34-site **Wish Poosh Campground** (eight miles northwest of town on the eastern shore of Cle Elum Lake, $14–28). Continue up Cle Elum Valley Road to find three more campgrounds. The 23-site **Cle Elum River** (Cle Elum Valley Road #903, 15 miles north of Cle Elum, $11–22) has potable water, but pit-toilet facilities raise the level of adventure here. **Red Mountain** (Cle Elum Valley Road #903, 16 miles north of Cle Elum, $8) is even a little rougher—its 10 sites have vault toilets and you must pack your own drinking water. Your compensation is the cheap nightly rate. At the end of the line is **Salmon la Sac** (518/885-3639 or 877/444-6777, www.reserveusa.com, $14–28, $7 reservation fee), a 99-site mega-campground, complete with flush toilets, shared kitchens, public horse corrals, and a guard station. More campgrounds are northeast of town on Highway 97 over Blewett Pass en route to Leavenworth.

About 15 miles west of Cle Elum and just off I-90, **Lake Easton State Park** (509/656-2586 or 888/226-7688, www.parks.wa.gov, $19 for tents, $26 RV hookups, $7 reservation fee, late April to mid-October) has additional camping.

Sun Country Golf Resort (841 St. Andrews Dr., 509/674-2226, www.golfsuncountry.com, full hookups $23 weekdays, $27 weekends, $150 per week), six miles west of Cle Elum, has an RV park and a nine-hole golf course.

Accommodations

Sleep in a converted railway caboose without having to share it with hobos at the **Iron Horse Inn Bed and Breakfast** (526 Marie Ave., 509/674-5939 or 800/228-9246, www.ironhorseinnbb.com, $80–145 s or d). The main building here was built in 1909 by the Chicago, Milwaukee, Pacific, and St. Paul Railroads to house railroad workers. The 10 rooms are all photo- and memorabilia-rich lessons in railroad history. And comfortable, too! A hot tub on the deck makes a nice place to relax. Some rooms have private baths; others share. The four cabooses are beautifully appointed and all have private baths. Iron Horse State Park Trail is just a few feet from here, making this a great place for cross-country skiers or cyclists. Two-night minimum on holiday weekends.

Adventursome cowpokes will find something more their speed at **Flying Horseshoe Ranch** (3190 Red Bridge Rd., 509/674-2366, www.flyinghorseshoeranch.com), a sprawling property that is like summer camp for families. There's just about every kind of rustic lodging under the sun (and snow) available: teepees ($90 for 4), platform tents ($90 d), sleeping bunkhouses ($100 for 8), and better-appointed wrangler cabins ($115 for 4) all with two shared shower houses and cookhouses for cookin' and cleanin'. There's also two private cabins, one larger one with kitchen and bath ($270 for 6) and a smaller honeymooner cabin ($165 d) with just a private bath. The grounds include a stable where you can ride horses, a playfield and ball house with tons of outdoors equipment free for use, and an outdoor pool.

Closer into town, Cle Elum has a spate of cheap hotels good for those just passing through town along I-90. One of the cleanest and most affordable is **Aster Inn** (521 E. 1st St., 509/674-2551, www.asterinn.com, $55–85 s or d), a quaint little rambler of a motel with individual rooms all decorated uniquely, from Western to floral. Some rooms have kitchenettes, others Jacuzzi tubs.

And out in Roslyn, just a block from downtown on a small hill, **Huckleberry House** (301 W. Pennsylvania, 509/649-2900, www.huckleberryhouse.com, $125 d) has four lovely rooms decorated with antiques in this beautifully restored early 1900s-era house.

Food

CLE ELUM

Get cinnamon rolls and espresso for the road, or a crusty loaf of Dutch crunch bread fresh from the brick oven (in use since 1906) at **Cle Elum Bakery** (501 E. 1st St., 509/674-2233, Mon.–Sat. 7 A.M.–5:30 P.M., Sun. 7 A.M.–2 P.M.).

MaMa Vallone's Steak House and Inn (302 W. 1st St., 509/674-5174, daily 4:30–8 P.M.) serves a large selection of steaks, as well as Italian dishes with homemade pasta. A country buffet is offered on Sunday. **El Caporal** (107 W. 1st St., 509/674-4284, daily 11 A.M.–10 P.M.) has quite good Mexican meals and margaritas.

ROSLYN

For such a small town, Roslyn has surprisingly good food. Very good breakfasts at **Roslyn Café** (201 W Pennsylvania Ave., 509/649-2763, www.roslyncafe.com, Mon.–Sat. 11 A.M.–3 P.M., Thurs.–Sat. 5–8 P.M., Sun. 9 A.M.–3 P.M.) best known for its colorful mural (altered to say "Roslyn's" for the television show).

For more than 80 years, people have been coming to **Carek's Meat Market** (502 E. 1st St., 509/649-2930, daily 10 A.M.–5 P.M.) to purchase fresh and smoked meats. Today, folks make the pilgrimage all the way from Seattle for the Polish sausages, beef jerky, and pepperoni.

The Brick Tavern (100 W. Pennsylvania Ave., 509/649-2643, Sun.–Thurs. 11:30 A.M.–9 P.M., Fri.–Sat. 11 A.M.–9 P.M.) features live music and dancing on weekends—generally the bar stays open until at least 11 P.M., sometimes until 2 A.M. on busy weekends. **Roslyn Brewing Company** (509/649-2232, www.roslynbrewery.com, Fri.–Sat. 1–7 P.M., Sun. noon–6 P.M.) brews two fine beers and is open for tours and tastings on the weekend.

Information

For local information, stop by the **chamber of commerce** (401 West 1st St., 509/674-5958, Mon.–Fri. 8 A.M.–4 P.M.).

Getting There

Kittitas County Connector (509/674-2251) has bus service to Ellensburg, Thorp, Roslyn, and Vantage.

ENUMCLAW AND VICINITY

Enumclaw (EE-num-claw) occupies a low plateau surrounded by dairy farms. The views of Mt. Rainier are outstanding from just about anywhere in town. Situated along Highway 410, Enumclaw is a portal for summer approaches to Mount Rainier's Sunrise area, as well as a jumping-off point to the remote northeastern corner of the park near Carbon River.

Sights

MUD MOUNTAIN DAM PARK

Mud Mountain Dam Park (seven miles southeast of Enumclaw off Hwy. 410, 360/825-3211) contains one of the nation's highest earth-and-rock flood-control dams. The park is a fun place to take the young kids to toddle. There is a wading pool, playground, picnic areas, and scenic overlooks. Older kids with more stamina will appreciate a scramble over at least part of the 10 miles of hiking trails that unravel on the grounds.

FEDERATION FOREST STATE PARK

Federation Forest State Park (18 mi. west of Enumclaw on Hwy. 410, 360/663-2207, www.parks.wa.gov) has 619 acres of old-growth forest along the White River. Amid the virgin timber, an interpretive center (summer Wed.–Sun. 9 A.M.–4 P.M., closed winters) houses displays on plants and animals in the forest. The park contains 11 miles of hiking trails, including two short interpretive paths and remnants of the historic Naches Trail, a pioneer trail that connected eastern Washington with Puget Sound. Federation Forest is also popular for fishing and picnicking; there's no camping in the park.

GREEN RIVER GORGE

A dozen miles northeast of Enumclaw on Highway 169, **Green River Gorge Conservation Area** is a 14-mile-long protected area that includes narrow gorges, white-water rapids, wildflowers, fossils, and caves along the Green River. Several state parks have been developed along the river, the most dramatic being the **Hanging Gardens Area** (access is via S.E. 386th St. /Franklin-Enumclaw Rd., ask rangers at Flaming Geyser State Park for specific directions), where a trail leads to the fern-covered cliffs lining the river.

Flaming Geyser State Park (S.E. Green Valley Rd. and S.E. Flaming Geyser Rd., www.parks.wa.gov) occupies several big bends in the Green River four miles southeast of Black Diamond on Flaming Geyser Road. Old coal-mining test holes produced two geysers, one burning an eight-inch flame and the other sending methane gas bubbling up through a stream. Enjoy hiking, picnicking, fishing, boating, and a playground; no camping is allowed. This is a take-out point for kayakers and rafters floating the Green River Gorge, and the quiet waters below here (at least in the summer) are popular with inner tubers.

Kanaskat-Palmer State Park (eleven miles northeast of Enumclaw on Farman Rd., www.parks.wa.gov) is another popular play area on the Green River, with fishing (especially for steelhead in the winter), camping, and trails through the riverside forests. Several access points in the park are used by river rafters and kayakers heading down the gorge. Because of several Class III–IV stretches, this part of the river is not for beginners.

Nolte State Park (six miles northeast of Enumclaw, www.parks.wa.gov, open mid-Apr.–Sept.) is a favorite hangout for picnicking, swimming, and fishing. The main attraction is Deep Lake and the 1.4-mile trail that offers a pleasant stroll around this 39-acre lake.

Entertainment and Events

The oldest county fair in the state, **King County Fair** (360/825-7777, www.kingcountyfair.com) is held the second and third week of July at Enumclaw's fairgrounds. A rodeo, top-billed live music acts, 4-H exhibits, food, crafts, racing pigs, and a logging show highlight this popular event.

See loggers in action at the **Buckley Log Show** on the last full weekend of June. Another big summertime activity at the fairgrounds is the **Pacific Northwest Highland Games,** held the last weekend in July. In addition to the tests of brute strength that are the main attraction, the games include bagpipe and dance competitions, animal exhibits, and vendors selling Scottish crafts, clothing, and foods. That same weekend brings the **Enumclaw Street Fair,** also dubbed "the Ice Cream and Pickle Festival," with a children's art festival, street dancing, and a food court.

In August, in the little nearby town of Wilkeson, the **National Handcar Races** are held in mid-July each year. In addition to the railroad handcar races, a parade, antique show, and arts and crafts festival provide diversions.

In early December, Enumclaw's **Christmas Parade and Tree Lighting** is popular.

Shopping

Stop by **MacRae's Indian Bookstore** (1605 Cole St., 360/825-3737, Tues.–Sat. 10 A.M.–6 P.M., Sun. 1–6 P.M., closed Mon.), where you'll find a remarkable collection of books on the original inhabitants of this land. It's said to be the largest bookstore of its kind anywhere; a mail-order catalog is available.

Sports and Recreation

For an especially pretty drive, head south from Enumclaw through Buckley and then on to minuscule Kapowsin, where the winding road takes you past small lakes, old dairy barns, and newer homes on a tree-draped valley floor. Get a taste of the Enumclaw Plateau's rich farming land by heading north from town toward Black Diamond on Highway 169. Spot lots of cows and horses along the way, including Rainier Stables' resident thoroughbred racehorses.

The Mt. Baker-Snoqualmie National Forest's **White River Ranger District** (450 Roosevelt Ave. E in Enumclaw, 360/825-6585, www.

fs.fed.us.r6/mbs, Mon.–Fri. 8 A.M.–4:15 P.M. year-round, plus Sat. 8 A.M.–4:15 P.M. in summer) has information on nearby hiking trails.

Rent bikes and skis or just gear up for a hike at **Enumclaw Ski and Mountain Company** (414 Roosevelt E, 360/825-6910, www.tx3.net/~enumsk).

GREEN RIVER RAFTING

The Green River Gorge is a 14-mile stretch of river north of Enumclaw rated Class III–IV, including many well-known rapids with names like Nozzle, Pipeline, and Ledge Drop. The river has a short spring season, generally March and April, since a dam holds the water back for Tacoma's water supply the rest of the year. Catch a ride aboard the guided tours offered by **River Recreation** (800/464-5899, www.riverrecreation.com), which offers 12-mile trips down the gorge from Kanasket-Palmer State Park to Flaming Geyser State Park, plus a riverside lunch spread.

CAMPING

Pound in your tent stakes ($17) or hook up the RV ($23) along the Green River at **Kanaskat-Palmer State Park** (11 miles northeast of Enumclaw on Farman Rd., 360/886-0148). Then you are ready to hop in a rental boat to explore the river. It's open all year, but with limited winter facilities. Make reservations ($7 extra) at 888/226-7688 or www.parks.wa.gov.

Accommodations

Stop in at **Park Center Hotel** (1000 Griffin, 360/825-4490 or 800/528-1234) before or after your Mount Rainier jaunt to unwind in the hot tub or clean up hike-muddied clothes in the laundry room. Also on-site is a restaurant, exercise room, and lots of parking space for RVs and boat trailers. The property is a bit run-down but clean, and you'll get free breakfast and Wi-Fi. Plus you can bring Rover with you.

Over in Buckley, stay at the **Mountain View Inn** (29405 Hwy. 410 E, 360/829-1100 or 800/582-4111, $89 s or $99 d). It has an outdoor pool, hot tub, and outdoor spa, plus a continental breakfast.

Food

Carb up before that long wilderness sojourn at Enumclaw's long-running breakfast favorite, ☾ **The Kettle** (1666 Garrett St., 360/825-7033, Tues.–Sat. 5 A.M.–2 P.M., Sun. 7 A.M.–2 P.M., closed Mon.). You can't go wrong with the house specialty omelettes, biscuits and gravy, or a towering stack of flapjacks. All servings are enough to stuff an elephant, so don't be afraid to split a plate.

The funky painted redbrick and green trim exterior draws you into the lively din at **The Mint Alehouse** (1608 Cole St., 360/825-8361, Mon.–Thurs. 11 A.M.–11 P.M., Fri.–Sat. 11 A.M.–midnight, Sun. noon–10 P.M.), a local watering hole and eatery guaranteed to fill you up. The menu is big on pizzas, salads, and sandwiches, with a few nacho and quesadilla options thrown into the mix as well. Beer connoisseurs will appreciate the 31 different brews on tap, as well as the proudly displayed tap handle collection, prized for its diversity.

Get fresh produce, flowers, and arts and crafts at the **Enumclaw Country Market** (1421 N. Cole St., 253/939-1707, 9:30 A.M.–3 P.M. Sat. late Apr.–mid-Oct.) next to the visitors center.

If you're hankering for real old-fashioned burgers and fries, keep driving south past Enumclaw into Buckley and swing into **Wally's White River Drive-In** (282 Hwy. 410 N, 360/829-0871, Sun.–Thurs. 8 A.M.–9 P.M., Fri.–Sat. 8 A.M.–10 P.M.). They serve up the best hunks o' beef in the area.

Information

The **Enumclaw Visitors Center** (1421 Cole St., 360/825-7666, www.enumclawchamber.com) is open Mon.–Fri. 9 A.M.–5 P.M., Saturday 10 A.M.–2 P.M., closed Sunday.

Getting There

Metro Transit (425/447-4800 or 800/542-7876, http://transit.metrokc.gov, $2.25 one-way) runs two routes in Enumclaw. Route 912 motors to Covington, while route 915 travels to Auburn station, which offers connections to Seattle via Sounder light rail.

Eatonville and Elbe

EATONVILLE

Rural Eatonville is located in farming and logging country in the foothills 25 miles west of Mt. Rainier. In recent years, Eatonville has attracted a number of artists and craftspeople, and several small galleries dot downtown.

Sights

NORTHWEST TREK WILDLIFE PARK

One of the region's biggest attractions is Northwest Trek Wildlife Park (360/832-6116, www.nwtrek.org, $15 adults, $13.50 seniors, $10 ages 5–17, $7 ages 3–4, free under three). Located on Highway 161 near Eatonville, this 600-acre wildlife park is a refuge for grizzly and black bears, wolves, mountain goats, moose, bighorn sheep, elk, and even a herd of bison. A tram transports visitors on a six-mile, hour-long tour of the park; also available are five miles of nature trails. Join in a park-sponsored weekend festival, salmon bake, or photo tour. The park opens at 9:30 A.M. daily Feb.–Oct. and on weekends the rest of the year. Closing times vary between 3 P.M. and 6 P.M. The trams leave hourly beginning at 10 A.M.

PIONEER FARM MUSEUM AND OHOP INDIAN VILLAGE

Experience what pioneer life was really like as you grind grain, churn butter, and milk a cow at the Pioneer Farm Museum and Ohop Indian Village (three miles north of Eatonville, between Highways 7 and 161, 360/832-6300, closed Thanksgiving through February, $7.50 adults, $6.50 seniors and kids). Ninety-minute guided tours are available daily 11 A.M.–4 P.M. in the summer, with reduced hours in the spring and fall. The farm is also home to a replica Native American village where you can learn about traditional hunting and fishing, tool making, and foods. Hour-long tours of the village are available only on summer weekends at 1 and 2:30 P.M. and cost an additional $7 for adults and $6 for kids. A trading post sells old-fashioned candy, trinkets, books, and rabbit skins.

PACK EXPERIMENTAL FOREST

Pack Experimental Forest (9010 453rd St. E., 360/832-6534, www.cfr.washington.edu/facility.pack) is on University of Washington land just west of Eatonville. The roads across Pack Forest are open weekdays only, but hiking trails are open daily. Short hiking trails crisscross the forest, taking you through stands of trees of varying ages, including a 42-acre preserve of old-growth Douglas fir, cedar, and hemlock.

Events

Local events of note include the **Fourth of July** with all the fun of a small-town festival, and the very popular **Eatonville Arts Festival,** held in mid-August.

Camping

Camp at **Alder Lake Park** (seven miles south of Eatonville, 360/569-2778, www.tacomapower.com), where both tent sites ($19) and RV spaces ($26 full hookups) are available, along with showers. The seven-mile-long lake was created by a dam that produces hydroelectric power for Tacoma City Light. Reservations are advised for summer weekends. The lake also has a popular sandy beach for sunbathing and swimming.

Accommodations

Stay at the spacious and modern **Mill Village Motel** (210 Center St., 360/832-3200 or 800/832-3248, $80 s or $90 d). Rooms come with fridges, microwaves, coffee pots, and TVs with satellite service. Continental breakfast is included.

Food

Dining options are limited in Eatonville, but there are a couple of little eateries worth a pit stop before tackling Rainier. **Mountain View Cafe** (106 Washington Ave. S., 360/832-8646, Wed.–Fri. 11 A.M.–8 P.M., Sat. 8 A.M.–8 P.M., Sun. 8 A.M.–3 P.M., closed Mon.–Tues.) grills up slow food fast, preparing tasty sandwiches, burgers with freshly formed patties, and fish and chips dipped in homemade batter. Eat in the dining room within the old converted house, or ask them to box it up so you can get to the park more quickly.

Or you can enjoy chips and salsa, yummy tacos, and other good Mexican food at **Puerto Vallarta** (220 Center St., 360/832-4033, daily 11 A.M.–9 P.M.).

The **Eatonville Farmers Market** (Washington and Center Streets, May to early October Saturday 10 A.M.–4 P.M.) features fresh produce, flowers, and local crafts.

Information

For more information about the town, visit the **Eatonville Visitor Information Center** (220 Center St., 360/832-4000, www.eatonville.com, Mon.–Fri. 9 A.M.–5 P.M., Sat. 10 A.M.–2 P.M.). Wonderland Trail hikers and other Rainier explorers will be happy to note that you can take a shower at the coin laundry next door to the information center.

ELBE

Fourteen miles from Mount Rainier National Park, Elbe is a wide spot in the road and a pleasant place to enjoy the foothill sights with a dose of railroad memorabilia. Visitors can eat dinner aboard the Cascadian Dinner Train, spend a night in a caboose at Hobo Inn, or peek inside Elbe's **Evangelische Lutherische Kirche,** a tiny white clapboard church measuring just 18 by 24 feet.

Sights and Recreation

MOUNT RAINIER SCENIC RAILROAD

One way to view the area west of Mt. Rainier is from the Mt. Rainier Scenic Railroad (49 Mineral Creek Rd., 360/569-2588 or 888/783-2611, www.mrsr.com, $20 adults, $18 seniors, $15 ages 4–12). Buy tickets for the vintage steam train at Elbe Station or at Mineral Lake station, where the 90-minute tour has been departing since massive floods in 2006 washed out a few key bridges along the old line. You'll still get to run through forests and over impressive bridges while being regaled with folksy live music and impressive views—especially when the mountain is out. The train runs twice daily in July and August, and on weekends from Memorial Day to early July and in September.

MINERAL LAKE

Rumor has it that oft-lucky trout anglers at **Mineral Lake** (three miles south of Elbe on Mineral Hill Rd.) regularly hook enormous 10-pound rainbows and brownies. This hidden glacial lake offers some impressive views of the mountain when it decides to peek out from under its pillow of clouds. Rent boats, fishing poles, and crayfish traps at **Mineral Lake Resort** (148 Mineral Hill Rd., 360/492-5367, www.minerallakeresort.com). Zip around in a pontoon ($105 full day, $85 half day) or slowly paddle yourself around in a rowboat ($20 daily). Or just fish from the dock for $6; poles can be had for $5 daily. Non-anglers can also play in the water in a paddleboat ($7 per hour).

Accommodations

Elbe's most unusual accommodations are at the **Hobo Inn** (360/569-2500, $115 s). You can set your bindles down in one of eight antique cabooses—some date back to 1916—that have been completely reconditioned, with beds and bathrooms added. One even features a hot tub. Rates include breakfast at the Mt. Rainier Dining Company right next door. Make reservations a month ahead in the summer to be assured of your own caboose—there are no stowaways allowed on this train.

You can make Mineral Lake your home base for Rainier expeditions and lazy fishing days from one of two spots along the lake. Families will dig the summer camp vibes at **Mineral Lake Resort** (148 Mineral Hill Rd., 360/492-5367, www.minerallakeresort.com), where they can borrow boats to explore the waters. Guests can either camp in their RVs or cozy up in one of the cabins on the property. The rustic studio cabins ($90–100) sleep up to six and include kitchenettes, outside barbeques and fire pits, and patios. The only catch is that you'll have to share the central bathrooms with the campers

© ERICKA CHICKOWSKI

Mineral Lake Lodge

and there are no showers on the property. For a bit more space and comfort, the bunkhouse ($180) can fit up to eight, includes all of the amenities of the studio cabins, and has a full bathroom.

Couples in search of a romantic getaway may prefer the historic **Mineral Lake Lodge** (195 Mineral Hill Rd., 360/492-5253, www.minerallakelodge.com, $115–145 s or d), a three-story log lodge built in 1906. The property has over 200 feet of grassy waterfront with the best view of Rainier on the whole lake. There's a bonfire area, private sauna, sunroom with a view, and an inviting porch swing all on the premises. Rooms are done up in themed Americana decor, and continental breakfast is served each morning.

Food

If you don't sleep in a caboose, at least eat in one. Right next door to the Hobo Inn, the **Mount Rainier Dining Company** (54106 Hwy. 7 E., 360/569-2500) is known for hearty breakfasts and finger-lickin' barbecue. Try the smoky, hearty servings of homemade stew served in bread bowls. This house specialty is made from leftovers from the barbecue.

The other old standard in Elbe is across the street. **Scale Shack Burger** (54109 Hwy. 7, 360/569-2247, daily 10 A.M. to 7 P.M.) flips its enormous "scaleburgers" from a converted truckers' weigh station shack. Sit out on one of the picnic tables clustered around the shack and enjoy the colorful tractor tire flowerpots while you munch on behemoth burgers and crispy fries.

Ashford

Ashford is your last chance for food, lodging, and gas before you enter Mount Rainier National Park from the most popular Nisqually entrance. Rather than being a "last resort," some of the hotels, cabins, and restaurants here are as good or better than park facilities. Established in 1891, Ashford began as an end-of-the-line town where tourists stepped off the Tacoma Eastern Railroad cars to enter the park.

For incredible views of Mt. Rainier, head north from Ashford on Copper Creek Road (Forest Road 59). The road also provides access to the Glacier View Wilderness.

SPORTS AND RECREATION

Mount Tahoma Trails

Halfway between Elbe and Ashford is Mount Tahoma Trails (www.skimtta.com), featuring 75 miles of groomed cross-country skiing in the winter, and mountain biking, horseback riding, and hiking on the trails in the summer. A series of three huts and a yurt provide overnight accommodations for six people (up to 14 in some of these), making it possible to ski or hike from hut to hut. There's no charge to stay in the huts, but a $25 per-person per-night damage deposit is required in advance, and you'll need a Sno-Park ($11) permit to park your vehicle. Buy one at Ashford Valley Grocery (29716 Hwy. 706 E, 360/569-2560, 6 A.M.–10 P.M.).

Campgrounds

Avoid driving the camper on the busy national park roads and instead opt to park at the peaceful **Mounthaven Resort** (38210 Hwy. 706 E, 360/569-2594, $30 full), which offers pretty sites under tall cedars, some near a gurgling creek. Mounthaven offers coin-op laundry facilities, pay phones, showers, and restrooms, and it is pet friendly.

ACCOMMODATIONS

Ashford has quite a few comfortable cabins, B&Bs, and lodges. Because of their popularity, reserve space at least two weeks ahead for midsummer.

Under $100

Built in 1912 as loggers' quarters, **Whittaker's Bunkhouse** (30205 Hwy. 706 E., 360/569-2439, dorm bed $35 s, motel $85–115 s or d) is a favorite among climbers seeking affordable lodging and comfortable camaraderie in the cozy shared dorm rooms here. The recently renovated private motel rooms also make a great launch pad for active families with little ones who don't quite feel up for camping. Warm up in the hot tub, or head to the espresso shop for a cup of java or to check your email.

Another affordable option is **Nisqually Lodge** (31609 Hwy. 706 E., 360/569-8804 or 888/674-3554, $95–105 s or d), which has large motel rooms and a hot tub. Rate includes continental breakfast.

$100-150

Literally a stone's throw from the park entrance, **Stone Creek Cabins** (38624 Hwy. 706 E., 360/569-2355 or 800/678-3942, www.destination-rainier.com/stone, $115–150) offers some of the best bargain cabins in Ashford. You can't beat the location, and the cabins themselves are modern, hip-roofed cedar cottages with kitchenettes and fireplaces on lightly wooded grounds.

Also near the park entrance, but not nearly as nice, **Gateway Inn Motel** (38820 Hwy. 706 E, 360/569-2506, $109–149) works for those in a pinch during the high season or just stopping over for the night. The cabin interiors are spacious and clean, but dated—in a late 1960s kind of way. But they all have fireplaces and the staff is friendly.

$150-200

A mile west of the park entrance, **Alexander's Country Inn** (37515 Hwy. 706 E., 360/569-2300 or 800/654-7615, www.alexanderscountryinn.com, $125–179) is the mainstay of elegant Rainier lodging. Constructed in 1912, the inn was visited by presidents Theodore Roosevelt and William Howard Taft. Guests will enjoy antique furnishings, fireplaces, stained-glass windows, and the modern addition of a hot tub. A full breakfast is served at the gourmet restaurant on-site — roundly lauded as Ashford's best.

Those who would prefer to get in touch with their chi would likely better appreciate **Wellspring** (54922 Kernahan Rd. E., 360/569-2514, $115–195 s or d). This attractive forested property hidden from the main road welcomes guests to cozy up inside its various log cabins. The property is host to a hot tub amidst a beautifully maintained zen garden with a running stream and two spa treatment rooms with their own wood-fired saunas, all of which are available on an hourly basis along with massage therapy. The cabins all come loaded with fridges, microwaves, and wood-burning stoves. Some also have kitchens. More adventurous guests can also choose to stay in the well-appointed platform tents open during the summer months.

Choose from a dozen different classic chalets with private hot tubs at **Jasmer's B&B and Cabins** (30005 Hwy. 706 E, 360/569-2682, www.jasmers.com, $150–195). These retreats also come with kitchens, patios, barbecues, fire pits, and picnic tables. Some are pet friendly and include laundry facilities. Jasmer's also offers fireplace rooms in the main guesthouse that include continental breakfast and a shared hot tub.

A classic old 1910 home, **Mountain Meadows Inn B&B** (28912 Hwy. 706 E, 360/569-2788, www.mtn-meadows-mt-rainier.com, $149–169) opens the doors to six spacious guest rooms with private baths in a lovely country setting. Breakfast is a scrumptious sit-down affair perfect for exchanging stories about the great outdoors. Be sure to ask the innkeepers for their own stories—they've traveled all over the world. They'll also be happy to show you their extensive collection of John Muir memorabilia. The inn also has a sauna, fishing pond, and nature trails.

$200-250

The pinnacle of Rainier luxury can be found three miles from the park entrance in **Stormking Cabin and Spa** (360/569-2964, www.stormkingspa.com, $190–205, no kids). This cluster of four cabins all offer private hot tubs and secluded privacy that make them a favorite among honeymooners. Three of the four are uniquely constructed round cabins with sixteen-sided walls, and all of them have unique walk-in showers—one made with impressive slate stonework, two with river rock, and one two-person greenhouse shower. On site is a luxury spa offering massage, aromatherapy soaks, and time to sweat in the sauna.

Food

The finest food in the Mt. Rainier area (priced accordingly) is served at **Alexander's Country Inn** (37515 Hwy. 706 E., 360/569-2300), where specialties include salmon, fresh trout (catch your own from the backyard pond), home-baked bread, and famous wild blackberry pie. They also offer a large wine list.

Rainier Overland Lodge (31811 Hwy. 706, 360/569-0851) serves big family-style breakfasts, a good chicken BLT sandwich, and a choice of all-American faves.

Get espresso coffees and sweets at **Whittaker's Bunkhouse** (30205 Hwy. 706 E, 360/569-2439).

The Highlander Steakhouse and Lounge (30319 Hwy. 706 E, right in the center of town, 360/569-2953) has a standard menu of well-prepared Americana, including very tasty homemade soups, breads, and pies.

Information and Services

Get maps, current weather conditions, and lodging information from the **Mt. Rainier Visitor Center** inside Whittaker Mountaineering (360/569-2451, Wed.–Sun. 9 A.M.–5 P.M.).

After a weekend of hiking in the park, head

to **Wellspring** (360/569-2514) or **Stormking Cabin and Spa** (360/569-2964) for a relaxing massage, sauna, and hot tub.

Summit Haus (next to Whittaker, 360/569-2142, www.rmiguides.com) sells and rents a wide range of camping and outdoor clothing and gear. This is also home to Rainier's longest-running climbing guide service, RMI Guides.

Highlander Tavern and Laundry (360/569-2953) offers an unusual mix: suds on tap, suds in the launderette, and showers to suds up after a backcountry trip.

Mount Rainier National Park

With 300 miles of hiking trails covering terrain from the lowland forests all the way to the ice-topped summit at 14,411 feet, Mt. Rainier is a recreational paradise. More than two million people visit Mount Rainier National Park annually, soaking up towering waterfalls vistas from the winding mountain roads, strolling through flower-filled mountain meadows at Paradise, camping beneath old-growth Douglas fir forests, climbing the mountain's glacier-clad slopes, listening to the bugling of elk on a fall evening, and skiing backcountry trails in the winter.

History

Although various tribes made seasonal fishing, hunting, and berry-picking forays into the foothills around Mt. Rainier, they apparently avoided the mountain itself, either in reverence for the great mountain, or because of its severe weather. The Klickitat who lived near present-day Ashford called the peak "Ta-ho-ma" (The Mountain, or Snowiest Peak). The city of Tacoma gained its name from the mountain that rises so tall behind it. Unfortunately, the Native American name for the peak itself was supplanted by an English name. As he was wont to do, Capt. George Vancouver named it after his friend, Rear Admiral Peter Rainier, in 1792. Thus Rainier—a minor character in British naval history—lives on in an American mountain that he never even saw.

In 1883, James Longmire—who had guided climbers to the base of Mt. Rainier for many years—discovered a mineral springs near the Nisqually River and staked a mining claim on the site. Longmire recognized the land for its true value—as a place to enjoy the wild beauty and grand mountain views. His Longmire Springs Resort was built in 1906 on what is now national park land in the park's oldest developed area: Longmire.

Mount Rainier became the nation's fifth national park in 1899, due in large part to pressure from a prominent group of Northern Pacific Railroad stockholders who not only appreciated the beauty of the mountain, but also saw money to be made in the proposition. The railroad had earlier been given alternating square-mile chunks of land in a checkerboard pattern as part of the federal government's incentive to promote building a transcontinental railroad. To allow the park to be created, the company exchanged land around Mt. Rainier—most of which lacked trees—for federal government parcels that just happened to contain commercially valuable timber. The Northern Pacific Railroad then proceeded to log its new land while simultaneously hauling visitors to the new park that it helped create. Not a bad business deal! The awesome beauty of this sleeping volcano has been drawing visitors ever since.

Geology

The volcanic summit of Mt. Rainier—fifth highest in the Lower 48 states—was created over a period of many millennia. A series of massive lava flows and sometimes-explosive eruptions over a million years created the volcanic cone of Mt. Rainier, scraping the clouds at more than 16,000 feet high. Around 5,700 years ago, something happened—perhaps an earthquake—that triggered an enormous

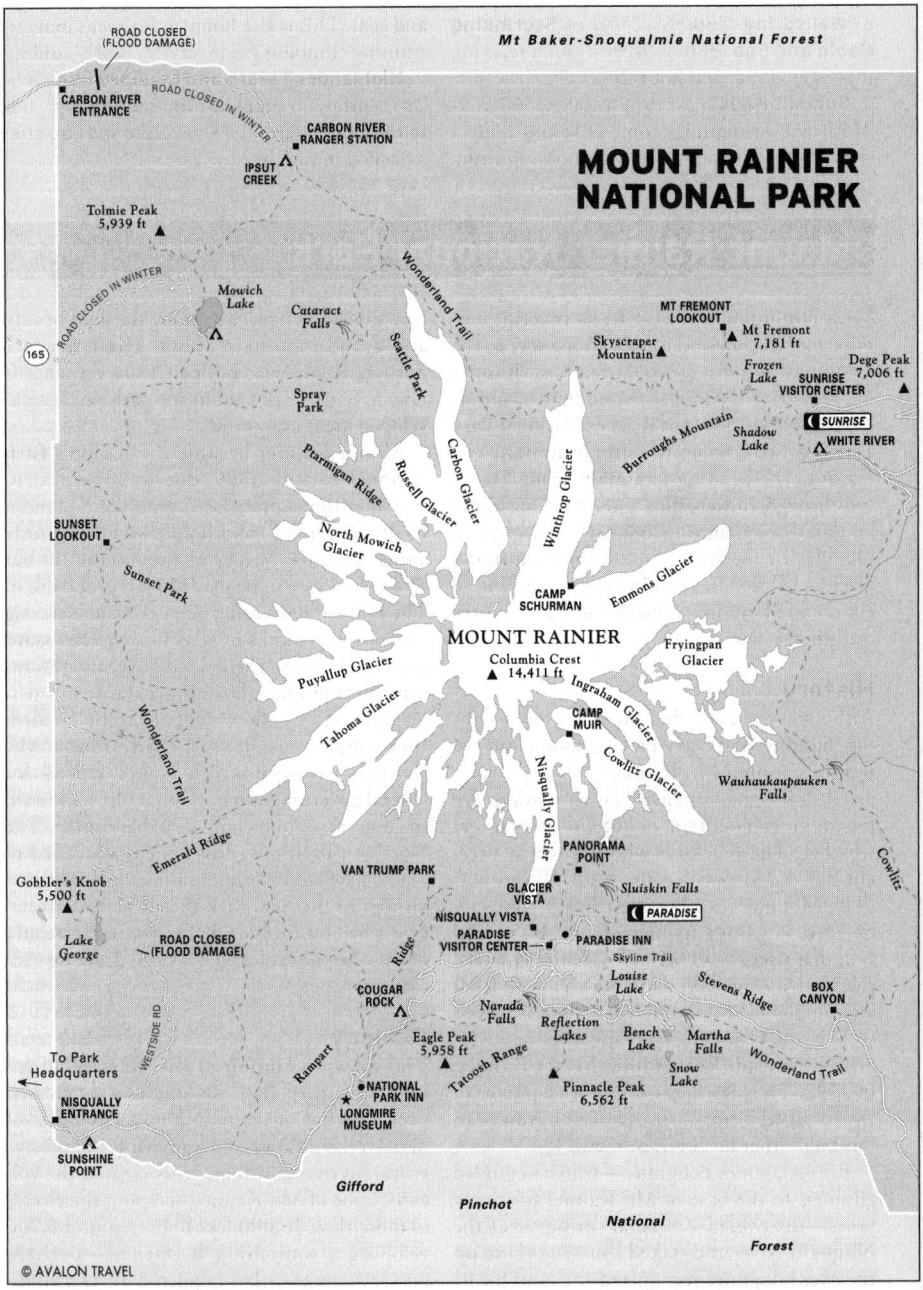
Mt Baker-Snoqualmie National Forest
MOUNT RAINIER NATIONAL PARK
ROAD CLOSED (FLOOD DAMAGE)
CARBON RIVER ENTRANCE
ROAD CLOSED IN WINTER
CARBON RIVER RANGER STATION
IPSUT CREEK
Tolmie Peak 5,939 ft
ROAD CLOSED IN WINTER
165
Mowich Lake
Cataract Falls
Wonderland Trail
Seattle Park
Spray Park
MT FREMONT LOOKOUT
Mt Fremont 7,181 ft
Skyscraper Mountain
Frozen Lake
Dege Peak 7,006 ft
SUNRISE VISITOR CENTER
SUNRISE
Burroughs Mountain
Shadow Lake
WHITE RIVER
Ptarmigan Ridge
Russell Glacier
Carbon Glacier
Winthrop Glacier
SUNSET LOOKOUT
North Mowich Glacier
Sunset Park
CAMP SCHURMAN
Emmons Glacier
MOUNT RAINIER
Columbia Crest
14,411 ft
Fryingpan Glacier
Puyallup Glacier
Ingraham Glacier
Tahoma Glacier
CAMP MUIR
Cowlitz Glacier
Wonderland Trail
Nisqually Glacier
Wauhaukaupauken Falls
Emerald Ridge
PANORAMA POINT
Cowlitz
Gobbler's Knob 5,500 ft
VAN TRUMP PARK
GLACIER VISTA
Sluiskin Falls
PARADISE
NISQUALLY VISTA
Lake George
ROAD CLOSED (FLOOD DAMAGE)
Ridge
PARADISE VISITOR CENTER
PARADISE INN
Skyline Trail
Louise Lake
Stevens Ridge
BOX CANYON
COUGAR ROCK
Narada Falls
Reflection Lakes
Bench Lake
Martha Falls
WESTSIDE RD
Eagle Peak 5,958 ft
Tatoosh Range
Snow Lake
Wonderland Trail
To Park Headquarters
Rampart
NATIONAL PARK INN
Pinnacle Peak 6,562 ft
NISQUALLY ENTRANCE
LONGMIRE MUSEUM
SUNSHINE POINT
Gifford
Pinchot
National
Forest
© AVALON TRAVEL

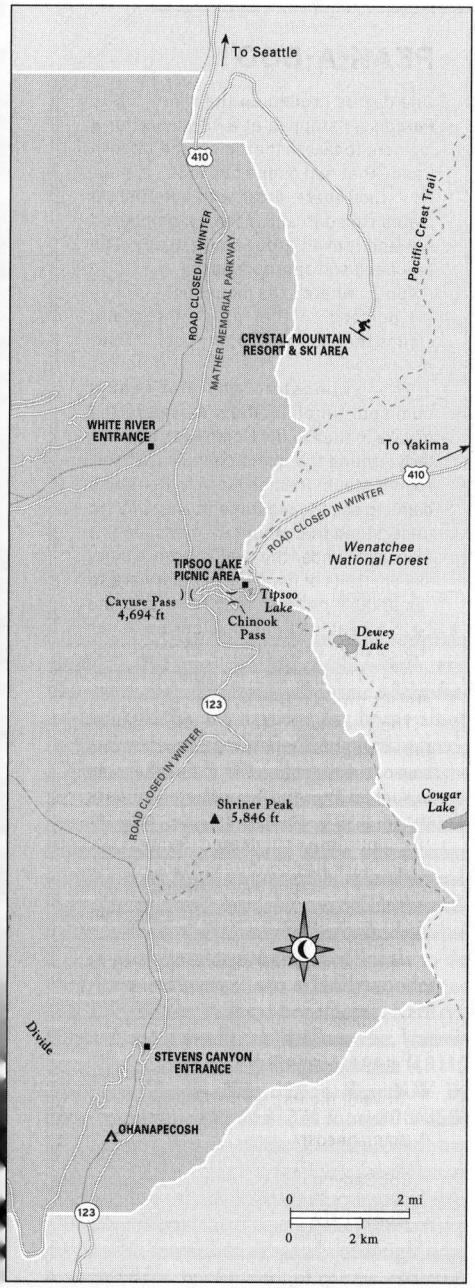

RAINIER'S GLACIERS

While forces from within the earth have created massive Mt. Rainier, the forces from above have worked to wear it down. Glaciers – created when more snow falls than melts off – have proven one of the most important of these erosive processes. After a period of several years and under the weight of additional snow, the accumulated snow crystals change into ice. Gravity pulls this ice slowly downhill, creating essentially a frozen river that grinds against whatever lies in the way, plucking loose rocks and soil and polishing hard bedrock. This debris moves slowly down the glacier as if on a conveyer belt, eventually reaching its terminus.

During the last ice age, which ended around 10,000 years ago, the glaciers flowing out from Rainier stretched for up to 40 miles into lowland valleys, while smaller glaciers filled the mountain cirques. Since that time, several thousand years of warming was followed by a period of cooling – the Little Ice Age – that caused the glaciers to expand. Geologists say that we are still in that cooler period, although a long warming trend has caused Mt. Rainier's glaciers to retreat considerably since the 1930s.

Spreading out from Mt. Rainier are some 40 glaciers, 25 that have names. Together, they represent the largest single-peak glacial system in the U.S. outside Alaska. The largest, **Emmons Glacier,** heads down the northeast side and is visible from Sunrise, while Paradise Visitor Center showcases the **Nisqually Glacier.**

collapse of one side of the mountain. More than a half cubic mile of debris (the Osceola Mudflow) roared down the White River valley in a mudflow that reached almost to Puget Sound. The collapse knocked nearly 2,000 feet off the summit of Mt. Rainier, and the mud and debris inundated areas where the cities of Enumclaw, Buckley, Puyallup, and Kent are now located. Additional large mudflows have continued to occur every 500 to 1,000 years, and geologists say that they may well return without warning, engulfing cities in their path. Smaller mudflows have occurred within the last century, including one in 1947 that created a "ghost forest" of trees along Kautz Creek.

The volcano has been relatively quiet for the past 2,500 years, but an eruption approximately 150 years ago released a plume of pumice, and steam explosions in the 1960s and 1970s show that the mountain is still very much alive.

Climate

Because of its incredible height, Rainier creates its own weather by interrupting the air flow around it and causing wet air blowing off the Pacific Ocean to release its moisture. This produces massive amounts of snowfall on the western slopes of the mountain; a world-record 1,122 inches (more than 93 feet!) fell at Paradise in 1971–1972. The mountain's height also accounts for its lenticular clouds—the upside-down-saucer-shaped clouds that obscure or hover just above the summit on otherwise clear days.

Although it can rain or snow any month of the year on Rainier, most of the precipitation arrives between October and early May, and nearly all of this falls as snow at the higher elevations. July and August are the driest and sunniest months. At Paradise (5,400 feet in elevation), the snowpack often tops 15 feet by late March, remaining on the ground until early July. Down the mountain at Longmire (2,761 feet in elevation), snow averages four feet deep in mid-winter and is generally gone after early May.

Throughout most of the park, temperatures are not much different from those around

PEAK-A-BOO

One day as I rolled up the windy hill to Paradise, I stopped at a viewpoint for a moment to take in the view of the Tatoosh Range that had opened up in the clouds. As I stood there, a car with out-of-state plates rolled in and a family clambered out and looked around quizzically. The teenaged son approached me.

"So . . . where's the mountain?"

I pointed to the mass of fog and clouds that had been at my back. "That-a-way."

The youngster was noticeably bummed. Unfortunately, those are the breaks in the Pacific Northwest, particularly around the damp country that surrounds Mount Rainier. Many tourists who come to see the monumental peak fail to understand that Mount Rainier spends a lot of time under the clouds – those blue-sky portraits of her in all her glory are so remarkable because they're hard to line up. Sometimes Rainier might be under the weather even when everywhere else is clear. The mountain is so big that it creates its own weather system.

The trick is to stay flexible – sometimes weather might be better on one side of the mountain while the other side is socked in – and appreciate the park for what it is. Sure, you might come for the mountain, but Mount Rainier National Park has countless trails, meadows, and riversides that would wow you if you could just let go of the weather disappointment.

Here are just a few of my favorite spots to chase away the cloud-cover blues:

- Narada Falls
- Paradise Visitor Center
- Grove of the Patriarchs Trail
- Ohanapecosh
- Box Canyon
- Tipsoo Lake

Puget Sound in all but winter. The average summer day at Longmire is in the 70s, with nights dipping into the high 40s. Temperatures at Paradise are commonly around 10°F cooler than this during the summer. Spring and fall are the times to be careful; rain at Longmire can very often translate to snow at Paradise. But fall weather also means fewer people and the brilliant yellow and red leaves of cottonwoods, vine maples, bigleaf maples, Sitka mountain ash, and blueberry bushes.

SIGHTS

Driving through Mount Rainier National Park provides numerous sightseeing and photographic opportunities; the surrounding mountains, waterfalls, forests, and canyons alone justify the trip. Several easily accessible places are especially noteworthy and are highlights of many travelers' journeys in Washington. The following descriptive tour begins in the southwest corner of the park and follows the main roads to the northeast corner.

Longmire Area

Longmire is seven miles from the Nisqually entrance in the southwest corner of the park. Named for James Longmire, whose Longmire Springs Resort first attracted large numbers of travelers to the park, Longmire is home to the National Park Inn (housed in an old Longmire Mineral Springs Resort building), and the **Longmire Museum** (360/569-2211 ext. 3314, daily 9 A.M.–4:30 P.M.) one of the oldest national park museums in existence. The small museum—located in the original park headquarters—contains displays on the park's natural history, along with exhibits of basketry, a small totem pole, and photos from the early days of the park. Nearby is a small transportation history museum inside the historic **Longmire Gas Station.**

Several nearby hiking trails cover the gamut, from easy strolls through the woods to steep mountain climbs. The **Wilderness Information Center** at Longmire (360/569-4453, June–mid-Oct. daily 7:30 A.M.–5 P.M.) can provide you with all the options.

Less than a mile in length, the **Trail of the Shadows** takes you on a stroll around the meadow where Longmire's resort stood, with views of the mountain. A longer loop hike continues from here up Rampart Ridge to a majestic view over the Nisqually River far below, and then joins the Wonderland Trail. Follow this back to Longmire for a total distance of five miles.

More adventurous hikers can climb the many switchbacks to the summit of 5,958-foot **Eagle Peak,** a distance of seven miles round-trip. The route passes through a wide range of vegetation, from dense old-growth stands along the Nisqually River to flowery alpine meadows offering extraordinary vistas across to Mt. Rainier. The mountain-encircling Wonderland Trail also passes through Longmire, making this a favorite starting point for backcountry hikes of varying lengths.

Paradise

The 13-mile drive from Longmire to Paradise is a delightful climb through tall evergreen forests where periodic openings provide down-valley and up-mountain vistas. Three miles before you reach Paradise is a pullout overlooking **Narada Falls,** where a steep trail leads to the plunge pool at its base. At an elevation of 5,400 feet, and with views across to the nearby mountain, Paradise Valley is appropriately named. When Virinda Longmire first visited this gorgeous area in the summer of 1885, the abundant wildflowers created a colorful contrast to the snowy summit of Mt. Rainier. "This must be what paradise is like!" she exclaimed, and thousands of tourists have concurred ever since. Get here in late July and August to see the peak of the floral display (and to join the throngs of fellow visitors who jam the parking lots and mountain trails on weekends). Paradise is easily the most popular place in the park, with an abundance of short and long hiking trails, grand scenery, and ample winter recreation opportunities.

In October 2008 park officials cut the ribbon on the new **Paradise Visitor Center** (360/569-2211, ext. 2328, daily 9 A.M.–7 P.M.

in the summer, and 10 A.M.–6 P.M. in spring and fall, open weekends and holidays only Oct. 15–early May), which replaced the distinctive but out-of-place flying saucer–shaped Henry M. Jackson Visitor Center. The gorgeous new facility matches the steep-roofed, stone-and-shingle architecture of Paradise Inn, while offering visitors up-to-date multimedia presentations, museum displays, and access to park rangers who are ready to answer questions and suggest hikes. During the summer, naturalists lead walks and give talks on a daily basis, and in winter they lead weekend snowshoe treks. Check the information desk for upcoming activities.

Built in 1917, Paradise Inn offers mountain-vista accommodations and meals mid-May through September only. Paradise visitors should do themselves a favor and take a peek inside before tromping away on a hike. The lobby hall and its massive fireplaces surrounded by rustic furniture are the best part of the inn.

A spiderweb of trails spins out over the subalpine forests and high-country meadows at Paradise; see the visitors center for a detailed map. Easiest is the **Nisqually Vista Trail,** a 1.2-mile loop hike that leads through flamboyantly floral high-country meadows west of the visitors center. Almost everyone in decent physical condition takes the oft-crowded **Skyline Trail,** a five-mile romp above the tree line to Glacier Vista and Panorama Point. Needless to say, the views are extraordinary. Be sure to carry water and stay on the path. Far too many folks wander off, creating damage to the meadows that takes years to restore.

Heading east from Paradise toward Stevens Canyon, the road passes **Reflection Lakes,** where on a calm and clear day the mirror-like surface reflects Mt. Rainier and a rim of forest. The **Pinnacle Peak Trail** starts at the Reflection Lakes parking lot; hike this 1.5-mile trail to the saddle between Pinnacle and Plummer Peaks for Mt. Rainier vistas. You'll gain 1,100 feet in elevation along the way.

An easier trail takes you uphill to **Bench and Snow Lakes.** The trailhead is a mile east of Reflection Lakes on Stevens Canyon Road, and the path goes 1.25 miles each way, through late-summer meadows filled with bear grass and flowers.

Stevens Canyon/ Ohanapecosh Area

East of Paradise, the road passes 100-foot-high **Martha Falls** and cuts across the slopes of Stevens Canyon as it follows Stevens Creek downhill. At **Box Canyon** a short trail leads to a footbridge spanning the deep but narrow gorge created by the Muddy Fork of the Cowlitz River. By the time you reach the junction with Highway 123, the road is deep within old-growth forests of Douglas fir and western hemlock at an elevation of just 2,200 feet.

The **Ohanapecosh Visitor Center** (360/569-2211, ext. 2352) is open daily 9 A.M.–6 P.M. late June through September, and daily 9 A.M.–5 P.M. late May to mid-June and in early October. It is closed mid-October to late May. Rangers lead two-hour walks several times a week during the summer months.

The **Grove of the Patriarchs Trail** starts just west of the Stevens Canyon entrance station and covers 1.5 miles of virgin forest terrain. This easy loop trail circles an island in the crystalline Ohanapecosh (oh-HAH-na-pee-kahsh) River, passing thousand-year-old Douglas firs, western hemlocks, and western red cedars that tower over a verdant fern-filled understory.

A longer hike, the **Silver Falls Trail,** follows the river in a three-mile loop that takes you to the 75-foot cataract of Silver Falls, passing a side trail to the site of Ohanapecosh Hot Springs Resort along the way. The resort was a popular Roaring '20s vacation place, but the badly dilapidated building was closed in the 1960s and torn down by the Park Service. It's illegal to enter the shallow springs here, and there are no pools anyway. The trail begins at the Ohanapecosh Campground.

The **Shriner Peak Trail** starts from Highway 123, 3.5 miles north of the Stevens Canyon entrance; park on the west side of the road about a half mile from the Panther Creek bridge. This eight-mile hike—about five hours round-trip—is almost completely devoid of shade and ends up at a lookout/ranger station at Shriner Peak (5,846 feet).

Cayuse Pass

North from Ohanapecosh, Highway 123 follows the Ohanapecosh River and Chinook Creek upstream, reaching 4,694 feet at Cayuse Pass, 11 miles from the Stevens Canyon entrance station. Here the road meets Highway 410, which continues north past the White River entrance and east over Chinook Pass, where Tipsoo Lake creates a picture-postcard image. Yakima is another 64 miles to the east.

Sunrise

The Sunrise area occupies a high subalpine plateau showcasing the northeast side of Mt. Rainier. Getting here is half the fun; a long series of switchbacks takes you 11 miles up from Highway 410, past the White River entrance station and through tall evergreen forests along the river before finally emerging into subalpine meadows offering all-encompassing vistas. Because of the rain-shadow effect, this side of Mt. Rainier gets far less precipitation than the western side, and the vegetation reflects this: grasses, sedges, and even whitebark pine are common here. The Sunrise area is home to large numbers of elk during the summer and fall. Elk are not native to the park but were brought here from Yellowstone and other parts of the West between 1903 and 1933; around 1,500 of them now inhabit the park.

Located at 6,400 feet, the log cabin **Sunrise Visitor Center** (360/569-2211, ext. 2357, July–early Sept. daily 9 A.M.–6 P.M.) houses natural history displays and has viewing telescopes where you can check out Mt. Rainier's glaciers, including massive Emmons Glacier, largest in the Lower 48. The interpretive staff leads daily nature walks; stop by the information desk for times and destinations. Not far away is **Sunrise Lodge** (July–Sept. only) with food and gifts, but no lodging.

Many trails head out from the Sunrise area, including sections of the Wonderland Trail

© ERICKA CHICKOWSKI

You can get a good look at Tahoma from Sunrise.

and shorter hikes to nearby lakes and mountains. The **White River Hiker Information Center** (at the entrance station, daily late May–Sept.) has backcountry and climbing permits, along with maps and other information. **Shadow Lake Trail** is one of the most popular, a three-mile jaunt that departs from Sunrise parking lot, drops to a rim overlooking the White River Valley, and then follows that ridge to Shadow Lake. Return via Frozen Lake and Sourdough Ridge.

To get to **Mt. Fremont Lookout** from the Sunrise parking lot, follow the trails to Sourdough Ridge and Frozen Lake, then branch off to the north. The mountain is 7,181 feet high, a gain of 1,200 feet. This well-marked six-mile path takes about three hours round-trip.

For **Dege Peak,** start between Sunshine Point and the Sunrise parking area; this one-mile trail climbs 7,006-foot Dege Peak in the Sourdough Mountains.

Carbon River Area

Because of its location in the far northwest corner of the park, this part of Mount Rainier National Park sees considerably less visitation than others. The region is named for the coal deposits that once attracted miners, but it is best known today for its magnificent temperate rainforest. Access is via Highway 165 south from Enumclaw and Buckley. Unfortunately, the 4.8-mile Carbon River Road leading from the park boundary past the Carbon River Ranger Station (360/829-9639) to Ipsut Creek Campground, was badly blown out by the river due to heavy storms that hit the Cascades in fall of 2006. Park officials are still figuring out what to do with the road and it could be years before damage is repaired.

A second (intact) gravel road enters the park south of here and climbs to Mowich Lake, located in a high glacial cirque. Get details at the **Information Center** (360/829-5127) in the town of Wilkeson.

The Carbon River Road is still open to hikers and bikers, so consider schlepping your stuff into the Ipsut Creek Campground and planning to explore via day hikes. From there, take the quarter-mile **Carbon River Rain Forest Trail** for a quick taste of Mt. Rainier's only true rain forest. The **Carbon Glacier** extends northwest from Mt. Rainier, reaching just 1,100 feet in elevation at its terminus, the lowest of any glacier in the U.S. outside Alaska. A section of the Wonderland Trail leads from Ipsut Creek Campground to the snout of the glacier, 3.5 miles each way. Watch out for rocks falling off the glacier.

From Mowich Lake, hike the three-mile trail past pretty Eunice Lake and on to the historic **Tolmie Peak** fire lookout at 5,939 feet in elevation.

SPORTS AND RECREATION

Backcountry Hiking

Rainier's hiking season is quite short: most trails are snow-free only from mid-July to mid-October, though trails at the lower elevations may open earlier and remain snow-free later in the year. It's always advisable to dress in layers for *all* seasons when hiking in the Cascades, wearing cool synthetics, wool, and rain gear. About 300 miles of hiking trails crisscross the park, many miles of which are suitable for day hikes. More than a dozen of the most popular hikes are described under *Sights*; drop by one of the hiking or visitors centers upon your arrival for up-to-date trail information. The park has a helpful *Wilderness Trip Planner* available by mail; get a copy from the park's backcountry desk (360/569-2211, ext. 3317). A number of companies lead guided hikes in the park, including REI Adventures (800/622-2236, www.rei.com). Contact the park for other concessionaires with similar services.

BACKCOUNTRY REGULATIONS

Backcountry permits are required for all overnight trips in the park throughout the year and are available for free if you wait until 24 hours before leaving on your trip, or $20 to reserve the permit ahead of time. Get them from the wilderness information centers and ranger stations in Longmire, White River, Wilkeson, Ohanapecosh, and Paradise, or print out a reservation from the Web (www.nps.gov/mora) and send it in with the fee. Permits are available up to 24 hours before you depart. If you're heading into a popular area on a busy weekend, your first choice may be full. Sunday–Thursday nights are far less crowded, so head out on these days if possible.

Fires are not allowed in the backcountry, so bring a stove along. Be sure to filter or otherwise treat any drinking water, since the protozoan Giardia and other harmful microorganisms may be present. Always practice no-trace camping and haul out any garbage. Hikers in backcountry meadows should stay on the trails at all times; plants here have only a brief growing season, and damaged areas take a long time to recover. Pets are not allowed on any park trails.

There are three types of backcountry camps within the park. **Trailside camps** are located every 3–7 miles along backcountry trails, including the mountain-circling Wonderland Trail. Trailside camps all contain a nearby water source and pit toilet, and five people (in two tents) are allowed at an individual campsite. The vast majority of hikers use these established campsites. If you choose to camp away from these, you'll need to stay at **cross-country camps,** hiker-chosen sites located a quarter mile away from the trail and other camps and at least 100 feet from water sources. Hikers are not allowed to establish cross-country camps along the Wonderland. Climbers generally curl up in **alpine camps,** in areas above 6,000 feet. The rule here is that tents must only be set on permanent snow or ice or on bare-ground areas previously used as a campsite. Don't clear new tent sites or build windbreaks on rocky areas. The rocks you pull up could be protecting fragile alpine plant root systems.

WONDERLAND TRAIL

The Wonderland Trail is a backpacker's dream: 93 miles of passes, forests, streams, and alpine meadows that completely encircle the mountain. The trail has lots of ups and downs, including 3,500-foot changes in elevation in several stretches of the route. Allow 10–14 days for the entire trip. Food (but not fuel) can be cached at ranger stations along the way by mailing packages to yourself; contact the Park Service (360/569-2211) for addresses and other specifics.

You can start your Wonderland hike almost anywhere—Mowich Lake, Longmire, White River, Box Canyon, or Ipsut Creek among the possibilities. A wide range of shorter one-way and loop hikes are also possible along the Wonderland Trail.

Also for marathon packers, the **Pacific Crest Trail** touches the east edge of the park at Tipsoo Lake on Highway 410, continuing north to British Columbia and south to Mexico.

OTHER TRAILS

The **Mother Mountain Loop** is a rewarding two- or three-night trip in the northwest section of the park. Begin at the Ipsut Creek Campground, making sure to allow time to hike in and out 4.8 miles each way along the washed-out Carbon River Road to this trailhead. Then follow the Wonderland Trail up the Carbon River, and then turn onto the **Spray Park Trail.** The trail approaches Cataract Falls (a quick side trip) and crosses Marmot Creek. Camping is permitted about one mile below Seattle Park in Cataract Valley with a permit. Hike across a permanent snowfield into Spray Park (where avalanche lilies carpet the meadows late in the summer), and continue to Mowich Lake, turning northeast to follow the Wonderland Trail down Ipsut Creek and back to your starting point. It's about 16 miles round-trip.

Another good overnighter, though not a circular route, is **Indian Bar.** This hike starts at Box Canyon on Stevens Canyon Road, crosses Nickel Creek, then turns left to follow the Cowlitz Divide. At Indian Bar, the Ohanapecosh River divides a meadow; the shelter is on the west side, just above Wauhaukaupauken Falls. Return by the same route for a total of 15 miles.

Gobbler's Knob is a fire lookout (5,500 feet) that can be reached from Round Pass on Westside Road near the Nisqually entrance.

This 2.5-mile trail passes Lake George. Westside Road is closed at Fish Creek, three miles up, due to recurring floods that have washed out the road, so you may need to wade across (sometimes this is not safe). The area is always prone to floods and mudflows. Bikes are allowed on the road (but not off the road) beyond here, but be sure to get current conditions from the Park Service before heading up. The lookout is also accessible from outside the park via the tiny Glacier View Wilderness.

Climbing

Because of its many glaciers and rocky faces, Mt. Rainier has long been one of the premier training peaks for American climbers. More than 4,500 people reach Mt. Rainier's summit every year—of some 9,000 who attempt it. Two days are usually required for the trek: the first day involves a four- to five-hour hike over trails and snowfields to Camp Muir, the south-side base camp at 10,000 feet, or Camp Schurman, on the northeast side at 9,500 feet. The second day starts early (about 2 A.M.) for the summit climb and the return to the Paradise starting point. Reservations are not accepted for the high camps, so be prepared to camp outside: Muir's 25-person capacity is frequently filled, and Schurman has no public shelter—your only luxury is a pit toilet.

All climbers must be in top physical condition before heading out, and experience in glacier travel is highly recommended. Rainier is a difficult climb, and before heading up, you need to undertake a rigorous conditioning program. Above the high camps climbers are roped, using ice axes and crampons to inch their way over glaciers to the summit. All climbers must register and get a **climbing card** ($30 annually) at a hiker information center, visitors center, or ranger station before their climb. Solo climbers need the park superintendent's approval. Climbers can reserve camping privileges on the mountain for an additional $20 fee.

GUIDED CLIMBS

Even inexperienced climbers can conquer the mountain if they are in excellent physical condition. Currently three park-sanctioned guide companies operate on Rainier.

Each service offers a number of guided climb routes, from the most accessible Camp Muir route to the path over the vast white Emmons Glacier on up to the extremely challenging Liberty Ridge route.

Founded in part by famed Everest climber Louis Whittaker and his twin brother Jim in 1968, **Rainier Mountaineering, Inc.** (summer 360/569-2227, winter 253/627-6242, www.rmiguides.com) offers guided treks up Mt. Rainier, along with snow- and ice-climbing seminars for climbers of all skill levels ($180 one-day snow- and ice-climbing school, no reservations necessary). Most popular is the four-day summit climb package ($926). RMI also offers crevasse rescue seminars, private lessons, and six-day winter mountaineering seminars ($1,850). Some of the required equipment—including boots, crampons, ice ax, and pack—is available for rent at the Guide House in Paradise.

Some beginners may appreciate the personal attention offered by either **Alpine Ascents** (206/378-1927, www.alpineascents.com) or **International Mountain Guides** (360/569-2609, http://mountainguides.com/); both run slightly more expensive than RMI but have a maximum 2:1 climber-to-guide ratio on their expeditions through Camp Muir. Alpine Ascents runs three-day summit climb packages for $1,280, which includes round-trip transportation from Seattle, a helpful benefit for out-of-towners wishing to avoid renting a car to get up to base camp. International Mountain Guides runs a longer, 4.5-day Muir summit that is the least-rushed guided climb up the mountain offered by any company. Similar to RMI, both companies also offer more challenging route options and a range of clinics and classes to improve climbing skills. Climbing programs operate from late May to late September.

Other Summer Recreation

Fishing is generally disappointing at Rainier (www.nps.gov/mora); the fish, if you wrangle any, are small. Or, as the Park Service

FIRST TO THE TOP

It is said that the Native American inhabitants of the area viewed "Tahoma" as sacred ground, inhabited by a vengeful deity who didn't welcome visitors. Although there are stories that a Native American guide led two white men to the summit as early as 1855, the men's names are long forgotten. Hazard Stevens, the Union's youngest Civil War general, was determined to be the first to (officially) reach Mt. Rainier's summit. So in 1870 he began assembling his climbing party. An unemployed miner, Philomon Beecher Van Trump, and landscape artist Edward T. Coleman would accompany him to the summit; James Longmire, a local farmer, would guide them as far as Bear Prairie, at 2,630 feet. But the group needed someone with expertise. They found it in Sluiskin, a nomad who had taken up residence at Bear Prairie, and whose grandfather, going against tribal tradition, had once attempted a summit climb – without success.

The first day out after Bear Prairie, Coleman turned back. He'd found himself in a precarious position on a precipice where he could go neither forward nor back with his 40-pound pack; so he chucked it, along with most of the party's food. Stevens, Van Trump, and Sluiskin continued.

As the climbers progressed, Sluiskin began losing his nerve. Stevens wrote about him in an article for *Atlantic Monthly* in 1876:

> *Takhoma, he said, was an enchanted mountain, inhabited by an evil spirit who dwelt in a fiery lake on its summit. No human being could ascend it or even attempt its ascent and survive . . . at first, indeed, the way was easy . . . but above [the broad snowfields] the rash adventurer would be compelled to climb up steeps of loose, rolling rocks, which would turn beneath his feet and cast him headlong into the deep abyss below.... Moreover, a furious tempest continually swept the crown of the mountain, and the luckless adventurer, even if he wonderfully escaped the perils below, would be torn from the mountain and whirled through the air by this fearful blast.*

Begging off, Sluiskin promised to wait three days for the climbers to return; then he'd go to Olympia to tell their friends they were dead.

Sluiskin's description of the mountain wasn't far from the truth. Stevens wrote:

> *Our course . . . brought us first to the southwest peak. This is a long, exceedingly sharp, narrow ridge springing out from the main dome for a mile into mid-air. The ridge affords not over ten or twelve feet of foothold on top, and the sides descend almost vertically.... The wind blew so violently that we were obliged to brace ourselves with our Alpine staffs and use great caution to guard against being swept off the ridge.*

After reaching the true summit of the mountain, Stevens and Van Trump found a volcanic steam cave where they huddled for warmth. In spite of the rotten-egg stench of the sulfuric steam, they spent the night. The next day the two men returned to Sluiskin, who was *really* surprised to see them and expressed his deep admiration for the men who had conquered Takhoma: "Strong men," he said, "stout hearts."

The first woman to top the summit was a schoolteacher named Fay Fuller, who climbed the mountain in 1890.

notes, "anglers' success is often less than anticipated."

The fish in park lakes are nonnative—all here are survivors of previous stocking efforts that have long since subsided. As a result, there are no limits or restrictions to what you catch on the lakes, with the exception of Frozen, Reflection, Shadow and Tipsoo Lakes, which are all closed water. Within park streams, park officials ask that you use barbless hooks to protect native fish. Fishing for bull trout and chinook salmon is prohibited, and there's a six-pound limit for all other fish, not to exceed 12 fish. No fishing is allowed on Klickitat Creek above the White River entrance supply intake, Ipsut Creek above the campground water intake, and Laughingwater Creek above the Ohanapecosh intake. Only fly-fishing is allowed on Ohanapecosh.

No fishing license is required. The park's lakes and ponds are ice-free from July to October; rivers, streams, and beaver ponds are usually fishable from late-May through late-October.

Nonmotorized boating is allowed on all park lakes except Frozen Lake, Reflection Lakes, Ghost Lake, and Tipsoo Lake; canoes are a great way to view the wildlife.

Horses are allowed on 100 miles of park trails; contact the Park Service for a horse trail map.

Cyclists find Mt. Rainier's roads to be steep, winding, and narrow—a prescription for trouble due to the heavy automobile traffic. Use extreme caution when cycling in the park, since RVers have a reputation for not always knowing the width of their vehicles. None of the backcountry trails in the park are open to mountain bikes, although nearby Forest Service land has hundreds of miles of such trails.

Cross-Country Skiing

Mount Rainier is famous for its abundant backcountry, where the snow seems to reach out forever, and the Telemark skiing is unmatched in Washington. Many beginners head to the Paradise parking lot to ski up the unplowed road, or out the trails to Nisqually Vista, Narada Falls, or Reflection Lake. None of these are groomed, but it generally doesn't take long for other folks to set down tracks in the new snow. The area gets an incredible 630 inches of snow in a typical year!

The east-side roads provide other skiing options, including, of course, the groomed slopes at Crystal Mountain Ski Area, just a few miles outside the park's northeast corner. For a quieter experience, the Ohanapecosh area is a good bet. Park near the ranger station and ski up the roads toward Cayuse Pass or Box Canyon if you are ambitious, but be sure to check about avalanche dangers before heading up. Easier skiing can be found in the unplowed Ohanapecosh Campground loops.

Rent skis, avalanche beacons, snowshoes, and other winter gear from the **Longmire** store (360/526-2411). They also provide ski lessons and tours. Ski rentals are not available at Paradise. If you plan to overnight in the backcountry be sure to get a permit before heading out; they are required year-round (but free in winter). Call 425/526-6677 for current avalanche conditions, or talk with Park Service folks in Longmire before heading up the hill.

Facilities are open for winter sports at Paradise from December to April. The park constructs a supervised snow play area here in early December; no snow sliding is allowed before that time to protect the vegetation. The area is a very popular place for inner tubes, saucers, or other soft sliding toys (no wooden toboggans or sleds with metal runners are allowed), but bring your own, since they are not available for rent.

Ranger-led **snowshoe walks** are offered at the Paradise Visitor Center on winter weekends and holidays. Snowshoes are free to use during these walks and can be rented from the lodge gift shop or the Longmire Store at other times.

Camping

There are hundreds of sites to pitch a tent or park an RV within Mount Rainier National Park's campgrounds (800/365-2267, http://reservations.nps.gov), all with running water and flush or pit toilets but no RV hookups. Coin-op showers are available at the Paradise Visitor Center when it is open, but you'll need to head to Ashford or other towns for laundry facilities. Gathering firewood is prohibited in the park, but it can be purchased at the Cougar Rock and Ohanapecosh campgrounds, as well as the Longmire General Store.

Currently only three of the five major park campgrounds are fully operational; **Sunshine Point Campground** (near the Nisqually entrance) is closed due to damage sustained from flooding in 2006 and **Ipsut Creek Campground** (at the end of the Carbon River Rd. in the northwest corner, $8) is only accessible to walk-in campers due to the washout of Carbon River Road in the same storm surge. A filter is a must here, as there is no running water.

Easier places to stake the tent or roll up the camper are **Cougar Rock Campground** (2.5 miles northeast of Longmire, $12–15) or **Ohanapecosh Campground** (near the southeast entrance on Highway 123, $12–15). Both are open late May to mid-October and can accommodate RVs up to 32 feet. Reservations are highly recommended from July 1 to Labor Day at these two grounds.

Those making the sojourn up to Sunrise and hikers planning on bivouacking up at Camp Schurman before an Emmons Glacier attempt like to stop in at **White River Campground** (on the east side in the Sunrise area, open late June– late Sept., $12).

The road is bumpy leading to the free **Mowich Lake Campground** (open mid-July–mid-Nov.) walk-in sites, the facilities are primitive, and there's no running water. But you'll be rewarded for your trouble by smaller crowds and pretty lakefront spots. Camping is not permitted in the Paradise area or along park roads in the summer, but winter camping is allowed at Paradise once the snow depth tops five feet. Get permits and details on locating your camp from the visitors center.

ACCOMMODATIONS

There are two inns within the park itself; both are run by the park concessionaire, **Mount Rainier Guest Services** (360/569-2275, www.guestservices.com/rainier). Each has a storied history and offers unparalleled access to the park, but for real comfort and relaxation the cabins and B&Bs in Ashford really are the way to go. Prices at both inns within the park are through the roof, and neither can quite shake that bit of institutionalized dreariness that lingers around many lodges within the national park system.

The **National Park Inn** ($107–197 s or d) at Longmire is open daily year-round. This inn has a central stone fireplace and decent rooms with shared or private baths. Built in 1917, **Paradise Inn** ($99–228 s or d) is an imposing wooden lodge with high ceilings, stone fireplaces, and unsurpassed mountain views from its elevation of 5,400 feet. The lodge underwent a $22 million renovation in 2008, but even after that the units are still not exactly up to luxury levels. The lodge is open daily from late May through September; rooms have shared or private baths.

FOOD

Longmire has a sit-down restaurant inside the **National Park Inn** (360/569-2411, open year-round). The dining room at **Paradise Inn** (360/569-2413, late May–Sept.) serves three meals a day and a big Sunday brunch during its season of operation. For something less formal, the **Paradise Visitor Center** (open daily May–early Oct., weekends and holidays year-round) operates a snack bar with typical fast food.

The cafeteria at **Sunrise Lodge** operates only between late June and early September. Limited groceries are available year-round at Longmire General Store and during the summer at Sunrise.

Call ahead, as hours vary from month to month at all of these venues.

INFORMATION AND SERVICES

Admission

Entrance to Mount Rainier National Park is $15 per vehicle, and $5 per person for folks arriving by foot and on bikes, motorcycles, buses, or horses. Your entrance fee is good for seven days. If you plan to visit several parks, or surrounding national forests or other federal recreation lands, get an $80 America the Beautiful National Parks and Federal Recreational Lands Annual Pass. Seniors over age 62 can pay a one-time fee of $10 for a lifetime version of this pass, and disabled visitors can obtain one for free at the park's entrance.

Information

Information and assorted publications are available at visitors centers in Longmire,

Paradise, Ohanapecosh, and Sunrise, and from the various entrance stations. The park's quarterly newspaper, ***Tahoma,*** is packed with up-to-date details on park activities, camping, hiking, climbing, and facilities. Request a copy in advance of your visit, along with a park map and other brochures, from the Park Service (360/569-2211). The **Northwest Interpretive Association** (360/569-2211, ext. 3320) sends out a mail-order catalog of publications and topographic maps. Park headquarters (360/569-2211, www.nps.gov/mora) are located nine miles outside the park in Ashford's Tahoma Woods area.

Services

Gift shops are found at Sunrise, Paradise, and Longmire. Camping supplies are limited in the park; it's better to bring yours in from the outside. Climbing supplies—including boots, crampons, ice axes, and packs—can be rented from the RMI Guide House at Paradise or Summit Haus in Ashford.

Park **post offices** are in Paradise Inn (summer) and Longmire's National Park Inn (all year). Short on cash? The closest ATM is located in Ashford at Ashford Valley Grocery (29716 Hwy. 706 E).

Interpretive Programs

The National Park Service schedules nature walks, campfire programs, and children's activities from July to late September. Program schedules are posted at visitors centers and campgrounds, as well as in the park newspaper, *Tahoma.* Come winter, naturalists offer snowshoe walks at Paradise.

GETTING THERE AND AROUND

By Car

In 1911, the first automobile to reach Mount Rainier National Park carried president William H. Taft aboard. Since then, the car has become the primary means of transportation to the park, with many visitors following the roads along the park's southern and eastern margins. Gasoline is not available inside the park, so be sure to fill your tank in surrounding towns.

Winter snow closes most of Mt. Rainier's roads, with the exception of the section between the Nisqually entrance and Paradise. This road closes each night and reopens in the morning after the plows have cleared any new-fallen snow. Chains are frequently required and should always be carried. The road between Paradise and Ohanapecosh is generally open Memorial Day to early November, while Highways 123 and 410 over Cayuse Pass usually open in late April and remain open till the first heavy snowfall (November). Chinook Pass is open from early June to November, and the road to Sunrise generally opens by the first of July and closes once the snow gets too deep, frequently in early October. Early snows can close any of these, so be sure to call ahead (360/569-2211) to see which roads are open. The Longmire store sells tire chains.

Bus Tours

Unfortunately, there are no bus or van shuttle services operating from Sea-Tac airport to Mt. Rainier—those looking for longer explorations must at least make it by car to Ashford.

In recent years the parks service has started experimenting with a free summertime passenger shuttle running between Paradise and Longmire every half hour 9 A.M.–5 P.M. Friday–Sunday, with extended service to Ashford Saturday and Sunday. Contact the Longmire visitors station for info.

Gray Line (206/626-5208 or 800/426-7532, www.graylineofseattle.com, $59 adults, $29.50 kids) leads hurried day trips to the park from Seattle. **Scenic Bound Tours** (206/433-6907 or 888/293-1404, www.seattlecitytours.com, $80) runs similar tours that depart from Seattle and take you to Mt. Rainier and back in 10 hours.

MOUNT RAINIER WILDERNESS AREAS

Outside of the park, half a dozen wilderness areas cover more than 356,000 acres of mountainous Forest Service terrain in the Mt. Rainier area. The largest of these—Norse

Peak, William O. Douglas, and Goat Rocks Wilderness Areas—form an almost continuous reach of wild country along the crest of the southern Cascades, broken only by Highway 410 near Chinook Pass and Highway 12 at White Pass.

A fee of $5 per vehicle per day is charged at all Forest Service trailheads. A better option is the $30 annual **Northwest Forest Pass** (800/270-7504, www.fs.fed.us/r6/feedemo), which can be used at most Washington national forests and is available at any Forest Service office. Or, if you plan on traveling the park, pick up an $80 America the Beautiful National Parks and Federal Recreational Lands Annual Pass. Seniors over age 62 can pay a one-time fee of $10 for a lifetime pass, and disabled visitors can obtain one for free at the park's entrance.

Also be sure to pick up a free, self-issued wilderness permit at all wilderness trailheads before hiking out.

Norse Peak Wilderness

This 50,923-acre wilderness reaches north from Highway 410 and just west of the Crystal Mountain Ski Area and covers rocky ridges, steep valleys, and forests of Douglas fir, western red cedar, and western hemlock. The **Pacific Crest Trail** climbs across the backbone of these ridges for approximately 27 miles from Government Meadow (accessible via Forest Road 70) on the north end, to Highway 410 near Chinook Pass on the south end. Along the way it cruises over high ridges, including two that top 6,400 feet; a popular side path leads to the summit of 6,856-foot Norse Peak for extraordinary views across to Mt. Rainier. The **Fifes Peaks** area on the east side of the wilderness is popular with rock climbers, but the rock can be weak in places. Some of the easiest access to the Pacific Crest Trail comes from near the Crystal Mountain Ski Area. Several paths leave from this area, including the **Silver Creek Trail** (No. 1192) and **Bullion Basin Trail** (No. 1156), both of which reach the PCT in a bit over two miles of hiking.

For a short hike with excellent views of Mt. Rainier, head 32 miles east from Enumclaw on Highway 410 to Corral Pass Road (No. 7174), and follow it seven miles to a parking area just before the Corral Pass Campground. From here, the appropriately named **Rainier View Trail** climbs for a mile to a 6,080-foot ridge overlooking the mountain. This is a popular camping place, but carry water since none is available at the ridge. The trail continues beyond this, connecting with the Castle Mountain Trail, 2.2 miles from your starting point. An additional five miles of hiking brings you to the Pacific Crest Trail near Martinson Gap. Check with the Forest Service for the condition of Castle Mountain Trail; at last check it was difficult to follow.

William O. Douglas Wilderness

Covering 167,195 acres, the William O. Douglas Wilderness is a delightful slice of wild mountain country that includes hundreds of small lakes, more than 250 miles of trails, and grand ridges that offer panoramic views. The wilderness is named for the Supreme Court Justice whose environmental stands helped create areas such as this, and who spent considerable time hiking in these mountains.

William O. Douglas Wilderness is accessible via Highway 410 on the north side, Highway 12 on the south, and the Bumping River Road in the center, along with various Forest Service roads on the east side. Bumping Lake Road leads past eight Forest Service campgrounds, the little settlement of Goose Prairie, and Bumping Lake. Boats can be rented and RV spaces are available at **Bumping Lake Marina** (509/575-0417). **Goose Prairie Inn** (509/837-3767) has a restaurant and cabin rentals, but these are generally only available in the fall and winter.

The **Pacific Crest Trail** heads through the southwest side of the wilderness for 14 miles; access it from Highways 12 and 410 on either end. Within the wilderness, the PCT passes many small lakes, marshes, tarns, and meadows, topping out on a 5,740-foot ridge where you can enjoy the mountain spectacle.

For an interesting loop trip that includes a section of the PCT, take Bumping River Road past Bumping Lake, and turn onto Road 18 to its end, where the **Bumping Lake Trail** (No. 971) climbs the headwaters of the Bumping River to Fish Lake. Here you turn north on the PCT, follow it to the **American Ridge Trail** (No. 958), and then hike two miles to the **Swamp Lake Trail** (No. 970), where you turn again to reach your starting point. The round-trip distance of this loop hike is approximately 27 miles.

A long one-way trek is the **American Ridge Trail** (No. 958), which starts just off Highway 410 and eventually meets the PCT after coursing over 27 miles of forests, ridges, and mountaintops, including 7,473-foot Goat Peak. At the PCT, you can turn north to reconnect with Highway 410, but you'll need to catch a ride back to your starting point or set up a vehicle shuttle.

Goat Rocks Wilderness

At 105,633 acres, Goat Rocks Wilderness occupies a long stretch of rocky volcanic peaks, alpine meadows, and open mountain country. The wilderness sits just south of Highway 12 (William O. Douglas Wilderness is on the north side of this route) and is also accessible from the southeast side via Forest Road 21, along with a myriad of other logging roads on the northeast and northwest margins.

A new backcountry permit system is being discussed for Goat Rocks Wilderness; contact **Cowlitz Valley Ranger Station** (in Randle, 360/497-1100) for details. They can also provide details on snow levels and trail conditions.

The **Pacific Crest Trail** (PCT) intersects White Pass as it continues north to Chinook Pass and south through the Goat Rocks Wilderness on its long path to Canada and Mexico. The PCT follows the crest of the Cascades for 36 miles through the Goat Rocks Wilderness, passing through some alpine meadows but generally following rough terrain 4,200–7,500 feet in elevation. The two miles between Elk Pass and Packwood Glacier are the most hazardous, but the scenery here is also the most spectacular. The trail is usually snow-free from late July

© ERICKA CHICKOWSKI

Tatoosh Wilderness from a distance

to mid-September, but even in late August you can expect to cross snowfields up to a half mile across, so bring your ice ax and warm clothing—several hikers have died from hypothermia on these exposed ridges.

For a fine but oft-crowded 13-mile loop trip, begin at the Berry Patch trailhead near Chambers Lake Campground at the end of Forest Road 2150 on the southwest side of the wilderness. The **Snowgrass Trail** (No. 96) climbs past high meadows near Snowgrass Flat, well known for its summertime wildflowers; there is no camping here. From here, you can connect with the PCT, or follow **Lily Basin Trail** (No. 86) along the ridge, and then return via exposed **Goat Ridge Trail** (No. 95) to your starting point.

Tatoosh Wilderness

This 15,800-acre wilderness abuts the southeast flank of Mount Rainier National Park and is one of the few remaining parcels of unlogged Forest Service land for miles. The nine-mile **Tatoosh Trail** (No. 161) is a strenuous forest and alpine hike but has outstanding views, especially if you take the side route to the 6,310-foot mountain that was formerly topped by Tatoosh Lookout. Another enjoyable side trail leads a half mile to Tatoosh Lakes. Get to the trailhead by turning off Highway 12 at the Packwood Ranger Station and following Forest Road 52 to Road 5270, which takes you to the trailhead, 11 miles from the Ranger Station.

Glacier View Wilderness

Tiny Glacier View Wilderness covers just over 3,000 acres on the southwest side of Mount Rainier National Park near the town of Ashford. The **Puyallup Trail** (No. 248) ascends from Forest Road 59 for 2.5 miles to the park boundary, continuing eastward an equal distance to the park's Westside Road. A side route climbs 5,485-foot **Gobbler's Knob** for a grand view of Mt. Rainier.

Clearwater Wilderness

This 14,300-acre wilderness occupies an oddly shaped parcel of unlogged land near the northern edge of Mount Rainier National Park. Much of the surrounding lands have been clear-cut. Access is from Forest Service roads off Highway 410 along the West Fork White River and from the Carbon River Road area. The **Carbon Trail** (No. 1179) cuts across this small wilderness for 9.4 miles, with a mile-long spur to the summit of 6,089-foot Bearhead Mountain, which provides views across the alpine meadows to still-wild Mt. Rainier and the heavily logged slopes of adjacent private and Forest Service lands. Get to the eastern end of Carbon Trail by following Forest Road 74 from Highway 410, and turning up Road 7450 to its end at the trailhead. From the west, take the Carbon River Road from Wilkenson, and turn up Road 7810 to its end beyond Copley Lake at the trailhead.

Chinook Pass and Highway 410

From Enumclaw, the winding route of Highway 410 cuts through the northeast corner of the park until it hooks east at Crystal Mountain, threading through Chinook Pass over to Naches and the Yakima Valley on the eastern side of the mountains. Highway 410 southeast of Crystal is a fair-weather route, closed in winter and often dusted with snow as late as June.

CRYSTAL MOUNTAIN AND GREENWATER

Sports and Recreation

CRYSTAL MOUNTAIN SKI AREA

Most Washington skiers will agree that nothing makes their hearts pitter-patter like standing in front of bluebird skies and freshly fallen powder at Crystal Mountain (360/663-2265, snow conditions 888/754-6199, www.skicrystal.com, lifts open daily 9 A.M.–4 P.M. mid-Nov.–mid-Apr.). This is Washington's largest and highest-elevation ski area, with some of the nicest lifts and lodges in the Northwest. On clear days you can take in views of Mount Rainier while carving up the slopes, no matter what your skill level—there's everything from bunny slopes to double black diamond routes to get the old ticker pounding. Even cross-country skiers can get into the act on miles of groomed trails.

Adult lift tickets are $60 all day, $55 half day. Students age 11–17 cost $55 all day, $50 half day. Kids 7–10 years old can wriggle their legs over the chairlift all day for $30 and half a day for $25. Little snowplowers six and under get in free. Seniors over 70 can buy one level of lift ticket for $35 all day. And beginners of any age can pick up a lift ticket good only for the bunny slope for $35.

Other services at Crystal Mountain include rentals, ski and snowboard schools, day care, and several restaurants.

Crystal Mountain is 76 miles from Seattle. The **Crystal Mountain Express** (800/665-2122) provides bus service from Seattle, Bellevue, and Tacoma on weekends and holidays late December–February. The cost is $85 adult round-trip, including an all-day lift ticket.

HIKING

Several popular hiking trails lead from the Crystal Mountain area to the **Pacific Crest Trail** in the nearby Norse Peak Wilderness Area. Another favorite is the **Crystal Mountain Trail** (No. 1163), a 12-mile loop hike (or mountain bike ride) that follows the ridge along Crystal Mountain. Unfortunately, the resort does not run a summer lift program, so you'll have to crank it out on your own.

CAMPING

Get regional camping and hiking information from the **Naches Ranger District** (509/653-2205). The Forest Service operates many popular campgrounds along Highway 410 between Enumclaw and Crystal Mountain, including **The Dalles Campground** (26 miles southeast of Enumclaw on Hwy. 410, 518/885-3639 or 877/444-6777, www.reserveusa.com, $14). The short and easy **Dalles River Trail** leaves from the campground and follows the White River. The main attraction here is a Douglas fir tree that reaches almost 10 feet in diameter. Also along the highway is **Silver Springs Campground** (35 miles southeast of Enumclaw on Hwy. 410, 518/885-3639 or 877/444-6777, www.reserveusa.com, $14), near the turnoff to Crystal Mountain Resort on Highway 410. Both of these are open mid-May to mid-October.

Accommodations

Crystal Mountain Lodging Suites (33000 Crystal Mountain Blvd., 360/663-2558 or 888/668-4368, www.crystalmountainlodging.com, $275–545 for four) has one- and two-bedroom condos within walking distance of the lifts. All condos have kitchens; some have fireplaces and share an outdoor heated pool. Save considerably on weekdays, in summer, or with ski-package deals.

Crystal Mountain Hotels (33818 Crystal Mountain Blvd., 360/663-2262 or 888/754-6400, www.crystalhotels.com) has rooms at the Village Inn ($200–215 d), Alpine Inn ($185–230 d), and Quicksilver Lodge ($280 for 4) near the base of the mountain.

Just five minutes away from the turnoff to the White River entrance to the national park and the steep ascent to Sunrise, **Alta Crystal Resort** (68317 Hwy. 410 E, 360/663-2500 or 800/277-6475, www.altacrystalresort.com, $219–269 d) is one of the more popular year-round lodging picks near Crystal. The property features a hot tub and swimming pool, plus hiking and Nordic skiing trails. Kids love the nightly bonfires in the summer. Choose between one- and two-bedroom condo units in the central lodge or a luxurious honeymoon cabin.

Food

Food of all types is available at on-the-mountain and base eateries. The highlight among them is **Summit House** (360/663-2300).

Accessible only by chairlift, this is the highest restaurant in the state and offers a phenomenal view of Mt. Rainier; watch for climbers approaching the summit. Open for lunch and dinner, the Summit House is a favorite place to watch the sunset over Mt. Rainier. Reservations are strongly recommended on weekends. In the summer, Crystal Mountain serves a special sunset dinner at Summit House. For $79 per person you'll be whisked up the chairlift before twilight and served a choice of soup or salad, an entrée, dessert, and a nonalcoholic beverage as the sun fades over the mountain.

As you're headed back toward Enumclaw after a day of skiing, do as the locals do and stop at **Naches Tavern** (58411 Hwy. 410 E, 360/663-2267, daily 11 A.M.–2 A.M., closes early in shoulder seasons, call for hours) in the tiny village of Greenwater. This is a cozy country place with a friendly atmosphere and good food served in large quantities. Order up an entrée or buy a hot dog and roast it over the crackling fire in their fireplace.

CHINOOK PASS

The highest of the Cascade mountain passes, Chinook Pass rises more than a mile above sea level (5,440 feet) on Highway 410. Just west of the pass, the highway enters Mount Rainier National Park, passing **Tipsoo Lake,** one of the most beautiful and easily accessed Cascade alpine lakes. Enjoy a picnic lunch here against a striking Mt. Rainier backdrop. More adventurous folks will enjoy the **Naches Peak Loop,** a 3.5-mile hike that skirts the lakeshore and then circles this mountain. Part of this loop follows the Pacific Crest Trail.

Boulder Cave is up a forest road just west of the little settlement of Cliffdell on Highway 410. Take a flashlight to explore this tunnel-like cavern.

More than a dozen other Forest Service campgrounds can be found just off Highway 410 between the national park and the town of Naches. Some are free; others charge $8–12. These are only available on a first-come, first-camp basis.

Accommodations

Whistlin' Jack Lodge (25 miles northwest of Naches (Na-CHEEZ) on Highway 410, 509/658-2433 or 800/827-2299, www.whistlinjacklodge.com) is on the sunny side of the mountains, with just 15 inches of precipitation annually and over 300 days of sunshine. Open year-round, the lodge includes a motel ($110), cabins ($160–265), restaurant, lounge with live music on weekends, gas, and groceries. If you are already hungry heading over Chinook Pass, be sure to stop at the diner here—it is a long haul to Yakima on an empty stomach and the choices in Naches are sparse.

Choose between classic motel rooms or cabins with fireplaces and kitchens at **Squaw Rock Resort** (20 miles northwest of Naches on Hwy. 410, 509/658-2926, www.squawrockresort.net, $85–140 s or d). Situated along the Naches River, this resort has a heated pool, hot tub, restaurant, store, and public showers.

Stay in one of two guests rooms in a small mountain cottage at **The Cozy Cat B&B** (12604 Hwy. 410, 509/658-2953, $70 s or $80 d) Rooms include private baths, and a full breakfast is griddled up each morning. The location is close to a small pond and offers fine mountain vistas.

Closer in to Naches and Yakima, **Apple Country Inn B&B** (4561 Old Naches Hwy., 509/965-0344, $79–95 d) is a remodeled 1911 farm house and working ranch positioned perfectly between Rainier and wine country in the Yakima Valley. Two guest rooms have private baths, a continental breakfast is served, and kids are welcome.

White Pass Scenic Byway

Winding its way east from I-5 through farmland, old growth forests and one of the state's prettiest alpine passes, White Pass Scenic Byway (US Hwy. 12) runs between Mount Rainier and Mount St. Helens. This makes it an ideal route for wanderlust-filled wayfarers hoping to spend a week or two exploring the state's two biggest volcanic attractions and the vast stretches of wilderness areas that span between them.

MOSSYROCK AND VICINITY

Mossyrock occupies farming country along the Cowlitz River northwest of Mount St. Helens and east of Chehalis. The primary crops raised here are tulips, blueberries, and Christmas trees. Two dams have created nearby Riffe and Mayfield Lakes, choice territory for anglers, boaters, and picnickers.

Sights

MARYS CORNER AND JACKSON HIGHWAY

Twenty miles west of Mossyrock on Highway 12 and just three miles east from I-5 is the crossroads called Marys Corner. Just south of the intersection on Jackson Highway is the **John R. Jackson House,** a log cabin built in 1845 that was a popular stopping place for Oregon Trail travelers. Jackson was one of the first American settlers north of the Columbia River, and this building served as the first U.S. District Court in what would become the state of Washington. Just north of Marys Corner on Jackson Road is a monument to John Jackson's wife, Matilda. (Technically, this five-acre plot of land is **Matilda N. Jackson State Park.**)

Two miles south of Marys Corner, the road passes **Lewis and Clark State Park** (360/864-2643), which preserves a proudly standing grove of old-growth evergreen. Several short trails provide loop hikes through the tall Douglas fir, western red cedar, western hemlock, and grand fir trees. The west side of Lewis and Clark State Park emphasizes horseback use.

© LEWIS COUNTY CONVENTION & VISITOR BUREAU/SANDY BALTAZAR

pink tulips at a bulb farm in Mossyrock

Camp beneath the forest for $17 (no hookups or reservations) April–September.

EAST TO MOSSYROCK

A pullout four miles east of Mossyrock leads to a viewpoint offering a glimpse—on clear days—of Mount St. Helens, 24 miles to the south. The **Cowlitz Salmon Hatchery** is on the Cowlitz River just below the Mayfield Lake dam, providing a good chance to watch salmon returning up a fish ladder in the spring and fall. Get there by following the signs from the Highway 12 turnoff, nine miles west of Mossyrock.

Mayfield Lake County Park (180 Beach Rd., 360/985-2364), off Highway 12 just west of Mossyrock, has a campground (open May–Sept.), swimming beach, boat launch, small picnic area, and playground. Follow the highway east to Mossyrock—there's a nice roadside viewpoint about three miles east of town.

Recreation

To reach **Mossyrock Park** (202 Ajlune Rd., 360/983-3900), turn south at the Mossyrock flashing light and follow the signs three miles east. Here you'll find walk-in tent sites ($14), RV sites with no hookups ($19) electric-only RV spots ($23), and full RV hookups ($25). Also on the property are picnic tables and boat launches on the green-blue Riffe Lake. The 24-mile-long lake was created in 1968; it was named Riffe Lake to honor the settlement of Riffe, founded in 1898 and now covered by about 225 feet of water.

If you turn north at the Mossyrock light you'll eventually get to **Ike Kinswa State Park** (360/983-3402), about three miles off the highway. This 454-acre park is open year-round for trout fishing on Mayfield Lake, with swimming, picnicking, lakeside campsites ($17), and RV sites ($23). In the winter, look for bald eagles on the trees along the shore. Make reservations ($7 extra) at 888/226-7688 or www.parks.wa.gov. Another place for RVs on the road to Ike Kinswa Park, two miles north of the highway, is **Harmony Lakeside RV** (360/983-3804, $35–49 with hookups).

In addition to its enclosed cabin and condo units, **Lake Mayfield Resort** (350 Hadlaller Rd. in Silver Creek, 360/985-2357) also offers camping. RV owners can roll in ($28–48), and campers can unfurl their tents onto sites with water ($35) or the primitive sites at the resort's secluded Adventure Island ($25).

For a little more solitude, **Barrier Dam Campground** (273 Fuller Rd., 360/985-2495) offers wooded tent ($18) and RV sites with full hookups ($28). The property also has a convenience and tackle store.

Accommodations

Sprawling along the southern shores of the lake, Lake Mayfield offers a spate of lodging options at its full-service property. The waterfront resort is well positioned for boat-owners, with a marina that includes a boat ramp and eight docks. You can choose between one- and two-bedroom condo units ($150–189), all with full kitchens, satellite television, and air conditioning. The resort also offers a large cabin it likes to call The Best Little Oarhouse ($255), which features a view of the lake on its patio with barbecue, plus a full kitchen and four bedrooms outfitted with queen beds. If that is a bit much for your taste, you can also choose between two rustic one-room cabins ($30–70). Neither have bathrooms, but there are public bathrooms and coin-op showers on the property.

Seven miles west of Mossyrock in Salkum, **The Shepherd's Inn B&B** (168 Autumn Heights Dr., 360/985-2434 or 800/985-2434, www.theshepherdsinn.com, $85–105 d) is an attractive, quiet, country home with five guest rooms (shared or private baths), including an indoor hot tub and full breakfast. Cozy and clean rooms are also available at Salkum's **Country Cabins** (2527 Hwy. 12, 360/985-2737, $60 s or d).

MORTON TO RANDLE

Passing the glinting waters of Riffe Lake you're likely to see timber-burdened semis zooming in either direction as you approach a string of small logging towns framed with a checkered mix of freshly cut and second growth forested slopes. Among these hamlets is Randle, which sits at the Highway 12 junction with Forest Road 25, the northeastern gateway to Mount St. Helens. Here too is where the highway begins banking north toward Rainier's southeastern corner.

Sights

The **Old Settlers Museum** (710 Main Ave., Morton, 360/496-5497, Memorial Day–Labor Day Sat. 1–4 P.M. or by appt.) displays local pioneer exhibits. When closed, stop by city hall for access to the museum. Three miles west of Morton on Short Road is a great binocular-view of Mount St. Helens' crater opening and lava dome.

Events

The **Morton Loggers Jubilee,** held the second weekend in August, is one of the largest timber carnivals in Washington. In addition to the standard ax throwing, log rolling, and other contests, you'll discover a riding lawnmower race, parades, barbecues, and dancing, along with an arts and crafts fair.

Sports and Recreation

HIKING

The **Woods Creek Watchable Wildlife Trail,** is an easy 1.5-mile path through mixed forests, a meadow, and past several beaver ponds. It leaves from the Woods Creek Information Station. Two other easy walks are the quarter-mile **Iron Creek Old-Growth Trail** and the 1.5-mile **Iron Creek Campground Trail,** both of which depart from Iron Creek Campground and offer treks though tall stands of cedar and Douglas fir. Also nearby—at the end of a quarter-mile path—is beautiful 60-foot **Iron Creek Falls.**

CAMPING

Public campsites can be found south of Randle in the Gifford Pinchot National Forest, along the east side of Mount St. Helens. Nearest is **Iron Creek Campground** (12 miles south on Forest Rd. 25, 518/885-3639 or 877/444-6777, www.reserveusa.com, open mid-May to late October, $18–20 for tents, $36 for RVs). Campfire programs are given at Iron Creek Friday and Saturday evenings in the summer. **Tower Rock Campground** is six miles east of Iron Creek on Road 76 (open mid-May to late September, $18–20). A good place for primitive camping in the national forest is along paved Forest Road 23, leading southeast from Randle toward Trout Lake. Just past North Fork Campground (group-camping site only) are several spots right along the Cispus River, 12 miles from Randle.

RV owners will likely be more comfortable at one of Randle's RV parks. Families can break out the fishing poles at **Tower Rock U-Fish RV Park** (137 Cispus Rd., 360/497-7680, www.towerrocktv.com, $22 with full hookups, $20 electric), which allows guests to cast into its waters without a license. You pay for what you catch, $4.25 per pound. Tent sites are also available for $16. This place is recommended. **Shady Firs Campground** (107 Young Rd., 360/497-6108, $27 full hookups) also offers a nice respite from the sun. The property has laundry and shower facilities.

Accommodations

Hikers headed for a big day around north Gifford Pinchot Forest will appreciate the gourmet breakfasts served by the French chef owner of **St. Helens Manor House B&B** (7476 Hwy. 12, 360/498-5243 or 800/551-3290, www.sthelensmanorhousebab.com, $85–95 s or d). He'll delight you with creations such as smoked salmon omelettes. The house itself has a little back story as well; this 1910 three-story abode is said to be haunted by two female ghosts that slam doors, appear in hallways, and toy with the security system. Kids are not allowed here.

For more basic accommodations, **Stiltner Motel** (250 Hwy. 7, 360/496-5103, $60 s or d) rents simple cabins with kitchenettes. The rooms at **Susan's Motel** (161 N. 2nd St., 360/496-5000, $80 s, $90 d) don't have kitchens, but guests do benefit from complimentary continental breakfast and Wi-Fi. **The Seasons Motel** (200 Westlake, 360/496-6835, $87 s or $98 d) is a good place, with a friendly staff and a warm breakfast served each morning.

The liveliest spot in Randle is **Tall Timber Motel** (one mile east of Randle on Hwy. 12, 360/497-2991, www.talltimbersrestaurantloungemotel.com, $75–113 s or d), which plays host to a homespun diner and a lounge that attracts local barflys, as well as a collection of comfortable motel rooms. **Woodland Motel** (11890 Hwy. 12, 360/494-6766, $40 s or $50 d) offers a few more in-room amenities, including satellite TV, microwave, and fridge, and even full kitchens in some units.

Food

Big Bottom Bar & Grill (9791 Hwy. 12, 360/497-0561) is a fun place for lunch or dinner with great service and dependably good all-American steaks and burgers. Hours are flexible, but usually doors will open at 10 A.M. daily and the kitchen turns off the burners at around 10 P.M. The bar keeps pouring until 2 A.M. most nights.

Information

The **Morton Chamber of Commerce** (2nd and Westlake, 360/496-6086, www.lewiscounty.com/morton) operates a summer-only log cabin visitors center. Randle's **Cowlitz Valley Ranger Station** (three miles east of town, 360/497-1100, May–Sept. daily 8 A.M.–4:30 P.M., Oct.–Apr. Mon.–Fri. 8 A.M.–4:30 P.M.) has detailed information on local hiking and mountain biking trails.

PACKWOOD

The small logging town of Packwood rubs elbows with some of the best scenery in the west. Situated where it is along Highway 12, it is within easy striking distance of Mount St. Helens' back side, White Pass, and all of the major stops within Mt. Rainier National Park. It is also literally an oasis amid a sea of wilderness areas—Tatoosh to the west, Goat Rocks to the east, William O. Douglas to the northeast, and Trapper Creek to the south. Much of the remaining land around the town is still publicly owned by the Forest Service, giving mountain bikers, snowmobilers, and other recreational enthusiasts an opportunity to enjoy the views as well.

Sports and Recreation

One of the quintessential hikes around this area is up Packwood Lake trail (trail No. 78, from trailhead at end of Forest Road 1260) to the so-named lake. This gentle climb starts in a few harvested forest areas before hitting the Goat Rocks Wilderness area. It might not be pretty to walk through, but the Forest Service is in the business of managing our timber resources—how else are we going to build roofs over our heads? Besides, in this instance the clearings offer a great peek at Rainier on clear days. Once you hit the wilderness boundary you'll be surrounded by plenty of old-growth forest all the way until the trail meets trail No. 81, when Packwood Lake Trail leads just outside the wilderness boundary down

© LEWIS COUNTY CONVENTION & VISITOR BUREAU/LOREN LANE

a view of Mount Rainier with the community of Packwood in the foreground.

to the lake (4.2 miles from trailhead), which provides good summertime fishing. You can continue up in elevation along the trail past Packwood Lake to Mosquito Lake and Lost Lake until it ends 9.6 miles later. Because this trail does lead through the wilderness area, mountain bikes are not allowed, but horses are. Bikers should consider the parallel Pipeline Trail (trail No. 74, from trailhead at end of Forest Road 1260), which runs 4.5 miles up to the lake.

The lake itself reflects Mount Rainier on clear days and is home to a thriving rainbow trout fishery that anglers can take a crack at by shore or float tube. This is one of the best fishing holes around Packwood, but far from the only—other favorites include Dog Lake, Leech Lake for fly fishers, and Skate Creek, accessible from the small and virtually unknown **Packwood State Park** (www.parks.wa.gov). This park has tall trees and decent fishing, but no facilities. Access is via Forest Road 52 across the Cowlitz River.

Packwood is also great fun in the winter. Cross-country skiers and snowmobilers flock to the **Packwood Winter Recreation Area** to slip and slide on the white stuff. Go about seven miles southwest of Packwood on Forest Road 21 to reach **Johnson Creek Sno-Park,** from which miles of groomed trails extend. You must have a Sno-Park Pass to access the park. Get one at Tatoosh Food Mart (13053 Hwy. 12, 360/494-7001).

CAMPING

The closest Forest Service camping can be found at **La Wis Wis Campground** ($18–20 tents, $36 RVs), seven miles northeast of town on Highway 12. Also fairly close is the primitive and free **Summit Creek Campground,** 12 miles north of town, and just east of the Highway 12 and Highway 123 junction on Forest Road 2160. No trailers are allowed here. Instead, park and hook up at **Packwood RV Park** (12985 Hwy. 12, 360/494-5145, $30). This wooded property is within walking distance of Packwood and has on-site laundry and showers, plus cable TV.

Accommodations

Cozy and friendly, **Hotel Packwood** (104 Main St., 360/494-5431, www.packwoodwa.com) is a renovated 1912 hotel that sends its guests back in time with its big veranda and lobby featuring a brick fireplace and antique piano. Stay in modest rooms with shared ($30 s or d) or private ($49) baths. Or opt for the Roosevelt Suite, which hosted T.R. back in the hotel's heyday.

Enjoy the heated outdoor pool in the summer and gazebo hot tub when the white stuff falls at **Mountain View Lodge & Motel** (13163 Hwy. 12, 360/494-5555, www.mtvlodge.com, $45–150 s or d), a favorite stopover for Seattle skiers headed up to White Pass Ski Resort.

Crest Trail Lodge (12729 Hwy. 12, 360/494-4944 or 800/477-5339, www.cresttraillodge.com, $80 s or 90 d) offers standard motel rooms, plus a hot tub, continental breakfast, and free wireless Internet. Another good place to get out of the elements, **Inn of Packwood** (12032 Hwy. 12, 360/494-5500, www.innofpackwood.com, $50 s or d) also sports an outdoor pool and hot tub. The inn has kitchenette units available for $145 for up to six people.

Food

Peters Inn (13051 Hwy. 12, 360/494-4000, Sun.–Thurs. 6 A.M.–9 P.M., Fri.–Sat. 6 A.M.–10 P.M.) has good breakfasts, seafood in season, steaks and prime rib, and homemade pies.

Information

Get information on nearby Gifford Pinchot National Forest from **Packwood Work Center** (13068 Hwy. 12, 360/494-0600, www.fs.fed.us/gpnf).

WHITE PASS

Highway 12 between Yakima and Mt. Rainier traverses 4,500-foot White Pass. The route climbs westward along the Tieton River through heavily forested areas with a few clear views of Rainier along the way.

White Pass Ski Area

Located off Highway 12 about 55 miles west of Yakima, and 12 miles southeast of Mount

Rainier National Park, White Pass Ski Area (509/672-3100, www.skiwhitepass.com, weekend rates $45 adults, $28 kids and seniors) offers a 1,500-foot vertical drop and 650 acres of skiing, served by five chairlifts (including a high-speed quad chair) and two Poma tows. The base elevation is 4,500 feet. Amenities include ski and snowboard lessons and rentals, child care, cafeteria, and bar. The resort also operates a small Nordic ski center; you can rent cross-country skis and get a pass for $16.

Near the ski area, **White Pass Village Inn** (48933 Hwy. 12, 509/672-3131, $80 d in winter) has condos of various sizes, with a winter-only heated outdoor pool. Nearby, find a store, gas station, and the **Summit House Restaurant** (509/672-3111, open in winter only).

Eight miles east of White Pass Ski Area on Highway 12, **Indian Creek Corral** (509/672-2400) offers one-hour ($70), overnight ($250, two-person minimum) and multi-day horseback rides in the summer. Hikers can also take advantage of their drop-camp service.

Rimrock Lake Area

Traveling along Highway 12, you can't miss **Rimrock Lake,** just a few miles east of White Pass. This massive blue-green lake was created in 1927 by what was then one of the largest earth-filled dams in the country. Today Rimrock is popular with anglers in search of good-sized silvers mid-May to late June, and with boaters, swimmers, and campers.

On the lake, **Twelve West** (509/672-2460, $30 with full hookups, $25 electric, year-round) has RV hookups, a marina, and hot showers.

Silver Beach Resort (40350 Hwy. 12, 509/672-2500) has rustic cabins with kitchenettes ($80, sleeps four), RV hookups ($20 with water, electric, and dump privileges), and a boat dock. **Trout Lodge** (27090 Hwy. 12, 509/672-2211, $75 d) has a four-unit motel, store, and restaurant (Fri. 9 A.M.–7:30 P.M., Sat. 8 A.M.–7:30 P.M., Sun. 8 A.M.–7:30 P.M., Mon. 9 A.M.–6:30 P.M.).

Tieton River-Rafting

In September, when most of the rivers in Washington have slowed to a trickle, river rats from around the Pacific Northwest gather around the normally quiet Tieton River for the big yearly event they call the "flip flop." That's when the engineers over at Rimrock Dam push a button and unleash a torrent of water that drains through the Tieton out to the greater Yakima River drainage area to provide Yakima Valley farmers valuable irrigation supplies. Rafters reap the benefits with an exciting class III (intermediate) ride that starts high in the mountains and descends at a rapid 50-feet-per-mile pace down through basalt canyons and into the dry valley on the east side of the Cascades, where the Tieton meets Naches River. The flip-flop only lasts about a month, but some rafting companies will still take you out through October.

There are dozens of rafting companies with encampments up and down the river. Get the most bang for your buck from **Blue Sky Outfitters** (800/228-7238, www.blueskyoutfitters.com), which paddles an epic 21-mile run along the river—longest among all guide services out there. Blue Sky also serves up a generous gourmet barbecue dinner after all is said and done aboard the rafts. Other respected services include **Downstream River Runners** (800/234-4644, www.riverpeople.com, $75), which employs some of the most experienced guides on the Tieton and provides snacks before and after your trip, and **Alpine Adventures** (800/723-8386, www.alpineadventures.com, $84), which has arranged special weekend packages with Yakima innkeepers.

Elk and Bighorn Sheep

During most winters, the large White Pass elk population and a small herd of bighorn sheep are fed at the **Oak Creek Wildlife Recreation Area** (two miles west of the intersection of Highways 410 and 12, and 17 miles west of Yakima, 509/575-2740) Best times to see them are early morning or late afternoon, when the animals are most active.

Approaching Mount St. Helens

CASTLE ROCK AND SPIRIT LAKE MEMORIAL HIGHWAY

The west side of Mount St. Helens offers the quickest access and has some of the finest views and the most developed facilities. Nearly 900,000 visitors take this route each year. With five elaborate visitors centers and a wide paved road reaching the center of the monument, this is the place most folks view the volcano. The main access route to the west side is Highway 504, the **Spirit Lake Memorial Highway.** Starting from the town of Castle Rock (exit 49 from I-5), Highway 504 offers a 54-mile scenic climb right to the heart of the volcanic destruction that resulted from the 1980 eruption. A secondary access is Highway 505, which cuts east from I-5 at the tiny town of **Toledo** (exit 60) and joins Highway 504 after 16 miles near the town of **Toutle** (TOOT-ul). The route below follows Spirit Lake Memorial Highway from I-5 to its terminus inside the national monument.

Castle Rock

Castle Rock (pop. 2,100) lies just west of I-5 along the Cowlitz River. The town is named for a 150-foot-high rocky knob that can be climbed by an easy-to-find path. The town was hit hard by the eruption of Mount St. Helens in 1980, when mud flows turned the Cowlitz into a raging torrent that washed out bridges and damaged or destroyed more than 200 homes. In town is a memorial to Harry Truman, the old-timer who died at his Spirit Lake home when the volcano erupted and buried the lake in hundreds of feet of debris.

SIGHTS

The **Castle Rock Exhibit Hall and Visitor Information Center** (147 Front Ave. NW, 360/274-6603, summer daily 9 A.M.–6 P.M., year-round Wed.–Sat. 10 A.M.–2 P.M., free) details the town and its connection to the Cowlitz River, the importance of the timber industry to the economy, and the impact of the 1980 eruption of Mount St. Helens.

EVENTS

The **Castle Rock Fair** on the fourth weekend of July is the big annual event, with a parade, stage shows, games, and carnival. The Mount St. Helens Motorcycle Club sponsors **Pro-Am TT Motorcycle Races** (www.mshmc.org) all summer at Castle Rock racetrack. Bicyclists come here for the **Tour de Blast** race in June and the **Seattle to Portland** bike race each July.

ACCOMMODATIONS

Castle Rock is the place to go for cheap Mount St. Helens–area lodging. Suitable motels include **7 West Motel** (864 Walsh Ave. NE, 360/274-7526, $48 s or $55 d), which has the cheapest rooms in Castle Rock, **Timberland Inn & Suites** (206 Spirit Lake Hwy., 360/274-6002 or 800/900-6335, www.timberland-inn.com,$79 s or $89 d), and **Mount St. Helens Motel** (227 Spirit Lake Hwy., 360/274-7721, www.mountsainthelensmotel.com, $65 s or 85 d).

Silver Lake

Your first big stop should be the comprehensive **Silver Lake Visitor Center** (five miles from I-5 on Spirit Lake Memorial Hwy., 360/274-2100, May–Sept. daily 9 A.M.–6 P.M., Oct.–Apr. daily 9 A.M.–5 P.M., $3), where the focus is on the eruption and its impacts. The centerpiece is a walk-in volcano that reveals the geological forces at work, but the other exhibits are equally well done, including models comparing the 1980 eruption with other volcanic eruptions (it was puny compared to the eruption that created Crater Lake), descriptions of the buildup to the eruption and images of the volcano in action, a working seismograph to see the latest shakers, and newspaper front pages from 1980. The mountain is 30 miles from here, but can be seen—on a clear day—through the spotting scopes outside. An extraordinary 10-minute slide show and a 22-minute movie alternate every half hour throughout the day. In addition to maps, books, and current trail and road

© WASHINGTON STATE TOURISM/LEVY SHECKLER

Silver Lake offers boat rentals and a view of Mount St. Helens.

information, the center offers daily interpretive programs throughout the year.

Seaquest State Park (888/226-7688, www.parks.wa.gov, $17 tents, $23 RVs) is right next to the visitors center, within a beautiful stand of gigantic old-growth Douglas firs and hemlocks. Camping is available here year-round. Silver Lake is one of the best bass fishing lakes in the state, and a public boat ramp is a mile east of the park. RV owners can also stop by **Mount St. Helens RV Park** (167 Schaffran Rd., 360/274-8522, $30 for full hookups).

ACCOMMODATIONS

Silver Lake Motel and Resort (3201 Spirit Lake Hwy., 360/274-6141, www.silverlakeresort.com, $75–175 s or d) has motel rooms with a balcony over the water and full kitchens, rustic two-bedroom cabins with full kitchens, and RV and tent sites. They also rent fishing boats.

Five miles up from I-5, the spacious **Blue Heron Inn B&B** (2846 Spirit Lake Hwy., 360/274-9595, www.blueheroninn.com, $159 s or d, $215 d for the hot tub suite) has seven guest rooms, all with private baths. A full breakfast and dinner are served. Not suitable for kids under five.

Hoffstadt Bluffs and Creek

As you continue east on Spirit Lake Highway from Silver Lake, the road slips past the trailer homes of **Toutle** at the juncture of the South and North Fork of the Toutle River, and then up along the North Fork into the mountains. Much of the route is on private timberland, with Weyerhaeuser tree plantations lining both sides of the road. A few miles west, signs point to the famous buried A-frame, another place to purchase souvenirs. Continue east through the Weyerhaeuser tree farms to **Hoffstadt Bluffs Visitor Center** (360/274-7750 or 800/752-8439, May–Oct. daily 10 A.M.–6 P.M.) at milepost 27. Owned by Cowlitz County, this timber-frame building houses two gift shops, a demonstration glass blowing studio, and a restaurant (June and Sept. daily 11:30–5 P.M., July–Aug. 11:30–6 P.M.) whose menu lists barbecue, burgers, and home-style blackberry cobbler among its other treats. Eat inside and enjoy the picture-window panorama, or outside on the patio overlooking the North Toutle Valley and Mount St. Helens. A picnic area is also available, with telescopes to watch the several hundred elk below and the mountain above.

Hillsboro Helicopters (360/274-7750 or 800/752-8439, www.hillsboro-aviation.com) sends scenic helicopter flights from Hoffstadt Bluffs over the dramatic crater and **Eco Park Adventure Trails** (360/274-7007, $30 per hour) offers horseback adventures within the blast zone around the bluffs.

ACCOMMODATIONS AND FOOD

Stay as close to the mountain as you can get from the west side at **Eco Park at Mount St. Helens** (just past mile marker 24, 360/274-6542). Owned by the same family who once ran the Spirit Lake Lodge in pre-eruption days, Eco Park offers the only accommodations inside the blast zone. The resort has summertime basic cabins ($100–125 d), yurts ($75 d), and campsites ($17.50) in a remote area on the northeast side. RVs are accepted on the site, but there are no hookups.

Toutle Diner and RV Park (5037 Spirit Lake Memorial Hwy, Toutle, 360/274-6208) offers full hookups ($21), some sites with cable TV. The diner (Sun.–Thurs. 8 A.M.–9 P.M., Fri.–Sat. 8 A.M.–10 P.M.) offers typical roadhouse fare, along with espresso and free Wi-Fi. The property also has shower and laundry facilities.

Upper Toutle Valley

From here eastward, Spirit Lake Memorial Highway climbs steadily uphill, with wide shoulders for bikes and numerous turnouts to take in the scenery. RVers should park at Hoffstadt Bluffs and those towing trailers should leave them there, since the road has some 7 percent grades ahead.

Next stop is the **Hoffstadt Creek Bridge,** one of 14 bridges that had to be reconstructed on Highway 504 after the eruption. The new bridge rises 370 feet above the canyon and stands near the edge of the blast zone—an incredible 14.8 miles from the crater. Everything from here on was killed by the heat of the explosion. Also, from here on you can see a sharp contrast between what private companies did after the eruption and what took place on Forest Service land. Weyerhaeuser salvage-logged its lands and immediately replanted millions of trees. With fertilization, the new stands are coming back surprisingly fast; some trees are already 40 feet tall! As a public agency, the Forest Service had a rather different mandate, and no logging or replanting took place within the national volcanic monument. Instead, the area has become a natural laboratory where scientists can study the recovery process, and where visitors can marvel at the power of nature. (Salvage logging and replanting were, however, done on Forest Service lands outside the monument boundaries.)

Today the upper Toutle River Valley is home to over 500 Roosevelt elk, many of which are visible by hiking two miles down Road 3100 near the Hoffstadt Creek Bridge. Despite harsh conditions, the elk survive on the nutritious grasses and clover that were planted in the mudflow following the eruption.

North Fork Ridge

The **Forest Learning Center** (Spirit Lake Memorial Hwy. milepost 33, 360/414-3439, 10 A.M.–6 P.M. daily May–Oct., closed in winter, free) highlights some of the differences between public management and that of Weyerhaeuser Company, with emphasis on Weyerhaeuser's salvage and recovery efforts after the eruption. The center sits on a 2,700-foot-high bluff over the North Fork of the Toutle River. Elaborate exhibits take you through a diorama of the forest prior to the 1980 eruption, an "eruption chamber" where a you-are-there multimedia program surrounds you, and then past additional exhibits extolling the salvage, reforestation, and recovery efforts, plus the benefits of private forestry practices and conservation. The Forest Learning Center is especially popular with families; kids can climb aboard a toy helicopter or play in the seven-foot-high rubber volcano outside. Telescopes provide a chance to watch elk in the valley below, and a one-mile trail descends into the valley. Other facilities include a gift shop and picnic area.

Be sure to stop at the **Elk Rock Viewpoint** at the entrance to the Mount St. Helens National Monument for magnificent views of the crater to the south and the deep river valley below, filled with a 700-foot-deep layer of rock, ash, and debris. Don't forget to look below for Roosevelt elk.

WOODLAND TO COUGAR

Woodland

Woodland acts as the southern gateway to Mount St. Helens, with Highway 503 heading northeast to the volcano. The area was first settled in the 1840s, and the town was incorporated in 1906. A 32-mile scenic climb into the hills along the highway cuts through second-growth forests, with periodic glimpses of Lake Merwin and Yale Lake—reservoirs that were created by dams on the Lewis River.

SIGHTS

There isn't a lot to the town of Woodland, but be sure to follow the signs to **Hulda Klager Lilac Gardens** (360/225-8996, donation requested) where you'll discover an 1889 farmhouse surrounded by three acres of grounds filled with colorful flowers and trees of all descriptions. Hulda Klager began hybridizing lilacs in 1903 and developed more than 250 new varieties, including 10 that can be found in the gardens here. The gardens are open year-round, and lilac starts (rooted lilac cuttings) are available weekdays, but the lovely Victorian-era home is open only for Lilac Week (the week preceding Mothers Day).

The **Cedar Creek Grist Mill** (10 miles east of Woodland off N.E. Cedar Creek Rd., 360/225-5832, www.cedarcreekgristmill.com, donation requested) is one of the few 19th-century water-powered gristmills remaining in the Northwest. Built in 1876, it has been carefully restored, with water fed in by a 650-foot log flume. Volunteers grind wheat here Saturday 1–4 P.M. and Sunday 2–4 P.M. Upstairs is a small museum detailing the reconstruction process.

D. B. COOPER

On November 24, 1971, a man known only as Dan Cooper jumped out of a Boeing 727 midflight and into the history and imagination of Washington state. After using what he claimed was a bomb to hijack a Seattle-bound Northwest Orient flight out of Portland, Cooper forced the pilot to land the airliner at Sea-Tac airport. Once his demands for $200,000 and four parachutes were met, he released the passengers and ordered the pilot to fly him to Reno, Nevada. While 10,000 feet over southern Washington, Cooper forced open the rear stairs of the aircraft, clutched his ransom money tightly, and jumped out into the dark night, never to be heard from again. In 1980, an eight-year-old child found nearly $6,000 of the ransom money, verified by serial number, by the banks of the Columbia River near Vancouver, Washington. Was the money left there by Cooper himself? Did it wash there from a tributary deep in the woods? Only one man knows, and for over 30 years, he's kept the secret.

EVENTS

Planter's Day is billed as the state's oldest continuously running festival. The four-day event celebrates the building of dikes to prevent flooding of Woodland and includes a carnival, fun run, pancake breakfast, firemen's barbecue, frog-jumping contest, and car show.

SPORTS AND RECREATION

The lilac gardens sit near **Horseshoe Lake,** formerly part of the Lewis River. It was created in 1940 when the river was rerouted to construct what is now I-5. The lake is a popular place to fish for trout and largemouth bass. Anglers may also want to stop at the Lake Merwin and Lake Speelyai. Merwin is known for some large tiger muskies, while Speelyai attracts fishing poles with its kokanee population. Both lakes make for pleasant picnicking and swimming, as does the Yale Park Recreation Area on Yale Lake.

Paradise Point State Park (five miles southeast of Woodland just off I-5, 360/263-2350 or 888/226-7688, www.parks.wa.gov, $12 tent, $7 reservation fee) has fishing, boating, and swimming in the East Fork Lewis River, a two-mile hiking trail, and camping. Open for day use and camping April–Sept., plus weekends and holidays the rest of the year. Because of its location right along I-5, this isn't a particularly quiet place to spend a night, but at least the highway makes for easy access.

More camping is available at **Woodland Special Campground** (N.W. 389th St., 800/527-3305, mid-May–mid-Oct., free) in dense forests three miles east of Woodland, run by the Department of Natural Resources.

RV drivers can also choose among several private grounds, including **Columbia Riverfront RV Park** (1881 Dike Rd., 360/225-8051, $35–42 full hookups), which affords river views from some of its sites, and **Lewis River RV Park** (3125 Lewis River Rd., 360/225-9556, $30 full hookups, $25 partial), which has a pool on-site.

ACCOMMODATIONS

There are several lodging choices in the Woodland area. Stay locally at **Lewis River Inn** (1100 Lewis River Rd., 360/225-6257 or 800/543-4344, $69–91 s or $77–99 d). It's located along the river, with balconies offering a view from the more expensive rooms.

Cheapest is **Lakeside Motel** (785 Lakeshore Dr., 360/225-8240, $48 s or $52 d). **Scandia Motel** (1123 Hoffman St., 360/225-8006, $40 s or $55 d) is similar but has the added benefit of an outdoor hot tub.

FOOD

Oak Tree Restaurant (1020 Atlantic St., 360/225-8446, Sun.–Thurs. 7 A.M.–10 P.M., Fri.–Sat. 7 A.M.–11 P.M.) is a popular place for steaks.

Cougar

The highway eventually leads you to the hamlet of Cougar, which serves as a jumping-off point for access to the southern and eastern sides of Mount St. Helens National Volcanic Monument.

ACCOMMODATIONS

Stay at the comfortable, kid-friendly **Monfort's B&B** (132 Cougar Rd., 360/238-5229, $60–90 s or d) with two guest rooms, private baths, and full breakfasts. The biggest property around Cougar is **Lone Fir Resort** (16806 Lewis River Rd., 360/238-5210, www.lonefirresort.com, $60–70 s or d), which offers motel rooms and a cabin in a wooded location with an outdoor pool. RV spaces are also available here ($27 full hookup).

Another good choice is **Cougar RV Park** (16730 Lewis River Rd., 360/238-5224), an eight-acre property staffed by a friendly bunch of folks. You'll find RV hookups ($25) and rustic camping cabins ($35 for up to five), basic shelters and beds on which to unroll the ol' sleeping sacks.

Information

A small trailer at Lakeshore Drive and Goerig Street houses the **Woodland Chamber of Commerce Information Center** (360/225-9552, daily 8 A.M.–4 P.M. year-round, and Fri.–Mon. until 7 P.M. Apr.–Oct.).

Mount St. Helens National Volcanic Monument

Prior to May 18, 1980, Mount St. Helens had the most perfectly shaped cone in the Pacific Northwest volcanic chain. The momentous plume of pumice and smoke Mount St. Helens spewed that day transformed a quiet and beautiful landscape into a moonscape wasteland. Today plants and animals are returning to the land as it recovers, but lingering fields of devastation continue to amaze and astound visitors. Mount St. Helens has become one of Washington's must-see sights, and a fine set of visitor facilities, access roads, and trails now offer ample opportunities to learn about the power of this active volcano.

Visiting Mount St. Helens

In 1982, the 110,000-acre **Mount St. Helens National Volcanic Monument** was created, and the area has been gradually opened to visitors as roads, bridges, visitors centers, and trails are built. The government still keeps parts of it off-limits to serve as a natural laboratory for scientists. They have learned one basic fact so far: nature heals itself more quickly than anyone expected. Plant and animal life is returning quite rapidly considering the extent of the destruction.

The Forest Service has imposed stringent regulations on activity within the National Monument, both to protect visitors from potential hazards and to protect the area as a natural laboratory of ecological change. Visitors must stay away from certain areas and not venture off trails; a minimum $100 fine, stringently enforced, awaits those who travel off-trail.

Roads approach Mount St. Helens from the east and west sides, offering dramatic views into its center, while more adventurous visitors can climb to the summit from the south side. The vast majority of visitors arrive from the west, turning off I-5 and following Spirit Lake Highway 54 miles past a series

© WASHINGTON STATE TOURISM/JIM POTH

Mount St. Helens in the distance

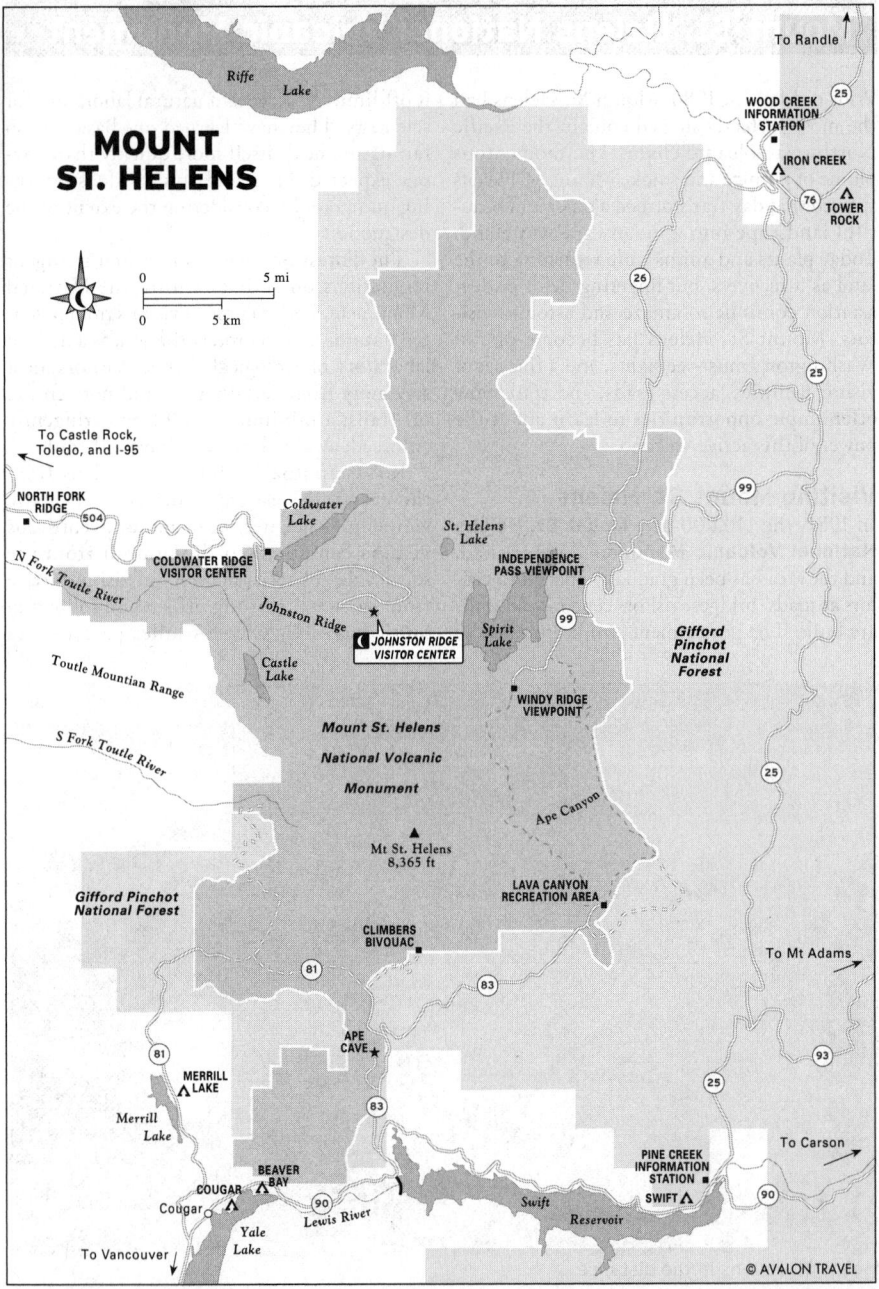
MOUNT ST. HELENS
0 5 mi
0 5 km
To Randle
Riffe Lake
WOOD CREEK INFORMATION STATION
IRON CREEK
TOWER ROCK
To Castle Rock, Toledo, and I-95
NORTH FORK RIDGE
Coldwater Lake
St. Helens Lake
COLDWATER RIDGE VISITOR CENTER
INDEPENDENCE PASS VIEWPOINT
N Fork Toutle River
Johnston Ridge
JOHNSTON RIDGE VISITOR CENTER
Spirit Lake
Gifford Pinchot National Forest
Castle Lake
Toutle Mountian Range
WINDY RIDGE VIEWPOINT
Mount St. Helens National Volcanic Monument
S Fork Toutle River
Ape Canyon
Mt St. Helens 8,365 ft
LAVA CANYON RECREATION AREA
Gifford Pinchot National Forest
CLIMBERS BIVOUAC
To Mt Adams
APE CAVE
MERRILL LAKE
Merrill Lake
To Carson
PINE CREEK INFORMATION STATION
BEAVER BAY
COUGAR
Cougar
Lewis River
Swift Reservoir
SWIFT
Yale Lake
To Vancouver
© AVALON TRAVEL

of visitors centers and ending at Johnston Ridge, where you can peer into the volcano's crater. Be sure to fill your gas tank before you start out on any of the Mount St. Helens access roads; gas stations are few and far between, especially on the east side. Specific access routes are described below from the east, south, and west. From the north side you are limited to distant views from a roadside pullout near Mossyrock Dam.

Visitors stopping in at Johnston's Ridge will need to pay a monument fee of $8 per person. If you just want to drive around or go for a hike, all that's required is a Northwest Forest Pass (800/270-7504, www.fs.fed.us/r6/feedemo, $5 daily, $30 annual). Get passes from any of the local visitors centers.

Camping

Specific campgrounds are described below for each side of Mount St. Helens. Dispersed camping is allowed only outside the restricted areas around the volcano. No camping is permitted within the upper North Fork of the Toutle River drainage, around Coldwater Lake and Spirit Lake, or around the volcano itself; check with the Forest Service for specifics.

Information

The **Mount St. Helens Volcanic Headquarters** (360/247-3900 www.fs.fed.us/gpnf/mshnvm or www.mountsthelens.com) is three miles north of Amboy on Highway 503. The office has brochures and the latest on conditions at Mount St. Helens, including the status of volcanic activity and trail closures.

Scenic Flights

Several aviation companies offer scenic flights over Mount St. Helens, affording passengers a view of the crater and lava dome that you can't get otherwise. Helicopter flights over the volcano are provided by **Hillsboro Helicopters** (360/274-7750 or 800/752-8439, www.hillsboro-aviation.com, $165) from Hoffstadt Bluffs and **Applebee Aviation** (503/647-0404, 15 minutes for $396, up to three passengers) from Eco Park Resort.

WEST SIDE ACCESS

Sights

COLDWATER RIDGE

Once the home of St. Helens' premier man-made attraction, Coldwater Ridge Visitor Center shuttered its doors in late 2007. Mountain oglers should still stop here to get a good look at the peak from the quarter-mile **Winds of Change Interpretive Trail,** just outside the closed visitors center. For another short hike, head two miles downhill to five-mile-long Coldwater Lake, where the quarter-mile **Birth of a Lake Trail** takes you by boardwalk past the debris avalanche left behind by the eruption. The lake is known for excellent rainbow and cutthroat trout fishing, with a minimum size of 16 inches for keepers. Rafts or float tubes are recommended to lessen the damage from bankside anglers, and gasoline-powered motorboats are prohibited. There's no camping, and be sure to stay on the trails or risk a $100 fine.

JOHNSTON RIDGE VISITOR CENTER

Spirit Lake Memorial Highway ends eight miles uphill from Coldwater Lake at the 4,300-foot level and the Johnston Ridge Visitor Center (360/274-2140, daily 10 A.M.–6 P.M. mid-May through September, daily 10 A.M.–4 P.M. the rest of the year). This facility emphasizes the geology of Mount St. Helens and ongoing scientific research work and is named for Dr. David Johnston, the geologist who was working here in 1980 when the volcano erupted. His last radio transmission, sent out as the mountain gave way, still haunts anyone who hears it: "Vancouver, Vancouver, this is it!" This visitors facility peers directly into the lava dome—just three miles away—that formed after the eruption (encased in clouds 200 days each year). Step inside to find a large model of the volcano that shows how the eruption progressed, geological monitoring equipment, and displays on the landscape both before and after the explosion. The highlight is a 16-minute film that re-creates the eruption in gripping, wide-screen detail. A half-mile **Eruption Trail** loops past a marker commemorating the 57 people killed by the 1980 blast.

ERUPTION!

At 8:32 A.M. on May 18, 1980, Mount St. Helens blew her top in an eruption that had the explosive power of several atomic bombs. The eruption was triggered by an earthquake measuring 5.1 on the Richter scale that sent a massive avalanche of rock, snow, and ice down the mountain's north slope at 200 mph, filling Spirit Lake – whose surface was instantly raised by 200 feet – and cresting over a 1,200-foot ridge. A second debris avalanche blasted down the North Fork of the Toutle River, and additional flows sent muddy water, rocks, and logs down the river, destroying bridges and homes along the way.

The landslide allowed pressure inside the volcano to escape explosively in an eruption that blew 1,312 feet (8.8 *billion* cubic yards) off the volcano's summit. A lateral blast shot northeast at 670 miles an hour, searing surrounding forests and flattening them up to 15 miles away. Temperatures 15 miles away reached an incredible 572°F, and the blast was followed by a plume of ash that rose 16 miles into the atmosphere. This explosion, along with the intense heat and landslides, killed 57 people within the blast zone, destroyed hundreds of homes, and ravaged the wildlife population. Spirit Lake was a virtual logjam of timber that had been swept away like matchsticks.

The damage wasn't limited to the area of the blast itself; 60,000 acres not destroyed by the blast were covered with more than eight inches of ash. Six hours after the eruption, river water at Castle Rock, 40 miles downstream, was over 100°F, and towns in eastern Washington – 150 miles away – were coated with up to three inches of ash, clogging carburetors and shrouding the towns in thick darkness at noon. Traces of ash were detected as far away as Montana, Denver, and Vancouver, British Columbia.

Sports and Recreation

HIKING AND CAMPING

For a spectacular hike with commanding views into Spirit Lake, begin at the Johnston Ridge Observatory and follow **Boundary Trail** four miles to Harry's Ridge. For an overnight hike, continue along this path to the summit of Mount Margaret and down before returning via the 5.5-mile **Lakes Trail.** You can camp at several small high-country lakes here (permit required). This is a research area, and scientists are attempting to keep human impacts to a minimum, so hikers need to stick within 10 feet of the trails.

There are no developed campsites within Mount St. Helens National Volcanic Monument. Camping is prohibited along the Spirit Lake Memorial Highway inside the monument boundaries.

SOUTH SIDE ACCESS

The south side of Mount St. Helens was not impacted nearly as much by the 1980 eruption and is best known as the access route to climb the summit, for Ape Cave, and for various hiking trails, including the Loowit System that circles the mountain. These sites are all accessible from Cougar.

Ape Cave

This 12,810-foot lava tube is one of the longest such caves in the nation, and one of the most popular visitor attractions at Mount St. Helens. The cave is 10 miles northeast of Cougar at the junction of Forest Roads 83 and 90 and is open all the time. From the entrance a staircase leads down to a chamber where the route splits. The downhill arm ends after an easy 0.75-mile walk, while the uphill route is more difficult and rocky, continuing 1.5 miles to an exit where an above-ground trail leads back to the starting point. Forest Service interpreters lead half-hour tours of Ape Cave twice a day in the summer. Be sure to bring drinking water and two flashlights and extra batteries (or rent a lantern for $2). Wear hiking boots, gloves, and warm clothes (the air is a steady 42°F all year). A small visitors center (daily 9 A.M.–6 P.M., mid-June through Labor Day) can provide assistance, publications, and lantern rentals. A Northwest Forest Pass ($5) is required for access to the cave. The road is plowed to the Trail of Two Forests, a half mile away, in the winter.

Sports and Recreation

CLIMBING MOUNT ST. HELENS

Mount St. Helens is the second-most-climbed peak on the planet, exceeded only by Japan's Mt. Fuji. With 16,000 people making the pilgrimage each year up Mount St. Helens, you're bound to have company on your trip to the top.

All climbing routes up Mount St. Helens are from the south side of the peak, and a permit ($15 Apr.–May 15, $22 May 15–Oct., free the rest of the year) is required for travel above the 4,800-foot level. From May 15 through October, 100 permits per day are issued on a first-come, first-served basis, with up to 60 of these available by advance reservation via the Mount St. Helens Institute webpage (www.mshinstitute.org). Make reservations as early as possible after February 1, since most summer weekends are reserved by late March. The other 40 permits are issued on a first-come, first-served basis starting at 6 P.M. each evening for the next day's climb. Stop by **Lone Fir Resort** (16806 Lewis River Road, Cougar, 360/238-5210) to purchase these. You'll need to sign in at Lone Fir both before and after the climb, whether you booked in advance or not. These confusing rules may change, so check with the monument (360/247-3900, 360/247-3961 for a recorded message) before planning a climb.

The climb begins past the entrance to Ape Cave. Follow Forest Road 83 a mile beyond the cave, then turn left on Road 8100 for another mile, and finally right on Road 830 for the final three miles to Climbers Bivouac at an elevation of 3,750 feet. Even though the climb is not technically difficult, don't underestimate the steep slopes and severe weather. The first stretch ascends through the forest at a gradual pace, but above the 4,800-foot level the pole-marked route is a scramble over boulder fields, volcanic pumice, ash, and snowfields (often present till mid-July). The crater itself is off-limits to the general public because steam explosions can create extremely dangerous conditions. Avoid the edge of the crater when snow tops the peak, since you may be stepping on a cornice that could give way.

Watch the weather reports before heading up the mountain; it can snow at any time of year, and low clouds can drastically reduce visibility. Call 503/808-2400 for the latest weather forecast. Listen to the report for Mt. Hood, as the weather on the two mountains is invariably similar. Climbing boots, sunscreen, and plenty of water are requirements (no water is available on the route or at Climbers Bivouac), and you need to start early—by 7 A.M.—to have enough time to get up and back before nightfall. Most folks take around eight hours for the nine-mile (round-trip) trek. Take an ice ax when snow is present, along with plenty of warm clothes and rain gear. Gaiters will help keep the snow and ash out of your boots. Primitive camping is available in the woods at the trailhead. Some climbers prefer to get a head start the night before, camping three miles up at the 4,800-foot level, where you'll find a composting toilet. Camping is not allowed above this point.

HIKING

A very easy path is the **Trail of Two Forests,** a brief boardwalk that takes you past the molds left when trees were immersed in lava flows 2,000 years ago. You can even crawl through two of these ancient impressions. The trail is right across from Ape Cave on Road 8303.

One of the most interesting hikes on the south end of Mount St. Helens is the 2.5-mile **Lava Canyon Trail,** which drops 1,400 feet along the Muddy River. This canyon was scoured out by a mudflow during the 1980 eruption, revealing sharp cliffs and five tall waterfalls. Although the upper end is wheelchair-accessible, the lower part crosses a long suspension bridge and then descends a cliff face by a steel ladder. Great for the adventurous, not fun if you have a case of acrophobia. Get to the trail by following Forest Road 83 nine miles (paved the entire way) beyond Ape Cave to the trailhead.

The **Loowit System** (No. 216) is a difficult 29-mile trail that circles Mount St. Helens and is accessible from trailheads on all sides of the mountain. Plan on three days to get all the way around, and be prepared for lots of up-and-down hiking and faint trails in places. Camping is available at various points along the way, but contact the Forest Service for specifics since some areas are off-limits.

For an enjoyable loop hike, head to the end of Forest Road 8123 on the southwest side of the mountain and the start of **Sheep Canyon Trail** (No. 240). This path climbs through old-growth forests and drainages that were ravaged by volcanic mudflows and into a flower-filled alpine meadow along the Loowit Trail before returning downhill on the Toutle Trail (No. 238), which connects to the Sheep Canyon Trail and your starting point. Total distance is approximately seven miles.

The **Lewis River Trail** (No. 31) follows along this beautiful river from the Curly Creek Falls to Lower Falls (a fun swimming hole), a distance of more than 10 miles. Between Curly Creek Falls and Lower Falls on Road 99 is **Big Creek Falls,** plummeting 125 feet into a pool that makes a popular place for a summer dip. Above Lower Falls, you can follow the road to a series of roadside falls, including the scenic Middle Falls and Upper Falls.

WINTER SPORTS

Forest Service Road 83's two Sno-Parks offer a wide area for winter activities, including cross-country skiing, snowshoeing, and snowmobiling. Most popular is the **Marble Mountain Sno-Park,** located seven miles east of Cougar on Forest Rd. 90, and another six miles up Road 83. Get a Sno-Park permit ($11) and ski trail maps at Cougar Store (16842 Lewis River Rd., 360/238-5228, winter Sun.–Thurs. 6 A.M.–8 P.M., Fri.–Sat. 6 A.M.–9 P.M.). Snowmobilers must also purchase an additional $30 annual permit. A large log **warming shelter** is open here in the winter months and includes a woodstove. Rent it as a summertime cabin (June–Oct., $100 for up to 10 people) from the Forest Service (360/247-3900).

CAMPING

The Forest Service's **Lower Falls Campground** (15 miles east of the Pine Creek Information Station on Forest Road 90, 518/885-3639 or 877/444-6777, www.reserveusa.com, mid-May–mid-Oct., $15 tents, $35 RVs, $5 extra for reservations) is a fine camping place, with views of three large falls along the Lewis River and a hiking trail that heads downriver for 10 miles.

Several other non–Forest Service public campgrounds provide camping on the south side of Mount St. Helens. Near the town of Cougar, **Cougar Campground** and **Beaver Bay Campground** offer tent camping ($17) and showers on the Yale Reservoir along Forest Road 90. Go north on Road 8100 to **Merrill Lake Campground,** a free Department of Natural Resources camping area, or head east on Road 90 to **Swift Campground** (just south of the Pine Creek Information Station, $17). Reserve a spot through Pacific Power and Light (503/464-5035). They also have very popular summer-only campgrounds at **Cresap Bay Park** (seven miles north of Amboy on Hwy. 503, $17) and **Saddle Dam Park** (near the Yale Lake dam on Frasier Rd., $17). Cresap Bay and Swift Campgrounds have campfire programs on Friday and Saturday nights June–August.

Information

Three miles north of Amboy on Highway 503, **Mount St. Helens Volcanic Headquarters** (42218 N.E. Yale Bridge Rd., 360/247-3900) is open Monday–Friday 7:30 A.M.–5 P.M. year-round. The Forest Service's **Pine Creek Information Station** (17 miles east of Cougar on Forest Rd. 90) is open daily 9 A.M.–6 P.M. from mid-June through September.

EAST SIDE ACCESS

Unlike the west side, where a wide, new highway passes four visitors centers that seem to compete with each other to see which one can offer the most wows per minute, visitors to Mount St. Helens' eastern flanks will discover narrow, winding one-lane routes, simple information stations, and more basic facilities. This is the wild side of the mountain, where the crowds are less and you're allowed to draw your own conclusions without being inundated with flashy multimedia shows and elaborate computer animations. Information, maps, and monument passes ($3–6) are available at the **Woods Creek Information Station** (approximately seven miles south of Randle) and the **Pine Creek Information Station** on the east end of Swift Reservoir (20 miles east of Cougar).

The east side of Mount St. Helens is accessed by Forest Road 25, which heads south from the town of Randle. This paved but steep one-lane road (with turnouts) continues all the way to Pine Creek Ranger Station on Swift Creek Reservoir, south of the mountain. It is closed due to snow from late October to Memorial Day weekend and is not recommended for trailers or RVs. For easier driving, drop off your trailer at the Woods Creek Information Station or Iron Creek Picnic Site on Forest Service Road 25 if traveling from the north, or at the Pine Creek Information Station if you're coming from the south.

To Windy Ridge

Forest Roads 25, 26, and 99 provide access to the east side of Mount St. Helens. The primary destination on the east side is Windy Ridge, where you can see Spirit Lake and a magnificent up-close view of the volcano. Take Roads 25 and 99 to reach the viewpoint. Forest Road 26 turns south from Iron Creek Campground and leads to **Quartz Creek Big Trees** area, where a half-mile path takes you through old-growth Douglas firs that escaped the eruption. Just a mile away is the edge of the zone where trees were flattened in the blast (trees in this area were salvaged after the eruption). From here on, everything was destroyed by the force of the eruption. Road 26 is blocked south of here due to washouts.

At **Ryan Lake** another short trail provides views of the lake filled with downed trees. This area is usually accessible year-round, with open, flat areas for cross-country skiing. **Meta Lake**—at the junction of Forest Roads 26 and 99—has a paved trail and the famous **Miner's Car,** destroyed in the blast. Three people had driven here the night before the volcano gave way on May 18, 1980 and were killed in a nearby cabin by the superheated explosion. Meta Lake is coming back surprisingly fast from the destruction, in part because ice and snow protected fish and other animals from the heat. Nature walks are offered here daily during the summer months.

Windy Ridge stands at the end of Road 99, 4,000 feet above sea level and 34 miles southwest of Randle. It is just five miles from the crater itself. Climb the 361 steps for an incredible view into the volcano, across the devastated pumice plain, and over log-choked Spirit Lake. Forest Service interpretive personnel are here daily May–October, providing frequent talks about the volcano from the amphitheater.

There are no improved campgrounds along Forest Roads 25 or 99 between Iron Creek Campground in Randle and Cougar.

Hiking

For something strenuous, follow the 2.5-mile **Norway Pass Trail** (No. 1) through blowndown forests to the 4,500-foot pass, gaining 900 feet in elevation along the way. You can continue beyond to the Coldwater Lake area, return the same way you came, or return to Independence Pass along Road 99 via **Independence Pass Trail** (No. 227), with extraordinary views over Spirit Lake. The round-trip distance for this is six miles. The Norway Pass Trailhead is just a mile north of Meta Lake; a water pump is also here.

Harmony Trail drops 570 feet in just a mile, offering the only legal access to the shore of Spirit Lake. Most living things were killed when pyroclastic flows filled it in 1980, causing water temperatures to reach almost 100°F. The trailhead is halfway between the Independence Pass trailhead and Windy Ridge.

At Windy Ridge you can hike the six-mile **Truman Trail** (No. 207) for up-close-and-personal views of the lava dome inside the crater, and to connect with the round-the-mountain **Loowit Trail** (No. 216). A spur of this (216 E) leads to Loowit Falls, where 100°F water pours out of the crater (no swimming).

Information

Get information on Mount St. Helens at the Forest Service's **Woods Creek Information Station** (six miles south of Randle on Forest Rd. 25, daily 9 A.M.–5 P.M. mid-May–Sept.)—they even offer drive-through service! **Cowlitz Valley Ranger Station** (three miles east of Randle on Hwy. 12, 360/497-1100) is open daily 8 A.M.–4:30 P.M. Memorial Day through September, and weekdays the rest of the year. **Pine Creek Information Station** (17 miles east of Cougar on Forest Rd. 90 and 45 miles south of Randle, daily 9 A.M.–6 P.M. mid-May–Sept.) has information for the southeast side of St. Helens.

Mount Adams and Gifford-Pinchot

If it stood alone, 12,276-foot Mt. Adams would be a prime recreation site, silhouetted on license plates and key chains. But from a Seattle viewpoint, Adams is geographically behind and below its limelight-hogging neighbors. The distance from main towns and roads make Mt. Adams an ideal spot to escape civilization.

Geology

Like its more active neighbors, Mt. Adams is of volcanic origins; unlike its neighbors, the mountain is believed to have been formed by a congregation of volcanic cones instead of a single large one. The mountain has been relatively quiescent for 10,000 years, and large glaciers crown its summit, including the Klickitat Glacier, second biggest of all Cascadian glaciers.

Getting There

There are two ways to approach Mt. Adams: from Seattle, take I-5 south to I-205 near Vancouver, then follow I-205 to Highway 14 and head east. At Underwood, take Highway 141 north to Trout Lake. An alternative is to take I-5 south past Chehalis, then east on Highway 12 to Randle and take the Randle Road (Forest Service Road 23) south for 56 miles to Trout Lake. This isolated road is definitely the scenic route, and the entire length is paved. Approaching from the east, you can drive down Highway 97 to Goldendale and west on Highway 142 to Klickitat and take the Glenwood-Trout Lake Road, or follow Highway 14 from Maryhill to Underwood and drive north. The roads into the Mt. Adams area are closed each winter due to heavy snowfall.

MOUNT ADAMS WILDERNESS

This 42,280-acre wilderness covers the summit of Mt. Adams, along with the entire eastern and northern flanks. The east side of the peak lies within the Yakama Reservation and is termed "Tract D." Trails—including the Pacific Crest Trail—provide a semicircular path through the heart of the wilderness. A new backcountry permit system is being discussed for Mt. Adams Wilderness; check with Mt. Adams Ranger District in Trout Lake (509/395-3400) for details.

Climbing Mount Adams

Mount Adams is one of the easiest Northwest volcanic peaks to climb; in fact, it's often used as a first climb by area mountaineering clubs. Before you begin, be sure to register with the Mt. Adams Ranger Station in Trout Lake (509/395-2501, June 1–Sept. 30 Mon.–Thurs. $10, Fri.–Sun. $15). The south slope route is least difficult: It begins at 6,000 feet at the end of Forest Roads 8040 and 500 at Cold Springs Camp, climbing up the old road for several miles, then ascending **South Climb Trail** (No. 183), crossing snowfields and zigzgging up pumice to the peak. Climbers should carry an ice ax, rope, crampons, warm clothing, sunglasses, and other basic supplies.

Hiking

The most heavily used trail in the Mount Adams Wilderness is **South Climb,** a 2.2-mile trail from Cold Springs Campground to timberline, from where climbers depart for routes to the summit. Those who prefer to stay low

BIGFOOT IN WASHINGTON?

Washington state is home to the widest expanse of primordial forest in the Lower 48. Much of the North Cascades forest is trackless and closed to all vehicles. It is this dense, mountainous wilderness that many believe is home to a thriving community of Sasquatches, more commonly known as bigfoots.

Cryptozoology – the study of animals that have not yet been categorized – may be more popular than ever now, but there's nothing new about belief and interest in the disputed creature. Northwestern American Indians such as the Coast Salish people have passed along legends about Sasquatch for centuries, and a superhuman beast appears frequently in their artwork. Reports of apelike hominids roaming the vast forests of Washington date back to the first days of white settlement and still trickle in today.

Most scientific observers write off such sightings as misidentification, tending to think that excitable hikers have seen a bear standing on its hind legs or something equally mundane. Regardless of the truth, Sasquatch has captivated the imaginations of Washingtonians. For the time that the Sonics played basketball in Seattle, their mascot was the enormous, hair-covered, high-energy 'Squatch. One of the largest regional publishers is known as Sasquatch Books. With spring comes the annual Sasquatch! Music Festival, held at the Gorge Amphitheater. And closing out the fair and carnival season is late August's Bigfoot Daze conference and fair held at Bigfoot Park in Carson. Despite the hoopla and doubters, many "cryptid-hunters" still quietly and humbly go about their business stalking the mythical beast through the woods and mountains of Washington's Cascade Range.

can follow the **Around the Mountain Trail** (No. 9) northwest for about six miles to the **Pacific Crest Trail** (PCT).

The 21 miles of the PCT that pass through Mt. Adams Wilderness are accessible from Forest Service Road 23, near its intersection with Forest Service Road 8810, on the south; on the north, the PCT crosses Forest Service Road 5603 near Potato Hill. Subalpine meadows, glacial streams, dense forest, wildflowers, and scenic viewpoints reward the adventurous hiker.

Beginning at Morrison Creek Horse Camp on the south side of Mt. Adams, 2.7-mile **Crofton Butte Trail** (No. 73) follows the mountain's lower slopes for scenic views of the butte. Take Forest Service Roads 80 and 8040 for about 10 miles from Trout Lake. The southeastern portion of the wilderness lies within the Yakama Reservation (509/865-5121, ext. 657), and hikers will need a separate camping permit.

Camping

The Mount Adams Ranger District has 17 developed campgrounds on the south side of Mt. Adams. Most are free, but there is an $17 fee at the larger campgrounds, including **Moss Creek** and **Peterson Prairie.** The historic **Peterson Prairie Guard Station,** west of Trout Lake, can be rented (Dec.–Apr., $59 d) and is popular with skiers, snowshoers, and snowmobilers. Contact the Mount Adams Ranger Station in Trout Lake (509/395-3400) for reservations.

Other Forest Service campgrounds line Forest Road 23, the route that connects the town of Randle with the northwest side of Mt. Adams. These are managed by the Cowlitz Valley Ranger District in Randle (360/497-1100) and range from free to $17 a night. Best among them is Takhalakh Lake Campground, which affords a gorgeous view of Mt. Adams.

TRAPPER CREEK WILDERNESS

Located halfway between Mount St. Helens and the Columbia River and covering just 6,050 acres, this is one of the smaller wilderness areas in Washington. It is also one of the few places in this part of the state where the forests have been spared from logging. Several trails provide access; longest is the **Observation Trail** (No. 132), which takes you through dense old-growth stands of timber, across a ridge, and to a spur trail that edges up 4,207-foot Observation Peak for panoramic views. From here, you can continue down to the junction with **Trapper Creek Trail** (No. 192), which takes you back along this pretty creek to your starting point. This loop hike is approximately 12 miles long. Call the Mt. Adams Ranger District (509/395-3400) for details.

INDIAN HEAVEN WILDERNESS

The 20,960-acre Indian Heaven Wilderness offers miles of little-used hiking trails; you won't find Mt. Rainier's crowds here because the average day hiker isn't willing to drive this far into the woods on beat-up forest roads. The wilderness covers a high plateau that is split through by the Pacific Crest Trail and dotted with small ponds, evergreen forests, meadows, and mosquitoes. It is located due west of Trout Lake and north of Carson. Call the Mt. Adams Ranger District (509/395-3400) in Trout Lake for details.

Hiking

Thomas Lake Trail is a well-used 3.3-mile path that starts on the west side of the wilderness from Forest Road 65 and passes Dee, Thomas, Naha, Umtux, and Sahalee Tyee lakes before intersecting with the Pacific Crest Trail near Blue Lake. Head north on the main road from Carson, then turn right onto Forest Service Road 65 for about 17 miles to the trailhead.

The Pacific Crest Trail traverses Indian Heaven Wilderness from south to north. Start at Crest Horse Camp, just south of the wilderness boundary on Forest Road 60 (right off Forest Service Road 65); the trail passes lakes, meadows, and forest for 17 miles through the wilderness area, then connects with Forest Service Road 24 near Surprise Lakes on the north side.

TROUT LAKE AND GLENWOOD

Trout Lake is a tiny agricultural settlement with dairy and horse farms (along with a llama ranch), found approximately 30 miles north of the Columbia Gorge town of White Salmon. Mt. Adams Orchards, the world's largest D'Anjou pear orchard, is just a few miles south of here on the way to White Salmon. Trout Lake is the main access point for the Mt. Adams area but has minimal services—a pair of restaurants, a grocery store, and a gas station. For more dining variety and other services, head south to the Columbia River or east to Goldendale.

The town does have the Forest Service's **Mt. Adams Ranger Station** (509/395-3400, year-round Monday–Friday 8 A.M.–4:30 P.M.), where you can get maps, camping information, and current trail conditions. Mountain climbers must register here to climb Mt. Adams (June 1–Sept. 30, Mon.–Thurs. $10, Fri.–Sun. $15). Just east of Trout Lake is a magnificent view of Mt. Adams, with a foreground of ripening huckleberry bushes in late August.

The equally small town of Glenwood is approximately 10 miles east of Trout Lake and six miles north of **Conboy Lake National Wildlife Refuge** (509/364-3489; http://pacific.fws.gov/ridgefield). This 5,800-acre refuge provides a feeding and resting area for thousands of geese, ducks, and swans during their spring and fall migrations. It's the only place in Washington where sandhill cranes nest. A two-mile loop makes for a nice shoreline and forest hike, with the chance to view the waterfowl.

Sights

Approaching Trout Lake from the south on Highway 141, the **Indian Sacred Viewpoint** provides a spectacular view of Mt. Adams. For a closer look, take Forest Service Road 23—the main Mt. Adams access road—about eight miles north from Trout Lake. Just before the pavement gives way to gravel, you'll have a fine view of the mountain to the east.

Events

The main local events are Glenwood's **Ketchum Kalf Rodeo** on the third weekend of July, and the **Trout Lake Fair and Dairy Show** on the first weekend of August. In mid-July, the **Trout Lake Festival of the Arts** (www.gorgearts.org/tlarts.htm) attracts local artisans of all types.

Sports and Recreation

GULAR ICE CAVE

Ancient volcanic activity formed this 650-foot-long, four-section lava tube cave, which during pioneer times supplied ice for the towns of The Dalles and Hood River. Accessible from Ice Caves Campground, six miles west of Trout Lake, the cave entrance is a collapsed sink, 15 feet across and 14 feet deep, connected to three other collapsed sinks by passageways. Wear warm clothing and sturdy boots, and bring at least two dependable flashlights. A helmet is also a good idea. The cave is managed by the Forest Service.

MOUNTAIN BIKING

The areas of the Gifford Pinchot National Forest north and west of Trout Lake, toward Mount St. Helens and Mt. Rainier, are crisscrossed with hundreds of dirt roads and single-track trails, a veritable paradise for adventurous mountain bikers. One great ride is up **Table Mountain,** located on Forest Road 90, three miles southwest of the intersection with Forest Road 23. Bikers can either bite the bullet and slog up the steep trail, or take the easier logging road to the top and bomb down the trail. Either way, a round-trip ride will take 3–4 hours. Another popular ride is the **Blue Lake Trail,** which branches off Forest Road 23 approximately three miles south of the North Fork Campground. A second trail reaches Blue Lake leaving Forest Road 23 just south of North Fork Campground, meaning bikers can take a longer loop ride if time permits. For information on these and other rides, ask at the Mt. Adams Ranger Station in Trout Lake or at the Randle Ranger Station in Randle.

CAMPING

The Forest Service maintains several fee campsites in the area around Trout Lake, including **Tahklakh Lake** ($17) and **Ollalie Lake** ($14). The section of the Gifford Pinchot National Forest surrounding Trout Lake, roughly between Mt. Adams, Mount St. Helens, and Mt. Rainier, is dotted with all manner of great spots for dispersed camping. Forest Roads 23, 25, and 90 are good places to begin looking.

Accommodations and Food

Kelly's Bed and Breakfast (Forest Road 23 just past the Chevron in Trout Lake, 509/395-2769, www.kellysbnb.com, $75–100 s or d) offers comfortable accommodations in a restored 1940s farmhouse, with excellent breakfasts. You can also rent the entire house for $230.

The Farm B&B (490 Sunnyside Rd. in Trout Lake, 509/395-2488, www.thefarmbnb.com, $95–115 s or d) is a classic three-story farmhouse constructed in 1890. Two cozy guest rooms share a bath, kids are accepted, and a full farm breakfast is served. More basic rooms are available for mountain climbers. Also in Trout Lake is **Serenity's** (2291 Highway 141, 509/395-2500 or 800/276-7993, www.serenitys.com, $99–129 d), with cabins with kitchenettes and hot tubs ; there is a two-night minimum. The restaurant here serves prime rib to die for.

Glenwood's 80-acre **Mt. Adams Lodge at Flying L Ranch** (509/364-3488 or 888/682-3267, www.mt-adams.com, $95–190 d) sits in a secluded valley on the eastern slope of the Cascades, with a spectacular skyline dominated by Mt. Adams. The lodge is a favorite place for family reunions and other groups, but there are also more private cabins. All include a full breakfast. Guests enjoy the hot tub and one-mile hiking trail.

Right next to the Chevron gas station in Trout Lake is **KJ's Bear Creek Café** (2376 Hwy. 141, 509/395-2525, summer daily 6 A.M.–9 P.M., fall and spring 6 A.M.–8 P.M., winter 6 A.M.–7 P.M.), serving up tasty breakfasts like huckleberry pancakes, when they're in season, and standard lunches and dinners to hungry hikers and travelers out of a small dining room. This is Trout Lake's only eatery, so gobble that food while it is hot.

Trout Lake has a popular **Saturday market** in July and August, with fresh produce, arts and crafts, and baked treats.

EASTERN WASHINGTON

When you cross the Columbia River on I-90 headed toward Spokane, you are entering the northernmost reaches of the Great American Desert, which runs through portions of eastern Washington, Oregon, Nevada, and California, and down into Arizona and Mexico. It ends with the trees of the Spokane area and the Okanogan Highlands. The Columbia River, in its huge S-shaped turn across the state, helps define the desert's northern and western boundaries.

Despite open country that freezes in the winter and sears in the summer, scarce rainfall, and precious few year-round streams, this basaltic desert has always had several small, scattered natural lakes. Their numbers increased dramatically when the enormous Columbia Basin Irrigation Project created Lake Roosevelt, Moses Lake, and Banks Lake and raised the water table to create hundreds of small ponds. Much of the region receives less than 10 inches of rain a year and sees 300-plus days of sunshine. Wind can sometimes be a problem, especially in the spring when blinding dust storms can arise.

GEOLOGY

Probably the most exciting event in eastern Washington history was witnessed by no one: the **Spokane Flood,** which occurred 18,000–20,000 years ago. As the last ice age came to an end, the glaciers melted and water backed up behind the ice-dammed Clark Fork River in the great basin where Missoula, Montana, now stands. The ice-and-earthen dam created an enormous lake covering more than 3,000

© WASHINGTON STATE TOURISM/LEVY SHECKLER

HIGHLIGHTS

Gingko Petrified Forest State Park: Come see this forest made of stone and you'll understand why petrified wood is the official state gem (page 601).

Grand Coulee Dam: Come see America's crowning engineering achievement, the largest concrete dam in the country (page 610).

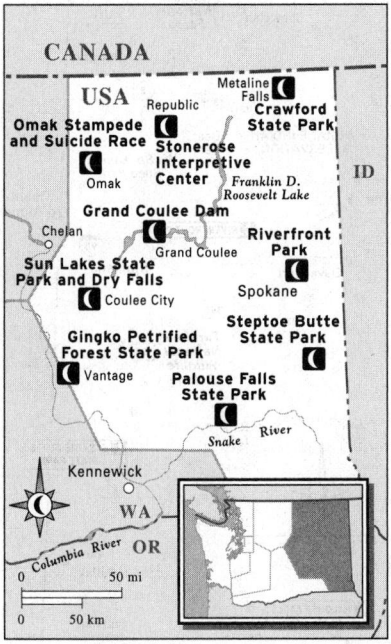

Sun Lakes State Park and Dry Falls: Turbulent waters carved the cliffsides here during the ice age, when, for a time, this was a waterfall four times the size of Niagara Falls (page 618).

Omak Stampede and Suicide Race: Athletes and horses train for years in this traditional Native American competition, where riders hoof pell-mell down a steep embankment and over the Okanogan River (page 623).

Stonerose Interpretive Center: Kids and adults alike get a kick out of digging for fossils at this Eocene-era fossil bed (page 630).

Crawford State Park: At this park it is a spelunker's delight inside Gardner Cave, the third-longest limestone cave in the state (page 638).

Riverfront Park: Downtown Spokane's centerpiece park, the site of Expo '74, ambles along the Spokane River, with numerous attractions, including a dramatic gondola ride over the Spokane Falls (page 646).

Steptoe Butte State Park: Enjoy views of the low-slung Palouse hills atop what the Native Americans once called "power mountain" (page 659).

Palouse Falls State Park: Peer over the basaltic edge as the waters thunder down the state's most dramatic falls (page 673).

LOOK FOR TO FIND RECOMMENDED SIGHTS, ACTIVITIES, DINING, AND LODGING.

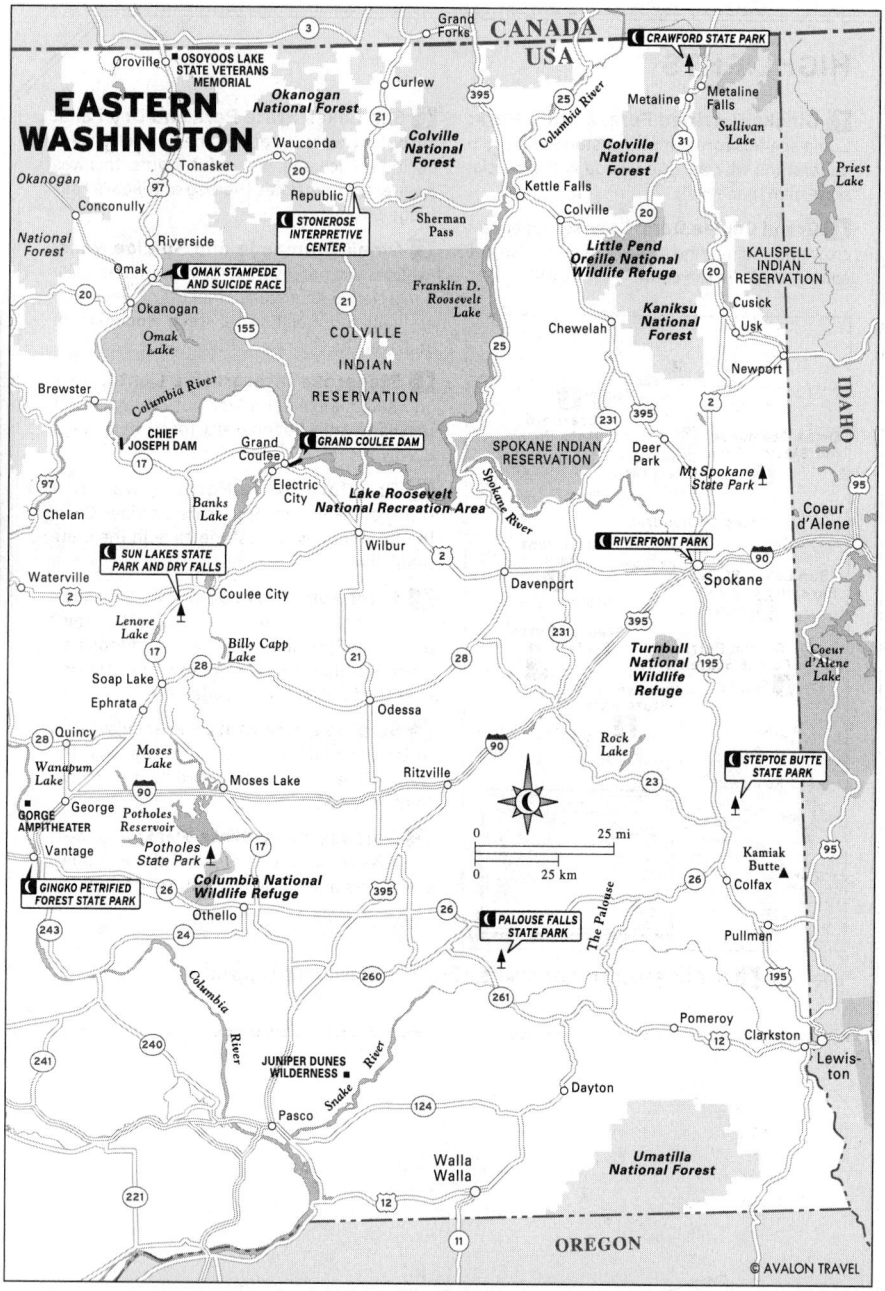
EASTERN WASHINGTON
CANADA
USA
Grand Forks
CRAWFORD STATE PARK
Oroville
OSOYOOS LAKE STATE VETERANS MEMORIAL
Okanogan National Forest
Curlew
Columbia River
Metaline
Metaline Falls
Sullivan Lake
Wauconda
Colville National Forest
Colville National Forest
Priest Lake
Okanogan
Tonasket
Conconully
Republic
STONEROSE INTERPRETIVE CENTER
Sherman Pass
Kettle Falls
Colville
Little Pend Oreille National Wildlife Refuge
KALISPELL INDIAN RESERVATION
National Forest
Riverside
Omak
OMAK STAMPEDE AND SUICIDE RACE
Franklin D. Roosevelt Lake
Okanogan
Omak Lake
COLVILLE INDIAN RESERVATION
Chewelah
Kaniksu National Forest
Cusick
Usk
Newport
IDAHO
Brewster
Columbia River
CHIEF JOSEPH DAM
Grand Coulee
GRAND COULEE DAM
SPOKANE INDIAN RESERVATION
Deer Park
Mt Spokane State Park
Electric City
Lake Roosevelt National Recreation Area
Spokane River
Banks Lake
Chelan
Coeur d'Alene
SUN LAKES STATE PARK AND DRY FALLS
Wilbur
RIVERFRONT PARK
Spokane
Waterville
Coulee City
Davenport
Lenore Lake
Billy Capp Lake
Turnbull National Wildlife Refuge
Coeur d'Alene Lake
Soap Lake
Ephrata
Odessa
Quincy
Moses Lake
Rock Lake
Wanapum Lake
Moses Lake
Ritzville
STEPTOE BUTTE STATE PARK
George
GORGE AMPITHEATER
Potholes Reservoir
Vantage
Potholes State Park
0 25 mi
0 25 km
Kamiak Butte
Colfax
GINGKO PETRIFIED FOREST STATE PARK
Columbia National Wildlife Refuge
Othello
PALOUSE FALLS STATE PARK
The Palouse
Pullman
Columbia River
Pomeroy
Clarkston
Lewiston
JUNIPER DUNES WILDERNESS
Snake River
Dayton
Pasco
Walla Walla
Umatilla National Forest
OREGON
© AVALON TRAVEL

THE CATASTROPHIST

It is much easier to understand the Channeled Scabland when you fly over it in a small plane. This geological oddity is a series of dry channels that run south-southwest out of the Spokane area, then fan out toward the Columbia River in the Tri-Cities area. Geologists always assumed the channels were created over a period of centuries by normal erosion, until a University of Chicago professor named **J. Harlen Bretz** became interested in the area while visiting Spokane in the early 1920s.

He got the idea from a topographic map and soon formulated the theory that the Channeled Scabland was not created by glacial activity and normal water erosion but by one or more catastrophic floods that originated from a vast lake dammed by earth and ice in the valley where Missoula, Montana, stands.

Bretz found more and more evidence to support his theory. He found lap marks high on the cliffs around Missoula, and erratics (boulders found far from their place of origin) high on the mountainsides along the Columbia River Gorge. He believed the flood occurred as the Ice Age waned, and snow and ice melt went over the top of an earth-and-ice dam that might have been as high as 2,000 feet. When it broke, it released a 3,000-square mile lake that contained 500 cubic miles of water, nearly half the volume of Lake Michigan.

The catastrophic flood Bretz envisioned headed due west from Missoula across the Idaho Panhandle, down the Spokane Valley, where the natural contour of the land turned it south and west. He believed the Palouse River originally flowed down the Washtucna Coulee where the towns of Washtucna and Kahlotus are now and emptied into the Snake River about 70 miles farther downstream from its present confluence at Lyons Ferry. Bretz also believed that the first floods ponded in the Pasco Basin and formed what he called Lake Lewis; eventually filled the Yakima, Walla Walla, and Snake River valleys; and finally bore into the Columbia River at Wallula Gap. He theorized that the floods came through the gap up to 800 feet deep and at 1.66 cubic miles of water an hour for two or three weeks, or 190 times the volume of the greatest Columbia River flood on record.

The floods scoured the sides of the Columbia Gorge up to 1,000 feet, and carried boulders embedded in ice that were stranded on the mountainsides and up valleys. When the waters hit the Willamette River, they headed upriver as far as Eugene and formed a temporary lake that covered up to 3,000 square miles.

This sounded pretty wild to his colleagues and went completely against the grain; nearly all geologic theory evolved in the 19th century and was based in part on religion which held strictly to the version of creation given in the Bible. When the Ivy Leaguers heard of Bretz's theory, some referred to his school, the University of Chicago, as "that Western trade school."

They picked on the wrong man. Bretz was tenacious and enjoyed a good academic brawl. For several summers he worked in eastern Washington, gathering more ammunition for the battle. One by one he gained converts to his cause, especially from those who actually toured the area with him and geologists already there.

It took 42 years for Bretz to be vindicated. In 1965, the International Geophysical Year conference was held in Denver; Bretz couldn't attend because of health problems, but he was well represented by a band of disciples who were determined that their point of view at least be seriously considered by on-site examination.

They arranged a trip across the west by chartered bus through the Rockies and into Montana, then down the course of the floods. At Missoula a Bretz believer began lecturing on what they were seeing from the bus windows and at specific stops. This continued all along the flood route. Finally, when the group stopped at a site near Kahlotus, all the pieces of Bretz's theory fell into place: dry cataracts, the rerouting of the Palouse River, the stream beds that haven't had running water in them in centuries, the ripple marks on canyon and coulee walls.

On that day most of his most outspoken opponents began backpedaling, and the group sent Bretz a dramatic telegram of congratulations. It ended with these words:

"We are all catastrophists."

square miles—larger than Puget Sound—and marks from its shoreline can still be seen along the mountains above the basin.

As the ice dam melted, the great pressure from the backed-up water caused it to suddenly collapse, sending an unimaginable rush of water over all of eastern Washington, flattening the landscape, gouging out coulees, washing away soil, and emptying the great lake in as little as two days. It is said to have been the greatest flood ever recorded on the planet. Evidence of the flood is shown on the landscape between Spokane and the Columbia River around the Tri-Cities area, a region known as the **Channeled Scablands.** Most protruding rocks and mesas are ship-shaped, all pointing in a northeasterly direction, and there's no evidence that the erosion process was caused by streams, the normal source of such erosion. The prevailing geological theory is that there may have been many of these floods.

PRACTICALITIES

A **Northwest Forest Pass** ($5 daily, $30 annual) is required for trailhead parking in Colville, Okanogan, Umatilla, and other Washington National Forests.

Columbia Basin

QUINCY AND GEORGE

The almost-flat Quincy Valley is a study in contrasts: although receiving just eight inches of rainfall, it contains some of the most productive farms in Washington, producing potatoes, apples, wheat, alfalfa, corn, and many other vegetable crops. This is possible because of the West Canal that feeds water from the Columbia River via Banks Lake to irrigate these fields. The valley was first settled in the late 19th century; it

© WASHINGTON STATE TOURISM/LEVY SHECKLER

Quincy wilderness

struggled along until 1951, when irrigation waters first reached here. Today the town of Quincy contains 4,000 people and is the primary agricultural center in the area. It has frozen-food processing plants, massive apple warehouses, a diatomaceous earth chemical plant, and even a still to extract mint flavoring. There are good views across Quincy Valley from the top of **Monument Hill** north of town.

For a look at one of the more unusual geologic features in the area, take exit 143 (six miles southwest of George) from I-90, and follow Old Vantage Road west down Frenchman Coulee to the basaltic rock **Pillars,** a favorite rock-climbing spot.

Gingko Petrified Forest State Park

Fifteen to 20 million years ago, this part of Washington was first covered by lush forests and then by molten lava that poured out of fissures in the earth's crust. Logs that had washed into nearby lakes were preserved intact by the lava cover; water eventually leaked through to the logs, and the silica in the groundwater replaced the natural structure of the wood. The tremendous erosion during the last ice age exposed 259 species of petrified trees in this area, including the prehistoric gingko, a "living fossil" that still grows in Japan and has been planted in city parks throughout America.

An **interpretive center** (509/856-2700, www.parks.wa.gov, mid-May to Aug. daily 10 A.M.–6 P.M.) just north of the town of Vantage (exit 136 of I-90) houses displays on the geologic history of the area and a slide show about gingkoes. Outside are large pieces of petrified wood and several petroglyphs.

For a beautiful country drive, head west from the interpretive center along the Vantage Highway that connects Vantage to Ellensburg. This is the back way and makes a good bike ride (narrow shoulders, alas). Sagebrush, rugged land, cattle, and ranches give this a Western appeal. Tune in the AM radio for cowboy or Mexican music to fit the mood. Two miles west on Vantage Highway are several interpretive trails that lead uphill past more samples of various petrified tree species beneath wire cages. A 2.5-mile trail leads across the dry, windblown hills past an assortment of scrappy wildflowers, sagebrush, and broad views. Watch for bald eagles, hawks, deer, elk, coyote, and a variety of lizards and snakes, including the poisonous northern Pacific rattlesnake.

Camping is available at **Wanapum State Recreation Area** (4.5 miles south of the Gingko Visitor Center, 888/226-7688, www.parks.wa.gov, mid-May to mid-Sept. daily, Nov.–Mar weekends only, $27 hookups, $7 extra reservation fee).

Entertainment, Events, and Recreation

Located 14 miles southwest of Quincy and seven miles northwest of George, the **Gorge Amphitheatre** (206/464-2000, www.hob.com) is an outstanding natural amphitheatre in the basaltic bluffs overlooking the Columbia River. Operated by House of Blues, the amphitheatre is home each summer to Saturday concerts by internationally known musicians that attract upwards of 20,000 people. Past performers have included R.E.M., Tina Turner, Sting, Vince Gill, and many more. Get tickets from TicketMaster (509/735-0500, www.ticketmaster.com). These shows fill motels as far away as Wenatchee and Moses Lake, so reserve ahead. Camping and RV spaces are available on adjacent grounds, and food services are offered.

Other than the amphitheatre concerts, the main local event is **Farmer Consumer Awareness Day** on the second Saturday of September in Quincy. It includes a fun run, parade, food booths, exhibits, live music, and guided tours of local food-processing plants.

An outdoor **swimming pool and aquatic park** is also in Quincy at Jaycee Municipal Park.

The tiny town of George is known for its **George Washington** celebration on the 4th of July (pretty obvious where the town name originated). Each year, locals bake the "world's largest cherry pie," and light the fireworks when evening comes. More nighttime fun happens at Christmas, when local farmers put lights on their rotating pivot-irrigation lines. Look for them along I-90 east of George.

Accommodations

There are three basic places to stay in Quincy: **Traditional Inns** (509/787-3525, www.traditionalinns.com, $120 d), **Sundowner Motel** (509/787-3587, $55 s or $65 d) and **Country Cabin** (711 2nd Ave. SW, 509/787-3515, $60 d). All of these have kitchenettes.

Eight miles west of Quincy off Highway 28, **Crescent Bar Resort** (509/787-1511, www.crescentbarresort.com, $100–210 d condo, $34 tent, $40 RV) on Wanapum Reservoir offers a restaurant, condos, and camping, plus a wide choice of recreation, from swimming to golf.

Information and Services

Get local information from the **Quincy Valley Chamber of Commerce** (119 F St. SE, 509/787-2140, www.quincyvalley.org) or from the seasonal **George Visitor Center** (509/785-3831). The **library** (108 B St. SW) has Internet access.

Getting There

Quincy is served by **Northwestern Trailways** (509/624-9863 or 800/366-3830, www.nwadv.com/northw) with service east to Spokane and west to Everett.

MOSES LAKE AND OTHELLO

The bustling small city of Moses Lake (pop. 15,000) is a growing desert settlement with all the usual trappings of American "progress": Wal-Mart, Kmart, McDonald's, strip malls, and developments spreading across the landscape. It isn't especially attractive but will do as a stopping point. The main attractions are nearby Moses Lake and Potholes Reservoir, along with the immensely popular summertime concerts at the Gorge Amphitheatre near George on the Columbia River. Like most of eastern Washington, the Moses Lake area gets little rainfall—about eight inches a year—and some of the state's highest summer temperatures.

History

Moses Lake is named for Chief Moses of the Sinkiuse tribe. Early white settlers came on the promises of developers and the Northern Pacific Railroad but found a hardscrabble existence in this desert country. One wrote of it being "100 miles to town, 20 miles to water, six inches to hell!" Two major government developments changed this. The first was the construction of Grand Coulee Dam in the 1930s, and more importantly, the completion of the Columbia Basin Irrigation Project in 1952. This brought large quantities of cheap water to the region and transformed it into some of the most productive fields in Washington. During World War II, a major army air base was developed on the flat lands near Moses Lake; eventually this became Larson Air Force Base. It closed in 1966, but the citizens of Moses Lake turned it into a training center for Boeing where the pilots and crews of various international airlines—most notably Japan Air Lines—flight-test new planes. Visitors to the area are likely to see jumbo jets circling slowly overhead, practicing maneuvers.

Sights

COLUMBIA NATIONAL WILDLIFE REFUGE

The Columbia National Wildlife Refuge (headquarters at 44 S. 8th St., Othello, 509/488-2668, http://pacific.fws.gov) covers 23,000 acres of scenic desert land between Moses Lake and the Othello area. The refuge contains a rugged jumble of cliffs, wide-open sagebrush grasslands, eroded canyons, and a scattering of more than 50 lakes and ponds created by rising groundwater due to irrigation. Most impressive of all are the **Drumheller Channels,** just south of Potholes Reservoir. They are visible from a viewpoint along McManamon Road, approximately nine miles northwest of Othello. The refuge is home to more than 100,000 birds each fall and is a vital winter resting area for mallards and Canada geese. Although the refuge is closed to public entry during the peak season to protect the birds, it is open for bird-watching, hiking, camping, and fishing in the spring and summer. Several short trails lead through.

POTHOLES RESERVOIR AND O'SULLIVAN DAM

When Columbia River water was pumped onto the fields, reclamation engineers didn't know exactly what to expect from the water—whether it would stand and create lakes, or flow underground. It did both. The irrigation water in the Moses Lake area and farther north toward Grand Coulee generally seeps southward—following the natural slope of the land—and collects in Potholes Reservoir behind O'Sullivan Dam.

The O'Sullivan Dam, on Highway 17 at the south end of Potholes Reservoir (halfway between Moses Lake and Othello) is one of the largest earth-filled dams in the nation. The reservoir collects overflow from irrigated lands to the north, transferring the water into the Potholes East Canal and feeding farms to the south. South of the dam are more than 50 seep lakes within Columbia National Wildlife Refuge. In the winter, Potholes Reservoir is a major resting place for waterfowl—thousands of ducks are visible. The area has a number of interesting rock formations, including striking columnar basalt formations in the Crab Creek Marsh area.

PARKS

Located at the southwest end of O'Sullivan Dam, **Potholes State Park** (O'Sullivan Dam Road, 509/765-7271 or 888/226-7688, www.parks.wa.gov, $17 tent, $23 full hookups, $7 extra reservation fee) is a popular spot for launching a boat to catch the reservoir's trout, walleye, and perch. Water-skiers, picnickers, and swimmers also enjoy the sunny east-of-the-mountains weather at this 2,500-acre park. The park offers summertime slide shows and nature hikes. Tent and RV sites are available year-round.

The city-run **Cascade Park** (Valley Rd., 509/766-9240, mid-April through mid-October) at Moses Lake offers swimming, boating, waterskiing, showers, and camping and RV hookups. **Cascade Water Rentals** (509/766-7075) rents personal watercraft, canoes, and fishing boats out of Cascade Marina.

© WASHINGTON STATE TOURISM/LEVY SHECKLER

Potholes Reservoir

Moses Community State Park (I-90 exit 175, www.parks.wa.gov) has swimming; fishing for trout, crappie, and catfish; a grassy picnic area; and a snack bar—but no camping. In the winter, this is a favorite ice-skating spot.

SAND DUNES

Hike, slide, or ride your off-road vehicle on over 3,000 acres of sand dunes south of the city of Moses Lake. Go four miles south on Division St., then follow the signs—and six miles of gravel road—to the ORV park. Camping is permitted here, but there are no facilities.

OTHER SIGHTS

Eighteen-mile-long **Moses Lake** is two miles west of town and popular with boaters and anglers.

Moses Lake Museum and Art Center (226 W. 3rd Ave., 509/766-9395, www.mlrec.com, Tues.–Sat. 11 A.M.–5 P.M., free) displays fossils, geological specimens, old photos, a fine collection of pipes and pottery, and changing art exhibits.

Monty Holm's House of Poverty and Mon Road Railroad (228 S. Commerce, 509/765-6342, summers only Mon.–Fri. 8 A.M.–3:45 P.M., free) contains things Monty collected over the years, including entire trains, gasoline engines, antique cars, fire engines, and just plain stuff. The yard out front is packed with vehicles of all types, from sheep wagons to a steam engine.

Armed forces buffs may want to check out the small **Schiffner Military and Police Museum** (4840 Westshore Dr., 509/765-6374, open by appointment) with over a hundred uniforms on display.

Entertainment and Events

McCosh Park Amphitheater along Moses Lake is the home to the free **Centennial Concert** series, with a range of styles. The concerts are held on Saturday July–September. Past performers have included The Platters, Glenn Yarbrough, and Ranch Romance.

Several local bars have live music on weekends, including **The Porterhouse** (217 N. Elder, 509/766-0308) and **El Papagayo** (Hwy. 17 and Stratford Rd., 509/765-1265).

The Memorial Day weekend **Spring Festival** features a carnival, arts and crafts displays, kids' and regular parades, restored rods and low-riders, fireworks, ATV races, and a 10K run. There is also an event called the Pickleball Tournament (509/765-8248) featuring miniature tennis matches with Wiffle balls named after a dog who loved to chase them.

A popular rodeo is the highlight of the **Grant County Fair** (off Hwy. 17, 509/765-3581, www.grantcountyfair.com) held the third week of August at the fairgrounds just north of town.

Sports and Recreation

Moses Lake Family Aquatic Center in McCosh Park (4th and Dogwood, 509/766-9246, www.mlrec.com, open mid-May through mid-Sept., $9 adults, $7 kids 5–12, free under 4) has an Olympic-size outdoor swimming pool, two 200-foot water slides, a tube slide, sand volleyball courts, concession stands, and lots of fun places for kids to play.

Play golf in the sunshine at **Sage Hills Golf Course** (15 miles south of Moses Lake on Hwy. 17, 509/2603) **Highlander Greens Golf Course** (1475 E. Nelson Rd., 509/766-1228) and **Potholes Golf Course** (6897 O'Sullivan Dam SE, 509/346-2447).

CAMPING AND RV PARKS

The city-run **Cascade Park** (Valley Rd. and Cascade Valley, 509/766-9240, $15 tent, $18 full hookups, $7 extra reservation fee) along Moses Lake has camping and RV hookups; open mid-April through mid-September. **Potholes State Park** (at the west end of O'Sullivan Dam, 509/765-7271) has tent sites ($14) and RV spaces ($20); open year-round. Make reservations ($7 extra) at 888/226-7688, www.parks.wa.gov.

The Moses Lake private RV parks are **Big Sun Resort** (2300 W. Marina Dr., 509/765-8294) **Suncrest Resort** (303 Hansen Rd., 509/765-0355) and **Willows RV Park** (2.5 miles south of I-90 exit 179 off Hwy. 17, 509/765-7531).

Public campsites are also available in **Scooteney Park** (11 miles south of Othello along Hwy. 17, 509/234-0527, $8 no hookups) and at **Soda Lake Campground** within Columbia National Wildlife Refuge.

Accommodations

If you're coming to one of the popular summertime concerts at the Gorge Amphitheatre, be sure to reserve at least two weeks ahead of time; things sometimes fill up all the way to Wenatchee. The chamber of commerce (800/992-6234) keeps track of who has space.

Located just off Highway 17, **Sage 'N' Sand Motel** (1011 S. Pioneer Way, 509/765-1755, $50 s or $55 d) has some of the cheapest rooms in town.

Sunland Motor Inn (309 E. 3rd Ave., 509/765-1170 or 800/220-4403, www.sunlandinn.com, $65–79 d) also rents basic motel rooms and serves a tasty breakfast with biscuits and gravy.

If you don't mind the drive, **Mar Don Resort** (8198 Hwy. 262 SE, Othello, 509/756-5061 or 800/416-2736, www.mardonresort.com, $60 d, $210 for 6) is a popular spot for fishing and waterskiing, 16 miles south of Moses Lake on Potholes Reservoir. Nestled in a grove of trees, it has a swimming beach, marina, and boat rentals.

Lakeshore Resort Motel (3396 W. Lakeshore Drive, 509/765-9201, $65 s or $68 d) has cottages, cabins, and an outdoor heated swimming pool right on Moses Lake.

Inn at Moses Lake (1741 E. Kittleson, 509/576-7500 or 800/576-7500, $90 d) is the nearest motel to Moses Lake and has a continental breakfast bar. Guests are offered access to a pool at the inn's sister property.

Holiday Inn Express (1735 E. Kittleson, 509/766-2000 or 800/465-4329, $150 d) is one of the nicer local places, with an indoor/outdoor pool, sauna, and weight room. All rooms come with microwave and fridge, plus you'll be treated to those delicious Holiday Inn Express cinnamon buns in the morning. You can also rent kayaks and bikes during the week.

Best Western Lake Front Hotel (3000 Marina Dr., 509/765-9211 or 800/235-4255, $119 s or $129 d) is a sizable resort right on the lake. Amenities include an outdoor pool, hot tub, health spa, exercise facility, and tennis courts. In Othello, **Lincoln Inn Best Western** (1020 E. Cedar St., 509/488-5671 or 800/528-1234, www.bestwestern.com, $80 s or d) has a heated outdoor pool and kitchenette units.

Food

MOSES LAKE

Michael's on the Lake (910 W. Broadway Ave., 509/765-1611, www.michaelsonthelake.com, Mon.–Thurs. 10:30 A.M.–10 P.M., Fri.–Sat. 8 A.M.–11 P.M., Sun. 8 A.M.–10 P.M.) is a good place for breakfast, with a choice of dining inside or on the deck overlooking Moses Lake.

Thai Cuisine (601 S. Pioneer Way, 509/766-1489, Mon.–Sat. 11 A.M.–9 P.M., closed Sun.) has an inexpensive lunch buffet.

For Chinese cooking in a range of styles, head to **Eddie's Restaurant** (801 N. Stratford Rd., 509/765-5334, Tues.–Sun. 4–9 P.M., closed Mon.).

Inca Mexican Restaurant (404 E. 3rd, 509/766-2426, Sun.–Thurs. 11 A.M.–10 P.M., Fri.–Sat. 11 A.M.–11 P.M.) offers authentic south-of-the-border fare.

Chico's Pizza (Vista Village Shopping Center, 509/765-4589, Su.–Thurs. 4–9:30 P.M., Fri.–Sat. 4–10:30 P.M.) makes distinctive and dense pizzas with unusual toppings. For steaks and pastas in an upscale setting, try **Paradise Restaurant** at the Best Western (3000 Marina Dr., 509/765-9211, daily 4–10 P.M.).

The **Columbia Basin Farmers Market** (509/762-5500) takes place downtown at the Civic Center Park Saturday mornings and Wednesday afternoons June–October.

OTHELLO

Like many other eastern Washington farming centers, Othello has a large number of migrant workers and a growing community of immigrants from Mexico and Central America. Because of this, you'll find a tortilla factory and several authentic Mexican restaurants here, including **El Caporal Restaurant** (1244 E. Main, 509/488-0487, Thurs.–Tues. 11 A.M.–9 P.M., Wed. 11 A.M.–3 P.M.) and the recommended **Casa Mexican** (1224 E. Main, 509/488-6163, daily 8 A.M.–9 P.M.).

You'll find the **Othello Farmers Market** (Main St. and 4th Ave., 509/488-2728, Saturday 8 A.M.–noon from mid-May to mid-Oct.) in Pioneer Park, with fresh fruits and veggies, honey, baked goods, and local crafts.

Information

For local information, contact the **Moses Lake Chamber of Commerce** (324 S. Pioneer Way, 509/765-7888 or 800/992-6234, www.moseslakechamber.org, Mon.–Fri. 8 A.M.–noon and 1–4 P.M.).

Getting There

Both **Greyhound** (509/765-6441 or 800/231-2222, www.greyhound.com) and **Northwestern Trailways** (509/624-9863 or 800/366-3830, www.nwadv.com) have bus service throughout the Northwest from Shilo Inn (1819 E. Kittleson Rd.). The nearest **Amtrak** station is in Ephrata.

ODESSA

Odessa is a tiny agricultural and retirement center of fewer than 1,000 folks. Wheat is the primary crop grown here. Like neighboring Ritzville, Odessa was settled by Volga Germans in the late 19th century, and more than three-quarters of the people are still of that heritage. The wide main street (1st Avenue) passes neat small homes of brick and wood, along with a handful of German-style buildings, including city hall. Odessa gets blazing hot in the summer.

Geology

Much of the land surrounding Odessa is raw, rough-edged desert, the heart of two cataclysmic geologic episodes. The first was a series of 150 volcanic eruptions starting 17 million years ago that covered much of the Northwest in lava up to three miles thick, followed by the ice ages that led to massive Columbia River floods. These floods carved enormous gouges in the basalt, creating the dry coulees prominent in eastern Washington. The Odessa area has dozens of shallow craters of varying sizes; some reach 2,000 feet across. There are as many theories on their origin as there are geologists who have studied these odd features.

To tour the Channeled Scablands around Odessa, stop by the information booth and pick up a detailed brochure. The tour takes you west of town along the bizarre formations of Crab Creek, past the ghost town of Irby, and on to the fascinating region around **Lakeview Ranch** on BLM land. Nearby are a series of large craters to explore, a picnic area, a few primitive campsites, and shady trees. Keep your eyes open for rattlesnakes, however.

Sights

The **Odessa Historisches Museum** (509/982-2539, 1–4 P.M.) on the west edge of town has exhibits on the Germans from Russia who settled the area and a replica of a barn from early Odessa. Nine miles west of Odessa off Highway 28 is the ghost town of **Irby,** where the 90-year-old Irby Hotel stands surrounded by desolate desert country. Immediately north of here are rich Palouse soils—prime wheat-growing areas—that escaped the massive floods of the ice ages. South of town are several Hutterite colonies; for tours, call **Schoonover Farms** (509/982-2257).

Events and Recreation

Odessa's Germanic heritage comes out in **Deutschesfest** on the third weekend of September. The festival includes a parade, homemade German food, arts and crafts, a carnival, and fun run, but the main attraction is a *biergarten* with polka, country and western, and bluegrass music from the Oom Pas and Mas band. Deutschesfest attracts retired folks by the busload, and more than 700 RVs fill the athletic field. Other Odessa events include a quilt show in late April, and a Christmas arts and crafts festival.

The **Odessa Tourist Park** (1st Ave. and 2nd St.) has free camping. **Odessa Golf Course**

(13080 28th St., 509/982-0093, $12 tent, $18 full hookups) is a nine-hole course on the west end of town and has space for RV hookups.

Accommodations and Food

Lodging is available at **Lacollage Inn** (509/982-2412, www.lacollageinn.com, $50–60 s or d), a kitschy hotel featuring themed rooms with artfully done murals splashing the walls from floor to ceiling.

For a taste of the area's German heritage, visit **Voise Sausage** (7 S. 1st St., 509/982-2956), where the sausage, bratwurst, and bologna are all made on the premises.

Information

Get information from a kiosk in Record Square (3 West 1st Ave.), or contact the **Odessa Chamber of Commerce** (509/982-0049, www.odessachamber.com).

EPHRATA

Ephrata (ee-FRAY-ta) is a tidy town set amidst a sprinkling of trees and surrounded by miles of flat and desolate desertscape with short grasses and sage, alternating with irrigated fields of verdant crops. The town stretches for over a mile along Basin Street and is headquarters to the Columbia Basin Reclamation Project, the irrigation arm of the Grand Coulee Dam project. Few towns in Washington were more desolate than Ephrata before the irrigation project arrived in the 1950s. The name comes from the Biblical village where Christ was born, Bethlehem Ephratah; it supposedly originated when a traveler on the Great Northern Railway stopped here and found a prospering orchard irrigated by a spring. It reminded him of the Holy Land, and the name stuck. (Ephratah means fertile region.)

Grant County Historical Museum and Pioneer Village

Ephrata is home to an outstanding collection of Native American and pioneer artifacts, clothing, tools, diaries, documents, and relics at Grant County Historical Museum and Pioneer Village (742 N. Basin St., 509/754-3334, May–Sept.

© WASHINGTON STATE TOURISM/LEVY SHECKLER

Grant County Historical Museum and Pioneer Village

Mon., Tues., and Thurs.–Sat. 10 A.M.–5 P.M. and Sunday 1–4 P.M., closed Wed. and Oct.–Apr., $3.50 for adults, $2.50 for ages 6–15, and free for kids under six). One of the finest historical collections in Washington, this museum covers almost four acres of downtown. The 30-building pioneer village includes a saloon, dress shop, barbershop, watch repair shop, Catholic church, jail, printing office, blacksmith, and even a house built from polished petrified wood. The buildings are both original structures and reproductions. Guided tours are available until 3 P.M.

In the crowded main museum, be sure to find the 1895 Rockaway carriage, a beautifully refurbished glass-enclosed carriage used by the local postmaster, who also happened to be Scottish nobleman Lord Thomas Blythe. An aimless young man, Blythe was sent to America by his father in an attempt to force him into maturity; it obviously worked, because Thomas Blythe went on to become a highly successful cattle rancher. Also surprising are the live snakes that occupy a back room, including a northern Pacific rattlesnake. Downstairs is an amusing collection of carved wooden creatures.

Demonstrations of pioneer crafts are given during both the **Living Museum** on the second weekend of June and **Pioneer Day,** the last weekend of September. During these events, Pioneer Village comes alive with costumed participants in every building—from apple pressing to wool spinning and cowboy poetry. Kids get to make their own horseshoes at the blacksmith shop. Ephrata also has a **Christmas Celebration** on the second weekend in December.

Events and Recreation

Ephrata's annual **Sage and Sun Festival,** held the second weekend of June, features a parade, arts and crafts, antique cars, and a carnival.

No public campsites are nearby, but travelers can pitch tents or park RVs at **Oasis RV Park** (a mile south of town, 509/754-5102, $26 full hookups), noteworthy for its big shade trees, swimming pool, and miniature golf. The city park next to Oasis has a popular fishing pond.

Accommodations and Food

Ephrata has a couple of decent chain motels, including **Travelodge** (31 Basin St. SW, 509/754-4651 or 800/255-3050, www.travelodge.com, $50 s or $55 d), which has a heated pool, and **Best Western Ephrata** (1257 Basin SW, 509/754-7111, $115 d), with rooms featuring microwaves and fridges, plus some with full kitchen units ($160 d).

Creative types will prefer **Ivy Chapel Inn B&B** (164 D St. SW, 509/754-0629, www.theivychapelinn.com, $85–110 d). Originally a Presbyterian Church, it is now a distinctive and friendly B&B. The ivy-covered redbrick building contains six guest rooms with private baths and full breakfasts; no kids under 10.

Downtown Ephrata is no bustling commercial hub, but you can get sandwiches and pies from **The Country Deli** (245 Basin St. NW, 509/754-3143, Tues.–Sat. 6:30 A.M.–8 P.M., Sun.–Mon. 6:30 A.M.3 P.M.) or pizzas from **Time Out Pizza** (1695 Basin St. SW, 509/754-1111, daily 11 A.M.–9 P.M.).

Information

For local information, contact the **Ephrata Chamber of Commerce** (90 Alder St. NW, 509/754-4656, www.ephratawachamber.com, Mon.–Fri. 9 A.M.–4 P.M.), which also has a visitor's pamphlet lobby open all weekend.

Getting There

Amtrak (800/872-7245, www.amtrak.com) provides service west to Wenatchee, Everett, Edmonds, and Seattle, and east to Spokane and Chicago. The Amtrak depot is on 1st Street. **Northwestern Trailways** (509/624-9863 or 800/366-3830, www.nwadv.com/northw) stops in front of the Chamber of Commerce, with daily bus service east to Spokane and west to Everett and Seattle.

SOAP LAKE

Located five miles northeast of Ephrata, Soap Lake is a small body of salty, highly alkaline water surrounded by the deserts of the Columbia Basin. The town of Soap Lake occupies the south shore of the lake and has long

© GRANT COUNTY TOURISM/J. CRAIG SWEAT

Soap Lake has the cure for what ails you.

been a place for "taking the cure" for such ailments as psoriasis and arthritis. Other folks come to soak in the warm sunshine; it shines 310 days a year over Soap Lake and only rains eight inches annually.

History

Though you'd never suspect it today, Soap Lake was once a bustling resort area surrounding the Soap Lake Sanitorium, a health retreat that capitalized on the lake's legendary medicinal qualities. The Tsincayuse sent their sick to soak in the *smokiam* (healing waters); early white explorers called it Soap Lake because its 17 natural minerals and oils give the water a soft soapy feel and create a sudslike foam on windy days. The only other place on earth with similar water is said to be Baden Baden, Germany.

In the early 1900s, great crowds of people from around the country came here to drink and bathe in the alkaline water to cure joint, skin, digestive, and circulatory ailments. Most of the visitors weren't too sick; they found time for drinking, dancing, and general hell-raising, leading the local newspaper to admonish them to "be more careful" about remembering their swimsuits! The drought and Depression of 1933 brought an end to the revelry, turning Soap Lake into a curiosity in the midst of a desolate region. It has been making a comeback, though, and the chamber of commerce actively promotes the curative powers of the lake's water with testimonials from satisfied customers ("After only nine days, the pain has gone, and I feel like a new person. . . ").

Events

Several local events attract out-of-towners to Soap Lake. The town celebrates **Smokiam Days** with a big fireworks show and parade on the **4th of July,** and a popular **Great Canoe Race** the second weekend of July. The latter covers almost 18 miles of paddling and portaging, and ends with a sprint across Soap Lake to the finish line. The second weekend of August brings the **Soap Lake Rod Run & Pig Feed,** an odd combination that includes a fun run, pig barbecue, and classic car show.

Sports and Recreation

East Beach has play equipment, lake access, and restrooms (the Soap Lake Chamber of Commerce is also here if you need maps or directions). **West Beach** is on the other side of town. One warning: Swim in loose-fitting suits to avoid chafing that can be aggravated by the highly alkaline water. Also be careful to rinse off at the showers and to put on sunscreen after bathing since the minerals in the water act to increase tanning and burning.

Smokiam Campground (509/246-1211, open April–October, $10 tents, $20 RVs) has waterfront camping. Well, it is actually just a gravel lot sandwiched between the lake and the highway. Another option is the **Soap Lake RV Resort** (22818 Highway 17 N., 509/246-0413, $20 full hookups).

Accommodations

The main draw at the spacious log **Notaras Lodge** (231 Main St., 509/246-0462, www.notaraslodge.com, $75–108 d) are the more expensive units featuring in-room whirlpools with Soap Lake water piped in, bathroom phones, skylights, and balconies. Also ask about massages and a one-night pass to the local members-only club.

The Inn at Soap Lake (226 Main Ave. E, 509/246-1132, www.innsoaplake.com, $59–125 d) was built in 1905 from rounded river stones. Rooms are nicely furnished with antiques and have kitchenettes and mineral water soaking tubs. Rates include a continental breakfast. Canoe and paddleboat rentals are available here.

Food

Don's Steak House (14 Canna St. across from Notaras Lodge, 509/246-1217, Mon.–Thurs. 11 A.M.–9:30 P.M., Fri. 11 A.M.–10 P.M., Sat. 4–10 P.M., Sun. noon–8 P.M.) specializes in delicious steak, seafood, and Greek dishes.

Information

The summer-only **Soap Lake Chamber of Commerce** (509/246-1821, www.soaplakcoc.org) is right along the lake in a small building. Next door is East Beach, a favorite swimming, picnic, and camping area.

Grand Coulee Dam and Vicinity

If you've been driving through the desert country of central Washington, Grand Coulee Dam comes as quite a surprise. Instead of barren sage, grass, and rock, you're suddenly in a cluster of small towns with lush green lawns and split-level suburban homes. This oasis in the desert is the result of one of the largest construction projects ever undertaken. The Grand Coulee is a 50-mile-long gorge carved by the Columbia River during the ice ages, when glaciers forced the river south of its current path. Much of the carving took place during the cataclysmic Spokane Floods thousands of years ago. By the way, the word coulee means dry ravine.

The dam is surrounded by a confusing cluster of towns with similar names. Electric City and Grand Coulee are south of the dam, Coulee Dam and Elmer City are north of the dam. All but Elmer City have services. Coulee City sits adjacent to Dry Falls Dam on Banks Lake, 30 miles south of Grand Coulee Dam.

GRAND COULEE DAM

Massive Grand Coulee Dam is the main destination for travelers in this part of Washington. The dam and surrounding facilities serve a variety of functions, including irrigation, power production, and flood control. Twice as high as Niagara Falls and nearly a mile long, the dam is one of the world's greatest producers of electricity, generating an incredible 22,000 megawatts of energy annually for cities in several states. Only Guri Dam in Venezuela and Itaipu Dam between Paraguay and Brazil generate more electricity. The dam stands 550 feet above bedrock—taller than the Washington

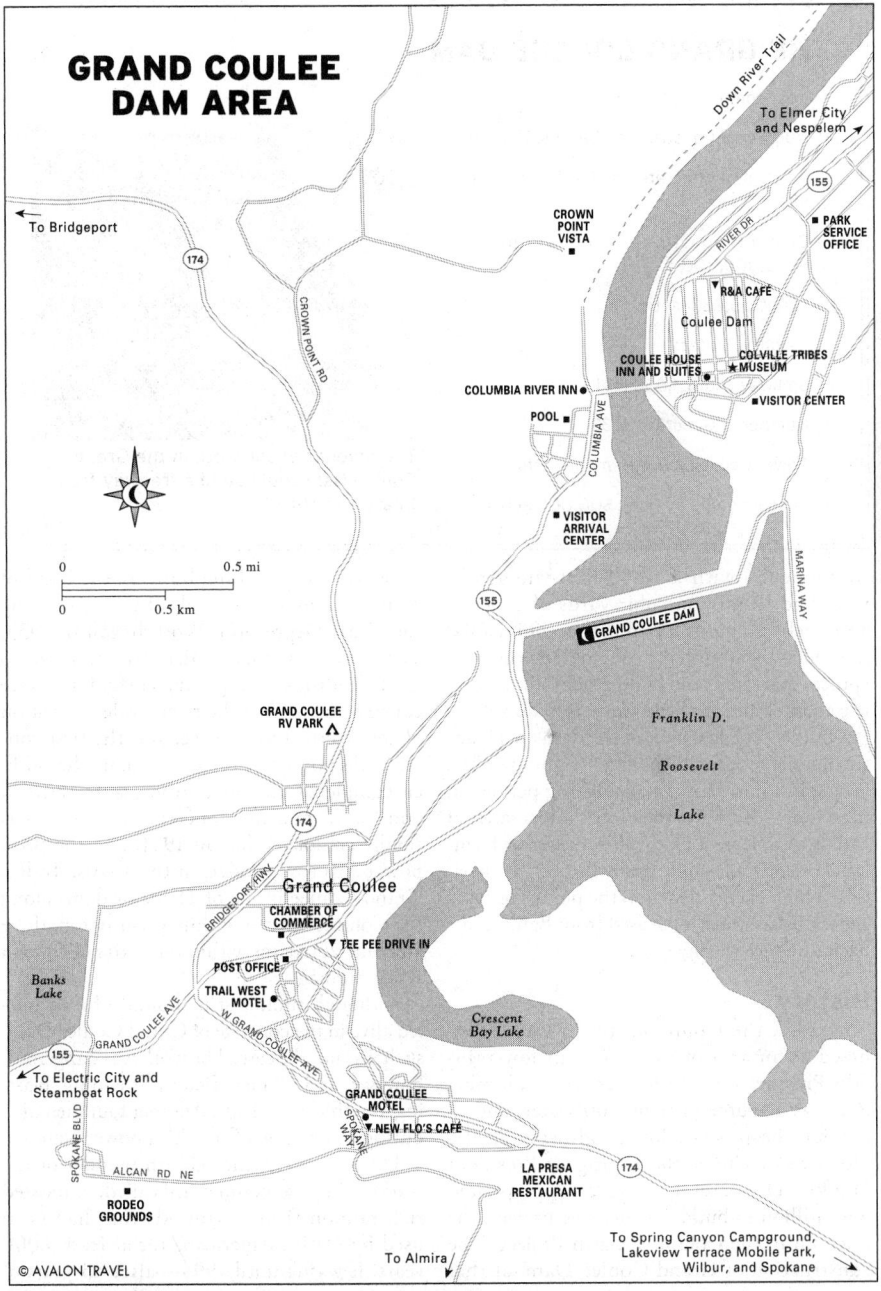
GRAND COULEE DAM AREA
Down River Trail
To Elmer City and Nespelem
155
To Bridgeport
174
CROWN POINT VISTA
PARK SERVICE OFFICE
RIVER DR
R&A CAFÉ
Coulee Dam
CROWN POINT RD
COULEE HOUSE INN AND SUITES
COLVILLE TRIBES MUSEUM
COLUMBIA RIVER INN
VISITOR CENTER
POOL
COLUMBIA AVE
VISITOR ARRIVAL CENTER
0 0.5 mi
0 0.5 km
155
MARINA WAY
GRAND COULEE DAM
GRAND COULEE RV PARK
Franklin D. Roosevelt Lake
174
Grand Coulee
BRIDGEPORT HWY
CHAMBER OF COMMERCE
TEE PEE DRIVE IN
POST OFFICE
Banks Lake
TRAIL WEST MOTEL
Crescent Bay Lake
GRAND COULEE AVE
W GRAND COULEE AVE
155
To Electric City and Steamboat Rock
GRAND COULEE MOTEL
NEW FLO'S CAFÉ
SPOKANE WAY
SPOKANE BLVD
ALCAN RD NE
LA PRESA MEXICAN RESTAURANT
174
RODEO GROUNDS
To Spring Canyon Campground, Lakeview Terrace Mobile Park, Wilbur, and Spokane
To Almira
© AVALON TRAVEL

THE GRAND COULEE DAM

- Year completed: 1951
- Number of Construction Deaths: 77 men
- Amount of Concrete Used: 11,975,521 cubic yards
- Cost of Construction (2007 dollars): $970,000,000
- Length: 5,223 feet
- Height: 550 feet
- Spillway Width: 1,650 feet
- Number of Generators: 33
- Power Capacity: 6,480 megawatts
- Land Irrigated by Dam: 500,000 acres

© ERICKA CHICKOWSKI

The amount of concrete in the Grand Coulee Dam could build a freeway from Seattle to Miami.

Monument—with a 1,650-foot-wide spillway. The 12 million cubic yards of concrete and steel it contains are enough to build a six-foot sidewalk around the equator (assuming, of course, that you could build a sidewalk around the equator and that you wanted to do so).

On the slope just west of the dam are gigantic pipes through which water is pumped 280 feet uphill into Banks Lake during periods of high flow. This water then feeds into a series of canals to irrigate a half million acres of farmland in the Columbia Basin Project. In periods of high energy demand, the pumps become generators as water is released from Banks Lake back down these pipes.

History

For years, the Columbia Basin was recognized as an area of rich soils but low rainfall. Pressure built to harness the Columbia River as a source of irrigation water, and to provide cheap power for the growing Pacific Northwest. Under the urging of President Franklin D. Roosevelt, Congress appropriated $60 million to build this massive project, the linchpin in the Columbia Basin Project. The construction of Grand Coulee Dam, at that time "the biggest thing built by the hand of man," employed thousands of workers during the Great Depression. Work began in 1933, as massive amounts of dirt were removed to get to bedrock. Temporary cofferdams were constructed to shift the river while excavation of the riverbed took place, and the first concrete was poured in 1935. Gradually the workers completed a foundation across the riverbed and began pouring concrete. The dam was finally completed late in 1941, and the third power plant was added in the 1970s. Today, Grand Coulee is one of 11 major dams along the Columbia River within Washington; there are some 200 dams within the entire Columbia River drainage.

Although rumors still abound of men buried alive in the concrete of Grand Coulee Dam, such was not the case. The work was dangerous, however, and 77 men died in drowning, blasting, or vehicle accidents. Another four men died during completion of the third power plant.

Unfortunately, the "eighth wonder of the world," as it is sometimes still called, inundated rich salmon fishing grounds that had been used by Native Americans for at least 9,000 years. It wasn't until 1994—after 43 years of contentious litigation—that the U.S. Congress finally agreed to pay the Colville Tribe $53 million (plus additional annual payments of $15 million) as compensation for the loss of this way of life.

Tours and Information

Start your visit with a stop at the Bureau of Reclamation's **Visitor Arrival Center** (just north of the dam on Hwy. 155, 509/633-9265, www.grandcouleedam.org, late May–Sept. daily 8:30 A.M.–9:30 P.M., Oct.–Apr. 9 A.M.–5 P.M.). Self-guided tours of the dam are available throughout the year when the center is open, and documentary movies are shown in the auditorium all day. The Visitor Arrival Center also houses one of the world's most advanced computer-controlled laser projection systems, used for spectacular summertime shows. A gift shop sells books about the dam and local natural history.

Guided tours are usually available; see the Visitor Arrival Center for the current status. A highlight of the dam tour is riding the glass incline elevator to the face of the power plant for a spectacular view of the spillway from an outside balcony. An artifact room displays the Native American tools and arrowheads uncovered during the construction of the dam, along with agate stones.

Laser Light Show

Each summer evening (at 10 P.M. Memorial Day–July, 9:30 P.M. in August, 8:30 P.M. in September) brings a most unusual and immensely popular event to Grand Coulee Dam: an elaborate high-tech laser light show that paints 300-foot figures on the face of the dam and tells the history of the Columbia River, of the Native American people who first lived here, and of the dam and how it transformed the desert land.

This program packs the house, even though the "house" can sit on surrounding hillsides or in their vehicles. Best vantage points are from the Visitor Arrival Center, from the parking lot just below here, from the park at the east end of the bridge in Coulee Dam, and from Crown Point Vista (farther away, but overlooking the entire area). If you're planning to park at the visitors center, get there an hour early to be sure of a spot, especially on weekends. Thousands of other folks are looking for the same vista point.

If you're too far away to hear the sound from the speakers, tune to 89.9 FM or 1490 AM for nightly broadcasts of the music and story. It's all done in an entertaining and patriotic way, ending in a Neil Diamond song.

Trails

Several local paths provide a chance to get away from the dam and explore. The **Candy Point Trail** was first built by the CCC in the 1930s, and their hand-laid stone is still in evidence. The path begins from a trailhead 300 feet down the hill behind the Coulee Dam Credit Union in the town of Coulee Dam and climbs steeply to Crown Point overlook, then over Candy Point, before returning to the river near Coulee Dam City Hall.

The **Down River Trail** is a gentle 6.5-mile path along the river north from the bridge, with several tree-lined rest areas. A less developed trail heads south from the dam to the towns of Grand Coulee and Electric City.

LAKE ROOSEVELT

Enormous Franklin D. Roosevelt Lake—stretching more than 150 miles from the dam almost to the Canadian border—is popular with boaters, water-skiers, swimmers, anglers, and campers.

Much of Franklin D. Roosevelt Lake—from Grand Coulee Dam to just below the town of Northport—has been designated the sprawling **Lake Roosevelt National Recreation Area** (509/633-9441, www.nps.gov/laro). The reservoir backs up not just the Columbia River waters, but also parts of the Spokane, Kettle, Colville, and Sanpoil Rivers. At more than 150 miles long, it is said to be the second-largest human-created lake in the world.

The dry, sunny climate is perfect for lake activities; summer temperatures range from the mid-70s to 100°F, with evenings cooling off to the 50s or 60s. The area is a popular winter recreation spot as well, with cross-country skiers, ice fishermen, and snowmobilers enjoying the off-season, along with the many bald eagles that winter here before heading north to British Columbia for the spring. You won't be the only one around if you visit in the summer; more than 1.8 million folks pass through the area each year.

Sports and Recreation

No lifeguards on the lake, but popular swimming beaches are found at **Spring Canyon** and **Keller Ferry** in lower Lake Roosevelt, and at **Fort Spokane** and **Porcupine Bay** on the Spokane River arm. The water in the Spokane River arm tends to be five to eight degrees warmer than the rest of the lake, where it averages in the 60s in June, rising to the 70s in August. If you're swimming outside a protected area, keep an eye out for boats!

Twenty-three public boat launches line Lake Roosevelt. All boats must have a launch permit ($6 for a permit covering seven consecutive days); call the Park Service (509/633-9441) for more info including annual permits. From April through June only a few of the launches are usable because the lake is lowered about 100 feet to accommodate the spring runoff. Call the reservoir hotline (800/824-4916) for an estimate of current and future water levels. Be sure to steer clear of protected swimming beaches and the waters near the dam.

A state fishing license is required to fish in the recreation area; you can pick one up—along with current fishing regulations—at most area hardware or sporting goods stores or marinas. The 30-plus species of fish inhabiting these waters include walleye (more than 90 percent of the annual catch), rainbow trout, and enormous white sturgeon, averaging 100–300 pounds but growing up to 20 feet long and to 1,800 pounds. Other residents include the kokanee salmon, yellow perch, bass, cutthroat trout, perch, and pike. The best months for fishing are September through November and May through June. In midsummer the fish retreat to cooler waters in streams or deep in the lake. Popular fishing spots are at the points where rivers and streams meet the lake—the Sanpoil River, Wilmont Creek, Hunters Creek, Kettle River, and others—or the waters near high shoreline cliffs, such as those near Keller Ferry.

Campers can stay at one of 35 campgrounds (10 of these are accessible only by boat) that line both sides of Lake Roosevelt and the Spokane River arm. None of the campgrounds offer hookups, showers, or reservations, but all have restrooms and most have running water. A $10 fee is charged for all but the boat-accessible campsites, which are free. Summer **campfire programs** are offered Friday and Saturday evenings at Evans, Fort Spokane, Spring Canyon, Kettle Falls, Keller Ferry, and Porcupine Bay campgrounds. Most campgrounds are open year-round; Porcupine Bay is open May–October. There is a 14-day camping limit.

Accommodations

One of the best ways to explore the reaches of Lake Roosevelt is aboard a rented houseboat. Swimming and fishing are just outside your bedroom window; there are no noisy neighbors to contend with; and you'll see parts of the lake you just can't reach by car. Each houseboat is at least 46 feet long and comes equipped with a kitchen, bath, sleeping areas for up to 13, swim slide and ladder, and gas grill. You can also rent 18-foot ski boats or 14-foot fishing boats to take along. Weekend rates in the summer (two nights and three days) are steep, around $1,000–2,500; save money by renting in the off-season or for longer periods. During the busy season, the rentals go quickly. For more information, contact **Lake Roosevelt Resort and Marina** (509/738-6121 or 800/635-7585, www.lakeroosevelt.com), **Roosevelt Recreational Enterprises** (509/633-0136 or 800/648-5253, www.colville.tribal.com/rre), or **Dakota Columbia Houseboat Adventures** (509/835-5647 or 800/816-2431, www.dakotacolumbia.com).

Information and Services

The best place for information is the **Grand Coulee Dam Visitor Arrival Center** (at the dam, 509/633-9265, www.grandcouleedam.org). Stop by the **Lake Roosevelt National Recreation Area Headquarters** (1008 Crest Dr. in Coulee Dam, 509/633-9441, www.nps.gov/laro, Mon.–Fri. 7:30 A.M.–4 P.M.) for additional details. Ranger stations are in Kettle Falls and Fort Spokane, and chamber of commerce visitors centers are in Grand Coulee and Coulee City.

There are small stores with groceries and supplies at Daisy Station, and in the marinas at McCoys, Seven Bays, Keller Ferry, and Kettle Falls. The surrounding towns of Kettle Falls, Coulee Dam, Grand Coulee, Colville, and Northport have food, lodging, and other services. Rent boats at **Keller Ferry Marina** (509/647-2253), **Seven Bays Marina** (509/633-0201 or 800/648-5253) or **Kettle Falls Marina** (509/738-6121 or 800/635-7585).

Getting There and Around

Two ferries cross Lake Roosevelt year-round: the **Keller Ferry** (daily 6 A.M.–11 P.M., free) connects with Highway 21 in the south part of the recreation area, and, farther north, the **Gifford Ferry** (6 A.M.–9:30 P.M. in summer, free) joins Highway 25 near Inchelium. Both ferries carry passengers and vehicles and take about 15 minutes for the crossing.

ELECTRIC CITY, GRAND COULEE, AND COULEE DAM

The towns of Electric City, Grand Coulee, and Coulee Dam surround the Grand Coulee Dam. In addition to accommodations and food, they provide a launching place to explore the dam, along with nearby Lake Roosevelt and Banks Lake Reservoirs. A fourth settlement, **Elmer City,** has 300 people and sits two miles north of the dam.

Sights

The **Colville Tribal Museum** (512 Mead Way in Coulee Dam, 509/633-0751, www.colvilletribes.com, 10 A.M.–6 P.M. Mon.–Sat. April–Dec., closed the rest of the year, free) has excellent exhibits relating to all 12 bands of the Colville, including old photos, cedar root and bear grass baskets, fine old cornhusk bags, and a Thomas Jefferson peace medal given to the Nez Percé by the Lewis and Clark expedition in 1804. A gift shop sells locally made moccasins, beaded goods, turquoise jewelry, baskets, and blankets. Nearby **Grand Gallery** (509/633-7187) exhibits local artists.

The well-known **Gehrke Windmills** can be found at Bicentennial Park in the town of Grand Coulee. These amusing, brightly colored pieces of folk art were created by the late Emil Gehrke from scraps of iron.

One of the best views of the dam is from **Crown Point Vista,** on a bluff 626 feet above the river, and two miles west of the Grand Coulee on Highway 174.

Entertainment and Events

The second weekend in May, the **Colorama Festival** brings a rodeo, parade, flea market, and carnival to the Coulee Dam area. Also in mid-May, the **Sunbanks Blues Festival** (509/633-3786) includes three full days of live blues acts. The **Memorial Day Festival** (800/268-5332) features arts and crafts, music, food, a fun run, and the grand opening of the laser light show followed by a big fireworks display off the top of the dam. This festival attracts some 75,000 visitors. More fireworks from the dam, along with arts and crafts, food, and entertainment mark the **4th of July.**

Bring some coin for the slots and the blackjack tables at **Coulee Dam Casino** (515 Birch St., Coulee Dam, 800/556-7492, www.colvillecasinos.com).

Sports and Recreation

The Park Service (509/633-9444) has free guided canoe trips around **Crescent Bay Lake** behind the town of Grand Coulee. These 90-minute paddles take place June–August and offer a good opportunity to see wildlife. Canoes, paddles, and life jackets are provided.

There are no lifeguards, but popular swimming places are Spring Canyon Campground along Lake Roosevelt and Steamboat Rock State Park, eight miles south on Banks Lake. **Sunbanks Resort** (509/633-3786, www.sunbanksresort.com) rents personal watercraft on Banks Lake.

About a mile south of Electric City, **Banks Lake Golf and Country Club** (Grand Coulee Airport Road, 509/633-0163) is an 18-hole public course.

CAMPING AND RV PARKS

The Park Service operates campgrounds (no showers, reservations, or RV hookups) all along Lake Roosevelt. Closest to the dam is **Spring Canyon** (three miles east of the town of Grand Coulee, open year-round, $10). Saturday evening campfire programs are held here during the summer.

The best camping on Banks Lake is at **Steamboat Rock State Park** (eight miles southwest of the dam on Hwy. 155, 888/226-7688, www.parks.wa.gov, $12 primitive, $17 standard tent, $23 full hookups, $7 extra reservation fee). Pull up an RV or throw a tent down on a grassy loop site, or hike a little less than a mile to a primitive and private spot right by the lake. These primitive sites can also be accessed by boat. If you stay, be sure to hike to the top of the rock over the steep but short trail that offers windswept vistas of the coulees.

The region is awash in private RV parks, with top honors split between **Coulee Playland Resort** (Banks Lake in Electric City, 509/633-2671, www.couleeplayland.com, $28–34 full hookups) and **Sunbanks Resort** (on Banks Lake just south of Electric City, 509/633-3786 or 888/822-7195, $22 tent or RV with water and electric, ask for sewer). Coulee Playland has the nicer waterfront and campsites, with a fully stocked marine and fishing store that is mighty convenient for those prone to losing tackle. Meanwhile, Sunbanks offers a nice restaurant, recreational rentals, a miniature golf course, espresso shop, and even an art gallery.

Accommodations

Lodging is mostly unpretentious in the Coulee area. Advance reservations are a good idea for the busy summer weekends; one or two months ahead should get you weekend lodging at the better motels. Winter rates can really plummet. Call the **Grand Coulee Dam Area Chamber of Commerce** (509/633-3074 or 800/268-5332, www.grandcouleedam.org) to see who has space.

Overlooking the dam, the pet-friendly **Coulee House Inn and Suites** (110 Roosevelt Way in Coulee Dam, 509/633-1101 or 800/715-7767, www.couleehouse.com, $89–159 d) has nice facilities that include an outdoor pool, hot tub, sauna, and exercise room. Kitchenettes are available. **Columbia River Inn** (10 Lincoln St. in Coulee Dam, 509/633-2100 or 800/633-6421, www.columbiariverinn.com, $105 d) is another nice place, with an outdoor pool and hot tub. The rooms provide views of the laser light show on summer evenings. Splurge a little and take advantage of the suites here, some with Jacuzzi tubs and balconies ($115) and others with two bedrooms and full kitchens ($210).

Sky Deck Motel (138 Miller Ave., Electric City, 509/633-0290, $75 d) is an attractive motel along Banks Lake with an outdoor pool and hot tub.

You won't find cookie-cutter rooms at **Grand Coulee Motel** (Spokane Way in Grand Coulee, 509/633-0770, www.grandcouleemotel.com, $55–145 d). All the rooms are different, ranging from simple one-bed units to three-room suites with kitchens. All rooms at least have a fridge and coffeemaker, and everyone gets a free continental breakfast in the morning. Guests can also take advantage of barbecues and laundry facilities on-site.

Another option in Grand Coulee is the simple **Trail West Motel** (108 Spokane Way in Grand Coulee, 509/633-3155, www.trailwestmotel.com, $55–122 d), which keeps an outdoor pool open in the summer months.

Food

The Coulee Dam area is not for gourmands, but you will find good food, generous portions, and friendly service. **New Flo's Café** (316 Spokane Way in Grand Coulee, 509/633-3216, daily 5:30 A.M.–1 P.M., closed Mon. in winter) has a strange name but serves big solid American breakfasts and lunches for a reasonable price. It's a great place to meet the locals.

Tee Pee Drive In (in Grand Coulee, 509/633-2111, daily 7 A.M.–7 P.M.) makes the best local burgers in a straight-from-the-'60s setting.

R & A Café (514 Birch St. in Coulee Dam, 509/633-2233, Mon.–Sat. 6 A.M.–2 P.M., closed Sun.) serves generous portions of family-style home cooking for breakfast and lunch.

La Presa Mexican Restaurant (in Coulee Dam, 509/633-3173, Mon.–Sat. 10 A.M.–9 P.M., closed Sun.) has authentic Mexican meals.

Information

For information on the surrounding area, contact the **Grand Coulee Dam Area Chamber of Commerce** (306 Midway in Grand Coulee, 509/633-3074 or 800/268-5332, www.grandcouleedam.org, summer Mon.–Sat. 8 A.M.–8 P.M., fall–spring Mon.–Fri. 8 A.M.–5 P.M.). A summer-only **visitors center** (509/632-5713) is located in Mason City Park (just uphill from the grocery store) in Coulee City. The Bureau of Reclamation's big **Visitor Arrival Center** is just north of the dam on Highway 155.

COULEE CITY AND VICINITY

Sights and Recreation

Banks Lake, which lies outside Lake Roosevelt National Recreation Area on the southwest side of the dam, is a 27-mile-long, clear-blue beauty surrounded by the deep sides of the coulee. In the early '50s, the coulee was dammed on both ends and filled with water from the Columbia. To get here, the water must be pumped 280 feet uphill from Lake Roosevelt through enormous pipes visible on the north side of Grand Coulee Dam. In addition to being a popular recreational alternative to Lake Roosevelt for anglers and water-skiers, Banks Lake water irrigates over a half million acres of farmland stretching south to the Oregon border. RVs and tent campers often camp for free in roadside access points along the lakeshore.

Cruising along Highway 155, you can't miss **Steamboat Rock State Park,** a scenic volcanic butte rising 700 feet above Banks Lake. You can hike a mile to the top for a panoramic view and then explore the 640 acres on the flat top. The trail starts near the north campground. Bring repellent to combat the vicious mosquitoes. Winter sports are also popular here, from ice fishing to snowmobiling and cross-country skiing.

Other places to camp include in town at **Coulee City Community Park** ($12 for tents, $17 for RVs). There's also a good swimming beach here. Another option is **Sun Lakes State Park** (Hwy. 17, 888/226-7688, www.parks.wa.gov, $17 tents, $23 RVs, $7 extra reservation fee), seven miles southwest of Coulee City. You can park RVs at **Coulee Lodge Resort** (509/632-5565, Apr.–Sept., $25), which also offers cabins ($60–85 d) and mobile homes ($80–120 d), six miles south along Blue Lake. The boatless can also rent watercraft here.

Entertainment and Events

Coulee City is home to the PRCA **Last Stand Rodeo** held on Memorial Day weekend for over 45 years.

Branding Iron Saloon has an antique bar, pool tables, and good pub grub, including the best burgers in town.

Accommodations

Most Coulee City accommodations are on the dowdy side—fine for hunters and anglers, but not so great for people who want more than a bed and shower. **Sun Lakes Park Resort** (seven miles south of Coulee City, 509/632-5291, www.sunlakesresort.com, $90–169 d) rents cabins and mobile homes on its lakeshore property. Splash in the lake or in the pool on property, or rent a rowboat to go farther afield. The resort is open mid-April to mid-October. **Ala Cozy Motel** (509/632-5703, $52 s or $62 d) is a little less elaborate and half as expensive. Kids can still enjoy the outdoor pool in the summer. Kitchenettes are available. **Banks Lake Lodge** (509/632-5596, $60–75 d) also has lakefront rentals. Choose between standard units or those with full kitchens. All units have a microwave and fridge.

LOWER GRAND COULEE AREA

Sun Lakes State Park and Dry Falls

Sun Lakes State Park (seven miles southwest of Coulee City on Hwy. 17, 888/226-7688, www.parks.wa.gov, $17 tent, $23 full hookups, $7 extra reservation fees) is famous for its "dry falls." The main part of Sun Lakes Park boasts 3,300 acres with year-round camping along Park Lake, plus horse trails, boating, swimming, and rainbow trout fishing. Concessions offer snacks, fishing supplies, horse rentals, and groceries. At least 10 smaller lakes dot the park; they are ancient plunge pools from a stupendous waterfall that once raged through here. A road leads east from Park Lake along the basalt cliff walls lining Meadow Creek to Deep Lake, and hiking trails provide access to other parts of this fascinating park.

Dry Falls Interpretive Center (four miles north of the main park entrance along Hwy. 17, 509/632-5583, mid-May–mid-Sept. daily 10 A.M.–6 P.M.) describes the incredible geologic history of this area. Outside, the cliff-edge viewpoints reveal a cluster of lakes bordered by green plants set against stark basalt cliffs. There is a certain strange beauty about this place, especially at dusk. A steep path leads a half mile down from the overlook to Dry Falls Lake. Look around the 400-foot cliff face and you may find the entrance to a small cave.

The Columbia River ran through this ancient volcanic landscape for eons, but during the ice ages that began a million years ago, glaciers forced the river to change course through the now-dry canyons called coulees. The ice also dammed the Columbia River in northern Idaho, creating an enormous body of water, Lake Missoula. When this ice dam burst around 17,000 years ago, a 2,000-foot-high wall of water rushed downstream, carving the land in a way that is almost beyond imagination. Today's Dry Falls was once the mightiest waterfall on the planet, reaching 400 feet high and over three miles across! This massive rush of water—at an estimated 386 million cubic feet per second, its volume was 10 times that of the combined flow of all rivers on earth—probably lasted but a few days or weeks but was repeated many times, as glaciers advanced and blocked the river, and as the ice dam broke again. The ripple marks left by the flood are up to 35 feet high and 350 feet apart. Over time, the periodic floods (geologists refer to these as the **Spokane Floods**) eroded the lip of the falls for a distance of almost 20 miles. Below this lip is Lower Grand Coulee, a deep 50-mile-long gorge that held the Columbia River during the ice ages. To get an idea of the magnitude of the flood, imagine this 900-foot deep, three-mile wide canyon filled with rushing water! After the glaciers retreated, the river returned to its old channel, leaving behind the dry coulees.

Lake Lenore Caves

Approximately nine miles south of Sun Lakes State Park, Highway 17 passes a series of four shallow caves, located high up the coulee cliffs. A trail leads from an information sign to several of these rock openings, which were created by the erosive action of floods that swept through the canyon during the ice ages. The caves were occupied by nomadic prehistoric peoples. Across the highway is a sign describing the Lahontan cutthroat trout that have been planted in the creek here.

Summer Falls State Park

Nine miles south of Coulee City on Pinto Ridge Road, Summer Falls State Park (www.parks.wa.gov) is an appropriately named park, since the falls created by the irrigation project exist only in the summer when irrigation water is needed. (The water reaches here from Banks Lake via an irrigation canal.) This is a cool spot for a picnic or fishing, but there's no camping. Pay attention to sirens, they'll warn of sudden flow increases that make it very dangerous to swim.

COLVILLE RESERVATION

The Colville Reservation covers more than 1.4 million acres of forested mountains, rolling rangeland, and rich farms in the Okanogan Highlands and Valley. They also have hunting, fishing, and mineral rights to an equal area to the north that was originally included in the reservation but was later opened to settlement.

The Native American peoples on the Colville subsist on income from various tribal businesses: a sawmill, grocery stores, fish hatchery, wood treatment plant, houseboat rentals, marina, and prosperous casinos in Okanogan, Coulee Dam, and Manson. The reservation has a population of 8,000 people; tribal headquarters are just south of Nespelem. The Colville Tribal Museum is located in Grand Coulee. Anglers will need to purchase special reservation permits (509/634-2112) from stores in nearby towns. Camping on the reservation also requires a permit (509/634-3145, www.colvilletribes.com).

History

The Colville Reservation is home to a dozen different tribes—Southern Okanogan, Lakes, Colville, San Poil, Nespelem, Methow, Entiat, Chelan, Wenatchi, Moses/Columbia, Palus, and Nez Percé—all shoehorned together by President Grant's executive order of 1872. The reservation was greatly reduced in 1886, when the Moses-Columbia tribe refused to be placed on land west of the Okanogan River—away from their home along the Columbia River—and these lands were opened to settlement by non-Native Americans. The tribes' traditional lands once reached from the Cascades to the Rockies, and from southern British Columbia to Oregon. The tribes have some similarities in language and cultural background, but many people still retain a clear tribal identity. Ironically, the term Colville comes from Fort Colville, named for Andrew Colville—a London financier who never even reached America!

Scenic Drives

Two very scenic country drives are Highway 21 between Keller and Republic, and Bridge Creek/Twin Lakes Road connecting Inchelium to Highway 21. The latter of these climbs west from Inchelium into remote hills covered with ponderosa pine and other evergreens, and

© WASHINGTON STATE TOURISM/LEVY SHECKLER

wilderness near the Colville Reservation

past **Rainbow Beach Resort** (509/722-5901) which offers cabins, tent and RV sites, boat rentals, and a store on mile-wide North Twin Lake. West of the lake, the narrow, winding road climbs through rounded mountains dense with trees but sliced by periodic clear-cuts. It eventually descends from the trees into rolling hills covered in grass and sage as you reach the Nespelem area.

St. Mary's Mission

This Jesuit mission (509/826-2097, open daily) was founded in 1896 by Father Steven DeRouge to bring Catholicism to the Okanogan and Chelan. DeRouge's presence met stiff resistance until he saved a Native American child who had fallen into the swift waters of Omak Creek. This act of mercy led Native American leaders to change their minds, and Chief Smitkin provided land to construct the mission. It began as a log cabin and gradually grew until two fires destroyed nearly everything early in the 20th century.

A new church was completed in 1915, with local settlers and Native Americans cooperating in the building of the altar; the side altars were shipped around the Horn from France. Today the mission contains a mix of old and new buildings, including the Paschal Sherman Indian School, now run by the Colville tribe, not the Jesuits. Up the hill, behind the church, is an old graveyard decorated with a thicket of wooden crosses and a carved wooden burro. The surrounding rocky, dry hills are covered with grass and sage.

To reach the mission, take Highway 155 east of Omak for four miles, then go 1.5 miles south. The **Sunflower Festival** takes place in late May, with food and games.

Inchelium

The free **Gifford Ferry** crosses Lake Roosevelt between Gifford and Inchelium, operating daily between 6:30 A.M. and 11 P.M. in summer. **Hartmans Log Cabin Resort** (509/722-3543, www.hartmanslogcabin.com, $45–70 d) has cabin and motel units, plus RV hookups in a quiet wooded plot by a glassy mountain lake.

Nespelem Area

Chief Joseph, leader of the Nez Percé during the famous retreat of 1877 is buried in Nespelem (nes-PEEL-em). He, along with 150 other tribal members, was exiled here in 1884. The cemetery is on the north end of town; follow 10th St. uphill to reach it. The **Chief Joseph grave** is a simple white obelisk with a few offerings and bandannas decorating a nearby tree; the monument notes that Hin-Mah-Too-Yah-Lat-Kekt (Thunder Rolling in the Mountains) died here September 21, 1904. He was approximately 60 years old. The nearby land is not greatly changed from the day of his passing—wide-open spaces of rolling grassy hills.

South of Nespelem is the **Colville Indian Agency** (509/634-2200, www.colvilletribes.com), headquarters for the reservation. Stop here for information on the reservation and the names of local artisans. Local beadwork is sold in the nearby **Trading Post Store.** Out front is the **Skolaskin Church,** built in 1874 at the behest of Chief Skolaskin, renowned for predicting a large earthquake in 1872 that caused a rock slide that briefly halted the flow of the Columbia. The log building was the first church on the Colville Reservation.

Events

Across the highway from the tribal offices is the Nespelem Community Center and a powwow circle that comes to life during the **4th of July Nespelem Powwow and All-Indian Rodeo,** a 10-day event with dance competitions—some involving full regalia—along with drumming, "stick" gambling, and delicious fry bread. The compound is bordered with dozens of tepees during the festivities. Do not enter the dance circle or take photos without asking. Another powwow is held in Nespelem on Veteran's Day and New Year's Day.

CHIEF JOSEPH DAM AREA

Chief Joseph Dam

Though overshadowed by the Grand Coulee to the east, the Chief Joseph Dam boasts a 2,000-foot-long powerhouse—largest in the

THE NEZ PERCÉ WAR

In 1877, the federal government tried to force the Nez Percé under Chief White Bird and Chief Joseph onto a reservation so that white ranchers could have their lands in Washington's Blue Mountains and Oregon's Wallowa Valley. The tribe refused, and tensions quickly mounted. A few drunken young men killed four whites, and subsequent raids led to the deaths of at least 14 more. The Army retaliated but was turned back by the Nez Percé. Rather than face government reinforcements, more than 1,000 Nez Percé began an 1,800-mile flight in a desperate bid to reach Canada. A series of running battles followed as the Nez Percé managed to confound the inept Army using their geographic knowledge and battle skills.

East of the newly established Yellowstone National Park in Wyoming, the Nez Percé plotted a masterful escape from two columns of Army forces, feinting a move down the Shoshone River and then heading north along a route that left their pursuers gasping in amazement – straight up the narrow Clarks Fork Canyon, "where rocks on each side came so near together that two horses abreast could hardly pass." Finally, less than 40 miles from the international border with Canada, the Army caught up with the Nez Percé, and after a fierce battle, the tribe was forced to surrender (although 300 did make good their escape).

Chief Joseph's haunting words at the surrender still echo through the years: "Hear me, my chiefs, I am tired; my heart is sick and sad. From where the sun now stands, I will fight no more forever." Despite promises that they would be allowed to return home, the Nez Percé were hustled onto remote reservations in Oklahoma, Kansas, South Dakota, and Washington, while whites remained on their rich ancestral lands. Chief Joseph spent the rest of his life on the Washington's Colville Reservation and died in 1904, reportedly of a broken heart.

world—and reaches over a mile across the Columbia River. It is the second biggest producer of hydropower in the nation (after Grand Coulee), supplying the electrical needs of 1.5 million people throughout the West. The dam was built in the 1950s, with a major addition in the 1970s. Water backed up behind the dam forms Rufus Woods Lake. The dam itself was named for Chief Joseph, famous leader of the Nez Percé in the 1870s, who is buried on the nearby Colville Reservation. One has to wonder how he would respond to having a dam named in his "honor." In late summer you may see Native Americans from the area fishing below the dam; unfortunately, no fish ladder was built around this massive dam, so all salmon runs above this point were wiped out.

You'll find vantage points of the dam from both sides of the river. A **visitors center** (509/686-5501, www.nws.usace.army.mil, daily 9 A.M.–5 P.M. Apr.–Oct.) is located near the center of the dam and is accessible from the north bank. From here you can peer through windows across the lineup of 27 massive generators and feel the rumble as they spin. A slide show describes the dam, and exhibits reveal the history of the region with an emphasis on hydropower. Most of the time it's a strange and sterile place with surveillance cameras watching your every move. Park rangers lead free hour-long tours of the dam at 10 A.M. and 2 P.M. from Memorial Day to Labor Day. A big wall map shows the 200 dams that block the Columbia River at points all along its basin. Outside, be sure to visit the trunnion bridge, where you get an up-close view of the massive spillway gates.

Bridgeport State Park

Three miles northeast of Bridgeport on Rufus Woods Lake, Bridgeport State Park (509/686-723, www.parks.wa.gov) offers boating, fishing, swimming, campsites ($14 for tents, $20 for RVs), and showers. The 750-acre park is an oasis of cottonwood and aspen trees surrounded by dark, beehive-shaped volcanic formations. Keep your eyes open for rattlesnakes. The park is open April–Oct. and includes the nine-hole **Lakewood Golf Course** within its boundaries. During the summer, Army Corps of Engineers rangers give Saturday night campfire programs.

Fort Okanogan State Park

Nine miles north of Bridgeport on Highway 17 near the intersection with Highway 97, Fort Okanogan State Park (509/923-2473, www.parks.wa.gov) is open daily 10 A.M.–6 P.M. from mid-May to mid-September (no camping, alas). Enjoy a picnic lunch on the grassy lawn overlooking Lake Pateros and step inside the **interpretive center** (10 A.M. to 5 P.M.) filled with interesting artifacts, displays, and dioramas of this historic fort.

Beneath the waters of Lake Pateros lies the site of Fort Okanogan, a historic fur-trading post established near the juncture of the Okanogan and Columbia Rivers. Begun in July of 1811 by David Thompson and other trappers working for John Jacob Astor's Pacific Fur Company, this was the first place to hoist the American flag in what would become Washington. The business proved lucrative at first; Okanogans were given trade items worth $160 in exchange for pelts that brought $10,000 in the East! Despite this, supply problems, stiff competition, and the threat of war with England forced Astor to sell his operation to Canadian interests. In 1821, the fort joined the vast Hudson's Bay Company holdings, operating as a major shipping point for buffalo hides down the Columbia River. Hudson's Bay continued to operate the fort until 1860, when an influx of settlers and the waning fur trade led them to pull out. The fort sites were excavated by archaeologists in the 1950s and early '60s, prior to completion of Wells Dam. The old fort location—as with many historic and cultural sites—is now buried beneath a Columbia River reservoir. So history becomes a collection of artifacts in a small museum.

Brewster

The town of Brewster (pop. 2,200) sits right on Lake Pateros (Columbia River), a couple of miles west from the mouth of Okanogan River. This is a rich agricultural area, with expansive apple, pear, and cherry orchards on the flats near the river mouth, plus additional orchards lining Highway 97 southwest of town. The region is also crowded with fruit processing plants. Stay at the appropriately named and modern **Apple Avenue Motel** (509/689-3000, $62 s or $76 d). Cheaper digs (but the same owners) are at **Brewster Motel** (806 Bridge St., 509/689-2625, $38 s or $56 d). RV spaces are also available here. **Columbia Cove RV Park** has tent and RV spaces in town. Head to **Rock Gardens Park,** halfway between Brewster and Bridgeport on Highway 173, for more camping.

Because of an abundance of Spanish-speaking farm workers, Brewster is gaining a distinctly south-of-the-border flavor. **La Milpa Grocery** has fresh corn tortillas and delicious Mexican pastries made in their bakery across the street. Brush up on your Spanish at the unpretentious **Los Camperos** restaurant (301 E. Main, 509/689-2183 Mon.–Sat. 11 A.M.–9:30 P.M., Sun. 11 A.M.–9 P.M.). If this isn't authentic enough, try one of the local taco wagons.

The main local event is **Bonanza Days,** held the first weekend of June, with hydroplane races, street dancing, and three-on-three basketball. In addition to swimming in Lake Pateros, Brewster has an impressive outdoor **swimming pool** in the grassy city park along the lake. Contact the **Brewster Chamber of Commerce** (509/689-3589, www.brewsterchamber.org) for additional information.

Omak and Okanogan

Omak and Okanogan (oh-ka-NO-gan), the valley's largest cities, are strung along the west bank of the Okanogan River, separated only by name. The Colville Reservation comes down to the river on the opposite bank, with Highway 97 following that side of the river.

Nestled between the east and west sections of the Okanogan National Forest, the twin towns serve as the commercial hub for a sparsely populated area dominated by apple orchards along the river valleys, plus logging, cattle grazing, and recreation in the national forest. Okanogan, the older of the two towns, serves as the county seat, while thriving Omak is the place for groceries, gas, and other necessities. Both Omak and Okanogan are conservative, rough-at-the-edges towns. Recent years have seen an influx of migrant workers and a growing Hispanic influence.

History

The city of Okanogan came about shortly after this region was opened to non-Native American settlers in 1886. Frank Cummings built a trading post at the mouth of Salmon Creek, and the town grew up around him. Omak was established in 1907 when Dr. J. I. Pogue, a disgruntled resident of Okanogan (they refused to name the town after him), moved north to found his own settlement. The two towns have had a low-level feud ever since, and despite their proximity, local voters have steadfastly refused to combine operations. Because of this, Omak and Okanogan have separate schools, city governments, and services.

Omak was chartered in 1910, but was slow to develop until the Biles-Coleman Lumber Company built a sawmill in 1922; it eventually became today's Omak Wood Products. You can't miss the plume of white smoke billowing into the air at their lumber and plywood mill. Recent years have seen less timber harvesting on nearby Okanogan National Forest due to the spotted owl and salmon controversies, but Omak still runs on timber. The Native-owned Colville Precision Pine Mill uses timber from the adjacent Colville Reservation.

Both town names are from native words. Okanogan is derived from the Salish term, *Ocanuckane* (rendezvous), while Omak comes from the word *Omache* (good medicine).

SIGHTS

Check out displays depicting pioneer life in the area at **Okanogan County Historical Museum** (1410 2nd N in Okanogan, 509/422-4272, www.omakchronicle.com/ochs, Memorial Day to Labor Day daily 10 A.M.–4 P.M., donation). Outside, find a replica of an Old West village, along with a replica of the old firehall.

Built in 1915, the **Okanogan County Courthouse** (3rd and Oak in Okanogan) has a Mediterranean-style red-tile roof and a gothic castlelike exterior. A **mural** on the side of Main Street Market features a painting of the Suicide Race. A walking trail—marked by big horseshoes denoting past Suicide Race winners—leads from downtown Omak to East Side Park.

ENTERTAINMENT AND EVENTS

Omak Stampede and Suicide Race

Omak is world-famous for its annual Stampede and Suicide Race (509/826-1002 or 800/933-6625, www.omakstampede.org), held the second weekend in August at East Side Park. Festivities include two parades, a big Western art show, carnival, and a major professional rodeo. During the week of the Stampede, a major attraction is the **Indian Encampment** in East Side Park. Hundreds of Native Americans come from all over the West to live in tepees, take part in traditional dance contests, or play stick games—a form of gambling. (Be sure to request permission before taking photos at the encampment.) The **Omak Western and Native Art Show** runs during the stampede and includes a quick-draw and salmon barbecue.

The main event features four chaotic horse races down a steep slope, across the Okanogan River, and into the crowded arena. Most of the 20 or so participants come from the nearby Colville Reservation, and this is a tradition that has gone on for more than 60 years. The dangerous downhill section often creates pile-ups that injure both riders and horses, sometimes leading to the death of the horse. This has led to vocal opposition from animal-rights organizations. Locals defend the race as a part of Native American and Western traditions. A shuttle bus provides service between Omak and Okanogan during the Stampede.

Entertainment

The Omak Performing Arts Center is the site of all sorts of events through the year, including concerts by **Okanogan Valley Orchestra and Chorus.** The **Breadline Café** (102 S. Ash in Omak, 509/826-5836) has folk, jazz, rock, or R&B most nights. For country music, head to **Cariboo Inn** (233 Queen St. in Okanogan, 509/422-6109) or **The Western Restaurant** (1930 N. 2nd Ave. in Okanogan, 509/422-6769). Empty your wallet in the slot machines at **Okanogan Bingo & Casino** (Hwy. 97, 800/559-4646).

Other Events

Okanogan Days on the first weekend of May features a parade, music, and airport fly-in. **Art in the Park** in the downtown park on the third weekend in June brings together artists and craftspeople along with tasty snacks at food booths. The **Okanogan County Fair** (509/422-1621, www.okanogancountyfair.org) at the fairgrounds in Omak brings more rodeo action, horse racing, a livestock auction, and musical entertainment in early September. Another popular Omak event is the **Cowboy Poetry Jubilee** in mid-March.

SPORTS AND RECREATION

Swim at the Olympic-size outdoor pools in Omak's East Side Park, or in Okanogan's Alma Park. The Okanogan River is a popular place for tubing in the summer months. **The Bike Shop** (137 S. 2nd Ave. in Okanogan, 509/422-0710) rents bikes.

Play golf at the **Okanogan Valley Golf Club** (509/826-6937) just west of town.

Loup Loup Ski Bowl (www.skitheloup.com) in the Methow Valley between Okanogan and Twisp on Highway 20, offers Alpine skiing on a 1,250-foot vertical drop.

Camping and RV Parks

Riverside camping ($3) and RV hookups ($12) are available at Okanogan's **Legion Park** on the north end of town and at **East Side Park** (509/826-1170), in Omak, next to the visitors center. Both are open all year. Park RVs at **Ponderosa RV Park** (1034 2nd Ave. S in Okanogan, 509/422-0400).

ACCOMMODATIONS

There are no B&Bs in the Omak and Okanogan area. Be sure to make motel reservations far in advance if you plan to attend the Omak Stampede and Suicide Race in August.

Fill up with a free hot breakfast at **Rodeway Inn** (122 N. Main in Omak, 509/826-0400 or 888/700-6625, www.rodeway.com, $54–59 s or $59–64 d), which features no-frills motel rooms right in town. When the summer sun shines, cool off in the outdoor pool here. Or try **Motel Nicholas** (half mile north of Omak on Hwy. 215, 509/826-4611, $49 s or $53 d), with rooms that have fridges, microwaves, and free Wi-Fi.

Find some of the nicest rooms in the Omak and Okanogan region at **Omak Inn** (912 Koala Dr. in Omak, 509/826-3822 or 800/204-4800, www.omakinnwa.com, $70 s or $75 d), which offers comfortable beds and leather sofas, as well as the option for a whirlpool suite for a little extra scratch. The property has an indoor pool, hot tub, and fitness center, plus an on-site restaurant and lounge.

Ponderosa Motor Lodge (1034 S. 2nd Ave., Okanogan, 509/422-0400, www.ponderosamotorlodge.com, $50 s or $60 d) is a nice mom-and-pop establishment with a small outdoor pool. All rooms come with refrigerators and microwaves, and kitchenette units are also available. For just a little bit more, **Okanogan**

Inn and Suites (the junction of Highways 97 and 20, Okanogan, 509/422-6431, www.okanoganinn.com, $65 d) features slightly nicer rooms, plus free Internet and continental breakfast. There's an outdoor pool, plus a modest workout room.

FOOD

Omak's **Breadline Café** (102 S. Ash St., 509/826-5836, Tues.–Sat. 11 A.M.–9 P.M., closed Sun.–Mon.) is *the* place for lunch in the area, with soups, salads, sandwiches, and espresso. The restaurant is also popular for breakfast and dinner. The decor in this old soda pop–bottling warehouse is funky mismatched chairs and tables, aging signs, and painted exposed beams.

For Mexican lunches and dinners, head to **Tequila's** (635 Okoma Dr. in Omak, 509/826-5417, Tues.–Thurs. and Sun. 11 A.M.–9 P.M., Fri.–Sat. 11 A.M.–10 P.M., closed Mon.).

Legion Park in Okanogan has a **farmers market** (509/826-1259) May to mid-October on Tuesday 4–7 P.M. and Saturday 9 A.M.–noon.

INFORMATION, SERVICES, AND TRANSPORTATION

The **Omak Visitor Information Center** (401 Omak Ave., 509/826-4218 or 800/225-6625, www.omakchronicle.com/omakvic, Mon.–Fri. 9 A.M.–5 P.M. year-round, plus Sat.–Sun. 10 A.M.–1 P.M. in the summer) has a ton of local information, along with videos on the Suicide Race. Okanogan has a summer-only **visitor information center** (509/422-9882) in Legion Park on the north end of town. The Okanogan National Forest **Supervisors Office** (1240 S. 2nd Ave. in Okanogan, 509/684-7000, www.fs.fed.us/r6/oka, Mon.–Fri. 7:45 A.M.–4:30 P.M.) has hiking and camping information for the Okanogan highland country.

I can't vouch for their hair-trimming ability, but **Wak N' Yak Beauty Salon** in Okanogan wins first prize in the odd name category.

Looking for local transportation? Try hitchhiking. The Omak/Okanogan area has neither bus service nor commercial air service of any kind!

Okanogan Valley

Okanogan Valley is a dry area surrounded by mountains, with 28 inches of annual snowfall and a sizzling hot, dry summer. Major irrigation projects make this an ideal place to grow apples, pears, peaches, and cherries. The valley served as a major route to British Columbia's Cariboo gold fields in 1857–1858, and in later years the 800-mile "Cariboo Trail" was used by cowboys to drive beef from the Yakima Valley to the mining towns. The old trail is now Highway 97, a busy north–south route along the wide Okanogan Valley. The highway cuts through most of the major towns—Okanogan, Omak, Tonasket, and Oroville—before entering Canada at a 24-hour border station. East of the valley are the Okanogan Highlands, a low range of mountains and hills covered with forests and rangeland. The highlands are essentially unpeopled, with a few small towns; only Republic is large enough to have all the services.

CONCONULLY

The pretty little burg of Conconully is 22 miles northwest of Omak and sits at an elevation of 2,300 feet, making for summertime temperatures much cooler than in the steamy Okanogan Valley. Conconully (derived from the Okanogan word for "money hole," a reference to the valuable beaver pelts found here) has a couple of stores and restaurants, along with several popular lakeside resorts.

Conconully sits between the natural Conconully Lake and the unnatural Conconully Reservoir. Built in 1910, the latter was the first Bureau of Reclamation irrigation project in America. The **Snow Dog Super Mush Race** in January is one of those wacky events that attracts folks to Conconully from around the region. The town also has a fun **4th of July** parade and street fair.

Recreation

Conconully State Park (509/826-7408, www.parks.wa.gov) sits along the shore of Conconully Reservoir and contains a log cabin and a sod-roofed replica of the first Okanogan County courthouse; Conconully was the county seat from 1889 to 1914. The reservoir is a popular place for boating, fishing, and swimming. Trees surround spacious grassy lawns that make fine picnicking spots; take the half-mile nature trail for a relaxing stroll. Cozy campsites are $14 (no RV hookups); open mid-April through October, and on weekends and holidays the rest of the year.

Five free Forest Service campgrounds are within nine miles of Conconully; closest is **Cottonwood Campground,** just two miles out Forest Road 38. The others are **Sugarloaf, Oriole, Kerr, and Salmon Meadows.**

Accommodations

There are two comfortable cabin resorts around Conconully: **Liar's Cove Resort** (509/826-1288, www.liarscr.com, $73–73 d) and **Shady Pines Resort** (509/826-2287, $55–60 d).

Other lodging can be found at the huntin' and fishin' favorite, **Kozy Kabins & RV Park** (509/826-6780 or 888/502-2246, $22 RV with full hookups, $42 d), which offers bare-bones huts with fridges and stoves. Bring your own cooking gear. There are shared bathrooms and showers, plus a community fire pit. Hunting dogs and other hounds are welcome.

Food

Try the pizza or roasted chicken at the **Tamarack Inn** (Lake and Main St., 509/846-8137, Sun.–Thurs. 11 A.M.–9 P.M., Fri.–Sat. 11 A.M.–2 A.M.). Tuesday is taco night and Thursday is steak night at Tamarack.

OROVILLE AND TONASKET

Oroville lies four miles south of the Canadian border on Highway 97, near the south shore of Lake Osoyoos, in a region of orchards and pine-topped hills. It was first settled in 1858, shortly after gold was discovered in British Columbia's Cariboo region, and its name was based on the Spanish word for gold *(oro).* The "Cariboo Trail" passed right through town, and this became the last chance to get American supplies before crossing the border.

Apple trees grow well here, and orchards are still a prominent feature in the valley; some 10,000 acres of farmland are irrigated along the Okanogan River from Oroville to Tonasket. An old irrigation flume follows the highway north from Oroville to the border. Local farmers have diversified in recent years, also planting nectarines, pears, apricots, peaches, and cherries. (By the way, the Okanogan River is called the Okanagan River once it crosses into Canada, another of the strange spelling quirks that pop up throughout this region.)

Sights and Recreation

A mile north of Oroville on Highway 97, **Osoyoos Lake State Veterans Memorial Park** offers fishing, swimming, waterskiing, and concessions on a natural lake shared with our Canadian neighbors. The east side of Osoyoos Lake has apple and pear trees planted in the early 1860s by Hiram F. "Okanogan" Smith, the first permanent white resident of the area. Smith brought his trees in from Fort Hope, British Columbia, by backpack. Several of the 135-plus-year-old trees are still bearing fruit.

Palmer Lake, 18 miles west of Oroville, a popular spot with ice-fishermen, is managed by the Bureau of Land Management; a boat launch and picnic area are at the south end of the lake.

About 12 miles northeast of Tonasket, **Sitzmark** (509/486-1027 or 509/486-2700, Wed.–Sun. and winter holidays) is a family place with a 680-foot vertical drop served by chair and Poma lifts and a rope tow, plus six kilometers of groomed cross-country trails. The area generally opens just after Christmas. The snow can be marginal at times, so be sure to call ahead. **Highland Park Sno-Park** (10 miles northeast of Tonasket) has 12 kilometers of groomed cross-country trails.

RV slots can be found at **Orchard RV Park, Eisen's RV Park,** or the parking lot at **Prince's Center.** Tent campers will do much better at **Osoyoos Lake State Veterans Memorial Park** (509/476-3321 or 888/226-7688, www.parks.wa.gov, $12, $7 extra reservation fee) a mile north of town, with tent sites but no RV hookups. Open April through October, plus weekends and holidays the rest of the year. The campground is often full all summer long.

Entertainment and Events

Fao's (1412 Main, 509/476-4142) has live music most weekends.

The second weekend of May means **Oroville May Festival,** a two-day party featuring a parade, pancake breakfast, Maypole dancing, bass tournament, arts and crafts, and basketball.

Tonasket Founders Day Rodeo the first weekend of June includes a big PRCA-sanctioned rodeo, parade, fun run, and cowboy breakfast, followed later that month by the **Tonasket Bluegrass Festival.** The main event of the summer is the **Sagebrush Loggers' Tourney** with all sorts of logging contests on the last weekend of August. In late May or early June, a **Friendship Pony Express Ride** takes place between Tonasket and Princeton, British Columbia.

Accommodations

Camaray Motel (509/476-3684, $46 s or d) has comfortable rooms and an outdoor pool, as does **Red Apple Inn** (Hwy. 97 and 18th, 509/476-3694, $46 s or $49 d), which also features a riverfront picnic area.

Visit **Sun Cove Resort** (11 miles southwest of Oroville, 509/476-2223, April–October, $65 d) on two-mile-long Wannacut Lake for a delightful family retreat with cozy cabins, hiking, swimming, and fishing, plus tent and RV spaces. Enjoy a swimming pool, guided horse-trail rides, and boat, kayak, and canoe rentals.

Spectacle Lake Resort (12 miles northwest of Tonasket on Loomis Hwy., 509/223-3433, www.spectaclelakeresort.com, $30–130 d) has rustic cabins, motel rooms, and a three-bedroom house.

Food

The dining options in Oroville are not especially noteworthy. Start out with a cup of java at **Espresso Expressions** (Main and Appleway, 509/476-2970, Mon.–Fri. 6 A.M.–5:30 P.M., Sat. 7:30 A.M.–4:30 P.M., Sun. 8:30 A.M.–2:30 P.M.). Sample freshly brewed German beer with smoked and barbecued entrées at **Alpine Brewing Company** (821 14th Ave., 509/476-9662).

Oroville is home to the huge **Prince's Center** grocery store, popular with Canadians in search of lower prices. Get fresh local fruits and juices from the cooler at **Golddigger Apples** (1220 Ironwood, 509/476-3646, Mon.–Fri. 8 A.M.–5 P.M.).

Oroville also has a **Farmers Market** across from the visitors center in the city park on Saturday 9 A.M.–noon, May through August.

In Tonasket, **Okanogan River Co-op** (21 W. 4th, 509/486-4188, Mon.–Fri. 9 A.M.–6 P.M., Sat. 9 A.M.–5 P.M., Sun noon–4 P.M.) sells natural foods, local organic produce, bulk foods, sandwiches, and coffees. Picnic tables next to the store make a nice place to munch. This is the center for the counterculture crowd in the area.

Information and Services

The **Washington State Information Center** (509/476-2739, www.orovillewashington.com) is along Highway 97 on the north end of town and is open daily in the summer, with reduced hours the rest of the year.

Get local facts at the **Tonasket Visitor Information Center** (215 S. Whitcomb, 509/486-4429, www.toasket.org) where you'll also find an RV park, restrooms, and a small interpretive center. Ask here about tours of local apple warehouses. Stop at the **Tonasket Ranger Station** (509/486-2186, www.fs.fed.us/r6/oka, Mon.–Fri. 7:45 A.M.–4:30 P.M.) for a guide to local hiking trails.

Highland Stage Company (509/486-4699) has two- and five-day stagecoach rides over the Okanogan Highlands.

Okanogan Highlands

OKANOGAN NATIONAL FOREST

The 1.7-million acre Okanogan National Forest reaches from the Methow Valley to the Canadian border and offers a plethora of recreational activities, including 1,600 miles of hiking trails, dozens of campgrounds, and hundreds of miles of cross-country skiing and mountain biking trails. Included within these boundaries are vast reaches of ponderosa pine, Douglas fir, and western larch forests, plus numerous peaks topping 7,000 feet. Two wilderness areas, Pasayten and Lake Chelan-Sawtooth are found within the forest boundaries. Forest headquarters is in Okanogan (1240 S. 2nd Ave., 509/662-4335, www.fs.fed.us/r6/oka). Stop here for backcountry permits, maps, or other information. Ranger district offices are located in Tonasket (509/486-2186) and Twisp (509/997-2131).

MOLSON AND CHESAW

The Oroville-Toroda Creek Road cuts east from Oroville to Chesaw, climbing a canyon and emerging into open rolling grass hills with caps of western larch, Douglas fir, and ponderosa pine. Scattered ranch houses dot these hills.

Tiny Chesaw consists of something like 30 people in a smattering of homes, along with a store, café, and abandoned old buildings. The town was named for Joe "Chee-saw," a Chinese settler who, with his Native American wife, constructed a cabin along Meyers Creek in the 1880s. An influx of gold miners and prospectors led to establishment of a town around this cabin. Today Chesaw is in the center of summer homes, recreational cabins, and ranches.

After eight miles, a side road leads five miles north to Molson, Washington's best known almost-ghost town, a delightful place in a wildly remote setting. Only a handful of folks still live here, surrounded by pieces of the past and the expansive land.

In the early 1900s, Molson became a major shipping point along the Great Northern Railroad, providing supplies for ranchers and miners, and sending their production to market. A spat over land—a local farmer claimed the town was entirely on his property—forced everyone to move a half mile north, leaving behind the buildings of Old Molson. New Molson declined when the railroad stopped running in the late 1920s.

Sights and Events

Old Molson town consists of eight weathered log and clapboard structures from the early 1900s, including a false-fronted bank, shingle mill, homestead cabin, and assay office. Inside are collections of antiques and historic photos from the area; outside are old wagons, threshers, and fascinating aging farm equipment.

Molson Museum (www.omakchronicle.com/ochs, Memorial Day–Labor Day daily 10 A.M.–5 P.M.) is housed in a three-story brick schoolhouse a quarter mile up the road. Inside, find antique hand tools, historic photos, and a collection of artifacts from the area's rich mining history. Volunteers serve cookies and tea and will tell you about the area's rich past.

Be sure to stop in the false-fronted **Chesaw Tavern,** where the ceiling is covered with dollar bills, the signs are pro-logging, and the beer is always cold. Hang around awhile and you're bound to meet "Chesaw Charlie," a former accountant who gave up the city life, grew a long white beard, rides around on a burro, and formed the "Church of the Utterly Indifferent." He'll be happy to perform marriage ceremonies.

Stop at **Kettle River Pottery** (99 Toroda Creek, Curlew, 509/779-4695, by appointment) for fine handmade pieces (some of their work is in the Smithsonian), or take a break by cutting north to see the Ranald MacDonald's Grave State Heritage Park (18 miles north of Curlew Lake State Park).

The very popular **Chesaw Rodeo** and fireworks occur on 4th of July weekend.

RANALD MACDONALD GRAVE

Hidden away in this remote corner of Washington, and just two miles south of the Canadian border station at **Ferry** (open 9 A.M.-5 P.M. daily), is a hillside Native American cemetery overlooking the narrow Kettle River Valley. A monument marks the grave of Ranald MacDonald, an explorer who helped change history. MacDonald was born in 1824 at a Hudson's Bay Company fur-trading post near Astoria. His parents were Princess Raven – daughter of a Chinook Chief – and the Scottish-American pioneer Archibald MacDonald. In Fort Vancouver, the young man became fascinated with Japan – a nation closed to all foreigners – and learned the language from a pair of sailors.

While sailing off the coast of Japan in 1848, he intentionally capsized his sailboat. After making it to shore, he was taken prisoner but eventually gained acceptance by the Japanese people and was allowed to travel and teach English. He was "rescued" from Japan a year later and continued his travels around the globe to Asia and Europe, as well as gold mining settlements in Australia and Alaska, before returning to Fort Colvile in Washington. MacDonald died in 1894, in the arms of his favorite niece; his last words were "Sayonara, Sayonara."

Ranald MacDonald's heritage was as the first foreigner to teach English to the Japanese and the first to promote ties between it and the United States. One of his students, Monyama Einsouke, served as interpreter for Commander Matthew Perry's vital trip to Japan in 1854. Although Ranald MacDonald is virtually unknown in America, he is revered in Japan, and pilgrims occasionally come to this remote gravesite to pay homage. A memorial to him now stands on Rishiri Island, Japan – the place he came ashore. For details on this man's life, pick up *Ranald MacDonald: Pacific Rim Adventurer* by Jo Ann Roe (Washington State University Press, www.wsu.edu).

Recreation

Four Forest Service campgrounds—**Beth Lake, Lost Lake, Bonaparte,** and **Beaver Lake**—are located south of Chesaw on the back way to Wauconda. They are open mid-May to mid-September and cost $8. **Big Tree Botanical Area** is a mile northeast of Lost Lake Campground (seven miles south of Chesaw) and includes enormous western larch (tamarack) trees. A short interpretive trail leads through the forest.

East of Chesaw, quiet country roads take you along bucolic Toroda Creek and Kettle River lined with tall riparian forests and populated by hunters each fall. The land is marked with country homes and farmsteads, irrigated pastures, hilltop pine trees, open meadows, and grazing cattle. It's a fantastic place for bike riding, especially in the fall when leaves turn a brilliant yellow. During Prohibition, this part of Washington was a major center for smuggling Canadian liquor across the border.

Information

East of here is the **Danville Port of Entry** (8 A.M.–midnight daily), where a single building is occupied by both U.S. and Canadian customs agents. For details on points north, get a copy of Andrew Hempstead's ***Moon British Columbia*** (Avalon Travel).

CURLEW

Curlew is another tiny burg surrounded by grand country, 10 miles from the Canadian border. Canadian radio stations dominate the airwaves in this part of Washington; tune in for a different perspective on the world.

Sights

Located on the eastern shore of Curlew Lake, halfway between Curlew and Republic, **Curlew Lake State Park** is a pretty little park offering shady picnic spots, along with good fishing and swimming.

Four miles south of Curlew is the surprising **Auto and Truck Museum** (509/779-4204, open by appointment, admission by donation). A commodious aluminum building houses dozens of old vehicles, including a beautifully restored 1928 Ford Phaeton owned by Walter Brennen (and used in several movies), a 1925 Howard Cooper (built in Spokane, and one of four in existence), and the smallest legal car ever built—the Orange Peel. All sorts of other oddities add to this wonderful collection maintained by local car buffs—the only such museum in Washington. Even more amazing is that all the cars still run.

Practicalities

Lake Curlew is the place to stay around these parts. For a roof over your head, check out the duplex and cabin units at **Black Beach Resort** (80 Black Beach Rd., Republic, 509/775-3989, $55–91 d). Or stay underneath the Milky Way at Curlew Lake State Park's attractive shady campsites (509/775-3592, www.parks.wa.gov, Apr.–Oct., $17 for tents, $20 for RVs), with good fishing and swimming.

For something a little closer to Curlew proper, hit **Wolfgang's Riverview Inn** (509/779-4252, www.televar.com/wolfgang, $45–60 d), two miles north of town center. This Bavarian-style lodge is a favorite among hunters and anglers and offers guided fly-fishing tours.

Dine on big steaks, prime rib, and sweet desserts at the **Riverside** (6 River Street, 509/779-4813, Fri–Sun. 4–8 P.M.). Curlew's best eatery, it's open for dinners only. It's also a popular resting place for road-weary bikers and road-trippers.

WAUCONDA

The drive east from Tonasket on Highway 20 follows Bonaparte Creek past old ranches into a beautiful valley bordered by wooded mountains. It's a great drive with little traffic, and one of the few places in Washington without the uglification that rapid development brings. Wauconda—about halfway between Tonasket and Republic—is a blink-and-you-missed-it town, with just a couple of buildings clustered around the combination restaurant, general store, video shop, gas station, and post office. Join the locals at a table in the **Wauconda Café** (509/486-4010, Mon.–Sat. 9 A.M.–7 P.M., Sun. 9 A.M.–5 P.M. in summer, call for winter hours), a small dining room overlooking the valley below. Surprisingly good food is served three meals a day, including burgers, shakes, steaks, prime rib, and even Chinese meals on weekends. Well worth the drive!

Bonaparte Lake Resort (509/486-2828, www.bonaparte-lake-resort.com, $45–65 d) features rustic cabins, as well as RV and tent camping. Get to the lake by heading three miles west from Wauconda on Highway 20, and then six miles north on Forest Road 32. Bring your own linens, towels, and kitchen utensils. The restaurant here makes the finest steaks in the area.

REPUBLIC

Stonerose Interpretive Center

A popular place for visitors is the Stonerose Interpretive Center (509/775-2295, www.stonerosefossil.org, May–Oct. Tues.–Sat. 10 A.M.–5 P.M., also Sundays mid-June–mid-Sept.), named for a 50-million-year-old fossil of an extinct rose found at a nearby rock pit. Many other plants, fish, and insects have been found here; they were deposited in an ancient lake bed. Stonerose has displays of fossils found at the site, along with literature on fossils. Also in the same building is the **Republic Historical Center,** with old photos lining the walls and a fine small gift shop selling local arts and crafts.

The public is invited to dig fossils at the **Boot Hill Fossil Site** ($3 adults, $2 ages 12–18 and seniors, free for children under 12) on the northern edge of town. You must get permission through the Stonerose Center and can only keep three fossils. Hammers and chisels may be rented for $3.

Events

Prospector's Days, held the second weekend of June, is the main local event, with a parade, golf tournament, crafts show, pancake feed, rodeo, stock car races, and even a cattle drive.

Republic's **4th of July** festivities include a big picnic in the park.

The **Ferry County Fair** is held on the fairgrounds 3.5 miles east of Republic on Labor Day weekend. This is one of the oldest fairs in the state, begun in the early 1900s as a chance to race horses. Today it includes 4-H demonstrations, livestock auctions, a parade, live entertainment, and, of course, horse racing.

Sports and Recreation

The Colville National Forest **Republic Ranger District** (180 N. Jefferson, 509/775-3305, www.fs.fed.us/r6/colville) office has detailed brochures on hiking and mountain biking routes in the area, including the popular **Lakes Area Mt. Bike Loop** south of town and the Sherman Pass area to the east. Ask here about the "Mystery Man Trees" on North Namankin Creek, images of a man emblazoned on trees.

For an easy and very scenic walk, take the half-mile hike to **Nine Mile Falls.** The trailhead is southeast of Republic; get directions from the Forest Service.

Camp at **Ferry County Fairgrounds** (3.5 miles east of town on Hwy. 20, summers only), with showers available. More RV sites are at **Miller RV Park** (584 W. Curlew Lake Rd., 509/775-1039). The nearest Forest Service sites are approximately 15 miles southwest of town: **Ferry Lake Campground** and **Swan Lake Campground,** both open May–September. There are groomed **cross-country ski trails** here during the winter months. Closer camping can be found at **Curlew Lake State Park,** nine miles north.

Accommodations

Northern Inn (852 S. Clark, 509/775-3371 or 888/801-1068, $66 s or $74 d) is an attractive place with clean and comfortable rooms. Kitchenettes are also available, as is wireless Internet for an extra charge. **Klondike Motel** (150 N. Clark Ave., 509/775-3555, $44–68 d) offers standard motel units, as well as kitchenette rooms. The **Prospector Inn** (979 S. Clark Ave., 509/775-3361, www.theprospectorinn.com, $51 or $64 d) is a clean little motel with the added amenities of with a sauna and hot tub.

Ride horses all day long at **K-Diamond-K Ranch** (509/775-3536, www.kdiamondk.com, $180 per person), a friendly, family-owned cattle ranch on 30,000 acres where guests go on horseback rides and hikes or just enjoy being outdoors. Stay in four large rooms with shared bath and savor three hearty meals a day. Meals, lodging, and rides are all included in the rate.

Food

One place stands out on the Republic eating scene: **Ferry County Co-op** (34 N. Clark Ave., 509/775-3754, Mon.–Fri. 7:45 A.M.–6 P.M., Sat. 10 A.M.–4 P.M., closed Sun.) is a counterculture store with an earthy bakery and a surprisingly good serve-yourself deli. Come here for a filling buffet breakfast or lunch, or to stock up on groceries and the latest environmental news.

The **Republic Drug Store** (6 N. Clark Ave., 509/775-3351, Mon.–Sat. 9 A.M.–6 P.M.) at 6th and Clark has a genuine old-fashioned corner drug store; they've been in business since 1904. Good Mexican meals in a fun setting can be had at **Esther's Restaurant** (90 N. Clark, 509/775-2088, 11:30 A.M.–9 P.M. Sat., closed Sun.).

Information

Republic's **visitors center** (509/775-3387, Tues.–Sat. 10 A.M.–4 P.M. mid-April through Oct.) is next to the Stonerose Center.

OVER SHERMAN PASS

From Republic, Highway 20 climbs easily into Colville National Forest through mixed forests of western larch (these turn a brilliant yellow each fall), Douglas fir, ponderosa pine, lodgepole pine, and aspen. The ascent tops out at **Sherman Pass,** the state's highest at 5,575 feet. In spite of the elevation, you won't see dramatic snowcapped peaks, just thousands of acres of forested hills. A 10-minute hike leads to fine views of lands to the east. Stop here for a pleasant picnic among the larch trees.

Hiking

At the pass, a side road leads to a trailhead for the **Kettle Crest Trail,** an excellent 30-mile-long hike that cuts north over the summit of the Kettle River Range. The area is popular with backcountry skiers in the winter.

Two miles up the Kettle Crest Trail is a spur to the top of 6,782-foot Columbia Mountain. Take this Forest Service path—**Columbia Mountain Trail**—for a wonderful short (but steep) climb to the summit, where you'll find a decrepit CCC lookout cabin and wide-angle vistas. It's a bit over five miles round-trip from the trailhead to the top of the mountain, making a fine chance to stretch your legs and enjoy the quiet, forested land and the ravens playing in the thermals. Water is available from a spring along the trail.

The Northeast Corner

Washington's northeast corner, north of Spokane and east of Lake Roosevelt, is dominated by Stevens and Pend Oreille (pon-der-RAY) Counties. (Pend Oreille is French for "pendant" or "earring," and is believed to have originated from French trappers who used the term for the earring-wearing Native American people of this area.) The region is a paradise of good fishing in lakes and rivers, all-season recreation from swimming to snow skiing, an abundance of wildlife, and very few people.

This uninhabited forest land gives wildlife photographers plenty of opportunities: the Pend Oreille River attracts ospreys, ducks, cranes, and geese, plus bighorn sheep, bears, cougars, elk, and an occasional moose or grizzly. This corner of the state isn't on the way to anywhere else in Washington, so only a determination to escape civilization or a strong exploratory drive brings visitors out here.

Several small towns serve the area: Kettle Falls, Colville, Chewelah, Ione, Metaline Falls, and Newport. They are unpretentious and friendly places and, although all have overnight accommodations and places to eat, most things of interest to visitors are out in the forests and along the rivers and lakes. Except for a bus that connects Colville with Spokane, there are no buses, trains, or planes servicing this part of Washington.

Politically, the northeast corner is Washington's outback. In many places the only radio voices you'll hear are right-wing talk shows, religious broadcasts, or country-western tunes. The remote and undeveloped beauty of this corner of the state also makes it popular with organic farmers, retirees, and escape-the-rat-race telecommuters, not to mention marijuana growers.

Rivers and Lakes

Pend Oreille River is one of just two rivers in North America that flow northward; it enters Canada north of Metaline Falls before circling back south to join the Columbia River near the town of Boundary. Small lakes are scattered throughout northeast Washington. Many are encircled by summer cabins, modest year-round homes, or low-budget resorts and RV parks. As is common in eastern Washington, the natural features here aren't played up or exploited to the degree they would be on the more crowded, beach-hungry East Coast or other more populous areas of the country; yours is likely to be the only boat on the lake. With this serenity comes a corresponding lack of services, so keep the fuel tank and ice chest full.

COLVILLE NATIONAL FOREST

Colville National Forest spreads over 1.1 million acres in half a dozen scattered puzzle pieces, reaching from Metaline Falls to Wauconda, 67 air-miles away. Abutting it on both sides are additional public lands: Okanogan National Forest to the west and Kaniksu National Forest reaching eastward into Idaho. The eastern portions of the Colville are capped by the Selkirk Mountains, one of the last places in the Lower 48 where grizzlies survive. The forests are a true mixture of evergreen and deciduous species, with grand fir, subalpine fir, lodgepole pine, aspen, Douglas fir, western white pine, western red cedar, western larch, birch, and cottonwood trees.

Hiking and Camping

Contact any Colville National Forest ranger station for a map and detailed descriptions of day hikes and longer treks. This is bear country, so make noise, store your food safely, and don't be too proud to choose another route if you encounter bears, bear tracks, or droppings.

Abercrombie Mountain Trail is a three-mile one-way hike to a ridge top with panoramic views of the Pend Oreille and Columbia River Valleys from 7,300 feet. From Colville, take Aladdin Highway north for 23 miles to Deep Creek Road, turn north onto Deep Creek Road for seven miles, then turn right on Silver Creek Road 4720 to the junction with Road 7078. Take 7078 north to Road 300, then follow it to the road's end where the trail begins. Most of the three miles is wooded, crossing several streams and huckleberry bushes on the way to the ridge. This trail is also popular with hunters because of the abundant deer—so look conspicuous!

In addition to the many hiking trails, the Forest Service maintains 27 campgrounds on the Colville. A number of Colville National Forest campgrounds and hiking trails are described elsewhere in this chapter.

Information

For more specific information on hiking, camping, and other recreational activities in the Colville National Forest, contact **Colville National Forest Headquarters** (765 S. Main, 509/684-7000, www.fs.fed.us/r6/colville). District offices are in Colville, Kettle Falls, Sullivan Lake, and Newport.

KETTLE FALLS

As you enter Kettle Falls, you're greeted by a sign proclaiming, Welcome to Kettle Falls—Home of 1,540 Friendly People and One Grouch. Ask around town and you'll find that the grouch is elected each year by the local citizenry, with each vote costing $0.25. Using the vote-early, vote-often method, it's possible to buy the election for a particularly deserving individual each year. (All the "election" proceeds go to promoting the town.)

Kettle Falls runs on a spectrum of businesses, including a large Boise Cascade lumber mill and two other wood products mills, orchards, and tourism, especially at nearby Lake Roosevelt. A large wood-fired power plant produces electricity near Kettle Falls, burning wood waste and chips.

History

The town of Kettle Falls was originally located three miles west of the current site along the Columbia River falls of the same name. The waterfalls were named *Les Chaudieres* (The Kettles) by French-Canadian fur traders in reference to the bowl-shaped rocks carved by the water's force. They were actually a series of cascades that dropped 33 feet in a half mile, enough to slow the upstream salmon movement, making them easier to catch in baskets or to spear with poles. When the fish were running, a person could catch over a thousand fish in a single day, providing a major source of winter food for the various tribes that used the site. The summer fishing site—said to have been the richest run of salmon on the planet—was used by Native Americans for more than 9,000 years. More and more people came to the area, and by the early 19th century, Kettle Falls was a summer home for over a thousand people from the surrounding region. It was a natural site for a trading post.

The Hudson's Bay Company established **Fort Colvile** here in 1826. (Note that the fort name was spelled "Colvile," unlike the city, National Forest, reservation, and other regional features spelled "Colville.") Fort Colvile grew rapidly into a small town, with barns, a windmill, coal kilns, and a water-powered gristmill. Farmers here supplied food for other Hudson's Bay forts along the Columbia River, and traders purchased and shipped furs from throughout the region; in 1840 they processed 18,000 furs. The arrival of missionaries—who emphasized farming rather than traditional Native American ways—and a shift away from beaver fur hats in England during the 1840s led to the fort's demise. It remained in existence until 1871 when Hudson's Bay abandoned all their land south of the Canadian border. A fire destroyed the structure in 1910.

The filling of Lake Roosevelt behind Grand Coulee Dam in 1941 forced the residents of Kettle Falls to move eastward to a place originally called Meyers Falls and subsequently renamed Kettle Falls. The falls themselves, along with the fort site and 9,000 years of history, now lie under the placid waters of this enormous reservoir. No fish pass was ever built around the dam; it wasn't worth the effort, officials said. Thus ended the world's richest salmon run.

Sights

The small **St. Paul's Mission,** in a grove of tall pines near old Kettle Falls, was built in 1847 and is one of the oldest churches in Washington. Jesuit missionaries held services here for the Native Americans who often fished for salmon in these waters. The Catholic chapel was closed 1858–1862 when gold fever brought an influx of white settlers and their booze, but it reopened for the summer salmon runs in the 1870s, after which it fell into disrepair. Reconstructed in 1939 using hand-hewn logs, the structure was turned over to the National Park Service in 1974.

Not far away is the **Kettle Falls Historical Center** (509/738-6627, weekends in May and Wed.–Sun. 11 A.M.–5 P.M. June 1 to Labor Day, closed winters, donation), a small building that houses murals, artifacts, and exhibits portraying the old ways of life before Lake Roosevelt flooded the falls and ended salmon fishing here.

Meyers Falls—the oldest continually used source of industrial power in the Pacific Northwest—has a small log building housing the **Meyers Falls Interpretive Center,** where historic photos line the walls. Outside is a replica of the 16-foot-high water wheel that operated here for many decades, along with the original stone wheels used to grind the grain. The cascades are a few feet distant, dropping 20 feet into a pretty plunge pool below a small dam that has been producing electrical power here since 1903. Prior to its completion, the falls turned three gristmills; the first built in 1826 by the Hudson's Bay Company. It milled wheat, oats, barley, and corn for their trading posts along the upper Columbia River and is said to have produced the first patented flour in the United States. The old mill was destroyed by a fire in 1916. The falls are located a mile south of town on Juniper Street; follow the signs from the highway.

Entertainment and Events

Town & Country Days is the big summer event in Kettle Falls, arriving the first weekend of June and featuring a parade, fun run, and local arts and crafts. This is also when the town grouch is chosen. The **Governor's Cup Walleye Tournament** on the third weekend of June is followed by the **Lake Roosevelt Regatta** on the second weekend of July.

Kettle Falls' **Woodland Theatre** (120 W. 3rd Ave., 509/738-6430) features plays, concerts, and musicals throughout the year.

Sports and Recreation

Fishing is a favorite activity in Lake Roosevelt. A net pen project near Kettle Falls produces rainbow trout, and the **Sherman Creek Hatchery** (four miles west of Kettle Falls, 800/824-4916) raises kokanee salmon for Lake Roosevelt. Call for the current lake elevation.

Lake Roosevelt is a feeding area for more than 200 **bald eagles** during the winter months, particularly the stretch from Kettle Falls south to Gifford Ferry. Best time to see these birds is late November to mid-February.

The National Park Service operates the wonderful **Kettle Falls Campground** (two miles south of Hwy. 395/20 on Boise Rd., 509/738-6266, www.nps.gov/laro, year-round, $10, no RV hookups) in tall ponderosa pines along Lake Roosevelt. Campfire programs take place most summer evenings; check at the Ranger Station for offerings. No reservations, so get here early for summer holiday weekends. Take showers at the Chevron station on the west end of town.

The Park Service maintains a very popular campground, boat ramp, and swimming beach (no lifeguard) along the shore of Lake Roosevelt just south of Highway 395/20.

Private RV parks around Kettle Falls include **Circle Up RV Park** (on Boise Rd. south of the Park Service office, 509/738-6617, $22 full hookups), **Grandview Inn and RV Park** ($25), and **North Lake Roosevelt Resort** (Roosevelt Road, 509/738-2593, $13 tent, $21 RV).

Accommodations

Grandview Inn Motel (978 Hwy. 395, 509/738-6733, $52 d, $60 d for kitchenette) has a delightful woodsy location overlooking Lake Roosevelt and comfortable rooms, some with kitchenettes. A more homey option is **Blue Moose Cabin Rentals** (five miles west of Kettle Falls, 509/738-6950, www.bluemoosecabins.com, $65 d), which has three cabins with kitchenettes.

Food

Little Gallea (270 W. 3rd, 509/738-6776, Mon.–Sat. 5 A.M.–2 P.M., 5–11 P.M., closed Sun.) is the local breakfast and lunch joint with well-prepared and inexpensive American food. For good steaks and seafood, stop by **Hudson Bay Co.** (2 Columbia Dr., 509/738-6164, daily 11 A.M.–9 P.M.).

More than a dozen local orchards produce cherries, apricots, peaches, pears, apples, and other fruits. Many of these operate fruit stands or have U-pick operations near the site of old Kettle Falls along Lake Roosevelt. Get a brochure from the chamber of commerce, or just head down Peachcrest Road till a place looks interesting.

China Bend Vineyards & Winery (3751 Vineyard Way, 509/732-6123 or 800/700-6123, www.chinabend.com) offers tastings of its organic wines and salsas. The grounds are gorgeous and right on the Columbia River. They also have a popular 4th of July celebration here each summer.

Information and Services

Find restaurant and lodging information at the **Kettle Falls Area Chamber of Commerce** (downtown along Hwy. 395/20, 509/738-2300, www.kettlefalls.org, daily 1–3 P.M. in summer). Hours are hit or miss in the off-season.

Stop by the Park Service's **Kettle Falls Ranger Station** (S. 1230 Boise Rd., 509/738-6266, www.nps.gov/laro) to view the displays of Native American artifacts and other items found at old Kettle Falls. Get Colville National Forest information at **Kettle Falls Ranger District** (255 W. 11th St., 509/738-6111, www.fs.fed.us/r6/colville).

COLVILLE

Like many of its neighbors in this part of Washington, Colville (pop. 5,000) depends on timber, mining, farming, and tourism to survive. There are still three sawmills in Colville fed by timber from Colville National Forest and private lands. The town began as a U.S. Army post called Fort Colville (not to be confused with the older Fort Colvile run by Hudson's Bay Company). The fort was abandoned in the early 1880s, but the settlement survived to become today's Colville, the largest "city" in northeastern Washington. Downtown Colville is a prosperous slice of middle America, and the surrounding area shows even more evidence: a sparkling new high school on the edge of town and the only Wal-Mart in this corner of the state.

Sights

Stevens County Historical Museum (700 N. Wynne St., 509/684-5968, June–Aug. daily 10 A.M.–4 P.M., May and Sept. daily 1–4 P.M., donation) contains an extensive collection of items from Fort Colville and Fort Colvile, along with Native American artifacts (a dugout canoe, headdresses, intricately woven baskets, and more), plus many historic photos. Be sure to ask the docents to play the old music box for you.

Outside the museum you'll find spacious grounds containing the three-story **Keller House,** completed in 1912 and essentially unchanged today. Walk down the hill under tall walnut trees to a collection of farm machinery and old buildings, including a sawmill, farmstead cabin, schoolhouse, fire lookout, and trapper's cabin.

Entertainment and Events

The **Colville Rodeo** (509/684-4849) comes to town in mid-June, with a parade and PRCA rodeo. **Colville Rendezvous** on the first weekend of August features food, arts and crafts, entertainment, and various sporting contests. Early August or September brings the **Northeast Washington Fair** with a parade, animal judging, carnival, and live music.

Sports and Recreation

Swim at the outdoor swimming pool in City Park, or just hang out under the beautiful tall ponderosa pines and Douglas fir trees that cover the grassy lawns. Colville is one of the few places that still has a drive-in movie theater; it's three miles west of town. Golfers can enjoy **Colville Elks Golf Course** (509/684-5508), an 18-hole course.

Nine miles east of Chewelah, **49° North** (509/935-6649, www.ski49n.com, $28 adults) has day and night skiing on 1,900 vertical feet of slope from four chairlifts. It's about an hour north of Spokane off Highway 395. Sixteen runs offer beginner through expert skiing; terrain is set aside for powder skiing on weekends. Be sure to drive to the ski area from Highway 395 on the Chewelah (west) side; the road in from Highway 20 on the east is a narrow gravel logging road, impassable in winter and no fun the rest of the year.

Tent camping and RV spaces are available at the **Northeast Washington Fairgrounds** on Columbia Street. Four Forest Service campgrounds are located in **Little Pend Oreille Lakes Recreation Area,** 25 miles northeast of Colville along Highway 20. Several more remote campgrounds are free, including **Big Meadow Lake Campground** (27 miles northeast of Colville on Meadow Creek Road). Here you'll find three miles of hiking trails (partly wheelchair-accessible), a replica of a homestead cabin, and a 35-foot wildlife-viewing tower where you may see moose, beavers, ospreys, or even black bears.

Accommodations

Bennie's Colville Inn (915 S Main St., 509/684-2517, www.colvilleinn.com, $48 to $102 s) has a range of rooms plus an indoor pool, hot tub, and a fitness center pass. **Comfort Inn** (166 N.E. Canning Dr., 509/684-2010 or 800/228-5150, www.comfortinn.com, $89 d) has an indoor pool and hot tub and serves a continental breakfast.

Food

Talk 'N' Coffee (119 E. Astor, 509/684-2373, Mon.–Fri. 7 A.M.–4:30 P.M., closed Sat.–Sun.) next to the chamber office is Colville's version of hip, with homemade scones and good espressos.

Head to **Rancho Chico** (S. Main) for Mexican-style meals. **Cafe Italiano** (153 W. 2nd St., 509/684-5957, Mon.–Fri. 11 A.M.–2 P.M. and 4–8 P.M., Sat.–Sun. 4–8 P.M.) is a cheery place with good pasta, chicken, veal, and seafood. **Barman's Country Store** (230 S. Main, 509/684-9710, Mon.–Sat. 10 A.M.–6 P.M., Sun. 11 A.M.–5 P.M.) has an old-fashioned soda fountain with sandwiches and homemade ice cream floats.

Colville has **farmers markets** (509/684-2326) on Wednesday noon–6 P.M. May–October at the corner of Hawthorne and Elm, and Saturday 8:30 A.M.–1 P.M. at 3rd and Main.

Information

Ask the **Colville Chamber of Commerce Visitor Information Center** (121 E. Astor, 509/684-5973, www.colville.com, Mon.–Fri. 10 A.M.–noon and 1–4 P.M.) for directions to the big "C" on Colville Mountain overlooking town.

For Forest Service information, visit the **Colville Ranger District** (755 S. Main, 509/684-7000, www.fs.fed.us/r6/colville, Mon.–Fri. 7:30 A.M.–4:30 P.M.) behind the Federal Building.

LITTLE PEND OREILLE LAKES RECREATION AREA

Heading east from Colville on Highway 20, the road cuts through beautiful mixed forests.

Be sure to stop at **Crystal Falls,** 12 miles east of Colville, where the waters of Little Pend Oreille River drop over a 30-foot cascade. It's a fine place for a picnic beneath the trees.

Approximately 25 miles northeast of Colville on Highway 20 is a chain of eight glacially formed bodies of water: the Little Pend Oreille Lakes. These are favorite getaway spots for folks from Spokane, offering more than 75 miles of multiuse trails open to hiking, motorcycles, mountain bikes, and horses. In winter, the Forest Service maintains 15 miles of groomed cross-country ski trails here. The lakes themselves are popular for swimming, sailing, boating, fishing, and canoeing. The country around here is a beautiful mix of open meadows and dense forests with plenty of larch trees (bright yellow in the fall).

Recreation

The Little Pend Oreille trail system has seven trails to satisfy all kinds of users—hikers and cross-country skiers. A popular 2.4-mile loop, the **Springboard Trail** begins at the east end of the Gillette Campground. This self-guided interpretive trail relates the history of an early homesteader and leads to a viewing platform.

Sherry Trail is a set of three short loops that total four miles in length and begin at the trailhead just west of Lake Sherry. This hike or ski route passes through lodgepole pine and Douglas fir and provides views of the lake and Little Pend Oreille River.

Frater Lake Trail has three ski/hike loops that start at Frater Lake on the east end of the recreation area. The two-mile Tiger Loop cuts through Douglas fir close to the lake on gentle terrain. The longer and steeper Coyote Rock Loop crosses a stream and meadow and has a viewpoint from Coyote Rock. Across on the south side of Highway 20 is the 2.6-mile **Lake Leo Trail,** popular with beginning cross-country skiers because of its gentle terrain.

You'll find four Forest Service campgrounds in the Little Pend Oreille Lakes area ($10). **Lake Leo, Lake Thomas, Gillette,** and **Lake Gillette** campgrounds are open Memorial Day to Labor Day (Lake Leo is open until the snow flies).

Practicalities

Beaver Lodge Resort (509/684-5657, $55 d) is a fun family place on Lake Gillette, with comfortable cabins, tent ($20) and RV ($30 full hookups) spaces, and boat and canoe rentals. There's also a store, deli, and laundry.

IONE

Ione (pop. 500) is a lumber and tourism town along the Pend Oreille River 35 miles north of Usk. Steamboats plied the Pend Oreille River in the 1880s; today nearby Box Canyon Dam backs up the river to create a popular place to water ski and fish. The Vaagen Brothers sawmill is Ione's main employer.

Sights and Recreation

Three miles north of Ione is **Box Canyon Dam,** the source of electrical power for much of the county. Stop at the visitors center (509/447-6700, open daily in summer) for summer tours only. The small pond here (complete with float) makes a great swimming hole and picnic area.

Ione City Park along the lake has a picnic area, boat launch, and outdoor swimming pool; open summers.

A few miles south of Ione is the crossroads called Tiger, where the **Tiger Historical Center** (summer only) has a small collection of memorabilia, along with local crafts.

The U.S. Forest Service's **Edgewater Campground** ($6–10; open mid-May through Sept.) sits across the Pend Oreille River and two miles north up Box Canyon-LeClerc Road (County Road 3669).

Events

Ione's **Down River Days** at the end of July features boat races, a parade, fun run, and street dance.

Accommodations and Food

The friendly and clean **Ione Motel and RV Park** (509/442-3213, $40–85 s or d) is right on the river and has rooms with microwaves and fridges, as well as RV hookups available.

On Highway 20 between Cusick and Ione,

© DEANA EDMISTON

Ione bridge from LeClerc Road, crossing the Pend Oreille River

Outpost Resort (509/445-1317, $45–100 d, $25 hookups, $15 tent) has rooms, a restaurant, groceries, boat launch, and camping. They also offer pontoon boat tours of the Pend Oreille River.

Box Canyon Resort (five miles north of Ione, 509/442-3728 or 800/676-8883, $50 s or $55 d, $72 d kitchenettes) offers simple accommodations near Ione.

Information

To get information on Ione, Metaline, and Metaline Falls, call the Cutter Theatre in Metaline Falls (509/446-4108, Mon.–Fri. 9 A.M.–5 P.M.).

Getting There

The North Pend Oreille Valley Lions Club **Excursion Train** (509/442-5466, $7) chugs between Ione and Metaline Falls, crossing Box Canyon Dam along the way. Trains leave Ione at 11 A.M., 1 P.M., and 3 P.M., with a stop in Metaline Falls before returning. They generally run six weekends each summer from mid-June to mid-October. Call for reservations.

METALINE AND METALINE FALLS

The twin towns of Metaline and Metaline Falls—jointly home to 500 people—sit across the Pend Oreille River from each other and just 10 miles from Canada. Metaline began as a mining camp around 1865 and was named for the metals the miners found here; Metaline Falls came later as the site of a big cement plant (now closed). There's still lead and zinc mining going on north of Metaline. Metaline Falls is a delightful little burg with quiet streets and small frame homes with neatly trimmed lawns. Stop at **Metaline City Park** where the spacious lawns provide a place to picnic, toss a Frisbee, or just hang out by the water.

Crawford State Park

You can tour one of the largest limestone caves in the state, **Gardner Cave,** at Crawford State Park (12 miles northwest of Metaline Falls off Hwy. 31, 509/446-406, www.parks.wa.gov). The cave is open late May to mid-September, with free guided tours Thurs.–Mon. between 10 A.M. and 4 P.M. Tours take you almost 500 feet into this 1,055-foot cavern, past fanciful (and fancifully named) stalactites, stalagmites, and columns. Dress warmly, as it's always cold inside. As you drive up to the cave, **mountain goats** are visible March to early June from a marked pullout along Flume Creek near the park; bring your binoculars.

Boundary Dam (509/446-3083, Thurs.–Mon. 10:30 A.M.–4:30 P.M. in summer), just east of Gardner Cave, has a visitors center next to the 340-foot arched concrete dam that is jammed between two tall cliffs. Its spray deck was used as a set in the 1997 post-apocalyptic film *The Postman,* starring Kevin Costner. Free tours of the dam and tunnels are given; call for reservations. A deck 500 feet above the river provides impressive vistas. Magnificent **Peewee Falls** plunges 200 feet into the south end of the reservoir; ask at the dam for directions.

Entertainment and Events

All summer long, the historic **Cutter Theatre** (509/446-4108) in Metaline Falls (an old school named for a famous Spokane architect, Kirtland Cutter) features live—and surprisingly good—summer weekend performances. In the winter you'll find more plays, lectures, and concerts at the Cutter. For first-run films in a small town, head down the block to the **Showhouse.**

The North Pend Oreille Valley Lions Club **Excursion Train** (509/442-5466, $7) rolls into Metaline Falls from Ione between mid-June and mid-October. Performances at the Cutter Theatre are often coordinated with rides so you can see a play during your stop in Metaline Falls.

On Labor Day Weekend, **Affair on Main Street** brings a downtown arts and crafts show. If you're in the region around Christmas, be sure to visit Metaline Falls for a display of 50 amusing **Christmas sculptures.**

Practicalities

Built in 1910, the historic **Washington Hotel** (509/446-4415, $40 d) is home to 18 restored rooms with handmade quilts, rugs, book-swap shelves, original furnishings, and bath down the hall. A studio and gallery include her works in progress. Be sure to ask about the "Santa's workshop" sculptures, a collection of 50 figures that are displayed around town each Christmas.

Circle Motel (two miles north of Metaline Falls on Highway 31, 509/446-4343, www.circlemotel.com 53 63 83) has rooms with microwaves, fridges, and satellite TV. **Mt. Linton RV Park** (509/446-4553, $18 tent, $25 full hookups) offers RV and tent spaces in Metaline.

Next to the Washington Hotel is **Cathy's Café** (Mon.–Fri. 5:30 A.M.–2 P.M., Sat.–Sun. 7 A.M.–2 P.M.), a down-home eatery that honors students who design a placemat with their choice of a sundae.

Find information in the summer at the **Metaline Falls Visitor Center** (www.povn.com/cutter, daily 10 A.M.–5 P.M. Memorial Day to Labor Day only); stop by the Washington Hotel at other times.

SULLIVAN LAKE AREA

Four-mile-long Sullivan Lake anchors a large section of Forest Service land within Colville National Forest, providing outstanding camping and hiking opportunities. A feeding station at the south end of Sullivan Lake is a good place to look for **bighorn sheep** in the winter. Much of this country has been clear-cut, but the Salmo-Priest Wilderness is here, along with Grassy Top Roadless Area. The Forest Service's **Sullivan Lake Ranger District** office (509/446-7500, www.fs.fed.us/r6/colville) is at the north end of the lake.

Hiking

Sullivan Lake Trail is a four-mile one-way hike along the eastern shore of Sullivan Lake through forested areas, connecting Sullivan Lake Campground with Noisy Creek Campground. The clear blue lake is the main attraction, but watch for bighorn sheep, black bear, and white-tailed deer. This is a very nice hike, especially in the fall. For a short historical hike, head to **Mill Pond Historical Site,** where a wheelchair-accessible trail leads past displays on the 1910 hydroelectric project.

© WASHINGTON STATE TOURISM//LEVY SHECKLER

Sullivan Lake is tucked away in the hills just east of Metaline Falls.

Camping

Four Forest Service campgrounds are along the shore of Sullivan Lake and nearby Mill Pond: **Sullivan Lake East, Sullivan Lake West, Mill Pond,** and **Noisy Creek.** All are open Memorial Day to Labor Day. Find good swimming beaches at Noisy Creek and the two Sullivan Lake campgrounds. All can also be reserved (518/885-3639 or 877/444-6777, www.recreation.gov, $10, $9 extra reservation fee).

Salmo-Priest Wilderness

One of Washington's least-known wilderness areas, the 39,937-acre Salmo-Priest Wilderness sits in the northeasternmost corner of the state, bordering Idaho and Canada. Much of the surrounding land has been heavily logged, but this small corner reveals the land as it once was: dense old-growth western red cedar, Douglas fir, grand fir, and western larch forests at the middle elevations, and subalpine openings atop the mountains. This is not a place for beginners, but a number of trails provide hiking opportunities for the adventurous. The weather is fickle and often wet, so bring your rain gear. Best times to hike are mid-July to mid-August. No backcountry permits are required.

The Salmo-Priest Wilderness is home to a number of endangered animals, including gray wolves, grizzly bears, and the last woodland caribou in the Lower 48 states; approximately 30 of them are here. In addition, the wilderness has a large black bear population. For your safety, pick up free food storage containers from the Sullivan Lake Forest Service office before heading out, and be sure you know how to stay safe in bear country!

A fine loop trip begins from the east end of Forest Road 2220 that leaves Forest Road 9345 just north of Sullivan Lake. The **Salmo Basin Trail** climbs up through virgin evergreen forests and crosses into Idaho (and almost into Canada) before joining the **Shedroof Divide Trail** near 7,572-foot Snowy Top (a rough but rewarding side trip). Follow Shedroof Divide Trail back across into Washington and its junction with **Salmo Divide Trail,** which will take you back to your starting point, a total distance of approximately 19 miles. Much of the trail is at 6,000 feet in elevation, so sea-level dwellers should expect to hike a little more slowly than usual.

USK, CUSICK, AND KALISPEL LANDS

Thirty-five miles south of Ione is the little settlement of Usk, home to the enormous Ponderay Valley Fibre newsprint factory (509/445-1732 or 800/638-4996 for tours). Usk is named for the town of Usk, England, and you can see "sister-town" photos inside the country store. The pilings visible all along the Pend Oreille River near here were used to corral logs as they floated downstream to local sawmills.

Cusick (Q-sick) is just two miles north of here and is home to the county fairgrounds.

The Kalispel Tribe (approximately 200 people) own a small section of land along the east side of the Pend Oreille River; they originally lived on a three-million-acre spread. The tribal lands were made official in 1934; this is one of the few non-reservation Native American homelands in the Lower 48.

Sights

Manresa Grotto is a 70-foot-wide cavern on Kalispel Tribal lands, right along LeClerc Creek Road and five miles north of the Pend Oreille River bridge at Usk. This spacious rock grotto was used by Father Jean Pierre DeSmet in the 1840s as a combination home and church to preach to local Native Americans. A stone altar and pews (of a sort) are still inside, and mass is held in mid-September every year. Osprey nest near here along the shore of the lake.

The Kalispel Tribal offices and the **Our Lady of Sorrows** church (built in 1914) are two miles south of here. Stop in to see who is making Native crafts in the area. Also ask to see the enormous mounted buffalo head (in a back room); the herd of 100 buffalo is immediately south of the office. Behind here is the powwow grounds used for the Salish Fairs.

Events

The first weekend of August brings the unusual **Salish Fair** at the Kalispel powwow grounds. It includes a buffalo barbecue, arts and crafts, stick games (gambling), war dancing, and a baseball tournament. Also enjoyable are the **Salish Barter Fairs** held here in August, where you can purchase or trade Native American crafts and other works. The **Pend Oreille County Fair & Rodeo** comes to Cusick in late August.

Accommodations and Food

Blueslide Resort (400041 Hwy. 20, Cusick, 509/445-1327, $45 d motel, $70–80 four-person cabin) is a nice family-oriented place with a motel and cabins, along with tent camping and RV spots on the Pend Oreille River. Facilities include a boat ramp and dock, swimming pool, and store, but no TVs. This is the only place where boaters can buy fuel along the river.

Just south of Usk at the junction of Highways 211 and 20 is **Crossroads Café** (509/445-1515, daily 6 A.M.–8 P.M.), a large bar and all-American eatery with live music on weekends. The **Usk Bar & Grill** makes good burgers.

NEWPORT AND VICINITY

The town of Newport is the Pend Oreille County seat and the largest settlement in these parts. It sits along the Pend Oreille River; the smaller Oldtown, Idaho, is on the other side of the bridge. The town was founded in Oldtown in 1889, but most everyone moved across the river when the Great Northern Railway built a depot on the Washington side three years later. There is nothing particularly notable about Newport, but it is a pleasant old-fashioned town with an attractive and bustling main drag.

Sights

The **County Historical Society Museum** (Washington and 4th, 509/447-5388, mid-May–Sept. daily 10 A.M.–4 P.M., voluntary donation) sits in Centennial Plaza Park with a 1909 Corliss steam engine and two historic cabins out front. Originally built as a train depot along the Idaho & Washington Northern Railroad, the museum now contains all sorts of obscure flotsam and jetsam, including a pencil collection. Next door is another old depot, which was used for many years by the competing Great Northern Railway and now houses Plum Creek Timber Company.

Just two miles east of Newport in Idaho is the **Albeni Falls Dam** (208/437-3133), where tours are given daily in the summer.

Built in 1915, the **Pend Oreille County Courthouse** occupies the block at 4th Street and Warren Avenue. It is on the National Register of Historic Places.

Events

Start the summer at **American Heritage Days** in early May at the fairgrounds. Events include old-time demonstrations, dancing, food, and crafts. The **Newport Rodeo** in late June includes a parade, carnival, cowboy breakfast, food and craft booths, and the main attraction, a PRCA-sanctioned rodeo.

The annual **Poker Paddle,** held the third weekend in July, consists of a 40-mile canoe trip down the Pend Oreille River; participants collect poker cards at various stops along the two-day route. A crowd congregates at the finish to greet the paddlers and enjoy food and game booths.

Sports and Recreation

The wheelchair-accessible **Pioneer Park Heritage Trail** begins at the Pioneer Park Campground and leads past interpretive signs that detail the life of the Kalispel tribe. **Lower Wolf Trail,** a short loop trail beginning from the north edge of town, passes through forest and wildflowers, affording views of Ashenfelder Bay. To reach it, turn north on Warren Ave. at its junction with Highway 20, continuing about a mile to the trailhead. The path is actually a series of short loops totaling 1.5 miles; half of them are wheelchair-accessible (but graveled).

The **Upper Wolf Trail System** consists of 2.5 miles of loop trails located just north of Newport off Laurel-Hurst Street. The trail system is popular with mountain bikers in the summer and cross-country skiers in winter.

A longer ski/bike/hike trail is the **Geophysical Trail System,** located approximately nine miles northwest of town on Indian Creek Road. In the winter, the Forest Service grooms six miles of trails. You'll need a Sno-Park permit to park here for skiing. The **Geophysical Observatory** was originally used for earthquake monitoring but now serves to detect the detonation of nuclear weapons. It is one of three such sites in America. It's closed to the public; the instruments are too sensitive!

Four Forest Service campgrounds are close to Newport: **Brown's Lake, South Skookum Lake, Pioneer Park,** and **Panhandle.** They charge $10 and are open Memorial Day to September. Pioneer Park Campground is two miles north of town on LeClerc Road; cross the bridge over the Pend Oreille River, and turn left. Campsites are also available two miles east at the Priest River Recreation Area in Idaho.

Practicalities

Your best local lodging option is **Golden Spur Motor Inn** (924 W. Highway 2, 509/447-3823, $50 s or $60 d).

Set along a crystal-clear mountain lake deep in the country, **Marshall Lake Resort** (seven miles north of Newport on Leclerc Rd., 509/447-4158, $35–70 d) is a favorite with hunters, anglers, and city-crazed stress-balls looking to unwind under the stars. The property offers rustic trailer cabins, as well as tent campsites ($15) and RV hookups ($18 electric). Cabins include kitchens and everyone shares restrooms with showers. Rent a variety of boats and canoes to explore the lake or ply its waters for fat cutthroat trout, or explore trails on more than 1,000 private acres.

Owen's Grocery and Deli (4th and Washington) has a deli and old-fashioned soda fountain with malts and banana splits. Get fresh produce and handicrafts at Newport's **Earth Market** on summer Saturdays 9 A.M.–1 P.M.

Information

The museum at the old depot houses the **Newport Visitor Center** (509/447-5812, summer daily 9 A.M.to 5 P.M., fall–spring Mon.–Fri. 9 A.M.–noon). Stop by the

Newport Ranger District (315 N. Warren Ave., 509/447-7300) for brochures on local trails and campgrounds. Ask here for directions to the South Baldy Lookout and the Roosevelt Grove of Ancient Cedars.

HUCKLEBERRY MOUNTAIN AND THE SPOKANE RIVER AREA

For a beautiful country drive, head west from Chewelah along the paved road connecting the one-store towns of Bluecreek and Cedonia. It takes you through lush valleys with big old dairy barns in varying stages of disrepair, and over gentle Huckleberry Mountain, covered with forests of ponderosa pine and western larch.

Highway 25 is another delightful drive, following the shore of Lake Roosevelt from Northport all the way to Fort Spokane, 90 miles to the south. The dark blue lake waters contrast sharply with hills of pine and grass. Numerous campsites line this shore (see *Lake Roosevelt* for specifics).

Gifford Ferry (6:30 A.M.–9:30 P.M.) crosses the reservoir every day, taking you to the town of Inchelium on the Colville Reservation.

Spokane Reservation

South of the tiny town called Fruitland, Highway 25 heads away from Lake Roosevelt and across the Spokane Reservation to Fort Spokane and Davenport. **Wellpinit,** the only settlement on the reservation, has a community store, post office, and big high school with "Wellpinit Redskins" emblazoned on the front. The essentially undeveloped reservation is scenic, hilly land covered in open ponderosa pine, large sections of which have been logged.

Fort Spokane

From 1880 to 1898, the U.S. Army post at Fort Spokane served to keep the peace between the Native Americans on the Colville Reservation in the forested hills to the north and the white settlers on the grassy plains to the south. The fort was built at the confluence of the Spokane River and the Columbia River and had 45 buildings at its peak in the 1890s. Those were peaceful years, in this area at least, so the soldiers practiced their drills and played a lot of baseball. They also drank more than a little, and many of the soldiers treated in the fort hospital were there because of bad whiskey or drunken brawls. The fort was closed at the outbreak of the Spanish-American War in 1898 and was later used as headquarters for the Colville Indian Agency and as a tuberculosis sanitorium. The grounds were abandoned in 1929 and transferred to the National Park Service in 1960, which has restored the remaining structures.

Take a walking tour through the grounds to see four of the original buildings, including an 1884 stable that housed the dozens of mules needed to haul supplies from the nearest railroad depot in Sprague. Trailside displays relate the fort's history, and the brick guardhouse (1892) has a **visitors center** (509/725-2715, daily 9:30 A.M.–5:30 P.M. from mid-May to early September). Rangers in 19th-century costumes offer hour-long tours of the fort on Sunday mornings in the summer.

The Park Service maintains a nearby swimming beach, campgrounds ($10), and amphitheater for Saturday campfire programs from mid-June to early September. Across the river on reservation land you'll find the **Two Rivers Casino** (800/722-4031), with roulette, craps, and blackjack; RV hookups are also available. Nearby is a stand selling Indian tacos. Heading south toward Davenport, Highway 25 passes through an open landscape of rolling wheat fields with scattered old red barns and two-story white houses. Side roads off the highway provide access to **Seven Bays Marina** and **Porcupine Bay,** popular camping, fishing, swimming, and boating areas within Lake Roosevelt National Recreation Area.

Long Lake Area

Long Lake Dam spans the Spokane River near the east edge of the Spokane Reservation. The grounds here offer a pleasant picnic spot beneath ponderosa pines; free lakeside summer-only campsites are available at **Long Lake Camp,** five miles east on Long Lake Dam Road.

Approximately five miles east of the junction between Highways 291 and 231 are a couple of large boulders surrounded by a chain-link fence. Behind the fence are several red-painted figures of unknown age, the **Long Lake petroglyphs.** Nothing special if you've seen the far more impressive petroglyphs of Utah and Wyoming, but they are worth a stop. East from here on Highway 291 the road follows the beautiful shore of Long Lake for quite a few miles, passing several small resorts and the podunk settlement called **Tumtum.** Forested hills climb away from the blue lake waters. The road continues past Riverside State Park and then on to Spokane, 35 miles from the junction with Highway 231.

Spokane

Spokane's population of 195,000 makes it the largest city between Seattle and Minneapolis and the second-largest city in Washington. Though Spokane is less than half as large as Seattle and has less urban sprawl, the two cities have had much in common from their earliest days: Both were leveled by great fires, after which both towns were rebuilt in brick; both cities attribute some of their early growth to outfitting gold and silver miners; both have impressive park systems designed by the same firm; and both cities hosted a world's fair. The legacy of that fair remains Spokane's centerpiece: the 100-acre Riverfront Park.

Known as the "Lilac City" for its bountiful springtime blooms, Spokane has the friendly, comfortable atmosphere of a small city in the Midwest. As it's located just 18 miles from the Idaho border, its tall downtown buildings and spreading suburbs seem an odd apparition among the undeveloped landscape of eastern Washington. The surrounding landscape is a mixture of rich agricultural lands, especially in the Palouse to the south, and piney hills as you head north toward the Selkirk Mountains. Slicing through it all is the Spokane River, or at least the dammed version; seven hydroelectric dams hold back the river waters between its origin in Coeur d'Alene Lake, Idaho, and its junction with the Columbia River near old Fort Spokane.

Spokane is the driest city east of the Cascades; it gets less than 17 inches of rain a year. Summers days frequently reach into the 80s, and winters are fairly mild, though it does snow.

History

The name Spokane comes from the Native American word "Spokan" (Sun People). The area around Spokane Falls has been occupied for thousands of years and was a favorite place to fish for salmon each summer. The first white settlers came to this area around 1810—very early in Washington's history—when David Thompson built Spokan House, the first trading post in the state along the Spokan River. (The "e" in Spokane was added later.) The War of 1812 and turbulent times that followed led to abandonment of the post in 1826, and white settlers didn't return until 1838, when Elkanah Walker and Cushing Eels established a Protestant mission that lasted until 1847. Though Spokane County was created in 1859, including all of the land between the Columbia River and Rocky Mountains north of the Snake River, the first permanent settlers didn't arrive at "Spokane Falls" until 1872. The first real settler was James N. Glover, the "Father of Spokane" and a strong proponent of the region's benefits.

By 1880, Spokane's population had grown to only 350, and the town competed hotly with neighboring Cheney for the county seat. Vote counters announced Spokane as the winner, but Cheney residents suspected the officials of lying about the results, so they came at night, kidnapped the election official and his records, and proclaimed Cheney the winner of the vote. Spokane's population grew dramatically by the next election—partly due to the arrival of the Northern Pacific Railway—and

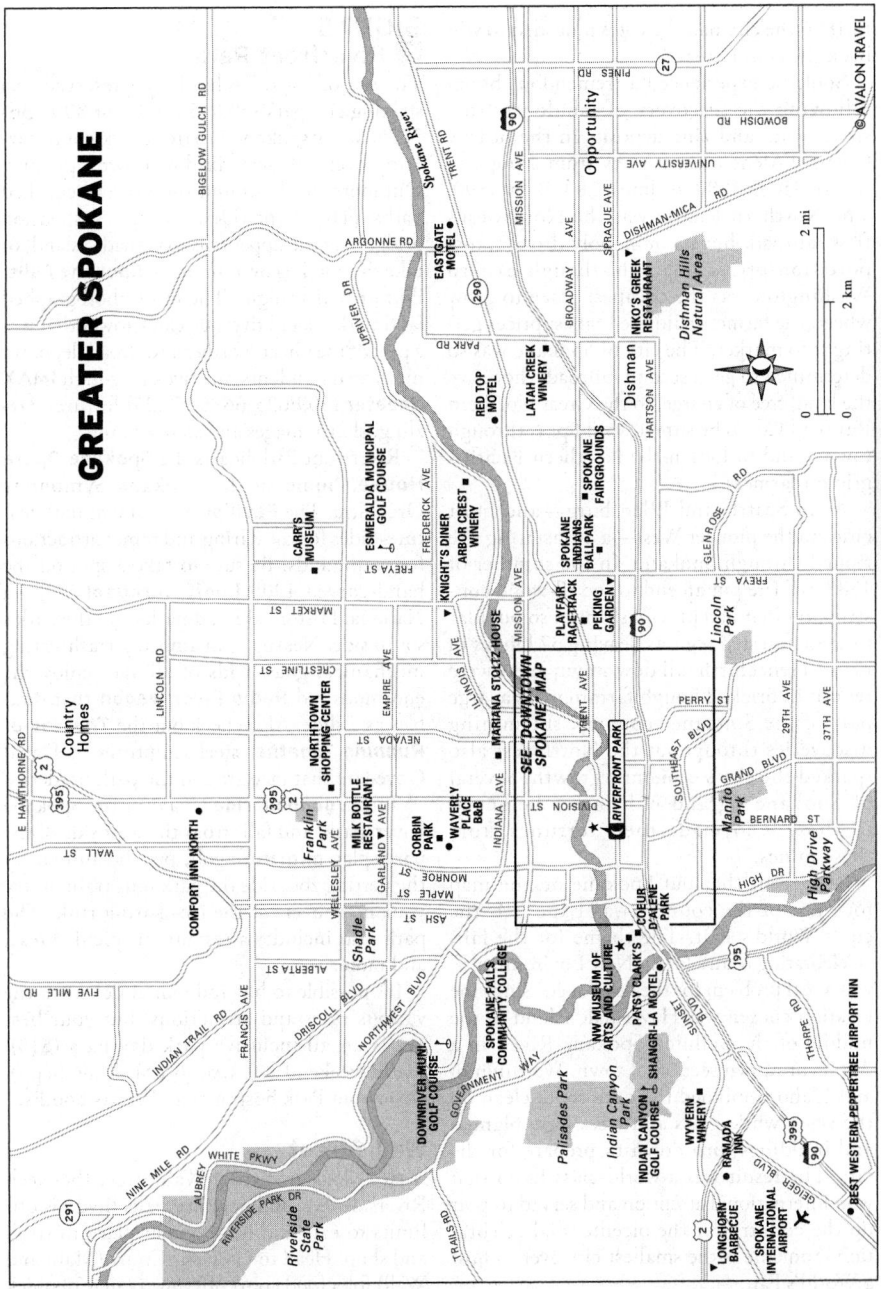
GREATER SPOKANE
SEE "DOWNTOWN SPOKANE" MAP
Country Homes
Franklin Park
Shadle Park
Riverside State Park
Palisades Park
Indian Canyon Park
Lincoln Park
Manito Park
High Drive Parkway
Dishman Hills Natural Area
Opportunity
Dishman
Spokane River
COMFORT INN NORTH
NORTHTOWN SHOPPING CENTER
MILK BOTTLE RESTAURANT
CORBIN PARK
WAVERLY PLACE B&B
CARR'S MUSEUM
ESMERALDA MUNICIPAL GOLF COURSE
KNIGHT'S DINER
ARBOR CREST WINERY
MARIANA STOLTZ HOUSE
RIVERFRONT PARK
SPOKANE FALLS COMMUNITY COLLEGE
DOWNRIVER MUNI. GOLF COURSE
NW MUSEUM OF ARTS AND CULTURE
PATSY CLARK'S
COEUR D'ALENE PARK
INDIAN CANYON GOLF COURSE
SHANGRI-LA MOTEL
WYVERN WINERY
RAMADA INN
LONGHORN BARBECUE
SPOKANE INTERNATIONAL AIRPORT
BEST WESTERN PEPPERTREE AIRPORT INN
PLAYFAIR RACETRACK
PEKING GARDEN
SPOKANE INDIANS BALLPARK
SPOKANE FAIRGROUNDS
LATAH CREEK WINERY
RED TOP MOTEL
EASTGATE MOTEL
NIKO'S GREEK RESTAURANT
© AVALON TRAVEL

in 1886 the city had the votes it needed to win back the county seat.

Spokane experienced a tremendous boom following the discovery of fabulously rich silver, lead, and zinc deposits in the nearby Coeur d'Alene area: it grew from a population of 350 in 1880 to almost 20,000 by 1890. The Northern Pacific was the Northwest's first railroad, but its monopoly drove transportation prices sky-high; though eastern Washington was the cheapest place to grow wheat, the farmers paid the highest prices getting it to market. The city of Spokane was so determined to get a second railroad, they gave the land, free of charge, to the Great Northern Railroad Co. to be sure it would pass through town—and to loosen the Northern Pacific's grip on farmers.

As in Seattle and Ellensburg—and most cities in the pioneer West—a devastating fire ripped through Spokane. In the summer of 1889, the fire put an end to the all-wood construction that had previously been so popular in these forested regions, leaving 32 blocks in ruins. Henceforth, all downtown areas were rebuilt in brick. Though farming was a large part of the Spokane economy, the mining discoveries throughout the Northwest also sparked the city's economic growth. Several of Spokane's grand old homes belonged to those who made their fortunes from these mines.

The event that put Spokane on the map for most of the country was Expo '74, the city's World's Fair. The theme for the fair, "Celebrating Man's Fresh, New Environment," was a real problem for the developers, since the location chosen was Havermale Island in the middle of the polluted Spokane River, in a dirty, run-down section of town. Washington and Idaho combined their efforts to clean up the river, while grass and trees were planted and buildings torn down to prepare for the fair. The result was a world-class Expo that won international attention and served to gear up the country for the bicentennial celebration. Spokane is the smallest city ever to host a World's Fair.

SIGHTS

Riverfront Park

The site of Expo '74 has been preserved as a striking city park (509/456-4386 or 800/336-7275, www.spokaneriverfrontpark.com) covering over 100 acres in downtown Spokane. Outdoors, stroll around the flower-bedecked paths, play on the rides, walk the suspension bridge over the upper falls to Canada Island, or take the gondola over dramatic **Spokane Falls,** illuminated at night. The most-photographed landmark is a tall riverside clock tower that was a part of the Great Northern Railroad depot for many years. Indoors, the five-story-high **IMAX Theater** (509/625-6686, $8.25) features dazzling, sharp images and stereo sound.

Riverfront Park boasts the **Spokane Opera House,** home to the Spokane Symphony Orchestra. The **Pavilion** amusement park features rides for the daring and tamer attractions for young kids. Be sure to take a spin on the hand-carved 1909 **Looff Carousel** ($2)—a National Historical Landmark—on the park's south side. Nearby is an amusing trash-eating mechanical goat. Kids of all ages enjoy the enormous red **Radio Flyer wagon** that doubles as a slide. Also check out the ***The Joy of Running Together*** steel sculptures by David Govedare that race around the park borders.

Take a **gondola ride** ($7) over the Spokane River, park, and falls from the west side of the park, play miniature golf, pet the animals at the petting zoo, ride the park tour train, or try your maneuvers at the ice-skating rink. The park also includes a restaurant, picnic areas, and more.

It's possible to buy individual tickets to the various rides and attractions, but your best bet is an all-inclusive park day pass ($13). Every weekend (10 A.M.–6 P.M. May–Sept.), Riverfront Park hosts arts and crafts booths.

Wall Street

A two-block section of Wall Street (between Riverside Ave. and Spokane Falls Blvd.) is off-limits to cars and is a popular place to stroll and shop. Head to Crescent Court (Main and Wall) for a food court offering a range of quick

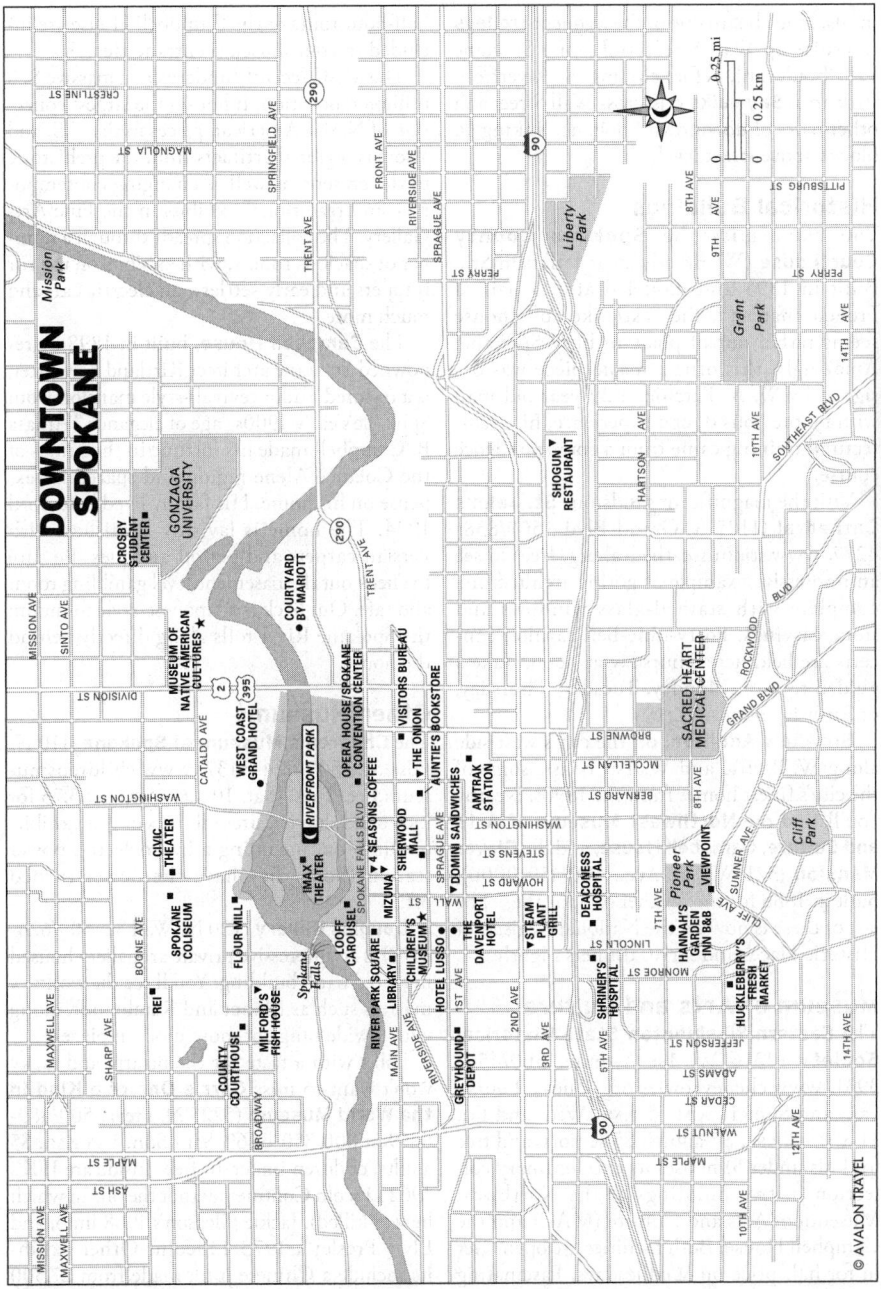
DOWNTOWN SPOKANE
Mission Park
CRESTLINE ST
MAGNOLIA ST
SPRINGFIELD AVE
FRONT AVE
RIVERSIDE AVE
SPRAGUE AVE
TRENT AVE
PERRY ST
Liberty Park
PITTSBURG ST
8TH AVE
9TH AVE
0 0.25 mi
0 0.25 km
MISSION AVE
SINTO AVE
DIVISION ST
CROSBY STUDENT CENTER
GONZAGA UNIVERSITY
MUSEUM OF NATIVE AMERICAN CULTURES
COURTYARD BY MARIOTT
CATALDO AVE
WEST COAST GRAND HOTEL
WASHINGTON ST
CIVIC THEATER
IMAX THEATER
RIVERFRONT PARK
OPERA HOUSE/SPOKANE CONVENTION CENTER
VISITORS BUREAU
4 SEASONS COFFEE
THE ONION
AUNTIE'S BOOKSTORE
SHERWOOD MALL
SPOKANE FALLS BLVD
SHOGUN RESTAURANT
HARTSON AVE
10TH AVE
SOUTHEAST BLVD
14TH AVE
Grant Park
BROWNE ST
MCCLELLAN ST
BERNARD ST
SACRED HEART MEDICAL CENTER
ROCKWOOD BLVD
GRAND BLVD
8TH AVE
SUMNER AVE
CLIFF AVE
Cliff Park
Pioneer Park
VIEWPOINT
HANNAH'S GARDEN INN B&B
HUCKLEBERRY'S FRESH MARKET
7TH AVE
MONROE ST
LINCOLN ST
DEACONESS HOSPITAL
SHRINER'S HOSPITAL
6TH AVE
JEFFERSON ST
ADAMS ST
CEDAR ST
WALNUT ST
MAPLE ST
12TH AVE
10TH AVE
14TH AVE
AMTRAK STATION
DOMINI SANDWICHES
STEVENS ST
HOWARD ST
STEAM PLANT GRILL
DAVENPORT HOTEL
HOTEL LUSSO
1ST AVE
2ND AVE
3RD AVE
WALL ST
CHILDREN'S MUSEUM
MIZUNA
LIBRARY
RIVER PARK SQUARE
LOOFF CAROUSEL
Spokane Falls
GREYHOUND DEPOT
MAIN AVE
RIVERSIDE AVE
SPOKANE COLISEUM
FLOUR MILL
BOGNE AVE
REI
MILFORD'S FISH HOUSE
COUNTY COURTHOUSE
BROADWAY
SHARP AVE
MAXWELL AVE
ASH ST
MISSION AVE
MAXWELL AVE
90
290
395
2
© AVALON TRAVEL

meals. Hop aboard one of the frequent **trolleys** to cruise up Wall Street and along Spokane Falls Boulevard, before circling the Riverfront Park area. **Skywalks** crisscross Wall Street and other parts of downtown Spokane, linking 14 blocks above street level.

Historical Buildings

You can't miss the **Spokane County Courthouse** (W. Broadway at Jefferson St.). Built in 1895 and modeled after a pair of French chateaux, the castlelike courthouse seems rather out of place in busy Spokane. Amazingly, this ornate masterpiece was designed by W. A. Ritchie, a 29-year-old man with no previous design experience; his architectural training came from a correspondence course.

Visit the magnificent sandstone **St. John's Cathedral** (1125 S. Grand Blvd., 509/838-4277, www.stjohns-cathedral.org, free) to see an impressive example of gothic architecture, complete with stained-glass windows and stone carvings. Forty-nine-bell carillon concerts are held here Thursday at noon. Take a guided tour on Monday, Tuesday, Thursday, or Saturday noon–3 P.M.

Browne's Addition, on the city's west side along W. Pacific and W. 1st, boasts some of the city's finest homes from the 1890s. Nearby you'll find the **Northwest Museum of Arts and Culture, Campbell House,** and the **Glover Mansion** (321 W. 8th Ave., 509/459-0000), built in 1888 for the "Father of Spokane." The last of these is now on the National Register of Historic Places and serves dinners nightly.

Museum of Arts and Culture

The **Eastern Washington State Historical Society** (2316 W. 1st Avenue, 509/456-3931, www.cheneycowles.org, Tues., Thurs., Sat., and Sun. 11 A.M.–5 P.M., Wed. and Fri. 11 A.M.–8 P.M., $7 adults, $5 seniors, and free for kids under 5) houses its extraordinary collection in two buildings at the Northwest Museum of Arts and Culture (MAC) and the Campbell House. Both facilities are open. Get in for half price on Wednesdays. Fascinating half-hour tours of the Campbell House are included in your museum entrance fee.

The MAC recently underwent a massive $28 million renovation. It houses the largest collection of Native American pieces in the U.S. and also has regional artifacts from the prehistoric to the present, as well as changing contemporary and traditional exhibits in the Fine Arts Gallery. The collection spreads through a number of spacious rooms, with exhibits on the fur trappers and early settlers, an electric car, and much more.

The **Campbell House,** built in 1898 by renowned Spokane architect Kirtland K. Cutter, is a restored Tudor revival–style mansion from Spokane's early 1900s "age of elegance." Amasa B. Campbell made his fortune in the mines of the Coeur d'Alene region and spared no expense on his home. His family lived here until 1924. The home is lavishly furnished with Persian carpets and period antiques. Be sure to check out the basement-level gambling room and safe. Out back is a Japanese-style fountain; the Spokane River rolls along directly behind the house.

Other Museums

The **Children's Museum of Spokane** (110 N. Post St., 509/624-5437, www.childrensmuseum.net, Tues.–Sat. 10 A.M.–5 P.M., $3.75 for kids or adults) features all sorts of fun exhibits to climb on, including a hydroelectric power station (hope they have the power turned off!).

Douglas Gallery (120 N. Wall St., 509/624-4179) is an impressive private art gallery housed in an old bank building. You'll see the works of masters such as Manet and Rembrandt, along with a wide range of more modern pieces.

Folks with a taste for the bizarre and tacky won't want to miss **Carr's One of a Kind in the World Museum** (5225 N. Freya, 509/489-8859 or 800/350-6469, Sat.–Sun. 1–4 P.M., $5 adults, children under 10 free. Inside are JFK's 1962 Lincoln Continental (not the one in which he was killed), Jackie Gleason's 1968 limo, and Elvis Presley's 1973 Lincoln. Other exhibits include a Chinese junk made from 27,500 matchsticks, plus a Cheyenne chief mannequin atop a papier-mâché horse! Only in America.

Located just 35 miles from bustling Spokane, Davenport is the seat for Lincoln County and a minor farming and ranching center in this open land of cattle ranches and wheat fields. There you can find the **Lincoln County Historical Museum** (Park and 7th Streets, 509/725-6711 or 800/326-8148, Mon.–Sat. 9 A.M.–5 P.M. May–Sept., plus Sunday 1–4 P.M. June–Aug.) for local memorabilia and a fine collection of agricultural equipment in the back building. The strangest sight here is the death mask of the outlaw Harry Tracy, a member of the Hole-in-the-Wall gang who lived in Spokane for a couple of years and then committed suicide after being cornered by lawmen nearby. The museum also serves as the local visitors center. Bird-watchers will want to ask where burrowing owls can be seen right in town.

Riverside State Park

This delightful park (www.parks.wa.gov) six miles northwest of town has open ponderosa pine forests with a grassy understory. As the name suggests, it sits along the Spokane River. Access is from Nine Mile Road on the north side of the river or several convoluted routes along the south shore. The 7,655-acre park is a popular place for camping, hiking, horseback riding (guided horseback rides are offered by a concessionaire), bird-watching, and kayaking (class III rapids).

A favorite hiking destination is the **"Bowl and Pitcher"** area, where a trail leaves the campground and crosses a suspension bridge to connect with a network of enjoyable paths. These unusual volcanic formations stand along the fast-flowing river and are visible from a dramatic overlook; the resemblance to a bowl and pitcher is vague. Get here by heading northwest from town on Highway 291 (Nine Mile Road) and turning left onto Rifle Club Road, then left again on Aubrey L. White Parkway after a half mile. The park entrance and the Bowl and Pitcher are on the right after 1.7 miles.

Another feature of Riverside State Park is the **Spokane House Interpretive Center** (12 miles

© WASHINGTON STATE TOURISM/LEVY SHECKLER

Riverfront Park is downtown Spokane's centerpiece attraction.

northwest of Spokane on Hwy. 291, 509/466-4747 Wed.–Sun. 10 A.M.–6 P.M. summers only, free) on the site of the first structure built by white men in the Pacific Northwest. Erected in 1810 by the Northwest Fur Company, this fur-trading post sat at the confluence of the Spokane and Little Spokane Rivers. After 16 years of use, the post was moved to a better site at Kettle Falls. No evidence remains of the trading post, but the interpretive center relates its history in a diorama, exhibits, and artifacts. It is located a half mile north of the bridge (on the northeast bank).

Mt. Spokane State Park

This sprawling park (www.parks.wa.gov) 30 miles northeast of the city on Highway 206 encompasses 5,881-foot Mt. Spokane and 5,306-foot Mt. Kit Carson. Enjoy hiking, mountain biking, and camping in the summer, downhill or cross-country skiing in the winter. A narrow, winding road (no RVs) climbs to the summit of Mt. Spokane, where you can stop for a picnic at the CCC-built Vista House. The incredible 360-degree vista encompasses the entire region, including parts of Idaho, Montana, British Columbia, and Alberta. Dirt roads lead to other areas, and trails crisscross the park offering day hikes for all levels of ability.

Other Gardens and Parks

Manito Park and Gardens (4 W. 21st Ave., 509/625-6622, daily 8 A.M.–dusk) contains immaculate old-fashioned floral and botanical displays, plus a duck pond that makes a delightful picnic spot. The park was created by the famous Olmsted Brothers, who also designed New York's Central Park. Features include the **Gaiser Conservatory,** which houses tropical plants and floral displays, a formal European-style garden with plantings that change with the seasons (May to early October), and the **Japanese Garden,** a tranquil place to relax. The last of these is supported by Spokane's sister city, Nishinomiya, Japan. In addition to these, you'll find a rose garden with 150 varieties of roses, and a perennial garden containing native plants.

Stroll through the **John A. Finch Arboretum** (3404 Woodland Blvd., 509/624-4832, daily dawn to dark, free) to see 65 acres of maples, rhododendrons, and ornamental trees along Garden Springs Creek, or walk the interpretive trail. Unfortunately, the attractive setting is marred by the rush of I-90 traffic just a few feet to the south.

For a great view across Spokane, head to Cliff St. above the south side of Pioneer Park. This is a neighborhood with some of Spokane's most impressive homes. Not far away is the city's highest point in **Cliff Park** (13th Ave. and Grove Street). The rock, a half acre wide at the base, was once a volcanic island. For more on Spokane city parks, visit www.spokaneparks.org.

Cat Tales Endangered Species Conservation Park (17020 N. Newport Hwy., 509/238-4126, www.cattales.org, Tues.–Sun. 10 A.M.–6 P.M. April–Sept., and Wed.–Sun. 10 A.M.–4 P.M. the rest of the year, $6 for adults, $5 for seniors, and $4 for kids under 12) has 44 rare or endangered big cats, including tigers, leopards, and pumas. Guided tours are offered.

Universities and Colleges

The Spokane area is home to four colleges and universities, along with two community colleges. Largest of these is Eastern Washington University in nearby Cheney. Other area schools include the private Whitworth College, a branch of Washington State University, and the Community Colleges of Spokane.

One of 28 Jesuit colleges in the U.S., **Gonzaga University** (Hamilton St. at Centennial Trail, www.gonzaga.edu) is an independent liberal arts school with a wide range of degree programs. The law school at Gonzaga is one of three in Washington. Also here is the **Jundt Art Center** (509/328-4220) with changing exhibits, along with an extraordinary glass chandelier by Dale Chihuly.

Wineries

Although the Spokane area doesn't have vineyards, several local wineries produce wines from

DER BINGLE

One of America's best-known crooners, **Bing Crosby** grew up in Spokane and attended Gonzaga College as a pre-law student. (His real name was Harry Lillis Crosby; while still a child, he picked up the nickname from a comic-strip character.) Gonzaga claims that he "left school" just a semester short of his degree "to pursue his singing career," but he was actually kicked out for throwing a piano through a fourth-floor window. Nevertheless, Crosby received an honorary doctorate from Gonzaga in 1937 (after he had become a star). Crosby gained fame in such films as *White Christmas* and *High Society*, and his performance in *Going My Way* won an Oscar in 1945. He went on to appear in or narrate 100 films. Bing died in 1979 at the age of 74 while playing golf in Spain; a posthumous biography by one of his sons was less than flattering, to put it mildly.

The **Crosby Student Center** on the campus of Gonzaga University (www.gonzaga.edu) houses a collection of Bing Crosby gold records, trophies (the Oscar is actually a duplicate), awards, pipes, and other memorabilia. The building was Bing's gift to his alma mater, and the Crosbyana Room is open daily till midnight during the school year. A bronze statue of Bing stands outside the student center, and his boyhood home is now the Gonzaga Alumni Association, across the street (508 E. Sharp); there's more memorabilia here. Also check out photos of Bing and his classmates inside the Administration Building.

grapes grown in Yakima Valley and elsewhere. Most of these offer tours and free tastings. Enjoy a picnic with a bottle of award-winning wine at **Wyvern Winery** (W. 7217 45th, 509/455-7835, www.wyverncellars.com, daily noon–5 P.M.) located in a log cabin on the outskirts of Spokane and open for tours and tastings.

Washington's largest producer of merlot wines, **Latah Creek Wine Cellars** (I-90 exit 289 at E. 13030 Indiana Ave., 509/926-0164, www.latahcreek.com, Mon.–Sat. 10 A.M.–5 P.M. and Sunday noon–5 P.M.) is an attractive Spanish mission–style winery that features tours, tastings, an art gallery, and a picnic courtyard.

Arbor Crest Wine Cellars (4705 N. Fruithill Rd., 509/927-9463, www.arborcrest.com, daily noon–5 P.M.) also has a tasting room and gift shop. The building, Cliff House, is a National Historic Site with a magnificent view and parklike grounds.

The small **Caterina Winery** (905 N. Washington, 509/328-5069, www.caterina.com, daily noon–5 P.M.) is downtown in the historic Broadview Dairy Building.

ENTERTAINMENT AND EVENTS

Nightlife

Spokane's surprisingly active club scene has spawned a number of national acts. You'll find something going on every night of the week, from garage band grunge to poetry readings. Pick up a free copy of *The Inlander* newspaper for information on upcoming events.

Clubs with live bands and DJs include **Sunset Junction** (1801 W. Sunset Blvd., 509/455-9131), **Thudpucker's** (43 W. Riverside, 509/747-5547), and **The Rocket Downtown** (18 S. Monroe, 509/455-5282).

Hang out with the college crowd at **Jack & Dan's Tavern** (1226 N Hamilton St., 509/487-6546). Owned by Gonzaga alum and former NBA star John Stockton's dad, this is a decades-old classic. Another popular sports-and-boozing bar is **The Viking** (1221 N. Stevens, 509/326-2942). On Sunday nights the scene shifts to **Mootsy's Tavern** (406 W. Sprague, 509/838-1570), where the poetry readings often pack the house.

Bayou Brewing Company (1003 E. Trent, 509/484-4818) is the most packaged place in town, with a re-created New Orleans' atmosphere (created by movie set designers), fresh-brewed beers, Cajun cooking, pool tables, and dance bands or comedy acts nightly. This is *the* place to be on Fat Tuesday. **O'Doherty's Irish**

Grille (W. 525 Spokane Falls Blvd., 509/747-0322) often has live Irish music and always has Guinness on draught.

The Arts

Riverfront Park (509/625-6685 or 800/336-7275, www.spokaneriverfrontpark.com) sponsors concerts and other entertainment during the summer.

The **Spokane Symphony**—in existence for nearly 60 years—presents classical, pops, and chamber concerts, plus *The Nutcracker* at the Spokane Opera House (334 W. Spokane Falls Blvd., 509/624-1200, www.spokanesymphony.org). The opera house is also home to music, dance, and dramatic productions throughout the year, including a popular **Best of Broadway** series of musicals.

The **Spokane Civic Theater** (1020 N. Howard, 509/325-2507, www.spokanecivictheatre.com) hosts performances from drama to comedy year-round. Also in town is the **Spokane Interplayers Ensemble** (509/455-7529, www.interplayers.com), a resident professional theater group performing seven productions each year.

There are plenty of places to catch a flick in Spokane, including the 20-plex theater downtown, **AMC River Park Square** (808 W. Main Ave # 334, 509/747-3456, www.riverparksquare.com), but only the **Garland** (924 W. Garland, 509/327-1050, www.garlandtheater.com) has films for $3.50.

Festivals and Events

The **Lilac Bloomsday Run** (509/838-1579, www.bloomsdayrun.org) held the first Sunday in May, attracts over 60,000 runners with a downtown 12-kilometer course. It's called the world's largest timed race; all competitors are given finishing times. Simultaneously, Spokane hosts one of America's largest fitness and running trade shows.

After Bloomsday, Spokane blossoms with two weeks of activity called the **Lilac Festival** (509/535-4554, www.lilacfestival.org), culminating in the Armed Forces Day Torchlight Parade on the third Saturday of May. The lilac garden at Manito Park is usually in full bloom for the festival; other events include entertainment, concerts, and an amateur golf tournament. The first weekend in June brings **ArtFest,** a kid-oriented hands-on event with arts, crafts, and food at MAC.

Basketball players from all over the Western U.S. descend on Spokane for **Hoopfest** (509/624-241, www.hoopfest.org) in late June, a weekend of three-on-three basketball games. More than 4,600 teams compete in this double-elimination tournament that spreads over 300 courts. In addition to the hoops, you'll find a food fair and other activities at Riverfront Park.

On the fourth Saturday in July Spokane comes to life with the **Royal Fireworks Concert and Festival** (509/455-6865, www.allegrobaroque.org), an extravaganza of food, entertainment, and an open-air symphony concert at Riverfront Park. Fireworks follow the music. **Pig Out in the Park,** on the week before Labor Day, is four days of food, live music, and a beer garden in Riverfront Park. The **Spokane Interstate Fair** (509/477-1766, www.spokanecounty.org/fair), held for nine days in mid-September at the fairgrounds at Broadway and Havana, features big name musical entertainment and a PRCA rodeo.

In late November, **Christmas Tree Elegance** features the lighting of an enormous metallic tree, a giant snowman, strolling carolers, carriage rides, and decorations.

SHOPPING

Downtown, skywalks link 14 blocks of shopping and dining on two levels, including two shopping malls plus several large department stores. The **Flour Mill** (621 W. Mallon) adjacent to the Riverfront Park was the most modern mill west of the Mississippi when it was built in 1890. Today the restored brick building is home to 17 shops, including galleries, restaurants, gifts, and candy stores.

Book lovers should be sure to stop by **Auntie's Bookstore** (402 W. Main, 509/838-0206, www.auntiesbooks.com, Mon.–Sat. 9 A.M.–9 P.M., Sun. 11 A.M.–6 P.M.). This excellent and spacious store has frequent poetry and prose readings, along with a fun game and puzzle shop.

SPORTS AND RECREATION

Spokane is surrounded by a diversity of recreation opportunities. Located just 33 miles from Spokane is **Coeur d'Alene Lake,** one of the most beautiful in the mountain west with the world's longest floating boardwalk and an 18-hole shoreline golf course with a floating green. Immediately north of Spokane are the **Selkirk Mountains,** where you'll find all sorts of wild country and a string of small towns along the Pend Oreille River. To the south are the wide-open spaces of the Palouse farmlands; to the west lies a massive desert in the Columbia Basin, along with famous Grand Coulee Dam.

Spectator Sports

The Northwest League's **Spokane Indians** (www.spokaneindiansbaseball.com) play Class-A baseball at the Interstate Fairgrounds Stadium on Havana Street. The 10,000-seat stadium is the classiest ballpark in the league. In the winter, the **Spokane Chiefs** (700 W. Mallon Ave., 509/535-7825, www.spokanechiefs.com) slap the puck around in the Spokane Veterans Memorial Arena, competing in the Western Hockey League. Concerts, ice shows, rodeos, circuses, and other major events also take place here.

Spokane Raceway Park (509/244-3663, www.spokaneracewaypark.com) puts on drag and stock car races on Saturday nights May–September.

Skiing

Thirty miles northeast of town on Highway 206 at Mt. Spokane State Park, **Mt. Spokane Ski & Snowboard Park** (tickets 509/238-2220, snow report 509/443-1397, www.mtspokane.com, $42 adult, $36 college and military, $33 youth) offers alpine skiing and snowboarding, including five chairlifts, and a 2,000-foot vertical drop. It's uncrowded and friendly, with a small-town atmosphere. Night skiing draws the crowds here, as does the dry snow and 360-degree view of the Cascade, Selkirk, and Rocky Mountains. Other features include ski and snowboard school and rentals, restaurant, and bar, but no child care. Bus transportation from Spokane is available on weekends.

Some 24 kilometers of groomed **cross-country ski trails** are adjacent to the downhill area; get Sno-Park permits at local sporting goods stores before heading up to ski. The 10-kilometer **Langlauf Cross-Country Ski Race** takes place here in early February; it's the biggest such race in the Northwest. Other nearby places with cross-country ski trails are **Downriver Golf Course** (509/327-5259), **Indian Canyon Golf Course** (509/747-5353), and **Hills Resort** (208/443-2551) in Priest Lake, Idaho.

Other nearby ski areas include **49° North** (509/935-6649, www.ski49n.com) near Chewelah, along with two Idaho resorts: **Schweitzer Mountain Resort** (800/831-8810, www.schweitzer.com) and **Silver Mountain** (800/204-6428, www.silvermt.com).

Golf

Spokane is justly proud of its numerous public and private golf courses, and is considered one of the five best golfing cities in America. More than a dozen can be found in the area, including **Indian Canyon** (S. Assembly and West Dr., 509/747-5353), one of the top public courses in the U.S. and the site of many major golf tournaments. Golfers who love the sport for its outdoorsy aspects will also appreciate **The Creek at Qualchan Golf Course** (301 E. Meadow Lane, 509/448-9317), which boasts its own bird and wildlife sanctuary, along with well-manicured fairways and greens.

Other Sports and Recreation

Hikers and cyclists should be sure to check out the excellent **Centennial Trail,** a nearly level paved path that extends 60 miles along the river from Coeur d'Alene, Idaho, to the confluence of the Spokane and Little Spokane Rivers in Riverside State Park.

Swim at one of more than half a dozen outdoor pools around Spokane; call the city's parks and rec department (509/625-6960) for details. In winter, visit the **YWCA** (W. 829 Broadway, 509/326-1190) indoor pool. More swimming can be had at **Liberty Lake,** near the Idaho border. Contact **Wiley E. Waters White Water Rafting** (888/502-1900, www.riverrafting.net) for nearby white-water rafting opportunities on the Spokane River.

The local **REI** store (1125 N. Monroe, 509/328-9900) has all sorts of classes and guides trips throughout the year. They also rent a range of camping and other outdoor gear.

Wild Walls (202 W. Sprague, 509/455-9596) has an indoor rock-climbing wall with instruction and gear rentals.

Enjoy a trail ride with **Indian Canyon Riding Stable** at Indian Canyon Park (4812 W. Canyon Dr., 509/624-4646). **Rockin' B Ranch** (509/891-9016) has a chuck wagon barbecue and cowboy singing at Liberty Lake, near the Idaho border.

Camping

The closest public campgrounds are in **Riverside State Park** (509/456-3964, www.parks.wa.gov) six miles northwest of town. Tent sites ($14; no RV hookups) are available year-round. **Mt. Spokane State Park** (509/456-4169, www.parks.wa.gov, $14), 30 miles northeast of Spokane, has tent sites and is open May–October.

Private RV parks include **Alpine Motel RV Park** (18815 E. Cataldo, 509/928-2700), **Alderwood RV Resort** (14007 N. Newport Hwy., 509/467-5320 or 888/847-0500), and **Yogi Bear's Camp Resort** (7520 Thomas Mallen Rd., 509/747-9415 or 800/494-7275).

ACCOMMODATIONS

Spokane has accommodations for nearly every taste and budget, from urbane boutiques to cozy country inns. During major summer events, such as the Lilac Bloomsday Run in May and Hoopfest in June, travelers should make reservations well in advance.

Under $100

Road dogs hightailing it along I-90 can save some scratch by stopping at **Shangri-La Motel** (2922 W. Government Way, 509/747-2066, $45), a bare-bones but clean and safe crash pad perfect for a night or two's rest. For slightly more comfortable budget digs, try **Comfort Inn North** (7111 N. Division, 509/467-7111 $75 d), one of the better chain motels in town. This place is immaculate, it's got a pool, and you'll be greeted with fresh cookies upon check-in.

Or, for a little touch of home, stay at ☾ **Marianna Stoltz House** (427 E. Indiana, 509/483-4316 or 800/978-6587, www.mariannastoltzhouse.com, $89–109 s). Set in a classic American foursquare home built in 1908, this affordable bed-and-breakfast stands on a tree-lined street near Gonzaga University. A wide veranda, spacious parlor, and antique furnishings add to the allure. The four antique-furnished guest rooms have private baths.

$100-150

Families with active kids are in for a treat at the ☾ **Ramada Inn** (next to Spokane International Airport, 509/838-5211 or 800/272-6232, www.theramada.com, $112 d) near the airport. You can let the little fishes loose on the inn's fantastic water park with four indoor pools and a giant twisty, turny water slide. There's a hot tub for the adults, too. The hotel also offers a free hotel shuttle. Rooms come equipped with high-speed Internet, but you've got to pay for it.

Within walking distance of the Spokane River and Riverside Park, **Courtyard by Marriott** (401 N. Riverpoint Blvd., 509/456-7600 or 800/321-2211, www.courtyard.com, $139 s or d) features an indoor pool, hot tub, and exercise room.

Hannah's Garden Inn B&B (820 W. 7th Ave., 509/747-6235, www.hannahsgardeninn.com, $110–150 d) is another grand historic home with an attractive garden and five guest rooms with shared or private baths. It's close to downtown and Manitou Park.

Waverly Place B&B (709 W. Waverly

Place, 509/328-1856, www.waverlyplace.com, $105–135 d) is a Victorian-era home on Corbin Park. Built in 1902, this gorgeous B&B features hardwood floors, gas chandeliers, a wraparound porch, and an outdoor swimming pool. The four guest rooms have private or shared baths, and kids are welcome. A gourmet breakfast is served.

$150-200

Unquestionably the nicest hotel in Eastern Washington, **The Davenport Hotel** (10 S. Post St., 509/455-8888 or 800/899-1482, www.thedavenporthotel.com, $169–209 d, suites $349–599 d) will spoil you to the point where you'll feel like Robin Leach should be nipping at your heels. The lobby says it all, with an interior chiseled in marble and a skylight ceiling accented with amazingly ornate and gilded crown moldings. It is decorated with luxe sofas, a trickling water fountain, and a baby grand piano. It just keeps getting better once you check in and dive into your plush bed. Rooms in the main hotel building are decorated with antique-style furnishings and floral linens, while rooms in the new tower feature hipper modern decor, including suede bedspreads and leopard-print chairs. All rooms come with marble walk-in showers, ultra-comfortable mattresses, and big flat-screen TVs. Housekeeping offers turndown service each night, leaving behind the hotel's signature soft peanut butter brittle. Wander the property and you'll find a fitness center, business center, indoor pool, and hot tub. It is also a pet-friendly establishment, and they'll even walk your dog for you.

Hotel Lusso (808 W. Sprague Ave., 509/747-9750 or 800/426-0670, www.hotellusso.com, $149–159 d, suites $179–295) is another snazzy alternative for those with refined tastes. Built in 1890, this luxury boutique hotel offers elegantly classic rooms, though the standard queen rooms are on the smallish size. All rooms come with deep soaking tubs, big desks, and free wireless Internet. The hotel bar is everything it should be, with dark wood paneling and a denlike atmosphere perfect for nursing a drink with some pals after a long day sightseeing or making sales calls. There's also a fitness center on property.

FOOD

Cafés and Diners

For all-American breakfast "comfort food" served in an old railroad car, don't miss **Knight's Diner** (2909 N. Market, 509/484-0015, Tues.–Sat. 6:30 A.M.–2 P.M., Sun. 7:30 A.M.–2 P.M., closed Mon.) a Spokane landmark for over 40 years. Sit at the long mahogany counter to watch the chef working a mountain of hash browns and catch the banter slung by the speedy waitresses. You'll find a cross-section of Spokane folks at this immensely popular, noisy, and hectic morning eatery any day of the week. **Café Marrone** (144 S. Cannon St., 509/456-8660, 8–3 9 8–3, www.cafemarronebrowns.com) is an excellent local breakfast place. Good lunches, too.

The **Milk Bottle Restaurant** (802 W. Garland, 509/325-1772, Mon.–Sat. 11 A.M.–4 P.M., closed Sun.) has been around since 1932 and is locally famous for burgers, shakes, and homemade ice cream. The building's shape is easy to guess.

Domini Sandwiches (703 W. Sprague, 509/747-2324, Mon.–Fri. 6:30 A.M.–5 P.M., Sat. 8:30 A.M.–3:30 P.M., closed Sun.) has been in business for 90 years. This family-run place has a great chaotic atmosphere and huge sandwiches with thick slices of meat.

Also well worth a visit for pastas, sandwiches, salads, desserts, and espresso is **Lindaman's Gourmet-to-Go** (1235 S. Grand Blvd., 509/838-3000 Mon.–Sat. 11 A.M.–9 P.M., closed Sun).

The Onion (302 W. Riverside, 509/747-3852, open at 11 A.M. daily) is a Spokane institution with fast and friendly service, a convivial atmosphere, and justly famous gourmet burgers, barbecue ribs, fajitas, and salads. Huckleberry milk shakes are another favorite, and beer drinkers will find plenty of offerings and a weekday happy hour. The location is within one of Spokane's classic old buildings, originally the St. Regis Hotel; many of its original furnishings are still present. Take heed of the name—this place has killer onion rings.

If you just want a great inexpensive burger without the frills, head to **Dick's Hamburgers** (10 E. 3rd Ave., 509/747-2481, Mon.–Thurs. 9 A.M.–midnight, Fri.–Sat. 9 A.M.–1 A.M., Sun. 8 A.M.–midnight). Similarly, **Longhorn Barbecue** (7611 W. Sunset Hwy., 509/838-8372, Sun.–Thurs. 6 A.M.–9 P.M., Fri.–Sat. 6 A.M.–8 P.M.) in the valley is the place for beefy ribs, steaks, and good milk shakes, minus the pretension.

Contemporary Northwest

Steam Plant Grill (159 S. Lincoln, 509/777-3900, www.steamplantgrill.com, Sun.–Thurs. 11 A.M.–9 P.M., Fri.–Sat. 11 A.M.–10 P.M.) is a stylish grill and lounge housed by a steam plant with 225 smokestacks.

Mizuna (214 N. Howard, 509/747-2004, www.mizuna.com, daily 5–10 P.M. and Mon.–Fri. 11:30 A.M.–2:30 P.M.), a classy enclave with exposed brick walls, wood floors, and marble tables, serves up beautifully presented dishes that feature fresh seasonal ingredients.

Asian

A showy, Benihana-style Japanese steak, seafood, and sushi place is **Shogun Restaurant** (821 E. 3rd Ave., 509/534-7777, daily 5–9 P.M.). Much smaller is the always-crowded sushi bar at **Suki Yaki** (119 N. Bernard, 509/624-0022, daily 4–10 P.M.). Reservations advised.

Peking Garden (3420 E. Sprague, 509/534-2525, Mon.–Thurs. 11 A.M.–10 P.M., Fri.–Sat. 11 A.M.–11 P.M., closed Sun.) is among the city's better Chinese restaurants—and inexpensive to boot. Try the big Mongolian barbecue where you select the food and watch them cook with flair (and flare).

Taste of India (3110 N. Division St., 509/327-7313, Mon.–Thurs. 11 A.M.–9:30 P.M., Fri.–Sat. 11 A.M.–10 P.M., Sun. 11 A.M.–9 P.M.) has very good Indian food.

Italian

For pizza, pastas, calzones, and desserts in a comfortable downtown setting, head to **Europa Pizzeria and Bakery** (125 S. Wall St., 509/455-4051, daily 11 A.M.–midnight).

An Italian place with great specials, including a smoked salmon lasagna, is **Luigi's** (245 W. Main, 509/624-5226, Tues.–Fri. 11 A.M.–10 P.M., Sat.–Mon. 4–11 P.M.). **Rock City** (W. 505 Riverside, 509/455-4400, Sun.–Thurs. 11:15 A.M.–9 P.M., Fri.–Sat. 11:15 A.M.–9:30 P.M.) is a very popular Italian eatery with calzones, pastas, unusual pizzas, and such specialties as chicken al forno and Jack Daniel's whiskey steak.

Other International

Enjoy delicious Greek food at **Niko's Greek and Middle Eastern Restaurant** downtown at (725 W. Riverside, 509/624-7444, 4–10 411). In addition to traditional faves such as spanakopita, lamb dishes, and baklava, the restaurant has a number of Indian specialties.

Luna (5620 S Perry St., 509/448-2383, www.lunaspokane.com, daily 8 A.M.–2 P.M. and 5–9 P.M.) is a delightful and trendy little bistro with noteworthy meals, including Sunday brunch. The menu changes often. Make reservations to be sure of a table. **Marrakesh Restaurant** (W. 2008 Northwest Blvd., 509/328-9733, daily 5–10 P.M.) serves Middle Eastern meals, including five-course Moroccan feasts.

Steak and Seafood

Milford's Fish House (719 N. Monroe St., 509/326-7251, Tues.–Fri. 5–9:45 P.M., Sat.–Sun. 4–9 P.M.) is Spokane's favorite place for fresh seafood. Be sure to check the specials and fresh oysters. It has excellent food, friendly service, and an attractive exposed-brick setting. Reservations are advised. **C. I. Shenanigan's Seafood Chophouse and Brewery** (332 N. Spokane Falls Court, 509/455-6690, Mon.–Sat. 11:30 A.M.–10 P.M., Sun. noon–10 P.M.) combines beer and seafood in a pleasant riverside location. The patio is especially popular on sunny afternoons.

In the Old Flour Mill near Riverfront Park, **Clinkerdagger's Restaurant** (621 W. Mallon Ave., 509/328-5965, www.clinkerdagger.com, daily 9 A.M.–2:30 P.M. and 4:30–9:45 P.M.) serves up a well-prepared menu that combines steaks, fresh seafood, and Northwest cuisine with a view of Spokane Falls.

Bakeries

Find good atmosphere, along with tasty muffins, cookies, scones, and espresso at **Rocket Bakery** (1325 W. 1st Ave., 509/747-1834, Sun.–Thurs. 6 A.M.–6 P.M., Fri.–Sat. 6 A.M.–8 P.M.). Rocket Bakery has three other local locations, including one in Pasadena Park (3315 N. Argonne Rd., 509/927-2340, same hours). **4 Seasons Coffee** (222 N. Howard St., 509/747-2315) is a great espresso and pastry shop, with a big brick-walled space and friendly service.

Markets

For upscale grocery shopping at its best, head to **Huckleberry's Fresh Market** (926 S. Monroe St., 509/624-1349, daily 7 A.M.–10 P.M.), the largest organic market in the inland Northwest and an excellent place to get produce, healthy foods, and wine. The first-rate deli features salads, soups, sandwiches, sushi, and baked goods, all to eat here or take away.

Spokane MarketPlace (1100 N. Ruby St., 509/482-2627) is an outdoor market with fresh produce, seafood, ethnic specialties, flowers, and pottery every Wednesday and Saturday in the summer. The **Spokane Farmers Market** (Division and 2nd Ave., 509/685-1548, www.spokanefarmersmarket.com) takes place 9 A.M.–1 P.M. Saturday and Wednesday mid-May through October.

INFORMATION AND SERVICES

Visit the **Spokane Regional Convention and Visitors Bureau** (201 W. Main, 509/747-3230 or 888/776-5263, www.visitspokane.com, May–Sept. Mon.–Fri. 9 A.M.–4:30 P.M., Sat. 8 A.M.–4 P.M., Sun. 10 A.M.–3 P.M., Oct.–Apr. Mon.–Fri. 9 A.M.–4:30 P.M.) for maps, brochures, and other information.

Check your email for free on the computers at the main **Spokane Public Library** (906 W. Main, 509/838-6757, http://splnet.spokpl.lib.wa.us). Half a dozen branch libraries are scattered around town, not to mention the local colleges and university libraries.

GETTING THERE AND AROUND

By Air

Spokane International Airport (www.spokaneairports.net), just west of town, is served by several major airlines, including Delta, Horizon, Northwest, Southwest, and United, along with **Central Mountain Air** (800/776-3000, www.flycma.com) with service to Calgary, Alberta.

By Train

Amtrak's Empire Builder (221 W. 1st St., 509/624-5144 or 800/872-724, www.amtrak.com) has daily service to Spokane from Chicago and Minneapolis, continuing west to Ephrata, Wenatchee, Everett, Edmonds, and Seattle or southwest to Pasco, Wishram, Bingen, Vancouver, and Portland.

By Bus

Spokane Transit (509/328-7433, www.spokanetransit.com, $1) serves downtown Spokane and the Cheney area. It offers a **trolley** (the Plaza Arena Shuttle) that circles the Riverfront Park area, with a side trip down Wall Street.

Greyhound (221 W. 1st Ave., 509/624-5251 or 800/231-2222, www.greyhound.com) provides nationwide connections from the Spokane bus terminal (221 W. 1st Ave.), as does **Northwestern Trailways** (509/838-5262 or 800/366-6975, www.nwadv.com/northw).

Palouse Country

The Palouse is a broad area of low hills and wide-open land that begins just south of Spokane and runs south to the Snake River and the Blue Mountains; you'll see an occasional fringe of trees (particularly in the northern portion), but mostly these hills are nothing but soil—deep and rich. This soil is so rich and the climate so stable that the area, Whitman County particularly, is known as the best wheat-growing area in the world.

Tourism is not a major factor in most of the small towns here, so expect lower prices for straightforward food, and motels that are plain, clean, and cheap.

SIGHTS

Cheney

Just 13 miles southwest of Spokane, Cheney is home to **Eastern Washington University,** where 8,000 undergraduates and 1,600 graduate students study in over 100 majors, both on the 300-acre campus and by extension in downtown Spokane. The **Gallery of Art** (509/359-6200, www.ewu.edu) here has changing exhibits throughout the school year.

The small **Cheney Historical Museum** (614 3rd St., Tuesday and Saturday 1–3 P.M., free) houses local memorabilia. While here, pick up a brochure describing the town's many historical buildings.

Turnbull National Wildlife Refuge

Just south of Cheney, 17,000-acre Turnbull National Wildlife Refuge (509/235-4723, www.r1.fws.gov) has miles of trails and roads for walking, cross-country skiing, horseback riding, mountain biking, or driving through the protected lake area. This refuge, unlike others in eastern Washington, is not open to hunting; this is strictly an observation-only area, and nature lovers will be rewarded with sightings of grebes, hawks, shorebirds, deer, coyote,

© ERICKA CHICKOWSKI

Palouse Country is the breadbasket of Washington.

owls, badgers, herons, and an occasional bald eagle or peregrine falcon. The refuge is open every day during daylight hours, and a $3 per vehicle fee is charged March–October.

Steptoe Butte State Park

Follow the signs from Highway 195 and drive to the top of Steptoe Butte State Park (509/549-3551, www.parks.wa.gov), about 50 miles south of Spokane, for panoramic views of the Palouse River farmland and Idaho's mountains to the east. The park has picnic areas, but no water or overnight facilities. Landscape photographers love Steptoe Butte because it serves as a 1,170-foot tripod for photos of the rolling hills of Washington and Idaho's Palouse Country. Almost a perfect pyramid—its original name was Pyramid Peak—it is also a popular place for kite flyers because of the almost-constant wind.

The peak has another distinction: it is the top of a quartzite mountain more than 600 million years old, part of the Selkirk Range rising above the 15 million-year-old basalt that covered the rest of the range. In geological vocabulary, any remnant of an older formation protruding out of a newer formation now is called a "steptoe." The hill is named for Colonel Edward J. Steptoe, who was soundly defeated in the area in a running battle with the Cayuse on May 17, 1858. It was only with the assistance of the Nez Percé Chief Timothy that Steptoe's men were able to escape down a narrow canyon through the middle of the Cayuse lines.

The state park has a day-use area at the foot of the peak with a well and picnic tables (open year-round). Several publicly and privately owned radio and television antennas bristle from the summit but don't interfere with the views from the road that corkscrews around and around to the summit. The best time to visit Steptoe Butte is early in the morning and late in the evening, when the low sunlight defines the rolling Palouse hills and you can see far into Idaho, south to the Blue Mountains of Washington and Oregon, west to the Cascade Range, and north past Spokane into Canada.

THE PALOUSE NAME

The Palouse begins just south of Spokane and runs south all the way to the Snake River and the Blue Mountains. It is bounded on the east by the Selkirk Mountains in western Idaho, and on the west by the Channeled Scablands.

Early French fur traders called this area of green grassland *pelouse* (lawn). The name was soon given to the land, the Native Americans who lived here, and the river that runs through it. The Native Americans rode spotted horses that the white settlers dubbed palouse or palousey horses; "a palousey" eventually became Appaloosa. Today, the national headquarters of the Appaloosa Horse Club is right across the Washington line in Moscow, Idaho.

The park is east of Highway 195 on Hume Road. Follow the signs from the town of Steptoe if you're coming from Spokane; if you're driving north from Colfax and Pullman, the signs for the butte and Hume Road are a short distance south of Steptoe.

EVENTS

Palouse Days Community Festival is on the third weekend of September.

Cheney's mid-July **Rodeo Days** (509/235-8480 or 509/235-4848) features bronc and bull riding, calf roping, and a parade at one of the largest amateur rodeos in the Northwest.

The main event in Oaksdale is **Old Mill Days** on the third weekend of June, with a fun run, parade, fine arts show, and more. Over in nearby Rosalia, **Battle Days** comes the first weekend of June, with a rodeo, parade, fun run, and dancing.

Colfax Summer Festival on the second weekend of July includes a parade, car show, food fest, fun run, basketball tournament, and live music. The Palouse Empire Fairground near Colfax has rodeos, horse shows, and fairs all summer long, including **Palouse Empire Plowing Bee** in April and **Palouse Empire Threshing Bee** in September. In between is the **Colfax Jr. Rodeo** on Memorial Day weekend. The main event is the four-day **Palouse Empire Fair** beginning the weekend after Labor Day. It features a rodeo, demonstrations of antique harvesting equipment, a carnival, and all the standard country fair activities.

PRACTICALITIES

Near Cheney are more than a dozen small recreation lakes, many with resorts. You can also park RVs or pitch tents at **Peaceful Pines Campground,** a mile southwest of Cheney on Hwy. 904, 509/235-4966. Several small resorts in the area have cabins, camping, RV parking, boat rentals, and fishing: **Williams Lake Resort** (509/235-2391 or 800/274-1540), **West Medical Lake Resort** (509/299-3921), **Four Seasons Campground & Fishing Resort** (on Sprague Lake, 509/257-2332), and **Rainbow Cove RV & Fishing Resort** (on Clear Lake, 509/299-3717). **Palouse Lions Park** also has riverside campsites.

Three-hundred-acre **Kamiak Butte County Park** (four miles southwest of Palouse along Hwy. 27, 509/397-6238) has camping and picnicking. A steep, one-mile hiking trail leads through evergreen forests to the top of this 3,641-foot butte, providing views of the Palouse Hills.

Siesta Motel (509/397-3417) in Colfax has lodging.

Northwestern Trailways (610 S. Main, 509/397-4102 or 800/366-3830, www.nwadv.com/northw) stops in Colfax.

Pullman

Pullman is a typical small college town with an abundance of pizza delivery joints, sub-sandwich shops, and beer-by-the-keg outlets. The prosperous downtown is an attractive, tidy place with redbrick buildings and a wide range of shops. The diverse student body helps make Pullman a surprisingly open and culturally mixed small city. Surrounding Pullman are agricultural lands that make up the heart of the rich Palouse country and contribute to Pullman's reputation as "lentil capital of the world." (Despite this claim, much of the pea and lentil industry is actually based just across the border in Moscow, Idaho.) One minor drawback to Pullman is the city's convoluted layout, which makes it easy to find yourself looping past the same buildings again and again.

History

Pullman was founded by Bolin Farr, who came from Missouri to settle at the confluence of Dry Fork Creek, Missouri Flat Creek, and the south fork of the Palouse in 1876. Thus, the town was first called "Three Forks." By 1881, it had grown—to a population of three. Hoping to attract financial aid from Chicago industrialist George Pullman (of Pullman sleeping-car fame), the citizens decided to name their "city" Pullman. It's still a matter of controversy whether he contributed anything, but the name stuck. A railroad branch extended to the town, the "crossroads of the Palouse," in 1883; by then Pullman had two stores, a hotel, a post office, and a blacksmith shop.

Following the common pattern of the West, fires devastated the wooden downtown district in 1887 and again in 1890; structures were rebuilt in brick, and many of these buildings are still standing. In 1892, the Washington Agricultural College opened in Pullman. There were just 21 students that first semester, but the school would grow into Washington State University, and the focal point for the city. Today, the local economy is dominated by academia; the university employs over 4,700 people.

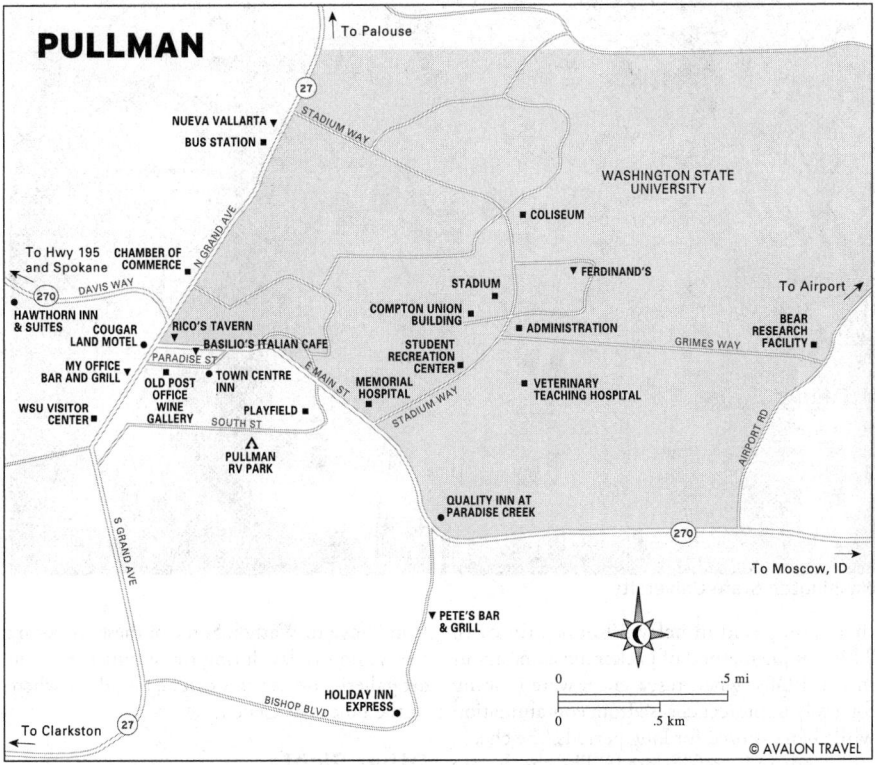

WASHINGTON STATE UNIVERSITY

Washington State University has a student body of more than 17,000 distributed throughout one graduate school and seven undergraduate colleges offering more than 100 major fields of study. The school is well known as an agricultural research center, but facilities also include an Electron Microscopy Center, Nuclear Radiation Center, Water Research Center, and an International Marketing Program for Agricultural Commodities. Students live in 23 residence halls, in the community, or in 24 fraternities and 14 sororities.

Ferdinand's Dairy Bar

The Food Quality Building is home to Ferdinand's (509/335-2141 or 800/457-5442, www.wsu.edu/creamery, Mon.–Fri. 9:30 A.M.–4:30 P.M., and on special event weekends, including home football games), a soda fountain run by the university's agricultural school, and the most popular tourist attraction on campus. As part of its agricultural research work, the university has maintained a dairy herd for more than 70 years; today, most of the milk produced goes into cheeses and ice cream. The cheese is made at a state-of-the-art plant in the Food Quality Building, and you can watch the operation and a 10-minute cheesy video upstairs from Ferdinand's. The soda fountain has delicious ice cream and shakes, making this a popular stopping place for students and visitors. On football Saturdays, you may have to wait 45 minutes for a cone!

The most famous product at Ferdinand's is **Cougar Gold,** a delicious cheddarlike cheese

© WASHINGTON STATE TOURISM/LEVY SHECKLER

Washington State University

that is only sold in hefty 30-ounce tin cans. This unique method of packaging came about in the 1930s, when researchers were looking for a way to protect cheese from contamination while being stored for long periods (the cheese still needs to be refrigerated). The cheeses are aged for up to a year to develop the proper flavor and texture. Technological advances have allowed plastic wrap to serve the same function, but Cougar Gold and other WSU Creamery cheeses still come in their distinctive tins. They aren't cheap, however, around $18 a tin.

Museum of Art

Although not impressive by Seattle standards, the Museum of Art in the Fine Arts Center (509/335-1910 or 509/335-6607, www.wsu.edu/artmuse, Tuesday 10 A.M.–10 P.M., Mon. and Wed.–Fri. 10 A.M.–4 P.M., Sat.–Sun. 1–5 P.M.) houses Washington's finest arts exhibition space east of the Cascades, with changing exhibits throughout the year. Also here is a permanent collection of works by well-known 19th- and 20th-century American and European painters, from Goya to Warhol. Some of these works are always on display during the summer. Student art galleries on campus can be found elsewhere in the Fine Arts Center.

Other Sights

The **Museum of Anthropology** (on the first floor of College Hall, 509/335-3441, Mon.–Thurs. 9 A.M.–4 P.M., Friday 9 A.M.–3 P.M.) has traveling exhibits from all over the globe and Northwest Native American artifacts (mostly from Snake River sites now inundated by reservoirs). Certainly the most unusual items are the plaster casts of what are purportedly Sasquatch footprints.

My favorite WSU museum is the **Jacklin Collection** (inside the Physical Sciences Building, weekdays 8 A.M.–5 P.M.). Here you'll discover the largest petrified wood collection in the western states, many pieces of which have been beautifully polished. In the entryway are several fun (and maybe even educational) science exhibits to play with.

WSU's **Veterinary Teaching Hospital** (509/335-0711) is a state-of-the-art animal care facility covering three acres on the south side of campus. Call two days ahead for tours.

Connors Museum of Zoology (in the Science Building, open by appointment only) claims the largest public collection of animals and birds in the Pacific Northwest. There's also an impressive **Nez Percé Music Archive** in Kimbrough Hall featuring tribal songs by historic leaders, including the voice of Chief Joseph. (You can also hear the recordings in the Kemble A. Stout Music Listening Library on campus.)

In addition to the larger exhibits at WSU, visitors will discover a big herbarium collection in Heald Hall for botanists, fungi and insects in Johnson Hall, and even the Smith Soil Monolith Collection, donated by a pedagogical philanthropist. Get a brochure describing these and other on-campus collections at the visitors center.

Bear Research Facility

Don't miss the fenced-in bear research facility along Airport Road on the east edge of campus. The WSU Bear Research Center (509/332-1511, www.natural-resources.wsu.edu) is an important facility for research on bruins from all over the world, particularly brown and black bears. This is the only place where adult grizzlies are housed for nutritional, physiological, and ecological research by graduate students and visiting scientists. The facility typically houses six grizzlies and four black bears, visible behind a stout fence. The resident bears were orphaned as cubs and would not have otherwise survived. In the winter, they hibernate in special temperature-controlled dens. Tours are available by reservation.

ENTERTAINMENT AND EVENTS

Nightlife

The best dancing and boozin' bars are in nearby Moscow, Idaho, but Pullman has a couple of options. **Rico's Tavern** (200 E. Main St., 509/332-6566, Sat.–Fri. 11:30 A.M.–2 A.M., Sun. 1 P.M.–2 A.M.) is a great rockin' place with blues and jazz bands, imported beers, and homemade wine coolers.

The college co-eds and jocks flock to **Cougar Cottage** (900 NE Colorado St., 206/332-1265), a divey joint with cheap brew and a definite frat vibe—no surprise considering its proximity to Greek Row.

If that scene isn't your thing, mingle with the locals, grad students, and professors at **My Office Bar and Grill** (215 S. Grand Ave., 509/334-1202), or take in a little vino at **Old Post Office Wine Gallery** (245 S.E. Paradise, 509/338-9463, www.opowines.com), a classy joint with leather chairs and plenty of tasty bites to pair with the wine.

The Arts

The university's 12,000-seat **Beasley Performing Arts Coliseum** (information 509/335-1514, tickets 800/325-7328, www.wsu.edu/BPAC) stages events from rock concerts to comedy shows. The university has theaters in Daggy Hall where you can attend Shakespearean plays, student productions, and a summer repertory season in June and July called **Summer Palace** (509/335-7236). Many other musical recitals and theatrical performances (509/335-8525) take place on campus all year.

Established in 1969, the **Washington-Idaho Symphony** (509/332-3408, www.c-5.com/symphony) puts on a number of productions a year. You can also hear free **summer outdoor concerts** at Reaney Park on Wednesday evenings from the third weekend of June through July.

Events

Pullman's annual **4th of July** celebration actually covers three towns. It begins in Johnson, 10 miles south of Pullman, where a silly parade features the weirdest and wackiest floats and costumes. Then it's on to Albion, six miles north of Pullman, for a big potluck meal at Community Hall. In the afternoon, head back to Pullman for a barbecue, live music, and after-dark fireworks show.

Pack your bottle of Beano for Pullman's main event in late August, the venerable **National Lentil Festival** (800/365-694, www.lentilfest.com). Over 200 gallons of lentil chili is simmered and served at the event, which also features a street fair, big parade, arts and crafts fair, live entertainment, a kids fishing derby, and a cook-off with such specialties as lentil pizza and even lentil ice cream.

The big **Holiday Arts and Crafts Show** comes to Beasley Coliseum in early November and is followed by the **Downtown Holiday Celebration,** complete with carolers and Santa Claus on the first Saturday of December.

The **Lionel Hampton Jazz Festival** (208/885-6765, www.jazz.uidaho.edu) in nearby Moscow is one of the biggest area events. Held the third weekend in February, it features many of the greats in jazz.

SPORTS AND RECREATION

Spectator Sports

The **WSU Cougars** (509/335-9626 or 800/462-6847, www.wsucougars.com) field teams in football, basketball, baseball, gymnastics, and track and field. The 40,000-seat **Martin Stadium** really rocks in even-numbered years when the Cougars play the arch-rival University of Washington Huskies in the annual Apple Cup.

Parks

Lawson Gardens (Derby St. near Dilke St.) covers 11 acres of land and features a formal rose and flower garden with a reflecting pool and gazebo. On the west side of town, **Sunnyside Park** has hiking trails, picnic areas, tennis and basketball courts, and playgrounds; this is the site of Pullman's annual 4th of July picnic and fireworks. **Reaney Park** on Reaney Way and Gray Lane has a swimming pool, gazebo, and playground.

The paved **Bill Chipman Palouse Trail** follows a gentle old railroad grade for eight miles, connecting Pullman with Moscow, Idaho. It's a great place for in-line skating or bike riding. The trail starts next to Quality Inn at the intersection of Highway 270 and Bishop Boulevard.

Outdoor Recreation Center

Located in the university's Hollingberry Field House, the Outdoor Recreation Center (509/335-2651) offers excellent non-credit classes in kayaking, cross-country skiing, rock climbing, wilderness survival, backpacking, and other subjects. Most of these are open to the public for a fee. They also have a **climbing wall** and rent a wide range of equipment to both students and the public, including backpacks, tents, rafts, canoes, skis, and snowboards.

Other Sports and Recreation

The **Student Recreation Center** (next to coliseum, 509/335-8732, http://urec.wsu.edu, $8 day pass) is a modern facility with lots to offer: a swimming pool, a 50-person hot tub, indoor hockey rink, basketball court, elevated track, Olympic weight room, and racquetball courts.

Camping

Campers can stay at the tiny city-run **Pullman RV Park** (509/334-4555, Apr.–Nov., $20 full hookups, $6 tents) next to the city playfield at South and Riverview Streets. Visitors can also find camping at **Kamiak Butte County Park** (13 miles northeast of Pullman on Hwy. 27, 509/397-6238, $15 tent and RV, no hookups), which offers more natural digs, including a 3.5-mile trail through a wooded setting, but it isn't as convenient to the university.

ACCOMMODATIONS

If you're planning to be in town for WSU football games or graduation, reserve several months, and maybe a year, ahead of time. The busiest time is when the Apple Cup Game (against arch-rival University of Washington) comes to Pullman. Late folks end up staying in Clarkston and "commuting" to the game. The chamber of commerce keeps track of available accommodations (800/365-6948).

Tucked into a gleaming white 1908 farm home, **Hazelton House** (210 N.W. Olsen St., 509/334-0408, www.hazeltonhousebb.com, $120–170) offers all of the special touches one expects of a cozy bed-and-breakfast. Wake up to a big hearty breakfast, relax over a cup of coffee on the deck when the weather warms up, and munch on cookies in the afternoon. This comfortable establishment is popular with visiting professors and families coming for special events such as graduation.

The following local motels are arranged by price. **Cougar Land Motel** (120 W. Main, 509/334-3535 or 800/334-3574, $50 s or $60 d) offers access to an outdoor pool. One of the nicest motels in town, **The Town Centre Inn** (445 S.E. Paradise, 509/334-2511, www.thetowncentreinn.com, $97–113 d) is a two-story, outdoor-entry motel with renovated rooms that all include refrigerators and microwaves, plus free Internet access. For $5 more, rent a unit with a dining room table and equipped kitchen. Families with large pets or small children and limited-mobility guests should ask for a ground floor room, as the spiral staircases are a bit difficult to navigate.

The **Hawthorn Inn and Suites** (928 N.W. Olson St., 509/332-0928 or 800/527-1133, www.hawthorn.com, $149 s or $159 d) has an indoor pool, hot tub, sauna, exercise room, and hot buffet breakfast.

Facilities include an outdoor pool, sauna, hot tub, fitness center, and breakfast buffet at **Quality Inn Paradise Creek** (1050 S.E. Bishop, 509/332-0500 or 800/669-3212, www.qualityinn.com, $124–164 d). **Holiday Inn Express** (1190 S.E. Bishop Blvd., 509/334-4437 or 800/465-4329, www.hi.com, $84 s or d) has an indoor pool, hot tub, fitness center, and continental breakfast.

FOOD

Cafés and Delis

The cheapest eats are found on campus at the **Compton Union Building** (http://cub.wsu.edu). Find five different eateries here, from cafeteria fare to sit-down comestibles. Also be sure to check out the ever-popular **Ferdinand's Dairy Bar** at WSU for ice cream, milk shakes, and cheeses. **Dissmores IGA** (1205 N. Grand Ave., 509/332-2918, daily 24 hours) has a good deli.

American

Pete's Bar & Grill (1100 Bishop Blvd., 509/334-4200, Mon.–Fri. 4 P.M.–2 A.M., Sat. 11 A.M.–2 A.M., Sun. 10 A.M.–2 A.M.) serves inexpensive burgers, pasta, and chicken and has a big salad bar. **Hilltop Restaurant** (Colfax Hwy., 509/334-2555, Sun.–Thurs. 4–9 P.M., Fri. 4–10 P.M., Sat. 5–10 P.M.) features a panoramic city view, decent steaks, and a popular Sunday brunch.

Swilly's Café (200 Kamiaken, 509/334-3395, Mon.–Fri. 11 A.M.–3 P.M. and 5–9:30 P.M., Sat. 5–9:30 P.M.) is a popular yuppified bistro with excellent lunches and dinners made from the freshest produce, baked goods, seafood, and meats. Riverside outdoor seating adds to the charm. Dinner reservations are recommended.

International

You won't go wrong at **Basilio's Italian Café** (337 E. Main St., 509/334-7663, Sun.–Thurs. 11 A.M.–9 P.M., Fri.–Sat. 11 A.M.–10 P.M.), a big brick-walled space where you order at the counter and then wait for the surprisingly good pasta dishes. Quick service and reasonable prices, too; entrées are popular with students. The best local place for pizzas is **Sella's Calzones & Pizza** (1115 E. Main St., 509/334-1895, Tues.–Sat. 11 A.M.–10 P.M., Sun.–Mon. 11 A.M.–9 P.M.).

Enjoy authentic Mexican cuisine at **Nuevo Vallarta** (1110 N. Grand Ave., 509/334-4689, daily 11 A.M.–10:30 P.M.) and good Chinese food at **The Emerald** (1140 N. Grand Ave., 509/334-5427, daily 10:30 A.M.–11 P.M.).

INFORMATION AND SERVICES

Start your campus visit at the very helpful WSU Visitor Center in the historic train depot (Hwy. 270 and Grand Avenue, 509/335-8633, www.wsu.edu/visitor, Mon.–Fri. 7 A.M.–4 P.M., plus some Saturdays). Football and other sports tickets are sold in the visitors center.

Public parking is available at a number of lots around campus; get a parking day-pass from the visitors center or on campus at the Public Safety Building.

Free **campus tours** (509/335-8633, Mon.–Fri. at 10:30 A.M. and 1 P.M.) depart the University Relations Office in Room 370 of the Lighty Student Service Building. These hour-long walking tours are offered year-round.

The **Pullman Chamber of Commerce** (415 N. Grand Ave., 509/334-3565 or 800/365-6948, www.pullman-wa.com, Mon.–Fri. 9 A.M.–5 P.M.) has all sorts of local brochures, including a walking tour of historic buildings.

For books, visit **Neill Public Library** (210 N. Grand Ave., 509/334-4555, www.neill-lib.org) or one of the seven on-campus libraries at WSU. **Brused Books** (105 N. Grand Ave., 509/334-7898, Mon.–Fri. 11 A.M.–6 P.M., Sat. 10 A.M.–6 P.M., Sun. noon–5 P.M.) is a fun place to browse for used books.

GETTING THERE AND AROUND

By Air

Horizon Airlines (800/547-9308, www.horizonair.com) has daily service between Moscow-Pullman Airport (in Pullman) and Seattle. **Inter-State Aviation** (509/332-6596 or 800/653-8420) offers flightseeing and air charter services.

By Bus

Pullman Transit (509/334-4555, www.pullmantransit.com, Mon.–Fri.) provides bus service throughout town.

Wheatland Express Commuter Bus (509/334-2200 or 800/334-2207, www.wheatland express.com) has Mon.–Sat. shuttle bus service between Pullman and Moscow, Idaho. Bikes are carried. **Link Transportation Services** (208/882-1223 or 800/359-4541, www.linktrans.com) provides shuttle bus service from Pullman and Moscow to Spokane Airport, as well as bus charters. **Northwestern Trailways,** 1002 Nye St., 509/334-1412 or 800/366-6975, www.nwadv.com/northw, has bus service north to Spokane, and south to Boise, Idaho.

PULLMAN VICINITY

Moscow

Although it's across the state line, the town of Moscow, Idaho, is a twin to Pullman. Moscow is just 10 miles away and has a number of attractions worth visiting: the **University of Idaho,** the **Appaloosa Museum and Heritage Center,** and many historic structures, including the **McConnell Mansion.** The country around here rises quickly into forested mountains, quite a change from the rolling grasslands of the Palouse.

The weekly **farmers market** in downtown Moscow runs all summer long on Saturday 8 A.M.–noon. Contact the **Moscow Chamber of Commerce** (208/882-1800 or 800/380-1801, www.moscowchamber.com) for more information.

Uniontown

Tiny Uniontown (pop. 350), a dozen miles south of Pullman, was first settled by German immigrants in the 1880s. Today, agriculture is the main support, as evidenced by the big grain elevator on the north side of town and the rolling farmland all around. Constructed in 1904, **St. Boniface Church** is Washington's oldest consecrated Catholic church.

The most distinctive feature—it's pretty hard to miss—is Steve Dahmen's old barn surrounded by an ever-expanding (600 feet at last measuring) fence of **iron wheels.** The wheels came from steam engines, threshing machines, hay rakes, tractors, wagons, and even sewing machines. Stop by to talk to the fence's friendly creator and to sign his guest book.

The Churchyard Inn B&B (206 St. Boniface, 509/229-3200, $75–180 d) contains seven guest rooms with private baths in a gorgeous brick 1905 inn listed on the National Register of Historic Places. The B&B was originally built as a rectory and later served as a convent. No kids are allowed.

Premier Alpaca Ranch & Guest Home (401 S. Railroad Ave., 509/229-3655, www.premieralpacas.com, $100 d, $130 for 4) is a restored century-old home with a guesthouse, plus an indoor lap pool. Guests will love to touch the alpacas.

Clarkston and Vicinity

Clarkston lies in the southeast corner of Washington along the Snake River, and right across the bridge from its larger neighbor, Lewiston, Idaho. The names reflect two famous explorers who traveled through here more than two centuries ago, Meriwether Lewis and William Clark. Clarkston is in the portion of eastern Washington often referred to as "The Banana Belt," because it has, as early Native Americans put it, "no wind, no snow." Some may take exception to the "no snow" part, but the climate is generally milder than that of other areas east of the Cascades. Clarkston is Washington's most inland seaport, more than 450 miles east of the Pacific via the Columbia River and its chief branch, the Snake.

History and Industry

On October 10, 1805, the Lewis and Clark expedition camped here en route to the Pacific. The region's first Anglo settlers were cattle ranchers, taking advantage of the nearly endless grazing lands. The Asotin Creek irrigation project of 1895 brought much-needed water to this parched region, and a wagon bridge built in 1896 between Clarkston (originally called Vineland) and Lewiston provided access to Lewiston's railroad. These projects, as well as dams constructed in the 1960s and '70s that turned the wild lower Snake into a navigable waterway, paved the way for agriculture, industry, and population growth. Unfortunately, these dams also destroyed magnificent stretches of wild river and buried countless archaeological sites.

Clarkston's first containerized shipment departed for Japan in 1975; today's primary exports are peas to Europe and paper products to Japan. Despite this, agriculture and forest products, not international shipping, are the mainstay of the city's economy. The largest (and stinkiest) local employer—by far—is Lewiston's **Potlatch Corporation** (509/799-0123). Tours of the sawmill and paperboard plant are available Monday–Friday by appointment.

SIGHTS AND RECREATION

Scenic Drives

To reach Pullman and other points north, you need to cross into Lewiston, Idaho, and traverse the Clearwater River bridge. From here, you can follow the heavily trafficked Highway 95, which connects into Highway 195, or follow the **Old Spiral Highway** instead. The latter road, which has been repaved, switchbacks and corkscrews its way up a shorter and considerably more interesting route, with spectacular views into Washington, Idaho, and Oregon from the 2,750-foot summit. A less extraordinary but still very scenic drive is along Highway 129 south from Clarkston to the Oregon border.

Asotin

The pretty little town of Asotin (as-O-tin) is six miles south of Clarkston along the Snake River. Visit the **Asotin County Historical Museum** (3rd and Filmore, 509/243-4659, Mon.–Sat. 1–5 P.M. in summer, Sat. 1–5 in winter, no charge) to see early artifacts and buildings and one of the largest collections of branding irons in existence. Ask here for directions to several petroglyphs visible south of Asotin. Also in Asotin is the **Full Gospel Church.** Built in 1889, it is on the National Register of Historic Places and houses the original oak pump organ. The Steamboat ***Jean*** is also here; it towed log rafts on the Willamette and Columbia Rivers from 1938 to 1957. Across the river in Lewiston is **Luna House Museum** (3rd and C Streets, 208/743-2535).

Parks and Trails

Five miles south of Clarkston, **Chief Looking Glass Park** provides boat access to the Snake River, with launch ramps, docks, and moorage, plus picnic tables and a playground. The paved 16-mile **Clearwater and Snake River National Recreation Trail** starts here and follows the levees north to Clarkston, over the bridge to Lewiston, and then back south along the river to Hells Gate State Park (which has a big swimming beach). The trail is a favorite bike riding, in-line skating, and walking route. South of Clarkston, the path cuts through **Swallows Park,** where a basalt rock is crowded with cliff swallow nests each spring. Swallows Park has river access for boating, swimming, and picnicking.

Eight miles west of town on Highway 12, **Chief Timothy State Park** (www.parks.wa.gov) sits on Silcott Island in the middle of Lower Granite Lake (the dammed-up Snake River). The park was named for a Nez Percé chief who befriended early white settlers. He is buried in Clarkston's Beachview Park. The area's history and geology are depicted at the small **Alpowai Interpretive Center** (intermittent hours). Also here are campsites, a boat launch, playground, swimming beach, and summertime concession stand. The nearby landscape is of sage and grass hills, with trees along the creek bottoms.

A more interesting destination is **Fields Spring State Park** (4.5 miles past Anatone on Hwy. 129, 509/256-3332, www.parks.wa.gov). This 445-acre park centers on 4,500-foot **Puffer Butte,** where the ridge-top vistas stretch over three states, down the deep gorge of Grand Ronde Canyon, and across the Wallowa Mountains. Get to the top on a mile-long trail from the day-use parking lot, passing summertime fields of wildflowers, and forests of ponderosa pine and other evergreens. Campsites are available, and winter visitors will enjoy the miles of cross-country ski trails and a lighted sledding hill.

Hells Canyon Recreation

Quite a few local companies offer float trips and jetboat excursions through the deepest river gorge in North America, the Snake River's **Hells Canyon,** separating Oregon and Idaho. The canyon lacks the steep cliffs of the Grand Canyon but is nevertheless an extraordinary place. From the summit of He Devil Peak to the Snake River—five air miles distant—the terrain plummets more than 8,000 feet. (A Nez Percé legend tells how their ancestors were threatened by seven devils. Using a very big stick, Coyote dug out the canyon, leaving the devils in what is now Idaho. Perhaps this could explain some of the right-wing militia mania that festers in parts of that state.)

Approximately 68 miles of the river—from Hells Canyon Dam in Oregon to the Washington border—is a National Wild and Scenic River. This is something of a miracle, since it represented a rare victory for conservationists over the electric power and agricultural interests that have managed to dam up lengthy portions of the Snake River. In 1964, a license was granted to build the High Mountain Sheep Dam in the middle of this undeveloped country. After years of litigation, congress finally voted to protect the river in 1975.

The Snake River features several class IV rapids (class V in high water), along with many class II and III rapids. In addition to the wild water of the canyon, along the way you'll see mysterious petroglyphs, an ancient lava flow, abundant wildlife, and rugged canyon scenery. Some outfitters use only inflatable rafts or dories, while the others use jet-powered boats. Most offer overnight trips as well as day trips.

For a complete list of commercial guides and outfitters, contact the Forest Service's **Hells Canyon Office** (three miles south of Clarkston on Hwy. 129, 509/758-0616, www.fs.fed.us/r6/w-w, Mon.–Fri. 7:30–11:30 A.M. and 12:30–4:30 P.M. year-round, plus summer weekends). For a 24-hour recording of current river conditions and other information, call 800/422-3143, or visit the USGS website (http://water.usgs.gov). The **Clarkston Chamber of Commerce** (502 Bridge St., 509/758-7712 or 800/933-2128, www.clarkstonchamber.org) also has information on local river-running companies. Expect to pay around $80–100 per person for the standard all-day canyon trip.

It is also possible to run the Snake River yourself if you have the equipment and skills, but you'll need to get permits for the summer season through a lottery system; contact the Hells Canyon office for its detailed *Floater's Guide.*

Other Recreation

Several local parks offer Snake River swimming, and the Clearwater River—just over the Idaho border—is a popular summertime inner-tubing spot. Nearby reservoirs offer a variety of boating opportunities, including windsurfing. The Snake River is famous for its rainbow trout, bass, steelhead, salmon, and monster sturgeon.

The local public links is **Quail Ridge Golf Course** (1725 Swallow's Nest Loop, 509/758-8501).

Camping

The closest public campground lies across the bridge to Idaho and three miles south of Lewiston along the Snake River at **Hells Gate State Park** (www.idahoparks.org/parks, 208/799-5015, $12–18).

Eight miles west of town on Highway 12, **Chief Timothy State Park** (8 miles west of Clarkston on US 12, 509/758-9580 or 888/226-7688, www.parks.wa.gov, $17 tents, $23 full hookups, $7 extra reservation fee) also has campsites with coin-operated showers. Open March to early December. **Fields Spring State Park** (30 miles south of Clarkston on Hwy. 129, 509/256-3332, $12 primitive, $17 tent) has primitive and standard campsites with showers and is open all year. No reservations. Because it is at 4,000 feet in elevation, Fields Spring offers a cool break on hot summer days.

RV campers will probably be happiest at **Granite Lake RV Resort** (306 Granite Lake Dr., 509/751-1635 or 800/989-4572, $29–42), a grassy lakeside resort that offers fancy touches such as paved sites, satellite TV, wireless Internet, and complimentary continental breakfast and newspapers served to your door each morning. The pet-friendly property also has laundry facilities and showers. In addition to the lake, there is also an adjacent 18-hole putting golf course and a 16-mile walking path along the Snake River that goes right by the property.

ENTERTAINMENT AND EVENTS

The Arts

The best place for live music (rock and pop tunes) is **Boomer's** (301 2nd St. in Lewiston, 509/746-2005).

Valley Art Center (842 6th St., 509/758-8331) features rotating exhibits and sales and also offers workshops and classes in all media.

Events

The **Asotin County Fair,** held the last weekend in April, features a rodeo, parade, cowboy breakfast, and stock show and sale. Also in late April, Lewiston's **Dogwood Festival** celebrates spring's flowering dogwoods with concerts, art in the park, and historical walking tours. Clarkston's **Sunflower Days** take place in mid-August. Several events in neighboring Lewiston complete the summer calendar: **Hot August Nights** with concerts in the park and an antique car show in late August, **Lewiston Roundup Rodeo and Parade** in early September, and **Nez Perce County Fair** in late September. **Lewis and Clark Days** is a celebration of history and adventure, including canoe carving, held in Clarkston in mid-October. Mid-December's **Christmas on the Confluence** is a lighted boat parade on the Snake River. A lighted Christmas twilight parade takes place at the same time in Clarkston.

SHOPPING

Meacham Mills (1305 Main St. in Lewiston, 208/743-0505) is a unique family-owned flour mill that uses stones to grind various types of grains. They also sell a variety of gourmet food products. The old Clarkston Airport hanger houses **The Hanger Antique Emporium** (935 Port Way, 509/758-0604), with some 100 dealers.

ACCOMMODATIONS

In addition to the properties here, you can also find respite just across the river in Lewiston, Idaho.

Clarkston offers a handful of budget motels, but the best among them is **Golden Key Motel** (1376 Bridge St., 509/758-5566, $53 d), which has clean—if spartan—rooms with the added perk of an outdoor pool. The **Motel 6** (222 Bridge St., 509/758-1631 or 800/466-8356, www.motel6.com, $46) is cleaner than most, also with an outdoor pool.

The **Best Western RiverTree Inn** (1257 Bridge St., 509/758-9551 or 800/597-3621, www.bestwestern.com, $110 d) sports the nicest property in Clarkston. Rooms are well updated with comfortable furnishings, they're clean, and they have wireless Internet. You'll also find amenities such as an outdoor pool, indoor hot tub, sauna, and exercise room onsite, plus a well-stocked continental breakfast served each morning.

Cliff House B&B (1227 Westlake Dr., 509/758-1267, www.cliffhouseclarkston.com $135–145 s or d) is eight miles west of Clarkston, atop a cliff high over the Snake River. Needless to say, the views are impressive from the B&B's deck. This spacious contemporary home has two guest rooms with private baths and a hot tub. A full breakfast is served at this adults-only lodging house.

FOOD

Sit down for a coffee and big breakfast with the Clarkston locals at **Come Inn Café** (508 Diagonal St., 509/758-2884). Get reasonable family meals at **South Shore Landing** (in the Quality Inn, 700 Port Dr., 509/758-9500).

If you're looking for something more exotic, **Bamboo Gardens** (907 6th St., 509/758-8898, Sun.–Thurs. 11 A.M.–9 P.M., Fri.–Sat. noon–10 P.M.) has Chinese food.

Fazzari's (1281 Bridge St., 509/758-3386, daily 11 A.M.–10 P.M.) features very good pizza, spaghetti, and sandwiches. Another popular Italian place is **Tomato Brothers** (200 Bridge St., 509/758-7902, Sun.–Thurs. 11 A.M.–9 P.M., Fri.–Sat. 11 A.M.–10 P.M.). **Rooster's Landing** (1550 Port Dr., 509/751-0155, Sun.–Thurs. 11 A.M.–9 P.M., Fri.–Sat. 11 A.M.–10 P.M.) has a big patio right on the river and a menu of steaks, seafood, burgers, and sandwiches.

INFORMATION

For maps or other information, contact the **Clarkston Chamber of Commerce** (502 Bridge St., 509/758-7712 or 800/933-2128, www.clarkstonchamber.org, Mon.–Fri. 9 A.M.–5 P.M.) or the **Lewiston Chamber of Commerce** (111 Main St., 208/743-3531 or 800/473-3543, www.lewistonchamber.com). Although Clarkston and Lewiston have different area codes, it's a local call from Clarkston to Lewiston, and you don't need to dial the area code for these calls.

GETTING THERE

Horizon Airlines (800/547-9308, www.horizonair.com) has service from Lewiston Airport to Seattle, Spokane, Boise, and Portland. **Empire Airlines** (800/392-9233, www.empirecoe.com) also serves this area. **Northwestern Trailways** (509/624-9863 or 800/366-3830, www.nwadv.com/northw) has bus connections north to Pullman and Spokane and south to Boise, Idaho, from the bus stop at Don's Chevron in Lewiston.

Snake River and Blue Mountains Country

As you drive Highway 12 from Clarkston to Walla Walla, the country offers up a hilly palette of grassland, sage, and strip-cropped wheat fields. Harvesting these rolling fields requires special self-leveling combines. The wide, easy highway sails over an easy 2,785-foot pass at Alpowa Summit, and then drops slowly down to the town of Pomeroy on the western side. Not much development out here, just a few weathered homesteads set against the big land and the even bigger sky. The Selkirk Mountains of Washington and Idaho are visible to the northeast, and the Blue Mountains of Washington and Oregon occupy the southern horizon.

POMEROY

Thirty-one miles west of Clarkston is the farming town of Pomeroy, the county seat—and only real settlement—in Pomeroy County. It's also the only county seat to have been established by an act of congress. A bitter rift with neighboring Pataha City—now essentially a ghost town—was finally resolved when congress awarded the seat to Pomeroy in 1884. Today Pomeroy is an agricultural center with half a dozen big grain elevators in use (or disuse). Not far away is the world's largest producer of Kentucky bluegrass lawn seed, Dye Seed Ranch.

Sights and Recreation

Pataha Flour Mill (509/843-3799), just east of Pomeroy, is a fully intact milling museum. It also houses the local chamber of commerce, a restaurant, gift shop and old-time photo parlor.

The city park has an outdoor summer-only swimming pool. The **Garfield County Fair** comes to Pomeroy in mid-September.

The **Pomeroy Ranger Station** (120 Main St., 509/843-1891, www.fs.fed.us/r6/uma) of Umatilla National Forest is on the west end of town. Stop here for information on the nearby Wenaha-Tucannon Wilderness, and for the scoop on camping, hiking, and mountain biking in the area. While here, pick up a map of the 70-mile **Kendall Skyline Drive.** The loop takes you through the Blue Mountains along rough but scenic forest roads.

The closest Forest Service campsite is **Alder Thicket Campground,** 18 miles south of Pomeroy on Forest Road 40. No charge (and no running water), and open till closed by snow in the fall.

Accommodations and Food

Pioneer Motel (1201 Main St., 509/843-1559, $45–70 d) offers simple rooms suitable for an overnight stay.

Head to **Donna's Drive-In** for breakfast and burgers.

The Forest Service rents out two historic cabins for $25 a night: **Clearwater Lookout Cabin** and **Wenatchee Guard Station.** The larger **Godman Guard Station** rents for $25–40, and the **Clearwater Big House** is $30–50. Contact the Pomeroy ranger station (120 Main St., 509/843-1891, www.fs.fed.us/r6/uma) for details.

WENAHA-TUCANNON WILDERNESS

This 177,000-acre wilderness (pronounced wen-NA-ha two-CAN-un) straddles the Washington/Oregon border within Umatilla (YOU-ma-til-la) National Forest. The wilderness is named for the two major rivers that cut through the Blue Mountains: the Wenaha and the Tucannon. The rugged terrain consists of deep canyons, narrow basaltic ridges, and mountains (2,000 to 6,400 feet in elevation) covered with lodgepole pine and other conifers. Some 200 miles of maintained trails cross the wilderness, with access from all sides, but the area is primarily used by elk hunters.

Hiking

The **Mt. Misery Trail** (No. 3113) starts from the end of Diamond Peak Road (42 miles south of Pomeroy) off Forest Road 40, at an elevation of 5,900 feet. This 16-mile-long trail follows Horse Ridge for several miles, providing dramatic vistas into the wilderness and good camping spots with nearby springs. A number of loop trips of varying lengths are possible from this trail, or you can simply hike out as far as you want and return back down this relatively easy route. Snow is likely to cover the trails until mid-June.

A popular lower-elevation path is the five-mile-long **Panjab Trail** (No. 3127) that begins at the end of Forest Road 4713, approximately 60 miles south of Dayton. Starting at 2,900 feet in elevation, this path climbs 5.6 miles to the Indian Corral area at an elevation of 5,600 feet. It ends on a ridge top offering breathtaking vistas, and from here you can continue deeper into the wilderness on several other trails. Because of the lower elevation, this trail is accessible earlier in the summer.

A fine day hike begins from the Teepee Campground, 32 miles south of Dayton at the end of Forest Road 4608. The **Oregon Butte Trail** (No. 3134) climbs for three miles into the wilderness—gaining 900 feet as you go—and ends at a fire lookout built in 1931. There's a good campsite on the ridge and a cold spring down the hill a short distance.

LOWER SNAKE RIVER AREA

Reservoir Recreation

The once-mighty Snake River through southeastern Washington is now just a series of placid reservoirs behind massive dams built in the 1960s and '70s. The lakes are popular with boaters, and locks make it possible for barge traffic to travel from the mouth of the Columbia all the way to Clarkston. Farthest east of these in Washington is Lower Granite Dam, which creates Lower Granite Lake. Downstream from here are the others: Little Goose Dam holding back Lake Bryan, Lower Monumental Dam creating Lake Herbert G. West, and Ice Harbor Dam creating Lake Sacajawea.

A number of parks and boat launches provide year-round recreation on these reservoirs. **Wawawai County Park** (509/397-6238 or www.whitmancounty.org) has camping ($10), picnic areas, a playground, rock climbing, and hiking trails. Get here by heading north from Clarkston on Highway 195 to tiny Colton, and turning left on Wawawai Road. Follow the road approximately 15 miles to the park. The last stretch is called Wawawai Grade Road. Just south of the park, **Wawawai Landing** has a launch ramp and dock on Lower Granite Lake. **Lower Granite Dam** and reservoir are accessible by driving 25 miles north from Pomeroy. The dam has a visitor center and a fish ladder with underwater windows. The locks are a good place to watch barges loaded with wheat heading downriver for Portland.

Just west of this dam on Lake Bryan is **Boyer Park and Marina** (509/397-3208, www.portwhitman.com) with launch ramps, moorage, docks, swimming beach and bathhouse, picnic area, and camping.

Central Ferry State Park (Hwy. 127 about 12 miles north of Dodge, 509/549-3551 or 888/226-7688, www.parks.wa.gov, $12 primitive, $23 full hookups, $7 extra reservation fee) features a swimming area with lifeguards, boat launches and docks, bass and catfish fishing, a picnic area, snack bar, camping and showers. The park is open mid-March to mid-November.

The **Lower Monumental Dam,** about six miles from Kahlotus on Devils Canyon Road, has a visitors center, fish ladder, picnic area, and boat dock. **Windust Park,** three miles downstream of the dam on the north shore, has free primitive campsites (open all year), swimming, a picnic area, and boat launch facilities.

Little Goose Dam, the creator of Lake Bryan, is about a mile west of Starbuck on Highway 261. Facilities here include a boat dock, fish-viewing area, and visitors center.

For information on Ice Harbor Dam and Lake Sacajawea near the mouth of the Snake River, see *Tri-Cities* in the *Columbia River Gorge and Wine Country* chapter.

Lyons Ferry State Park

Located in remote and desolate country at the confluence of the Snake and Palouse Rivers, this popular park (509/646-3252, www.parks.wa.gov) has fishing, swimming, and boating. It's eight miles northwest of Starbuck on Highway 261. The campground has out-in-the-sun primitive ($8) and standard ($13) sites; open April to mid-November.

In 1968, Washington State University researchers discovered human bones in what came to be known as the **Marmes Rockshelter.** Carbon-14 dating showed the bones to be at least 10,000 years old, making this one of the earliest known human occupation sites in North America. Unfortunately, the Lower Monumental Dam inundated both this important site and a Palouse burial area; the graves were moved to a nearby hill. A 0.75-mile trail leads from the campground to the new gravesite.

The Army Corps of Engineers has free dispersed camping along the reservoir, approximately two miles north of Starbuck. Near the state park is **Lyons Ferry Hatchery** (509/549-3551), where self-guided tours are available. **Lyons Ferry Marina** (509/399-2001) has additional campsites, a launch ramp for the Snake River, and a small store. A towering **Union Pacific railroad trestle** spans the river nearby.

Palouse Falls State Park

About six miles north of Lyons Ferry and another two miles in along a gravel road is Palouse Falls (www.parks.wa.gov), one of the most incredible waterfalls in Washington. It's particularly impressive in the spring when the flow reaches its peak. Here, the Palouse River hurdles over a wide semicircle of volcanic rock into an enormous plunge pool almost 200 feet below. The dark basalt and dry sage-and-grass landscape seem stunned by the powerful roar of water in this remote place. On sunny days, you're likely to see a rainbow in the spray. Acrophobics should stay away from the cliff-top overlook that affords views of the pool far below.

The state park has picnic tables and on-the-lawn campsites ($8; open mid-March to early October). Primitive, unmaintained trails lead to the top of the falls and down into the gorge below. Watch your step if you take these steep and sometimes dangerous paths.

DAYTON

The landscape east of Dayton is a striped Pendleton blanket of undulating wheat-covered hills, scattered farms, and an over-arching sky. Home to some 2,500 people, the small farming town of Dayton has a Blue Mountains backdrop, a number of interesting historical buildings, and even a four-star restaurant. Lewis and Clark passed through the area in 1806, but the Cayuse had long lived here, using present-day Main Street as a racetrack for their horses. The town was established in 1871 by Jesse Day (Dayton's namesake) and prospered as a crossroads town and agricultural center. The main business today is the Green Giant/Pillsbury plant, where more than a third of the world's asparagus is canned. The plant also processes seed peas. The lazy Touchet (TWO-shay) River flows right through town.

Sights

DEPOT MUSEUM

Built in 1881 by the Oregon Railroad & Navigation Company, Dayton's train depot—oldest in the state—is now the town museum (222 E. Commercial St., 509/382-2026, www.daytonhistoricdepot.org, Nov.–Apr. Wed.–Sat. 11 A.M.–4 P.M., May–Oct. Wed.–Sat. 10 A.M.–noon and 1–5 P.M., Sun. 1–4 P.M., $5 adults, free 12 and under). The immaculate and beautifully restored wooden structure originally had quarters for the stationmaster upstairs, with passenger rooms below. The museum contains the original depot furnishings and woodstove downstairs, along with a fascinating collection of memorabilia that includes century-old photos upstairs. The volunteer staff is happy to offer tours of the museum.

HISTORIC BUILDINGS

Dayton's impressive **Columbia County Courthouse** was built in 1887, making it the oldest in the state of Washington. The restored Italianate-style courthouse features

© WASHINGTON STATE TOURISM/LEVY SHECKLER

Dayton's train depot

a tall central tower capped by wrought iron railings. It is one of more than 80 local buildings listed on the National Register of Historic Places. Pick up a walking tour brochure of the others from the Depot Museum, or just saunter down any of the tree-lined streets to enjoy the many turn-of-the-20th-century Victorian homes (many of these remain unrestored).

The **Bruce Memorial Museum** (318 Main St., Waitsburg, 509/337-6221 or 509/337-6157, summer Fri.–Sat. 1–4 P.M.) occupies a gorgeous, antique-filled Victorian home and carriage house in Waitsburg built in 1883. Call for an appointment in the off-season.

LEWIS AND CLARK TRAIL STATE PARK

Five miles west of Dayton, Lewis and Clark Trail State Park (36149 Hwy. 12, 509/337-6457, www.parks.wa.gov) is a choice stopping place for travelers—it was, after all, a resting point for the ultimate cross-country wanderers in 1806, when Lewis and Clark stopped there. The park's tall ponderosa pines and cooling waters of the Touchet River are a welcome break from the sizzling summer heat of the encircling wheat fields. There are always fish in the adjacent Touchet River, and you can walk the mile-long nature trail.

Events

The main local summer festival is **Dayton Days** on Memorial Day weekend, which includes three days of pari-mutuel horse racing, a rodeo, parade, arts and crafts displays, and dancing. In mid-July, the **Dayton Summer Hoopla** is a three-on-three basketball tournament. There are more local activities—a parade, wine-tasting, auction, and dancing—at **Depot Days Festival,** held in mid-September. The **Columbia County Fair** comes 'round on the second weekend in September and always includes big-name country music, a rodeo, livestock auction, and demolition derby. On the second Sunday in October, the Dayton Historical Society sponsors a **Historic Homes Tour** (509/382-2026). On the day after Thanksgiving the town erupts in the **Christmas Kickoff,** with fireworks, hay rides, Santa, and caroling at the community tree.

Sports and Recreation

The town has an Olympic-size outdoor **swimming pool** open summers in the city park, as well as a nine-hole **golf course.**

SKIING

Ski Bluewood (262 E. Main St., 509/382-4725, www.bluewood.com, $39 adult, $35 kids, $31 seniors), 22 miles southeast of Dayton and 52 miles from Walla Walla, offers downhill skiing on 1,125 vertical feet in the Umatilla National Forest. It has the second highest base elevation in Washington (5,670 feet), and because Bluewood is over 300 miles from the coast, conditions here are generally drier than on most Washington slopes. The ski area has two triple chairlifts and a Poma. Slopes cover a spectrum from beginner through expert terrain.

CAMPING

The closest public campsites are in **Lewis and Clark Trail State Park** (36149 Hwy. 12, 509/337-6457, www.parks.wa.gov, $12–17, no hookups). A campground here has space for tents and vehicles and is open early May to mid-September. In the off-season you can camp in the day-use area. Coin-operated showers are available.

The Umatilla National Forest's **Godman Campground** (25 miles southeast of Dayton on Forest Rd. 26) offers high-country camping up at an elevation of 6,050 feet. This free site has no running water and remains open until closed by snow. At the campground is a trailhead for the West Butte Creek Trail into Wenaha-Tucannon Wilderness Area.

Accommodations

There are a surprising number of lodging choices in Dayton. Least expensive is **Blue Mountain Motel** (414 W. Main St., 509/382-3040, www.bluemountainmotel.net, $44–99 d), popular for its country-style rooms. The pet-friendly property offers free wireless Internet, and guests can munch on complimentary cookies in the lobby throughout the day. The **Weinhard Hotel** (235 E. Main St., 509/382-4032, www.weinhard.com, $125–180 d) offers the finest accommodations in town. The building was built in 1890 by the nephew of Henry Weinhard, the brewer of that delicious ale. Beautifully restored and furnished with antiques, the hotel exudes a classy elegance. Be sure to check out the art gallery on premises that features local artists' work.

The Purple House B&B (415 E. Clay St., 509/382-3159 or 800/486-2574, www.purplehousebnb.com, $95–135 d) is in a white-trimmed, baby-blue Queen Anne home. It has four guest rooms with private or shared baths, plus a separate carriage house. Lounge by the outdoor pool in the summer or curl up with a book in the library when a cold snap hits. Guests with disabilities will be happy to note that the home has wheelchair access.

Food

Dayton's claim to fame is **Patit Creek Restaurant** (725 E. Main St., 509/382-2625, Wed.–Thurs. 11:30 A.M.–1 P.M. and 4:30–6:30 P.M., Fri. 11:30 A.M.–1 P.M. and 4:30–7:30 P.M., Sat. 4:30–7:30 P.M., closed Sun.–Tues.), the only four-star French restaurant east of the Cascades. The decor is simple, but the changing menu features regional dishes made from fresh local ingredients. Reservations are strongly advised.

Information

The **Dayton Chamber of Commerce** (166 E. Main St. 509/382-4825 or 800/882-6299, www.historicdayton.com) offers local information.

BACKGROUND

In Washington, the traveler can find some of America's most diverse and fascinating country. The lush verdant forests are remarkable, but they are not nearly the only noteworthy attraction here. There is the sophisticated city of Seattle; the dramatic Cascade Mountains with glacier-clad summits and active volcanoes; the arid plains, giant dams, and rolling wheat fields of eastern Washington; the long sandy beaches and rugged rocky coastline bordering the Pacific; the justly famous gorge of the mighty Columbia River; hundreds of islands of all sizes and shapes in Puget Sound; and, of course, the lush rainforests of the Olympic Peninsula for which the state is so famous.

Washington's acclaimed "livability" has made it a favored destination for American, European, and Asian visitors. Increased tourism has been a boon to some of the smaller towns in the Cascades and along the Olympic Peninsula, where the drastic reduction in timber harvesting has cost thousands of jobs. Tourism hasn't completely replaced logging and sawmill work, but it has provided some new economic vistas.

Washington may be tucked away in the northwest corner of America, but it stands at the front door of the Pacific. The state's access to Asian markets has made it a major player in Pacific Rim trade. Boeing and Microsoft have huge stakes here: Boeing airplanes are one of the nation's most important exports, and Microsoft's software sells to a global market—and has made Bill Gates the richest human on the planet.

© WASHINGTON STATE TOURISM/LEVY SHECKLER

The Land

GEOGRAPHY AND CLIMATE

A State Divided

To the surprise of many first-time visitors, who are expecting only evergreen forests, natural lakes, and lots of saltwater towered over by snowcapped mountains, Washington has a dual personality. It is divided into the dramatically different eastern and western halves by the Cascade Range, which extends 600 miles from Canada through Washington and Oregon before flattening out and disappearing in Northern California. The Cascade Range has a powerful effect on the state's climate and scenery. The mountains wring moisture from the clouds, dumping rain and snow on the western flanks but leaving little for the dry and sunny east side. Those who expect to see only the evergreen land of the state's promotional campaigns are surprised when they travel through the broad wheat fields of eastern Washington. This country has its own beauty, and in places resembles the wide-open spaces of Wyoming or Montana—not an image commonly associated with Washington.

Much smaller but with an equally dramatic silhouette, the Olympic Range is quite different from the ancient and volatile Cascades. The Olympics (the backbone of Olympic National Park) are some of the world's youngest mountains, just one or two million years old. Though not exceptionally tall (Mount Olympus is the highest at 7,965 feet), the Olympics produce dramatically varied weather. Storms spawned over the Pacific dump 70–100 inches of annual rainfall on the coastal plains, and 150 inches or more (with a record of 184 inches at Wynoochee Oxbow) in the rainforests on the western and southwestern slopes—the heaviest precipitation in the contiguous United States. But on the northeast slopes of this range, Port Angeles, Sequim, Port Townsend, Whidbey Island, and the San Juans are in the driest area of western Washington, receiving only 12–20 inches annually. The most familiar example of this is Sequim, which sits in the rain shadow of the Olympics and is so dry that farmers must irrigate their crops.

LIGHTS, CAMERA, ACTION

Washington makes a great background for movies and TV programs, and quite a few of both have filmed here. The most popular show filmed in Washington was *Northern Exposure*, a lighthearted fish-out-of-water story that followed a New York doctor's move to harsh, slow-paced Alaska. The show was filmed in the lovely little town of Roslyn, and fans of the show can still find many familiar sights here. Fans of the films *Sleepless in Seattle* and *Singles* will also recognize plenty of scenery from these love stories as they explore the Seattle area.

It's not all young love and cuteness, though. David Lynch's mind-twisting murder mystery series *Twin Peaks* also affords Washington a star-turn, with Snoqualmie and North Bend especially prominent and including an unforgettable shot of Snoqualmie Falls and the Salish Lodge. The 1999 film adaptation of local author David Gunderson's *Snow Falling on Cedars* uses the Puget Sound islands on which it was based as backdrop, and Stephen King's 2002 miniseries *Rose Red* uses Thornwood Castle in Steilacoom as its setting. Notching up the creepiness factor just a bit more, blockbuster show *The X Files* frequently did shoots in northern Washington, and who could forget the bleak and drizzly Seattle of the 2002 U.S. version of Japanese horror flick *The Ring?*

Western Washington

Aside from the Olympic rainforests, most of the "wet side of the mountains" actually isn't all that wet: Seattle's annual rainfall of 38 inches is less than that of Chicago or New York. Winter snowfalls are generally light and melt quickly; a real snowstorm paralyzes the city for days due to the lack of snow-removal equipment and snow-driving expertise among natives.

Typical western Washington weather is mild and wet in the winter, warm and dry in the summer. Semipermanent high- and low-pressure systems in the North Pacific create predictable patterns of clouds and light rain beginning in October, with daytime temperatures in the 40s throughout most of the winter; December and January are the region's wettest months. In spring, the clouds give way to partly sunny days, and it's not unusual to have six weeks of cloudless skies in July and August. Summer daytime temperatures are usually in the 70s and 80s, with perhaps half a dozen 90°F days each year. Thunderstorms are rare, and tornadoes even more so; the humidity is low despite the area's moisture.

Seattle averages about an inch of snow per month in winter, though many winters are snow-free. Mount Rainier is the place to go for snow—in the winter of 1955–1956, the Paradise ranger station (elev. 5,500 feet) received 1,000 inches (83 feet) of snow. Winters with at least 70 feet are the norm. Cascade ski areas usually open in November and remain open through early spring, beginning and ending with Mt. Baker's eight-month ski season.

Eastern Washington

Compared with western Washington, the "dry side of the mountains" has hotter summers, colder winters, more snow, and less rain. The area from the Cascade Range east across the Columbia Basin to the Palouse hills has hot, dry weather with an average of only 7–15 inches of annual rainfall. Summer daytime temperatures are in the 90s, with many days each year over 100°F; the state's record high of 118°F occurred at Ice Harbor Dam (near Pasco) in 1961. July and August are the driest months, often devoid of any precipitation at all; what rain they do receive generally comes packaged in thunderstorms. Winters bring 10–35 inches of snowfall and daytime temperatures in the 20s and 30s.

The Okanogan and Methow Valleys, in the north-central part of the state, are a cross-country skier's paradise. Annual winter snowfalls range 30–70 inches, beginning in November and staying on the ground through March or April. January maximum temperatures hover around 30°, with some nighttime below-zero temperatures recorded each year. In summer, the Okanogan Valley is another eastern Washington hot spot, with temperatures averaging 85–90°F including several 100°F days each season, plus occasional thunderstorms and hailstorms.

Much of this part of Washington, from the Columbia River east to the Spokane area and the Palouse hills south of Spokane, is technically a desert because the rainfall is less than 12 inches a year; in a few places no more than eight inches can be measured. In fact, this is the northern end of the Great American Desert, which runs from the Mexican border north almost to the Canadian border. Today it doesn't look like the Sahara or Death Valley because of the vast irrigation systems that have been built there, turning the desert into a cross-hatched garden.

The largest irrigation project is the massive **Columbia Basin Project,** created by Grand Coulee Dam, which puts water on a half million acres of farms and vineyards. The mighty Columbia—the second-biggest river in America—drains an area of 259,000 square miles within parts of seven states and Canada. With the dams backing water over the river's rapids, barges can now travel all the way to Clarkston and Lewiston along the Washington/Idaho border.

As you travel toward the state's eastern boundary with Idaho, the elevation gradually rises and the more extreme desert weather returns to a cool dampness. The farms in the Palouse Country near Pullman are among the most productive wheat farms in the world, and because the climate is usually so predictable, eastern Washington wheat farmers have never had a complete crop failure in history.

Summer temperatures in central and eastern Washington are in the upper 80s and winter averages in the 30s, with a few extremes of plus 100°F and minus 20°F recorded every year. The Blue Mountains in the southeast corner get up to 40 inches of precipitation, while Pend Oreille County in the northeast corner receives 28 inches of rain and 40–80 inches of snow.

Flora and Fauna

Washington has a widely varied assortment of flora and fauna that reflects its richly diverse climate and geography. The Pacific Ocean and Puget Sound, the Olympic rainforest, the mountainous regions of the Cascades and Olympics, and the arid land of eastern Washington each support a unique population of birds, animals, and plants.

THE FORESTS

Washington's state tree, the western hemlock, is widely used in the forest industry as a pulpwood species, and it and Douglas fir are two of the most abundant low-elevation trees in the state. Above 3,000 feet in elevation, Pacific silver fir and mountain hemlock take over. Bigleaf maples are distinguished by—you got it—their enormous leaves, up to a foot across. The Pacific madrona is found along the coast and characterized by waxy, evergreen leaves and peeling reddish bark that exposes a smooth underskin. Other common trees are the western red cedar, Sitka spruce, grand fir, black cottonwood, red alder, and vine maple. Northeast Washington and parts of the Cascades have other species, including lodgepole pine, western larch, western white pine, ponderosa pine, and Engelmann spruce.

Olympic Rain forest

At Olympic National Park, the Hoh, Queets, and Quinault River Valleys constitute the better part of the Olympic rain forest, an

© WASHINGTON STATE TOURISM/JIM POTH

wild flowers on Dog Mountain, near Stevenson

area unique in the world. The largest known western hemlock and Sitka spruce grow in the Quinault Valley, the largest Douglas fir is in Queets, and the largest red alder is in the Hoh. The four major species here—the Sitka spruce, western red cedar, Douglas fir, and western hemlock—all grow very tall: trees average 200 feet, with many topping 300 feet.

The height of the trees isn't the only fascinating aspect of the rain forest: The visitor is immediately struck by how green everything is, and how pristine. These areas have never been logged; what you see is nature, pure and simple. Enormous trees spring out of the long-since-decayed "nursery logs" that gave them life, with club moss eerily draping the branches; ferns and mosses cover nearly every inch of available ground in a thick carpet. Though most rainfall occurs from fall to spring, even summer days feel damp from high humidity and ocean fog. And it isn't just trees that one finds in these rainforests, but an incredible diversity of ferns, mosses, shrubs, herbs, and other plants, along with many kinds of birds, mammals, insects, and amphibians.

Old-Growth Forests

Old-growth forests are defined as being at least 250 years old, though some stands are actually far older, approaching 1,000 years. Because of the tall overstory trees that moderate temperatures and hold much of the snow, original forests are more stable than cutover areas and less susceptible to climatic extremes. This helps the survival of forest animals by allowing them to browse at all times of the year. It also allows for a multilayered understory of trees, bushes, and herbs that can support a larger variety of animal life. In addition, defects in the old trees and standing dead trees—called snags—provide nesting sites for birds, flying squirrels, and other animals, while the fallen trees create nutrient-rich mulch as they decay. In many old-growth forests, these fallen giants become "nursery logs," with new trees sprouting in a straight line along the trunk.

FLOWERS

Rhododendrons

Washington's state flower—the coast rhododendron—is found from British Columbia south to northern California and east to the foothills of the Cascades. About 500 pure rhododendron species are hardy to this climate, along with several hundred more greenhouse varieties, which are combined and cross-pollinated to produce thousands of hybrids.

Rhodies are standard fare in western Washington gardens, relatively easy to grow and beautiful to behold, in colors from yellows to pinks to bright reds and whites. The best-known rhododendron gardens are on Whidbey Island, Bainbridge Island, and in the towns of Federal Way and Brinnon. Visit in spring and early summer to enjoy them at their peak.

MARINELIFE

Killer Whales (Orcas)

The orca, or killer whale, is the largest member of the family Delphinidae, a classification that includes toothed whales and dolphins. Named "killer whales" because they take warm-blooded prey, these cetaceans eat anything from harbor and ringed seals to seabirds, otters, dolphins, fish, and squid, depending on the local food supply. In Puget Sound, they generally eat only fish—mostly salmon, rockfish, and cod—and leave the other species alone.

Orcas are highly social, traveling in packs or "pods" of up to 40 individuals. Families stay together, protecting the young and mourning their dead. There are three resident pods in Puget Sound and along the Washington coast, with a total of about 75 members; other transient pods occasionally swim into the area but don't stay long. The most frequent sightings are around the San Juan Islands, especially at Lime Kiln State Park on the west side of San Juan Island. Unfortunately, the resident population of orcas around the San Juans has declined sharply in recent years. Get the latest at the San Juan Island-based **Whale Museum** website (www.whale-museum.org).

© WASHINGTON STATE TOURISM/JIM POTH

orca pod swimming near the San Juan Islands

Gray Whales

Every spring, tour boats leave the docks at Westport and a few other coastal towns for a close-up look at the migrating California gray whales. These enormous whales—up to 42 feet in length and upward of 30 tons—migrate from the Bering and Chukchi seas to the warm breeding lagoons off Baja California in winter, passing the Washington coast southbound in November and December and northbound from April to June. Occasionally a group of gray whales comes into Puget Sound, and several have beached themselves and died for thus-far-unknown reasons. Most, however, follow the outer coastline. After a 70-year hiatus, the Makah tribe in the far northwest corner of Washington again started hunting gray whales in 1998. They are allowed to take a maximum of five each year for food.

Gray whales are easily identified by their gray color, the absence of a dorsal fin, and bumpy ridges on their backs; their faces are generally covered with patches of barnacles and orange whale lice. Unconcerned with their appearance, gray whales often lift their faces out of the water up to about eye level in a motion referred to as spyhopping.

Porpoises

Commonly seen in the Strait of Juan de Fuca alongside the ferry *Coho* from Port Angeles to Victoria, B.C., **Dall's porpoises** frequently travel south through the Admiralty Inlet and, on rare occasions, as far south as Tacoma. Dall's porpoises reach lengths of 6.5 feet and can weigh up to 330 pounds; they feed primarily on squid and small fish.

The **harbor porpoise** is Puget Sound's smallest cetacean, ranging to nearly six feet in length and 150 pounds. Although similar in appearance to the Dall's porpoise, the harbor porpoise is much more shy and rarely spotted in the wild. Accurate counts are impossible, but the population around the San Juan Islands has been estimated at fewer than 100; none live in Puget Sound anymore, though resident populations were spotted there in the 1940s.

In summer and early fall, schools of up to 100

Pacific white-sided dolphins enter the Strait of Juan de Fuca, traveling as far inshore as Port Angeles but rarely any farther east. Reaching up to seven feet in length and 200 pounds, these dolphins are common off Japan and along the continental shelf from Baja California to the Gulf of Alaska. They have black backs, white shoulders and bellies, and hourglass-shaped streaks that run from their foreheads to their tails; the rear halves of their dorsal fins are light gray. Like the Dall's porpoise, white-sided dolphins enjoy riding bow waves and often leap full-length out of the water alongside a boat.

Seals and Sea Lions

Harbor seals are numerous throughout Puget Sound and the Strait of Juan de Fuca, with their statewide population estimated at 7,000. They can be seen at low tide sunning themselves on rocks in isolated areas, but they will quickly return to the water if approached by humans. Though they appear clumsy on land, these 100- to 200-pound seals are poetry in motion underwater; they flip, turn, and glide with little apparent effort, staying underwater for as long as 20 minutes.

The **California sea lion** is a seasonal visitor to the Strait of Juan de Fuca and northern Puget Sound, though on some mornings in winter and early spring their barking can be heard in shoreline communities as far south as Tacoma. These dark brown sea lions breed off the coast of California and Mexico in the early summer, and then some adventurous males migrate as far north as British Columbia for the winter. A large group of them collects just offshore from Everett, where a commercial tour boat takes visitors out for a closer look.

The lighter-colored **Steller sea lions** are more numerous in the Puget Sound area, numbering up to several hundred in winter, primarily around Sucia Island in the northern Sound. The males of the species are much larger than the females, growing to almost 10 feet in length and weighing over a ton, while the females are a dainty six feet long and 600 pounds. Both are almost white when wet; the male has a yellow mane.

Other Marine Creatures

Puget Sound is home to the largest species of **octopus** in the world. Though it grows to 12 feet across the arms and weighs 25–30 or more pounds, it's not dangerous and, in fact, often plays with divers.

Another peculiar Puget Sound inhabitant is the **geoduck** (pronounced GOOey-duck, from the Native American *gweduck,* meaning dig deep). These large clams can burrow as deep as five feet and weigh in at four or five pounds, with reports of some clams exceeding 15 pounds. The fleshy part of the body is so large that neither the entire body nor the siphon can be completely withdrawn into the shell. Geoducks are generally cut up and used in chowder, but some quality restaurants serve them as regular menu items or specials.

The **horse clam** is the second-largest Pacific Northwest clam, weighing up to five pounds. Horse clams only dig about two feet deep, so they're much easier to gather and can be found in Cultus and Useless bays at the south end of Whidbey Island. Both geoducks and horse clams prefer sandy or sand-gravel beaches.

For information on clamming, contact the **Washington Department of Fish and Wildlife** (360/902-2700, www.wa.gov/wdfw/fish-sh.htm). Some years, the overabundant growth of microorganisms causes the clams to build up dangerous levels of toxins. So, before digging, it's practically mandatory to call the **Shellfish Hotline** (360/796-3215 or 800/562-5632) for the latest on the edibility of clams.

LAND ANIMALS

Washington is home to a wide variety of land mammals, some of which have been brought back from the edge of extinction. Federal and state wildlife agencies alike have worked to preserve habitats for all forms of wildlife, and the state has become a richer place to live as a result.

Mule deer, the rare Columbia white-tailed deer, Rocky Mountain and Roosevelt elk, bighorn sheep, mountain goats, black bears (and a few grizzly bears), and a wide variety of smaller mammals, such as marmots, beavers, badgers, muskrats, nutrias, rabbits, and squirrels, are

SLUGS

If western Washington had an official invertebrate creature, it could easily be the common slug; the region is famous for them. Slugs look like snails that have lost their shells – or little green or brown squirts of slime about three to five inches long. They do well in the region; the damp climate is just what slugs need to thrive. Slugs can curl up into a ball to protect themselves, or flatten and elongate themselves to squeeze into tight places. They move on one long foot by secreting mucus that gets firm where the foot must grab hold and stays slimy under the part that must slide. The native **banana slug,** light green or yellowish with dark spots, has been rapidly outnumbered by the imported European **black slug,** which is now far more common in area gardens than the native variety.

Getting rid of slugs is no easy matter. Traditional home remedies include salting and beer traps; both require a strong stomach. Most residents just try to avoid stepping on them – unless, of course they own the gardens. Then it's war!

some of the animals you can expect to see, especially in the numerous wildlife refuges scattered across the state. The last remaining herd of woodland caribou in the Lower 48 can be found in the Selkirk Mountains of northeast Washington. Even the timber wolf—exterminated from Washington in the 1930s—has made a comeback. The first wolf call was heard in the summer of 1990, and small numbers have now moved into the North Cascades and Selkirks from British Columbia.

Columbian White-Tailed Deer

Lewis and Clark were the first explorers to comment on this subspecies of mule deer, which evolved along the lower Columbia River between the Willamette River and the Pacific Ocean. These deer look much like their larger cousins but are smaller and have a slightly longer tail and a white underside. By the 1960s, their numbers had dwindled to just 230. The population has rebounded, but they remain endangered. Find them at the **Julia Butler Hansen National Wildlife Refuge** (just west of Cathlamet on Hwy. 4, 360/795-3915, www.r1.fws.gov).

Roosevelt Elk

The Roosevelt elk live on the Olympic Peninsula, mostly inside the boundaries of Olympic National Park, where they are not hunted. They are a subspecies of their Rocky Mountain relatives, which were almost killed off in the Cascades, and have smaller antlers than their cousins. Roosevelt elk are named for President Theodore Roosevelt, who was instrumental in their preservation.

Cougars

Attitudes toward these big cats have changed dramatically over the years. Cougar populations are increasing in Washington at the same time as human developments push homes and people onto land that was previously wild. This combination has led to an increase in cougar attacks throughout the West; of 14 fatal cougar attacks in the last century, four took place in the last decade. None of the fatalities occurred in Washington, but brazen attacks have taken place in recent years, particularly on small children. If you come face to face with a mountain lion, maintain eye contact while backing slowly away. Try to appear larger than you are by raising your arms or by spreading a jacket or shirt. If you have children with you, pick them up. Talk loudly. But never, never run. Wildlife officials say compressed-air horns and pepper spray may ward off cougar attacks, and cougars are less likely to attack more than one person traveling together. The North Cascades National Park website (www.nps.gov/noca/cougar.htm) has additional safety tips for travel in mountain lion country.

Bears

Black bears are fairly widespread in Washington, with large populations on the Olympic Peninsula and in the northeast

© ERICKA CHICKOWSKI

Don't kid yourself, they're out there. Always exercise caution in the wilderness.

corner of the state. All of the black bears on the Olympic Peninsula are black; in other areas they may be black, brown, or honey-colored. They'll eat anything, from carpenter ants to berries to dead elk to salmon, plus anything you pack in from the supermarket.

Grizzly bears are rare in Washington, but there are a few in the North Cascades and in the Selkirk Mountains. Grizzlies once roamed throughout the western states, but now they are a threatened species with a total population of fewer than 1,000 in the Lower 48. Most of these survive in remote parts of Wyoming, Idaho, and Montana, with just a handful in Washington, so encounters are rare.

Avoid unexpected confrontations with bears by letting them know you're there. If you walk with a breeze hitting your back, any bears ahead of you will know you are coming. If you're unable to see everything around you for at least 50 yards, warn any hidden animals by talking, singing, clapping your hands, tapping a cup, rattling a can of pebbles, or wearing a bell. Safety is also in numbers: the more people hiking together, the more likely a bear is to sense you and stay away. Don't let your dog run free—it may sniff out a bear and lead it back to you. When camping in the backcountry, store all food, soap, garbage, and clothes worn while cooking in a sack hung from a tree branch at least 10 feet up and four feet out from the tree trunk. In an established campground, keep those items in your car's trunk. Don't sleep where you cooked dinner, and keep sleeping bags and gear away from cooking odors.

If you do encounter a bear, here's how to identify it: A grizzly is generally lighter in color than a black bear, though color alone can't be used for identification. Look for the grizzly's shoulder hump (behind its head) and a concave ("dish face") profile from its eyes to the end of its nose, with a distinct snout. (Black bears have no hump and a straight profile.) While you're looking for identifying marks, slowly detour out of the bear's path and stay upwind so the bear will know you're there; don't make abrupt noises or movements.

While retreating, look for a tree to climb—one in which you can get at least 12 feet up and stay there until you're certain that the bear has left the area. If no tree is close, your best bet is to back slowly away. Don't try to outrun the bear—grizzlies can hit 40 mph in short bursts, and you can't beat that, no matter how scared you are. Sometimes dropping an item such as a hat or jacket will distract the bear, and talking also seems to have some value in convincing bears you're a human. If the bear sniffs the air or stands on its hind legs it is probably trying to identify you. When it does, it will usually run away. If a bear woofs and postures, don't imitate, as this is a challenge. Keep retreating! Most bear charges are a bluff; the bear will often stop short and amble off.

Bear authorities now recommend against dropping to the ground if you are attacked by a **black bear,** since they tend to be more aggressive in such situations and are more likely to prey on humans. If a black bear attacks, fight back with whatever weapons are at hand; large rocks and branches can be surprisingly effective deterrents, as can yelling and shouting.

In the rare event of a night attack in your tent, defend yourself *very* aggressively. Never play dead under such circumstances, since the bear probably views you as prey; it may give up if you make it a fight. Before you go to bed, try to plan escape routes should you be attacked in the night, and be sure to have a flashlight and pepper spray handy. Keeping your sleeping bag partly unzipped also allows the chance to escape should a bear attempt to drag you away. If someone is attacked in a tent near you, yelling and throwing rocks or sticks may drive the bear away.

The Washington Department of Fish and Wildlife's website (www.wa.gov/wdfw) has additional safety tips for travel in bear country.

BIRDS

The **National Audubon Society's** Washington state office (360/786-8020, www.wa.audubon.org) has detailed information on birds and bird-watching in the state.

Eagles

Approximately 300 pairs of bald eagles make their year-round home in Washington, primarily west of the Cascades. In winter that number swells to over 1,600 birds, drawn to rivers throughout the state by the carcasses of spawned-out salmon. Several white-water rafting companies operating in the North Cascades offer midwinter Skagit float trips just for the thrill of seeing these majestic birds.

The adult bald eagle's distinctive white head and tail make it easy to spot. But it takes four years for it to acquire distinctive markings, making the immature eagle confusing to identify, as it may show whitish markings anywhere on its body. In contrast, the somewhat similar golden eagle has distinct white patches on its tail and underwings.

Their large nests, sometimes measuring over eight feet wide and 12 feet high, are often found in old-growth spruce and fir; snags are popular for sunning, resting, and watching for their next meal.

The state's heaviest concentration of breeding bald eagles can be seen on the San Juan Islands, enjoying the warm updrafts around Mt. Constitution on Orcas Island and Mt. Findlayson and Mt. Dallas on San Juan Island, and along the Strait of Juan de Fuca. The annual "salmon festival" brings the resident and migrating birds to the inland reaches of the Skagit, Sauk, Nooksack, and Stillaguamish rivers, with some enterprising pairs seen along southern Puget Sound and the lower Columbia River.

Owls

Washington's most famous nighttime aerial hunter is the **northern spotted owl,** which nests in old-growth forests along the Pacific Coast—forests that are filled with snags and broken trees that provide ideal nesting spots and smaller, sheltered trees for young owls who can't yet fly properly and must use their feet to climb from tree to tree. These forests are full of spotted-owl food: flying squirrels, snowshoe hares, and wood rats. Spotted owls are big eaters and quite territorial; 2,200

THE SPOTTED OWL VS. THE TIMBER INDUSTRY

The northern spotted owl is a Pacific Northwest forest dweller that lives only in tall, dense old-growth forests. More than a century of logging in Western Washington has taken a major toll on the habitat for these owls, and in the late 1980s and early 1990s, environmental groups successfully petitioned the U.S. Fish and Wildlife Service to list the owl as a threatened species. As a result, loggers are required to leave 40 percent of old-growth forest intact within 1.3 miles of any reported spotted owl activity or nesting. Since then, the region has lost thousands of jobs in the logging industry, although some studies suggest that other forces are at least partially to blame. Ironically, spotted owl populations have also continued to decline, perhaps because the barred owl, a fierce competitor, has begun invading the territory of the spotted owl. Loggers and their allies tend to regard the whole episode as part of a leftist agenda that puts the survival of a largely insignificant species over the economic livelihood of people. Environmentalists see the plight of the owl as a microcosm for the environment as a whole and a call to reform and conserve. Despite the heated controversy that rages on below, the unassuming spotted owl seems personally disinterested in all of the fuss.

acres of old-growth forest will support but a single pair of owls. Because suitable forest is being greatly reduced by logging, the spotted owls' numbers are diminishing—only an estimated 2,500 pairs remain in the Pacific Northwest's old-growth forests, though the population appears to have stabilized somewhat in recent years.

Other Birds

Other noteworthy birds in western Washington include the great blue heron, frequently seen along harbors or suburban lakes. The belted kingfisher is a common year-round resident of Puget Sound and the Strait of Juan de Fuca. Red-tailed hawks are often perched along I-5 and other highways, waiting for a meal. Noisy Steller's jays, blue with a black head, are common in picnic areas and neighborhoods.

In the Cascades and east of the mountains, the beautiful mountain bluebird is sometimes spotted in snags in open areas, and the town of Bickleton in the Horse Heaven Hills of southern Washington maintains hundreds of bluebird houses that stand on fence posts, in trees, and in front of the church. East of the mountains, striking black-and-white magpies are frequently seen flitting over the highway.

History

PREHISTORY

Although Washington is one of the more recent additions to the United States, archaeological evidence suggests that the Pacific Northwest was one of the first populated areas in North America. In recent years, animal and human remains as much as 13,000 years old have been found across the state.

In the late 1950s and early 1960s, archaeologists uncovered numerous artifacts and partial skeletons of people known as Marmes Man in a cave overlooking the Palouse River near its confluence with the Snake River. Dated at more than 10,000 years old, this is one of the earliest known human occupation sites in North America.

At Ozette in the northwest corner of the state, an ancient village was covered by a mudflow, perhaps triggered by an earthquake some 500 years ago. More than 50,000 well-preserved artifacts have been found and cataloged; many are now on display at the Makah Cultural and Research Center in Neah Bay. Other sites have also revealed how long people have been here: Thumbnail-sized quartz knife blades found at the Hoko River site near Clallam Bay are believed to be 2,500 years old.

One of the most fascinating discoveries occurred in 1977, when Emanuel Manis, retired on a farm outside of Sequim, was digging a pond on a back corner of his land and found two enormous tusks. A Washington State University archaeological team, led by zoologist Carl Gustafson, concluded that these were 12,000-year-old mastodon tusks. The group discovered other mastodon bones, including a rib that contained the bone point of some prehistoric weapon used to kill the animal. These bones are now on display at the Sequim-Dungeness Museum in Sequim.

Native Americans

According to one theory (hotly disputed right now), Native Americans originally crossed over to Alaska from Asia at the end of the last Ice Age, when the sea was 300 or more feet below present levels and the strait was a walkable passage. As these peoples spread throughout the Pacific Northwest, they adopted significantly different lifestyles on each side of the Cascades. West of the mountains, salmon, shellfish, whales, and other seafood made up a large part of the Native American diet; western red cedars provided ample wood for canoes, houses, and medicinal teas and ointments. A mild climate and plentiful food allowed these coastal tribes to stay in one place for most of the year, and in fact the north coast tribes were among the wealthiest in America. They often built longhouses—wooden structures up to 100 feet long and 40 feet wide that housed several families.

Coastal tribes were skilled canoe carvers and could travel up the Columbia as far as The Dalles, where rapids prohibited further progress. Inland tribes would meet them here for an annual fair with trading, dancing, gambling, and general hell-raising. Haidas and Tlingits

WHAT'S IN A NAME?

Many place names in Washington are based on American Indian words and can be difficult to pronounce for the uninitiated. Here are correct pronunciations of a few of the trickiest for travelers.

- Anacortes – anna-CORT-ess
- Bingen – BIN-jin
- Chehalis – chuh-HAY-less
- Cle Elum - clee-EL-uhm
- Chelan – SHELL-an
- Dosewallips – DOSE-wallops
- Duvall - DU-vall
- Enumclaw - EE-nuhm-claw
- Issaquah – IS-ah-qwah
- Hyak – HI-yak
- Methow - MET-how
- Mukilteo – MUCK-ill-tee-oh
- Puyallup – pyoo-ALL-up
- Queets – KWEETS
- Sammamish – suh-MAM-ish
- Sequim – SKWIM
- Skagit – SKA-jiht
- Snoqualmie – snow-QUAL-mee
- Toutle – TOOTLE
- Tyee – TIE-e
- Washougal – wah-SHOO-guhl
- Wenatchee – wuh-NACH-ee
- Yakima – YAK-i-maw

WASHINGTON NATIVE AMERICAN TRIBES

- Cathlamet
- Cathlapotle
- Cayuse
- Chehalis
- Chelan
- Chilluckittequaw
- Chimakum
- Chinook
- Clackamas
- Clallam
- Clalskanie
- Columbia
- Colville
- Copalis
- Cowlitz
- Duwamish
- Hoh
- Humptulips
- Kalispel Klickitat
- Kwaiailk
- Kwalhioqua
- Lummi
- Makah
- Methow
- Mical
- Muckleshoot
- Nez Percé
- Nisqually
- Nooksack
- Ntlakyapamuk
- Okanagon
- Ozette
- Palouse
- Pshwanwapam
- Puyallup
- Queets
- Quileute
- Quinault
- Sahehwamish
- Samish
- Sanpoil
- Satsop
- Semiahmoo
- Senijextee
- Sinkaietk
- Sinkakaius
- Skagit
- Skilloot
- Snohomish
- Snoqualmie
- Spokan
- Squaxon
- Suquamish
- Swinomish
- Taidnapam
- Twana
- Wallawalla
- Wanapam
- Watlala
- Wenatchee
- Wishram
- Yakama

from Alaska and British Columbia thought nothing of paddling hundreds of miles to trade—or raid.

East of the Cascades, particularly near the Columbia River, salmon was an important part of the diet, though dependence on deer, elk, bear, squirrel, and rabbit led these tribes to live seminomadic lives. The introduction of the horse to eastern Washington in the mid-1700s made hunting, especially for large bison, much easier. Native Americans in eastern Washington lived in caves or rock shelters while hunting, as well as in well-insulated pit houses that could hold several families.

The Europeans' arrival was met with reactions ranging from tolerant acceptance to swift murder. Relations between the races are still strained today; the interpretation of peace treaties signed in the 1850s is being hotly debated, with many lawsuits concerning property, water, and especially fishing rights pending. Tribes have also caused considerable consternation among some local and state governmental agencies by building casinos on their reservations and earning millions of dollars each year for their members. Most Native Americans do not live on reservations, though there are 22 reservations scattered throughout Washington, the largest being the Yakama and Colville.

A NEW WORLD

The first foreigners to land on Washington's shores were probably Chinese and Japanese fishermen who arrived weeks or months after they were blown off course. None of the Asian nations was interested in expanding across the Pacific in those days, and nobody particularly cared about the land to the east. Records, if any, were skimpy and ignored. That was definitely not the case in southern Europe.

Spanish Explorers

In 1592, exactly a century after Columbus made his landfall in the Caribbean, a Greek explorer using the Spanish name Juan de Fuca sailed along Washington's coast and claimed to have discovered the fabled "Northwest Passage," an inland waterway crossing North America from the Pacific to the Atlantic. Later explorers did find a waterway close to where de Fuca indicated, but it led only into today's Puget Sound, not all the way to the Atlantic Ocean.

Spain, hoping to regain some of its diminishing power and wealth, sent an expedition out in the 1700s to explore the Northwest Coast. In 1774, Juan Perez explored as far north as the Queen Charlotte Islands off Vancouver Island and was the first European to describe the Pacific Northwest coastline and Olympic Mountains, before he was forced to turn back by sickness and storms.

In 1775, a larger Spanish expedition set out, led by Bruno de Heceta and Juan Francisco de la Bodega y Quadra. Heceta went ashore at Point Grenville, just north of Moclips on the Washington coast, and claimed all of the Northwest for Spain. Farther south, Bodega y Quadra sent seven men ashore in a small metal craft for wood and water; they were quickly killed and their boat torn apart in the whites' first encounter with coastal Native Americans. The two ships sailed away without further incident; Quadra named the island Isla de Dolores (Isle of Sorrows), today's Destruction Island. Quadra continued his explorations as far north as present-day Sitka, Alaska, while Heceta sailed north to Nootka Sound. Heceta failed to note the Strait of Juan de Fuca, but he did come across "the mouth of some great river," presumably the Columbia, though the death or illness of much of his crew prevented further exploration and robbed Spain of an important claim.

Russian Voyages

Russian exploration of the Pacific Northwest began in the mid-1700s, when Vitus Bering led two expeditions to determine whether a land bridge connected Russia with North America. Bering sailed as far south as the Columbia River before turning back. The abundance of sea otters and beavers led Russian fur traders to establish posts from Alaska to northern California, which posed a serious threat to other nations hoping to stake a claim.

Early English and American Exploration

England was the force to be reckoned with in the battle for the Northwest. In 1776, Captain James Cook took two ships, the *Discovery* and the *Resolution,* and 170 men on an expedition that brought him to the Hawaiian Islands, the Oregon coast, and Vancouver Island's Nootka Sound. Cook was killed by hostile Hawaiians in a dispute over a boat in 1779, and his crew returned to England.

Other English sailors continued in Cook's footsteps. In 1787, Charles Barkley and his wife Frances explored and named the Strait of Juan de Fuca. In 1788, John Meares named Mount Olympus and other features of the Olympic Peninsula.

An American, Robert Gray, sailed out of Boston to explore and trade along the Northwest Coast in 1792. Stopping first at Nootka Sound—the hot spot to trade on

Vancouver Island—Gray worked his way south and spent three days anchored in today's Grays Harbor. Continuing south, Gray discovered the mouth of the Columbia River and traded there with the Chinook people before heading home.

Best known today, however, is the expedition led by George Vancouver in 1792. His goal was to explore the inland waters and make one last attempt at finding the Northwest Passage. The names of Vancouver's lieutenants and crew are a list of Washington place-names: Baker, Rainier, Whidbey, Puget. The expedition carefully charted and thoroughly described all navigable waterways and named every prominent feature. When Vancouver heard of Gray's discovery of the Columbia River, he sent William Broughton upriver to a point east of Portland to strengthen England's claim on the land.

Lewis and Clark Expedition

The best-known overland expedition began in St. Louis in 1804, led by Meriwether Lewis and William Clark. President Thomas Jefferson sent these men and their party to study the geology, animals, and plantlife of the 827,000 square miles acquired in the Louisiana Purchase, which extended as far west as the Rocky Mountains, and to explore and map the rivers and lands west of the Rockies that were still more or less up for grabs as the new country competed with England, Russia, and Spain for all the land between the two oceans.

Lewis and Clark's group left St. Louis in

THE WHITMAN MASSACRE

Following the Lewis and Clark expedition of 1805-1806, American interest in the "Oregon Country" began to rise exponentially. Some of the earliest to travel westward as settlers were missionaries seeking to convert the Native Americans to Christianity, and one of the first of these pioneers was a young medical missionary, Dr. Marcus Whitman. Whitman had been lured west in part by new reports (mostly fraudulent) that the Northwest tribes were seeking men to teach them about the Bible. In 1835, he and another missionary, Samuel Parker, headed west to locate sites for Protestant missions in the Oregon Territory. Convinced of a need, Whitman hurried back, married Narcissa Prentiss, and recruited three other missionaries. By 1836, this small entourage was heading westward in covered wagons; it was the first time white women ventured across the continent overland.

The success of this trek helped establish the Oregon Trail as a way westward. Whitman played another crucial role in 1843 when he led the largest wagon train ever assembled – the Applegate Wagon Train of almost 900 people – from Independence, Missouri, to the mouth of the Columbia River. This six-month trip fired the public's imagination and helped open the gates to a flood of some 350,000 later emigrants. This is not why he is remembered today, though it certainly had an impact on what followed.

THE MISSION

The Whitmans settled along the Walla Walla River in a spot the Cayuse called Waiilatpu (wy-EE-la-poo; Place of the Rye Grass). The home they built was the first permanent home whites had built in the Northwest, and their new daughter was the first white girl born west of the Rockies and north of California. Their new mission was intended to convert the Cayuse, but these efforts met with minimal success; the Cayuse had little interest in religious worship, books, schooling, or farming. They did, however, appreciate Dr. Whitman's medical knowledge and assistance. Despite setbacks, the Whitmans persevered, and their mission became a vital Oregon Trail stopping point until 1844, when most emigrants shifted to a more southerly route. One day a wagon train arrived carrying the seven Sager children, whose parents died on the way west; the Whitmans took them in as their own.

Historians have forever after argued over the attitude the Whitmans and other mission-canoes and keelboats, heading north on the Missouri River to present-day North Dakota. After wintering there with the Mandan people, the party, whose numbers were reduced to 28 for the final push, set out again on the Missouri River, crossed the Rockies on foot, and headed down the Clearwater River to the Snake River, in search of the Columbia River they knew would lead them to the ocean. In October 1805, the party got their first view of the Columbia and followed it downriver for many a "cloudy, rainey, disagreeable morning" until they reached the Pacific Ocean.

They built a winter camp, Fort Clatsop, south of the river and spent a cold, wet winter there, plagued by sickness. In spring they headed for home. The two leaders split up, with Lewis returning much the way they had come and Clark exploring the Yellowstone River to the south. They met up again in North Dakota where the Yellowstone enters the Missouri and returned to St. Louis in September 1806.

The First White Settlers

During the time between the early exploration and the permanent settlement of the Northwest, British and American trading posts emerged to take advantage of the area's abundant supply of beaver and sea-otter pelts. Two English companies, the North West Company and Hudson's Bay Company, merged in 1821; American fur-trading outfits included many small, independent companies as well as John

aries had toward the Native Americans, but most agree that they treated them with courtesy. One basic fact remains: The missionaries of that era showed little respect for the natives' culture and beliefs, an attitude that led to suspicion and distrust. To compound matters, some Native Americans became ill from medicines Whitman gave them, while others ate some of the poisons Whitman used to keep coyotes away from his gardens.

END OF A DREAM

The Native Americans of Oregon Territory lived in relative peace with the emigrants, although there were scattered raids on wagon trains, along with thefts of equipment, horses, and cattle. But as the trickle of wagons turned to a westward deluge, and as settlers began to occupy their ancestral lands, anger began to boil inside. The breaking point came in 1847 when a devastating measles epidemic – brought by the emigrants – swept through the region, killing fully half of the Cayuse. Dr. Whitman's medicines worked for whites, but not for the Native Americans, who had no natural resistance to the disease. Cayuse leaders feared that it was all a ruse, and that Whitman was poisoning their people to make room for more Anglo settlers.

On November 29, 1847, a band of Cayuse raided the mission, killing Marcus and Narcissa Whitman, two of the Sager children, and nine others. They then took 50 people captive; most of them were eventually ransomed for $500 worth of goods, but three more children died of measles while in captivity. The murders provoked a war between the Cayuse and emigrant settlers, and when news of the massacre reached Washington DC it created a national uproar that led to the official establishment of Oregon Territory the following year and the closure of the country to settlers until 1859. Thus in life – as a leader in establishing the Oregon Trail – and in death – as the inspiration for the first territorial government west of the Rockies – Marcus Whitman changed American history. Three years after the massacre, five Cayuse warriors were turned over to Washington territorial officials; all five were baptized, given Christian names, and quickly hanged. The tomahawk that Chief Tomahas apparently used to kill Dr. Whitman is at the Oregon Historical Society in Portland; anthropologists exhumed Whitman's body and matched the fracture in his skull to this tomahawk.

Astor's Pacific Fur Company and the Rocky Mountain Fur Company.

The most influential of them, the Hudson's Bay Company, built its temporary headquarters on the north side of the Columbia, 100 miles inland at Fort Vancouver, across the river from its confluence with the Willamette.

The settlers planted crops (including the apples and wheat that are so important to Washington's economy today), raised livestock, and made the fort as self-sufficient as possible. At its peak, 500 people lived at or near the fort. Fort Vancouver served as a model for other Hudson's Bay Company posts at Spokane, Okanogan, and Nisqually. When settlers began arriving in droves and the beaver population diminished in the late 1840s, the Hudson's Bay Company was crowded out and moved its headquarters elsewhere.

Missions were another important method of establishing white settlements in the Washington Territory. The first missionary, Jason Lee, was sent by the Methodist Church in 1834 to introduce Christianity to the native peoples, but instead he spent much of his time and resources ministering to whites at Fort Vancouver.

The promise of free land under the Organic Act of 1843 and the Donation Land Law of 1850 fueled the "Great Migration" of 1843, in which almost 900 settlers traveled to the Oregon Country, six times the number of the previous year. More pioneers followed: 1,500 in 1844 and 3,000 in 1845. Most settlers came by way of the Oregon Trail from St. Joseph, Missouri, along the North Platte River, through southern Wyoming and southern Idaho into Oregon, then north to the Columbia River. Soon the route looked like a cleared road; traces of it can still be seen where the wagon tires dug ruts in stone and where wheels packed the ground so hard that grass still cannot grow. Washington's early settlers congregated around five fledgling cities: Seattle, Port Townsend, Oysterville, Centralia, and Walla Walla; other smaller communities developed at Tumwater, Steilacoom, Olympia, and Fairhaven, now part of Bellingham. In eastern Washington the major communities were Spokane and Walla Walla.

Settling the Claims

By 1846, only the U.S. and England retained claims to the Oregon Country; Spain and Russia had sold or lost their North American possessions. Negotiators brought the U.S. and England to agreement on a division at the 49th parallel from the Rockies to the main channel between Vancouver Island and the mainland, running through the center of the Strait of Juan de Fuca to the Pacific Ocean.

The unspecified "main channel" was viewed to be either the Rosario Strait or the Haro Strait, leaving the San Juan Islands in the middle of the disputed waterway. Both nations claimed the islands. The British maintained a Hudson's Bay Company fort, but American settlers began moving in and establishing farms. In 1859, an American shot and killed a British-owned pig that had repeatedly rooted in his garden, and the resulting uproar nearly started a war. The British demanded payment for the pig, the American refused, and soon both sides began bringing in soldiers and heavy weapons. Within three months the English had a force of 2,140 troops, five warships, and 167 heavy guns arrayed against the American army's 461 soldiers and 14 cannons. Fortunately, calmer heads prevailed, and no further shots were fired in the "Pig War." Soldiers of both nations remained on the islands for the next 13 years, and in 1872, Germany's Kaiser Wilhelm was chosen to conduct arbitration. He awarded the islands to the Americans and pronounced the Haro Strait the dividing channel.

In spite of all this arbitration, one small piece of real estate managed to be overlooked. A peninsula hung down from the Canadian mainland into the Strait of Georgia south of the 49th parallel, making it American land. Rather than settling the matter when it was discovered, the appendix still dangles there and is known as Point Roberts, a bit of America attached to Canada.

Growth of a New State

In 1848, President James Polk created Oregon Territory and appointed Joseph Lane as the first territorial governor a year later. In the

THE MERCER GIRLS

In the 1860s, Seattle faced a major crisis. As was the case with many still-rough frontier towns, the nascent city just wasn't attracting many single women. As one may imagine, a city populated with hundreds of male fishermen and lumberjacks and very few available women can find itself the scene of trouble. If nothing else, it makes it rather tough to establish and grow a permanent city. It was this problem that local businessman and professor Asa Mercer set out to rectify.

In 1864, Mercer scraped together some money from the local citizenry and set out back East to round up some ladies. In Massachusetts, he eagerly recruited single women and widows of fallen Civil War soldiers to come back to Seattle. This first trip resulted in the relocation of 11 women, an event much celebrated by at least 11 Seattle men. Mercer made a second trip in 1865, this time convincing nearly a hundred women to make the journey. Despite the higher numbers, the trip was counted as a failure – Mercer had promised at least 500 marriageable women.

Asa Mercer went on to marry one of the girls he met on his second trip and move to Wyoming to write and raise cattle. His family left its name on Mercer Island, a swanky Seattle suburb. His maidens, meanwhile, all married locals, with the single exception of Elizabeth Ordway, a dedicated teacher, activist, and early feminist. Today, many longtime Seattleites can trace their origins to one of the Mercer Girls, whose modern descendants hold occasional receptions around town.

early 1840s, most Americans lived south of the Columbia River. By 1849, only 304 people lived north of the river, but in the next year that number tripled as more and more settlers ventured northward. As they moved farther away from the territorial government, the settlers felt left out of governmental matters and decided to separate from Oregon. Delegates met at the Monticello Convention in 1852 to list reasons for the proposed separation, and Congress found little opposition to the bill. Washington Territory—named, of course, for George Washington—was created in 1853. The initial territory included much of present-day Idaho and Montana. In 1863, Idaho Territory was carved off the whole, followed by Montana Territory in 1864, giving the territories much the same boundaries that the states now occupy.

When Washington became a territory, its population was under 4,000 people; by 1880 it had grown to over 125,000 and was considered a serious candidate for statehood. Washington was admitted as the 42nd state in 1889, with Olympia as its capital and a growing population of over 173,000. When the news was telegraphed to Washington officials in Olympia, they discovered one problem; the telegraph had been sent collect, and they could not read it until the cost was paid. Welcome to the United States!

Into the 20th Century

The 40 years between 1870 and 1910 marked a period of tremendous growth in Washington. In 1870, the territory's population was just shy of 24,000; in 1910, the new state, created with the same boundaries, had 1,142,000 residents. Much of this growth was a direct result of the arrival of the Northern Pacific and Great Northern railways in the late 1880s, bringing industry and settlers to Puget Sound and creating new towns all along their routes. Spokane saw rapid economic growth during the 1880s, outfitting miners for the gold, silver, and lead rush in Idaho.

The 1880s also spelled disaster for Spokane, Ellensburg, and Seattle, when major portions of these cities' thriving downtown areas were destroyed by fire. Though the cities were rebuilt quickly in brick, the state was hit hard by a nationwide depression, the Panic of 1893, when growth slowed on both sides of the mountains and businesses failed. A gold rush in the Yukon and the emergence of hydroelectric power helped get the state back on its feet. At the end of this period of growth, the Alaska-Yukon-Pacific Exposition of 1909 brought nationwide attention and over 3.7 million visitors to what is now the University of Washington campus in Seattle to promote the ties between Washington, the far north, and Pacific Rim countries.

The first and second World Wars changed Washington's economy from one based largely on mining, farming, logging, and fishing to manufacturing and ship and airplane building, highlighted by Boeing's B-17; over 13,000 of the "Flying Fortresses" were built for World War II. Boeing continues to be one of the state's largest employers and most important industries and in the 1990s became America's biggest exporter.

Seattle's 1962 World's Fair was the first such exposition to be an economic success, drawing almost 10 million people during its six-month run and creating a permanent addition to the city's culture with the Seattle Center. Spokane followed suit 12 years later with Expo '74, emphasizing environmental concerns and cleaning up its own Spokane River in the process.

Industry and Economy

Washington's earliest industries—fishing, mining, farming, and logging—depended upon the abundant natural resources that the pioneers found here. Today only farming and logging are major industries, although logging has taken a severe hit from the spotted owl and marbled murrelet controversy, as areas are set aside from logging to preserve their habitat. Farming remains the basis for much of Washington's economy, and hydroelectric power creates jobs and low electricity costs from the state's plentiful resources. Over the years, though, manufacturing, shipping, and other industries have become increasingly important to the state's economy, particularly the trio of Boeing, Microsoft, and Weyerhaeuser.

Mining

Coal was first discovered east of Bellingham in 1849, and mining began in 1855. Discoveries of coal in the Cascades in the late 1800s gave rise to a number of small mining towns (such as Black Diamond, Carbonado, Wilkeson, Newcastle, Cle Elum, and Roslyn) on both sides of the Cascades. Though coal was plentiful—geologists today believe there are 6–65 billion tons in the state—it was soft and therefore limited in its uses. Often found in steep ravines or streams, it was also difficult to extract and transport. Underground explosions and other accidents gave Washington more mining fatalities per number of miners than any other state for several years in the late 1800s. By the turn of the 20th century, coal from the Rocky Mountains had become a cheaper and more practical fuel source, and by 1930 coal mining had virtually disappeared. Today, coal mining is seeing a minor revival; for the past several years, over five million tons of coal per year have been strip-mined near Centralia for use in a thermal-electric power plant there.

Other minerals begat industries that met with varying degrees of success. Discoveries of gold and silver in the mountains of Washington's northeastern corner caused short-lived rushes—and Indian wars, as whites crossed onto reservation lands—but outfitting miners for the gold rushes of Idaho and the Yukon yielded better returns. A successful silver, gold, and lead refinery in Tacoma was started in 1890 by William R. Rust; he later sold the plant to the American Smelting and Refining Company (ASARCO) for processing copper.

A gold mine still operates in Republic, but Washington's most valuable minerals are the least exotic: 60 percent of the money made from mineral production is derived from cement, stone, and gravel pits in the western half of the state.

Lumber

The Pacific Northwest states of Washington, Oregon, and Idaho supply about half of the total lumber in the United States. Washington is generally the third- or fourth-largest producer of the 50 states, with Oregon taking the lead since 1938. Douglas fir, western hemlock, and western red cedar are some of the commercially important trees native to the area west of the Cascades.

Wood and wood products have been a vital part of Washington's economy ever since the coastal Native Americans first began using cedar for longhouses, totem poles, and canoes—they even made clothing from cedar bark. The first white settlers and missionaries used wood for construction of their forts, homes, and blockhouses, and British explorer John Meares was the first to ship lumber to the Orient in 1788. Seattle's founding fathers depended on lumber sales to San Francisco for much of their income; Yesler's waterfront sawmill was an important part of the city's early economy. The lumber business boomed with the cheaper transportation provided by the arrival of the railroads in Puget Sound in the late 1880s and 1890s.

In 1900, Frederick Weyerhaeuser purchased 900,000 acres of prime forest land from the Northern Pacific Railroad for $6 an acre, later increasing his holdings to over two million acres by 1913. With over six million acres today, the Weyerhaeuser Corporation is the largest lumber company in the country.

Forests cover over 23 million Washington acres, 18 million of which are commercial forests. It's difficult to look at the shaved hillsides of the Cascades and not think it offensive, but all of us use wood, the trees are replanted, and logging and wood products still employ a substantial number of Washington's workers.

Farming

Washington's Native Americans relied on hunting and food gathering rather than agriculture to supply their families' needs. It wasn't until Fort Vancouver was established in the 1820s that commercial agriculture took hold in Washington, as Hudson's Bay Company acquired a surplus of cattle to sell to the early settlers. Farming developed slowly west of the Cascades, as the heavily forested land first had to be cleared, and the acidic soils produced minimal yields. As settlers spread east of the Cascades, the wide-open spaces were perfect for cattle ranching, sheep herding, and grain growing.

Agriculture grew rapidly through the early 20th century, when the arrival of the railroads created markets and irrigation projects. Agriculture flourished during the first and second World Wars and quickly rebounded after the Depression, when refrigeration allowed Washington farmers to compete on a national scale.

In 1952, the Columbia Basin Irrigation Project opened up a half million parched acres for farming around Ephrata and Moses Lake. Today, Washington farmers and ranchers produce crops worth billions of dollars annually, over 80 percent of which is derived from agriculture east of the Cascades. The biggest money crop is wheat, grown on three million acres in eastern Washington, especially in the famous Palouse hills near Pullman. Nearly all the state's wheat is shipped overseas to Japan, Korea, Taiwan, the Philippines, and other Asian markets. Other important crops are hay, potatoes, livestock, apples, pears, cherries, grapes, onions, and other fruits and vegetables. Washington is one of the few states that grows cranberries, in the southeast corner in bogs near Willapa Bay.

Washington is probably best known for its apples, some 10 *billion* of which are grown annually, approximately 40 percent of the nation's total apple production. The center of apple growing is between Wenatchee and Chelan, but orchards can be found in many parts of the state. A majority of the apples grown in Washington are of the Red Delicious variety, though other varieties such as Gala, Braeburn, and Fuji have gained greatly in popularity within the last few years.

One of the state's fastest-growing crops is wine grapes. In 1972, Washington had just six

SALMON

Few things are as inseparably a part of the persona of the Northwest as the noble salmon. For thousands of years, coastal Native Americans such as the Salish people have relied heavily on these fish for their livelihood. The fact that salmon are born in rivers, spend much of their lives in saltwater, then return to rivers to spawn make them the perfect focus of seasonal Native rituals and ceremonies. Traveling through Washington, you're bound to spot many representations of these hook-billed fish in Native paintings, art, and totem poles.

When white settlers arrived, salmon made up a large part of their diet and economy, as well. For the better part of a century, commercial salmon fisheries operated throughout the region. Declining stocks due to overfishing and the disappearing freshwater habitats so critical to these fish have forced a shutdown of this activity to protect the very existence of local salmon species.

People here have always relied on salmon, but it's crucial to look at the role they play in the ecosystem as a whole. Salmon are absolutely critical to the survival of many local animals, such as brown bears, eagles, orcas, harbor seals, and porpoises. They serve as an excellent bellwether species, demonstrating the overall health of the estuary systems.

SALMON SPECIES IN WASHINGTON

- chinook
- chum
- coho
- pink
- sockeye
- cutthroat trout
- steelhead

wineries; today there are more than 170, and visitors come to tour the Columbia and Yakima Valleys much as they would California's wine-producing regions. Washington is now recognized as one of the prime wine producers in the country, with many award-winning wines and ten official wine-growing regions. Washington boosters point out that these valleys lie at the same latitude as France's Burgundy and Bordeaux regions. The state's largest producer of wines is Chateau Ste. Michelle, with wineries in both the Yakima Valley and Woodinville.

Fishing

Fishing is one of the state's oldest industries, as the original Native Americans on both sides of the Cascades depended on Columbia River salmon and other fish for much of their diet, and coastal Native Americans from the Neah Bay area were whalers. Commercial fishing, less important to the early settlers than logging and other industries, wasn't firmly established until the 1860s, when canneries, new salmon-fishing techniques, and new markets at home and abroad led to the industry's rapid expansion.

Until the 1980s, the Pacific Northwest salmon industry harvested more than 250,000 pounds of salmon annually, worth more than $100 million. In the 1990s, the runs collapsed due to a combination of warm oceanic currents, the destruction of spawning habitat by dams and logging, overfishing, and droughts. Ocean fishing was banned off the coast of Washington and Oregon, and except for certain tribal fisheries and a few short openings, it has remained closed.

Shipping

From the time Seattle's earliest settlers dropped a horseshoe on a clothesline into Elliott Bay to determine its depth, shipping has played an important role in the development of Puget Sound communities. Today, Seattle and Tacoma are among the most important seaports in the world.

The first goods shipped from Seattle were logs that would be used as dock pilings in San Francisco. Lumber and wood products still account for a good portion of the area's exports, particularly from smaller ports such as Everett, Port Gamble, Port Angeles, Hoquiam, Olympia, and Bellingham. Seattle and Tacoma are important containerized shipping ports, where bulk and manufactured goods from airplanes to wheat are exported to Japan, China, Taiwan, Canada, and Australia. Telecommunications equipment, cars and trucks, clothing, and petroleum products are the primary imports, arriving from Canada, Japan, Taiwan, and Hong Kong. Both the ports of Tacoma and Seattle continue to be national trade leaders, and the future for containerized shipping in Washington looks bright. Oil tankers also arrive from Alaska to supply four oil refineries in Anacortes and Ferndale.

While Seattle and Tacoma get most of the shipping attention, Columbia River ports have been doing very well, thank you, especially the deep water ports of Portland, Vancouver, Longview, and Kalama, which do a big business as terminals for wheat, corn, soda ash, logs, and other materials coming down the Columbia River bound for Pacific Rim nations. These same ports import massive amounts of alumina from Australia, limestone from Canada, and cement from China, along with countless other products.

ESSENTIALS

Getting There

The **Washington State Department of Transportation's** website (www.wsdot.wa.gov) is a good one-stop place for links to the various auto, ferry, bus, air, bike, and train options around the state.

BY AIR

Washington's two major airports are **Seattle-Tacoma International (Sea-Tac)** and **Spokane International,** served by nearly all the major carriers and a handful of smaller airlines. **Horizon Air** (a subsidiary of Alaska Airlines) (800/252-7522, www.horizonair.com) is the big "little" airline, connecting many Washington cities including Seattle, Spokane, Bellingham, Lewiston, Pasco, Port Angeles, Pullman, Walla Walla, Wenatchee, and Yakima.

BY TRAIN

Amtrak (800/872-7245, www.amtrak.com) serves Washington with two routes. The north–south route along the West Coast is aboard the **Coast Starlight,** which has service several times a day to Seattle, Tacoma, Olympia/Lacey, Centralia, Longview/Kelso, Vancouver, Portland, and south to Los Angeles. The modern and stylish **Cascades** provides daily

© WASHINGTON STATE TOURISM/JIM POTH

train connections north to Vancouver, B.C., via Edmonds, Everett, Mount Vernon, and Bellingham. The east–west route to Chicago is on the **Empire Builder,** which has daily service to Spokane, then turns southwest to Portland with stops at Pasco, Wishram, Bingen/White Salmon, and Vancouver, or to Seattle via Ephrata, Wenatchee, Everett, and Edmonds.

Note that Amtrak requires advance reservations; you can't just go down to the station and climb aboard.

BY CAR

Highways and roads are generally well maintained in Washington. The main approaches to Washington are I-5 from the north or south in the coastal area, I-90 from parts east, and I-84 from eastern Oregon.

Getting Around

BY CAR

Car Rentals

All the major car rental agencies operate at or near Seattle's Sea-Tac Airport, and any of them can be reached via their toll-free numbers or online. When reserving a car, be sure to mention if you are a member of AAA or Costco; you can often save substantially on the rates. The best deals are sometimes from locations away from the airport where the taxes are lower, but you'll need to get there from the airport and that can add to your costs. I've found that **Thrifty Car Rental** (800/847-4389, www.thrifty.com) often has some of the lowest rates; it's a good starting point for price comparisons. For wheelchair-friendly van rentals, contact **Wheelchair Getaways** (425/788-7318 or 800/642-2042, www.wheelchairgetaways.com).

Safety on the Road

From late fall to early spring, expect snow at Interstate 90's Snoqualmie Pass (between North Bend and Cle Elum in central Washington), Stevens Pass on US Highway 2, and White Pass on State Highway 12. Closures often affect Cayuse Pass on State Highway 410 and Rainy and Washington Passes on State Highway 20 (the North Cascades Highway) after the first snowfall each winter.

Snow tires or chains are frequently required on the passes, but even when they're not, it's always a good idea to carry a set of chains and emergency equipment (flares, shovel, blankets, food, and cell phone). Before you set out, call the Department of Transportation's **Mountain Pass Report** (800/695-7623, www.wsdot.wa.gov/traffic/passes); it gives road and weather conditions for all of the Cascade passes from October 15 through April 15. The website also has live cameras showing current conditions at a dozen passes in the Cascades and elsewhere.

BY BUS

Transportation Connections (www.transconnect.org) is a private, nonprofit agency whose excellent website contains links to a wide range of public transportation companies in Washington. In addition to buses, they include car sharing, cycling organizations, Amtrak, and the state ferries.

Intercity Buses

Greyhound (206/628-5526 or 800/231-2222, www.greyhound.com) serves most major cities in Washington, providing nationwide connections. Its main routes are along I-5 from Canada to Oregon, along I-90 from Seattle to Spokane, and I-82 from Ellensburg to Pendleton, Oregon.

Public Transit Buses

Washington's public buses offer a comprehensive system, with low-priced service throughout all of western Washington. The coverage is less complete east of the Cascades, but still good. Many buses have bike racks. On the Web, visit www.wsdot.wa.gov/transit/for a complete listing of buses, trains, and other travel options.

DRIVING IN DEER COUNTRY

Mule deer, white-tailed deer, and black-tailed deer thrive throughout Washington, from the woods of Western Washington to the deserts of the East. Even neighborhoods within the city of Seattle sometimes see a deer or two. Driving through deer country requires certain precautions, as even low-speed collisions can be expensive and potentially deadly.

- Be attentive during dawn and dusk. That's when deer are most active.
- Pay attention to Deer Crossing signs.
- Watch the driver ahead of you. When his brake lights come on, it could be because he's spotted a deer.
- Deer are prone to leaping out of roadside swales into the road.
- When you see one deer, be cautious – others are usually nearby.
- If you do hit a deer, try to move the carcass off of the road. If the deer was merely injured, call the nonemergency police number for your locality.

Bus Tours

A number of companies offer multi-day motor coach tours throughout the Pacific Northwest. Two of the largest are **Gray Line of Seattle** (206/626-5208 or 800/426-7532, www.graylineofseattle.com) and **Tauck World Discovery** (800/788-7885, www.tauck.com).

BY FERRY

Washington State Ferries

The Washington state ferry system (206/464-6400, www.wsdot.wa.gov/ferries) is the largest mass transit system in the state, carrying more than 26 million passengers and 11 million vehicles each year. This is the most scenic way to see the Sound, but the system also serves many commuters who ride the ferry to work each day in Seattle, Tacoma, or Everett. Ferries operate every day, including holidays.

The best sightseeing is on the Anacortes–San Juan Islands route, which once a day continues to Sidney, British Columbia. Ferries also connect Port Townsend with Keystone (Whidbey Island); Clinton (Whidbey Island) with Mukilteo (southwest of Everett); Edmonds with Kingston (on the Kitsap Peninsula); Seattle with Winslow (Bainbridge Island) and Bremerton; Fauntleroy (southwest Seattle) with Southworth (southeast of Bremerton) and Vashon Island; and Tacoma (at Point Defiance) with Tahlequah (at the south end of Vashon Island).

The ferry system operates on a first-come, first-served basis, with reservations available only for the international routes from Anacortes to Sidney, B.C., and from Orcas Island or San Juan Island to Sidney. Foot passengers never need to wait, but those in vehicles may find themselves watching several ferries come and go before they can get onboard at peak hours.

The larger ferries have food service, vending machines dispensing candy bars and junk food, and beer; the smaller boats have vending machines only. Pets on leashes are allowed on the car decks or in carrying containers on passenger decks. Bikes, kayaks, and canoes are also allowed onboard for a small surcharge.

Other Ferries

A number of small Washington ferries provide service around the state, including service to Anderson Island, Guemes Island, and Lummi Island within Puget Sound, along with three Columbia River ferries.

Several private companies offer ferry connections to Vancouver Island. Take the MV *Coho* (360/457-4491, www.cohoferry.com) from Port Angeles to Victoria, B.C., across the Strait of Juan de Fuca. From Seattle, the *Victoria Clipper* (800/888-2535, www.clippervacations.com) has passenger-only service to Victoria daily in summer.

Independent tour and charter boat companies in Seattle, Tacoma, Everett, Bellingham, the San Juan Islands, Westport, and other coastal cities offer sight-seeing, fishing, and whale-watching tours throughout the year.

BY BICYCLE

Something about cycling makes a visit seem so much more intimate than just breezing through in a car. If you're willing to make the effort, Washington offers almost limitless rewards for the two-wheeled. Whidbey Island, for example, offers miles of under-traveled roads, sunnier weather than Seattle, and great state parks where you can rest. Many of the other Puget Sound islands, such as the San Juans, Vashon, Bainbridge, Mercer, and Camano Islands, are also easy to get to, are as challenging a ride as you choose to tackle, and have little automobile traffic.

Even the more populated city centers strive for bike friendliness, perhaps best embodied by Seattle's Burke-Gilman Trail. The 14-mile paved path runs from the scenic industrial ruins at Gasworks Park all the way to Kenmore at the north end of Lake Washington. There, it hooks up with the Sammamish River Trail, which goes right past Woodinville's Chateau Ste. Michelle and Columbia wineries—great places to stop for lunch with a bottle of wine.

In West Seattle, the road and bike path from Alki Beach to Lincoln Park is a popular 12-mile loop. Five Mile Drive in Tacoma's Point Defiance Park is open to cars as well, but cyclists are given a wide berth; the road passes through an impressive old-growth forest.

The Washington State Department of Transportation (360/705-7000, www.ci.seattle.wa.us) publishes bicycle maps and guidelines, including a very helpful statewide map showing traffic data and road widths to help determine which roads are the safest.

Sports and Recreation

The beauty of Washington is that you can surf on a Westport beach one day, go horseback riding the next, and be on the edge of a Mt. Rainier glacier the following day. The Pacific coast has long beaches for playing in the sand, fishing, or beachcombing; the various national parks and forests offer backcountry hiking at its finest in the Olympics, Cascades, and northeast Washington; Puget Sound is a haven for sea kayaking and sailing; Columbia Gorge offers some of the finest windsurfing on the planet; anglers love the countless lakes, reservoirs, and rivers; river rafters and kayakers head down the state's white-water rivers throughout the summer; and cyclists discover roads and trails of every description. In the winter, the options shift to snow sports, and Washington has 'em all, including skiing of all types, snowboarding, sledding, skating, and snowmobiling.

ORGANIZATIONS

The Mountaineers

Established in 1906, The Mountaineers (bookstore at 300 3rd Ave. W, Seattle, 206/284-6310, www.mountaineers.org) is a 15,000-member organization of outdoor enthusiasts with a strong environmental bent. Based in Seattle, the club organizes hiking, climbing, cycling, skiing, snowshoeing, sea kayaking, and many other activities and events throughout the year. They even have a singles group where you can meet others with similar interests. Membership costs $50 per year (plus an initiation fee of $35), and members receive *The Mountaineer,* a monthly magazine listing local activities, along with 20 percent discounts on their many excellent books.

Washington Department of Fish and Wildlife

This state agency (360/902-2200, www.wdfw.wa.gov) is in charge of fishing, hunting, and clamming in Washington. Contact them for current game fish regulations, or pick up the fat ***Fishing in Washington*** booklet at sporting goods or other stores that sell fishing licenses.

© WASHINGTON STATE TOURISM/JIM POTH

deep sea fishing on the Washington coast

PUBLIC LANDS

Almost 45 percent of Washington's 42.6 million acres are publicly held. The rules, regulations, permit requirements, and fees on public lands change constantly, especially Forest Service and Park Service lands, so check with a local ranger station before heading out or purchase *Washington's Backcountry Access Guide,* an excellent booklet that explains regulations in each area. Buy it online at www.mountaineers.org.

National Parks

Washington's three major national parks attract millions of visitors each year and offer must-see sights. **North Cascades National Park** (www.nps.gov/noca) covers a half million acres of wild mountain country that includes more than 300 glaciers, hundreds of miles of hiking trails, and the 55-mile long Lake Chelan. **Mount Rainier National Park** (www.nps.gov/mora) contains the state's tallest and best summit: 14,411-foot Mt. Rainier. Hiking trails encircle the peak, and scenic mountain roads provide lingering views of the mountain meadows, subalpine forests, and glaciers that make this one of the nation's crown jewels. **Olympic National Park** (www.nps.gov/olym) is famous for the lush west-side rainforests with enormous old-growth trees, but it also has dramatic mountainous country and the incomparable Pacific coastline.

Forest Service Lands

United States Forest Service lands cover more than nine million acres in Washington state within seven national forests. These forests are managed for multiple uses, but the emphasis has—until recently at least—been on logging. Concerns over spotted owl survival led to a moratorium on timber harvesting in many areas. The National Forests of Washington also contain 24 wilderness areas that cover more than 2.5 million acres. Over half of the total acreage falls within the three largest: Glacier Peak Wilderness (576,900 acres), Pasaytan Wilderness (530,000 acres), and Alpine Lakes Wilderness (393,360 acres). The Forest Service

FOREST ROAD NUMBERING SYSTEM

The way the Forest Service numbers its roads can be inscrutable to outsiders, who might find it a bit esoteric. Here's all you need to know: If you see a road with two numbers, say Forest Service Road 25, that is a main arterial. These are typically well maintained, either paved or very level gravel roads that are passable to passenger vehicles. A road with a four- or three-digit number is a collector or local road. These are the more rugged roads that you would typically think of when you imagine a Forest Service road. Try these only with high-clearance and four-wheel-drive vehicles. And be careful! There aren't usually any guardrails on forest roads.

also manages Mount St. Helens National Volcanic Monument and the Columbia River Gorge National Scenic Area, two of the state's most interesting natural areas.

Many Forest Service trailheads now charge user fees. Day use is generally $5 per vehicle per day, or pay $30 for an annual **Northwest Forest Pass** (877/874-6775, www.discovernw.org), which can be used in most national forests in Washington. The plus side is that 80 percent of this money is used to maintain local recreation areas and trails. For details on recreation in the forests, contact the headquarters offices below or stop by a local ranger station.

Colville National Forest (Colville, 509/684-7000, www.fs.fed.us/cvnf)

Gifford Pinchot National Forest (Vancouver, 360/750-5000, www.fs.fed.us/gpnf)

Columbia River Gorge National Scenic Area (Hood River, Oregon, 541/386-2333, www.fs.fed.us/r6/Columbia)

Mount St. Helens National Volcanic Monument (Amboy, 360/247-3900, www.fs.fed.us/gpnf)

Mount Baker/Snoqualmie National Forest (Mountlake Terrace, 425/775-9702 or 800/627-0062, www.fs.fed.us/r6/mbs)

Okanogan National Forest (Okanogan, 509/826-3275, www.fs.fed.us/r6/Okanogan)

Olympic National Forest (Olympia, 360/956-2402, www.fs.fed.us/r6/Olympic)

Wenatchee National Forest (Wenatchee, 509/662-4335, www.fs.fed.us/r6/Wenatchee)

Umatilla National Forest (Walla Walla, 509/522-6290, www.fs.fed.us/r6/uma)

State Parks

The state of Washington manages 125 state parks covering over 230,000 acres. State park facilities are surprisingly diverse, including several historic forts (Fort Townsend, Fort Flagler, Fort Ebey, Fort Worden, and others), many miles of sandy ocean beaches (including Grayland Beach, Fort Canby, Long Beach, Ocean City, and Pacific Beach), one of the largest public telescopes in the region (Goldendale Observatory), a park devoted to whale-watching (Lime Kiln), a campground where Lewis and Clark spent a night (Lewis and Clark Trail), and an incredible waterfalls surrounded by desolate eastern Washington land (Palouse Falls). In addition, the state park system includes numerous historic sites, environmental learning centers for school kids, and 40 marine parks, many of which are accessible only by boat.

A fine source for state park information is the *Parks Guide* produced by Washington State Parks. For this publication, park brochures, or reservation information, contact the Washington State Parks and Recreation Commission (360/902-8844, www.parks.wa.gov).

WINTER SPORTS

Downhill Skiing and Snowboarding

Washington's best ski and snowboard areas are stretched along the Cascades from Mt. Baker to Mt. Rainier. Snow on the western slopes of the Cascades is usually wet and heavy, but some ski areas on the eastern slopes, such as

Mission Ridge, have powdery snow. Visitors centers carry the *Washington State Winter Recreation Guide.*

Cross-Country Skiing

Cross-country, or Nordic, skiing is particularly popular on the eastern slopes of the mountains, in part because the snow is more powdery and the weather is usually sunny and clear. Some of the best cross-country skiing is in the Methow Valley, with close to 100 miles of trail marked, the majority of which are groomed. The **Methow Valley Sports Trail Association** (509/996-3287, www.mvsta.com) provides a hotline for ski-touring information and a brochure showing the major trails. Other popular cross-country skiing areas include Mount Tahoma Trails (near Mount Rainier National Park), Echo Valley (near Lake Chelan), Hurricane Ridge (Olympic National Park), Leavenworth Winter Sports Club, Stevens Pass Nordic Center, White Pass Nordic Center, and Summit Nordic Center. Most of these areas groom trails for both traditional and skate-skiing.

The state maintains more than 40 **Sno-Parks** in the Cascades and eastern mountains, with nearby skiing trails (sometimes groomed, sometimes not). The permits required to park at these plowed areas are available from retail outlets throughout the state. The cost is $9 for a one-day pass, or $21 for the entire winter season, with the money helping to pay for plowing, signs, trail grooming, and maintenance. The State Parks and Recreation Commission (360/902-8844, www.parks.wa.gov/winter) sells Sno-Park permits and has maps and brochures of groomed cross-country ski trails and other ski areas.

For the current snow avalanche danger in the backcountry, contact the Forest Service (206/526-6677) or the **Northwest Weather and Avalanche Center** (www.nwac.noaa.gov).

Snowmobiling

The state maintains over 2,200 miles of groomed snowmobile trails, primarily in the Cascades and northeast corner of the state. For a map showing snowmobile trails and a publication on snowmobile use in the state, contact Washington State Park Recreation Division (360/902-8844, www.parks.wa.gov/winter).

CAMPING

State Parks

Washington maintains more than 80 state parks with campgrounds, offering clean and scenic accommodations across the state. Tent sites are around $14, RV hookups (not available in all campgrounds) cost around $20. Note: if you pitch a tent in a site with electricity, you will be charged the RV rate. Some state parks also offer more primitive campsites for $6 that attract hikers and cyclists. Most park sites include a picnic table, barbecue grill, nearby running water, garbage removal, a flush toilet, and coin-operated hot showers. Many state parks are closed October–March; those that remain open often have limited winter camping facilities. Most campground gates close at 10 P.M., so get there early!

Campground reservations (888/226-7688, www.parks.wa.gov) can be made for nearly half of the state parks and are available as little as two days in advance, or as much as 11 months ahead of time. A $7 reservation fee is charged in addition to the first night's campground fee and can be paid by credit card or check. The general state parks phone number is 360/902-8844.

The state also maintains 40 or so marine state parks in the San Juan Islands and around Puget Sound. Moorage occupancy is limited to 72 hours and cannot be reserved in advance. The **Cascadia Marine Trail System** includes more than 35 campsites around Puget Sound available to sea kayakers and users of other small human-powered or sailing vessels. Get maps and information from the **Washington Water Trails Association** (206/545-9161, www.wwta.org).

Other Public Campgrounds

Campsites at national forests and parks are scattered across Washington. Some sites are free, but most campgrounds charge $8–12. More than 60 Forest Service campgrounds are reservable for an extra fee of $9. Call **ReserveUSA** (877/444-6777) or make reservations on the Web at www.recreation.gov. With a few exceptions, Park Service campgrounds are not reservable, so get there early on busy summer weekends!

Washington's Department of Natural Resources (DNR; 800/527-3305, www.dnr.wa.gov) manages millions of acres of public lands in the state, primarily on a multiple-use basis. Campsites can be found at DNR forests throughout the state; DNR produces a helpful map showing more than 80 free public campgrounds on its land.

Private RV Parks

Every town of any size has at least one private RV park. These private campgrounds generally charge $3–5 for showers if you're not camping there. People traveling in RVs often find that they prefer private parks to state and national parks, since they have better amenities.

Accommodations and Food

ACCOMMODATIONS

Lodging in Washington covers the complete spectrum, from five-star luxury accommodations where a king would feel pampered all the way down to seedy motels so tawdry that even the roaches think twice. The law of supply and demand holds fairly true when it comes to motel rates. You'll pay the least at motels in rural areas away from the main tourist track, and the most at popular destinations in peak season. This is especially true on midsummer weekends for such places as the San Juan Islands, Chelan, Leavenworth, Whidbey Island, or Long Beach, and for Seattle and vicinity year-round. At many of the resort towns, you may need to reserve months ahead of time for the peak season, and a minimum stay of two or more nights may be required. It always pays to call ahead.

Throughout this book I have listed only two prices for most lodging places: one person (single, or s) and two people (double, or d). The rates do not include state tax (eight percent) and local taxes, which can sometimes be substantial. These prices are not set in stone. If a convention is in town or the motel is nearly full, they may rise; if the economy is tight, or it's late February at a beach resort, you may pay considerably less.

For a complete listing of motels, hotels, and bed-and-breakfasts in Washington, request a copy of the free ***Washington State Visitors Guide*** (877/906-1001, www.stayinwashington.com) or pick it up at larger visitors centers around the state.

Hostels

Hostels offer the cheapest lodging options in Washington, with bunk bed accommodations for just $15–30 per person. They are a good choice for single travelers on a budget, or anyone who wants to meet other independent travelers. Although commonly called youth hostels, these really are not just for high school and college folks; you're likely to meet adventurous people of all ages. The official versions are managed by **Hostelling International** (also known as AYH), with statewide headquarters at the Seattle hostel (206/281-7306, www.hiayh.org). At these hostels, guests stay in dormitory-style rooms, have access to a kitchen, and generally do a cleanup chore. You'll need to bring your own sleeping bag or linens, and an annual membership fee is required (nonmembers pay an introductory membership and higher overnight rates). A variety of restrictions may put a crimp in your plans: many hostels kick you out around 10 A.M. and remain closed till 5 P.M. or so, and no alcohol is allowed. Some also have a curfew. Most have a few spaces for couples who want their own room, but you may need to reserve these in advance. Instead of turning on the TV set, you'll meet travelers from all over the world and discover must-see sights and great out-of-the way cafés.

Private hostels are less predictable, with fewer rules. Alcohol is generally allowed, and you won't have to be back before the witching hour, but they can be more chaotic, noisy, and even downright grungy at times. These range all over the place, from the rambling old school hostel at Bingen that is now a destination for windsurfers to the funky Doe Bay Village Resort where the clothing-optional hot tub is filled most evenings. Seattle has a private hostel, and others are found in Port Angeles and south of Forks on the Olympic Peninsula, in Republic in the northeast corner of the state, in the town of Eldon on Hood Canal, and at Ashford near Mt. Rainier. All these official and unofficial hostels are described in accommodations sections of this book. A good website for AYH and private hostel information is www.hostels.com.

Motels and Hotels

The largest cities—Seattle, Spokane, Tacoma, Bellevue, Olympia—obviously have the greatest range of accommodations. All of these cities, without exception, have reasonably priced lodging just outside city limits, so you can stay a half hour or less away and spend the extra money having fun. If you're staying at the pricier chains, be sure to always ask about discounts such as AAA member rates, senior discounts, corporate or government rates, business travel fares, military rates, or other special deals.

In Seattle or Spokane, you can stay at the budget chains near the airport; in Tacoma, stay up the road in Fife. Make reservations ahead of time whenever possible; the least expensive rooms fill up fast. Finding a room—any room—can be extremely difficult in summer (even on weekdays) at popular resort areas such as Lake Chelan, the San Juan Islands, the national parks, or along the ocean. Again, staying a half hour from the action can better your chances of finding a room as well as saving you money—try the motels in Wenatchee when Lake Chelan is filled up, or stay in Forks or Port Angeles instead of at Olympic National Park lodges.

Bed-and-Breakfasts

More than 500 bed-and-breakfasts are scattered around the state of Washington. Some parts of the state, particularly Port Townsend, are filled with restored turn-of-the-20th-century Victorian homes that have been converted to B&Bs. Other B&Bs are old farmhouses, lodges, cottages, or modern homes with private entrances. In most cases, a room at a B&B will cost as much as one of the better motel rooms. You may miss the cable TV and room service, but you'll get a filling breakfast, a chance to spend time with a local, plus peace and quiet.

Many B&Bs don't allow kids, and almost none allow pets or smoking; probably a third of the rooms won't have a private bath (though one is probably just a few steps away). Bed-and-breakfasts are a fine way to get acquainted with a new area and a good choice for people traveling alone, since you'll have opportunities to meet fellow travelers. Note, however, that there is often little or no difference between the price a single person pays and that paid by a couple.

The **Washington Bed and Breakfast Guild** (800/647-2918, www.wbbg.com) produces a brochure describing its members. **Seattle B&B Association** (206/547-1020 or 800/348-5630, www.seattlebandbs.com) also has a brochure, and you'll find links to many of Seattle's better places at its website. **A Pacific Reservation Service** (206/439-7677 or 800/684-2932, www.seattlebedandbreakfast.com) offers reservations at 225 B&Bs, houses, cottages, houseboats, condos, and lodges throughout the Pacific Northwest.

FOOD AND DRINK

Over the years, local produce and preferences have come to define "Northwest cuisine." Fresh salmon is popular and can be found on virtually every restaurant's menu. Red snapper, halibut, and cod are also served fresh almost everywhere in western Washington. Less common are the local Olympia oysters and geoduck clams. As you head east, the seafood is generally frozen, though some restaurants pride themselves on their fresh fish. Steaks are often imported from the Midwest and are generally very good.

© KITSAP PENINSULA VISITORS BUREAU/JEAN BOYLE

Roadside stands and farmers markets display the many local products available.

Farm Fresh

Western Washington is also known for its strawberries, blackberries, and various other kinds of berries. For a detailed directory of organic farms, natural foods grocers, and organic restaurants, and a complete listing of 70 or so farmers markets, contact the **Washington State Farmers Market Association** (206/706-5198, www.wafarmersmarkets.com). The many farms around Puget Sound are listed in a free ***Farm Fresh Guide*** available in local visitors centers or online at www.pugetsound-fresh.org.

Eastern Washington is the place to go for fresh fruit and produce. Washington apples are mostly of the Red and Golden Delicious, Gala, Braeburn, Fuji, and Granny Smith varieties. Many other kinds of fruit are grown along the central corridor—cherries, peaches, and apricots. The Walla Walla sweet onion is reputedly mild enough to bite into raw, like an apple, and it is sold in gift packs. Asparagus, pears, and berries of all kinds are also big eastern Washington crops.

Beer and Wine

Washington is home to several microbreweries. The larger ones—such as the Redhook Ale Brewery in Woodinville—offer tours and tasting.

Washington wines have become world-class in the last decade or so, winning awards and gaining in popularity across the country. Most of Washington's wine grapes come from vineyards in Yakima Valley and Columbia River Valley, and wineries line the highway between Yakima and the Tri-Cities and into Walla Walla.

For details on the state's 170 wineries, see the ***Touring the Washington Wine Country*** booklet, available in visitors centers around the state or directly from the Washington Wine Commission (206/667-9463, www.washingtonwine.org).

Tips for Travelers

ACCESS FOR TRAVELERS WITH DISABILITIES

In existence since 1977, the nonprofit **Alliance of People with disAbilities** (206/545-7055 or 877/539-0212, www.disabilitypride.org) works to provide advocacy, education, and other assistance for people with significant disabilities. The **Washington Department of Transportation's** website (www.wsdot.wa.gov/choices) has details on accessible transportation choices. **Wheelchair Getaways** (888/376-1500, www.wheelchairgetaways.com) rents wheelchair-friendly vans in Seattle.

Washington is a leader in developing barrier-free recreation sites on federal and state lands, and the state publishes a detailed ***Accessible Outdoor Recreation Guide.*** Find it at visitors centers, by calling 360/902-3000, or on the Web at www.parks.wa.gov/ada-rec. See also ***Accessible Trails in Washington's Backcountry,*** published by The Mountaineers (www.mountaineers.org).

GAY AND LESBIAN TRAVELERS

Gay and lesbian travelers will find Washington as open-minded as it is beautiful. It's home to a populous LGBT community, particularly in the Seattle metropolitan area. Even in most rural parts of the state, gay and lesbians will feel safe and accepted by Washingtonians.

While there's not really any kind of "lavender line" in Seattle, much of the LGBT nightlife and cultural pulse is centered around the colorful Capitol Hill neighborhood. Here you'll find a wide variety of gay and lesbian bars, as well as the **Seattle LGBT Center** (1122 East Pike St., 206/323-5428, www.seattlelgbt.org), a community center that frequently holds cultural events and whose volunteers are quite willing

DOG PARKS

Washington is a tremendously dog-friendly state, with its open trails, pet-friendly hotels, and millions of birds and squirrels to chase. You and your best friend never have to go far to have an adventure – Washington is full of truly excellent dog parks.

Marymoor Park is the premier pooch park west of the Cascades, featuring 40 leash-free acres of canine recreation. Play fetch in the grassy fields or splash around in the mellow Sammamish Slough. This well-landscaped and flawlessly maintained park is sure to set tails wagging.

I-5 Colonnade Dog Park is near downtown Seattle. This unique park is nestled underneath a lofty I-5 overpass, although it's easy to forget about the hustle and bustle a hundred feet over your head. This long, terraced park is a great place for socializing or fetch, and even provides complete shelter from the rain.

The **SCRAPS Dog Park** in Spokane is the first off-leash park in Spokane County. A repurposed rest-area, the park is a three-acre dog party by the East's big city.

Fort Steilacoom Park in Lakewood near Tacoma hosts a great park, divided into sections for big dogs and little dogs. Near the former site of an historic mental hospital, the park features open areas for running as well as shady groves and sniff-tastic brush.

When in Yakima, check out the **Norman & Nellie Byrd Off-leash Dog Park** along the Yakima Greenway Path. It can seem a bit deserted at times, so be sure to bring a few toys if you go.

The city of **Vancouver** has a fascinating policy on off-leash dogs, featuring over 30 parks and areas that have off-leash hours at least part of the day. From beaches to fields, there is something for any sort of dog here. Check vancouver.ca/parks/info/dogparks for the latest hours and locations.

to offer referrals and other information about the city and region to area visitors.

Seattle is also home to one of the largest Pride (www.seattlepride.org) parades in the West. Held each June, the parade typically winds through downtown along 4th Avenue.

TRAVELING WITH PETS

With its wide open spaces, mountainous trails, and temperate weather, Washington is a rewarding place to travel with your furry companions. Where appropriate, I've tried to include information about pet-friendly lodging, parks, and trails. In Seattle, I'd have to say my personal favorite pet-friendly lodging is at the attentive **Alexis Hotel,** which not only accepts pups with open paws but also offers pet sitting.

As you venture further afield, you'll find that the state is fairly liberal about its wilderness pet policies when compared to other western states, such as California. Leashed dogs are allowed at campgrounds and trails within the state park system and banned only from designated swimming areas at those parks. You can also bring your leashed dog throughout all national forest land except designated wilderness areas.

Though leashed dogs can visit Mount Rainier, Olympic, and North Cascades National Parks, they are only allowed in paved areas and developed campgrounds, not on trails. The sole exception is along the Pacific Crest Trail, which allows dogs on leashes no longer than six feet.

Health and Safety

GIARDIA

Although Washington's backcountry lakes and streams may appear clean, you could be risking a debilitating sickness by drinking untreated water. The protozoan Giardia lamblia is found throughout the state, spread by both humans and animals (including beaver, hence the nickname "Beaver Fever"). This parasite usually takes up to a week after contact to present itself, and the cramping, nausea, and diarrhea can last up to 25 days.

The disease is curable with drugs, but it's always best to carry safe drinking water on any trip, or to boil any water taken from creeks or lakes. Bringing water to a full boil is sufficient to kill Giardia and other harmful organisms. Another option—most folks choose this one—is to use a water filter (available in camping stores). Note, however, that these may not filter out other organisms such as Campylobactor jejuni, bacteria that are just 0.2 microns in size. Chlorine and iodine are not always reliable, taste foul, and can be unhealthy.

If you think you have picked up Giardia, be sure to see a medical professional immediately. It's seldom life-threatening but can cause long-term health damage if left untreated.

HYPOTHERMIA

Anyone who has spent time in the outdoors knows the dangers of exposure to cold, wet, and windy conditions. Even at temperatures well above freezing, hypothermia—the reduction of the body's inner core temperature—can prove fatal. The ailment can strike during the summer as well, so always be prepared! In the higher elevations of the Cascades and Olympics the weather is unpredictable, and the temperature can drop dramatically in a matter of hours or even minutes.

In the early stages, hypothermia causes uncontrollable shivering, followed by a loss of coordination, slurred speech, and then a rapid descent into unconsciousness and death. Always travel prepared for sudden changes in the weather. Wear clothing that insulates well and that holds its heat when wet. Wool and polypropylene are far better than cotton, and clothes should be worn in layers to provide better trapping of heat and a chance to adjust to conditions more easily. Always carry a wool hat, since your head loses more heat than any other part of the body. Bring a waterproof shell to cut the wind. Put on rain gear *before* it starts raining; head back or set up camp when the weather looks threatening; eat candy bars, keep active, or snuggle with a friend in a down bag to generate warmth.

If someone in your party begins to show signs of hypothermia, don't take any chances, even if the person denies needing help. Get the victim out of the wind, strip off his clothes, and put him in a dry sleeping bag on an insulating pad. Skin-to-skin contact is the best way to warm a hypothermic person, and that means you'll also need to strip and climb in the sleeping bag. Do not give the victim alcohol or hot drinks, and do not try to warm the person too quickly since it could lead to heart failure. Once the victim has recovered, get medical help as soon as possible. Ideally, you're far better off keeping close tabs on everyone in the group and seeking shelter *before* exhaustion and hypothermia set in.

TICKS

Ticks can be an annoyance in parts of Washington, particularly lower-elevation brushy and grassy areas in the spring and early summer. They drop onto unsuspecting humans and other animals to suck blood and can spread Lyme disease or relapsing fever, although this is rare in Washington.

When hiking, avoid ticks by tucking pant legs into boots and shirts into pants, using insect repellents containing DEET, and carefully inspecting your clothes while outside. Light-colored clothing (easier to see the ticks) and broad hats may also help. Check your body while hiking and immediately after the trip. If possible, remove ticks before they become embedded in your skin. If one does become attached, use tweezers to gently remove the tick, being sure to get the head. Try not to crush the body since this may release more bacteria. Apply a triple antibiotic ointment such as Neosporin to the area, and monitor the bite area for two weeks. You may want to save the tick in a jar with some damp tissue paper for later identification.

OTHER BACKCOUNTRY SAFETY TIPS

The most important part of surviving—and enjoying—the backcountry is to be prepared. Know where you're going: Get maps, camping information, and weather and trail conditions from a ranger before setting out. Don't hike alone. Two are better than one, and three are better than two—if someone gets hurt, one person can stay with the injured party and one can go for help. Bring more than enough food so hunger won't cause you to continue when weather conditions say stop. Tell someone where you're going and when you'll be back.

Always carry the **10 essentials:** map, compass, water bottle, first-aid kit, flashlight, matches (or lighter) and fire starter, knife, extra clothing (a full set, in case you fall in a stream) including rain gear, food, and sunglasses—especially if you're hiking on snow. In addition, many hikers now carry cellular phones in areas where the coverage allows for communication.

Check your ego at the trailhead; stop for the night when the weather gets bad—even if it's 2 P.M.—or head back. Don't press on when you're exhausted—tired hikers are sloppy hikers, and even a small injury can be disastrous in the woods.

Information and Services

MONEY

Foreign currency can be changed at Sea-Tac airport or in downtown Seattle exchange bureaus. **Travelers checks** are the safest way to carry money, but buy them from a well-known U.S. company such as American Express, Bank of America, or Visa. They are accepted without charge in most stores and businesses. It's not a good idea to travel with travelers checks in non-U.S. currency, since they are only accepted at a few banks and are a time-consuming hassle.

Automated teller machines are ubiquitous in Washington state. Find an up-to-date listing of Cirrus system ATMs at 800/424-7787 or www.mastercard.com; for the Plus system, 800/843-7587 or www.visa.com/atms.

The major **credit cards**—especially Visa and Master Card—are accepted virtually everywhere. For many travelers this is the easiest way to access funds while traveling.

COMMUNICATIONS AND MEDIA

Telephone

Washington is broken up into five distinct area codes. Numbers within Seattle bear 206 prefixes, while those in the Eastside and Seattle's surrounding suburbs use the 425 area code. In and around Tacoma and Olympia, numbers start with 253. The rest of Western Washington bears the catch-all 360 area code, while Eastern Washington numbers use the 509 prefix.

Currently the state only requires 10-digit dialing between area codes, not within them. When placing a long distance call, be sure to dial a 1 first. Otherwise, as is the case when calling between Seattle and the Eastside, simply dial the 10 digits and you'll be patched through.

Internet

Washington is an extremely technologically savvy state, so finding an open internet connection in your travels should be a fairly easy task. Most hotels, motels, and bed-and-breakfasts offer some sort of internet connectivity, though many still charge for the privilege. The luxury hotels in Seattle are particularly guilty of doing so, which is funny considering most chain motels offer Wi-Fi at no extra cost.

Similarly, most coffee shops and many restaurants in town also offer Wi-Fi gratis, though it will usually set you back at least the cost of a latte. If you're pinching pennies or if you're traveling without a computer, lean on the local library systems, many of which across the state provide free Wi-Fi connectivity or the use of an Internet-enabled PC for non-cardholders.

The city of Seattle also provides free Wi-Fi connectivity in limited areas of town as part of an ongoing pilot project. One can access the free network, which is named "seattlewifi" in the SSID, from the U District and Columbia City neighborhoods, and within City Hall, Occidental Park in Pioneer Square, Westlake Park downtown, and Victor Steinbrueck Park near the market.

Frequent ferry travelers can also find Wi-Fi aboard Washington State Ferries, though there is a fee for the service (www.boingo.com/ferrywifi, $7.95 per connection).

Newspapers and Magazines

Maybe it's the rain, but Seattleites and Washingtonians in general are big readers. As a result, you'll likely encounter a full spectrum of newspapers, magazines, pamphlets, and newsletters in your travels.

In Seattle, the paper of record is *The Seattle Times.* Alternative papers, *The Stranger* and *Seattle Weekly,* give their mainstream journalism sisters and brothers hell with a more edgy breed of features and a pretty robust rundown of entertainment happenings.

Seattle is also home to not one, but two slick city glossies, *Seattle Magazine* and *Seattle Metropolitan Magazine,* the latter of which I prefer for its quirky storytelling and imaginative photography and art direction.

In Tacoma, the locals are informed by *The News Tribune,* while in Olympia they read *The Olympian.*

Across the mountains, *The Spokane Spokesman Review* is the biggest name in media, along with the *Yakima Herald.*

The state is also home to numerous other hometown weeklies. To get the scoop on which towns produce a paper, visit www.usnpl.com/wanews.php for a cheat sheet.

MAPS AND TOURIST INFORMATION

For a free travel packet that includes the very helpful ***Washington State Visitors Guide,*** contact Washington State Tourism (800/544-1800, www.experience washington.com). Its website provides comprehensive details and links on Washington travel. You can also pick up maps and brochures in person at the larger visitors centers around Washington.

For details on Washington's federal lands, visit the **Outdoor Recreation Information Center** inside the Seattle REI store (222 Yale Ave. N, 206/470-4060). It is staffed by National Park Service and Forest Service personnel who can answer your questions on hiking trails, campgrounds, and backcountry access. Ranger stations at the national parks and forests can sell you forest and topographic maps and provide campground and trail information and other printed material.

RESOURCES

Suggested Reading

FOOD AND WINE

Calcott, Katy. *The Food Lover's Guide to Seattle* Seattle: Sasquatch Books, 2004. A comprehensive look at the city's rich crop of greengrocers, bakeries, cheese shops, wine specialists, and much more.

Gregutt, Paul. *Washington Wines and Wineries: The Essential Guide.* Berkeley: University of California Press, 2007. A refreshing primer on the state's favorite libation, with details on varietals, growers, and tasting rooms.

Matthews, Sara. *Washington: The State of Wine.* Portland, OR: Graphic Arts Center Publishing Company, 2006. A vivid pictorial of Washington's vitocultural scenery.

Rex-Johnson, Braiden and Jackie Johnston. *Pacific Northwest Wining and Dining.* Indianapolis: Wiley, 2007. A storytelling cookbook featuring regional recipes, stories about area dining institutions and a collection of photos that will satisfy the eyes if not the stomach.

HISTORY AND CULTURE

Clark, Ella. *Indian Legends of the Pacific Northwest.* Berkeley: University of California Press, 2003. Learn the folktales of regional natives.

Hayes, Derek. *Historical Atlas of the Pacific Northwest.* Seattle: Sasquatch Books, 2002. Very informative atlas depicting the many faces of the Northwest in map form, from the earliest explorers to the present day.

Kirk, Ruth, and Carmela Alexander. *Exploring Washington's Past: A Road Guide to History.* Seattle: University of Washington Press, 1996. A town-by-town description of hundreds of historical sights around the state.

Roe, Joann *Ranald MacDonald: Pacific Rim Adventurer.* Pullman: Washington State University Press, 1997. The incredible story of a man almost unknown in America but revered in Japan. MacDonald was an adventurer whose daring exploits helped open Japan to the outside world.

Speidel, William. *Sons of the Profits.* Seattle: Nettle Creek Publishing Co., 2003. Written by the quirky founder of the Seattle Underground Tour, this is an offbeat look at the colorful characters of Seattle's past.

Swan, James G. *The Northwest Coast Or, Three Years' Residence in Washington Territory. 1857.* Seattle: University of Washington Press, 1992. A fascinating report of life on the frontier with both whites and Native Americans depicted.

NATURAL SCIENCES

Alt, David D., and Donald W. Hyndman. *Roadside Geology of Washington.* Missoula, MT: Mountain Press Publishing Co., 1986. A great book for anyone with an interest in geology, with easy-to-understand descriptions of how volcanoes, glaciers, floods, and other processes shaped the state's topography over the eons.

Duane, J. *The Beachcomber' S Guide to Seashore Life in the Pacific Northwest.* Vancouver, British Columbia:Harbour Publishing, 1999. Identify shells, rocks and other seaside finds with this handy tome.

Kozloff, Eugene N. *Plants and Animals of the Pacific Northwest.* Seattle: University of Washington Press, 1978. It may be older than this author, but still the most thorough book of its kind.

Whitney, Stephen and Rob Sandelin. *Field Guide to the Cascades & Olympics.* Seattle: The Mountaineers, 2004. An easily-packable, waterproof guide to flora and fauna perfect for long hikes and camping trips.

HIKING AND CLIMBING

Beckey, Fred. *Cascade Alpine Guide: Climbing and High Routes.* Seattle: The Mountaineers, 2000-2009. Four volumes of very detailed Cascade climbing routes, plus historical information and photos.

Burton, Joan and Ira Spring. *Best Hikes with Children in Western Washington.* Seattle: The Mountaineers, 2006. Having kids doesn't have to mean the end of your days on the trail. A two-volume guide to short hikes, all featuring lakes, waterfalls, views, or other points of interest that will motivate kids of all ages.

Copeland, Craig and Kathy. *Hiking from Here to Wow North Cascades.* Berkeley: Wilderness Press. Skip the standard hikes and go straight to the ones that make you say "Wow" by perusing the lineup in this guide.

Landers, Rich. *100 Hikes in the Inland Northwest.* Seattle: The Mountaineers, 2003. Descriptions, photos, and maps of hikes in eastern Washington plus parts of Idaho, Montana, and Oregon.

Manning, Harvey and Penny Manning. *Walks & Hikes in the Foothills and Lowlands Around Puget Sound.* Seattle: The Mountaineers, 1995. No recent updates, but still a classic. This is a great guide to easy summer strolls and snow-free winter hikes.

Molvar, Erik. *Hiking Olympic National Park* Helena: Falcon Press, 2008. A popular guide to the Olympics.

Wood, Robert L. *Olympic Mountains Trail Guide.* Seattle: The Mountaineers, 2000. Detailed trail descriptions, maps, and photos of national park and national forest trails on the Olympic Peninsula.

OTHER OUTDOOR RECREATION

Blair, Seabury. *Backcountry Ski! Washington: The Best Trails and Descents for Free-Heelers and Snowboarders.* Seattle: Sasquatch Books, 2002. Telemark skiers and other backcountry ski afficianados on the hunt for the best drops would do well to flip through this book.

Landers, Rich, Dan Hensen, Vern Huser and Doug North. *Paddling Washington: 100 Flatwater and Whitewater Routes in Washington State and the Inland Northwest.* Seattle: The Mountaineers, 2008. Whether you're looking for a quiet canoe trip or a roaring raft ride, this volume is for you.

Mueller, Marge, and Ted Mueller. *Exploring Washington's Wild Areas.* Seattle: Mountaineers, 2002. This book provides an overview of Washington's wilderness areas and national parks, with brief descriptions of hiking and climbing in each. An excellent introduction to these wild places. Nicely illustrated, too.

Mueller, Marge, and Ted Mueller. *North Puget Sound: Afoot & Afloat.* Seattle: The Mountaineers, 2006. Painstakingly detailed guide to North Puget Sound, from Point Roberts to Whidbey Island and west to Neah Bay, helpful to both boaters and landlubbers. Boat launches, parks, points of interest, plus photos and maps.

Mueller, Marge, and Ted Mueller. *The San Juan Islands: Afoot & Afloat.* Seattle: The Mountaineers, 2004. A thorough guide to "the big four" and numerous lesser islands in the San Juan chain. Includes boating, biking, sightseeing, and more, with maps and photos.

Poffenbarger, Amy and Mark. *Mountain Bike America: Washington.* Guilford, CT: Globe Pequot, 2001.

Spring, Vicky and Tom Kirkendall. *100 Best Cross Country Ski Trails in Washington.* Seattle: The Mountaineers, 2002.

Stienstra, Tom. *Moon Washington Camping.* Berkeley: Avalon Travel, 2006. The authoritative guide to public and private campgrounds around the state.

Woods, Erin, and Bill Woods. *Bicycling the Backroads.* Seattle: The Mountaineers, 1994-97. Three volumes—Around Puget Sound, of Northwest Washington, and of Southwest Washington—provide in-depth information on bike routes, terrain, elevation gain, and points of interest, plus explicit directions and plenty of maps.

SEATTLE IN DEPTH

Bergman, Ann. *Out and About Seattle with the Kids.* Seattle: Sasquatch Books, 2009. Family places around Seattle.

Dwyer, Jeff. *Ghost Hunter's Guide to Seattle and Puget Sound.* Gretna, LA: Pelican Publishing Company, 2008. Hang around Seattle's best haunts with help from this eccentric book.

Elenga, Maureen. *Seattle Architecture: A Walking Guide to Downtown.* Seattle: Seattle Architecture Foundation, 2008. Architecture buffs and urban explorers are sure to enjoy the site histories and descriptions detailed in here.

Fischer, Monica. Seattle Best Places. Seattle: Sasquatch Books, 2008. The list format can be a bit wearing, but this book offers a very comprehensive compendium of Seattle dining choices.

Lucas, Eric. Seattle Survival Guide. Seattle: Sasquatch Books, 2005. This guide offers useful info and a great overview for those recently relocated to the Puget Sound.

Moon Metro Seattle. Berkeley: Avalon Travel, 2003. A handy map-based guide offering tips on Seattle's hotspots.

ONWARD TRAVEL

The following is a shameless promotion for other Moon Handbooks in which Washington visitors may be interested. All of these are authoritative guides for their respective regions. Find out more on the web at www.moon.com.

Hempstead, Andrew. *Moon British Columbia.* Berkeley: Avalon Travel, 2008.

Morris, Elizabeth and Mark. *Moon Coastal Oregon.* Berkeley: Avalon Travel, 2007.

Morris, Elizabeth and Mark. *Moon Oregon.* Berkeley: Avalon Travel, 2007.

Pitcher, Don. *Moon San Juan Islands.* Berkeley: Avalon Travel, 2008.

Root, Don. *Moon Idaho.* Berkeley: Avalon Travel, 2004.

Internet Resources

ABOUT WASHINGTON

Official City Sites
www.officialcitysites.org

You may need to click through a few pages to find the Washington homepage, but this is a very helpful way to locate official city websites and chambers of commerce.

State of Washington
www.access.wa.gov

The official Washington website is a great starting point for those interested in the state, with a multitude of links, including to state, local, and federal agencies. You'll find everything from public libraries to the Cemetery Board here, plus photos of Washington, employment information, traffic reports, and news releases.

Washington Chambers of Commerce
www.wcce.org

A good place to find links to regional chambers of commerce websites.

Washington State Department of Transportation
www.wsdot.wa.gov

This site contains links to the public ferry, bus, air, bike, and train options around the state.

TRAVEL

Seattle B&B Association
www.seattlebandbs.com

Find most of the city's better B&Bs at this useful site.

Seattle/King County Convention & Visitors Bureau
www.seeseattle.org

Head to this website for links to hundreds of member businesses—including many motels and hotels—along with info on the city and surrounding areas.

The Map Company
www.wamaps.com

This site features detailed maps from all over the state, available to view for free online or for purchase.

Transportation Connections
www.transconnect.org

This private non-profit agency's website features links to a wide range of public transportation companies in Washington. In addition to buses, they also include car sharing, cycling organizations, Amtr
ak, and the state ferries.

Washington Bed and Breakfast Guild
www.wbbg.com

The state B&B association's website has links to homepages run by its many members.

Washington State Hotel and Lodging Association
www.stayinwashington.com

This private association has hundreds of member hotels, motels, and B&Bs on their website. They also produce a very useful free visitors' guide available in most visitor centers.

Washington State Tourism
www.experiencewashington.com

This is the state's tourism department site, and a good source for anyone planning to visit.

OUTDOOR RECREATION

National Park Service
www.nps.gov

Washington is home to nine different national parks, from the miniscule Klondike Gold Rush National Historical Park in downtown Seattle, to the half-million acres of land within North Cascades National Park. Learn about them at the official Park Service homepage.

Outdoor Recreation Information Center
www.nps.gov/ccso/oric.htm
This is a good one-stop place to learn about outdoor recreational opportunities on federal and state lands around Washington. Their information desk is inside the big Seattle REI store.

Recreation.gov
www.recreation.gov
This is the place to reserve campsites at public campsites around Washington.

Ski Washington
www.skiwashington.com
Nine of the state's largest downhill ski areas are accessible through this web portal.

The Mountaineers
www.mountaineers.org
Established in 1906, this Seattle-based organization sponsors thousands of outdoor trips and events throughout the year, publishes books, and works on a variety of environmental issues.

U.S. Forest Service Pacific Northwest Region
www.fs.fed.us/r6/r6nf.htm
This site contains links to National Forests throughout the Pacific Northwest.

Washington Department of Fish and Wildlife
http://wdfw.wa.gov/
Head to this official website for details on fishing licenses and seasons. You can even purchase your license online.

Washington State Accessible Outdoor Recreation Guide
www.parks.wa.gov/ada-rec
This site has details on barrier-free recreation sites on federal and state lands.

Washington State Parks and Recreation Commission
www.parks.wa.gov
Filled with details on 125 state parks. You can also make campground reservations here for the parks.

NEWS AND EVENTS

Art Guide Northwest
www.artguidenw.com
This is the online version of a free publication that details gallery openings and exhibits throughout the Pacific Northwest.

Hometown News
www.hometownnews.com/wa.htm
This site contains links to websites for virtually all of Washington's newspapers.

Saturdaymarkets.com
www.saturdaymarkets.com
This site lists information on farmers markets around Washington.

Washington Festivals and Events Association
www.wfea.org
An online source for upcoming activities of all types.

Washington State Fairs
www.wastatefairs.com
Want to learn more about the dozens of county, regional, and state fairs around Washington? This is a great place to start your search.

Index

A

Abercrombie Mountain Trail: 633
Aberdeen: 356-359
Aberdeen Museum of History: 357
accommodations: 705-706; *see also specific place*
Acme: 479
ACT (A Contemporary Theatre): 51
Admiralty Point Lighthouse Interpretive Center: 135
Affair on Main Street: 639
Agate Beach: 283
agriculture: 695-696
Ahtanum Mission: 430
Airfield Estates: 435
Air Force One: 47
air travel: 698; *see also specific place*
Albeni Falls Dam: 642
Alder Creek Pioneer Picnic and Rodeo: 410
Alder Lake Park: 550
Alexander Blockhouse: 135
Alki Beach Park: 15, 46
Alki Point Lighthouse: 46
Alki Trail: 58
All Fool's Day Parade and Basset Bash: 116
Alpine Falls: 530
Alpine Lakes Wilderness Area: 527-528, 543
Alpowai Interpretive Center: 668
Alta Lake State Park: 501
Altapes Creek Trail: 447
Alverson Boulevard: 145
American Camp: 16, 256-258
American exploration and settlement: 689-692
American Heritage Days: 642
American Hop Museum: 430
American Lake Park: 210
American Legion Park: 223
American Museum of Radio and Electricity: 170
American Ridge Trail: 570
amusement/water parks: Columbia Gorge/Wine Country 418; Eastern Washington 646; North Cascades 507; North Puget Sound 182-183; South Puget Sound 239
Anacortes: 249-255
Anacortes Community Forest Lands: 252
Anacortes Community Theatre: 251
Anacortes Farmers Market: 255
Anacortes Museum: 249
Anacortes Waterfront Festival: 251
Anderson Cabin: 349
Anderson Island: 227
Anderson Island Historical Museum: 227
Anderson Lake State Park: 310
Andreas Keller: 519
animal life: 680-686; *see also specific place*
animal safety: 490, 684-685
Ann Starrett Mansion: 308, 312
An-O-Chords Annual Barbershop Concert and Salmon Barbecue: 251-252
Antique Auto Rally: 494
Antique Power Show: 436
antiques: Columbia Gorge/Wine Country 406, 436; Eastside 95, 101; North Cascades 505; North Puget Sound 122, 129, 146, 152, 172; Olympic Peninsula 297, 309; South Puget Sound 208, 219
Ape Cave: 588-589
Aplets and Cotlets: 515
Appaloosa Museum and Heritage Center: 666
Apple Blossom Festival (Chelan): 505
Apple Blossom Festival (Wenatchee): 454
Apple Capital Recreation Loop: 454-455
Apple Pie Jamboree: 501
Apple Squeeze Festival: 208
aquariums: Columbia Gorge/Wine Country 389; North Puget Sound 170; Olympic Coast 353; Olympic Peninsula/Coast 322; Seattle 14, 34; South Puget Sound 203, 223
Arbor Crest Wine Cellars: 651
arboretums: Columbia Gorge/Wine Country 432; Eastern Washington 650; North Puget Sound 167; Seattle 45
archaeology: 335, 417, 673, 686-687
architecture: Eastern Washington 648; North Cascades 504; North Puget Sound 167; Olympic Peninsula/Coast 376; Seattle 28-29, 35-36, 39, 86; South Puget Sound 14, 189, 191, 205; *see also* historic houses and districts
Arco Exhibits Building: 167
Arctic Park: 358
Ardenvoir: 514
Arlington: 154-155
Arlington Festival: 151
Armed Forces Day Torchlight Parade (Spokane): 652
Armed Forces Festival and Parade (Bremerton): 216
Around the Mountain Trail: 593

Arroyo Park: 172
art classes/workshops: 91, 101, 139, 225, 297, 370, 445
art fairs/festivals: Columbia Gorge/Wine Country 417, 446; Eastern Washington 624, 639, 652, 664, 669; Eastside 94, 101, 122; North Cascades 519; North Puget Sound 122, 129, 136, 161, 171; Olympic Peninsula/Coast 303, 309, 380; San Juan Islands 252, 261, 273; Seattle 53; South Cascades 550, 594-595; South Puget Sound 194, 225, 230; *see also specific place*
ArtFest: 652
Arthur D. Feiro Marine Laboratory: 322
Art in the Park (Leavenworth): 519
Art in the Park (Okanogan): 624
Artist Point: 465
Artist Ridge Trail: 466
art museums and galleries: Columbia Gorge/Wine Country 399, 407, 408-409, 425, 430, 436, 437, 445; Eastern Washington 604, 615, 623, 648, 650, 658, 662; Eastside 91, 101, 112; North Cascades 500, 505; North Puget Sound 122, 129, 145, 146, 160, 167, 171; Olympic Peninsula/Coast 297, 309, 324, 326, 370; San Juan Islands 251, 260, 272-273, 283; Seattle 32-33, 39, 40, 44-45, 55; South Puget Sound 15, 195, 202, 216, 218, 225
Art's Alive!: 161
Arts Council Gift Gallery: 146
Art Walk (Kirkland): 101
Art Walks (Whidbey Island): 129
Ashford: 553-555
Asotin: 667
Asotin County Fair: 669
Asotin County Historical Museum: 667
Astoria, Oregon: 377
astronomy: 12, 406
Auburn: 238, 239
Auburn Avenue Dinner Theater: 237
Aurora Bridge Troll: 42
Auto and Truck Museum: 629-630
automobile travel: 699; *see also* scenic drives; *specific place*
auto racing: *see* car racing
aviation attractions: Columbia Gorge/Wine Country 11, 389, 418; North Cascades 482; North Puget Sound 139, 144-145, 151; Olympic Peninsula/Coast 380; San Juan Islands 273; Seattle 14, 46-47; South Puget Sound 206

B

Badger Mountain: 453
Bagley Wright Theater: 38
Bainbridge Farmers Market: 235
Bainbridge Gardens: 233-234
Bainbridge Island: 233-236
Bainbridge Island Historical Museum: 233
Bainbridge Island Vineyards and Winery: 234
Baker Boyer Bank: 423
bakeries: *see specific place*
Baker Lake: 480-481
Baker River: 481
Bald Eagle Interpretive Center: 482
Bald Eagle Mountain Trail: 529
Ballard: 13, 40-41
Ballard Locks: 42
ballet: 52, 207, 417, 453
balloon rides: *see* hot-air balloon rides
Banks Lake: 617
Barclay Lake Trail: 532
Barnard Griffin Winery: 417
Barnes Point: 18, 333
Baron Manfred Vierthaler Winery: 239
Battle Days: 659
Battle Ground Lake State Park: 391
Bavarian Ice Fest: 519
Bavarian Village: 518
Bay Pavilion: 34
Bays Street Playhouse: 219
Bayview Farmers Market: 132
Bay View State Park: 158, 162
Beachcombers Driftwood Show: 364
Beachcombers Fun Fair: 353
beach driving: 353, 375
beaches: Columbia Gorge/Wine Country 405; Eastern Washington 610, 614, 617, 640, 643, 672; Eastside 93, 96, 100, 101, 113; North Cascades 506, 508; North Puget Sound 121, 129, 130, 133, 137, 140, 142, 151, 153, 165, 180; Olympic Peninsula/Coast 19, 20, 298, 309, 314, 315, 322, 324, 335, 336, 341, 344, 345, 349, 353, 354, 361, 364, 368-369, 371, 378; San Juan Islands 257, 272, 281, 283, 284, 288, 289; Seattle 15, 42, 46; South Cascades 550, 574; South Puget Sound 196, 208, 209-210, 216, 221, 225, 228, 230, 232, 233, 240, 241
Beacon Rock State Park: 12, 397-398
Bear Research Facility: 663
bears: 490, 663, 683-685
Beasley Performing Arts Coliseum: 663
Beaver Lake Trail: 473
bed-and-breakfasts: 706; *see also specific place*

Beebe Bridge Park: 508
Bellevue: 91-99
Bellevue Arts Fair: 94
Bellevue Arts Museum: 91
Bellevue Botanical Garden: 92-93
Bellevue Chamber Chorus: 94
Bellevue Civic Theatre: 94
Bellevue Philharmonic Orchestra: 94
Bellingham: 166-179
Bellingham Chalk Art Festival: 171
Bellingham Farmers Market: 177
Bellingham Festival of Music: 171
Bellingham Railway Museum: 170
Bellingham Theatre Guild: 171
Bellis Fair Mall: 172
Bell Point: 258
Belltown: 13, 35-38
Belvedere Viewpoint: 46
Benaroya Hall: 15, 52
Bench Lake: 560
Benson Beach: 371
Benson Farmstead B&B: 13, 158
Benton City: 435
Benton Franklin Fair and Rodeo: 418
Berlin Wall: 38
Berry Dairy Days: 157
Berthusen Park: 182
Best of Broadway: 652
Bickleton: 410
Big Cedars County Park: 401
Big Creek Falls: 590
Big Creek Viewpoint: 301
Bigelow House: 191-192
Bigfoot Daze: 401
Big Four Ice Cave: 19, 471, 474
Big Lava Bed Geologic Area: 400-401
Big Quilcene Trail: 304
Big Rock Garden Park: 172
Big Tree Botanical Area: 629
bike races: 105, 107, 234, 494, 580
bike rentals: Columbia Gorge/Wine Country 399, 403, 418, 438, 447, 454; Eastern Washington 624; Eastside 95, 102, 108; North Cascades 494, 495, 507, 511, 522; North Puget Sound 157, 174; Olympic Peninsula/Coast 310, 319, 327, 354, 372, 378; San Juan Islands 261, 264, 273, 283; Seattle 58-59; South Cascades 549; South Puget Sound 230, 234
biking: 701; Columbia Gorge/Wine Country 391, 399, 401, 415, 418, 426, 438, 447, 454-455; Eastern Washington 601, 628, 629, 631, 637, 642, 650, 653, 658, 664, 668; Eastside 96, 101, 102, 108, 112; North Cascades 473, 492, 494-495, 507, 522, 531, 533; North Puget Sound 19, 123, 147, 152, 157, 173; Olympic Peninsula/Coast 319-320, 335-336, 338, 348, 368, 376, 378; San Juan Islands 16, 250, 283; Seattle 46, 58-59; South Cascades 545, 553, 562, 564, 566, 578, 595; South Puget Sound 195-196, 208, 209, 228, 230
Bill Chipman Palouse Trail: 664
Billy Goat Loop Trail: 491
Bingen: 402-404
Birch Bay: 181
Birch Bay Discovery Days: 181
Birch Bay State Park: 173, 180, 182
birds/bird-watching: 685-686; Columbia Gorge/Wine Country 391, 409, 410, 412, 421, 432; Eastern Washington 601, 602, 603, 614, 634, 649, 658-659; North Cascades 465, 479, 480, 482, 483, 512, 519; North Puget Sound 123, 133, 137, 143, 145, 146, 151, 158, 161; Olympic Peninsula/Coast 292, 301, 309, 317, 336, 341, 345, 349, 353, 357, 361, 371, 376, 378; San Juan Islands 252, 257, 259, 281, 283; Seattle 40, 45; South Cascades 575, 594; South Puget Sound 192-193, 209, 233
Birth of a Lake Trail: 587
Bite of Seattle: 54
Blackberry Festival: 216
Blackman Historic Museum: 150
Blackwood Canyon: 435
Blaine: 20, 181
Blake Island: 17, 232
Blakely Island: 289
Blessing of the Fleet: 361
Blewett Pass: 519
Blewett Pass Interpretive Trail: 519
Blind Island State Park: 288
Bloedel Donovan Park: 172, 173
Bloedel Reserve: 233
Bluebird Inn: 410-411
Bluegrass Festival and Street Fair: 476
Blue Lake: 491
Blue Lake Trail: 595
Blue Mountains: 671-675
Blues by the Bay: 146
boatbuilding: 38, 305, 307
boat cruises and tours: Columbia Gorge/Wine Country 396, 399, 421; Eastern Washington 615, 638; Eastside 96, 102, 113; North Cascades 479, 483, 487, 513, 514, 530; North Puget Sound 138, 142-143, 160, 161,

173, 182–183; Olympic Coast 378; Olympic Peninsula/Coast 309–310, 319, 331, 341; San Juan Islands 248, 252, 262–263, 273, 274, 275, 283–284; Seattle 17, 86; South Puget Sound 215, 218, 223, 225, 230, 232, 234
boating: Columbia Gorge/Wine Country 409, 411, 416, 438, 451; Eastern Washington 19, 603, 614, 615, 617, 618, 621, 626, 637, 643, 668, 669, 672, 673; Eastside 101–102; North Cascades 19, 474, 480, 495, 496, 505, 507, 508; North Puget Sound 130, 137, 141, 142, 151, 152, 161–162, 165, 182; Olympic Peninsula/Coast 314, 315, 319, 332, 338, 353, 357, 378; South Cascades 543, 545, 548, 566, 574, 575, 579, 581, 584; South Puget Sound 216, 228, 233; *see also* kayaking; river rafting; *specific place*
boat museums: 34, 38, 216
boat rentals: Columbia Gorge/Wine Country 399, 404, 418, 438, 447, 455; Eastern Washington 603, 615–616, 617, 620, 642; Eastside 96, 102, 113; North Cascades 488, 495, 507, 520, 522; North Puget Sound 137, 140, 147, 161, 172, 173; Olympic Peninsula/Coast 300, 309, 319, 327, 333, 354, 378; San Juan Islands 252, 262, 263, 264, 270, 272, 273–274, 275, 283–284; Seattle 43, 57–58; South Cascades 549, 551; South Puget Sound 196, 208, 223, 225, 230, 232, 234
boat tours: 146, 215, 249, 356, 667
Boehms Candies: 110–111
Boeing Tour: 144–145
Bogachiel River: 19, 338
Bogachiel River Trailhead: 338
Bogachiel State Park: 338, 339
Bonair Winery: 433
Bonanza Days: 622
Bonneville Dam: 398
Bonneville Lock and Dam: 398
Bonneville Second Powerhouse: 398
Book-It Repertory Theatre: 51
bookstores: *see specific place*
Bookwalter Winery: 417
Boot Hill Fossil Site: 630
Bothell: 115–117
Bothell Historical Society: 115
Bothell Landing: 115
Boulder Cave: 572
Boulder River Trail: 473
Boulder River Wilderness: 471
Boundary Dam: 639
Boundary Trail: 588
Bow: 13, 164
"Bowl and Pitcher" area: 649
Bowman Bay: 141–142
Box Canyon: 560
Box Canyon Dam: 637
Boy and Dog: 129
Boyer Park and Marina: 672
Brackett's Landing Park: 121
Brady's Oyster Feed: 361
Breazeale Interpretive Center: 157–158
Bremerton: 215–218
Bremerton Community Theatre: 216
Bremerton Naval Museum: 216
Bremerton Symphony Orchestra: 216
Bretz, J. Harlen: 599
breweries: 707; Columbia Gorge/Wine Country 394, 397, 420, 429, 442; Eastern Washington 627, 651; Eastside 101, 114, 116; North Cascades 468, 499, 534; North Puget Sound 149, 159, 164, 170, 177; Olympic Peninsula 313; San Juan Islands 251, 254–255; Seattle 47–48; South Cascades 540, 547; South Puget Sound 213
Brewster: 622
Brick Tavern: 544–545
Bridal Veil Falls: 530
Bridge of Glass: 14, 200
Bridge of the Gods: 398, 400
Bridgeport State Park: 621–622
bridges: Columbia Gorge/Wine Country 398, 400, 437; Eastside 91; North Cascades 481; North Puget Sound 13, 141; Olympic Peninsula/Coast 296, 297, 377, 378; Seattle 42; South Cascades 582; South Puget Sound 214
Bridle Crest Trail: 96
Bridle Trails State Park: 96
Brinnon: 301
British Camp: 16, 258
Broadway: 39
Broadway Center for the Performing Arts: 207
Brooks Memorial State Park: 406
Brothers Wilderness: 302–303
Brown Bag Concert (Orcas Island): 272
Brown Bag Music Series (Bellingham): 171
Browne's Addition: 648
Browns Point Lighthouse Park: 204–205
Bruce Memorial Museum: 674
Bruceport County Park: 376
Bubble Festival: 37, 54
Buckhorn Wilderness: 304
Buckley Log Show: 548
Buckskin Ridge Trail: 491
Bullion Basin Trail: 569

Bumbershoot: 54
Bumping Lake Trail: 570
Burke-Gilman Trail: 39, 58, 115
Burke Museum: 44
Burlington: 164-166
Burlington Farmers Market: 159
Burton Acres Park: 230
Bush Pioneer County Park: 376
bus travel: 699-700; *see also specific place*

C

Cabin Creek Nordic Ski Area: 546
Cama Beach State Park: 153
Camano Island: 155
Camano Island State Park: 150-151, 153
Camas: 397
Camas Days: 397
Camlann Medieval Village: 538-539
Campbell House: 648
Camp Cushman: 300-301
Camp Seven Logger's Museum: 481
Camp 6 Logging Museum: 204
Canada: 20, 84, 179-185, 629
candy factory tours: 110-111, 515
Candy Point Trail: 613
canoeing: Columbia Gorge/Wine Country 399; Eastern Washington 615, 637, 642; Eastside 93, 96, 113; North Cascades 474, 507, 520, 522; North Puget Sound 142, 147, 172, 173; Olympic Peninsula 317, 333, 353, 359; Seattle 43, 57-58; South Cascades 566; South Puget Sound 196
Canoe Ridge Vineyard: 425
Canyon Lake: 474
Cape Alva: 336
Cape Disappointment Lighthouse: 367
Cape Disappointment State Park: 20, 366-367, 371
Cape Flattery: 20, 335
Cape Flattery Lighthouse: 335
Cape Flattery Trail: 335
Cape Horn Viewpoint: 397
Cape Loop Road: 335
Cape St. Mary Ranch: 281
Capitol Campus: 189, 191
Capitol Forest: 195, 196
Capitol Hill: 39
Capitol Playhouse '24: 194
Capitol Theater: 435
Cap Sante Park: 250
Carbon Glacier: 562
Carbon River Area: 562
Carbon River Rain Forest Trail: 562
Carbon Trail: 571
Carkeek Park: 42
Carl S. English Jr. Botanical Gardens: 42
Carnegie Art Center: 425
Carnell House Museum: 359
carousels: 410, 646
Carpenter Museum: 544
car racing: Columbia Gorge/Wine Country 418, 436; Eastern Washington 653; North Cascades 534; North Puget Sound 157; Olympic Peninsula/Coast 326-327, 359; South Puget Sound 207, 237
car rentals: 699
Carr Inlet: 227-228
Carr's One of a Kind in the World Museum: 648-649
car shows: Columbia Gorge/Wine Country 411, 436; Eastern Washington 604, 608, 609, 629-630, 659, 669; Eastside 107; North Cascades 494, 499, 505, 533; North Puget Sound 152; Olympic Peninsula/Coast 370, 380; South Puget Sound 203, 219; *see also specific place*
Carson: 400-402
Carson Hot Springs Resort: 400-401
car travel: 699; *see also* scenic drives; *specific place*
Cascade Cliffs Winery: 407
Cascade Falls: 16, 272
Cascade Loop: 478
Cascade Park: 603, 604
Cascade Pass: 488, 489
Cascade Railroad Tunnel: 527
Cascadia Marine Trail System: 704
Case Inlet: 228
Cashmere: 515-516
Cashmere Apple Days: 516
casinos: *see* gambling
Casino Snoqualmie: 539
Castle Rock: 580
Castle Rock Exhibit Hall and Visitor Information Center: 580
Castle Rock Fair: 580
castles: 307, 311, 356-357
Caterina Winery: 651
Cat Tales Endangered Species Conservation Park: 650
Cattle Point Interpretive Area: 258
Causland Park: 249-250
caves: Eastern Washington 618, 638-639, 641; Eastside 112; North Cascades 471, 474; South Cascades 573, 588-589, 595
Cayuse Pass: 561

CCC Interpretive Center: 142
Cedarbrook Herb Farm: 318
Cedar Creek Grist Mill: 583
Cedar Creek Trail: 494
Cedar Rock Biological Preserve: 288
Celebrate Hoodsport Days: 300
Celebrate Lavender Festival: 319
Celebration of Chocolates and Red Wine: 436
cemeteries: Columbia Gorge/Wine Country 422, 423; Eastern Washington 620; North Puget Sound 137; San Juan Islands 258, 259; Seattle 39-40; South Cascades 545; South Puget Sound 240
Centennial Concert series: 604
Centennial Park: 123
Centennial Trail (Snohomish): 152
Centennial Trail (Spokane): 653
Center Church: 281
Center for Wooden Boats: 38
Center House: 37-38
Central Ferry State Park: 672
Central Park: 389
Central Sundries: 544
Central Washington Agricultural Museum: 431
Central Washington State Fair: 436
Central Washington University: 445
Centrum Foundation: 309
Chain Lakes Trail: 467
Channeled Scablands: 600, 606
Charbonneau Park: 415-416
Chateau Ste. Michelle Winery: 115
Chehalis Indian Reservation: 194
Chehalis Valley Historical Museum: 359
Chelan: 502-511
Chelan Butte Lookout: 504
Chelan County Fair: 516
Chelan County Historical Museum: 515-516
Chelan Valley Farmers Market: 510
Cheney: 658
Cheney Historical Museum: 658
Chesaw: 628-629
Chesaw Rodeo: 628
Chesaw Tavern: 628
Chetzemoka Park: 309
Chief Joseph: 620, 621
Chief Joseph Dam: 620-621
Chief Looking Glass Park: 667
Chief Taholah Day Celebration: 349
Chief Timothy State Park: 668
Chihuly, Dale: 203
Chihuly Bridge of Glass: 14, 200
Children's Museum (Bellingham): 167
Children's Museum of Spokane: 648
Children's Museum of Tacoma: 203
Children's Museum of Walla Walla: 423
Chilly Hilly: 234
Chimpanzee & Human Communication Institute: 445
Chimposiums: 445
China Bend Vineyards & Winery: 635
Chinese New Year: 53
Chinook Pass: 573
Chinook Salmon Derby: 505
Chinook Wines: 434
Chism Beach Park: 96
Chito Beach Bluegrass Jamboree: 335
Chittenden Locks: 13, 42
Chkalov Monument: 389
Choochokam Festival of the Arts: 129
Chris Craft Rendezvous: 219
Christianson's Nursery: 156
Chuckanut Drive: 164-165
Chuckanut Manor: 17, 165
Chuckanut Mountain: 165
Cinco de Mayo: 417
City Beach Park: 140
CityPass: 28
Civil War Re-enactment: 181
Clallam Bay Spit: 335
Clallam County Fair: 326
clam farms: 189, 303
Clam Lights: 240
Clark County Historical Museum: 390
Clarkston: 667-670
Clearwater and Snake River National Recreation Trail: 667-668
Clearwater Wilderness: 571
Cle Elum: 544-547
Cle Elum Historical Telephone Museum: 544
Cle Elum River: 547
Cliff Park (Spokane): 650
Cliffs Park (Columbia Gorge): 410
climate: 677-679; *see also specific place*
climbing: *see* mountaineering; rock climbing
Clinkerdagger's Restaurant: 12, 656
Clinton: 127, 129-132
Clipper: 479
Clyde and Mary Harris Gallery: 425
Clyde Theatre: 129
Clymer Museum: 443, 445
Coal Lake: 474
Coal Miner Days Festival: 545
Coastal Forest Trail: 371
Coast Artillery Museum: 308
Coast Guard Museum: 34
Coeur d'Alene Lake: 653

Colbert House: 367
Coldwater Ridge: 587
Coleman Glacier: 466
Colfax Jr. Rodeo: 660
Colfax Summer Festival: 659-660
colleges: see universities and colleges
Colonel Bob Trail: 346
Colonel Bob Wilderness: 346
Colorama Festival: 615
Columbia Basin: 600-610
Columbia Basin College Performing Arts: 417
Columbia Basin Farmers Market: 605
Columbia Center: 28-29, 418
Columbia County Courthouse: 673-674
Columbia County Fair: 674
Columbia Crest: 411
Columbia Cup: 418
Columbia Gorge: 395-412
Columbia Gorge Bluegrass Festival: 399
Columbia Gorge Interpretive Center: 398-399
Columbia Mountain Trail: 632
Columbia National Wildlife Refuge: 602
Columbia Park: 415, 418, 419
Columbia Park Family Fishing Pond: 415
Columbia River Exhibition of History, Science, and Technology: 415
Columbia River Gorge National Scenic Area: 395-412
Columbia River Waterfront Trail: 391
Columbia Theatre: 380
Columbia Valley Wineries Barrel Tasting: 417
Columbia Winery: 115
Colville: 635-636
Colville National Forest: 17, 632-633
Colville Rendezvous: 636
Colville Reservation: 618-620
Colville Rodeo: 636
Colville Tribal Museum: 615
Commander's House (Fort Clatsop): 377
Commanding Officer's House (Fort Worden State Park): 308
Commencement Park: 209, 210
Commons at Federal Way: 240-241
Conboy Lake National Wildlife Refuge: 594
Concerts in the Park (Bainbridge): 234
Concerts in the Parks (Bellingham): 171
Concerts on the Boardwalk: 216
Concerts on the Cove: 136
Concerts on the Pier: 326
Conconully: 625-626
Conconully State Park: 626
Concrete: 481-482
Concrete Fly-In: 482
Connors Museum of Zoology: 663
conservatories: 39, 205, 650
Cook, James: 689
Coon Lake: 512
Cooper, D. B.: 583
Copalis Days: 349
Copper Ridge-Chilliwack Loop Trail: 466
Cougar: 584
Cougar Mountain Regional Wildland Park: 112
Cougar Mountain Zoo: 18, 111
Coulee City: 617
Coulee City Community Park: 617
Coulee Dam (city): 615-617
Coulee Dam Casino: 615
Country Christmas Lighted Farm Implement Parade: 437
Country Village Farmers Market: 117
County Historical Society Museum: 641-642
County Line Park: 378
Coupeville: 13, 19, 134-139
Coupeville Arts and Crafts Festival: 136
Coupeville Arts Center: 139
Coupeville Farmers Market: 136
Cowboy Poetry Jubilee: 624
Cowiche Canyon: 438
Cowlitz Community Farmers Market: 382
Cowlitz County Fair: 380
Cowlitz River Canoe Race: 380
Cowlitz Salmon Hatchery: 574
crabbing: 130, 299, 314, 361
Craftfair: 519
Cranberrian Fair: 370
cranberry attractions: 368
Cranberry Coast: 364-365
Cranberry Harvest Festival: 364
Cranberry Lake: 142
Crawford State Park: 638-639
Cresap Bay Park: 590
Crescent Bay Lake: 615
Crofton Butte Trail: 593
Crosby House: 193
Crosby Student Center: 651
Crow Butte State Park: 411-412
Crown Point Vista: 615
Crow Valley School Museum: 272
Cruz, The: 219
Crystal Falls: 637
Crystal Mountain: 20, 571-573
Crystal Mountain Trail: 572
culinary tours: 17
Curlew: 629-630
Curlew Lake State Park: 629, 631
Cushman Falls: 301

Cusick: 641
Cutter Theatre: 639

D

Dacres Hotel: 423
Daffodil Festival: 207
Dahlia Trial Garden: 204
Dakota Creek Shipyard: 252
Dalby Waterwheel: 298
Dalles, The: 404-405
Dalles Dam: 404
Dalles River Trail: 572
Damfino Lakes: 466
Damon Point: 353
Dancers Series: Steps: 39
Daroga State Park: 508
Darrington: 469-476
Dash Point State Park: 210, 240, 241
Dave Mackie County Park: 130
Davenport Hotel: 12, 655
Davis Blockhouse: 137
Daybreak Star Arts and Cultural Center: 40
Dayton: 673-675
Dayton Days: 674
Dayton Summer Hoopla: 674
Decatur Island: 289
Deception Creek Trail: 530
Deception Falls: 530
Deception Pass Bridge: 13, 141
Deception Pass State Park: 13, 140, 141-144
Deer Creek: 474
Deer Harbor: 270
Deer Lake Park: 130, 334
Dege Peak: 562
Deming: 463, 479
Deming Logging Show: 463
Denny Hall: 44
Denny Park: 101
Depot Arts Center: 251
Depot Days Festival: 674
Desert Wind Winery: 435
Des Moines: 241
Des Moines Beach Park: 241
Desolation Peak: 13, 488-489
Destiny Ridge Vineyard: 411
Destruction Island: 344
Deutschesfest: 606
Diablo: 487
Diablo Lake: 13, 485
Dick & Jane's Spot: 445
Dirtyface Trail: 522
disabilities, travelers with: 708
Discovery Park: 17, 40
Discovery Trail: 368
diving: *see specific place*
Dixieland Jazz Festival: 354, 357
Doe Island State Park: 288
Dog Mountain Trail: 402
dog parks: 708; *see also specific place*
dog show: 436
dogsledding: 522, 625-626
Dogwood Festival: 669
doll museum: 91-92
Don Morse Memorial City Park: 507
Dosewallips Falls: 302
Dosewallips Recreation Area: 302
Dosewallips State Park: 18, 301
Double Bluff Beach Park: 133
Douglas County Courthouse: 452
Douglas County Historical Museum: 453
Douglas Gallery: 648
Doug's Beach State Park: 405
Down Home 4th of July Parade: 111
Down River Days: 637
Down River Trail: 613
Downtown Holiday Celebration: 664
Driftwood Players: 357
Drumheller Channels: 602
Dry Falls: 618
Duckabush Recreation Area: 302
Duckabush River Trail: 303
Duck Lake: 353
Dune Interpretive Trail: 361
Dune Trail: 368
Dungeness National Wildlife Refuge: 317
Dungeness Recreation Area: 319
Dungeness Spit: 18, 316-317
Dutch Sinterklaas Celebration: 181-182

E

Eagle Creek Trail: 500
Eagle Falls: 530
Eagle Harbor Waterfront Park: 233
Eagle Peak: 559
East Bank Trail: 488
East Beach: 610
East Benton County Historical Museum: 415
Eastern Washington State Historical Society: 648
Eastern Washington University: 658
East Side Park: 624
Eastsound: 270
East Tiger Mountain: 112
Eastward: 484-485
Easy Pass: 489
Eaton Hill Winery: 434

Eatonville: 550-551
Eatonville Arts Festival: 550
Eatonville Farmers Market: 551
Ebey's Landing National Historical Reserve: 13, 135
Ebey's Landing State Park: 135
Echo Ridge: 507
Echo Valley Ski Area: 507
Eco Park at Mount St. Helens: 11, 582
Edgewater Park: 156
Edison: 164
Ediz Hook: 322, 324
Edmonds: 121-126
Edmonds Art Festival: 122
Edmonds Art Walk: 122
Edmonds Fishing Pier: 121
Edmonds Historical Museum: 121-122
Edmonds Marina Beach Park: 121
Edmonds Marsh: 123
Edmonds Underwater Park: 121, 123
Edridge: 170
Elbe: 551-552
Eldon: 301
Electric City: 615-617
Elip Creek Trail: 346
Elk Rock View Point: 583
Ellensburg: 443-449
Ellensburg Bull: 445
Ellensburg National Art Show and Auction: 446
Ellensburg Rodeo: 445-446
Elma: 360
Elmer City: 615
Elwha River Trail: 19, 331
Elwha River Valley: 331-332
Emerald Downs: 237
Emerald Queen Casino: 207
Emmanuel Episcopal Church: 272
Emmons Glacier: 557
Empty Space Theatre: 51
Enatai Beach Park: 96
Enchanted Valley Trail: 346
Enchantment Lakes: 528
English Camp: 16, 258
English land claims: 689, 690, 692
Entiat: 514
Entiat City Park: 514
Entiat Historical Museum: 514
Entiat National Fish Hatchery: 514
Enumclaw: 547-549
Enumclaw Street Fair: 548
Ephrata: 607-608
equestrian attractions: see horseback riding
Erickson's Bay: 337
Erie View Trail: 252
Eruption Trail: 587
Eschbach Park: 438
Esther Short Park: 389
Jesus of Nazareth: 237
Evangelische Lutherische Kirche: 551
Everett: 144-150
Everett Center for the Arts: 145
Everett Farmers Market: 149
Everett Marina: 145, 147
Everett Symphony: 146
Evergreen Classic Horse Show: 107
Evergreen Mountain: 531
Evergreen Speedway: 534
Evergreen State Fair: 533-534
Evergreen State Fairgrounds: 533-534
Everson-Nooksack Summer Festival: 463
Excelsior Pass: 466
Experience Music Project: 37
explorers: 689-691; *see also specific place*
Ezra Meeker Mansion: 236

F

Facelli Winery: 115-116
Fairhaven: 166-167, 170
Fairhaven Farmers Market: 177
Fall Harvest and Community Festival: 426
Falls Creek: 347
Falls View Canyon Trail: 304
Family Fest: 240
Farmer Consumer Awareness Day: 601
farmers markets: 707; *see also specific place*
farming: 695-696
farm visits: Columbia Gorge/Wine Country 423, 441-442, 451-452, 457; Eastern Washington 606; Eastside 93; North Cascades 501, 505, 533; North Puget Sound 13, 133, 151, 155-156, 180; Olympic Peninsula 318, 319; San Juan Islands 281; South Cascades 539; South Puget Sound 228, 230, 237; *see also* fruit orchards
Farrel-McWhirter Park: 105-106
Fathoms O' Fun Carnival: 219
fauna: 680-686; *see also specific place*
Fauntleroy: 46
Fay-Bainbridge State Park: 65, 233
Federal Way: 242-243
Federation Forest State Park: 547
Ferdinand's Dairy Bar: 661-662
Ferndale: 181
ferries: *see specific place*
Ferry County Fair: 631
Festival of American Fiddle Tunes: 309

Festival of Colors: 353
Festival of Lights: 359
festivals: *see specific festival; place*
Fields Spring State Park: 668, 669
Fiery Floods Festival: 418
Fifes Peaks: 569
5th Avenue Theatre: 51
film festivals: 52
film/TV productions: 677; Eastern Washington 639; North Cascades 465, 512; North Puget Sound 135; Olympic Peninsula/Coast 307, 308, 311, 318, 339; San Juan Islands 263, 274; Seattle 15, 63; South Cascades 18, 536, 544, 545; South Puget Sound 211, 214
Fire and Ice Trail: 466
Fireman's Museum: 161
Fire O'er the Water: 349
Fireworks on the Beach: 370
First Night: 207
First Saturday Art Walk: 55
Fish Creek Trail: 489
Fishermen's Terminal: 42
fish hatcheries: Columbia Gorge/Wine Country 402; Eastern Washington 634, 673; Eastside 111; North Cascades 482-483, 494, 501, 514, 518, 532; North Puget Sound 170, 172; Olympic Peninsula 297, 304; South Cascades 538, 574
Fishhook Park: 416
fishing: *see specific place*
fishing charters: 147, 161, 173, 263, 310, 362, 371-372
fish ladders: Columbia Gorge/Wine Country 398, 410, 415, 451; Eastern Washington 672; North Cascades 475, 482, 501; Seattle 13, 42; South Cascades 574; South Puget Sound 192, 193
Five-Mile Drive: 208
Flaming Geyser State Park: 18, 548
Flapjacks Lake: 301
Fletcher Canyon Trail: 346
flightseeing tours: Columbia Gorge/Wine Country 458; Eastern Washington 666; North Cascades 511, 513, 516; North Puget Sound 152, 160; Olympic Peninsula 298, 331; San Juan Islands 248, 249, 280; Seattle 85; South Cascades 582, 587; South Puget Sound 243
flora: 679-680; *see also specific place*
Flour Mill: 652
flower festivals: 156-157, 207, 237, 319, 620, 652, 669
Flowing Lake Park: 534
fly-fishing: Columbia Gorge/Wine Country 447; Eastern Washington 19, 630; North Puget Sound 142; South Cascades 538, 541, 566, 578
food: 706-707; *see also specific place*
food tours: 17
Fordefjord Lutheran Church: 223
Forest Learning Center: 582-583
forests: *see specific place*
Forest Service lands: 702-703, 704-705
Forest Storytelling Festival: 326
Forks: 337-338, 339
Forks Farmers Market: 340
Forks Timber Museum: 338
Fort Canby: 315, 367
Fort Cascades: 398
Fort Casey State Park: 135, 137, 315
Fort Clatsop: 377
Fort Columbia State Park: 315, 377
Fort Ebey State Park: 136, 137, 315
Fort Flagler State Park: 314, 315, 316
Fort Lawton: 40
Fort Lewis Military Museum: 206
Fort Nez Percé: 424
Fort Nisqually: 204
Fort Okanogan State Park: 622
Fort Simcoe State Park: 431-432
Fort Spokane: 614, 643
Fort Steilacoom: 206
Fort Vancouver Brigade Encampment: 390
Fort Vancouver Candlelight Tours: 391
Fort Vancouver National Historic Reserve: 11, 388
Fort Walla Walla: 422
Fort Walla Walla Museum Complex: 422
Fort Walla Walla Park: 423
Fort Ward State Park: 233
Fort Worden State Park: 18, 308, 310, 312, 315
49° North: 636, 653
49er Days: 494
Founders' Day (Sedro-Woolley): 480
Founders' Days (Cashmere): 516
Fox Island: 227-228
Fox Island Historical Society and Museum: 227
Fragrance Garden: 182
Franklin County Museum: 415
Franklin Park: 438
Frater Lake Trail: 637
Fraternity Snoqualmie Nudist Park: 113
Fred Remon Memorial Bridge: 437
Freedom Fair: 207-208
Freeland: 132-134
Freeland Park: 133
Freeway Park: 29

Freeze Yer Buns Run: 499
Freighthouse Square: 208
Fremont: 42, 53
Fremont Drawbridge: 42
French Creek Road 2010: 474
Frenchman's Bar Park: 391
Friday Harbor: 16, 256
Friendship Pony Express Ride: 627
Front Street Park: 518
fruit orchards: 695; Columbia Gorge/Wine Country 12, 17, 408, 441-442, 451-452, 457; Eastern Washington 635; North Cascades 501, 505; South Puget Sound 228
Frye Art Museum: 32-33
Full Gospel Church: 667
Funhouse, The: 272
Future of Flight Center: 144-145

G

Gaches Mansion: 161
Gaiser Conservatory: 650
Gallery of Art: 658
"Galloping Gertie": 214
Gardens at La Conner Flats, The: 156
Gardner Cave: 638-639
Garfield County Fair: 671
Garlic Festival: 370
Gasworks Park: 15, 39
Gatton Creek: 347
gays and lesbians: 48-49, 708-709
G'day Goldendale Community Days: 406
Gehrke Windmills: 615
General Motors Cup Hydroplane Races: 54
geography: 677-679
Geophysical Observatory: 642
Geophysical Trail System: 642
George: 601-602
George Washington celebration: 601-602
Giardia: 709
Gifford-Pinchot: 592-595
Gig Harbor: 224-227
Gig Harbor Art Festival: 225
Gig Harbor Farmers Market: 226
Gilman Town Hall Museum: 110
Gilman Village: 112
Gingko Petrified Forest State Park: 12, 601
Glacier: 463
Glacier Basin Trail: 472
Glacier Peak Wilderness: 472-473
glaciers: 466, 557, 562
Glacier View Wilderness: 571
glassblowing: North Puget Sound 151, 160; San Juan Islands 272, 283; Seattle 55; South Cascades 581; South Puget Sound 14, 15, 208, 230
glass museum: 14, 200, 202
Glenwood: 594-595
glockenspiels: 402, 520
Glover Mansion: 648
Goat Ridge Trail: 571
Goat Rocks Wilderness: 570-571
Goat Wall: 492
Gobbler's Knob: 563-564, 571
Go 4th Celebration: 380
Gold Bar Museum: 532
Goldendale: 405-407
Goldendale Observatory State Park: 12, 406
Golden Gardens Park: 42
golfing: Columbia Gorge/Wine Country 415, 418, 426, 438, 455; Eastern Washington 604, 606-607, 616, 622, 636, 653, 669, 675; Eastside 96, 108; North Cascades 495, 502, 506, 523; North Puget Sound 123, 140, 147, 152, 172, 174, 182; Olympic Peninsula/Coast 297, 301, 310, 320, 354, 372, 381; San Juan Islands 253, 264, 275, 284; South Cascades 546; South Puget Sound 196, 210, 219, 241
gondola rides: 646
Gonzaga University: 650
Good Olde Days: 482
Goose Rock: 143
Gorge Amphitheatre: 601
Gorge Crest Winery: 402
Gorge Heritage Museum: 402
Gorge Lake: 485
Gorge Powerhouse: 485
Governor's Cup Walleye Tournament: 634
Governor's Mansion: 191
Grand Avenue Park: 145
Grand Central Hotel: 110
Grand Coulee (city): 615-617
Grand Coulee Dam: 12, 610-613
Grand Forest: 234
Grand Gallery: 615
Grandview Grape Stomp: 436
Grandy Lake County Park: 481
Granite Falls: 469-476
Granite Falls Farmers Marketplace: 476
Granite Falls Fish Ladder: 475
Granite Falls Museum: 475
Grant County Fair: 604
Grant County Historical Museum and Pioneer Village: 607-608
Grant House: 389
Grant's Grill: 11, 393

Grasser's Hill: 137
Grasshopper Pass: 492
Graves Creek: 347
Graves Creek Nature Trail: 346
Gray, Robert: 356, 689-690
Grayland Beach State Park: 364
Grays Harbor: 356-359
Grays Harbor County Fair: 359
Grays Harbor Discovery Days Celebration: 357
Grays Harbor Historical Seaport: 356
Grays Harbor Shorebird Festival: 357
Grays Harbor Wildlife Refuge: 357
Grays River Covered Bridge: 378
Grays River Covered Bridge Festival: 378
Great Canoe Race: 609
Greenbank: 132-134
Greenbank Farm: 13, 133
Greening of Coupeville: 136
Green Lake: 43, 58, 59
Green Mountain: 216
Green River Gorge Conservation Area: 18, 548, 549
Greenwater: 571-573
Griffiths-Priday State Park: 18, 349
Grove of the Patriarchs: 11, 560
Gular Ice Cave: 595

H

Hadlock Manor: 315-316
Haller Fountain: 305
Hall of Mosses Trail: 342
Hamilton Mountain: 397
Hamilton Viewpoint: 46
Hamma Hamma Recreation Area: 301-302
Hands Across the Border Peace Arch Celebration: 181
Hands On Children's Museum: 192
Hanford Reach National Monument: 415
Hanford Site: 412, 414-415
hang gliding: 506
Hanging Gardens Area: 548
Hannegan Pass: 466
Harbor Days Festival: 195
Harbor History Museum: 224-225
harbor history museum: 224-225
harbor tours: 170, 215, 218
Harley Owners Group Sun & Surf Run: 354
Harmony Trail: 591
Harold E. LeMay Museum: 203
Harper Joy Theatre: 425
Hart Lake Trail: 512
Harts Pass: 12, 492
Hartstene Island: 228
Harvest Festival (Lynden): 181
Harvest Festival (Whidbey Island): 136
Hawaiian Chieftain: 356
Hazel Wolf Bird Sanctuary: 432
health/safety: 709-710
Heather Lake: 470-471
Heather Meadows: 19, 465, 466-467
Hedges Cellars: 435
helicopter tours: *see* flightseeing tours
Heliotrope Ridge Trail: 466
Hells Canyon Recreation: 668
Hells Gate State Park: 669
Henderson House Museum: 193
Hendrix, James M. "Jimi": 240
Henry Art Gallery: 44-45
Henry M. Jackson Wilderness Area: 471-472, 529
Henry Thompson Bridge: 481
Herbfarm: 17, 117
Heritage Festival: 107
Heritage Fountain: 14, 192
Heybrook Lookout: 532
High Divide Trail: 466
Highland Games & Scottish Fair: 157
Highland Park Sno-Park: 626-627
Highway 410: 571-573
Highway 20: 477-478
hiking: 333; Columbia Gorge/Wine Country 12, 390, 391, 396, 397, 399, 401, 402, 426, 438; Eastern Washington 602, 603, 613, 617, 628, 631-632, 633, 636, 637, 639, 640-641, 642, 649, 650, 653, 664, 667-668, 671-672; Eastside 18, 93, 96, 101, 106, 112-113, 115, 116; North Cascades 12, 13, 19, 465, 466-467, 470-473, 479, 480-481, 483, 487, 488-491, 492, 494, 495, 499-500, 501, 505-506, 511-512, 514, 519, 522-523, 527-529, 531, 532; North Puget Sound 133, 135, 136, 137, 143, 151, 157-158, 165, 172, 173, 182, 315; Olympic Peninsula/Coast 18, 19, 20, 292, 294, 299, 301, 302-303, 304, 308, 314, 315, 317, 319, 327, 331-332, 334, 335, 336, 337, 338, 341, 343, 345, 346, 359, 368, 371, 376; San Juan Islands 252-253, 258, 270, 275, 281, 284, 288-289; Seattle 39, 40, 42, 45, 46; South Cascades 19, 540-541, 543, 545-546, 547, 548, 549, 550, 553, 559, 560-564, 569-571, 572, 573, 574, 577-578, 579, 584, 587, 588, 589-590, 591, 592-594; South Puget Sound 193, 195, 208, 216, 219, 228, 230, 232, 234, 240
Hill, Sam: 408-409
Hing Hay Park: 35

Hiram M. Chittenden Locks: 13, 42
Historic Everett Theatre: 146
Historic Homes Tour: 674
historic houses and districts: Columbia Gorge/Wine Country 389, 406, 407, 408-409, 422-423, 424, 452-453; Eastern Washington 607-608, 628, 635-636, 648, 666, 673-674; Eastside 110; North Cascades 471-472, 476, 479, 493, 504, 511, 515-516; North Puget Sound 121, 136, 145, 150, 161, 166-167, 170, 180; Olympic Peninsula/Coast 307-308, 314, 322, 324, 331, 349, 356-357, 367, 369, 377, 379; San Juan Islands 250, 258-259; South Cascades 574, 583; South Puget Sound 16, 191-192, 193, 205, 218, 227, 236
Hoffstadt Bluffs and Creek: 581-582
Hoffstadt Creek Bridge: 582
Hoh Indian Reservation: 344
Hoh Rain Forest: 18-19, 342-344
Hoh Rain Forest Visitor Center: 342
Hoh River Trail: 343
Hoh River Valley: 342-344
Holden Village: 511
Holiday Arts and Crafts Show: 664
Holland Days: 181
Holland Happening: 139
Home: 228
Home Tour: 136
Home Valley County Park: 401
Hood Canal: 18, 295-296
Hood Canal Floating Bridge: 296
Hood Canal Hatchery: 299
Hood Canal Salmon Derby: 300
Hood Canal ShrimpFest: 303
Hood Park: 416
Hoodsport: 18, 299-300
Hoodsport Winery: 299
Hoopfest: 652
Hoquiam: 356-359
Hoquiam Aquatic Center: 357
Hoquiam-Grays Harbor Farmers Market: 358
Hoquiam's Castle: 356-357
horseback riding: *see specific place*
horse-drawn carriages: 523
horse racing: 237, 359, 418, 623-624, 631
Horseshoe Lake: 583
horse shows: 107, 533, 659
Horsethief Lake State Park: 404-405
hot-air balloon festivals: 195, 425-426, 436-437
hot-air balloon rides: 108, 116, 152, 495
Hot August Nights: 669
Hotel Murano: 14, 211
hot springs: 331, 334, 400-401
houseboat rentals: 63, 303, 614
Hovander Homestead Park: 180
Howard Miller Steelhead Park: 484
Howe Art Gallery & Kinetic Sculpture Garden: 273
Hoypus Point: 142
Huckleberry Fest: 402
Huckleberry Mountain: 643
Hulda Klager Lilac Gardens: 583
Humes Ranch: 331
hunting: 297-298, 310, 546, 701
Hurricane Ridge: 18, 324
Hurricane Ridge Trail: 327
Hurricane Ridge Visitor Center: 324
Husky Union Building: 44
Hyatt Vineyards Winery: 433
hypothermia: 709-710

I

ice caves: 19, 471, 474
Ice Harbor Lock and Dam: 415
ice skating: 174, 454, 496, 507, 508, 604
Icicle Creek Interpretive Trail: 518-519
Icicle Creek Music Center: 519
Icicle River Trail: 521
Idylwood Park: 105
IKEA Renton River Days: 240
Ike Kinswa State Park: 575
Illahee State Park: 216
Ilwaco: 367, 372-373
Ilwaco Heritage Museum: 367
Imagine Children's Museum: 145
Imus Creek Nature Trail: 512
Inchelium: 620
Independence Pass Trail: 591
Index: 531
Index Town Wall: 532
Indian Bar: 563
Indian Encampment: 623
Indian Heaven Wilderness: 594
Indian Painted Rocks: 430
Indian Sacred Viewpoint: 594
information and services: 711-712; *see also specific place*
International District: 17, 34-35
International Folk Dance Festival: 519
International Fountain: 38
International Glass Museum: 14, 200, 202
International Kite Challenge: 353
International Nautical Chainsaw Carving Contest: 361

Internet: 711
Interrorem Nature Trail: 302
Interurban Trail: 123, 147, 165, 173
Intiman Theatre Company: 51
Ione: 637-638
Ione City Park: 637
Irby: 606
Irely Lake: 346
Irene Rinehart Riverfront Park: 445
Iris Garden: 204
Iron Creek Campground Trail: 576
Iron Creek Falls: 576
Iron Creek Old-Growth Trail: 576
Iron Horse State Park: 541, 545
Iron Horse Trail: 447
Iron Triangle: 315
Island County Fair: 129
Island County Historical Museum: 136
Island Earth Fair: 230
Islands Certified Local: 267
Island Wine Company, The: 261
Issaquah: 110-114
Issaquah Alps: 18, 112
Issaquah Reindeer Festival: 111-112
Issaquah Salmon Days: 111
Issaquah State Salmon Hatchery: 111
Issaquah Train Depot Museum: 110
itineraries: 9, 11-20

J

Jackie's Lagoon: 257
Jacklin Collection: 662
Jack Pass: 531
Jackson Highway: 574
Jacob Durr Wagon Road: 437
James Island State Park: 288
Japanese Garden (Ellensburg): 445
Japanese Garden (Spokane): 650
Japanese Garden (Tacoma): 204
Japanese Gulch: 123
Japanese Tea Garden (Seattle): 45
Jarrell Cove State Park: 228
Jazz Port Townsend: 309
Jean: 667
Jefferson County Courthouse: 307
Jefferson County Fair: 309
Jefferson County Historical Society: 307
Jennings Nature Park: 151
Jetty Island: 145
Jetty Island Days: 146
Joemma State Park: 228
John A. Finch Arboretum: 650
John Day Lock and Dam: 410
John M. Morrison Loop Trail: 253
John R. Jackson House: 574
Johnson Creek Sno-Park: 578
Johnson Farm: 227
Johnston Ridge Visitor Center: 11, 587
John Wayne Marina: 319
John Wayne Trail: 447
Jolly Mountain: 546
Jones Island State Park: 289
Joseph Whidbey State Park: 140
Joy of Running Together, The: 646
Juan de Fuca Festival: 326
Juanita Bay Park: 101
Juanita Beach Park: 101
Julia Butler Hansen National Wildlife Refuge: 378
July Creek: 347
Jumper Spring Nationals: 533
Jundt Art Center: 650
Juniper Dunes Wilderness: 416-417

K

Kachess Ridge: 545
Kah Tai Lagoon Nature Park: 309
Kalaloch: 19, 344
Kalispel: 641
Kamiak Butte County Park: 660, 664
Kanaskat-Palmer State Park: 18, 548, 549
Karpeles Manuscript Library Museum: 205
kayaking: Columbia Gorge/Wine Country 399, 438, 447; Eastern Washington 649; Eastside 93, 96, 102, 113; North Cascades 479, 507, 522, 530; North Puget Sound 137, 140, 142-143, 172, 173; Olympic Coast 378; Olympic Peninsula/Coast 300, 309, 310, 314, 319, 331, 345, 361, 378; San Juan Islands 19, 252, 261-262, 273-274, 275, 283, 288-289; Seattle 43, 57-58, 86; South Cascades 548; South Puget Sound 223, 225, 228, 230, 234, 240
Kayak Point County Park: 152
Kelcema Lake Ski Route: 474
Keller Ferry: 614
Keller House: 635-636
Kelsey Creek Farm and Park: 93
Kelso: 379-382
Kelso Highlander Festival: 380
Kendal Katwalk: 543
Kendall Katwalk: 19, 463
Kendall Skyline Drive: 671
Kennewick Farmers Market: 421
Kennewick Man: 417
Kent: 238, 239

Kent Farmers Market: 239
Kepler's Parade & Shake Rat Olympics: 349
Kerouac, Jack: 489
Kerry Park: 40
Ketchum Kalf Rodeo: 594
Kettle Crest Trail: 631-632
Kettle Falls: 633-635
Kettle Falls Historical Center: 634
Kettle Falls Ranger Station: 635
Key City Public Theatre: 308
Key Peninsula: 228
Keyport: 221
Keystone Jetty underwater park: 137
Kinderfest: 519
Kinetic Sculpture Race: 309
King County Fair: 548
King 5 Winterfest: 52
King Ludwig's Gasthaus: 519
King Street Station: 29
Kiona Vineyards Winery: 435
Kirkland: 100-104
Kirkland Arts Center: 101
Kirkland Farmers Market: 101
Kirkland Marina: 102
Kirkland Performance Center: 101
Kirkman House: 422-423
Kirland Uncorked: 101
Kite Festival: 361
kites: 353, 361, 368, 370; *see also specific place*
Kitsap County Fair and Rodeo: 216
Kitsap County Historical Museum: 216
Kitsap Memorial State Park: 223
Kitsap Peninsula: 215-227
Kittitas County Fair: 446
Kittitas County Farmers Market: 449
Kittitas County Historical Museum: 443
Klahanee Ridge Trail: 327
Kla Ha Ya Days: 151-152
Klickitat Canyon Winery: 402
Klickitat County Fair and Rodeo: 406
Klickitat County Historical Museum: 406
Klondike Gold Rush National Historical Park: 15, 32
Kobe Terrace Park: 35
Kopachuck State Park: 210, 225
KVI Beach: 230

L

Labor Day Rodeo: 494
La Conner: 160-164
La Conner Flats Display Garden: 156
La Conner Quilt Museum: 161
Ladder Creek Falls and Rock Gardens: 485, 487
Lady Washington: 356
Lake Aberdeen: 357
Lake Ann (Heather Meadows area): 466
Lake Ann (Liberty Bell Roadless Area): 490
Lake Chelan: 19, 504, 505
Lake Chelan Bach Feste: 505
Lake Chelan Golf Course: 507
Lake Chelan Museum: 504
Lake Chelan-Sawtooth Wilderness: 500, 512
Lake Chelan State Park: 505, 506, 508
Lake Chelan Western Days: 505
Lake Chelan Winterfest: 505
Lake Crescent: 18, 332-333
Lake Easton State Park: 545, 547
Lakefair: 195
Lake Hills Greenbelt: 96
Lake Leland Park: 304
Lake Lenore Caves: 618
Lake Leo Trail: 637
Lake Padden Park: 172, 173
Lake Pondilla: 137
Lake Quinault: 19, 345-348
Lake Quinault Resort: 19, 347
Lake Roesiger Park: 534
Lake Roosevelt: 613-615
Lake Roosevelt National Recreation Area: 613
Lake Roosevelt Regatta: 634
Lake Sacajawea: 415-416
Lake Sacajawea Park: 379
Lake Samish: 173
Lake Sammamish State Park: 113
Lakes Area Mt. Bike Loop: 631
Lakeshore Trail: 512
Lakes Trail: 588
Lake Street: 100
Lake Sutherland: 327
Lake Sylvia State Park: 357, 359
Lake Terrell Wildlife Area: 182
Lake to Lake Parkway Trail: 96
Lake 22: 471
Lake Union: 38-39
Lake Union Wooden Boat Festival: 53
Lakeview Cemetery: 39-40
Lakeview Ranch: 606
Lake Wallula: 416
Lake Washington: 45-46
Lake Washington Boulevard: 58
Lake Washington Floating Bridge: 91
Lake Wenatchee: 522
Lake Wenatchee State Park: 520, 521
Lakewold Gardens: 204
Lakewood Park: 209
Lake Wynoochee: 359

Langlauf Cross-Country Ski Race: 653
Langley: 19, 127, 129-132
Langley Mystery Weekend: 129
La Push: 18, 340-342
Larrabee State Park: 165, 173
laser light shows: 12, 613
Last Stand Rodeo: 617
Last Trading Post: 494
Latah Creek Wine Cellars: 651
lava beds: 401
Lava Canyon Trail: 589
Lawson Gardens: 664
Leadbetter Point State Park: 371
Leavenworth: 516-527
Leavenworth Farmers Market: 526
Leavenworth Golf Course Trail: 521
Leavenworth International Accordion Celebration: 519
Leavenworth National Fish Hatchery: 518
Leavenworth Ski Hill: 521
Leavenworth Summer Theater: 519
L'Ecole No. 41 Winery: 425
LeFeber Bulb Company: 156
Legislative Building: 14, 191
Lenin: 43
Levey Park: 415
Lewis and Clark Days: 669
Lewis and Clark expedition: 690-691
Lewis and Clark Interpretive Center: 367
Lewis and Clark State Park (South Cascades): 574
Lewis and Clark Trail State Park (Columbia Gorge/Wine Country): 426
Lewis and Clark Trail State Park (Eastern Washington): 674, 675
Lewis River Trail: 590
Lewiston Roundup Rodeo and Parade: 669
Liberty Bay Park: 223
Liberty Bell Roadless Area: 490-491
Liberty Lake: 654
Liberty Orchards: 515
Liberty Theatre: 423
Library Fair: 273
Lighted Boat Parade (Bellingham): 171
Lighted Boat Parade (Gig Harbor): 225
Lighted Boat Parade (Poulsbo): 223
Lighted Ships of Christmas Boat Parade (Anacortes): 252
Lighter than Air Hot Air Balloon Festival: 195
lighthouses: North Puget Sound 121, 135; Olympic Peninsula/Coast 308, 314, 317, 319, 335, 344, 361, 367, 371; San Juan Islands 258, 259; Seattle 46; South Puget Sound 204-205, 230
Lilac Bloomsday Run: 652
Lilac Festival: 652
Lilliwaup: 299
Lily Basin Trail: 571
Lime Kiln Point State Park: 259
Lincoln County Historical Museum: 649
Lincoln Park: 46, 327
Lincoln Rock State Park: 455-456
Lincoln Theatre: 156
Ling Shen Ching Tze Temple: 105
Lionel Hampton Jazz Festival: 664
Little Creek Casino: 297
Little Goose Dam: 672
Little Huckleberry Mountain: 401
Little Mountain Park: 158
Little Pend Oreille Lakes Recreation Area: 636-637
Little Red Schoolhouse: 288
Little Si: 540-541
Little White Salmon: 402
Living Museum: 608
llama farms: 230
llama pack trips: 489-490, 491
locks: 13, 42, 410, 672
Loganberry Festival: 133
Log Cabin Museum: 218
Loggerodeo: 480
Loggers Playday: 357
Long Beach: 368, 371, 373, 374-375
Long Beach Peninsula: 366-379
Longboard Classic Surf Festival: 361
Long Island: 376
Long Lake: 643-644
Long Lake County Park: 219
Long Lake Dam: 643
Longmire Area: 559
Longmire Gas Station: 559
Longmire Museum: 559
Longview: 379-382
Looff Carousel: 646
Lookout Mountain Lookout: 500
Loomis Lake State Park: 369
Loowit System: 590
Loowit Trail: 591
Lopez Historical Museum: 281
Lopez Island: 16, 281-287
Lopez Island Community Church: 281
Lopez Island Farmers Market: 286
Lopez Island Vineyards: 281
Lopez Library: 281
Lopez Village: 281
Lost Mountain Winery: 318
Lovers Lane Trail: 334

Lowell Riverfront Trail: 147
Lower Grand Coulee Area: 618
Lower Granite Dam: 672
Lower Monumental Dam: 672
Lower Snake River: 672-673
Lower Wolf Trail: 642
Lucky Dog Casino: 299
Lucky Eagle Casino: 194
lumber industry: 695
Lummi Island: 179-180, 181
Lummi Stommish Water Festival: 181
Luna House Museum: 667
Lundeen Park: 151
Luther Burbank Park: 93
Lyle: 402
Lyman Lake Trail: 512
Lynden: 180-182
Lynden in Lights: 182
Lynden Pioneer Museum: 181
Lynnwood: 122
Lyons Ferry Hatchery: 673
Lyons Ferry State Park: 672-673
Lyre River Recreation Area: 336

M

MacDonald, Ranald: 629
Madison Park: 45-46
Madrona Farms: 281
magazines: 712
Magnolia: 40
Magnolia Park: 40
Maiden of Deception Pass: 142
Maifest: 519
Makah Days: 335
Makah Indian Reservation: 334
Makah Museum: 335
Maloney-Sobieski Mountain Road: 531
Manatash Ridge Viewpoint: 437
Manchester State Park: 219
Manito Park and Gardens: 650
Manresa Castle: 307, 311
Manresa Grotto: 641
Manzanita Park: 234
Maple Falls: 463
Maple Glade Rain Forest Trail: 346
Maple Hall: 161
Maple Pass: 490
Marblemount: 13, 482-484
Marblemount Fish Hatchery: 482-483
Marcus Whitman Hotel: 423
Mardi Gras: 53
Marhut Falls Trail: 302
Marina Park: 100
marinelife-watching: 680-682; North Cascades 479; North Puget Sound 142, 145, 173; Olympic Peninsula/Coast 336, 341, 356, 361, 362, 371; San Juan Islands 16, 252, 259, 261-263, 274, 283; *see also* aquariums
Marine Park: 209, 210, 389
Marine Science Center: 223
Marine Supply & Hardware Co.: 252
Maritime Gig: 225
Maritime Heritage Center (Bellingham): 170
Maritime Heritage Center (Seattle): 38
Marmes Rockshelter: 673
Marrowstone Island: 314-315, 316
Marrowstone Point Lighthouse: 314
Marshall House: 389
Marsh's Free Museum: 370
Martha Falls: 560
Maryhill: 407-409
Maryhill Museum of Art: 407, 408-409
Maryhill State Park: 409
Maryhill Winery: 12, 407-408
Marymere Falls Trail: 333
Marymoor Amphitheater: 106-107
Marymoor Park: 105
Marys Corner: 574
Marysville: 154-155
Mason County Fair: 297
Mason County Forest Festival: 297
Mason County Historical Museum: 297
Masterworks Choral Ensemble: 194
Matilda N. Jackson State Park: 574
Mayfield Lake County Park: 574
McChord Air Museum: 206
McCleary: 360
McCleary Bear Festival: 359
McConnell Mansion: 666
McCosh Park Amphitheater: 604
McGregor Mountain: 512
McLane Creek Nature Trail: 196
McNary Dam: 412
McNary National Wildlife Refuge: 412
Meacham Mills: 669
Meerkerk Rhododendron Gardens: 133
Memorial Day (San Juan Island): 261
Memorial Day Festival (Grand Coulee Dam): 615
Memorial Day Weekend (Index): 532
Mercer girls: 693
Mercer Island: 91-99
Mercer Slough: 93
Merriman Falls: 348
Meta Lake: 591
Metaline: 638-639
Metaline City Park: 638

Metaline Falls: 638-639
Methow: 501-502
Methow Music Festival: 494
Methow Valley: 491-502
Methow Valley Mountain Bike Festival: 494
Methow Valley Sport Trails Association: 20, 494, 495-496
Meydenbauer Center: 94
Meyers Falls: 634
Microsoft Museum: 105
Mid-Columbia Regional Ballet: 417
Mid-Columbia Symphony: 417
Mike's Dive Resort: 18, 300
Milbrandt Vineyards: 435
military attractions: Columbia Gorge/Wine Country 11, 386, 388-389, 390, 391, 398, 422, 424, 431-432, 436; Eastern Washington 604, 643, 652; North Puget Sound 135-136, 137, 146, 315; Olympic Peninsula/Coast 18, 20, 296, 308, 314, 315, 335, 367, 377; San Juan Islands 256-258; Seattle 40; South Puget Sound 204, 206, 215, 216, 219, 221, 233
Mill Bay Casino: 508
Millersylvania State Park: 193, 196
Mill Pond Historical Site: 639
Mima Mounds: 193-194
Mindport: 167, 170
Mineral Lake: 551
Mineral Springs Resort: 519
Miner's Car: 591
mining industry: 694
Mission Creek Players: 453-454
Mission Ridge Ski Area: 20, 455, 521, 543
Moclips: 348-351
Model Railroad Show: 37
Molson: 628
Molson Museum: 628
Monroe: 533
Monroe Historical Society Museum: 533
Monte Cristo: 471-472
Montesano: 359-360
Monty Holm's House of Poverty and Mon Road Railraod: 604
Monument Hill: 601
Moosefest: 545
Moran State Park: 16, 270, 272, 274
Morton: 575-577
Morton Loggers Jubilee: 575-576
Moscow: 666
Moses Community State Park: 604
Moses Lake (lake): 604
Moses Lake (town): 602-605
Moses Lake Family Aquatic Center: 604
Moses Lake Museum and Art Center: 604
Mossyrock: 574-575
Mossyrock Park: 575
Mother Mountain Loop: 563
Mother Nature's Window: 151
motorcycles: 202-203, 252, 354, 580
Mount Adams Wilderness: 19, 592-593
mountaineering: North Cascades 466, 470; North Puget Sound 172; Olympic Peninsula/Coast 343; Seattle 59; South Cascades 19, 564, 589, 592
Mountaineers, The: 701
Mountaineers' Forest Theater: 221
Mountain Loop Highway: 469-476
Mountain View Cemetery: 423
Mount Baker: 20, 463-469
Mount Baker Vineyards: 463-464
Mount Constitution: 16, 270
Mount Forgotten Meadows: 471
Mount Pilchuck State Park: 470
Mount Rainier National Park: 11, 19, 555-571, 702
Mount Rainier Scenic Railroad: 551
Mount Rainier Wilderness Areas: 568-571
Mount Si: 540-541
Mount Skokomish Wilderness: 302
Mount St. Helens National Volcanic Monument: 11, 19, 585-592
Mount Tahoma Trails: 20, 553
Mount Vernon: 155-160
Mount Vernon-Skagit Valley Farmers Market: 159
movies: *see specific place*
Mt. Baker Highway: 463
Mt. Baker Ski Area: 464, 467
Mt. Baker Theatre: 170
Mt. Constitution: 272
Mt. Ellinor Trail: 301
Mt. Erie: 250
Mt. Fremont Lookout: 562
Mt. Misery Trail: 671-672
Mt. Olympus: 343
Mt. Spokane Ski & Snowboard Park: 653
Mt. Spokane State Park: 650, 654
Mt. Storm King Trail: 333
Mt. Townsend Trail: 304
Mt. Walker: 304
Mt. Young Trail: 258
Muckleshoot Indian Casino: 237
Mud Mountain Dam Park: 547
Mukilteo: 13, 121-126
Mukilteo Historical Museum: 121

Mukilteo Lighthouse Festival: 122
Mukilteo Lighthouse Park: 121
Mural-in-a-Day: 430, 436
Museum and Arts Center: 316
Museum of Anthropology: 662
Museum of Art: 662
Museum of Flight: 14, 46-47
Museum of Flight Restoration Center: 145
Museum of History and Industry: 45-46
Museum of Northwest Art: 160
Museum on Bulb History: 156
music festivals: Columbia Gorge/Wine Country 399, 436; Eastern Washington 615, 627, 652, 664; Eastside 107, 113; North Cascades 476, 494, 505, 519; North Puget Sound 146, 171; Olympic Peninsula/Coast 304, 309, 335, 354, 357, 370; San Juan Islands 273; Seattle 54; South Puget Sound 207, 219, 230, 234, 240
Music in the Park (Bothell): 116
Music in the Park (Olympia): 195
Music in the Park (SeaTac): 240
Music in the Parks (Everett): 146
Music Theatre of Wenatchee: 453
M.V. Plover: 179
Myrtle Edwards Park: 34
Mystery Bay State Park: 314-315

N

Naches Peak Loop: 572
Narada Falls: 559
Nason Ridge Trail: 522-523
National Championship Chukar Field Trials: 436
National Handcar Races: 548
National Lentil Festival: 663-664
national wildlife refuges: Columbia Gorge/Wine Country 389-390, 412, 432; Eastern Washington 602, 658-659; Olympic Coast 357, 376, 378; Olympic Peninsula 317; South Cascades 594; South Puget Sound 192-193
Native Americans: 687-689, 691; Columbia Gorge/Wine Country 431, 436, 437; Eastern Washington 618-620, 623-624, 641, 642, 643, 663; Olympic Peninsula/Coast 298-299, 334, 335, 340, 341, 344, 345, 349; Seattle 17, 40, 86; South Cascades 550; South Puget Sound 205-206, 232
Naval Submarine Base: 221
Naval Undersea Museum: 221
Naval Undersea Warfare Center: 221
Neah Bay: 20, 334, 336-337
Necklace Valley Trail: 528
Neely Mansion: 236
Neil Barn: 140
Nels Bruseth Memorial Garden: 476
Nespelem: 620
Newcastle Beach Park: 96
New Dungeness Lighthouse: 317
Newhalem: 484-485
Newport: 641-643
Newport Rodeo: 642
newspapers: 711-712
New Year's Eve: 52
Nez Percé County Fair: 669
Nez Percé Music Archive: 663
nightlife: *see specific place*
Nike missile bases: 111
Nine Mile Falls: 631
Nippon Kan Theater: 51
Nisqually Glacier: 557
Nisqually National Wildlife Refuge: 192-193
Nisqually Reach Nature Center: 193
Nisqually Vista Trail: 560
Nolte State Park: 548
Nooksack City Park: 468
Nooksack Falls: 464
Nooksack River Casino: 463
Nooksack Valley: 464-465, 479
Nordic Heritage Museum: 41
Norse Peak Wilderness: 569
North Beach: 348-356
North Bend: 540-542
North Cascades Highway: 477-478
North Cascades Institute: 479
North Cascades Loop: 478
North Cascade Smokejumper Base: 494
North Cascades National Park: 13, 485-491, 702
North Central Washington Fair: 453
Northeast Corner: 632-644
Northeast Washington Fair: 636
Northern Pacific Railway Museum: 431
Northern Snohomish County: 150-155
North Fork Ridge: 582-583
North Fork Sauk Falls: 475
North Fork Sauk Trail (Glacier Peak Wilderness): 473
North Fork Trail (Colonel Bob Wilderness): 346
North Fork Trail (Elwha River Valley): 331
North Fork Trail (Henry M. Jackson Wilderness Area): 529
North Head Lighthouse: 371
North Jetty: 353
Northwest Experimental Aircraft Association Fly-In: 151

Northwest Folklife Festival: 53
Northwest Forest Pass: 703
Northwest Museum of Arts and Culture: 648
Northwest Native Garden: 204
Northwest Outdoor Center: 15, 57
Northwest Puppet Center: 46
Northwest Railway Museum: 538
Northwest School of Wooden Boatbuilding: 305, 307
Northwest Trek Wildlife Park: 550
Northwest Washington Fair: 181
Norway Pass Trail: 591
Norwegian Memorial: 336
nuclear power: 412, 414-415, 642
Nudestock: 113
nudist resorts: 533
Nugents Corner: 463, 479
Nutcracker Museum: 520
Nutty Narrows: 379

O

Oak Bay: 314-316
Oak Creek Wildlife Recreation Area: 579
Oak Harbor: 139-141
Oak Harbor Public Market: 141
Oaks to Wetlands Wildlife Trail: 390
Observation Trail: 593-594
observatories: 12, 406
Obstruction Pass State Park: 272, 274
Obstruction Point Road: 324, 326
Occidental Square Park: 29
Ocean Beach Highway: 378
Ocean City: 348-351
Ocean City State Park: 349, 353
Ocean Park: 368-369, 374, 375
Ocean Shores: 18, 351-356
Ocean Shores Environmental Interpretive Center: 353
Octoberfest: 494
Odd Fellows Hall: 110
Odessa: 606-607
Odessa Historisches Museum: 606
Odlin County Park: 281, 284
Odyssey, the Maritime Discovery Center: 34
Officers' Row: 389
Ohanapecosh Area: 560
Ohme Gardens: 449, 451
Oil City: 341, 344
Okanogan: 623-625
Okanogan Bingo & Casino: 623-624
Okanogan County Courthouse: 623
Okanogan County Fair: 624
Okanogan County Historical Museum: 623
Okanogan Days: 624
Okanogan Highlands: 628-632
Okanogan National Forest: 17, 628
Okanogan Valley: 625-627
Okanogan Valley Orchestra and Chorus: 623-624
Oktoberfest: 261
Olallie State Park: 541
Old Apple Tree Festival: 391
Old Apple Tree Park: 389
Old City Hall: 205
Olde Fashioned Christmas at Pioneer Park: 181
Old Fort Townsend State Park: 308
Old Mill Days: 659
Old Molson: 628
Old Number Six: 485
Old Sauk Trail: 473
Old Settlers Museum: 575
Old Snohomish Village Museum: 150
Old Spiral Highway: 667
Old State Capitol Building: 191
Old Time Threshing Bee: 533
Old Townsend State Park: 310
Ollalie Lake: 595
Olmstead Place State Park: 445
Olympia: 14, 15, 189-199; traveling to: 359-360
Olympia Arts Walk: 194
Olympia Farmers Market: 199
Olympia Little Theater: 194
Olympia Symphony Orchestra: 194
Olympia Watershed Park: 195-196
Olympic Beach: 121
Olympic Cellars: 317
Olympic Coast National Marine Sanctuary: 337
Olympic Game Farm: 318
Olympic Hot Springs: 331
Olympic Music Festival: 304
Olympic National Park: 292, 294, 702
Olympic National Park Visitor Center: 18, 324
Olympic Sculpture Park: 14, 34
Omak: 623-625
Omak Stampede and Suicide Race: 623-624
Omak Western and Native Art Show: 623
On the Boards: 51
Opening Day of Boating Season: 53
opera: Eastern Washington 646; Olympic Peninsula 326; Seattle 15, 38, 52; South Puget Sound 207
Opera House: 38
Orcas Island: 16, 270-280
Orcas Island Chamber Music Festival: 273
Orcas Island Farmers Market: 280
Orcas Island Fly-In: 273

Orcas Island Historical Museum: 272
Orcas Theatre & Community Center: 272
Orcas Village: 270
orchards: see fruit orchards
Oregon, driving from: 377
Oregon Butte Trail: 672
Oregon Trail Days: 195
Oroville: 626-627
Oroville May Festival: 627
Osoyoos Lake State Veterans Memorial Park: 626, 627
O'Sullivan Dam: 603
Othello: 605-606
Othello Farmers Market: 606
Otto Farm, The: 180
Our Lady of Good Voyage Chapel: 259
Our Lady of Sorrows: 641
outdoor gear: Columbia Gorge/Wine Country 399, 447; Eastern Washington 654; Eastside 95; North Cascades 495, 513; North Puget Sound 123; Olympic Peninsula/Coast 310, 326, 342-343; San Juan Islands 252, 273; Seattle 55-56; South Cascades 546, 549, 555, 566, 568; South Puget Sound 209
Outdoor Music Festival: 234
Outdoor Recreation Center: 664
Outdoor Sculpture Garden: 167
Outdoor Summer Musical: 425
Oval Creek Trail: 500
Owen Beach: 208
Oyhut Wildlife Recreation Area: 353
Oyster Bar, The: 17, 165-166
oyster farms: 189, 303
Oysterfest: 297
oyster gathering: 221
Oyster Run: 252
Oyster Stampede: 376
Oysterville: 369
Oysterville Baptist Church: 369
Oysterville National Historic District: 369
Ozette Lake: 336, 337
Ozette Ranger Station: 336

P

Pacific Arts Center Wenatchee: 453
Pacific Beach State Park: 19, 349
Pacific County Courthouse: 376
Pacific Crest Trail: 19, 472-473, 489, 492, 527, 528, 563, 569-571, 572, 593
Pacific Northwest Ballet: 52
Pacific Northwest Highland Games: 548
Pacific Northwest Quarter Horse Shows: 533
Pacific Rim Bonsai Collection: 240
Pacific Science Center: 36-37
Pack Experimental Forest: 550
Packwood: 577-578
Packwood State Park: 578
Packwood Winter Recreation Area: 578
Palmer Lake: 626
Palouse Country: 20, 658-660
Palouse Days Community Festival: 659
Palouse Empire Fair: 660
Palouse Empire Plowing Bee: 660
Palouse Empire Threshing Bee: 660
Palouse Falls: 20
Palouse Falls State Park: 673
Palouse Lions Park: 660
Panjab Trail: 672
Pantages Theater: 207
Parade of Lighted Ships: 195
Paradise: 11, 559-560
Paradise Point State Park: 391, 584
Paradise Theater: 225
paragliding: 506
Parallax Gallery: 532
Paramount Theater: 51
Parego Lagoon: 137
Park Butte: 481
Park on the Lid, The: 93
Park Pass: 489, 512
Pasayten Wilderness: 491
Pasco Farmers Market: 421
Pasco Village Marketplace: 418
Pass Lake: 142
Pataha Flour Mill: 671
Pateros: 501-502
Pateros Hydro Classic: 501
Paterson: 409, 412
Patrick M. Paul Vineyards: 425
Pavilion: 646
Paws on Parade: 545
P. D. Q. & K. Railroad: 204
Peace Arch State Park: 20, 179
Pearrygin Lake State Park: 495, 496
Pearson Air Museum: 11, 389
Peewee Falls: 639
Pendleton Woolen Mill: 397
Pend Oreille: 20, 632
Pend Oreille County Courthouse: 642
Pend Oreille County Fair & Rodeo: 641
Pend Oreille River: 19, 20, 632
Peninsula Jazz Festival: 219
Peninsula Park: 501
Penn Cove Mussel Festival: 136
Penn Cove Water Festival: 136
Penrose Point State Park: 210, 228

Percival Landing Park: 192
Percival Landing Tower: 192
performing arts: Columbia Gorge/Wine Country 390, 417, 425, 435-436, 453-454; Eastern Washington 624, 634, 639, 646, 652, 663; Eastside 94, 101, 111, 116; North Cascades 519; North Puget Sound 129, 139, 146, 156, 170-171; Olympic Peninsula/Coast 304, 308-309, 326, 357, 370, 380; San Juan Islands 251, 260, 272; Seattle 15, 38, 51-52; South Cascades 539; South Puget Sound 194, 195, 207, 216, 219, 221, 225, 237
Perry Creek Falls: 471
Peshastin Pinnacles State Park: 520
Pete's Flying Aces: 240
petroglyphs/pictographs: Columbia Gorge/Wine Country 404, 430; Eastern Washington 601, 644, 667, 668; North Cascades 501; Olympic Peninsula 336
pets, traveling with: 708, 709
Phelps Creek Trail: 523
photography supplies: 57
Picket Range: 490
Pickett Historical Museum: 531
Picture Lake: 464-465
Piety Flats Winery: 434
Pig Out in the Park: 652
"Pig War": 257, 692
Pig War Museum: 258
Pike Place Fish: 33, 70-71
Pike Place Market: 13, 14, 33, 54, 70-71
Pike Place Market Festival: 53
Pike Place Market tours: 17, 33
Pilchuck Glass School: 151
Pillar Point County Park: 335
Pillars: 601
Pilot Ridge Trail: 473
Pine Lake: 113
Pine Ridge Loop Trail: 252
Pinnacle Peak Trail: 560
Pioneer Day (Ephrata): 608
Pioneer Days (Cle Elum): 545
Pioneer Farm Museum and Ohop Indian Village: 550
Pioneer Motorcycle Museum: 202-203
Pioneer Park (Bellevue): 93
Pioneer Park (Ferndale): 180
Pioneer Park (La Conner): 161
Pioneer Park (Walla Walla): 423
Pioneer Park Heritage Trail: 642
Pioneer Skate Park: 455
Pioneer Square (Seattle): 15, 29
Pioneer Square Fire Festival: 53
planning tips: 8-10
Planter's Day: 583
plants: 679-680; *see also specific place*
Playground of Dreams: 415
Pleasant Harbor State Park: 301
Point Defiance Park: 203-204
Point Defiance Park Natural Areas: 208
Point of Arches: 336
Point Robinson Lighthouse: 230
Point Whitney Shellfish Lab: 303
Point Wilson Lighthouse: 308
Poker Paddle: 642
Polar Bear Swim: 181
Polson Museum: 357
Pomeroy: 671
Poodle Dog Pass: 472
Porcupine Bay: 614, 643
Port Angeles: 18, 322-331
Port Angeles Community Players: 326
Port Angeles Farmers Market: 330
Port Angeles Fine Arts Center: 324
Port Angeles Light Opera Association: 326
Port Angeles Speedway: 326-327
Port Angeles Symphony Orchestra: 326
Port Hadlock: 315-316
Port Ludlow: 315
Port Ludlow Farmers Market: 315
Port Orchard: 218-221
Port Orchard Farmers Market: 220
Portteus Vineyards: 434
Port Townsend: 18, 305-314
Port Townsend Blues Festival: 309
Port Townsend Community Orchestra: 309
Port Townsend Farmers Market: 313
Port Townsend Marine Science Center: 308
Posey Island State Park: 289
Possession Beach County Park: 130
Potholes Reservoir: 603
Potholes State Park: 603, 604
Potlatch: 299
Potlatch Corporation: 667
Potlatch State Park: 299
Poulsbo: 221-224
Pow Wow & Rodeo: 436
Presby Mansion: 406
Press Room Theatre: 453
Preston Premium Wines: 417
Priest Point Park: 192, 196
Prince Creek Trail: 512
Pro-Am TT Motorcycle Races: 580
Procession of the Species: 194
Prospector's Days: 630
Prosser: 434-435, 442

Prosser Balloon Rally and Harvest Festival: 436-437
Prosser Farmers Market: 442
Prosser Wine & Food Fair: 436
public art: Columbia Gorge/Wine Country 445; Eastern Washington 646; Eastside 101; North Puget Sound 129, 167; San Juan Islands 259; Seattle 33, 34, 39, 42-43
public lands: 702, 704-705
Puffer Butte: 668
Puget Power-Redmond Trail: 108
Puget Sound Energy Visitors Center: 481
Puget Sound Maritime Museum: 38
Puget Sound Naval Shipyard: 216
Pullman: 660-666
Purdy Spit: 225
Putvin Trail: 302
Puyallup: 236-239
Puyallup Fair: 237
Puyallup Farmers Market: 239
Puyallup Trail: 571
Puyallup Valley: 236-239

Q

Quartz Creek Big Trees: 591
Queen Anne: 40
Queets Loop Trail: 345
Queets River: 345
Queets Trail: 345
Quilceda Creek Vintners: 154
Quilcene: 304-305
Quilcene Historical Museum: 304
Quilcene National Fish Hatchery: 304
Quileute Days: 341
Quileute Indian Reservation: 340
Quileute Tribe Museum: 341
Quinault Indian Reservation: 345
Quinault National Recreation Trail System: 346
Quinault Rain Forest Nature Trail: 346
Quincy: 600-602

R

Ragtime Rhodie Dixieland Jazz Festival: 370
Railroad Days: 476
Railroad Depot: 110
railroad excursions: 204, 538, 551, 638, 639
Rails to Trails: 376, 545
railway museums: 170, 431, 538, 604, 673
Rainbow Falls: 480, 512
rain forests: 679-680; Olympic National Park 292, 294; Olympic Peninsula/Coast 338, 342, 346; South Cascades 562
Rainier Tower: 29
Rainier View Trail: 569
Rainy Lake: 490
R. A. Long Park: 379
Randle: 575-577
Ranger Hole Trail: 302
Rasar State Park: 480
Rattlesnake Hills: 12, 433-434
Rattlesnake Lake: 541
Rattlesnake Ledge: 541
Rattlesnake Mountain Scenic Area: 541
Ravenna Park: 45
Raymond: 375-377
Reaney Park: 664
Red, White & Blues Festival: 240
Red Barn: 47
Redhook Ale Brewery: 116
Redmen Hall: 378
Redmond: 105-109
Redmond Bicycle Derby Days: 107
Redmond Saturday Market: 107
Red Wind Casino: 194
Reed Park: 445
Reflection Lakes: 560
Renaissance Faires: 195, 417, 538-539
Renton: 242, 243
Reptile Serpentarium: 532
Republic: 630-631
Republic Historical Center: 630
Return of the Orcas Festival: 260-261
Reynolds-Day Building: 423
Rhododendron Festival: 309
Rhododendron Garden: 204
Rhododendron Park: 137-138
Rhododendron Species Foundation Garden: 240
Rialto Beach: 341
Rialto Theater: 207
Rich Passage Winery: 234
Rick Steves' Europe Through the Backdoor: 122-123
Ridgefield National Wildlife Refuge: 389-390
Ridge to River Relay: 454
Rimrock Lake Area: 579
Riverbend Park: 158
Riverfront Park (Spokane): 12, 646, 652
Riverfront Park (Wenatchee): 454
River Life Interpretive Center: 378
River Meadows County Park: 152
River Raft Challenge Race: 482
river rafting: Columbia Gorge/Wine Country 19, 402-403, 455; Eastern Washington 654, 668-669; North Cascades 13, 465-466, 473, 483-484, 495, 511, 522, 529-530;

Olympic Peninsula 331, 345; South Cascades 18, 19-20, 548, 549, 579
Riverside State Park: 649, 654
River Trail: 538
Riverwalk Park: 506
Roche Harbor: 258-259
rock climbing: Columbia Gorge/Wine Country 404, 430; Eastern Washington 601, 654, 664, 672; North Cascades 490, 495, 520, 532; North Puget Sound 172; Seattle 59; South Cascades 569; South Puget Sound 196
Rock Creek Park: 398
Rocket City Neon Museum: 397
Rock Gardens Park: 622
rock hunting: 361, 446, 447, 519
Rockin' B Ranch: 654
Rock Island Hydro Park: 455
Rock N Tomahawk Ranch: 447
Rockport: 482-484
Rockport Ferry: 484
Rockport State Park: 483
Rocky Brook Falls: 302
Rocky Reach Dam: 451
Rodeo Days: 659
rodeos: Columbia Gorge/Wine Country 390, 406, 410, 418, 426, 436, 445-446; Eastern Washington 604, 617, 620, 623, 624, 627, 628, 630, 636, 641, 642, 652, 659, 660, 669, 674; North Cascades 476, 480, 494, 505; Olympic Peninsula/Coast 359; South Cascades 594; South Puget Sound 216; *see also specific place*
Rod Run to the End of the World: 370
Roosevelt: 409, 412
Roozengaarde: 155
Rosalie Whyel Museum of Doll Art: 91-92
Rosario Beach: 142
Rose Garden: 204
Rose Theatre: 308
Roslyn: 544-545, 547
Roslyn Museum: 545
Ross Lake: 13, 487-488
Ross Lake Resort: 13, 488
Rotary Park: 250
Rothschild House: 307
Royal Fireworks Concert and Festival: 652
Royal Theatre: 260
Ruby Beach: 344
Ruby Theater: 504
Russian explorers: 689
Russian rocket: 42-43
Rust Mansion: 205
Ryan House Museum: 236
Ryan Lake: 591

S

Sacajawea State Park: 416
Saddle Dam Park: 590
Safeco Field: 59
safety/health: 709-710
safety tips: 710
Sage and Sun Festival: 608
Sagebrush Loggers' Tourney: 627
Sagelands Vineyard: 433
Saint Edward State Park: 100-101
Salish Barter Fairs: 641
Salish Fair: 641
Salish Lodge: 18, 539
Salmo Basin Trail: 640
Salmo Divide Trail: 640-641
salmon: 696; *see also* fish hatcheries; *specific place*
Salmon Bakes: 208
Salmon Creek Park: 379, 391
Salmo-Priest Wilderness: 640-641
Salsbury Point County Park: 296
Salt Creek County Park: 335, 336
Saltwater State Park: 240, 241
Salty Sea Days: 146
Salty's on Alki: 15, 80-81
Samish Park: 172
Sammamish River Trail: 58, 108, 115, 116
Samuel Benn Park: 357
sandcastle/sand sculpture contests: 181, 349, 370
Sandcastle Sculpture Contest: 349
sand dunes: 416-417, 604
Sand Point: 336
Sandsations Sand Sculptures: 370
Sandsculpture Contest: 349
San Juan Community Theatre & Arts Center: 260
San Juan County Fair: 261
San Juan County Park: 263
San Juan Farmers Market: 269
San Juan Historical Museum: 258
San Juan Island: 256-269
San Juan Island National Historical Park: 16, 256-259
San Juan Vineyards: 16, 261
Santa Train: 204
Sarah Spurgeon Art Gallery: 445
Satus Pass: 406
Sauk Mountain Road: 483
Sauk River: 473

Sauk River County Park: 476
Scandia Midsommarfest: 223
Scandinavian Language Institute: 41
Scenic Beach State Park: 221
scenic drives: Columbia Gorge/Wine Country 396, 437; Eastern Washington 601, 619-620, 643, 667, 671; North Cascades 464-465, 469, 477-478, 501, 504, 527, 531, 533; North Puget Sound 137, 153, 164-165; Olympic Coast 334, 335-336, 348; San Juan Islands 250; South Cascades 548, 559, 580, 583; South Puget Sound 208
Schafer State Park: 360
Schiffner Military and Police Museum: 604
Schweitzer Mountain Resort: 653
Scooteney Park: 605
Scottish Highland Games: 181
Seabeck: 221
Seafair: 53, 54
Seafoodfest: 54
Seafood Store: 303
Seagull Calling Contest: 219
sea kayaking: *see* kayaking
Seaquest State Park: 581
Seasons Performance Hall, The: 435-436
Sea-Tac Corridor: 239-243
SeaTac Farmers Market: 242
Seattle: 21-87; accommodations 60-65; entertainment/events 47-54; food 65-81; information and services 81-82; itineraries 13, 14-15; maps 26-27, 30-31; shopping 54-56; sights 28-47; sports/recreation 57-60; tours 15, 17, 32, 33, 35, 85-87; transportation 82-87
Seattle Aquarium: 14, 34
Seattle Art Museum: 32
Seattle Asian Art Museum: 39
Seattle Center: 14, 35-38
Seattle Children's Museum: 38
Seattle Children's Theater: 51
Seattle City Light Tours: 487
Seattle International Film Festival: 52
Seattle International Raceway: 237
Seattle Monorail: 35
Seattle Music Fest: 54
Seattle Opera: 15, 52
Seattle Police Museum: 33
Seattle Public Theater: 51
Seattle Repertory Theatre: 51
Seattle Symphony: 52
Seattle to Portland bike race: 580
Seattle Underground Tour: 15, 32
Seattle Youth Symphony: 52
Seaview: 373-375
Sea View Theatre: 272
Second Beach: 341
Sedro-Woolley: 478-480
Sedro-Woolley Museum: 479
Sehome: 170
Sehome Hill Arboretum: 167
Selkirk Moutains: 653
Semiahmoo County Park: 179
Semiahmoo Spit: 179
Sequim: 18, 316-321
Sequim Aquatic Recreation Center: 320
Sequim Bay State Park: 319
Sequim Irrigation Festival: 319
Seven Bays Marina: 643
7 Cedars Casino: 319
Seward Park: 46
Shadow Lake Trail: 562
Shadow of the Sentinels Trail: 480
Shafer Museum: 12, 493
Shakespeare Festival: 194, 195
Shark Reef Recreation Area: 283
Shaw Island: 287-288
Shaw Island Historical Museum: 287-288
Shedroof Divide Trail: 640
Sheehan Gallery: 425
Sheep Canyon Trail: 590
Shelton: 296-298
Shelton Farmers Market: 298
Shelton Trout Hatchery: 297
Sheri's Sweet Shop: 12, 499
Sherman Creek Hatchery: 634
Sherman Pass: 631-632
Sherry Trail: 637
Shilshole Bay: 40-41
Shilshole Marina: 42
Shine Tidelands State Park: 314
shipping industry: 696-697
Shi Shi Beach: 20, 336
Shoalwater Bay Bingo and Casino: 364
shopping: *see specific place*
Shores Mall: 354
Show 'N Shine Festival: 476
Shriner Peak Trail: 560-561
Sidewalk Art Show: 417
Sidney Art Gallery and Museum: 218
Silvana: 153
Silver Creek Trail: 569
Silver Falls: 514
Silver Falls Trail: 560
Silver Lake: 580-581
Silver Lake County Park: 467-468
Silver Lake Winery (Woodinville): 115

Silver Lake Winery (Zillah): 434
Silver Mountain: 653
Sitzmark: 626
Six to Sunset: 390
Skagit County Fair: 157
Skagit County Historical Museum: 160-161
Skagit Display Gardens: 156
Skagit River: 13, 483-484
Skagit River Bald Eagle Natural Area: 483
Skagit Speedway: 157
Skagit Valley: 155-160
Skagit Valley Casino Resort: 165
Skagit Valley Gardens: 156
Skagit Valley Tulip Festival: 156-157
Skagit View Trail: 483
Skagit Wildlife Recreation Area: 161
Skamania County Fair and Timber Carnival: 399
Skamokawa Center: 378
Skamokawa Vista Park: 378, 379
Ski Hill Trail: 521
skiing/snowboarding: 703; Columbia Gorge/Wine Country 20, 453, 455, 521, 543; Eastern Washington 624, 636, 653, 675; Eastside 95; North Cascades 20, 467, 496, 507-508, 519, 521, 529; North Puget Sound 174; Olympic Peninsula 324, 327; South Cascades 20, 571-572, 579
Ski to Sea Marathon: 171, 173, 463, 467
Skokomish Indian Reservation: 298-299
Skolaskin Church: 620
Skykomish: 531
Skykomish State Salmon Hatchery: 532
Skykomish Valley: 530-533
Skyline Divide: 466
Skyline Trail: 560
Slate Peak Lookout: 492
sleigh rides: 496, 521-522
Slocum House Theater: 390
slugs: 683
Smith Park: 140
Smith Tower: 29
Smokiam Days: 609
Snake River: 671-675
Snohomish Classic Car and Hot Rod Display: 152
Snohomish Farmers Market: 154
Snoqualmie: 538
Snoqualmie Falls: 18, 538
Snoqualmie Falls Forest Theater: 539
Snoqualmie Pass: 20, 542-544
Snoqualmie Valley: 538-544
Snoqualmie Valley Museum: 540
Snoqualmie Valley Railroad: 538
Snow Dog Super Mush Race: 625-626
Snowgrass Trail: 571
Snow Lake: 560
Snow Lake Trail: 528
snowmobiling: 704; Eastern Washington 614, 617; North Cascades 474, 501, 507, 508, 519, 522; South Cascades 545, 578, 590, 593
snowshoeing: Columbia Gorge/Wine Country 399; North Cascades 474, 513, 521; Olympic Peninsula 324, 327; South Cascades 566, 590, 593
Soap Lake: 608-610
Soap Lake Rod Run & Pig Feed: 609
Sol Duc: 333-334
Sol Duc Falls: 18, 334
Sol Duc Hot Spring Resort: 18, 334
Sol Duc Hot Springs: 334
Sol Duc River Trail: 334
Sons of Norway Hall: 222
Sourdough Mountain: 487
South Beach: 257
South Beach County Park: 288
Southcenter Mall: 240
South Climb Trail: 592-593
South Hill Mall: 237
South Jetty: 361
South Kitsap Community Park: 219
South Lake Union: 15, 38
South Lake Union Discovery Center: 38
South Lake Union Park: 38
South Seattle: 46-47
Southwest Washington Symphony: 380
South Whidbey Historical Museum: 129
South Whidbey State Park: 133
South Whidbey Tilth Farmers Market: 131-132
Space Needle: 13, 14, 35-36
Spaghetti Feed: 208
Spanaway Speedway: 207
Spanish explorers: 689
Spearfish Park: 404
Spencer Spit State Park: 281, 284
Spirit Lake Memorial Highway: 580-583, 585, 587
Spokane: 12, 644-657
Spokane Civic Theater: 652
Spokane County Courthouse: 648
Spokane Falls: 646
Spokane Farmers Market: 657
Spokane Floods: 596, 618
Spokane House Interpretive Center: 649-650
Spokane Interplayers Ensemble: 652
Spokane Interstate Fair: 652
Spokane Opera House: 646

Spokane Raceway Park: 653
Spokane Reservation: 643
Spokane River: 643
sports venues: Columbia Gorge/Wine Country 418-419, 437, 454; Eastern Washington 653, 664; North Puget Sound 146; Seattle 59-60; South Puget Sound 206
Spray Park Trail: 563
Springboard Trail: 637
Spring Canyon: 614
Spring Creek National Fish Hatchery: 402
Spring Fair and Daffodil Festival: 237
Spring Festival (Moses Lake): 604
Spring Festival (White Salmon): 402
Spruce Nature Trail: 343
Spruce Railroad Trail: 333
Squak Mountain State Park: 112-113
Squalicum Harbor: 170
Squire Creek County Park: 476
Stadium High School: 205
stagecoach rides: 627
St. Andrew's Episcopal Church: 504
Stanwood: 155
Stanwood-Camano Community Fair: 153
Starbucks: 17, 66
statehood: 692-693
State Library: 16, 191
State Route 520 Evergreen Floating Bridge: 91
State Supreme Court: 191
St. Boniface Church: 666
Steamboat Rock State Park: 19, 616, 617
Steel Arch Bridge: 297
Stehekin: 511-514
Steilacoom: 205-206
Steilacoom 4th of July: 208
Steilacoom Town Hall and Museum: 205
Steilacoom Tribal Cultural Center and Museum: 205-206
Stephen Mather Wilderness: 485
Steps Winebar: 261
Steptoe Butte State Park: 659
Stevens Canyon: 560
Stevens County Historical Museum: 635
Stevenson: 398
Stevens Pass: 20, 521, 527-530
Stevens Pass Ski Area: 529
St. James Church: 390
St. John's Cathedral: 648
St. Joseph's Catholic Church: 452
St. Mary's Mission: 620
Stonerose Interpretive Center: 630
Stormy Mountain: 504
St. Paul's Mission: 634
Strait of Juan de Fuca: 334-337
Strawberry Festival (Snohomish): 151
Strawberry Festival (Tukwila): 240
Strawberry Festival (Vashon Island): 230
street fairs: Eastern Washington 626; Eastside 94, 99, 107; North Cascades 476, 480, 501, 505; North Puget Sound 139, 157, 171; Olympic Peninsula 300; Seattle 53, 54; South Cascades 548; South Puget Sound 208, 234
Stretch Point Island: 228
Stretch Point State Park: 228, 298
Student Recreation Center: 664
Sucia Island State Park: 288
Sugarloaf Trail: 252-253
Suiattle River: 473
Suiattle River Road 26: 474
Sullivan Lake: 639-641
Sullivan Lake Trail: 639
Sultan: 533
Sultan Farmers Market: 533
Sultan Summer Shindig: 533
Summer Arts Fair (Friday Harbor): 261
Summer Arts Festival (Longview/Kelso): 380
Summer Celebration: 99
Summer Concerts on the Green: 116
Summer Falls State Park: 618
Summerfest (Kirkland): 101
Summer Festival on the Green (Bothell): 115
Summer Palace: 663
Summer Solstice Parade and Fair: 53
Summit at Snoqualmie: 542, 543
Summit Nordic Center: 542
Summit Trail: 500, 512
Summit Tubing Area: 542
Sunbanks Blues Festival: 615
Sundial Park: 210
Sunfest: 417
Sunflower Days (Clarkston): 669
Sunflower Festival (Colville Reservation): 620
Sun Lakes State Park: 617, 618
Sunnyside Cemetery: 137
Sunnyside Park: 664
Sunrise: 11, 561-562
Sunset Avenue: 121
Supermall of the Great Northwest: 237
Super Saturday: 194-195
Surf Frolic Festival: 341
surfing: 341, 361, 362
Swallows Park: 668
Swamp Lake Trail: 570
Swauk Forest Discovery Trail: 519
swimming: Columbia Gorge/Wine Country 391,

397, 411-412, 415, 416, 418, 426, 438, 447, 453, 454, 455; Eastern Washington 601, 603-604, 610, 614, 615, 617, 618, 621, 622, 624, 626, 629, 636, 637, 640, 643, 654, 664, 668, 672, 673, 675; Eastside 93, 96, 101, 105, 113; North Cascades 480, 495, 496, 499, 501, 505, 506, 508, 520, 530; North Puget Sound 129, 130, 137, 140, 142, 145, 147, 151, 152, 172, 180; Olympic Peninsula/Coast 299, 301, 327, 332, 338, 357, 359, 378; San Juan Islands 253, 270, 272; Seattle 43, 46, 59; South Cascades 543, 545, 548, 550, 574, 575, 579, 583, 584; South Puget Sound 193, 195, 196, 209-210, 216, 219, 225, 232, 240, 241
Swinomish Northern Lights Casino & Bingo: 252
Sylvester Park: 192
symphony: Columbia Gorge/Wine Country 390, 417, 425, 435-436, 453; Eastern Washington 652, 663; Eastside 94, 101; North Puget Sound 146, 170-171; Olympic Peninsula 326, 380; Seattle 52; South Puget Sound 194, 207, 216
Syttende Mai Parade: 41

T

Table Mountain: 466
Table Mountain (Gifford Pinchot National Forest): 595
Tacoma: 14, 200-215
Tacoma Actors Guild: 207
Tacoma Art Museum: 15, 202
Tacoma Dome: 206
Tacoma Farmers Market: 214
Tacoma Glassblowing Studio: 15, 208
Tacoma Little Theater: 207
Tacoma Mall: 208
Tacoma Master Chorale: 207
Tacoma Musical Playhouse: 207
Tacoma Nature Center: 209
Tacoma Opera: 207
Tacoma Philharmonic: 207
Tacoma Symphony: 207
Tacoma Youth Symphony: 207
Tahklakh Lake: 595
Taste of Chelan Street Fair: 505
Taste of Edmonds Festival: 122
Taste of Tacoma: 208
Tasting Room Yakima, The: 433
Tatoosh Trail: 571
Tatoosh Wilderness: 571
teahouses: 70
Teddy Bear Cove: 165
telephone service: 711
Temple Theater: 207
Tenino City Park: 193
Tennant Lake Interpretive Center: 182
Terra Blanca: 435
Thanksgiving in Yakima Valley Wine Country: 437
theater, live: *see* performing arts
Theater on the Square: 207
Theatre Arts series: 171
Thomas Lake Trail: 594
Thorp Grist Mill: 445
Thorp Lake: 545
Three Fingers Mountain: 471
Three Lakes Trail: 346
Three Rivers Air Show: 380
Three Rivers Children's Museum: 415
Three Rivers Mall: 380
Three Rivers Winery: 424
Threshing Bee: 446
Thurston County Fair: 195
Thurston Wolfe Winery: 435
ticks: 710
Tieton River: 19-20, 579
Tiger Historical Center: 637
Tiger Mountain: 18, 112
Tiger Mountain State Forest: 112
Tillicum Village: 17, 86, 232
Timber Bowl Rodeo: 476
Tin Pan Gap: 471
Tipsoo Lake: 572
Titlow Park: 209
Tivoli Festival: 41
Tlingit totem: 29
Tokul Creek State Fish Hatchery: 538
Toleda: 580
"Tollie" locomotive: 297
Tolmie Peak: 562
Tolmie State Park: 195
Tolt McDonald Park: 538, 540
Tolt Pipeline Trail: 116
Tonasket: 626-627
Tonasket Bluegrass Festival: 627
Tonasket Founders Day Rodeo: 627
Toppenish: 12, 430-431, 442
Toppenish National Wildlife Refuge: 432
Tour de Blast: 580
Tour de Lopez: 283
tourist information: 712; *see also specific place*
Toutle: 580, 581
Town & Country Days: 634
Town Toyota Center: 454

Traditional Lutefisk Dinner: 223
Trafton School: 476
Trail of the Shadows: 559
Trail of Two Forests: 589
train excursions: 204, 538, 551, 638, 639
train travel: 698-699
transportation: 698-701; *see also specific place*
Trapper Creek Trail: 594
Trapper Creek Wilderness: 593-594
Treaty Days and the All-Indian Rodeo and Pow Wow: 436
Tribal Jam: 437
Tri-Cities: 412-421
Tri-Cities Children's Festival: 417
Tri-Cities Water Follies: 418
Tri-Cities Wine Festival: 418
Tri-City Raceway: 418
Troll Haven: 318-319
Troublesome Creek Nature Trail: 531
Trout Lake: 594-595
Trout Lake Fair and Dairy Show: 594
Trout Lake Festival of the Arts: 594-595
Truman Trail: 591
Tucker Cellars: 434
Tukwila Days: 240
Tulalip Casino: 151
tulip festival: 156-157, 160
Tulip Town: 157
Tumtum: 644
Tumwater Falls: 14, 193, 199
Tumwater Falls Park: 193
Tumwater Historical District: 16, 193
Turlo: 474
Turnbull National Wildlife Refuge: 658-659
Turn Island State Park: 289
Twanoh State Park: 299
Twenty-Five Mile Creek State Park: 505, 508
Twin Falls: 541
Twin Harbors State Park: 361, 362
Twin Rivers Park: 151
Twisp: 499-500
Twisp River Valley Trail: 494
Twisp Show 'N' Shine: 499
Two Rivers Casino: 643
Two Rivers County Park: 416
Two Rivers Heritage Museum: 397
Two Sisters: 424

U

Umatilla National Wildlife Refuge: 412
Union: 298-299
Union Station: 205
Uniontown: 666
Unique Tin Weekend: 380
universities and colleges: Columbia Gorge/Wine Country 423, 445; Eastern Washington 650, 658, 661, 666; North Puget Sound 167; Seattle 43-45; South Puget Sound 205
University District (Seattle): 43-45
University District Street Fair: 53
University of Idaho: 666
University of Washington: 43-44
University of Washington (Tacoma): 205
University of Washington Arboretum: 45
Unlimited hydroplane races: 418
Upper Lena Lake: 303
Upper Oak Bay Jefferson County Park: 314
Upper Skagit Bald Eagle Festival: 482
Upper Toutle Valley: 582
Upper Wolf Trail System: 642
US Bank Centre: 29
Usk: 641
USS *Turner Joy:* 215

V

Vance Creek County Park: 359
Vancouver: 11, 386-395
Vancouver Barracks: 384, 388-389
Vancouver Farmers Market: 394
Vancouver Lake Park: 391
Vancouver National Historic Reserve: 11, 388-389
Vancouver Rodeo: 390
Vancouver Symphony Orchestra: 390
VanLierop Bulb Farms: 237
Van Zandt: 479
Vashon Farmers Market: 230
Vashon Island: 228-232
Vela Luka Croatian Dancers: 251
Velodrome: 105
Verlot: 470-471, 474
Veterinary Teaching Hospital: 662-663
Victoria, Canada: 84
Victorian Village: 454
View Point Park: 454-455
Viking Fest: 223
Viking Union: 167
Vintage and Classic Boat Show: 161
Vinters' Village complex: 434-435
Vintiques Northwest Nationals: 436
Volunteer Park: 39

W

Wagonwheel Lake: 301
Wahkiakum Museum: 378
Waikiki Beach: 371

Waldron Island: 289
walking tours: Columbia Gorge/Wine Country 423, 451; Eastern Washington 643; North Puget Sound 167; Olympic Peninsula/Coast 307, 322, 369; Seattle 86-87; *see also specific place*
Wallace Falls State Park: 532
Walla Walla: 20, 421-429
Walla Walla Balloon Stampede: 425-426
Walla Walla Community College: 423
Walla Walla Frontier Days Fair & Rodeo: 426
Walla Walla Little Theatre: 425
Walla Walla Point Park: 454
Walla Walla Sweet Onion Harvest Festival: 426
Walla Walla Symphony Orchestra: 425
Walla Walla University: 423
Wallingford: 43
Wall Street: 646, 648
Wallula: 424
Wanapum State Recreation Area: 601
Wapato Lake Park: 209-210
Washaway Beach: 365
Washington Center for the Performing Arts: 194
Washington Hunter: 533
Washington-Idaho Symphony: 663
Washington Mutual Tower: 29
Washington Park: 250-251, 253
Washington Pass Viewpoint: 13, 485
Washington State Apple Commission Visitor Center: 452
Washington State Autumn Leaf Festival: 519
Washington State Capitol Museum: 16, 191
Washington State History Museum: 14, 202
Washington State International Kite Festival: 370
Washington State Railroads Historical Society Museum: 415
Washington State University: 661; sports 664; tours 665
Washington Summer Microbrew Festival: 101
Washougal: 397
Waterbrook Winery: 425
waterfalls: Columbia Gorge/Wine Country 397; Eastern Washington 618, 634, 637, 639, 642, 646, 673; North Cascades 464, 471, 472, 473, 475, 480, 485, 490, 512, 514, 530, 532; Olympic Peninsula/Coast 18, 301, 302, 304, 333, 334, 346, 348; San Juan Islands 16, 270; Seattle 32; South Cascades 18, 538, 541, 559, 560, 576, 590; South Puget Sound 14, 193
Waterfront (Eastside): 93, 100
Waterfront (North Puget Sound): 121
Waterfront (Seattle): 14, 33-34
Waterfront Park (Leavenworth): 518, 521
Waterfront Park (Seattle): 34
Water Music Festival: 370
water parks: 182-183, 239, 418, 507
Water Resources Education Center: 389
Waterville: 452-453
Waterville Days: 453
Waterville Historic Hotel: 452-453
Wauconda: 630
Waverly Beach Park: 101
Wawawai County Park: 672
Wawawai Landing: 672
weather: 677-679; *see also specific place*
Webb Lookout: 302
Welcome Pass: 466
Wellpinit: 643
Wells Dam: 501
Wellspring: 11, 554
Wenaha-Tucannon Wilderness: 671-672
Wenatchee: 17, 20, 449-458
Wenatchee Confluence State Park: 454, 455
Wenatchee River County Park: 455, 516
Wenatchee Valley Farmers Market: 457-458
Wenatchee Valley Mall: 454
Wenatchee Valley Museum and Cultural Center: 451
Wenatchee Valley Super Oval: 454
Wenatchee Youth Circus: 454
Wenberg State Park: 152
Wescott Bay Sculpture Park: 259
West Beach: 610
West End Farmers Market: 421
Western Washington University: 167
West Fork Foss River Trail: 528
West Fork Humptulips River Trail: 346
Westhaven State Park: 361
Westlake Center: 14, 35
Westport: 360-364
Westport Fishing Pier: 362
Westport Light State Park: 361
Westport Maritime Museum: 360-361
Westport Seafood Festival: 361
West Seattle: 46
West Sound: 270
West Wind Trail: 371
Weyerhaeuser King County Aquatic Center: 241
Whale Museum, The: 258
whale-watching: 680-681; North Cascades 479; North Puget Sound 173; Olympic Peninsula/Coast 336, 341, 356, 362, 371; San Juan Islands 16, 252, 259, 261-263, 274
Whatcom County Old Settlers Picnic: 181

Whatcom Falls Park: 172
Whatcom Symphony Orchestra: 170-171
Whidbey Island: 13, 19, 126-144
Whidbey Island Center for the Arts: 129
Whidbey Island Greenbank Farm: 13, 133
Whidbey Island Naval Air Station: 139
Whidbey Island Race Week: 139-140
Whidbey Island Winery: 129
Whisky Dick Triathlon: 446
Whistle Lake Shore Loop: 252
White Buck Museum: 494
White Buck Trading Co.: 493-494
White Chuck Trail: 472
White Pass: 543, 578-579
White Pass Scenic Byway: 574-579
White Pass Ski Area: 578-579
White River Hiker Information Center: 562
White River Valley: 236-239
White River Valley Historical Museum: 236
White Salmon: 402-404
white settlement: 691-692
whitewater rafting: *see* river rafting
Whitman massacre: 690-691
Whitman Mission National Historic Site: 424
Whitman University: 423
Whitney Gardens & Nursery: 303
Whoop-N-Holler Ranch Museum: 411
Wickersham: 479
Wilbert Trail: 133
Wild Blackberry Festival: 359
Wildcat Lake: 216
wilderness areas: Columbia Gorge/Wine Country 416-417; Eastern Washington 640-641, 671-672; North Cascades 471-473, 485, 491, 500, 512, 527-529; Olympic Peninsula/Coast 302-303, 304, 346; South Cascades 19, 543, 568-571, 592-594
wilderness use permits: 294
Wild Goose Trail: 467
wildlife/wildlife-watching: 680-686; Eastern Washington 601, 636, 639, 650, 658-659, 663; North Cascades 472, 490, 491; North Puget Sound 133, 151; Olympic Peninsula/Coast 292, 302, 324, 348, 376, 378; South Cascades 550, 561, 579, 582-583; South Puget Sound 193; *see also* birds/bird-watching; marinelife-watching; *specific place*
Wild Waves: 239
Wildwood Chapel: 482
Willaby: 347
Willapa Bay: 369-370
Willapa Bay Interpretive Center: 369
Willapa National Wildlife Refuge: 376
Willard National Fish Hatchery: 402
William O. Douglas Wilderness: 569-570
William Shore Memorial Pool: 327
Winchester Mountain: 466
Windermere Cup Races: 53
Wind Mountain: 401
Wind River Cellars: 402
Winds of Change Interpretive Trail: 587
windsurfing: Columbia Gorge/Wine Country 391, 398, 399, 405, 409; Eastern Washington 669; North Cascades 507; North Puget Sound 180; Olympic Peninsula/Coast 299, 314, 319; Seattle 43; South Puget Sound 225
Windust Park: 672
Windy Pass Trail: 492
Windy Ridge: 591
Winemakers' Loft, The: 434
wine/wineries: 695-696, 707; Columbia Gorge/Wine Country 12, 17, 390, 393, 402, 407-408, 411, 417, 418, 424-425, 432-435, 436, 437, 449, 457; Eastern Washington 635, 650-651, 663; Eastside 101, 106, 111, 115-116; North Cascades 463-464; North Puget Sound 129, 154; Olympic Peninsula 299, 317-318, 380; San Juan Islands 16, 261, 281; South Puget Sound 234, 239
Wing Luke Asian Museum: 35
Winslow: 233
Winterfest in Historic Tenino: 195
Wintergrass: 207
Winthrop: 12, 492-499
Winthrop National Fish Hatchery: 494
Winthrop Rhythm and Blues Festival: 494
Winthrop Rodeo Days: 494
Wolf Haven: 193
Wolf Tree Nature Trail: 40
Wonderland Trail: 19, 563
Wooden Boat Festival (Olympia): 194
Wooden Boat Festival (Port Townsend): 309
Woodfest: 480
Woodinville: 17, 115-117
Woodinville Farmers Market: 116
Woodinville Wine Festival: 116
Woodland: 583-584
Woodland Park Rose Garden: 43
Woodland Park Zoo: 43
Woodland Theatre: 634
Woods Creek Watchable Wildlife Trail: 576
Woodward Canyon Winery: 424-425
World Class Crab Races & Feed: 361
World Kite Museum: 368
World of Music Arts and Dance (WOMAD): 107

World's Largest King Salmon Barbecue: 252
"World's Longest Beach" arch: 368
Wreckage: 369
Wright Park: 205
W. T. Preston: 249
W. W. Seymour Botanical Conservatory: 205
Wyatt Park: 151
Wyvern Winery: 651

XYZ

Yakama Cultural Heritage Center: 431
Yakama Reservation: 431
Yakima: 12, 430, 431
Yakima Area Arboretum: 432
Yakima River: 447
Yakima River Canyon: 19, 438
Yakima River Greenway: 438
Yakima Speedway: 436
Yakima Sportsman State Park: 438
Yakima Symphony Orchestra: 435
Yakima Valley: 17, 430–443
Yakima Valley Community Band: 435
Yakima Valley Museum: 431
Yakima Valley Spring Barrel Tasting: 436
Yakima Valley Wine Growers Association: 432
Yashiro Japanese Garden: 192
Yelm-Tenino Trail: 196
Ye Merrie Greenwood Renaissance Faire: 417
Ye Olde Curiousity Shop: 14, 34
Yule Fest (Poulsbo): 223
Yulefest (Seattle): 41
Zabel's Rhododendrons: 192
Zoolights: 204, 208
zoos: Eastside 18, 111; Seattle 43; South Puget Sound 203
Zoo Sounds: 204, 208

List of Maps

Anacortes: 250
Anacortes, Downtown: 251
Bellevue and Mercer Island: 92
Bellingham: 168-169
Chelan: 503
Columbia Gorge and Wine Country: 385
Eastern Washington: 598
Eastside: 90
Ellensburg: 444
Friday Harbor: 260
Grand Coulee Dam Area: 611
Leavenworth: 517
Lopez Island: 282
Mount Baker Hiking: 464
Mount Rainier National Park: 556
Mount St. Helens: 586
North Cascades: 461
North Cascades National Park: 486
North Puget Sound: 120
Ocean Shores: 352
Olympia: 190
Olympic National Park: 325
Olympic Peninsula: 293
Orcas Island: 271
Port Angeles: 323
Port Townsend: 306
Pullman: 661
San Juan Islands: 246
Seattle: 26-27
Seattle, Downtown: 30-31
Sequim: 317
South Cascades: 537
South Puget Sound: 188
Spokane, Downtown: 647
Spokane, Greater: 645
Tacoma: 201
Tacoma, Downtown: 202
Tri-Cities: 413
Vancouver: 387
Vashon Island: 229
Washington: 2-3
Wenatchee: 450
Whidbey Island: 128
Yakima Valley Wineries: 432

Acknowledgments

First and foremost, I have to thank and acknowledge my husband, Paul, for his full partnership in producing this book. Paul spent hours upon hours editing and writing copy, confirming contact and price information and researching facts. His help was essential to the completion of the project and his mark was particularly indelible upon the Seattle, Olympic, South Cascades, Essentials and Resources chapters, as well as a number of callouts. I quite literally couldn't have done it without him!

I'd also like to thank Annie Blakely for her patience and helpful suggestions throughout the process, as well as Shari Husain for the finishing touches at the end of the editorial cycle. Thanks, too, to Domini Dragoone in production and Brice Ticen in cartography for the bang-up work they did in making all those words look pretty.

Acknowledgments

www.moon.com

DESTINATIONS | ACTIVITIES | BLOGS | MAPS | BOOKS

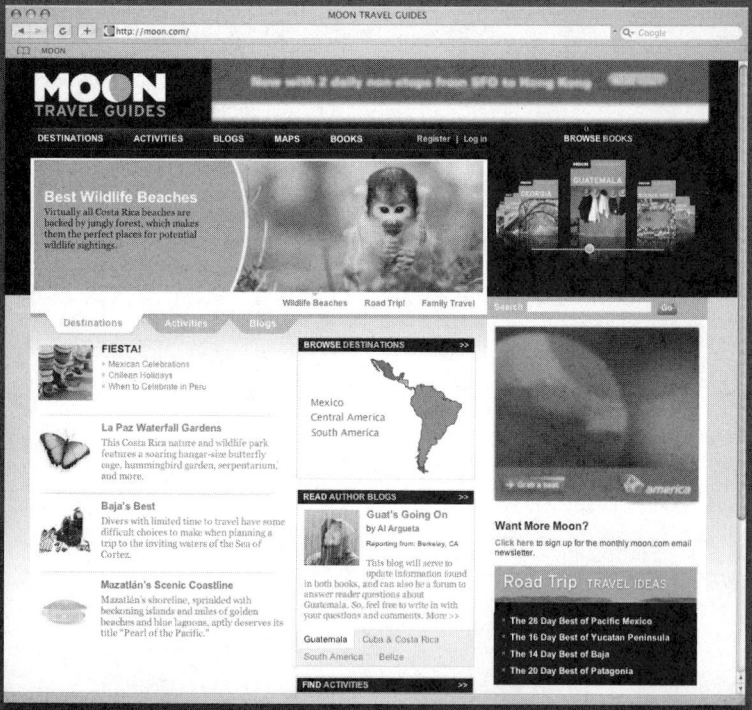

MOON.COM is all new, and ready to help plan your next trip! Filled with fresh trip ideas and strategies, author interviews, informative blogs, a detailed map library, and descriptions of all the Moon guidebooks, Moon.com is all you need to get out and explore the world—or even places in your own backyard. As always, when you travel with Moon, expect an experience that is uncommon and truly unique.

MAP SYMBOLS

- Expressway
- Primary Road
- Secondary Road
- Unpaved Road
- Trail
- Ferry
- Railroad
- Pedestrian Walkway
- Stairs
- Highlight
- City/Town
- State Capital
- National Capital
- Point of Interest
- Accommodation
- Restaurant/Bar
- Other Location
- Campground
- Airfield
- Airport
- Mountain
- Unique Natural Feature
- Waterfall
- Park
- Trailhead
- Skiing Area
- Golf Course
- Parking Area
- Archaeological Site
- Church
- Gas Station
- Glacier
- Mangrove
- Reef
- Swamp

CONVERSION TABLES

°C = (°F - 32) / 1.8
°F = (°C x 1.8) + 32
1 inch = 2.54 centimeters (cm)
1 foot = 0.304 meters (m)
1 yard = 0.914 meters
1 mile = 1.6093 kilometers (km)
1 km = 0.6214 miles
1 fathom = 1.8288 m
1 chain = 20.1168 m
1 furlong = 201.168 m
1 acre = 0.4047 hectares
1 sq km = 100 hectares
1 sq mile = 2.59 square km
1 ounce = 28.35 grams
1 pound = 0.4536 kilograms
1 short ton = 0.90718 metric ton
1 short ton = 2,000 pounds
1 long ton = 1.016 metric tons
1 long ton = 2,240 pounds
1 metric ton = 1,000 kilograms
1 quart = 0.94635 liters
1 US gallon = 3.7854 liters
1 Imperial gallon = 4.5459 liters
1 nautical mile = 1.852 km

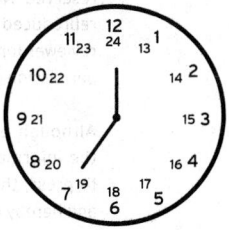

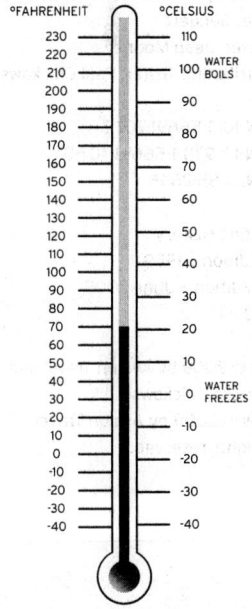

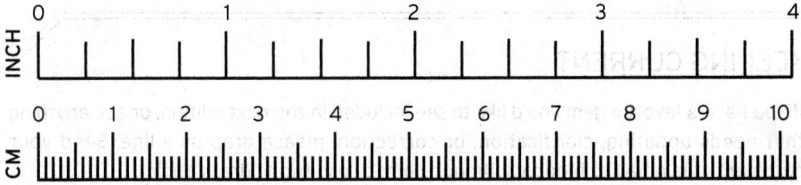

MOON WASHINGTON

Avalon Travel
a member of the Perseus Books Group
1700 Fourth Street
Berkeley, CA 94710, USA
www.moon.com

Editors: Annie M. Blakley & Shaharazade Husain
Series Manager: Kathryn Ettinger
Copy Editor: Valerie Sellers Blanton
Graphics Coordinators: Kathryn Osgood
Production Coordinators: Domini Dragoone
Cover Designer: Domini Dragoone
Map Editor: Brice Ticen
Cartographers: Jon Twena, Lohnes & Wright, Kat Bennett
Indexer: Jean Mooney
Contributing Writer: Paul Chickowski

ISBN-10: 1-56691-707-7
ISBN-13: 978-1-56691-707-0
ISSN: 1085-2646

Printing History
1st Edition – 1989
8th Edition – June 2009
5 4 3 2 1

Text © 2009 by Avalon Travel and Ericka Chickowski
Maps © 2009 by Avalon Travel.
All rights reserved.

Some photos and illustrations are used by permission and are the property of the original copyright owners.

Front cover photo: weathered barn with fields of red, orange, and yellow tulips in Skagit County, © Terry Donnelly.

Title page photo: Mount Rainier from Sunrise, © Ericka Chickowski.

Interior color photos: pages 4–20, all photos © Ericka Chickowski.

Printed in the United States by RR Donnelley

Moon Handbooks and the Moon logo are the property of Avalon Travel. All other marks and logos depicted are the property of the original owners. All rights reserved. No part of this book may be translated or reproduced in any form, except brief extracts by a reviewer for the purpose of a review, without written permission of the copyright owner.

Although every effort was made to ensure that the information was correct at the time of going to press, the author and publisher do not assume and hereby disclaim any liability to any party for any loss or damage caused by errors, omissions, or any potential travel disruption due to labor or financial difficulty, whether such errors or omissions result from negligence, accident, or any other cause.

KEEPING CURRENT

If you have a favorite gem you'd like to see included in the next edition, or see anything that needs updating, clarification, or correction, please drop us a line. Send your comments via email to feedback@moon.com, or use the address above.